STANDARD VOLUME

# INTERMEDIATE
# ACCOUNTING
## ELEVENTH EDITION

Jay M. Smith, PhD, CPA
Brigham Young University

K. Fred Skousen, PhD, CPA
Brigham Young University

*Consulting Editors:*

Earl K. Stice, PhD
Rice University

James D. Stice, PhD
Brigham Young University

COLLEGE DIVISION South-Western Publishing Co.

Cincinnati Ohio

Publisher: Mark Hubble
Developmental Editor: Linda A. Spang
Project Editor: Mary H. Draper
Production Editors: Leslie Kauffman, Mark D. Sears
Associate Editor: Malvine Litten
Designer: Joseph M. Devine
Marketing Manager: Jim S. Enders
Cover Photo: Carla A. Sansone Photography

AC93KA

Library of Congress Cataloging-in-Publication Data

Smith, Jay M.
    Intermediate accounting : standard volume / Jay M. Smith,
K. Fred Skousen. -- 11th ed.
        p.   cm.
    Includes bibliographical references and indexes.
    "AC93KA."
    ISBN 0-538-81357-1 (acid-free paper)
    1. Accounting.   I. Skousen, K. Fred.    II. Title.
HF5635.S645  1991
657'.044--dc20
                                                91-38101
                                                  CIP


Material from Uniform CPA Examination Questions and Unofficial
Answers, Copyright © 1974, 1976, 1978, 1979, 1981, 1983, 1984,
1985, 1986, 1988, and 1989 by the American Institute of
Certified Public Accountants, Inc., is reprinted or adapted
with permission.

3 4 5 KI 5 4 3

Printed in the United States of America

 This book is printed on recycled, acid-free paper that meets Environmental Protection Agency standards.

# PREFACE

As we write this edition of INTERMEDIATE AC-COUNTING, we are impressed with the significant changes occurring in accounting education. In response to the American Accounting Association's call for change in accounting education in its 1986 report, "Future Accounting Education: Preparing for the Expanded Profession," curriculum revision is occurring at scores of universities and colleges. Some of these changes are being sponsored by the Accounting Education Change Commission (AECC), a body established to administer a $4 million grant from the national CPA firms as their commitment to improving the way accountants are being educated. Both the accounting profession and the accounting academic community recognize that the demands being placed on accountants today and in the future will require substantial changes in emphasis in the accounting curriculum. These changes include more emphasis on such key factors as developing students' abilities to solve broad unstructured problems, to communicate more effectively, to work in a world of changing technology that involves international communities, and to exhibit leadership skills.

We teach at a school (Brigham Young University) that received one of the initial curriculum grants from the AECC. Many significant changes are occurring in our program, and they are affecting the way intermediate accounting is being taught. We have therefore considered these changes in preparing the eleventh edition of our text. We have found that any one classification scheme for teaching intermediate accounting is not perfect. For decades, intermediate accounting texts have followed a "balance sheet" approach, and this edition continues that tradition. At BYU, however, we are experimenting with a transaction cycle, or events, approach. This approach involves identifying the basic events of a business and studying the financial, tax, managerial, audit, and systems issues related to each event during one period of time. We have found it possible to use our text in this nontraditional way by selecting those text and problem materials that emphasize the concepts we want to stress in our junior year core. For those who may be interested, a more detailed description of the integrated junior year for the accounting program at Brigham Young University is included in the Instructor's Resource Manual that accompanies the text.

We encourage adopters to experiment in their use of our text. We have never felt that our book necessarily should be taught by starting with Chapter 1 and proceeding to Chapter 22. Indeed, we have not always used it this way in our teaching. Although we recommend using Chapters 1 and 2 before the remaining chapters because we refer to the conceptual framework throughout the text, we have tried to make the chapter material as independent from other chapters as possible.

## SIGNIFICANT CHANGES IN THE ELEVENTH EDITION

The eleventh edition of INTERMEDIATE AC-COUNTING is being published one year early because of some significant additions and changes that we feel reflect the atmosphere of change in accounting education. We invite careful examination of these changes and the philosophical reasons for them. We believe that this edition not only carries on the tradition of providing the most teachable and student-oriented text on the market, but includes material that will assist instructors and students alike in meeting the challenge of improving accounting education. The following significant changes in the eleventh edition are highlighted.

### Movement of Chapter on Cash Flows to Part One of Text

Although we commented above that the order of text topics is not fixed, we feel that the movement of the cash flows chapter from the back of the text to the front is very significant. For several years, especially since the FASB adopted its conceptual framework, the importance of reporting cash flows has been stressed. No longer can the statement of cash flows be looked upon as a "supplemental statement." It reports information that is vital for many decisions, and the usefulness of this information has been enhanced significantly by the revised format prescribed by FASB Statement No. 95. We feel that placement of the statement of cash flows with the income statement and the balance sheet conveys this importance to students and assists them in gaining a broader understanding of the impact of business events, not only on net income and the balance sheet, but also on cash flows.

We did not just "move" the chapter, but rewrote it recognizing that students would have difficulty understanding some complex transactions at this early stage of their study of intermediate accounting. We have omitted unnecessary complexities from Chapter 6, and have included a discussion of their impact on cash flows as appropriate throughout the text. Thus, the discussion of different treatments of allowance for doubtful accounts is covered in Chapter 9, the cash effects of bond premium and discount amortization are included in Chapter 16, and the complexities of cash flows for lease arrangements are explained in Chapter 20. With these complexities removed from Chapter 6, we feel that the format for the statement of cash flows, which is more understandable than the old funds statement, makes it possible to teach both the indirect and direct methods at this earlier time. We have elected to stress the T-account approach in the chapter because it is less complicated than the work sheet approach. The latter approach is retained, however, in an appendix to Chapter 6 for those who wish to use it.

We recognize that some users of our text will want to continue teaching the statement of cash flows later in the course. As many of our reviewers have pointed out, the eleventh edition provides flexibility that allows individual instructors to determine when their students should study the statement of cash flows. The Instructor's Resource Manual that accompanies the text explains how the cash flow material in Chapter 6 and subsequent chapters can be used by those who prefer later coverage.

## Introduction of International Issues

Accounting and business students need more exposure to international issues. This conclusion is stressed by all groups that have been studying accounting and business education. In the past, international issues have been taught mainly in the advanced accounting course. Because many accounting graduates do not take an advanced course, we feel it is important that some international issues be covered in an intermediate text. We have carefully added many examples and topics to achieve this goal. Specific international topics added to this edition of the text are described below.

**International Standards and Harmonization**   The movement to coordinate the establishment of accounting standards internationally is presented in Chapter 1. Throughout the text, examples of international variations in the treatment of business events, such as inventory valuation and goodwill reporting, are included.

**International Transaction Accounting**   In Chapter 11, we have added a section dealing with the accounting for sales and purchases of goods in foreign markets, and the foreign exchange adjustments necessary at the time of sale or purchase, subsequent reporting, and settlement of the transaction.

In addition to these specific topics, some of the "real-world" opening scenarios and boxed items, as discussed below, reflect international events.

## New Opening Scenarios and Boxed Items

Previous editions have included examples of actual financial statements and references to specific company illustrations, and we have expanded and updated this material in the eleventh edition. Much more "real-world" material has been added in the form of opening scenarios and boxed items. Each chapter of the text has a real-world opening scenario that suggests why the topics included in the chapter are relevant to what the students will be doing when they graduate. Each chapter of the text also includes at least one boxed item, derived from current literature, that describes recent events and asks the student to consider various policy and conceptual issues related to the material. Students can consider these "asides" as they read the text material, and instructors can use this material in class discussion to broaden the student's understanding. Issues such as the Gulf War, the S&L crisis, athletes' deferred compensation arrangements, and the merger of national CPA firms all add a high degree of realism to the traditional material. Suggested solutions to the questions in the boxed items are included in the Solutions Manual.

## Annotated Instructor's Edition

We are introducing an Annotated Instructor's Edition of our text. Four types of annotated notes are included throughout the text: (1) enrichment examples, (2) points to stress, (3) teaching tips, and (4) historical notes. We have included in these annotations ideas we have tried as teachers and further enrichment material that could be useful for instructors as they use our text. We also have tried to alert instructors to areas that might be especially difficult for students to grasp. We feel the material in the annotations will be of considerable value in the classroom.

## Expanded and Updated End-of-Chapter Material

New cases, exercises, and problems have been added to each chapter of the text. Many of these end-of-chapter materials refer to topics that have been added to the text. Because the AECC has urged accounting educators to stress student analysis and judgment as opposed to application of detailed rules, we have added more open-ended cases and problems in this edition.

## SUPPLEMENTARY MATERIALS

A comprehensive package of supplementary materials is provided with the eleventh edition to assist both instructors and students.

## Available to Instructors

**Solutions Manual.** This manual contains the answers to all end-of-chapter questions, cases, exercises, and problems, and suggested solutions to questions that accompany the boxed items in the text.

**Solutions Transparencies.** Transparencies of solutions for all end-of-chapter exercises and problems are available to adopters. A larger and heavier typeface has been used in preparing transparencies for the eleventh edition to improve their readability.

**Instructor's Resource Manual.** This manual contains objectives, chapter outlines, teaching suggestions and strategies, topical overviews of end-of-chapter materials, assignment classifications with level of difficulty and estimated completion time, suggested readings on chapter topics, and teaching transparency masters. The text of the Instructor's Resource Manual is available on diskette.

**Test Bank, prepared by Jay M. Smith and James D. Stice, Brigham Young University, and Earl K. Stice, Rice University.** A test bank is available in both printed and computer (MicroSWAT III) versions. The test bank, which has been significantly revised and expanded, includes true-false, matching, and multiple-choice questions and several short examination problems for each chapter, accompanied by solutions.

**Template Diskette.** The template diskette is used with Lotus® 1-2-3®* for solving selected end-of-chapter exercises and problems that are identified in the textbook with the symbol at the right. ▪▪ The diskette may be ordered free of charge from South-Western Publishing Co.

**Key for Practice Case.** The key provides a complete solution for *SporTime Inc. II*.

## Available to Students

**Study Guide, prepared by Frank J. Imke, Arizona State University West.** The study guide provides review and reinforcement materials for each chapter, including learning objectives, a glossary of key terms in the chapter, chapter review outlines, objective questions, and short problems. Answers for all questions and problems are provided in a separate section at the end of the study guide.

**Practice Case, prepared by Donald C. Dwyer, Berkshire Community College.** The practice case, *SporTime Inc. II*, provides a comprehensive review of accounting principles. It is available in both manual and computer versions.

**Electronic Spreadsheet Applications for Intermediate Accounting, prepared by Gaylord N. Smith, Albion College.** This supplemental text-workbook with template diskette includes intermediate accounting applications and a Lotus 1-2-3 tutorial. It requires approximately 25-30 hours for completion.

**Working Papers.** Forms for solving end-of-chapter exercises and problems are contained in a single bound volume and are perforated for easy removal.

**Check Figures.** Instructors may order check figures for students to use in verifying their solutions to end-of-chapter problems.

## ACKNOWLEDGEMENTS

We have been ably assisted in the extensive additions to the eleventh edition of the text by Professor

---

*Lotus® 1-2-3® are registered trademarks of the Lotus Development Corporation. Any reference to Lotus or 1-2-3 refers to this footnote.

James D. Stice of Brigham Young University and Professor Earl K. Stice of Rice University. Their insight and creativity have been extremely valuable to us as we have sought to make changes in the spirit of the Accounting Education Change Commission's charge.

Relevant pronouncements of the Financial Accounting Standards Board and other authoritative publications are paraphrased, quoted, discussed, and referenced throughout the text. We are indebted to the American Accounting Association, the American Institute of Certified Public Accountants, the Financial Accounting Standards Board, and the Securities and Exchange Commission for material from their publications. Also, we gratefully acknowledge the American Institute of Certified Public Accountants for permission to use questions from the Uniform CPA Examination.

We wish to thank the following faculty who reviewed manuscript for this edition and provided many helpful suggestions.

Bruce Bradford
LaSalle University

Barney R. Cargile
The University of Alabama

Henry H. Davis
Eastern Illinois University

Allen J. Frank
University of West Florida

Gary R. Freeman
The University of Tulsa

Debra Goorbin
Westchester Community College

Scott I. Jerris
West Virginia University

Jerry G. Kreuze
Western Michigan University

William J. Kross
Purdue University

Kenneth R. Lambert
Memphis State University

Brenda Jill Radcliff
Indiana Vocational Technical College, Bloomington

William Staats
Hudson Valley Community College

We thank Brenda Hester of Volunteer State Community College and Dorthy Steinsapir of Middlesex County College for their valuable comments in verifying solutions for the Solutions Manual.

We also wish to thank the many instructors and students who have used INTERMEDIATE ACCOUNTING and volunteered their comments and suggestions.

Jay M. Smith
K. Fred Skousen

# ABOUT THE AUTHORS

## THE AUTHORS

Jay M. Smith, PhD, CPA, is Professor of Accounting at the School of Accountancy, Brigham Young University. He holds a bachelor's and master's degree from BYU and a PhD from Stanford University. He has over thirty years' teaching experience at BYU, Stanford, the University of Minnesota, and the University of Hawaii. In 1984 he was a faculty resident at Arthur Andersen & Co.'s St. Charles, Illinois, professional education center. He has received several awards and recognitions in accounting, including fellowships from the Danforth and Sloan Foundations and teaching excellence awards from Brigham Young University and the Utah Association of Certified Public Accountants. He has served as a member of the Faculty Advisory Group working with Coopers & Lybrand in their Excellence in Auditing educational project. This group received the 1991 "Innovation in Accounting Education" award from the American Accounting Association. Currently, Professor Smith is serving as project coordinator for the AECC grant received by BYU to restructure the accounting junior year curriculum. He is a member of the American Institute of CPAs and the American Accounting Association and has served on numerous committees of these organizations, including the Practice Subcommittee of the AICPA Board of Examiners with responsibility for writing the practice section of the CPA examination (1986-89).

K. Fred Skousen, PhD, CPA, holds the J. Willard and Alice S. Marriott Chair of Management and is Dean of the Marriott School of Management, Brigham Young University. He was director of the School of Accountancy at BYU for nine years prior to becoming Dean. He has a bachelor's degree from BYU and the master's and PhD degrees from the University of Illinois. Professor Skousen has taught at the University of Illinois, the University of Minnesota, the University of California at Berkeley, and the University of Missouri. He received Distinguished Faculty Awards at the University of Minnesota and at BYU and was recognized as the National Beta Alpha Psi Academic Accountant of the Year in 1979. Professor Skousen is the author or coauthor of over 50 articles, research reports, and books. He served as Director of Research and a member of the Executive Committee of the American Accounting Association and is a member of the American Institute of CPAs and the Utah Association of CPAs. He has served as president of the UACPA and on Council for the AICPA. Dr. Skousen also has served as a consultant to the Controller General of the United States, the Federal Trade Commission, the California Society of CPAs, and several large companies. He was a Faculty Resident on the staff of the Securities and Exchange Commission and a Faculty Fellow with Price Waterhouse and Co.

## THE CONSULTING EDITORS

Earl K. Stice, PhD, is Assistant Professor of Accounting at the Jones Graduate School of Administration, Rice University. He holds bachelor's and master's degrees from Brigham Young University and a PhD from Cornell University. Professor Stice previously taught at the University of Arizona where he was selected Professor of the Year in the College of Business and Public Administration in 1988. His research interests lie in identifying the factors that influence accounting choices and in measuring the capital market effects of accounting information. He has published papers in the *Journal of Financial and Quantitative Analysis* and *The Accounting Review* and is coauthor of *Readings and Applications in Financial Accounting*.

James D. Stice, PhD, is Price Waterhouse Research Fellow and Assistant Professor at the School of Accountancy and Information Systems (SOAIS) at Brigham Young University. He holds a bachelor's and master's degree from BYU and a PhD from the University of Washington. He received the Outstanding Faculty Award from the SOAIS in 1990. Articles by Professor Stice have appeared in *The Accounting Review*, *The CPA Journal*, and other professional journals. He serves as a consultant for companies in the computer and banking industries.

# BRIEF CONTENTS

# CONTENTS

---

# PART ONE

## Overview of Accounting and Its Theoretical Foundation

# CHAPTER 1

# Financial Reporting and the Accounting Profession

The time has arrived for United Exploration Inc.'s annual stockholders' meeting. The purpose of the meeting is to elect members to the Board of Directors, to take care of miscellaneous corporate matters, and to answer stockholders' questions concerning the recently issued financial statements. The attendance at this year's meeting is unusually large because of a significant decline in net income reported for the current year.

Three groups are represented at the meeting: (1) management, (2) independent auditors, and (3) stockholders. Much of the technical discussion involves the impact of changing the method of depreciation used for the financial statements. Management explains to the stockholders that the new method makes United's statements more comparable to those of competitors. The stockholders are especially concerned because the decline in net income has had a negative effect in the stock market. There is some expressed concern that management is purposely manipulating income. The stockholders are interested in the impact of the accounting change because they must decide whether to buy additional shares in the company, sell the shares they have, or maintain their present position.

The above scenario describing a stockholders' meeting is repeated hundreds of times each year as various interested parties meet to discuss the financial affairs of their companies. The audited financial statements contained in annual reports are the primary, and sometimes the only, source of financial information available to stockholders about the profitability and financial soundness of a corporation. The accountants who are responsible for preparing these financial statements play a vital role in the functioning of national and international economies. This chapter will discuss that role along with other aspects of the accounting profession.

## ACCOUNTING AND FINANCIAL REPORTING

As implied in the introductory scenario and as indicated in the following quotation, the overall objective of accounting* is to provide information that can be used in making economic decisions.

> Accounting is a service activity. Its function is to provide quantitative information, primarily financial in nature, about economic entities that is intended to be useful in making economic decisions—in making reasoned choices among alternative courses of action.[1]

Several key features of this definition should be noted. First, accounting provides a vital service in today's business environment. Economists and environmentalists remind us constantly that we live in a world with limited resources. We must use our natural resources, our labor, and our financial wealth wisely so as to maximize their benefits to society. The better the accounting system that measures and reports the costs of using these resources, the better the decisions that are made for allocating them. Second, accounting is concerned primarily with quantitative financial information that is used in conjunction with qualitative evaluations in making judgments. Finally, although accountants place much emphasis on reporting what has already occurred, this past information is intended to be useful in making economic decisions about the future.

### Users of Accounting Information

If accounting is to meet its objective of providing useful information for economic decision making, the following questions must be answered: (1) Who are the users of accounting information? and (2) What information do they require to meet their decision-making needs?

User groups are normally divided into two major classifications: (1) **internal users**, who make decisions directly affecting the internal operations of the enterprise, and (2) **external users**, who make decisions concerning their relationship to the enterprise. Major internal and external user groups are listed in Exhibit 1—1.

---

*A glossary of key terms appears in Appendix B at the end of the text. The terms included in the glossary are printed in color and are listed at the end of each chapter.

[1]*Statement of the Accounting Principles Board No. 4,* "Basic Concepts and Accounting Principles Underlying Financial Statements of Business Enterprises" (New York: American Institute of Certified Public Accountants, 1970), par. 40.

Internal users need information to assist in planning and controlling enterprise operations and managing (allocating) enterprise resources. The accounting system must provide timely information needed to control day-to-day operations and to make major planning decisions, such as: Do we make this product or another one? Do we build a new production plant or expand existing facilities? Must we increase prices or can we cut costs?

**Exhibit 1—1     Internal and External Users of Accounting Information**

| Internal users | External users |
|---|---|
| Company management | Creditors and potential creditors |
| Company employees | Investors and potential investors |
| Board of directors | Financial analysts |
| | Governmental agencies |
| | Other interested parties |

The types of decisions made by external users vary widely; thus, their information needs are highly diverse. Considerable time and effort have been devoted to studying the information needs of external users. As a result, two groups, creditors and investors, have been identified as the principal external users of financial information. Two reasons cited for the importance of these groups are:[2]

1. Their decisions significantly affect the allocation of resources in the economy.
2. Information provided to meet investors' and creditors' needs is likely to be generally useful to members of other groups who are interested in essentially the same financial aspects of business enterprises as investors and creditors.

Creditors need information about the profitability and stability of the enterprise to answer such questions as: Do we lend the money? And, if so, with what provisions? Investors (both existing stockholders and potential investors) need information concerning the safety and profitability of their investment. As noted in the introduction to this chapter, stockholders must decide whether to increase, decrease, terminate, or maintain their interest in an enterprise.

## Financial Reporting

The two major classifications of users, internal and external, have led to a distinction between two major areas of accounting. Management accounting (sometimes referred to as managerial or cost accounting) is concerned primarily with financial reporting for internal users. Internal users, especially management, have control over the accounting system and can specify precisely what information is needed and how the information is to be reported. Financial accounting focuses on the development and communication of financial information for external users primarily in the form of general-purpose financial statements. These statements include a balance sheet, income statement, statement of cash flows, and usually a statement of changes in retained earnings or in owners' equity.

Most accounting systems are designed to generate information for both internal and external reporting. Generally, the external information is much more highly summarized than the information reported internally. The internal decisions made by management

[2]*Statement of Financial Accounting Concepts No. 1,* "Objectives of Financial Reporting by Business Enterprises" (Stamford: Financial Accounting Standards Board, 1978), par. 30.

require information regarding, for example, specific product lines, specific financing alter-natives, individual sales territories, detailed expense classifications, and differences be-tween actual and budgeted revenues and costs. The decisions made by external users require broader indications of overall profitability and financial stability.

While internal financial reporting is governed by the needs of management, external financial reporting is governed by an established body of standards or principles[3] that are designed to reflect the external users' needs. The development of these standards is dis-cussed in some detail later in this chapter.

This textbook focuses on financial accounting and external reporting. The remaining chapters present the concepts, standards, and procedures applied in the development of the basic financial statements.

## THE ACCOUNTING PROFESSION

Professional accountants perform their work in many different roles and environments. To meet its various reporting needs, a business enterprise may employ **financial accoun-tants,** who are primarily concerned with external financial reporting; **management ac-countants,** who are primarily concerned with internal financial reporting; and **tax ac-countants,** who prepare the necessary federal, state, and local tax returns and advise management in matters relating to taxation. In smaller organizations, there is less speciali-zation and more combining of responsibility for the various accounting functions.

Larger business enterprises typically employ **internal auditors** who review the work performed by accountants and others within the enterprise and report their findings to management. In addition to auditing financial reports generated by the accounting sys-tem, they review the operational policies of the company and make recommendations for improving efficiency and effectiveness. Although internal auditors are employees of the enterprise, they must be independent with respect to the employees whose work they review. Thus, internal auditors generally report to top management or a special audit committee of the board of directors.

Some accountants, known as **Certified Public Accountants (CPAs),** do not work for a single business enterprise. Rather, they provide a variety of services for many different individual and business clients. With respect to external financial reporting, the most important service provided by CPAs is the independent audit of financial statements.

### The Independent Audit Function

As independent auditors, CPAs play a critical role in the reporting of financial informa-tion to external users. In performing an **independent audit,** their responsibility is to examine the financial statements to be furnished to external users and to express an opinion as to the fairness of the statements in adhering to generally accepted accounting principles. The auditor's opinion is communicated in a report that accompanies the financial statements. The opinion is based on evidence gathered by the auditor from the detailed records and documents maintained by the company and from a review of the controls over the accounting system. A revised three-paragraph auditor's report was adopted by the accounting profession effective July 15, 1988. The new report form re-placed a standard two-paragraph report that had been used for forty years. The revision emphasizes the separate responsibilities that management and the auditors have for the accounting system and for the information in the financial statements. An example of the

[3]The terms "standards" and "principles" are used interchangeably by the accounting profession and in this text.

new report form is included in the 1990 annual report of The Procter & Gamble Company and is reproduced in Exhibit 1—2.[4] Modifications to the standard report are required in some cases, for example, when the auditor determines that the financial statements contain a departure from generally accepted accounting principles. Another type of modification is necessary when, because of circumstances, no opinion is possible. As an example, an excerpt from the 1988 auditor's report for Great American Corporation (a multi-bank holding company headquartered in Baton Rouge, Louisiana) is shown below.

> During 1988, the Corporation's financial difficulties have continued, and its net loss in 1988 was approximately $10 million. This loss has further eroded the Corporation's capital position and its ability to meet debt terms with two major creditors. . . The accompanying financial statements were prepared by management in conformity with generally accepted accounting principles on a going-concern basis and do not reflect any adjustments relating to the recoverability of recorded asset amounts or the amounts and classifications of liabilities that might be necessary if the Corporation is unable to obtain a restructured agreement with a creditor. . .
>
> Because of the significant effects of the uncertainties discussed in the preceding paragraph, we are unable to express an opinion on the financial statements. . .

The need for independent audits resulted from the emergence of the corporate form of business and the resulting separation of ownership and management. A significant proportion of the productive activity in the United States is conducted by publicly held corporations; that is, by corporations whose securities are sold to the general public. The stockholders who own the corporations are primarily investors and are generally not involved in enterprise operations. These investor-owners rely on management to operate the business and report periodically on the performance and financial status of the enterprise. Those companies registered nationally with the Securities and Exchange Commission are *required* to have an annual independent audit as an assurance to the stockholders.

Management has control over the information reported to stockholders and other external users and is responsible for the content of the financial statements. A statement emphasizing this responsibility is included in the annual report to stockholders, as illustrated for The Procter & Gamble Company in Exhibit 1—3. Management is also accountable for the profitability and financial condition of the enterprise as reflected in the statements. Obviously, there is a motivation on the part of management to present the financial information in the most favorable manner possible. It is the responsibility of the auditors to review management's reports and to independently decide if the reports are indeed representative of the actual conditions existing within the enterprise. The auditor's opinion adds credibility to the financial statements of enterprises, whether large or small, or privately or publicly held.

## Other Services Provided by CPAs

In addition to performing independent audits, CPAs assist clients in **tax planning** and reporting to various government entities. CPAs also function as management consultants, offering advice to clients in such areas as systems design, organization, personnel, finance, internal control, and employee benefits. These services are frequently referred to as **management advisory services.** Various accounting services are also provided for smaller, privately owned businesses.

---

[4]See also the auditor's report that accompanies the financial statements of IBM Corporation, reproduced in Appendix A at the end of the book. Note that Price Waterhouse, the firm that audits IBM's financial statements, uses a one-paragraph standard report that begins with the auditor's opinion. This variation is acceptable as it contains all the ingredients of the standard three-paragraph report.

**Exhibit 1—2    The Procter & Gamble Company—Auditors' Report**

## Report Of Independent Accountants

**Deloitte &
    Touche**
⟁

250 East Fifth Street
Cincinnati, Ohio 45202

To the Board of Directors and Shareholders of The Procter & Gamble Company:

We have audited the accompanying consolidated balance sheets of The Procter & Gamble Company and subsidiaries as of June 30, 1990 and 1989, and the related consolidated statements of earnings, retained earnings, and cash flows for each of the three years in the period ended June 30, 1990. These financial statements are the responsibility of the companies' management. Our responsibility is to express an opinion on these financial statements based on our audits.

We conducted our audits in accordance with generally accepted auditing standards. Those standards require that we plan and perform the audits to obtain reasonable assurance about whether the financial statements are free of material misstatement. An audit includes examining, on a test basis, evidence supporting the amounts and disclosures in the financial statements. An audit also includes assessing the accounting principles used and significant estimates made by management, as well as evaluating the overall financial statement presentation. We believe that our audits provide a reasonable basis for our opinion.

In our opinion, the financial statements referred to above present fairly, in all material respects, the financial position of the companies at June 30, 1990 and 1989, and the results of their operations and their cash flows for each of the three years in the period ended June 30, 1990, in conformity with generally accepted accounting principles.

*Deloitte & Touche*

August 9, 1990

**Exhibit 1—3    The Procter & Gamble Company—Statement of Management Responsibility**

## Responsibility For The Financial Statements

The financial statements of The Procter & Gamble Company and its subsidiaries are the responsibility of, and have been prepared by, the Company, in accordance with generally accepted accounting principles. To help insure the accuracy and integrity of its financial data, the Company has developed and maintains internal accounting controls which are designed to provide reasonable assurances that transactions are executed as authorized and accurately recorded, and that assets are properly safeguarded. These controls are monitored by an extensive program of internal audits.

The financial statements have been audited by the Company's independent public accountants, Deloitte & Touche. Their report is shown on page 33.

The Board of Directors has an Audit Committee composed entirely of outside Directors. The Committee meets periodically with representatives of Deloitte & Touche and financial management to review accounting, control, auditing, and financial reporting matters. To help assure the independence of the public accountants, Deloitte & Touche regularly meets privately with the Audit Committee.

## The Practice of Public Accounting

CPAs practice either individually or in firms. Because of the importance of personal liability for professional conduct, public accounting firms are generally organized as either proprietorships or partnerships. Most state laws now permit CPAs to be organized as professional corporations. These corporations provide many of the benefits of the corporate structure, but still retain personal liability for the professionals involved.

Almost all big, publicly held corporations are audited by a few large CPA firms. Listed in alphabetical order, the six largest firms are Arthur Andersen & Co.; Coopers & Lybrand; Deloitte & Touche; Ernst & Young; KPMG Peat Marwick; and Price Waterhouse & Co. Each of these firms is an international organization with many offices in the United States and abroad.

Many small businesses and nonprofit entities are serviced by regional and local CPA firms, including a large number of sole practitioners. In these firms, the role of auditing is often less important than the areas of tax reporting and planning and systems consulting. A CPA in a smaller firm is expected to be something of an accounting generalist, as opposed to the more specialized positions of CPAs in large regional and national firms. A vital role is played by the smaller public accounting firms in serving the thousands of small entities in the United States that are crucial to the nation's economy.[5]

## THE DEVELOPMENT OF ACCOUNTING STANDARDS

Accounting principles and procedures have evolved over hundreds of years. The formal standard-setting process that exists today, however, has developed in the past fifty years. Because accounting grew so rapidly with the advent of the Industrial Revolution, accounting procedures were often developed without extended debate or discussion. Accountants developed methods that seemed to meet the needs of their respective companies, resulting in diverse procedures among companies in accounting for similar activities. The comparability of the resulting financial reports, therefore, was often questionable.

During the 1920s, these differences led to financial statements that were often inflated in value. Market values of stocks rose higher than the underlying real values warranted until the entire structure collapsed in the stock market crash of 1929. The government of the United States, under the leadership of President Franklin D. Roosevelt, vigorously attacked the ensuing depression and, among other things, created the Securities and Exchange Commission (SEC). This new agency was given the responsibility to protect the interests of investors by ensuring full and fair disclosure in the regulation of the capital markets. The broad power granted to the SEC by Congress will be more fully discussed in a separate section. The emergence of the SEC forced the accounting profession in the U.S. to unite and to become more diligent in developing accounting principles and ethics to govern the profession. This led over time to the formation of several different private sector organizations, each having the responsibility of issuing accounting standards. These organizations, their publications, and the time they were in existence are identified in Exhibit 1—4 and discussed in subsequent sections of the chapter.

In the previous pages, three important groups that are involved with general-purpose financial statements were identified: users, managers of business enterprises, and independent auditors. As has been demonstrated, each of these groups has its own specific function to perform in the complex business environment that constitutes our economy. In

---

[5]According to a newsnote in *Forbes*, 98% of all the businesses in the United States are private proprietorships or partnerships. They account for one-third of the U.S. output, and 65 of them have revenues over $1 billion. "Who Needs Stockholders?" *Forbes* (November 18, 1985), p. 6.

## The Public Accounting Profession

Litigation, consulting, and internationalization are three areas of challenge facing the public accounting profession. Litigation is not a new concern; the number of suits filed against accountants during the 1970s and 1980s exceeded the number filed in the entire previous history of the profession. The suits can be especially expensive because auditors are sometimes held to be "jointly and severally liable" for the entire loss suffered by the plaintiffs. This means that if the stockholders of a bankrupt company win a $20 million judgment against the management and auditors of the company, the auditors may be held responsible to pay the whole $20 million if the other defendants (the management) do not have the means to pay.

Another challenge facing the public accounting profession is the slow growth in the market for audit services. Because of this, accounting firms are earning an increasing share of their revenues from performing consulting services. In fact, it has been suggested (only partly in jest) that the large accounting firms are becoming consulting firms that do a little auditing on the side. Increased consulting has both good and bad aspects. Consulting work typically is more profitable than are traditional audit services, but when accounting firms provide consulting services for the same clients that they audit, the auditors' independence is called into question.

The increased importance of consulting was partly responsible for the accounting firm mergers of the late 1980s. Increased size allowed the merged firms to offer a broad array of consulting services to their clients. Another factor in the mergers was the trend toward internationalization. In 1987 Peat Marwick, whose major operations were in the United States, merged with KMG Main Hurdman, which at the time had the biggest European accounting operations of any firm. The combined firm, KPMG Peat Marwick, was able to draw away several multinational clients from other accounting firms. One German client was quoted as saying: "They not only know German tax law and accounting backwards and forwards but speak German and give us guidance literature in German and English. The other Big Eight accounting firms can do this, but Peat has prepared itself earlier and better." International competitiveness was one reason given for the subsequent 1989 mergers of Ernst & Whinney with Arthur Young (now Ernst and Young) and Deloitte Haskins and Sells with Touche Ross (now Deloitte and Touche). These latter mergers reduced the Big Eight to the Big Six.

### Questions:

1. *Why would shareholders of a bankrupt company sue the auditors of the company?*
2. *Do you see anything wrong with independent public accountants doing consulting work? Let's say that one division of an accounting firm has a $30 million consulting contract with a client and that another division of the same accounting firm audits the financial statements of that client. Is there a conflict of interest?*
3. *Do you think it makes any difference how many large accounting firms there are? What if there were only four? Or two? Or one?*

Sources:

Lee Berton, "Peat Experience Shows Why Accountants Are Rushing to Merge," *The Wall Street Journal*, July 17, 1989: p. A1.

Stephen H. Miller, "Avoiding Lawsuits," *Journal of Accountancy*, September 1988: p. 57.

Richard Greene, "Blood on the Ledger," *Forbes*, May 18, 1987: p. 202.

many instances, these functions may be in conflict with each other. This condition provides another reason for the establishment of accounting standards—to resolve those different points of view that lead to different accounting methods being applied in similar circumstances.

**Exhibit 1—4    U.S. Accounting Standard-Setting Bodies**

| Standard-Setting Body | Date | Authoritative Publications |
|---|---|---|
| AICPA Committee on Accounting Procedures | 1939-1959 | Accounting Research Bulletins |
| Accounting Principles Board | 1959-1973 | APB Opinions |
| Financial Accounting Standards Board | 1973-present | Statements of Financial Accounting Standards Interpretations |

Standards are designed to help accountants apply consistent principles for different businesses. They are recognized by the profession as representing the generally accepted position of the profession, and must be followed in the preparation of financial statements unless circumstances warrant an exception to a standard. These standards are commonly referred to as **generally accepted accounting principles (GAAP)**. If the management of an enterprise feels the circumstances do not warrant compliance with the standard, an exception can be taken. Under these circumstances, the auditor's report must clearly disclose the nature of and the reason for the exception in the financial statements.[6]

## Financial Accounting Standards Board

The **Financial Accounting Standards Board (FASB)** is an independent organization consisting of seven full-time members drawn from professional accounting, business, government, and academia.[7] The members are required to sever all connections with their firms or institutions prior to assuming membership on the Board. Members are appointed for five-year terms and are eligible for reappointment to one additional term. Headquartered in Norwalk, Connecticut, the Board has its own research staff and an annual budget in excess of $13 million.

Funding for the FASB is obtained through the **Financial Accounting Foundation (FAF)**, an organization that is also responsible for selecting members of the FASB and its Advisory Council. (See Exhibit 1—5 for Financial Accounting Foundation organization chart.) The **Financial Accounting Standards Advisory Council** consults with the Board on major policy questions, selects task forces to work on specific major projects, and conducts such other activities as may be requested by the FASB. The Foundation is administered by a Board of Trustees whose 16 members are made up of representatives from eight sponsoring institutions as follows:

- American Accounting Association (AAA)
- American Institute of Certified Public Accountants (AICPA)
- Financial Analysts Federation (FAF)
- Financial Executives Institute (FEI)
- Institute of Management Accountants (IMA)

[6]American Institute of Certified Public Accountants, *Code of Professional Conduct*, Rule 203.

[7]Maintaining neutrality is sometimes difficult when complex issues affect so many groups in material ways. For example, in 1985, executives of business enterprises openly expressed their desire for more business representation on the FASB to assure that their interests were being considered. In a newspaper article, "The F.A.S.B. Comes Under Fire," Eric Berg, writing for *The New York Times*, stated that "It [business] has deluged foundation members with telephone calls and letters and has formed a committee with some of the most powerful financial executives in America to make sure more business executives get on the Board." *The New York Times*, August 18, 1985, Section 3, page 4.

- Securities Industry Associates (SIA)
- National Association of State Auditors, Comptrollers, and Treasurers (NASACT)
- Government Finance Officers Association (GFOA)

The latter two organizations were added in 1984 when the Foundation assumed responsibility for selecting members for a newly established organization, the **Governmental Accounting Standards Board (GASB)**. This Board was organized to establish standards in the governmental area.

**Exhibit 1—5    Financial Accounting Foundation Organizational Chart**

### The Standard-Setting Process

The major function of the FASB is to study accounting issues and establish accounting standards. These standards are published as **Statements of Financial Accounting Standards.** The FASB also issues **Statements of Financial Accounting Concepts.** The concepts identified in the statements are intended as guides for establishing standards. That is, they provide a framework within which specific accounting standards can be developed.[8]

Because the actions of the FASB have an impact on many individuals and groups within the economy, the Board follows a standard-setting process that is open to public observation and participation. The Board separates the topics it deals with into two areas: (1) Major Projects and (2) Implementation and Practice Problems. The process for the first area is very extensive and often requires from two to four years or more to complete. For example, significant events in the development of FASB Statement No. 87, "Employers' Accounting for Pensions," issued in 1985, and FASB Statement No. 106, "Employers' Accounting for Postretirement Benefits Other Than Pensions," issued in 1990, are listed in Exhibit 1—6.

Controversial issues, such as accounting for pensions, generate extensive debate and lobbying on the part of firms. As might be expected, the lobbying behavior of firms for and

[8]The conceptual framework of the FASB is discussed fully in Chapter 2.

**Exhibit 1—6    Significant Events in the Development of FASB Statements No. 87, "Employers' Accounting for Pensions," and No. 106, "Employers' Accounting for Postretirement Benefits Other Than Pensions"**

| | |
|---|---|
| 1974 | Pensions added to FASB agenda |
| 1975 | Task force appointed |
| 1975 | Discussion Memorandum #1 issued |
| 1976 | Public hearing #1 held |
| 1977 | Exposure Draft #1 issued |
| 1979 | Exposure Draft #1 revised; other postretirement benefits added to project |
| 1980 | FASB background paper issued |
| 1981 | Discussion Memorandum #2 issued |
| 1981 | Public hearing #2 held |
| 1982 | Preliminary Views document issued |
| 1983 | Supplement to Discussion Memorandum #2 issued |
| 1984 | Public hearing #3 held; other postretirement benefits made a separate project |
| 1985 | Exposure Draft #2 issued |
| 1985 | Public hearing #4 held |
| 1985 | Statement No. 87 issued in December |
| 1989 | Exposure Draft on other postretirement benefits issued and public hearing held |
| 1990 | Statement No. 106 issued in December |

against proposed accounting standards is not random; firms lobby against standards that they perceive will have a negative impact on their financial statements. For example, 218 industrial companies that submitted letters opposing the FASB's 1982 Preliminary Views document relating to pensions were compared with 582 similar companies that did not submit opposing letters. The comparison revealed that the companies opposed to the proposed pension accounting standard were more likely to be adversely affected by it (in terms of lower earnings or higher liabilities). One letter read: "Including the net pension liability on the balance sheet . . . could result in even higher borrowing costs and possibly jeopardize loan covenants and other regulatory requirements."[9]

While the sixteen years required to complete the pensions project exceed the normal period for Major Projects, this example illustrates how difficult it is to resolve some of the more complex accounting issues. The process for the second area, Implementation and Practice Problems, though still subject to public input, is designed for completion within a six- to twelve-month period.

**Major Projects**    For each major project undertaken by the Board, a task force of outside experts is appointed to study the existing literature. When available literature is deemed insufficient, additional research is conducted. Subsequently, the Board issues a **Discussion Memorandum** that identifies the principal issues involved with the topic. This document includes a discussion of the various points of view as to the resolution of the issues, but does not include specific conclusions. An extensive bibliography is usually included. Readers of the discussion memorandum are invited to comment either in writing or orally at a public hearing. Sometimes a topic is not identified well enough to issue a discussion memorandum, and the FASB issues a preliminary document identified as an "Invitation to Comment." The topic is briefly discussed in the document, and readers are encouraged to send their comments to the FASB for more definite formulation of specific issues.

---

[9]Jere R. Francis, "Lobbying Against Proposed Accounting Standards: The Case of Employers' Pension Accounting," *Journal of Accounting and Public Policy*, (Spring 1987), p. 35.

After a Discussion Memorandum has been issued and comments from interested parties have been evaluated, the Board meets as many times as necessary to resolve the issues. These meetings are open to the public, and the agenda is published in advance. From these meetings, the Board develops an **Exposure Draft** of a Statement that includes specific recommendations for financial accounting and reporting. Prior to 1991, a majority of the 7-member board (4 members) was the minimum requirement for approval of an exposure draft or a final statement of standards. This requirement was changed effective January 1, 1991, to a minimum approval of 5 members, or to what has been referred to as a "super majority."[10] After the exposure draft has been issued, reaction to the new document is again requested from the accounting and business community. At the end of the exposure period, usually 60 days or more, all comment papers are reviewed by the Staff and the Board. Further deliberation by the Board leads to either the issuance of a **Statement of Financial Accounting Standards**, to a revised Exposure Draft, or in some cases to abandonment of the project.

The final statement not only sets forth the actual standards, but also establishes the effective date and method of transition, and gives pertinent background information and the basis for the Board's conclusions, including reasons for rejecting significant alternative solutions. If any members dissent from the majority view, they may include the reasons for their dissent as part of the document.

**Implementation and Practice Problems**   The second category of issues dealt with by the Board involves implementation and practice problems that relate to previously issued standards. Depending on the nature of a problem, the Board may issue a Statement of Financial Accounting Standards or an **Interpretation of a Statement of Financial Accounting Standards**. The interpretation may be issued without appointing a task force, issuing a Discussion Memorandum, or holding public hearings. Exposure of these publications, however, to either the public or the Advisory Council is required as part of the due process followed by the Board.

Problems that arise in practice are also addressed in **Technical Bulletins** prepared and issued by the staff of the FASB. The Bulletins, which are reviewed by the Board prior to being issued, provide guidance for particular situations that arise in practice. In contrast with Standards and Interpretations, the staff Technical Bulletins do not have the authority of GAAP.

**Emerging Issues Task Force**   The long-term nature of the standard-setting process has been one of the principal points of criticism of the FASB. There seems to be no alternative to the lengthy process, however, given the philosophy that arriving at a consensus among members of the accounting profession and other interested parties is important to the Board's credibility.

In an effort to overcome this criticism and provide more timely guidance on issues, in 1984 the FASB established the **Emerging Issues Task Force (EITF)**. The Task Force assists the FASB in the early identification of emerging issues that affect financial reporting. The EITF consists of 14 members who include the senior technical partners of the major national CPA firms plus representatives from major associations of preparers of financial statements, such as the Institute of Management Accountants (IMA) and the Financial Executive Institute (FEI). They meet approximately every six weeks.

As an emerging issue is discussed, an attempt is made to arrive at a consensus treatment for the issue. If no more than two members disagree with a position, a consensus is

---

[10]A number of close 4-3 votes that resulted in standards not favored by many businessmen led to strong pressure on the Financial Accounting Foundation to change the voting requirements. Although not favored by members of the FASB, the change was made in 1990.

reached that defines the generally accepted accounting treatment until the FASB considers the issue. The EITF not only helps the FASB and its staff to better understand emerging issues, but in some cases the Task Force determines that no immediate FASB action is necessary because a diversity in practice is not likely to evolve.[11]

Abstracts of the FASB Emerging Issues Task Force are published periodically. They are identified by a two-part number; the first part represents the year the issue was discussed, and the second part identifies the issue number for that year. Over 220 issues were considered by the EITF during the period 1984-1989 and are summarized in the abstracts. Although many of the issues are very specialized by topic and industry, the importance of the EITF to the standard-setting process cannot be overemphasized. Because discussions rarely last more than a day or two, and a consensus is reached on a majority of the issues discussed, timely guidance is provided to the accounting profession without the often lengthy due process of the FASB.

The standard-setting procedures of the FASB are intended to help accomplish its mission, which is to establish and improve standards of financial accounting and reporting. The credibility of the Board has fluctuated through the years as different issues have been resolved. The FASB has no legislative power, but must depend on the general acceptance of its pronouncements by the accounting profession and other interested groups. This acceptability is directly influenced by two other organizations: the AICPA and the SEC.

## American Institute of Certified Public Accountants

The American Institute of Certified Public Accountants (AICPA) is the professional organization of practicing CPAs in the United States. The organization was founded in 1887, and it publishes a monthly journal, the *Journal of Accountancy*. Membership in the AICPA is voluntary, and over 300,000 CPAs are members. The AICPA has several important responsibilities including standard-setting, quality control, and certification and continuing education for CPAs.

**Standard-Setting Responsibilities**     Prior to the formation of the FASB, accounting principles were established under the direction of the AICPA. From 1939-1959, principles were formed by the AICPA's Committee on Accounting Procedures (CAP). Their pronouncements were known as Accounting Research Bulletins (ARBs). From 1959 to 1973, accounting principles were formed by another AICPA committee, the Accounting Principles Board (APB), and issued as Opinions. Dissatisfaction with the part-time nature of these committees, their failure to react quickly to some issues, and the lack of broad representation on the committees because of their direct relationship to the AICPA led to the formation of the FASB in 1973.

Although the FASB replaced the APB as the official standard-setting body for the profession, the AICPA continues to influence the establishment of accounting standards through its issuance of Accounting and Audit Guides and Statements of Position (SOPs). The Guides are issued by specially appointed committees of the AICPA and relate to specific industries, such as construction, insurance, banking, and real estate. These Guides contain information concerning the auditing of these entities, and also discuss alternative accounting methods that may be employed by the industry. The Guides often recommend a preferred accounting method. The SOPs were issued by the Accounting Standards Executive Committee (AcSEC), an AICPA committee established when the FASB assumed the standard-setting role. SOPs often dealt with emerging issues that had not yet been placed on the FASB agenda but needed to be addressed by the

[11]*EITF Abstracts*, October 26, 1989 (Norwalk: Financial Accounting Standards Board, 1989), p. i.

professions for improved comparability in financial reporting. Although the Guides and SOPS are not part of GAAP, they are considered Preferable Accounting Principles and may be looked upon as another important source of standards guidance.

The FASB became concerned about this growing volume of "other" standards, and in 1979 adopted the Guides and SOPs as officially preferred accounting principles subject to their review and possible subsequent issuance as FASB Statements.[12] Beginning in the early 1980s, many specialized industry guides were adopted as FASB standards. (See list of FASB standards in Appendix C of the text). Although SOPS are now being issued only to amend audit guides, AcSEC still helps the FASB identify emerging issues and communicates the concerns of CPAs on accounting issues to the FASB. Thus, the AICPA continues to influence the establishment of accounting standards.

In addition to influencing the establishment of accounting standards, the AICPA assumes direct responsibility for the establishment of auditing standards. The Auditing Standards Board is a part-time board of 15 members from public accounting practice with responsibility for establishing guidelines for the proper conduct of audits. Similar committees of the AICPA are responsible for establishing standards for the performance of tax and consulting services.

**Quality Control**   The AICPA is also concerned with maintaining the integrity of the profession through its Code of Professional Conduct and through a quality control program that includes a process of peer review of CPA firms conducted by other CPAs. Although membership in the AICPA traditionally has been individual, the influence of the firm has become increasingly important. In the late 1970s, the AICPA instituted a firm membership in one of two sections: (1) the **SEC Practice Section (SECPS)** for firms that have clients subject to government regulation through the Securities and Exchange Commission (SEC), and (2) the **Private Companies Practice Section (PCPS)** for firms that do not have clients regulated by the SEC. The SEC practice firms are subject to more stringent regulation than the private companies practice firms, although a high quality of performance is expected of all firms.

In late 1989, the AICPA membership voted by a more than six-to-one margin to make membership in the SECPS a requirement for all firms that audit any companies that are SEC registrants. Before this vote, membership in both sections was voluntary. A firm may belong to both sections, and most of the larger firms do. Both sections require periodic peer reviews of all its members. In addition, since 1988, the AICPA has required a quality review program of all its members. While this review is not as extensive as a peer review, it is designed to upgrade the quality of work done in the profession. Thus, those members without SEC clients who do not join the PCPS must still submit to periodic quality reviews.

The quality review requirement was only one of several requirements approved by the AICPA membership to address an issue that arose primarily in the 1980s referred to as the "expectation gap." This gap is identified as the difference between how users of financial statements interpreted the auditor's responsibilities and how auditors themselves viewed their responsibilities. Users felt auditors should alert them earlier to a firm's financial difficulties, and thus protect their investments from loss. The auditing profession addressed this problem and issued a group of ten new auditing standards in mid-1988 to identify more clearly the auditor's responsibilities for detection of fraud, evaluation of a company's internal control, and identification of companies unlikely to be able to con-

---

[12]*Statement of Financial Accounting Standards No. 32,* "Specialized Accounting and Reporting Principles and Practices in AICPA Statements of Position and Guides on Accounting and Auditing Matters" (Stamford: Financial Accounting Standards Board, 1979).

tinue operations. These new regulations and standards are having a significant impact on the auditing profession.

**Certification and Continuing Education**    Another important function of the AICPA is preparation and grading of the Uniform CPA examination. This examination is given simultaneously in all fifty states and the U.S. territories twice each year—in May and November. Currently, the CPA examination covers two and one-half days; however, beginning in May 1994, this will be reduced to 2 days and a revised format will be implemented. In addition to passing the examination, an individual must meet the state education and experience requirements in order to obtain state certification as a CPA. Most states now require CPAs to meet continuing education requirements in order to retain their licenses to practice. The AICPA assists its members in meeting these requirements through an extensive Continuing Professional Education (CPE) program that includes courses offered throughout the United States.

## Securities and Exchange Commission

The Securities and Exchange Commission (SEC) was created by an act of Congress in 1934. Its primary role is to regulate the issuance and trading of securities by corporations to the general public. Prior to offering securities for sale to the public, a company must file a registration statement with the Commission that contains financial and organizational disclosures. In addition, all publicly held companies are required to furnish annual and other periodical information to the Commission and to have their external financial statements examined by independent accountants.

The Commission's intent is not to prevent the trading of speculative securities, but to insist that investors have adequate information. As a result, the SEC is vitally interested in financial reporting and the development of accounting standards. The Commission carefully monitors the standard-setting process and responds to Discussion Memorandums and Exposure Drafts issued by the FASB. The Commission also brings to the Board's attention emerging problems that need to be addressed and sends observers to meet with the Emerging Issues Task Force.

When the Commission was formed, Congress gave it power to establish accounting principles as follows:

> The Commission may prescribe, in regard to reports made pursuant to this title, the form or forms in which the required information shall be set forth, the items or details to be shown in the balance sheet and the earning statement, and the methods to be followed in the preparation of reports, in the appraisal or valuation of assets and liabilities . . .[13]

The Commission has generally refrained from fully using these powers, preferring to work through the private sector in the development of standards. Throughout its existence, however, the Commission has issued statements pertaining to accounting and auditing issues. Most of them are quite specific in nature and deal with a particular company or a specific situation. At present, SEC statements are referred to as either **Financial Reporting Releases (FRRs)** or **Accounting and Auditing Enforcement Releases (AAERs)**. Prior to 1982, they were referred to as **Accounting Series Releases (ASRs)**. Although the SEC is generally supportive of the FASB, from time to time the Commission intervenes in the standard-setting process. The SEC has been credited, for example, with requiring experimentation with current value disclosure when it appeared

[13]Securities Exchange Act of 1934, Section 13(b).

that the FASB was going to recommend an alternative approach to reporting inflation information.[14]

## American Accounting Association

The **American Accounting Association** is primarily an organization for accounting academicians, although practicing professional accountants also belong in large numbers. The oldest regular publication of the AAA is a quarterly research journal, *The Accounting Review*. It has been published since 1926. In 1983, a second journal was added, *Issues in Accounting Education*. Although this educator's journal began as an annual publication, it is now published semiannually. Beginning in March 1987, the AAA began publishing another quarterly general-audience journal, *Accounting Horizons*. This newest journal is designed to address issues of wide interest to both educators and practitioners that stress real-world accounting problems and practices and thus attract a wider readership than *The Accounting Review*.

Several specialized sections have been organized within the AAA, and many of these also publish journals. Accounting academicians are very interested in the development of accounting standards. They have the unique position of being professionals not directly involved with the preparation or audit of financial statements. Thus, they are able to consider objectively the needs of users as well as business enterprises and auditors. The AAA was instrumental in encouraging development by the FASB of a conceptual framework for accounting that would assist in the development of standards to govern financial reporting. AAA committee members review FASB Discussion Memorandums and Exposure Drafts and respond to the proposals of the FASB. Individual members of the association participate actively in research projects that are used by the FASB as the basis for many of its recommendations.[15]

The members of the American Accounting Association hold many different opinions and points of view. One of the major roles of the AAA is to serve as a forum within which educators can express their views, either individually or in specially appointed committees. The AAA, however, does not claim to serve as a majority voice for accounting academicians and, until recently, had a firm policy against taking positions on accounting issues as an association. A new policy was adopted in 1988 that permits the Executive Committee of the AAA to take positions representing its membership as needed. The impact of the academic arm of accounting on the establishment of accounting standards has increased through the years, as evidenced by inclusion of an educator as a member of the FASB and the large number of educators included on FASB task forces and the FASB staff.

## Other Organizations

Although the preceding groups have traditionally exercised the most direct influence upon the regulation of accountants and the development of accounting principles, the influence of other groups has also been felt. Professional accountants from business enterprises are represented on the Board of Trustees of the Financial Accounting Foundation by two organizations, the **Financial Executives Institute (FEI)** and the **Institute of Management Accountants (IMA),** formerly National Association of Accountants.

---

[14]For additional information on the SEC, see K. Fred Skousen, *An Introduction to the SEC*, 5th edition (Cincinnati: South-Western Publishing Co., 1990).

[15]Indicative of this type of research is the following report issued as background for a specific standard. Dennis R. Beresford, Lawrence C. Best, Paul W. Craig, and Joseph V. Weber, *Accounting for Income Taxes: A Review of Alternatives* (Stamford: Financial Accounting Standards Board, 1983).

The FEI is a national organization composed of financial executives employed by large corporations. The FEI membership includes treasurers, controllers, and financial vice-presidents. The FEI has sponsored several research projects through the years related to financial reporting problems.

The IMA is more concerned with the information needs of internal users than with external reporting. Its monthly publication, *Management Accounting,* has traditionally dealt mainly with problems involving information systems and the development and use of accounting data within the business organization. It awards the **Certificate of Management Accounting (CMA)** to those management accountants who pass a 2½-day qualifying examination and meet specified experience requirements. Because a firm's information system usually provides data for both internal and external reporting, the NAA is also concerned about the activities of the FASB and responds to its invitations to comment on issues that are related to internal reporting.

The users of external financial reports are also represented on the Financial Accounting Foundation's Board of Trustees by two organizations. The **Financial Analysts Federation** represents the large number of analysts who advise the investing public on the meaning of the financial reports issued by America's businesses. Members of this group have often been critical of corporate financial reporting practices and have continually requested increased disclosure of pertinent financial data. The **Securities Industry Associates** is the organization that represents the investment bankers who manage the portfolios of the large institutional investors that have affected the stock market so dramatically in the past decade. The large amount of investment capital controlled by insurance companies and banks has significantly diminished the influence of the small investor in the market. Institutional investors represent a major group of external users of financial information and have become increasingly vocal with regard to financial reporting and the establishment of accounting standards.

Although the preceding discussion of accounting standards has focused on reporting by business enterprises, the accounting profession is also concerned with the reporting by the numerous government institutions in our economy. This includes not only the Federal Government and its agencies, but also the large number of states, counties, and municipal governments. It is estimated that the total expenditures by these government organizations exceed 1.5 trillion dollars per year. Two government organizations were added to the list of sponsors of the FAF in 1984—the **National Association of State Auditors, Treasurers, and Controllers** and the **Government Finance Officers Association.** These organizations are especially interested in the standards issued by the **Governmental Accounting Standards Board,** a companion board to the FASB organized in 1984 to focus on reporting by the public sector of our economy. Although the statements issued by governmental organizations do not have a direct impact on investors, the magnitude of their impact on such vital economic factors as interest rates, tax policies, and employment rates cannot be ignored in any financial planning. Creditors are especially affected by the financial activities of governmental units that require funding through various forms of bonds and long-term notes.

Although the FASB and the GASB are independent boards, their jurisdictional bounds at times have been subject to much discussion. Some types of entities, such as hospitals and universities, exist in both the private and public (government) sectors of our economy. Because the FASB is responsible for establishing accounting standards for these institutions in the private sector, and the GASB is responsible for those in the government sector, a lack of comparability can exist on several issues. In 1989, the Financial Accounting Foundation decided that in these areas with conflicting jurisdictions, the FASB would govern. When the government sector objected strenuously to this proposal, the Foundation reversed itself and left the jurisdiction divided, with a commitment from the public sector to consider more carefully the problem of differing standards for essentially the same type of organization.

Another government unit of great interest to the accounting profession is the **Internal Revenue Service**. Although tax accounting and financial accounting impact one another only indirectly in most cases, the popular perception is that they are one and the same. However, it must be kept in mind that tax accounting and financial accounting were designed with different purposes in mind. In the Thor Power Tool Case (1979), the Supreme Court stated:

> The primary goal of financial accounting is to provide useful information to management, shareholders, creditors, and others properly interested; the major responsibility of the accountant is to protect these parties from being misled. The primary goal of the income tax system, in contrast, is the equitable collection of revenue. . .

### International Standard-Setting

While the FASB establishes accounting standards for U.S. entities, other countries have their own standard-setting bodies. Often, because of cultural and historical differences, the standards developed in these countries differ from those developed by the FASB for the United States. This creates many reporting problems for foreign companies doing business in the United States and domestic companies doing business in foreign countries. In an attempt to harmonize conflicting standards, the **International Accounting Standards Committee (IASC)** was formed in 1973 to develop worldwide accounting standards. This body now represents more than 100 accountancy bodies from 75 countries. It serves to the world community what the FASB does to the U.S. business community. The globalization of the business community makes these cooperative efforts increasingly important if financial reporting is to achieve on a worldwide basis the objectives discussed in the previous pages.[16]

---

## IMPACT OF ACCOUNTING STANDARDS

As discussed earlier in this chapter, accounting information plays a critical role in the economic decision-making process. Thus, the standards applied in financial reporting have a significant impact on the allocation of resources in our economy.

### Professional Judgment

Many accounting standards provide general guidelines rather than precise rules. The accountant, therefore, must exercise professional judgment in interpreting and applying standards. For example, FASB Statement No. 5, "Accounting for Contingencies," states that a contingent loss and the related liability should be recognized in the financial statements only if it is "probable" that an actual future loss will be sustained. It is up to the accountant and the auditor to decide whether it is "probable" that an event, such as a lawsuit, will result in a definite liability. The accountant's decision has a direct impact on the information reported on the financial statements.

Texaco Inc. provides an interesting example of the difficulty in applying the contingent liability standards. On December 10, 1985, a Texas district court entered judgment for Pennzoil Company against Texaco Inc. for $11 billion. This was only $3 billion less

[16]Dennis Beresford, "Commentary on Internationalization of Accounting Standards," *Accounting Horizons*, March 1990, pp. 99-106.

than Texaco's total stockholders' equity at the time of the judgment. Texaco appealed the ruling, which arose from a conflict over attempts to acquire Getty Oil Company, claiming it was excessive and would destroy the company. In its 1985 and 1986 financial statements, Texaco included a lengthy note describing the litigation and the appeal process. The note stated that because Texaco Inc. "believes that there is no legal basis for the judgment, which it believes is contrary to the evidence and applicable law,"[17] no provision for the judgment was included in the balance sheet or the income statement at December 31, 1985 or 1986. On April 12, 1987, Texaco filed a petition for relief under Chapter 11 bankruptcy laws, and agreed to a restructuring of its assets and liabilities. On December 19, 1987, after failing to obtain a reversal of the judgment, Texaco Inc. reached an agreement with Pennzoil. The agreed settlement included a $3 billion cash payment to Pennzoil from Texaco as full settlement of the earlier judgment.

The 1987 financial statements included the agreed settlement of $3 billion as an expense. The 1987 statements also included a lengthy note on "Chapter 11—Plan of Reorganization." The auditor's report that accompanied the 1987 financial statements included the following explanatory paragraph and conclusion:

### Exhibit 1—7     Texaco Inc.

As more fully described in Notes 1 and 16 to the consolidated financial statements, a judgment, which may be subject to further appeal, has been rendered against Texaco Inc. in the Pennzoil litigation. On April 12, 1987, Texaco Inc. and two of its subsidiaries (the Debtor Companies) each filed a Voluntary Petition for Relief under Chapter 11, Title 11 of the United States Code. The Debtor Companies are operating their businesses as debtors-in-possession subject to the jurisdiction of the U.S. Federal Court. The accompanying financial statements have been prepared on a going-concern basis which contemplates the realization of assets and payment of liabilities in the ordinary course of business. The financial statements do not give effect to all reclassifications and may not give effect to all adjustments that could result from any plans, arrangements or actions which might arise out of the reorganization proceedings, as the eventual outcome of these proceedings is not presently determinable.

In our opinion, subject to the effect, if any, that might have been required had the outcome of the uncertainties referred to in the preceding paragraph been known, the financial statements referred to above present fairly the financial position of Texaco Inc. and subsidiary companies as of December 31, 1987 and 1986, and the results of their operations and the changes in their financial position for each of the three years in the period ended December 31, 1987, in conformity with generally accepted accounting principles applied on a consistent basis.

### Alternative Accounting Principles

In many areas, there is more than one generally accepted principle or standard for reporting events or transactions. Examples include depreciation of plant assets, inventory valuation, and costs of long-term construction contracts. The choice of one standard rather than another can have a material effect on financial statements.

For example, in 1988 The Penn Central Corporation changed its method of valuing some of its inventories from FIFO to LIFO. The income statement for the year reported net income of $103.4 million and earnings per share of $1.46. Had Penn Central continued to value its inventories under the FIFO method, net income would have decreased by $7.4 million and earnings per share by $.10. The inventory reported on the balance sheet would have declined by $20 million, or by 8%.

[17]Texaco Inc. and Subsidiary Companies 1986 Consolidated Financial Statements, Note 17.

Reported financial information can have far-reaching effects. The announcement of net income which is lower than expected has been shown to lead to a decline in stock price. A decrease in reported earnings may also restrict a company's ability to pay dividends. Also, employees may suffer since many companies tie employee bonuses to reported net income. Increased levels of liabilities may cause a company to be in violation of existing debt agreements, leading to costly renegotiation, and may also restrict the company's ability to borrow in the future. Reported poor financial condition can also adversely affect a company's relationship with its suppliers, dealers, and even its customers.

These are just a few examples of the impact of accounting standards and their application. They are intended to underscore the importance of accounting information and the standards applied in developing that information.

## FINANCIAL REPORTING IN A COMPLEX BUSINESS ENVIRONMENT

The environment within which business and accounting function has become increasingly complex. One of its characteristic features is its state of continual change due to the many social, political, legal, and economic influences. Technology has developed new products that have led to a dramatic shift from a capital-intensive industrial economy in the United States to a labor-intensive information technology economy. Government continues to influence the economy through its budget deficits, tax regulations, international trade policy, and actions to control inflation. World markets have become closer as businesses have increased their international involvement and funds have become increasingly fluid in movement around the world. If accounting is to continue to be the "language of business," it must adapt to these complex, changing relationships.

This dynamic environment means that financial reporting must reflect these environmental factors. For example, the technological revolution of the past few years has included a significant increase in the use of computers, both in business and in the home. Thousands of companies, many quite small, have been formed to produce wide varieties of computer software for public consumption. The financial reporting issue involved concerns the treatment of costs to develop the software. There is always uncertainty as to whether the cost to develop the software will be recovered in the marketplace. Should these costs be reported as assets before the judgment of the marketplace is known, or should they be charged to expense and written off against revenue?[18]

Another example of how our complex environment affects financial reporting is the financial marketplace. It is continuing to develop new instruments that adapt to the rapid changes in the economy. Interest-rate swaps, zero-coupon bonds, interest-only strips, and mandatory redeemable preferred stock are a few of the financial instruments that have emerged in the past few years. Some have suggested that the financial activities of businesses are being revolutionized by these new instruments, and that financial reporting is having trouble keeping up. To address these complex issues, the FASB is reexamining some of the fundamental notions underlying financial reporting, such as how to distinguish between debt and equity.

The changing business environment creates the need to review existing standards to see if they require revision. The FASB, which has issued over 100 standards in its 20 years of existence, has adopted a policy of continually reviewing its pronouncements to see if modification is needed.

---

[18]The FASB responded to this question by issuing *Statement of Financial Accounting Standards No. 86,* "Accounting for Computer Software Costs" (Stamford: Financial Accounting Standards Board, 1985). See Chapter 12 for detailed discussion of this topic.

## The FASB: What's Right and What's Wrong With It

The FASB frequently has been the center of considerable controversy. FASB Statement No. 94, "Consolidation of All Majority-Owned Subsidiaries," mandated that the consolidated financial statements of parent companies include financing subsidiaries (GMAC, for example, must now be included in the statements of its parent corporation, General Motors). Many users claim that key financial ratios have been rendered meaningless by this requirement. FASB Statement No. 96, "Accounting for Income Taxes," has drawn more criticism than any other statement since the FASB's inception. Because of continuing complaints about FASB Statement No. 96, its effective date was delayed first by one year, and then again by another two years. Critics have also complained that the FASB's new Statement No. 106, "Employers' Accounting for Postretirement Benefits Other Than Pensions," will add hundreds of billions of dollars in liabilities to corporate balance sheets. The outcry against the FASB reached its pinnacle in an article in *Business Week* entitled "First Thing We Do Is Kill All the Accountants."

It is certainly the case that some of the criticism aimed at the FASB has been self-serving. Opposition to the postretirement benefits proposal seems to stem more from a concern over its effect on income than from any disagreement with the underlying rationale. However, some of the criticisms are well founded. Tom Jones, Citicorp's senior vice president—finance, was quoted as saying: "The FASB's tax standard is requiring us to figure out complex tax schedules for operations in 90 countries and at least 30 states and has taken up to 15 people at the bank almost 12 months to calculate." Mr. Jones estimated that it cost Citicorp about $3 million to implement the provisions of FASB Statement No. 96.

In all its deliberations, the FASB must walk a fine line between practicality and technical soundness. It has been suggested that excessive meddling by outside groups helped lead to the death of the FASB's predecessor, the Accounting Principles Board. Similar pressures are now being brought to bear on the FASB.

The FASB and the Financial Accounting Foundation have responded to the criticism. A standing trustee committee has been appointed by the FAF to review FASB operations on a continuing basis. This review process includes periodic meetings between Foundation trustees and individual FASB members to discuss performance.

Some financial executives have run out of patience with the FASB and are ready to trust the setting of accounting standards to Congress or the SEC. However, most people involved still favor retaining the standard-setting power in the private sector. According to John Burton, professor of accounting at Columbia University and former chief accountant at the SEC: "As faulty as accounting rule-making may be, it's still better to keep Congress out of the act. Otherwise, politics would take over and there'd be no chance for standard-setters to come to their senses now and then."

### Questions:

1. *The assertion that implementation of an accounting rule would cost a company $3 million seems to be a good argument against that rule. What other reasons might a company have for opposing a new accounting rule?*
2. *What factors would favor entrusting the setting of accounting standards to the SEC? To the FASB?*
3. *What do you think should be the FASB's most important consideration when setting accounting standards?*

Sources:

Lee Berton, "Accounting-Board Rulings Make Business See Red," *The Wall Street Journal*, March 21, 1989: p. A24.

Lee Berton, "FASB Group, Stung by Firms' Criticism. To Keep Tighter Rein on Rule Making," *The Wall Street Journal*, June 13, 1989: p. A5.

Dennis R. Beresford, "What's Right With the FASB," *Journal of Accountancy*, January 1990: p. 81.

## CONFLICT BETWEEN PUBLIC AND PRIVATE SECTOR

As indicated previously, the SEC has historically left the standard-setting process to the private sector. The Commission's influence, however, has often been felt on specific issues. From time to time, Congress has urged the SEC to exercise a more direct role in setting financial accounting standards and in evaluating the independence and quality control of CPA firms. Over the past two decades, there have been many legal actions brought against CPA firms for failure to disclose fairly the financial condition of a company. These legal actions have become more common, and as they arise, Congress, through its committee structure, again raises difficult questions about whether the standard-setting system in the private sector is working for the benefit of the public.

In 1978 there were two significant congressional committees that conducted hearings concerning the accounting profession: the Metcalf Committee, chaired by Senator Lee Metcalf (Montana), and the Moss Committee, chaired by Representative John E. Moss (California). A Senate staff report entitled "The Accounting Establishment" was used extensively by the committees as they probed such issues as the possible monopoly position of the largest U.S. accounting firms; the independence of auditors whose firms employ tax consultants and management advisory consultants who work directly with audit clients; and the poor quality of audit work being performed in some instances. Although no definite legislative action was taken, these committees attracted a great deal of attention from the profession, and several changes were made by the AICPA as a result of these hearings, including its establishment of the firm membership divisions. Also, as a result of these hearings, annual reports from the SEC on the auditing profession are now required by Congress. These reports have generally been positive; however, another increase in business failures in the mid and late 1980s, including many savings and loan failures, led to another round of hearings under the direction of Representative John Dingell of Michigan. The SEC commissioned a blue ribbon committee to study the issue of fraudulent financial reporting. Their report, known as the Treadway Report after its chairman Robert Treadway, made several specific recommendations to management, auditors, and educators to help detect and deter management fraud.[19] The congressional Dingell Committee urged the various sectors to study the Treadway Report carefully, and generally agreed with the recommendations to improve audit quality.

Although much attention is paid to the audit function by these congressional committees, there also has been concern over the establishment of accounting standards. Critics of standard-setting in the private sector ask if it is realistic to assume that the profession can establish and administer standards and still retain an independent posture. Congress

[19]Several large fraud cases emerged in the late 1980s. Among the more prominent were EMS Securities, a case where the auditor accepted money to issue fraudulent reports, and ZZZZ Best, a case where millions of dollars of phony business were not detected by the auditors before fraudulent reports were issued. As the 1990s begin, several multimillion dollar suits have been brought against CPA firms involved in audits of savings and loan institutions. The magnitude of these suits threatens the financial stability of even the largest of these firms.

continues to prod the SEC to exercise a more active role in assuring that financial reporting is adequately measuring and disclosing the true status of companies and their activities. The FASB has responded to this pressure by its open discussion policy and its attempt to arrive at standards that balance theory and varying user needs.

Regardless of who sets accounting standards, the task is difficult. As will be discussed in the next chapter, there are very few absolutes in accounting principles. As evidenced by the voluminous tax legislation and the extreme difficulty in achieving tax simplification, passing the responsibility for accounting standard-setting to the SEC or a similar governmental agency would probably lead to even greater complexity in financial reporting. If accountants are to retain their role as professionals, they must be able to exercise judgment in applying general guidelines to specific problems. Financial statement users, managers of business enterprises, and professional auditors must balance their needs and views and continue to work toward more meaningful accounting and financial reporting. If these users cannot obtain meaningful reports through private sector organizations such as the FASB, there will be increased demand from the public through Congress to do it by legislation.

## OVERVIEW OF INTERMEDIATE ACCOUNTING

This first chapter is designed to emphasize the importance of accounting and financial reporting in today's complex business environment and the challenges that face those who are members of the accounting profession. The remaining chapters of the text cover in depth the elements contained in the basic financial statements presented to external users. To help students realize that the issues discussed are not just textbook issues, extensive examples of actual businesses are included throughout the book.

Although there has been a growing body of standards that constitute GAAP, there are many unresolved areas. In some cases, the existing standards have been questioned, and recommendations for revision of the standards have been made. It is important that those who plan to enter the profession of accounting have a foundation as to not only what GAAP currently is, but also have a theoretical understanding of why it developed to its present state.

## KEY TERMS

Accounting 3
Accounting and Audit Guides 14
Accounting and Auditing
  Enforcement Releases (AAERs)
  16
Accounting Principles Board (APB)
  14
Accounting Research Bulletins
  (ARBs) 14
Accounting Series Releases (ASRs)
  16
American Accounting Association
  (AAA) 17
American Institute of Certified
  Public Accountants (AICPA) 14

Certified Public Accountants
  (CPAs) 5
Committee on Accounting
  Procedures (CAP) 14
Discussion Memorandum 12
Emerging Issues Task Force (EITF)
  13
Exposure Draft 13
Financial accounting 4
Financial Accounting Foundation
  (FAF) 10
Financial Accounting Standards
  Advisory Council 10
Financial Accounting Standards
  Board (FASB) 10

Financial Analysts Federation 18
Financial Executives Institute (FEI)
  17
Financial Reporting Releases (FRRs)
  16
Generally accepted accounting
  principles (GAAP) 10
General-purpose financial
  statements 4
Governmental Accounting
  Standards Board (GASB) 11
Independent audit 5
Institute of Management
  Accountants (IMA) 17

---

# QUESTIONS

1. Accounting has been defined as a service activity. Who is served by accounting and how are they benefited?
2. Accounting is sometimes characterized as dealing only with the past. Give three examples of how accounting information can be of value in dealing with the future.
3. How does the fact that there are limited resources in the world relate to accounting information?
4. Distinguish between management accounting and financial accounting.
5. Contrast the roles of an accountant and an auditor.
6. Why are independent audits necessary?
7. How has the merger of several large accounting firms improved the ability of these firms to deal with international clients?
8. What conditions led to the establishment of accounting standard-setting bodies?
9. What are the differences in purpose and scope of the FASB's Statements of Financial Accounting Standards, Statements of Financial Accounting Concepts, Interpretations of Statements of Financial Accounting Standards, and Technical Bulletins?
10. What characteristics of the standard-setting process are designed to increase the acceptability of standards established by the FASB?
11. (a) What role does the Emerging Issues Task Force play in establishing accounting standards? (b) Why can it meet this role more efficiently than the FASB?
12. What are the relationships of the AICPA and the AAA to the FASB?
13. What is the purpose of the AICPA peer review program and which firms are required to submit to such a review?
14. How does the SEC influence the accounting profession?
15. Why is standard setting such a difficult and complex task?
16. Why is Congress conducting hearings on the accounting profession? What type of legislation has been proposed to increase control over accounting?

---

# DISCUSSION CASES

### Case 1—1    (How should I invest?)

Recent projections suggest that members of the "baby boom" generation will inherit as much as $8 trillion from their parents. Assume that you just inherited $1 million. You are aware that numerous studies have shown that investments in equity securities (stocks) give the highest rate of return over the long run. However, you are not sure which companies you should invest in. You send for and receive the annual reports of several companies in three growth industries.

In making your investment decision, what useful information would you expect to find in:

(a) the balance sheet?
(b) the income statement?
(c) the statement of cash flows?

### Case 1—2    (And then there were six!)

The existence of relatively few large CPA firms that service virtually all of the major industrial and financial companies and thus dominate the accounting profession has led to criticism through the years. During 1989, mergers among the large public accounting firms in the United States changed the Big Eight into the Big Six.

(a) What dangers do you see from the emergence of relatively few large CPA firms? What advantages?

(b) One reason offered for the mergers is that they improved the ability of merging firms to provide the broad array of consulting services that provide an increasing share of the revenues of the large accounting firms. What problems might intensify as public accounting firms earn an ever-larger share of their income from consulting?

### Case 1—3  (What do users need?)

The definition of accounting quoted in this chapter stresses that information generated by an accounting system should be useful for making decisions. There are two basic types of users: those outside the company (external users) and those within the company (internal users). Distinguish between the types of information these two user groups would need in order to make their decisions.

### Case 1—4  (SEC: A necessary evil?)

Annette Wilson and Henry Wall were selected to compete with students from other universities in presenting a case dealing with the need for a government agency with oversight responsibility to monitor the quality of accounting in the private sector.

Draft an outline showing the points you think Annette and Henry should make.

### Case 1—5  (How can accounting standards be taught?)

The FASB issues statements of standards, statements of concepts, interpretations, positions, and technical bulletins. The FASB's Emerging Issues Task Force issues consensus statements. The SEC issues releases. The AICPA produces position statements and audit guides. With this proliferation of authoritative material, some see the practice of accounting becoming more like the practice of law.

Describe some of the difficulties in accounting education that are caused by the complex nature of accounting standards.

### Case 1—6  (We aren't getting what we expect.)

Quality Enterprises Inc. issued its 1992 financial statements on February 22, 1993. The auditors expressed a "clean" opinion in the audit report. On July 14, 1993, the company filed for bankruptcy as a result of an inability to meet currently maturing long-term debt obligations. Reasons cited for the action include (1) large losses on inventory due to overproduction of product lines that did not sell, (2) failure to collect on a large account receivable due to the customer's bankruptcy, and (3) a deteriorating economic environment caused by a severe recession in the spring of 1993. Joan Stevens, a large stockholder of Quality, is concerned about the fact that a company with a clean audit opinion could have financial difficulty leading to bankruptcy just four months after the audit report was issued. "Where were the auditors?" she inquired. In reply, the auditors contend that on December 31, 1992, the date of the financial statements, the statements were presented in accordance with GAAP.

What is the auditor's responsibility for protecting users from losses? How does this case illustrate the "expectation gap" issue?

### Case 1—7  (Does lobbying improve the quality of accounting standards?)

The "due process" system of the FASB encourages public input into the standard-setting process. Written comments are invited, public hearings are held, and proposed standards are often changed in response to this input. However, some observers have suggested that this process makes the setting of accounting standards less a technical exercise and more a political one. Parties are known to lobby for or against proposed standards according to their economic interests.

(a) How would accounting standard-setting be improved by eliminating lobbying?

(b) How would accounting standard-setting be harmed by eliminating lobbying?

# CHAPTER 2

# A Conceptual Framework of Accounting

---

---

In 1987, General Motors elected to change the estimated useful life of its tools and dies. The change resulted in an increase in income from operations of over $1.2 billion, accounting for approximately 25% of earnings for that year. If accounting rules allow such flexibility and judgment in the reporting of revenues and expenses, is accounting more of an art or a science? Should accounting standards allow management such discretion in reporting financial information?

Contrary to the preceding example, the general public often views accounting as a scientific discipline based on a fixed set of rules and procedures. This is a natural perception since the public's exposure to accounting generally relates to financial statements, tax returns, and other reports showing dollar amounts that give an impression of exactness. Those within the profession, however, recognize that accounting is more an art than a science and that the operating results and other accounting measurements are based on estimates and judgments relative to the measurement and communication of business activity.

Even though accounting professionals must rely on their judgment, accounting and financial reporting are governed by a well-established body of "generally accepted accounting principles," referred to as GAAP. As explained in Chapter 1, GAAP includes standards and interpretations issued by the FASB and those pronouncements issued by previous standard-setting bodies that have not been suspended or superseded. Underlying these principles or standards are several fundamental concepts and assumptions that collectively provide a theoretical or conceptual framework of accounting. This chapter focuses on the need for such a framework and examines the major components of the FASB's conceptual framework.

## NEED FOR A CONCEPTUAL FRAMEWORK

Much has been written about the theoretical foundation or **conceptual framework** that underlies accounting practice. There are several reasons why such a framework is important. One major purpose is to provide broad definitions of the objectives, terms, and concepts involved in the practice of accounting. This definitional aspect of the framework prescribes the boundaries of accounting and financial reporting.

A strong theoretical foundation is essential if accounting practice is to keep pace with a changing business environment. Accountants are continually faced with new situations, technological advances, and business innovations that present new accounting and reporting problems. These problems must be dealt with in an organized and consistent manner. If their impact is sufficiently broad, specific issues may be resolved through the FASB's standard-setting process. The conceptual framework plays a vital role in the development of new standards and in the revision of previously issued standards. Recognizing the importance of this role, the FASB stated that fundamental concepts "guide the Board in developing accounting and reporting standards by providing . . . a common foundation and basic reasoning on which to consider merits of alternatives."[1] In a very real sense, then, the FASB itself is a primary beneficiary of a conceptual framework.

A conceptual framework also brings together the objectives and fundamentals of existing accounting practice and financial reporting. This helps users to better understand the purposes, content, and characteristics of information provided by accounting.

A conceptual framework not only helps in understanding existing practice, but it also provides a guide for future practice. When accountants are confronted with new developments that are not covered by GAAP, a conceptual framework provides a reference for analyzing and resolving emerging issues.

A conceptual framework is also useful in selecting the most appropriate methods for reporting enterprise activity. Often, there is more than one justifiable or generally accepted reporting alternative for a particular transaction or event, and accountants must use their judgment in selecting among available alternatives. Fundamental concepts provide guidance in choosing the alternative that most accurately reflects the financial position and results of operations for the entity given the specific circumstances involved. If businesses and their activities were identical, reporting alternatives could be eliminated. However, that is not the case. Even within a particular industry, companies are not organized in exactly the same way. They do not produce identical products nor provide identical services, and their accounting systems and the reports generated therefrom are not uniform. Thus, accountants must exercise professional judgment in fulfilling their role as suppliers of useful information for decision makers. A conceptual framework helps make the results of the reporting process more comparable than they would be otherwise.

[1]*Statement of Financial Accounting Concepts No. 6,* "Elements of Financial Statements" (Stamford: Financial Accounting Standards Board, December 1985), p. i.

In summary, a conceptual framework of accounting should:

1. Define the boundaries of accounting by providing definitions of basic objectives, key terms, and fundamental concepts;
2. Assist the FASB in the standard-setting process by providing a basis for developing new and revised accounting and reporting standards;
3. Provide a description of current practice and a frame of reference for resolving new issues not covered by GAAP; and
4. Assist accountants and others in selecting from among reporting alternatives the method that best represents the economic reality of the situation.

If these purposes are accomplished, the overall result should be a reporting of the most useful information for decision-making purposes, which is the ultimate goal of accounting.

## NATURE AND COMPONENTS OF THE FASB'S CONCEPTUAL FRAMEWORK

Serious attempts to develop a theoretical foundation of accounting can be traced to the 1930s. Among the leaders in such attempts were accounting educators, both individually and collectively as a part of the American Accounting Association (AAA). In 1936, the Executive Committee of the AAA began issuing a series of publications devoted to accounting theory, the last of which was published in 1965 and entitled "A Statement of Basic Accounting Theory." During the period from 1936 to 1973, there were several additional publications issued by the AAA and also by the American Institute of Certified Public Accountants (AICPA), each attempting to develop a conceptual foundation for the practice of accounting.[2]

While these publications made significant contributions to the development of accounting thought, no unified structure of accounting theory emerged from these efforts. When the Financial Accounting Standards Board was established in 1973, it responded to the need for a general theoretical framework by undertaking a comprehensive project to develop a "conceptual framework for financial accounting and reporting." This project has been described as an attempt to establish a constitution for accounting. The goal of the FASB was to provide "a coherent system of interrelated objectives and fundamentals that is expected to lead to consistent standards and that prescribes the nature, function, and limits of financial accounting and reporting."[3]

The conceptual framework project was one of the original FASB agenda items. It was viewed as a long-term, continuing project to be developed in stages. Because of its significant potential impact on many aspects of financial reporting, and therefore its controversial nature, progress was deliberate. The project had high priority and received a large share of FASB resources. In December 1985, the FASB issued the last of six Statements of

---

[2]Among the most prominent of these publications were: Maurice Moonitz, *Accounting Research Study No. 1*, "The Basic Postulates of Accounting" (New York: American Institute of Certified Public Accountants, 1961); William A. Paton and A. C. Littleton, *An Introduction to Corporate Accounting Standards*, Monograph 3 (Evanston, Ill.: American Accounting Association, 1940); Thomas H. Sanders, Henry R. Hatfield, and W. Moore, *A Statement of Accounting Principles* (New York: American Institute of Accountants, Inc., 1938); Robert T. Sprouse and Maurice Moonitz, *Accounting Research Study No. 3*, "A Tentative Set of Broad Accounting Principles for Business Enterprises" (New York: American Institute of Certified Public Accountants, 1962); *Statement of the Accounting Principles Board No. 4*, "Basic Concepts and Accounting Principles Underlying Financial Statements of Business Enterprises" (New York: American Institute of Certified Public Accountants, October 1970), *Report of the Study Group on the Objectives of Financial Statements*, "Objectives of Financial Statements" (New York: American Institute of Certified Public Accountants, October 1973).

[3]*Statement of Financial Accounting Concepts No. 6*, p. i.

**Financial Accounting Concepts (frequently referred to as Concepts Statements),** which provide the basis for the conceptual framework.[4]

The FASB's framework incorporates many widely accepted concepts and principles developed in earlier works. In addition, several traditional assumptions underlying accounting practice are explicitly or implicitly recognized in the framework. The assumptions are discussed later in the chapter and include economic entity, going concern, arm's-length transactions, stable monetary unit, accounting periods, and accrual accounting. The main components of the FASB's conceptual framework, including the underlying assumptions, are presented in Exhibit 2—1.

The first area addressed by the FASB was the basic purposes or **objectives** of financial reporting. The Board sought answers to the questions: Who are the users of accounting information? What kinds of information do they require for decision making? Based on the objectives, the FASB proceeded to develop fundamental concepts that define the important **qualitative characteristics** of useful information and the specific **elements** to be included in financial statements.

Building on the objectives and fundamental concepts, the FASB addressed the issues of **recognition, measurement,** and **reporting.** In this final phase of the framework project, the Board established broad implementation guidelines relating to the questions: When should revenues and expenses be recognized? How should revenues and expenses and other financial statement elements be measured (valued)? How should financial information be reported or displayed?

Each of the framework components is discussed in the following sections. In considering the individual components, the interrelationships become apparent. Decisions concerning one part of the framework influence other parts.

## Objectives of Financial Reporting

The starting point for the FASB's conceptual framework was to establish the objectives of financial reporting. Without identifying the goals for financial reporting (e.g., who needs what kind of information and for what reasons), accountants cannot determine the recognition criteria needed, which measurements are useful, or how best to report accounting information.

The financial reporting objectives discussed in this chapter and listed in Exhibit 2—2 are summarized and adapted from FASB Concepts Statement No. 1. Some general observations regarding these objectives should be made. First, because the FASB is currently the primary standard-setting body for accounting in the private sector, the Board's objectives should be considered carefully. However, it should also be recognized that another group might identify somewhat different objectives for financial reporting. The objectives, as well as the other components of the conceptual framework, should, therefore, not be interpreted as "universal truths."

A second and related point is that the objectives of financial reporting are directly connected with the needs of those for whom the information is intended and must be considered in their environmental context. Financial reporting is not an end in itself, but

[4]The six Concepts Statements issued by the FASB are:

1. Objectives of Financial Reporting by Business Enterprises
2. Qualitative Characteristics of Accounting Information
3. Elements of Financial Statements of Business Enterprises
4. Objectives of Financial Reporting by Nonbusiness Organizations
5. Recognition and Measurement in Financial Statements of Business Enterprises
6. Elements of Financial Statements (a replacement of No. 3, broadened to include not-for-profit as well as business enterprises).

## Exhibit 2—1    A Conceptual Framework for Accounting

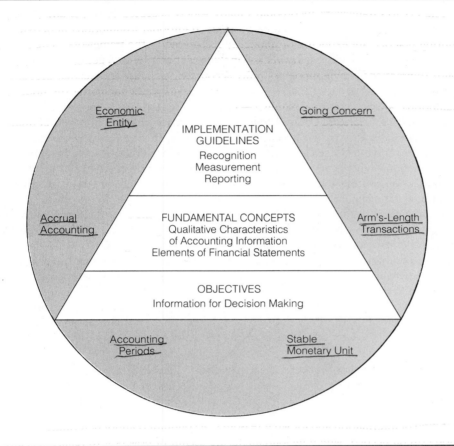

## Exhibit 2—2    Objectives of Financial Reporting

**Overall Objective:**    Provide useful information for decision making

**Primary Objectives:**    Provide information:
a. for assessing cash flow prospects
b. about financial condition
c. about performance and earnings
d. about how funds are obtained and used

**Additional Objectives:**    Provide information:
a. that allows managers to make decisions in the best interest of owners
b. that allows owners to assess management's performance
c. as explanations and interpretations to help users understand the financial information provided

Source: *Statement of Financial Accounting Concepts No. 1*

is directed toward satisfying the need for useful information in making business and economic decisions. Thus, the objectives of financial reporting may change due to changes in the information needs of decision makers and because of changes in the economic, legal, political, and social aspects of the total business environment.

Third, the objectives of financial reporting are intended to be broad in nature. The objectives must be broadly based to satisfy a variety of user needs. Thus, they are objectives for general-purpose financial reporting, attempting to satisfy the common interests of various potential users rather than to meet the specific needs of any selected group.

While there are many potential users of financial reports, the objectives are directed primarily toward the needs of those external users of accounting data who lack the authority to prescribe the information they desire. For example, the Internal Revenue Service or the Securities and Exchange Commission can require selected information from individuals and companies. Investors and creditors, however, must rely to a significant extent on the information contained in the periodic financial reports supplied by management and, therefore, are the major users toward which financial reporting is directed.

A fourth point is that the objectives pertain to financial reporting in general, which encompasses not only disclosures in financial statements, but also other information concerning an enterprise's financial condition and earnings ability. While financial statements are a primary means of communicating information to external parties, other forms and sources are also used for decision making. The total information spectrum relative to investment, credit, and similar decisions is presented in Exhibit 2—3. This illustrates the overall focus of financial reporting and, more specifically, the areas of primary concern for financial accounting—the financial statements, the notes to financial statements, and supplementary disclosures directly affected by generally accepted accounting principles.

**Information for Decision Making**    As discussed in Chapter 1, the **overall objective** of financial reporting is **to provide information that is useful for decision making.** The FASB states:

> Financial reporting should provide information that is useful to present and potential investors and creditors and other users in making rational investment, credit, and similar decisions. The information should be comprehensible to those who have a reasonable understanding of business and economic activities and are willing to study the information with reasonable diligence.[5]

The emphasis in this overall objective is on investors and creditors as the primary external users, because in satisfying their needs, most other general-purpose needs of external users will be met. This objective also recognizes a fairly sophisticated user of financial reports, one who has a reasonable understanding of accounting and business and who is willing to study and analyze the information presented.

**Cash Flow Prospects**    Investors and creditors are interested primarily in a company's future cash flows. Thus, financial reporting should **provide information that is useful in assessing cash flow prospects.** Investment and lending decisions are made with the expectation of eventually increasing cash resources. An investor hopes to receive a return on the investment in the form of cash dividends and ultimately to sell the investment for more than it cost. Creditors seek to recover their cash outlays by repayments of the loans and to increase cash resources from interest payments. In making decisions, investors and creditors must consider the amounts, timing, and uncertainty (risk) of these prospective cash flows.

[5]*Statement of Financial Accounting Concepts No. 1,* par. 34.

**Exhibit 2—3    Information Spectrum**

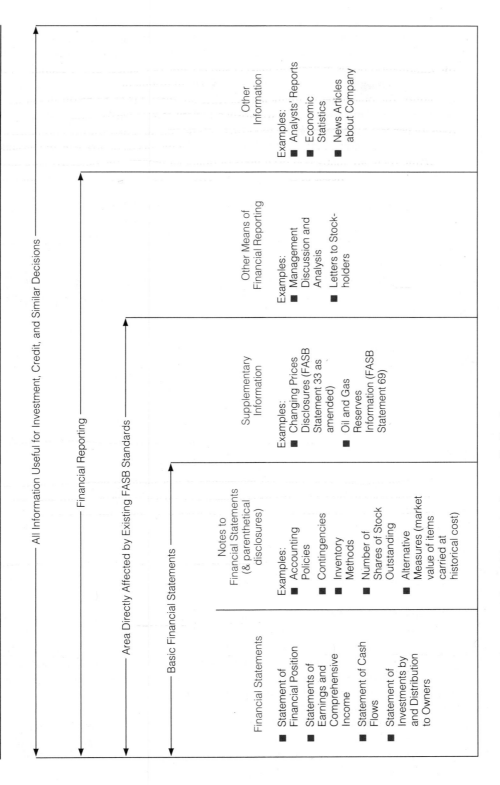

Source: *Adapted from Statement of Financial Accounting Concepts No. 5, p. 5.*

A company is similar to an investor in desiring to recover its investment plus receive a return on that investment. A company invests cash in noncash resources in order to produce a product or service that it expects to sell for an amount greater than the amount invested, thereby increasing cash resources. To the extent that a company is successful in generating favorable cash flows, it can pay dividends and interest, and the market price of its securities will increase. Thus, as illustrated in Exhibit 2—4, the cash flows to investors and creditors are directly related to the cash flows of business enterprises, and financial reporting should provide information that is useful in assessing the enterprise's prospective cash flows.

**Exhibit 2—4    Enterprise Cash Flows To and From Investors and Creditors**

**Enterprise Financial Condition**    Financial reporting should **provide information about an enterprise's assets, liabilities, and owners' equity** to help investors, creditors, and others evaluate the financial strengths and weaknesses of the enterprise and its liquidity and solvency. Such information will help users determine the financial condition of a company, which, in turn, should provide insight into the prospects of future cash flows. It may also help users who wish to estimate the overall value of a business.

**Enterprise Performance and Earnings**    Another important objective of financial reporting is to provide **information about an enterprise's financial performance during a period.** Performance is evaluated mainly on the basis of enterprise earnings. In fact, the FASB states that "the primary focus of financial reporting is information about an enterprise's performance provided by measures of earnings and its components."[6] There are

---

[6]*Statement of Financial Accounting Concepts No. 1*, par. 43.

several aspects of this important objective. Clearly, investors and creditors are concerned mostly with expectations of future enterprise performance. However, to a large degree, they rely on evaluations of past performance as measures of future performance. The FASB recognizes that investors and creditors want information about earnings primarily as an indicator of future cash-flow potential. The Board concluded, however, that information about enterprise earnings, measured by accrual accounting, generally provides a better indicator of performance than does information about current cash receipts and disbursements.

Investors and creditors use reported earnings and information concerning the components of earnings in a variety of ways. For example, earnings may be interpreted by users of financial statements as an overall measure of managerial effectiveness, as a predictor of future earnings and long-term "earning power," and as an indicator of the risk of investing or lending. The information may be used to establish new predictions, confirm previous expectations, or change past evaluations.

**How Funds Are Obtained and Used**    Notwithstanding the emphasis on earnings, another objective of financial reporting is to **provide information about an enterprise's cash flows during a period.** This objective encompasses information about the enterprise's borrowing and repayment of borrowed funds; its capital transactions, such as the issuance of stock and payment of dividends; and any other factors that may affect its liquidity and solvency. Much of the information to satisfy this objective is provided in the statement of cash flows, although information about earnings and about assets, liabilities, and owners' equity is also useful in evaluating the liquidity and solvency of a firm.

**Additional Objectives**    Although the objectives of financial reporting are aimed primarily at the needs of external users, financial reporting should also **provide information that allows managers and directors to make decisions that are in the best interest of the owners.** A related objective is that sufficient **information should be provided to allow the owners to assess how well management has discharged its stewardship responsibility** over the entrusted resources. This requires an additional objective—**financial reporting should include explanations and interpretations to help users understand the financial information provided.**

In summary, if the objectives discussed in the preceding paragraphs are fully attained, the FASB believes those who make economic decisions will have better information upon which to evaluate alternative courses of action and the expected returns, costs, and risks of each. The result should be a more efficient allocation of scarce resources among competing uses by individuals, enterprises, markets, and the government.

## Qualitative Characteristics of Accounting Information

Individuals who are responsible for financial reporting should continually seek to provide the best, i.e., most useful, information possible within reasonable cost constraints. The problem is very complex because of the many choices among acceptable reporting alternatives. For example, what items should be capitalized as assets or which items reported as liabilities? Which revenues and costs should be assigned to a particular reporting period and on what basis? What are the attributes to be measured: historical costs, current values, or net realizable values? At what level of aggregation or disaggregation should information be presented? Where should specific information be disclosed—in the financial statements, in the notes to the financial statements, or perhaps not at all? These and similar choices must be made by policymakers, such as members of the FASB or SEC; by management as they fulfill their stewardship roles; and by accountants as they assist management in reporting on a company's activities.

To assist in choosing among financial accounting and reporting alternatives, several criteria have been established by the FASB. These criteria relate to the qualitative characteristics of accounting information. A hierarchy of these qualities is presented in Exhibit 2—5 and will be used as a frame of reference in discussing them.

**Exhibit 2—5        A Hierarchy of Accounting Information Qualities**

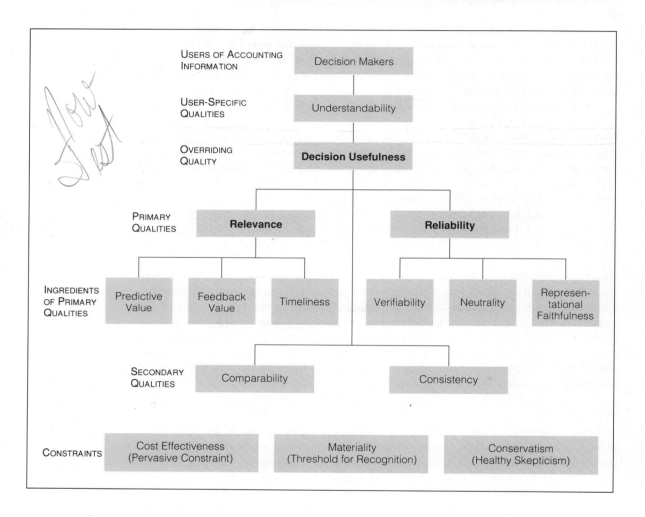

Source: Adapted from FASB *Statement of Financial Accounting Concepts No. 2*, p. 15.

**Decision Usefulness**    The overriding quality or characteristic of accounting information is **decision usefulness,** which is central to the hierarchy presented in Exhibit 2—5. All other qualities are viewed in terms of their contribution to decision usefulness. The illustrated hierarchy distinguishes user-specific qualities, such as **understandability,** from qualities inherent in accounting information, such as relevance and reliability. The quality of understandability is essential to decision usefulness. Information cannot be useful to decision makers if it is not understood even though the information may be relevant and reliable. The understandability of information depends on the characteristics of users, e.g., their prior knowledge, and also on the inherent characteristics of the information presented. Hence, understandability can be evaluated only with respect to specific classes of decision makers. As indicated earlier, financial reporting is directed toward those users who have a reasonable understanding of business and economic activities and who are willing to study the information provided with reasonable diligence.

**Primary Qualities**    In the following statement, the FASB identified **relevance** and **reliability** as the primary qualities inherent in useful accounting information:

> The qualities that distinguish "better" (more useful) information from "inferior" (less useful) information are primarily the qualities of relevance and reliability, with some other characteristics that those qualities imply.[7]

*Relevance*    The relevance of information may be judged only in relation to its intended use. If information is not relevant to the needs of decision makers, it is useless regardless of how well it meets other criteria. The objective of relevance, then, is to select methods of measuring and reporting that will aid those individuals who rely on financial statements to make decisions.

The FASB defines relevant information as that which will "make a difference." Relevant information may confirm expectations or change them. Thus, relevance is related to the **feedback value** and the **predictive value** of information. If the decision maker's expectations are neither confirmed nor changed by certain information, that information is not relevant and therefore is not useful to the decision maker. If a user can better predict future consequences based on information about past events and transactions, then such information is relevant.[8]

Relevant information normally provides both feedback and predictive value at the same time. Feedback on past events helps confirm or correct earlier expectations. Such information can then be used to help predict future outcomes. For example, when General Motors presents comparative income statements, an investor has information to compare last year's operating results with this year's. This provides a general basis for evaluating prior expectations and for estimating what next year's results might be. The information therefore provides both feedback and predictive value concerning General Motors. As stated by the FASB, "Without a knowledge of the past, the basis for prediction will usually be lacking. Without an interest in the future, knowledge of the past is sterile."[9]

Timeliness is another key ingredient of relevance, relating directly to decision usefulness. Again using General Motors as an example, when the company issues interim financial reports, it is attempting to provide information on a timely basis so that the information will be more relevant. Thus, to be relevant, information must offer predictive or feedback value, and it must be presented to users in a timely manner.

*Reliability*    The second primary quality of accounting information is reliability. Accounting information is reliable if users can depend on it to be reasonably free from error or bias and to be a faithful representation of the economic conditions or events that it purports to represent.[10] Reliability does not mean absolute accuracy. Information that is based on judgments and that includes estimates and approximations cannot be totally

---

[7]*Statement of Financial Accounting Concepts No. 2*, "Qualitative Characteristics of Accounting Information" (Stamford: Financial Accounting Standards Board, May 1980), par. 15.

[8]*Ibid.*, pars. 46-50.

[9]*Ibid.*, par. 51.

[10]*Ibid.*, par. 63.

accurate, but it should be reliable. The objective, then, is to present the type of information in which users can have confidence. Such information must contain the key ingredients of reliability: verifiability, neutrality, and representational faithfulness.

**Verifiability** implies objectivity and consensus. Accountants seek to base their findings on facts that are determined objectively and that can be verified by other trained accountants using the same measurement methods. For example, assume that the amount of depreciation expense reported in the current year's income statement for the SAVE-ON Company is $125,000. That amount can be verified if it is known that the straight-line method of depreciation was applied to depreciable assets totaling $1,250,000 and that the assets had an estimated useful life of 10 years with no salvage value.

**Neutrality** relates to information being communicated in an unbiased manner. If financial statements are to satisfy a wide variety of users, the information presented should not be biased in favor of one group of users to the detriment of others. In this sense, the concept of neutrality is similar to the all-encompassing concept of "fairness."

The ingredient of **representational faithfulness** means that there is agreement between the information being reported and the actual results of economic activity being measured. Thus, the amounts and descriptions reported in the financial statements should reflect the economic reality of what is being represented. For a company to report sales of $3.4 million when they actually had sales of $2.5 million would not be a faithful representation and would cause the information to be unreliable.

**Secondary Qualities**   In addition to the primary qualities of relevance and reliability, there are two secondary qualities that affect the usefulness of accounting information: comparability and consistency.

*Comparability*   The essence of **comparability** is that information becomes much more useful when it can be related to a benchmark or standard. The comparison may be with data for other firms or it may be with similar information for the same firm but for other equivalent periods of time. To illustrate how comparable data can increase the usefulness of information, consider the situation where a company reports current assets of $350,000 and current liabilities of $275,000. The current ratio is 1.27, but does this information reflect a favorable or unfavorable liquidity position? Without knowing comparable data for other companies in the industry or the current ratio of this company for other years, the information is of somewhat limited value. If data were available to show that the average current ratio of all companies in this particular industry is 1.22 and further that this company's current ratio was 1.10 for the previous year, then it would appear that the company's liquidity position has improved and that it is in relatively good shape.

Given that comparability increases the usefulness of information, financial reports should provide data permitting comparisons among companies and comparisons of results of the same company over different time periods. This requires that similar events be accounted for in the same manner on the financial statements of different companies and for a particular company for different periods. It should be recognized, however, that uniformity is not always the answer to comparability. Different circumstances may require different accounting treatment.

Still, one of the greatest unsolved problems in accounting is the present acceptance of alternative accounting methods under situations that do not appear to be sufficiently different to warrant different accounting practices. The goal is for basic similarities and differences in the activities of companies to be apparent from the financial statements.

Research in accounting is currently being directed toward identifying circumstances that justify the use of a given method of accounting. If this research is successful, alternative methods can be eliminated where circumstances are found to be the same. In the meantime, current practice requires disclosure of the accounting methods used, as well as the impact of changes in methods when a change can be justified. Although the disclosures currently made do not generally provide enough information for a user to convert the published financial information from one accounting method to another, they do provide information that can assist the user in determining the degree of comparability among enterprises.

**Consistency**    Consistency is another important ingredient of useful accounting information. In view of the number of reporting alternatives, the methods adopted by an enterprise should be consistently employed if there is to be continuity and comparability in the financial statements. In analyzing statements, users seek to identify and evaluate the changes and trends within the enterprise. Conclusions concerning financial position and operations may be materially in error if, for example, accelerated depreciation is applied against the revenue of one year and straight-line depreciation against the revenue of the next year, or if securities are reported under long-term investments in one year and under current assets in the following year.

This is not to suggest that methods once adopted should not be changed. A continuing analysis of the business activities, as well as changing conditions, may suggest changes in accounting methods and presentations leading to more informative statements. These changes should be incorporated in the accounting system and the financial statements. The statements should be accompanied by a clear explanation of the nature of the changes and their effects, where they are material, so that current reporting can be properly interpreted and related to past reporting.

**Constraints**    Underlying the informational qualities identified in Exhibit 2—5 are three important constraints: (1) cost effectiveness, (2) materiality, and (3) conservatism.

**Cost Effectiveness**    Information is like other commodities in that it must be worth more than the cost of providing it to consumers. This concept is referred to as **cost effectiveness.** Too often government regulators and others assume that information is a "free" good. Obviously, it is not, and the relationship between costs and benefits must always be kept in mind when selecting or requiring reporting alternatives. To illustrate, in the early 1970s the Federal Trade Commission proposed that large companies be required to disclose information about lines of business. A group of companies brought court action to prohibit the proposed requirement. A major argument of the companies was that the information would be very costly to prepare, because it was not normally generated by the accounting system. The companies also argued that the line-of-business disclosures in the form proposed by the FTC would not be beneficial to users, because the reported segments would be artificial and not those the companies normally used to report on a less-than-company-wide basis. Although the FTC prevailed, primarily because of perceived benefits in regulating anti-trust situations, this case underscores an important point—the cost of producing information (including, for example, modification to the existing accounting system, or even additional printing and mailing costs) must be compared to the extra benefits (generally meaning an improvement in specific decisions of users) to determine if the information should be reported.

The difficulty in assessing cost effectiveness is that the costs and benefits, especially the benefits, are not always evident or easily measured. Notwithstanding this difficulty, cost effectiveness is an important constraint and should be considered when selecting reporting alternatives.

***Materiality***    Contrary to the belief of many readers of financial statements, the amounts reported in the statements are not always complete and are often not exact. While for many decisions completeness and exactness are not required, there is a point at which information that is incomplete or inexact does influence a decision. This point defines the boundary between information that is material and information that is immaterial.

**Materiality** is an overriding concept related to, but distinguishable from, the primary qualities of relevance and reliability. Materiality determines the threshold for recognition of accounting items and is primarily a quantitative consideration. While relevance is directed toward the nature of the information, materiality focuses on the size of a judgment item in a given set of circumstances. Materiality deals with the specific question: Is the item large enough or the degree of the accuracy precise enough to influence the decision of a user of the information? Of course, the degree of influence caused by the size of an item also depends on the nature of the item and the circumstances in which a judgment must be made. For example, a $1 million loss from a product-related lawsuit might be financially devastating for some enterprises, but may not even warrant separate disclosure on Ford Motor Company's financial statements.

At the present time, there are few guidelines to assist preparers of financial reports in applying the concept of materiality. Where materiality guidelines do exist, they are often not uniform. For example, the materiality guideline for reporting by segments of a company suggests that certain information be disclosed for any major segment that accounts for 10% or more of total company sales. On the other hand, for determining the significance of dilution in earnings-per-share computations, the materiality guideline is 3%. Thus for these two different reporting areas, the materiality guideline varies from 10% to 3%. Since quantitative guidance concerning materiality is often lacking, managers and accountants must exercise judgment in determining whether a failure to disclose certain data will influence the decisions of the users of financial statements.

Past court cases can help determine what is material by providing examples of where the lack of disclosure of certain information in the financial statements has been considered a material misstatement. The failure to disclose proper inventory values or pending sales of large amounts of assets, the failure to disclose the imminence of a highly profitable transaction or to disclose a significant downward readjustment of reported earnings are a few examples.[11]

In summary, the following point should be kept in mind in making judgments concerning materiality:

> The omission or misstatement of an item in a financial report is material if, in the light of surrounding circumstances, the magnitude of the item is such that it is probable that the judgment of a reasonable person relying upon the report would have been changed or influenced by the inclusion or correction of the item.[12]

***Conservatism***    Another constraint associated with the characteristics of useful information is **conservatism.** This means that when accountants have genuine doubt concerning which of two or more reporting alternatives should be selected, users are best served by adopting a conservative approach, that is, by choosing the alternative with the least favorable impact on owners' equity. However, conservatism does not mean deliberate and arbitrary understatement of assets and earnings. On the contrary, use of conservative

---

[11]For additional examples of quantitative materiality considerations, see *Statement of Financial Accounting Concepts No. 2,* Appendix C, par. 165.

[12]*Ibid.,* par. 132.

procedures is motivated by not wanting to overstate assets and earnings when dealing in "gray areas."

Conservatism should be used when a degree of skepticism is warranted. For example, generally accepted accounting principles require the expensing of research and development costs on the basis that the future benefits cannot be accurately determined. Since there is often reasonable doubt as to the existence or amount of future benefits, the costs are expensed, and the amount of income reported currently is reduced. Another example of conservatism in accounting practice is reporting short-term marketable equity securities at a lower-of-cost-or-market value. If IBM held short-term marketable equity securities and the market value dropped below cost, the company should report those securities at the lower market value. To continue to report the securities at cost would overstate current assets and might imply to statement users that current assets exceed current liabilities by more than is actually the case.

The constraint of conservatism is a useful one, but one that should be applied carefully and used only as a moderating and refining influence on the information reported. Essentially, conservatism means prudence in financial accounting and reporting.

## Elements of Financial Statements

Having identified the qualitative characteristics of accounting information, the FASB in Concepts Statement No. 3 established definitions for the ten basic elements of financial statements of business enterprises. In Concepts Statement No. 6, the FASB expanded the scope of Statement No. 3 to encompass not-for-profit organizations as well. These elements comprise the building blocks upon which financial statements are constructed. The elements are interrelated and collectively report the performance and status of an enterprise. For reference purposes, the FASB definitions of the ten basic elements are listed on page 43. These definitions and the issues surrounding them are discussed in detail as the elements are introduced in later chapters.

## Recognition, Measurement, and Reporting

FASB Concepts Statement No. 5 builds on the foundation laid by the previously issued concepts statements and provides broad guidelines for implementing or applying the objectives and fundamental concepts discussed thus far. It provides guidance in determining *what* information should be formally incorporated into financial statements and *when*. Specifically, Statement No. 5 sets forth recognition criteria and discusses certain measurement issues that are closely related to recognition. In addition, this statement addresses financial reporting and identifies the financial statements that should be presented in light of the objectives of financial reporting.

**Recognition Criteria**    Recognition is the process of formally recording an item and eventually reporting it as one of the elements in the financial statements. Recognition involves both the initial recording of an item and any subsequent changes related to that item. To qualify for recognition, an item should meet four fundamental criteria: (1) definition, (2) measurability, (3) relevance, and (4) reliability.[13] For an item to be formally recognized, it must meet one of the definitions of the elements of financial statements, as defined in Concepts Statement No. 6. For example, a receivable must meet the definition of an asset to be recorded and reported as such on a balance sheet. The same is true of liabilities, owners' equity, revenues, expenses, and other elements.

---

[13]*Statement of Financial Accounting Concepts No. 5,* "Recognition and Measurement in Financial Statements of Business Enterprises" (Stamford: Financial Accounting Standards Board, December 1984), par. 63.

## Accounting for an Oil Spill

On March 24, 1989, the Exxon Valdez, an oil tanker, hit a reef near Alaska. This accident resulted in over 11 million gallons of oil being spilled into the ocean and onto the coast of Alaska. Although Exxon carries insurance against such events, damage from the Alaskan oil spill, estimated at over $2 billion, far exceeds policy limits.

The federal government has budgeted funds for cleaning up oil spills and other environmental accidents. However, a federal appeals court in Washington ruled, just four months following the Valdez accident, that companies responsible for environmental damage are responsible for restoring the environment to its condition prior to the damage.

### Questions:

1. *Does the Valdez oil spill meet the definition of a liability?*
2. *If the cleanup of the spill takes several years, would it be likely that Exxon could make damage estimates at the end of 1989 that would be reliable enough to allow the liability to be recorded at the end of 1989?*
3. *If Exxon determines that the liability cannot be reliably estimated, should some other type of disclosure be required?*

Sources:

*The Wall Street Journal,* March 30, 1989, p. A3.

*The Wall Street Journal,* July 17, 1989, p. B12.

In addition to qualifying as an element, an item must be objectively measurable in monetary terms to be recognized. Sometimes an item clearly meets the definition criterion but cannot be measured objectively. For example, in the letter to shareholders in the 1990 annual report of IBM Corporation, the chairman of the board mentions the significant value of IBM's more than 370,000 employees. (See Appendix A at the end of the book.) These employees have future benefit to IBM and may be considered assets of high value to that company. Yet, that value is not recognized as an asset on IBM's balance sheet, since it cannot be measured in a reliable manner.

Information about an item must be both relevant and reliable in order for the item to be recognized. Since there are often trade-offs between relevance and reliability, consideration of these primary qualities may affect the timing of recognition. For example, information about a pending lawsuit may be relevant, but its recognition usually is delayed until the amounts and circumstances can be determined with sufficient reliability.

The four fundamental recognition criteria apply to all elements of financial statements. However, since one of the major tasks of accounting is to measure and report net income (loss), proper application of the recognition criteria is particularly important when recognizing revenues and expenses. Generally, under the **revenue recognition principle**, revenues for a period are recorded when two conditions are met: (1) the earnings process is substantially complete, and (2) there is receipt of cash or a near-cash asset. These two criteria have led to the conventional recognition of revenue at the point of sale, i.e., at the specific point in the earning process when assets are sold or services are rendered. According to the **matching principle**, expenses for a period are determined by association with specific revenues or a particular time period. The revenue recognition and expense matching principles are discussed and illustrated in Chapter 4.

## The 10 Elements of Financial Statements

- **Assets** are probable future economic benefits obtained or cont
  entity as a result of past transactions or events.
- **Liabilities** are probable future sacrifices of economic benefits ε
  obligations of a particular entity to transfer assets or provide servi
  in the future as a result of past transactions or events.
- **Equity** or **net assets** is the residual interest in the assets of an entity
  deducting its liabilities.
- **Investments by owners** are increases in equity of a particular bu
  resulting from transfers to it from other entities of something valu
  increase ownership interests (or equity) in it. Assets are most comm
  investments by owners, but that which is received may also include ε
  faction or conversion of liabilities of the enterprise.
- **Distributions to owners** are decreases in equity of a particular busi
  resulting from transferring assets, rendering services, or incurring liε
  enterprise to owners. Distributions to owners decrease ownership intere
  in an enterprise.
- **Comprehensive income** is the change in equity of a business enterprise during a period from transactions and other events and circumstances from nonowner sources. It
  includes all changes in equity during a period except those resulting from investments
  by owners and distributions to owners.
- **Revenues** are inflows or other enhancements of assets of an entity or settlement of its
  liabilities (or a combination of both) from delivering or producing goods, rendering services, or other activities that constitute the entity's ongoing major or central operations.
- **Expenses** are outflows or other using-up of assets or incurrences of liabilities (or a
  combination of both) from delivering or producing goods, rendering services, or carrying out other activities that constitute the entity's ongoing major or central
  operations.
- **Gains** are increases in equity (net assets) from peripheral or incidental transactions of
  an entity and from all other transactions and other events and circumstances affecting
  the entity except those that result from revenues or investments by owners.
- **Losses** are decreases in equity (net assets) from peripheral or incidental transactions
  of an entity and from all other transactions and other events and circumstances affecting the entity except those that result from expenses or distributions to owners.

Source: *Statement of Financial Accounting Concepts No. 6*, pp. ix-x.

**Measurement Attributes**    Closely related to recognition is measurement. There are five
different measurement attributes currently used in practice and specifically mentioned in
Concepts Statement No. 5.[14]

Historical cost is the cash equivalent price exchanged for goods or services at the date
of acquisition. Land, buildings, equipment, and most inventories are common examples
of items recognized using the historical cost attribute.

Current replacement cost is the cash equivalent price that would be exchanged currently to purchase or replace equivalent goods or services. Some inventories are recognized at their current replacement costs.

Current market value is the cash equivalent price that could be obtained by selling an
asset in an orderly liquidation. Some investments in marketable securities are reported
using current market values.

Net realizable value is the amount of cash expected to be received from the conversion of assets in the normal course of business. Generally, this attribute is equal to the sales
price less normal costs to sell. Net realizable value is used for recognizing short-term
receivables and some inventories.

[14]*Ibid.*, par. 67.

sent (or discounted) value is the amount of net future cash inflows or outflows counted to their present value. Long-term receivables and long-term payables use this measurement attribute.

It should be noted that different measurement attributes often have the same monetary value, especially at the point of initial recognition. For example, the historical cost and the current replacement cost of a piece of land are the same at the date of acquisition. The amount would also be the current market value of the land at that point in time, assuming an arm's-length transaction.

The trade-off between relevance and reliability mentioned earlier is also evident in considering which measurement attribute to use. Current accounting practice is said to be based on historical costs, since that is the attribute generally used in the initial recording of transactions. Historical cost is used because it is objective (reliable), being based on an exchange that has taken place between presumably independent parties. In effect, the historical cost is the fair market price of the item involved in the transaction at that date. Many accountants feel that current replacement costs or market values are more relevant than historical costs for future-oriented decisions; yet, those attributes often lack reliability. Because it is both reliable and relevant, historical cost has been the valuation basis most commonly used in accounting practice. However, as indicated above, other measurement attributes are used at times and are expected to continue to be used in the future. The "proper" measurement attribute is the one that under the circumstances provides the most useful (relevant and reliable) information at a reasonable cost.

In using historical cost as one (and perhaps the dominant) measurement attribute, the FASB indicated in Concepts Statement No. 5 that it expects nominal units of money to continue to be used in recognizing items in financial reporting. Nominal units of money are unadjusted for general price changes and therefore fluctuate over time in terms of purchasing power. If there is little or no inflation, measurement using nominal dollars is satisfactory. However, if general price levels change significantly, the FASB will probably have to reconsider this decision.

**Financial Reporting**   For financial reporting to be most effective, all relevant information should be presented in an unbiased, understandable, and timely manner. This is sometimes referred to as the **full disclosure principle.** Because of the cost-benefit constraint discussed earlier, however, it would be impossible to report *all* relevant information. Further, too much information would adversely affect understandability and, therefore, decision usefulness. Those who provide financial information must use judgment in determining what information best satisfies the full disclosure principle within reasonable cost limitations.

Although guidelines in this area are not well defined, Concepts Statement No. 5 indicates that a "full set of financial statements" is necessary to meet the objectives of financial reporting. Included in the recommended set of general-purpose financial statements are reports that would show:[15]

- Financial position at the end of the period
- Earnings (net income) for the period
- Comprehensive income (total nonowner changes in equity) for the period
- Cash flows during the period
- Investments by and distributions to owners during the period

Current practice generally includes a set of financial statements consisting of: (1) a balance sheet reporting the financial position of a business at a certain date; (2) an **income statement** presenting the results of operations of an entity for a reporting period; and (3) a **statement of cash flows** identifying the net cash flows from operating, investing, and

[15]*Statement of Financial Accounting Concepts No. 5,* par. 13.

financing activities during the reporting period. The three primary statements are referred to as general-purpose financial statements because they are intended for use by a wide variety of external users. Although there has been some discussion as to the need for special-purpose statements directed to specific external users, there has been no significant movement toward this in practice.

Sometimes a **retained earnings statement** is provided, or combined with the income statement, showing the changes in retained earnings for the period. When there are changes in owners' equity other than those affecting retained earnings, a supplemental **statement of changes in owners' equity** may be presented to provide a complete reconciliation of the beginning and ending equity balances.

The current general-purpose statements would seem to satisfy the recommendations of Concepts Statement No. 5 with one exception. **Comprehensive income** is a concept specifically defined in Statement No. 5 as including all changes in owners' equity except investments by and distributions to owners. This concept, which is explained and illustrated in Chapter 4, may eventually require a new statement.

In general, the FASB and other standard-setting bodies have been reluctant to specify exact formats for reporting. Instead, they have allowed and encouraged companies to experiment with various reporting (display) techniques. The results are sometimes quite encouraging as companies voluntarily seek new and better ways to present information. For example, many companies present graphic and various types of pictorial displays in their annual reports to assist users in understanding the information provided in financial statements. The graphs reproduced in Exhibit 2—6 were included in the 1989 annual report of Albertson's, Inc., to supplement the information presented in the income statement. This is one example of the many ways in which companies are attempting to enhance the usefulness of their financial statements.

## TRADITIONAL ASSUMPTIONS OF THE ACCOUNTING MODEL

The FASB's Conceptual Framework described in the preceding sections is influenced by several underlying assumptions. While not addressed explicitly, these traditional assumptions are implicit in the conceptual framework. They, too, help establish generally accepted accounting practice. The following paragraphs briefly describe the six basic assumptions that were identified in Exhibit 2—1 on page 31.

First, the business enterprise is viewed as a specific **economic entity** separate and distinct from its owners and any other business unit. It is the entity and its activities that receive the focus of attention for accounting and reporting purposes.

Second, in the absence of evidence to the contrary, the entity is viewed as a **going concern.** This continuity assumption provides support for the preparation of a balance sheet that reports costs assignable to future activities rather than market values of properties that would be realized in the event of voluntary liquidation or forced sale. This same assumption calls for the preparation of an income statement reporting only such portions of revenues and costs as are allocable to current activities.

Third, the transactions and events of an entity provide the basis for accounting entries, and any changes in resources and equity values are generally not recorded until a transaction has taken place. Furthermore, transactions are assumed to be **arm's-length transactions.** That is, they occur between independent parties, each of whom is capable of protecting its own interests. If Entity A is selling goods to Entity B, it will try to sell at a sufficiently high price to make a profit. Entity B, on the other hand, will try to purchase those goods at a reasonably low price. The bargained price arrived at in this arm's-length transaction is assumed to be an objective market valuation at that date, and is considered an objective value for measurement purposes.

**Exhibit 2—6     Supplemental Disclosure of Operating Data**

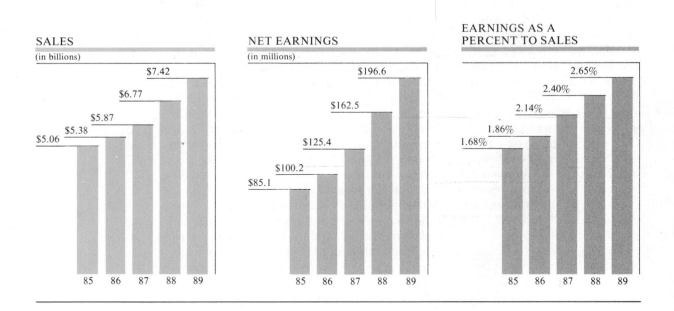

Fourth, transactions are assumed to be measured in **stable monetary units.** Because of this assumption, changes in the dollar's purchasing power have traditionally been ignored. Thus, financial statements reflect items that are measured in terms of nominal dollars. To many accountants, this is a serious limitation of the accounting model.

Fifth, because accounting information is needed on a timely basis, the life of a business entity is divided into specific **accounting periods.** By convention, the year has been established as the normal period for reporting. Annual statements, as well as statements covering shorter intervals, such as quarters, are provided by entities to satisfy the needs of those requiring timely financial information.

Finally, for each time period, an income measure is determined using **accrual accounting.** This means that revenues are recognized when earned, not necessarily when cash is received; and expenses are recognized when incurred, not necessarily when cash is paid. For most financial reporting purposes, accrual accounting is considered preferable to the cash-basis system of accounting.

In total, these assumptions as well as the concepts discussed earlier in the chapter comprise the current accounting model. They help determine what will be accounted for and in what manner. In effect, they set the boundaries of accounting practice. If these boundaries are violated, additional disclosure in the financial statements is typically required. An example of the disclosure relating to the violation of the going-concern assumption was illustrated in Chapter 1 on page 19.

## CONCEPTUAL FRAMEWORK SUMMARIZED

Exhibit 2—7 summarizes the major components of a conceptual framework of accounting. Such a framework provides a basis for consistent judgments by standard-setters, preparers, users, auditors, and others involved in financial reporting. A conceptual framework will not solve all accounting problems, but if used on a consistent basis over time, it should help improve financial reporting. The framework discussed in this chapter will be a reference source throughout the text. In studying the remaining chapters, you will see many applications and a few exceptions to the theoretical framework established here. An understanding of the overall theoretical framework of accounting should make it easier for you to understand specific issues and problems encountered in practice.

## Exhibit 2—7    A Conceptual Framework of Accounting

### I. Objectives of Financial Reporting
A. Overall—Provide useful information for decision making
B. Primary—Provide information:
   1. For assessing cash flow prospects
   2. About financial condition
   3. About performance and earnings
   4. About how funds are obtained and used
C. Additional—Provide information:
   1. That allows managers to make decisions in the best interest of owners
   2. That allows owners to assess management's performance
   3. As explanations and interpretations to help users understand the information provided

### II. Fundamental Concepts
A. Qualitative Characteristics of Accounting Information
   1. Overriding quality—decision usefulness
   2. Primary qualities
      a. Relevance
         • predictive value
         • feedback value
         • timeliness
      b. Reliability
         • verifiability
         • neutrality
         • representational faithfulness
   3. Secondary qualities
      a. Comparability
      b. Consistency
   4. Constraints
      a. Cost effectiveness (pervasive constraint)
      b. Materiality (recognition threshold)
      c. Conservatism (healthy skepticism)
B. Elements of Financial Statements
   1. Assets
   2. Liabilities
   3. Equity
   4. Investments by owners
   5. Distributions to owners
   6. Comprehensive income
   7. Revenues
   8. Expenses
   9. Gains
   10. Losses

### III. Implementation Guidelines
A. Recognition Criteria
1. Definition
2. Measurability
3. Relevance
4. Reliability
B. Measurement Attributes
1. Historical cost
2. Current replacement cost
3. Current market value
4. Net realizable value
5. Present (or discounted) value
C. Financial Reporting
1. Full disclosure
2. Set of general-purpose financial statements
   a. Financial position
   b. Earnings (net income or loss)
   c. Comprehensive income
   d. Cash flows
   e. Investments by and distributions to owners

### IV. Traditional Assumptions of the Accounting Model
A. Economic entity
B. Going concern
C. Arm's-length transactions
D. Stable monetary unit
E. Accounting periods
F. Accrual accounting

---

## KEY TERMS

Accounting periods 46
Accrual accounting 46
Arm's-length transactions 45
Balance sheet 44
Comparability 38
Comprehensive income 45
Conceptual framework 28
Conservatism 40
Consistency 39
Cost effectiveness 39
Current market value 43
Current replacement cost 43
Decision usefulness 36
Economic entity 45

Feedback value 37
Full disclosure principle 44
Going concern 45
Historical cost 43
Income statement 44
Matching principle 42
Materiality 40
Net realizable value 43
Neutrality 38
Predictive value 37
Present (or discounted) value 43
Recognition 41
Relevance 37

Reliability 37
Representational faithfulness 38
Retained earnings statement 45
Revenue recognition principle 42
Stable monetary units 46
Statement of cash flows 44
Statement of changes in owners' equity 45
Statements of financial accounting concepts 30
Timeliness 37
Understandability 36
Verifiability 38

---

## QUESTIONS

1. List and explain the main reasons why a conceptual framework of accounting is important.
2. Why is judgment required by accountants in fulfilling their role as suppliers of information?
3. The FASB's Conceptual Framework project has received considerable attention. What is the project expected to accomplish? What is it not likely to do?
4. Identify the major objectives of financial reporting as specified by the FASB.

5. The overriding quality of accounting information is decision usefulness. How does the user-specific quality of "understandability" affect decision usefulness?
6. Distinguish between the primary informational qualities of relevance and reliability.
7. Does reliability imply absolute accuracy? Explain.
8. Define comparability. How does comparability relate to uniformity?
9. Of what value is consistency in financial reporting?

10. Why is it so difficult to measure the cost effectiveness of accounting information?
11. What is the current materiality standard in accounting?
12. Is it possible for information to be immaterial and yet relevant? Explain.
13. What is conservatism in accounting? When does it become a relevant issue? What are some examples of conservatism in accounting practice?
14. Identify the criteria that an item must meet to qualify for recognition.
15. Identify and describe five different measurement attributes.
16. FASB Concepts Statement No. 5 indicates that a full set of financial statements is needed to meet the objectives of financial reporting. What should the reports that constitute a set of general-purpose financial statements show?
17. Identify the six traditional assumptions that influence the conceptual framework, and briefly explain how they affect it.

## DISCUSSION CASES

### Case 2—1   (The establishment of a conceptual framework)

As a student of accounting, you have noticed that a substantial portion of the literature deals with establishing a theoretical framework upon which accounting practice can be based. This is currently the case and has been for the past 50 years. Yet, in discussions with colleagues and friends, you have to admit that the accounting profession has found it difficult to establish an authoritative set of accounting concepts and principles that are universally accepted within the business community. As you think about this problem, at least two questions come to mind: (1) Is an overall conceptual framework of accounting even needed? and (2) What has the FASB done differently, if anything, to succeed in establishing a conceptual framework for accounting where others have failed? Discuss possible answers to these questions.

### Case 2—2   (How important are the economic consequences of accounting principles?)

During the 1960s, and again in the 1980s, corporate merger activity increased significantly in the United States. Many of the early mergers involved companies in completely unrelated fields. Sometimes a company in a weak financial position merged with a stronger company. The combined financial statements would then postpone the disclosure of poor management to statement users. In an attempt to clarify the accounting rules and to eliminate financial statement manipulation that did not truly present the entity's financial status, the Accounting Principles Board proposed a change in accounting for mergers. One business executive involved in merger activity commented publicly that the Board had no right to issue such pronouncements. If the accounting requirements were changed, the executive argued, merger activity would decline and economic growth in our economy would stagnate.

More recently, the FASB has issued standards that require companies to account for unfunded pension costs as liabilities. Executives of several large companies have argued that such accounting will seriously limit the ability of many companies to borrow and will have a serious, negative impact on business activity and, therefore, on society.

Recognizing that accounting rules have an impact on business activity and may affect economic growth, should this result influence the decision by accounting standard-setting bodies as to how transactions should be recorded and reported? Should the impact on society be an important consideration for an accounting principle?

### Case 2—3   (Cash flow vs. accrual-basis earnings)

The Financial Accounting Standards Board concluded in Concepts Statement No. 1 that investors and creditors are interested "in an enterprise's future cash flows and its ability to generate favorable cash flows [that] leads primarily to an interest in information about its earnings rather than information directly about its cash flows." The Board further states that "information about enterprise earnings and its components measured by accrual accounting generally provides a better indication of enterprise performance than information about current cash receipts and payments." If an investor or creditor is interested in future cash flows, why isn't the focus on an examination of a firm's past cash flows? What are the limitations associated with using cash flows to measure the perform-ance of an enterprise? Conversely, what are the risks to an investor or creditor of focusing solely on accrual-based earnings figures?

## Case 2—4 (Trade-offs in providing useful accounting information)

The FASB's conceptual framework is intended to provide guidance in selecting from alternative accounting methods those that are most appropriate under the circumstances. Accountants must exercise judgment in applying the general guidelines in each specific set of circumstances. Often trade-offs exist between different qualitative characteristics of accounting information. For each of the following situations, identify the qualitative characteristics involved and discuss the possible trade-offs that exist.

1. Benavides Company charges to expense all items under $1,000.
2. Do-It-Now Company has recently decided to change its depreciation method to straight line from declining balance.
3. Future, Inc., has decided to use the allowance method for bad debts rather than the direct write-off method.
4. Nights Inn is trying to convince its auditors to allow a restatement of all asset values to their current market values.

## Case 2—5 (Elements of financial statements)

Conserv Corporation, a computer software company, is trying to determine the appropriate accounting procedure to apply to its software development costs. Management is considering capital-izing the development costs and amortizing them over several years. Alternatively, they are consider-ing charging the costs to expense as soon as they are incurred. You, as an accountant, have been asked to help settle this issue. Which definitions of financial statement elements would apply to these costs? Based on this information, what accounting procedure would you recommend and why?

## Case 2—6 (Recognition, measurement, and reporting considerations in financial reporting)

Several years ago, the SEC adopted amendments to Regulation S-X, requiring separate disclosure of preferred stock subject to mandatory redemption requirements, often called "redeemable preferred stock." In taking such action, the SEC noted an increase in the use of complex securities—such as redeemable preferred stock—that exhibit both debt and equity characteristics. The question subse-quently considered by the FASB was whether or not such securities should be classified as liabilities rather than as equity securities. How might the FASB's guidelines for recognition, measurement, and reporting assist in resolving this or similar issues?

## Case 2—7 (Measurement attributes: historical costs vs. current values)

Financial statements rely heavily on historical cost information. In fact, the FASB, in Concepts Statement No. 5, states:

> Present financial statements frequently are characterized as being based on the historical cost (histori-cal proceeds) attribute. That no doubt reflects the fact that, for most enterprises, a great many of the individual events recognized in financial statements are acquisitions of goods or services for cash or equivalent that are recorded at historical cost.

However, several industries feel that the information provided using historical costs is not rele-vant for investors and creditors. As an example, The Rouse Company, a national real estate develop-ment firm, provides financial statements using both a historical cost and a current-value basis. In its 1988 annual report, The Rouse Company reported property with a current value of just under $1.5 billion. The property's historical cost was $67 million. Why do accountants focus primarily on historical cost figures? If the $1.5 billion figure is more relevant for investors and creditors, why don't traditional financial statements reflect current values? What are the risks to investors, creditors, and auditors of presenting current-value information in the body of financial statements?

### Case 2—8 (Financial reporting: the difficult task of satisfying diverse informational needs)

Teri Green has recently been promoted. She is now the chief financial officer of Teltrex, Inc., and has primary responsibility for the external reporting function. During the past three weeks, Green has met with: Jeff Thalman, the senior vice president of Westmore First National Bank, where Teltrex has a $1,000,000 line of credit; Susan Davis, a financial analyst for Stubbs, Jones, and McConkie, a brokerage firm; and Brian Ellis, who is something of a corporate gadfly and who owns 2 percent of the outstanding common stock of Teltrex. Each of these individuals has commented on last year's annual report of Teltrex, pointing out deficiencies and suggesting additional information they would like to see presented in this year's annual report. From Green's point of view, explain the nature of general-purpose financial statements and indicate the informational qualities of the accounting data that she must be concerned with in fulfilling the corporation's external reporting responsibility.

### Case 2—9    (Responsibility for financial reporting)

It is apparent from reading *The Wall Street Journal* and other financial publications that an increasing number of lawsuits are being filed each year against independent accountants (CPAs). Most cases involve accountants who audited the financial statements of companies that subsequently went bankrupt. Who is responsible for a company's financial statements, and how might preparers and others use a conceptual framework to fulfill their responsibilities?

### Case 2—10    (The trade-off between relevance and reliability)

The cable television industry is facing competition from companies using advanced technologies. The use of microwave allows programs to be beamed, at low cost, to locations not accessed by cable. This technology, if successful, could eliminate the need for the current high-fixed-cost, physically-intrusive cable systems. What information do cable companies need in order to evaluate the potential of microwave TV? What is a limitation associated with estimating demand for microwave TV? Why don't cable companies just wait and see if microwave TV is a success?

### Case 2—11    (Measurement issues associated with a specific liability)

Companies regularly obtain money through the issuance of bonds. The market value of bonds changes daily and on any given day is a function of many factors including economic variables, industry developments, and firm-specific information. How should bonds be reported on the books of the issuer: at their market value on the balance sheet date? at their historical selling price? at their discounted present value? or at their eventual maturity value? For each of the above measurement attributes, identify and discuss the issues associated with each attribute.

---

## EXERCISES

### Exercise 2—1    (Aspects of the FASB's conceptual framework)

Determine whether the following statements are true or false. If a statement is false, explain why.

1. Comprehensive income includes changes in equity resulting from distributions to owners.
2. Timeliness and predictive value are both characteristics of relevant information.
3. The tendency to recognize favorable events early is an example of conservatism.
4. Objectives of Concepts Statement No. 1 focus primarily on the needs of internal users of financial information.

5. Statements of Financial Accounting Concepts are considered authoritative pronouncements.
6. The overriding objective of financial reporting is to provide information for making economic decisions.
7. Concepts Statement No. 1 seeks to clarify *how* financial statement reporting should be accomplished, and succeeding Concepts Statements clarify *what* should be reported in financial statements.
8. Certain modifying constraints, such as conservatism, can justify departures from GAAP.
9. Under Concepts Statement No. 5, the term "recognized" is synonymous with the term "recorded."
10. Once an accounting method is adopted, it should never be changed.

### Exercise 2—2  (Conceptual framework terminology)

Match the statements on the left with the letter of the terms on the right. An answer (letter) may be used more than once and some terms require more than one answer (letter).

1. Key ingredients in quality of relevance.
2. Basic assumptions that influence the FASB's Conceptual Framework.
3. The idea that information should represent what it purports to represent.
4. An important constraint, relating to costs and benefits.
5. An example of conservatism.
6. The availability of information when it is needed.
7. Associating expense with a particular revenue or time period.
8. Determines the threshold for recognition.
9. Implies objectivity and consensus.
10. Transactions between independent parties.

a. Cost effectiveness
b. Representational faithfulness
c. Matching principle
d. Verifiability
e. Time periods
f. Unrealized
g. Completeness
h. Timeliness
i. Materiality
j. Predictive value
k. Economic entity
l. Lower-of-cost-or-market rule
m. Accrual accounting
n. Arm's-length

### Exercise 2—3  (Objectives of financial reporting)

For each of the following independent situations, identify the relevant objective(s) of financial reporting that the company may be overlooking. Discuss each of these objectives.

1. The president of Coventry, Inc., feels that the financial statements should be prepared for use by management only, since they are the primary decision makers.
2. Cascade Carpets Co. feels that financial statements should only reflect the present financial standing and cash position of the firm and should not provide any future-oriented data.
3. The vice president of Share Enterprises, Inc., believes that the financial statements are to present only current-year revenues and expenses and not disclose assets, liabilities, and owners' equity.
4. Cruz Co. has a policy of providing disclosures of only its assets, liabilities, and owners' equity.
5. Marty Manufacturing, Inc., always discloses the assets, liabilities, and owners' equity of the firm along with the revenues and expenses. Marty's management believes that these items provide all the information relevant to investing decisions.

### Exercise 2—4  (Applications of accounting characteristics and concepts)

For each situation listed, indicate by letter the appropriate qualitative characteristic(s) or accounting concept(s) applied. A letter may be used more than once, and more than one characteristic or concept may apply to a particular situation.

(a) Understandability
(b) Verifiability
(c) Timeliness

(d) Representational faithfulness
(e) Neutrality
(f) Relevance

| | | | |
|---|---|---|---|
| (g) | Going concern | (k) | Materiality |
| (h) | Economic entity | (l) | Comparability |
| (i) | Historical cost | (m) | Conservatism |
| (j) | Quantifiability | | |

1. Goodwill is only recorded in the accounts when it arises from the purchase of another entity at a price higher than the fair market value of the purchased entity's tangible assets.
2. Marketable securities are valued at the lower of cost or market.
3. All payments out of petty cash are debited to Miscellaneous Expense.
4. Plant assets are classified separately as land or buildings, with an accumulated depreciation account for buildings.
5. Periodic payments of $1,500 per month for services of H. Hay, who is the sole proprietor of the company, are reported as withdrawals.
6. Small tools used by a large manufacturing firm are recorded as expenses when purchased.
7. Marketable securities are initially recorded at cost.
8. A retail store estimates inventory, rather than taking a complete physical count, for purposes of preparing monthly financial statements.
9. A note describing the company's possible liability in a lawsuit is included with the financial statements even though no formal liability exists at the balance sheet date.
10. Depreciation on plant assets is consistently computed each year by the straight-line method.

## Exercise 2—5 (Trade-off between qualitative characteristics)

In each of the following independent situations, an example is given requiring a trade-off between the qualitative characteristics discussed in the text. For each situation, identify the relevant characteristics and briefly discuss how satisfying one characteristic may involve not satisfying another.

1. The book value of an office building is approaching its originally estimated salvage value of $200,000. However, its current market value has been estimated at $20 million. The company's management would like to disclose to financial statement users the current value of the building on the balance sheet.
2. MMM Industries has used the FIFO inventory method for the past twenty years. However, all other major competitors use the LIFO method of accounting for inventories. MMM is contemplating a switch from FIFO to LIFO.
3. Stocks Inc. is negotiating with a major bank for a significant loan. The bank has asked that a set of financial statements be provided as quickly after the year-end as possible. Because invoices from many of the company's suppliers are mailed several weeks after inventory is received, Stocks Inc. is considering estimating the amounts associated with those liabilities to be able to prepare their financial statements more quickly.
4. Satellite Inc. produces and sells satellites to government and private industries. The company provides a warranty guaranteeing the performance of the satellites. A recent space launch placed one of their satellites in orbit, and several malfunctions have occurred. At year-end, Satellite Inc.'s auditors would like the company to disclose the potential liability in the notes to the financial statements. Officers of Satellite Inc. believe that the satellite can be repaired in orbit and that disclosure of a contingency such as this would unnecessarily bias the financial statements.

## Exercise 2—6 (Elements of financial reporting)

For each of the following items, identify the financial statement element being discussed.

1. Changes in equity during a period, except those resulting from investments by owners and distributions to owners.
2. The net assets of an entity.
3. The result of a transaction requiring the future transfer of assets to other entities.
4. An increase in assets from the delivery of goods that constitute the entity's ongoing central operations.

5.  An increase in an entity's net assets from incidental transactions.
6.  An increase in net assets through the issuance of stock.
7.  Decreases in net assets from peripheral transactions of an enterprise.
8.  The payment of a dividend.
9.  Outflows of assets from the delivery of goods or services.
10. An item offering future value to an entity.

### Exercise 2—7   (Assumptions of financial reporting)

In each of the following independent situations, an example is given involving one of the traditional assumptions of the accounting model. For each situation, identify the assumption involved (briefly explain your answer).

1.  A subsidiary of Parent Inc. was exhibiting poor earnings performance for the year. In an effort to increase the subsidiary's reported earnings, Parent Inc. purchased products from the subsidiary at twice the normal markup.
2.  Johnson Corp. required additional funding to introduce a new product line. Management prepared cash-basis financial statements and presented them to bank officials in order to obtain the loan.
3.  When preparing the financial statements for MacNeil & Sons, the accountant included certain personal assets of MacNeil and his sons in preparing the statements.
4.  The operations of Uintah Savings & Loan are being evaluated by the federal government. During their investigations, government officials have determined that numerous loans made by top management were unwise and have seriously endangered the future existence of the savings and loan.
5.  Pine Valley Ski Resort has experienced a drastic reduction in revenues because of a light snowfall for the year. Rather than produce financial statements at the end of the fiscal year, as is traditionally done, management has elected to wait until next year and present results for a two-year period.
6.  Colobri Inc. has inventory that was purchased in 1990 at a cost of $150,000. Because of inflation, that same inventory, if purchased today, would cost $225,000. Management would like to report the asset on the balance sheet at its current value.

### Exercise 2—8   (Theoretical support for corrected balance sheet)

G. Nielsen prepared the following balance sheet for Nielsen Inc. as of December 31, 1993. Review each item listed, and considering the additional data given, prepare a corrected, properly classified balance sheet. Where a change is made in reporting an item, disclose in a separate note the theoretical support for your suggested change. Record any offsetting adjustments in the Retained Earnings account, except for possible contributed capital changes.

Additional data:

(a) Cash included a bank checking account of $20,000, current checks and money orders on hand of $5,000, and a $5,000 check that could not be cashed. The check was from Davis Co., a customer that had gone out of business. Nielsen feels this $5,000 will probably not be recovered.
(b) Marketable securities are listed at year-end market values. They were purchased early in 1993 for $46,800.
(c) Nielsen estimates that all receivables are collectible except for a three-year-old, past-due note of $8,000. Past collection experience indicates that two percent of current notes and accounts prove uncollectible.
(d) Land and buildings are recorded at initial cost. At date of acquisition, land was valued at $70,000 and buildings at $450,000. Building depreciation has been correctly recorded.
(e) Goodwill was recorded when Nielsen received an offer of $40,000 more for the business than the recorded asset values.
(f) Of the notes payable, $30,000 will be due in 1994 with the remainder of the notes coming due in 1995 and 1996.

(g) The mortgage is payable in annual payments of $19,500 plus interest.

(h) The capital stock has a par value of $100 per share; 2,500 shares are issued and outstanding.

### Assets

| | |
|---|---:|
| Cash ............................................... *25,000* | $ 30,000 |
| Marketable securities ............................. *46,800* | 55,000 |
| Notes receivable ................................... *32,000* | 40,000 |
| Accounts receivable ............................... | 130,000 |
| Inventories ........................................ | 195,000 |
| Land and buildings ................................ | 520,000 |
| Accumulated depreciation—buildings ............... | (27,000) |
| Goodwill ........................................... | ~~40,000~~ |
| | $983,000 |

### Liabilities

| | |
|---|---:|
| Accounts payable ................................. | $ 85,000 |
| Taxes payable .................................... | 65,000 |
| Notes payable .................................... | 120,000 |
| Mortgage payable ................................. | 273,000 |
| Capital stock .......................... *250,000* | 300,000 |
| Retained earnings ................................ | 140,000 |
| | $983,000 |

## Exercise 2—9  (Theoretical support for corrected income statement)

Hillstead prepared the following income statement for the calendar year 1993.

| | |
|---|---|
| Revenues .............. | $80,000 |
| Expenses.............. | 50,000 |
| Net income............ | $30,000 |

An examination of the records reveals the following:

(a) Hillstead is the sole proprietor.

(b) Business operations include:
   1. A catering service
   2. An equipment rental shop
   3. Rental of a part of Hillstead's home for small receptions

(c) Revenues include:

| | |
|---|---:|
| 1. Catering service sales..................................... | $50,000 |
| 2. Equipment rentals ........................................ | 12,500 |
| 3. Reception rental space.................................... | 17,500 |
| | $80,000 |

(d) Expenses consisted of:

| | |
|---|---:|
| 1. Cost of goods sold (catering) ............................. | $15,000 |
| 2. Other costs (catering) .................................... | 11,500 |
| 3. Depreciation—equipment rental .......................... | 1,500 |
| 4. Repairs and other costs—equipment rental .............. | 2,500 |
| 5. Depreciation, $2,000; cleaning, $4,500; and miscellaneous costs, $1,000—reception rental space..................... | 7,500 |
| 6. Living expenses—family ................................. | 12,000 |
| | $50,000 |

Based on the FASB's Conceptual Framework, indicate what changes, if any, you would make in the income statement format and amount of Hillstead's income for 1993 and give theoretical support for your conclusions.

# CHAPTER 3

# Review of the Accounting Process

---

**CHAPTER TOPICS**

**Overview of the Accounting Process**

**Recording Phase**

**Summarizing Phase**

**Accrual Versus Cash-Basis Accounting**

**Computers and the Accounting Process**

**Special Journals and Subsidiary Ledgers (Appendix 3—1)**

**Closing Method for Inventory (Appendix 3—2)**

---

In 1986, TravelCenter was the largest Alaskan travel agency and one of Alaska's ten largest companies. Total revenue was $100 million. In 1987, TravelCenter was in Chapter 11 bankruptcy. Major factors in the bankruptcy were a downturn in the Alaskan economy because of falling oil prices and TravelCenter's own overextension into other lines of business (including a limousine service and a fishing resort). In addition, according to documents filed in bankruptcy court, TravelCenter's demise was partly a result of disastrous financial recordkeeping. As an example, receivables were grossly overstated because cash collections on customer accounts were never recorded. According to a court-appointed examiner, the cash was collected and its receipt recorded, but "the accounts were never taken off the [receivables] list."[1] It seems that TravelCenter forgot the cardinal rule of bookkeeping: debits = credits.

[1]Laura Del Rosso, "TravelCenter's Road to Collapse," *Travel Weekly*, September 7, 1987: p. 47.

As indicated by the TravelCenter example, all business enterprises, regardless of size or the nature of their operations, need accurate records of business transactions. Businesses that do not keep accurate records will not operate as efficiently and profitably as they could otherwise. In addition, the Foreign Corrupt Practices Act of 1977 requires publicly held companies to keep accurate books and records that fairly reflect business activity.

A variety of reports are prepared from accounting records to assist users in making better economic decisions. As explained in Chapters 1 and 2, general-purpose financial statements are prepared for external user groups, primarily current or potential investors and creditors, who are involved financially with an enterprise but who are not a part of its management team. User groups within organizations, especially those in managerial positions, receive reports to assist them in planning and controlling the day-to-day operations of their organizations. Tax returns and similar reports must be prepared to comply with Internal Revenue Service (IRS) requirements. Special reports are required by various regulatory agencies such as the Securities and Exchange Commission (SEC).

Each of these reports is based on data that are the result of an accounting system and a set of procedures collectively referred to as the **accounting process**, or the **accounting cycle.** While this process follows a fairly standard set of procedures, the exact nature of the **accounting system** used to collect and report the data will depend on the type of business, its size, the volume of transactions processed, the degree of automation employed, and other related factors. The various routines in each system are developed to meet the special needs of the business unit. Every accounting system, however, should be designed to provide accurate information on a timely and efficient basis. At the same time, the system must provide controls that are effective in preventing mistakes and guarding against dishonesty.

Historically, accounting systems were maintained by hand and referred to as **manual systems.** Such systems continue to be used effectively in many situations. In today's business environment, however, most companies use at least some type of automated equipment, such as cash registers or other special-purpose business machines, and many companies have **electronic data processing (EDP) systems** that utilize the capabilities of high-speed computers. Furthermore, the advent of microcomputers has put EDP systems within the reach of almost all smaller companies that previously had to rely on manual or partially mechanized systems. As explained later in the chapter, an EDP system has many advantages and some disadvantages. The important point is that all accounting systems are designed to serve the same information gathering and processing functions. There is no difference in the underlying accounting concepts involved, only in some mechanical aspects of the process and in the appearance of the records and reports. Since it is easier to understand and to illustrate, a manual system will be used for the examples in this chapter and throughout the text.

The purpose of this chapter is to review the basic steps of the accounting process, including a brief review of the mechanics of double-entry accounting. A number of basic accounting terms are presented in the chapter and are included in the glossary at the end of the book.

## OVERVIEW OF THE ACCOUNTING PROCESS

The accounting process consists of two interrelated parts: (1) the recording phase and (2) the summarizing phase. The recording phase is concerned with the collection of information about economic transactions and events. For most businesses, the recording function is based on double-entry accounting procedures. In the summarizing phase, the recorded information is organized and summarized, using various formats for a variety of decision-making purposes. There is an overlapping of the two phases, since the recording of transactions is an ongoing activity that does not cease at the end of an accounting period but continues uninterrupted while events of the preceding period are being summarized. The recording and summarizing phases of the accounting process are reviewed and illustrated in this chapter. The form and content of the basic financial statements are discussed in depth and illustrated in Chapters 4, 5, and 6.[2] The accounting process, illustrated in Exhibit 3—1, generally includes the following steps in well-defined sequence:

### Recording Phase

1. Business documents are analyzed. Analysis of the documentation of business activities provides the basis for making an initial record of each transaction.
2. Transactions are recorded. Based on the supporting documents from Step 1, transactions are recorded in chronological order in books of original entry, or journals.
3. Transactions are posted. Transactions, as classified and recorded in the journals, are posted to the appropriate accounts in the general and, where applicable, subsidiary ledgers.

### Summarizing Phase

4. A trial balance of the accounts in the general ledger is prepared. The trial balance, usually prepared on a work sheet, provides a summary of the information as classified in the ledger, as well as a general check on the accuracy of recording and posting.
5. Adjusting entries are recorded. Before financial statements can be prepared, all relevant information that has not been recorded must be determined. Often, adjustments are first made on a work sheet and may be formally recorded and posted at any time prior to closing (Step 7). If a work sheet is not used, the adjusting entries must be recorded and posted at this point so the accounts are current prior to the preparation of financial statements.
6. Financial statements are prepared. Statements summarizing operations and showing the financial position and cash flows are prepared from the information on the work sheet or directly from the adjusted accounts.
7. Nominal accounts are closed. Balances in the nominal (temporary) accounts are closed into appropriate summary accounts. As determined in summary accounts, the results of operations are transferred to the appropriate owners' equity accounts.
8. A post-closing trial balance may be taken. A post-closing trial balance is taken to determine the equality of the debits and credits after posting the adjusting and closing entries.
9. Selected accounts may be reversed. Accrued and prepaid balances that were established by adjusting entries may be returned to the nominal accounts that are to be used in recording and summarizing activities involving these items in the new period. This step is not required, but may be desirable as a means of facilitating recording and adjusting routines in the succeeding period.

### Recording Phase

Accurate financial statements can be prepared only if transactions have been properly recorded. A **transaction** is an event that involves the transfer or exchange of goods or

---

[2]Appendix A, at the end of the book, provides an illustrated set of financial statements from the 1990 annual report of IBM Corporation.

**Exhibit 3—1    The Accounting Process**

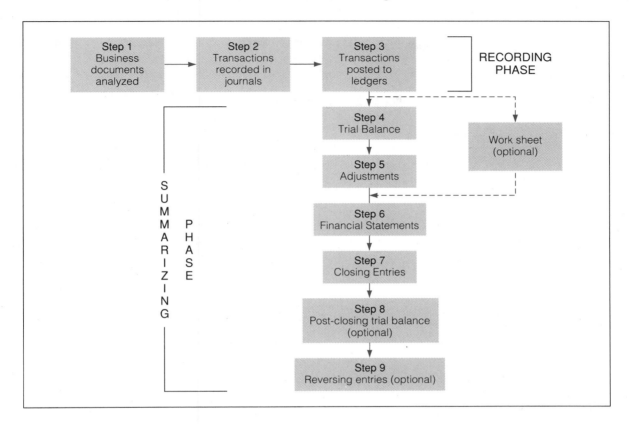

services between two or more entities. Examples of business transactions include the purchase of merchandise or other assets from suppliers and the sale of goods or services to customers. In addition to transactions, other events and circumstances may affect the assets, liabilities, and owners' equity of the business. Some of those events and circumstances also must be recorded. Examples include the recognition of depreciation on plant assets, a decline in the market value of inventories and investments, or a loss suffered from a flood or an earthquake.

As indicated, the recording phase involves analyzing business documents, journalizing transactions, and posting to the ledger accounts. Before discussing these steps, the system of double-entry accounting will be reviewed, since most businesses use this procedure in recording their transactions.

**Double-Entry Accounting**    As explained in Chapters 1 and 2, financial accounting rests on a foundation of basic assumptions, concepts, and principles that govern the recording, classifying, summarizing, and reporting of accounting data. **Double-entry accounting** is an old and universally accepted system for recording accounting data. With double-entry accounting, each transaction is recorded in a way that maintains the equality of the basic accounting equation:

**Assets  =  Liabilities  +  Owners' Equity**

To review how double-entry accounting works, recall that a debit is an entry on the left side of an account and a credit is an entry on the right side. The debit/credit relationships of accounts were explained in detail in your introductory accounting course. Exhibit 3—2 summarizes these relationships for a corporation. You will note that assets, expenses, and dividends are increased by debits and decreased by credits. Liabilities, owners' equity accounts (capital stock and retained earnings), and revenues are increased by credits and decreased by debits.

### Exhibit 3—2    Debit and Credit Relationships of Accounts

| Assets | | = | Liabilities | | + | Owners' Equity | |
|---|---|---|---|---|---|---|---|
| DR | CR | | DR | CR | | DR | CR |
| (+) | (−) | | (−) | (+) | | (−) | (+) |

| Capital Stock | | Retained Earnings | |
|---|---|---|---|
| DR | CR | DR | CR |
| (−) | (+) | (−) | (+) |

| Expenses | | Revenues | |
|---|---|---|---|
| DR | CR | DR | CR |
| (+) | (−) | (−) | (+) |

| Dividends | |
|---|---|
| DR | CR |
| (+) | (−) |

To illustrate double-entry accounting, consider the transactions and journal entries shown in Exhibit 3—3 and their impact on the accounting equation. In studying this illustration, you should note that for each transaction, total debits equal total credits and the equality of the accounting equation is maintained.

To summarize, you should remember the following important features of double-entry accounting:

1. Assets are always increased by debits and decreased by credits.
2. Liability and owners' equity accounts are always increased by credits and decreased by debits.
3. Owners' equity for a corporation includes capital stock accounts and the retained earnings account.

4. Revenues, expenses, and dividends relate to owners' equity through the retained earnings account.
5. Expenses and dividends are increased by debits and decreased by credits.
6. Revenues are increased by credits and decreased by debits.
7. The difference between total revenues and total expenses for a period is net income (loss), which increases (decreases) owners' equity through Retained Earnings.

**Exhibit 3—3    Double-Entry Accounting: Illustrative Transactions and Journal Entries**

| Transaction | Journal Entry | | Impact of Transactions on Accounting Equation Assets = Liabilities + Owners' Equity | | |
|---|---|---|---|---|---|
| 1. Investment by shareholder in a corporation, $10,000 | Cash . . . . . . . . . . . . . Capital Stock . . . . | 10,000 | 10,000 | +10,000 = | +10,000 |
| 2. Purchase of supplies on account, $5,000 | Supplies . . . . . . . . Accts. Payable . . . | 5,000 | 5,000 | + 5,000 = + 5,000 | |
| 3. Payment of wages expense, $2,500 | Wages Expense . . . Cash . . . . . . . . . . . | 2,500 | 2,500 | − 2,500 = (Increase in an expense reduces Retained Earnings and, therefore, Owners' Equity) | − 2,500 |
| 4. Collection of accounts receivable, $1,000 | Cash . . . . . . . . . . . . . Accts. Receivable | 1,000 | 1,000 | + 1,000 − 1,000 = | |
| 5. Payment of account payable, $500 | Accts. Payable . . . . Cash . . . . . . . . . . . | 500 | 500 | − 500 = − 500 | |
| 6. Sale of merchandise on account for $20,000 | Accts. Receivable Sales . . . . . . . . . . | 20,000 | 20,000 | +20,000 = (Increase in revenue increases Retained Earnings and, therefore, Owners' Equity) | +20,000 |
| 7. Purchase of equipment: $15,000 down payment plus $40,000 long-term note | Equipment . . . . . . . Cash . . . . . . . . . . . Note Payable . . . . | 55,000 | 15,000 40,000 | +55,000 − 15,000 = +40,000 | |
| 8. Payment of cash dividends, $4,000 | Dividends . . . . . . . . Cash . . . . . . . . . . . | 4,000 | 4,000 | − 4,000 = (Dividends reduce Retained Earnings and, therefore, Owners' Equity) | − 4,000 |

**Analyzing Business Documents**    The basic accounting records of a business consist of:

1. Original source materials evidencing transactions, called business documents or source documents,
2. Records for classifying and recording transactions, known as journals or "books of original entry" and,
3. Records for summarizing the effects of transactions upon individual accounts, known as ledgers.

The recording phase begins with an analysis of the documentation showing what business activities have occurred. Normally, a business document is the first record of each transaction. Such a document offers detailed information concerning the transaction and also fixes responsibility by naming the parties involved. The business documents provide support for the data to be recorded in the journals. Copies of sales invoices or cash register tapes, for example, are the evidence in support of sales transactions; purchase invoices support purchase transactions; debit and credit memorandums support adjustments in debtor and creditor balances; check stubs and canceled checks provide data concerning cash disbursements; the corporation minutes book supports entries authorized by action of the board of directors; journal vouchers prepared and approved by appropriate officers are a source of data for adjustments or corrections that are to be reported in the accounts. Documents underlying each recorded transaction provide a means of verifying the accounting records and thus form a vital part of the information and control system.

**Journalizing Transactions**    Once the information provided on business documents has been analyzed, transactions are recorded in chronological order in the appropriate journals. In some small businesses, all transactions are recorded in a single journal. Most business enterprises, however, maintain various special journals, designed to meet their specific needs, as well as a general journal. A special journal is used to record a particular type of frequently recurring transaction. Special journals are commonly used, for example, to record each of the following types of transactions: sales, purchases, cash disbursements, and cash receipts. A general journal is used to record all transactions for which a special journal is not maintained. As illustrated below, a general journal shows the transaction date and the accounts affected, and allows for a brief description of each transaction. It also provides Debit and Credit columns and a Posting Reference column. When transactions are posted, as explained in the next section, the appropriate ledger account numbers are entered in the Posting Reference column. Special journals are illustrated and explained in Appendix 3—1 at the end of this chapter.

**GENERAL JOURNAL** Page 24

| Date | | Description | Post. Ref. | Debit | Credit |
|---|---|---|---|---|---|
| 1993 July | 1 | Dividends...................................... | 330 | 25,000 | |
| | | Dividends Payable ........................... | 260 | | 25,000 |
| | | *Declared semiannual cash dividend on common stock.* | | | |
| | 10 | Equipment.................................... | 180 | 7,500 | |
| | | Notes Payable................................ | 220 | | 7,500 |
| | | *Issued note for new equipment.* | | | |
| | 31 | Payroll Tax Expense .......................... | 418 | 2,650 | |
| | | Payroll Taxes Payable........................ | 240 | | 2,650 |
| | | *Recorded payroll taxes for month.* | | | |

**Posting to the Ledger Accounts**    An account is used to summarize the effects of transactions on each element of the expanded accounting equation. A ledger is a collection of all the accounts maintained by a business and may be in the form of a book or computer files. The specific accounts required by a business unit vary depending on the nature of the business, its properties and activities, the information to be provided on the financial statements, and the controls to be employed in carrying out the accounting functions. The accounts used by a particular business are usually expressed in the form of a chart of accounts. This chart lists all accounts in systematic form with identifying numbers or symbols that provide the framework for summarizing business operations.

Information recorded in the journals is transferred to appropriate accounts in the ledger. This transfer is referred to as posting. Ledger accounts for Equipment and Notes Payable are presented below, illustrating the posting of the July 10 transaction from the general journal on page 62. The posting reference (J24) indicates that the transaction was transferred from page 24 of the general journal. Note that the account numbers for Equipment (180) and Notes Payable (220) are entered in the Posting Reference column of the journal.

## GENERAL LEDGER

**Account Equipment**                                                         **Account No. 180**

| Date | | Item | Post. Ref. | Debit | Credit | Balance |
|------|--|------|-----------|-------|--------|---------|
| 1993 July | 1 | Balance............................ | | | | 10,550 |
| | 10 | Purchase Equipment................ | J24 | 7,500 | | 18,050 |

**Account Notes Payable**                                                     **Account No. 220**

| Date | | Item | Post. Ref. | Debit | Credit | Balance |
|------|--|------|-----------|-------|--------|---------|
| 1993 July | 1 | Balance............................ | | | | 5,750 |
| | 10 | Purchase Equipment................ | J24 | | 7,500 | 13,250 |

It is often desirable to establish separate ledgers for detailed information in support of balance sheet or income statement items. The general ledger includes all accounts appearing on the financial statements, while separate subsidiary ledgers afford additional detail in support of certain general ledger accounts. For example, a single accounts receivable account is usually carried in the general ledger, and individual customer accounts are recorded in a subsidiary accounts receivable ledger. Also, the capital stock account in the general ledger is normally supported by individual stockholder accounts in a subsidiary stockholders ledger. The general ledger account that summarizes the detailed information in a subsidiary ledger is known as a control account. Subsidiary ledger accounts are illustrated in Appendix 3—1 at the end of this chapter.

Depending primarily on the number of transactions involved, amounts may be posted to ledger accounts on a daily, weekly, or monthly basis. If a computer system is being used, the posting process may be done automatically as transactions are recorded. At the end of an accounting period, when the posting process has been completed, the balances in the ledger accounts are used for preparing the trial balance.

## Summarizing Phase

As noted earlier, the objective of the accounting process is to produce financial statements and other reports that will assist various users in making economic decisions. Once the recording phase is completed, the data must be summarized and organized into a useful format. The remaining steps of the accounting process are designed to accomplish this purpose. These steps will be illustrated using data from Rosi, Inc., a hypothetical merchandising company, for the year ended December 31, 1993.

**Preparing a Trial Balance**    After all transactions for the period have been posted to the ledger accounts, the balance for each account is determined. Every account will have either a debit, credit, or zero balance. A trial balance is a list of all accounts and their balances. The trial balance, therefore, indicates whether total debits equal total credits

## Luca Pacioli

The earliest systematic explanation of modern double-entry accounting is contained in a book on mathematics written in 1494. *Summa de Arithmetica, Geometria, Proportioni et Proportionalita* (Everything about Arithmetic, Geometry, and Proportion) was written by Luca Pacioli, a noted mathematician and a monk of the order of St. Francis. Pacioli was no obscure writer; he once collaborated on a book with Leonardo da Vinci. The bookkeeping portion of *Summa* is called *De Computis et Scripturis* (Of Reckonings and Writings). Pacioli did not invent double-entry accounting; he simply provided an organized treatment of the "method of Venice," which had developed during the fourteenth and fifteenth centuries.

In most respects, the double-entry method explained by Pacioli is the same as that used today. One difference was the use of a third book—the memorial—in addition to the journal and the ledger, which we currently use. The memorial was the book of original entry. Since transactions occurred in a variety of currencies, and also because money was rarely worth its face value, amounts recorded in the memorial were converted to a common working currency before being entered in the journal. In addition, Pacioli didn't outline procedures for the production of periodic financial statements. Business was seen as a succession of individual ventures (like a voyage to trade textiles for spice), and the revenues and expenses for each venture were accounted for separately. Instead of a periodic closing of the nominal accounts, the profit or loss from an individual venture was transferred to the capital account when the venture was completed.

One notable feature of Pacioli's work is that it contains no worked-out examples; the topic of bookkeeping is dealt with strictly in the abstract. Since Pacioli's day, quite a number of accounting students have unsuccessfully tried the same approach in preparing for accounting exams.

Sources:

J. Row Fogo, "History of Bookkeeping" in *A History of Accounting and Accountants*, Richard Brown, editor, (London: Frank Cass and Company Limited, 1968): pp. 93-170.

Henry Rand Hatfield, "An Historical Defense of Bookkeeping," *The Journal of Accountancy*, April 1924: pp. 241-253.

and thus provides a general check on the accuracy of recording and posting. A trial balance for Rosi, Inc., is presented on page 65.

**Preparing Adjusting Entries**     In order to report information on a timely basis, the life of a business is divided into relatively short time periods, such as a year, a quarter, or a month. While this is essential for the information to be useful, it does create problems for the accountant who must summarize the financial operations for the designated period and report on the financial position at the end of that period. Transactions during the period have been recorded in the appropriate journals and posted to the ledger accounts. At the end of the period, many accounts require adjustments to reflect current conditions. At this time, too, other financial data, not recognized previously, must be entered in the accounts to bring the books up to date. This requires analysis of individual accounts and various source documents. Based on this analysis, adjusting entries are made, and financial statements are prepared using the adjusted account balances.

This part of the accounting process is illustrated using the adjusting data for Rosi, Inc., presented on page 66. The data are classified according to the typical areas requiring adjustment at the end of the designated time period, in this case the year 1993. The accounts listed in the trial balance below do not reflect the adjusting data. The adjusting data must be combined with the information on the trial balance if the resulting financial statements are to appropriately reflect company operating results and financial position.

**Rosi, Inc.**
**Trial Balance**
**December 31, 1993**

|  | Debit | Credit |
|---|---|---|
| Cash | $ 83,110 | |
| Accounts Receivable | 106,500 | |
| Allowance for Doubtful Accounts | | $ 1,610 |
| Inventory | 45,000 | |
| Prepaid Insurance | 8,000 | |
| Interest Receivable | 0 | |
| Notes Receivable | 28,000 | |
| Land | 114,000 | |
| Buildings | 156,000 | |
| Accum. Depr.—Buildings | | 39,000 |
| Furniture & Equipment | 19,000 | |
| Accum. Depr.—Furniture & Equipment | | 3,800 |
| Accounts Payable | | 37,910 |
| Unearned Rent Revenue | | 0 |
| Salaries and Wages Payable | | 0 |
| Interest Payable | | 0 |
| Payroll Taxes Payable | | 5,130 |
| Income Tax Payable | | 0 |
| Dividends Payable | | 3,400 |
| Bonds Payable | | 140,000 |
| Common Stock, $15 par | | 150,000 |
| Retained Earnings | | 126,770 |
| Dividends | 13,600 | |
| Sales | | 479,500 |
| Purchases | 162,600 | |
| Purchase Discounts | | 3,290 |
| Cost of Goods Sold | 0 | |
| Salaries and Wages Expense | 172,450 | |
| Heat, Light, and Power | 32,480 | |
| Payroll Tax Expense | 18,300 | |
| Advertising Expense | 18,600 | |
| Doubtful Accounts Expense | 0 | |
| Depr. Exp.—Buildings | 0 | |
| Depr. Exp.—Furniture & Equipment | 0 | |
| Insurance Expense | 0 | |
| Interest Revenue | | 1,100 |
| Rent Revenue | | 2,550 |
| Interest Expense | 16,420 | |
| Income Tax Expense | 0 | |
| Totals | $994,060 | $994,060 |

***Asset Depreciation*** Charges to operations for the use of buildings, furniture, and equipment must be recorded at the end of the period. In recording asset depreciation, operations are charged with a portion of the asset's cost, and the carrying value of the asset is reduced by that amount. A reduction in an asset for depreciation is usually recorded by a

Adjusting Data for Rosi, Inc.
December 31, 1993

Asset Depreciation:
  (a) Buildings, 5% per year.
  (b) Furniture and equipment, 10% per year.
Doubtful Accounts:
  (c) The allowance for doubtful accounts is to be increased by $1,100.
Accrued Expenses:
  (d) Salaries and wages, $2,150.
  (e) Interest on bonds payable, $5,000.
Accrued Revenues:
  (f) Interest on notes receivable, $250.
Prepaid Expenses:
  (g) Prepaid insurance, $3,800.
Deferred Revenues:
  (h) Unearned rent revenue, $475.
Income taxes:
  (i) Federal and state income taxes, $8,000.
Inventory:
  (j) A periodic inventory system is used; the ending inventory balance is $51,000.

credit to a contra account, Accumulated Depreciation. A contra account (or offset account) is set up to record subtractions from a related account. For example, Allowance for Doubtful Accounts is a contra account to Accounts Receivable. Certain accounts relate to others, but must be added rather than subtracted on the statements, and are referred to as adjunct accounts. Examples include Freight-In, which is added to Purchases, and Additional Paid-In Capital, which is added to the capital stock account balance.

Adjustments at the end of the year for depreciation for Rosi, Inc., are as follows:

| | | | |
|---|---|---|---|
| (a) | Depreciation Expense—Buildings | 7,800 | |
| | Accumulated Depreciation—Buildings | | 7,800 |
| | *To record depreciation on buildings at 5% per year.* | | |
| (b) | Depreciation Expense—Furniture & Equipment | 1,900 | |
| | Accumulated Depreciation—Furniture & Equipment | | 1,900 |
| | *To record depreciation on furniture and equipment at 10% per year.* | | |

**Doubtful Accounts**    Invariably, when a business allows customers to purchase goods and services on credit, some of the accounts receivable will not be collected, resulting in a charge to income for bad debt expense. Under the accrual concept, an adjustment should be made for the estimated expense in the current period, rather than when specific accounts actually become uncollectible. This produces a better matching of revenues and expenses and therefore a better income measurement. Using this procedure, operations are charged with the estimated expense, and receivables are reduced by means of a contra account, Allowance for Doubtful Accounts. To illustrate, the adjustment for Rosi, Inc., at the end of the year, assuming the allowance account is to be increased by $1,100, would be as follows:

| | | | |
|---|---|---|---|
| (c) | Doubtful Accounts Expense | 1,100 | |
| | Allowance for Doubtful Accounts | | 1,100 |
| | *To adjust for estimated doubtful accounts expense.* | | |

Throughout the accounting period, when there is positive evidence that a specific account is uncollectible, the appropriate amount is written off against the contra account. For example, if a $150 receivable were considered uncollectible, that amount would be written off as follows:

| | | |
|---|---|---|
| Allowance for Doubtful Accounts . . . . . . . . . . . . . . . . . . . . . . . . . . | 150 | |
| Accounts Receivable  . . . . . . . . . . . . . . . . . . . . . . . . . . . . . . . . . | | 150 |
| *To write off an uncollectible account.* | | |

No entry is made to Doubtful Accounts Expense, since the adjusting entry has already provided for an estimated expense based on previous experience for all receivables.

**Accrued Expenses**    During the period, certain expenses may have been incurred for which payment is not to be made until a subsequent period. At the end of the period, it is necessary to determine and record any expenses not yet recognized. In recording an accrued expense, an expense account is debited and a liability account is credited. The adjusting entries to record accrued expenses for Rosi, Inc., are:

| | | | |
|---|---|---|---|
| (d) | Salaries and Wages Expense . . . . . . . . . . . . . . . . . . . . . . . . . . . . . | 2,150 | |
| | Salaries and Wages Payable . . . . . . . . . . . . . . . . . . . . . . . . . . . . | | 2,150 |
| | *To record accrued salaries and wages.* | | |
| (e) | Interest Expense  . . . . . . . . . . . . . . . . . . . . . . . . . . . . . . . . . . . . . | 5,000 | |
| | Interest Payable . . . . . . . . . . . . . . . . . . . . . . . . . . . . . . . . . . . . . | | 5,000 |
| | *To record accrued interest on bonds.* | | |

**Accrued Revenues**    During the period, certain amounts may have been earned, although collection is not to be made until a subsequent period. At the end of the period, it is necessary to determine and record the earnings not yet recognized. In recording accrued revenues, an asset account is debited and a revenue account is credited. The illustrative entry recognizing the accrued revenue for Rosi, Inc., is as follows:

| | | | |
|---|---|---|---|
| (f) | Interest Receivable . . . . . . . . . . . . . . . . . . . . . . . . . . . . . . . . . . . . . | 250 | |
| | Interest Revenue . . . . . . . . . . . . . . . . . . . . . . . . . . . . . . . . . . . . . . | | 250 |
| | *To record accrued interest on notes receivable.* | | |

**Prepaid Expenses**    During the period, expenditures may have been recorded on the books for commodities or goods that are not to be received or used up currently. At the end of the period, it is necessary to determine the portions of such expenditures that are applicable to subsequent periods, and hence require recognition as assets.

The method of adjusting for prepaid expenses depends on how the expenditures were originally entered in the accounts. They may have been recorded originally as debits to (1) an asset account or (2) an expense account.

**Original Debit to an Asset Account.** If an asset account was originally debited, the adjusting entry requires that an expense account be debited for the amount applicable to the current period and the asset account be credited. The asset account remains with a debit balance that shows the amount applicable to future periods. An adjusting entry for prepaid insurance for Rosi, Inc., illustrates this situation as follows:

| | | | |
|---|---|---|---|
| (g) | Insurance Expense  . . . . . . . . . . . . . . . . . . . . . . . . . . . . . . . . . . . . | 4,200 | |
| | Prepaid Insurance . . . . . . . . . . . . . . . . . . . . . . . . . . . . . . . . . . . . | | 4,200 |
| | *To record expired insurance ($8,000 − $3,800 = $4,200).* | | |

Since the asset account Prepaid Insurance was originally debited, as shown in the trial balance, the amount of the prepayment ($8,000) must be reduced to reflect only the $3,800 that remains unexpired.

**Original Debit to an Expense Account.** If an expense account was originally debited, the adjusting entry requires that an asset account be debited for the amount applicable to future periods and the expense account be credited. The expense account then remains with a debit balance representing the amount applicable to the current period. For example, if Rosi, Inc., had originally debited Insurance Expense for $8,000, the adjusting entry would be:

| | | |
|---|---|---|
| Prepaid Insurance ($8,000 − $4,200) . . . . . . . . . . . . . . . . . . . . . . . | 3,800 | |
| Insurance Expense . . . . . . . . . . . . . . . . . . . . . . . . . . . . . . . . . | | 3,800 |

### Deferred Revenues

Payments may be received from customers prior to the delivery of goods or services. Amounts received in advance are recorded by debiting an asset account, usually Cash, and crediting either a revenue account or a liability account. At the end of the period, it is necessary to determine the amount of revenue earned in the current period and the amount to be deferred to future periods. The method of adjusting for deferred revenues depends on whether the receipts for undelivered goods or services were recorded originally as credits to (1) a revenue account or (2) a liability account.

**Original Credit to a Revenue Account.** If a revenue account was originally credited, this account is debited and a liability account is credited for the revenue applicable to a future period. The revenue account remains with a credit balance representing the earnings applicable to the current period. As indicated in the trial balance for Rosi, Inc., rent receipts are recorded originally in the rent revenue account. Unearned revenue at the end of 1993 is $475 and is recorded as follows:

| | | |
|---|---|---|
| (h)  Rent Revenue . . . . . . . . . . . . . . . . . . . . . . . . . . . . . . . . . . . . . . . | 475 | |
| Unearned Rent Revenue . . . . . . . . . . . . . . . . . . . . . . . . . . . . . | | 475 |
| *To record unearned rent revenue.* | | |

**Original Credit to a Liability Account.** If a liability account was credited originally, this account is debited and a revenue account is credited for the amount applicable to the current period. The liability account remains with a credit balance that shows the amount applicable to future periods. For example, if Rosi, Inc., had originally credited Unearned Rent Revenue for $2,550, the adjusting entry would be:

| | | |
|---|---|---|
| Unearned Rent Revenue . . . . . . . . . . . . . . . . . . . . . . . . . . . . . . . | 2,075 | |
| Rent Revenue ($2,550 - $475) . . . . . . . . . . . . . . . . . . . . . . . . . . | | 2,075 |

### Income Taxes

When a corporation reports earnings, adjustments must be made for federal and state income taxes. Income Tax Expense is debited and Income Tax Payable is credited. The entry to record income taxes for Rosi, Inc., is as follows:

| | | |
|---|---|---|
| (i)  Income Tax Expense . . . . . . . . . . . . . . . . . . . . . . . . . . . . . . . . . . | 8,000 | |
| Income Tax Payable . . . . . . . . . . . . . . . . . . . . . . . . . . . . . . . . . | | 8,000 |
| *To record income taxes.* | | |

Note that the above entry assumes a single year-end accrual of income taxes. Most companies record income taxes monthly when estimated payments are made to federal and state taxing authorities.

### Adjusting the Inventory Account

The type of adjustment required for the inventory account depends on whether a periodic or a perpetual inventory system is used. When the periodic inventory system is used, physical inventories must be taken at the end of the period to determine the inventory to be reported on the balance sheet and the cost of goods sold to be reported on the income statement. When perpetual inventory records are maintained, the ending inventory and the cost of goods sold balances appear in the ledger. An adjustment is necessary only to correct the recorded balances for any spoilage or theft or bookkeeping errors that may have occurred, as determined by a physical count of the inventory. The inventory procedures for merchandising companies are reviewed in the following paragraphs. Accounting for inventories of manufacturers is explained in a later chapter.

**Periodic (Physical) Inventories.** When using the **periodic inventory system**, all purchases of merchandise during a period are recorded in a purchases account. At the end of the period, before adjustments are made, the inventory account still reflects the beginning inventory balance. The ending balance, based on a physical count, may be recorded in the inventory account by an adjusting entry. At the same time the inventory account is adjusted, the balance in Purchases and related accounts, such as Purchase Discounts or Freight-In, are transferred to Cost of Goods Sold. In this way, the amount of Cost of Goods Sold is established through a single adjusting entry.

Using the method just described, an adjustment for Rosi, Inc., would be made to the inventory account by debiting it for $6,000 ($51,000 − $45,000), debiting Purchase Discounts for $3,290, crediting Purchases for $162,600, and debiting Cost of Goods Sold for the net amount, $153,310. This would increase Inventory to its ending balance of $51,000, close Purchase Discounts and Purchases, and reflect the amount of Cost of Goods Sold to be reported on the income statement. The adjusting entry would be as follows:

| | | | |
|---|---|---|---|
| (j) | Inventory | 6,000 | |
| | Purchase Discounts | 3,290 | |
| | Cost of Goods Sold | 153,310 | |
| | Purchases | | 162,600 |
| | *To adjust inventory, cost of goods sold, and related accounts.* | | |

An alternative to the above procedure is illustrated in Appendix 3—2 at the end of this chapter. This alternative is sometimes referred to as the "closing method," while the preceding approach is referred to as the "adjusting method" for a periodic inventory system.

**Perpetual Inventories.** When a **perpetual inventory system** is maintained, a separate purchases account is not used. The inventory account is debited whenever goods are acquired. When a sale takes place, two entries are required: (1) the sale is recorded in the usual manner, and (2) the merchandise sold is recorded by a debit to Cost of Goods Sold and a credit to Inventory. At any time during the period, Inventory reflects the inventory on hand, and Cost of Goods Sold shows the cost of merchandise sold. At the end of the period, no adjustment is needed for inventory, except to adjust for spoilage or theft as noted earlier. Cost of Goods Sold would be debited and Inventory would be credited for the cost of the spoiled or stolen goods.

***Preparing Financial Statements*** Once all accounts have been brought up to date through the adjustment process, **financial statements** may be prepared. The data may be taken directly from the adjusted account balances in the ledger, or a work sheet may be used.

***Using a Work Sheet*** An optional step in the accounting process is to use a **work sheet** to facilitate the preparation of adjusting entries and financial statements. A work sheet is an accounting tool that is often used in organizing large quantities of data. However, preparing a work sheet is not a required step. As indicated, financial statements can be prepared directly from data in adjusted ledger account balances.

When a work sheet is constructed, trial balance data are listed in the first pair of columns. The adjusting entries are listed in the second pair of columns. Sometimes a third pair of columns is included to show the trial balance after adjustment. Account balances, as adjusted, are carried forward to the appropriate financial statement columns. A work sheet for a merchandising enterprise will include a pair of columns for the income statement accounts and a pair for the balance sheet accounts. There are no columns for the statement of cash flows, because this statement requires additional analysis of changes in account balances for the period. The income statement, balance sheet, and statement of cash flows are discussed and illustrated in subsequent chapters. A work sheet for Rosi, Inc., is shown on pages 72 and 73. All adjustments illustrated previously are included.

**Closing the Nominal Accounts**      Once adjusting entries are formally recorded in the general journal and posted to the ledger accounts, the books are ready to be closed in preparation for a new accounting period. During this closing process, the **nominal (temporary) account** balances are transferred to a **real (permanent) account**, leaving the nominal accounts with a zero balance. Nominal accounts include all income statement accounts plus the dividends account for a corporation or the drawings account for a proprietorship or partnership. The real account that receives the closing amounts from the nominal accounts is Retained Earnings for a corporation or the respective capital accounts for a proprietorship or partnership. Since they are real accounts, these and all other balance sheet accounts remain open and carry their balances forward to the new period.

The mechanics of closing the nominal accounts are straightforward. All revenue accounts with credit balances are closed by being debited; all expense accounts with debit balances are closed by being credited. This reduces these temporary accounts to a zero balance. The difference between the closing debit amounts for revenues and the credit amounts for expenses is net income (or net loss) and is an increase (or decrease) to Retained Earnings. The closing of Dividends reduces Retained Earnings. Thus, the closing entries for revenues, expenses, and dividends may be made directly to Retained Earnings, as follows:

| | | |
|---|---|---|
| Revenues . . . . . . . . . . . . . . . . . . . . . . . . . . . . . . . . . . . . . . . . . . . . . . . . . . . . . . . | xx | |
|     Retained Earnings . . . . . . . . . . . . . . . . . . . . . . . . . . . . . . . . . . . . . . . . . . | | xx |
|     *To close revenues to Retained Earnings.* | | |
| Retained Earnings . . . . . . . . . . . . . . . . . . . . . . . . . . . . . . . . . . . . . . . . . . . . . . | xx | |
|     Expenses . . . . . . . . . . . . . . . . . . . . . . . . . . . . . . . . . . . . . . . . . . . . . . . . . . . | | xx |
|     *To close expenses to Retained Earnings.* | | |
| Retained Earnings . . . . . . . . . . . . . . . . . . . . . . . . . . . . . . . . . . . . . . . . . . . . . . | xx | |
|     Dividends . . . . . . . . . . . . . . . . . . . . . . . . . . . . . . . . . . . . . . . . . . . . . . . . . . . | | xx |
|     *To close the dividends account to Retained Earnings.* | | |

An alternative to the closing method described above is to use an income summary account. Income Summary is a temporary "clearing" account that is used only to accumulate amounts from the closing entries for revenues and expenses and therefore summarizes the net income or net loss for the period. After revenues and expenses are closed to Income Summary, the balance in that account is then closed to Retained Earnings. Dividends must still be closed directly to Retained Earnings, since dividends do not affect net income and are not closed to Income Summary. If a work sheet is prepared, the balances in the Income Statement columns provide the data for closing revenues and expenses. The **closing entries** for Rosi, Inc., are presented on the following page, assuming that an income summary account is used. Note that with the adjusting method illustrated for Inventory, Cost of Goods Sold is already computed. It can then be closed to Income Summary (or directly to Retained Earnings if an income summary account is not used) just like any other operating expense.

### Closing Entries

| | | | |
|---|---|---:|---:|
| **1993** | | | |
| Dec. 31 | Sales | 479,500 | |
| | Interest Revenue | 1,350 | |
| | Rent Revenue | 2,075 | |
| | Income Summary | | 482,925 |
| | *To close revenue accounts to Income Summary.* | | |
| | | | |
| 31 | Income Summary | 441,710 | |
| | Cost of Goods Sold | | 153,310 |
| | Salaries and Wages Expense | | 174,600 |
| | Heat, Light, and Power | | 32,480 |
| | Payroll Tax Expense | | 18,300 |
| | Advertising Expense | | 18,600 |
| | Interest Expense | | 21,420 |
| | Doubtful Accounts Expense | | 1,100 |
| | Depreciation Expense—Buildings | | 7,800 |
| | Depreciation Expense—Furniture and Equipment | | 1,900 |
| | Insurance Expense | | 4,200 |
| | Income Tax Expense | | 8,000 |
| | *To close expense accounts to Income Summary.* | | |
| | | | |
| 31 | Income Summary | 41,215 | |
| | Retained Earnings | | 41,215 |
| | *To transfer the balance in Income Summary to Retained Earnings.* | | |
| | | | |
| 31 | Retained Earnings | 13,600 | |
| | Dividends | | 13,600 |
| | *To close Dividends to Retained Earnings.* | | |

***Preparing a Post-Closing Trial Balance***    After the closing entries are posted, a post-closing trial balance may be prepared to verify the equality of the debits and credits for all real accounts. The post-closing trial balance for Rosi, Inc., is presented on page 74.

***Reversing Entries***    At the beginning of a new period, the following types of adjusting entries may be reversed:

1. Accrued expenses
2. Accrued revenues
3. Prepaid expenses when the original debit was to an expense account
4. Deferred revenues when the original credit was to a revenue account

Reversing entries are not necessary, but they make it possible to record the expense payments or revenue receipts in the new period in the usual manner. For example, if a reversing entry is not made for accrued expenses, payments in the subsequent period would have to be analyzed as to (1) the amount representing payment of the accrued

Rosi,
Work
December

| | Account Title | Trial Balance Debit | Trial Balance Credit | |
|---|---|---|---|---|
| 1 | Cash | 83,110 | | 1 |
| 2 | Accounts Receivable | 106,500 | | 2 |
| 3 | Allowance for Doubtful Accounts | | 1,610 | 3 |
| 4 | Inventory | 45,000 | | 4 |
| 5 | Prepaid Insurance | 8,000 | | 5 |
| 6 | Interest Receivable | 0 | | 6 |
| 7 | Notes Receivable | 28,000 | | 7 |
| 8 | Land | 114,000 | | 8 |
| 9 | Buildings | 156,000 | | 9 |
| 10 | Accumulated Depreciation—Buildings | | 39,000 | 10 |
| 11 | Furniture & Equipment | 19,000 | | 11 |
| 12 | Accumulated Depreciation—Furniture & Equipment | | 3,800 | 12 |
| 13 | Accounts Payable | | 37,910 | 13 |
| 14 | Unearned Rent Revenue | | 0 | 14 |
| 15 | Salaries and Wages Payable | | 0 | 15 |
| 16 | Interest Payable | | 0 | 16 |
| 17 | Payroll Taxes Payable | | 5,130 | 17 |
| 18 | Income Taxes Payable | | 0 | 18 |
| 19 | Dividends Payable | | 3,400 | 19 |
| 20 | Bonds Payable | | 140,000 | 20 |
| 21 | Common Stock, $15 par | | 150,000 | 21 |
| 22 | Retained Earnings | | 126,770 | 22 |
| 23 | Dividends | 13,600 | | 23 |
| 24 | Sales | | 479,500 | 24 |
| 25 | Purchases | 162,600 | | 25 |
| 26 | Purchase Discounts | | 3,290 | 26 |
| 27 | Cost of Goods Sold | 0 | | 27 |
| 28 | Salaries and Wages Expense | 172,450 | | 28 |
| 29 | Heat, Light, and Power | 32,480 | | 29 |
| 30 | Payroll Tax Expense | 18,300 | | 30 |
| 31 | Advertising Expense | 18,600 | | 31 |
| 32 | Doubtful Accounts Expense | 0 | | 32 |
| 33 | Depreciation Expense—Buildings | 0 | | 33 |
| 34 | Depreciation Expense—Furniture & Equipment | 0 | | 34 |
| 35 | Insurance Expense | 0 | | 35 |
| 36 | Interest Revenue | | 1,100 | 36 |
| 37 | Rent Revenue | | 2,550 | 37 |
| 38 | Interest Expense | 16,420 | | 38 |
| 39 | Income Tax Expense | 0 | | 39 |
| 40 | Totals | 994,060 | 994,060 | 40 |
| 41 | Net Income | | | 41 |
| 42 | | | | 42 |

Inc.
Sheet
31, 1993

| # | Adjustments Debit | | Adjustments Credit | | Income Statement Debit | Income Statement Credit | Balance Sheet Debit | Balance Sheet Credit | # |
|---|---|---|---|---|---|---|---|---|---|
| 1 | | | | | | | 83,110 | | 1 |
| 2 | | | | | | | 106,500 | | 2 |
| 3 | | | (c) | 1,100 | | | | 2,710 | 3 |
| 4 | (j) | 6,000 | | | | | 51,000 | | 4 |
| 5 | | | (g) | 4,200 | | | 3,800 | | 5 |
| 6 | (f) | 250 | | | | | 250 | | 6 |
| 7 | | | | | | | 28,000 | | 7 |
| 8 | | | | | | | 114,000 | | 8 |
| 9 | | | | | | | 156,000 | | 9 |
| 10 | | | (a) | 7,800 | | | | 46,800 | 10 |
| 11 | | | | | | | 19,000 | | 11 |
| 12 | | | (b) | 1,900 | | | | 5,700 | 12 |
| 13 | | | | | | | | 37,910 | 13 |
| 14 | | | (h) | 475 | | | | 475 | 14 |
| 15 | | | (d) | 2,150 | | | | 2,150 | 15 |
| 16 | | | (e) | 5,000 | | | | 5,000 | 16 |
| 17 | | | | | | | | 5,130 | 17 |
| 18 | | | (i) | 8,000 | | | | 8,000 | 18 |
| 19 | | | | | | | | 3,400 | 19 |
| 20 | | | | | | | | 140,000 | 20 |
| 21 | | | | | | | | 150,000 | 21 |
| 22 | | | | | | | | 126,770 | 22 |
| 23 | | | | | | | 13,600 | | 23 |
| 24 | | | | | | 479,500 | | | 24 |
| 25 | | | (j) | 162,600 | | | | | 25 |
| 26 | (j) | 3,290 | | | | | | | 26 |
| 27 | (j) | 153,310 | | | 153,310 | | | | 27 |
| 28 | (d) | 2,150 | | | 174,600 | | | | 28 |
| 29 | | | | | 32,480 | | | | 29 |
| 30 | | | | | 18,300 | | | | 30 |
| 31 | | | | | 18,600 | | | | 31 |
| 32 | (c) | 1,100 | | | 1,100 | | | | 32 |
| 33 | (a) | 7,800 | | | 7,800 | | | | 33 |
| 34 | (b) | 1,900 | | | 1,900 | | | | 34 |
| 35 | (g) | 4,200 | | | 4,200 | | | | 35 |
| 36 | | | (f) | 250 | | 1,350 | | | 36 |
| 37 | (h) | 475 | | | | 2,075 | | | 37 |
| 38 | (e) | 5,000 | | | 21,420 | | | | 38 |
| 39 | (i) | 8,000 | | | 8,000 | | | | 39 |
| 40 | | 193,475 | | 193,475 | 441,710 | 482,925 | 575,260 | 534,045 | 40 |
| 41 | | | | | 41,215 | | | 41,215 | 41 |
| 42 | | | | | 482,925 | 482,925 | 575,260 | 575,260 | 42 |

**Rosi, Inc.**
**Post-Closing Trial Balance**
**December 31, 1993**

|  | Debit | Credit |
|---|---|---|
| Cash ............................................................. | $ 83,110 |  |
| Accounts Receivable ......................................... | 106,500 |  |
| Allowance for Doubtful Accounts ............................. |  | $ 2,710 |
| Inventory ....................................................... | 51,000 |  |
| Prepaid Insurance ............................................ | 3,800 |  |
| Interest Receivable .......................................... | 250 |  |
| Notes Receivable............................................. | 28,000 |  |
| Land ........................................................... | 114,000 |  |
| Buildings ...................................................... | 156,000 |  |
| Accumulated Depreciation—Buildings ........................ |  | 46,800 |
| Furniture and Equipment ..................................... | 19,000 |  |
| Accumulated Depreciation—Furniture and Equipment ........... |  | 5,700 |
| Accounts Payable ............................................. |  | 37,910 |
| Unearned Rent Revenue ...................................... |  | 475 |
| Salaries and Wages Payable .................................. |  | 2,150 |
| Interest Payable.............................................. |  | 5,000 |
| Payroll Taxes Payable ........................................ |  | 5,130 |
| Income Tax Payable .......................................... |  | 8,000 |
| Dividends Payable ............................................ |  | 3,400 |
| Bonds Payable ................................................ |  | 140,000 |
| Common Stock, $15 par ...................................... |  | 150,000 |
| Retained Earnings............................................ |  | 154,385 |
|  | $561,660 | $561,660 |

liability, and (2) the amount representing the expense of the current period. Alternatively, the accrued and deferred accounts could be left unadjusted until the close of the subsequent reporting period when they would be adjusted to their correct balances.

The adjustments establishing accrued and prepaid balances for Rosi, Inc., were illustrated earlier in the chapter. The appropriate reversing entries are shown below.

**Reversing Entries**

| 1994 |  |  |  |
|---|---|---|---|
| Jan. 1 | Salaries and Wages Payable ......................... | 2,150 |  |
|  | Salaries and Wages Expense ...................... |  | 2,150 |
| 1 | Interest Payable..................................... | 5,000 |  |
|  | Interest Expense ................................. |  | 5,000 |
| 1 | Interest Revenue .................................... | 250 |  |
|  | Interest Receivable ............................... |  | 250 |
| 1 | Unearned Rent Revenue ............................. | 475 |  |
|  | Rent Revenue ..................................... |  | 475 |

To illustrate accounting for an accrued expense when (1) reversing entries are made and (2) reversing entries are not made, assume that accrued salaries on December 31,

1993, are $350 and on December 31, 1994, are $500. Payment of salaries for the period ending January 4, 1994, is $1,000. Adjustments are made and the books are closed annually on December 31. The possible entries are shown below:

| | (1) Assuming Liability Account Is Reversed | | (2) Assuming Liability Account Is Not Reversed | | |
|---|---|---|---|---|---|
| | | | (a) Transaction in Next Period Is Analyzed. | | (b) Transaction in Next Period Is Not Analyzed. Adjustment at Close of Next Reporting Period. |
| **December 31, 1993** Adjusting entry to record accrued salaries. | Salaries Exp. .... 350 Salaries Payable....... | 350 | Salaries Exp..... 350 Salaries Payable ...... | 350 | Salaries Exp. .... 350 Salaries Payable....... 350 |
| **December 31, 1993** Closing entry to transfer expense to the income summary account. | Income Summary....... xxx Salaries Exp. .. | xxx | Income Summary ...... xxx Salaries Exp... | xxx | Income Summary....... xxx Salaries Exp. .. xxx |
| **January 1, 1994** Reversing entry to transfer balance to the account that will be charged when payment is made. | Salaries Payable ........ 350 Salaries Exp. .. | 350 | No entry | | No entry |
| **January 4, 1994** Payment of salaries for period ending January 4, 1994. | Salaries Exp. .... 1,000 Cash ........ | 1,000 | Salaries Payable ........ 350 Salaries Exp..... 650 Cash ........ | 1,000 | Salaries Exp. .... 1,000 Cash ......... 1,000 |
| **December 31, 1994** Adjusting entry to record accrued salaries. | Salaries Exp. .... 500 Salaries Payable....... | 500 | Salaries Exp..... 500 Salaries Payable ...... | 500 | Salaries Exp. .... 150 Salaries Payable....... 150 |

## ACCRUAL VERSUS CASH-BASIS ACCOUNTING

The procedures described in the previous sections are those required in a double-entry system based on accrual accounting. Accrual accounting recognizes revenues as they are earned, not necessarily when cash is received. Expenses are recognized and recorded when they are incurred, not necessarily when cash is paid. This provides for a better matching of revenues and expenses during an accounting period and generally results in financial statements that more accurately reflect a company's financial position and results of operations.[3]

Some accounting systems are based on cash receipts and cash disbursements instead of accrual accounting. Cash-basis accounting procedures frequently are found in organizations not requiring a complete set of double-entry records. Such organizations might include smaller, unincorporated businesses, and some nonprofit organizations. Professionals engaged in service businesses, such as CPAs, dentists, and engineers, also have traditionally used cash accounting systems. Even many of these organizations, however, periodically use professional accountants to prepare financial statements and other required reports on an accrual basis.

---

[3]In Concepts Statement No. 6, the FASB discusses the concept of accrual accounting and relates it to the objectives of financial reporting. *Statement of Financial Accounting Concepts No. 6*, "Elements of Financial Statements" (Stamford: Financial Accounting Standards Board, December 1985).

### Triple-Entry Bookkeeping

It has been said that the system of double-entry bookkeeping is "like Euclid's theory of ratios, an absolutely perfect one." Evidence for this comes from the fact that the fundamentals of the system remain largely unchanged after 500 years of use. However, Professor Yuji Ijiri of Carnegie-Mellon University has suggested an improvement—triple-entry bookkeeping.

Professor Ijiri uses the notion from Newtonian physics that the three important aspects of an object are its position, its velocity, and its acceleration. Applying this to a firm's financial statements, one gets the following concepts: wealth, income, and force. Wealth, as shown on the balance sheet, indicates a firm's financial position. Income shows a firm's rate of change in wealth, just as the velocity of a car describes the rate of change in the position of the car. Force, a term put into a new context by Professor Ijiri, describes the rate of change in income, just as acceleration tells how fast the velocity of a car is changing. Professor Ijiri has designed a triple-entry bookkeeping system that tracks a firm's wealth, its periodic income, and its force.

It might be suggested that techniques already exist for examining the rate of change in income; financial statement analysis involves determining the causes of changes in income statement amounts from one year to the next. However, this "variance" analysis is not a systematic part of the bookkeeping system. The advantage of Ijiri's triple-entry system is that variance analysis would become routine, something to be performed by all and not just by specialists. The situation is similar to that which existed in relation to the computation of income before double-entry accounting. The concept of income certainly existed before the development of double-entry accounting; a contribution of the double-entry system was to make the computation of income routine.

Source: Yuji Ijiri, "Triple-Entry Bookkeeping and Income Momentum," *Studies in Accounting Research #18* (Sarasota: American Accounting Association, 1982).

Discussion continues as to the appropriateness of using cash accounting systems, especially as a basis for determining tax liabilities.[4] The FASB, in *Concepts Statement No. 1*, indicates that accrual accounting provides a better basis for financial reports than does information showing only cash receipts and disbursements. The AICPA's position, however, is that the cash basis is appropriate for some smaller companies and especially for companies in the service industry. Until this issue is settled, accountants will continue to be asked on occasion to convert cash-based records to generally accepted accrual-based financial statements. The concepts involved are described and illustrated in Chapter 6, which explains the statement of cash flows.

## COMPUTERS AND THE ACCOUNTING PROCESS

The usual procedures for recording transactions and the sequence of activities leading to the preparation of financial statements have been briefly reviewed in this chapter. These procedures and activities are referred to collectively as the accounting process or accounting cycle.

[4]For an argument on retaining the cash basis of accounting, see Ronnie G. Flippo, "The President's Tax Proposals: A View from Capitol Hill," *Journal of Accountancy* (September 1985), pp. 86-88.

As an organization grows in size and complexity, the recording and summarizing processes become more involved, and means are sought for improving efficiency and reducing costs. Some enterprises may find that a system involving primarily manual operations is adequate in meeting their needs. Others find that information processing needs can be handled effectively only through electronic data processing (EDP) equipment.

Companies requiring great speed and accuracy in processing large amounts of accounting data often utilize a computer system capable of storing and recalling data, performing many mathematical functions, and making certain routine decisions based on mathematical comparisons. These systems normally include various other machines that can "read" data from disks, magnetic tapes, or punched cards and print information in a variety of forms, all under the control of a computer.

Modern computer systems have vast capabilities. The individual steps involved in recording and summarizing may be combined into one process. The information traditionally recorded in journals and ledgers may be stored in memory banks or on computer disks and recalled as needed. On-line, real-time systems have the capability of continuous updating of all relevant files. This makes it possible for reports to be produced on a much more timely basis.

Since the early 1960s, society has been caught in the midst of an ongoing computer revolution. Technological advances in integrated circuitry and microchips led to one of the most significant phenomena of the 1980s—the development of *personal computers (PCs)*. These compact, relatively inexpensive computers have changed the way in which many companies and individuals keep track of their business activities. These computers are being used for a variety of activities, including: financial analysis, accounting functions, word processing, data base management, inventory control, and credit analysis of customers. As uses have expanded, software packages have been developed to meet current and future demand. The impact of PCs is felt not only in business, but in education and in family life. Several colleges now require entering freshmen to purchase their own PCs for use in a variety of business, mathematics, and science courses. Exposure to computers, and especially the PC, is also very common in elementary and secondary school curricula.

This computer revolution is rapidly changing society and, along with it, the way business is conducted and, therefore, the way accounting functions are performed. However, despite their tremendous capabilities, computers cannot replace skilled accountants. In fact, their presence places increased demands on the accountant in directing the operations of the computer systems to assure the use of appropriate procedures. Although all arithmetical operations can be assumed to be done accurately by computers, the validity of the output data depends on the adequacy of the instructions given the computer. Unlike a human accountant, a computer cannot think for itself but must be given explicit instructions for performing each operation. This has certain advantages in that the accountant can be sure every direction will be carried out precisely. On the other hand, this places a great responsibility on the accountant to anticipate any unusual situations requiring special consideration or judgment. Various control techniques also must be developed for checking and verifying data recorded in electronic form.

The significance of the accounting process in our society and its applicability to every business unit, regardless of size, must be appreciated. Although the procedures may be modified to meet special conditions and may be performed through a variety of manual or computer systems, the process reviewed in this chapter is fundamental to the accounting systems of all enterprises.

# APPENDIX 3-1

## Special Journals and Subsidiary Ledgers

In recording transactions, many companies use **special journals** in addition to the general journal. Special journals eliminate much of the repetitive work involved in recording routine transactions. In addition, they permit the recording functions to be divided among accounting personnel, each individual being responsible for a separate record. This specialization often results in greater efficiency and increased accuracy, as well as a higher degree of control.

Some examples of special journals are the sales journal, the purchases journal, the cash receipts journal, the cash disbursements journal, the payroll register, and the voucher register.

Sales on account are recorded in the **sales journal**. The subsequent collections on account, as well as other transactions involving the receipt of cash, are recorded in the **cash receipts journal**. Merchandise purchases on account are entered in a **purchases journal** or a **voucher register**. Subsequent payments on account, as well as other transactions involving the payment of cash, are recorded in a **cash payments journal** or a **check register.** A payroll register may be employed to accumulate payroll information, including payroll deductions and withholdings for taxes.

Column headings in the various journals specify the accounts to be debited or credited; account titles and explanations may therefore be omitted in recording routine transactions. A Sundry column is usually provided for transactions that are relatively infrequent, and account titles must be entered in recording such transactions.

The use of special journals facilitates recording and also simplifies the posting process, because the totals of many transactions, rather than separate data for each transaction, can be posted to the ledger accounts. Certain data must be transferred individually—data affecting individual accounts receivable and accounts payable and data reported in the Sundry columns—but the overall volume of posting is substantially reduced.

The format of a particular journal must satisfy the needs of the individual business unit. For example, with an automated or computerized system, the general journal, any specialized journals, and subsidiary ledgers may be modified or eliminated. Recognizing that modifications are necessary for individual systems, the following sections discuss a voucher system and illustrate some special journals that are commonly used with manual accounting systems.

### VOUCHER SYSTEM

Relatively large organizations ordinarily provide for the control of purchases and cash disbursements through adoption of some form of a voucher system. With the use of a voucher system, checks may be drawn only upon a written authorization in the form of a **voucher** approved by some responsible official.

A voucher is prepared, not only in support of each payment to be made for goods and services purchased on account, but also for all other transactions calling for payment by check, including cash purchases, retirement of debt, replenishment of petty cash funds, payrolls, and dividends. The voucher identifies the person authorizing the expenditure, explains the nature of the transaction, and names the accounts affected by the transaction. For control purposes, vouchers should be prenumbered, checked against purchase invoices, and compared with receiving reports. Upon verification, the voucher and the related business documents are submitted to the appropriate official for final approval. When approved, the prenumbered voucher is recorded in a voucher register. The voucher register is a book of original entry and takes the place of a purchases journal. Charges on each voucher are classified and recorded in appropriate Debit columns, and the amount to be paid is listed in an Accounts Payable or Vouchers Payable column. After a voucher is entered in the register, it is placed in an unpaid vouchers file together with its supporting documents.

Checks are written in payment of individual vouchers. The checks are recorded in a check register, which is used in place of a cash payments journal, as debits to Accounts Payable or Vouchers Payable and credits to Cash. Since charges to the various asset, liability, or expense accounts were recognized when the payable was recorded in the voucher register, these accounts need not be listed in the payments record. When a check is issued, payment of the voucher is reported in the voucher register by entering the check number and the payment date. Paid vouchers and supporting documents are removed from the unpaid file, marked "paid," and placed in a separate paid vouchers file. The balance of the payable account, after the credit for total vouchers issued and the debit for total vouchers paid, should be equal to the sum of the unpaid vouchers file. The voucher register, while representing a journal, also provides the detail in support of the accounts payable or vouchers payable total.

## ILLUSTRATION OF SPECIAL JOURNALS AND SUBSIDIARY LEDGERS

Assume that Central Valley, Inc., maintains the following books of original entry: sales journal, cash receipts journal, voucher register, check register, and general journal. As noted, the format of a particular journal must satisfy the needs of the individual business unit. Those presented for Central Valley, Inc., are illustrative only.

### Sales Journal

The sales journal for the month of July 1993 appears as follows:

SALES JOURNAL — Page 6

| Date | | Invoice No. | Account Debited | Post. Ref. | Accts. Rec. Dr. Sales Cr. |
|------|---|---------|-----------------|------------|---------------------------|
| 1993 | | | | | |
| July | 2 | 701 | The Chocolate Factory .................... | ✓ | 3,450 |
| | 6 | 702 | Huffman Company ....................... | ✓ | 6,510 |
| | 10 | 703 | Stocks and Co. .......................... | ✓ | 1,525 |
| | 12 | 704 | Bennet, Inc. ............................ | ✓ | 4,860 |
| | 15 | 705 | The Chocolate Factory .................... | ✓ | 2,000 |
| | 18 | 706 | Ridnour Corporation ..................... | ✓ | 5,940 |
| | 20 | 707 | Hillcrest Sales Co. ...................... | ✓ | 1,910 |
| | 23 | 708 | Kirstein, Inc. ........................... | ✓ | 7,650 |
| | 27 | 709 | DataMark Systems Inc. .................. | ✓ | 1,280 |
| | 29 | 710 | Fuller Distributing Co. ................... | ✓ | 2,925 |
| | 31 | 711 | Stocks and Co. .......................... | ✓ | 2,100 |
| | | | | | 40,150 |
| | | | | | (116) (41) |

As illustrated, credit sales are recorded by debits to Accounts Receivable and credits to Sales. The sales invoice number provides a reference to the original source document for each transaction. Debits are posted to individual customers' accounts in the accounts receivable subsidiary ledger as indicated by a check (√) in the Posting Reference column. The total sales for the month ($40,150) are posted to Accounts Receivable and Sales (accounts #116 and #41, respectively).

## Cash Receipts Journal

The cash receipts journal for Central Valley, Inc., for July 1993 appears as follows:

CASH RECEIPTS JOURNAL                                      Page 8

| Date | | Account Credited | Post. Ref. | Sundry Accounts Cr. | Accounts Receivable Cr. | Sales Discounts Dr. | Cash Dr. |
|------|---|------|------|------|------|------|------|
| 1993 | | | | | | | |
| July | 3 | Hamilton Sign Co. ....... | √ | | 5,650 | 113 | 5,537 |
| | 7 | DataMark Systems Inc.... | √ | | 1,400 | 28 | 1,372 |
| | 8 | Sales ................... | 41 | 365 | | | 365 |
| | 10 | The Chocolate Factory ... | √ | | 3,450 | 69 | 3,381 |
| | 11 | Sawyer Co. ............. | √ | | 2,735 | | 2,735 |
| | 14 | Rohas, Inc.............. | √ | | 4,875 | | 4,875 |
| | 16 | Milo Company ......... | √ | | 920 | | 920 |
| | 17 | Poynter Corp. .......... | √ | | 6,100 | | 6,100 |
| | 21 | Earnst Co. ............. | √ | | 6,870 | | 6,870 |
| | 22 | Tax Refund Receivable ... | 120 | 5,780 | | | 5,780 |
| | 25 | Sales ................... | 41 | 440 | | | 440 |
| | 29 | Hillcrest Sales Co. ....... | √ | | 1,900 | 38 | 1,862 |
| | 31 | The Chocolate Factory ... | √ | | 2,000 | | 2,000 |
| | 31 | Notes Receivable ........ | 113 | 8,500 | | | 8,565 |
| | | Interest Revenue ........ | 72 | 65 | | | |
| | | | | 15,150 | 35,900 | 248 | 50,802 |
| | | | | (√) | (116) | (42) | (111) |

The cash receipts journal records all receipts of cash. Collections of cash from previously recorded credit sales are posted in total as a credit to Accounts Receivable (account #116) and as debits to Sales Discounts (account #42) and Cash (account #111). The credits to Accounts Receivable are posted to the individual customer accounts in the subsidiary ledger as noted by the check (√) in the Posting Reference column. Cash sales, e.g., as shown for July 8 and July 25, are posted individually as a credit to Sales (account #41) and as a part of the total debit to Cash. Other transactions involving cash receipts, e.g., the collection of a note receivable on July 31, are posted individually as credits and as a part of the total debit to Cash.

## Voucher Register

As noted, the voucher register takes the place of a purchases journal, providing a record of all authorized payments to be made by check. A partial voucher register appears on the next page. For illustrative purposes, separate debit columns are provided for two accounts—Purchases and Payroll. Other items are recorded in the Sundry Dr. column. Additional separate columns could be added for other items, such as advertising, if desired. The total amount of each column is posted to the corresponding account, with the exception of the Sundry Dr. and Cr. columns, which are posted individually.

**VOUCHER REGISTER**

| Date | Vou. No. | Payee | Paid Date | Paid Ck. No. | Accounts Payable Cr. | Purchases Dr. | Payroll Dr. | Account | Post. Ref. | Sundry Amount Dr. | Sundry Amount Cr. |
|---|---|---|---|---|---|---|---|---|---|---|---|
| 31 | 7132 | Security National Bank ......... | 7/31 | 3106 | 9,120 | | | Notes Payable... | 211 | 9,120 | |
| 31 | 7133 | Payroll .......... | 7/31 | 3107 | 1,640 | | 2,130 | FICA Taxes Payable ...... | 215 | | 90 |
| | | | | | | | | Income Taxes Payable ...... | 214 | | 400 |
| 31 | 7134 | Far Fabrications .. | | | 3,290 | 3,290 | | | | | |
| 31 | 7135 | Midland Inc...... | | | 1,500 | 1,500 | | | | | |
| 31 | 7136 | Nyland Supply Co............ | | | 5,550 | 5,550 | | | | | |
| 31 | | Total .......... | | | 55,375 | 24,930 | 2,130 | | | 33,645 | 5,330 |
| | | | | | (213) | (51) | (620) | | | (√) | (√) |

## Check Register

A partial check register is illustrated below. It accounts for all the checks issued during the period. Checks are issued only in payment of properly approved vouchers. The payee is designated together with the number of the voucher authorizing the payment.

**CHECK REGISTER**

| Date | Check No. | Account Debited | Vou. No. | Accounts Payable Dr. | Purchase Discounts Cr. | Cash Cr. |
|---|---|---|---|---|---|---|
| 31 | 3106 | Security National Bank .... | 7132 | 9,120 | | 9,120 |
| 31 | 3107 | Payroll ................... | 7133 | 1,640 | | 1,640 |
| 31 | 3108 | Pat Bunnell ............... | 7005 | 1,500 | 30 | 1,470 |
| 31 | | Total .................... | | 61,160 | 275 | 60,885 |
| | | | | (213) | (52) | (111) |

## General Journal

Regardless of the number and nature of special journals, certain transactions cannot appropriately be recorded in the special journals and are recorded in the general journal. A general journal with an illustrative entry during the month of July is illustrated below. This general journal is prepared in two-column form. A pair of Debit and Credit columns is provided for the entries that are to be made to the general ledger accounts.

**GENERAL JOURNAL**                                              Page 3

| Date | Description | Post. Ref. | Debit | Credit |
|---|---|---|---|---|
| 1993 July 31 | Allowance for Doubtful Accounts ............... | 117 | 1,270 | |
| | Accounts Receivable ........................ | 116 | | 1,270 |
| | *To write off uncollectible account. (Rit-Z Shop)* | | | |

## Subsidiary Ledgers

As explained in the chapter, subsidiary ledgers provide the detail of individual accounts in support of a control account in the general ledger. Whenever possible, individual postings to subsidiary accounts are made directly from the business documents evidencing the transactions. This practice saves time and avoids errors that might arise in summarizing and transferring this information. If postings to the subsidiary records and to the control accounts are made accurately, the sum of the detail in a subsidiary record will agree with the balance in the control account. A reconciliation of each subsidiary ledger with its related control account should be made periodically, and any discrepancies found should be investigated and corrected.

As an illustration of the relationship of a general ledger control account to its subsidiary ledger accounts, the accounts receivable control account is shown below. Three of the subsidiary accounts are also shown.

### GENERAL LEDGER

**Account: Accounts Receivable**                                                                 Account No. 116

| Date | | Item | Post. Ref. | Debit | Credit | Balance |
|---|---|---|---|---|---|---|
| 1993 | | | | | | |
| July | 1 | Balance............................ | | | | 9,200 |
| | 31 | Sales on account .................. | S6 | 40,150 | | 49,350 |
| | 31 | Collections on account ............. | CR8 | | 35,900 | 13,450 |
| | 31 | Write-off of uncollectible account .... (Rit-Z Shop) | J3 | | 1,270 | 12,180 |

### ACCOUNTS RECEIVABLE SUBSIDIARY LEDGER

**Name: Stocks and Co.**
**Address: 546 South Fox Rd., Chicago, IL 60665**

| Date | | Item | Post. Ref. | Debit | Credit | Balance |
|---|---|---|---|---|---|---|
| 1993 | | | | | | |
| July | 1 | Balance............................ | | | | 1,000 |
| | 10 | Purchase ......................... | S6 | 1,525 | | 2,525 |
| | 31 | Purchase ......................... | S6 | 2,100 | | 4,025 |

**Name: The Chocolate Factory**
**Address: 7890 Redwood Dr., Pittsburgh, PA 15234**

| Date | | Item | Post. Ref. | Debit | Credit | Balance |
|---|---|---|---|---|---|---|
| 1993 | | | | | | |
| July | 2 | Purchase ......................... | S6 | 3,450 | | 3,450 |
| | 10 | Payment.......................... | CR8 | | 3,450 | -0- |
| | 15 | Purchase ......................... | S6 | 2,000 | | 2,000 |
| | 31 | Payment.......................... | CR8 | | 2,000 | -0- |

**Name: The Rit-Z Shop**
**Address: 789 Cotton Drive, Phoenix, AZ 85090**

| Date | | Item | Post. Ref. | Debit | Credit | Balance |
|---|---|---|---|---|---|---|
| 1993 | | | | | | |
| July | 1 | Balance............................ | | | | 1,270 |
| | 31 | Write-off of uncollectible account (6 months old)........................ | J3 | | 1,270 | -0- |

# APPENDIX 3-2

## Closing Method for Inventory

In the work sheet presented on pages 72 and 73, Inventory and related accounts are adjusted through a cost of goods sold account. An alternative approach is to "close" beginning and ending inventory amounts to Income Summary. With this procedure, cost of goods sold appears only as a calculated figure in the income statement; it does not appear in the accounts. This method is illustrated in the work sheet on pages 84 and 85. Adjusting entries (a) through (i) are the same as those in the earlier example for Rosi, Inc. Using the closing procedure, however, the following entries would be made for Inventory:

| | | | |
|---|---|---|---|
| (j) | Income Summary ................................... | 45,000 | |
| | Inventory ........................................ | | 45,000 |
| | *To close beginning inventory to Income Summary.* | | |
| | | | |
| (k) | Inventory ......................................... | 51,000 | |
| | Income Summary.................................. | | 51,000 |
| | *To record ending inventory.* | | |

Note that Income Summary shows both a debit and a credit on the income statement section of the work sheet, and no adjustment is made for Purchases and Purchase Discounts. The balances in these accounts are extended to the Income Statement columns in the work sheet. Subsequently, these accounts would be closed to Income Summary as part of the normal closing process.

Other variations of the closing approach to merchandise inventory can be found in practice. Regardless of the approach used, financial statements will reflect the same ending inventory and cost of goods sold amounts.

| | Account Title | Trial Balance | | |
|---|---|---|---|---|
| | | Debit | Credit | |
| 1 | Cash | 83,110 | | 1 |
| 2 | Accounts Receivable | 106,500 | | 2 |
| 3 | Allowance for Doubtful Accounts | | 1,610 | 3 |
| 4 | Inventory | 45,000 | | 4 |
| 5 | Prepaid Insurance | 8,000 | | 5 |
| 6 | Interest Receivable | 0 | | 6 |
| 7 | Notes Receivable | 28,000 | | 7 |
| 8 | Land | 114,000 | | 8 |
| 9 | Buildings | 156,000 | | 9 |
| 10 | Accumulated Depreciation—Buildings | | 39,000 | 10 |
| 11 | Furniture & Equipment | 19,000 | | 11 |
| 12 | Accumulated Depreciation—Furniture & Equipment | | 3,800 | 12 |
| 13 | Accounts Payable | | 37,910 | 13 |
| 14 | Unearned Rent Revenue | | 0 | 14 |
| 15 | Salaries and Wages Payable | | 0 | 15 |
| 16 | Interest Payable | | 0 | 16 |
| 17 | Payroll Taxes Payable | | 5,130 | 17 |
| 18 | Income Taxes Payable | | 0 | 18 |
| 19 | Dividends Payable | | 3,400 | 19 |
| 20 | Bonus Payable | | 140,000 | 20 |
| 21 | Common Stock, $15 par | | 150,000 | 21 |
| 22 | Retained Earnings | | 126,770 | 22 |
| 23 | Dividends | 13,600 | | 23 |
| 24 | Income Summary | | 0 | 24 |
| 25 | Sales | | 479,500 | 25 |
| 26 | Purchases | 162,600 | | 26 |
| 27 | Purchase Discounts | | 3,290 | 27 |
| 28 | Salaries and Wages Expense | 172,450 | | 28 |
| 29 | Heat, Light, and Power | 32,480 | | 29 |
| 30 | Payroll Tax Expense | 18,300 | | 30 |
| 31 | Advertising Expense | 18,600 | | 31 |
| 32 | Doubtful Accounts Expense | 0 | | 32 |
| 33 | Depreciation Expense—Buildings | 0 | | 33 |
| 34 | Depreciation Expense—Furniture & Equipment | 0 | | 34 |
| 35 | Insurance Expense | 0 | | 35 |
| 36 | Interest Revenue | | 1,100 | 36 |
| 37 | Rent Revenue | | 2,550 | 37 |
| 38 | Interest Expense | 16,420 | | 38 |
| 39 | Income Tax Expense | 0 | | 39 |
| 40 | Totals | 994,060 | 994,060 | 40 |
| 41 | Net Income | | | 41 |
| 42 | | | | 42 |

Inc.
Sheet
31, 1993

| | Adjustments | | | Income Statement | | Balance Sheet | | |
| | Debit | Credit | | Debit | Credit | Debit | Credit | |
|---|---|---|---|---|---|---|---|---|
| 1 | | | | | | 83,110 | | 1 |
| 2 | | | | | | 106,500 | | 2 |
| 3 | | (c) | 1,100 | | | | 2,710 | 3 |
| 4 | (k) 51,000 | (j) | 45,000 | | | 51,000 | | 4 |
| 5 | | (g) | 4,200 | | | 3,800 | | 5 |
| 6 | (f) 250 | | | | | 250 | | 6 |
| 7 | | | | | | 28,000 | | 7 |
| 8 | | | | | | 114,000 | | 8 |
| 9 | | | | | | 156,000 | | 9 |
| 10 | | (a) | 7,800 | | | | 46,800 | 10 |
| 11 | | | | | | 19,000 | | 11 |
| 12 | | (b) | 1,900 | | | | 5,700 | 12 |
| 13 | | | | | | | 37,910 | 13 |
| 14 | | (h) | 475 | | | | 475 | 14 |
| 15 | | (d) | 2,150 | | | | 2,150 | 15 |
| 16 | | (e) | 5,000 | | | | 5,000 | 16 |
| 17 | | | | | | | 5,130 | 17 |
| 18 | | (i) | 8,000 | | | | 8,000 | 18 |
| 19 | | | | | | | 3,400 | 19 |
| 20 | | | | | | | 140,000 | 20 |
| 21 | | | | | | | 150,000 | 21 |
| 22 | | | | | | | 126,770 | 22 |
| 23 | | | | | | 13,600 | | 23 |
| 24 | (j) 45,000 | (k) | 51,000 | 45,000 | 51,000 | | | 24 |
| 25 | | | | | 479,500 | | | 25 |
| 26 | | | | 162,600 | | | | 26 |
| 27 | | | | | 3,290 | | | 27 |
| 28 | (d) 2,150 | | | 174,600 | | | | 28 |
| 29 | | | | 32,480 | | | | 29 |
| 30 | | | | 18,300 | | | | 30 |
| 31 | | | | 18,600 | | | | 31 |
| 32 | (c) 1,100 | | | 1,100 | | | | 32 |
| 33 | (a) 7,800 | | | 7,800 | | | | 33 |
| 34 | (b) 1,900 | | | 1,900 | | | | 34 |
| 35 | (g) 4,200 | | | 4,200 | | | | 35 |
| 36 | | (f) | 250 | | 1,350 | | | 36 |
| 37 | (h) 475 | | | | 2,075 | | | 37 |
| 38 | (e) 5,000 | | | 21,420 | | | | 38 |
| 39 | (i) 8,000 | | | 8,000 | | | | 39 |
| 40 | 126,875 | | 126,875 | 496,000 | 537,215 | 575,260 | 534,045 | 40 |
| 41 | | | | 41,215 | | | 41,215 | 41 |
| 42 | | | | 537,215 | 537,215 | 575,260 | 575,260 | 42 |

## KEY TERMS

Account 62
Accounting process (cycle) 57
Accounting system 57
Accrual accounting 75
Adjunct accounts 66
Adjusting entries 64
Business (source) documents 61
Cash-basis accounting 75
Chart of accounts 62
Closing entries 70
Contra account 66
Control account 63

Credit 59
Debit 59
Double-entry accounting 59
Electronic data processing (EDP) systems 57
General journal 62
General ledger 63
Income summary 70
Journals 61
Ledgers 61
Nominal (temporary) account 70
Periodic inventory system 69

Perpetual inventory system 69
Post-closing trial balance 71
Posting 62
Real (permanent) account 70
Reversing entries 71
Special journal 62
Subsidiary ledgers 63
Transaction 58
Trial balance 63
Voucher system 78
Work sheet 69

## QUESTIONS

1. What type of reports are generated from the accounting system?
2. What are the main similarities and differences between a manual and an automated accounting system?
3. Distinguish between the recording and summarizing phases of the accounting process.
4. List and describe the steps in the accounting process. Why is each step necessary? Which steps are optional?
5. Under double-entry accounting, what are the debit/credit relationships of accounts?
6. Distinguish between: (a) real and nominal accounts, (b) general journal and special journals, and (c) general ledger and subsidiary ledgers.
7. As Beechnut Mining Company's independent certified public accountant, you find that the company accountant posts adjusting and closing entries directly to the ledger without formal entries in the general journal. How would you evaluate this procedure in your report to management?
8. Explain the nature and the purpose of (a) adjusting entries, (b) closing entries, and (c) reversing entries.
9. Give three common examples of contra accounts. Explain why contra accounts are used.
10. Payment of insurance in advance may be recorded in either (a) an expense account or (b) an asset account. Which method would you recommend? What periodic entries are required under each method?
11. Distinguish between the procedures followed by a merchandising enterprise using a periodic (physical) inventory system and one using a perpetual inventory system.
12. Describe the nature and purpose of a work sheet.
13. What effect, if any, does the use of a work sheet have on the sequence of the summarizing phase of the accounting process?
14. The accountant for the Miller Hardware Store, after completing all adjustments except for the merchandise inventory, makes the following entry to close the beginning inventory, to set up the ending inventory, to close all nominal accounts, and to report the net result of operations in the capital account.

| | | |
|---|---:|---:|
| Inventory (Dec. 31, 1993) .... | 22,500 | |
| Sales ..................... | 250,000 | |
| Purchase Discounts ......... | 2,500 | |
|   Inventory (Jan. 1, 1993) ... | | 25,000 |
|   Purchases .............. | | 175,000 |
|   Selling Expense .......... | | 25,000 |
|   General and Administrative | | 18,750 |
|   Expenses ............... | | |
|   Interest Expense.......... | | 1,875 |
|   M. Miller, Capital ......... | | 29,375 |

  (a) Would you regard this procedure as being acceptable?
  (b) What alternate procedure could you have followed to close the nominal accounts?
15. From the following list of accounts, determine which ones should be closed and whether each would normally be closed by a debit or by a credit entry.

Cash
Rent Expense
Accounts Receivable
Land
Depreciation Expense
Sales Revenue
Sales Discounts

Purchases
Freight-In
Retained Earnings
Capital Stock
Interest Revenue
Advertising Expense
Purchase Discounts
Notes Payable
Dividends
Accounts Payable

16. Distinguish between accrual and cash-basis accounting.
17. Is greater accuracy achieved in financial statements prepared from double-entry accrual data as compared with cash data? Explain.
18. What are the major advantages of electronic data processing as compared with manual processing of accounting data?
19. One of your clients overheard a computer manufacturer sales representative saying the computer will make the accountant obsolete. How would you respond to this comment?
*20. What advantages are provided through the use of: (a) special journals, (b) subsidiary ledgers, and (c) the voucher system?
*21. The Tantor Co. maintains a sales journal, a voucher register, a cash receipts journal, a cash disbursements journal, and a general journal. For each account listed below, indicate the most common journal sources of debits and credits.

(a) Cash
(b) Marketable Securities
(c) Notes Receivable
(d) Accounts Receivable
(e) Allowance for Doubtful Accounts
(f) Merchandise Inventory
(g) Land and Buildings
(h) Accumulated Depreciation
(i) Notes Payable
(j) Vouchers Payable
(k) Capital Stock
(l) Retained Earnings
(m) Sales
(n) Sales Discounts
(o) Purchases
(p) Freight-In
(q) Purchase Returns
(r) Purchase Discounts
(s) Salaries
(t) Depreciation

**22. How does the closing method differ from the adjusting method for Inventory and related accounts in a periodic inventory system?

* Relates to Appendix 3—1

** Relates to Appendix 3—2

---

## DISCUSSION CASES

### Case 3—1  (What do the terms "debit" and "credit" mean?)

Following are two quotes from magazine articles:

Retiree health benefits have become the most controversial, misunderstood issue that U.S. corporations face today. Propelling the benefits issue to the forefront is a set of proposed accounting standards that will force companies to reckon the cost of their current and future retiree health benefits and post this cost as a debit.

Source: William H. Sharkey, Jr., "Coping With Retiree Health Care Costs," *Business Insurance*, (January 9, 1989): p. 20.

[Basketball] center Mario Credit has been something of a debit throughout the tournament, but the emergence of his understudy, the corpulent and loose-lipped Oliver Miller, has largely obscured Credit's subpar performances.

Source: Alexander Wolff, "The Hogs Were in Heaven," *Sports Illustrated*, (April 2, 1990): p. 28.

Describe how the accounting terms "debit" and "credit" have been misused in each of the above quotes.

### Case 3—2   (Where is your cash box?)

Consider the following account of a veterinarian attempting to hire his first bookkeeper:

Miss Harbottle, the prospective bookkeeper, paused at the desk, heaped high with incoming and outgoing bills and circulars from drug firms with here and there stray boxes of pills and tubes of udder ointment.

Stirring distastefully among the mess, she extracted the dog-eared old ledger and held it up between finger and thumb. "What's this?"

Siegfried trotted forward. "Oh, that's our ledger. We enter the visits into it from our day book, which is here somewhere." He scrabbled about on the desk. "Ah, here it is. This is where we write the calls as they come in."

She studied the two books for a few minutes with an expression of amazement that gave way to a grim humor. She straightened up slowly and spoke patiently. "And where, may I ask, is your cash box?"

"Well, we just stuff it in there, you know." Siegfried pointed to the pint pot on the corner of the mantelpiece. "Haven't got what you'd call a proper cash box, but this does the job all right."

Miss Harbottle looked at the pot with horror. Crumpled cheques and notes peeped over the brim at her; many of their companions had burst out on the hearth below. "And you mean to say that you go out and leave that money there day after day?"

"Never seems to come to any harm." Siegfried replied.

"And how about your petty cash?"

Siegfried gave an uneasy giggle. "All in there, you know. All cash—petty and otherwise."

(Excerpted from: James Herriot, *All Creatures Great and Small*, 1972, St. Martin's Press: New York.)

Situations similar to the one described above are not unusual for small businesses. How does a business survive with such bad bookkeeping?

### Case 3—3   (To record or not to record)

Explain why each of the following hypothetical events would *not* be recorded in a journal entry.

1. A famous and much-beloved movie star is secretly filmed by an investigative news team using your company's product when she in fact has an endorsement contract with your company's major competitor.
2. Two of your firm's top vice presidents have a bitter argument and will probably never speak to one another again.
3. Your company's chief research chemist is killed in a plane crash.
4. Because of unfavorable economic news, consumer confidence is shaken and the stock market falls by 10 percent.
5. You, a small business owner, buy a sofa for your home. You pay with a check drawn on your personal, not your business, checking account.
6. Disney decides to build the next Walt Disney World near a large piece of property you own.

### Case 3—4   (When cash basis is different from accrual)

Alice Guth operates a low-impact aerobics studio. Alice has been in business for three years and has always had her financial statements prepared on a cash basis. This year, Alice's accountant has suggested that accrual-based financial statements would give a more accurate picture of the performance of the business. Alice's friend Frank Geller tells her that, in his experience, accrual-based financial statements tell pretty much the same story as cash-basis statements.

Under what circumstances would the cash basis and the accrual basis of accounting yield quite different pictures of a firm's operating performance? Under what circumstances would the cash basis and the accrual basis show approximately the same picture?

## Case 3—5  (The impact of computers on financial reporting)

Computers have drastically altered the way accounting records are maintained. Almost all businesses now keep at least some of their accounting records on computer. However, the most visible output of the accounting system, the financial information included in the Annual Report, is still prepared and disseminated the old-fashioned way—on paper. What types of changes in companies' annual reports are likely to occur over the next 10 to 15 years as a result of the increasingly widespread use of computers?

# EXERCISES

## Exercise 3—1  (Journal entries)

Alaska Supply Company, a merchandising firm, engaged in the following transactions during October 1993. The company records inventory using the perpetual system.

Oct.  1  Sold merchandise on account to the Plough Corporation for $15,000; terms 2/10, n/30, FOB shipping point. Plough paid $200 freight on the goods. The merchandise cost $7,450.

5  Purchased inventory costing $8,350 on account; terms n/30.

7  Received payment from Plough for goods shipped October 1.

15  The payroll paid for the first half of October was $18,000. (Ignore payroll taxes.)

18  Purchased a machine for $10,400 cash.

22  Declared a dividend of $.75 per share on 45,000 shares of common stock outstanding.

27  Purchased building and land for $150,000 in cash and a $250,000 mortgage payable, due in 30 years. The land was appraised at $150,000 and the building at $350,000.

Record the above transactions in general journal form.

## Exercise 3—2  (Posting to Accounts)

Refer to the data in Exercise 3—1. Below is Alaska Supply's trial balance as of October 1:

|  | Debit | Credit |
|---|---|---|
| Cash | $200,000 | |
| Accounts Receivable | 21,540 | |
| Inventory | 32,680 | |
| Land | 15,400 | |
| Building | 9,000 | |
| Accounts Payable | | $ 9,190 |
| Mortgage Payable | | 23,700 |
| Common Stock | | 185,000 |
| Retained Earnings | | 60,730 |
| | $278,620 | $278,620 |

1. Prepare T-accounts for all items in the October 1 trial balance and enter the initial balances.
2. Post the journal entries made in Exercise 3—1 and determine ending balances.

## Exercise 3—3  (Adjusting entries)

In analyzing the accounts of Loma Corporation, the adjusting data listed below are determined on December 31, the end of an annual fiscal period.

(a)  The prepaid insurance account shows a debit of $3,600, representing the cost of a 2-year fire insurance policy dated July 1.

(b) On September 1, Rent Revenue was credited for $3,750, representing revenue from subrental for a 5-month period beginning on that date.
(c) Purchase of advertising materials for $2,475 during the year was recorded in the advertising expense account. On December 31, advertising materials costing $275 are on hand.
(d) On November 1, $3,000 was paid on rent for a 6-month period beginning on that date. The rent expense account was debited.
(e) Miscellaneous Office Expense was debited for office supplies of $1,350 purchased during the year. On December 31, office supplies of $320 are on hand.
(f) Interest of $352 is accrued on notes payable.

1. Give the adjusting entry for each item.
2. What sources would provide the information for each adjustment?

### Exercise 3—4  (Adjusting and correcting entries)

Upon inspecting the books and records for Beardall Company for the year ended December 31, 1993, you find the following data.

(a) A receivable of $380 from Clarke Realty is determined to be uncollectible. The company maintains an allowance for doubtful accounts for such losses.
(b) A creditor, E. J. Stanley Co., has just been awarded damages of $2,200 as a result of breach of contract during the current year by Beardall Company. Nothing appears on the books in connection with this matter.
(c) A fire destroyed part of a branch office. Furniture and fixtures that cost $10,200 and had a book value of $7,800 at the time of the fire were completely destroyed. The insurance company has agreed to pay $6,500 under the provisions of the fire insurance policy.
(d) Advances of $1,150 to salespersons have been previously recorded as sales salaries expense.
(e) Machinery at the end of the year shows a balance of $18,460. It is discovered that additions to this account during the year totaled $4,460, but of this amount, $800 should have been recorded as repairs. Depreciation is to be recorded at 10% on machinery owned throughout the year, but at one-half this rate on machinery purchased or sold during the year.

Record the entries required to adjust and correct the accounts. (Ignore income tax consequences.)

### Exercise 3—5  (Adjusting and closing entries and post-closing trial balance)

Accounts of Pioneer Heating Co. at the end of the first year of operations show the balances listed below. The end-of-the-year physical inventory is $50,000. Prepaid operating expenses are $4,000 and accrued sales commissions payable are $5,900. Investment revenue receivable is $1,000. Depreciation for the year on buildings is $4,500 and on machinery, $5,000. Federal and state income taxes for the year are estimated at $18,100.

|  | Debit | Credit |
|---|---|---|
| Cash | $ 39,000 | |
| Investments | 50,000 | |
| Land | 70,000 | |
| Buildings | 180,000 | |
| Machinery | 100,000 | |
| Accounts Payable | | $ 65,000 |
| Common Stock | | 320,000 |
| Additional Paid-In Capital | | 40,000 |
| Sales | | 590,000 |
| Purchases | 280,000 | |
| Sales Commissions | 200,000 | |
| General Operating Expenses | 101,000 | |
| Investment Revenue | | 5,000 |
| | $1,020,000 | $1,020,000 |

1. Prepare the necessary entries to adjust and close the books, assuming use of an income summary account and the adjusting method for inventory.
2. Prepare a post-closing trial balance.

### Exercise 3—6 (Adjusting and closing entries and post-closing trial balance)

Below is the trial balance for Feigenbaum Company as of December 31.

|  | Debit | Credit |
|---|---|---|
| Cash | $ 38,000 | |
| Marketable Securities | 20,000 | |
| Accounts Receivable | 402,000 | |
| Inventory | 57,000 | |
| Prepaid Expenses | 54,000 | |
| Land | 65,000 | |
| Plant and Equipment | 1,167,000 | |
| Other Assets | 1,563,000 | |
| Accounts Payable | | $ 147,000 |
| Wages, Interest, and Taxes Payable | | 215,000 |
| Unearned Revenue | | 33,000 |
| Long-Term Debt | | 1,201,000 |
| Other Liabilities | | 336,000 |
| Common Stock | | 185,000 |
| Retained Earnings | | 1,112,000 |
| Sales | | 2,801,000 |
| Interest Revenue | | 23,000 |
| Cost of Goods Sold | 1,565,000 | |
| Selling, General, and Administrative Expenses | 640,000 | |
| Interest Expense | 79,000 | |
| Income Tax Expense | 264,000 | |
| Dividends | 139,000 | |
| | $6,053,000 | $6,053,000 |

Consider the following additional information:

(a) Feigenbaum uses a perpetual inventory system.
(b) The prepaid expenses were paid on September 1 and relate to a 3-year insurance policy that went into effect on September 1.
(c) The unearned revenue relates to rental of an unused portion of the corporate offices. The $33,000 was received on April 1 and represents payment in advance for one year's rental.
(d) Plant and Equipment includes $10,000 for equipment repairs that were erroneously recorded as equipment purchases. The repairs were made on December 30.
(e) Other Assets include $8,000 for miscellaneous office supplies, which were purchased in mid-October. An end-of-year count reveals that only $6,500 of the office supplies remain.
(f) Selling, General, and Administrative Expenses incorrectly includes $15,000 for office furniture purchases (Other Assets). The purchases were made on December 30.
(g) Inventory wrongly includes $6,000 of inventory that Feigenbaum had purchased on account but that was returned to the supplier on December 28 because it was of unsatisfactory quality.

Based on the above information:

1. Record the entries necessary to adjust the books.
2. Record the entries necessary to close the books. Use an Income Summary account. Assume the adjustments in (1) do not affect Income Tax Expense.
3. Prepare a post-closing trial balance.

### Exercise 3—7 (Analysis of journal entries)

For each of the journal entries below, write a description of the underlying event.

| | | | |
|---|---|---:|---:|
| 1. | Cash | 300 | |
| | Accounts Receivable | | 300 |
| 2. | Accounts Payable | 400 | |
| | Inventory | | 400 |
| 3. | Cash | 5,000 | |
| | Loan Payable | | 5,000 |
| 4. | Cash | 200 | |
| | Accounts Receivable | 700 | |
| | Sales Revenue | | 900 |
| | Cost of Goods Sold | 550 | |
| | Inventory | | 550 |
| 5. | Prepaid Insurance | 200 | |
| | Cash | | 200 |
| 6. | Dividends | 250 | |
| | Dividends Payable | | 250 |
| 7. | Retained Earnings | 1,000 | |
| | Dividends | | 1,000 |
| 8. | Insurance Expense | 50 | |
| | Prepaid Insurance | | 50 |
| 9. | Inventory | 600 | |
| | Cash | | 150 |
| | Accounts Payable | | 450 |
| 10. | Allowance for Doubtful Accounts | 46 | |
| | Accounts Receivable | | 46 |
| 11. | Interest Expense | 125 | |
| | Interest Payable | | 125 |
| 12. | Wages Payable | 130 | |
| | Wages Expense | 75 | |
| | Cash | | 205 |
| 13. | Accounts Payable | 500 | |
| | Cash | | 490 |
| | Purchase Discounts | | 10 |

### Exercise 3—8 (Adjusting entries)

The following accounts were taken from the trial balance of Cristy Company as of December 31, 1993. Given the information below, make the necessary adjusting entries.

| | |
|---|---:|
| Sales Revenue | $90,000 |
| Interest Revenue | 5,000 |
| Equipment | 46,000 |
| Accumulated Depreciation—Equipment | 12,000 |
| Beginning Inventory | 20,000 |
| Advertising Expense | 2,000 |
| Selling Expense | 6,000 |
| Interest Expense | 1,000 |

(a)  The equipment has an estimated useful life of 5 years and a salvage value of $1,000. Depreciation is calculated using the straight-line method.
(b)  Ending inventory is $28,000. The adjusting method for inventory is used.
(c)  $1,000 of selling expense has been paid in advance.
(d)  Interest of $500 has accrued on notes receivable.
(e)  $400 of advertising expense was incorrectly debited to selling expense.

### Exercise 3—9   (Adjusting and reversing entries)

On May 16, 1993, Lisa Anderson paid insurance for a 3-year period beginning June 1. She recorded the payment as follows:

Prepaid Insurance .......................................... 1,224
    Cash .................................................... 1,224

1. What adjustment is required on December 31? What reversing entry, if any, would you make?
2. What nominal account could be debited instead of Prepaid Insurance? What adjusting entry would be needed under these circumstances? What reversing entry, if any, would you make?

### Exercise 3—10   (Adjusting entries)

The data listed below were obtained from an analysis of the accounts of Noble Distributor Company as of March 31, 1993, in preparation of the annual report. Noble records current transactions in nominal accounts and *does not* reverse adjusting entries. What are the appropriate adjusting entries?

(a) Prepaid Insurance has a balance of $14,100. Noble has the following policies in force:

| Policy | Date | Term | Cost | Coverage |
|--------|------|------|------|----------|
| A | 1/1/93 | 2 years | $ 3,600 | Shop equipment |
| B | 12/1/92 | 6 months | 1,800 | Delivery equipment |
| C | 7/1/92 | 3 years | 12,000 | Buildings |

(b) Unearned Subscription Revenue has a balance of $56,250. The following subscriptions were collected in the current year. There are no other unexpired subscriptions.

| Effective Date | Amount | Term |
|----------------|--------|------|
| July 1, 1992 ............................. | $27,000 | 1 year |
| October 1, 1992 ........................ | 22,200 | 1 year |
| January 1, 1993 ........................ | 28,800 | 1 year |
| April 1, 1993 ........................... | 20,700 | 1 year |

(c) Interest Payable has a balance of $825. Noble owes a 10%, 90-day note for $45,000 dated March 1, 1993.
(d) Supplies has a balance of $2,190. An inventory of supplies revealed a total of $1,410.
(e) Salaries Payable has a balance of $9,750. The payroll for the 5-day workweek ended April 3 totaled $11,250.

### Exercise 3—11   (Analyzing adjusting entries)

Computer Consulting Company uses the asset-and-liability approach in accounting for prepaid expenses and unearned revenues. Selected account balances at the end of the current and prior year are presented below. The company does not make reversing entries, and accrued expenses and revenues are adjusted only at year-end.

| | Adjusted Balances Dec. 31, 1992 | Adjusted Balances Dec. 31, 1993 |
|---|---|---|
| Prepaid Rent ........................ | $ 4,800 | $3,600 |
| Salaries and Wages Payable ........... | 2,500 | 4,500 |
| Unearned Consulting Fees ............ | 13,000 | 6,400 |
| Interest Receivable ................. | 1,200 | 1,800 |

During 1993 Computer Consulting paid $10,000 for rent and $50,000 for wages. $108,000 was received for consulting fees and $2,400 was received as interest.

1. Provide the entries that were made at December 31, 1993, to adjust the accounts to the year-end balances above.
2. Determine the proper amount of Rent Expense, Salaries and Wages Expense, Consulting Fees Revenue, and Interest Revenue to be reported on the current-year income statement.

### Exercise 3—12 (Closing entries)

An accountant for Jolley, Inc., a merchandising enterprise, has just finished posting all the year-end adjusting entries to the ledger accounts and now wishes to close the appropriate account balances in preparation for the new period.

1. For each of the accounts listed, indicate whether the year-end balance should be: (a) carried forward to the new period, (b) closed by debiting the account, or (c) closed by crediting the account. Assume Jolley uses a perpetual inventory system.

| | | | | | |
|---|---|---|---|---|---|
| (a) | Cash | $ 25,000 | (k) | Accounts Payable | $ 12,000 |
| (b) | Sales | 50,000 | (l) | Accounts Receivable | 140,000 |
| (c) | Dividends | 3,000 | (m) | Prepaid Insurance | 16,000 |
| (d) | Inventory | 7,500 | (n) | Interest Receivable | 1,500 |
| (e) | Selling Expenses | 6,000 | (o) | Sales Discounts | 2,500 |
| (f) | Capital Stock | 100,000 | (p) | Interest Revenue | 3,500 |
| (g) | Income Summary | 0 | (q) | Supplies | 8,000 |
| (h) | Wages Expense | 10,000 | (r) | Retained Earnings | 6,500 |
| (i) | Dividends Payable | 4,000 | (s) | Accumulated Depr. | 2,000 |
| (j) | Cost of Goods Sold | 22,500 | (t) | Depreciation Exp. | 1,000 |

2. Give the necessary closing entries.
3. What was Jolley's net income (loss) for the period?

### Exercise 3—13 (Closing entries—proprietorship, partnership, and corporation)

Lennon's Tannery shows a credit balance in the Income Summary account of $67,600 after the revenue and expense items have been transferred to this account at the end of the fiscal year. Give the remaining entries to close the books assuming:

(a) The business is a sole proprietorship: the owner, D. H. Lennon, has made withdrawals of $14,000 during the year, and this is reported in a drawing account.
(b) The business is a partnership: the owners, D. H. Lennon and B. L. Oster, share profits 5:3; they have made withdrawals of $25,000 and $16,000, respectively, and these amounts are reported in drawing accounts.
(c) The business is a corporation: the ledger reports Additional Paid-In Capital, $250,000, and Retained Earnings, $100,000; dividends during the year amounting to $32,500 were recorded in a dividends account.

### Exercise 3—14 (Determining income from equity account analysis)

On November 1, the capital of J. Hale was $85,000, and on November 30, the capital was $95,100. During the month, Hale withdrew merchandise costing $5,000 and, on November 25, paid a $10,000 note payable of the business with interest at 10% for three months with a check drawn on a personal checking account. What was Hale's net income or loss for the month of November?

### Exercise 3—15 (Determining income from equity account analysis)

An analysis of the records of J. L. Kane disclosed changes in account balances for 1993 and the supplementary data listed below. From these data, calculate the net income or loss for 1993.

| | |
|---|---|
| Cash | $ 3,000 decrease |
| Accounts receivable | 2,000 increase |
| Inventory | 16,000 increase |
| Accounts payable | 4,000 increase |

During the year, Kane borrowed $30,000 in notes from the bank and paid off notes of $20,000 and interest of $1,000. Interest of $375 is accrued as of December 31, 1993. There was no interest payable at the end of 1992.

In 1993, Kane also transferred certain marketable securities to the business, and these were sold for $8,000 to finance the purchase of merchandise. Kane made weekly withdrawals in 1993 of $500.

## *Exercise 3—16   (Special journals)

Caddy's Inc. uses a general journal, sales journal, cash receipts journal, cash disbursements journal, and a voucher register. For each transaction below, indicate the appropriate journal(s) or register to be used.

(a)  Make a credit sale.
(b)  Collect cash on an account receivable.
(c)  Record bad-debt expense.
(d)  Write a check for payroll expense.
(e)  Purchase materials on account.
(f)  Give a discount on a sale.
(g)  Sell equipment on credit.
(h)  Make a cash sale.
(i)  Borrow $3,000 from the bank.
(j)  Record adjusting and closing entries.
(k)  Pay a supplier with a check.
(l)  Record accrued interest payable.
(m) Sell truck for cash.
(n)  Record depreciation expense.
(o)  Pay back loan.

*Relates to Appendix 3—1

## *Exercise 3—17   (Voucher register)

On July 15, vouchers for payment of the following items were approved by the chief financial officer of Lorenz Company:

| Amount | Payee | Purpose |
|---|---|---|
| $1,530 | Outland Hardware | Payment for inventory received |
| 4,000 | Locker Bank | Repayment of loan principal |
| 350 | Thom Insurance | Payment in advance for insurance |
| 8,790 | Payroll | Gross pay = $10,000; taxes payable = $1,210 |
| 1,240 | Better Electric | Last month's utilities |
| 2,600 | Rands Supply | Payment for inventory received |
| 670 | Frank Elsholz | Customer refund for sales return |
| 1,210 | U.S. Government | Remittance of taxes withheld |
| 3,000 | Thurston Howell | Advance on salary |

Prepare a voucher register and record the approved vouchers described above. The last voucher prepared on July 14 had the number 1022. Lorenz uses a periodic inventory system.

*Relates to Appendix 3—1

## *Exercise 3—18   (Voucher register and check register)

All of the vouchers described in Exercise 3—17 were paid by check on July 16, starting with check number 439. A 2 percent purchase discount was taken on the payment to Rands Supply. Based on the information provided:

1. Complete the voucher register prepared in Exercise 3—17 showing the payment of the vouchers by check.
2. Prepare a check register and enter the checks paid on July 16.

*Relates to Appendix 3—1

## *Exercise 3—19   (Cash receipts journal)

Mandelbrot Graphics makes most of its sales on credit. Data from the October sales journal are given below:

| Date | Invoice No. | Account Debited | Acct. Rec. (Dr) Sales (Cr) |
|---|---|---|---|
| 10/2 | 9045 | Franklin Printing | $1,200 |
| 10/8 | 9046 | Simpson Company | 2,350 |
| 10/15 | 9047 | Midstate University | 4,780 |
| 10/18 | 9048 | Topper Oil, Inc. | 565 |
| 10/24 | 9049 | Julia Company | 1,700 |
| 10/29 | 9050 | Fractal Design | 3,675 |

During November, Mandelbrot received payment for all of the credit sales made in October. Julia Company was given a 3 percent sales discount. Mandelbrot's cash sales during November totaled $380. In addition, during November Mandelbrot received full payment on a $5,000 note receivable, along with $450 in interest. Also, Mandelbrot received a $750 refund for an insurance policy that had been canceled. Prepare a cash receipts journal for Mandelbrot Graphics for November.

*Relates to Appendix 3—1

## *Exercise 3—20   (Closing method for inventory)

The unadjusted balances for inventory and related accounts for Button-Down Corporation as of December 31, 1993, are as follows:

| | |
|---|---|
| Beginning Inventory | $26,750 |
| Ending Inventory | 32,425 |
| Purchases | 59,400 |
| Purchase Discounts | 2,650 |
| Freight-In | 3,115 |

1. Give the necessary adjusting and closing entries for Inventory and related accounts assuming the "closing method" is used.
2. Determine the amount of cost of goods sold to be reported on the Income Statement.

*Relates to Appendix 3—2

## PROBLEMS

### Problem 3—1   (Journal entries)

Selfish Gene Company is a merchandising firm. The following events occurred during the month of May. Note: Selfish Gene maintains a perpetual inventory system.

May  1   Received $40,000 cash as new stockholder investment.
     3   Purchased inventory costing $8,000 on account from Dawkins Company; terms 2/10, n/30.

May 4    Purchased office supplies for $500 cash.

4    Held an office party for the retiring accountant. Balloons, hats, and refreshments cost $150 and were paid for with office staff contributions.

5    Sold merchandise costing $7,500 on account for $14,000 to Richard Company; terms, 3/15, n/30.

8    Paid employee wages of $2,000. Gross wages were $2,450; taxes totaling $450 were withheld.

9    Hired a new accountant; agreed to a first-year salary of $28,000.

9    Paid $1,500 for newspaper advertising.

10    Received payment from Richard Company.

12    Purchased a machine for $6,400 cash.

15    Declared a cash dividend totaling $25,000.

18    Sold merchandise costing $13,000 for $3,000 cash and $21,000 on account to Feynman Company; terms, n/30.

19    Paid Dawkins Company account in full.

22    Company executives appeared on the cover of a national newsmagazine. Related article extolled Selfish Gene's labor practices, environmental concerns, and customer service.

23    Market value of Selfish Gene's common stock rose by $150,000.

25    Purchased a building for $15,000 cash and a $135,000 mortgage payable.

29    Paid dividends declared on May 15.

### Instructions:

1. Record the preceding events in general journal form.
2. Which event do you think had the most significant economic impact on Selfish Gene Company? Are all economically relevant events recorded in the financial records?

### Problem 3—2   (Adjusting and reversing entries)

The trial balance of Kohler's Diamonds shows, among other items, the following balances on December 31, 1993, the end of a fiscal year:

|  | Debit | Credit |
|---|---|---|
| Accounts Receivable | $150,000 | |
| 9% Century City Bonds | 225,000 | |
| Land | 275,000 | |
| Buildings | 450,000 | |
| Accumulated Depreciation—Buildings | | $173,250 |
| 8% First-Mortgage Bonds Payable | | 600,000 |
| Rent Revenue | | 71,500 |
| Office Expense | 7,500 | |

The following facts are ascertained on this date upon inspection of the company's records:

(a)    It is estimated that approximately 2% of accounts receivable may prove uncollectible.

(b)    Interest is received semiannually on the Century City bonds on March 1 and September 1.

(c)    Buildings are depreciated at 5% a year; however, there were building additions of $50,000 during the year. The company computes depreciation on asset acquisitions during the year at one-half the annual rate.

(d)    Interest on the First-Mortgage bonds is payable semiannually on February 1 and August 1.

(e)    Rent revenue includes $5,100 that was received on November 1, representing rent on part of the buildings for the period November 1, 1993, to October 31, 1994.

(f)    Office supplies of $2,000 are on hand at December 31. Purchases of office supplies were debited to the office expense account.

**Instructions:**

1. Prepare the journal entries to adjust the books on December 31, 1993.
2. Give the reversing entries that may be appropriate at the beginning of 1994.

## Problem 3—3  (Account classification and debit/credit relationship)

**Instructions:**   Using the format provided, identify for each account:

1. Whether the account will appear on a balance sheet (B/S), income statement (I/S), or neither (N);
2. Whether the account is an asset (A), liability (L), owners' equity (OE), revenue (R), expense (E), or other (0);
3. Whether the account is real or nominal;
4. Whether the account will be "closed" or left "open" at year-end; and
5. Whether the account *normally* has a debit (Dr) or a credit (Cr) balance.

| Account Title | (1) B/S I/S N | (2) A,L,OE, R,E,O | (3) Real or Nominal | (4) Closed or Open | (5) Debit (Dr) or Credit (Cr) |
|---|---|---|---|---|---|
| Example: Cash | B/S | A | Real | Open | Dr |

(a)  Unearned Rent Revenue
(b)  Accounts Receivable
(c)  Inventory
(d)  Accounts Payable
(e)  Prepaid Rent
(f)  Mortgage Payable
(g)  Sales
(h)  Cost of Goods Sold
(i)  Dividends
(j)  Dividends Payable

(k)  Interest Receivable
(l)  Wages Expense
(m)  Drawings
(n)  Supplies
(o)  Income Summary
(p)  Accumulated Depreciation
(q)  Retained Earnings
(r)  Discount on Bonds Payable
(s)  Goodwill
(t)  Additional Paid-In Capital

## Problem 3—4  (Adjusting entries)

On December 31, the Philips Company noted the following transactions that occurred during 1993, some or all of which might require adjustment to the books.

(a)  Payment to suppliers of $1,200 was made for purchases on account during the year and was not recorded.
(b)  Building and land were purchased on January 2 for $175,000. The building's fair market value was $100,000 at the time of purchase. The building is being depreciated over a 20-year life using the straight-line method, and assuming no salvage value.
(c)  Of the $34,000 in Accounts Receivable, 2.5% is estimated to be uncollectible. Currently, the Allowance for Doubtful Accounts shows a debit balance of $290.
(d)  On August 1, $25,000 was loaned to a customer on a 6-month note with interest at an annual rate of 12%.
(e)  During 1993, Philips received $2,500 in advance for services, 80% of which will be performed in 1994. The $2,500 was credited to sales revenue.
(f)  The interest expense account was debited for all interest charges incurred during the year and shows a balance of $1,100. However, of this amount, $300 represents a discount on a 60-day note payable, due January 30, 1994.

**Instructions:**

1. Give the necessary adjusting entries to bring the books up to date.
2. Indicate the net change in income as a result of the foregoing adjustments.

## Problem 3—5  (Analysis of adjusting entries)

The accountant for Save More Company made the following adjusting entries on December 31, 1993:

| | | | |
|---|---|---:|---:|
| (a) | Prepaid Rent | 1,200 | |
| | Rent Expense | | 1,200 |
| (b) | Advertising Materials | 2,000 | |
| | Advertising Expense | | 2,000 |
| (c) | Rent Revenue | 500 | |
| | Unearned Revenue | | 500 |
| (d) | Office Supplies | 1,000 | |
| | Office Expense | | 1,000 |
| (e) | Prepaid Insurance | 1,050 | |
| | Insurance Expense | | 1,050 |

Further information is provided as follows:

(a)  Rent is paid every October 1.
(b)  Advertising materials are paid at one time (June 1) and are used evenly throughout the year.
(c)  Rent is received in advance every March 1.
(d)  Office supplies are purchased every July 1 and used evenly throughout the year.
(e)  Yearly insurance premium is payable each August 1.

**Instructions:**   For each adjusting entry, indicate the original transaction entry that was recorded.

## Problem 3—6  (Adjusting entries)

The bookkeeper for the Irwin Wholesale Electric Co. prepares no reversing entries and records all revenue and expense items in nominal accounts during the period. The following balances, among others, are listed on the trial balance at the end of the fiscal period, December 31, 1993, before accounts have been adjusted:

| | Dr (Cr) |
|---|---:|
| Accounts Receivable | $152,000 |
| Allowance for Doubtful Accounts | (1,000) |
| Interest Receivable | 2,800 |
| Discounts on Notes Payable | 300 |
| Prepaid Real Estate and Personal Property Tax | 1,800 |
| Salaries and Wages Payable | (4,000) |
| Discounts on Notes Receivable | (2,800) |
| Unearned Rent Revenue | (1,500) |

Inspection of the company's records reveals the following as of December 31, 1993:

(a)  Uncollectible accounts are estimated at 3% of the accounts receivable balance.
(b)  The accrued interest on investments totals $2,400.
(c)  The company borrows cash by discounting its own notes at the bank. Discounts on notes payable at the end of 1993 are $1,600.
(d)  Prepaid real estate and personal property taxes are $1,800, the same as at the end of 1992.
(e)  Accrued salaries and wages are $4,300.
(f)  The company accepts notes from customers, giving its customers credit for the face of the note less a charge for interest. At the end of each period, any interest applicable to the succeeding period is reported as a discount. Discounts on notes receivable at the end of 1993 are $1,500.
(g)  Part of the company's properties had been sublet on September 15, 1992, at a rental of $3,000 per month. The arrangement was terminated at the end of one year.

**Instructions:**   Give the adjusting entries required to bring the books up to date.

## Problem 3—7 (Preparation of work sheet and adjusting and closing entries)

Account balances taken from the ledger of the Builders' Supply Corporation on December 31, 1993, are listed below. Information relating to adjustments on December 31, 1993, follows:

(a) The inventory on hand is $87,570. Inventory and related accounts are adjusted through Cost of Goods Sold.
(b) Allowance for Doubtful Accounts is to be increased to a balance of $3,000.
(c) Buildings are depreciated at the rate of 5% per year.
(d) Accrued selling expenses are $3,840.
(e) There are supplies of $780 on hand.
(f) Prepaid insurance relating to 1994 totals $720.
(g) Accrued interest on long-term investments is $240.
(h) Accrued real estate and payroll taxes are $900.
(i) Accrued interest on the mortgage is $480.
(j) Income tax is estimated to be 20% of the income before income tax.

| | |
|---|---:|
| Cash | $ 24,000 |
| Accounts Receivable | 72,000 |
| Allowance for Doubtful Accounts | 1,380 |
| Inventory, Dec. 31, 1992 | 62,000 |
| Long-Term Investments | 15,400 |
| Land | 69,600 |
| Buildings | 72,000 |
| Accumulated Depreciation—Buildings | 19,800 |
| Capital Stock, $10 par | 180,000 |
| Retained Earnings, Dec. 31, 1992 | 14,840 |
| Dividends | 13,400 |
| Accounts Payable | 35,000 |
| Mortgage Payable | 68,800 |
| Sales | 246,000 |
| Sales Returns | 4,360 |
| Sales Discounts | 5,400 |
| Interest Revenue | 660 |
| Purchases | 138,480 |
| Purchase Discounts | 2,140 |
| Freight-In | 3,600 |
| Selling Expense | 49,440 |
| Office Expense | 21,680 |
| Insurance Expense | 1,440 |
| Supplies Expense | 5,200 |
| Taxes—Real Estate and Payroll | 7,980 |
| Interest Expense | 2,640 |

### Instructions:

1. Prepare a trial balance.
2. Journalize the adjustments.
3. Journalize the closing entries.
4. Prepare a post-closing trial balance.

Although not required, the use of a work sheet is recommended for the solution of this problem.

## Problem 3—8 (Adjusting and closing entries and post-closing trial balance)

Data for adjustments at December 31, 1993, are as follows:

(a) Kwon International uses a perpetual inventory system.
(b) An analysis of Accounts Receivable reveals that the appropriate year-end balance in the Allowance for Doubtful Accounts is $700.

(c)  Equipment depreciation for the year totaled $45,000.

(d)  A recheck of the inventory count revealed that goods costing $4,300 were wrongly excluded from ending inventory. The goods in question were not shipped until January 3, 1994. A related receivable for $6,000 was also mistakenly recorded.

(e)  Interest on the note payable has not been accrued. The note was issued on March 1, 1993, and the interest rate is 15 percent.

(f)  The balance in Insurance Expense represents $2,000 that was paid for a one-year policy on October 1. The policy went into effect on October 1.

(g)  Dividends totaling $5,600 were declared on December 25. The dividends will not be paid until January 15, 1994.

**Kwon International Corporation**
**Unadjusted Trial Balance**
**December 31, 1993**

|  | Debit | Credit |
|---|---|---|
| Cash | $ 22,500 | |
| Accounts Receivable | 24,000 | |
| Allowance for Doubtful Accounts | | $     240 |
| Inventory | 45,300 | |
| Equipment | 210,000 | |
| Accumulated Depreciation—Equipment | | 42,000 |
| Accounts Payable | | 28,000 |
| Notes Payable | | 80,000 |
| Wages Payable | | 10,000 |
| Income Taxes Payable | | 8,900 |
| Common Stock | | 50,000 |
| Retained Earnings | | 27,310 |
| Sales Revenue | | 270,000 |
| Interest Revenue | | 8,000 |
| Cost of Goods Sold | 171,250 | |
| Wages Expense | 28,000 | |
| Interest Expense | 1,500 | |
| Utilities Expense | 5,000 | |
| Insurance Expense | 2,000 | |
| Advertising Expense | 6,000 | |
| Income Tax Expense | 8,900 | |
| | $524,450 | $524,450 |

**Instructions:**

1. Journalize the necessary adjusting entries.
2. Journalize the necessary closing entries using an income summary account.
3. Prepare a post-closing trial balance.
4. Can a company pay dividends in a year in which it has a net loss? Can a company owe income taxes in a year in which it has a net loss?

**\*Problem 3—9  (Preparation of work sheet and adjusting, closing, and reversing entries)**

The following account balances are taken from the general ledger of the Whitni Corporation on December 31, 1993, the end of its fiscal year. The corporation was organized January 2, 1990.

| | |
|---|---|
| Cash | $ 40,250 |
| Notes Receivable | 16,500 |
| Accounts Receivable | 63,000 |
| Allowance for Doubtful Accounts (credit balance) | 650 |

| | |
|---|---:|
| Inventory, January 1, 1993 | 88,700 |
| Land | 80,000 |
| Buildings | 247,600 |
| Accumulated Depreciation—Buildings | 18,000 |
| Furniture and Fixtures | 15,000 |
| Accumulated Depreciation—Furniture and Fixtures | 9,000 |
| Notes Payable | 18,000 |
| Accounts Payable | 72,700 |
| Common Stock, $100 par | 240,000 |
| Retained Earnings | 129,125 |
| Sales | 760,000 |
| Sales Returns and Allowances | 17,000 |
| Purchases | 479,650 |
| Purchase Discounts | 7,850 |
| Heat, Light, and Power | 16,700 |
| Property Tax Expense | 10,200 |
| Salaries and Wages Expense | 89,000 |
| Sales Commissions | 73,925 |
| Insurance Expense | 18,000 |
| Interest Revenue | 2,600 |
| Interest Expense | 2,400 |

Data for adjustments at December 31, 1993, are as follows:

(a)  Merchandise inventory, $94,700.
(b)  Depreciation (to nearest month for additions): Furniture and fixtures, 10%; Buildings, 4%. Additions to the buildings costing $150,000 were completed June 30, 1993.
(c)  Allowance for Doubtful Accounts is to be increased to a balance of $2,500.
(d)  Accrued expenses:
     Sales commissions, $700
     Interest on notes payable, $45
     Property tax, $6,000
(e)  Prepaid expenses: insurance, $3,200.
(f)  Accrued revenue: interest on notes receivable, $750.
(g)  The following information is also to be recorded:
     (1) On December 30, the board of directors declared a quarterly dividend of $1.50 per share on common stock, payable January 25, 1994, to stockholders of record January 15, 1994.
     (2) Income tax for 1993 is estimated at $15,000.
     (3) The only charges to Retained Earnings during the year resulted from the declaration of the regular quarterly dividends.

**Instructions:**  Using either the adjusting method for inventory or the closing method illustrated in Appendix 3—2:

1. Prepare an eight-column work sheet. There should be a pair of columns each for trial balance, adjustments, income statement, and balance sheet.
2. Prepare all the journal entries necessary to record the effects of the foregoing information and to adjust and close the books of the corporation.
3. Prepare the reversing entries that may appropriately be made.

*Closing method (Appendix 3—2) is optional for this problem.

### *Problem 3—10   (Using special journals)

West Mountain Inc., a fruit wholesaler, records business transactions in the following books of original entry: general journal (J); voucher register (VR); check register (CR); sales journal (SJ); and cash receipts journal (CRJ). West Mountain recorded and filed the following business documents:

(a) Sales invoices for sales on account totaling $4,600.
(b) The day's cash register tape showing receipts for cash sales at $700.
(c) A list of cash received on various customers' accounts totaling $2,930. Sales discounts taken were $30.
(d) The telephone bill for $60 payable in one week.
(e) Vendors' invoices for $5,000 worth of fruit received.
(f) Check stub for payment of last week's purchases from All-Growers Farms, $5,940. Terms were 1/10, n/30, and payment was made within the discount period.
(g) Check stub for repayment of a $10,000, 90-day note to Mercantile Bank, $10,300.
(h) A letter notifying West Mountain that Littex Markets, a customer, has declared bankruptcy. All creditors will receive 10 cents on every dollar due. Littex owes West Mountain $1,300.

## Instructions:

1. Indicate the books of original entry in which West Mountain recorded each of the business transactions. (Use the designated abbreviations.)
2. Record the debits and credits for each entry as though only a general journal were used. Use account titles implied by the voucher system.

*Relates to Appendix 3—1

## *Problem 3—11  (Using special journals)

A fire destroyed Fong Company's journals. However, the general ledger and accounts receivable subsidiary ledger were saved. An inspection of the ledgers reveals the following information:

### GENERAL LEDGER

| Cash (Acct. No. 11) | | | |
|---|---|---|---|
| May 1 | Bal. 8,200 | | |
| 31 | 7,338 | | |

| Sales (Acct. No. 41) | | | |
|---|---|---|---|
| | | May 31 | 5,050 |
| | | 31 | 4,500 |

| Sales Discounts (Acct. No. 42) | | | |
|---|---|---|---|
| May 3 | 12 | | |

| Accounts Receivable (Acct. No. 12) | | | |
|---|---|---|---|
| May 1 | Bal. 3,100 | May 31 | 2,850 |
| 31 | 5,050 | | |

### ACCOUNTS RECEIVABLE LEDGER

| Customer A | | | |
|---|---|---|---|
| May 1 | Bal. 290 | | |
| 5 | 500 | | |

| Customer B | | | |
|---|---|---|---|
| May 1 | Bal. 1,250 | May 13 | 1,000 |
| 5 | 400 | | |

| Customer C | | | |
|---|---|---|---|
| May 2 | 1,450 | | |

| Customer D | | | |
|---|---|---|---|
| May 1 | Bal. 1,560 | May 11 | 650 |

| Customer E | | | |
|---|---|---|---|
| May 2 | 1,200 | May 3 | 1,200 |
| 12 | 1,500 | | |

Fong's credit terms are 1/10, n/30.

**Instructions:**   Reconstruct the sales and cash receipts journals from the information given.

*Relates to Appendix 3—1

## *Problem 3—12   (Voucher and check registers)

Prepare a voucher register and a check register for Bethe Company and record the following transactions. The last voucher used was #9847, and the last check used was #562.

June   1   Paid voucher #9846 (for office supplies from JOK Supplies), $560. No discount was taken. (Record this in the check register only.)

      2   Purchased inventory on account from Nimitz Company, $1,800; terms, 1/10, n/30. Bethe uses the periodic inventory method.

      2   Received utilities bill from NiStar Electric for May, $985; terms, 3/15, n/30.

      4   Paid voucher #9847 to the *Archer Journal* for advertising, $400. No discount was taken. (Record this in the check register only.)

      8   Paid Nimitz Company account in full.

      8   Authorized customer refund to Spruance Company, $1,150.

      8   Paid refund to Spruance Company.

      9   Authorized payment of cash dividends previously declared, $2,500. (No voucher was prepared at declaration date.)

     10   Received notice of mortgage payment due to ATP Financial, $5,000; $4,600 represents interest and $400 represents principal. Payment was authorized.

     12   Paid utility bill.

     12   Made mortgage payment.

     13   Approved loan to Ken Nelson, an officer of the company, $6,000.

     15   Disbursed loan to Ken Nelson.

     15   Approved payroll: gross pay, $11,000; taxes withheld, $2,000; health insurance premiums withheld, $980.

     15   Paid net payroll.

     17   Signed a contract for a fire insurance policy with Halsey Casualty. The policy is for one year, costs $4,000, and goes into effect on June 18.

     18   Paid for fire insurance.

     19   Purchased inventory on account from Wainwright Company, $2,300; terms, 2/10, n/30.

     22   Paid cash dividend.

     30   Approved payroll: gross pay, $11,500; taxes withheld, $2,200; health insurance premiums withheld, $980.

     30   Paid net payroll.

     30   Authorized and paid taxes withheld for June to U.S. Government.

     30   Authorized and paid health insurance premiums withheld for June to Unicare Insurance.

*Relates to Appendix 3—1

# CHAPTER 4

## The Income Statement

---

---

The title of *The Wall Street Journal* article was eye-catching: "Sears Net Had Fivefold Rise in 4th Period."[1] Sears reported a net income for the fourth quarter of 1989 of $602.1 million compared to net income of $117.4 million for the fourth quarter of 1988. However, in the fourth quarter of 1988, Sears had one-time expenses of $442 million related to restructuring and a $58.6 million loss related to the disposal of a business segment. When these two factors are considered, and comparable numbers are generated, how well did Sears do for the fourth quarter of 1989? When comparing financial statements across time as well as across companies, what factors must be considered?

[1]*The Wall Street Journal*, February 6, 1990, p. A4.

## IMPORTANCE OF RECOGNIZING, MEASURING, AND REPORTING INCOME

The recognition, measurement, and reporting (display) of business income and its components are considered by many to be the most important tasks of accountants. The users of financial statements who must make decisions regarding their relationship with the company are almost always concerned with a measure of its success in using the resources committed to its operation. Has the activity been profitable? What is the trend of profitability? Is it increasingly profitable, or is there a downward trend? What is the most probable result for future years? Will the company be profitable enough to pay interest on its debt and dividends to its stockholders and still grow at a desired rate? These and other questions all relate to the basic question—What is income?

For many users, only one figure, the "bottom line," is meaningful. They feel uncomfortable trying to analyze additional information. To others, information about the components of income is important and can be used to help predict future income and cash flows. Not only can this information be helpful to a specific user, but it is also of value to the economy. As discussed in Chapter 1, one of the principal tasks facing accountants is to provide information that will assist in allocating scarce resources to the most efficient and effective organizations. If reported income is overstated when compared with the actual underlying situation, a poor allocation will be made. Resources will flow to inefficient entities, while the more efficient entities will suffer due to a lack of resources.

Income figures are also used for purposes other than resource allocation by creditors and investors. Governments, both federal and state, rely heavily on income taxes as a source of their revenues. The income figure used for assessing taxes is based on laws passed by Congress and regulations applied by the IRS and various courts. The income determined for financial reporting, however, is determined by adherence to accounting standards (GAAP) developed by the profession. Thus, the amount of income reported to creditors and investors may not be the same as the income reported for tax purposes. Many items are the same for both types of reporting, but there are some significant differences. Most of these differences relate to the specific purposes Congress has for taxing income. Governments use an income figure as a base to assess taxes, but they must use one that relates closely with the ability of the taxpayer to pay the computed tax. For example, accrual accounting requires companies to defer recognition of revenues that are received before they are earned. Income tax regulations, however, require these unearned revenues to be reported as income as soon as they are received in cash.

This text focuses on principles of accounting that are the supporting foundation for financial accounting and reporting. Income for tax purposes will be discussed, but only as it is used to determine the income tax expense and other tax-related amounts reported in the financial statements.

## INCOME DETERMINATION

Although there are varying ways to measure income, all of them share a common basic concept: income is a return over and above the investment. One of the more widely accepted definitions of income states that it is the amount that an entity could return to its investors and still leave the entity as well-off at the end of the period as it was at the beginning.[2] But what does it mean to be "as well-off," and how can it be measured? Most measurements are based on some concept of capital or ownership maintenance. Two

---

[2]Although many economists and accountants have adopted this view, a basic reference is J. R. Hicks' widely accepted book, *Value and Capital,* 2nd edition (Oxford University Press, 1946).

concepts of capital maintenance were considered by the FASB in its conceptual framework: **financial capital maintenance** and **physical capital maintenance**.

The financial capital maintenance concept assumes that an enterprise has income "only if the dollar amount of an enterprise's net assets (assets − liabilities, or owners' equity) at the end of a period exceeds the dollar amount of net assets at the beginning of the period *after* excluding the effects of transactions with owners."[3] To illustrate, assume that Kreidler, Inc., had the following assets and liabilities at the beginning and the end of a period:

|  | Beginning of Period | End of Period |
|---|---|---|
| Total assets | $510,000 | $560,000 |
| Total liabilities | 430,000 | 390,000 |
| Net assets (owners' equity) | $ 80,000 | $170,000 |

If there were no investments by owners or distributions to owners during the period, income would be $90,000, the amount of the increase in net assets. Assume, however, that owners invested $40,000 in the business and received distributions (dividends) of $15,000. Income for the period would be $65,000, computed as follows:

| | |
|---|---|
| Net assets, end of period | $170,000 |
| Net assets, beginning of period | 80,000 |
| Change (increase) in net assets | $ 90,000 |
| Deduct investment by owners | (40,000) |
| Add distributions (dividends) to owners | 15,000 |
| Income | $ 65,000 |

Another way of defining capital maintenance is in terms of **physical capital maintenance**. Under this concept, income occurs "only if the physical productive capacity of the enterprise at the end of a period . . . exceeds the physical productive capacity at the beginning of the same period, also after excluding the effects of transactions with owners."[4] This concept requires that productive assets (inventories, buildings, and equipment) be valued at current cost. Productive capital is maintained only if the current costs of these capital assets are maintained. Thus, if the beginning net assets value of $80,000 in the above example rose to $100,000 by the end of the year because of rising prices, and new investments and dividends were as shown, income would be $45,000 rather than $65,000. The $20,000 difference would be the amount necessary to "maintain physical productive capacity" and would not be part of income.

The Financial Accounting Standards Board considered carefully these two ways of viewing income, and adopted the financial capital maintenance concept as part of its conceptual framework.

Even with the acceptance of the financial capital maintenance concept, the question of how the net asset balance should be valued must be considered. Many suggest that net assets should be measured at their unexpired historical cost values as is currently being done. Others feel that replacement values or disposal values should be used. Some would include as assets intangible resources, such as human resources, goodwill, and geographical location, that have been attained over time without specifically identified payments.

---

[3]*Statement of Financial Accounting Concepts No. 5,* "Recognition and Measurement in Financial Statements of Business Enterprises" (Stamford: Financial Accounting Standards Board, 1984) par. 47.

[4]*Ibid.*

Others feel that only resources that have been acquired in arm's-length exchange activities should be included.

Likewise, controversy has developed over the recognition and measurement of liabilities. Should future claims against the entity for items such as pensions, warranties, and deferred income taxes be valued at their discounted values, at their future cash flow values, or eliminated completely from the financial statements until events clearly define the existence of a specific liability? The reported income under the financial maintenance concept will vary widely depending on when and how the assets, liabilities, and changes in the valuation of assets and liabilities are measured.

Comparing the net assets at two points in time, as was done above, yields a single net income figure. However, no detail concerning the components of income is disclosed. To provide this detail, accountants have adopted a transaction approach to measuring income that stresses the direct computation of revenues and expenses. As long as the same measurement method is used, income will be the same under the transaction approach as with a single income computation.

## Transaction Approach to Income Determination

The **transaction approach**, sometimes referred to as the "matching method," focuses on business events that affect certain elements of financial statements, namely, revenues, expenses, gains, and losses. Income is measured as the difference between resource inflows (revenues and gains) and outflows (expenses and losses) over a period of time. Definitions for the four income elements were presented in Chapter 2 and are repeated below as an aid to the following discussion.

As can be seen from studying these definitions, by defining gains and losses in terms of changes in equity after providing for revenues, expenses, and investments and distributions to the owners, income determined by the transaction approach will be the same income as that determined under financial capital maintenance. However, by identifying intermediate income components, the transaction approach provides detail to assist in predicting future cash flows.

The key problem in recognizing and measuring income using the transaction approach is deciding when an "inflow or other enhancement of assets" has occurred and how to measure the "outflows or other using-up of assets." As discussed in Chapter 2, the first issue is identified as "the revenue recognition" problem, and the second issue is identified as the "expense recognition" or "matching" problem.

### Component Elements of Income

- **Revenues** are inflows or other enhancements of assets of an entity or settlements of its liabilities (or a combination of both) from delivering or producing goods, rendering services, or other activities that constitute the entity's ongoing major or central operations.
- **Expenses** are outflows or other using-up of assets or incurrences of liabilities (or a combination of both) from delivering or producing goods, rendering services, or carrying out other activities that constitute the entity's ongoing major or central operations.
- **Gains** are increases in equity (net assets) from peripheral or incidental transactions of an entity and from all other transactions and other events and circumstances affecting the entity except those that result from revenues or investments by owners.

- Losses are decreases in equity (net assets) from peripheral or incidental transactions of an entity and from all other transactions and other events and circumstances affecting the entity except those that result from expenses or distributions to owners.

Source: *Statement of Financial Accounting Concepts No. 6*, "Elements of Financial Statements" (Stamford: Financial Accounting Standards Board, 1985), p. x.

**✗Revenue and Gain Recognition**    The transaction approach requires a clear definition of when income elements should be recognized, or recorded, in the financial statements. Under the generally accepted accounting principle of accrual, revenue recognition does not necessarily occur when cash is received. The conceptual framework identifies two factors that should be considered in deciding when revenues and gains should be recognized: **realization** and the **earnings process.** Revenues and gains are generally recognized when:[5]

1. They are realized or realizable, and
2. They have been earned through substantial completion of the activities involved in the earnings process.

In order for revenues and gains to be **realized,** inventory or other assets must be exchanged for cash or claims to cash. Revenues are **realizable** when assets held or assets received in an exchange are readily convertible to known amounts of cash or claims to cash. The **earnings process** criterion relates primarily to revenue recognition. Most gains result from transactions and events, such as the sale of land or a patent, that involve no earnings process. Thus, being realized or realizable is of more importance in recognizing gains.

Application of these two criteria to certain industries and companies within these industries has resulted in recognition of revenue at different points in the revenue-producing cycle. This cycle can be a lengthy one. For a manufacturing company, it begins with the development of proposals for a certain product by an individual or by the research and development department and extends through planning, production, sale, collection, and finally expiration of the warranty period. All of these steps are involved in generating sales revenue. If there is a failure at any step, revenue may be seriously curtailed or even completely eliminated. Yet, there is only one aggregate revenue amount for the entire cycle, the selling price of the product.

For a service company, the revenue-producing cycle begins with an agreement to provide a service and extends through the planning and performance of the service to the collection of the cash and final proof through the passage of time that the service has been adequately performed. With increasing legal actions being taken against professionals, such as doctors and accountants, one could argue that the revenue-producing cycle does not end until the possibility of legal claims for services performed is remote.

Although some accountants have argued for recognizing revenue on a partial basis over these extended production or service periods, the prevailing practice has been to select one point in the cycle that best meets the revenue recognition criteria. Both of these criteria are generally met at the **point of sale,** which is generally when goods are delivered or services are rendered to customers. Thus, revenue for automobiles sold to dealers by Ford Motor Company will be recognized when the cars are shipped to the dealers. Similarly, Price Waterhouse and Co. will record its revenue from audit and tax work when the services have been performed and billed. In both examples, the earnings process is deemed to be substantially complete, and the cash or receivable from the

[5]*Statement of Financial Accounting Concepts No. 5*, par. 83.

## Revenue Recognition

A common method for inflating revenues and profits is to ship more inventory to customers than they order. *Business Week* illustrates two instances where the revenue recognition criteria may have been compromised. Using a practice known as "trade loading," RJR Nabisco, the second largest cigarette producer in America, would ship more inventory to wholesalers than the wholesalers could resell. The excess inventory would eventually be returned, but RJR would book the revenue and profit when the cigarettes were originally shipped. Management stopped this practice in 1988, and the result was a $360 million decrease in operating profits for 1989.

Another company, Regina Co., took trade loading several steps further. In a hurried effort to compete in the upright vacuum cleaner market, Regina skipped proper testing of its product, the Housekeeper. The result: 40,000 units, or 16% of sales, were returned. Regina's solution: lease a building to store the returned items and make no entries to record the returns. In a continued effort to make Regina's stock attractive, the firm began to record sales when goods were ordered, not when they were shipped. Further, to ensure that projected sales figures were achieved for the fiscal year ending June 30, 1988, the company generated $5.4 million of fictitious sales invoices for the last three business days of the year.

### Questions:

1. *Do the above transactions of RJR Nabisco and Regina satisfy the revenue recognition criteria as set forth by the FASB?*
2. *If RJR Nabisco has open contracts with distributors that require distributors to attempt to sell all inventory shipped to them, does trade loading violate the revenue recognition criteria?*
3. *Regina recorded revenue when goods were ordered rather than when the goods were shipped. Does it really make a difference when the journal entry is made?*
4. *As Regina's accountant, what could you do if the president of the company (who was fined $50,000 and sentenced to one year in jail) asked for your assistance in "cooking the books?"*

Sources:

Walecia Konrad, "RJR Nabisco," *Business Week*, February 19, 1990.

John A. Byrne, "Regina," *Business Week*, February 12, 1990.

customer meets the realization criterion. Although the "point-of-sale" practice is the most common revenue recognition point, there are notable variations to this general rule.

1. If products or other assets are readily realizable because they can be sold at reliably determined prices without significant selling effort, revenues may be recognized at the **point of completed production.** Examples of this situation may occur with certain precious metals and agricultural products that are supported by government price guarantees. In these situations, the earnings process is considered to be substantially complete when the mining or production of the goods is complete.
2. If a product or service is contracted for in advance, revenue may be recognized as production takes place or as services are performed, especially if the production or performance period extends over more than one fiscal year. The **percentage-of-completion** and **proportional performance** methods of accounting have been developed to recognize revenue at several points in the production or service cycle rather than waiting until the final delivery or performance takes place. This exception to the

general point-of-sale rule is necessary if the qualitative characteristics of relevance and representational faithfulness are to be met. Construction contracts for buildings, roads, and dams and contracts for scientific research are examples of situations where these methods of revenue recognition occur. In all cases where this revenue recognition variation is employed, a firm, enforceable contract must exist to meet the realizability criterion, and an objective measure of progress toward completion must be attainable.

3. If collectibility of assets received for products or services is considered doubtful, revenues and gains may be recognized as the cash is received. Although the earnings process has been substantially completed, the questionable receivable fails to meet the realization criterion. The **installment sales** and **cost recovery methods** of accounting have been developed to recognize revenue under these conditions. Sales of real estate, especially speculative recreational property, are often recorded using this variation of the general rule.

The general point-of-sale rule will be assumed unless specifically stated otherwise. The variations introduced above are discussed fully in a later chapter.

**Expense and Loss Recognition**    In order to determine income, not only must criteria for revenue recognition be established, but the principles for recognizing expenses and losses must be clearly defined. Some expenses are directly associated with revenues and can thus be recognized in the same period as the related revenues. Other expenses are not associated with specific revenues and are recognized in the time period when paid or incurred. Still other expenditures are not recognized currently as expenses because they relate to future revenues and, therefore, are reported as assets. Expense recognition, then, can be divided into three categories: (1) direct matching, (2) systematic and rational allocation, and (3) immediate recognition.

***Direct Matching***    Relating expenses to specific revenues is often referred to as the "matching" process. For example, the cost of goods sold is clearly a direct expense that can be matched with the revenues produced by the sale of goods and reported in the same time period as the revenues are recognized. Similarly, shipping costs and sales commissions usually relate directly to revenues.[6]

Direct expenses include not only those that have already been incurred, but should also include anticipated expenses related to revenues of the current period. After delivery of goods to customers, there are still costs of collection, bad debt losses from uncollectible receivables, and possible warranty costs for product deficiencies. These expenses are directly related to revenues and should be estimated and matched against recognized revenues for the period.

***Systematic and Rational Allocation***    The second general expense recognition category involves assets that benefit more than one accounting period. The cost of assets such as buildings, equipment, patents, and prepaid insurance are spread across the periods of expected benefit in some systematic and rational way. Generally, it is difficult if not impossible to relate these expenses directly to specific revenues or to specific periods, but it is clear that they are necessary if the revenue is to be earned. Examples of expenses that are included in this category are depreciation and amortization.

[6]*Statement of Financial Accounting Concepts No. 6,* par. 144.

The methods adopted for recognizing expenses and losses should appear reasonable to an unbiased observer and should be followed consistently unless the underlying conditions surrounding the asset change. Some expenses are related to the goods being produced, and thus may be deferred in inventory values if the goods are unsold at the end of an accounting period. Examples include depreciation on production machinery and plant insurance. Other expenses are related to periods, and are allocated directly as an expense of the immediate time period. Examples include depreciation of delivery trucks and amortization of bond discount.[7]

**Immediate Recognition**    Many expenses are not related to specific revenues, but are incurred to obtain goods and services that indirectly help to generate revenues. Because these goods and services are used almost immediately, their costs are recognized as expenses in the period of acquisition. Examples include most administrative costs, such as office salaries, utilities, and general advertising and selling expenses.

Immediate recognition is also appropriate when future benefits are highly uncertain. For example, expenditures for research and development may provide significant future benefits, but they are usually so uncertain that the costs are written off in the period in which they are incurred.

Most losses also fit in the immediate recognition category. Because they arise from peripheral or incidental transactions, they do not relate directly to revenues. Examples include losses from disposition of used equipment, losses from natural catastrophes such as earthquakes or tornadoes, and losses from disposition of investments.

**Changes in Estimates**    In reporting periodic revenues and in attempting to properly match those expenses incurred to generate current-period revenues, accountants must continually make judgments. The numbers reported in the financial statements reflect these judgments and are based on estimates of such factors as the number of years of useful life for depreciable assets, the amount of uncollectible accounts expected, or the amount of warranty liability to be recorded on the books. These and other estimates are made using the best available information at the statement date. However, conditions may subsequently change, and the estimates may need to be revised. Naturally, if either revenue or expense amounts are changed, the income statement is affected. The question is whether the previously reported income measures should be revised or whether the changes should impact only current and future periods.

The Accounting Principles Board stated in Opinion No. 20 that changes in estimates should be reflected in the current period (the period in which the estimate is revised) and in future periods, if any, that are affected. No retroactive adjustments are to be made for a change in estimate.[8] These changes are considered a normal part of the accounting process and not errors made in past periods. For example, Mattel Inc. extended the life of its tools, dies, and molds from two years or less to three years. Extending the life reduced tooling expense by $9 million and increased net income by $8.6 million or $.18 per share in the year of the change.

To illustrate the computations for a change in estimate, assume that Springville Manufacturing Co., Inc., purchased a milling machine at a cost of $100,000. At the time of purchase, it was estimated that the machine would have a useful life of 10 years and no salvage value. Assuming no salvage value and the straight-line method is used, the depreciation expense is $10,000 per year ($100,000 ÷ 10). At the beginning of the fifth year,

[7]*Ibid.*, par. 147.

[8]*Opinions of the Accounting Principles Board No. 20*, "Accounting Changes" (New York: American Institute of Certified Public Accountants, 1971), par. 31.

**Accrual Accounting**

The stock market crash of October 1987 caused many businesses to rethink the manner in which they operate. The crash caused at least one business to consider the way it recognized revenues and expenses. The Boston Company, Inc., a money managing unit of Shearson Lehman Hutton Holdings Inc., reported that pretax profits for the first nine months of 1988 had been overstated by an estimated 40%. Being a subsidiary of another company, Boston does not disclose separate earnings. However, the company admits that 1988 profits were overstated by $44 million.

In danger of not meeting corporate performance goals, top executives at Boston deferred many expenses "beyond accepted accounting norms, and revenue was inappropriately booked far in advance." These practices had the effect of "making the current quarter look more profitable." Boston Co. was hoping that a decline in short-term interest rates would provide additional profits to cover the deceptive accounting practices. (Boston Co. funds its long-term mortgages with short-term deposits in its banking unit, so the firm benefits when short-term rates drop.)

**Questions:**

1. How are expenses deferred and revenues booked (recorded) in advance? What would the journal entries be?
2. Why would top executives encourage these misleading accounting practices?
3. None of the top executives who ordered the misstatements actually made the journal entries. If you were Boston Co.'s accountant, what would you have done?
4. Is Boston's independent auditor responsible for detecting these types of misstatements?

Sources:

George Anders, *The Wall Street Journal*, January 23, 1989.

Christopher J. Chipello & George Anders, *The Wall Street Journal*, January 30, 1989.

however, conditions indicated that the machine would only be used for 3 more years. Depreciation expense in the fifth, sixth, and seventh years should reflect the revised estimate, but depreciation expense recorded in the first four years would not be affected. Since the book value at the end of four years is $60,000 ($100,000 − $40,000 accumulated depreciation), annual depreciation charges for the remaining 3 years of estimated life would be $20,000 ($60,000 ÷ 3). The following schedule summarizes the depreciation charges over the life of the asset:

| Year | Depreciation |
|------|--------------|
| 1 | $ 10,000 |
| 2 | 10,000 |
| 3 | 10,000 |
| 4 | 10,000 |
| 5 | 20,000 |
| 6 | 20,000 |
| 7 | 20,000 |
| | $100,000 |

**Effects of Changing Prices**    The preceding presentation of revenue and expense recognition has not addressed the question of how, if at all, changing prices are to be recognized under the transaction approach. As indicated in Chapter 2, accountants have traditionally ignored this phenomenon, especially when gains would result from recognition. When an economy experiences high rates of inflation, users of financial statements become concerned that the statements do not reflect the impact of these changing prices. When the inflation rates are lower, this user concern decreases. Sears, Roebuck and Co. addresses this concern in its 1988 annual report:

> Reported earnings have been impacted by inflation; however, there is no simple way of separating those effects. Competitive conditions permitting, the company modifies the prices charged for its goods and services in order to recognize cost changes as incurred or as anticipated. By also attempting to control costs and efficiently utilize resources, the company strives to minimize the effects of inflation on its operations.

The Financial Accounting Standards Board in Statement No. 33 required certain large publicly held companies to disclose selected information about price changes on a supplemental basis. The Board did not require this recognition to be reported in the basic financial statements, but in a supplemental note to the financial statements that did not have to be audited. Subsequently, some of the disclosure requirements were eliminated in Statement No. 82, and all price-level disclosures were made voluntary in Statement No. 89.

Generally accepted accounting principles are still based primarily on historical exchange prices, and the transaction approach to income determination recognizes price changes only when losses in value are indicated.

## REPORTING OF INCOME

After recognition and measurement criteria are established, the manner in which income is to be reported (displayed) must be determined. Although GAAP requires disclosure of many specific items of information, there is no standardized form of the income statement or other general-purpose financial statements. The reporting of income thus raises many questions regarding, for example, the format of the income statement, terminology used to describe the items presented, the level of detail in the statement, and income-related disclosures to be presented in notes to the financial statements. In answering these and other questions regarding the reporting of income, the overriding consideration should be the usefulness of the information for decision making.

In the following sections, current practices in reporting income will be examined and illustrated. Subsequently, the implications of the FASB's conceptual framework for future reporting practices will be considered.

### Form of the Income Statement

The income statement traditionally has been prepared in either single-step or multiple-step form. Under the **single-step form,** all revenues and gains that are identified as operating items are placed first on the income statement followed by all expenses and losses that are identified as operating items. The difference between total revenues and total expenses represents income from operations. If there are no nonoperating, irregular, or extraordinary items, this difference is also equal to net income. The income statement for The Procter & Gamble Company, reproduced on page 115, illustrates the single-step form. Note that income taxes are reported separately from other expenses, which is a common variation of the basic single-step form.

Under the **multiple-step form,** the income statement is divided into separate sections (referred to as "intermediate components" in Concepts Statement No. 5), and various subtotals are reported that reflect different levels of profitability. Some of those sections, especially those reported *after* operating income, are specified by FASB pronouncements. Others have become standardized by wide usage. The income statement of The Coca-Cola Company, reproduced on page 116, illustrates one form of a multiple-step income statement. Since the FASB has chosen not to be too specific about display, it is understandable that wide variations of reporting can be found in practice.[9]

### Exhibit 4—1   The Procter & Gamble Company—Single-Step Income Statement

## Consolidated Statement Of Earnings

The Procter & Gamble Company And Subsidiaries

| Years Ended June 30 (Millions of Dollars Except Per Share Amounts) | 1990 | 1989 | 1988 |
|---|---|---|---|
| **Income** | | | |
| Net sales | **$24,081** | $21,398 | $19,336 |
| Interest and other income | **561** | 291 | 155 |
| | **24,642** | 21,689 | 19,491 |
| **Costs and Expenses** | | | |
| Cost of products sold | **14,658** | 13,371 | 11,880 |
| Marketing, administrative, and other expenses | **7,121** | 5,988 | 5,660 |
| Interest expense | **442** | 391 | 321 |
| | **22,221** | 19,750 | 17,861 |
| **Earnings Before Income Taxes** | **2,421** | 1,939 | 1,630 |
| **Income Taxes** | **819** | 733 | 610 |
| **Net Earnings** | **$ 1,602** | $ 1,206 | $ 1,020 |
| **Net Earnings Per Common Share*** | **$4.49** | $3.56 | $2.98 |
| **Net Earnings Per Common Share Assuming Full Dilution*** | **$4.27** | $3.47 | $2.96 |
| **Dividends Per Common Share*** | **$1.75** | $1.50 | $1.38 |
| **Average shares outstanding* (in millions)** | **346.1** | 334.4 | 338.6 |

*Adjusted for two-for-one stock split effective October 20, 1989

A multiple-step income statement for Techtronics Corporation, a hypothetical company, is illustrated on page 118. It will be referred to in discussing the content of a multiple-step income statement. To comply with SEC requirements, income statements are usually presented in comparative form for three years (see Exhibits 4—1 and 4—2). To simplify the illustration, only one year is presented. The illustrated income statement contains more detail than is usually found in actual published financial statements. It has

[9]*Accounting Trends & Techniques* reports that the multiple-step format is becoming increasingly popular. Of the companies surveyed in 1989, 61% used the multiple-step approach compared to 53% in 1985.

become common practice to issue highly condensed statements, with details and supporting schedules provided in notes to the statements. The potential problem with this practice is that the condensed statements may not provide as much predictive and feedback value as statements that provide more detail about the components of income directly on the statement.

### Exhibit 4—2    The Coca-Cola Company—Multiple-Step Income Statement

**Consolidated Statements of Income**
(In thousands except per share data)

THE COCA-COLA COMPANY AND SUBSIDIARIES

| Year Ended December 31, | 1989 | 1988 | 1987 |
|---|---|---|---|
| **Net Operating Revenues** | $8,965,786 | $8,337,831 | $7,658,341 |
| Cost of goods sold | 3,892,069 | 3,701,472 | 3,633,159 |
| **Gross Profit** | 5,073,717 | 4,636,359 | 4,025,182 |
| Selling, administrative and general expenses | 3,347,932 | 3,038,058 | 2,665,022 |
| Provisions for restructured operations | – | – | 36,370 |
| **Operating Income** | 1,725,785 | 1,598,301 | 1,323,790 |
| Interest income | 205,035 | 199,333 | 232,032 |
| Interest expense | 308,034 | 230,513 | 296,772 |
| Equity income | 75,490 | 92,542 | 64,393 |
| Other income (deductions)–net | 4,847 | (33,243) | 531 |
| Gain on sale of Belmont Springs Water Co., Inc. | 61,187 | – | – |
| Gain on sale of stock by T.C.C. Beverages Ltd. | – | – | 39,654 |
| **Income from Continuing Operations Before Income Taxes** | 1,764,310 | 1,626,420 | 1,363,628 |
| Income taxes | 571,471 | 537,434 | 496,348 |
| **Income from Continuing Operations** | 1,192,839 | 1,088,986 | 867,280 |
| Equity income (loss) from discontinued operation | 21,537 | (44,283) | 48,856 |
| Gain on sale of discontinued operation (net of income taxes of $421,021) | 509,449 | – | – |
| **Net Income** | 1,723,825 | 1,044,703 | 916,136 |
| Preferred stock dividends | 21,392 | 6,426 | – |
| **Net Income Available to Common Shareholders** | $1,702,433 | $1,038,277 | $ 916,136 |
| **Income (Loss) Per Common Share** | | | |
| Continuing operations | $    3.39 | $    2.97 | $    2.30 |
| Discontinued operation | 1.53 | (0.12) | 0.13 |
| **Net Income Per Common Share** | $    4.92 | $    2.85 | $    2.43 |
| **Average Common Shares Outstanding** | 345,981 | 364,612 | 377,372 |

See Notes to Consolidated Financial Statements.

## Content of a Multiple-Step Income Statement

The Techtronics Corporation income statement has two major categories of income and nine separate sections as follows:

**I. Income from continuing operations:**
   1. Net sales
   2. Cost of goods sold
   3. Operating expenses
   4. Other revenues and gains
   5. Other expenses and losses
   6. Income taxes on continuing operations
**II. Irregular or extraordinary items:**
   7. Discontinued operations
   8. Extraordinary items
   9. Cumulative effects of changes in accounting principles

There are several important points about this categorization. Only one income tax amount is reported for all items included in the income from continuing operations category; it is presented as the last section in the category. In contrast, each item in the irregular or extraordinary items category is reported net of its income tax effect, referred to as "net of tax." This separation of income tax expense into different sections of the income statement is referred to as "intraperiod income tax allocation."

The various types of gains and losses are not reported entirely in one section of an income statement. Some are reported as part of income from continuing operations, and others are included in irregular or extraordinary items. If a gain or loss is considered part of the ongoing operations of the company, and if its measurement is not too uncertain, it should be included in the continuing operations category. If a gain or loss relates to operations, but is too irregular to classify with the normal recurring items, it is reported separately in the second category. In addition, some gains and losses have been identified by the FASB as not affecting the income statement at all, but are recorded as direct adjustments to owners' equity. In this category are certain foreign currency translation adjustments and market value declines in long-term securities.

Regardless of where gains and losses are reported, they are usually presented as a net figure, i.e., the difference between gross sales price and cost. This differs, of course, from operating revenues and expenses that are usually reported separately at their gross amounts.

Although the FASB has been very specific about how the irregular and extraordinary items should be displayed, the Board has said little about the display of income from operations. The Techtronics Corporation illustration, although more detailed than most published statements, demonstrates the use of operating income categories commonly found in practice. As the concepts in the FASB's conceptual framework are incorporated into the accounting standards, some increased standardization of an operating income format is likely.

A review of the multiple-step income statement discloses several subtotals, especially in the operating category. These subtotals are identified as follows:

1. Gross profit (Net sales − Cost of goods sold)
2. Operating income (#1 − Operating expenses)
3. Income from continuing operations before income taxes (#2 + Other revenues and gains − Other expenses and losses)
4. Income from continuing operations (#3 − income taxes)
5. Net income (#4 + or − irregular and extraordinary items)

Each of the major sections of the income statement and related subtotals will be discussed separately as a way to better understand current practices in reporting income.

**Techtronics Corporation**
**Income Statement**
**For the Year Ended December 31, 1993**

| | | | |
|---|---:|---:|---:|
| Revenue from net sales: | | | |
| Sales | | $800,000 | |
| Less: Sales returns and allowances | $ 12,000 | | |
|     Sales discounts | 8,000 | 20,000 | $780,000 |
| Cost of goods sold: | | | |
| Beginning inventory | | $125,000 | |
| Net purchases | $630,000 | | |
| Freight-in | 32,000 | 662,000 | |
| Cost of goods available for sale | | $787,000 | |
| Less ending inventory | | 296,000 | 491,000 |
| Gross profit on sales | | | $289,000 |
| Operating expenses: | | | |
| Selling expenses: | | | |
| Sales salaries | $ 46,000 | | |
| Advertising expense | 27,000 | | |
| Miscellaneous selling expenses | 12,000 | $ 85,000 | |
| General and administrative expenses: | | | |
| Officers' and office salaries | $ 44,000 | | |
| Taxes and insurance | 26,500 | | |
| Depreciation and amortization expense | 30,000 | | |
| Doubtful accounts expense | 8,600 | | |
| Miscellaneous general expense | 9,200 | 118,300 | 203,300 |
| Operating income | | | $ 85,700 |
| Other revenues and gains: | | | |
| Interest revenue | | $ 12,750 | |
| Gain on sale of investment | | 37,000 | 49,750 |
| Other expenses and losses: | | | |
| Interest expense | | $ (18,250) | |
| Loss on sale of equipment | | (5,250) | (23,500) |
| Income from continuing operations | | | |
| before income taxes | | | $111,950 |
| Income taxes | | | 44,780 |
| Income from continuing operations | | | $ 67,170 |
| Discontinued operations: | | | |
| Loss from operations of discontinued business segment (net of income tax savings of $14,000) | | $ (21,000) | |
| Loss on disposal of business segment (net of income tax savings of $6,400) | | (9,600) | (30,600) |
| Extraordinary gain from early debt extinguishment (net of income taxes of $10,160) | | | 15,240 |
| Cumulative effect of changing inventory method (net of income tax savings of $3,000) | | | (4,500) |
| Net income | | | $ 47,310 |
| Earnings per common share: | | | |
| Income from continuing operations | | | $     1.34 |
| Discontinued operations | | | (0.61) |
| Extraordinary gain | | | 0.31 |
| Cumulative effect of accounting change | | | (0.09) |
| Net income | | | $     0.95 |

**Net Sales**     Revenue from net sales reports the total sales to customers for the period less any sales discounts or returns and allowances. This total should not include additions to billings for sales and excise taxes that the business is required to collect on behalf of the government. These billing increases are properly recognized as current liabilities. Sales returns and allowances and sales discounts should be subtracted from gross sales in arriving at net sales revenue. When the sales price is increased to cover the cost of freight to the customer and the customer is billed accordingly, freight charges paid by the company should also be subtracted from sales in arriving at net sales. Freight charges not passed to the buyer are recognized as selling expenses.

**Cost of Goods Sold**    In any merchandising or manufacturing enterprise, the cost of goods relating to sales of the period must be determined. As illustrated in the Techtronics Corporation income statement, **cost of goods available for sale** is first determined. This is the sum of the beginning inventory, net purchases, and all other buying, freight, and storage costs relating to the acquisition of goods. The net purchases balance is developed by subtracting purchase returns and allowances and purchase discounts from gross purchases. Cost of goods sold is then calculated by subtracting the ending inventory from the cost of goods available for sale.

When the goods are manufactured by the seller, additional elements enter into the cost of goods sold. Besides material costs, a company incurs labor and overhead costs to convert the material from its raw material state to a finished good. A manufacturing company has three inventories rather than one: raw materials, goods in process, and finished goods. The Techtronics Corporation is a merchandising company. The cost of goods sold for a manufacturing company is illustrated in Chapter 10.

**Operating Expenses**    Operating expenses may be reported in two parts: (1) selling expenses and (2) general and administrative expenses. **Selling expenses** include such items as sales salaries and commissions and related payroll taxes, advertising and store displays, store supplies used, depreciation of store furniture and equipment, and delivery expenses. **General and administrative expenses** include officers' and office salaries and related payroll taxes, office supplies used, depreciation of office furniture and fixtures, telephone, postage, business licenses and fees, legal and accounting services, contributions, and similar items. For manufacturing companies, charges related jointly to both production and administrative functions should be allocated in some equitable manner between manufacturing overhead and operating expenses.

**Other Revenues and Gains**    This section usually includes items identified with the peripheral activities of the company. Examples include revenue from financial activities, such as rents, interest, and dividends, and gains from the sale of assets such as equipment or investments.

**Other Expenses and Losses**    This section is parallel to the previous one, but results in deductions from, rather than increases to, operating income. Examples include interest expense and losses from the sale of assets.

**Income Tax on Continuing Operations**    As explained earlier in this chapter, total income tax expense for a period is allocated to various components of income. One amount is computed for income from continuing operations, and separate computations are made for any irregular or extraordinary items. In the Techtronics illustration, an income tax rate of 40% was assumed. Thus, the amount of income tax related to continuing operations is $44,780 ($111,950 × .40).

The same tax rate is applied to all income components in the Techtronics illustration. In practice, however, intraperiod income tax allocation may involve different rates for different components of income. This results from graduated tax rates and special or alternative rates for certain types of gains and losses.

**Discontinued Operations**   An increasingly common irregular item involves the disposition of a major segment of a business either through sale or abandonment. In 1989, 81 of the 600 surveyed companies in *Accounting Trends & Techniques* reported discontinued operations in their statements. The segment of the company disposed of may be a major line of business, a major class of customer, or a subsidiary company. To qualify as discontinued operations for reporting purposes, the assets and related activities of the segment must be clearly distinguishable from other assets, operating results, and general activities of the company, both physically and operationally, as well as for financial reporting purposes. For example, closing down one of three plants making the same product, eliminating *part* of a line of business, or shifting the production or marketing functions from one location to another would not be classified as discontinued operations.

There are many reasons why management may decide to dispose of a segment. For example:

1. The segment may be unprofitable.
2. The segment may be too isolated geographically.
3. The segment may not fit into the long-range plans for the company.
4. Management may need funds to reduce long-term debt or to expand into other areas.
5. Management may be fearful of a corporate take-over by new investors desiring to gain control of the company.

In the 1980s, management of many companies adopted anti-takeover strategies to try to protect their companies. One of the more popular techniques was to sell peripheral operational segments, especially unprofitable ones, that had been acquired during earlier conglomerate years, and to consolidate the company around its principal business operations. As mentioned in the introduction of this chapter, one company that decided to divest itself of some peripheral activities was Sears, Roebuck and Co. During the fourth quarter of 1988, the company adopted plans to divest itself of the group life-health business of the Allstate Insurance Group and the commercial division of the Coldwell Banker Real Estate Group, Inc. Sears' 1988 income statement is reproduced in Exhibit 4—3 on page 121, and the note explaining the divestiture is reproduced in Exhibit 4—4, page 123.

Many successful takeovers are financed by financial institutions willing to lend billions of dollars to support the buyout of current stockholders. After the new management assumes control of the company, a common strategy is to sell parts of the company to reduce the debt incurred in the takeover. For example, Allied Corporation purchased Bendix Corporation, a $4.1 billion (revenues) automotive parts, aerospace, and machine tool conglomerate. Within two years, Allied liquidated a machine tool company, an earthmoving machine business, and a large pipe-bending business. Similarly, in 1985 W. R. Grace & Co. purchased a 26% interest in a West German group and then made plans to sell over $1 billion of assets, including its retail operations that included sporting goods, home centers, and western wear.[10]

Regardless of the reason, the discontinuance of a substantial portion of company operations is a significant event. Therefore, information about discontinued operations should be presented explicitly to readers of financial statements.

---

[10]"W. R. Grace Plans Asset Sales in 1986 Totaling $1 Billion," *The Wall Street Journal*, February 12, 1986, p. 33.

**Exhibit 4—3    Sears, Roebuck and Co.—Income Statement**

## SEARS, ROEBUCK AND CO.
## CONSOLIDATED STATEMENTS OF INCOME

| millions, except per common share data | 1988 | 1987 | 1986 |
|---|---|---|---|
| **Revenues** | $50,251.0 | $45,904.1 | $42,302.8 |
| **Expenses** | | | |
| Costs and expenses | 45,616.5 | 41,222.5 | 38,138.8 |
| Nonrecurring expenses (note 3) | 751.1 | 105.2 | — |
| Interest | 2,937.4 | 2,720.6 | 2,653.3 |
| Total expenses | 49,305.0 | 44,048.3 | 40,792.1 |
| Operating income | 946.0 | 1,855.8 | 1,510.7 |
| Other income | 156.8 | 239.4 | 282.2 |
| Income from continuing operations before income taxes, minority interest and equity in net income of unconsolidated companies | 1,102.8 | 2,095.2 | 1,792.9 |
| Income taxes (notes 1, 7) | | | |
| Current operations | 53.5 | 520.5 | 443.8 |
| Fresh start and deferred tax benefits | — | (172.4) | — |
| Minority interest and equity in net income of unconsolidated companies | (17.0) | (20.9) | (13.5) |
| **Income from continuing operations** (note 1) | 1,032.3 | 1,726.2 | 1,335.6 |
| Discontinued operations (note 2): | | | |
| Operating income (loss), less income tax benefit (expense) of $34.7, $97.0 and $(8.6) | (64.2) | (93.4) | 3.0 |
| Loss on disposal, less income tax benefit of $30.2 | (58.6) | — | — |
| Income before cumulative effect of accounting change | 909.5 | 1,632.8 | 1,338.6 |
| Cumulative effect of change in accounting for income taxes (note 1) | 544.2 | — | — |
| **Net income** | $1,453.7 | $1,632.8 | $1,338.6 |
| **Net income per common share:** | | | |
| Income from continuing operations | $2.72 | $4.55 | $3.57 |
| Discontinued operations | (.32) | (.25) | .01 |
| Income before cumulative effect of accounting change | 2.40 | 4.30 | 3.58 |
| Cumulative effect of change in accounting for income taxes | 1.44 | — | — |
| Net income | $3.84 | $4.30 | $3.58 |
| Average common shares outstanding | 378.8 | 377.9 | 368.8 |

See accompanying notes and the summarized Group financial statements.

**Reporting Requirements for Discontinued Operations**    When a company discontinues operating a segment of its business, future comparability requires that all elements that relate to the discontinued operation be identified and separated from continuing operations. Thus, in the Techtronics Corporation income statement illustrated on page 118, the first category after Income From Continuing Operations is Discontinued Operations. The category is further separated into two subdivisions: (1) the current-year income or loss from operating the discontinued segment, or a $21,000 loss, and (2) disclosure of the gain or loss on the actual disposal of the business segment, or a further $9,600 loss.

As previously indicated, the irregular items are all reported net of their respective tax effects. If the item is a gain, it is reduced by the tax on the gain. If the item is a loss, it is deductible against other income and thus its existence *saves* income taxes. The overall company loss can thus be reduced by the tax savings arising from being able to deduct the loss from otherwise taxable income.

The income statement for Techtronics Corporation on page 118 discloses both of these subdivisions. The income tax rate is 40% on all items. Analysis of the income statement shows that Techtronics had an operating loss for the current year of $35,000, but that after a tax savings of $14,000 was deducted, only $21,000 is reported as a loss. The second item discloses that the segment was sold and a loss of $16,000 was experienced on the sale. Application of the income tax rate of 40% reduces this loss to $9,600. If comparative statements are prepared, the same separation between continued and discontinued operations for prior years should be made.

Often a company will decide on a particular date (the **measurement date**) to dispose of a business segment, but will have a phase-out period between that date and the date the segment is actually sold (**disposal date**). The gain or loss on disposal will include any income or loss from operating the segment during the phase-out period. To illustrate using the income statement on page 118, assume Techtronics Corporation decided on July 1, 1993, to phase out a segment of its operation. This date is the measurement date and marks the beginning of the phase-out period. Assume also that the segment was disposed of on November 17, 1993.

The $9,600 loss on disposal reflects both the operating results during phase-out and the gain or loss on final disposal, net of income taxes. The $21,000 loss represents the operating loss (net of income tax savings of $14,000) for the period January 1, 1993, to July 1, 1993. If the accounting year ends before the disposal is completed, estimates must be made of the expected gain or loss from final disposal. If the computation indicates an expected loss on disposal, the accounting constraint of conservatism dictates that the loss should be recognized in the current period, not in the later period when the loss actually occurs. If the computation indicates an expected gain on disposal, the gain will not be recognized until it is actually realized in the subsequent period. The time line presented below uses the Techtronics example to illustrate the relevant time periods to be considered when accounting for discontinued operations.

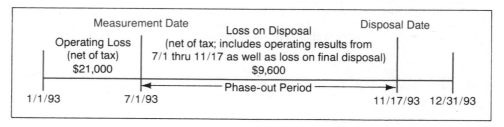

The Sears, Roebuck and Co. income statement in Exhibit 4—3 illustrates how the two components of discontinued operations (income or loss from operating the segment and gain or loss on disposal) are reported. The first line in the discontinued operations section reports the operating income or loss, net of income taxes, for the discontinued operations for all 3 years. The second line indicates the loss on disposal in 1988. The separation of income from discontinued operations from regular income enhances the comparability of this year's results with those of prior years. It also enables financial statement users to assess future cash flows with more authority.

Further disclosure of discontinued operations can be made in notes to the financial statements. For example, the Sears note reproduced in Exhibit 4—4 explains that the loss on disposal includes "future operating losses" of the disposed business during the phase-out period. Sears also provides additional disclosure relating to the assets and liabilities that will be sold.

The reporting requirements for discontinued operations are contained in APB Opinion No. 30, "Reporting the Results of Operations."[11] The reporting of discontinued operations can become complex, and only a summary of the guidelines provided by APB Opinion No. 30 is covered here. Application of the guidelines requires judgment. The goal should be to report information that will assist external users in assessing future cash flows by clearly distinguishing normal, recurring earnings patterns from those activities that are irregular, yet significant in assessing the total company results of operations.

**Exhibit 4—4    Sears, Roebuck and Co.—Note Disclosure for Discontinued Operations**

### 2. Discontinued operations

During the fourth quarter of 1988, the company adopted plans to divest the group life-health business of Allstate Insurance Group and the commercial division of Coldwell Banker Real Estate Group. Certain portions of the group life-health operation have been terminated and other portions were sold effective January 1, 1989. Under the sales contract, the company remains responsible for the run-off of certain group medical contracts through approximately January, 1990. A $58.6 million after tax loss was recorded in 1988 for disposal costs and future operating losses of the group life-health business. The commercial division of Coldwell Banker will be sold during 1989.

Prior year Statements of Income and related footnotes have been restated for the results of the discontinued operations. Revenues of the discontinued businesses, net of intercompany amounts, were $1.2, $1.3 and $1.1 billion in 1988, 1987 and 1986, respectively. The Statements of Financial Position include the following assets and liabilities of the discontinued operations which will be sold:

| | December 31 | |
| --- | --- | --- |
| millions | 1988 | 1987 |
| Investments | $345.1 | $275.1 |
| Property and equipment, net | 52.0 | 50.5 |
| Other assets | 130.8 | 154.4 |
| Total assets | 527.9 | 480.0 |
| Insurance reserves | 306.1 | 264.4 |
| Other liabilities | 74.1 | 65.4 |
| Total liabilities | $380.2 | $329.8 |

**Extraordinary Items**    According to APB Opinion No. 30, extraordinary items are events and transactions that are both **unusual in nature and infrequent in occurrence**. Thus, to qualify as extraordinary, an item must "possess a high degree of abnormality and

[11]*Opinions of the Accounting Principles Board No. 30*, "Reporting the Results of Operations" (New York: American Institute of Certified Public Accountants, 1973), par. 20.

be of a type clearly unrelated to, or only incidentally related to, the ordinary and typical activities of the entity . . . [and] be of a type that would not reasonably be expected to recur in the foreseeable future. . . .[12]

The intent of the Accounting Principles Board was to restrict the items that could be classified as extraordinary. The presumption of the Board was that an item should be considered ordinary and part of the company's usual activity unless evidence clearly supported its classification as an extraordinary item. The Board offered certain examples of gains and losses that should *not* be reported as extraordinary items. These include:

1. The write-down or write-off of receivables, inventories, equipment leased to others, or intangible assets.
2. The gains or losses from exchanges or translation of foreign currencies, including those relating to major devaluations and revaluations.
3. The gains or losses on disposal of a segment of a business.
4. Other gains or losses from sale or abandonment of property, plant, or equipment used in the business.
5. The effects of a strike.
6. The adjustment of accruals on long-term contracts.

The standard-setting bodies have identified only one major item as extraordinary regardless of whether it meets the dual criteria: a gain or loss from early extinguishment of debt.[13] An example would be a gain or loss on the retirement of bonds before their maturity date. Besides early extinguishment of debt, companies have reported as extraordinary items litigation settlements, write-offs of assets in foreign countries where expropriation risks were high, and pension plan terminations.

Some items may not meet both criteria for extraordinary items, but may meet one of them. Although these items do not qualify as extraordinary, they should be disclosed separately as part of income from continuing operations, either before or after operating income. Examples of these items include strike-related costs, obsolete inventory write-downs, and gains and losses from liquidation of investments. Another example is included in Sears' income statement on page 121. Sears reported its restructuring charges in 1987 and 1988 as "nonrecurring expenses" in its 1988 income statement. Because these charges were included as part of operating income, they were reported before income taxes.

**Cumulative Effects of Changes in Accounting Principles**     The last item included in the irregular category of the income statement is the effect of changing accounting principles. Although the profession has recognized the desirability of consistency in application of accounting principles, there are occasions where conditions justify a change from one principle to another. Sometimes this condition arises because the standard-setting body issues a new pronouncement requiring a change in principle. If GAAP is to be followed, the company has no choice but to change to conform with the new standard. Both IBM (Appendix A) and Sears (page 121) reported such a change when they adopted the new FASB standard for deferred income taxes. Sometimes economic conditions change, and a company changes accounting principles so that reporting can be more representative of the actual conditions. For example, when there was double-digit inflation during the late 1970s, many companies changed their inventory methods to LIFO to reduce their income and thus reduce the actual cash payments for income taxes.

[12]*Ibid.*, par. 20.

[13]*Statement of Financial Accounting Standards No. 4,* "Reporting Gains and Losses From Extinguishment of Debt" (Stamford: Financial Accounting Standards Board, 1975).

When a change in accounting principle occurs, management may have the option of deciding to reflect the new principle retroactively or only in the current and future periods. If the change arises because of a new FASB standard, the Board designates how the change must be implemented. If the change is made at management's discretion, however, the implementation decision is made by management. For example, a company may decide to change its depreciation method from straight-line to declining balance for only new acquisitions. Under this condition, no special accounting entries are required in the period of the accounting change. If, however, the company decides to apply the new depreciation method to all existing assets, an entry is needed in the current year to adjust the statements for the cumulative effect of the change. The Board has recognized two different ways to adjust current statements to reflect the cumulative effect of a change in accounting principle. (1) Generally, income statements should report the cumulative effect of the change in the current year with no restatement of prior years' figures. (2) Special cases require the restatement of financial statements for all prior years. In these special cases, the beginning balance of retained earnings for the current year reflects the cumulative effect of the prior years' changes. As with discontinued operations and extraordinary items, the adjustment in either case should be net of income taxes.

In the income statement on page 118, the Techtronics Corporation recorded a $4,500 cumulative loss due to changing inventory principles as the last of the irregular or extraordinary items. The pretax loss to Techtronics was $7,500, but income tax savings reduced the reported loss by $3,000.

If Techtronics Corporation had followed the other method of reporting the cumulative effects of the change in accounting principles, there would have been no adjustment to income; instead, the loss would have been recorded as a charge directly to Retained Earnings. The Accounting Principles Board specified different criteria to help accountants determine which approach should be applied under what circumstances. Further discussion of these criteria is included in a later chapter.

**Earnings Per Share**    In 1969, the Accounting Principles Board issued Opinion No. 15 that required all companies to include a section in the income statement converting certain income components to earnings per share. Separate earnings-per-share amounts are computed by dividing income from continuing operations and each irregular or extraordinary item by the weighted average number of shares of common stock outstanding for the reporting period.[14]

For example, the Techtronics Corporation income statement illustrated on page 118 shows earnings per share of $1.34 for income from continuing operations, $.61 for loss from discontinued operations, $.31 for extraordinary gain, and a loss of $.09 for the cumulative effect of a change in accounting principle, for a total of $.95 for net income. These figures were derived by dividing each identified component of net income by 50,000 shares of common stock outstanding during the period.

## REPORTING CHANGES IN RETAINED EARNINGS

Many corporations include a statement identifying the changes in retained earnings as one of their financial statements. This statement generally begins with the opening balance in the retained earnings account and then shows the additions and deductions to arrive at the ending balance. In many cases, this statement is very simple. Net income is

---

[14]*Opinions of the Accounting Principles Board No. 15,* "Earnings Per Share" (New York: American Institute of Certified Public Accountants, 1969), par. 47.

included as an addition, dividend distributions as a deduction, and any special credits or charges are added or subtracted as appropriate. There are two general types of retained earnings adjustments: (1) **prior-period adjustments**, and (2) as indicated earlier, adjustments arising from some changes in accounting principles. Prior-period adjustments arise primarily when an error occurs in one period and is not discovered until a subsequent period.

The retained earnings statement for Techtronics Corporation is illustrated below.

**Techtronics Corporation**
**Retained Earnings Statement**
**For the Year Ended December 31, 1993**

| | |
|---|---:|
| Retained Earnings, January 1, 1993 | $286,590 |
| Add prior-period adjustment—correction of inventory understatement (net of income taxes of $10,000) | 15,000 |
| Adjusted retained earnings, January 1, 1993 | $301,590 |
| Add net income from income statement | 47,310 |
| | $348,900 |
| Deduct dividends declared | 40,000 |
| Retained earnings, December 31, 1993 | $308,900 |

Prior-period adjustments for errors are not reported often, because most errors are discovered and corrected in the year they occur. In some cases, however, a considerable amount of time may elapse before an error is discovered. As an example, in 1987 Matrix Science Corp. discovered revenue recognition errors arising from fraudulent actions by its former management. As a result, the following adjustment was made to restate retained earnings as of June 30, 1984:

| | |
|---|---:|
| Retained earnings, June 30, 1984 | $28,534,300 |
| Less prior-period adjustment (see accompanying note) | 1,207,500 |
| Adjusted retained earnings, June 30, 1984 | $27,326,800 |

The accompanying note presented in the 1987 annual report, and reproduced in Exhibit 4—5, is revealing in its specificity as to the cause of the prior-period errors.

## REPORTING IMPLICATIONS OF THE CONCEPTUAL FRAMEWORK

The Financial Accounting Standards Board recommended new terminology to report the changes in owners' equity. One of the ten elements defined in Concepts Statement No. 6 and presented in Chapter 2 was "Comprehensive income." The Board defined this term as follows:

> Comprehensive income is the change in equity of a business enterprise during a period from transactions and other events and circumstances from nonowner sources. It includes all changes in equity during a period except those resulting from investments by owners and distributions to owners.[15]

The Board also defined a new term for the bottom line of an income statement. As discussed in the chapter, the last figure on an income statement is usually labeled "Net income." The Board did not define net income; however, they did recommend adoption

[15]*Statement of Financial Accounting Concepts No. 6*, par. 70.

**Exhibit 4—5    Matrix Science Corp.—Disclosure of Prior-Period Adjustment**

## NOTES TO CONSOLIDATED FINANCIAL STATEMENTS

*2. Special Investigation and Accounting Practices*

In August 1987, it became known that the Company had followed a practice of recording sales prior to the shipment of goods. In connection therewith, the Board of Directors engaged special legal counsel and the Company's auditors to conduct an investigation of the Company's accounting practices. Additionally, in September 1987, it was determined that substantial amounts of credit memorandums, primarily for customer returns, had not been processed in a timely manner.

The above practices involved certain senior officers and other employees of the Company. In October 1987, the former president, executive vice president, and chief financial officer resigned their positions and entered into consulting agreements as of the date of their resignations with the Company. The consulting agreement with the former president ended on January 8, 1988, and the other two agreements are on a month-to-month basis.

The results of the investigation concluded that the sales recording and credit memo practices discussed above resulted in the incorrect recording of sales. While the Company does not believe the resulting adjustments were material to its financial statements, when taken as a whole in any prior year, the Company has determined that a restatement of prior years' financial statements is appropriate. . . .

At June 30, 1984, retained earnings as previously reported, was $28,534,300. Retained earnings, as restated, was $27,326,800.

---

of the term "earnings." As defined in the Statement, **earnings** is identical with net income as that term is used in practice except that the last irregular item discussed, "Cumulative Effects of Changes in Accounting Principles," is not included in earnings. Thus, the earnings amount for the Techtronics Corporation would be $51,810 ($47,310 + $4,500). In addition to an earnings statement, the Board suggested that a new comprehensive income statement should be prepared. This statement would start with the earnings amount and include all other nonowner changes to owners' equity. This statement would include the cumulative effects of changes in accounting principles. Also included would be any recognized changes in values, such as write-downs of long-term equity investments and foreign currency translation adjustments.

The Board did not include a display of a suggested statement of comprehensive income in Concepts Statement No. 5, but stated: "This Statement does not consider details of displaying those different kinds of information and does not preclude the possibility that some entities might choose to combine some of that information in a single statement."[16] An example of how a statement of comprehensive income might appear for Techtronics Corporation is included on the next page.

It is important to recognize that the terms "earnings" and "comprehensive income" recommended in the concepts statements are not presently part of GAAP. Not until they are incorporated into a statement of standards will they be required of business management and auditors.

A review of the 1990 edition of *Accounting Trends & Techniques* indicates very little change in terminology has occurred as a result of Concepts Statement No. 5. "Income" is

---

[16]*Statement of Financial Accounting Concepts No. 5*, par. 14.

still the most widely used, with "earnings" being only half as popular. None of the 600 reporting companies surveyed by *Accounting Trends & Techniques* in 1989 adopted the comprehensive income concept.

**Techtronics Corporation**
**Statement of Comprehensive Income**
**For the Year Ended December 31, 1993**

| | |
|---|---|
| Earnings per earnings statement.................................... | $51,810 |
| Cumulative effect of changing inventory method (net of income tax savings of $3,000) ............................................. | (4,500) |
| Prior-period adjustment—correction of inventory understatement (net of income taxes of $10,000) ......................................... | 15,000 |
| Foreign currency translation adjustment............................. | 30,000 |
| Comprehensive income ............................................ | $92,310 |

## SUMMARY

As indicated in the short case situation that began this chapter, one "bottom line" figure for income can often be misleading and result in an inefficient allocation of resources. Standard-setting bodies have been concerned with the ingredients that enter an income measurement. The FASB has tried to address the related problems of income recognition, measurement, and reporting in their concepts statements. Decision usefulness will be improved if some of these recommendations are incorporated into practice. However, change is always slow, especially when the changes involve entrenched terminology and formats. Many of the income components introduced in this chapter will be explored in greater depth in later chapters of the text. A summary of the treatment of the special items discussed in this chapter is included on page 129.

## KEY TERMS

Comprehensive income 126
Cumulative effect of a change in accounting principle 125
Discontinued operations 120
Earnings 127
Expense recognition 111

Expenses 108
Extraordinary items 123
Financial capital maintenance 107
Gains 108
Losses 109

Physical capital maintenance 107
Prior-period adjustments 126
Revenue recognition 109
Revenues 108
Transaction approach 108

**Exhibit 4—6    Summary of Procedures for Reporting Irregular, Nonrecurring, or Unusual Items***

| Where Reported | Category | Description | Examples |
|---|---|---|---|
| Part of income from continuing operations | Changes in estimates | Normal recurring changes in estimating future amounts. Included in normal accounts. | Changes in building and equipment lives, changes in estimated loss from uncollectible accounts receivable, changes in estimate of warranty liability. |
| | Unusual gains and losses, not considered extraordinary | Unusual or infrequent, but not both. Related to normal business operations. Material in amount. Shown in other revenues and gains or other expenses and losses. | Gains or losses from sale of assets, investments, or other operating assets. Write-off of receivables as uncollectible, inventories as obsolete. |
| On income statement, but after income from continuing operations | Discontinued operations | Disposal of completely separate line of business. Include gain or loss from operating segment, and gain or loss from sale or abandonment. | Sale by conglomerate company of separate line of business, such as milling company selling restaurant segment. |
| | Extraordinary items | Both unusual and nonrecurring. Not related to normal business operations. Material in amount. | Material gains and losses from early extinguishment of debt, from some casualties or legal claims if meet criteria. |
| | Changes in accounting principles— general case | Change from one accepted principle to another. | Change from one method of inventory pricing to another, change in depreciation method. |
| As adjustment to retained earnings on the balance sheet | Prior-period adjustments and special case changes in accounting principles | Material correction of errors, changes in accounting principles that require retroactive adjustment. | Failure to depreciate fixed assets, mathematical error in computing inventory balance, retroactive adjustment for new FASB standard. |

*This chart describes the usual case. Exceptions to the descriptions occasionally do occur.

# QUESTIONS

1. FASB Concepts Statement No. 1 states, "The primary focus of financial reporting is information about an enterprise's performance provided by measures of earnings and its components." Why is it unwise for users of financial statements to focus too much attention on the income statement?

2. Income as determined by income tax regulations is not necessarily the same as income reported to external users. Why might there be differences?

3. After the necessary definitions and assumptions have been made that support the determination of income, what are the two methods of income measurement that may be used to determine income? How do they differ?

4. What different measurement methods may be applied to net assets in arriving at income under the capital maintenance approach?

5. How are revenues and expenses different from gains and losses?

6. What two factors must be considered in deciding the point at which revenues and gains should be recognized? At what point in the revenue cycle are these conditions usually met?

7. Name three exceptions to the general rule that assumes revenue is recognized at the point of sale. What is the justification for these exceptions?

8. What guidelines are used to match costs with revenues in determining income?

9. What are some possible disadvantages of a multiple-step income statement and of a single-step statement?

10. Identify the major sections (components of income) that are included in a multiple-step income statement.

11. What is the meaning of "intraperiod" income tax allocation?

12. The Pop-Up Company has decided to sell its lid manufacturing division even though the division is expected to show a small profit this year. The division's assets will be sold at a loss of $10,000 to another company. What information (if any) should Pop-Up disclose in its financial reports with respect to this division?

13. Which of the following would *not* normally qualify as an extraordinary item?
   (a) The write-down or write-off of receivables.
   (b) Major devaluation of foreign currency.
   (c) Loss on sale of plant and equipment.
   (d) Gain from early extinguishment of debt.
   (e) Loss due to extensive flood damage to an asphalt company in Las Vegas, Nevada.
   (f) Loss due to extensive earthquake damage to a furniture company in Los Angeles, California.
   (g) Farming loss due to heavy spring rains in the Northwest.

14. Explain briefly the difference in accounting treatment of (a) a change in accounting principle, and (b) a change in accounting estimate.

15. What is the general practice in reporting earnings per share?

16. Define comprehensive income. How does it differ from net income?

---

## DISCUSSION CASES

### Case 4—1   (Are we really better off?)

The Plath Company Board of Directors finally receives the income statement for the past year from management. Board members are initially pleased to see that after three loss years, the company will be reporting a profit for the current year. Further investigation reveals that depreciation expense is significantly lower than it was last year. Company management, concerned by the losses, decided to change its method of reporting depreciation from an accelerated method to straight-line. If the depreciation method had not been changed, a loss would have resulted for the fourth consecutive year. When questioned by the Board about the accounting change, management replied that the majority of companies in the industry use the straight-line depreciation method, and thus the change makes Plath's income statement more comparable to the other companies.

Since comparability is an important qualitative characteristic of accounting information, should the Board accept the explanation of management? How should the information about the change in the depreciation method be displayed in the financial statements?

### Case 4—2   (How can my company have income but no cash?)

Max Stevenson owns a local drug store. During the past few years the economy has experienced a period of high inflation. Stevenson has had the policy of withdrawing cash from his business equal to 80% of the company's reported net income. As the business has grown, he has had a CPA prepare the company's financial statements and tax returns. The following is a summary of the company's income statement for the current year:

| | |
|---|---:|
| Revenue | $565,000 |
| Cost of goods sold (drugs, etc.) | 395,000 |
| Gross profit on items sold | $170,000 |
| Operating expenses (including taxes) | 110,000 |
| Net income | $ 60,000 |

Even though the business has reported net income each year, it has experienced severe cash flow shortages. The company has had to pay higher prices for its inventory as the company has tried to maintain the same quantity and quality of its goods. For example, last year's cost of goods sold had a historical cost of $250,000 and a replacement cost of $295,000. The current year's cost of goods sold has a replacement cost of $440,000. Stevenson's personal cash outflows have also grown faster than his withdrawals from the company due to increasing personal demands.

Stevenson asks you as a financial advisor how the company can have income of $60,000, but how he and the company can still have a shortage of cash.

### Case 4—3  (When should revenue be recognized?)

Stan Crowfoot is a renowned sculptor who specializes in American Indian sculptures. Typically, a cast is prepared for each work to permit the multiple reproduction of the pieces. A limited number of copies are made for each sculpture, and the mold is destroyed after the number is reached. Limiting the number of pieces enhances the price, and most of the pieces have initially sold for $2,000 to $4,000. To encourage sales, Stan has a liberal return policy that permits customers to return any unwanted piece for a period of up to one year from the date of sale and receive a full refund.

Do you think Stan should recognize revenue: (1) when the piece is produced and cast in bronze, (2) when the goods are delivered to the customer, or (3) when the period of return has passed? Justify your answer in terms of the conceptual framework.

### Case 4—4  (When should revenue be recognized?)

You are engaged as a consultant to Skyways Unlimited, a manufacturer of satellite dishes for television reception. Skyways sells its dishes to dealers who in turn sell them to customers. As an inducement to carry sufficient inventory, the dealers are not required to pay for the dishes until they have been sold. There is no formal provision for return of the dishes by the dealers; however, Skyways has requested returns when a dealer's sales activity is considered to be too low. Overall, returns have amounted to less than 10% of the dishes sent to dealers. No interest is charged to the dealers on their balances unless they do not remit promptly upon the sale to a customer.

At what point would you recommend that Skyways recognize the revenue from the sale of dishes to the dealers?

### Case 4—5  (We just changed our minds.)

Management for Marlowe Manufacturing Company decided in 1993 to discontinue one of its unsuccessful product lines. The line was not large enough for it to meet the definition of a business segment. The planned discontinuance involved obsolete inventory, assembly lines, and packaging and advertising supplies. It was estimated that a loss of $250,000 would result from the decision, and this estimate was recorded as a loss in the 1993 income statement. In 1994, new management was appointed and it was decided that maybe the unsuccessful product line could be turned around with a more aggressive marketing policy. The change was made, and indeed the product began to make money. The new management wants to reverse the adjustment made the previous year and remove the liability for the estimated loss.

How should the 1993 estimated loss be reported in the 1993 income statement? How should the 1994 reversal of the 1993 action be reported in the 1994 financial statements?

### Case 4—6  (The sure-fire computer software)

The Flexisoft Company has had excellent success in developing business software for microcomputers. Management has followed the accounting practice of deferring the development costs for the software until sufficient sales have developed to cover the software cost. Because of past successes, management feels it is improper to charge software costs directly to expense as current GAAP requires.

What are the pros and cons of deferring or expensing immediately these developmental costs?

### Case 4—7  (Deferred initial operating losses)

Small loan companies often experience losses in the operation of newly opened branch loan offices. Such results usually can be anticipated by management prior to making a decision on expansion. It has been recommended by some accountants that the operating losses of newly opened branches should be reported as deferred charges during the first twelve months of operation or until the first profitable month occurs. Such deferred charges would then be amortized over a five-year period.

Would you support this recommendation? Justify your answer.

### Case 4—8  (What was last year's income?)

The Walesco Corporation has decided to discontinue an entire segment of its business effective November 1, 1993. It hopes to sell the assets involved and convert the physical plant to other uses within the manufacturing division. The CPA auditing the books indicates that GAAP requires separate identification of the revenues and expenses related to the segment to be sold and their removal from the continuing revenue and expense amounts. The controller objects to this change. "We have already distributed widely last year's numbers. If we change them now, one year later, confidence in our financial statements will be greatly eroded."

What are the pros and cons of identifying separately the costs related to the discontinued segment?

### Case 4—9  (Analysis of Financial Statements—IBM Corporation)

Refer to the financial statements of IBM Corporation in Appendix A in answering the following questions:

1. Of IBM's four divisions—Sales, Support Services, Software, and Rentals and Financing—which had the highest gross profit in 1990? Which had the highest gross profit percentage, i.e., gross profit divided by revenues? Which division was the most profitable?
2. IBM's operating income declined from $8.746 million in 1988 to $6.893 million in 1989. Identify the major reason for the decline. (Search the notes to the financial statements for additional information.)
3. Does IBM generate most of its revenue within the United States or outside the United States? What is the trend for IBM regarding international sales?
4. How does IBM recognize revenue: Upon completion of goods? Upon shipment of goods? Over time?
5. Does IBM expense its software costs using direct matching, systematic and rational allocation, or immediate recognition?
6. How does IBM expense depreciation, goodwill, and selling expenses?
7. In 1988, IBM disclosed a cumulative effect from the change in accounting for income tax. Where is additional information regarding that change disclosed?

---

## EXERCISES

### Exercise 4—1  (Calculation of net income)

Changes in the balance sheet account balances for the Smite Sales Co. during 1993 are shown below. Dividends declared during 1993 were $40,000. Calculate the net income for the year assuming there were no transactions, other than the dividends, affecting retained earnings.

|  | Increase (Decrease) |
|---|---|
| Cash ......................................................... | $  95,500 |
| Accounts Receivable ....................................... | 92,000 |
| Inventory ................................................... | (30,000) |

|  | Increase (Decrease) |
|---|---|
| Buildings and Equipment (net) | $190,000 |
| Patents | (5,000) |
| Accounts Payable | (75,000) |
| Bonds Payable | 150,000 |
| Capital Stock | 100,000 |
| Additional Paid-In Capital | 50,000 |

## Exercise 4—2  (Revenue recognition)

For each of the following transactions, events, or circumstances, indicate whether the recognition criteria for revenues and gains are met and provide support for your answer.

(a) An order of $25,000 for merchandise is received from a customer.
(b) The value of timberlands increases by $40,000 for the year due to normal growth.
(c) Accounting services are rendered to a client on account.
(d) A 1985 investment was made in land at a cost of $80,000. The land currently has a fair market value of $107,000.
(e) Cash of $5,600 is collected from the sale of a gift certificate that is redeemable in the next accounting period.
(f) Cash of $7,500 is collected from subscribers for subscription fees to a monthly magazine. The subscription period is 2 years.
(g) You owe a creditor $1,500, payable in thirty days. The creditor has cash flow difficulties and has agreed to allow you to retire the debt in full with an immediate payment of $1,200.

## Exercise 4—3  (Revenue recognition)

Indicate which of the following transactions or events gives rise to the recognition of revenue in 1993 under the accrual basis of accounting. If revenue is not recognized, what is the account, if any, that is credited?

(a) On December 15, 1993, Howe Company received $20,000 as rent revenue for the six-month period beginning January 1, 1994.
(b) Monroe Tractor Co., on July 1, 1993, sold one of its tractors and received $10,000 in cash and a note for $50,000 at 12% interest, payable in one year. The fair market value of the tractor is $60,000.
(c) Oswald, Inc., issued additional shares of common stock on December 10, 1993, for $30,000 above par value.
(d) Balance Company received a purchase order in 1993 from an established customer for $10,200 of merchandise. The merchandise was shipped on December 20, 1993. The company's credit policy allows the customer to return the merchandise within 30 days, and a 3% discount is allowed if paid within 20 days from shipment.
(e) Gloria, Inc., sold merchandise costing $2,000 for $2,500 in August 1993. The terms of the sale are 15% down on a 12-month conditional sales contract, with title to the goods being retained by the seller until the contract price is paid in full.
(f) On November 1, 1993, Jones & Whitlock entered into an agreement to audit the 1993 financial statements of Lehi Mills for a fee of $35,000. The audit work began on December 15, 1993, and will be completed around February 15, 1994.

## Exercise 4—4  (Expense recognition)

For each of the following items, indicate whether the expense should be recognized using (1) direct matching, (2) systematic and rational allocation, or (3) immediate recognition. Provide support for your answer.

(a) Johnson & Smith, Inc., conducts cancer research. The company's hope is to develop a cure for the deadly disease. To date, their efforts have proven unsuccessful. They are testing a new drug, Ebzinene, which has cost $400,000 to develop.

(b) Sears, Roebuck and Co. warranties many of the products it sells. Although the warranty periods range from days to years, Sears can reasonably estimate warranty costs.

(c) Stocks Co. recently signed a two-year lease agreement on a warehouse. The entire cost of $15,000 was paid in advance.

(d) John Clark assembles chairs for the Stone Furniture Company. The company pays Clark on an hourly basis.

(e) Hardy Co. recently purchased a fleet of new delivery trucks. The trucks are each expected to last for 100,000 miles.

(f) Taylor Manufacturing Inc. regularly advertises in national trade journals. The objective is to acquire name recognition, not to promote a specific product.

### Exercise 4—5   (Change in estimate)

The Swalberg Corporation purchased a patent on January 2, 1988, for $375,000. The original life of the patent was estimated to be 15 years. However, in December of 1993, the controller of Swalberg received information proving conclusively that the product protected by the Swalberg patent would be obsolete within three years. Accordingly, the company decided to write off the unamortized portion of the patent cost over four years beginning in 1993. How would the change in estimate be reflected in the accounts for 1993 and subsequent years?

### Exercise 4—6   (Classification of income statement items)

Where in a multiple-step income statement would each of the following items be reported?

(a) Purchase discounts
(b) Gain on early retirement of debt
(c) Interest revenue
(d) Loss on sale of equipment
(e) Casualty loss from hurricane
(f) Sales commissions
(g) Loss on disposal of segment
(h) Income tax expense
(i) Gain on sale of land
(j) Sales discounts
(k) Loss from long-term investments written off as worthless
(l) Depletion expense
(m) Cumulative effect of change in depreciation method
(n) Vacation pay of office employee
(o) Ending inventory

### Exercise 4—7   (Analysis and preparation of income statement)

The selling expenses of Caribou Inc. for 1993 are 13% of sales. General expenses, excluding doubtful accounts, are 25% of cost of goods sold, but only 15% of sales. Doubtful accounts are 2% of sales. The beginning inventory was $136,000, and it decreased 30% during the year. Income from operations for the year before income tax of 30% is $160,000. Extraordinary gain, net of tax of 30%, is $21,000. Prepare an income statement, including earnings-per-share data, giving supporting computations. Caribou Inc. has 110,000 shares of common stock outstanding.

### Exercise 4—8   (Intraperiod income tax allocation)

The Brigham Corporation reported the following income items before tax for the year 1993:

| | |
|---|---|
| Income from continuing operations before income tax................. | $210,000 |
| Loss from operations of a discontinued business segment ............. | 50,000 |
| Gain from disposal of a business segment........................... | 20,000 |
| Extraordinary gain on retirement of debt ........................... | 100,000 |

The income tax rate is 35% on all items. Prepare the portion of the income statement beginning with "Income from continuing operations before income tax" for the year ended December 31, 1993, after applying proper intraperiod income tax allocation procedures.

### Exercise 4—9   (Discontinued operations)

On June 30, 1993, top management of Garrison Manufacturing Co. decided to dispose of an unprofitable business segment. A loss of $80,000 associated with the segment was incurred during the first six months of 1993, prior to management's decision. Between July 1 and November 30, an additional $20,000 loss was incurred in phasing out the segment. The plant facilities associated with the business segment were sold on December 1, and a $15,000 gain was realized on the sale of the plant assets.

(a)   Assuming a 30% tax rate, what will be the gain or loss from operating the discontinued segment?
(b)   What will be the gain or loss on disposal of the business segment?
(c)   Prepare the discontinued operations section of Garrison Manufacturing Co.'s income statement for the year ending December 31, 1993.

### Exercise 4—10   (Change in accounting principle)

In 1988, Sears, Roebuck and Co. changed its method of accounting for income taxes. The FASB required the new principle to be applied retroactively, but prior years' financial statements were not required to be restated. The change decreased 1988 income from continuing operations by $177.6 million. However, the cumulative effect on prior years was a gain of $544.2 million.

Assuming income from continuing operations for 1988 was $1,032.3 million, complete Sears' income statement for 1988, assuming no other irregular or extraordinary items. Assume 400 million shares of common stock were outstanding during the period.

### Exercise 4—11   (Reporting items on financial statements)

Under what classification would you report each of the following items on the financial statements?

(a)   Revenue from sale of obsolete inventory.
(b)   Loss on sale of the fertilizer production division of a lawn supplies manufacturer.
(c)   Material penalties arising from early payment of a mortgage.
(d)   Gain resulting from changing asset balances to adjust for the effect of excessive depreciation charged in error in prior years.
(e)   Loss resulting from excessive accrual in prior years of estimated revenues from long-term contracts.
(f)   Costs incurred to purchase a valuable patent.
(g)   Net income from the discontinued dune buggy operations of a custom car designer.
(h)   Costs of rearranging plant machinery into a more efficient order.
(i)   Error made in capitalizing advertising expense during the prior year.
(j)   Gain on sale of land to the government.
(k)   Loss from destruction of crops by a hailstorm.
(l)   Cumulative effect of changing depreciation method.
(m)   Additional depreciation resulting from a change in the estimated useful life of an asset.
(n)   Gain on sale of long-term investments.
(o)   Loss from spring flooding.

(p) Sale of obsolete inventory at less than book value.
(q) Additional federal income tax assessment for prior years.
(r) Loss resulting from the sale of a portion of a line of business.
(s) Costs associated with moving an American business to Japan.
(t) Loss resulting from a patent that was recently determined to be worthless.

## Exercise 4—12  (Multiple-step income statement)

From the following list of accounts, prepare a multiple-step income statement in good form showing all appropriate items properly classified, including disclosure of earnings-per-share data. (No monetary amounts are to be recognized.)

Accounts Payable
Accumulated Depreciation—Office Building
Accumulated Depreciation—Delivery Equipment
Accumulated Depreciation—Office Furniture and Fixtures
Advertising Expense
Allowance for Doubtful Accounts
Cash
Common Stock, $20 par (10,000 shares outstanding)
Delivery Salaries
Depreciation Expense—Office Building
Depreciation Expense—Delivery Equipment
Depreciation Expense—Office Furniture and Fixtures
Dividend Revenue
Dividends Payable
Dividends Receivable
Doubtful Accounts Expense
Extraordinary Gain (net of income taxes)
Freight-In
Federal Unemployment Tax Payable
Goodwill
Income Taxes
Income Tax Payable
Insurance Expense
Interest Expense—Bonds

Interest Expense—Other
Interest Payable
Interest Receivable
Interest Revenue
Inventory
Loss From Discontinued Operations (net of income taxes)
Miscellaneous Delivery Expense
Miscellaneous General Expense
Miscellaneous Selling Expense
Office Salaries
Office Supplies
Office Supplies Used
Officers' Salaries
Property Taxes
Purchases
Purchase Discounts
Purchase Returns and Allowances
Retained Earnings
Royalties Received in Advance
Royalty Revenue
Salaries and Wages Payable
Sales
Sales Discounts
Sales Returns and Allowances
Sales Salaries and Commissions
Sales Tax Payable

## Exercise 4—13  (Single-step income statement and statement of retained earnings)

The Pensacola Awning Co. reports the following for 1993:

| | |
|---|---:|
| Retained earnings, January 1 | $ 444,500 |
| Selling expenses | 287,000 |
| Sales revenue | 1,360,000 |
| Interest expense | 13,390 |
| General and administrative expenses | 236,400 |
| Cost of goods sold | 765,000 |
| Dividends declared this year | 32,000 |
| Tax rate for all items | 35% |
| Average shares of common stock outstanding during the year | 25,000 |

Prepare a single-step income statement (including earnings-per-share data) and a statement of retained earnings for Pensacola.

### Exercise 4—14   (Correction of retained earnings statement)

M. Taylor has been employed as a bookkeeper at the Losser Corporation for a number of years. With the assistance of a clerk, Taylor handles all accounting duties, including the preparation of financial statements. The following is a statement of earned surplus prepared by Taylor for 1993.

**Losser Corporation**
**Statement of Earned Surplus**
**For 1993**

| | | |
|---|---:|---:|
| Balance at beginning of year .......................... | | $ 85,949 |
| Additions: | | |
| Change in estimate of 1992 amortization expense ....... | $  2,800 | |
| Gain on sale of land .................................. | 18,350 | |
| Interest revenue ..................................... | 4,500 | |
| Profit and loss for 1993 ............................. | 13,680 | |
| Total additions ...................................... | | 39,330 |
| Total ......................................... | | $125,279 |
| Deductions: | | |
| Increased depreciation due to change in estimated life ... | $  5,000 | |
| Dividends declared and paid ......................... | 10,000 | |
| Loss on sale of equipment .......................... | 3,860 | |
| Loss from major casualty (extraordinary) .............. | 27,730 | |
| Total deductions .................................... | | 46,590 |
| Balance at end of year ................................. | | $ 78,689 |

**Instructions:**

1. Prepare a schedule showing the correct net income for 1993. (Ignore income taxes.)
2. Prepare a retained earnings statement for 1993.
3. Explain why you have changed the retained earnings statement.

## PROBLEMS

### Problem 4—1   (Single-step income statement)

The Payette Co. on July 1, 1993, reported a retained earnings balance of $1,525,000. The books of the company showed the following account balances on June 30, 1994:

| | |
|---|---:|
| Sales ....................................................... | $2,500,000 |
| Inventory: July 1, 1993............................................ | 160,000 |
| June 30, 1994 ........................................ | 165,000 |
| Sales Returns and Allowances .................................... | 30,000 |
| Purchases ................................................... | 1,536,000 |
| Purchase Discounts............................................. | 24,000 |
| Dividends Paid ................................................ | 260,000 |
| Selling and General Expenses .................................... | 250,000 |
| Income Taxes ................................................ | 249,550 |

**Instructions:**   Prepare a single-step income statement and a retained earnings statement. The Payette Co. has 400,000 shares of common stock outstanding.

### Problem 4—2   (Revenue recognition and preparation of income statement)

The Richmond Company manufactures and sells robot-type toys for children. Under one type of agreement with the dealers, Richmond is to receive payment upon shipment to the dealers. Under another type of agreement, Richmond receives payments only after the dealer makes the sale. Under this latter agreement, toys may be returned by the dealer. The president of Richmond desires to know how the income statement would differ under these two methods over a two-year period.

The following information is made available for making the computations:

| | |
|---|---|
| Sales price per unit: | |
| If paid after shipment ........................................... | $5 |
| If paid after sale, with right of return ............................. | $6 |
| Cost to produce per unit (assume fixed quantity of toys is produced)... | $3 |
| Expected bad debt percentage of sales if revenue recognized at time of shipment ................................................................. | 5% |
| Expected bad debt percentage of sales if revenue recognized at time of sale ...................................................................... | ½% |
| Selling expense—1993........................................... | $25,000 |
| Selling expense—1994........................................... | $15,000 |
| General and administrative expenses—1993 and 1994 ............... | $20,000 |

| | Quantity Shipped and Sold | |
|---|---|---|
| | 1993 | 1994 |
| Units shipped to dealers ............................. | 25,000 | 30,000 |
| Units sold by dealers ................................ | 14,000 | 22,000 |

**Instructions:**

1. Prepare comparative income statements for 1993 and 1994 for each of the two types of dealer agreements assuming the company began operations in 1993.
2. Discuss the implications of the revenue recognition method used for each of the dealer agreements.

## Problem 4—3 (Revenue and expense recognition)

On December 31, 1993, The Hadley Company provides the following pre-audit income statement for your review:

| | |
|---|---|
| Sales ..................................................... | $185,000 |
| Cost of goods sold ...................................... | (94,000) |
| Gross margin ............................................. | $ 91,000 |
| Rent expense ............................................. | (18,000) |
| Advertising expense ...................................... | (6,000) |
| Warranty expense ........................................ | (8,000) |
| Other expenses .......................................... | (20,000) |
| Net income .............................................. | $ 39,000 |

The following information is also available:

(a)  Many of Hadley's customers pay for their orders in advance. At year-end, $18,000 of orders paid for in advance of shipment have been included in the sales figure.
(b)  Hadley introduced and sold several products during the year with a 30-day, money-back guarantee. During the year, customers seldom returned the products. Hadley has not included in revenue or in cost of goods sold those items sold within the last 30 days that included the guarantee. The revenue is $16,000, and the cost associated with the products is $7,500.
(c)  On January 1, 1993, Hadley prepaid its building rent for 18 months. The entire amount paid, $18,000, was charged to Rent Expense.
(d)  On July 1, 1993, Hadley paid $24,000 for general advertising to be completed prior to the end of 1993. Hadley's management estimates that the advertising will benefit a two-year period and, therefore, has elected to charge the costs to the income statement at the rate of $1,000 a month.
(e)  Hadley has collected current cost information relating to its inventory. The cost of goods sold, if valued using current costing techniques, is $106,000.

(f)   In past years, Hadley has estimated warranty expense using a percentage of sales. Hadley estimates future warranty costs relating to 1993 sales will amount to five percent of sales. However, during 1993, Hadley elected to charge costs to warranty expense as costs were incurred. Hadley spent $8,000 during 1993 to repair and replace defective inventory sold in current and prior periods.

**Instructions:**

1. For each item of additional information, identify the revenue or expense recognition issue.
2. Prepare a revised income statement using the information provided.

### Problem 4—4   (Intraperiod income tax allocation)

The following information relates to Delaney Manufacturing Inc. for the fiscal year ended July 31, 1994. Assume there are no tax rate changes, a 30% tax rate applies to all items reported in the income statement, and there are no differences between financial and taxable income.

| | |
|---|---:|
| Taxable income, year ending July 31, 1994 | $ 975,000 |
| Nonoperating items included in taxable income: | |
|   Extraordinary gain | 101,000 |
|   Loss from disposal of a business segment | (140,000) |
| Prior-year error resulting in income overstatement for fiscal year 1993; tax refund to be requested | 75,000 |
| Retained earnings, August 1, 1993 | 2,750,000 |

**Instructions:**   Prepare the income statement for Delaney Manufacturing Inc. beginning with "Income from continuing operations before income taxes" and the retained earnings statement for the fiscal year ended July 31, 1994. Apply intraperiod income tax allocation procedures to both statements.

### Problem 4—5   (Reporting special income items)

Radiant Cosmetics Inc. shows a retained earnings balance on January 1, 1993, of $620,000. For 1993, the income from continuing operations was $210,000 before income tax. Following is a list of special items:

| | |
|---|---:|
| Income from operations of a discontinued cosmetics division | $18,000 |
| Loss on the sale of the cosmetics division | 50,000 |
| Gain on extinguishment of long-term debt | 25,000 |
| Correction of sales understatement in 1992 (net of income taxes of $21,000 to be paid when amended 1992 return is filed) | 39,000 |
| Omission of depreciation charges of prior years (a claim has been filed for an income tax refund of $8,000) | 20,000 |

Income tax paid during 1993 was $82,000, which consisted of the tax on continuing operations, plus $8,000 resulting from operations of the discontinued cosmetics division and $10,000 from the gain from extinguishment of debt, less a $20,000 tax reduction for loss on the sale of the cosmetics division. Dividends of $30,000 were declared by the company during the year (50,000 shares of common stock are outstanding).

**Instructions:**   Prepare the income statement for Radiant Cosmetics Inc. beginning with "Income from continuing operations before income taxes." Include an accompanying retained earnings statement.

### Problem 4—6   (Income and retained earnings statements)

Selected account balances of Connell Company for 1993 along with additional information as of December 31 are as follows:

| | |
|---|---:|
| Contribution to Employee Pension Fund | $  290,000 |
| Delivery Expense | 425,000 |
| Depreciation Expense—Delivery Trucks | 29,000 |
| Depreciation Expense—Office Building | 25,000 |
| Depreciation Expense—Office Equipment | 10,000 |
| Depreciation Expense—Store Equipment | 25,000 |
| Dividends | 150,000 |
| Dividend Revenue | 5,000 |
| Doubtful Accounts Expense | 32,000 |
| Freight-In | 145,000 |
| Gain on Sale of Office Equipment | 10,000 |
| Income Taxes, 1993 | 344,700 |
| Interest Revenue | 1,500 |
| Loss on Sale of Marketable Securities | 50,000 |
| Loss on Write-Down of Obsolete Inventory | 75,000 |
| Inventory, January 1, 1993 | 850,000 |
| Miscellaneous General Expenses | 45,000 |
| Miscellaneous Selling Expenses | 50,000 |
| Officers' and Office Salaries | 850,000 |
| Property Taxes | 100,000 |
| Purchase Discounts | 47,700 |
| Purchases | 4,133,200 |
| Retained Earnings, January 1, 1993 | 550,000 |
| Sales | 8,125,000 |
| Sales Discounts | 55,000 |
| Sales Returns and Allowances | 95,000 |
| Sales Salaries | 521,000 |
| Stores Supplies Expense | 60,000 |

(a) Inventory was valued at year-end as follows:

| | |
|---|---:|
| Cost | $825,000 |
| Write-down of obsolete inventory | 75,000 |
| | $750,000 |

(b) Number of Connell shares of stock outstanding: 50,000

**Instructions:** Prepare statements of income and retained earnings in multiple-step format for the year ended December 31, 1993.

## Problem 4—7 (Corrected income statement)

The following pre-audit income statement for Jericho Recreation, Inc., was prepared by a newly hired staff accountant for the year ending December 31, 1993.

| | | |
|---|---:|---:|
| Net revenues | | $797,000 |
| Cost of goods sold | | 320,800 |
| Gross profit | | $476,200 |
| Expenses: | | |
| Sales salaries and commissions | $160,000 | |
| Officers' and office salaries | 210,000 | |
| Depreciation | 56,000 | |
| Advertising expense | 13,400 | |
| Other general and administrative expenses | 38,800 | |
| | | 478,200 |
| Net loss from continuing operations | | (2,000) |
| Discontinued operations: | | |
| Gain on disposal of business segment | | 40,000 |
| Income before income taxes | | $  38,000 |
| Income taxes (30%) | | 11,400 |
| Net income | | $  26,600 |
| Earnings per common share (10,000 shares outstanding) | | $2.66 |

The following information was obtained by Jericho's independent auditor:

(a) Net revenues in the income statement included the following items:

| | |
|---|---:|
| Sales returns and allowances ................... | $ 9,500 |
| Interest revenue .............................. | 6,600 |
| Interest expense.............................. | 10,600 |
| Loss on sale of short-term investment .......... | 3,000 |
| Gain on early extinguishment of debt .......... | 16,000 |

(b) Jericho changed its method of inventory costing in 1993. The staff accountant correctly determined that the cumulative effect of the change, before any tax considerations, was a reduction in current-year income of $18,000. In preparing the income statement, the accountant added the $18,000 to cost of goods sold.

(c) Of the total depreciation expense reported in the income statement, 60% relates to stores and store equipment, 40% to office building and equipment.

(d) At the beginning of 1993, management decided to close one of Jericho's retail stores. The inventory and equipment were moved to another Jericho store, and the land and building were sold on July 1, 1993, at a pretax gain of $40,000. This amount has been reported under discontinued operations.

(d) The income tax rate is 30%.

**Instructions:**   Prepare a corrected multiple-step income statement for the period ended December 31, 1993.

**Problem 4—8   (Analysis of income items—multiple-step income statement preparation)**

On December 31, 1993, analysis of the Dille Sporting Goods' operations for 1993 revealed the following:

(a) Total cash collections from customers, $107,770.
(b) December 31, 1992, inventory balance, $10,020.
(c) Total cash payments, $96,350.
(d) Accounts receivable, December 31, 1992, $20,350.
(e) Accounts payable, December 31, 1992, $9,870.
(f) Accounts receivable, December 31, 1993, $10,780.
(g) Accounts payable, December 31, 1993, $5,175.
(h) General and administrative expenses total 20% of sales. This amount includes the depreciation on store and equipment.
(i) Selling expenses of $11,661 total 30% of gross profit on sales.
(j) No general and administrative or selling expense liabilities existed at December 31, 1993.
(k) Wages and salaries payable at December 31, 1992, $3,750.
(l) Depreciation expense on store and equipment total 13.5% of general and administrative expenses.
(m) Shares of stock issued and outstanding, 6,000.
(n) The income tax rate is 30%.

**Instructions:**   Prepare a multiple-step income statement for the year ended December 31, 1993.

**Problem 4—9   (Corrected income and retained earnings statements)**

Selected preadjustment account balances and adjusting information of Sunset Cosmetics Inc. for the year ended December 31, 1993, are as follows:

| | |
|---|---:|
| Retained Earnings, January 1, 1993 ............................... | $440,670 |
| Sales Salaries and Commissions.................................... | 25,000 |
| Advertising Expense ............................................. | 16,090 |
| Legal Services .................................................. | 2,225 |

| | |
|---|---:|
| Insurance and Licenses | 7,680 |
| Travel Expense—Sales Representatives | 4,560 |
| Depreciation Expense—Sales/Delivery Equipment | 6,100 |
| Depreciation Expense—Office Equipment | 4,200 |
| Interest Revenue | 550 |
| Utilities | 6,400 |
| Telephone and Postage | 1,475 |
| Supplies Inventory | 2,180 |
| Miscellaneous Selling Expenses | 2,740 |
| Dividends | 33,000 |
| Dividend Revenue | 5,150 |
| Interest Expense | 4,520 |
| Allowance for Doubtful Accounts (Cr. balance) | 160 |
| Officers' Salaries | 36,600 |
| Sales | 451,000 |
| Sales Returns and Allowances | 3,900 |
| Sales Discounts | 880 |
| Gain on Sale of Assets | 7,820 |
| Inventory, January 1, 1993 | 89,700 |
| Inventory, December 31, 1993 | 20,550 |
| Purchases | 141,600 |
| Freight-In | 5,525 |
| Accounts Receivable, December 31, 1993 | 261,000 |
| Gain From Discontinued Operations (before income taxes) | 40,000 |
| Extraordinary Loss (before income taxes) | 72,600 |

Shares of common stock outstanding, 39,000

Adjusting information:

(a) Cost of inventory in the possession of consignees as of December 31, 1993, was not included in the ending inventory balance ... **$18,600**

(b) After preparing an analysis of aged accounts receivable, a decision was made to increase the allowance for doubtful accounts to a percentage of the ending accounts receivable balance ... **2%**

(c) Purchase returns and allowances were unrecorded. They are computed as a percentage of purchases (not including freight-in) ... **6%**

(d) Sales commissions for the last day of the year had not been accrued.
Total sales for the day ... **$ 3,050**
Average sales commissions as a percent of sales ... **3%**

(e) No accrual had been made for a freight bill received on January 3, 1994, for goods received on December 29, 1993 ... **$ 570**

(f) An advertising campaign was initiated November 1, 1993. This amount was recorded as "prepaid advertising" and should be amortized over a six-month period. No amortization was recorded ... **$ 1,818**

(g) Freight charges paid on sold merchandise were netted against sales.
Freight charge on sales during 1993 ... **$ 3,500**

(h) Interest earned but not accrued ... **$ 560**

(i) Depreciation expense on a new forklift purchased March 1, 1993, had not been recognized. (Assume all equipment will have no salvage value and the straight-line method is used. Depreciation is calculated to the nearest month.)
Purchase price ... **$ 7,800**
Estimated life in years ... **10**

(j) A "real" account is debited upon the receipt of supplies.
Supplies on hand at year-end ... **$ 1,225**

(k) Income tax rate (on all items) ... **30%**

**Instructions:**   Prepare a corrected multiple-step income statement and a retained earnings statement for the year ended December 31, 1993. Assume all amounts are material.

## Problem 4—10  (Comprehensive income statement)

The Blacksburg Company decides to follow the FASB recommendations and prepare both an earnings statement and a statement of comprehensive income. The following information for the year ending December 31, 1993, has been provided for the preparation of the statements:

| | | |
|---|---:|---|
| Sales | $450,000 | |
| Cost of goods sold | 263,000 | |
| Foreign translation adjustment (net of income taxes) | 33,000 | (cr.) |
| Selling expenses | 63,900 | |
| Extraordinary gain (net of income taxes) | 39,400 | |
| Correction of inventory error (net of income taxes) | 28,680 | (cr.) |
| General and administrative expenses | 58,720 | |
| Cumulative effect of change in depreciation method (net of income tax savings) | 18,380 | (dr.) |
| Income tax expense | 21,500 | |
| Gain on sale of investment | 6,700 | |
| Proceeds from sale of land at cost | 75,000 | |
| Dividends | 8,900 | |

**Instructions:**  Prepare the two statements for the company. Use a single-step approach for the earnings statement.

# CHAPTER 5

## The Balance Sheet

---

**CHAPTER TOPICS**

**Usefulness of the Balance Sheet**

**Elements of the Balance Sheet**

**Form of the Balance Sheet**

**Additional Disclosure to the Balance Sheet**

**Limitations of the Balance Sheet**

---

Apple Computer began its 1985 Annual Report as follows:

> 1985 was a turbulent year.
>
> It was a year that began with
> record profits and sales.
>
> It was also a year in which
> we reported the first quarterly
> loss in Apple's history.

As of January 1, 1985, a focus on Apple's income statement alone would have given no indication that 1985 would be a turbulent year. For Apple's fiscal year ending September 30, 1985, sales during the first quarter (October 1984 through December 1984) were a record $698 million, and quarterly earnings were a record $0.75 per share. On the other hand, an analysis of balance sheet information would have disclosed that the post-Christmas dealer inventories of Apple computers were disturbingly high—unsold Apple computers in the hands of dealers at the end of 1984 represented 7.2 weeks of sales, compared to the average dealer inventory of 4.1 weeks. This excess dealer inventory was a signal of a sales slowdown that eventually resulted in the following: a major corporate restructuring to cut costs, a decrease in the number of Apple employees by 1,200, the closing of two factories and the sale of another, and the temporary interruption of some research and development.

For many years, the income statement has been the dominant financial statement for external decision making. Earnings per share, placement of extraordinary items, and revenue recognition have all been topics of great interest to standard-setting bodies. The financial press has regularly reported quarterly earnings of large corporations as newsworthy events. The income statement, however, tells only part of the financial story. It does not answer questions such as: What is the company doing with the income? How is the company being financed? How far in debt is the company? How liquid are its assets? To answer these questions, an external user has to consider the balance sheet, or statement of financial position. This statement reports information that is very important for a user in evaluating the ability of a company to continue in operation.

Over the past several years the financial community has expressed increased interest in the financial conditions of reporting entities, especially their liquidity. The Financial Accounting Standards Board also has devoted considerable attention to evaluating how its standards affect the balance sheet.[1] The increased interest in the balance sheet is partially related to the significant number of companies that have been experiencing financial difficulty. By concentrating too much on profitability at the expense of financial strength, some companies find they have insufficient cash to pay their debts. This chapter focuses on the strengths and limitations of the balance sheet and describes how companies report their assets, liabilities, and owners' equity.

## USEFULNESS OF THE BALANCE SHEET

The balance sheet reports as of a given point in time the resources of a business (**assets**), its obligations (**liabilities**), and the residual ownership claims against its resources (**owners' equity**). By analyzing the relationships among these items, investors, creditors, and others can assess a firm's liquidity, i.e., its ability to meet short-term obligations, and solvency, i.e., its ability to pay all current and long-term debts as they come due. The balance sheet also shows the composition of assets and liabilities, the relative proportions of debt and equity financing, and how much of a firm's earnings have been retained in the business. Collectively, this information can be used by external parties to help assess the financial status of a firm at a particular date.

Following the traditional accounting model, the balance sheet is a historical report presenting the cumulative results of all past transactions of a business measured in terms of historical costs. It is an expression of the basic accounting equation: **Assets = Liabilities + Owners' Equity.** The balance sheet shows both the character and the amount of the assets, liabilities, and owners' equity.

Balance sheets, especially when compared over time and with additional data, provide a great deal of useful information to those interested in analyzing the financial well-being of a company. Specific relationships, such as a company's current ratio, its debt-to-equity ratio, and its rate of return on investment can be highlighted.[2] Future commitments, favorable and unfavorable trends, problem areas in terms of collection patterns, and the relative equity positions of creditors and owners can also be analyzed, all of which assist in evaluating the financial position of a company.

---

[1]See, for example, David E. Hawkins, "Toward the New Balance Sheet," *Harvard Business Review* (November-December 1984), pp. 156-163.

[2]These ratios and relationships are discussed in detail in the last chapter of the text.

Of special interest to both creditors and investors in analyzing the balance sheet is the company's **financial flexibility**. For example, how well could the company weather unexpected losses in assets, damage claims arising from its operations, or significant reductions in sales? Often, the negative impact on net assets from such events is so material that the existence of the company is threatened unless it can enter the capital markets for additional funds from either creditors or investors. The problem is that obtaining funds becomes difficult once a company is in trouble. Terms for borrowing, including high interest rates, may be so unfavorable that they create further difficulty for a company. Additional stock issues may only sell at decreased prices, diluting the equity of existing shareholders.

Even large companies are not immune to financial crisis. In January 1990, two giant U.S. retailing corporations, Allied Stores Corp. and Federated Department Stores, Inc., filed for bankruptcy protection. These corporations were part of Canadian Robert Campeau's real estate and investment holdings. Extensive borrowing by Campeau to acquire such prominent retail chains as Bloomingdale's and Abraham & Straus in New York and Seattle's Bon Marche led to a $7.5 billion debt that required massive cash payments for principal and interest.[3] Other prominent companies, such as Greyhound, Inc., Circle K, and the many holdings of New York real estate developer Donald Trump, were faced with burgeoning debt and extremely high cash flow requirements in the early 1990s. Severe restrictions by creditors were necessary to try to save these companies from collapse. The impact of high debt was observable on the balance sheets as companies lost their financial flexibility.

## ELEMENTS OF THE BALANCE SHEET

The three elements found on the balance sheet were defined in Chapter 2. These definitions, which are part of FASB Concepts Statement No. 6, are repeated below.[4]

- **Assets** are probable future economic benefits obtained or controlled by a particular entity as a result of past transactions or events.
- **Liabilities** are probable future sacrifices of economic benefits arising from present obligations of a particular entity to transfer assets or provide services to other entities in the future as a result of past transactions or events.
- **Equity** or **net assets** is the residual interest in the assets of an entity that remains after deducting its liabilities. In a business enterprise, the equity is the ownership interest.

Assets are the resources owned or controlled by an entity. They include cash and other highly liquid resources, such as claims against others (receivables) and temporary investments. Assets also include costs that are expected to provide future economic benefits. For example, expenditures made for inventories, prepaid insurance, equipment, and patents are recoverable costs that will be recognized as expenses and matched against revenues of future periods.

Liabilities measure the claims of creditors against entity resources. As indicated by the FASB's definition, the method for settlement of liabilities varies. A liability may call for settlement by cash payment or settlement through goods to be delivered or services to be performed.

Owners' equity measures the interest of the ownership group in the total resources of the enterprise. It equals the net assets of an enterprise, or the difference between total

---

[3]"It'll Be a Hard Sell," *Business Week*, January 29, 1990, pp. 30-31.

[4]*Statement of Financial Accounting Concepts No. 6*, "Elements of Financial Statements" (Stamford: Financial Accounting Standards Board, 1985), p. ix.

assets and total liabilities. This interest arises from investment by owners, and is increased by net income and decreased by net losses and distributions to owners. An ownership interest does not call for settlement on a certain date; in the event of business dissolution, it represents a claim on assets only after creditors have been paid in full.

### Classified Balance Sheets

Balance sheet items are generally classified in a manner that facilitates analysis and interpretation of financial data. Information of primary concern to all parties is the business unit's liquidity and solvency—its ability to meet current and long-term obligations. Accordingly, assets and liabilities are classified as (1) **current** or **short-term** items and (2) **noncurrent** or **long-term** items. When assets and liabilities are so classified, the difference between current assets and current liabilities may be determined. This is referred to as the company's **working capital**—the liquid buffer available in meeting financial demands and contingencies of the future.

The importance of an adequate working capital position cannot be minimized. A business may not be able to survive in the absence of a satisfactory relationship between current assets and current liabilities. Furthermore, its ability to prosper is largely determined by the compostion of the current asset pool. There must be a proper balance between liquid assets in the form of cash and temporary investments, and receivables and inventories. Activities of the business revolve around these assets. Cash and temporary investments, representing immediate purchasing power, are used to meet current claims and purchasing, payroll, and expense requirements; receivables are the outgrowth of sales effort and provide cash in the course of operations; inventory is also a source of cash as well as the means of achieving a profit. Management, in setting policies with respect to selling, purchasing, financing, expanding, and the paying of dividends, must work within the limitations set by the company's working capital position.

Some writers have questioned the usefulness of the current/noncurrent distinction for all companies. For example, Loyd Heath argues that since any classification scheme is arbitrary, the classification between current and noncurrent should be abolished. Assets and liabilities could then be listed in the order of their liquidity without arbitrary subtotals.[5] Although there is some arbitrariness in the detailed classifications, the popularity among users of the current ratio (current assets divided by current liabilities) as a measure of liquidity suggests that the classification does meet the test of decision usefulness and should be retained.

Although there are no standard categories that must be used, the general framework for a balance sheet shown in Exhibit 5—1 is representative and will be used in this chapter.

The different sections of the classified balance sheet will be discussed in detail below. The components of working capital, current assets and current liabilities, will be discussed first, followed by noncurrent assets and noncurrent liabilities. The hypothetical balance sheet of Techtronics Corporation will be used to illustrate each section.

### Current Assets

**Current assets** include cash and resources that are reasonably expected to be converted into cash during the normal operating cycle of a business or within one year, whichever period is longer. As depicted on the next page, the **normal operating cycle** is the time required for cash to be converted to inventories, inventories into receivables, and receivables ultimately into cash. When the operating cycle exceeds twelve months, for example, in the tobacco, distillery, and lumber industries, the longer period is used.

---

[5]Loyd Heath, "Is Working Capital Really Working?" *Journal of Accountancy* (August 1980), pp. 55-62.

**Exhibit 5—1    General Form for a Classified Balance Sheet**

### Assets

Current assets:
    Cash
    Marketable securities and other short-term investments
    Accounts and notes receivable
    Inventories
    Other current assets, such as prepaid expenses
Noncurrent assets:
    Investments
    Land, buildings, and equipment
    Intangible assets
    Other noncurrent assets

### Liabilities

Current liabilities:
    Accounts and notes payable
    Accrued expenses
    Current portion of long-term obligations
    Other current liabilities, such as unearned revenues
Noncurrent liabilities:
    Long-term debt, such as notes, bonds, and mortgages payable
    Long-term lease obligations
    Deferred income tax liability
    Other noncurrent liabilities

### Owners' Equity

Contributed capital:
    Capital stock
    Additional paid-in capital
Retained earnings

Some exceptions to the general definition of current assets should be noted. Cash that is restricted as to use, e.g., designated for the acquisition of noncurrent assets or for the liquidation of noncurrent debts, should not be included in current assets. Also, in classifying assets not related to the operating cycle, a one-year period is always used as the basis for current classification. For example, a note receivable due in 15 months that arose from the sale of land previously held for investment would be classified as noncurrent even if the normal operating cycle exceeds 15 months.

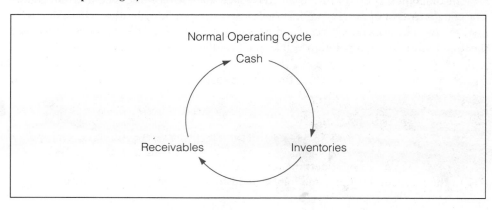

In addition to cash, receivables, and inventories, current assets typically include such resources as prepaid expenses and marketable securities. Prepayments of such items as insurance and rent are not current assets in the sense that they will be converted into cash but on the basis that, if they had not been prepaid, the use of cash or other current assets during the operating cycle period would have been required. Long-term prepayments should be reported as noncurrent assets and charged to the operations of several years. If securities of other companies, whether marketable or not, are acquired for purposes of control rather than conversion back to cash during the normal operating cycle, they should not be designated as current assets.

Current assets are normally listed on the balance sheet in the order of their liquidity. These assets, with the exception of marketable securities and inventories, are usually reported at their estimated realizable values. Thus, current receivable balances are reduced by allowances for estimated uncollectible accounts. Marketable equity securities should be reported at the lower of aggregate cost or market.[6] Inventories may be reported at cost or on the basis of "cost or market, whichever is lower."

The current asset section of the balance sheet for Techtronics Corporation is illustrated below.

| Current assets: | | |
|---|---:|---:|
| Cash | $ 52,650 | |
| Marketable securities (reported at market; cost, $72,600) | 67,350 | |
| Receivables (net of allowance for doubtful accounts) .... | 363,700 | |
| Inventories (reported at FIFO cost or market, whichever is lower) | 296,000 | |
| Prepaid expenses and other | 32,900 | |
| Total current assets | | $812,600 |

## Current Liabilities

Current liabilities are those obligations that are reasonably expected to be paid using current assets or by creating other current liabilities. Generally, if a liability is reasonably expected to be paid within 12 months, it is classified as current. As with receivables, payables arising from the normal operating activities may be classified as current even if they are not to be paid within 12 months, as long as they are to be paid within the operating cycle which may exceed 12 months.

In addition to accounts payable and short-term borrowings, current liabilities also include amounts for accrued expenses. Common accruals include salaries and wages, interest, and taxes. The current liabilities section also includes amounts representing the portion of the long-term obligations due to be satisfied within one year, or within one operating cycle if the length of the cycle exceeds one year.

Other current liabilities include unearned revenues arising from advance payments by customers. Examples include revenue collected in advance by publishers on magazine subscriptions and rent collected in advance by landlords. These advances are recognized as revenue when the earning process is substantially complete, i.e., when an issue of the magazine is mailed to customers or when the rental period passes. While some unearned revenues may represent noncurrent obligations to provide goods or services, the majority of advance receipts are earned within one year or less and are thus reported as current liabilities.

The current liability classification generally does not include the following items, since these do not require the use of resources classified as current.

---

[6]*Statement of Financial Accounting Standards No. 12*, "Accounting for Certain Marketable Securities" (Stamford: Financial Accounting Standards Board, 1975), par. 8.

1. Debts to be liquidated from funds that have been accumulated and are reported as noncurrent assets. These funds are often called "sinking funds."
2. Short-term obligations to be refinanced, assuming certain criteria are met as discussed below.[7]

**Short-Term Obligations to Be Refinanced**     The FASB has concluded that short-term obligations that are expected to be refinanced, i.e., replaced by the issuance of new obligations, should be excluded from current liabilities if the following conditions are met: (1) the intent of the company is to refinance the obligations on a long-term basis, and (2) the company's intent is evidenced by an actual refinancing after the balance sheet date but before the financial statements are finalized, or by the existence of an explicit refinancing agreement.[8] In effect, the FASB is recognizing that certain short-term obligations will not require the use of current assets during a period even though they are scheduled to mature during that period. Thus, they should not be classified as current liabilities.

**Callable Obligations**     Classification problems can arise when an obligation is **callable** by a creditor, because it is difficult to determine exactly when the obligation will be paid. A callable obligation is one that is either (1) payable on demand (has no specified due date) or (2) has a specified due date, but is callable if the debtor violates the provisions of the debt agreement. Any obligation that is due on demand or will become due on demand within one year from the balance sheet date (or operating cycle if longer) should be classified as current.[9]

In addition, a long-term obligation should be classified as current if it is callable at the balance sheet date because the debtor is in violation of a contract provision. For example, some instruments have a specific clause identifying conditions that can cause the debt to be immediately callable, e.g., failure to earn a certain return on assets or failure to make an interest payment. These clauses are referred to as objective acceleration clauses. The FASB has stated that if conditions that make the obligation callable have occurred, the debt should be classified as a current debt unless (1) the creditor has waived the right to demand payment for more than one year (or normal operating cycle if longer) from the balance sheet date, or (2) the debtor has cured the deficiency after the balance sheet date but before the statements are issued, and the debt is not callable for a period that extends beyond the debtor's normal operating cycle.[10]

In some cases, the contract does not specifically identify the circumstances under which a payment will be accelerated, but it does indicate some general conditions that permit the lender to unilaterally accelerate the due date. This type of provision is known as a subjective acceleration clause because, although the clause may specify certain conditions under which the obligation may be called, the violation of the conditions cannot be objectively determined. Examples of the wording in such clauses might be, "if the debtor fails to maintain satisfactory operations," or "if a material adverse change occurs." The FASB has recommended that if invoking of the clause is deemed probable, the liability should be classified as a current liability. If invoking of the clause is considered to be

---

[7]*Statement of Financial Accounting Standards No. 6,* "Classification of Short-Term Obligations Expected to Be Refinanced" (Stamford: Financial Accounting Standards Board, 1975).

[8]*Statement of Financial Accounting Standards No. 6,* pars. 9-11.

[9]*Statement of Financial Accounting Standards No. 78,* "Classification of Obligations That Are Callable by the Creditor" (Stamford: Financial Accounting Standards Board, 1983), par. 5.

[10]*Ibid.*

reasonably possible but not probable, only a footnote disclosure is necessary, and the liability continues to be classified as noncurrent.[11]

The current liability section of the balance sheet for Techtronics Corporation is illustrated below:

Current liabilities:

| | |
|---|---:|
| Notes payable........................................ | $ 75,000 |
| Accounts payable .................................... | 312,700 |
| Accrued expenses .................................... | 46,200 |
| Current portion of long-term debt ..................... | 62,000 |
| Other current liabilities............................... | 28,600 |
| Total current liabilities ............................... | $524,500 |

## Noncurrent Assets

Assets not qualifying for presentation under the current heading are classified under a number of noncurrent headings. Noncurrent assets may be listed under separate headings, such as "Investments," "Land, buildings, and equipment," "Intangible assets," and "Other long-term assets."

**Investments**    Investments held for such long-term purposes as regular income, appreciation, or ownership control are reported under the heading "Investments." Examples of items properly reported under this heading are stocks, bonds, and mortgage holdings; securities of affiliated companies and advances to such companies; fund assets consisting of cash and securities held for the redemption of bonds or stocks, the replacement of buildings, or the payment of pensions; land held for investment purposes; the cash surrender value of life insurance; and other miscellaneous investments not used directly in the operations of the business. Although many long-term investments are reported at cost, there are modifications to the valuation of some investments that will be discussed in later chapters.

**Land, Buildings, and Equipment**    Properties of a tangible and relatively permanent character that are used in the normal business operations are reported under "Land, buildings, and equipment" or other appropriate headings, such as "Property and equipment." Land, buildings, machinery, tools, furniture, fixtures, and vehicles are included in this section of the blance sheet. Most tangible properties, except land, are normally reported at cost less accumulated depreciation.

**Intangible Assets**    The long-term rights and privileges of a nonphysical nature acquired for use in business operations are often reported under the heading "Intangible assets." Included in this class are such items as goodwill, patents, trademarks, franchises, copyrights, formulas, leaseholds, and organization costs. Intangible assets are normally reported at cost less amounts previously amortized.

**Other Noncurrent Assets**    Those noncurrent assets not suitably reported under any of the previous classifications may be listed under the general heading "Other noncurrent assets" or may be listed separately under special descriptive headings. Such assets include, for example, long-term advances to officers, long-term receivables, deposits made with taxing authorities and utility companies, and deferred income tax assets.

---

[11]FASB Technical Bulletin, 79-3, "Subjective Acceleration Clauses in Long-Term Debt Agreements" (Stamford: Financial Accounting Standards Board, December 1979), par. 003.

Prepayments for services or benefits to be received over a number of periods are properly regarded as noncurrent. Among these are such items as plant rearrangement costs and developmental and improvement costs. These long-term prepayments are frequently reported under a "Deferred costs" or "Deferred charges" heading. However, objection can be raised to a deferred costs category since this designation could be applied to all costs assignable to future periods including inventories, buildings and equipment, and intangible assets. The deferred costs heading may be avoided by reporting long-term prepayments within the other noncurrent assets section or under separate descriptive headings.

A deferred income tax asset account may be shown under "Other noncurrent assets" or may be reported separately. In general, deferred income tax balances result from temporary differences between taxable income (the income subject to tax on the tax return) and income before taxes reported on the income statement. Deferred income tax assets arise when taxable income exceeds reported income for the period and the difference is expected to "reverse" in future periods. These assets are similar to prepaid expenses, but the computation and reporting of deferred income tax assets is much more complex.

The noncurrent assets section of the balance sheet for Techtronics Corporation is illustrated below:

| Noncurrent assets: | | |
|---|---:|---:|
| Investments | $128,000 | |
| Land | 76,300 | |
| Buildings and equipment (net of accumulated depreciation of $228,600) | 732,900 | |
| Intangible assets | 165,000 | |
| Other noncurrent assets | 37,800 | |
| Total noncurrent assets | | $1,140,000 |

## Noncurrent Liabilities

Obligations not reasonably expected to be paid or otherwise satisfied within 12 months (or within the operating cycle if it exceeds 12 months) are classified as noncurrent liabilities. Noncurrent liabilities are generally listed under separate headings, such as "Long-term debt," "Long-term lease obligations," "Deferred income tax liabilities," and "Other noncurrent liabilities."

**Long-Term Debt**    Long-term notes, bonds, mortgages, and similar obligations not requiring the use of current funds for their retirement are generally reported on the balance sheet under the heading "Long-term debt."

When an amount borrowed is not the same as the amount ultimately required in settlement of the debt and the debt is stated in the accounts at its maturity amount, a discount or premium is reported. The discount or premium should be related to the debt item; a discount, then, should be subtracted from the amount reported for the debt, and a premium should be added to the amount reported for the debt. The debt is thus reported at its present value as measured by the proceeds from its issuance.

When a note, a bond issue, or a mortgage formerly classified as a long-term obligation becomes payable within a year, it should be reclassified and presented as a current liability, except when the obligation is to be refinanced, as discussed earlier, or is to be paid out of a fund classified as noncurrent.

**Long-Term Lease Obligations**    Some leases of land, buildings, and equipment are financially structured so that they are in substance debt-financed purchases. The FASB has established criteria to determine which leases are in effect purchases, or capital leases, rather than ordinary operating leases. In accounting for capital leases, the present value of the future minimum lease payments is recorded as a long-term liability. That portion of the present value due within the next year or normal operating cycle, whichever is longer, is classified as a current liability.

**Deferred Income Tax Liability**    The credit balance in this account indicates that, due to temporary differences between taxable income and financial income, a future tax liability may have to be paid. The most common temporary difference occurs in computing depreciation expense for book and tax purposes. Generally, the tax regulations permit a faster write-off of asset cost than is allowable for financial reporting purposes.

Almost all large companies include a **deferred income tax liability** in their balance sheets. In 1988, the FASB issued a controversial standard, FASB Statement No. 96, that altered accounting for deferred tax liabilities. The implementation of this standard has been postponed twice, pending further consideration of criticism from preparers and users of financial statements. Some companies adopted FASB Statement No. 96 when it was first issued in 1988, but the majority have waited for a final FASB decision. This situation has created a lack of comparability in issued financial statements. In addition, since the liability is not reported at its present (discounted) value, some analysts disregard it when evaluating a company's debt position. In summary, the accounting for deferred income taxes is very complex and controversial and has been the subject of considerable debate in recent years.

**Other Noncurrent Liabilities**    Those noncurrent liabilities not suitably reported under the separate headings may be listed under this general heading or may be listed separately under special descriptive headings. Such liabilities could include long-term obligations to company officers or affiliated companies, matured but unclaimed bond principal and interest obligations, long-term liabilities under pension plans, unearned revenues, and obligations for advance collections on contracts that will not be completed within one year.[12]

**Contingent Liabilities**    Past activities or circumstances may give rise to possible future liabilities, although legal obligations do not exist on the date of the balance sheet. These possible claims are known as **contingent liabilities**. They are potential obligations involving uncertainty as to possible losses. As future events occur or fail to occur, this uncertainty will be resolved. Thus, a contingent liability is distinguishable from an **estimated liability**. The latter is a definite obligation with only the amount of the obligation in question and subject to estimation at the balance sheet date. There may not be any doubt as to the amount of a contingent liability, for example, a pending lawsuit, but there is considerable uncertainty as to whether the obligation will actually materialize.

In the past, contingent liabilities were not recorded in the accounts nor presented on the balance sheet. When they were disclosed, it was in the notes to the financial statements. As indicated in Chapter 1, FASB Statement No. 5 states that if a future payment is considered probable, the liability should be recorded by a debit to a loss account and a credit to a liability account. Otherwise, the contingent nature of the loss may be disclosed in a note to the financial statements as discussed on page 161. The noncurrent liabilities section of Techtronics Corporation's balance sheet is illustrated on the next page.

---

[12]*Accounting Research and Terminology Bulletins—Final Edition, No. 43,* "Restatement and Revision of Accounting Research Bulletins" (New York: American Institute of Certified Public Accountants, 1961), Chapter 3, par. 8 and footnotes 2 and 3.

[13]*Statement of Financial Accounting Standards No. 5,* "Accounting for Contingencies" (Stamford: Financial Accounting Standards Board, 1975), pars. 8-13.

Noncurrent liabilities:

| | | |
|---|---:|---:|
| Notes payable | $ 75,000 | |
| Bonds payable | 165,000 | |
| Long-term lease obligations | 135,000 | |
| Deferred income tax liability | 126,700 | |
| Other noncurrent liabilities | 72,500 | |
| Total noncurrent liabilities | | $574,200 |

## Owners' Equity

The method of reporting the owners' equity varies with the form of the business unit. Business units are typically divided into three categories: (1) **proprietorships**, (2) **partnerships**, and (3) **corporations**. In the case of a proprietorship, the owner's equity in assets is reported by means of a single capital account. The balance in this account is the cumulative result of the owner's investments and withdrawals as well as past earnings and losses. In a partnership, capital accounts are established for each partner. Capital account balances summarize the investments and withdrawals and shares of past earnings and losses of each partner, and thus measure the partners' individual equities in the partnership assets.

In a corporation, the difference between assets and liabilities is referred to as **owners' equity, shareholders' equity,** or simply, **capital**. In presenting the owners' equity on the balance sheet, a distinction is made between the equity originating from the stockholders' investments, referred to as **contributed capital** or **paid-in capital**, and the equity originating from earnings, referred to as **retained earnings**.

The relationship and distinction between the amount of capital contributed or paid in by the owners of the corporation relative to the amount the company has earned and retained in the business is a significant one. Such disclosure helps creditors and investors assess the long-term ability of a company to internally finance its own operations. If the contributed capital of a corporation is large relative to the total owners' equity, it means the corporation has been financed primarily from external sources, usually from the sale of stock to investors. If the earned capital of a corporation is large relative to the total owners' equity, it means the company has been profitable in the past and has retained those earnings in the business to help finance its activities. This distinction between earned and contributed capital is not as important for a proprietorship or partnership because the owners of those types of businesses generally are also involved in their management and therefore are aware of how the company activities are being financed.

**Contributed Capital**    Contributed (or paid-in) capital is generally reported in two parts: (1) **capital stock** and (2) **additional paid-in capital**. The amount reported on the balance sheet as **capital stock** usually reflects the number of shares issued multiplied by the par value or stated value per share. When the stock does not have a par or stated value, capital stock is reported at the amount received on its original sale or at some other value as stipulated by law or assigned by the corporation's board of directors. When more than one class of stock has been issued, the stock of each class is reported separately.

**Additional paid-in capital** represents investments by stockholders in excess of the amounts assignable to capital stock. It may also reflect transactions other than the sale of stock, such as the acquisition of property as a result of a donation or the sale of treasury stock at more than cost. **Treasury stock** is stock that has been issued but subsequently reacquired by the corporation and is being held for possible future reissuance or retirement.

Additional paid-in capital balances are added to capital stock so that the total amount of contributed capital is reported on the balance sheet. Treasury stock is usually subtracted from the sum of contributed capital and retained earnings balances. Contributed capital is discussed in detail in Chapter 17.

**Retained Earnings**   The amount of undistributed earnings of past periods is reported as **retained earnings**. The total amount thus shown will probably not represent cash available for payment as dividends since past years' earnings will usually already have been reinvested in other assets. An excess of dividends and losses over earnings results in a negative retained earnings balance called a **deficit**. The balance of retained earnings is added to the contributed capital total in summarizing the stockholders' equity; a deficit is subtracted.

Portions of retained earnings are sometimes reported as restricted and unavailable as a basis for dividends. Restricted earnings may be designated as *appropriations*. Appropriations are sometimes made for such purposes as sinking funds, plant expansion, loss contingencies, and the reacquisition of capital stock. Often such appropriations are disclosed in a note rather than in the accounts. When appropriations have been made in the accounts, retained earnings on the balance sheet consists of an amount designated as appropriated and a balance designated as *unappropriated* or *free*. The term "reserve" should not generally be used to designate appropriations. Retained earnings are discussed in detail in Chapter 18.

The Owners' Equity section of the balance sheet of Techtronics Corporation is illustrated as follows:

| | | |
|---|---:|---:|
| Contributed capital: | | |
| Preferred stock, $50 par, 20,000 shares authorized, | | |
| 2,500 shares issued and outstanding .................. | $125,000 | |
| Common stock, $5 par, 100,000 shares authorized, | | |
| 50,000 shares issued and outstanding ................. | 250,000 | |
| Additional paid-in capital............................ | 170,000 | $545,000 |
| Retained earnings ....................................... | | 308,900 |
| Total owners' equity ..................................... | | $853,900 |

## Offsets on the Balance Sheet

As illustrated in the preceding discussion, a number of balance sheet items are frequently reported at gross amounts calling for the recognition of offset balances in arriving at proper valuations. Such offset balances are found in asset, liability, and owners' equity categories. In the case of assets, for example, an allowance for doubtful accounts is subtracted from the sum of the customer accounts in reporting the net amount estimated as collectible; accumulated depreciation is subtracted from the related buildings and equipment balances in reporting the costs of the assets still assignable to future revenues. In the case of liabilities, reacquired bonds or *treasury* bonds are subtracted from bonds issued in reporting the amount of bonds outstanding; a bond discount is subtracted from the face value of bonds outstanding in reporting the net amount of the debt. In the stockholders' equity section of the balance sheet, treasury stock is deducted in reporting total stockholders' equity.

The types of offsets described above, utilizing contra accounts, are required for proper reporting of particular balance sheet items. Offsets are improper, however, if applied to different asset and liability balances or to asset and owners' equity balances even when there is some relationship between the items. For example, a company may accumulate cash in a special fund to discharge certain tax liabilities; but as long as control of the cash is retained and the liabilities are still outstanding, the company should continue to report both the asset and the liabilities separately. Or a company may accumulate cash in a special fund for the redemption of preferred stock outstanding; but until the cash is applied to the reacquisition of the stock, the company must continue to report the asset as well as the owners' equity item. A company may have made advances to certain salespersons while at the same time reporting accrued amounts payable to others; but a net figure cannot be justified here, just as a net figure cannot be justified for the offset of trade receivables against trade payables.

The offset criteria came under scrutiny in the mid 1980s when a new standard for pension accounting was issued by the FASB. The FASB faced a major question concerning whether pension assets should be reported separately from pension liabilities or whether the past practice of allowing pension assets to be offset against pension liabilities should be continued. The Board elected to allow offsets of pension assets and liabilities, but also decided to add the topic of offsetting to its agenda.

## FORM OF THE BALANCE SHEET

The form of the balance sheet presentation varies in practice. Its form may be influenced by the nature and size of the business, by the character of the business properties, by requirements set by regulatory bodies, or by display preferences in presenting key relationships. The balance sheet is prepared in one of two basic forms: (1) the account form, with assets being reported on the left-hand side and liabilities and owners' equity on the right-hand side, or (2) the report form, with assets, liabilities, and owners' equity sections appearing in vertical arrangement.[14]

The order of asset and liability classifications may vary, but most businesses emphasize working capital position and liquidity, with assets and liabilities presented in the order of their liquidity. An exception to this order is generally found in the land, buildings, and equipment section where the more permanent assets with longer useful lives are listed first. The balance sheet for Techtronics Corporation reproduced on page 158 illustrates the account form reported in the order of liquidity. The balance sheet of IBM Corporation, reproduced in Appendix A, is an example of the report form. The categories used by individual companies vary widely; however, the basic format and structure remain the same.

In some industries, the investment in plant assets is so significant that these assets are placed first on the balance sheet. Also, the equity capital and long-term debt obtained to finance plant assets are listed before current liabilities. The utility industry is a good example of this situation. A balance sheet for the Southwestern Public Service Company is illustrated in Exhibit 5—2.

Balance sheets are generally presented in comparative form. With comparative reports for two or more dates, information is made available concerning the nature and trend of financial changes taking place within the periods between balance sheet dates. Currently, a minimum of two years of balance sheets and three years of income statements and cash flow statements are required by the SEC to be included in the annual report to shareholders.

## ADDITIONAL DISCLOSURE TO THE BALANCE SHEET

Regardless of which form of balance sheet is used, the basic statement does not provide all the information desired by users. Among other things, creditors and investors need to know what methods of accounting were used by the company to arrive at the balances in the accounts. The users often feel they need more information than just account titles and

---

[14]These two forms have been equally popular; however, the report form has been increasing in popularity. *Accounting Trends & Techniques* reported that in 1989, 404 of 600 companies used the report form and 195 the account form. *Accounting Trends & Techniques* (New York: AICPA, 1990), p. 87.

## Today's Balance-Sheet Tilt

The following is condensed from an article by Ray Groves, Co-Chief Executive of Ernst & Young, one of the six largest U.S. public accounting firms.

If there is a theme for the future for financial executives, public accountants, and the users of financial statements, it may be summed up in two words: complexity and volatility. A major reason for the increase in complexity and volatility is the shift that has been in process for some time and promises to accelerate—the shift in emphasis from the income statement to the balance sheet.

The FASB spent a good bit of its first decade developing a conceptual framework. This conceptual framework has a significant leaning toward the balance sheet. There is a feeling that any changes in valuation of assets and liabilities should be reflected in the financial statements, regardless of whether there has been a transaction that causes that change. The result is a movement toward more market-value accounting and reporting. In the view of some, the emphasis today on balance-sheet accounting recalls a similar emphasis of 50 years ago.

This balance-sheet tilt shows up in recent FASB statements on pensions and on income taxes. We are moving toward an era in which the income statement reflects not just operating results, but all changes in the values of assets and liabilities.

This shift in emphasis is not only from the income statement to the balance sheet; it is also away from supplemental disclosure off the balance sheet and toward integrated disclosure on the balance sheet. For example, automotive and other large manufacturing companies that have financial subsidiaries must now fully disclose the assets and liabilities of those subsidiaries on the parent balance sheets.

The theme of complexity and volatility is reflective of the society in which we live. It is an increasingly complex world in which money moves in different forms very quickly. Obviously, given this volatility, our financial reporting does have to mirror what is going on, whether it's in the economic environment or the political environment. What we need is realistic and useful financial information that is complete but not too complex, and subject to change but not too volatile. We have an accounting model that, with continual improvements, will achieve just that.

### Questions:

1. *How might the balance-sheet tilt affect the valuation of marketable securities owned by a company?*
2. *How can the balance sheet reflect changes in value without greatly affecting the income statement?*
3. *Does an emphasis on balance-sheet valuation automatically mean a change in the income statement?*

Source: Ray Groves, "What Today's Balance-Sheet Tilt Means," *Financial Executive,* September/October 1989: pp. 26-30.

amounts. Sometimes the additional information desired is descriptive and is reported in narrative form. In other cases, additional numerical data are reported.

There are at least three methods commonly used by companies to provide additional disclosure:

1. Parenthetical notations in the body of the statement.
2. Notes to the basic financial statements.
3. Separate schedules furnished by management that supplement the basic financial statements.

It is generally felt that readers of financial statements are more likely to see the additional information if it is included on the face of the financial statement in a paren-

### Techtronics Corporation
### Balance Sheet
### December 31, 1993

| Assets | | | Liabilities | | | |
|---|---|---|---|---|---|---|
| **Current assets:** | | | **Current liabilities:** | | | |
| Cash | $ 52,650 | | Notes payable | $ 75,000 | | |
| Marketable securities (reported at market; cost, 72,600) | 67,350 | | Accounts payable | 312,700 | | |
| | | | Accrued expenses | 46,200 | | |
| | | | Current portion of long-term debt | 62,000 | | |
| Receivables (net of allowance for doubtful accounts) | 363,700 | | Other current liabilities | 28,600 | | |
| | | | Total current liabilities | | $ 524,500 | |
| Inventories (reported at FIFO cost or market, whichever is lower) | 296,000 | | | | | |
| | | | **Noncurrent liabilities:** | | | |
| Prepaid expenses and other | 32,900 | | Notes payable | $ 75,000 | | |
| Total current assets | | $ 812,600 | Bonds payable | 165,000 | | |
| | | | Long-term lease obligations | 135,000 | | |
| **Noncurrent assets:** | | | Deferred income tax liability | 126,700 | | |
| Investments | $128,000 | | Other noncurrent liabilities | 72,500 | | |
| Land | 76,300 | | Total noncurrent liabilities | | 574,200 | |
| Buildings and equipment (net of accumulated depreciation of $228,600) | 732,900 | | Total liabilities | | $1,098,700 | |
| Intangible assets | 165,000 | | | | | |
| Other noncurrent assets | 37,800 | | **Owners' Equity** | | | |
| Total noncurrent assets | | 1,140,000 | **Contributed capital:** | | | |
| | | | Preferred stock, $50 par, 20,000 shares authorized, 2,500 shares issued and outstanding | $125,000 | | |
| | | | Common stock, $5 par, 100,000 shares authorized, 50,000 shares issued and outstanding | 250,000 | | |
| | | | Additional paid-in capital | 170,000 | $ 545,000 | |
| | | | Retained earnings | | 308,900 | |
| | | | Total owners' equity | | $ 853,900 | |
| Total assets | | $1,952,600 | Total liabilities and owners' equity | | $1,952,600 | |

thetical notation. However, if the data are lengthy or complex, it is generally better to provide the detail in notes that are recognized as being an integral part of the statements themselves. Unless specifically excluded, notes are covered by the auditor's opinion. In some instances, the notes include detailed schedules that provide additional information to the serious user. Several parenthetical notations are included in the balance sheet for Techtronics Corporation. For example, in current assets, there are parenthetical comments concerning valuation. In each case, the same data could have been disclosed in notes.

The following types of notes are typically included by management as support to the basic financial statements:

1. Summary of significant accounting policies.
2. Additional information (both numerical and descriptive) to support summary totals found on the financial statements, usually the balance sheet. This is the most common type of note used.

*Report*

**Exhibit 5—2     Southwestern Public Service Company—Balance Sheet**

## BALANCE SHEETS

*Southwestern Public Service Company*

|  | August 31, | |
|---|---|---|
|  | **1990** | 1989 |
|  | (In Thousands) | |

**ASSETS**

Utility Plant:

| | | |
|---|---|---|
| Utility plant in service (Note 5) | **$1,989,215** | $1,953,676 |
| Accumulated depreciation | **(604,397)** | (557,304) |
| Net plant in service | **1,384,818** | 1,396,372 |
| Construction work in progress | **16,409** | 13,711 |
| Net utility plant | **1,401,227** | 1,410,083 |
| Nonutility Property and Investments | **23,396** | 17,496 |

Current Assets:

| | | |
|---|---|---|
| Cash and temporary investments | **98,319** | 118,744 |
| Accounts receivable, net | **52,186** | 55,769 |
| Accrual for unbilled revenues | **29,746** | 30,647 |
| Materials and supplies, at average cost | **14,469** | 10,103 |
| Prepayments and other current assets | **3,481** | 4,058 |
| Total current assets | **198,201** | 219,321 |
| Deferred Debits | **36,015** | 34,411 |
| Total Assets | **$1,658,839** | $1,681,311 |

**CAPITALIZATION AND LIABILITIES**

Capitalization (See Consolidated Statements of Capitalization):

| | | |
|---|---|---|
| Common shareholders' equity | **$ 656,296** | $ 634,761 |
| Preferred stock — redemption not required | **72,680** | 72,680 |
| Preferred stock — redemption mandatory | **28,432** | 29,716 |
| Long-term debt | **519,674** | 563,992 |
| Total capitalization | **1,277,082** | 1,301,149 |

Current Liabilities:

| | | |
|---|---|---|
| Current maturities of long-term debt | **15,670** | 5,821 |
| Accounts and contracts payable | **7,924** | 6,730 |
| Liability for refunds to customers (Notes 2 and 3) | **22,217** | 17,224 |
| Interest accrued | **14,692** | 15,296 |
| Fuel and purchased power expense accrued | **29,803** | 39,462 |
| Taxes accrued | **14,512** | 14,248 |
| Dividends payable on common stock | **22,505** | 22,505 |
| Other current liabilities | **19,342** | 19,554 |
| Total current liabilities | **146,665** | 140,840 |

Deferred Credits:

| | | |
|---|---|---|
| Deferred income taxes | **220,933** | 209,772 |
| Unamortized investment tax credits | **7,305** | 20,945 |
| Other | **6,854** | 8,605 |
| Total deferred credits | **235,092** | 239,322 |

Commitments and Contingencies (Notes, 3, 7 and 10)

| | | |
|---|---|---|
| Total Capitalization and Liabilities | **$1,658,839** | $1,681,311 |

3. Information about items that are not reported on the basic statements because the items fail to meet the recognition criteria, but are still considered to be significant to users in their decision making.
4. Supplementary information required by the FASB or the SEC to fulfill the full-disclosure principle.

Each of these classifications is briefly discussed in the following paragraphs.

## Summary of Significant Accounting Policies

GAAP requires that information about the accounting principles and policies followed in arriving at the amounts in the financial statements be disclosed to the users. The Accounting Principles Board concluded in APB Opinion No. 22:

> . . . When financial statements are issued purporting to present fairly financial position, changes in financial position, and results of operations in accordance with generally accepted accounting principles, a description of all significant accounting policies of the reporting entity should be included as an integral part of the financial statements.[15]

The Board further stated:

> . . . In general, the disclosure should encompass important judgments as to appropriateness of principles relating to recognition of revenue and allocation of asset costs to current and future periods; in particular, it should encompass those accounting principles and methods that involve any of the following: (a) A selection from existing acceptable alternatives; (b) Principles and methods peculiar to the industry in which the reporting entity operates, even if such principles and methods are predominantly followed in that industry; (c) Unusual or innovative applications of generally accepted accounting principles (and, as applicable, of principles and methods peculiar to the industry in which the reporting entity operates).[16]

Examples of disclosures of accounting policies required by this opinion would include, among others, those relating to depreciation methods, amortization of intangible assets, inventory costing methods, the recognition of profit on long-term, construction-type contracts, and the recognition of revenue from leasing operations.[17]

The exact format for reporting the summary of accounting policies was not specified by the APB. However, the Board recommended such disclosure be included as the initial note or as a separate summary preceding the notes to the financial statements. The summary of significant accounting policies for IBM Corporation is presented in Appendix A.

## Additional Information to Support Summary Totals

In order to prepare a balance sheet that is brief enough to be understandable but complete enough to meet the needs of users, notes are sometimes added that provide either quantitative or narrative information to support the statement amounts. The IBM Corporation notes in Appendix A include a number of examples of this type of note, e.g., Marketable

---

[15]*Opinions of the Accounting Principles Board, No. 22,* "Disclosure of Accounting Policies" (New York: American Institute of Certified Public Accountants, 1972), par. 8.

[16]*Ibid.,* par. 12.

[17]*Ibid.,* par. 13.

Securities, Plant, Rental Machines and Other Property, and Long-Term Debt all provide additional numerical information to support the statement totals. Much of this detail is provided in response to specific disclosure requirements of either the SEC or the FASB. The specific format for the schedules is generally left to management's discretion. Some of the notes that support amounts in the financial statements are primarily descriptive in nature. Examples of this type in the IBM statements include notes on Retirement Plans, Postretirement Benefits, and the Stock Purchase Plan.

### Information About Items Not Included in Financial Statements

As discussed in Chapter 2, items included in the financial statements must meet certain recognition criteria. Even though an item might not meet the criteria for recognition in the statements, information concerning the item might be relevant to the users. Gain and loss contingencies are good examples of this type of item. A **gain contingency** exists when a company has a potential claim to receive assets, but the actual receipt of the assets is uncertain, pending the outcome of some future event, such as a possible favorable court settlement in a lawsuit. A **loss contingency** relates to a possible claim against the company that might require an outflow of assets. In Statement No. 5, the FASB indicated that if the incurrence of a loss is "reasonably possible," the contingency should be disclosed in the notes to the financial statements. The information provided should include as much data as possible to assist the user in evaluating the risk of the loss contingency.[18]

### Supplementary Information

The FASB and SEC both require supplementary information that must be reported in separate schedules. For example, the FASB requires the disclosure of quarterly information for certain companies. While the information in these notes is important to the users, it may not be covered by the auditors' opinion. A note that is not covered by the opinion should be clearly marked "unaudited."

### Subsequent Events

Although a balance sheet is prepared as of a given date, it is usually several weeks and sometimes even months after that date before the financial statements are issued and made available to external users. During this time, the accounts are analyzed, adjusting entries are prepared, and for many companies, an independent audit is completed. Events may take place during this "subsequent period" that have an impact upon the balance sheet and the other basic financial statements for the preceding year. Some of these events may even affect the amounts reported in the statements. These events are referred to in the accounting literature as subsequent events or post-balance sheet events.

---

[18]*Statement of Financial Accounting Standards No. 5.* Further discussion of loss contingencies and disclosure examples are presented in Chapter 15.

There are two different types of subsequent events that require consideration by management and evaluation by the independent auditor:[19]

1. Those that affect the amounts to be reported in one or more of the financial statements for the preceding accounting period.
2. Those that do not affect the amounts in the financial statements for the preceding accounting period, but that should be reported in the notes to these financial statements.

The first type of subsequent event usually provides additional information that affects the amounts included in the financial statements. The reported amounts in several accounts, such as Allowance for Doubtful Accounts, Warranty Liability, and Income Taxes Payable, reflect estimates of the expected value. These estimates are based on information available as of a given date. If a subsequent event provides information that shows that the conditions existing as of the balance sheet date were different from those assumed when making the estimate, a change in the amount to be reported in the financial statements is required.

To illustrate this type of event, assume that a month after the balance sheet date it is learned that a major customer has filed for bankruptcy. This information was not known as of the balance sheet date, and only ordinary provisions were made in determining the Allowance for Doubtful Accounts. In all likelihood, the customer was already in financial difficulty at the balance sheet date, but it was not general knowledge. The filing of bankruptcy reveals that the conditions at the balance sheet date were different than those assumed in preparing the statements, and a further adjustment to both the balance sheet and income statement is indicated.

The second type of subsequent event does not reveal a difference in the conditions as of the balance sheet date, but involves an event that is considered so significant that its disclosure is highly relevant to readers of the financial statements. These events will usually affect the subsequent year's financial statements and thus may affect decisions currently being made by users. Examples of such events include a casualty that destroys material portions of a company's assets, acquisition of a major subsidiary, sale of significant amounts of bonds or capital stock, and losses on receivables when the cause of the loss occurred subsequent to the balance sheet date. Information about this type of event is included in the notes to the financial statements and serves to notify the reader that the predictive value of the statements may be affected by the subsequent event. American Express Company reported this type of subsequent event in its 1987 financial statements as shown in Exhibit 5—3.

There are, of course, many business events that occur during this subsequent period that are related only to the subsequent year and therefore have no impact on the preceding year's financial statements.

The overall objective of note disclosure is clarification of the information presented in the financial statements. Disclosure requirements are so extensive that they cannot be completely discussed in any single chapter. Specific requirements will be noted as appropriate throughout the text.

## LIMITATIONS OF THE BALANCE SHEET

Notwithstanding its usefulness, the balance sheet has some serious limitations. External users often need to know a company's worth. The balance sheet, however, does not

[19]*AICPA Professional Standards*, AU Section 560, "Subsequent Events" (Chicago: Commerce Clearing House, 1985), pars. .02-.05.

## Exhibit 5—3    American Express Company—Disclosure of Subsequent Event

### 2 • Subsequent Event

In January 1988, Shearson Lehman Brothers Holdings Inc. (Holdings) completed its acquisition of The E. F. Hutton Group Inc. (Hutton). Pursuant to a tender offer commencing December 7, 1987, a wholly owned subsidiary of Holdings purchased 29.6 million shares of Hutton common stock at $29.25 per share in cash. The purchase was financed by borrowings of Shearson Lehman of approximately $800 million in senior subordinated debt at various interest rates and by working capital of Shearson Lehman of $66 million. Subsequently, approximately 3.3 million shares of Hutton common stock will be exchanged for approximately $96.5 million in face value of 10¾% Senior Subordinated Notes of Shearson Lehman. The combined company was renamed Shearson Lehman Hutton Inc.

The transaction will be accounted for as a purchase in January 1988. Accordingly, the acquisition is not reflected in the accompanying financial statements.

---

generally reflect the current values of a business. Instead, the entity's resources and obligations are usually shown at historical costs based on past transactions and events. The historical cost measurements represent market values existing at the dates the transactions or events occurred. However, when the prices of specific assets increase significantly after the acquisition date, as has certainly been the case recently in the United States, then the balance sheet numbers are not relevant for evaluating a company's current worth.

A related problem with the balance sheet is the instability of the dollar, the standard accounting measuring unit in the United States. Because of general price changes in the economy, the dollar does not maintain a constant purchasing power. Yet the historical costs of resources and equities shown on the balance sheet are not adjusted for changes in the purchasing power of the measuring unit. The result is a balance sheet that reflects assets, liabilities, and equities in terms of unequal purchasing power units. Some elements, for example, may be stated in terms of 1960 dollars and some in terms of current-year dollars. The variations in purchasing power of the amounts reported in the balance sheet make comparisons among companies, and even within a single company, less meaningful.

An additional limitation of the balance sheet, also related to the need for comparability, is that all companies do not classify and report all like items similarly. For example, titles and account classifications vary; some companies provide considerably more detail than others; and some companies with apparently similar transactions report them differently. Such differences make comparisons difficult and diminish the potential value of balance sheet analysis.

The balance sheet may be considered deficient in another respect. Due primarily to measurement problems, some entity resources and obligations are not reported on the balance sheet. For example, the employees of a company may be one of its most valuable resources; yet, they are not shown on the balance sheet because their future service potentials are not measurable in monetary terms. Similarly, a company's potential liability for polluting the air would not normally be shown on its balance sheet. The assumptions of the traditional accounting model identified in Chapter 2, specifically the requirements of arm's-length transactions or events measurable in monetary terms, add to the objectivity of balance sheet disclosures but at the same time cause some information to be omitted that is likely to be relevant to certain users' decisions.

One author, reflecting on these limitations, wrote the following:

> The current balance sheet published by most corporations is a pathetic financial representation of a company's real resources and obligations. It is a dumping ground for dangling debit and credit entries and a listing of dollar values determined by different, often outmoded, accounting concepts. Users find that the face of such statements often excludes more relevant data than it includes.[20]

This dim view of the balance sheet is not shared by many accountants and users of financial statements. The balance sheet is an important statement for investors and creditors. While its limitations must be understood, it can still provide a user with valuable information for decisions.

The conceptual framework established by the FASB stresses the objective of usefulness of accounting information. During the past few years, the Board has considered several issues that directly affect the balance sheet, using the conceptual framework as a guide in the development of new standards. In some instances, the new standards have a direct impact on the amounts reported on the balance sheet. Notable examples include pensions, receivables with right of return, deferred income tax accounting, and interest capitalization. In other instances, the impact has been on required disclosure in notes, such as the requirement for some companies to disclose segment data and off-balance-sheet financing arrangements. These and other examples will be discussed throughout the text.

[20]David E. Hawkins, "Towards the New Balance Sheet," *Harvard Business Review*, November-December 1984, p. 156.

## KEY TERMS

Account form [of balance sheet] 156
Additional paid-in capital 154
Assets 146
Balance sheet 145
Callable obligation 150
Capital stock 154
Contingent liabilities 153
Contributed capital 154
Current assets 147
Current liabilities 149

Deferred income tax assets 152
Deferred income tax liability 153
Deficit 155
Liabilities 146
Liquidity 145
Net assets 146
Normal operating cycle 147
Objective acceleration clause 150
Owners' equity 146

Paid-in capital 154
Post-balance sheet events 161
Report form [of balance sheet] 156
Retained earnings 154
Solvency 145
Subjective acceleration clause 150
Subsequent events 161
Treasury stock 154
Working capital 147

## QUESTIONS

1. In what way is the balance sheet useful to decision makers?
2. What three elements are contained in the balance sheet?
3. What are the major classifications of (a) assets, (b) liabilities, and (c) owners' equity? Indicate the nature of the items reported within each major classification.
4. (a) Why is the distinction between current assets/liabilities and noncurrent assets/liabilities considered to be important? (b) What arguments are there for not making a distinction?

5. What criteria are generally used (a) in classifying assets as current or noncurrent? (b) in classifying liabilities as current or noncurrent?
6. (a) What is a subjective acceleration clause? (b) An objective acceleration clause? (c) How do these clauses in debt instruments affect the classification of a liability?
7. Indicate under what circumstances each of the following can be considered noncurrent: (a) cash (b) receivables.

8. Distinguish between the following: (a) contingent liabilities and estimated liabilities (b) appropriated retained earnings and unappropriated retained earnings.
9. Under what circumstances may offset balances be properly recognized on the balance sheet?
10. What are the major types of notes attached to the financial statements?
11. Under what circumstances might a parenthetical notation on the balance sheet be preferred to a note?
12. What are some examples of supplementary information included in the notes to financial statements?
13. Under what circumstances does a subsequent event lead to a journal entry for the previous reporting period?

---

## DISCUSSION CASES

### Case 5—1 (What do the figures mean?)

Listed below are some of the largest corporations in the world.

| Company Name | Country | (in millions of U.S. dollars) | | |
| --- | --- | --- | --- | --- |
| | | Market Value | Total Assets | Net Income |
| Nippon Telegraph and Telephone (telecommunications) | Japan | 165,032 | 82,953 | 1,738  94.96 |
| Dai-Ichi Kangyo Bank (banking) | Japan | 66,558 | 375,390 | 1,096  60.73 |
| Toyota Motor Corp. (automobiles) | Japan | 54,553 | 41,156 | 2,319 |
| Tokyo Electric Power (utilities) | Japan | 54,847 | 78,907 | 936 |
| Royal Dutch/Shell (energy) | Netherlands | 54,706 | 85,734 | 5,237 |
| International Business Machines (computers) | U.S. | 71,822 | 73,037 | 5,491 |
| General Motors (automobiles) | U.S. | 30,852 | 163,820 | 4,632 |
| Exxon (energy) | U.S. | 56,703 | 74,293 | 5,260 |
| American Telephone and Telegraph (telecommunications) | U.S. | 30,868 | 35,152 | -1,669 |
| Citicorp (banking) | U.S. | 8,256 | 207,666 | 1,698 |

Sources: *Forbes,* May 1, 1989, and *Forbes,* July 24, 1989.

As an analyst for a securities broker, you are asked the following questions concerning some of the figures:

1. Nippon Telegraph and Telephone has total assets of $83 billion, but a stock market value of $165 billion. How can a company be worth more than its total assets?
2. Citicorp and Dai-Ichi Kangyo Bank have the highest total assets on the list and yet their net incomes are exceeded by many of the other companies. Why do you think this is?
3. The price/earnings ratio, often called the PE ratio, is defined as: market price per share ÷ earnings per share. Alternatively, the PE ratio can be computed as: total market value ÷ net income. Compute the PE ratios for the companies listed above. What factors do you think determine PE ratios?

## Case 5—2  (We've got you now!)

The Piedmont Computer Company has brought legal action against ATC Corporation for alleged monopolistic practices in the development of software. The claim has been pending for two years, with both sides accumulating evidence to support their positions. The case is now ready for trial. ATC Corporation has offered to settle out of court for $500,000, but Piedmont is asking for $5,000,000. Piedmont's attorneys feel an award of $2,500,000 from the court is very likely.

If financial statements must be issued prior to the court action, how should Piedmont reflect this contingent claim? Support your decision where possible from the conceptual framework.

## Case 5—3  (But what is our liability?)

The Ditka Engineering Co. has signed a third-party loan guarantee for Liberty Company. The loan is from the National Bank of Illinois for $500,000. Liberty has recently filed for bankruptcy, and it is estimated by the company's auditors that creditors can expect to receive no more than 40% of their claims from Liberty. The treasurer of Ditka feels that because of the high uncertainty of final settlement, a liability should be recorded for the entire $500,000. The chief accountant, on the other hand, feels the 40% collection figure is reasonable and proposes that a $300,000 liability be recorded. The president of Ditka does not think a reasonable estimate can be made at this time, and proposes that nothing be accrued for the contingent liability, but that a note be added to the financial statements explaining the situation.

As an independent outside auditor, what position would you take? Why?

## Case 5—4  (Aren't the financial statements enough?)

Excello Corporation's basic financial statements for the year just ended have been prepared in accordance with GAAP. During the current year, management changed the accounting method for computing depreciation; a major competitor constructed a new plant in the area; three separate lawsuits were brought against the corporation that are not expected to be settled for two years or more; and the corporation continued to use an acceptable revenue recognition principle that differs from that used by most other companies in the industry. Also, after the end of the year, but before the statements were issued, Excello issued additional shares of common stock.

Excello has recently applied for a large bank loan, and the bank has requested a copy of the financial statements. The auditors for Excello have prepared several notes, some quite lengthy, to accompany the financial statements, but Excello's management does not think the loan officer at the bank would understand them and therefore submits the statements without the notes. The bank accepts the statements as submitted.

Which of the events described above should be included in notes to the financial statements? Do you think it is acceptable to delete notes when submitting financial statements to third parties? Substantiate your position.

## Case 5—5  (Which company is which?)

On the next page are summaries of the balance sheets of five companies. The amounts are all stated as a percentage of total assets. The five companies are:

BankAmerica, a large bank.
Kelly Services, a firm that provides temporary employees.
Sears (just the merchandise group).
Sears (consolidated, including the financial subsidiaries).
Consolidated Edison, a utility serving New York City.

1. Match each of the balance sheet summaries (A through E) with the appropriate company. Justify your choices.
2. How does consolidation improve the usefulness of financial statements? What are some disadvantages of consolidated financial statements?

| | A | B | C | D | E |
|---|---|---|---|---|---|
| Receivables ................................ | 36.8 | 61.1 | 41.5 | 69.1 | 3.9 |
| Inventories .................................. | 4.8 | 15.7 | 0.0 | 0.0 | 3.3 |
| Other current assets ....................... | 9.7 | 4.9 | 48.0 | 25.0 | 4.6 |
| Land, buildings, and equipment ............. | 6.6 | 15.7 | 8.7 | 1.9 | 84.5 |
| Other long-term assets..................... | 42.1 | 2.6 | 1.8 | 4.0 | 3.7 |
| Short-term payables ....................... | 9.6 | 15.3 | 29.6 | 1.3 | 4.2 |
| Other current liabilities..................... | 37.0 | 26.2 | 0.0 | 89.3 | 3.2 |
| Long-term liabilities ....................... | 35.4 | 35.7 | 0.0 | 6.5 | 41.9 |
| Equity ..................................... | 18.0 | 22.8 | 70.4 | 2.9 | 50.7 |

## Case 5—6  (How can we live with debt covenant requirements?)

Bohr Company has a credit agreement with a syndicate of banks. In order to impose some limitations on Bohr's financial riskiness, the credit agreement requires Bohr to maintain a current ratio (current assets ÷ current liabilities) of at least 1.4 and a debt ratio (total liabilities ÷ total assets) of .55 or less. The following summary data reflect a projection of Bohr's balance sheet for the coming year-end:

| | |
|---|---|
| Current assets ............................................... | $1,200,000 |
| Long-term assets ............................................. | 1,800,000 |
| Current liabilities ............................................. | 900,000 |
| Long-term liabilities ........................................... | 800,000 |
| Equity ....................................................... | 1,300,000 |

The following information has also been prepared:

(a) If Bohr were to use FIFO instead of LIFO for inventory valuation, ending inventory would increase by $50,000.

(b) The amounts listed for long-term assets and liabilities include the anticipated purchase (and associated mortgage payable) of a building costing $100,000. Bohr can lease the building instead; the lease would qualify for treatment as an operating lease.

(c) The projected amounts include a planned declaration of cash dividends totaling $40,000 to be paid next year. Bohr has consistently paid dividends of equivalent amounts.

As a consultant to Bohr, you are asked to respond to the following two questions:

1. What steps can Bohr take to avoid violating the current-ratio constraint?
2. What steps can Bohr take to avoid violating the debt-ratio constraint?

Of the steps that you propose, which ones do you think the banks had in mind when they imposed the loan covenants? If you had assisted the banks in drawing up the loan covenants, how would you have written them differently to avoid unintended consequences?

## EXERCISES

### Exercise 5—1  (Balance sheet classification)

A balance sheet contains the following classifications:

(a) Current assets
(b) Investments
(c) Land, buildings, and equipment
(d) Intangible assets
(e) Other noncurrent assets
(f) Current liabilities

(g) Long-term debt
(h) Other noncurrent liabilities
(i) Capital stock
(j) Additional paid-in capital
(k) Retained earnings

Indicate by letter how each of the following accounts would be classified. Place a minus sign ( − ) for all accounts representing offset or contra balances.

1. Discount on Bonds Payable
2. Stock of Subsidiary Corporation
3. 12% Bonds Payable (due in six months)
4. U.S. Treasury Notes
5. Income Tax Payable
6. Sales Tax Payable
7. Estimated Claims Under Warranties for Service and Replacements
8. Par Value of Stock Issued and Outstanding
9. Unearned Rent Revenue (six months in advance)
10. Long-Term Advances to Officers
11. Interest Receivable
12. Preferred Stock Retirement Fund
13. Trademarks
14. Allowance for Doubtful Accounts
15. Dividends Payable
16. Accumulated Depreciation
17. Petty Cash Fund
18. Prepaid Rent
19. Prepaid Insurance
20. Organization Costs

## Exercise 5—2    (Balance sheet classification)

State how each of the following accounts should be classified on the balance sheet:

(a) Treasury Stock
(b) Retained Earnings
(c) Vacation Pay Payable
(d) Retained Earnings Appropriated for Loss Contingencies
(e) Allowance for Doubtful Accounts
(f) Liability for Pension Payments
(g) Marketable Securities
(h) Paid-In Capital From Sale of Stock at More Than Stated Value
(i) Leasehold Improvements
(j) Goodwill
(k) Receivables—U.S. Government Contracts
(l) Advances to Salespersons
(m) Premium on Bonds Payable
(n) Inventory
(o) Patents
(p) Unclaimed Payroll Checks
(q) Employees' Income Tax Payable
(r) Subscription Revenue Received in Advance
(s) Interest Payable
(t) Deferred Income Tax Asset
(u) Tools
(v) Deferred Income Tax Liability

## Exercise 5—3    (Asset definition)

Using the definition of an asset from FASB Concepts Statement No. 6, indicate whether each of the following should be listed as an asset by DeBroglie Company:

(a) DeBroglie has legal title to a silver mine in a remote location. Historically, the mine has yielded over $100 million in silver. Engineering estimates suggest that no further minerals are economically extractable from the mine.
(b) DeBroglie is currently negotiating the purchase of an oil field with proven oil reserves totaling 2 billion barrels.
(c) DeBroglie employs a team of five geologists who are widely recognized as the worldwide leaders in their field.
(d) DeBroglie claims ownership of a large piece of real estate in a foreign country. The real estate has a current market value of over $650 million. The country expropriated the land 35 years ago, and no representative of DeBroglie has been allowed on the property since.
(e) Several years ago, DeBroglie purchased a large meteor crater on the advice of a geologist who had developed a theory claiming that vast deposits of iron ore lay underneath the crater. The crater has no other economic use. No ore has been found and the geologist's theory is not generally accepted.

### Exercise 5—4   (Liability definition)

Using the definition of a liability from FASB Concepts Statement No. 6, indicate whether each of the following should be listed as a liability by Pauli Company:

(a) Pauli was involved in a highly publicized lawsuit last year. Pauli lost and was ordered to pay damages of $125 million. The payment has been made.

(b) In exchange for television advertising services that Pauli received last month, Pauli is obligated to provide the television station with building maintenance service for the next four months.

(c) Pauli contractually guarantees to replace any of its stain-resistant carpets if they are stained and can't be cleaned.

(d) Pauli estimates that its total payroll for the coming year will exceed $35 million.

(e) In the past, Pauli has suffered frequent vandalism at its storage warehouses. Pauli estimates that losses due to vandalism during the coming year will total $3 million.

### Exercise 5—5   (Balance sheet preparation—account form)

From the following list of accounts, prepare a balance sheet in account form showing all balance sheet items properly classified. (No monetary amounts are to be recognized.)

Accounts Payable
Accounts Receivable
Accumulated Depreciation—Buildings
Accumulated Depreciation—Equipment
Advertising Expense
Allowance for Decline in Value of Marketable Securities
Allowance for Doubtful Accounts
Bonds Payable
Buildings
Cash
Common Stock
Cost of Goods Sold
Deferred Income Tax Liability
Depreciation Expense—Buildings
Dividends
Doubtful Accounts Expense
Equipment
Estimated Warranty Expense Payable (current)
Gain on Sale of Land
Gain on Sale of Marketable Securities
Goodwill
Income Summary
Income Tax Expense
Income Tax Payable

Interest Receivable
Interest Revenue
Inventory
Investment in Bonds
Land
Loss on Purchase Commitments
Marketable Securities
Miscellaneous General Expense
Notes Payable
Paid-In Capital From Sale of Common Stock at More Than Stated Value
Paid-In Capital From Sale of Treasury Stock
Patents
Pension Fund
Premium on Bonds Payable
Prepaid Insurance
Property Tax Expense
Purchases
Purchase Discounts
Retained Earnings
Salaries Payable
Sales
Sales Salaries
Travel Expense

### Exercise 5—6   (Computation of working capital)

From the following data, compute the working capital for Benson Equipment Co. at December 31, 1993:

| | |
|---|---:|
| Cash in general checking account | $ 10,000 |
| Cash in fund to be used to retire bonds in 1997 | 50,000 |
| Cash held to pay sales taxes | 18,000 |
| Notes receivable—due February 1995 | 100,000 |
| Trade accounts receivable | 125,000 |
| Inventory | 75,000 |

| | |
|---|---:|
| Prepaid insurance—for 1994 and 1995 | $ 15,000 |
| Vacant land held as investment | 300,000 |
| Used equipment to be sold | 25,000 |
| Deferred tax asset—to be recovered in 1995 | 10,000 |
| Trade accounts payable | 80,000 |
| Note payable July 1994 | 33,000 |
| Note payable January 1995 | 10,000 |
| Bonds payable—maturity date 1997 | 210,000 |
| Salaries payable | 20,000 |
| Sales tax payable | 23,000 |
| Goodwill | 37,000 |

## Exercise 5—7   (Preparation of corrected balance sheet)

The following balance sheet was prepared for Kelvin Company as of December 31, 1993:

**Kelvin Company**
**Balance Sheet**
**December 31, 1993**

| Assets | | Liabilities and Owners' Equity | |
|---|---:|---|---:|
| **Current assets:** | | **Current liabilities:** | |
| Cash | $ 12,500 | Accounts payable | $ 3,750 |
| Marketable securities | 5,000 | Other current liabilities | 2,000 |
| Accounts receivable, net | 21,350 | Total current liabilities | $ 5,750 |
| Inventory | 35,000 | | |
| Other current assets | 14,200 | Long-term liabilities | $ 32,750 |
| Total current assets | $ 88,050 | Total liabilities | $ 38,500 |
| **Noncurrent assets:** | | | |
| Land, buildings, and equipment, | | **Owners' equity:** | |
| net | $ 64,800 | Common stock | $ 50,000 |
| Treasury stock | 4,500 | Retained earnings | 82,450 |
| Other noncurrent assets | 13,600 | Total owners' equity | $132,450 |
| Total noncurrent assets | $ 82,900 | | |
| Total assets | $170,950 | Total liabilities and owners' equity | $170,950 |

The following additional information relates to the December 31, 1993, balance sheet:

(a)  Cash includes $4,000 that has been restricted to the purchase of manufacturing equipment (a noncurrent asset).

(b)  Marketable securities include $2,750 of stock that was purchased in order to give the company significant ownership and a seat on the board of directors of a major supplier.

(c)  Other current assets include a $1,500 advance to the president of the company. No due date has been set.

(d)  Long-term liabilities include bonds payable of $10,000. Of this amount, $1,500 represents bonds scheduled to be redeemed in 1994.

(e)  Long-term liabilities also include a $7,000 bank loan. On May 15, the loan will become due on demand.

(f)  Retained earnings in the amount of $4,650 has been restricted and is unavailable for dividends.

(g)  On December 21, dividends in the amount of $15,000 were declared to be paid to shareholders of record on January 25. These dividends have not been reflected in the financial statements.

(h)  Cash in the amount of $19,000 has been placed in a restricted fund for the redemption of preferred stock in 1994. Both the cash and the stock have been removed from the balance sheet.

(i)  Land, buildings, and equipment includes land costing $6,500 that is being held for investment purposes and that is scheduled to be sold in 1994.

Based on the information provided, prepare a corrected balance sheet as of December 31, 1993.

### Exercise 5—8   (Balance sheet relationships)

For each of the items, (a) through (o) on the Crosby and Company Inc. balance sheet, indicate the amount that should appear on the balance sheet.

**Crosby and Company Inc.**
**Consolidated Balance Sheet**
**December 31, 1993**

*[handwritten: 437078]*

#### Assets

| | | |
|---|---:|---:|
| Current assets: | | |
| Cash | | $ (a) *13185* |
| Marketable securities | | 25,153 |
| Accounts and notes receivable | $ (b) *17535* | |
| Allowance for doubtful accounts and notes receivable | 9,622 | 165,693 |
| Inventories | | 235,813 |
| Other current assets | | 10,419 |
| Total current assets | | $ (c) *450263* |
| Noncurrent assets: | | |
| Land, buildings, and equipment, | $ (d) *771604* | |
| Accumulated depreciation | 352,186 | $419,418 |
| Other noncurrent assets | | 15,631 |
| Total noncurrent assets | | 435,049 |
| Total assets | | $885,312 |

#### Liabilities and Owners' Equity

| | | |
|---|---:|---:|
| Current liabilities: | | |
| Accounts payable | | $ 98,670 |
| Payable to banks | | 22,858 |
| Income taxes payable | | 8,328 |
| Current installments of long-term debt | | (e) *5720* |
| Accrued expenses | | 6,610 |
| Total current liabilities | | $142,186 |
| Noncurrent liabilities: | | |
| Long-term debt | | $ (f) *131754* |
| Deferred income tax liability | | 40,406 |
| Minority interest in subsidiaries | | 3,309 |
| Total noncurrent liabilities | | (g) *175469* |
| Total liabilities | | $317,655 |
| Contributed Capital: | | |
| Preferred stock, no par value (authorized 1,618 shares; issued 1,115 shares) | | $ 16,596 |
| Common stock, $1 par value per share (authorized 60,000 shares, issued 25,939 shares) | *25939* | $ (h) |
| Additional paid-in capital | | (i) *47066* (j) *73005* |
| Total contributed capital | | $ (k) *89601* |
| Retained earnings: | | |
| Appropriated | $100,000 | |
| Unappropriated | (l) *404744* | 504,744 |
| Total contributed capital and retained earnings | | $ (m) *594345* |
| Less treasury stock, at cost (1,236 shares) | | 26,688 |
| Total owner's equity | | (n) *567657* |
| Total liabilities and owners' equity | | $ (o) *885312* |

### Exercise 5—9   (Balance sheet schedules)

In its annual report to stockholders, Crantz Inc. presents a condensed balance sheet with detailed data provided in supplementary schedules. From the adjusted trial balance of Crantz, prepare the following schedules, properly classifying all accounts as to balance sheet categories:

(a) Current assets
(b) Land, buildings, and equipment
(c) Intangible assets
(d) Total assets

(e) Current liabilities
(f) Noncurrent liabilities
(g) Owners' equity
(h) Total liabilities and owners' equity

**Crantz Inc.**
**Adjusted Trial Balance**
**December 31, 1993**

|  | Debit | Credit |
|---|---|---|
| Cash | $ 28,900 | |
| Marketable Securities—at cost (market, $23,400) | 20,000 | |
| Notes Receivable—trade debtors | 18,000 | |
| Accrued Interest on Notes Receivable | 1,800 | |
| Accounts Receivable | 88,400 | |
| Allowance for Doubtful Accounts | | $ 4,300 |
| Inventory | 56,900 | |
| Prepaid Expenses | 6,100 | |
| Accounts Payable | | 26,500 |
| Notes Payable—trade creditors | | 16,000 |
| Accrued Interest on Notes Payable | | 800 |
| Land | 80,000 | |
| Buildings | 170,000 | |
| Accumulated Depreciation—Buildings | | 34,000 |
| Equipment | 48,000 | |
| Accumulated Depreciation—Equipment | | 7,600 |
| Patents | 15,000 | |
| Franchises | 10,000 | |
| Bonds Payable, 8%—issue 1 (mature 12/31/95) | | 50,000 |
| Bonds Payable, 12%—issue 2 (mature 12/31/99) | | 100,000 |
| Accrued Interest on Bonds Payable | | 8,000 |
| Premium on Bonds Payable—issue 1 | | 1,500 |
| Discount on Bonds Payable—issue 2 | 10,500 | |
| Mortgage Payable | | 57,500 |
| Accrued Interest on Mortgage Payable | | 2,160 |
| Capital Stock, par value $25, 10,000 shares authorized, 4,000 shares issued | | 100,000 |
| Additional Paid-In Capital | | 16,800 |
| Retained Earnings Appropriated for Bond Redemption | | 35,000 |
| Unappropriated Retained Earnings | | 104,440 |
| Treasury Stock—at cost (500 shares) | 11,000 | |
|  | $564,600 | $564,600 |

### Exercise 5—10   (Classification of subsequent events)

The following events occurred after the end of the company's fiscal year, but before the annual audit was completed. Classify each event as to its impact on the financial statements, i.e., (1) reported by changing the amounts in the financial statements, (2) reported in notes to the financial statements, (3) does not require reporting. Include support for your classification.

(a) Major customer went bankrupt due to a deteriorating financial condition.
(b) Company sustained extensive hurricane damage to one of its plants.
(c) Company settled a major lawsuit that had been pending for two years.
(d) Increasing U.S. trade deficit may have impact on company's overseas sales.
(e) Company sold a large block of preferred stock.
(f) Preparation of current year's income tax return disclosed an additional $25,000 is due on last year's return.
(g) Company's controller resigned and was replaced by an audit manager from the company's audit firm.

## Exercise 5—11   (Reporting financial information)

For each of the items below, indicate whether the item should be reflected in the 1993 financial statements for Rutherford Company. If the item should be reflected, indicate whether it should be reported in the financial statements themselves or by note disclosure.

(a) During 1993, the company had a gain on the sale of manufacturing assets.
(b) As of December 31, 1993, the company was in violation of certain loan covenants. The violation does not cause the loans to be callable immediately, but does increase the interest charge by 1.5%.
(c) The company uses straight-line depreciation for all tangible, long-term assets.
(d) As of December 31, 1993, accounts receivable in the amount of $6.7 million are estimated to be uncollectible.
(e) The Environmental Protection Agency is investigating the company's procedures for disposing of toxic waste. Outside consultants have estimated that the company may be liable for fines of up to $8 million.
(f) The company's reported Provision for Income Taxes includes $3.6 million in current taxes and $7.3 million in deferred taxes.
(g) During 1993, a long-term insurance agreement was signed. The company paid five years' insurance premiums in advance.
(h) As of December 31, 1993, the company holds $11.2 million of its own stock that it purchased in the open market and is holding for possible reissuance.
(i) During 1993, the company hired three prominent research chemists away from its chief competitor.
(j) Reported long-term debt is composed of senior subordinated debentures, convertible debentures, junior subordinated debentures, and capital lease obligations.
(k) Early in 1994, a significant drop in raw materials prices caused the company's stock price to rise in anticipation of sharply increased profits for the year.

## Exercise 5—12   (Preparation of notes to financial statements)

The following information was used to prepare the financial statements for Delta Chemical Company. Prepare the necessary notes to accompany the statements.

Delta uses the LIFO inventory method on its financial statements. If the FIFO method were used, the ending inventory balance would be reduced by $50,000, and net income for the year would be reduced by $35,000 after taxes. Delta depreciates its equipment using the straight-line method. Revenue is generally recognized when inventory is shipped unless it is sold on a consignment basis. The current value of the equipment is $525,000 as contrasted to its depreciated cost of $375,000.

Delta has borrowed $350,000 on 10-year notes at 14% interest. The notes are due on July 1, 2003. Delta's equipment has been pledged as collateral for the loan. The terms of the note prohibit additional long-term borrowing without the express permission of the holder of the notes. Delta is planning to request such permission during the next fiscal year.

The board of directors of Delta is currently discussing a merger with another chemical company. No public announcement has yet been made, but it is anticipated that additional shares of stock will be issued as part of the merger. Delta's balance sheet will report receivables of $126,000. Included in this figure is a $25,000 advance to the president of Delta, $30,000 of notes receivable from customers, $10,000 in advances to sales representatives, and $70,000 of accounts receivable from customers. The reported balance reflects a deduction for anticipated collection losses.

# PROBLEMS

## Problem 5—1   (Computing balance sheet components)

Crist Equipment Inc. furnishes you with the following list of accounts:

| | | | |
|---|---:|---|---:|
| Accounts Payable | $ 66,000 | Investment in Siebert Co. Stock | |
| Accounts Receivable | 40,000 | (current marketable securities) | $21,000 |
| Accumulated Depreciation | 44,000 | Paid-In Capital in Excess of Par | 42,500 |
| Advances to Salespersons | 5,000 | Premium on Bonds Payable | 6,000 |
| Advertising Expense | 72,000 | Prepaid Insurance Expense | 3,000 |
| Allowance for Doubtful Accounts | 10,000 | Rent Revenue | 37,000 |
| Bonds Payable | 70,000 | Rent Revenue Received in Advance | |
| Cash | 22,000 | (4 months) | 8,000 |
| Certificates of Deposit | 21,000 | Retained Earnings | 40,000 |
| Common Stock (par) | 150,000 | Retained Earnings Appropriated for | |
| Deferred Income Tax Liability | 53,000 | Loss Contingencies | 30,000 |
| Equipment | 215,500 | Taxes Payable | 10,000 |
| Inventory | 49,000 | Tools | 68,000 |
| Investment in Kaine Oil Co. Stock | | | |
| (40% of outstanding stock owned | | | |
| for control purposes) | 85,000 | | |

**Instructions:**  From the above list of accounts, determine working capital, total assets, total liabilities, and owners' equity per share of stock (75,000 shares outstanding).

## Problem 5—2   (Classified balance sheet)

Below is a list of account titles and balances for Johnson Investment Corporation as of January 31, 1993.

| | | | |
|---|---:|---|---:|
| Accounts Payable | $ 75,900 | Interest Payable | $  3,050 |
| Accounts Receivable | 116,000 | Interest Receivable | 900 |
| Accumulated Depreciation— | | Inventory | 184,300 |
| Buildings | 151,700 | Investments in Undeveloped | |
| Accumulated Depreciation— | | Properties | 197,000 |
| Machinery and Equipment | 27,000 | Land | 188,000 |
| Additional Paid-In Capital— | | Machinery and Equipment | 145,000 |
| Common Stock | 62,000 | Miscellaneous Supplies Inventory | 6,200 |
| Allowance for Doubtful Notes and | | Notes Payable (current) | 58,260 |
| Accounts Receivable | 5,800 | Notes Payable (due in 1998) | 38,000 |
| Buildings | 380,000 | Notes Receivable (current) | 22,470 |
| Cash in Banks | 8,880 | Preferred Stock, $5 par | 320,000 |
| Cash on Hand | 97,300 | Prepaid Insurance | 3,500 |
| Cash Fund for Stock Redemption | 17,500 | Retained Earnings (debit balance) | 11,740 |
| Claim for Income Tax Refund | 4,500 | Salaries and Wages Payable | 9,400 |
| Common Stock, $20 par | 650,000 | Temporary Investment in | |
| Employees' Income Tax Payable | 4,780 | Marketable Securities | 146,800 |
| Income Taxes Payable | 24,200 | | |

**Instructions:**  Prepare a properly classified balance sheet in report form.

## Problem 5—3   (Classified balance sheet—account form including notes)

Adjusted account balances and supplemental information for Brockbank Research Corp. as of December 31, 1993, are as follows:

| | | | |
|---|---:|---|---:|
| Accounts Payable | $ 32,160 | Cash Fund for Bond Retirement | $3,600 |
| Accounts Receivable—Trade | 57,731 | Common Stock | 175,000 |
| Accumulated Depreciation— | | Deferred Income Tax Liability | 45,000 |
| Leasehold Improvements and | | Dividends Payable | 37,500 |
| Equipment | 579,472 | Franchises | 12,150 |
| Additional Paid-In Capital | 125,000 | Leasehold Improvements | 65,800 |
| Furniture, Fixtures, and Store | | 7 1/2%-12% Mortgage Notes | 200,000 |
| Equipment | 769,000 | Notes Payable—Banks (due in | |
| Inventory | 201,620 | 1994) | 17,000 |
| Investment in Unconsolidated | | Notes Payable—Trade | 63,540 |
| Subsidiary | 80,000 | Patent Licenses | 57,402 |
| Insurance Claims Receivable | 120,000 | Prepaid Insurance | 5,500 |
| Land | 6,000 | Profit Sharing, Payroll, | |
| Allowance for Doubtful Accounts | 1,731 | and Vacation Payable | 40,000 |
| Automobiles | 132,800 | Retained Earnings | 225,800 |
| Cash | 30,600 | Tax Receivable—In Litigation | 13,000 |

Supplemental information:

(a) Depreciation is provided by the straight-line method over the estimated useful lives of the assets.

(b) Common stock is $5 par, and 35,000 of the 100,000 authorized shares were issued and are outstanding.

(c) The cost of an exclusive franchise to import a foreign company's ball bearings and a related patent license are being amortized on the straight-line method over their remaining lives: franchise, 10 years; patents, 15 years.

(d) Inventories are stated at the lower of cost or market; cost was determined by the specific identification method.

(e) Insurance claims based on the opinion of an independent insurance adjustor are for property damages at the central warehouse. These claims are estimated to be ⅔ collectible in the following year and ⅓ collectible thereafter.

(f) The company leases all of its buildings from various lessors. Estimated fixed lease obligations are $50,000 per year for the next ten years. The leases do not meet the criteria for capitalization.

(g) The company is currently in litigation over a claimed overpayment of income tax of $13,000. In the opinion of counsel, the claim is valid. The company is contingently liable on guaranteed notes worth $17,000.

**Instructions:** Prepare a properly classified balance sheet in account form. Include all notes and parenthetical notations necessary to properly disclose the essential financial data:

## Problem 5—4   (Classification of liabilities)

The bookkeeper for HiTone Corp. prepared the following schedule of liabilities as of December 31, 1993:

| | |
|---|---:|
| Accounts payable | $ 56,000 |
| Notes payable—trade | 12,000 |
| Notes payable—bank | 70,000 |
| Wages and salaries payable | 1,500 |
| Interest payable | 16,000 |
| Mortgage note payable—10% | 60,000 |
| Mortgage note payable—12% | 150,000 |
| Bonds payable | 100,000 |
| Total | $465,500 |

The following additional information pertains to these liabilities:

(a)   All trade notes payable are due within six months of the balance sheet date.
(b)   Bank notes payable include two separate notes payable to Second City Bank:
    (1) A $20,000, 13% note issued March 1, 1991, payable on demand. Interest is payable each six months.
    (2) A 1-year, $50,000, 11 1/2% note issued January 2, 1993. On December 30, 1993, HiTone negotiated a written agreement with Second City Bank to replace the note with a 2-year, $50,000, 12% note to be issued January 2, 1994.
(c)   The 10% mortgage note was issued October 1, 1990, with a term of 10 years. Terms of the note give the holder the right to demand immediate payment if the company fails to make a monthly interest payment within 10 days of the date the payment is due. As of December 31, 1993, HiTone is three months behind in paying its required interest payment.
(d)   The 12% mortgage note was issued May 1, 1987, with a term of 20 years. The current principal amount due is $150,000. Principal and interest are payable annually on April 30. A payment of $22,000 is due April 30, 1994. The payment includes interest of $18,000.
(e)   The bonds payable are 10-year, 8% bonds, issued June 30, 1984.

**Instructions:**   Prepare the liabilities section of the December 31, 1993, classified balance sheet for HiTone Corp. Include notes as appropriate. Assume the interest payable accrual has been computed correctly.

## Problem 5—5   (Corrected balance sheet)

The following balance sheet was prepared by the accountant for Rowley Company.

**Rowley Company**
**Balance Sheet**
**June 30, 1993**

### Assets

| | |
|---|---:|
| Cash ........................................................... | $ 25,500 |
| Marketable securities (includes 30% ownership in stock of Oak Mountain Developers, at cost of $250,000) ....................... | 312,000 |
| Inventories (net of amount still due suppliers of $85,000)............ | 624,600 |
| Prepaid expenses (includes a deposit of $10,000 made on inventories to be delivered in 18 months)...................................... | 33,000 |
| Land, buildings, and equipment (excluding $60,000 of equipment still in use, but fully depreciated) ...................................... | 220,000 |
| Goodwill (based on estimate by the president of Rowley Company).. | 70,000 |
| Total assets .................................................... | $1,285,100 |

### Liabilities and Owners' Equity

| | |
|---|---:|
| Notes payable ($75,000 due in 1995) ............................. | $ 135,000 |
| Accounts payable (not including amount due to suppliers of inventory—see above) ......................................... | 142,000 |
| Long-term liability under pension plan .......................... | 60,000 |
| Appropriation for building expansion ........................... | 105,000 |
| Accumulated depreciation....................................... | 73,000 |
| Taxes payable ................................................. | 44,500 |
| Bonds payable (net of discount of $10,000) ...................... | 290,000 |
| Deferred income tax liability.................................... | 68,000 |
| Common stock (10,000 shares, $20 par) ......................... | 200,000 |
| Additional paid-in capital....................................... | 50,500 |
| Unappropriated retained earnings ............................... | 117,100 |
| Total liabilities and owners' equity ............................. | $1,285,100 |

**Instructions:**  Prepare a corrected classified balance sheet in report form using appropriate account titles.

## Problem 5—6  (Classified balance sheet—report form)

The financial position of St. Charles Ranch is summarized in the following letter to the corporation's accountant.

Dear Dallas:

The following information should be of value to you in preparing the balance sheet for St. Charles Ranch as of December 31, 1993. The balance of cash as of December 31 as reported on the bank statement was $43,825. There were still outstanding checks of $9,320 that had not cleared the bank, and cash on hand of $5,640 was not deposited until January 4, 1994.

Customers owed the company $40,500 at December 31. We estimated 6% of this amount will never be collected. We owe suppliers $32,000 for poultry feed purchased in November and December. About 75% of this feed was used before December 31.

Because we think the price of grain will rise in 1994, we are holding 10,000 bushels of wheat and 5,000 bushels of oats until spring. The market value at December 31 was $3.50 per bushel of wheat and $1.50 per bushel of oats. We estimate that both prices will increase 15% by selling time. We are not able to estimate the cost of raising this product.

St. Charles Ranch owns 1,850 acres of land. Two separate purchases of land were made as follows: 1,250 acres at $200 per acre in 1976, and 600 acres at $400 per acre in 1981. Similar land is currently selling for $800 per acre. The balance of the mortgage on the two parcels of land is $250,000 at December 31; 10% of this mortgage must be paid in 1994.

Our farm buildings and equipment cost us $176,400 and on the average are 40% depreciated. If we were to replace these buildings and equipment at today's prices, we believe we would be conservative in estimating a cost of $300,000.

We have not paid property taxes of $5,500 for 1994 billed to us in late November. Our estimated income tax for 1993 is $18,500. A refund claim for $2,800 has been filed relative to the 1991 income tax return. The claim arose because of an error made on the 1991 return.

The operator of the ranch will receive a bonus of $9,000 for 1993 operations. It will be paid when the entire grain crop has been sold.

As you will recall, we issued 14,000 shares of $10 par stock upon incorporation. The ranch received $290,000 as net proceeds from the stock issue. Dividends of $30,000 were declared last month and will be paid on February 1, 1994.

The new year appears to hold great promise. Thanks for your help in preparing this statement.

Sincerely,
Frank K. Santiago
President—St. Charles Ranch

**Instructions:**  Based on this information, prepare a properly classified balance sheet in report form as of December 31, 1993.

## Problem 5—7  (Corrected balance sheet—report form)

The bookkeeper for Dependable Computers Inc. reports the following balance sheet amounts as of June 30, 1993:

| | |
|---|---:|
| Current Assets | $264,050 |
| Other Assets | 628,550 |
| Current Liabilities | 158,600 |
| Other Liabilities | 90,000 |
| Capital | 644,000 |

A review of account balances reveals the following data:

(a)  An analysis of current assets discloses the following:

| | |
|---|---:|
| Cash ...................................................... | $ 62,250 |
| Marketable securities held as temporary investment ...................... | 60,000 |
| Trade accounts receivable.............................................. | 56,800 |
| Inventories, including advertising supplies of $2,000 ...................... | 85,000 |
| | $264,050 |

(b)  Other assets include:

Land, buildings, and equipment:

| | |
|---|---:|
| Depreciated book value (cost, $656,000) ................................ | $549,000 |
| Deposit with a supplier for merchandise ordered for August delivery......... | 2,150 |
| Goodwill recorded on the books to cancel losses incurred by the company in prior years ...................................................... | 77,400 |
| | $628,550 |

(c)  Current liabilities include:

| | | |
|---|---:|---:|
| Payroll payable........................................... | | $  7,150 |
| Taxes payable............................................ | | 4,150 |
| Rent payable............................................. | | 11,400 |
| Trade accounts payable: | | |
| Total owed to suppliers on account ........................ | $101,400 | |
| Less 6-month note received from a supplier who purchased some used equipment on June 29, 1993 ..................... | 1,500 | 99,900 |
| Notes payable............................................ | | 36,000 |
| | | $158,600 |

(d)  Other liabilities include:

| | |
|---|---:|
| 9% mortgage on land, buildings, and equipment, payable in semiannual installments of $9,000 through June 30, 1998 ................... | $ 90,000 |

(e)  Capital includes:

| | |
|---|---:|
| Preferred stock: 19,000 shares outstanding ($20 par value) ................ | $380,000 |
| Common stock: 160,000 shares at stated value ........................... | 264,000 |
| | $644,000 |

(f)  Common shares were originally issued for full consideration, but the losses of the company for the past years were charged against the common stock balance.

| | |
|---|---:|
| Total consideration at time of issuance ................................... | $391,000 |

**Instructions:**  Using the account balances and related data, prepare a corrected balance sheet in report form showing individual asset, liability, and capital balances properly classified.

## ▣ Problem 5—8   (Corrected balance sheet—report form)

The balance sheet at the top of the next page is submitted to you for inspection and review. In the course of the review, you find the data listed below.

(a)  The possibility of uncollectible accounts on accounts receivable has not been considered. It is estimated that uncollectible accounts will total $4,800.

(b)  $45,000 representing the cost of a large-scale newspaper advertising campaign completed in 1993 has been added to the inventories, since it is believed that this campaign will benefit sales of 1994. It is also found that inventories include merchandise of $16,250 received on December 31 that has not yet been recorded as a purchase.

(c)  The books show that land, buildings, and equipment have a cost of $556,800 with depreciation of $180,000 recognized in prior years. However, these balances include fully depreciated equipment of $85,000 that has been scrapped and is no longer on hand.

**Appalachian Freight Company**
**Balance Sheet**
**December 31, 1993**

| Assets | | Liabilities and Owners' Equity | |
|---|---|---|---|
| Cash........................... | $ 45,050 | Miscellaneous liabilities.......... | $ 3,600 |
| Accounts receivable............. | 112,500 | Loan payable ................... | 76,200 |
| Inventories ..................... | 204,000 | Accounts payable .............. | 75,250 |
| Prepaid insurance............... | 8,800 | Capital stock ................... | 215,000 |
| Land, buildings, and equipment .. | 376,800 | Paid-in capital .................. | 377,100 |
| | $747,150 | | $747,150 |

(d) Miscellaneous liabilities of $3,600 represent salaries payable of $9,500, less noncurrent advances of $5,900 made to company officials.

(e) Loan payable represents a loan from the bank that is payable in regular quarterly installments of $6,250.

(f) Tax liabilities not shown are estimated at $18,250.

(g) Deferred income tax liability arising from temporary differences totals $44,550. This liability was not included in the balance sheet.

(h) Capital stock consists of 6,250 shares of preferred 6% stock, par $20, and 9,000 shares of common stock, stated value $10.

(i) Capital stock had been issued for a total consideration of $283,600, the amount received in excess of the par and stated values of the stock being reported as paid-in capital.

(j) Net income and dividends were recorded in Paid-In Capital.

**Instructions:**   Prepare a corrected balance sheet in report form with accounts properly classified.

### Problem 5—9   (Corrected balance sheet—report form)

The accountant for the Delicious Bakery prepares the following condensed balance sheet.

**Delicious Bakery**
**Condensed Balance Sheet**
**December 31, 1993**

| | |
|---|---|
| Current assets ............................................... | $53,415 |
| Less current liabilities....................................... | 29,000 |
| Working capital ............................................. | $24,415 |
| Add other assets ........................................... | 75,120 |
| | $99,535 |
| Deduct other liabilities ..................................... | 3,600 |
| Investment in business ..................................... | $95,935 |

A review of the account balances disclosed the following data:

(a) An analysis of the current asset grouping revealed the following:

| | |
|---|---|
| Cash ....................................................... | $10,600 |
| Trade accounts receivable (fully collectible) ................... | 12,500 |
| Notes receivable (notes of customer who has been declared bankrupt and is unable to pay anything on the obligations) ................................. | 1,000 |
| Marketable securities, at cost (market value $2,575)........................ | 4,250 |
| Inventory ................................................... | 20,965 |
| Cash surrender value of insurance on officers' lives ....................... | 4,100 |
| Total current assets......................................... | $53,415 |

The inventory account was found to include supplies costing $425, a delivery truck acquired at the end of 1993 at a cost of $2,100, and fixtures at a depreciated value of $10,400. The fixtures had been acquired in 1990 at a cost of $12,500.

(b)   The total for other assets was determined as follows:

| | |
|---|---:|
| Land and buildings at cost of acquisition, July 1, 1991 ...................... | $92,000 |
| Less balance due on mortgage, $16,000, and accrued interest on mortgage, $880 (mortgage is payable in annual installments of $4,000 on July 1 of each year together with interest for the year at that time at 11%) ................. | 16,880 |
| Total other assets ...................................................... | $75,120 |

It was estimated that the land, at the time of the purchase, was worth $30,000. Buildings as of December 31, 1993, were estimated to have a remaining life of 17½ years.

(c)   Current liabilities represented balances that were payable to trade creditors.
(d)   Other liabilities consisted of withholding, payroll, real estate and other taxes payable to the federal, state, and local governments. However, no recognition was given the accrued salaries, utilities, and other miscellaneous items totaling $350.
(e)   The company was originally organized in 1989 when 5,000 shares of no-par stock with a stated value of $5 per share were issued in exchange for business assets that were recognized on the books at their fair market value of $55,000.

**Instructions:**   Prepare a corrected balance sheet in report form with the items properly classified.

### ■ Problem 5—10   (Classified balance sheet—account form)

Tony Akea incorporated his concrete manufacturing operations on January 1, 1993, by issuing 10,000 shares of $10 par common stock to himself. The following balance sheet for the new corporation was prepared:

**Cornish Corporation**
**Balance Sheet**
**January 1, 1993**

| | | | |
|---|---:|---|---:|
| Cash.......................... | $ 10,000 | Accounts payable—suppliers ..... | $ 45,000 |
| Accounts receivable............. | 74,000 | Capital stock, $10 par ........... | 130,000 |
| Inventory ..................... | 75,000 | Additional paid-in capital ........ | 130,000 |
| Equipment .................... | 115,000 | | |
| | $275,000 | | $275,000 |

During 1993, Cornish Corporation engaged in the following transactions:

(a)   Cornish Corporation produced concrete costing $270,000. Concrete costs consisted of the following: $200,000, raw materials purchased; $25,000, labor; and $45,000, overhead. Cornish Corporation paid the $45,000 owed to suppliers as of January 1, and $130,000 of the $200,000 of raw materials purchased during the year. All labor, except for $1,500, and recorded overhead were paid in cash during the year. Other operating expenses of $15,000 were incurred and paid in 1993.
(b)   Concrete costing $290,000 was sold during 1993 for $380,000. All sales were made on credit, and collections on receivables were $365,000.

(c)  Cornish Corporation purchased machinery (fair market value = $190,000) by trading in old equipment costing $50,000 and paying $140,000 in cash. There is no accumulated depreciation on the old equipment as it was revalued when the new corporation was formed.

(d)  Cornish Corporation issued an additional 4,000 shares of common stock for $25 per share and declared a dividend of $3 per share to all stockholders of record as of December 31, 1993, payable on January 15, 1994.

(e)  Depreciation expense for 1993 was $27,000. The allowance for doubtful accounts after year-end adjustments is $2,500.

**Instructions:**  Prepare a properly classified balance sheet in account form for the Cornish Corporation as of December 31, 1993.

# CHAPTER 6

## Statement of Cash Flows

The case of W. T. Grant is a classic in cash flow analysis. During the 1960s and 1970s, Grant was one of the largest retailers in the United States, with over 1,200 stores nation-wide. Grant was a stable New York Stock Exchange firm that had paid cash dividends every year since 1907. However, the inability of Grant's operations to generate positive cash flow indicated the existence of serious problems. From 1966 through 1973, while Grant's net income was steady at about $35 million per year, cash flow from operations was negative in every year except 1968 and 1969, and even in those years the positive cash flow generated was insignificant in amount. The results for the fiscal year ended January 31, 1973, are the most striking. Net income for the year was $38 million. Working capital from operations (a measure often referred to as "cash flow") was $48 million. However, actual cash flow generated by operations for the year, after considering sharp increases in receivables and inventory, was *negative* $120 million. In October 1975, Grant filed for bankruptcy, and by early 1976, the company was liquidated and ceased to exist.[1]

Assessing the amounts, timing, and uncertainty of future cash flows is one of the primary objectives of financial reporting.[2] The statement that provides information needed to meet this objective is a statement of cash flows. This chapter provides an overview of reporting cash flows and outlines the techniques for preparing and analyzing a cash flow statement.

## HISTORICAL PERSPECTIVE

As discussed in Chapters 4 and 5, the primary financial statements for a business enterprise include the balance sheet, the income statement, and the statement of cash flows. The balance sheet reports the financial position of a business at a given time. The income statement reports the operating results for the period and may be accompanied by a statement summarizing the changes in retained earnings or stockholders' equity in successive periods. The statement of cash flows provides information about the cash receipts and cash payments of an entity during a period of time. It has replaced the previously required **statement of changes in financial position** or **funds statement**.

The funds statement went through several years of development in becoming one of the primary financial statements. In 1961, Accounting Research Study No. 2, sponsored by the AICPA, recommended that a funds statement be prepared and included with the income statement and balance sheet in annual reports to shareholders.[3] Two years later, APB Opinion No. 3 was issued to provide guidelines for the preparation of the funds statement.[4] Even though Opinion No. 3 did not require a funds statement, most businesses recognized the value of the funds statement and included it in their annual reports. Thus it was somewhat anticlimactic when, in 1971, the APB issued Opinion No. 19 officially requiring that a funds statement be included as one of the three primary financial statements in annual reports to shareholders and that it be covered by the auditor's report.[5]

Opinion No. 19 did not specify a single definition or concept of funds to be used in preparing the funds statement or a required format for the statement. Thus companies were allowed considerable flexibility in the reporting of funds flow information. In late 1987, the FASB issued Statement No. 95, which superseded APB Opinion No. 19. Instead of allowing various definitions of funds, such as cash or working capital, and a variety of formats, the FASB called for a statement of cash flows to replace the more general statement of changes in financial position. In addition, the FASB specified a format that highlights cash flows from operating, investing, and financing activities.[6] A major reason for the FASB's actions was the desire to help investors and creditors better predict future cash flows.

---

[1]See James A. Largay, III and Clyde P. Stickney, "Cash Flows, Ratio Analysis and the W. T. Grant Company Bankruptcy" *Financial Analysts Journal*, July/August 1980: pp. 51-54; and *Moody's Handbook of Common Stocks*, Second Quarterly 1973 Edition.

[2]*Statement of Financial Accounting Concepts No. 1*, "Objectives of Financial Reporting by Business Enterprises" (Stamford: Financial Accounting Standards Board, 1978), par. 37.

[3]Perry Mason, *Accounting Research Study No. 2*, "'Cash Flow' Analysis and the Funds Statement" (New York: American Institute of Certified Public Accountants, 1961).

[4]Opinions of the Accounting Principles Board, No. 3, "The Statement of Source and Application of Funds" (New York: American Institute of Certified Public Accountants, 1963).

[5]*Opinions of the Accounting Principles Board, No. 19*, "Reporting Changes in Financial Position" (New York: American Institute of Certified Public Accountants, 1971).

[6]*Statement of Financial Accounting Standards No. 95*, "Statement of Cash Flows" (Stamford: Financial Accounting Standards Board, November 1987).

## PURPOSES OF A STATEMENT OF CASH FLOWS

As previously noted, the major purpose of a statement of cash flows is to provide relevant information about the cash receipts and cash payments of an entity during a period of time. This information should help investors and creditors assess an entity's ability to generate positive future net cash flows and to meet its current and long-term obligations, including possible future dividend payments. In addition, the statement of cash flows should help users assess the reasons for the differences between net income and the related cash receipts and payments. Finally, the statement of cash flows should help to determine the effects of both cash and noncash investing and financing transactions on an entity's financial position.[7]

To achieve these objectives, the FASB concluded that a statement of cash flows should report the cash effects of an entity's operations, its investing transactions, and its financing transactions. Additional disclosures should be made of any significant investing or financing transactions that affect an enterprise's financial position but do not directly affect cash flows during the period. Finally, a reconciliation of accrual net income and net cash flow from operating activities also should be provided.

### Cash Equivalents

A statement of cash flows explains the change during the period in cash and cash equivalents—short-term, highly liquid investments that can be converted easily into cash. To qualify as a cash equivalent, an item must be:[8]

1. Readily convertible to cash, and
2. So near its maturity that there is insignificant risk of changes in value due to changes in interest rates.

Generally, only investments with original maturities of three months or less qualify as cash equivalents. **Original maturity** in this case is determined from the date an investment was acquired by the reporting entity, which may not coincide with the date of issuance of the security. For example, both a three-month U.S. Treasury bill and a three-year Treasury note purchased three months prior to maturity qualify as cash equivalents. However, if the Treasury note were purchased three years ago, it would not qualify as a cash equivalent during the last three months prior to its maturity.[9] In addition to U.S. Treasury obligations, cash equivalents can include such items as money market funds and commercial paper. Investments in marketable *equity* securities (common and preferred stock) normally would not be classified as cash equivalents, because such securities have no definite maturity date and are subject to fluctuations in value.

Not all investments qualifying as cash equivalents need be reported as such. Management is required to establish a policy concerning which short-term, highly liquid investments are to be treated as cash equivalents. Once a policy is established, management should disclose which items are being treated as cash equivalents in presenting its cash flow statement. Any change in the established policy would be considered a change in accounting principle.

### Major Classifications of Cash Flows

The funds statement required by APB Opinion No. 19 classified the flow of resources simply as sources and uses of funds. In the statement of cash flows, cash receipts and

[7] *Ibid.*, par. 5.

[8] *Ibid.*, par. 8.

[9] *Ibid.*

payments are classified according to three main categories: **operating activities, investing activities,** and **financing activities.** Exhibit 6—1 summarizes the major types of cash receipts and cash payments included in each category. Note that these are general classifications. Specific items might be classified differently for certain types of businesses. For example, activities normally classified as investing might be classified as operating activities for a bank or other financial institution.[10]

### Exhibit 6—1    Major Classifications of Cash Flows

**Operating Activities**
Cash receipts from:
  Sale of goods or services
  Interest revenue
  Dividend revenue
Cash payments to:
  Suppliers for inventory purchases
  Employees for services
  Governments for taxes
  Lenders for interest expense
  Others for other expenses (e.g., utilities, rent)

**Investing Activities**
Cash receipts from:
  Sale of plant assets
  Sale of a business segment
  Sale of investments in equity securities of other entities or debt securities (other than cash equivalents)
  Collection of principal on loans made to other entities
Cash payments to:
  Purchase plant assets
  Purchase equity securities of other entities or debt securities (other than cash equivalents)
  Make loans to other entities

**Financing Activities**
Cash receipts from:
  Issuance of own stock
  Borrowing (e.g., bonds, notes, mortgages)
Cash payments to:
  Stockholders as dividends
  Repay principal amounts borrowed
  Repurchase an entity's own stock (treasury stock)

**Operating Activities**    Operating activities include those transactions and events that normally enter into the determination of operating income. Cash receipts from selling goods or from providing services would be the major cash inflow for most businesses. Other cash receipts might come from interest, dividends, and similar items. Major cash

[10]With the issuance of Statement No. 102, the FASB has specifically modified Statement No. 95 with respect to the classification of certain securities or debt instruments held in a trading portfolio of a financial institution. Thus, the cash receipts or cash payments from acquisitions or sales of securities or other assets that are acquired specifically for resale and that are carried at market values in trading accounts should be classified as operating cash flows instead of investing cash flows. A similar reclassification should be made for loans that are acquired specifically for resale and that are carried at market or lower-of-cost-or-market values. See *Statement of Financial Accounting Standards No. 102,* "Statement of Cash Flows—Exemption of Certain Enterprises and Classification of Cash Flows From Certain Securities Acquired for Resale," (Norwalk: Financial Accounting Standards Board, February 1989), pars. 8-9.

outflows would include payments to purchase inventory and to pay wages, taxes, interest, utilities, rent, and similar expenses. The net amount of cash provided or used by operating activities is a key figure that should be highlighted on a statement of cash flows.

While cash inflows from interest or dividends logically might be classified as investing or financing activities, the FASB decided to classify them as operating activities, which conforms to their presentation on the income statement.

**Investing Activities**    Transactions and events involving the purchase and sale of securities (excluding cash equivalents), land, buildings, equipment, and other assets not generally held for resale, and the making and collecting of loans are classified as investing activities. These activities occur regularly and result in cash receipts and payments. They are not classified as operating activities, since they relate only indirectly to the central, ongoing operation of an entity, which is usually the sale of goods or services.

**Financing Activities**    Financing activities include transactions and events whereby cash is obtained from or repaid to owners (equity financing) and creditors (debt financing). For example, the cash proceeds from issuing capital stock or bonds would be classified under financing activities. Similarly, payments to reacquire stock (treasury stock) or to retire bonds and the payment of dividends are considered financing activities.

### Noncash Investing and Financing Activities

Some investing and financing activities affect an entity's financial position but not the entity's cash flows during the period. For example, equipment may be purchased with a note payable, or land may be acquired by issuing stock. Such noncash investing and financing activities were previously reported in a funds statement under the "all-financial-resources concept" as both a source and a use of funds. Now, according to FASB Statement No. 95, significant noncash investing and financing activities should be disclosed separately, either in the notes to the financial statements or in an accompanying schedule, not in the statement itself.[11] The statement of cash flows reports only operating, investing, and financing activities involving cash.

---

### REPORTING CASH FLOWS

Exhibit 6—2 illustrates the general format, with details and amounts omitted, for a statement of cash flows. The statement should report the net cash provided by, or used in, operating, investing, and financing activities and the net effect of total cash flows on cash and cash equivalents during the period. While the exact format of the statement is not specified by the FASB, the information is to be presented in a manner that reconciles beginning and ending cash and cash equivalent amounts.[12]

The preparation of the investing and financing activities sections of the statement of cash flows is straightforward. The operating activities section, however, is more complex, because it requires analysis of operating accounts to convert them from an accrual to a cash basis. In Chapter 4, the wide use of the accrual concept in recognizing revenues and expenses was discussed. Net income as defined by GAAP is an accrual concept. The

---

[11]*FASB Statement No. 95*, par. 32.

[12]Additional disclosures are required in reconciling the change in cash and cash equivalents for a company that has foreign currency transactions. Such entities must report the equivalent of foreign currency cash flows and should show the effect of any exchange rate fluctuations on the cash balances as a separate item in the cash flow statement. The complexities involved in reporting these foreign currency cash flows are considered beyond the scope of this text.

## Exhibit 6—2    General Format for a Statement of Cash Flows

| | |
|---|---:|
| Cash provided by (or used in): | |
|     Operating activities ................................................ | $XXX |
|     Investing activities ................................................ | XXX |
|     Financing activities................................................ | XXX |
| Net increase (decrease) in cash and cash equivalents .................. | $XXX |
| Cash and cash equivalents at beginning of year ....................... | XXX |
| Cash and cash equivalents at end of year ............................ | $XXX |

statement of cash flows, on the other hand, is designed to report the cash effects of these same revenue and expense items.

There are two methods that may be used in calculating and reporting the amount of net cash flow from operating activities: the indirect method and the direct method. The most popular method used in reported financial statements is the indirect method. A survey of 600 companies providing a statement of cash flows for 1989 revealed that 583 of the companies used the indirect method.[13]

The indirect method begins with net income as reported on the income statement and adjusts this accrual amount for any items that do not affect cash flows. The adjustments are of three basic types: (1) revenues and expenses that do not involve cash inflows or outflows, e.g., cost allocations such as depreciation and amortization, (2) gains and losses on events reported in other sections of the statement of cash flows, and (3) conversions of current operating assets and liabilities from the accrual to the cash basis. The operating activities section of the statement of cash flows for Pier 1 Imports, Inc., in Exhibit 6—3 illustrates the indirect method of reporting net cash flow from operations. IBM Corporation's statement of cash flows in Appendix A provides another illustration of the indirect method.

The direct method does not begin with reported net income, but instead analyzes the cash effects of operating activities and reports the total cash paid or received for each major type of activity. Because recorded accounting information normally reflects the accrual basis, a conversion of accounts, such as Sales, from the accrual basis to a cash basis is required. The direct method of reporting net cash flow from operating activities is illustrated by the partial statement of cash flows for United States Surgical Corporation in Exhibit 6—4.

Both methods produce identical results—that is, the same amount of net cash flow provided by (or used in) operations. The indirect method is favored and used by most companies, because it is relatively easy to apply and it reconciles the difference between net income and the net cash flow provided by operations. The direct method is favored by many users of financial statements, because it reports directly the sources of cash inflows and outflows without the potentially confusing adjustments to net income. The FASB considered the arguments for both methods, and although the Board favored the clarity of the direct method, they finally permitted either method to be used.[14]

Because the indirect method is so widely used, it will be explained first, and the preparation of a statement of cash flows using the indirect method will be illustrated. The

[13]*Accounting Trends & Techniques*—1990 (New York: American Institute of Certified Public Accountants, 1990), p. 350.

[14]*Statement of Financial Accounting Standards No. 95,* "Statement of Cash Flows" (Stamford: Financial Accounting Standards Board, November 1987), pars. 27-28.

**Exhibit 6—3        Pier 1 Imports, Inc.—Indirect Method of Reporting Cash Flow From Operating Activities**

Pier 1 Imports, Inc.
# Consolidated Statement of Cash Flows
*(in thousands)*

| | YEAR ENDED | | |
| --- | --- | --- | --- |
| | MARCH 3, 1990 | FEBRUARY 25, 1989 | FEBRUARY 27, 1988 |
| Cash flow from operating activities: | | | |
| Net income | $ 25,503 | $ 21,850 | $ 16,075 |
| Adjustments to reconcile to net cash provided by operating activities: | | | |
| Depreciation, amortization, deferred taxes and other | 18,908 | 12,687 | 8,309 |
| Increase in inventories | (26,034) | (26,698) | (20,954) |
| Increase in accounts receivable and other current assets | (8,579) | (19,980) | (2,472) |
| Change in other assets and other, net | 392 | 150 | (2,651) |
| Change in accounts payable and accrued expenses | (935) | 12,362 | 6,607 |
| Net cash provided by operating activities | 9,255 | 371 | 4,914 |

acceptable alternative —the direct method—will then be explained, and the reporting differences between the two methods will be highlighted.

## The Indirect Method of Reporting Cash Flow From Operations

The adjustments to net income required to compute cash flow from operations using the indirect method can be determined by careful analysis of the income statement and balance sheet. The three basic types of adjustments identified previously (noncash items, gains and losses, and current operating accounts) are explained in the following sections. It is important to recognize that these adjustments are not entered in the accounting records. They are simply additions to, and subtractions from, net income on the statement of cash flows in order to convert from an accrual to a cash basis.

**Adjustments for Noncash Income Statement Items**   Some items reported in the income statement do not affect cash, although they are properly recognized as revenues or expenses. These items must be removed from net income to determine the cash flow from operations. Examples of noncash items include depreciation on buildings and equipment, amortization of intangible assets such as goodwill, and revenues realized in the form of noncash assets. The most common adjustment to net income is for depreciation. Because the journal entry to record periodic depreciation involves an expense account and a contra asset account (Accumulated Depreciation), but no cash, depreciation expense is a noncash item and must be added to reported net income to compute cash flows from operating activities.

This adjustment is sometimes misinterpreted by financial statement users as indicating that depreciation expense is an important source of cash inflows. Only revenue produces cash inflows from operating activities. The depreciation adjustment recognizes that re-

**Exhibit 6—4    United States Surgical Corporation—Direct Method of Reporting Cash Flow From Operating Activities**

## UNITED STATES SURGICAL CORPORATION

### Consolidated Statements of Cash Flows

| In thousands | 1989 | 1988 | 1987 |
|---|---|---|---|
| Cash flows from operating activities: | | | |
| Cash received from customers ......................... | $327,199 | $284,026 | $238,204 |
| Cash paid to vendors, suppliers and employees....... | (274,131) | (227,168) | (183,100) |
| Interest paid (net of capitalized interest)................ | (7,289) | (7,254) | (7,904) |
| Income taxes paid.............. | (6,840) | (6,186) | (6,945) |
| Proceeds from legal settlement (Note B) ............... | 10,000 | | |
| Net cash provided by operating activities ................. | 48,939 | 43,418 | 40,255 |

*[handwritten annotation: Sale + Rev    change A/R]*

ported net income includes expenses that do not require cash outflows, and these types of expenses must be eliminated (added back) to determine net cash flow from operations.

**Adjustments for Gains and Losses From Sale of Assets**    The net income amount used as a starting point with the indirect method also may include gains or losses from the sale of assets, such as investments in securities or property, plant, and equipment. The sale of assets, other than inventory, is an incidental or peripheral activity and not part of the central operations of a business. Such transactions are therefore properly classified as investing activities rather than operating activities. The proceeds from the sale of an asset include any gain or loss; thus, if the cash inflows are reported in the investing section and no adjustment is made to net income in the operating section, a double counting of the gain or loss will occur. This is corrected by deducting the gain or adding the loss to net income in computing operating cash flow.

To illustrate, assume that Halifax Corporation sold for $75,000 land that cost $50,000. This land had been held for possible expansion, but was no longer needed. The entry for the sale would be:

| | | |
|---|---|---|
| Cash ...................................................... | 75,000 | |
| Land ...................................................... | | 50,000 |
| Gain on Sale of Land ..................................... | | 25,000 |

Since the $25,000 gain was included in net income, that amount would be subtracted in deriving cash flows from operating activities using the indirect method. The entire $75,000 is reported on the statement of cash flows under investing activities as cash received from the sale of land.

**Adjustments for Changes in Current Operating Accounts**    Net income under generally accepted accounting principles is reported on the accrual basis. This means that all revenues, expenses, current operating assets, and current operating liabilities are also recorded on an accrual basis. To convert net income from an accrual to a cash basis, adjustments must be made to net income for the increases or decreases in the balances of the current operating assets and liabilities.

*Changes in Current Operating Asset Accounts*    In general, increases in current operating assets are subtracted from net income and decreases in current operating assets are added to net income to adjust net income to net cash flow from operations. To illustrate, assume the ending balance in Accounts Receivable was $20,000 more than the beginning balance. This indicates that the amount of cash collected during the period was $20,000 less than the sales revenue reported in the income statement on an accrual basis. Thus, the $20,000 increase would be subtracted from net income to reflect the cash received for the period on the cash flow statement. If a receivable balance decreases, the opposite would be true; the decrease would be added to net income because more cash was collected than is reflected in the revenue reported in the income statement.[15]

As with receivables, an increase in inventory is subtracted from net income, because more cash was used for purchases than is reflected in cost of goods sold on the income statement. A decrease in inventory is added to net income, because less cash was used to acquire goods than is reflected in the income statement.

Adjustments also must be made for changes in prepaid asset accounts. An increase in a prepaid asset, such as Prepaid Insurance, is subtracted from net income to reflect the amount of cash paid for insurance. A decrease in a prepaid account is added to net income.

The changes in most current asset accounts affect operating income and require adjustment as described above. Changes in temporary investments, on the other hand, generally do not affect operating activities but are considered investing activities. Those short-term investments that qualify as cash equivalents would be included with cash. The changes in other temporary investments would be included under the category of investing activities. For brokerage firms and financial institutions, as mentioned earlier, purchases and sales of trading account securities would be considered operating activities. Nontrading account securities, even for these firms, would be classified as investing activities.

*Changes in Current Operating Liability Accounts*    Adjustments to reflect changes in current operating liabilities are just the opposite of the adjustments for changes in current operating assets. Increases in current operating liabilities are added to net income, and decreases in current operating liabilities are subtracted from net income to convert accrual net income to the cash basis. To illustrate, an increase in accounts payable means less cash was used than the amount of purchases or cost of goods sold recorded on an accrual basis. Thus an increase in accounts payable is added to net income in deriving cash flow from operations. A decrease in accounts payable is deducted from net income, because more cash was paid than is reflected in accrual net income.

Similar adjustments for other current payables that affect income would be required. For example, the amount of wages expense, interest expense, and taxes expense reported on the income statement would have to be adjusted for increases and decreases in related

---

[15]In this chapter, unless otherwise noted, it will be assumed that all accounts receivable amounts (as well as accounts payable amounts) are related to operations. Nontrade receivables and payables would be reported as investing and financing activities.

payable balances to report the net cash flow provided by (used in) operating activities. Adjustments for increases or decreases in other current payables that do not affect income (e.g., dividends payable) would also have to be made. These adjustments would be reflected in the investing and financing activities sections of the cash flow statement rather than in the operating section.

Adjustments also must be made for changes in unearned revenue accounts, such as Advances From Customers or Unearned Rent Revenue. An increase in an unearned revenue account is added to net income, while a decrease is subtracted to adjust the revenue reported on the income statement to a cash basis.

Exhibit 6—5 summarizes the procedures for determining net cash flow from operating activities using the indirect method.

### Exhibit 6—5    Cash Flows From Operating Activities—Indirect Method

| | | |
|---|---:|---:|
| **Net income reported on the income statement** . . . . . . . . . . . . . . . | | $XXX |
| Adjustments for noncash items: | | |
| + Depreciation . . . . . . . . . . . . . . . . . . . . . . . . . . . . . . . . . . . . . . | $XXX | |
| + Amortization of intangible assets . . . . . . . . . . . . . . . . . . . . . . . | XXX | |
| +/− Other noncash items included in net income . . . . . . . . . . . | XXX | XXX |
| Adjustments for gains and losses: | | |
| − Gains on sales of assets . . . . . . . . . . . . . . . . . . . . . . . . . . . . . | $XXX | |
| + Losses on sales of assets . . . . . . . . . . . . . . . . . . . . . . . . . . . . | XXX | XXX |
| Adjustments for changes in current operating accounts: | | |
| − Increases in current operating asset accounts (except cash and cash equivalents) . . . . . . . . . . . . . . . . . . . . . . . . . . . . | $XXX | |
| + Decreases in current operating asset accounts (except cash and cash equivalents) . . . . . . . . . . . . . . . . . . . . . . . . . . . . | XXX | |
| + Increases in current operating liability accounts . . . . . . . . . . . | XXX | |
| − Decreases in current operating liability accounts . . . . . . . . . . | XXX | XXX |
| **Net cash provided by (used in) operating activities** . . . . . . . . . . . . | | $XXX |

### Preparing a Statement of Cash Flows

Four steps are generally required in preparing a statement of cash flows:

1. *Determine the change in cash* (including cash equivalents). This is simply the difference between beginning and ending cash balances for the period being analyzed. The change in cash is the "target figure"—the amount that will be explained by the statement of cash flows.
2. *Determine the net cash provided by (used in) operating activities.* This step requires analysis of comparative balance sheet amounts, income statement data, and specific transactions that relate to company operations.
3. *Determine the net cash provided by (used in) investing and financing activities.* This step requires analysis of the cash flow impact of all accounts and transactions relating to investing and financing activities.
4. *Prepare a formal statement of cash flows,* classified according to operating, investing, and financing activities. Note that the amount determined in Step 1 should equal the total net increase (decrease) in cash reported on the statement of cash flows and will,

therefore, reconcile the beginning and ending cash balances for the period. Any significant noncash investing or financing transactions should be reported separately, not on the statement of cash flows.

## Illustration—Indirect Method

To illustrate the process of analyzing accounts and preparing a statement of cash flows, a simple example will be considered. The balance sheets, income statement, and additional information for the Taylor Company provide the necessary data for the illustrations. To emphasize the nature of the account analysis required in preparing a statement of cash flows, it is assumed that no other information is available. In practice, however, the data for preparing a cash flow statement can be taken directly from the accounting records.

**Taylor Company**
**Comparative Balance Sheet**
**December 31, 1993 and 1992**

|  | 1993 | 1992 |
|---|---|---|
| **Assets** | | |
| Cash and cash equivalents | $ 82,000 | $ 40,000 |
| Accounts receivable | 180,000 | 150,000 |
| Inventory | 170,000 | 200,000 |
| Equipment | 200,000 | 140,000 |
| Accumulated depreciation | (72,000) | (60,000) |
| Total assets | $560,000 | $470,000 |
| **Liabilities and Stockholders' Equity** | | |
| Accounts payable | $100,000 | $ 80,000 |
| Long-term notes payable | 100,000 | 50,000 |
| Common stock | 250,000 | 250,000 |
| Retained earnings | 110,000 | 90,000 |
| Total liabilities and stockholders' equity | $560,000 | $470,000 |

**Taylor Company**
**Income Statement**
**For the Year Ended December 31, 1993**

| | | |
|---|---|---|
| Sales revenue | | $345,000 |
| Cost of goods sold | | 120,000 |
| Gross margin | | $225,000 |
| Expenses: | | |
| Selling and general expenses | $58,000 | |
| Depreciation | 40,000 | |
| Interest expense | 2,000 | 100,000 |
| Operating income | | $125,000 |
| Gain from sale of equipment | | 5,000 |
| Income before income taxes | | $130,000 |
| Income tax expense | | 30,000 |
| Net income | | $100,000 |

Additional information:
1. Equipment costing $30,000, with a book value of $2,000, was sold for $7,000 during the year.
2. Retained Earnings was affected only by net income and cash dividends paid during the year.

Determining the change in cash and cash equivalents[16] is the first step in preparing a statement of cash flows. For Taylor Company, the cash balance has increased $42,000.

Since the primary purpose of the statement is to identify the cash receipts and payments for the period, and thus explain the change in the cash balance, the statement can be prepared by analyzing all noncash balance sheet accounts to determine what operating, investing, and financing transactions took place and what effect they had on cash flow.

To assist in the analysis of accounts, it is often helpful to use T-accounts, especially for certain accounts such as Retained Earnings, where the net change in the balance does not clearly show the total picture of the inflows and outflows of cash. To illustrate, the balance sheet shows that the December 31, 1992, balance in Retained Earnings for the Taylor Company was $90,000. It has increased $20,000 during 1993 to $110,000. Since the reported net income was $100,000 for 1993, there must have been reductions in Retained Earnings totaling $80,000. An analysis of the retained earnings account indicates a reduction of $80,000 for dividends.

**Retained Earnings**

| Dividends | 80,000 | Beginning balance | 90,000 |
|---|---|---|---|
| | | Net income | 100,000 |
| | | Ending balance | 110,000 |

Based on this analysis, the $100,000 of net income, prior to any adjustments, would be shown as an operating source of cash and the $80,000 of dividends as a use of cash for financing activities. These items would appear on a partially completed cash flow statement as shown below:

Cash flows from operating activities:
  Net income ............................................ $100,000

Cash flows from financing activities:
  Payment of dividends ...................................... $ (80,000)

Continuing the example, Taylor Company's net income of $100,000 must be adjusted for any noncash items and for any gains or losses. The entry to record depreciation has no effect on cash, so the depreciation expense for the period must be added to net income to arrive at cash provided by (used in) operations.

The amount of depreciation expense for the period for Taylor Company can be determined from the income statement. If limited information were available (e.g., if depreciation were included with other operating expenses in the income statement), an analysis of Accumulated Depreciation and the related equipment account would be necessary. The T-accounts on page 194 facilitate the analysis.

As illustrated, the net change in the equipment account is $60,000. Since $30,000 of equipment was sold, $90,000 of equipment must have been purchased, and this should be reflected on the cash flow statement as an investing activity. Similarly, the net change in Accumulated Depreciation is $12,000. The account was decreased by $28,000 due to the sale of equipment. The $40,000 of depreciation expense, a noncash item, should be added to net income as an adjustment to derive cash flow from operations.

In addition to adjustments for noncash items, net income must also be adjusted for gains and losses reported in the income statement. For Taylor Company, the $5,000 gain

[16]Throughout the remainder of the chapter, the term "cash" includes cash equivalents where appropriate.

from the sale of equipment (selling price of $7,000 less book value of $2,000) must be subtracted from net income. The proceeds from the sale of equipment, $7,000 in this illustration, provide the cash, and this amount should be included in the cash flow statement as part of cash flows from investing activities. Because the $5,000 gain on the sale is included in net income, it must be subtracted from net income to avoid counting the gain twice.

**Equipment**

| | | | |
|---|---|---|---|
| Beginning balance | 140,000 | Sale of equipment | 30,000 |
| Purchase of equipment | 90,000 | | |
| Ending balance | 200,000 | | |

**Accumulated Depreciation**

| | | | |
|---|---|---|---|
| Sale of equipment | 28,000 | Beginning balance | 60,000 |
| | | Depreciation expense | 40,000 |
| | | Ending balance | 72,000 |

The adjustments for Taylor Company for depreciation, to eliminate the gain on sale of equipment, and to record the increase and decrease in cash from the sale and purchase of equipment are illustrated in the developing statement of cash flows as follows:

**Cash flows from operating activities:**
| | |
|---|---|
| Net income .............................................. | $100,000 |
| Adjustments: | |
|     Depreciation expense ......................................... | 40,000 |
|     Gain on sale of equipment ...................................... | (5,000) |

**Cash flows from investing activities:**
| | |
|---|---|
| Sale of equipment ........................................... | $ 7,000 |
| Purchase of equipment ........................................ | (90,000) |

**Cash flows from financing activities:**
| | |
|---|---|
| Payment of dividends.......................................... | $ (80,000) |

In the Taylor Company example, the amount of net income adjusted for items not requiring cash is $135,000 ($100,000 net income + $40,000 depreciation − $5,000 gain). When preparing a cash flow statement, this amount must be further adjusted to reflect net income measured on a cash basis. As discussed previously in the chapter, with the indirect method, changes in current operating accounts are recognized as adjustments to accrual net income in deriving net cash flow from operations.

T-accounts for the current operating asset and liability accounts of Taylor Company are presented below:

**Accounts Receivable**

| | | | |
|---|---|---|---|
| Beginning balance | 150,000 | | |
| Net increase | 30,000 | | |
| Ending balance | 180,000 | | |

**Inventory**

| | | | |
|---|---|---|---|
| Beginning balance | 200,000 | Net decrease | 30,000 |
| Ending balance | 170,000 | | |

**Accounts Payable**

| | | | |
|---|---|---|---|
| | | Beginning balance | 80,000 |
| | | Net increase | 20,000 |
| | | Ending balance | 100,000 |

The $30,000 increase in receivables is deducted from net income, since cash receipts for goods and services sold were less than the revenue recognized in arriving at accrual net income. The $30,000 decrease in inventory is added to net income, since purchases were less than the charge made against revenue for cost of sales in arriving at net income. The $20,000 increase in accounts payable requires an addition to net income, since the cash disbursements for goods and services purchased were less than the charges made for these items in arriving at net income. These adjustments would result in the following presentation of cash flows from operating activities for Taylor Company:

| | |
|---|---|
| Cash flows from operating activities: | |
| Net income ........................................ | $100,000 |
| Adjustments: | |
| Depreciation expense ............................. | 40,000 |
| Gain on sale of equipment ........................ | (5,000) |
| Increase in accounts receivable .................... | (30,000) |
| Decrease in inventory ............................. | 30,000 |
| Increase in accounts payable ...................... | 20,000 |
| Net cash provided by operating activities .............. | $155,000 |

At this point, all noncash accounts have been analyzed except Long-Term Notes Payable and Common Stock. In the Taylor Company example, there is no change in the common stock account, but there is an increase of $50,000 in the long-term notes payable account. Unless there is contrary information, it is reasonable to assume that this increase resulted from additional borrowing, a financing activity. Thus the complete statement of cash flows, using the indirect method for operating activities, would appear as on page 196.

The completed statement highlights the major categories of inflows and outflows of cash. Taylor Company generated $155,000 from its operations. It used $83,000 for investments and another $30,000 for financing activities. The remaining $42,000 represents an increase in the cash balance and is the amount needed to reconcile the beginning-of-year and end-of-year cash and cash equivalent balances.

FASB Statement No. 95 requires disclosure of the amounts paid for interest expense and income taxes during the year. This supplemental disclosure can be presented with the statement of cash flows, as illustrated for Taylor Company, or in the notes to the financial statements. In the Taylor example, the amounts paid for interest and taxes are taken directly from the income statement. If the balance sheet had reported any beginning or ending payable balances for interest or taxes, the accrual-basis income statement amounts would have to be converted to a cash basis.

**Taylor Company**
**Statement of Cash Flows (Indirect Method)**
**For the Year Ended December 31, 1993**

| | | |
|---|---:|---:|
| **Cash flows from operating activities:** | | |
| Net income .......................................... | $100,000 | |
| Adjustments: | | |
| Depreciation expense .............................. | 40,000 | |
| Gain on sale of equipment ......................... | (5,000) | |
| Increase in accounts receivable ................... | (30,000) | |
| Decrease in inventory .............................. | 30,000 | |
| Increase in accounts payable ...................... | 20,000 | |
| Net cash provided by operating activities .............. | | $155,000 |
| **Cash flows from investing activities:** | | |
| Sale of equipment ................................... | $  7,000 | |
| Purchase of equipment .............................. | (90,000) | |
| Net cash used in investing activities................... | | (83,000) |
| **Cash flows from financing activities:** | | |
| Payment of dividends................................ | $ (80,000) | |
| Increase in long-term notes payable.................. | 50,000 | |
| Net cash used in financing activities.................. | | (30,000) |
| **Net increase in cash and cash equivalents** ............... | | $ 42,000 |
| Cash and cash equivalents at beginning of year ........... | | 40,000 |
| **Cash and cash equivalents at end of year**................ | | $ 82,000 |
| | | |
| **Supplemental Disclosure:** | | |
| Cash payments for: | | |
| Interest .................................. | $  2,000 | |
| Income taxes............................. | 30,000 | |

## The Direct Method of Determining Cash Flow From Operations

Unlike the indirect method, the direct method of determining cash flow from operations does not begin with net income, but reports *directly* the total cash inflows and outflows for each major category of operating activities. The inflows usually include cash receipts from (1) the sale of goods or services and (2) some peripheral activities, such as dividend and interest revenue. The outflows usually include cash payments made to (1) suppliers for inventory purchases, (2) employees for services, (3) governmental bodies for taxes, (4) lenders for interest expense, and (5) service providers for such items as rent and utilities. To determine these amounts, each cash transaction could be analyzed separately to derive the total cash receipts and payments for each category. Usually, however, summarized data provided in the financial statements can be analyzed to convert accrual-basis revenues and expenses to cash receipts and payments. No adjustment for noncash items, such as depreciation, is required under the direct method, since only cash events are reported.

To illustrate the analytical process that is used in preparing a cash flow statement with the direct method, consider sales revenue as an example. The amount of sales reported on the income statement must be adjusted for changes in accounts receivable balances to determine the cash collected during the period. The beginning receivables balance represents sales from the previous period. These receivables are assumed to have been collected in cash during the current period. The ending receivables represent sales of the current period that will be collected in a future period. Thus, to determine the cash collected from customers during the current period, the beginning receivables must be added to, and the ending receivables subtracted from, the accrual sales figure. If we assume reported sales of $500,000 and beginning and ending accounts receivable balances of $125,000 and $110,000 respectively, the computation would be:

| | |
|---|---|
| Sales (reported on income statement) ............................. | $500,000 |
| + Beginning accounts receivable .................................... | 125,000· |
| − Ending accounts receivable ...................................... | (110,000) |
| = Cash receipts from customers.................................... | $515,000 |

Rather than using the beginning and ending receivable balances, it is equally accepta-ble, and sometimes easier, to make the conversion using the increase or decrease in the accounts receivable balance. This method was illustrated when converting current operat-ing assets and liabilities under the indirect method. Thus, a decrease in the accounts receivable balance would be added to the reported sales amount and an increase would be deducted. In the above example, accounts receivable decreased by $15,000 during the year ($125,000 − $110,000). The cash receipts from customers would be $515,000 ($500,000 + $15,000), the same amount derived by using beginning and ending balances.

An assumption made in the above example (and throughout this chapter) is that all accounts receivable are collectible. The complications associated with uncollectible ac-counts, including the estimated expense for bad debts, will be addressed in Chapter 9, which covers receivables.

The conversion process applicable to sales also is required for other revenues and their related receivable balances. Revenues collected in advance require further explanation. For example, when rent revenue is collected in advance, the cash is received before it is earned. For these types of revenue items, the ending unearned rent balance is added to and the beginning unearned rent balance is subtracted from the reported rent revenue amount to compute the cash received for rent during the period.

A similar process and rationale are applicable for converting expenses reported on an accrual basis to the amount of cash paid during the period. To illustrate, if $150,000 of wages expense is reported on the income statement and the beginning and ending wages payable amounts are $40,000 and $45,000 respectively, the amount of cash paid for wages would be as follows:

| | |
|---|---|
| Wages expense (reported on income statement) .................... | $150,000 |
| + Beginning wages payable ....................................... | 40,000 |
| − Ending wages payable .......................................... | (45,000) |
| = Cash paid for wages during the period .......................... | $145,000 |

The conversion process would be the same for all expenses that are incurred prior to being paid, e.g., utilities, interest, property taxes, and income taxes. Prepaid expenses, however, are paid and recorded as assets prior to becoming an expense. An example would be prepaid insurance. For these types of expenses, the following calculation is required. Assume that insurance expense reported for the current period is $4,000 and the begin-ning and ending balances in Prepaid Insurance are $1,000 and $500, respectively. The amount of cash paid for insurance would be:

| | |
|---|---|
| Insurance expense (reported on income statement).................... | $4,000 |
| + Ending prepaid insurance......................................... | 500 |
| − Beginning prepaid insurance...................................... | (1,000) |
| = Cash paid for insurance ......................................... | $3,500 |

The amount of cash paid for inventory also must be calculated. If a company is using a periodic inventory system, the amount of purchases can be determined directly from the purchases accounts. That amount would then be adjusted by adding the beginning accounts payable balance and subtracting the ending accounts payable balance to determine the cash paid for inventory. If a perpetual inventory system is used, the cost of goods sold is known, but the amount of purchases would have to be calculated by adding the ending inventory and subtracting the beginning inventory amounts. Then, purchases would be adjusted to a cash basis by considering the beginning and ending accounts payable balances. The following calculations, with assumed numbers, illustrate this point:

| | |
|---|---:|
| Cost of goods sold (from perpetual inventory records) . . . . . . . . . . . . . . . | $240,000 |
| + Ending inventory . . . . . . . . . . . . . . . . . . . . . . . . . . . . . . . . . . . . . . . . . . | 43,000 |
| − Beginning inventory . . . . . . . . . . . . . . . . . . . . . . . . . . . . . . . . . . . . . . . | (38,000) |
| = Purchases . . . . . . . . . . . . . . . . . . . . . . . . . . . . . . . . . . . . . . . . . . . . . . . | $245,000 |
| + Beginning accounts payable . . . . . . . . . . . . . . . . . . . . . . . . . . . . . . . . . | 27,000 |
| − Ending accounts payable . . . . . . . . . . . . . . . . . . . . . . . . . . . . . . . . . . . . | (30,000) |
| = Cash paid for inventory . . . . . . . . . . . . . . . . . . . . . . . . . . . . . . . . . . . . . | $242,000 |

Exhibit 6—6 summarizes the adjusting procedures used to convert accrual amounts to the cash basis when using the direct method. The exhibit includes an example of each basic type of revenue and expense adjustment. If a company earns dividend revenue or incurs interest expense, FASB Statement No. 95 requires that those items be reported under operating activities. Dividend revenue is adjusted in the same manner as interest revenue. Interest expense is converted using the approach illustrated for wages expense.

## Illustration—Direct Method

To illustrate the preparation of the operating activities section of a statement of cash flows prepared using the direct method, an analysis will be made of the Taylor Company information presented on page 192.

To determine the amount of cash collected from customers for Taylor Company, the $345,000 of sales revenue reported on the income statement must be converted to a cash basis. Following the analytical approach described above, the computation is as follows:

| | |
|---|---:|
| Sales revenue . . . . . . . . . . . . . . . . . . . . . . . . . . . . . . . . . . . . . . . . . . . . . . . | $345,000 |
| + Beginning accounts receivable . . . . . . . . . . . . . . . . . . . . . . . . . . . . . . . | 150,000 |
| − Ending accounts receivable . . . . . . . . . . . . . . . . . . . . . . . . . . . . . . . . . . | (180,000) |
| = Cash receipts from customers . . . . . . . . . . . . . . . . . . . . . . . . . . . . . . . . | $315,000 |

Similar adjustments must be made to determine the cash paid for inventory purchases.

| | |
|---|---:|
| Cost of goods sold . . . . . . . . . . . . . . . . . . . . . . . . . . . . . . . . . . . . . . . . . . . | $ 120,000 |
| + Ending inventory . . . . . . . . . . . . . . . . . . . . . . . . . . . . . . . . . . . . . . . . . . . | 170,000 |
| − Beginning inventory . . . . . . . . . . . . . . . . . . . . . . . . . . . . . . . . . . . . . . . . | (200,000) |
| = Goods purchased during year . . . . . . . . . . . . . . . . . . . . . . . . . . . . . . . . . | $ 90,000 |
| + Beginning accounts payable . . . . . . . . . . . . . . . . . . . . . . . . . . . . . . . . . | 80,000 |
| − Ending accounts payable . . . . . . . . . . . . . . . . . . . . . . . . . . . . . . . . . . . . | (100,000) |
| = Cash paid for inventory purchases . . . . . . . . . . . . . . . . . . . . . . . . . . . . . | $ 70,000 |

For Taylor Company, the $58,000 of operating expenses (excluding depreciation and interest) does not require adjustment, since no related current asset or current liability

**Exhibit 6—6   Cash Flows From Operating Activities—Direct Method**

| Accrual Basis | ± Adjustments Required | = Cash Basis |
|---|---|---|
| Net sales | + Beginning accounts receivable<br>− Ending accounts receivable | = Cash receipts from customers |
| Other revenues (e.g., rent and interest):<br>  Rent revenue | + Ending unearned rent<br>− Beginning unearned rent | = Cash received for rent |
| Interest revenue | + Beginning interest receivable<br>− Ending interest receivable | = Cash received for interest |
| Cost of goods sold | + Ending inventory<br>− Beginning inventory<br>+ Beginning accounts payable<br>− Ending accounts payable | = Cash paid for inventory |
| Operating expenses (e.g., insurance and wages; excludes depreciation and other noncash items):<br>  Insurance expense | + Ending prepaid insurance<br>− Beginning prepaid insurance | = Cash paid for insurance |
| Wages expense | + Beginning wages payable<br>− Ending wages payable | = Cash paid for wages |
| Income tax expense | + Beginning income taxes payable<br>− Ending income taxes payable | = Cash paid for income taxes |
| | | Net cash provided by (used in) operating activities |

balances changed during this period. The same is true for Taylor Company's interest expense and income tax expense. Thus, the cash paid for operating expenses was $58,000; for interest, $2,000; for income taxes, $30,000. Note also that no adjustments are needed for noncash items, such as the $40,000 depreciation expense and the $5,000 gain, when using the direct method.

Based on the above analysis, the operating activities section of the statement of cash flows for Taylor Company, using the direct method, would be as follows:

**Taylor Company**
**Partial Statement of Cash Flows (Direct Method)**
**For the Year Ended December 31, 1993**

| | | |
|---|---:|---:|
| **Cash flows from operating activities:** | | |
| Cash receipts from customers ......................... | | $315,000 |
| Cash payments for: | | |
| Inventory ......................................... | $70,000 | |
| Operating expenses ............................... | 58,000 | |
| Interest .......................................... | 2,000 | |
| Income taxes...................................... | 30,000 | 160,000 |
| Net cash provided by operating activities ................ | | $155,000 |

Note that the amount of cash provided by operations, $155,000, is the same as the amount determined using the indirect method (page 196). The investing and financing sections of the statements would be identical. If the direct approach is used, the FASB requires that a schedule be included that reconciles net income to net cash provided by (used in) operations. A schedule to accompany Taylor Company's cash flow statement prepared using the direct method is provided below. If the indirect approach is used, this reconciliation is already part of the statement.

**Taylor Company**
**Schedule Reconciling Net Income to Net Cash**
**Provided by Operating Activities**
**For the Year Ended December 31, 1993**

| | | |
|---|---:|---:|
| Net income ............................................. | | $100,000 |
| Adjustments to reconcile net income to net cash provided | | |
| by operating activities: | | |
| Depreciation expense ............................... | $40,000 | |
| Gain on sale of equipment .......................... | (5,000) | |
| Increase in accounts receivable ...................... | (30,000) | |
| Decrease in inventory ............................... | 30,000 | |
| Increase in accounts payable ........................ | 20,000 | 55,000 |
| Net cash provided by operating activities ................ | | $155,000 |

## COMPREHENSIVE ILLUSTRATION OF STATEMENT OF CASH FLOWS

Examples in the preceding sections involved only a few accounts and were thus relatively simple. Ordinarily, however, more complex circumstances are encountered, and a more systematic approach is required in preparing a statement of cash flows. In the pages that follow, a comprehensive T-account approach for use with the indirect method is described first. The adjustments needed to prepare the operating activities section with the direct method are then discussed. The appendix to this chapter describes and illustrates a work sheet approach to preparing a statement of cash flows with the indirect method.

The illustrations and analysis that follow are based on the comparative balance sheet data and combined income and retained earnings statement for Western Resources, Inc., as shown on page 203, and the following information:

- Marketable securities that do not qualify as cash equivalents were purchased during the year at a cost of $2,000.

## Background of FASB Statement No. 95

Although Statement No. 95 has been around only since 1987, cash flow statements have a long history in the United States. In 1863, The Northern Central Railroad issued a summary of its financial transactions that included an outline of its cash receipts and cash disbursements for the year. Later, emphasis shifted away from cash flow and toward a broader definition of "funds." In 1902, United States Steel Corporation produced a report that listed the major causes of the change in "funds" during the year—funds being defined as current assets minus accounts payable. A working capital funds statement—reporting causes of changes in funds defined as current assets minus current liabilities—became increasingly popular after 1920. A funds statement was made mandatory in 1971 by APB Opinion No. 19. The definition of funds was left to the provider, with both a cash emphasis and a working capital emphasis being permissible.

During the early 1980s, the Financial Executives Institute (FEI) encouraged its members to adopt a cash emphasis in their funds statements. In 1980, only 10 percent of the Fortune 500 used a cash focus. By 1985, 70 percent used a cash focus. During this same period, the FASB issued *Statement of Financial Accounting Concepts No. 5*, which suggested that, conceptually, a cash flow statement should be part of a full set of financial statements. In April 1985 the FASB added a cash flow reporting project to its agenda.

The FASB cash flow pronouncement, *Statement of Financial Accounting Standards No. 95*, illustrates that the setting of accounting standards is not a science, but is a "balancing act" with the differing opinions of users and preparers being weighed against one another and the considerations of cost of implementation being weighed against the potential benefits. Since standard setting is a balancing act, not all interested parties will agree on the final outcome. In fact, three of the seven FASB members dissented to the final version of Statement No. 95.

One area of disagreement was in relation to the categorization of interest and dividend cash flows. Three of the Board members felt that interest and dividends paid are a cost of obtaining financing and should both be classified as cash outflows from financing activities. But, in Statement No. 95, dividend payments are included in the financing activities section, while interest payments are classified as cash outflows from operating activities. Similarly, the three Board members felt that interest and dividends received are returns on investments and therefore should be classified as cash inflows from investing activities. Statement No. 95 includes both these items in the operating activities section.

A more significant disagreement related to the permissibility of both the indirect and the direct methods of reporting cash flow from operations. Before the issuance of the Statement, a majority of the outside comments to the Board advocated requiring use of the direct method. Most of these comments were from commercial lenders who indicated that detailed cash flow information by category would help them to better assess a firm's ability to repay borrowing. Those opposed to this direct method requirement, and who instead advocated the permissibility of both methods, were mainly preparers and providers of financial statements. They argued that requiring use of the direct method would impose excessive implementation costs on some firms. They also argued that the indirect method provides more meaningful information because it is more similar to what has been used in the past. The final Statement allows both methods, but does "encourage" use of the direct method.

Statement No. 95 describes major change in financial reporting as "an evolutionary process." Conceptual purity is balanced against feasibility and cost of implementation. While it is likely that the standards of cash flow reporting will be further improved in the future, Statement No. 95 represents a significant incremental improvement over prior practice.

**Questions:**

1. *Interest and dividends paid are both costs of obtaining financing—interest is the cost of obtaining debt financing, and dividends are the cost of obtaining equity financing. Accordingly, some have advocated classifying both interest and dividends paid as cash outflows from financing activities. What arguments can you think of to support classifying interest paid as an operating cash outflow, as required by Statement No. 95?*
2. *Imagine that 10 years have gone by since the issuance of Statement No. 95 and that you are a member of the FASB. The Board is reconsidering the issue of whether both the direct and indirect methods should be allowed, or whether use of the direct method should be made mandatory. What evidence would you look at to help you make your decision?*

Sources:

James H. Thompson and Thomas E. Buttross, "Return to Cash Flow," *The CPA Journal*, March 1988: pp. 30-40.

Dennis R. Beresford, "The 'Balancing Act' in Setting Accounting Standards," *Accounting Horizons*, March 1988: pp. 1-7.

*Statement of Financial Accounting Standards No. 95*, "Statement of Cash Flows" (1987), pars. 88-90 and 106-121.

- A tornado totally destroyed a building costing $40,000 with a book value of $10,000. The insurance company paid $10,000 cash; a new building was then constructed at a cost of $105,000.
- Long-term investments, cost $96,000, were sold for $102,500.
- Land was acquired for $108,500, the seller accepting in payment $40,000 of common stock and $68,500 in cash.
- New machinery was purchased for $12,000 cash.
- The amortization of patent cost and depreciation expense on buildings and equipment were recorded as follows:

| | |
|---|---:|
| Depreciation—buildings | $ 5,600 |
| Depreciation—machinery and equipment | 15,300 |
| Amortization—patents | 5,000 |
| Total depreciation and amortization | $25,900 |

- Ten-year bonds were sold at their face value of $30,000 at the beginning of the year.

### Indirect Method—T-Account Approach to Preparing a Statement of Cash Flows

With a comprehensive T-account approach, special "cash flows" T-accounts are established. These accounts are used to summarize cash flows from operations and from investing and financing activities during the period. They provide the basis for preparing the formal cash flow statement. Individual T-accounts are also established for Cash and all other balance sheet accounts.

During the process of analysis, the change in each account is explained as providing or using cash. In the three T-accounts summarizing cash flows from operating, investing, and financing activities, a debit represents an increase in cash, while a credit reflects a decrease. Once the changes in all balance sheet accounts have been reconciled and the cash flows T-accounts balanced, the formal cash flow statement can be prepared.

In preparing a cash flow statement for Western Resources, Inc., we begin by determining the change in cash balance, in this case an $8,700 decrease. All noncash accounts may now be analyzed using the T-accounts illustrated on the following pages. As noted,

**Western Resources, Inc.**
**Statement of Income and Retained Earnings**
**For the Year Ended December 31, 1993**

| | | |
|---|---:|---:|
| Sales..................................................... | | $753,800 |
| Cost of goods sold ..................................... | | 524,100 |
| Gross margin ........................................... | | $229,700 |
| Expenses: | | |
| Selling and general expenses......................... | $146,400 | |
| Depreciation and amortization expense................ | 25,900 | |
| Interest expense....................................... | 3,600 | 175,900 |
| Operating income ...................................... | | $ 53,800 |
| Gain on sale of long-term investment ................... | | 6,500 |
| Income before income taxes............................ | | $ 60,300 |
| Income tax expense .................................... | | 24,000 |
| Net income ............................................ | | $ 36,300 |
| Retained earnings, December 31, 1992 ................. | | 234,300 |
| | | $270,600 |
| Cash dividends........................................ | | 25,100 |
| Retained earnings, December 31, 1993 ................. | | $245,500 |

**Western Resources, Inc.**
**Comparative Balance Sheet**
**December 31, 1993 and 1992**

| | 1993 | | 1992 | |
|---|---:|---:|---:|---:|
| **Assets** | | | | |
| Current assets: | | | | |
| Cash and cash equivalents ......... | $ 46,300 | | $ 55,000 | |
| Marketable securities .............. | 12,000 | | 10,000 | |
| Accounts receivable .............. | 60,000 | | 70,500 | |
| Inventories....................... | 75,000 | | 76,500 | |
| Prepaid operating expenses ........ | 16,500 | $209,800 | 12,000 | $224,000 |
| Investments (at cost) .............. | | 10,000 | | 106,000 |
| Land, buildings, and equipment: | | | | |
| Land .......................... | $183,500 | | $ 75,000 | |
| Buildings ......................... | 290,000 | | 225,000 | |
| Less accumulated depreciation .... | (130,600) | | (155,000) | |
| Machinery and equipment ......... | 132,000 | | 120,000 | |
| Less accumulated depreciation .... | (58,800) | 416,100 | (43,500) | 221,500 |
| Patents ........................... | | 35,000 | | 40,000 |
| Total assets........................ | | $670,900 | | $591,500 |
| **Liabilities** | | | | |
| Current liabilities: | | | | |
| Accounts payable ................. | $ 91,000 | | $ 97,700 | |
| Income taxes payable.............. | 10,000 | | 9,500 | |
| Dividends payable................. | 4,400 | $105,400 | — | $107,200 |
| Bonds payable ..................... | | 30,000 | | — |
| Total liabilities ..................... | | $135,400 | | $107,200 |
| **Stockholders' Equity** | | | | |
| Common stock ..................... | $290,000 | | $250,000 | |
| Retained earnings .................. | 245,500 | 535,500 | 234,300 | 484,300 |
| Total liabilities and stockholders' equity .............................. | | $670,900 | | $591,500 |

the cash flow statement is prepared directly from the cash flows T-accounts and is illustrated on page 208.

Generally, the most efficient approach to developing T-accounts for a statement of cash flows is to begin with an analysis of the change in Retained Earnings [see items (a) and (b)]. After the change in Retained Earnings has been accounted for, the remaining noncash accounts should be reviewed in conjunction with the income statement and supplementary information to determine what additional adjustments are required. Operating income should be adjusted to determine the actual amount of cash provided or used by operations [items (e), (i), (j), and (l)-(p)]. Analysis must also be made to determine all other cash flows from investing and financing activities [items (b), (c), (d), (e), (f), (h), (k), and (q)], and to reflect significant investing and financing activities that have no effect on cash [item (g)].

Explanations for individual adjustments for Western Resources, Inc., follow. The letter preceding each explanation corresponds with that used in the T-accounts, which are presented on pages 206-207. Entries are presented to help explain the preparation of a statement of cash flows. They are not journal entries that would be recorded in the accounting records.

(a)   Net income is recorded in the T-accounts as follows:

| | | |
|---|---:|---:|
| Cash Flows—Operating | 36,300 | |
|    Retained Earnings | | 36,300 |

(b)   The cash dividends declared and deducted from retained earnings are adjusted for the change in the dividends payable balance in arriving at the amount of dividends actually paid during the year. The entry would be:

| | | |
|---|---:|---:|
| Retained Earnings | 25,100 | |
|    Dividends Payable | | 4,400 |
|    Cash Flows—Financing | | 20,700 |

(c)   The destruction of the building and the subsequent insurance reimbursement have the effect of providing cash of $10,000, the proceeds from the insurance company. The entry would be:

| | | |
|---|---:|---:|
| Accumulated Depreciation—Buildings | 30,000 | |
| Cash Flows—Investing | 10,000 | |
|    Buildings | | 40,000 |

(d)   The buildings account was increased by the cost of constructing a new building, $105,000. The cost of the new building is reported separately as an investment of cash by the following entry:

| | | |
|---|---:|---:|
| Buildings | 105,000 | |
|    Cash Flows—Investing | | 105,000 |

(e)   The sale of long-term investments was recorded by a credit to the asset account at cost, $96,000, and a credit to a gain on sale of investment account. At the end of the period, the gain account was closed to retained earnings as part of income from continuing operations. Since the effect of the sale was to provide cash of $102,500, this amount is reported as cash provided by investing activities. The investments account balance is reduced, and cash provided by operations is decreased by the amount of the gain. The following adjustment is made:

| | | |
|---|---:|---:|
| Cash Flows—Investing | 102,500 | |
|    Investments | | 96,000 |
|    Cash Flows—Operating | | 6,500 |

(f) and (g) Land was acquired at a price of $108,500; payment was made in common stock valued at $40,000 and cash of $68,500. Two separate entries are made to segregate the cash and noncash components of this transaction:

| | | |
|---|---|---|
| (f) | Land ............................................... | 68,500 |
| | Cash Flows—Investing ............................ | | 68,500 |
| (g) | Land ............................................... | 40,000 |
| | Common Stock .................................... | | 40,000 |

The issuance of common stock for land has no effect on cash, but it is a significant transaction that should be disclosed separately. Recall that the body of the cash flow statement reports only transactions affecting cash, in accordance with FASB Statement No. 95.

(h) Machinery costing $12,000 was acquired during the year. Payment was made in cash and is reported as cash used for investing purposes. The adjustment for the acquisition of machinery is:

| | | |
|---|---|---|
| Machinery and Equipment ................................. | 12,000 | |
| Cash Flows—Investing .................................... | | 12,000 |

(i) and (j) The changes in the accumulated depreciation accounts and in the patents account result from the recognition of depreciation and amortization expense for the period. These noncash expenses are added in computing cash flows from operations by the following adjustments:

| | | |
|---|---|---|
| (i) | Cash Flows—Operating ............................. | 20,900 |
| | Accumulated Depreciation—Buildings ................ | | 5,600 |
| | Accumulated Depreciation—Machinery and Equipment | | 15,300 |
| (j) | Cash Flows—Operating ............................. | 5,000 |
| | Patents .......................................... | | 5,000 |

(k) During the year, bonds were issued at their face value of $30,000. The entry is:

| | | |
|---|---|---|
| Cash Flows—Financing .................................... | 30,000 | |
| Bonds Payable ......................................... | | 30,000 |

(l)-(p) In preparing a cash flow statement, operating income must be adjusted from an accrual basis to a cash basis, as explained earlier in the chapter. The entries (l) through (p) reflect that analysis for Western Resources, Inc.

| | | |
|---|---|---|
| (l) | Cash Flows—Operating ............................. | 10,500 |
| | Accounts Receivable ............................... | | 10,500 |
| (m) | Cash Flows—Operating ............................. | 1,500 |
| | Inventories ....................................... | | 1,500 |
| (n) | Prepaid Operating Expenses ........................ | 4,500 |
| | Cash Flows—Operating .............................. | | 4,500 |
| (o) | Accounts Payable .................................. | 6,700 |
| | Cash Flows—Operating .............................. | | 6,700 |
| (p) | Cash Flows—Operating ............................. | 500 |
| | Income Taxes Payable .............................. | | 500 |

(q) As noted earlier in the chapter, marketable securities are treated differently from other current assets in preparing a cash flow statement, since marketable securities transactions usually are investing rather than operating activities. The adjustment to reflect the purchase of $2,000 of marketable securities would be:

| | | |
|---|---|---|
| Marketable Securities ...................................... | 2,000 | |
| Cash Flows—Investing ..................................... | | 2,000 |

(r)    After all changes in account balances have been reconciled and the effects of the changes on cash flow have been recorded in the cash flow T-accounts, the balances of those T-accounts are determined and transferred to a Cash Flows Summary T-account as shown below. The excess of credits (decreases in cash) over debits (increases in cash) is equal to the net change in the cash balance for the period of $8,700. The following entry is made to reflect the net decrease in cash:

| | | |
|---|---|---|
| Net Decrease in Cash ..................................... | 8,700 | |
| Cash .................................................. | | 8,700 |

All T-accounts are now complete, and a statement of cash flows for Western Resources, Inc., can be prepared in an appropriate format, such as the one presented on page 208.

**Cash Flows—Operating**

| | | | |
|---|---|---|---|
| (a) | 36,300 | (e) | 6,500 |
| (i) | 20,900 | (n) | 4,500 |
| (j) | 5,000 | (o) | 6,700 |
| (l) | 10,500 | | |
| (m) | 1,500 | | |
| (p) | 500 | | |
| Net cash provided by operating activities .. | 57,000 | | |

**Cash Flows—Investing**

| | | | |
|---|---|---|---|
| (c) | 10,000 | (d) | 105,000 |
| (e) | 102,500 | (f) | 68,500 |
| | | (h) | 12,000 |
| | | (q) | 2,000 |
| Net cash used in investing activities ...... | | | 75,000 |

**Cash Flows—Financing**

| | | | |
|---|---|---|---|
| (k) | 30,000 | (b) | 20,700 |
| Net cash provided by financing activities... | 9,300 | | |

**Cash Flows Summary**

| | | | |
|---|---|---|---|
| Net cash provided—operating ........... | 57,000 | | |
| Net cash used—investing .............. | | | 75,000 |
| Net cash provided—financing ........... | 9,300 | | |
| Net decrease in cash ................. (r) | 8,700 | | |
| | 75,000 | | 75,000 |

**Cash and Cash Equivalents**

| | | | |
|---|---|---|---|
| Beginning bal. | 55,000 | (r) | 8,700 |
| Ending bal. | 46,300 | | |

**Marketable Securities**

| | | | |
|---|---|---|---|
| Beginning bal. | 10,000 | | |
| (q) | 2,000 | | |
| Ending bal. | 12,000 | | |

**Accounts Receivable**

| | | | |
|---|---|---|---|
| Beginning bal. | 70,500 | (l) | 10,500 |
| Ending bal. | 60,000 | | |

**Inventories**

| | | | |
|---|---|---|---|
| Beginning bal. | 76,500 | (m) | 1,500 |
| Ending bal. | 75,000 | | |

**Prepaid Operating Expenses**

| | | | |
|---|---|---|---|
| Beginning bal. | 12,000 | | |
| (n) | 4,500 | | |
| Ending bal. | 16,500 | | |

**Investments**

| | | | |
|---|---|---|---|
| Beginning bal. | 106,000 | (e) | 96,000 |
| Ending bal. | 10,000 | | |

**Land**

| | | | |
|---|---|---|---|
| Beginning bal. | 75,000 | | |
| (f) | 68,500 | | |
| (g) | 40,000 | | |
| Ending bal. | 183,500 | | |

**Buildings**

| | | | |
|---|---|---|---|
| Beginning bal. | 225,000 | (c) | 40,000 |
| (d) | 105,000 | | |
| Ending bal. | 290,000 | | |

**Accumulated Depreciation—Buildings**

| | | | |
|---|---|---|---|
| (c) | 30,000 | Beginning bal. | 155,000 |
| | | (i) | 5,600 |
| | | Ending bal. | 130,600 |

**Machinery and Equipment**

| | | | |
|---|---|---|---|
| Beginning bal. | 120,000 | | |
| (h) | 12,000 | | |
| Ending bal. | 132,000 | | |

**Accumulated Depreciation— Machinery and Equipment**

| | | | |
|---|---|---|---|
| | | Beginning bal. | 43,500 |
| | | (i) | 15,300 |
| | | Ending bal. | 58,800 |

**Patents**

| | | | |
|---|---|---|---|
| Beginning bal. | 40,000 | (j) | 5,000 |
| Ending bal. | 35,000 | | |

**Accounts Payable**

| | | | |
|---|---|---|---|
| (o) | 6,700 | Beginning bal. | 97,700 |
| | | Ending bal. | 91,000 |

**Income Taxes Payable**

| | | | |
|---|---|---|---|
| | | Beginning bal. | 9,500 |
| | | (p) | 500 |
| | | Ending bal. | 10,000 |

**Dividends Payable**

| | | | |
|---|---|---|---|
| | | Beginning bal. | 0 |
| | | (b) | 4,400 |
| | | Ending bal. | 4,400 |

**Bonds Payable**

| | | | |
|---|---|---|---|
| | | Beginning bal. | 0 |
| | | (k) | 30,000 |
| | | Ending bal. | 30,000 |

**Common Stock**

| | | | |
|---|---|---|---|
| | | Beginning bal. | 250,000 |
| | | (g) | 40,000 |
| | | Ending bal. | 290,000 |

**Retained Earnings**

| | | | |
|---|---|---|---|
| (b) | 25,100 | Beginning bal. | 234,300 |
| | | (a) | 36,300 |
| | | Ending bal. | 245,500 |

**Western Resources, Inc.**
**Statement of Cash Flows**
**For the Year Ended December 31, 1993**

| | | |
|---|---:|---:|
| **Cash flows from operating activities:** | | |
| Income from continuing operations ................... | $ 36,300 | |
| Adjustments: | | |
| Depreciation expense .............................. | 20,900 | |
| Amortization of patents ............................ | 5,000 | |
| Gain on sale of investments ........................ | (6,500) | |
| Decrease in accounts receivable .................... | 10,500 | |
| Decrease in inventories ............................ | 1,500 | |
| Increase in prepaid operating expenses.............. | (4,500) | |
| Decrease in accounts payable ...................... | (6,700) | |
| Increase in income taxes payable ................... | 500 | |
| Net cash provided by operating activities .............. | | $ 57,000 |
| | | |
| **Cash flows from investing activities:** | | |
| Involuntary conversion of building .................... | $ 10,000 | |
| Construction of building ............................ | (105,000) | |
| Sale of long-term investments ....................... | 102,500 | |
| Purchase of land ................................... | (68,500) | |
| Purchase of machinery and equipment ............... | (12,000) | |
| Purchase of marketable securities .................... | (2,000) | |
| Net cash used in investing activities................... | | (75,000) |
| | | |
| **Cash flows from financing activities:** | | |
| Issuance of bonds .................................. | $ 30,000 | |
| Payment of cash dividends .......................... | (20,700) | |
| Net cash provided by financing activities .............. | | 9,300 |
| | | |
| **Net decrease in cash and cash equivalents** .............. | | $ (8,700) |
| Cash and cash equivalents at beginning of year .......... | | 55,000 |
| **Cash and cash equivalents at end of year**................ | | $ 46,300 |
| | | |
| **Supplemental Disclosure:** | | |
| Cash payments for: | | |
| Interest ......................................... | $ 3,600 | |
| Income taxes..................................... | 23,500 | |
| Noncash transaction: | | |
| Land acquired by issuing common stock ........... | 40,000 | |

A reader analyzing the cash flow statement for Western Resources, Inc., can readily see that $57,000 cash was provided internally from operating activities. This amount was not sufficient to satisfy the investment needs of the company, and so additional cash was generated from external financing activities involving the issuance of bonds. The cash generated from operations clearly met the need for payment of cash dividends, but when other cash needs are considered, the total cash outflow exceeded the total inflow of cash for the period, causing the cash balance to decrease by $8,700, or 15.8%.

In addition to the formal statement of cash flows, supplemental disclosure is required for significant noncash investing and financing transactions. Thus, Western Resources would report the acquisition of land valued at $40,000 in exchange for common stock. When the indirect method is used to report operating activities, the amount of cash paid for interest and income taxes also must be disclosed. For Western Resources, the amount paid for interest, $3,600, is taken directly from the income statement, because there is no interest payable at the beginning or end of the year. The amount paid for taxes is determined as follows:

| | |
|---|---|
| Income tax expense (reported in the income statement) .............. | $24,000 |
| Deduct increase in income taxes payable ........................... | (500) |
| Amount of cash paid for income taxes ............................. | $23,500 |

In the Western Resources illustration, the supplemental disclosures are presented in a schedule accompanying the statement of cash flows. Alternatively, the information could be presented in the notes to the financial statements.

## Direct Method—Adjustments Required to Prepare the Operating Activities Section of a Statement of Cash Flows

As noted earlier, the direct and indirect methods differ only in their impact on the operating activities section of the statement of cash flows. When using the direct method, individual operating revenue and expense items reported on the income statement are converted from an accrual to a cash basis. The conversion procedures are summarized in Exhibit 6—6 on page 199.

The adjustments required to convert operating revenues and expenses for Western Resources, Inc., to a cash basis are presented below. In this illustration, net increases or decreases in the current operating accounts are used to make the conversion from accrual to cash rather than the beginning and ending balances as illustrated earlier in the chapter.

| | |
|---|---|
| Sales ...................................................... | $753,800 |
| Decrease in accounts receivable ............................... | 10,500 [1] |
| Cash receipts from customers .................................. | $764,300 |
| | |
| Cost of goods sold ........................................... | $524,100 |
| Decrease in inventory ......................................... | (1,500) [2] |
| Decrease in accounts payable .................................. | 6,700 [3] |
| Cash paid for inventory ....................................... | $529,300 |
| | |
| Selling and general expenses.................................. | $146,400 |
| Increase in prepaid operating expenses ........................ | 4,500 [4] |
| Cash paid for selling and general expenses ..................... | $150,900 |
| | |
| Interest expense............................................. | $ 3,600 |
| Adjustment required.......................................... | -0- [5] |
| Cash paid for interest ........................................ | $ 3,600 |
| | |
| Income tax expense ......................................... | $ 24,000 |
| Increase in income taxes payable ............................. | (500) [6] |
| Cash paid for income taxes.................................... | $ 23,500 |

Key to adjustments

[1]Decrease in accounts receivable (previous sales collected this period).
[2]Decrease in inventories (inventory sold this period but purchased last period).
[3]Decrease in accounts payable (purchases made last period but paid for this period).
[4]Increase in prepaid operating expenses (additional prepaid expenses paid for this period).
[5]No change in interest payable; therefore, no adjustment required.
[6]Increase in income taxes payable (income taxes of this period not yet paid).

With the direct method, only operating revenues and expenses involving cash are included in the conversion process. Noncash items, such as the depreciation and amortization expense of $25,900, are not relevant. Also, the $6,500 gain from the sale of an investment is ignored in the analysis, because it is an investing not an operating activity.

Cash flows from operating activities are presented on the statement of cash flows using the direct method as shown on page 210. The rest of the statement is identical to the one presented on page 208.

**Western Resources, Inc.**
**Statement of Cash Flows**
**For the Year Ended December 31, 1993**

| | | |
|---|---:|---:|
| **Cash flows from operating activities:** | | |
| Cash receipts from customers .......................... | | $764,300 |
| Cash payments for: | | |
|     Inventory .......................................... | $529,300 | |
|     Selling and general expenses....................... | 150,900 | |
|     Interest expense.................................... | 3,600 | |
|     Income taxes....................................... | 23,500 | 707,300 |
| Net cash provided by operating activities ................ | | $ 57,000 |

A reconciliation of net income to net cash flow from operations, similar to that illustrated for Taylor Company on page 200, would be presented along with the statement of cash flows prepared using the direct method. Supplemental disclosure of the noncash transaction (exchange of stock for land) would be presented separately. When the direct method is used, cash paid for interest and taxes is included in the operating activities section of the statement.

## SUMMARY

The FASB's conceptual framework suggests that a statement of cash flows is essential in meeting the informational needs of investors and creditors. Statement No. 95 now requires that such a statement be presented as one of the three primary financial statements prepared for external users. The cash flows for the period are to be classified according to three main categories: operating activities, investing activities, and financing activities. The statement reports the net cash provided by or used in each category and explains the net increase or decrease in cash and cash equivalents. Significant financing and investing transactions not involving cash are to be reported in notes to the financial statements or in separate schedules, not in the statement of cash flows.

Companies may use either the indirect or the direct method in presenting cash flows from operating activities. The indirect method, which is used by a vast majority of companies, begins with net income for the period and adjusts this amount to net cash provided by (used in) operating activities. In contrast, the direct method does not begin with net income, but reports directly the amount of cash received or paid for each major type of operating activity, e.g., cash received from customers and cash paid to suppliers. A separate schedule reconciling net income to net cash provided by (used in) operating activities is required when the statement of cash flows is prepared using the direct method. If the indirect method is used, supplemental disclosures of cash paid for interest and income taxes are required. With the direct method, these amounts are included in the operating activities section of the statement of cash flows.

As a result of the specific reporting guidelines in FASB Statement No. 95, external users can expect a considerable degree of uniformity and comparability in the presentation of the statement of cash flows. IBM Corporation's 1990 statement of cash flows, included in Appendix A at the end of the text, illustrates how this company is complying with Statement No. 95.

All of the basic aspects of cash flow reporting and disclosure have been covered in this chapter. Additional complexities are introduced in later chapters as appropriate. An expanded illustration, incorporating these complexities, is provided in an appendix to the last chapter of the text, which covers financial statement analysis.

## Cash Flow Versus Earnings

Picking stocks based on price-earnings (PE) ratios is a strategy that has been used for over 50 years. (A company's PE ratio equals stock price per share divided by earnings per share.) In general, the strategy involves buying stocks of firms with low PE ratios—low compared to the market average or low compared to the firm's average PE ratio in the past. This strategy places much emphasis on the usefulness of traditional reported net income based on accrual accounting.

Many analysts are now using cash flow as the basis for picking stocks. Operating cash flow is seen as a good indicator of how much money a company would have to respond to new expansion opportunities or to sustain itself in a crisis. Corporate raiders are attracted to firms with strong cash flow, because that cash can be used to pay interest on any debt used in an acquisition.

Cash flow analysis is sometimes hampered by inconsistency in the definition of "cash flow." Cash flow sometimes means: net income + depreciation + amortization. Increasingly, cash flow means the cash flow from operations reported in the statement of cash flows, which takes into account the changes in levels of operating receivables, inventories, and operating payables. Another measure of cash flow is sometimes called "free cash flow" and is defined as: operating cash flow + interest expense + income tax expense − capital expenditures − dividends. Free cash flow for a business has been compared to discretionary income for a family—that is, funds available for optional uses.

Real estate investments have long been evaluated based on cash flow. This same approach is increasingly being applied to all types of ventures. While Time Inc. and Warner Communications were negotiating their merger, J. Richard Munro, Chairman of Time Inc., told shareholders at the annual meeting: "When it comes to valuing media and entertainment companies like ours, what matters is not profits but cash flow."

### Questions:

1. *Having learned about the advantages of accrual accounting, what warnings would you give to someone using cash flow analysis to pick attractive investments?*
2. *What do you think makes cash flow analysis particularly useful for evaluating real estate investments?*

Sources:

John R. Dorfman, "Two Money Managers Duke It out in Debate on Stock-Value Theories," *The Wall Street Journal*, July 17, 1989: p. C1.

Jeffrey M. Laderman, "Earnings, Schmernings—Look at the Cash," *Business Week*, July 24, 1989: p. 56.

# APPENDIX

## Work Sheet Approach to Preparing a Statement of Cash Flows–Indirect Method

This appendix illustrates a work sheet approach to preparing a statement of cash flows using the indirect method. As shown, this approach produces the same results as the T-account approach illustrated in the chapter; only the format is different. To highlight the similarities in the two approaches, the information and account analysis used in the T-account illustration for Western Resources, Inc., will also be used for the work sheet illustration.

Using a work sheet, such as the one illustrated on page 213, facilitates the analysis of account changes when using the indirect method. The format of the work sheet is straightforward. The first amount column contains the beginning balances, then there are two columns for analysis of transactions to arrive at the ending balances in the fourth column.

In preparing a work sheet, accumulated depreciation balances, instead of being reported as credit balances in the debit (asset) section, may be more conveniently listed with liability and owners' equity balances in the credit section. Similarly, contra liability accounts and contra owners' equity balances may be separately recognized and more conveniently listed with assets in the debit section.

The lower portion of the work sheet shows the major categories of cash flows: operating, investing, and financing. A debit in the lower section means an increase in cash, while a credit is a decrease in cash. It is from the lower section of the work sheet that the formal statement of cash flows is prepared. In following the illustration, it may be helpful to refer to the detailed explanations for individual adjustments described on pages 204-206 of the chapter. Once the changes in all accounts have been reconciled and the work sheet is complete, the formal cash flow statement can be prepared, as illustrated on page 208.

**Western Resources, Inc.**
**Work Sheet for Statement of Cash Flows—Indirect Method**
**For the Year Ended December 31, 1993**

| Accounts | Balance Dec. 31, 1992 | Adjustments Debit | | Adjustments Credit | | Balance Dec. 31, 1993 |
|---|---|---|---|---|---|---|
| **Debits** | | | | | | |
| Cash and Cash Equivalents . . . . . . | 55,000 | | | (r) | 8,700 | 46,300 |
| Marketable Securities . . . . . . . . . . | 10,000 | (q) | 2,000 | | | 12,000 |
| Accounts Receivable . . . . . . . . . . . | 70,500 | | | (l) | 10,500 | 60,000 |
| Inventories . . . . . . . . . . . . . . . . . . . | 76,500 | | | (m) | 1,500 | 75,000 |
| Prepaid Operating Expenses . . . . . | 12,000 | (n) | 4,500 | | | 16,500 |
| Investments . . . . . . . . . . . . . . . . . | 106,000 | | | (e) | 96,000 | 10,000 |
| Land . . . . . . . . . . . . . . . . . . . . . . . | 75,000 | (f) | 68,500 | | | |
| | | (g) | 40,000 | | | 183,500 |
| Buildings . . . . . . . . . . . . . . . . . . . . | 225,000 | (d) | 105,000 | (c) | 40,000 | 290,000 |
| Machinery and Equipment . . . . . . | 120,000 | (h) | 12,000 | | | 132,000 |
| Patents . . . . . . . . . . . . . . . . . . . . . | 40,000 | | | (j) | 5,000 | 35,000 |
| | 790,000 | | | | | 860,300 |
| **Credits** | | | | | | |
| Accum. Depr.—Buildings . . . . . . . | 155,000 | (c) | 30,000 | (i) | 5,600 | 130,600 |
| Accum. Depr.—Mach. and Eq. . . . . | 43,500 | | | (i) | 15,300 | 58,800 |
| Accounts Payable . . . . . . . . . . . . . | 97,700 | (o) | 6,700 | | | 91,000 |
| Income Taxes Payable . . . . . . . . . | 9,500 | | | (p) | 500 | 10,000 |
| Dividends Payable . . . . . . . . . . . . . | | | | (b) | 4,400 | 4,400 |
| Bonds Payable . . . . . . . . . . . . . . . . | | | | (k) | 30,000 | 30,000 |
| Common Stock . . . . . . . . . . . . . . . . | 250,000 | | | (g) | 40,000 | 290,000 |
| Retained Earnings . . . . . . . . . . . . . | 234,300 | (b) | 25,100 | (a) | 36,300 | 245,500 |
| | 790,000 | | 293,800 | | 293,800 | 860,300 |

| | Adjustments Debit | | Adjustments Credit | |
|---|---|---|---|---|
| **Cash flows from operating activities:** | | | | |
| Net income . . . . . . . . . . . . . . . . . . . . . . . . . . . | (a) | 36,300 | | |
| Adjustments: | | | | |
| Depreciation expense . . . . . . . . . . . . . . . . . . | (i) | 20,900 | | |
| Amortization of patents . . . . . . . . . . . . . . . | (j) | 5,000 | | |
| Gain on sale of investments . . . . . . . . . . . . | | | (e) | 6,500 |
| Decrease in accounts receivable . . . . . . . . | (l) | 10,500 | | |
| Decrease in inventories . . . . . . . . . . . . . . . | (m) | 1,500 | | |
| Increase in prepaid operating expenses . . | | | (n) | 4,500 |
| Decrease in accounts payable . . . . . . . . . . | | | (o) | 6,700 |
| Increase in income taxes payable . . . . . . . | (p) | 500 | | |
| **Cash flows from investing activities:** | | | | |
| Involuntary conversion of building . . . . . . | (c) | 10,000 | | |
| Construction of building . . . . . . . . . . . . . . . | | | (d) | 105,000 |
| Sale of long-term investments . . . . . . . . . . | (e) | 102,500 | | |
| Purchase of land . . . . . . . . . . . . . . . . . . . . . | | | (f) | 68,500 |
| Purchase of machinery and equipment . . | | | (h) | 12,000 |
| Purchase of marketable securities . . . . . . . | | | (q) | 2,000 |
| **Cash flows from financing activities:** | | | | |
| Issuance of bonds . . . . . . . . . . . . . . . . . . . . | (k) | 30,000 | | |
| Payment of cash dividends . . . . . . . . . . . . | | | (b) | 20,700 |
| | | 217,200 | | 225,900 |
| **Net decrease in cash** . . . . . . . . . . . . . . . . . . | (r) | 8,700 | | |
| | | 225,900 | | 225,900 |

---

## KEY TERMS

Cash equivalents 184

Direct method 187

Financing activities 186

Indirect method 187

Investing activities 186

Noncash items 188

Noncash investing and financing
  activities 186

Operating activities 185

Statement of cash flows 183

---

## QUESTIONS

1.  (a)  Why is the statement of cash flows one of three primary financial statements required to be presented to external users?
    (b)  What are the major purposes of a cash flow statement?
2.  What information does the cash flow statement provide that is not provided by an income statement or by comparative balance sheets?
3.  Why has the statement of cash flows replaced the funds statement previously required by generally accepted accounting principles?
4.  What uses might each of the following find for a cash flow statement?
    (a)  Manager of a small laundry.
    (b)  Stockholder interested in regular dividends.
    (c)  Bank granting short-term loans.
    (d)  Officer of a labor union.
5.  What criteria must be met for an item to be considered a cash equivalent in preparing a statement of cash flows?
6.  Why does the FASB in Statement No. 95 treat dividend payments as a financing activity but treat the receipt of dividends as an operating activity?

7.  Either the direct method or the indirect method may be used to report cash flows from operating activities. What is the difference in approach for the two methods?
8.  Why do many users prefer the direct method? Why do the majority of preparers prefer the indirect method?
9.  What supplemental disclosures are required by FASB Statement No. 95 if a company elects to use the direct method in preparing its statement of cash flows? What disclosures are required if the indirect method is used?
10.  (a)  Why is it important to report cash flows from operating activities separately from investing and financing activities in the statement of cash flows?
    (b)  To compute net cash provided by (used in) operating activities, what adjustments are applied to net income when using the indirect method?
11.  How are significant noncash investing and financing transactions reported in connection with a statement of cash flows?
12.  What alternatives are there for developing the information needed for the statement of cash flows?

---

## DISCUSSION CASES

### Case 6—1  (Is depreciation a source of cash?)

Brad Berrett and Jim Wong are roommates in college. Berrett is an accounting major while Wong is a finance major. Both have recently studied the statement of cash flows in their classes. Wong's finance professor stated that depreciation is a major source of cash for some companies. Berrett's accounting professor indicated in class that depreciation cannot be a source of cash because cash is not affected by the recording of depreciation.

Berrett and Wong wonder which professor is correct. Explain the positions taken by both professors and indicate which viewpoint you support and why.

## Case 6—2  (Where does all the money go?)

Price Brothers Auto Parts has hired you as a consultant to analyze the company's financial position. One of the owners, David Price, is in charge of the financial affairs of the company. He makes all the deposits and pays the bills, but has an accountant prepare a balance sheet and an income statement once a year. The business has been quite profitable over the years. In fact, two years ago Price Brothers opened a second store and is now considering a third outlet. However, the economy has slowed and the cash position has become very tight. The company is having an increasingly difficult time paying its bills. David has not been able to satisfactorily explain to his brothers what is happening. What factors should you consider and what recommendations might you make to Price Brothers?

## Case 6—3  (Why do we have more cash?)

Hot Lunch Delivery Service has always had a policy to pay stockholders annual dividends in an amount exactly equal to net income for the year. Joe Alberg, the company's president, is confused because the cash balance has been consistently increasing ever since Hot Lunch began operations 5 years ago, in spite of their faithful adherence to the dividend policy. Assuming no errors have been made in the bookkeeping process, explain why this situation might occur.

## Case 6—4  (Which method should we use: the direct or the indirect method?)

As the assistant controller of Do-It-Right Company, you have been given the assignment to study FASB Statement No. 95 and make recommendations on how the company should prepare its statement of cash flows. Specifically, you are to indicate which method should be used in reporting cash flows from operating activities: the direct method or the indirect method. Which method do you recommend and why?

## Case 6—5  (Some kind of accountant you are!)

Early in 1994, Laura Dennis, a recent graduate of Southeast State College, delivers the following financial statements to John Roberts of Roberts, Inc. After a quick review, Roberts exclaims, "What do you mean I had net income of $20,000? I borrowed $40,000 from the bank and my cash balance decreased by $2,000. I must have had a loss! Some kind of accountant you are!" How should Ms. Dennis answer Mr. Roberts?

**Roberts, Inc.**
**Comparative Balance Sheet**
**December 31, 1993 and 1992**

|  | 1993 | 1992 |
|---|---|---|
| **Assets** | | |
| Cash | $ 3,000 | $ 5,000 |
| Accounts receivable | 18,000 | 8,000 |
| Inventory | 20,000 | 15,000 |
| Equipment (at cost) | 52,000 | 20,000 |
| Accumulated depreciation | (10,000) | (5,000) |
| Total assets | $83,000 | $43,000 |
| **Liabilities and Stockholders' Equity** | | |
| Accounts payable | $ 4,000 | $ 9,000 |
| Notes payable—long-term | 40,000 | — |
| Common stock, $10 par | 20,000 | 20,000 |
| Retained earnings | 19,000 | 14,000 |
| Total liabilities and stockholders' equity | $83,000 | $43,000 |

**Roberts, Inc.**
**Combined Statement of Income and Retained Earnings**
**For the Year Ended December 31, 1993**

| | | |
|---|---:|---:|
| Sales .................................................. | | $240,000 |
| Cost of goods sold ................................... | $150,000 | |
| Operating expenses (including depreciation of $5,000) ..... | 70,000 | 220,000 |
| Net income .......................................... | | $ 20,000 |
| Add retained earnings, January 1, 1993 ................. | | 14,000 |
| Deduct dividends paid ................................ | | (15,000) |
| Retained earnings, December 31, 1993 ................. | | $ 19,000 |

### Case 6—6 (How to generate cash)

Assume that you own and operate a small business. You have just completed your forecasts and budgets for next year and realize that you will need an infusion of $30,000 cash to get you through the year. You are reluctant to seek a partner because you do not want to dilute your control of the business. Preliminary talks with several lenders convince you that you probably won't be able to get a loan. What can you do to raise the $30,000 cash necessary to get you through the year?

### Case 6—7 (Cash flow per share)

In Statement No. 95, the FASB explicitly prohibited the reporting of "cash flow per share" in the financial statements. Cash flow per share is an amount often reported by firms outside the financial statements and also often included in financial analyses prepared by investment advisory services. Why do you think the FASB explicitly prohibited the inclusion of cash flow per share in the financial statements?

## EXERCISES

### Exercise 6—1 (Classification of cash flows)

Indicate whether each of the following items would be classified as (1) an operating activity, an investing activity, or a financing activity, or (2) as a noncash transaction or noncash item.

(a)  Cash collected from customers.
(b)  Cash paid to suppliers for inventory.
(c)  Cash received for interest on a nontrade note receivable.
(d)  Cash received from issuance of stock.
(e)  Cash paid for dividends.
(f)  Cash received from bank on a loan.
(g)  Cash paid for interest on a loan.
(h)  Cash paid to retire bonds.
(i)  Cash paid to purchase stock of another company as a long-term investment.
(j)  Cash received from the sale of a business segment.
(k)  Cash paid for property taxes.
(l)  Cash received for dividend revenue.
(m) Cash paid for wages.
(n)  Cash paid for insurance.
(o)  Preferred stock retired by issuing common stock.
(p)  Depreciation expense for the year.
(q)  Cash paid to purchase machinery.
(r)  Cash received from the sale of land.

## Exercise 6—2  (Cash flow analysis)

State how each of the following items would be reflected on a statement of cash flows.

(a)  Marketable securities (not cash equivalents) were purchased for $5,000.
(b)  Buildings were acquired for $187,500, the company paying $50,000 cash and signing a 12% mortgage note, payable in 5 years, for the balance.
(c)  Cash of $62,500 was paid to purchase business assets consisting of: merchandise, $22,500; furniture and fixtures, $7,500; land and buildings, $23,750; and goodwill, $8,750.
(d)  A cash dividend of $1,250 was declared in the current period, payable at the beginning of the next period.
(e)  Accounts Payable shows a decrease for the period of $3,750.

## Exercise 6—3  (Cash receipts and cash payments)

The accountant for Alpine Hobby Stores prepared the following selected information for the year ended December 31, 1993.

|  | Dec. 31, 1993 | Dec. 31, 1992 |
|---|---|---|
| (a)  Equipment.............................. | $25,000 | $30,000 |
| (b)  Accumulated depreciation ................. | 11,000 | 9,500 |
| (c)  Long-term debt .......................... | 11,000 | 20,000 |
| (d)  Common stock........................... | 20,000 | 15,000 |

Equipment with a book value of $20,000 was sold for $17,000 cash. The original cost of the equipment was $25,000.

Determine the cash inflows and outflows during 1993 associated with each of the accounts listed. Indicate how the cash flows for each item would be presented on the statement of cash flows.

## Exercise 6—4  (Format of statement of cash flows with indirect method)

From the following information for the Carter Corporation, prepare a statement of cash flows for the year ended December 31, 1993, using the indirect method.

| | |
|---|---|
| Amortization of patent ........................................... | $ 4,000 |
| Depreciation expense ............................................ | 7,000 |
| Issuance of common stock ....................................... | 25,000 |
| Issuance of new bonds payable................................... | 30,000 |
| Net income .................................................... | 55,000 |
| Payment of dividends............................................ | 22,500 |
| Purchase of equipment .......................................... | 33,200 |
| Retirement of long-term debt ..................................... | 40,000 |
| Sale of land (includes $6,000 gain) ............................... | 35,000 |
| Decrease in accounts receivable .................................. | 2,100 |
| Increase in inventory............................................ | 1,200 |
| Increase in accounts payable ..................................... | 1,500 |
| Increase in cash ............................................... | 56,700 |
| Cash balance, January 1, 1993 ................................... | 62,800 |

## Exercise 6—5  (Cash flow from operations—indirect method)

The following information was taken from the books of Tapwater Company. Compute the amount of net cash provided by (used in) operating activities during 1993 using the indirect method.

|                                                           | Dec. 31, 1993 | Dec. 31, 1992 |
|-----------------------------------------------------------|--------------:|--------------:|
| Accounts receivable ...........................           | $18,900       | $16,750       |
| Accounts payable ..............................          | 11,500        | 14,000        |
| Accumulated depreciation (no plant assets were            |               |               |
| retired during the year) .......................          | 26,000        | 22,000        |
| Inventories ...................................           | 24,500        | 20,000        |
| Other current liabilities.........................        | 5,000         | 3,000         |
| Prepaid insurance ..............................         | 1,200         | 2,000         |
| Net income ...................................            | 35,500        |               |

### Exercise 6—6   (Cash flow from operations—direct method)

A summary of revenues and expenses for Stanton Company for 1993 follows:

| | |
|---|---:|
| Sales ....................................................... | $6,000,000 |
| Cost of goods manufactured and sold ........................... | 2,800,000 |
| Gross profit .................................................. | $3,200,000 |
| Selling, general, and administrative expenses..................... | 2,000,000 |
| Income before income tax...................................... | $1,200,000 |
| Income tax.................................................... | 520,000 |
| Net income .................................................. | $ 680,000 |

Net changes in working capital accounts for 1993 were as follows:

|                                                              | Debit     | Credit    |
|--------------------------------------------------------------|----------:|----------:|
| Cash ......................................................   | $104,000  |           |
| Trade accounts receivable.............................       | 400,000   |           |
| Inventories .............................................     |           | $ 60,000  |
| Prepaid expenses (selling and general) ...................    | 10,000    |           |
| Accrued expenses (75% of increase related to manufactur-     |           |           |
| ing activities and 25% to general operating activities) ......|           | 32,000    |
| Income taxes payable....................................      |           | 48,000    |
| Trade accounts payable .................................      |           | 140,000   |

Depreciation on plant and equipment for the year totaled $600,000; 70% was related to manufacturing activities and 30% to general and administrative activities.

Prepare a schedule of net cash provided by (used in) operating activities for the year using the direct method.

### Exercise 6—7   (Cash flow from operations—indirect method)

The following information was taken from the comparative financial statements of Buttercup Corporation:

| | |
|---|---:|
| Net income for year ............................................ | $ 90,000 |
| Sales revenue................................................. | 500,000 |
| Cost of goods sold (except depreciation) ........................ | 300,000 |
| Depreciation expense for year ................................... | 60,000 |
| Amortization of goodwill for year ................................ | 10,000 |
| Interest expense on short-term debt for year ...................... | 3,500 |
| Dividends declared and paid during year ......................... | 65,000 |

Selected account balances:

|  | Beginning of Year | End of Year |
|---|---|---|
| Accounts Receivable . . . . . . . . . . . . . . . . . . . . . . . . . . . . . . . . . . | $43,000 | $30,000 |
| Inventory . . . . . . . . . . . . . . . . . . . . . . . . . . . . . . . . . . . . . . . . . . | 42,000 | 50,000 |
| Accounts Payable . . . . . . . . . . . . . . . . . . . . . . . . . . . . . . . . . . | 59,400 | 56,000 |
| Interest Payable . . . . . . . . . . . . . . . . . . . . . . . . . . . . . . . . . . . . | 1,000 | — |

Using the indirect method, compute the net amount of cash provided by (used in) operating activities for the year.

### Exercise 6—8   (Cash flow from operations—direct method)

Based on the information given in Exercise 6—7 and using the direct method, compute the net amount of cash provided by (used in) operating activities for the year.

### Exercise 6—9   (Cash computations)

A comparative balance sheet and income statement data for the Xavier Metals Company are presented below and on the next page.

**Xavier Metals Company**
**Comparative Balance Sheet**
**December 31, 1993 and 1992**

|  | 1993 | 1992 |
|---|---|---|
| **Assets** | | |
| Current assets: | | |
| Cash . . . . . . . . . . . . . . . . . . . . . . . . . . . . . . . . . . . . . . . . . . . | $ 119,000 | $ 98,000 |
| Marketable securities (not cash equivalents) . . . . . . . . . | 59,000 | — |
| Accounts receivable . . . . . . . . . . . . . . . . . . . . . . . . . . . . . | 312,000 | 254,000 |
| Inventory . . . . . . . . . . . . . . . . . . . . . . . . . . . . . . . . . . . . . . | 278,000 | 239,000 |
| Prepaid expenses. . . . . . . . . . . . . . . . . . . . . . . . . . . . . . . | 35,000 | 21,000 |
| Total current assets. . . . . . . . . . . . . . . . . . . . . . . . . . . . | $ 803,000 | $612,000 |
| Property, plant, and equipment . . . . . . . . . . . . . . . . . . . . . | $ 536,000 | $409,000 |
| Accumulated depreciation. . . . . . . . . . . . . . . . . . . . . . . . . | 76,000 | 53,000 |
|  | $ 460,000 | $356,000 |
| Total assets . . . . . . . . . . . . . . . . . . . . . . . . . . . . . . . . . . . | $1,263,000 | $968,000 |
| **Liabilities and Stockholders' Equity** | | |
| Current liabilities: | | |
| Accounts payable . . . . . . . . . . . . . . . . . . . . . . . . . . . . . . | $ 212,000 | $198,000 |
| Accrued expenses . . . . . . . . . . . . . . . . . . . . . . . . . . . . . . | 98,000 | 76,000 |
| Dividends payable . . . . . . . . . . . . . . . . . . . . . . . . . . . . . . | 40,000 | — |
| Total current liabilities . . . . . . . . . . . . . . . . . . . . . . . . . . | $ 350,000 | $274,000 |
| Notes payable—due 1995 . . . . . . . . . . . . . . . . . . . . . . . . . | 125,000 | — |
| Total liabilities . . . . . . . . . . . . . . . . . . . . . . . . . . . . . . . | $ 475,000 | $274,000 |
| Stockholders' equity: | | |
| Common stock . . . . . . . . . . . . . . . . . . . . . . . . . . . . . . . . | $ 600,000 | $550,000 |
| Retained earnings . . . . . . . . . . . . . . . . . . . . . . . . . . . . . | 188,000 | 144,000 |
| Total stockholders' equity . . . . . . . . . . . . . . . . . . . . . . . | $ 788,000 | $694,000 |
| Total liabilities and stockholders' equity . . . . . . . . . . . . . . | $1,263,000 | $968,000 |

**Xavier Metals Company**
**Condensed Comparative Income Statement**
**For the Years Ended December 31, 1993 and 1992**

|  | 1993 | 1992 |
|---|---|---|
| Net sales | $3,561,000 | $3,254,000 |
| Cost of goods sold | 2,789,000 | 2,568,000 |
| Gross profit | $ 772,000 | $ 686,000 |
| Expenses | 521,000 | 486,000 |
| Net income | $ 251,000 | $ 200,000 |

Additional information for Xavier:

(a)  All accounts receivable and accounts payable relate to trade merchandise.
(b)  The proceeds from the notes payable were used to finance plant expansion.
(c)  Capital stock was sold to provide additional working capital.

Compute the following for 1993:

1.  Cash collected from accounts receivable, assuming all sales are on account.
2.  Cash payments made on accounts payable to suppliers, assuming that all purchases of inventory are on account.
3.  Cash payments for dividends.
4.  Cash receipts that were not provided by operations.
5.  Cash payments for assets that were not reflected in operations.

### Exercise 6—10    (Statement of cash flows—indirect method)

Below is information for Boswell Manufacturing Company:

(a)  Long-term debt of $450,000 was retired at face value.
(b)  New machinery was purchased for $48,000.
(c)  Common stock with a par value of $120,000 was issued for $150,000.
(d)  Dividends of $18,000 declared in 1992 were paid in January 1993, and dividends of $27,000 were declared in December 1993, to be paid in 1994.
(e)  Included in net income for 1993 was a $2,000 loss on the sale of marketable securities. There were no other transactions affecting marketable securities in 1993.
(f)  Net income was $280,800. Included in the computation were depreciation expense of $60,000 and goodwill amortization of $30,000.

|  | Dec. 31, 1993 | Dec. 31, 1992 |
|---|---|---|
| Current assets: |  |  |
| Cash and cash equivalents | $108,100 | $ 80,000 |
| Marketable securities (at cost)* | 39,000 | 60,000 |
| Accounts receivable | 213,000 | 200,000 |
| Inventory | 192,000 | 162,000 |
| Current liabilities: |  |  |
| Accounts payable | 51,000 | 85,800 |
| Dividends payable | 27,000 | 18,000 |
| Interest payable | 11,100 | 3,000 |
| Wages payable | 84,000 | 12,000 |

*Not cash equivalents

Prepare a statement of cash flows for the year ended December 31, 1993, using the indirect method.

### Exercise 6—11   (Cash flow from operations—comparison of indirect and direct methods)

The statement of cash flows for Riker Company (prepared using the indirect method) is shown below.

**Riker Company**
**Statement of Cash Flows**
**For the Year Ended December 31, 1993**

| | | |
|---|---:|---:|
| **Cash flows from operating activities:** | | |
| Net income .......................................... | | $ 68,850 |
| Adjustments: | | |
| Depreciation ...................................... | $ 65,000 | |
| Amortization ...................................... | 10,000 | |
| Loss on sale of machine .......................... | 7,400 | |
| Gain on retirement of long-term debt................ | (2,330) | |
| Increase in accounts receivable .................... | (8,600) | |
| Decrease in inventory ............................. | 12,430 | |
| Decrease in prepaid operating expenses ............. | 1,680 | |
| Decrease in accounts payable ...................... | (2,400) | |
| Increase in interest payable ....................... | 500 | |
| Increase in income taxes payable ................... | 2,500 | 86,180 |
| Net cash provided by operating activities .............. | | $155,030 |
| **Cash flows from investing activities:** | | |
| Sale of machine .................................... | $ 12,000 | |
| Purchase of fixed assets ........................... | (78,000) | |
| Net cash used in investing activities.................. | | (66,000) |
| **Cash flows from financing activities:** | | |
| Retirement of long-term debt ....................... | $(65,000) | |
| Payment of dividends............................... | (27,000) | |
| Net cash used in financing activities.................. | | (92,000) |
| **Net decrease in cash** .................................. | | $ (2,970) |
| Cash at beginning of year ............................. | | 5,320 |
| **Cash at end of year**.................................... | | $ 2,350 |

Consider the following additional information:

(a)  Sales for the year totaled $812,350. Cost of goods sold was $500,000. Operating expenses were $100,000. Interest expense was $23,000. Income tax expense was $40,430.

(b)  80% of the increase in accounts payable related to inventory purchases; the remaining 20% related to operating expenses.

(c)  Depreciation and amortization are period costs; they do not enter into the computation of cost of goods sold.

Prepare the operating activities section of the statement of cash flows for Riker Company using the direct method.

### Exercise 6—12   (Statement of cash flows—indirect method)

The Sunnyvale Corporation prepared for 1993 and 1992 the following balance sheet data:

|                                                   | Dec. 31, 1993 | Dec. 31, 1992 |
|---------------------------------------------------|--------------:|--------------:|
| Cash and cash equivalents                         | $ 349,500     | $ 255,000     |
| Marketable securities                             | 69,000        | 420,000       |
| Accounts receivable                               | 360,000       | 345,000       |
| Merchandise inventory                             | 750,000       | 654,000       |
| Prepaid insurance                                 | 4,500         | 6,000         |
| Buildings and equipment                           | 5,515,500     | 4,350,000     |
| Accumulated depreciation—buildings and equipment ..| (2,235,000)  | (1,995,000)   |
| Total                                             | $4,813,500    | $4,035,000    |
|                                                   |               |               |
| Accounts payable                                  | $ 613,500     | $ 945,000     |
| Salaries payable                                  | 75,000        | 105,000       |
| Notes payable—bank (current)                      | 150,000       | 600,000       |
| Notes payable—bank (long-term)                    | 1,500,000     | —             |
| Capital stock, $5 par                             | 2,400,000     | 2,400,000     |
| Retained earnings (deficit)                       | 75,000        | (15,000)      |
| Total                                             | $4,813,500    | $4,035,000    |

Cash needed to purchase new equipment and to improve the company's working capital position was raised by selling marketable securities costing $351,000 for $360,000 and by borrowing from the bank with a long-term note. Equipment costing $75,000 with a book value of $15,000 was sold for $18,000; the gain on sale was included in net income. The company paid cash dividends of $90,000 during the year and reported earnings of $180,000 for 1993. There were no entries in the retained earnings account other than to record the dividend and the net income for the year. Marketable securities are reported at cost which is lower than market; these securities do not qualify as cash equivalents.

Prepare a statement of cash flows using the indirect method.

### Exercise 6—13   (Statement of cash flows—indirect method)

The following are financial statements for LaForge Company:

**LaForge Company**
**Comparative Balance Sheet**
**December 31, 1993 and 1992**
**(Dollars in thousands)**

|                                          | 1993    | 1992    |
|------------------------------------------|--------:|--------:|
| **Assets**                               |         |         |
| Cash                                     | $ 22    | $ 16    |
| Accounts receivable                      | 200     | 250     |
| Inventory                                | 125     | 95      |
| Prepaid general expenses                 | 18      | 10      |
| Plant assets                             | 1,019   | 1,000   |
| Accumulated depreciation—plant assets    | (527)   | (597)   |
| Total assets                             | $ 857   | $ 774   |
|                                          |         |         |
| **Liabilities and Stockholders' Equity** |         |         |
| Accounts payable                         | $ 75    | $ 50    |
| Interest payable                         | 10      | 8       |
| Income taxes payable                     | 90      | 107     |
| Bonds payable                            | 117     | 77      |
| Common stock                             | 338     | 300     |
| Retained earnings                        | 227     | 232     |
| Total liabilities and stockholders' equity| $ 857  | $ 774   |

**LaForge Company
Condensed Income Statement
For the Year Ended December 31, 1993
(Dollars in thousands)**

| | | |
|---|---:|---:|
| Sales | | $1,300 |
| Cost of goods sold | | 880 |
| Gross profit | | $ 420 |
| Operating expenses: | | |
| General expenses | $ 240 | |
| Interest expense | 15 | |
| Income tax expense | 35 | |
| Depreciation expense | 60 | 350 |
| Net income | | $ 70 |

The following information is also available for 1993:

(a)  Plant assets were sold for their book value of $200 during the year. The assets had an original cost of $330.
(b)  Cash dividends totaling $75 were paid during the year.
(c)  All accounts payable relate to inventory purchases.
(d)  All purchases of plant assets were cash transactions.

Prepare a statement of cash flows for 1993 for LaForge Company using the indirect method.

**Exercise 6—14   (Statement of cash flows—direct method)**

Using the information given in Exercise 6-13, prepare a statement of cash flows for 1993 for LaForge Company using the direct method.

**Exercise 6—15   (Preparation of income statement using balance sheet and cash flow data)**

The following are financial statements for Troi Company:

**Troi Company
Comparative Balance Sheet
December 31, 1993 and December 31, 1992**

| | 1993 | 1992 |
|---|---:|---:|
| **Assets** | | |
| Cash | $ 4,000 | $ 3,400 |
| Accounts receivable | 25,000 | 18,000 |
| Inventory | 30,000 | 34,000 |
| Prepaid general expenses | 5,700 | 5,000 |
| Property, plant, and equipment | 305,000 | 320,000 |
| Accumulated depreciation | (103,500) | (128,900) |
| Goodwill | 36,000 | 40,000 |
| Total assets | $302,200 | $291,500 |
| **Liabilities and Stockholders' Equity** | | |
| Accounts payable | $ 25,000 | $ 22,000 |
| Wages payable | 12,000 | 10,300 |
| Interest payable | 2,800 | 4,000 |
| Dividends payable | 14,000 | — |
| Income taxes payable | 1,600 | 1,200 |
| Bonds payable | 100,000 | 120,000 |
| Common stock | 50,000 | 50,000 |
| Retained earnings | 96,800 | 84,000 |
| Total liabilities and stockholders' equity | $302,200 | $291,500 |

**Troi Company**
**Statement of Cash Flows**
**For the Year Ended December 31, 1993**

| | | |
|---|---:|---:|
| **Cash flows from operating activities:** | | |
| Cash receipts from customers ........................ | | $685,300 |
| Cash payments for: | | |
| Purchases of inventory............................. | $300,000 | |
| General expenses ................................. | 102,000 | |
| Wage expense .................................... | 150,000 | |
| Interest expense................................... | 11,000 | |
| Income tax expense .............................. | 23,900 | 586,900 |
| Net cash provided by operating activities .............. | | $ 98,400 |
| **Cash flows from investing activities:** | | |
| Sale of property, plant, and equipment ................ | $ 27,200 | |
| Purchase of property, plant, and equipment............. | (60,000) | |
| Net cash used in investing activities.................... | | (32,800) |
| **Cash flows from financing activities:** | | |
| Retirement of bonds payable ........................ | $ (23,000) | |
| Payment of dividends................................ | (42,000) | |
| Net cash used in financing activities.................... | | (65,000) |
| **Net increase in cash** .................................... | | $      600 |
| Cash at beginning of year ............................... | | 3,400 |
| **Cash at end of year** .................................... | | $   4,000 |

Consider the following additional information:

(a)  All the accounts payable relate to inventory purchases.
(b)  Property, plant, and equipment sold had an original cost of $75,000 and a book value of $22,000.

Prepare the income statement for Troi Company for the year ended December 31, 1993.

---

# PROBLEMS

## Problem 6—1   (Statement of cash flows—indirect method)

Comparative balance sheet data for the Amber Company are presented below.

| | Dec. 31, 1993 | Dec. 31, 1992 |
|---|---:|---:|
| Cash ........................................... | $   2,000 | $ 10,000 |
| Marketable securities .................................. | 9,000 | 18,000 |
| Accounts receivable ................................... | 94,000 | 86,000 |
| Inventory ............................................. | 110,000 | 100,000 |
| Property, plant, and equipment ......................... | 550,000 | 500,000 |
| Accumulated depreciation—property, plant, and equipment | (277,500) | (250,000) |
| Total ...................................... | $487,500 | $464,000 |
| Short-term notes payable ............................. | $     — | $ 20,000 |
| Accounts payable ..................................... | 105,000 | 80,000 |
| Long-term notes payable............................... | 100,000 | 75,000 |
| Bonds payable ........................................ | 50,000 | 100,000 |
| Common stock, $5 par ................................. | 100,000 | 100,000 |
| Additional paid-in capital............................... | 75,000 | 75,000 |
| Retained earnings ..................................... | 57,500 | 14,000 |
| Total ...................................... | $487,500 | $464,000 |

The marketable securities qualify as cash equivalents. New equipment was purchased for $50,000, payment consisting of $25,000 cash and a long-term note for $25,000. Proceeds from the short-term notes payable were used for operating purposes. Cash dividends of $10,000 were paid in 1993; all other changes to retained earnings were caused by the net income for 1993, which amounted to $53,500.

**Instructions:**   Prepare a statement of cash flows for the year ended December 31, 1993, using the indirect method.

### Problem 6—2   (Statement of cash flows—indirect method)

The following information was taken from the records of Alderman Produce Company for the year ended June 30, 1993:

| | |
|---|---:|
| Borrowed on long-term notes | $20,000 |
| Issued capital stock | 50,000 |
| Purchased equipment | 27,000 |
| Net income | 47,000 |
| Purchased treasury stock | 1,500 |
| Paid dividends | 30,000 |
| Depreciation expense | 12,000 |
| Retired bonds payable | 70,000 |
| Goodwill amortization | 2,000 |
| Sold long-term investment (at cost) | 5,000 |
| Increase in cash | 11,000 |
| Decrease in inventories | 8,000 |
| Increase in accounts receivable | 8,500 |
| Increase in accounts payable | 4,000 |
| Cash balance, July 1, 1992 | 20,000 |

**Instructions:**

1. From the information given, prepare a statement of cash flows using the indirect method.
2. Briefly explain what an interested party would learn from studying the cash flow statement for Alderman Produce Company.

### Problem 6—3   (Statement of cash flows—indirect method)

The following information was obtained from analysis of selected accounts of Orlando Co. for the year ended December 31, 1993:

| | |
|---|---:|
| Increase in long-term debt | $ 57,000 |
| Purchase of treasury stock | 52,000 |
| Depreciation and amortization | 197,000 |
| Gain on sale of equipment (included in net income) | 6,000 |
| Proceeds from issuance of common stock | 184,000 |
| Purchase of equipment | 434,000 |
| Proceeds from sale of equipment | 20,000 |
| Payment of dividends | 49,000 |
| Net income | 375,000 |
| Increase (decrease) in working capital accounts: | |
| Cash | 45,000 |
| Accounts receivable | 229,000 |
| Inventories | 275,000 |
| Trade notes payable | 167,000 |
| Accounts payable | 124,000 |
| Taxes payable | (34,000) |
| Cash balance, January 1, 1993 | 120,000 |

**Instructions:**   From the information given, prepare a statement of cash flows using the indirect method.

## Problem 6—4  (Statement of cash flows—direct method)

Based on an analysis of Cash and other accounts, the following information was provided by the controller of Lumbercamp, Inc., a manufacturer of wood burning stoves, for the year 1993.

(a)  Cash sales for the year were $150,000; sales on account totaled $180,000.
(b)  Cost of goods sold was 50 percent of total sales.
(c)  All inventory is purchased on account.
(d)  Depreciation on equipment was $93,000 for the year.
(e)  Amortization of goodwill was $6,000.
(f)  Collection of accounts receivable was $114,000.
(g)  Payments on accounts payable for inventory equaled $117,000.
(h)  Rent expense paid in cash was $33,000.
(i)  60,000 shares of $10 par stock were issued for $720,000.
(j)  Land was acquired by issuance of a $300,000 bond that sold for $318,000.
(k)  Equipment was purchased for cash at a cost of $252,000.
(l)  Dividends of $138,000 were declared.
(m)  $45,000 of dividends that had been declared the previous year were paid.
(n)  A machine used on the assembly line was sold for $36,000. The machine had a book value of $21,000.
(o)  Another machine with a book value of $1,500 was scrapped and was reported as an ordinary loss. No cash was received on this transaction.
(p)  The cash account had a balance of $62,000 on January 1, 1993.

**Instructions:**  Use the direct method to prepare a statement of cash flows for Lumbercamp, Inc., for the year ending December 31, 1993.

## Problem 6—5  (Statement of cash flows—indirect method)

Comparative balance sheet data for the partnership of Young and Jones are as follows:

| | Dec. 31, 1993 | Dec. 31, 1992 |
|---|---|---|
| Cash ........................................... | $ 14,000 | $ 10,500 |
| Accounts receivable ........................... | 22,000 | 25,500 |
| Inventory ...................................... | 112,500 | 85,000 |
| Prepaid expenses .............................. | 3,500 | 4,250 |
| Furniture and fixtures ......................... | 64,500 | 42,000 |
| Accumulated depreciation...................... | (33,875) | (25,425) |
| Total ...................................... | $182,625 | $141,825 |
| | | |
| Accrued expenses ............................. | $ 7,000 | $ 5,200 |
| Accounts payable ............................. | 19,425 | 28,875 |
| Long-term note ............................... | 17,700 | — |
| Donna Young, capital ......................... | 51,375 | 50,875 |
| Diane Jones, capital .......................... | 87,125 | 56,875 |
| Total ...................................... | $182,625 | $141,825 |

Net income for the year was $43,000, and this was transferred in equal amounts to the partners capital accounts. Further changes in the capital accounts arose from additional investments and withdrawals by the partners. The change in the furniture and fixtures account arose from a purchase of additional furniture; part of the purchase price was paid in cash and a long-term note was issued for the balance.

**Instructions:**  Using the indirect method, prepare a statement of cash flows for 1993.

## Problem 6—6   (Statement of cash flows—indirect method)

Berclay Tile Co. reported net income of $6,160 for 1993 but has been showing an overdraft in its bank account in recent months. The manager has contacted you as the auditor for an explanation. The information that follows was given to you for examination.

**Berclay Tile Co.**
**Comparative Balance Sheet**
**December 31, 1993 and 1992**

| | 1993 | | 1992 | |
|---|---|---|---|---|
| **Assets** | | | | |
| Current assets: | | | | |
| Cash | | $ (960) | | $ 4,780 |
| Accounts receivable | | 4,000 | | 1,000 |
| Inventory | | 2,350 | | 750 |
| Prepaid insurance | | 70 | | 195 |
| Total current assets | | $ 5,460 | | $ 6,725 |
| Land, buildings, and equipment: | | | | |
| Land | | $12,500 | | $12,500 |
| Buildings | $25,000 | | $25,000 | |
| Accumulated depreciation | (15,000) | 10,000 | (14,000) | 11,000 |
| Equipment | $37,250 | | $30,850 | |
| Accumulated depreciation | (22,500) | 14,750 | (18,400) | 12,450 |
| Total land, buildings, and equipment | | $37,250 | | $35,950 |
| Total assets | | $42,710 | | $42,675 |
| **Liabilities and Stockholders' Equity** | | | | |
| Current liabilities: | | | | |
| Accounts payable | | $ 4,250 | | $ 3,500 |
| Taxes payable | | 1,400 | | 2,350 |
| Wages payable | | 750 | | 1,675 |
| Notes payable—current portion | | 1,500 | | 3,500 |
| Total current liabilities | | $ 7,900 | | $11,025 |
| Long-term liabilities: | | | | |
| Notes payable | | 10,500 | | 11,500 |
| Stockholders' equity: | | | | |
| Capital stock | $17,500 | | $15,000 | |
| Retained earnings | 6,810 | | 5,150 | |
| Total stockholders' equity | | 24,310 | | 20,150 |
| Total liabilities and stockholders' equity | | $42,710 | | $42,675 |

You also determine the following:

(a) Equipment was sold for $1,500, its cost was $2,500 and its book value was $500. The gain was reported as Other Revenue.
(b) Cash dividends of $4,500 were paid.

**Instructions:**   Prepare a statement of cash flows using the indirect method.

## Problem 6—7 (Statement of cash flows—direct method)

The following data show the account balances of Novations, Inc., at the beginning and end of the company's accounting period:

| Debits | Dec. 31, 1993 | Jan. 1, 1993 |
|---|---|---|
| Cash and Cash Equivalents | $176,400 | $ 58,000 |
| Accounts Receivable | 32,000 | 26,600 |
| Inventory | 21,000 | 25,400 |
| Prepaid Insurance | 5,600 | 4,000 |
| Long-Term Investments (at cost) | 6,000 | 16,800 |
| Equipment | 80,000 | 66,000 |
| Treasury Stock (at cost) | 10,000 | 20,000 |
| Cost of Goods Sold | 368,000 | |
| Operating Expenses | 185,000 | |
| Income Tax Expense | 37,600 | |
| Loss on Sale of Equipment | 1,000 | |
| Total debits | $922,600 | $216,800 |

| Credits | | |
|---|---|---|
| Accumulated Depreciation—Equipment | $ 19,000 | $ 18,000 |
| Accounts Payable | 7,000 | 11,200 |
| Interest Payable | 1,000 | 2,000 |
| Income Taxes Payable | 12,000 | 8,000 |
| Notes Payable—Long-Term | 16,000 | 24,000 |
| Common Stock | 110,000 | 100,000 |
| Paid-In Capital in Excess of Par | 32,000 | 30,000 |
| Retained Earnings | 19,600* | 23,600 |
| Sales | 704,000 | |
| Gain on Sale of Long-Term Investments | 2,000 | |
| Total credits | $922,600 | $216,800 |

*Preclosing balance

The following information was also available:

(a) All purchases and sales were on account.
(b) Equipment costing $10,000 was sold for $3,000; a loss of $1,000 was recognized on the sale.
(c) Among other items, the operating expenses included depreciation expense of $7,000; interest expense of $2,800; and insurance expense of $2,400.
(d) Equipment was purchased during the year by issuing common stock and by paying the balance ($12,000) in cash.
(e) Treasury stock was sold for $4,000 less than it cost; the decrease in owners' equity was recorded by reducing retained earnings. No dividends were paid during the year.

### Instructions:

1. Prepare a statement of cash flows for the year ended December 31,1993, using the direct method of reporting cash flows from operating activities.
2. Comment on the lack of dividend payment. Does a "no dividend" policy seem appropriate under the current circumstances for Novations, Inc.?

## Problem 6—8  (Income statement and statement of cash flows—indirect method)

Refer to the data for Novations, Inc., in Problem 6—7.

**Instructions:**

1. Prepare an income statement for Novations, Inc., for the year ended December 31, 1993.
2. Prepare a statement of cash flows for the year ended December 31, 1993, using the indirect method.

## Problem 6—9  (Analysis of cash flow data)

The following summary data are for Queue Company:

|  | 1993 | 1992 | 1991 |
|---|---|---|---|
| Cash .......................................... | $ 75,000 | $ 70,000 | $ 60,000 |
| Other current assets ......................... | 450,000 | 400,000 | 370,000 |
| Current liabilities ............................ | 335,000 | 240,000 | 250,000 |
| Depreciation expense........................ | 50,000 | 48,000 | 41,000 |
| Net income ................................. | 65,000 | 57,000 | 54,000 |

All current assets and current liabilities relate to operations.

**Instructions:**

1. Compute net cash provided by (used in) operating activities for 1992 and 1993.
2. How would the numbers you computed in (1) change if Queue had decided to delay payment of $50,000 in accounts payable from late 1992 to early 1993? This will increase both cash and accounts payable as of December 31, 1992; the December 31, 1993, amounts will be unaffected.
3. Ignore the change described in (2). How would the numbers you computed in (1) change if Queue had decided to delay purchase of $50,000 of inventory for cash from late 1992 to early 1993. This will increase cash but decrease inventory as of December 31, 1992; the December 31, 1993, amounts will be unaffected.
4. Can net cash from operations be manipulated? Explain your answer.

## Problem 6—10  (Definitions of cash flow)

The following summary information is for Data Company:

|  | 1993 | 1992 | 1991 | 1990 |
|---|---|---|---|---|
| Net income ................................... | $  50 | $  50 | $  50 | $  50 |
| Depreciation expense........................ | 30 | 30 | 30 | 30 |
| Change in accounts receivable................ | + 10 | 0 | + 20 | + 15 |
| Change in inventory ......................... | + 15 | − 30 | 0 | − 5 |
| Change in accounts payable.................. | + 20 | + 25 | − 15 | + 10 |

**Instructions:**

1. Compute net cash provided by (used in) operating activities for Data Company for the years 1990 through 1993.
2. One definition of "cash flow" often used in financial analysis is: net income + depreciation. Use this definition to compute "cash flow" for Data Company for the years 1990 through 1993.
3. Under what circumstances is the "net income + depreciation" measure of cash flow a good estimate of actual cash flow from operations? Under what circumstances is it a particularly misleading measure?

## Problem 6—11   (Cash flow from operations—direct method)

The following combined income and retained earnings statement, along with selected balance sheet data, are provided for the Timberdale Company.

**Timberdale Company**
**Combined Income and Retained Earnings Statement**
**For the Year Ended December 31, 1993**

| | | |
|---|---:|---:|
| Revenues: | | |
| Net sales revenue | | $170,000 |
| Other revenues | | 9,000* |
| Total revenues | | $179,000 |
| Expenses: | | |
| Cost of goods sold | $102,000 | |
| Selling and administrative expenses | 29,400 | |
| Depreciation expense | 6,400 | |
| Interest expense | 2,800 | |
| Total expenses | | 140,600 |
| Income before taxes | | $ 38,400 |
| Income taxes | | (11,520) |
| Net income | | $ 26,880 |
| Retained earnings, January 1, 1993 | | 67,000 |
| | | $ 93,880 |
| Dividends declared and paid | | (5,000) |
| Retained earnings, December 31, 1993 | | $ 88,880 |

*Gain on sale of equipment (cost, $19,000; book value, $12,000; sales price, $21,000).

| | Balance Sheet Amounts | |
|---|---|---|
| | Beginning of Year | End of Year |
| Accounts receivable | $21,000 | $22,000 |
| Inventory | 38,600 | 36,000 |
| Prepaid expenses | 1,900 | 1,400 |
| Accounts payable | 14,400 | 16,000 |
| Interest payable | 3,000 | 2,000 |
| Income taxes payable | 1,000 | 5,000 |

### Instructions:

1. Using the direct method, compute the amount of net cash provided by (used in) operating activities for Timberdale Company for 1993.
2. What is the impact of dividends paid on net cash from operations? Explain.

## Problem 6—12   (Statement of cash flows using T-accounts and indirect method)

The post-closing trial balances on page 231 are provided for the Dallas Department Store.

The following additional information was obtained from Dallas Department Store's accounting records:

- All accounts receivable were from sales to customers.
- The inventory and accounts payable were for merchandise purchased for resale.
- The prepaid expenses and accrued liabilities were for operating expenses.

- During the year, plant assets were purchased by paying $180,000 cash and signing a $24,000 mortgage.
- Plant assets with a cost of $60,000 and accumulated depreciation of $24,000 were sold for $48,000 cash.
- Depreciation expense for the year was included in operating expenses.
- Common stock was sold for $36,000 cash.
- Cash dividends of $12,000 were paid during the year.

| | Debit (Credit) | |
| --- | --- | --- |
| | Trial Balance Dec. 31, 1993 | Trial Balance Dec. 31, 1992 |
| Cash and Cash Equivalents ............................... | $ 28,800 | $ 12,000 |
| Accounts Receivable ...................................... | 24,000 | 36,000 |
| Inventory ................................................. | 144,000 | 96,000 |
| Prepaid Expenses ......................................... | 7,200 | 6,000 |
| Plant Assets .............................................. | 624,000 | 480,000 |
| Accumulated Depreciation—Plant Assets .................. | (122,400) | (48,000) |
| Accounts Payable ......................................... | (30,000) | (24,000) |
| Accrued Liabilities ....................................... | (12,000) | (9,600) |
| Mortgage Payable ........................................ | (84,000) | (60,000) |
| Bonds Payable............................................ | (240,000) | (240,000) |
| Common Stock ........................................... | (210,000) | (180,000) |
| Capital in Excess of Par................................... | (36,000) | (30,000) |
| Retained Earnings ........................................ | (93,600) | (38,400) |
| Total..................................................... | $   -0- | $   -0- |

**Instructions:**  Using T-accounts, prepare a statement of cash flows for Dallas Department Store for the year ended December 31, 1993, using the indirect method.

**\*Problem 6—13  (Statement of cash flows using a work sheet and indirect method)**

Refer to the information for Dallas Department Store in Problem 6—12.

**Instructions:**  Using a work sheet, prepare a statement of cash flows (indirect method) for the year ended December 31, 1993.

*Relates to Appendix

# CHAPTER 7

# Time Value of Money: Accounting Applications

---

**CHAPTER TOPICS**

**The Time-Value-of-Money Concept**

**Simple and Compound Interest**

**Future- and Present-Value Techniques**

**Business Applications**

**Converting to Annuity-Due Factor Values**

**Interpolation**

---

The Utah Jazz signed basketball star Karl "The Mailman" Malone to a 10-year, $18 million contract. However, "The Mailman" currently receives only $1.26 million per year, as 30% of his contract is deferred until after the year 2004. On the day Karl Malone signed the long-term contract, what was its value? $18 million? Does the fact that he does not receive 30% of his contract until the next century affect its valuation?

---

## THE TIME-VALUE-OF-MONEY CONCEPT

As pointed out quite dramatically by the Malone contract, the concept of the **time value of money** is becoming increasingly important in today's business world. Decision makers, whether professional basketball players or business executives, must try to adjust for the impact of interest and changing economic prices. Consider the following illustrative situations:

- You are in the market for a new car. A newspaper advertisement offers the vehicle you want with two payment options. You can choose between an immediate cash price of $12,500 or a 6% financing option with payments over two years of $532 at the end of each month. Which alternative purchase plan should you choose?
- You intend to provide income for your retirement. If you are 20 years old, how much must you invest now in order to establish a fund large enough to pay for your retirement in 45 years?
- Every month, millions of individuals make mortgage payments on their homes. Because part of each payment is interest, and therefore tax-deductible, a method is needed for calculating the interest portion of each payment. What are the procedures for determining the interest and principal portions of each payment over the life of the mortgage?

In each of the preceding situations, decisions must be made regarding inflows and outflows of money over an extended period of time. Making correct financial decisions requires that the time value of money be taken into account. This means that dollars to be received or paid in the future must be "discounted" or adjusted to their present values. Alternatively, current dollars may be "accumulated" or adjusted to their future values so that comparisons of dollar amounts at different time periods can be meaningful.

In the first example, you must decide whether to pay $12,500 cash now or make 24 monthly payments of $532. Assuming you have sufficient cash, wouldn't it be better to pay $12,500 for the car now instead of $12,768 (24 payments of $532) under the time-payment plan? The answer to that question is, "Not necessarily." This decision requires that the alternatives be made comparable in terms of the time value of money, that is, the two alternatives must be stated at their respective present values.

The present value of the first alternative, the cash purchase, is simply the amount of cash to be paid currently, or $12,500. The present value of the second alternative is equal to the present value of each of the 24 payments, as illustrated below.

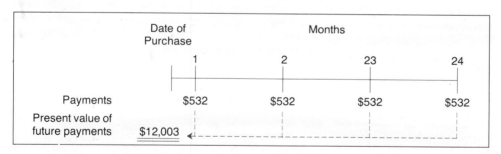

The total present value of the 24 payments of $532 each discounted to the date of purchase at 6% interest is approximately $12,003.[1] This amount is less than the $12,500 cash price the dealer is willing to accept. Therefore, assuming no other factors are relevant to your decision, you should purchase the car on the time-payment plan. This conclusion and the other examples in the chapter ignore any tax implications, which may modify the decision in actual practice.

There are many business situations where present or future value techniques must be used in making financial decisions. Common applications in accounting include the following categories:

---

[1]As will be explained later, the $12,003 is determined by discounting an annuity of $532 for 24 months at an annual interest rate of 6%.

1. Valuing long-term notes receivable and payable where there is no stated rate of interest or where the stated rate does not reflect existing economic conditions.
2. Determining bond prices and using the effective-interest method for amortizing bond premiums or discounts.
3. Determining appropriate values for long-term capital leases and measuring the amount of interest expense and principal applicable to the periodic lease payments.
4. Accounting for pension funds, including interest accruals and amortization entries.
5. Accounting for sinking funds, for example, when a fund is established to retire long-term debts.
6. Analyzing investment alternatives.
7. Establishing amortization schedules for mortgages and measuring periodic payments on long-term purchase contracts.
8. Determining appropriate asset, liability, and equity values in mergers and business combinations.

Since future and present value techniques are commonly used in business and have become increasingly important for accountants, this chapter explains these techniques and provides several illustrations of their use. The emphasis in the chapter is on present value techniques, since most applications in accounting require future amounts to be discounted to the present. The material presented may be a review for some students; for others, it will add to the theoretical foundation underlying current accounting practice. The techniques explained will be used throughout the text, especially in the chapters dealing with long-term investments and long-term liabilities. Before future and present value techniques can be explained, however, the concept of interest must first be defined.

## COMPUTING THE AMOUNT OF INTEREST

Money, like other commodities, is a scarce resource and a payment for its use is generally required. This payment (cost) for the use of money is interest. For example, if $100 is borrowed, whether from an individual, a business, or a bank, and $110 is paid back, $10 in interest has been paid for the use of the $100. Thus, interest represents the excess cash paid or received over the amount of cash borrowed or loaned.

### Simple Interest

Generally, interest is specified in terms of a percentage rate for a period of time, usually a year. For example, interest at 8% means the annual cost of borrowing an amount of money, called the principal, is equal to 8% of that amount. If $100 is borrowed for a period of one year at 8% annual interest, the total to be repaid is $108—the amount of the principal, $100, and the interest for a year, $8 ($100 × .08 × 1). Interest on a $1,000 note for 6 months at an annual rate of 8% is $40 ($1,000 × .08 × $\frac{6}{12}$). In this case, the annual rate of 8% is multipled by $\frac{6}{12}$ (or $\frac{1}{2}$ year) because interest is being computed for less than one year. Thus, the formula for computing simple interest is:

$$i = p \times r \times t,$$

where:

$i$ = Amount of simple interest
$p$ = Principal amount
$r$ = Interest rate (per period)
$t$ = Time (number of periods)

## The Difference Between Simple and Compound Interest

The preceding formula applies to the computation of simple interest. Most transactions, however, involve compound interest. This means that the amount of interest earned for a certain period is added to the principal for the next period. Interest for the subsequent period is computed on the new amount, which includes both principal and accumulated interest.

The difference between simple and compound interest can be quite significant, particularly over a long period of time. Consider, for example, the case of Christopher Columbus. On October 12, 1492, Columbus landed in the Americas and (although this is not well known) his first action was to deposit $100 in the First Bank of the Americas. The annual interest rate was 5%. On October 12, 1992, Columbus' heirs went to the bank to check the status of their ancestor's account. The bank manager informed them that certain records had been lost, and it was unknown whether Mr. Columbus had selected a simple or compound interest account. The heirs were given the option of making that choice now. After a few calculations, the heirs elected compound interest. Why? Using simple interest, the balance in Columbus' account had increased by $5 per year ($100 x .05) to a current total of $2,600 ($100 principal + $2,500 interest). Using compound interest, the money in Columbus' account (which had been earning interest on the interest) totaled $3,932,000,000,000, or approximately $4 trillion.

**Computing Compound Interest**    To illustrate the computation of compound interest, assume $100 is deposited in a bank and left for two years at 6% annual interest. At the end of the first year, the $100 has earned $6 interest ($100 × .06 x 1). At the end of the second year, $6 has been earned for the first year, plus another $6.36 interest (6% on the $106 balance at the beginning of the second year). Thus, the total interest earned is $12.36 rather than $12 because of the compounding effect. The table below, based on the foregoing example, illustrates the computation of simple and compound interest for four years.

| Year | Simple Interest Computation | Interest | Total | Compound Interest Computation | Interest | Total |
|------|------------------|----------|-------|------------------|----------|-------|
| 1 | ($100 × .06) | $6 | $106 | ($100.00 × .06) | $6.00 | $106.00 |
| 2 | ( 100 × .06) | 6 | 112 | ( 106.00 × .06) | 6.36 | 112.36 |
| 3 | ( 100 × .06) | 6 | 118 | ( 112.36 × .06) | 6.74 | 119.10 |
| 4 | ( 100 × .06) | 6 | 124 | ( 119.10 × .06) | 7.15 | 126.25 |

**The Effect of Compounding Periods**    The interest rate used in compound interest problems is the effective rate of interest and is generally stated as an annual rate, sometimes called "per annum." However, if the compounding of interest is for periods other than a year, the stated rate of interest must be adjusted. A comparable adjustment must be made to the number of periods. The adjustments required to the interest rate (i) and to the number of periods (n) for semiannual, quarterly, and monthly compounding of interest are as follows:

| Example | Annual Compounding | Semiannual Compounding | Quarterly Compounding | Monthly Compounding |
|---------|-------------------|-----------------------|----------------------|---------------------|
| 1. | i= 6%, n=10 | i= 3%, n=20 | i=1.5%, n=40 | i=.5%, n=120 |
| 2. | i=12%, n= 5 | i= 6%, n=10 | i= 3%, n=20 | i= 1%, n= 60 |
| 3. | i=24%, n= 3 | i=12%, n= 6 | i= 6%, n=12 | i= 2%, n= 36 |

As shown in the table, the semiannual compounding of interest requires the annual interest rate to be reduced by half and the number of periods to be doubled. Quarterly compounding of interest requires use of one-fourth the annual rate and 4 times the number of periods, and so forth. Because of this compounding effect, more interest is earned by an investor with semiannual interest than with annual interest, and more is earned with quarterly compounding than with semiannual compounding.

## FUTURE- AND PRESENT-VALUE TECHNIQUES

Since money earns interest over time, $100 received today is more valuable than $100 received one year from today. Future and present value analysis is a method of comparing the value of money received or expected to be received at different time periods.

Analyses requiring comparisons of present dollars and future dollars may be viewed from one of two perspectives, the future or the present. If a future time frame is chosen, all cash flows must be **accumulated** to that future point. In this instance, the effect of interest is to increase the amounts or values over time so that the future amount is greater than the present amount. For example, $500 invested today will accumulate to a future value of $1,079 (rounded) in 10 years if 8% annually compounded interest is paid on the investment.

If, on the other hand, the present is chosen as the point in time at which to evaluate alternatives, all cash flows must be **discounted** from the future to the present. In this instance, the discounting effect reduces the amounts or values. To illustrate, if an investor is earning 10% annual interest on a note receivable that will pay $10,000 in 3 years, what might the investor accept today in full payment, i.e., what is the present value of that note? The amount the investor should be willing to accept, assuming a 10% interest rate is satisfactory and that other considerations are held constant, is $7,513 (rounded), which is the discounted present value of the note. The rationale for the investor is that if the $7,513 could be invested at 10%, compounded annually, it would accumulate to $10,000 in 3 years.

As just illustrated, the future and present value situations involving lump-sum amounts are essentially reciprocal relationships, and both future and present values are based on the concept of interest. Thus, if interest can be earned at 8% per year, the future value of $100 one year from now is $108 [$100 x (1 + .08)]. Conversely, assuming the same rate of interest, the present value of a $108 payment due in one year is $100 [$108 ÷ (1 + .08)]. Similarly, $100 to be received in one year, at an 8% annual interest rate, is worth $92.59 today ($100 ÷ 1.08), because $92.59 invested at 8% will grow to $100 [$92.59 × (1 + .08)] in one year.

### Use of Formulas

There are four common future and present value situations, each with a corresponding formula. Two of the situations deal with one-time, lump-sum payments or receipts[2] (either future or present values), and the other two involve annuities (either future or present values). An annuity consists of a **series of equal payments** over a specified number of **equal time periods**. For example, a contract calling for three annual payments of $3,000 each would be an annuity. However, a similar contract requiring three annual payments of $2,000, $3,000, and $4,000, respectively, would not be an annuity since the payments are not equal.

Without going into the derivation of the formulas, the four common situations are as follows:

[2]Hereafter in this chapter, the terms *payments* and *receipts* will be used interchangeably. A payment by one party in a transaction becomes a receipt to the other party and vice versa.

1. Future Value of a Lump-Sum Payment: $FV = P(1 + i)^n$ where:    *Table 1*

$$FV = \text{Future value}$$
$$P = \text{Principal amount to be accumulated}$$
$$i = \text{Interest rate per period}$$
$$n = \text{Number of periods}$$

### Example

Future value of $1,500 to be accumulated at 10% annual interest for 5 years.

$$FV = \$1,500(1 + .10)^5$$
$$FV = \underline{\$2,416} \text{ (rounded)}$$

2. Present Value of a Lump-Sum Payment: $PV = A\left[\dfrac{1}{(1 + i)^n}\right]$ where:    *Table 2*

$$PV = \text{Present value}$$
$$A = \text{Accumulated amount to be discounted}$$
$$i = \text{Interest rate per period}$$
$$n = \text{Number of periods}$$

### Example

Present value of $2,416 to be discounted at 10% annual interest for 5 years.

$$PV = \$2,416\left[\dfrac{1}{(1 + .10)^5}\right]$$
$$PV = \underline{\$1,500} \text{ (rounded)}$$

3. Future Value of an Annuity: $FV_n = R\left[\dfrac{(1 + i)^n - 1}{i}\right]$ where:    *Table 3*

$$FV_n = \text{Future value of an annuity}$$
$$R = \text{Annuity payment to be accumulated}$$
$$i = \text{Interest rate per period}$$
$$n = \text{Number of periods}$$

### Example

Future value of annuity of $2,000 for 10 years to be accumulated at 12% annual interest.

$$FV_n = \$2,000\left[\dfrac{(1 + .12)^{10} - 1}{.12}\right]$$
$$FV_n = \underline{\$35,097} \text{ (rounded)}$$

4. Present Value of an Annuity: $PV_n = R\left[\dfrac{1 - \dfrac{1}{(1 + i)^n}}{i}\right]$ where:    *Table 4*

$$PV_n = \text{Present value of an annuity}$$
$$R = \text{Annuity payment to be discounted}$$
$$i = \text{Interest rate per period}$$
$$n = \text{Number of periods}$$

### Example

Present value of an annuity of $5,000 for 3 years to be discounted at 11% annual interest.

$$PV_n = \$5,000 \left[ \frac{1 - \frac{1}{(1 + .11)}}{.11} \right]$$

$$PV_n = \underline{\$12,219} \text{ (rounded)}$$

## Use of Tables

In the previous examples, formulas were used to make the computations. This is easily accomplished with most modern-day calculators or with microcomputers. Without such tools, however, use of the formulas may be time-consuming. Because of this, future and present value tables have been developed for each of the four situations. These tables, such as those provided on pages 253-256, are based on computing the value of $1 for various interest rates and periods of time. Consequently, future and present value computations can be made by multiplying the appropriate table value factor for $1 by the applicable lump-sum or annuity amount involved in the particular situation. Thus the formulas for the four situations may be rewritten as follows:

1. Future Value of a Lump-Sum Payment: *Table 1*

$$FV = P(1 + i)^n \text{ or } FV = P(FVF_{\overline{n}|i}) \text{ or simply}$$
$$FV = P(\text{Table I factor})$$

where:

$FVF_{\overline{n}|i}$ = Future value factor for a particular interest rate (i) and for a certain number of periods (n) from Table I.

### Example    (from page 237):

FV = $1,500 (1.6105 = Factor from Table I; n = 5; i = 10%)
FV = $\underline{\$2,416}$ (rounded)

2. Present Value of a Lump-Sum Payment: *Table 2*

$$PV = A \frac{1}{(1 + i)^n} \text{ or } PV = A(PVF_{\overline{n}|i}) \text{ or simply}$$
$$PV = A (\text{Table II factor})$$

where:

$PVF_{\overline{n}|i}$ = Present value factor for a particular interest rate (i) and for a certain number of periods (n) from Table II.

### Example    (from page 237):

PV = $2,416(0.6209 = Factor from Table II; n = 5; i = 10%)
PV = $\underline{\$1,500}$ (rounded)

3. Future Value of an Annuity:

$$FV_n = R\left[\frac{(1 + i)^n - 1}{i}\right] \text{ or } FV_n = R(FVAF_{\overline{n}|i}) \text{ or simply}$$

$$FV_n = R \text{ (Table III factor)}$$

where:

$PVAF_{\overline{n}|i}$ = Future value factor for a particular interest rate (i) and for a certain number of periods (n) from Table III.

***Example***   (from page 237):

$FV_n = \$2,000(17.5487 = \text{Factor from Table III}; n = 10; i = 12\%)$
$FV_n = \underline{\$35,097}$   (rounded)

4. Present Value of an Annuity:

$$PV_n = R\left[\frac{1 - \frac{1}{(1 + i)^n}}{i}\right] \text{ or } PV_n = R(PVAF_{\overline{n}|i}) \text{ or simply}$$

$$PV_n = R \text{ (Table IV factor)}$$

where:

$PVAF_{\overline{n}|i}$ = Present value factor for a particular interest rate (i) and for a certain number of periods (n) from Table IV.

***Example***   (from page 238):

$PV_n = \$5,000(2.4437 = \text{Factor from Table IV}; n = 3; i = 11\%)$
$PV_n = \underline{\$12,219}$ (rounded)

Note that the answers obtained in the examples by using the tables are the same as those obtained using the formulas with a calculator or microcomputer.

## Business Applications

The following examples demonstrate the application of future and present value computations in solving business problems, including each of the four situations previously described. Additional applications are provided in later sections as well as in the exercises and problems at the end of the chapter.

### Example 1    Future Value of a Lump Sum

Marywhether Company loans its president, Celia Phillips, $15,000 to purchase a car. Marywhether accepts a note due in 4 years with interest at 10% compounded semiannually. How much cash does Marywhether expect to receive from Phillips when the note is paid at maturity?

## Compensation for Loss of Income

In courts of law, attorneys commonly call on CPAs to assist in computing damages. For example, in cases where an individual is wrongly discharged and is prevented from continuing in a chosen profession, lost income must be computed and a settlement made.

Consider the case of Ann Hopkins. She was nominated for partnership at Price Waterhouse, an international CPA firm, in 1982. At the time, she was bringing more business into the firm than any of the other 87 partner candidates, who were all men. She was denied partnership and she subsequently resigned and sued the firm. A U.S. district judge ruled in 1990 that Hopkins was to be made a partner in Price Waterhouse and awarded back pay.

### Questions:

1. *How should the amount of back pay be computed? Should raises that might have been received be included? Should cost of living adjustments be factored in?*
2. *What assumptions should be made regarding the interest rate used in computing damages? Should the market rate of interest be used? Should the real interest rate be used (i.e., the market rate less the rate of inflation)?*
3. *If you were Ms. Hopkins, which interest rate would you argue for and why?*
4. *If you were Price Waterhouse, which interest rate would you argue for and why?*

*Source:   Public Accounting Report, June 15, 1990, pp. 1-2.*

### Solution:

This problem involves a lump-sum payment to be accumulated 4 years into the future. In many present and future value problems, a time line is helpful in visualizing the problem:

| | | (10% compounded semiannually) | | | | | | | |
|---|---|---|---|---|---|---|---|---|---|
| $15,000 – – – – – – – – – – – – – – – – – – – – – – – – – – – – – – – – – – ► $22,162 | | | | | | | | | |
| | | $16,538 | | $18,233 | | $20,102 | | | |
| | $15,750 | | $17,365 | | $19,145 | | $21,107 | | |
| Interest Amounts | $750 | $788 | $827 | $868 | $912 | $957 | $1,005 | $1,055 | |
| Interest Periods | 1 | 2 | 3 | 4 | 5 | 6 | 7 | 8 | |
| | Year 0 | | | | | | | Year 4 | |

The $15,000 must be accumulated for 4 years at 10% compounded semiannually. Table I may be used, and the applicable formula is:

$$FV = P(FVF_{\overline{n}|i})$$

where:

FV = The future value of a lump sum
P  = $15,000
n  = 8 periods (4 years × 2)
i  = 5% effective interest rate per period (10% ÷ 2)

$$FV = \$15,000(\text{Table I}_{\overline{8}|5\%})$$
$$FV = \$15,000(1.4775)$$
$$FV = \underline{\$22,162} \text{ (rounded)}$$

In 4 years, Marywhether will expect to receive $22,162, consisting of $15,000 principal repayment and $7,162 interest.

### Example 2    Present Value of a Lump Sum

Edgemont Enterprises holds a note receivable from a steady customer. The note is for $22,000, which includes principal and interest, and is due to be paid in exactly 2 years. The customer wants to pay the note now, and both parties agree that 10% is a reasonable annual interest rate to use in discounting the note. How much will the customer pay Edgemont Enterprises today to settle the obligation?

**Solution:**

The lump-sum future payment must be discounted to the present at the agreed upon annual rate of interest of 10%. Since this involves a present-value computation of a lump-sum amount, Table II is used, and the applicable formula is:

$$PV = A(PVF_{\overline{n}|i})$$

where:

$PV$ = The present value of a lump sum
$A$ = $22,000
$n$ = 2 periods
$i$ = 10% effective interest rate per period

$$PV = \$22,000(\text{Table II}_{\overline{2}|10\%})$$
$$PV = \$22,000(0.8264)$$
$$PV = \underline{\$18,181} \text{ (rounded)}$$

The customer will pay approximately $18,181 today to settle the obligation.

### Example 3    Present Value of Series of Unequal Payments

Casper Sporting Goods Co. is considering a $1 million capital investment that will provide the following expected net receipts at the *end* of each of the next six years.

| Year | Expected Net Receipts |
|------|----------------------|
| 1    | $195,000             |
| 2    | 457,000              |
| 3    | 593,000              |
| 4    | 421,000              |
| 5    | 95,000               |
| 6    | 5,000                |

Casper will make the investment only if the rate of return is greater than 12%. Will Casper make the investment?

**Solution:**

A series of unequal future receipts must be compared with a present lump-sum investment. For such a comparison to be made, all future cash flows must be discounted to the present.

If the rate of return on the investment is greater than 12%, then the total of all yearly net receipts discounted to the present at 12% will be greater than the amount invested. Since the future receipts are not equal, this situation does not involve an annuity. Each receipt must be discounted individually. Table II is used, and the applicable formula is: $PV = A(PVF_{\overline{n}|i})$ where:

| (1) Year = n | (2) A (Net Receipts) | (3) Table II $_{\overline{n}|12\%}$ | (2) × (3) = (4) PV (Discounted Amount) |
|---|---|---|---|
| 1 | $195,000 | .8929 | $  174,116 |
| 2 | 457,000 | .7972 | 364,320 |
| 3 | 593,000 | .7118 | 422,097 |
| 4 | 421,000 | .6355 | 267,546 |
| 5 | 95,000 | .5674 | 53,903 |
| 6 | 5,000 | .5066 | 2,533 |

Total $1,284,515 (Rounded)

The total discounted receipts are greater than the $1 million investment; thus, the rate of return is more than 12%. Therefore, other things being equal, Casper will invest.

### Example 4    Future Value of an Annuity

Boswell Co. owes an installment debt of $1,000 per quarter for 5 years. The creditor has indicated a willingness to accept an equivalent lump-sum payment at the end of the contract period instead of the series of equal payments made at the end of each quarter. If the money is worth 16% compounded quarterly, what is the equivalent lump-sum payment at the end of the contract period?

**Solution:**

The equivalent lump-sum payment can be found by accumulating the quarterly $1,000 payments to the end of the contract period. Since the payments are equal, this is an annuity. Table III is used, and the applicable formula is:

$$FV_n = R(FVAF_{\overline{n}|i})$$

where:

$FV_n$ = The unknown equivalent lump-sum payment
$R$    = $1,000 quarterly installment to be accumulated
$n$    = 20 periods (5 years × 4 quarters)
$i$    = 4% effective interest rate per period (16% ÷ 4)

$FV_n$ = $1,000 (Table III $_{\overline{20}|4\%}$)
$FV_n$ = $1,000(29.7781)
$FV_n$ = $29,778 (rounded)

The $29,778 paid at the end of 5 years is approximately equivalent to the 20 quarterly payments of $1,000 each plus interest.

### Example 5    Present Value of an Annuity

Mary Sabin, proprietor of Sabin Appliance, received two offers for her last, used, deluxe-model refrigerator. Jerry Sloan will pay $650 in cash. Elise Jensen will pay $700 consisting of a down payment of $100 and 12 monthly payments of $50. If the installment interest rate is 24% compounded monthly, which offer should Sabin accept?

**Solution:**

In order to compare the two alternative methods of payment, all cash flows must be accumulated or discounted to one point in time. As illustrated by the time line, the present is selected as the point of comparison.

Sloan's offer is $650 today. The present value of $650 today is $650. Jensen's offer consists of an annuity of 12 payments, plus $100 paid today, which is not part of the annuity. The annuity may be discounted to the present by using Table IV and the applicable formula:

$$PV_n = R(PVAF_{\overline{n}|i})$$

where:

$PV_n$ = Unknown present value of 12 payments
$R$ = $50 monthly payment to be discounted
$n$ = 12 periods (1 year × 12 months)
$i$ = 2% effective interest rate per period (24% ÷ 12)

$PV_n$ = $50 (Table IV$_{\overline{12}|2\%}$)
$PV_n$ = $50 (10.5753)
$PV_n$ = $529

| | |
|---|---:|
| Present value of Jensen's payments | $529 |
| Present value of Jensen's $100 down payment | 100 |
| Total present value of Jensen's offer | $629 |

Therefore, Sloan's offer of $650 cash is more desirable than Jensen's offer.

### Determining the Number of Periods, the Interest Rate, or the Amount of Payment

So far, the examples and illustrations have required solutions for the future or present values, with the other three variables in the formulas being given. Sometimes business problems require solving for the number of periods, the interest rate,[3] or the amount of payment instead of the future or present value amounts. In each of the formulas, there are four variables. If information is known about any three of the variables, the fourth (unknown) value can be determined. The following examples illustrate how to solve for these other variables.

### Example 6     Determining the Number of Periods

Rocky Mountain Survey Company wants to purchase new equipment at a cost of $100,000. The company has $88,850 available in cash but does not want to borrow the other $11,150 for the purchase. If the company can invest the $88,850 today at an interest rate of 12% compounded quarterly, how many years will it be before Rocky Mountain will have the $100,000 it needs to buy the equipment?

**Solution:**

As illustrated below, Rocky Mountain Survey Company can invest $88,850 now at 12% interest compounded quarterly and needs to know how long it will take for this amount to accumulate to $100,000.

In this situation, involving both present values and future values, either Table I or Table II may be used. If Table I is used, the applicable formula is:

$$FV = PVF_{\overline{n}|i}$$
$$FV = P(\text{Table I factor})$$

The problem would be solved as follows:

$$\frac{FV}{P} = \text{Table I factor}$$
$$\frac{\$100,000}{\$88,850} = 1.1255$$

Reading down the 3% column (12% ÷ 4) in Table I, the factor value of 1.1255 is shown for n = 4. Therefore, it would take 4 periods (quarters) or 1 year for Rocky Mountain to earn enough interest to have $88,850 accumulate to a future value of $100,000.

If Table II is used, the applicable formula is:

$$PV = FVF_{\overline{n}|i}$$
$$PV = A(\text{Table II factor})$$

---

[3]When the interest rate is not known, it is properly called the **implicit rate of interest**, that is, the rate of interest implied by the terms of a contract or situation. (See Examples 7 and 10 in this chapter.)

Solving,

$$\frac{PV}{A} = \text{Table II factor}$$

$$\frac{\$88,850}{\$100,000} = .8885$$

Reading down the 3% column in Table II, the factor of 0.8885 corresponds with n = 4 (quarters) or 1 year. This illustrates again the reciprocal nature of future and present values for lump-sum amounts.

### Example 7    Determining the Interest Rate

The Hughes family wishes to purchase a baby grand piano. The cost of the piano one year from now will be $5,800. If the family can invest $5,000 now, what annual interest rate must they earn on their investment to have $5,800 at the end of one year?

**Solution:**

The Hughes family can invest $5,000 now and needs it to accumulate to $5,800 in one year. The rate of annual interest they need to earn can be computed as shown below.
If Table I is used, the applicable formula is:

$$FV = PVF_{\overline{n}|i}$$
$$FV = P(\text{Table I factor})$$

$$\frac{FV}{P} = \text{Table I factor}$$

$$\frac{\$5,800}{\$5,000} = 1.1600$$

Reading across the n = 1 row, the factor value 1.1600 corresponds to an annual effective interest rate of 16%. Therefore, the Hughes family would have to earn 16% annual interest to accomplish their goal. The same result is obtained if Table II is used to solve this problem.

### Example 8    Determining the Amount of Payment

Provo 1st National Bank is willing to lend a customer $75,000 to buy a warehouse. The note will be secured by a 5-year mortgage and carry an annual interest rate of 12%. Equal payments are to be made at the end of each year over the 5-year period. How much will the yearly payment be?

**Solution:**

This is an example of an unknown annuity payment. Since the present value ($75,000) is known, as well as the interest rate (12%) and the number of periods (5), the annuity payment can be determined using Table IV. The applicable formula is:

$$PV_n = R(PVAF_{\overline{n}|i})$$
$$PV_n = R(\text{Table IV factor})$$
$$\$75,000 = R(3.6048) \ (\text{for n = 5 and i = 12\%})$$

$$\frac{\$75,000}{3.6048} = R$$

$$\underline{\$20,806} \ (\text{rounded}) = R$$

The payment on this 5-year mortgage would be approximately $20,806 each year.

---

## ADDITIONAL COMPLEXITIES

The illustrations up to this point have been fairly straightforward. In practice, however, complexities can arise that make it somewhat more difficult to use the future and present value tables. Two of these complexities involve: (1) converting ordinary annuity tables to annuity-due factor values, and (2) interpolation.

### Ordinary Annuity Vs. Annuity Due

Annuities are of two types: ordinary annuities (annuities in arrears) and annuities due (annuities in advance). The periodic receipts or payments for an **ordinary annuity** are made at the *end of each period,* and the last payment coincides with the end of the annuity term. The periodic receipts or payments for an **annuity due** are made at the *beginning of the period,* and one period of the annuity term remains after the last payment. These differences are illustrated below.

**Ordinary Annuity of $1 for 3 Years (10% annual interest)**

Therefore, assuming a 10% annual interest rate, the present value of an annuity of $1 per year to be received at the *end* of each of the next 3 years is $2.49 ($.91 + $.83 + $.75). Notice that the last $1 is received on the maturity date, or the end of the annuity term.

Again assuming a 10% annual interest rate, the present value of an annuity of $1 per year to be received at the *beginning* of each of the next 3 years is $2.74 ($1.00 + $.91 + $.83). Notice here that the last payment is received 1 year prior to the maturity date.

**Annuity Due of $1 for 3 Years (10% annual interest)**

The difference in the two annuities is in the timing of the payments, and, therefore, how many interest periods are involved. As shown below, both annuities require 3 payments. However, the ordinary annuity payments are at the end of each period, so there are only 2 periods of interest accumulation; the annuity-due payments are in advance or at the beginning of the period, so there are 3 periods of interest accumulation.

**Accumulation of Ordinary Annuity for 3 Years**

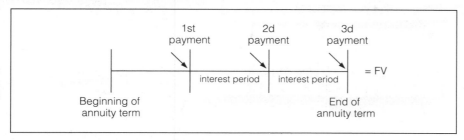

**Accumulation of Annuity Due for 3 Years**

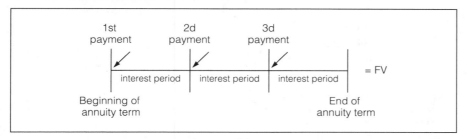

The preceding situation is exactly reversed when viewed from a present-value standpoint. The ordinary annuity has 3 interest or discount periods, while the annuity due has only 2 periods, as shown below.

**Present Value of Ordinary Annuity for 3 Years**

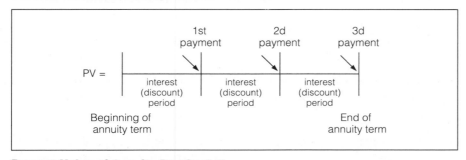

**Present Value of Annuity Due for 3 Years**

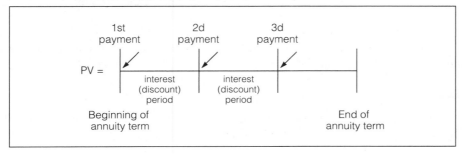

Even though most future- and present-value annuity tables are computed for ordinary annuities (payments at the end of the periods), these tables can be used for solving annuity-due problems where the payments are in advance. However, the following adjustments would be required:

1. To find the **future value of an annuity due** using ordinary annuity table values (Table III), select the appropriate table value for an ordinary annuity for one additional period (n + 1) and subtract the extra payment (which is 1.0000 in terms of the table value for rents of $1.00). The formula is:

$$FV_n = R(FVAF_{\overline{n+1}|i} - 1)$$

2. To find the **present value of an annuity due** using ordinary annuity table values (Table IV), select the appropriate table value for an ordinary annuity for one less period (n − 1) and add the extra payment (1.0000). The formula is:

$$PV_n = R(PVAF_{\overline{n-1}|i} + 1)$$

By making the above adjustments, when payments are in advance, ordinary annuity tables may be used for all annuity situations. There are special annuity-due tables available, but they are not needed if one understands how to convert from ordinary annuity factor values to annuity-due factor values.

For example, the table value (Table III) for the future amount of an annuity due for 3 periods at 10% is:

| | | |
|---|---|---|
| (1) | Factor for future value of an ordinary annuity of $1 for 4 periods (n + 1) at 10% ...................................................... | 4.6410 |
| (2) | Less one payment .................................................. | 1.0000 |
| (3) | Factor for future value of an annuity due of $1 for 3 periods at 10% ....... | 3.6410 |

The table value (Table IV) for the present value of an annuity due for 3 periods at 10% is:

| | |
|---|---|
| (1) Factor for present value of an ordinary annuity of $1 for 2 periods (n − 1) at 10% .................................................... | 1.7355 |
| (2) Plus one payment .................................................. | 1.0000 |
| (3) Factor for present value of an annuity due of $1 for 3 periods at 10% ....... | 2.7355 |

The following examples illustrate the application of converting from ordinary annuity table values to annuity-due table values.

### Example 9    Converting From Ordinary Annuity to Annuity-Due Table Values for Future Amounts

The Porter Corporation desires to accumulate funds to retire a $200,000 bond issue at the end of 15 years. Funds set aside for this purpose can be invested to yield 8%. What annual payment starting immediately would provide the needed funds?

**Solution:**

Annuity payments of an unknown amount are to be accumulated toward a specific dollar amount at a known interest rate. Therefore, Table III is used. Because the first payment is to be made immediately, all payments will fall due at the beginning of each period and an annuity due is used. The appropriate formula is:

$$FV_n = R(FVAF_{\overline{n+1}|i} - 1)$$

where:

$$
\begin{aligned}
FV_n &= \$200{,}000 \\
R &= \text{Unknown annual payment} \\
n &= \text{15 periods} \\
i &= \text{8\% annual interest}
\end{aligned}
$$

$$\$200{,}000 = R(\text{Table III}_{\overline{16}|8\%} - 1)$$
$$\$200{,}000 = R(29.3243)$$

$$\frac{\$200{,}000}{29.3243} = R$$

$$\underline{\$6{,}820} = R$$

Porter Corporation must deposit \$6,820 annually, starting immediately, to accumulate \$200,000 in 15 years at 8% annual interest.

### Example 10    Converting From Ordinary Annuity to Annuity-Due Table Values for Present Values

Utah Corporation has completed negotiations to lease equipment with a fair market value of \$45,897. The lease contract specifies semiannual payments of \$3,775 for 10 years beginning immediately. At the end of the lease, Utah Corporation may purchase the equipment for a nominal amount. What is the implicit annual rate of interest on the lease purchase?

**Solution:**

This is a common application of an annuity-due situation in accounting since most lease contracts require payments in advance, i.e., at the beginning of the period rather than at the end of the period. The implicit interest rate must be computed for the present value of an annuity due. The present value is the fair market value of the equipment, and the payment is the lease payment. Table IV is used, and the applicable formula is:

$$PV_n = R(PVAF_{\overline{n-1}|i} + 1)$$

where:

$$
\begin{aligned}
PV_n &= \$45{,}897 \\
R &= \$3{,}775 \\
n &= \text{20 periods (10 years} \times \text{2 payments per year)} \\
i &= \text{The unknown semiannual interest rate}
\end{aligned}
$$

$$\$45{,}897 = \$3{,}775(\text{Table IV}_{\overline{19}|i} + 1)$$

$$\frac{\$45{,}897}{\$3{,}775} = 12.1581 = \text{Table IV}_{\overline{19}|i} + 1$$

$$\underline{11.1581} = \text{Table IV}_{\overline{19}|i}$$

Examination of Table IV for 19 periods and a factor of 11.1581 shows Table IV $\overline{19}|_{6\%}$ = 11.1581. Therefore, $i$ = 6%. The implicit annual interest rate is twice the semiannual rate, or 2 × 6% = 12%.

## Interpolation

A difficulty in using future- and present-value tables arises when the exact factor does not appear in the table. One solution is to use the applicable formula. Interpolation is another solution. Interpolation assumes the change between two table values is linear. Although such an assumption is not totally correct, the margin of error is often insignificant, especially if the table value ranges are not too wide.

For example, determine the table value for the present value of $1 due in 9 periods at 4½%. The appropriate factor does not appear in Table II. However, the two closest values are Table II $\overline{9}|_{4\%}$ = .7026 and Table II $\overline{9}|_{5\%}$ = .6446. Interpolation relates the unknown value to the change in the known values. This relationship may be shown as a proportion:

The .0290 is the difference between the value for 5% and the value for 4½%. Therefore, the value needed is .0290 + .6446 = .6736. Using the mathematical formula for Table II,

$$\left\{ PV = A\left[ \frac{1}{(1 + i)^n} \right] \right\},$$

the present value of $1 at 4½% interest for 9 periods is .6729.

$$\left\{ PV = 1\left[ \frac{1}{(1 + .045)^9} \right] \right\}.$$

The difference (.6736 − .6729 = .0007) is insignificant for most business purposes.

Interpolation is useful in finding a particular unknown table value that lies between two given values. This procedure is also used in approximating the number of periods or unknown interest rates when the table value is known. The following examples illustrate the determination of these two variables.

## Example 11    Interpolation: Unknown Number of Periods

The Newbold Foundation contributes $600,000 to a university for a new building on the condition that construction will not begin until the gift, invested at 10% per year, amounts to $1,500,000. How long before construction may begin?

**Solution:**

This problem involves finding the time (number of periods) required for a lump-sum payment to accumulate to a specified future amount. Table I is used and the applicable formula is:

$$FV = P(FVF_{\overline{n}|}i)$$

where:

| | |
|---|---|
| FV | = $1,500,000 |
| P | = $600,000 |
| n | = Unknown number of periods |
| i | = 10% effective interest rate per year |

$$\$1,500,000 = \$600,000(\text{Table I}_{\overline{n}|10\%})$$

$$\frac{\$1,500,000}{\$600,000} = \text{Table I}_{\overline{n}|10\%}$$

$$\underline{2.5} = \text{Table I}_{\overline{n}|10\%}$$

Referring to Table I, reading down the $i = 10\%$ column:

| n | Table Factor |
|---|---|
| 9 = | 2.3579 |
| 10 = | 2.5937 |

Interpolating:

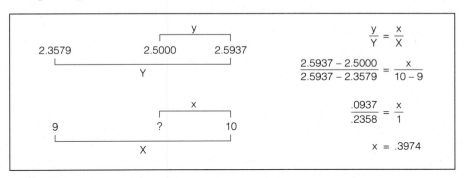

The .3974 is the difference between the number of periods at table factor 2.5937 and the number of periods at table factor 2.5000. Therefore, the number of periods needed is $10.0000 - .3974 = 9.6026$. In other words, about 9.6 periods (in this case, years) are required for $600,000 to amount to $1,500,000 at 10% annual interest.

**Example 12    Interpolation: Implicit Rate of Interest**

Fellmar, Inc., has entered into an automobile lease arrangement. The fair market value of the leased automobile is $15,815, and the contract calls for quarterly payments of $1,525 due at the end of each quarter for 3 years. What is the implicit rate of interest on the lease arrangement?

**Solution:**

The implicit interest rate must be computed for the present value of an ordinary annuity. The present value is the fair market value of the automobile, and the payment is the lease payment. Table IV is used, and the appropriate formula is given below.

$$PV_n = R(PVAF_{\overline{n}|i})$$

where:

$$PV_n = \$15,815$$
$$R = \$1,525$$
$$n = 12 \ (3 \text{ years} \times 4 \text{ payments per year})$$
$$= \text{The unknown quarterly interest rate}$$

$$\$15,815 = \$1,525(\text{Table IV}_{\overline{12}|i})$$

$$\frac{\$15,815}{\$1,525} = \text{Table IV}_{\overline{12}|i}$$

$$\underline{10.3705} = \text{Table IV}_{\overline{12}|i}$$

Reading across the $n = 12$ row of Table IV:

| i | | Table Factor |
|---|---|---|
| 2% | = | 10.5753 |
| 3% | = | 9.9540 |

Interpolating:

The .6704 is the difference between the interest rate at the table factor 9.9540 and the interest rate at the table factor 10.3705. Therefore, the quarterly implicit interest rate is $3.0000 - .6704 = 2.33\%$; and the annual implicit interest rate is 9.32% (2.33% × 4).

## CONCLUDING COMMENT

As noted in Chapter 2, the FASB's conceptual framework allows for various measurement attributes, one of which is discounted present values. This measurement attribute is receiving additional attention from the FASB. In October 1988, the FASB added to its agenda a project that is considering the use of present values and interest in accounting measurements. This chapter has illustrated a few of the many business applications of present- and future-value measurement techniques. As the FASB continues to debate issues with long-term financial impact, e.g., deferred income taxes and postretirement employment benefits, the importance of the time-value-of-money concept will increase. In the remaining chapters of this text, additional illustrations of this important concept will be presented.

TABLE I
Amount of $1 Due in n Periods

| | 1% | 2% | 3% | 4% | 5% | 6% | 7% | 8% | 9% | 10% | 11% | 12% | 14% | 16% | 20% |
|---|---|---|---|---|---|---|---|---|---|---|---|---|---|---|---|
| 1 | 1.0100 | 1.0200 | 1.0300 | 1.0400 | 1.0500 | 1.0600 | 1.0700 | 1.0800 | 1.0900 | 1.1000 | 1.1100 | 1.1200 | 1.1400 | 1.1600 | 1.2000 |
| 2 | 1.0201 | 1.0404 | 1.0609 | 1.0816 | 1.1025 | 1.1236 | 1.1449 | 1.1664 | 1.1881 | 1.2100 | 1.2321 | 1.2544 | 1.2996 | 1.3456 | 1.4400 |
| 3 | 1.0303 | 1.0612 | 1.0927 | 1.1249 | 1.1576 | 1.1910 | 1.2250 | 1.2597 | 1.2950 | 1.3310 | 1.3676 | 1.4049 | 1.4815 | 1.5609 | 1.7280 |
| 4 | 1.0406 | 1.0824 | 1.1255 | 1.1699 | 1.2155 | 1.2625 | 1.3108 | 1.3605 | 1.4116 | 1.4641 | 1.5181 | 1.5735 | 1.6890 | 1.8106 | 2.0736 |
| 5 | 1.0510 | 1.1041 | 1.1593 | 1.2167 | 1.2763 | 1.3382 | 1.4026 | 1.4693 | 1.5386 | 1.6105 | 1.6851 | 1.7623 | 1.9254 | 2.1003 | 2.4883 |
| 6 | 1.0615 | 1.1262 | 1.1941 | 1.2653 | 1.3401 | 1.4185 | 1.5007 | 1.5869 | 1.6771 | 1.7716 | 1.8704 | 1.9738 | 2.1950 | 2.4364 | 2.9860 |
| 7 | 1.0712 | 1.1487 | 1.2299 | 1.3159 | 1.4071 | 1.5036 | 1.6058 | 1.7138 | 1.8280 | 1.9487 | 2.0762 | 2.2107 | 2.5023 | 2.8262 | 3.5832 |
| 8 | 1.0829 | 1.1717 | 1.2668 | 1.3686 | 1.4775 | 1.5938 | 1.7182 | 1.8509 | 1.9926 | 2.1436 | 2.3045 | 2.4760 | 2.8526 | 3.2784 | 4.2998 |
| 9 | 1.0937 | 1.1951 | 1.3048 | 1.4233 | 1.5513 | 1.6895 | 1.8385 | 1.9990 | 2.1719 | 2.3579 | 2.5580 | 2.7731 | 3.2519 | 3.8030 | 5.1598 |
| 10 | 1.1046 | 1.2190 | 1.3439 | 1.4802 | 1.6289 | 1.7908 | 1.9672 | 2.1589 | 2.3674 | 2.5937 | 2.8394 | 3.1058 | 3.7072 | 4.4114 | 6.1917 |
| 11 | 1.1157 | 1.2434 | 1.3842 | 1.5395 | 1.7103 | 1.8983 | 2.1049 | 2.3316 | 2.5804 | 2.8531 | 3.1518 | 3.4785 | 4.2262 | 5.1173 | 7.4301 |
| 12 | 1.1268 | 1.2682 | 1.4258 | 1.6010 | 1.7959 | 2.0122 | 2.2522 | 2.5182 | 2.8127 | 3.1384 | 3.4985 | 3.8960 | 4.8179 | 5.9360 | 8.9161 |
| 13 | 1.1381 | 1.2936 | 1.4685 | 1.6651 | 1.8856 | 2.1329 | 2.4098 | 2.7196 | 3.0658 | 3.4523 | 3.8833 | 4.3635 | 5.4924 | 6.8858 | 10.6993 |
| 14 | 1.1495 | 1.3195 | 1.5126 | 1.7317 | 1.9799 | 2.2609 | 2.5785 | 2.9372 | 3.3417 | 3.7975 | 4.3104 | 4.8871 | 6.2613 | 7.9875 | 12.8392 |
| 15 | 1.1610 | 1.3459 | 1.5580 | 1.8009 | 2.0789 | 2.3966 | 2.7590 | 3.1722 | 3.6425 | 4.1772 | 4.7846 | 5.4736 | 7.1379 | 9.2655 | 15.4070 |
| 16 | 1.1726 | 1.3728 | 1.6047 | 1.8730 | 2.1829 | 2.5404 | 2.9522 | 3.4259 | 3.9703 | 4.5950 | 5.3109 | 6.1304 | 8.1372 | 10.7480 | 18.4884 |
| 17 | 1.1843 | 1.4002 | 1.6528 | 1.9479 | 2.2920 | 2.6928 | 3.1588 | 3.7000 | 4.3276 | 5.0545 | 5.8951 | 6.8660 | 9.2765 | 12.4677 | 22.1861 |
| 18 | 1.1961 | 1.4282 | 1.7024 | 2.0258 | 2.4066 | 2.8543 | 3.3799 | 3.9960 | 4.7171 | 5.5599 | 6.5436 | 7.6900 | 10.5752 | 14.4625 | 26.6233 |
| 19 | 1.2081 | 1.4568 | 1.7535 | 2.1068 | 2.5270 | 3.0256 | 3.6165 | 4.3157 | 5.1417 | 6.1159 | 7.2633 | 8.6128 | 12.0557 | 16.7765 | 31.9480 |
| 20 | 1.2202 | 1.4859 | 1.8061 | 2.1911 | 2.6533 | 3.2071 | 3.8697 | 4.6610 | 5.6044 | 6.7275 | 8.0623 | 9.6463 | 13.7435 | 19.4608 | 38.3376 |
| 21 | 1.2324 | 1.5157 | 1.8603 | 2.2788 | 2.7860 | 3.3996 | 4.1406 | 5.0338 | 6.1088 | 7.4002 | 8.9492 | 10.8038 | 15.6676 | 22.5745 | 46.0051 |
| 22 | 1.2447 | 1.5460 | 1.9161 | 2.3699 | 2.9253 | 3.6035 | 4.4304 | 5.4365 | 6.6586 | 8.1403 | 9.9336 | 12.1003 | 17.8610 | 26.1864 | 55.2061 |
| 23 | 1.2572 | 1.5769 | 1.9736 | 2.4647 | 3.0715 | 3.8197 | 4.7405 | 5.8715 | 7.2579 | 8.9543 | 11.0263 | 13.5523 | 20.3616 | 30.3762 | 66.2474 |
| 24 | 1.2697 | 1.6084 | 2.0328 | 2.5633 | 3.2251 | 4.0489 | 5.0724 | 6.3412 | 7.9111 | 9.8497 | 12.2392 | 15.1786 | 23.2122 | 35.2364 | 79.4968 |
| 25 | 1.2824 | 1.6406 | 2.0938 | 2.6658 | 3.3864 | 4.2919 | 5.4274 | 6.8485 | 8.6231 | 10.8347 | 13.5855 | 17.0001 | 26.4619 | 40.8742 | 95.3962 |
| 26 | 1.2953 | 1.6734 | 2.1566 | 2.7725 | 3.5557 | 4.5494 | 5.8074 | 7.3964 | 9.3992 | 11.9182 | 15.0799 | 19.0401 | 30.1666 | 47.4141 | 114.4755 |
| 27 | 1.3082 | 1.7069 | 2.2213 | 2.8834 | 3.7335 | 4.8223 | 6.2139 | 7.9881 | 10.2451 | 13.1100 | 16.7386 | 21.3249 | 34.3899 | 55.0004 | 137.3706 |
| 28 | 1.3213 | 1.7410 | 2.2879 | 2.9987 | 3.9201 | 5.1117 | 6.6488 | 8.6271 | 11.1671 | 14.4210 | 18.5799 | 23.8839 | 39.2045 | 63.8004 | 164.8447 |
| 29 | 1.3345 | 1.7758 | 2.3566 | 3.1187 | 4.1161 | 5.4184 | 7.1143 | 9.3173 | 12.1722 | 15.8631 | 20.6237 | 26.7499 | 44.6931 | 74.0085 | 197.8136 |
| 30 | 1.3478 | 1.8114 | 2.4273 | 3.2434 | 4.3219 | 5.7435 | 7.6123 | 10.0627 | 13.2677 | 17.4494 | 22.8923 | 29.9599 | 50.9502 | 85.8499 | 237.3763 |
| 35 | 1.4166 | 1.9999 | 2.8139 | 3.9461 | 5.5160 | 7.6861 | 10.6766 | 14.7853 | 20.4140 | 28.1024 | 38.5749 | 52.7996 | 98.1002 | 180.3141 | 590.6682 |
| 40 | 1.4889 | 2.2080 | 3.2620 | 4.8010 | 7.0400 | 10.2857 | 14.9745 | 21.7245 | 31.4094 | 45.2593 | 65.0009 | 93.0510 | 188.8835 | 378.7212 | 1,469.7716 |
| 45 | 1.5648 | 2.4379 | 3.7816 | 5.8412 | 8.9850 | 13.7646 | 21.0025 | 31.9204 | 48.3273 | 72.8905 | 109.5302 | 163.9876 | 363.6791 | 795.4438 | 3,657.2620 |
| 50 | 1.6446 | 2.6916 | 4.3839 | 7.1067 | 11.4674 | 18.4202 | 29.4570 | 46.9016 | 74.3575 | 117.3909 | 184.5648 | 289.0022 | 700.2330 | 1,670.7038 | 9,100.4382 |

## TABLE II
### Present Value of $1 Due in n Periods

| | 1% | 2% | 3% | 4% | 5% | 6% | 7% | 8% | 9% | 10% | 11% | 12% | 14% | 16% | 20% |
|---|---|---|---|---|---|---|---|---|---|---|---|---|---|---|---|
| 1 | 0.9901 | 0.9804 | 0.9709 | 0.9615 | 0.9524 | 0.9434 | 0.9346 | 0.9259 | 0.9174 | 0.9091 | 0.9009 | 0.8929 | 0.8772 | 0.8621 | 0.8333 |
| 2 | 0.9803 | 0.9612 | 0.9426 | 0.9246 | 0.9070 | 0.8900 | 0.8734 | 0.8573 | 0.8417 | 0.8264 | 0.8116 | 0.7972 | 0.7695 | 0.7432 | 0.6944 |
| 3 | 0.9706 | 0.9423 | 0.9151 | 0.8890 | 0.8638 | 0.8396 | 0.8163 | 0.7938 | 0.7722 | 0.7513 | 0.7312 | 0.7118 | 0.6750 | 0.6407 | 0.5787 |
| 4 | 0.9610 | 0.9238 | 0.8885 | 0.8548 | 0.8227 | 0.7921 | 0.7629 | 0.7350 | 0.7084 | 0.6830 | 0.6587 | 0.6355 | 0.5921 | 0.5523 | 0.4823 |
| 5 | 0.9515 | 0.9057 | 0.8626 | 0.8219 | 0.7835 | 0.7473 | 0.7130 | 0.6806 | 0.6499 | 0.6209 | 0.5935 | 0.5674 | 0.5194 | 0.4761 | 0.4019 |
| 6 | 0.9420 | 0.8880 | 0.8375 | 0.7903 | 0.7462 | 0.7050 | 0.6663 | 0.6302 | 0.5963 | 0.5645 | 0.5346 | 0.5066 | 0.4556 | 0.4104 | 0.3349 |
| 7 | 0.9327 | 0.8706 | 0.8131 | 0.7599 | 0.7107 | 0.6651 | 0.6227 | 0.5835 | 0.5470 | 0.5132 | 0.4817 | 0.4523 | 0.3996 | 0.3538 | 0.2791 |
| 8 | 0.9235 | 0.8535 | 0.7894 | 0.7307 | 0.6768 | 0.6274 | 0.5820 | 0.5403 | 0.5019 | 0.4665 | 0.4339 | 0.4039 | 0.3506 | 0.3050 | 0.2326 |
| 9 | 0.9143 | 0.8368 | 0.7664 | 0.7026 | 0.6446 | 0.5919 | 0.5439 | 0.5002 | 0.4604 | 0.4241 | 0.3909 | 0.3606 | 0.3075 | 0.2630 | 0.1938 |
| 10 | 0.9053 | 0.8203 | 0.7441 | 0.6756 | 0.6139 | 0.5584 | 0.5083 | 0.4632 | 0.4224 | 0.3855 | 0.3522 | 0.3220 | 0.2697 | 0.2267 | 0.1615 |
| 11 | 0.8963 | 0.8043 | 0.7224 | 0.6496 | 0.5847 | 0.5268 | 0.4751 | 0.4289 | 0.3875 | 0.3505 | 0.3173 | 0.2875 | 0.2366 | 0.1954 | 0.1346 |
| 12 | 0.8874 | 0.7885 | 0.7014 | 0.6246 | 0.5568 | 0.4970 | 0.4440 | 0.3971 | 0.3555 | 0.3186 | 0.2858 | 0.2567 | 0.2076 | 0.1685 | 0.1122 |
| 13 | 0.8787 | 0.7730 | 0.6810 | 0.6006 | 0.5303 | 0.4688 | 0.4150 | 0.3677 | 0.3262 | 0.2897 | 0.2575 | 0.2292 | 0.1821 | 0.1452 | 0.0935 |
| 14 | 0.8700 | 0.7579 | 0.6611 | 0.5775 | 0.5051 | 0.4423 | 0.3878 | 0.3405 | 0.2992 | 0.2633 | 0.2320 | 0.2046 | 0.1597 | 0.1252 | 0.0779 |
| 15 | 0.8613 | 0.7430 | 0.6419 | 0.5553 | 0.4810 | 0.4173 | 0.3624 | 0.3152 | 0.2745 | 0.2394 | 0.2090 | 0.1827 | 0.1401 | 0.1079 | 0.0649 |
| 16 | 0.8528 | 0.7284 | 0.6232 | 0.5339 | 0.4581 | 0.3936 | 0.3387 | 0.2919 | 0.2519 | 0.2176 | 0.1883 | 0.1631 | 0.1229 | 0.0930 | 0.0541 |
| 17 | 0.8444 | 0.7142 | 0.6050 | 0.5134 | 0.4363 | 0.3714 | 0.3166 | 0.2703 | 0.2311 | 0.1978 | 0.1696 | 0.1456 | 0.1078 | 0.0802 | 0.0451 |
| 18 | 0.8360 | 0.7002 | 0.5874 | 0.4936 | 0.4155 | 0.3503 | 0.2959 | 0.2502 | 0.2120 | 0.1799 | 0.1528 | 0.1300 | 0.0946 | 0.0691 | 0.0376 |
| 19 | 0.8277 | 0.6864 | 0.5703 | 0.4746 | 0.3957 | 0.3305 | 0.2765 | 0.2317 | 0.1945 | 0.1635 | 0.1377 | 0.1161 | 0.0829 | 0.0596 | 0.0313 |
| 20 | 0.8195 | 0.6730 | 0.5537 | 0.4564 | 0.3769 | 0.3118 | 0.2584 | 0.2145 | 0.1784 | 0.1486 | 0.1240 | 0.1037 | 0.0728 | 0.0514 | 0.0261 |
| 21 | 0.8114 | 0.6598 | 0.5375 | 0.4388 | 0.3589 | 0.2942 | 0.2415 | 0.1987 | 0.1637 | 0.1351 | 0.1117 | 0.0926 | 0.0638 | 0.0443 | 0.0217 |
| 22 | 0.8034 | 0.6468 | 0.5219 | 0.4220 | 0.3418 | 0.2775 | 0.2257 | 0.1839 | 0.1502 | 0.1228 | 0.1007 | 0.0826 | 0.0560 | 0.0382 | 0.0181 |
| 23 | 0.7954 | 0.6342 | 0.5067 | 0.4057 | 0.3256 | 0.2618 | 0.2109 | 0.1703 | 0.1378 | 0.1117 | 0.0907 | 0.0738 | 0.0491 | 0.0329 | 0.0151 |
| 24 | 0.7876 | 0.6217 | 0.4919 | 0.3901 | 0.3101 | 0.2470 | 0.1971 | 0.1577 | 0.1264 | 0.1015 | 0.0817 | 0.0659 | 0.0431 | 0.0284 | 0.0126 |
| 25 | 0.7798 | 0.6095 | 0.4776 | 0.3751 | 0.2953 | 0.2330 | 0.1842 | 0.1460 | 0.1160 | 0.0923 | 0.0736 | 0.0588 | 0.0378 | 0.0245 | 0.0105 |
| 26 | 0.7720 | 0.5976 | 0.4637 | 0.3607 | 0.2812 | 0.2198 | 0.1722 | 0.1352 | 0.1064 | 0.0839 | 0.0663 | 0.0525 | 0.0331 | 0.0211 | 0.0087 |
| 27 | 0.7644 | 0.5859 | 0.4502 | 0.3468 | 0.2678 | 0.2074 | 0.1609 | 0.1252 | 0.0976 | 0.0763 | 0.0597 | 0.0469 | 0.0291 | 0.0182 | 0.0073 |
| 28 | 0.7568 | 0.5744 | 0.4371 | 0.3335 | 0.2551 | 0.1956 | 0.1504 | 0.1159 | 0.0895 | 0.0693 | 0.0538 | 0.0419 | 0.0255 | 0.0157 | 0.0061 |
| 29 | 0.7493 | 0.5631 | 0.4243 | 0.3207 | 0.2429 | 0.1846 | 0.1406 | 0.1073 | 0.0822 | 0.0630 | 0.0485 | 0.0374 | 0.0224 | 0.0135 | 0.0051 |
| 30 | 0.7419 | 0.5521 | 0.4120 | 0.3083 | 0.2314 | 0.1741 | 0.1314 | 0.0994 | 0.0754 | 0.0573 | 0.0437 | 0.0334 | 0.0196 | 0.0116 | 0.0042 |
| 35 | 0.7059 | 0.5000 | 0.3554 | 0.2534 | 0.1813 | 0.1301 | 0.0937 | 0.0676 | 0.0490 | 0.0356 | 0.0259 | 0.0189 | 0.0102 | 0.0055 | 0.0017 |
| 40 | 0.6717 | 0.4529 | 0.3066 | 0.2083 | 0.1420 | 0.0972 | 0.0668 | 0.0460 | 0.0318 | 0.0221 | 0.0154 | 0.0107 | 0.0053 | 0.0026 | 0.0007 |
| 45 | 0.6391 | 0.4102 | 0.2644 | 0.1712 | 0.1113 | 0.0727 | 0.0476 | 0.0313 | 0.0207 | 0.0137 | 0.0091 | 0.0061 | 0.0027 | 0.0013 | 0.0003 |
| 50 | 0.6080 | 0.3715 | 0.2281 | 0.1407 | 0.0872 | 0.0543 | 0.0339 | 0.0213 | 0.0134 | 0.0085 | 0.0054 | 0.0035 | 0.0014 | 0.0006 | 0.0001 |

TABLE III
Amount of an Ordinary Annuity of $1 per Period

| | 1% | 2% | 3% | 4% | 5% | 6% | 7% | 8% | 9% | 10% | 11% | 12% | 14% | 16% | 20% |
|---|---|---|---|---|---|---|---|---|---|---|---|---|---|---|---|
| 1 | 1.0000 | 1.0000 | 1.0000 | 1.0000 | 1.0000 | 1.0000 | 1.0000 | 1.0000 | 1.0000 | 1.0000 | 1.0000 | 1.0000 | 1.0000 | 1.0000 | 1.0000 |
| 2 | 2.0100 | 2.0200 | 2.0300 | 2.0400 | 2.0500 | 2.0600 | 2.0700 | 2.0800 | 2.0900 | 2.1000 | 2.1100 | 2.1200 | 2.1400 | 2.1600 | 2.2000 |
| 3 | 3.0301 | 3.0604 | 3.0909 | 3.1216 | 3.1525 | 3.1836 | 3.2149 | 3.2464 | 3.2781 | 3.3100 | 3.3421 | 3.3744 | 3.4396 | 3.5056 | 3.6400 |
| 4 | 4.0604 | 4.1216 | 4.1836 | 4.2465 | 4.3101 | 4.3746 | 4.4399 | 4.5061 | 4.5731 | 4.6410 | 4.7097 | 4.7793 | 4.9211 | 5.0665 | 5.3680 |
| 5 | 5.1010 | 5.2040 | 5.3091 | 5.4163 | 5.5256 | 5.6371 | 5.7507 | 5.8666 | 5.9847 | 6.1051 | 6.2278 | 6.3528 | 6.6101 | 6.8771 | 7.4416 |
| 6 | 6.1520 | 6.3081 | 6.4684 | 6.6330 | 6.8019 | 6.9753 | 7.1533 | 7.3359 | 7.5233 | 7.7156 | 7.9129 | 8.1152 | 8.5355 | 8.9775 | 9.9299 |
| 7 | 7.2135 | 7.4343 | 7.6625 | 7.8983 | 8.1420 | 8.3938 | 8.6540 | 8.9228 | 9.2004 | 9.4872 | 9.7833 | 10.0890 | 10.7305 | 11.4139 | 12.9159 |
| 8 | 8.2857 | 8.5830 | 8.8923 | 9.2142 | 9.5491 | 9.8975 | 10.2598 | 10.6366 | 11.0285 | 11.4359 | 11.8594 | 12.2997 | 13.2328 | 14.2401 | 16.4991 |
| 9 | 9.3685 | 9.7546 | 10.1591 | 10.5828 | 11.0266 | 11.4913 | 11.9780 | 12.4876 | 13.0210 | 13.5795 | 14.1640 | 14.7757 | 16.0853 | 17.5185 | 20.7989 |
| 10 | 10.4622 | 10.9497 | 11.4639 | 12.0061 | 12.5779 | 13.1808 | 13.8164 | 14.4866 | 15.1929 | 15.9374 | 16.7220 | 17.5487 | 19.3373 | 21.3215 | 25.9587 |
| 11 | 11.5668 | 12.1687 | 12.8078 | 13.4864 | 14.2068 | 14.9716 | 15.7836 | 16.6455 | 17.5603 | 18.5312 | 19.5614 | 20.6546 | 23.0445 | 25.7329 | 32.1504 |
| 12 | 12.6825 | 13.4121 | 14.1920 | 15.0258 | 15.9171 | 16.8699 | 17.8885 | 18.9771 | 20.1407 | 21.3843 | 22.7132 | 24.1331 | 27.2707 | 30.8502 | 39.5805 |
| 13 | 13.8093 | 14.6803 | 15.6178 | 16.6268 | 17.7130 | 18.8821 | 20.1406 | 21.4953 | 22.9534 | 24.5227 | 26.2116 | 28.0291 | 32.0887 | 36.7862 | 48.4966 |
| 14 | 14.9474 | 15.9739 | 17.0863 | 18.2919 | 19.5986 | 21.0151 | 22.5505 | 24.2149 | 26.0192 | 27.9750 | 30.0949 | 32.3926 | 37.5811 | 43.6720 | 59.1959 |
| 15 | 16.0969 | 17.2934 | 18.5989 | 20.0236 | 21.5786 | 23.2760 | 25.1290 | 27.1521 | 29.3609 | 31.7725 | 34.4054 | 37.2797 | 43.8424 | 51.6595 | 72.0351 |
| 16 | 17.2579 | 18.6393 | 20.1569 | 21.8245 | 23.6575 | 25.6725 | 27.8881 | 30.3243 | 33.0034 | 35.9497 | 39.1899 | 42.7533 | 50.9804 | 60.9250 | 87.4421 |
| 17 | 18.4304 | 20.0121 | 21.7616 | 23.6975 | 25.8404 | 28.2129 | 30.8402 | 33.7502 | 36.9737 | 40.5447 | 44.5008 | 48.8837 | 59.1176 | 71.6730 | 105.9306 |
| 18 | 19.6147 | 21.4123 | 23.4144 | 25.6454 | 28.1324 | 30.9057 | 33.9990 | 37.4502 | 41.3013 | 45.5992 | 50.3959 | 55.7497 | 68.3941 | 84.1407 | 128.1167 |
| 19 | 20.8190 | 22.8406 | 25.1169 | 27.6712 | 30.5390 | 33.7600 | 37.3790 | 41.4463 | 46.0185 | 51.1591 | 56.9395 | 63.4397 | 78.9692 | 98.6032 | 154.7400 |
| 20 | 22.0190 | 24.2974 | 26.8704 | 29.7781 | 33.0660 | 36.7856 | 40.9955 | 45.7620 | 51.1601 | 57.2750 | 64.2028 | 72.0524 | 91.0249 | 115.3797 | 186.6880 |
| 21 | 23.2392 | 25.7833 | 28.6765 | 31.9692 | 35.7193 | 39.9927 | 44.8652 | 50.4229 | 56.7645 | 64.0025 | 72.2651 | 81.6987 | 104.7684 | 134.8405 | 225.0256 |
| 22 | 24.4716 | 27.2990 | 30.5368 | 34.2480 | 38.5052 | 43.3923 | 49.0057 | 55.4568 | 62.8733 | 71.4027 | 81.2143 | 92.5026 | 120.4360 | 157.4150 | 271.0307 |
| 23 | 25.7163 | 28.8450 | 32.4529 | 36.6179 | 41.4305 | 46.9958 | 53.4361 | 60.8933 | 69.5319 | 79.5430 | 91.1479 | 104.6029 | 138.2970 | 183.6014 | 326.2369 |
| 24 | 26.9735 | 30.4219 | 34.4265 | 39.0826 | 44.5020 | 50.8156 | 58.1767 | 66.7648 | 76.7898 | 88.4973 | 102.1742 | 118.1552 | 158.6586 | 213.9776 | 392.4842 |
| 25 | 28.2432 | 32.0303 | 36.4593 | 41.6459 | 47.7271 | 54.8645 | 63.2490 | 73.1059 | 84.7009 | 98.3471 | 114.4133 | 133.3339 | 181.8708 | 249.2140 | 471.9811 |
| 26 | 29.5256 | 33.6709 | 38.5530 | 44.3117 | 51.1135 | 59.1564 | 68.6765 | 79.9544 | 93.3240 | 109.1818 | 127.9988 | 150.3339 | 208.3327 | 290.0883 | 567.3773 |
| 27 | 30.8209 | 35.3443 | 40.7096 | 47.0842 | 54.6691 | 63.7058 | 74.4838 | 87.3508 | 102.7231 | 121.0999 | 143.0786 | 169.3740 | 238.4993 | 337.5024 | 681.8528 |
| 28 | 32.1291 | 37.0512 | 42.9309 | 49.9676 | 58.4026 | 68.5281 | 80.6977 | 95.3388 | 112.9682 | 134.2099 | 159.8173 | 190.6989 | 272.8892 | 392.5028 | 819.2233 |
| 29 | 33.4504 | 38.7922 | 45.2189 | 52.9663 | 62.3227 | 73.6398 | 87.3465 | 103.9659 | 124.1354 | 148.6309 | 178.3972 | 214.5828 | 312.0937 | 456.3032 | 984.0680 |
| 30 | 34.7849 | 40.5681 | 47.5754 | 56.0849 | 66.4388 | 79.0582 | 94.4608 | 113.2832 | 136.3075 | 164.4940 | 199.0209 | 241.3327 | 356.7868 | 530.3117 | 1181.8816 |
| 35 | 41.6603 | 49.9945 | 60.4621 | 73.6522 | 90.3203 | 111.4348 | 138.2369 | 172.3168 | 215.7108 | 271.0244 | 341.5896 | 431.6635 | 693.5727 | 1120.7130 | 2948.3411 |
| 40 | 48.8864 | 60.4020 | 75.4013 | 95.0255 | 120.7998 | 154.7620 | 199.6351 | 259.0565 | 337.8824 | 442.5926 | 581.8261 | 767.0914 | 1342.0251 | 2360.7572 | 7343.8578 |
| 45 | 56.4811 | 71.8927 | 92.7199 | 121.0294 | 159.7002 | 212.7435 | 285.7493 | 386.5056 | 525.8587 | 718.9048 | 986.6386 | 1358.2300 | 2590.5648 | 4965.2739 | 18281.3099 |
| 50 | 64.4632 | 84.5794 | 112.7969 | 152.6671 | 209.3480 | 290.3359 | 406.5289 | 573.7702 | 815.0836 | 1163.9085 | 1668.7712 | 2400.0182 | 4994.5213 | 10435.6488 | 45497.1908 |

TABLE IV
Present Value of an Ordinary Annuity of $1 per Period

| | 1% | 2% | 3% | 4% | 5% | 6% | 7% | 8% | 9% | 10% | 11% | 12% | 14% | 16% | 20% |
|---|---|---|---|---|---|---|---|---|---|---|---|---|---|---|---|
| 1 | 0.9901 | 0.9804 | 0.9709 | 0.9615 | 0.9524 | 0.9434 | 0.9346 | 0.9259 | 0.9174 | 0.9091 | 0.9009 | 0.8929 | 0.8772 | 0.8621 | 0.8333 |
| 2 | 1.9704 | 1.9416 | 1.9135 | 1.8861 | 1.8594 | 1.8334 | 1.8080 | 1.7833 | 1.7591 | 1.7355 | 1.7125 | 1.6901 | 1.6467 | 1.6052 | 1.5278 |
| 3 | 2.9410 | 2.8839 | 2.8286 | 2.7751 | 2.7232 | 2.6730 | 2.6243 | 2.5771 | 2.5313 | 2.4869 | 2.4437 | 2.4081 | 2.3216 | 2.2459 | 2.1065 |
| 4 | 3.9020 | 3.8077 | 3.7171 | 3.6299 | 3.5460 | 3.4651 | 3.3872 | 3.3121 | 3.2397 | 3.1699 | 3.1024 | 3.0373 | 2.9137 | 2.7982 | 2.5887 |
| 5 | 4.8534 | 4.7135 | 4.5797 | 4.4518 | 4.3295 | 4.2124 | 4.1002 | 3.9927 | 3.8897 | 3.7908 | 3.6959 | 3.6048 | 3.4331 | 3.2743 | 2.9906 |
| 6 | 5.7955 | 5.6014 | 5.4172 | 5.2421 | 5.0757 | 4.9173 | 4.7665 | 4.6229 | 4.4859 | 4.3553 | 4.2305 | 4.1114 | 3.8887 | 3.6847 | 3.3255 |
| 7 | 6.7282 | 6.4720 | 6.2303 | 6.0021 | 5.7864 | 5.5824 | 5.3893 | 5.2064 | 5.0330 | 4.8684 | 4.7122 | 4.5638 | 4.2883 | 4.0386 | 3.6046 |
| 8 | 7.6517 | 7.3255 | 7.0197 | 6.7327 | 6.4632 | 6.2098 | 5.9713 | 5.7466 | 5.5348 | 5.3349 | 5.1461 | 4.9676 | 4.6389 | 4.3436 | 3.8372 |
| 9 | 8.5660 | 8.1622 | 7.7861 | 7.4353 | 7.1078 | 6.8017 | 6.5152 | 6.2469 | 5.9952 | 5.7590 | 5.5370 | 5.3282 | 4.9464 | 4.6065 | 4.0310 |
| 10 | 9.4713 | 8.9826 | 8.5302 | 8.1109 | 7.7217 | 7.3601 | 7.0236 | 6.7101 | 6.4177 | 6.1446 | 5.8892 | 5.6502 | 5.2161 | 4.8332 | 4.1925 |
| 11 | 10.3676 | 9.7868 | 9.2526 | 8.7605 | 8.3064 | 7.8869 | 7.4987 | 7.1390 | 6.8052 | 6.4951 | 6.2065 | 5.9377 | 5.4527 | 5.0286 | 4.3271 |
| 12 | 11.2551 | 10.5753 | 9.9540 | 9.3851 | 8.8633 | 8.3838 | 7.9427 | 7.5361 | 7.1607 | 6.8137 | 6.4924 | 6.1944 | 5.6603 | 5.1971 | 4.4392 |
| 13 | 12.1337 | 11.3484 | 10.6350 | 9.9856 | 9.3936 | 8.8527 | 8.3577 | 7.9038 | 7.4869 | 7.1034 | 6.7499 | 6.4235 | 5.8424 | 5.3423 | 4.5327 |
| 14 | 13.0037 | 12.1062 | 11.2961 | 10.5631 | 9.8986 | 9.2950 | 8.7455 | 8.2442 | 7.7862 | 7.3667 | 6.9819 | 6.6282 | 6.0021 | 5.4675 | 4.6106 |
| 15 | 13.8651 | 12.8493 | 11.9379 | 11.1184 | 10.3797 | 9.7122 | 9.1079 | 8.5595 | 8.0607 | 7.6061 | 7.1909 | 6.8109 | 6.1422 | 5.5755 | 4.6755 |
| 16 | 14.7179 | 13.5777 | 12.5611 | 11.6523 | 10.8378 | 10.1059 | 9.4466 | 8.8514 | 8.3126 | 7.8237 | 7.3792 | 6.9740 | 6.2651 | 5.6685 | 4.7296 |
| 17 | 15.5623 | 14.2919 | 13.1661 | 12.1657 | 11.2741 | 10.4773 | 9.7632 | 9.1216 | 8.5436 | 8.0216 | 7.5488 | 7.1196 | 6.3729 | 5.7487 | 4.7746 |
| 18 | 16.3983 | 14.9920 | 13.7535 | 12.6593 | 11.6896 | 10.8276 | 10.0591 | 9.3719 | 8.7556 | 8.2014 | 7.7016 | 7.2497 | 6.4674 | 5.8178 | 4.8122 |
| 19 | 17.2260 | 15.6785 | 14.3238 | 13.1339 | 12.0853 | 11.1581 | 10.3356 | 9.6036 | 8.9501 | 8.3649 | 7.8393 | 7.3658 | 6.5504 | 5.8775 | 4.8435 |
| 20 | 18.0456 | 16.3514 | 14.8775 | 13.5903 | 12.4622 | 11.4699 | 10.5940 | 9.8181 | 9.1285 | 8.5136 | 7.9633 | 7.4694 | 6.6231 | 5.9288 | 4.8696 |
| 21 | 18.8570 | 17.0112 | 15.4150 | 14.0292 | 12.8212 | 11.7641 | 10.8355 | 10.0168 | 9.2922 | 8.6487 | 8.0751 | 7.5620 | 6.6870 | 5.9731 | 4.8913 |
| 22 | 19.6604 | 17.6580 | 15.9369 | 14.4511 | 13.1630 | 12.0416 | 11.0612 | 10.2007 | 9.4424 | 8.7715 | 8.1757 | 7.6446 | 6.7429 | 6.0113 | 4.9094 |
| 23 | 20.4558 | 18.2922 | 16.4436 | 14.8568 | 13.4886 | 12.3034 | 11.2722 | 10.3711 | 9.5802 | 8.8832 | 8.2664 | 7.7184 | 6.7921 | 6.0442 | 4.9245 |
| 24 | 21.2434 | 18.9139 | 16.9355 | 15.2470 | 13.7986 | 12.5504 | 11.4693 | 10.5288 | 9.7066 | 8.9847 | 8.3481 | 7.7843 | 6.8351 | 6.0726 | 4.9371 |
| 25 | 22.0232 | 19.5235 | 17.4131 | 15.6221 | 14.0939 | 12.7834 | 11.6536 | 10.6748 | 9.8226 | 9.0770 | 8.4217 | 7.8431 | 6.8729 | 6.0971 | 4.9476 |
| 26 | 22.7952 | 20.1210 | 17.8768 | 15.9828 | 14.3752 | 13.0032 | 11.8258 | 10.8100 | 9.9290 | 9.1609 | 8.4881 | 7.8957 | 6.9061 | 6.1182 | 4.9563 |
| 27 | 23.5596 | 20.7069 | 18.3270 | 16.3296 | 14.6430 | 13.2105 | 11.9867 | 10.9352 | 10.0266 | 9.2372 | 8.5478 | 7.9426 | 6.9352 | 6.1364 | 4.9636 |
| 28 | 24.3164 | 21.2813 | 18.7641 | 16.6631 | 14.8981 | 13.4062 | 12.1371 | 11.0511 | 10.1161 | 9.3066 | 8.6016 | 7.9844 | 6.9607 | 6.1520 | 4.9697 |
| 29 | 25.0658 | 21.8444 | 19.1885 | 16.9837 | 15.1411 | 13.5907 | 12.2777 | 11.1584 | 10.1983 | 9.3696 | 8.6501 | 8.0218 | 6.9830 | 6.1656 | 4.9747 |
| 30 | 25.8077 | 22.3965 | 19.6004 | 17.2920 | 15.3725 | 13.7648 | 12.4090 | 11.2578 | 10.2737 | 9.4269 | 8.6938 | 8.0552 | 7.0027 | 6.1772 | 4.9789 |
| 35 | 29.4086 | 24.9986 | 21.4872 | 18.6646 | 16.3742 | 14.4982 | 12.9477 | 11.6546 | 10.5668 | 9.6442 | 8.8552 | 8.1755 | 7.0700 | 6.2153 | 4.9915 |
| 40 | 32.8347 | 27.3555 | 23.1148 | 19.7928 | 17.1591 | 15.0463 | 13.3317 | 11.9246 | 10.7574 | 9.7791 | 8.9511 | 8.2438 | 7.1050 | 6.2335 | 4.9966 |
| 45 | 36.0945 | 29.4902 | 24.5187 | 20.7200 | 17.7741 | 15.4558 | 13.6055 | 12.1084 | 10.8812 | 9.8628 | 9.0079 | 8.2825 | 7.1232 | 6.2421 | 4.9986 |
| 50 | 39.1961 | 31.4236 | 25.7298 | 21.4822 | 18.2559 | 15.7619 | 13.8007 | 12.2335 | 10.9617 | 9.9148 | 9.0417 | 8.3045 | 7.1327 | 6.2463 | 4.9995 |

## KEY TERMS

Annuity 236
Annuity due 246
Compound interest 235
Effective rate of interest 235

Future value 236
Interest 234
Interpolation 250
Ordinary annuity 246

Present value 236
Principal 234
Simple interest 234

## QUESTIONS

1. Explain what is meant by the time-value-of-money concept and describe its impact on business decisions.
2. Identify some common accounting applications of the time-value-of-money concept.
3. Explain the difference between simple interest and compound interest.
4. Determine the amount of interest earned on the following:
   (a) $9,000 borrowed from a bank at 10% simple annual interest for 8 months.
   (b) $15,000 invested for 2 years at 15% simple annual interest.
   (c) $1,500 invested for 26 days at 12% simple annual interest. (Use a 360-day year.)
5. Indicate the rate per period and the number of periods for each of the following:
   (a) 10% per year, for 3 years, compounded annually.
   (b) 10% per year, for 3 years, compounded semiannually.
   (c) 10% per year, for 3 years, compounded quarterly.
   (d) 10% per year, for 3 years, compounded monthly.
6. What is meant by *discounting* cash flows?
7. Indicate the table and the table value that would be used in calculating the following:
   (a) The value today of $5,000 due in 3 years at 16% interest per year, compounded semiannually.
   (b) The value today of 5 future annual payments of $4,000 at 12% interest per year, compounded annually.
   (c) The value in 10 years of $6,000 deposited today at 10% interest per year, compounded semiannually.
   (d) The value in 5 years of quarterly payments of $1,500 for 5 years at 16% interest per year, compounded quarterly.
8. Determine how much interest is earned on the following (round to nearest dollar):
   (a) $10,500 invested for 5 years at 8% per year, compounded annually.
   (b) $7,500 invested for 10 years at 20% per year, compounded semiannually.
   (c) $12,000 invested for 4 years at 16% per year, compounded quarterly.
   (d) 1,750 invested for 1 year at 24% per year, compounded monthly.

9. Determine the table values that would be used for the following:
   (a) Present value of a single amount to be received at the end of 2 years at 10% interest compounded annually.
   (b) Present value of 14 semiannual payments made at the end of the period at 10% interest compounded semiannually.
   (c) Future value of a single amount invested for 5 years at 12% interest compounded annually.
   (d) Future value of 6 equal quarterly payments made at the end of the period at 16% interest compounded quarterly.
10. An accounting student bought an inexpensive computer for $260 to assist in homework assignments. The student financed the computer, agreeing to pay $26.12 at the end of each month for 12 months. What approximate monthly interest rate did the student pay?
11. Define an annuity. What is the difference between an "ordinary annuity" and an "annuity due"?
12. Explain how the table values for the future-value ordinary annuity table are converted to annuity-due values.
13. Explain how the table values for the present-value ordinary annuity table are converted to annuity-due values.
14. For each of the following, compute the future amount of an ordinary annuity (round to nearest dollar):
   (a) 12 annual payments of $100 at 6% per annum, compounded annually.
   (b) 8 semiannual payments of $50 at 8% per annum, compounded semiannually.
   (c) 19 quarterly payments of $125 at 12% per annum, compounded quarterly.
15. What are the future amounts in Question 14 if the annuities are annuities due?
16. For each of the following, compute the present value of an ordinary annuity:
   (a) $1,000 annually for 10 years at 8% per annum, compounded annually.
   (b) $2,050 semiannually for 6 years at 6% per annum, compounded semiannually.
   (c) $5,600 quarterly for 3 years at 8% per annum, compounded quarterly.

17. What are the present values in Question 16 if the annuities are annuities due?
18. What is interpolation, when is it used, and is it 100% accurate? Explain.
19. Determine by interpolation the table value that would be used for the following:
    (a) Future value of $1 in 6 years at 13% interest per year, compounded semiannually.
    (b) Future value of $1 paid annually for 10 years at 13% interest per year, compounded annually.
    (c) Present value of $1 due in 10 years at 9% interest per year, compounded quarterly.
    (d) Present value of semiannual payments of $1 for 10 years at 9% interest per year, compounded semiannually.
20. At what annual rate of interest would an investment of $20,000 accumulate to $38,000 at the end of 5 years? (Hint: Interpolation is needed.)

---

## EXERCISES

### Exercise 7—1  (Simple and compound interest)

Dietrick Corporation borrowed $30,000 from its major shareholder, the president of the company, at an annual interest rate of 12%.

1. Assuming simple interest,
   (a) How much will Dietrick have to pay to settle its obligation if the loan is to be repaid in 12 months?
   (b) How much of the payment is interest?
   (c) How much will Dietrick have to pay if the loan is due in 18 months?
2. If the loan is paid off in 18 months and interest is compounded annually, how much will the company have to pay?
3. Compare the answers for (1c) and (2) and explain why they differ.

### Exercise 7—2  (Reciprocal relationships: future and present values)

Determine the amount that would accumulate for the following investments:

(a)  $10,050 at 10% per annum, compounded annually, for 6 years.
(b)  $650 at 12% per annum, compounded quarterly, for 10 years.
(c)  $5,000 at 16% per annum, compounded annually, for 4 years, and then reinvested at 16% per annum, compounded semiannually, for 4 more years.
(d)  $1,000 at 8% per annum, compounded semiannually, for 5 years, an additional $1,000 added and then the entire amount reinvested at 12% per annum, compounded quarterly, for 3 more years.

### Exercise 7—3  (Reciprocal relationships: future and present values)

Determine the amount that must be deposited now at compound interest to provide the desired sum for each of the following:

(a)  Amount to be invested for 10 years at 6% per annum, compounded semiannually, to equal $17,000.
(b)  Amount to be invested for 2 1/2 years at 8% per annum, compounded quarterly, to equal $5,000.
(c)  Amount to be invested for 15 years at 12% per annum, compounded semiannually, then reinvested at 16% per annum, compounded quarterly, for 5 more years to equal $25,000.
(d)  Amount to be invested at 8% per annum, compounded semiannually, for 3 years, then $5,000 more added and the entire amount reinvested at the same rate for another 3 years, compounded semiannually, to equal $12,500.

## Exercise 7—4  (Choosing between alternative investments)

Heather Company has $10,000 to invest. One alternative will yield 10% per year, compounded annually, for 4 years. A second alternative is to deposit the $10,000 in a bank that will pay 8% per year, compounded quarterly. Which alternative should Heather select?

## Exercise 7—5  (Future values of ordinary annuity payments)

Compute the future values of the following periodic investments:

(a)  $1,500 semiannual payments for 6 years at 10% per annum, compounded semiannually.
(b)  $800 monthly payments for 1 year at 24% interest per annum, compounded monthly.
(c)  $1,705 quarterly payments for 4 years at 16% per annum, compounded quarterly.

## Exercise 7—6  (Determining ordinary annuity deposits)

Determine the amount of the periodic deposit for the following. Assume deposits are made at the end of the period.

(a)  The monthly deposit invested at 24% per annum, compounded monthly, that will accumulate to $500,000 at the end of 1 year.
(b)  The quarterly deposit invested at 8% per annum, compounded quarterly, that will accumulate to $1,050 at the end of 2 years.
(c)  The annual deposit invested at 6% per annum, compounded annually, that will accumulate to $50,500 at the end of 4 years.

## Exercise 7—7  (Unknown annuity amount)

Ryan Henry wants to buy his son a BMW for his 21st birthday. If Ryan's son is turning 16 today, and interest is 8% per annum, compounded semiannually, what would Ryan's semiannual investment need to be if the car will cost $26,000 and the first payment is made six months from today?

## Exercise 7—8  (Unequal payments)

Joe Sluggo signed a contract to play baseball for the Rocky Mountain Whirlwinds. His 5-year contract calls for annual payments at the end of each year as shown below:

| Year | Payment |
|------|---------|
| 1 | $100,000 |
| 2 | 150,000 |
| 3 | 200,000 |
| 4 | 250,000 |
| 5 | 300,000 |

If interest is compounded at 12% annually, what is the present value of Mr. Sluggo's contract?

## Exercise 7—9  (Unknown investment periods)

Determine the number of periods for which the following amounts would have to be invested, under the terms specified, to accumulate to $10,000. Convert the number of periods to years.

(a)  $5,051 at 10% per annum, compounded semiannually.
(b)  $5,002 at 8% per annum, compounded annually.
(c)  $5,134 at 16% per annum, compounded quarterly.

### Exercise 7—10   (Unknown interest rates)

Determine the annual interest rate that is needed for the following investments to accumulate to $50,000.

(a)  $10,414 for 20 years, interest compounded semiannually.
(b)  $7,102 for 10 years, interest compounded quarterly.
(c)  $33,778 for 10 years, interest compounded annually.

### Exercise 7—11   (Unknown investment periods—annuities)

Determine the number of periods for which the following annuity payments would have to be invested to accumulate to $20,000. Assume payments are made at the end of each period. Convert the number of periods to years.

(a)  Annual payments of $5,927 at 12% per annum, compounded annually.
(b)  Semiannual payments of $3,409 at 16% per annum, compounded semi-annually.
(c)  Quarterly payments of $4,640 at 20% per annum, compounded quarterly.

### Exercise 7—12   (Unknown interest rates—annuities)

Determine the annual interest rate that is needed for the following annuities to accumulate to $25,000. Assume payments are made at the end of each period.

(a)  Annual payments of $4,095 for 5 years, interest compounded annually.
(b)  Semiannual payments of $5,715 for 2 years, interest compounded semiannually.
(c)  Quarterly payments of $1,864 for 3 years, interest compounded quarterly.

### Exercise 7—13   (Determining ordinary annuity payments)

Determine the amount of the periodic payments needed to pay off the following purchases. Payments are made at the end of the period.

(a)  Purchase of a waterbed for $1,205. Monthly payments are to be made for 1 year with interest at 24% per annum, compounded monthly.
(b)  Purchase of a motor boat for $26,565. Quarterly payments are to be made for 4 years with interest at 8% per annum, compounded quarterly.
(c)  Purchase of a condominium for $65,500. Semiannual payments are to be made for 10 years with interest at 10% per annum, compounded semiannually.

### Exercise 7—14   (Determining annuity-due payments)

Compute the amount of the periodic payments for Exercise 7—13 if the payments are made at the beginning of the period.

### Exercise 7—15   (Unknown purchase price for ordinary annuity payments)

Determine the purchase price for the different payment plans. Payments are at the end of the period.

(a)  $25.12 monthly payments for 1 year, with 36% interest per annum, compounded monthly.
(b)  $1,010.75 semiannual payments for 8 years, with 8% interest per annum, compounded semiannually.
(c)  $5,801.69 annual payments for 20 years with 12% interest per annum, compounded annually.

### Exercise 7—16   (Unknown purchase price for annuity-due payments)

Determine the purchase price for the payment plans in Exercise 7—15 if payments are made at the beginning of the period.

### Exercise 7—17  (Interpolation—unknown interest rate)

On July 17, 1992, Jerry Sloan borrowed $40,000 from his rich Uncle George to open a sporting goods store. Starting July 17, 1993, Jerry has to make 5 equal annual payments of $10,500 each to repay the loan. What interest rate is Jerry paying?

### Exercise 7—18  (Interpolation—unknown interest rate)

Demo Company has decided to purchase a new office building. Management signs a bank note to pay the Second State Bank $10,000 every 6 months for 10 years. At the date of purchase, the office building costs $120,000. The first payment is 6 months later. What is the approximate annual rate of interest on the note?

### Exercise 7—19  (Interpolation—unknown interest rate)

If the payments in Exercise 7—18 began on the date the papers were signed, what would the annual interest rate be?

---

## PROBLEMS

### Problem 7—1  (Determining unknown quantities)

Determine the unknown quantity for each of the following independent situations using the appropriate interest tables:

1. Jeff and Nancy want to start a trust fund for their newborn son, Mark. They have decided to invest $5,000 today. If interest is 8% compounded semiannually, how much will be in the fund when Mark turns 20?
2. Nixon Corporation wants to establish a retirement fund. Management wants to have $1,000,000 in the fund at the end of 40 years. If fund assets will earn 12%, compounded annually, how much will need to be invested now?
3. How many payments would Star, Inc., need to make if it purchases a new building for $100,000 with annual payments made at the end of each year of $16,401.24 and interest of 16%, compounded annually?
4. An investment broker indicates that an investment of $10,000 in a CD for 10 years at the current interest rate will accumulate to $21,589. What is the current annual rate of interest if interest is compounded annually?

### Problem 7—2  (Determining unknown quantities)

Determine the unknown quantity for each of the following independent situations using the appropriate interest tables:

1. Sue wants to have $10,000 saved when she begins college. If Sue enters college in 4 years and interest is 8% compounded annually, how much will Sue need to save each year assuming equal deposits at the end of each year?
2. XYZ Company has obtained a bank loan to finance the purchase of an automobile for one of its executives. The terms of the loan require monthly payments at the end of each month of $585. If the interest rate is 18% compounded monthly, and the car costs $15,850, for how many months will XYZ have to make payments?
3. Diaz Company is offering the following investment plan. If deposits of $250 are made semiannually for the next 9 years, $7,726 will accrue. If interest is compounded semiannually, what is the approximate annual rate of interest on the investment?
4. Jack wants to buy a rental unit. For how many periods will he have to make annual deposits of $5,000 in order to accumulate $50,445, the price of the rental unit, if interest is 12% compounded annually? Assume deposits are made at the end of each year.

### Problem 7—3   (Comparing the value of two contracts)

John Jock and Sam Sport, world famous football players, signed multi-year contracts with their respective teams. Now they are in a dispute over who is getting paid the most. John signed a 5-year, $15 million contract, while Sam's 5-year contract totals only $14 million but includes a signing bonus paid at the beginning of the 5-year contract term. The annual salary payments and the signing bonus are as follows:

|  | John Jock | Sam Sport |
|---|---|---|
| Signing bonus | $ -0- | $ 1,000,000 |
| Salaries: Year 1 | 1,500,000 | 2,600,000 |
| Year 2 | 2,000,000 | 2,600,000 |
| Year 3 | 2,750,000 | 2,600,000 |
| Year 4 | 3,750,000 | 2,600,000 |
| Year 5 | 5,000,000 | 2,600,000 |
| Totals | $15,000,000 | $14,000,000 |

1. If salaries are paid at the end of each year and interest is 12% annually, which player received the larger contract in terms of present value?
2. If salaries are paid at the end of each year and interest is 8% annually, which player received the larger contract in terms of present value?
3. What factors affect the present values of the above contracts?

### Problem 7—4   (Determining the implicit interest rate)

Valley Technical College needs to purchase some computers. Because the college is short of cash, Computer Sales Company has agreed to let Valley have the computers now and pay $2,500 per computer 6 months from now. If the current cash price is $2,404, what is the rate of interest Valley would be paying?

### Problem 7—5   (Choosing between purchase alternatives)

Foot Loose, Inc., needs to purchase a new shoelace-making machine. Machines Ready has agreed to sell them the machine for $22,000 down and 4 payments of $5,700 to be paid in semiannual installments for the next 2 years. Do-It-Yourself Machines has offered to sell Foot Loose a comparable machine for $10,000 down and 4 semiannual payments of $9,000. If the current interest rate is 16%, compounded semiannually, which machine should Foot Loose purchase?

### Problem 7—6   (Choosing between rent payment alternatives)

Park City Construction is building a new office building, and management is trying to decide how rent payments for the office space should be structured. The alternatives are:

(a) Annual payment of $15,000 at the end of each year.
(b) Monthly payments of $1,200 at the end of each month.

Assuming an interest rate of 12% compounded monthly, which payment schedule should Park City use?

### Problem 7—7   (Computing mortgage payments with the use of formulas)

George and Barbara Shrub would like to purchase a large white house and are evaluating their financing options. Bank A offers a 10-year mortgage at 12% annual interest, compounded monthly, with payments made at the end of each month. Bank B is offering a 10-year mortgage at 13% annual interest, compounded annually, with payments made at the end of each year. The purchase price of the white house is $250,000.

1. Use formulas to compute the following amounts:
   (a) The monthly payment for the Bank A mortgage.
   (b) The annual payment for the Bank B mortgage.
2. Which financing alternative would you advise the Shrubs to select?

### Problem 7—8  (Future value of annuity-due deposits)

Rose Sanchez plans to save $1,000 each year to pay for a 2-week trip to Mexico. If Rose makes her first deposit on July 1, 1992, and her last deposit on July 1, 1994, how much will she have for her trip on July 1, 1995? Assume that the annual interest rate is 8%.

### Problem 7—9  (Determining number and amount of payments on retirement plan)

Ed Anderson has $250,000 accumulated in a retirement account and plans to receive annual payments of $40,360 at the end of each year.

(a) If interest is 12% annually, how many payments will Ed receive?
(b) If payments are made at the beginning of the year, how many full payments would he receive, and how much would the last payment be?
(c) What would the payments have to be if Ed wants to receive 20 payments, each at the end of the year?
(d) What would the payments have to be if Ed wants to receive 20 payments, each at the beginning of the year?

### Problem 7—10  (Planning for the future)

John Seymor turned 20 years old today and is trying to plan for his future. He would like to ensure that he has enough money to care for himself when he retires. If John plans on retiring when he turns 60 years old, and interest is 10%:

1. How much money would he need to invest at the end of every year in order to have $1,000,000 on his 60th birthday?
2. How much money would he need to invest at the end of every year in order to be able to withdraw $100,000 at the end of each year for 10 years, with the first withdrawal being on his 61st birthday?
3. In both of the above scenarios, John wants to have $1,000,000 available for his retirement. Why aren't the answers to (1) and (2) identical?

### Problem 7—11  (Choosing among alternative payment plans)

The following payment plans are offered on the purchase of a new freezer:

(a) $375 cash.
(b) 8 monthly payments of $55.
(c) $100 cash down and 6 monthly payments of $50.

Which payment plan would you choose if interest is 24% annually, compounded monthly, if you are the purchaser? if you are the seller? (Assume ordinary annuities where applicable.)

### Problem 7—12  (Determining sinking fund payments)

Payback Company wants to start a sinking fund to cover the retirement of a serial bond issuance. The bonds begin maturing in 15 years at a rate of $30,000 per year for 15 years. Payback Company can earn annual interest of 6% for the first 15 years and 10% for the remaining years. How much will Payback Company have to deposit annually under the following assumptions?

(a) Payments into the fund are made at the end of the year, and bonds are retired at the end of the year.

(b) Payments into the fund are made at the beginning of the year, and bonds are retired at the beginning of the year.
(c) Payments into the fund are made at the beginning of the year, and bonds are retired at the end of the year.

### Problem 7—13 (Determining amount of annuity-due payments and interest)

Briercliff Inc. borrowed $4,000 on a 10%, 1-year note due on August 1, 1993. On that date, Briercliff was unable to pay the obligation but arranged for Western Loan Company to pay the holder $4,000. Briercliff agreed to pay Western Loan Company a series of 5 equal annual payments beginning August 1, 1993. Each payment is in part a reduction of principal and in part a payment of interest at 12% annually. (a) What is the amount of each payment? (b) What is the total amount of interest on the obligation?

### Problem 7—14 (Determing purchase price)

Big Company purchased a machine on February 1, 1993, and will make 7 semiannual payments of $14,000 beginning 5 years from the date of purchase. The interest rate will be 12%, compounded semiannually. Determine the purchase price of the machine.

### Problem 7—15 (Estimating the value of a company)

Cline Corporation is considering the acquisition of a company and wants to determine the value of the company based on the following information. (Assume revenues and expenses are received and incurred evenly throughout the year.)

| Years | Estimated Interest Rate | Estimated Annual Revenues | Estimated Annual Expenses |
|-------|-------------------------|---------------------------|---------------------------|
| 1-5   | 16% compounded annually | $170,000 | $140,000 |
| 6-10  | 12% compounded quarterly | 215,000 | 155,000 |
| 11-15 | 14% compounded semiannually | 245,000 | 185,000 |

Based on estimated net profit, discounted to the present, what is the value of the company?

### Problem 7—16 (Choosing among insurance options)

Dr. Philips is considering the purchase of a life insurance policy. The following options are available for payment to the beneficiary upon the death of Dr. Philips:

(a) $100,000 immediately.
(b) $8,000 at the end of each quarter for 4 years.
(c) $30,000 immediately and $5,000 in quarterly payments for 4½ years.
(d) Quarterly payments of $4,350 for the next 10 years.

Given an annual interest rate of 12%, compounded quarterly, which option would you recommend to Dr. Philips?

### Problem 7—17 (Buy or lease—implicit interest rate)

An equipment company representative has a machine for sale or lease. If you purchase the machine for cash, the cost is $7,596. If you lease the machine, you will have to sign a noncancelable lease and make 5 annual payments of $2,000 each. The first payment will be paid on the first day of the lease contract. Determine the implicit interest rate of the lease contract.

# PART TWO

## Assets

# CHAPTER 8

# Cash and Temporary Investments

---

**CHAPTER TOPICS**

**Composition of Cash**

**Management and Control of Cash**

**Petty Cash Fund**

**Bank Reconciliations**

**Accounting for Temporary Investments**

**Valuation of Marketable Securities**

**Reporting Cash and Temporary Investments on the Balance Sheet**

**Reporting Marketable Securities on the Statement of Cash Flows**

---

In 64 minutes on Friday, May 13, 1988, an employee of First Chicago, a large bank holding company, transferred $70 million from the accounts of three major customers—Merrill Lynch, United Airlines, and Brown-Forman. Far from being a high-tech operation, the unauthorized transfers were accomplished by fake phone confirmations of the requested electronic transfers of funds. The First Chicago employee, while pretending to follow the required procedure of calling the customers to confirm the transfer requests, instead called his accomplices who were waiting at a south side Chicago home. Because the confirmation calls were often monitored, the accomplices had been coached on the correct coded responses. The confirmations were unquestioned and the electronic transfers were approved and made. The embezzlement was discovered later that day when First Chicago informed Merrill Lynch of an overdraft in its account. Merrill Lynch disagreed, an investigation ensued, the scheme was uncovered, and the funds were returned. Officials speculated at the time that the scheme might have gone uncovered longer if the schemers had not tried to take "a jillion dollars" in one bite.[1]

As the First Chicago example illustrates, liquid assets must be managed carefully. The first part of this book has established a perspective of accounting and its theoretical foundation. Part II explores items classified as assets, beginning with the most liquid assets: cash and temporary investments.

## CASH

Cash is perhaps the single most important item on a balance sheet. Since it serves as the medium of exchange in our economy, cash is involved directly or indirectly in almost all business transactions. Even when cash is not involved directly in a transaction, it provides the basis for measurement and accounting for all other items.

Another reason why cash is so important is that individuals, businesses, and even governments must maintain an adequate liquidity position; that is, they must have a sufficient amount of cash on hand to pay obligations as they come due if they are to remain viable operating entities. In the early stages of its conceptual framework project, the FASB identified the need to report information on cash and liquidity as one of the key objectives of financial reporting. This emphasis eventually led to the requirement of providing a statement of cash flows as one of the primary financial statements.

In striking contrast to the importance of cash as a key element in the liquidity position of an entity is its unproductive nature. Since cash is the measure of value, it cannot expand or grow unless it is converted into other properties. Cash kept under a mattress, for example, will not grow or appreciate, whereas land may increase in value if held. Excessive balances of cash on hand are often referred to as **idle cash**. Efficient cash management requires available cash to be continuously working in one of several ways as part of the operating cycle or as a short-term or long-term investment. The management of cash is therefore a critical business function.

### Composition of Cash

Cash is the most liquid of current assets and consists of those items that serve as a medium of exchange and provide a basis for accounting measurement. To be reported as "cash," an item must be readily available and not restricted for use in the payment of current obligations. A general guideline is whether an item is *acceptable for deposit at face value* by a bank or other financial institution.

Items that are classified as cash include coin and currency on hand and unrestricted funds available on deposit in a bank, which are often called demand deposits since they can be withdrawn upon demand. Demand deposits would include amounts in checking, savings, and money market deposit accounts. Petty cash funds or change funds and negotiable instruments, such as personal checks, travelers' checks, cashiers' checks, bank drafts, and money orders are also items commonly reported as cash. The total of these items plus undeposited coin and currency is sometimes called **cash on hand**. Also included as cash would be any company checks that have been written but that have not been mailed or delivered. Deposits that are not immediately available due to withdrawal or other restrictions are sometimes referred to as time deposits. These deposits are often separately classified as "restricted cash" or "temporary investments." Examples of time deposits in-

[1]Jeff Bailey, "U.S. Charges Seven in 'No-Tech' Attempt to Steal $70 Million From First Chicago," *The Wall Street Journal*, May 19, 1988, p. 2.

clude certificates of deposit (CDs) and money market savings certificates. CDs, for example, generally may be withdrawn without penalty only at specified maturity dates.

Deposits in foreign banks that are subject to immediate and unrestricted withdrawal generally qualify as cash and are reported at their U.S. dollar equivalents as of the date of the balance sheet. However, cash in foreign banks that is restricted as to use or withdrawal should be designated as receivables of a current or noncurrent character and reported subject to appropriate allowances for estimated uncollectibles.

Some items do not meet the "acceptance at face value on deposit" test and should not be reported as cash. Examples include postage stamps (which are office supplies) and postdated checks, IOUs, and not-sufficient-funds (NSF) checks (all of which are in effect receivables).

Cash balances specifically designated by management for special purposes should be reported separately. Those cash balances to be applied to some current purpose or current obligation are properly reported in the current section on the balance sheet. For example, cash funds for employees' travel may be reported separately from cash but still be classified as a current asset. However, restricted cash should be reported as a current item only if it is to be applied to some current purpose or obligation. Classification of the cash balance as current or noncurrent should parallel the classification applied to the liability. Cash balances not available for current purposes require separate designation and classification under a noncurrent heading on the balance sheet.

A credit balance in the cash account resulting from the issuance of checks in excess of the amount on deposit is known as a **cash overdraft** and should be reported as a current liability. When a company has two or more accounts with a single bank, an overdraft can be offset against an account with a positive balance. If the depositor fails to cover the overdraft, the bank has the legal right to apply funds from one account to cover the overdraft in another. However, when a company has accounts with two different banks and there is a positive balance in one account and an overdraft in the other, both an asset balance and a liability balance should be recognized in view of the claim against one bank and the obligation to the other; if recognition of an overdraft is to be avoided, cash should be transferred to cover the deficiency, because the legal right of offset does not exist between two banks.

In summary, cash is a current asset comprised of coin, currency, and other items that (1) serve as a medium of exchange and (2) provide the basis for measurement in accounting. Most negotiable instruments (e.g., checks, bank drafts, and money orders) qualify as cash because they can be converted to currency on demand or are acceptable for deposit at face value by a bank. Components of cash restricted as to use or withdrawal should be disclosed or reported separately and classified as an investment, a receivable, or other asset. Exhibit 8—1 summarizes the classification of various items that have been discussed. The objective of disclosure is to provide the user of financial statements with information to assist in evaluating the entity's ability to meet obligations (i.e., its liquidity and solvency) and in assessing the effectiveness of cash management.

Since the concept of cash embodies the standard of value, few valuation problems are encountered in reporting those items qualifying as cash. When cash is comprised solely of cash on hand and unrestricted demand deposits, the total generally appears on the balance sheet as a single item—Cash. When other components of cash are significant, they should be disclosed or reported as separate items.

## Compensating Balances

In connection with financing arrangements, it is common practice for a company to agree to maintain a minimum or average balance on deposit with a bank or other lending

**Exhibit 8—1    Classification of Cash and Noncash Items**

| Item | Classification |
|---|---|
| Undeposited coin & currency . . . . . . . . . . . . . . . . . . . . . . . . | Cash |
| Unrestricted funds on deposit at bank (demand deposits) . . . . . . . . . . . . . . . . . . . . . . . . . . . . . . . . . . . . . . . . | Cash |
| Petty cash & change funds . . . . . . . . . . . . . . . . . . . . . . . . . | Cash |
| Negotiable instruments, such as checks, bank drafts, and money orders . . . . . . . . . . . . . . . . . . . . . . . . . . . . . . . | Cash |
| Company checks written but not yet mailed or delivered | Cash |
| Restricted deposits, such as CDs and money market savings certificates (time deposits) . . . . . . . . . . . . . . . . . . | Temporary Investments |
| Deposits in foreign banks: | |
| Unrestricted . . . . . . . . . . . . . . . . . . . . . . . . . . . . . . . . . | Cash |
| Restricted . . . . . . . . . . . . . . . . . . . . . . . . . . . . . . . . . . . . | Receivables |
| Postage stamps . . . . . . . . . . . . . . . . . . . . . . . . . . . . . . . . . | Office Supplies |
| IOUs, postdated checks, and not-sufficient-funds (NSF) checks . . . . . . . . . . . . . . . . . . . . . . . . . . . . . . . . . . . . . . | Receivables |
| Cash restricted for special purposes . . . . . . . . . . . . . . . . . . | Restricted Cash* |
| Cash overdraft . . . . . . . . . . . . . . . . . . . . . . . . . . . . . . . . . . | Current Liability |

*Separately reported as current or noncurrent asset depending on the purpose for which it is restricted.

institution. These compensating balances are defined by the SEC as ". . . that portion of any demand deposit (or any time deposit or certificate of deposit) maintained by a corporation . . . which constitutes support for existing borrowing arrangements of the corporation . . . with a lending institution. Such arrangements would include both outstanding borrowings and the assurance of future credit availability."[2]

Compensating balances provide a source of funds to the lender as partial compensation for credit extended. In effect, such arrangements raise the interest rate of the borrower because a portion of the amount on deposit with the lending institution cannot be used. These balances present an accounting problem from the standpoint of disclosure. Readers of financial statements are likely to assume the entire cash balance is available to meet current obligations, when, in fact, part of the balance is restricted.

The solution to this problem is to disclose the amount of compensating balances. The SEC recommends that any "legally restricted" deposits held as compensating balances be segregated and reported separately. If the balances are the result of short-term financing arrangements, they should be shown separately among the "cash items" in the current asset section; if the compensating balances are in connection with long-term agreements, they should be classified as noncurrent, either as investments or "other assets." In many instances, deposits are not legally restricted, but compensating balance agreements still exist as business commitments in connection with lines of credit. In these situations, the amounts and nature of the arrangements should be disclosed in the notes to the financial statements, as illustrated on page 270 for Patten Corporation.

## Management and Control of Cash

As noted earlier, a business enterprise must maintain sufficient cash for current operations and for paying obligations as they come due. Any excess cash should be invested tempo-

[2]Securities and Exchange Commission, *Accounting Series Release No. 148*, "Disclosure of Compensating Balances and Short-Term Borrowing Arrangements" (Washington: U.S. Government Printing Office, 1973).

---

**Exhibit 8—2    Patten Corporation—Disclosure of Compensating Balances**

---

## 5  Notes Payable, Lines of Credit and Commercial Paper

The Company has borrowings with various banks and commercial paper which are used to finance inventory purchases and notes receivable and to fund operations. Significant financial data related to the Company's bank and commercial paper facilities are as follows:

|  | Years ended | | |
|---|---|---|---|
|  | April 2, 1989 | April 3, 1988 | March 31, 1987 |
| Short-term lines of credit available ............ | $58,000,000 | $53,748,000 | $31,475,000 |
| Long-term lines of credit available ............ | — | 41,500,000 | 29,500,000 |
| Total lines of credit available ................ | $58,000,000 | $95,248,000 | $60,975,000 |

The Company's lines of credit constitute business commitments and, accordingly, are subject to continued creditworthiness and review by the lending banks. Approximately 41% of the aggregate amount available under the lines of credit requires the security of existing notes receivable and inventory. At April 2, 1989, the Company was required to maintain average compensating balances of approximately 3.9% of total available lines.

---

rarily to earn an additional return for the shareholders. Effective cash management also requires controls to protect cash from loss by theft or fraud. Since cash is the most liquid asset, it is particularly susceptible to misappropriation unless properly safeguarded. When computerized accounting systems are used, controls are still necessary, and are perhaps even more important than with a strictly manual system, in properly accounting for all inflows, outflows, and balances of cash.

The system for controlling cash must be adapted to a particular business. It is not feasible to describe all the features and techniques employed in businesses of various kinds and sizes. In general, however, systems of cash control deny access to the accounting records to those who handle cash. This reduces the possibility of improper entries to conceal the misuse of cash receipts and cash payments. The probability of misappropriation of cash is greatly reduced if two or more employees must conspire in an embezzlement. Further, systems normally provide for separation of the receiving and paying functions. The basic characteristics of a system of cash control are:

1. Specifically assigned responsibility for handling cash receipts.
2. Separation of handling and recording cash receipts.
3. Daily deposit of all cash received.
4. Voucher system to control cash payments.
5. Internal audits at irregular intervals.
6. Double record of cash—bank and books, with reconciliations performed by someone outside the accounting function.

These controls are more likely to be found in large companies with many employees. Small companies with few employees generally have difficulty in totally segregating accounting and cash-handling duties. Even small companies, however, should incorporate as many control features as possible.

To the extent that a company can incorporate effective internal controls, it can reduce significantly the chances of theft, loss, or inadvertent errors in accounting for and controlling cash. Even the most elaborate control system, however, cannot totally eliminate the possibilities of misappropriations or errors. The use of a petty cash fund can

## Electronic Funds Transfer

For years it has been forecast that we would soon be living in a cashless, paperless society with all transfers of funds being done electronically. Although banks and financial institutions routinely use electronic funds transfer (EFT), most consumers still make all their payments with cash, check, or credit card. The most recent innovation for consumers is called EFT/POS (electronic funds transfer at the point of sale). Typically this involves the use of a debit card, which is similar to a credit card, except that at the time of sale the funds are immediately transferred from the purchaser's bank account to the seller's account.

In 1989, only two percent of customers expressed a preference for electronic payment systems, like debit cards, over paying by cash, check, or credit card. However, the benefits of electronic payment have led to forecasts of rapid growth. Debit card transactions cost less for retailers to process than credit card transactions, the retailer receives the cash instantly, and the number of bad debts is greatly reduced. For customers, debit cards reduce delays and uncertainties at the point of sale.

The effects of debit card transactions are not uniformly positive. Some users complain that the use of debit cards eliminates "float," the extra use of funds during the interval between when a person writes a check or makes a charge and when the amount is actually subtracted from that person's bank account. With a debit card, there is no interval and thus there is no float. Also, most of the benefits of debit card use accrue to the receiver (prompt receipt, low bad debts, etc.), leaving users with little incentive to use the cards. Some retailers are beginning to extend cash discounts to debit card users.

Banks are not completely in favor of debit cards either. Some fear that use of debit cards will reduce banks' lucrative credit card business. Also, as individuals become more comfortable with electronic banking in general, banks fear that they will make fewer visits to the banks themselves, thereby decreasing the amount of "cross-services," like consumer loans, safety-deposit boxes, and savings plans.

Widespread electronic payments have also been met with some resistance by civil libertarians. With computerized registers already tabulating everything a customer purchases, payment by debit card completes the database by supplying the name and address of the purchaser. Use of this database makes possible the study of individual consumers' spending habits. Marketers are already talking about targeting product promotions at those customers who have demonstrated an interest in similar products.

In spite of these difficulties, debit card usage is fast catching on in some market segments. Rapid growth in use is expected in gasoline sales. And, among demographic groups, college students are the most frequent users. In fact, some college bookstores are rapidly approaching a cashless state. One cash customer at a college bookstore, in a long line with debit and credit card users who experienced no difficulty in making their purchases, was surprised when the beleaguered cashier asked for a picture ID before he would accept a $20 bill as payment.

### Questions:

1. *What obstacles must be overcome before electronic funds transfers become widespread among consumers?*
2. *How would bank reconciliations differ if most transactions were made electronically?*
3. *Why might debit cards reduce the use of credit cards?*

Sources:

Lauren Lekoski, "Is EFT Finally Ready to Lift Off?" *Supermarket Business*, October 1989, p. 38.

"Debit Cards, EFT Still Grasping for Toehold," *Chain Store Age Executive*, February 1989, p. 67.

facilitate control over small cash payments, and periodic bank reconciliations can help identify any cash shortages or errors that may have been made in accounting for cash.

## Petty Cash Fund

Immediate cash payments and payments too small to be made by check may be made from a petty cash fund. Under an **imprest petty cash system**, the petty cash fund is created by cashing a check for the amount of the fund. In recording the establishment of the fund, Petty Cash is debited and Cash is credited. The cash is then turned over to a cashier or some person who is solely responsible for payments made out of the fund. The cashier should require a signed receipt for all payments made. These receipts may be printed in prenumbered form. Frequently, a bill or other memorandum is submitted when a payment is requested. A record of petty cash payments may be kept in a *petty cash journal*.

Whenever the amount of cash in the fund runs low and also at the end of each fiscal period, the fund is replenished by writing a check equal to the payments made. In recording replenishment, expenses and other appropriate accounts are debited for petty cash disbursements and Cash is credited. When the fund fails to balance, an adjustment is usually made to a miscellaneous expense or revenue account, sometimes called "Cash Short and Over." Unless theft is involved, this will usually involve only a nominal amount arising, for example, from errors in making change.

As noted above, a petty cash fund is usually replenished at the end of each fiscal period. If replenishment does not occur at year-end, however, an adjustment to Petty Cash is required to properly record all expenditures from the fund during the period. The debit entries would be the same as those to record replenishment; the credit entry would be to Petty Cash, reflecting a reduction in that account.

To illustrate the appropriate entries in accounting for petty cash, assume that Keat Company establishes a petty cash fund on January 1 in the amount of $500. The following entry would be made.

| | | |
|---|---|---|
| Petty Cash | 500 | |
|     Cash | | 500 |
|     *To establish a $500 petty cash fund.* | | |

During the next six months, the person responsible for the fund made payments for office supplies ($245), postage ($110), and office equipment repairs ($25). Receipts for these items are maintained as evidence supporting the petty cash disbursements. On July 1 the fund is replenished. At that time the coin and currency in the fund totaled $115. The entry to record the expenses and replenish the fund would be:

| | | |
|---|---|---|
| Office Supplies Expense | 245 | |
| Postage Expense | 110 | |
| Repair Expense | 25 | |
| Cash Short and Over (or Misc. Expense) | 5 | |
|     Cash | | 385 |
|     *To record expenses and replenish the petty cash fund.* | | |

After this entry, the fund would be restored to its original amount, $500. If Keat Company decided to reduce the fund to $400, an entry would be required as follows:

| | | |
|---|---|---|
| Cash | 100 | |
|     Petty Cash | | 100 |
|     *To reduce the petty cash fund from $500 to $400.* | | |

Assume further that during the next six months, Keat Company used its petty cash fund to purchase additional office supplies ($136), purchase decorations and refreshments for an office party ($89), and pay freight charges ($55). Even though the fund was not replenished on December 31, an entry would be required to properly record the expenditures from the fund for that period, as follows:

| | | |
|---|---:|---:|
| Office Supplies Expense | 136 | |
| Misc. Expenses | 89 | |
| Freight | 55 | |
| Petty Cash | | 280 |

*To record expenses paid from the petty cash fund.*

The entry to increase a petty cash fund is the same as to establish the fund initially—a debit to Petty Cash and a credit to Cash. However, petty cash funds should only be large enough to cover small expenditures. Large amounts should be disbursed through an authorized voucher system.

## Bank Reconciliations

When daily receipts are deposited and payments other than those from petty cash are made by check, the bank's statement of its transactions with the depositor can be compared with the record of cash as reported on the depositor's books. A comparison of the bank balance with the balance reported on the books is usually made monthly by means of a summary known as a bank reconciliation. A bank reconciliation is prepared to disclose any errors or irregularities in either the records of the bank or those of the business unit. It is developed in a form that points out the reasons for discrepancies in the two balances. It should be prepared by an individual who neither handles nor records cash. Any discrepancies should be brought to the immediate attention of appropriate company officials.

When the bank statement and the depositor's records are compared, certain items may appear on one and not the other, resulting in a difference in the two balances. Most of these differences result from temporary timing lags and are thus normal. Four common types of differences arise in the following situations:

1. A deposit made near the end of the month and recorded on the depositor's books is not received by the bank in time to be reflected on the bank statement. This amount, referred to as a deposit in transit, has to be added to the bank statement balance to make it agree with the balance on the depositor's books.
2. Checks written near the end of the month have reduced the depositor's cash balance, but have not cleared the bank as of the bank statement date. These outstanding checks must be subtracted from the bank statement balance to make it agree with the depositor's records.
3. The bank normally charges a monthly fee for servicing an account. The bank automatically reduces the depositor's account balance for this bank service charge and notes the amount on the bank statement. The depositor must deduct this amount from the recorded cash balance to make it agree with the bank statement balance. The return of a customer's check for which insufficient funds are available, known as a not-sufficient-funds (NSF) check, is handled in a similar manner.
4. An amount owed to the depositor is paid directly to the bank by a third party and added to the depositor's account. Upon receipt of the bank statement (assuming prior notification has not been received from the bank), this amount must be added to the cash balance on the depositor's books. Examples include a direct payroll deposit by an individual's employer and interest added by the bank on a savings account.

If, after considering the items mentioned above, the bank statement and the book balances cannot be reconciled, a detailed analysis of both the bank's records and the depositor's books may be necessary to determine whether errors or irregularities exist on the records of either party.

**Preparing a Bank Reconciliation**    A common form of bank reconciliation is illustrated below. This form is prepared in two sections, the bank statement balance being adjusted to the corrected cash balance in the first section, and the book balance being adjusted to the same corrected cash balance in the second section. Any items not yet recognized by the bank (e.g., deposits in transit or outstanding checks) as well as any errors made by the bank are recorded in the first section. The second section contains any items the depositor has not yet recognized (e.g., direct deposits, NSF checks, or bank service charges) and any corrections for errors made on the depositor's books.

The reconciliation of bank and book balances to a corrected balance has two important advantages: it develops a corrected cash figure, and it shows separately all items requiring adjustment on the depositor's books.

An alternative form of reconciliation would be to reconcile the bank statement balance to the book balance. This form would not develop a corrected cash figure, however, and would make it more difficult to determine the adjustments needed on the depositor's books.

**Svendsen, Inc.**
**Bank Reconciliation**
**November 30, 1993**

| | | |
|---|---:|---:|
| Balance per bank statement, November 30, 1993 . . . . . . . . . | | $2,979.72 |
| Add: Deposits in transit . . . . . . . . . . . . . . . . . . . . . . . . . . . . | $658.50 | |
| Charge for interest made to depositor's account by bank in error . . . . . . . . . . . . . . . . . . . . . . . . . . . . . . | 12.50 | 671.00 |
| | | $3,650.72 |
| Deduct outstanding checks: | | |
| No. 1125 . . . . . . . . . . . . . . . . . . . . . . . . . . . . . . . . . . . . . | $ 58.16 | |
| No. 1138 . . . . . . . . . . . . . . . . . . . . . . . . . . . . . . . . . . . . . | 100.00 | |
| No. 1152 . . . . . . . . . . . . . . . . . . . . . . . . . . . . . . . . . . . . . | 98.60 | |
| No. 1154 . . . . . . . . . . . . . . . . . . . . . . . . . . . . . . . . . . . . . | 255.00 | |
| No. 1155 . . . . . . . . . . . . . . . . . . . . . . . . . . . . . . . . . . . . . | 192.07 | 703.83 |
| Corrected bank balance . . . . . . . . . . . . . . . . . . . . . . . . . . . | | $2,946.89 |
| Balance per books, November 30, 1993 . . . . . . . . . . . . . . . . | | $2,952.49 |
| Add: Interest earned during November . . . . . . . . . . . . . . . . | $ 98.50 | |
| Check No. 1116 to Ace Advertising for $46 recorded by depositor as $64 in error . . . . . . . . . . . . . . . . . . . . . | 18.00 | 116.50 |
| | | $3,068.99 |
| Deduct: Bank service charges . . . . . . . . . . . . . . . . . . . . . . . | $  3.16 | |
| Customer's check deposited November 25 and returned marked NSF . . . . . . . . . . . . . . . . . . . . . . . | 118.94 | 122.10 |
| Corrected book balance . . . . . . . . . . . . . . . . . . . . . . . . . . . | | $2,946.89 |

After preparing the reconciliation, the depositor should record any items appearing on the bank statement and requiring recognition on the company's books as well as any corrections for errors discovered on its own books. The bank should be notified immediately of any bank errors. The following entries would be required on the books of Svendsen, Inc., as a result of the November 30 reconciliation:

| | | |
|---|---:|---:|
| Cash . . . . . . . . . . . . . . . . . . . . . . . . . . . . . . . . . . . . . . . . . . . . . . . . . . . . . . | 98.50 | |
| Interest Revenue . . . . . . . . . . . . . . . . . . . . . . . . . . . . . . . . . . . . . . . | | 98.50 |
| *To record interest earned during November.* | | |

```
Cash ....................................................    18.00
    Advertising Expense ......................................              18.00
        To record correction for check in payment of advertising
        recorded as $64 instead of the actual amount, $46.

Accounts Receivable......................................    118.94
Miscellaneous General Expense ...........................      3.16
    Cash .................................................             122.10
        To record customer's uncollectible check and bank charges
        for November.
```

After these entries are posted, the cash account will show a balance of $2,946.89. If financial statements were prepared at November 30, this is the amount that would be reported on the balance sheet. It should be noted that the bank reconciliation is not presented to external users. It is used as a control procedure and as an accounting tool to determine the adjustments required to bring the cash account and related account balances up to date.

**Preparing a "Proof of Cash"**    A bank reconciliation is sometimes expanded to incorporate a proof of both receipts and disbursements as separate steps in the reconciliation process. This is often referred to as a **four-column bank reconciliation** or a **proof of cash**.

In a four-column reconciliation, columns are provided for the beginning reconciliation, deposits or receipts, withdrawals or disbursements, and the ending reconciliation. Thus the four-column approach is really two reconciliations in one. The first column contains a reconciliation as of the end of the preceding period. The deposits per bank statement or receipts per books for the period are added to the beginning balances, and the withdrawals per bank statement or disbursements per books are subtracted to arrive at the ending balances. Deposits/receipts are reconciled in the second column and withdrawals/disbursements in the third column. The amounts must reconcile both vertically and horizontally for the ending bank and book balances to agree.

In order to complete this type of reconciliation, each adjustment must be carefully analyzed. Note that two columns are always affected for each adjustment. For example, a deposit of $425.40 on October 31, 1993, was recorded by the bank in November and is included in the total bank deposits of $21,312.40 for November. However, the deposit was properly recorded on the books as a receipt in October; thus the $425.40 is not included in the book receipts of $21,457 for November, but is included in the beginning book balance of $5,406.22. The reconciliation accounts for this by deducting the in-transit deposit from the total bank deposits for November and by adding the deposit to the beginning October 31 bank statement balance. This is the same type of analysis that would have been made on October 31 for a regular bank reconciliation on that date. Similarly, the $658.50 deposit in transit at the end of November is already recorded in the book receipts and ending cash balance as of November 30, but must be added to the bank deposits and ending balance to reconcile to the correct balances as of November 30.

A similar analysis is needed for reconciling the timing differences for outstanding checks. Checks totaling $810.50 were outstanding (had not cleared the bank) on October 31 and therefore should be deducted from the October 31 bank balance. The bank records include those checks as withdrawals for November (that is, the $810.50 is included in the total bank withdrawals of $24,228.10), and so the $810.50 must be subtracted from the November withdrawals to reconcile with the corrected balances. On the other hand, the outstanding checks at the end of November are valid withdrawals for November, and so the $703.83 must be added to the bank withdrawals for November and subtracted from the bank cash balance as of November 30.

The adjustment for a "not-sufficient-funds" (NSF) check depends on how the company and bank records are kept. Typically, a company will periodically deposit its checks,

**Svendsen, Inc.**
**Proof of Cash**
**November 30, 1993**

| | Beginning Reconciliation October 31 | Deposits/ Receipts | Withdrawals/ Disbursements | Ending Reconciliation November 30 |
|---|---|---|---|---|
| Balance per bank statement .............. | $5,895.42 | $21,312.40 | $24,228.10 | $2,979.72 |
| Deposits in transit: | | | | |
| October 31 ............ | 425.40 | (425.40) | | |
| November 30 .......... | | 658.50 | | 658.50 |
| Outstanding checks: | | | | |
| October 31 ............ | (810.50) | | (810.50) | |
| November 30 .......... | | | 703.83 | (703.83) |
| NSF check redeposited during November; no entry made on books for return or redeposit ....... | | (100.00) | (100.00) | |
| Charge for interest made by bank in error .......... | | | (12.50) | 12.50 |
| Corrected bank balance ... | $5,510.32 | $21,445.50 | $24,008.93 | $2,946.89 |
| Balance per books........ | $5,406.22 | $21,457.00 | $23,910.73 | $2,952.49 |
| Bank service charges: | | | | |
| October ............... | (5.90) | | (5.90) | |
| November ............. | | | 3.16 | (3.16) |
| Customer's check deposited November 25 found to be uncollectible (NSF) .................. | | | 118.94 | (118.94) |
| Interest earned: | | | | |
| October .............. | 110.00 | (110.00) | | |
| November ............. | | 98.50 | | 98.50 |
| Check No. 1116 for $46 recorded by depositor as $64 in error ............. | | | (18.00) | 18.00 |
| Corrected book balance ... | $5,510.32 | $21,445.50 | $24,008.93 | $2,946.89 |

recording them as receipts and additions to the cash balance. The bank will similarly record the deposits as increases in cash for the company. However, when the bank determines that a particular check is not collectible from the maker (an NSF check), it usually will show the check as a withdrawal and thus a reduction in the company's cash balance. If, after checking with the customer, the company determines the check is now good, it may merely redeposit the check without making any entries on the books for the bank's return of the check or the redeposit. The bank, however, will again show the check as a deposit and an increase in the cash balance. After the redeposit, the bank will show the correct cash balance. However, the bank deposits included the check twice, once when originally deposited and a second time upon redeposit, and the bank withdrawals included the check once, when it became an NSF check. Therefore, to reconcile the bank and book deposits/receipts and withdrawals/disbursements, the NSF check ($100 in the example) is subtracted from both the bank deposits and withdrawals. (Alternatively, the $100 NSF check could be added to the book receipts and disbursements to make the books reconcile with the bank records.) The preceding discussion is illustrated in Exhibit 8—3 using ( + ) and ( − ) designations to reinforce this point.

If a company finds that an NSF check cannot be collected immediately, then instead of redepositing the check, it must record the check amount in accounts receivable on the

**Exhibit 8—3    Typical Treatment in Reconciling NSF Check**

| Bank | Balance (Oct. 31) | Deposits/ Receipts | Withdrawals/ Disbursements | Balance (Nov. 30) |
|---|---|---|---|---|
| 1. Original deposit .......... | | + | | + |
| 2. Check becomes NSF ..... | | | + | − |
| 3. Check redeposited ....... | | + | | + |
| 4. Adjustment to reconcile .. | | − | − | |
| Correct balance .......... | | + | | + |
| **Books** | | | | |
| 1. Original deposit .......... | | + | | + |
| 2. Check returned by bank (no book entry) .......... | | | | |
| 3. Check redeposited (no book entry) .............. | | | | |
| Correct balance .......... | | + | | + |

books. Such is the case for the $118.94 check for Svendsen, Inc., in the illustration. Since the bank will have already shown the check as a withdrawal and a reduction in the cash balance, a similar adjustment must be made to the company records.

Another common type of adjustment may be required for errors made either on the bank or book records. These have to be corrected as illustrated for Svendsen, Inc. Once all adjustments are made, the total corrected balances will be the same for both the bank and book records for all four columns.

The illustrations for Svendsen, Inc., assume adjustments of the book amounts are made in the month subsequent to their discovery. If the adjustments were made in the same month, as might be true at year-end, there would be no adjustments in the first column for the book amounts. For example, the $5.90 October bank service charge in the illustration is recognized on the books in November. If the adjustment had been made at the end of October, the beginning book balance would have already shown $5,400.32 ($5,406.22 - $5.90), and the total book disbursements for November would have been $5.90 less. A similar rationale exists for the $110 interest recorded by the bank for Svendsen in October.

The expanded proof of cash or four-column reconciliation procedure normally reduces the time and effort required to find errors made by either the bank or the depositor. In developing comparisons of both receipts and disbursements, the areas in which errors have been made, as well as the amounts of the discrepancies within each area, are immediately identified. This procedure is frequently used by auditors when there is any question of possible discrepancies in the handling of cash.

## TEMPORARY INVESTMENTS

Temporarily available excess cash can be invested to generate revenue that would not be available if cash were left idle. Investments made during seasonal periods of low activity can be converted into cash needed during periods of expanding operations. Assets acquired as temporary investments are reported in the current assets section of the balance sheet.

As mentioned previously in the chapter, temporary investments commonly include time deposit instruments, such as CDs and money market certificates. They also include

## Bank Account Manipulation

From July 1980 through February 1982, E. F. Hutton was able to create an extra $1 billion in available funds by aggressively manipulating and shuffling $10 billion in branch office bank accounts. These extra funds provided considerable interest revenue (or interest expense savings), because during that time period, short-term interest rates were often in the 18 to 20 percent range.

One technique used involved the intentional overdrafting of accounts held at small local banks. Large withdrawals, sometimes ten times as much as the account balance, were made from small local banks, with the funds being deposited in Hutton's central bank account. The funds would earn interest in the central account until the local bank required the overdraft to be covered, a period often extending for several days.

Another abuse involved the overaggressive use of float in the local bank accounts. Float is extra money in a bank account, money that has already been spent, by check, but that the bank has not yet deducted from the account because the check has yet to be presented at the bank for payment. For example, when a bank reconciliation is done, the total of the outstanding checks represents the amount of the float. Hutton intentionally opened accounts in small rural banks because the collection process of such banks is typically slower, allowing for more float. Hutton reportedly particularly liked doing business with banks in Watertown, New York on the eastern shore of Lake Ontario, where heavy winter snowstorms could be expected to delay the mails and thus slow down the check clearing process. Taking advantage of checking account float is not illegal, or even unethical; it is good business practice. However, Hutton misused the process by creating chains of bank accounts and transferring funds from one to another by writing a check on one bank and depositing the check in another. During the check clearing interval, the funds would be earning interest in both banks.

This wasn't the first instance of overaggressive use of float. In October 1978, the SEC warned brokers to stop trying to extend the check clearing period and thus increase the float by paying East Coast customers with checks drawn on West Coast banks, and vice versa. And, in October 1979, a New York state judge assessed damages to Merrill Lynch for paying New York customers with California checks.

In May 1985, Hutton pleaded guilty to 2,000 counts of mail and wire fraud and agreed to pay approximately $10 million in fines and restitution.

### Questions:

1.  *What ethical issues are involved in using float as E. F. Hutton did?*
2.  *How can manipulation, as described in this case, be controlled?*

Sources:

Andy Pasztor, Bruce Ingersoll, and Daniel Hertzberg, "Hutton Unit Pleads Guilty in Fraud Case," *The Wall Street Journal*, May 3, 1985, p. 3.

Andy Pasztor and Scott McMurray, "E. F. Hutton Scheme Involved More Cash Than Disclosed, U.S. Prosecutor Says," *The Wall Street Journal*, May 6, 1985, p. 3.

Anthony Bianco and G. David Wallace, "What Did Hutton's Managers Know—And When Did They Know It?" *Business Week*, May 20, 1985, p. 110.

short-term debt instruments such as **commercial paper** (high-yield notes issued by corporations and generally maturing within 30 days to nine months) and **Treasury Bills** (U.S. government obligations that are sold at a weekly auction and have maturities ranging from 13 weeks to one year).

Companies also invest funds in securities, including **debt securities** (corporate and government bonds) and **equity securities** (common and preferred stocks). Securities may be reported as current (temporary) or noncurrent investments, depending on their nature and the purpose for which they were acquired. Accounting and reporting considerations applicable to noncurrent investments are discussed later in this book.

## Criteria for Reporting Securities as Temporary Investments

Investments in securities qualify for reporting as temporary investments if (1) there is a ready market for converting such securities into cash *and* (2) it is management's intention to sell them if the need for cash arises. As indicated by the first criterion, only **marketable securities** qualify for reporting as temporary investments. Securities are considered marketable when a day-to-day market exists and when they can be sold on short notice. The volume of trading in the securities should be sufficient to absorb a company's holdings without materially affecting the market price. Securities having a limited market and fluctuating widely in price are not suitable for temporary investments.

Marketable securities may be converted into cash shortly after being acquired or they may be held for some time. In either case, however, they are properly classified as temporary investments as long as management intends to sell them if the need for cash arises. The deciding factor is management's intent, not the length of time the securities are held. Therefore, the following securities do not qualify as temporary investments even though they may be marketable: (1) reacquired shares of a corporation's own stock; (2) securities acquired to gain control of a company; (3) securities held for maintenance of business relations; and (4) any other securities that cannot be used or are not intended to be used as a ready source of cash.

## Recording Purchase and Sale of Marketable Securities

Stocks and bonds acquired as temporary investments are recorded at cost, which includes brokerage fees, taxes, and other charges incurred in their acquisition. Stocks are normally quoted at a price per single share; bonds are quoted at a price per $100 face value, although they are normally issued in $1,000 denominations. The purchase of 100 shares of stock at 5 1/8, then, would indicate a purchase price of $512.50; the purchase of a $1,000 bond at 104 1/4 would indicate a purchase price of $1,042.50.

When interest-bearing securities are acquired between interest payment dates, the amount paid for the security is increased by a charge for accrued interest to the date of purchase. This charge should not be reported as part of the investment cost. Two assets have been acquired—the security and the accrued interest receivable—and should be reported in two separate asset accounts. Upon the receipt of interest, the accrued interest account is closed and Interest Revenue is credited for the amount of interest earned since the purchase date. Instead of recording the interest as a receivable (**asset approach**), Interest Revenue may be debited for the accrued interest paid. The subsequent collection of interest would then be credited in full to Interest Revenue. The latter procedure (**revenue approach**) is usually more convenient.

To illustrate the entries for the acquisition of securities, assume that $100,000 in U.S. Treasury notes are purchased at 104 1/4, including brokerage fees, on May 1. Interest is 9% payable semiannually on January 1 and July 1. Accrued interest of $3,000 would thus be added to the purchase price. The entries to record the purchase of the securities and the subsequent collection of interest under the alternate procedures would be as follows:

### Asset Approach:

| | | | | |
|---|---|---|---|---|
| Apr. 1 | Marketable Securities (9% U.S. Treasury Notes) ..... | 104,250 | |
| | Interest Receivable ................................ | 3,000 | |
| | Cash ........................................... | | 107,250 |
| | | | |
| July 1 | Cash........................................... | 4,500 | |
| | Interest Receivable ............................. | | 3,000 |
| | Interest Revenue ............................... | | 1,500 |

### Revenue Approach:

| | | | | |
|---|---|---|---|---|
| Apr. 1 | Marketable Securities (9% U.S. Treasury Notes) ..... | 104,250 | |
| | Interest Revenue.................................. | 3,000 | |
| | Cash ........................................... | | 107,250 |
| | | | |
| July 1 | Cash........................................... | 4,500 | |
| | Interest Revenue ............................... | | 4,500 |

The important point is that under either approach, the interest revenue recorded for the period is equal to the interest earned, not the amount received. In this case, the company earned $1,500, representing interest for the period May 1 to June 30.

When debt securities are acquired at a higher or lower price than their maturity value and it is expected that they will be held until maturity, periodic amortization of the premium or accumulation of the discount with corresponding adjustments to interest revenue is required. However, when securities are acquired as a temporary investment and it is not likely they will be held until maturity, such procedures are normally not necessary. When a temporary investment is sold, the difference between the sales proceeds and the cost is reported as a gain or loss on the sale. For example, if the U.S. Treasury notes in the preceding illustration were sold on July 1 for $105,000, and the brokerage fees on the sale were $500, the transaction would be recorded as follows:

| | | | |
|---|---|---|---|
| July 1 | Cash........................................... | 104,500 | |
| | Marketable Securities (9% U.S. Treasury Notes).... | | 104,250 |
| | Gain on Sale of Marketable Securities............. | | 250 |

The gain would be reported on the income statement as "Other revenue." Note that the brokerage fees involved in the purchase increase the cost of a temporary investment, while the selling fees reduce the cash proceeds and any recognized gain on the sale.

## Valuing Marketable Securities Subsequent to Acquisition

Three different methods for the valuation of marketable securities have been advanced: (1) cost, (2) cost or market, whichever is lower, and (3) market.

**Valuation at Cost**     Valuation of marketable securities at cost refers to the original acquisition price of a marketable security, including all related fees, unless a new cost basis has been assigned to recognize a permanent decline in the value of the security. Cost is to be used unless circumstances require another method as is the case with marketable equity securities, to be explained in the next section. The recognition of gain or loss is deferred until the asset is sold, at which time investment cost is matched against investment proceeds. The cost basis is consistent with income tax procedures, recognizing neither gain nor loss until there is a sale or exchange.

**Valuation at Cost or Market, Whichever Is Lower**     When using the lower-of-cost-or-market (LCM) method, if market is lower than cost, security values are written down to the lower value; if market is higher than cost, securities are maintained at cost, gains awaiting confirmation through sale.

FASB Statement No. 12, "Accounting for Certain Marketable Securities," requires that **marketable equity securities** be carried at the **lower of aggregate cost or market**.[3] An equity security is defined by the FASB in Statement No. 12 as:

> . . . any instrument representing ownership shares (e.g., common, preferred, and other capital stock), or the right to acquire (e.g., warrants, rights, and call options) or dispose of (e.g., put options) ownership shares in an enterprise at fixed or determinable prices. The term does not encompass preferred stock that by its terms either must be redeemed by the issuing enterprise or is redeemable at the option of the investor, nor does it include treasury stock or convertible bonds.[4]

FASB Statement No. 12 deals only with marketable *equity* securities. **Marketable debt securities** still may be carried at cost unless there is a substantial decline that is not due to temporary conditions. It seems logical, however, to treat all short-term marketable securities similarly. All temporary investments are acquired for the same reason—utilization of idle cash to generate a short-term return. Both equity securities and debt securities must meet the same criteria to qualify as temporary investments, and their valuation should reflect a similar concept, i.e., the amount of cash that could be realized upon liquidation at the balance sheet date. Therefore, in the illustrations and end-of-chapter materials in this text, the lower-of-cost-or-market method is used for *all* short-term marketable securities (i.e., stocks and bonds). It should be recognized, however, that actual practice varies. Some companies interpret FASB Statement No. 12 strictly and account for only marketable equity securities on the lower-of-cost-or-market basis.

***Applying the Lower-of-Cost-or-Market Method***    FASB Statement No. 12 requires that the lower-of-cost-or-market method be applied to securities in the **aggregate** and not to individual securities. To illustrate the difference between lower of cost or market on an aggregate basis versus an individual item basis, assume Devon Corporation acquired marketable securities during 1993. The cost and market values of those securities on December 31, 1993, are as follows:

|  | Cost | Market | Lower of Cost or Market on Individual Basis |
|---|---|---|---|
| 1,000 shares of Carter Co. common ....... | $20,000 | $16,000 | $16,000 |
| $25,000 10% U.S. Treasury notes ......... | 25,000 | 26,500 | 25,000 |
| $10,000 U.S. Government 8% bonds ...... | 10,000 | 7,500 | 7,500 |
|  | $55,000 | $50,000 | $48,500 |

The lower-of-cost-or-market value on an aggregate basis is $50,000; on an individual basis, $48,500.

An important factor considered by the FASB in choosing the aggregate basis is that many companies view their marketable securities portfolios as collective assets. Further, the Board felt that applying the lower-of-cost-or-market procedure on an individual security basis would be unduly conservative.

---

[3]*Statement of Financial Accounting Standards No. 12,* "Accounting for Certain Marketable Securities" (Stamford: Financial Accounting Standards Board, 1975), par. 8.

[4]*Ibid,* par. 7a.

However, the FASB did recognize that many companies classify separately their current and noncurrent securities portfolios. Therefore, when a classified balance sheet is presented, the lower of aggregate cost or market is to be applied to the separate current and noncurrent portfolios. When an unclassified balance sheet is presented, the entire marketable equity securities portfolio is to be considered a noncurrent asset. The application of FASB Statement No. 12 to long-term marketable equity securities is discussed in detail in Chapter 15.

**Recognizing a Decline in Market Value**     In adopting the lower-of-aggregate-cost-or-market method for marketable equity securities, the FASB chose to recognize declines in the realizable value of short-term marketable equity securities portfolios as a charge against income of the current period. The possibility of a future recovery in the market value was not considered sufficient reason to maintain the carrying value at cost.

Recognition of a decline in value on the books calls for a reduction of the asset and a debit to a loss account. Various titles are used for the loss account: Unrealized Loss on Marketable Securities; Loss on Valuation of Marketable Equity Securities; Recognized Decline in Value of Current Marketable Securities. The authors prefer the last title to avoid confusion with the entry required upon the final sale of the securities or with the title used in accounting for long-term marketable equity securities. It should also be noted that the basis of the securities for measurement of the ultimate gain or loss on final disposition continues to be cost. Cost can be preserved on the books using a valuation account to reduce the securities to market. The following entry illustrates this procedure, using the cost and market value information for Devon Corporation at December 31, 1993:

| | | |
|---|---|---|
| Recognized Decline in Value of Current Marketable Securities .... | 5,000 | |
|    Allowance for Decline in Value of Current Marketable Securities | | 5,000 |

The balance sheet would show:

| | | |
|---|---|---|
| Current assets: | | |
|    Marketable securities (at cost) .......................... | $55,000 | |
|    Less allowance for decline in value of current marketable securities ........................................... | 5,000 | |
|    Marketable securities (at market, December 31, 1993) ...... | | $50,000 |

In practice, a shorter form is often used, such as the following:

| | |
|---|---|
| Current assets: | |
|    Marketable securities (reported at market; cost, $55,000) ... | $50,000 |

The $5,000 loss in the above example would be reported on Devon Corporation's 1993 income statement as an "other expense" after operating income.

**Recognizing a Recovery in Market Value**     If in the future there is an increase in the market value of the short-term marketable securities portfolio, the write-down should be reversed to the extent that the resulting carrying value does not exceed original cost. For example, assume that no securities were purchased or sold by Devon Corporation during 1994 and the aggregate market value of the portfolio at December 31, 1994, was $52,000. The $2,000 increase or "recovery" would be recognized as shown in the following entry:

| | | |
|---|---|---|
| Allowance for Decline in Value of Current Marketable Securities ................................................. | 2,000 | |
|    Recovery of Recognized Decline in Value of Current Marketable Securities ......................................... | | 2,000 |

This entry reduces the allowance account balance to $3,000 ($5,000 − $2,000), and the December 31, 1994, balance sheet would report marketable securities at their aggregate market value of $52,000 (cost of $55,000 − allowance of $3,000). The $2,000 credit to the recovery account would be reported as "Other revenue" after operating income on Devon Corporation's 1994 income statement.

The original write-down of $5,000 is viewed as a valuation allowance, representing an estimated decrease in the realizable value of the portfolio. The subsequent market increase reduces this valuation allowance. If market value exceeds cost at a subsequent valuation date, the allowance account would be eliminated, and the securities would be valued at cost, the lower of the two values. The reversal of a write-down is considered a change in accounting estimate of an unrealized loss, as was noted in Chapter 4.[5]

**Impact of Changes in Portfolio**    In subsequent periods, the portfolio of temporary investments will change through purchases and sales of individual securities. Because cost is the accepted basis for recognition of gain or loss on final disposition, the sale of marketable securities is recorded as though no valuation account existed, i.e., on a cost basis. At the end of each accounting period, an analysis is made of cost and aggregate market value for the existing securities in the portfolio, and the allowance account is adjusted to reflect the new difference between cost and market.

To illustrate accounting for subsequent years' transactions, refer again to the portfolio information for Devon Corporation at December 31, 1993, on page 281. Also recall that, as of December 31, 1994, the aggregate market value of the portfolio was $52,000 and the balance in the allowance account was $3,000. Assume that in 1995 the Carter Co. stock is sold for $17,000, and $25,000 of 9% U.S. Treasury notes are purchased for $24,500. The following entries are made:

| | | |
|---|---|---|
| Cash | 17,000 | |
| Loss on Sale of Marketable Securities | 3,000 | |
| Marketable Securities (Carter Co. Common) | | 20,000 |
| Marketable Securities (9% U.S. Treasury Notes) | 24,500 | |
| Cash | | 24,500 |

Assume that, as of December 31, 1995, the aggregate market value of the temporary investments is $59,000. When comparing the aggregate market value to the aggregate cost of $59,500 ($25,000 + $10,000 + $24,500), the following adjusting entry would be made at the end of 1995:

| | | |
|---|---|---|
| Allowance for Decline in Value of Current Marketable Securities | 2,500 | |
| Recovery of Recognized Decline in Value of Current Marketable Securities | | 2,500 |

This entry leaves the valuation account with a balance of $500 which, when subtracted from cost of $59,500, will report the marketable securities at their aggregate market value of $59,000.

If, instead of being $59,000, the aggregate market value of the securities portfolio had fallen during 1995 to $53,000 (compared to cost of $59,500), the adjusting entry would be:

| | | |
|---|---|---|
| Recognized Decline in Value of Current Marketable Securities | 3,500 | |
| Allowance for Decline in Value of Current Marketable Securities | | 3,500 |

[5]See *FASB Statement No. 5*, par. 2, and *APB Opinion No. 20*, par. 10.

This entry increases the allowance account balance from $3,000 to $6,500 which, when subtracted from cost of $59,500, will report marketable securities at their aggregate market value of $53,000.

On the other hand, if the aggregate market value of the securities portfolio had risen to $60,000 at December 31, 1995 (compared to cost of $59,500), the adjusting entry at year-end would be:

| | | |
|---|---|---|
| Allowance for Decline in Value of Current Marketable Securities ............................................................... | 3,000 | |
|     Recovery of Recognized Decline in Value of Current Marketable Securities ......................................... | | 3,000 |

This entry cancels the allowance account since the $59,500 original cost of securities is lower than their current $60,000 aggregate market value.

**Reclassification of a Marketable Security**    If the classification of a marketable equity security changes from current to noncurrent or vice versa, the security must be transferred to the applicable portfolio at the lower-of-cost-or-market value at date of transfer. If the market value is lower than cost, the market value becomes the new cost basis and a realized loss is to be included in determining net income.[6] In essence, this procedure recognizes the loss upon transfer as though it had been realized. This should reduce the likelihood of income being manipulated through the transfer of securities between current and long-term portfolios.

**Summary of Lower-of-Cost-or-Market Method**    To summarize the accounting for current marketable equity securities under FASB Statement No. 12, securities are originally recorded at cost. Subsequent valuation is at lower of cost or market on an aggregate basis. Any necessary adjustment is made at year-end through a valuation allowance account. A reduction in value is recognized as a current-period loss in the income statement; a recovery of a previous write-down, up to the original cost but no higher, is recognized as a current-period gain in the income statement. These gains or losses are usually presented after operating income as "Other revenues" or "Other expenses." The amount of gain or loss on the ultimate sale of a marketable security is measured as the difference between the sales price and the original cost of the security without consideration for any previous allowance adjustments. Then, at year-end, the allowance account is adjusted once again to reflect the lower-of-cost-or-market amount for the remaining securities in the portfolio.

FASB Statement No. 12 requires disclosure of specific information with respect to marketable equity securities, including aggregate cost and market values, gross unrealized gains and losses, and the amount of net realized gain or loss included in net income.[7] The information included by Masco Industries in its 1988 annual report, and reproduced on page 285, provides an example of the required disclosures for marketable securities.

**Valuation at Market**    Market value refers to the current market price of a marketable security. In applying the market value method, permanent declines in market prices of securities are recognized as losses in the current period. Temporary declines in market values are treated the same as under the lower-of-cost-or-market method. That is, security values are written down to market through a valuation adjustment at the end of the accounting period. Where the market method differs is in the valuation of securities whose prices have increased above cost. With the market method, current market prices are recognized as affording an objective basis for the valuation of marketable securities;

---

[6]*Statement of Financial Accounting Standards No. 12, op. cit.*, par. 10.

[7]*Ibid.*, par. 12.

**Exhibit 8—4    Masco Industries—Disclosures for Marketable Securities**

**MARKETABLE SECURITIES**

| | (In Thousands) At December 31 | |
| --- | --- | --- |
| | **1988** | **1987** |
| Marketable securities, principally equity, at cost | $ 68,120 | $266,240 |
| Valuation allowance | – | (44,750) |
| Marketable securities at carrying value | $ 68,120 | $221,490 |

Marketable securities (principally equity) had unrealized gains of approximately $9.2 million and $7.8 million, and unrealized losses of approximately $3.2 million and $52.6 million at December 31, 1988 and 1987, respectively.

As a result of the significant decline of the equity markets occurring in the fourth quarter of 1987, the market value of the Company's marketable securities portfolio incurred a substantial unrealized decline; accordingly, the Company charged income in the fourth quarter of 1987 by establishing a valuation allowance at December 31, 1987 to reflect then current market levels. This valuation allowance was recovered and included in income in 1988.

therefore, such securities would be reported on the balance sheet at their current values, whether higher or lower than cost.

Market value has been and continues to be an acceptable method for valuing marketable securities within certain industries that follow specialized accounting practices with respect to marketable securities. Enterprises within these industries, such as securities brokers and dealers who carry marketable equity securities at market value, are not required by FASB Statement No. 12 to change to lower of cost or market. *For most companies, however, the market value method is not presently considered generally accepted accounting practice, and the lower-of-cost-or-market method should be used.*

## Evaluation of Methods

Valuation at cost finds support on the grounds that it is an extension of the cost principle; the asset is carried at cost until a sale or exchange provides an alternative asset and confirms a gain or loss. The cost method offers valuation on a consistent basis from period to period. It is the simplest method to apply and it adheres to income tax requirements. However, certain objections to cost can be raised. The use of cost means investments may be carried at amounts differing from values objectively determinable at the balance sheet date, and the integrity of both balance sheet and income statement measurements can be challenged. The use of cost also means identical securities may be reported at different values because of purchases at different prices. A further objection is that management, in controlling the sale of securities, can determine the periods in which gains or losses are to be recognized even though the changes in values may have accrued over a number of periods.

The use of market value is advocated on the basis that there is evidence of the net realizable value of the marketable securities held at the balance sheet date and any changes from previous carrying values should be recognized as gains or losses in the current period. Assuming marketable securities are defined as having a readily available sales price or bid and ask price from one of the national securities exchanges or over-the-counter markets, this method is objective and relatively simple to apply. The major draw-back of this method is that gains or losses may be recognized prior to realization, i.e., prior to the actual sale of the securities. In addition, market values fluctuate, often significantly, which would require continual changing of the carrying value of marketable securities on the balance sheet. Market is also challenged as a departure from the cost principle and as lacking in conservatism. Furthermore, market is not acceptable for general accounting or income tax purposes.

The lower-of-cost-or-market procedure provides for recognizing market declines and serves to prevent potential mistakes arising in analyzing statements when these declines are not reported. The lower of cost or market is supported as a conservative procedure. This approach may be challenged on the basis that it may be the most complicated method to follow, and it fails to apply a single valuation concept consistently. Securities carried at cost at the end of one period may be reported at market value in the subsequent period. Critics argue that if net realizable value is a desirable measurement concept, its use should not depend on whether portfolio values are greater or less than original cost.

Regardless of the theoretical merits of the three methods, generally accepted accounting principles currently require use of the lower-of-cost-or-market method for marketable equity securities. With the emphasis in the conceptual framework on decision usefulness, the market valuation method may gain broader acceptance in the future.

## REPORTING CASH AND TEMPORARY INVESTMENTS ON THE BALANCE SHEET

In reporting cash and temporary investments, many companies follow the guidelines described in the chapter and report cash separately from restricted cash items and marketable securities. Other companies combine cash with time deposits or with marketable securities. When cash and certain types of temporary investment items are combined, an increasingly popular title is "Cash and cash equivalents."[8] **Cash equivalents**, as defined in Chapter 6, include time deposits and highly liquid debt instruments, usually having maturities of three months or less. Some examples of the varying methods used for reporting cash and temporary investments follow.

**Exhibit 8—5    Centel Corporation**

## CONSOLIDATED BALANCE SHEETS    Centel Corporation

| Thousands of Dollars                December 31, | **1988** | 1987 |
|---|---|---|
| **Assets** | | |
| **Current Assets** | | |
| Cash and Temporary Investments | $ **22,015** | $ 47,757 |

[8]Use of this term as a balance sheet caption has become increasingly common as companies have implemented FASB Statement No. 95, "Statement of Cash Flows," which requires that the cash flow statement report changes in cash and cash equivalents.

**Exhibit 8—6    General Electric Company**

# Statement of Financial Position

|  | General Electric Company and consolidated affiliates | |
|---|---|---|
| At December 31 (In millions) | 1988 | 1987 |
| Assets | | |
| Cash (note 12) | $  2,187 | $  2,543 |
| Marketable securities carried at cost (note 13) | 5,779 | 5,353 |
| Marketable securities carried at market (note 14) | 5,089 | 4,000 |

**Exhibit 8—7    Ametek, Inc.**

AMETEK, Inc.

## CONSOLIDATED BALANCE SHEET
(Dollars in thousands)

|  | December 31, | |
|---|---|---|
|  | 1988 | 1987 |
| **Assets** | | |
| **Current assets:** | | |
| Cash and cash equivalents (Note 1) | $  9,492 | $  29,997 |
| Marketable securities (Note 1) | 106,612 | 150,930 |

**Securities and Other Investments**

Marketable securities (primarily U.S. Government securities) and other fixed income investments are carried at cost plus accrued interest, which approximates market.

**Exhibit 8—8    HON INDUSTRIES Inc. and Subsidiaries**

HON INDUSTRIES Inc. and Subsidiaries
## Consolidated Balance Sheets

| As of Year-End | 1988 | 1987 | 1986 |
|---|---|---|---|
| **Assets** | | | |
| Current Assets | | | |
| Cash and cash equivalents | $  65,709,000 | $ 25,930,000 | $ 33,452,000 |
| Short-term investments | 2,390,000 | 2,404,000 | 2,958,000 |

## REPORTING MARKETABLE SECURITIES ON THE STATEMENT OF CASH FLOWS

Although reporting of cash flow data related to marketable securities is very straightforward in simple cases, sorting out the appropriate treatment of realized gains and losses, and also of unrealized losses and market value recoveries resulting from application of the lower-of-cost-or-market rule, can be more problematic. The key principles to remember are: (1) all the cash flow effects of purchases and sales of marketable securities (other than cash equivalents) should be disclosed in the investing activities section of the statement of cash flows and (2) cash flow from operating activities should *not* include amounts related to realized gains and losses or unrealized losses and market value recoveries.

To illustrate, assume that Garner Company purchased marketable securities for $47,000 during 1993. Also assume that, as of December 31, 1993, the securities have a market value of $44,000. The $47,000 purchase price will be shown in the 1993 statement of cash flows as a reduction in cash flow from investing activities. The 1993 income statement will show an unrealized loss of $3,000; however, this write-down to market has no cash flow implications. If the direct method is used, then the $3,000 loss is ignored in computing cash flow from operating activities. If the indirect method is used, then the $3,000 loss must be *added back* to net income, because it is a noncash item.

Assume that the securities are sold in 1994 for $46,000. The $46,000 sales price will be shown as an increase in cash flow from investing activities. Net income for the year will be increased by $2,000, the net effect of the realized loss of $1,000 ($46,000 sales price − cost of $47,000) and the $3,000 recovery to eliminate the allowance established in 1993. Again, if the direct method is used, both the $1,000 realized loss and the $3,000 recovery gain are ignored in computing operating cash flow, because they are noncash items. If the indirect method is used, the $1,000 loss must be *added to* and the $3,000 recovery gain must be *subtracted from* net income to avoid their double counting when computing operating cash flow.

## KEY TERMS

Bank reconciliation 273
Bank service charge 273
Cash 267
Cash equivalents 286
Cash overdraft 268
Compensating balances 269
Debt securities 279

Demand deposits 267
Deposit in transit 273
Equity securities 279
Imprest petty cash system 272
Lower-of-cost-or-market (LCM) method 280
Marketable securities 279

Not-sufficient-funds (NSF) check 273
Outstanding checks 273
Petty cash fund 272
Temporary investments 277
Time deposits 267

## QUESTIONS

1. Why is cash on hand both necessary and yet potentially unproductive?
2. The following items were included as cash on the balance sheet for the Lawson Co. How should each of the items have been reported?
   (a) Demand deposits with bank
   (b) Restricted cash deposits in foreign banks
   (c) Bank account used for payment of salaries and wages
   (d) Cash in a special cash account to be used currently for the construction of a new building
   (e) Customers' checks returned by the bank marked "Not Sufficient Funds"
   (f) Customers' postdated checks
   (g) IOUs from employees
   (h) Postage stamps received in the mail for merchandise
   (i) Postal money orders received from customers and not yet deposited
   (j) Notes receivable in the hands of the bank for collection

(k) Special bank account in which sales tax collections are deposited

(l) Customers' checks not yet deposited

3. On reconciling the cash account with the bank statement, it is found that the general cash fund is overdrawn $436 but the bond redemption account has a balance of $5,400. The treasurer wishes to show cash as a current asset at $4,964. Discuss.

4. The Melvin Company shows in its accounts a cash balance of $66,500 with Bank A and an overdraft of $1,500 with Bank B on December 31. Bank B regards the overdraft as in effect a loan to the Melvin Company and charges interest on the overdraft balance. How would you report the balances with Banks A and B? Would your answer be any different if the overdraft arose as a result of certain checks that had been deposited and proved to be uncollectible and if the overdraft was cleared promptly by the Melvin Company at the beginning of January?

5. Mills Manufacturing is required to maintain a compensating balance of $15,000 with its bank to maintain a line of open credit. The compensating balance is legally restricted as to its use. How should the compensating balance be reported on the balance sheet and why?

6. (a) What are the major advantages in using imprest petty cash funds? (b) What dangers must be guarded against when petty cash funds are used?

7. (a) Give at least four common sources of differences between depositor and bank balances. (b) Which of the differences in (a) require an adjusting entry on the books of the depositor?

8. (a) What purposes are served by preparing a four-column reconciliation of receipts and disbursements? (b) Why might this form be used by auditors?

9. Define *temporary investments*. What criteria must be met for a security to be considered a temporary investment?

10. What two methods may be used to record the payment for accrued interest on interest-bearing securities? Which method is preferable?

11. (a) What positions are held with respect to the valuation of marketable securities? (b) What arguments can be advanced in support of each, and which position do you feel has the greatest merit?

12. Cintech International reports marketable securities on the balance sheet at the lower of cost or market. What adjustments are required on the books at the end of the year in each situation below?

(a) Securities are purchased early in 1992, and at the end of 1992, their market value is more than cost.

(b) At the end of 1993, the market value of the securities is less than cost.

(c) At the end of 1994, the market value of the securities is greater than at the end of 1993, but is still less than cost.

(d) At the end of 1995, the market value of the securities is more than the amount originally paid.

13. FASB Statement No. 12 requires the use of lower-of-cost-or-market (LCM) valuation for marketable *equity* securities. Why might companies choose to apply LCM to *all* short-term marketable securities? If LCM is not used to value nonequity securities, what is the appropriate basis of valuation for those securities: cost, market, or some other basis?

14. Where are the cash flow effects of purchases and sales of marketable securities disclosed in the statement of cash flows? How should gains and losses associated with marketable securities be reflected in the statement of cash flows?

## DISCUSSION CASES

### Case 8—1    (Cash management)

Jack Wilson, manager of Expert Building Company, is a valued and trusted employee. He has been with the company from its start two years ago. Because of the demands of his job, he has not taken a vacation since he began working. He is in charge of recording collections on account, making the daily bank deposits, and reconciling the bank statement.

Early this year, clients began complaining to you, the president, about incorrect statements. As president, you check into this matter. Wilson tells you there is nothing to worry about. He attests, "The problem is due to the slow mail; customers' payments and statements are crossing in the mail." However, because clients were not complaining last year, you doubt that the mail is the primary reason for the problem.

What might be some of the reasons for the delay? What are some other problems that might begin to occur? What can be done to remedy the problem? What should be done to make sure the problems are avoided in the future?

## Case 8—2  (Float management)

Bunsen Company's cash collections average $10,000 per day. Because Bunsen's customers are scattered across the country, the average interval between when a customer writes a check and when the check clears and the amount is credited to Bunsen's account is 7 days. Bunsen could reduce this to 3 days by implementing a lockbox system. With a lockbox system, a company makes arrangements with a bank to retrieve customer checks from a post office box and deposit them directly into the company's account.

Bunsen's cash payments also average $10,000 per day. Bunsen's checks are drawn on a bank located in a major metropolitan area so the check-clearing time is very short—2 days. If Bunsen were to use a checking account in a small rural bank, the average check-clearing time would increase to 5 days.

1. How much would Bunsen's net interest income increase if it were to implement the lockbox system and switch its checking account to a small rural bank? Assume that the interest rate on checking accounts is 6% per annum based on the average daily balance.
2. What if the banking fee for operating the lockbox system were $4,000 per year—should the lockbox system be implemented?

## Case 8—3  (Allocation of cash and near-cash assets)

Bruno Johnson, Chief Financial Officer of Tollerud Company, has determined that Tollerud should keep on hand $35 million in cash or near-cash assets in order to maintain proper liquidity. Bruno is now trying to determine how to allocate the $35 million among the checking account, certificates of deposit, and marketable securities. What factors should influence Bruno's decision?

## Case 8—4  (Accounting for petty cash)

You have just accepted a job with Philodendron Co. Your duties include being cashier of the petty cash fund. Upon inspection of the fund, you find that it includes $143 in currency, $5 in postage stamps, $21 in IOUs, and $37 in various receipts. Since no written records are kept of the petty cash fund, you had to find out from the previous cashier that the approved amount of the fund is $215.

1. Discuss the elements of control necessary for effective maintenance of a petty cash fund.
2. Suggest changes that Philodendron Co. can make to improve the effectiveness of its petty cash fund.

## Case 8—5  (Unrealized losses and economic consequences)

There has been much disagreement about whether unrealized losses on short-term marketable securities should be recognized. The stock market crash of 1987 provided support for both opinions. Those who oppose recognition of unrealized losses point to the fact that the substantial decline in stock prices in 1987 was largely reversed in 1988, and many "paper losses" were never realized. However, others point out that the declines were in fact economic losses and that the earnings volatility reflected the volatile nature of the economy.

1. What effects on firm behavior and practice would you predict to be associated with the requirement that unrealized losses on short-term marketable securities be recognized? Are these consequences an appropriate economic response?
2. What accounting treatment for these unrealized losses seems most appropriate to you?

## Case 8—6  (Lower of cost or market and loan covenants)

Ingqvist Company has the following short-term marketable securities portfolio as of December 31. All securities were purchased during the current year.

|  | Cost | Market Value |
|---|---|---|
| Falconer Company .................................... | $ 50,000 | $ 95,000 |
| Berge Company ...................................... | 35,000 | 63,000 |
| St. Cloud Company ................................... | 40,000 | 44,000 |
| Chatterbox Company .................................. | 23,000 | 25,000 |
| Total ........................................... | $148,000 | $227,000 |

In addition to short-term marketable securities, Ingqvist has other current assets totaling $500,000. Total current liabilities as of December 31 are $350,000.

Ingqvist Company has a $700,000 long-term bank loan. One of the covenants associated with the loan is that Ingqvist must maintain a current ratio (current assets ÷ current liabilities) of at least 2.0. Failure to satisfy this constraint means that the loan becomes payable immediately, and Ingqvist must either pay it off in full or renegotiate the terms—almost certainly at a higher interest rate.

1. What action in relation to the short-term marketable securities portfolio could Ingqvist undertake on December 31 to avoid violating the current-ratio covenant?
2. What factors should Ingqvist consider before taking this action?
3. How fairly does the lower-of-cost-or-market rule reflect Ingqvist's financial position in this case?

## EXERCISES

### Exercise 8—1   (Reporting cash on the balance sheet)

1. Indicate how each of the items below should be reported using the following classifications: (a) cash, (b) restricted cash, (c) temporary investment, (d) receivable, (e) liability, or (f) office supplies.

| | | |
|---|---|---|
| 1. Checking account at First Security .... *A* | | $(20) |
| 2. Checking account at Second Security ... *A* | | 350 |
| 3. U.S. savings bonds ..... *C* | | 650 |
| 4. Payroll account ...... *B* | | 100 |
| 5. Sales tax account ...... *B* | | 150 |
| 6. Foreign bank account—restricted (in equivalent U.S. dollars) . *B* | | 750 |
| 7. Postage stamps ........ *F* | | 22 |
| 8. Employee's postdated check ... *B* | | 30 |
| 9. IOU from president's brother .... *B* | | 75 |
| 10. Credit memo from a vendor for a purchase return .. *D* | | 87 |
| 11. Traveler's check ..... *A* | | 50 |
| 12. Not-sufficient-funds check ... *A* | | 18 |
| 13. Petty cash fund ($16 in currency and expense receipts for $84) .. *A* | | 100 |
| 14. Money order ... *A* | | 36 |

2. What amount would be reported as unrestricted cash on the balance sheet?

### Exercise 8—2   (Accounting for petty cash)

An examination on the morning of January 2 by the auditor for the Pearson Lumber Company discloses the items on the following page in the petty cash drawer.

The ledger account discloses a $1,050 balance for Petty Cash. (1) What adjusting entries should be made so that petty cash is correctly stated on the balance sheet? (2) What is the correct amount of petty cash for the balance sheet? (3) How could the practice of borrowing by employees from the fund be discouraged?

| | | |
|---|---|---:|
| Stamps....................................................... | | $    22.00 |
| Currency and coin .......................................... | | 115.66 |
| IOUs from members of the office staff...................... | | 121.00 |
| An envelope containing collections for a football pool, with office staff names attached.................................... | | 35.00 |
| Petty cash vouchers for: | | |
|     Typewriter repairs ....................................... | $13.00 | |
|     Stamps ................................................... | 45.00 | |
|     Telegram charges ........................................ | 28.50 | |
|     Delivery fees ............................................ | 12.00 | 98.50 |
| Employee's check postdated January 15..................... | | 150.00 |
| Employee's check marked "NSF" ........................... | | 189.00 |
| Check drawn by Pearson Lumber Company to Petty Cash ..... | | 345.00 |
| | | $1,076.16 |

## Exercise 8—3   (Cash and internal control)

Explain why each of the following pairs of duties should *not* be performed by the same person:

(a)   Receiving cash payments from customers.
       Recording charges to customer accounts.
(b)   Replenishing cash in the petty cash fund.
       Controlling and recording payments from the petty cash fund.
(c)   Preparing the bank reconciliation.
       Recording daily cash receipt totals.
(d)   Daily depositing of cash in the bank.
       Preparing the bank reconciliation.
(e)   Mailing of computer-generated checks.
       Accessing the check-writing computer program.

## Exercise 8—4   (Composition of cash)

Warfield Company had the following cash balances at December 31, 1993:

| | |
|---|---:|
| Undeposited coin and currency .................................... | $    35,000 |
| Unrestricted demand deposits .................................... | 1,450,000 |
| Company checks written (and deducted from the demand deposits amount) but not scheduled to be mailed until January 2.............................................................. | 180,000 |
| Time deposits restricted for use (expected use in 1994) ............ | 3,000,000 |

In exchange for a guaranteed line of credit, Warfield has agreed to maintain a minimum balance of $150,000 in its unrestricted demand deposits account. How much should Warfield report as "Cash" in its December 31, 1993, balance sheet?

## Exercise 8—5   (Correct cash balance)

Sterling Company's bank statement for the month of March included the following information:

| | |
|---|---:|
| Ending balance, March 31 ......................................... | $28,046 |
| Bank service charge for March...................................... | 130 |
| Interest paid by bank to Sterling for March .......................... | 107 |

In comparing the bank statement to its own cash records, Sterling found the following:

| | |
|---|---:|
| Deposits made but not yet recorded by the bank ...................... | $3,689 |
| Checks written and mailed but not yet recorded by the bank ............ | 4,786 |

In addition, Sterling discovered that it had erroneously recorded a check for $46 that should have been recorded for $64. What is Sterling's correct cash balance at March 31?

### Exercise 8—6   (Correct cash balance)

Letterman Corporation's bank statement for the month of April included the following information:

| | |
|---|---|
| Bank service charge for April . . . . . . . . . . . . . . . . . . . . . . . . . . . . . . . . . . . . . | $130 |
| Check deposited by Letterman during April was not collectible and has | |
| been marked "NSF" by the bank and returned . . . . . . . . . . . . . . . . . . . . . . . . | 400 |

In comparing the bank statement to its own cash records, Letterman found the following:

| | |
|---|---|
| Deposits made but not yet recorded by the bank . . . . . . . . . . . . . . . . . . . . . . | $1,324 |
| Checks written and mailed but not yet recorded by the bank . . . . . . . . . . . . | 987 |

All the deposits in transit and outstanding checks have been properly recorded in Letterman's books. Letterman also found a check for $350, payable to Letterman Corporation, that had not yet been deposited and had not been recorded in Letterman's books. Letterman's books show a bank account balance of $4,112 (before any adjustments or corrections). What is Letterman Corporation's correct cash balance at April 30?

### Exercise 8—7   (Adjusting the cash account)

The accounting department supplied the following data in reconciling the bank statement for Thalman Auto:

| | |
|---|---|
| Cash balance per books . . . . . . . . . . . . . . . . . . . . . . . . . . . . . . . . . . . . . . . . . . | $14,692.71 |
| Deposits in transit . . . . . . . . . . . . . . . . . . . . . . . . . . . . . . . . . . . . . . . . . . . . . . | 2,615.23 |
| Bank service charge . . . . . . . . . . . . . . . . . . . . . . . . . . . . . . . . . . . . . . . . . . . . | 25.00 |
| Outstanding checks . . . . . . . . . . . . . . . . . . . . . . . . . . . . . . . . . . . . . . . . . . . . . | 3,079.51 |
| Note collected by bank including $45 interest (Thalman not yet notified) . . . . . . . . . . . . . . . . . . . . . . . . . . . . . . . . . . . . . . . . . . . . . . . . . . . . | 1,045.00 |
| Error by bank—check drawn by Thalerman Corp. was charged to Thalman's account . . . . . . . . . . . . . . . . . . . . . . . . . . . . . . . . . . . . . . . . . . . . | 617.08 |
| Sale and deposit of $1,729.00 was entered in the sales journal and cash receipts journal as $1,792.00 | |

Give the journal entries required on the books to adjust the cash account.

### Exercise 8—8   (Bank reconciliation)

On July 2, the Minnesota Manufacturing Co. received its bank statement for the month ending June 30. The bank statement indicates a balance of $5,680. The cash account as of the close of business on June 30 has a balance of $3,275. In reconciling the balances, the auditor discovers the following:

(a)   Receipts on June 30 of $9,500 were not deposited until July 1.
(b)   Checks outstanding on June 30 were $12,310.
(c)   Collection by bank of note for $150 less collection fees of $25, not recorded on the books.
(d)   The bank has charged the depositor for overdrafts, $80.
(e)   A canceled check to W. E. Lee for $9,618 was entered in cash payments incorrectly as $9,168.

Prepare the June 30 bank reconciliation.

### Exercise 8—9   (Bank reconciliation—analysis of outstanding checks)

The following information was included in the bank reconciliation for Rytton, Inc., for June. What was the total of outstanding checks at the beginning of June? Assume all other reconciling items are listed on page 294.

| | |
|---|---:|
| Checks and charges recorded by bank in June, including a June service charge of $10 ......... | $16,435 |
| Service charge made by bank in May and recorded on the books in June | 5 |
| Total of credits to Cash in all journals during June ................... | 19,292 |
| Customer's NSF check returned as a bank charge in June (no entry made on books) ......... | 100 |
| Customer's NSF check returned in May and redeposited in June (no entry made on books in either May or June) .......... | 250 |
| Outstanding checks at June 30 ...................... | 8,060 |
| Deposit in transit at June 30 ....................... | 600 |

## Exercise 8—10   (Four-column bank reconciliation)

Tyler Corporation began doing business with Security Bank on October 1. On that date the correct cash balance was $4,000. All cash transactions are cleared through the bank account. Subsequent transactions during October and November relating to the records of Tyler and Security are summarized below.

| | Tyler Corporation Books | Security Bank Books |
|---|---:|---:|
| October deposits ................................ | $7,360 | $7,110 |
| October checks................................ | 6,290 | 6,130 |
| October service charge ........................ | — | 10 |
| October 31 balance ..... | 5,070 | 4,970 |
| November deposits............................. | 8,220 | 8,280 |
| November checks .............................. | 9,410 | 9,220 |
| November service charge ...................... | — | 15 |
| Note collected by bank (included $15 interest) ......... | — | 1,015 |
| October service charge recorded in November ......... | 10 | — |
| November 30 balance.... | 3,870 | 5,030 |

On the basis of the foregoing data: (1) prepare a four-column reconciliation for the month ended November 30, reconciling both bank and book balances to a corrected balance, and (2) give entries that would be required on Tyler's books to adjust the cash account as of November 30.

## Exercise 8—11   (Journalizing marketable securities transactions)

Give the entries necessary to record the following transactions of Rexton, Inc.:

(a)  Purchased $80,000 U.S. Treasury 8% bonds, paying 102½ plus accrued interest of $1,500. Brokerage fees were $590. Rexton, Inc., uses the revenue approach to record accrued interest on purchased bonds.
(b)  Purchased 1,000 shares of Agler Co. common stock at 175 plus brokerage fees of $1,200.
(c)  Received semiannual interest on the U.S. Treasury bonds.
(d)  Sold 150 shares of Agler at 185.
(e)  Sold $20,000 of U.S. Treasury 8% bonds at 103 plus accrued interest of $275.
(f)  Purchased a $15,000, 6-month certificate of deposit.

## Exercise 8—12   (Valuation of marketable securities)

During 1993, Litten Company purchased marketable equity securities as a short-term investment. The cost of the securities, and their market values on December 31, 1993, are listed at the top of the next page.

| Security | Cost | Market Value (12/31/93) |
|---|---|---|
| A | $ 65,000 | $ 81,000 |
| B | 100,000 | 54,000 |
| C | 220,000 | 226,000 |

As of the beginning of 1993, Litten had a zero balance in Allowance for Decline in Value of Marketable Securities. Before any adjustments related to these marketable securities, Litten had net income of $300,000. (1) What is net income after making any necessary marketable securities adjustments? (Ignore income taxes.) (2) What would net income be if the market value of Security B were $95,000?

### Exercise 8—13  (Accounting for marketable securities)

During 1993, Sunshine Inc. purchased the following marketable securities:

| | Cost | Year-End Market |
|---|---|---|
| Wexler Co. Common | $12,000 | $14,000 |
| 10% U.S. Treasury Notes | 18,000 | 11,000 |
| TexCo Bonds | 25,000 | 27,000 |

All marketable securities are to be reported on the balance sheet at the lower of aggregate cost or market. (1) What entry would be made at year-end assuming the above values? (2) What entry would be made during 1994 assuming one-half of the Wexler Co. common stock is sold for $7,000? (3) What entry would be made at the end of 1994 assuming: (a) the market value of remaining securities is $45,000? (b) the market value of remaining securities is $48,000? (c) the market value of remaining securities is $55,000?

### Exercise 8—14  (Valuation of marketable securities)

American Steel Corp. acquires marketable securities in 1992 at a cost of $200,000. Market values of the securities at the end of each year are as follows: 1992, $195,500; 1993, $219,000; 1994, $211,000. Give the entries at the end of 1992, 1993, and 1994 and indicate how the securities would be reported on the balance sheet at the end of each year under each of the following assumptions:

(a)  Securities are reported at cost.
(b)  Securities are reported at the lower of cost or market on an aggregate basis.

### Exercise 8—15  (Marketable securities and the statement of cash flows)

Indicate how each of the following transactions or events would be reflected in a statement of cash flows prepared using the indirect method. Each transaction or event is independent of the others, and none of the securities are classified as cash equivalents. For items (a) and (e), assume that the balance in the valuation allowance was zero at the beginning of the year.

(a)  At year-end, the marketable securities portfolio has an aggregate cost of $170,000 and an aggregate market value of $150,000.
(b)  During the year, marketable securities were purchased for $50,000 cash.
(c)  During the year, marketable securities with a cost of $90,000 were sold for $105,000 cash.
(d)  During the year, marketable securities with a cost of $90,000 were sold for $75,000 cash.
(e)  At year-end, the marketable securities portfolio has an aggregate cost of $170,000 and an aggregate market value of $190,000.

# PROBLEMS

### Problem 8—1   (Composition of cash and marketable securities)

The balance of $192,200 in the cash account of Thomson Inc. consists of the following items:

| | |
|---|---:|
| Petty cash fund ......................................... | $   1,000 |
| Receivable from an employee ......................... | 200 |
| Cash in bond sinking fund............................ | 15,000 |
| Cash in a foreign bank unavailable for withdrawal .............. | 40,000 |
| Cash in First Bank .................................... | 120,000 |
| Currency on hand ..................................... | 16,000 |

The balance in the marketable securities account consists of:

| | |
|---|---:|
| U.S. Treasury bonds ................................... | $ 52,600 |
| Voting stock of an affiliated company (15% interest) ................. | 425,000 |
| Advances to an affiliated company (no maturity date specified) ........ | 115,000 |
| A note receivable from a customer ................................ | 20,500 |
| The company's own shares held as treasury stock .................... | 25,000 |
| Stock of Midwest Telephone Co ................................. | 64,000 |

**Instructions:**  Calculate the correct cash and marketable securities balances and state what accounts and in what sections of the balance sheet the other items would be properly reported.

### Problem 8—2   (Compensating balance and effective interest rates)

Krebsbach Company is negotiating a loan with FIS Bank. Krebsbach needs $900,000. As part of the loan agreement, FIS Bank will require Krebsbach to maintain a compensating balance of 15% of the loan amount on deposit in a checking account at the bank. Krebsbach currently maintains a balance of $50,000 in the checking account. The interest rate Krebsbach will be required to pay on the loan will be 12%; the interest rate FIS pays on checking accounts is 4%.

**Instructions:**

1. Compute the amount of the loan.
2. Determine the effective interest rate on the loan. (Hint: Compute the net interest paid on the loan per year and the "take-home" amount of the loan.)

### Problem 8—3   (Restricted cash)

Club Med, Inc., operates Club Med resorts in the United States, Mexico, the Caribbean, Asia, the South Pacific, and the Indian Ocean Basin. Club Med routinely receives payment in advance from vacationers. In some countries, Club Med is required by law to deposit cash received as payment for future vacations in special accounts. Cash in these accounts is restricted as to its use.

Assume that on December 31 Club Med received cash totaling $6,000,000 as payment in advance for vacations at one of its resorts. The resort is in a country that requires the cash to be deposited in a special account.

**Instructions:**

1. Prepare the journal entry necessary to record receipt of the $6,000,000.
2. Explain how the $6,000,000 would be disclosed in the December 31 balance sheet.

### Problem 8—4   (Accounting for petty cash)

On December 1, 1993, LGA Corporation established an imprest petty cash fund. The operations of the fund for the last month of 1993 and the first month of 1994 are summarized as follows.

Dec.  1  The petty cash fund was established by cashing a company check for $1,500 and delivering the proceeds to the fund cashier.

21  A request for replenishment of the petty cash fund was received by the accounts payable department, supported by appropriate signed vouchers, summarized as follows:

| | |
|---|---:|
| Selling expenses | $ 324 |
| Administrative expenses | 513 |
| Special equipment | 122 |
| Telephone, telegraph, and postage | 48 |
| Miscellaneous expenses | 260 |
| Total | $1,267 |

A check for $1,294 was drawn payable to the petty cash cashier.

31  The company's independent certified public accountant counted the fund in connection with the year-end audit work and found the following:

| | | |
|---|---:|---:|
| Cash in petty cash fund | | $ 655 |
| Employees' checks with January dates (postdated) | | 85 |
| Expense vouchers properly approved as follows: | | |
| Selling expenses | $146 | |
| Administrative expenses | 412 | |
| Office supplies | 28 | |
| Telephone, telegraph, and postage | 48 | |
| Miscellaneous expenses | 120 | 754 |
| Total | | $1,494 |

The petty cash fund was not replenished at December 31, 1993.

Jan.  15  The employees' checks held in the petty cash fund at December 31 were cashed and the proceeds retained in the fund.

31  A request for replenishment was made and a check was drawn to restore the fund to its original balance of $1,500. The support vouchers for January expenditures are summarized below.

| | |
|---|---:|
| Selling expenses | $ 85 |
| Administrative expenses | 312 |
| Telephone, telegraph, and postage | 35 |
| Miscellaneous expenses | 220 |
| Total | $652 |

**Instructions:**  Record the transactions in general journal form.

## Problem 8—5  (Bank reconciliation)

The cash account of Delta, Inc., disclosed a balance of $17,056.48 on October 31. The bank statement as of October 31 showed a balance of $21,209.45. Upon comparing the statement with the cash records, the following facts were developed:

(a)  Delta's account had been charged on October 26 for a customer's uncollectible check amounting to $1,143.

(b)  A 2-month, 9%, $3,000 customer's note dated August 25, discounted on October 12, had been dishonored October 26, and the bank had charged Delta for $3,050.83, which included a protest fee of $5.83.

(c)  A customer's check for $725 had been entered as $625 by both the depositor and the bank but was later corrected by the bank.

(d)  Check No. 661 for $1,242.50 had been entered in the cash disbursements journal at $1,224.50 and Check No. 652 for $32.90 had been entered as $329.00. The company uses the voucher system.

(e)  There were bank service charges for October of $39.43 not yet recorded on the books.

(f) A bank memo stated that M. Sear's note for $2,500 and interest of $62.50 had been collected on October 29, and the bank had made a charge of $12.50 (No entry had been made on the books when the note was sent to the bank for collection.)

(g) Receipts of October 29 for $6,850 were deposited November 1.

The following checks were outstanding on October 31:

| | | | |
|---|---|---|---|
| No. 620 | $1,250.00 | No. 671 | $ 732.50 |
| No. 621 | 3,448.23 | No. 673 | 187.90 |
| No. 632 | 2,405.25 | No. 675 | 275.72 |
| No. 670 | 1,775.38 | No. 676 | 2,233.15 |

**Instructions:**

1. Prepare a bank reconciliation as of October 31.
2. Give the journal entries required as a result of the preceding information.

### Problem 8—6   (Bank reconciliation)

The books of Hawkins Company show a cash balance of $23,383 as of July 31. Hawkins' bank statement shows a cash balance for the company of $21,432. Additional information which might be useful in reconciling the disparity between the two balances follows:

(a) A deposit of $800 was recorded by the bank on July 3, but it should have been recorded for Hawker Company rather than Hawkins Company.

(b) Petty cash of $425 was included in the cash balance, but an actual count reveals $516 on hand.

(c) Check No. 315 in payment of electric bill for $125 was correctly recorded by the bank but was recorded in the cash disbursements journal of Hawkins as $215.

(d) The bank statement does not show receipts of $1,250 which were deposited on July 31.

(e) The bank statement indicated a monthly service charge of $35.

(f) A check for $372 was returned marked NSF. The check had been included in the July 24 deposit. As of July 31, the check had not been redeposited.

(g) Proceeds from cash sales of $1,530 for July 19 were stolen. The company expects to recover this amount from the insurance company. The cash receipts were recorded in the books, but no entry was made for the loss.

(h) A check for $2,560 cleared the bank on July 29. It was a transfer to the payroll account at the same bank. On July 31, all but $1,255 of payroll checks had been processed at the bank.

(i) Interest of $56 has accrued on funds the bank had invested for Hawkins for the month of July.

(j) Outstanding checks totaled $1,420 as of July 31.

(k) The July 22 deposit included a check for $705 that had been returned on July 15 marked NSF. Hawkins Company had made no entry upon return of the check. The redeposit of the check on July 22 was recorded in the cash receipts journal of Hawkins as a collection on account.

**Instructions:**

1. Prepare a bank reconciliation as of July 31.
2. Make the necessary journal entries for Hawkins Company with the information provided on the bank reconciliation.

### Problem 8—7   (Reconciliation of an individual's bank account)

The data at the top of the next page was taken from Sylvester Krueger's check register for the month of April. Sylvester's bank reconciliation for March showed one outstanding check, Check #78 for $43.00 (written on March 23), and one deposit in transit, Deposit #10499 for $87.00 (made on March 30).

**Instructions:** Prepare a reconciliation of Sylvester's bank account as of April 30. Show both a corrected balance per bank and a corrected balance per books. Assume that any errors or discrepancies you find are Sylvester's fault, not the bank's.

| Date | | Item | Checks | Deposits | Balance |
|---|---|---|---|---|---|
| 19— | | | | | |
| April | 1 | Beginning Balance . . . . . . . . . . . . . . . . . . . . . . | | | $123.00 |
| | 1 | Deposit #10500 . . . . . . . . . . . . . . . . . . . . . . . | | $523.34 | 646.34 |
| | 1 | Check #79 . . . . . . . . . . . . . . . . . . . . . . . . . . | $ 5.00 | | 651.34 |
| | 4 | Check #80 . . . . . . . . . . . . . . . . . . . . . . . . . . | 213.47 | | 437.97 |
| | 27 | Deposit #10501 . . . . . . . . . . . . . . . . . . . . . . . | | 235.48 | 673.45 |
| | 29 | Check #81 . . . . . . . . . . . . . . . . . . . . . . . . . . | 264.35 | | 409.80 |

The following is from Sylvester's bank statement for April:

| April | 1 | Beginning Balance . . . . . . . . . . . . . . . . . . . . . . | | | $ 79.00 |
|---|---|---|---|---|---|
| | 3 | Check #79 . . . . . . . . . . . . . . . . . . . . . . . . . . | $ 5.00 | | 74.00 |
| | 3 | Deposit #10499 . . . . . . . . . . . . . . . . . . . . . . . | | $ 87.00 | 161.00 |
| | 5 | Check #80 . . . . . . . . . . . . . . . . . . . . . . . . . . | 213.47 | | (52.47) |
| | 5 | Automatic Loan . . . . . . . . . . . . . . . . . . . . . . . | | 163.00 | 110.53 |
| | 8 | Deposit #10500 . . . . . . . . . . . . . . . . . . . . . . . | | 528.34 | 638.87 |
| | 20 | NSF Check . . . . . . . . . . . . . . . . . . . . . . . . . . | 20.00 | | 618.87 |
| | 20 | Service Charge . . . . . . . . . . . . . . . . . . . . . . . | 12.00 | | 606.87 |
| | 30 | Interest . . . . . . . . . . . . . . . . . . . . . . . . . . . . | | 1.65 | 608.52 |

## Problem 8—8  (Four-column bank reconciliation)

The following data is applicable to the Morgan Building Co.:

(a) The July 31 bank statement balance of $74,875 included a bank service charge of $235 not previously reported to the company but recorded on the company's books in August.
(b) The cash account balance in the general ledger on July 31 was $66,715.
(c) Outstanding checks at July 31 were $13,475. Deposits in transit on July 31 were $5,080.
(d) The bank statement on August 31 had a balance of $78,265, recognizing deposits of $105,360 and withdrawals of $101,970. The withdrawals included a service charge for August of $270 not yet reported to Morgan Building Co.
(e) The cash account balance in the general ledger on August 31 was $80,435, recognizing receipts of $104,405 for August and checks written during August of $90,450. Deposits in transit on August 31 were $4,125, and checks of $2,225 were outstanding as of that date.

## Instructions:

1. Prepare a four-column bank reconciliation as of August 31.
2. Give any entries at August 31 that may be required on the company's books.

## Problem 8—9  (Four-column bank reconciliation)

The following information is related to Downtown Company:

| | August | September |
|---|---|---|
| Bank statement balance—at month end . . . . . . . . . . . . . . . . | $ 2,412 | $ 2,782 |
| Cash account balance—at month end . . . . . . . . . . . . . . . . . . | 1,975 | 2,296 |
| Bank charges for NSF check returned (normally written off in month following return) . . . . . . . . . . . . . . . . . . . . . . . . . . | 38 | 80 |
| Outstanding checks—at month end . . . . . . . . . . . . . . . . . . . . | 600 | 865 |
| Deposits in transit—at month end . . . . . . . . . . . . . . . . . . . . | 300 | 470 |
| Bank service charges (normally recorded in month following bank charge) . . . . . . . . . . . . . . . . . . . . . . . . . . . . . . . . . . . . | 25 | 29 |
| Drafts collected by bank (not recorded by company until month following collection) . . . . . . . . . . . . . . . . . . . . . . . . . . | 200 | 150 |
| Total credits to cash account . . . . . . . . . . . . . . . . . . . . . . . . | 14,853 | 17,979 |
| Total deposits on bank statement . . . . . . . . . . . . . . . . . . . . . . | ? | 18,080 |

Check #411 was erroneously recorded in the company checkbook and journal as $286; the correct amount is $236. (This check was not outstanding on September 30.) All disbursements were made by check.

**Instructions:**   Prepare a four-column bank reconciliation for the month of September.

## Problem 8–10   (Four-column bank reconciliation with adjusting entries)

Asil Corporation received the following bank statement on August 1:

| Date | | Withdrawals | Deposits | Balance |
|---|---|---|---|---|
| July | 1 | | | $66,405 |
| | 2 | $ 2,502 | | 63,903 |
| | 3 | 2,240 | $ 1,050 | 62,713 |
| | 5 | | 2,106 | 64,819 |
| | 6 | | 5,535 | 70,354 |
| | 8 | | 5,817 | 76,171 |
| | 9 | 8,181 | | 67,990 |
| | 10 | | 4,317 | 72,307 |
| | 11 | 6,819 | | 65,488 |
| | 12 | 7,425 | 4,926 | 62,989 |
| | 13 | | | 62,989 |
| | 15 | | 3,509 | 66,498 |
| | 16 | 9,777 | | 56,721 |
| | 17 | 6,221 | 7,702 | 58,202 |
| | 18 | 6,484 | | 51,718 |
| | 19 | | 3,418 | 55,136 |
| | 20 | | 8,470 | 63,606 |
| | 22 | | 6,492 | 70,098 |
| | 23 | 5,546 | | 64,552 |
| | 24 | | | 64,552 |
| | 25 | 8,735 | | 55,817 |
| | 26 | | 8,246 | 64,063 |
| | 27 | | 9,385 | 73,448 |
| | 29 | 7,060 | | 66,388 |
| | 30 | | 5,827 | 72,215 |
| | 31 | 6,405 | | 65,810 |
| | Totals | $77,395 | $76,800 | |

At June 30, the balance in Asil's cash account in the general ledger was $62,150. The following transactions were posted to the cash account during the month of July:

| Date | | Disbursements | Receipts |
|---|---|---|---|
| July | 1 | $    165 | $ 3,729 |
| | 2 | | 5,535 |
| | 3 | 8,181 | |
| | 5 | | 5,817 |
| | 6 | | 4,317 |
| | 8 | 6,819 | |
| | 9 | 7,425 | 4,926 |
| | 10 | | |
| | 11 | | |
| | 12 | | 3,509 |
| | 13 | 9,391 | |
| | 15 | | 7,702 |
| | 16 | 6,221 | |
| | 17 | 6,484 | 3,418 |

| July 18 | | 5,310 |
|---|---|---|
| 19 | | 6,492 |
| 20 | 5,074 | |
| 22 | 8,735 | |
| 23 | | 8,246 |
| 24 | | |
| 25 | | |
| 26 | 6,885 | 8,913 |
| 27 | | |
| 29 | 5,913 | 5,152 |
| 30 | | 2,238 |
| 31 | 5,857 | |
| Totals | $77,150 | $75,304 |

Additional information:

(a)  Asil makes a journal entry for service charges, direct deposits, and interest earned in the month subsequent to the month the items are reflected on the bank statement.

(b)  Casper Co. makes a direct deposit of $675 to Asil's account at the bank on the 30th of every month. This payment, which is rent revenue to Asil, is not recorded by Asil until the bank statement is received.

(c)  On the 23rd of July an NSF check for $472 was returned by the bank. The check was redeposited on July 27th, and no entry was made by Asil.

(d)  Check No. 1145 dated July 29 was written for $1,492 of wages, but recorded by Asil on its books as $1,000.

(e)  On July 16, the bank recorded a withdrawal of $386 for Asil that should have been for Azil Company.

(f)  The bank service charge for June was $165 and for July was $175.

(g)  The interest earned in June was $3,054 and in July was $3,160.

(h)  During June, Asil wrote Check No. 1095 for $9,850 for rent expense but recorded the check on its books as $8,955. Asil discovered the mistake in July, when the canceled checks were returned with the June bank statement, but neglected to correct the error on the books at that time.

(i)  At the end of June, Asil had $3,156 of deposits in transit, and checks totaling $4,742 that had not cleared the bank. In addition, all of Asil's transactions with the bank after July 29 have not cleared the bank.

**Instructions:**

1.  Prepare a four-column bank reconciliation.
2.  Prepare any necessary adjusting journal entries on the books of Asil Corporation.
3.  Prepare any necessary notation to the bank for errors that should be corrected by the bank.

### Problem 8—11  (Accounting for marketable equity securities)

During 1993, Merz Company purchased 3,000 shares of ABC Company common stock for $16 per share and 2,000 shares of XYZ Company common stock for $33 per share. These investments are intended to be held as ready sources of cash.

On December 31, 1993, ABC common stock was trading for $20 per share and XYZ common stock was trading for $22 per share.

On March 23, 1994, the 2,000 shares of XYZ common stock were sold for $17 per share. On December 31, 1994, ABC common stock was trading for $19 per share.

**Instructions:**

1. Provide the journal entries to be made on December 31, 1993, March 23, 1994, and December 31, 1994.
2. Describe how the following items would be treated in Merz Company's statement of cash flows for the year ended December 31, 1994. Merz uses the indirect method of reporting cash flow from operating activities.
   - (a) The proceeds from the sale of the XYZ shares.
   - (b) Any realized gain or loss on the sale of the XYZ shares.
   - (c) Any unrealized gain or loss on the remaining marketable securities.

### Problem 8—12   (Recording and valuing temporary investments)

Myers & Associates reports the following information on the December 31, 1992, balance sheet:

| | | |
|---|---:|---:|
| Marketable securities (at cost) ........................... | $225,850 | |
| Less allowance for decline in value of marketable securities............................................... | 2,260 | $223,590 |

Supporting records of Myers' temporary holdings show marketable securities as follows:

| | Cost | Market |
|---|---:|---:|
| 200 shares of Conway Co. common ..................... | $ 25,450 | $ 24,300 |
| $80,000 U.S. Treasury 7% bonds ........................ | 79,650 | 77,400 |
| $120,000 U.S. Treasury 7½% bonds .................... | 120,750 | 121,890 |
| | $225,850 | $223,590 |

Interest dates on the Treasury bonds are January 1 and July 1. Myers & Associates makes reversing entries and uses the revenue approach to record the purchase of bonds with accrued interest. During 1993 and 1994, Myers & Associates completed the following transactions related to temporary investments:

**1993**

Jan.   1   Received semiannual interest on U.S. Treasury bonds. (The entry to reverse the interest accrual at the end of the last year has already been made.)

Apr.   1   Sold $60,000 of the 7½% U.S. Treasury bonds at 102 plus accrued interest. Brokerage fees were $200.

May   21   Received dividends of 25 cents per share on the Conway Co. common stock. The dividend had not been recorded on the declaration date.

July   1   Received semiannual interest on U.S. Treasury bonds, then sold the 7% treasury bonds at 97½. Brokerage fees were $250.

Aug.   15   Purchased 100 shares of Nieman Inc. common stock at 116 plus brokerage fees of $50.

Nov.   1   Purchased $50,000 of 8% U.S. Treasury bonds at 101 plus accrued interest. Brokerage fees were $125. Interest dates are January 1 and July 1.

Dec.   31   Market prices of securities were: Conway Co. common, 110; 7½% U.S. Treasury bonds, 101¾; 8% U.S. Treasury bonds, 101; Nieman Inc. common, 116¾. Myers & Associates reports all marketable securities at the lower of aggregate cost or market.

**1994**

Jan.   2   Recorded the receipt of semiannual interest on the U.S. Treasury bonds.

Feb.   1   Sold the remaining 7½% U.S. Treasury bonds at 101 plus accrued interest. Brokerage fees were $300.

**Instructions:**

1. Prepare journal entries for the foregoing transactions and to accrue required interest on December 31, 1993. Give computations in support of your entries.
2. Show how marketable securities would be presented on the December 31, 1993, balance sheet.

### Problem 8—13   (Accounting for marketable equity securities)

Fox Company made the following transactions in the common stock of NOP Company:

July 10, 1992   Purchased 10,000 shares at $45 per share.
Sep. 29, 1993   Sold 2,000 shares for $51 per share.
Aug. 17, 1994   Sold 2,500 shares for $33 per share.

The end-of-year market prices for the shares were as follows:

| | |
|---|---|
| December 31, 1992 ........................................... | $40 per share |
| December 31, 1993 ........................................... | $39 per share |
| December 31, 1994 ........................................... | $31 per share |

Fox views its holdings of the stock of NOP Company as an investment of idle cash resources.

**Instructions:**   Prepare the necessary entries for 1992, 1993, and 1994. Fox values the securities at lower of cost or market.

### Problem 8—14   (Journal entries and balance sheet presentation for marketable securities)

On December 31, 1992, Durst Company's balance sheet showed the following balance in its marketable securities account:

| | | |
|---|---|---|
| Current assets: | | |
| Marketable securities (at cost) ........................ | $155,000 | |
| Less allowance for decline in value of current marketable securities ........................................... | 7,250 | |
| Marketable securities ................................. | | $147,750 |

Durst's marketable securities portfolio on December 31, 1992, was made up of the following securities:

| | Cost | Market |
|---|---|---|
| 1000 shares of Herzog Corp. stock ....................... | $ 75,000 | $ 76,250 |
| 800 shares Taylor, Inc., stock ........................... | 55,000 | 52,825 |
| 10% New York City Water bonds (Interest payable semiannually on January 1 and July 1)........................ | 25,000 | 18,675 |
| | $155,000 | $147,750 |

During 1993, the following transactions took place:

Jan.   3   Received interest on the New York City Water bonds.
Mar.   1   Purchased 300 additional shares of Herzog Corp. stock for $22,950.
Apr.  15   Sold 400 shares of the Taylor, Inc., stock for $69 per share.
July   3   Received interest on the New York City Water bonds.
Oct.  30   Purchased 1,500 shares of Cook Co. stock for $83,250.

Durst makes reversing entries on January 1 for all year-end accrual entries. The values of the stocks and bonds on December 31, 1993, are as follows:

| | |
|---|---|
| Herzog Corp. stock .......................................... | $76.60/share |
| Taylor, Inc., stock.......................................... | $68.50/share |
| Cook Co. stock ............................................ | $55.25/share |
| New York City Water bonds .................................. | $20,555 |

**Instructions:**

1. Make all necessary journal entries for 1993, including any year-end accrual or adjusting entries.
2. Show how the marketable securities would be presented on the balance sheet at December 31, 1993.

### Problem 8—15  (Alternative methods of valuing marketable securities)

Dextron Co. made the following investments in marketable securities in 1992:

| | |
|---|---|
| Martin Inc. common stock, 1,400 shares @ 45¾ ..................... | $ 64,050 |
| Smith Corp. common stock, 1,750 shares @ 22½ ..................... | 39,375 |
| Walker Bros. first-mortgage 8% bonds, 105 $1000 bonds at par ........ | 105,000 |
| | $208,425 |

All of the Smith Corp. shares were sold at the end of 1994 for $29,750. The market values of the securities held at the ends of 1992, 1993, and 1994 were as follows:

| | 1992 | 1993 | 1994 |
|---|---|---|---|
| Martin Inc. ..................................... | $ 68,250 | $ 55,650 | $ 60,375 |
| Smith Corp...................................... | 35,700 | 30,100 | — |
| Walker Bros. ................................... | 108,500 | 110,250 | 105,350 |

**Instructions:**   Prepare the necessary entries for 1992, 1993, and 1994 for the valuation and the sale of securities, and show how the securities would be reported on the balance sheets prepared at the ends of 1992, 1993, and 1994 under each of the following assumptions:

(a)  Securities are valued at cost.
(b)  Securities are valued at the lower of cost or market (aggregate basis).

### Problem 8—16  (Journal entries for temporary investments)

During 1993 and 1994, the Kopson Co. made the following journal entries to account for transactions involving temporary investments:

```
       1993
(a) Nov.  1   Marketable Securities (10% U.S. Treasury Bonds) ...   106,883
                  Cash ........................................              106,883
                    To record the purchase of $100,000 of U.S. Trea-
                    sury bonds at 103¼. Brokerage fees were $300.
                    Interest is payable semiannually on January 1
                    and July 1.

(b) Dec. 31   Marketable Securities ............................   4,283
                  Allowance for Decline in Value of Current Market-
                  able Securities ................................              4,283
                    To record the decrease in market value of the
                    current marketable securities based on the fol-
                    lowing data:
```

| | Cost | Market |
|---|---|---|
| Fleming Co. stock ...................................... | $ 25,250 | $ 23,350 |
| Dobson Co. stock....................................... | 32,450 | 33,950 |
| 10% U.S. Treasury bonds .............................. | 106,883 | 103,000 |
| | $164,583 | $160,300 |

The beginning allowance account balance was $500. There were no other entries in 1993.

1994

(c) Jan. 1  Cash ........................................... 5,000
                Interest Revenue ............................. 5,000
                    *To record interest revenue for six months.*

(d) July 1  Cash ........................................... 5,000
                Interest Revenue ............................. 5,000
                    *To record interest revenue for six months.*

(e) Dec. 6  Marketable Securities ............................ 50,000
                Long-Term Investment in Equity Securities ........ 50,000
                    *To record the reclassification of 10,000 shares of*
                    *Braxton Co. stock, which was selected by manage-*
                    *ment for sale in 1995. Market price was $4.80 per*
                    *share at the date of reclassification.*

(f) Dec. 31 Recognized Decline in Value of Current Marketable Se-
                curities ........................................ 5,483
                Allowance for Decline in Value of Current Market-
                able Securities ................................ 5,483
                    *To record the decrease in the market value of the*
                    *current marketable securities based on the follow-*
                    *ing data:*

|  | Cost | Market |
|---|---|---|
| Fleming Co. stock ..................................... | $ 25,250 | $ 24,950 |
| Dobson Co. stock...................................... | 32,450 | 32,650 |
| 10% U.S. Treasury bonds ............................. | 106,883 | 103,500 |
| Braxton Co. stock..................................... | 50,000 | 48,000 |
|  | $214,583 | $209,100 |

There were no other entries.

**Instructions:**   For each incorrect entry, give the entry that should have been made. Assume the revenue approach and the lower-of-cost-or-market method.

# CHAPTER 9

# Receivables

In 1938, McKesson & Robbins, Inc., reported total assets of $87 million. Of that amount, $9 million represented fictitious accounts receivable. Certain company officials had responded to the desire to increase assets and revenue by making false entries for sales.

The most notorious accounting scandal of the 1970s was the Equity Funding case. Between 1964 and 1973, Equity Funding created $85 million of bogus revenue by falsely recording loans receivable from insurance customers. As the fraud deepened and the need for extra reported revenue increased, Equity Funding also began to create insurance policies for nonexistent customers. Overall, revenue was overstated by more than $140 million during the fraud period.

A much-publicized fraud of the 1980s involved ZZZZ Best, a carpet-cleaning concern started by young entrepreneur Barry Minkow. ZZZZ Best enhanced reported results by reporting revenue and receivables from imaginary fire-damage restoration jobs.

In these and many other cases involving fraudulent financial reporting, receivables have been a key element. Receivables continue to be a ripe area for fraud because the journal entry is so easy to make—debit Receivable, credit Revenue.

For most businesses, receivables are a significant item, often representing a major portion of the liquid assets of a company. Retail and merchandising companies, such as Sears, Roebuck and Co. or J. C. Penney Company, Inc., typically have 50 to 70 percent of total current assets tied up in receivables. For some service-type businesses, the percentage is even higher. Receivables also can provide a significant source of revenues from finance charges. For example, at December 31, 1988, Sears had approximately $4.5 billion of domestic accounts receivable. These receivables were expected to earn finance charge revenues at annual percentage rates ranging from 11 to 21 percent. On the other hand, a lack of control of receivables can result in substantial losses from uncollectible accounts. Even with good credit policies and collection procedures, bad debt losses often range from one to five percent of total credit sales. Finally, receivables can be used as collateral for a loan or sold to generate funds for operating purposes. During 1988, for example, The Goodyear Tire & Rubber Company sold $2.45 billion of receivables.

As the above examples illustrate, receivables can affect the profitability of company operations in a number of ways. This makes the management, control, and accounting for receivables important tasks. The major considerations in accounting for receivables involve their recognition, classification, valuation, and reporting. Collection of receivables and the use of receivables in financing company operations are also important considerations. These issues are addressed in this chapter.

## CLASSIFICATION OF RECEIVABLES

In its broadest sense, the term receivables is applicable to all claims against others for money, goods, or services. For accounting purposes, however, the term is generally employed in a narrower sense to designate claims expected to be settled by the receipt of cash.

In classifying receivables, an important distinction is made between trade and nontrade receivables. Usually the chief source of receivables is the normal operating activities of a business, i.e., credit sales of goods or services to customers. These trade receivables may be evidenced by a formal written promise to pay and classified as notes receivable. In most cases, however, trade receivables are unsecured "open accounts," often referred to simply as accounts receivable.

Accounts receivable represent an extension of short-term credit to customers. Payments are generally due within 30 to 90 days. The credit arrangements are typically informal agreements between seller and buyer supported by such business documents as invoices, sales orders, and delivery contracts. Normally trade receivables do not involve interest, although an interest or service charge may be added if payments are not made within a specified period. Trade receivables are the most common type of receivable and are generally the most significant in total dollar amount.

Nontrade receivables include all other types of receivables. They arise from a variety of transactions, such as: (1) the sale of securities or property other than inventory; (2) advances to stockholders, directors, officers, employees, and affiliated companies; (3) deposits with creditors, utilities, and other agencies; (4) purchase prepayments; (5) deposits to guarantee contract performance or expense payment; (6) claims for losses or damages; (7) claims for rebates and tax refunds; (8) subscriptions for capital stock; and (9) dividends and interest receivable. Nontrade receivables should be summarized in appropriately titled accounts and reported separately in the financial statements.

Another way of classifying receivables relates to the **current** or short-term versus **noncurrent** or long-term nature of receivables. As indicated in Chapter 5, the "Current assets" classification, as broadly conceived, includes all receivables identified as collectible within one year or the normal operating cycle, whichever is longer. Thus, for classification purposes, all trade receivables are considered **current receivables**; each nontrade item requires separate analysis to determine whether it is reasonable to assume that it will be collected within one year. **Noncurrent receivables** are reported under the "Investments" or "Other noncurrent assets" caption, or as a separate item with an appropriate description.

In summary, receivables are classified in various ways, e.g., as accounts or notes receivable, as trade or nontrade receivables, and as current or noncurrent receivables. These categories are not mutually exclusive. For example, accounts receivable are trade receivables and are current; notes receivable may be trade receivables and therefore current in some circumstances, but may be nontrade receivables, either current or noncurrent, in other situations. The classifications used most often in practice and throughout this book will be simply *accounts receivable, notes receivable,* and *other receivables.*

## ACCOUNTS RECEIVABLE

As indicated earlier, accounts receivable include all trade receivables not supported by a written agreement or "note." The following sections discuss the major accounting problems associated with accounts receivable: (1) when they are to be recognized; (2) how they are to be valued and reported; and (3) how they may be used as a source of cash in financing company operations.

### Recognition of Accounts Receivable

The recognition of accounts receivable is related to the recognition of revenue. Since revenues are generally recorded when the earning process is complete and cash is realized or realizable, it follows that a receivable arising from the sale of goods is generally recognized when title to the goods passes to the buyer. Because the point at which title passes may vary with the terms of the sale, it is normal practice to recognize the receivable when goods are shipped to the customer. It is at this point in time that the revenue recognition criteria are normally satisfied. Receivables should not be recognized for goods shipped on approval, where the shipper retains title until there is a formal acceptance, or for goods shipped on consignment, where the shipper retains title until the goods are sold by the consignee. Receivables for service to customers are properly recognized when the services are performed. The entry for recognizing a receivable from the sale of goods or services is:

| | | |
|---|---|---|
| Accounts Receivable | XXX | |
| Sales | | XXX |

When the account is collected, Accounts Receivable is credited and Cash is debited.

For department stores and major oil and gas companies, a significant portion of receivables arise from *credit card sales.* The recognition of such receivables is similar to recognition of other trade receivables.

The treatment of credit card sales for other companies, such as American Express or banks that handle VISA or MasterCard, is somewhat different. These companies are generally responsible for approving customers' credit and collecting the receivables. Consequently, they usually charge a service fee, normally 2% to 5% of net credit card sales. These companies generally follow one of two procedures in reimbursing the retail companies that accept their cards: (1) the retailer must submit the credit card receipts in order to receive payments, or (2) they allow retailers to deposit the receipts directly into a checking account. American Express, Diners Club, Carte Blanche, and other travel and entertainment card companies generally follow the first procedure; bank cards are accounted for with the second method.[1]

As an example of how a retail company would account for credit card sales under these two approaches, assume that Little Italy Pizza Parlor has American Express drafts that total $1,200 on November 20. The entry to record the sales would be:

| | | |
|---|---|---|
| Accounts Receivable—American Express | 1,200 | |
| Sales | | 1,200 |
| *To record American Express credit card sales for November 20.* | | |

Little Italy would then send the receipts to American Express, which would send a check to Little Italy for $1,200 less its service fees. Assuming a 5% service charge, which Little Italy would recognize as a selling expense, the entry to record the payment from American Express would be:

| | | |
|---|---|---|
| Cash | 1,140 | |
| Credit Card Service Charge | 60 | |
| Accounts Receivable | | 1,200 |
| *To record payment from American Express on credit card sales.* | | |

Continuing the example, assume Little Italy also had VISA charge sales of $2,000. These sales are handled under the second method and are treated like a cash sale. In effect, bank credit card sales, such as VISA and MasterCard, are a form of factoring receivables, which is discussed later in the chapter. The retail company makes out a regular, but separate, bank deposit slip and deposits the credit card receipts as though they were cash. The bank receives the deposit slip and credit card receipts and increases the retailer's checking account balance for the total amount less the bank credit card service charge. Assuming a 4% bank service charge, in our example Little Italy would make the following entry:

| | | |
|---|---|---|
| Cash | 1,920 | |
| Credit Card Service Charge | 80 | |
| Sales | | 2,000 |
| *To record VISA credit card sales for November 20.* | | |

Note that under this method a receivable is never established by the retail companies. The receivables from the customers are the responsibility of the bank that issued the credit card. The customers pay the bank directly and any uncollectibles are losses for the bank.

## Valuation and Reporting of Accounts Receivable

Theoretically, all receivables should be valued at an amount representing the present value of the expected future cash receipts. As explained in Chapter 7, the present value of a $1,000 receivable due in 1 year at a 10% interest rate is $909.10 ($1,000 × the present value factor of .9091 from Table II in Chapter 7). The difference in the present value and the amount to be received in the future ($90.90 in the example) is the implicit interest. Since accounts receivable are short-term, usually being collected within 30 to 90 days, the amount of interest is small relative to the amount of the receivable. Consequently, the

---

[1]The total number of credit cards in the U.S. exceeds one billion. Consumers currently use plastic to pay for $28 out of every $100 spent on consumable goods and services. (Reported in *The Wall Street Journal*, July 26, 1990, p. A.1 in "Business Bulletin" by Pamela Sabastian.)

accounting profession has chosen to ignore the interest element for these trade receivables.[2]

Instead of valuing accounts receivable at a discounted present value, they are reported at their **net realizable value**, i.e., their expected cash value. This means that accounts receivable should be recorded net of estimated uncollectible items and trade discounts. The objective is to report the receivables at the amount of claims from customers actually expected to be collected in cash.

**Uncollectible Accounts Receivable**     Invariably, some receivables will prove uncollectible. The simplest method for recognizing the loss from these uncollectible accounts is to debit an expense account, such as Bad Debt Expense or Uncollectible Accounts Expense, and credit Accounts Receivable at the time it is determined that an account cannot be collected. This approach is called the **direct write-off method** and is often used by small businesses because of its simplicity. While the recognition of uncollectibles in the period of their discovery is simple and convenient, this method does not provide for the matching of current revenues with related expenses and does not report receivables at their net realizable value. Therefore, use of the direct write-off method is considered a departure from generally accepted accounting principles. The following sections describe the procedures used in estimating uncollectibles with the **allowance method**, which is required by GAAP.[3]

*Establishing an Allowance for Doubtful Accounts*     When using the allowance method, the amount of receivables estimated to be uncollectible is recorded by a debit to Doubtful Accounts Expense and a credit to Allowance for Doubtful Accounts. The terminology for these account titles may vary somewhat. Other possibilities, besides Allowance for Doubtful Accounts, include Allowance for Uncollectible Accounts and Allowance for Bad Debts. The expense account title usually is consistent with that of the allowance account. A typical entry, normally made as an end-of-the-period adjustment, would be as follows:

```
Doubtful Accounts Expense ....................................     XXX
    Allowance for Doubtful Accounts ............................            XXX
        To record estimated uncollectible accounts receivable for the
        period.
```

The expense would be reported as a selling or general and administrative expense, and the allowance account would be shown as a deduction from Accounts Receivable, thereby reporting the net realizable amount of the receivables.

*Writing Off an Uncollectible Account Under the Allowance Method*     When positive evidence is available concerning the partial or complete worthlessness of an account, the account is written off by a debit to the allowance account, which was previously established, and a credit to Accounts Receivable. Positive evidence of a reduction in value is found in the bankruptcy, death, or disappearance of a debtor, failure to enforce collection legally, or barring of collection by the statute of limitations. Write-offs should be supported by evidence of the uncollectibility of the accounts from appropriate parties, such as courts, lawyers, or credit agencies, and should be authorized in writing by appropriate company officers. The entry to write off an uncollectible receivable would be:

---

[2]See *Opinions of the Accounting Principles Board No. 21,* "Interest on Receivables and Payables" (New York: American Institute of Certified Public Accountants, 1971), par. 3(a).

[3]As a result of the Tax Reform Act of 1986, the direct write-off method of determining bad debt expense is required for income tax purposes. Prior to the Act, taxpayers could use either the direct write-off or the allowance method.

```
Allowance for Doubtful Accounts ..............................    XXX
    Accounts Receivable ........................................        XXX
        To record the write-off of an uncollectible account.
```

Note that no entry is made to Doubtful Accounts Expense at this time. That entry was made when the allowance was established. The expense was thus recorded in the period when the sale was made, not necessarily in the period when the account became uncollectible, as with the direct write-off method.

Occasionally, an account that has been written off as uncollectible is unexpectedly collected. Entries are required to reverse the write-off entry and to record the collection. Assuming an account of $1,500 was written off as uncollectible but was subsequently collected, the following entries would be made at the time of collection:

```
Accounts Receivable ........................................    1,500
    Allowance for Doubtful Accounts ..........................        1,500
        To reverse the entry made to write off the account.

Cash ......................................................    1,500
    Accounts Receivable ....................................        1,500
        To record collection of the account.
```

**Estimating Uncollectibles Based on Sales Percentage**    The estimate for uncollectible accounts may be based on sales for the period or the amount of receivables outstanding at the end of the period. When a sales basis is used, the amount of uncollectible accounts in past years relative to total sales provides a percentage of estimated uncollectibles. This percentage may be modified by expectations based on current experience. Since doubtful accounts occur only with credit sales, it would seem logical to develop a percentage of doubtful accounts to credit sales of past periods. This percentage is then applied to credit sales of the current period. However, since extra work may be required in maintaining separate records of cash and credit sales or in analyzing sales data, the percentage is frequently developed in terms of total sales. Unless there is considerable periodic fluctuation in the proportion of cash and credit sales, the **percentage-of-total-sales method** will normally give satisfactory results.

To illustrate, if 2% of sales are considered doubtful in terms of collection and sales for the period are $100,000, the charge for Doubtful Accounts Expense would be 2% of the current period's sales, or $2,000. Note that any existing balance in the allowance account resulting from past-period charges to Doubtful Accounts Expense is ignored. The entry for this period would be simply:

```
Doubtful Accounts Expense ..................................    2,000
    Allowance for Doubtful Accounts ..........................        2,000
        ($100,000 × .02 = $2,000)
```

The sales percentage method for estimating doubtful accounts is widely used in practice because it is simple to apply. Companies often use this method to estimate doubtful accounts periodically during the year and then adjust the allowance account at year-end in relationship to the accounts receivable balance, as explained in the next section.

**Estimating Uncollectibles Based on Accounts Receivable Balance**    Instead of using a percentage of sales to estimate uncollectible accounts, companies may base their estimates on a **percentage of total accounts receivable outstanding**. This method emphasizes the relationship between the accounts receivable balance and the allowance for doubtful accounts. For example, if total accounts receivable are $50,000 and it is estimated that 3% of those accounts will be uncollectible, then the allowance account should have a balance of $1,500 ($50,000 × .03). If the allowance account already has a $600 credit balance from prior periods, then the current-period adjusting entry would be:

| Doubtful Accounts Expense ..................................... | 900 | |
| Allowance for Doubtful Accounts ........................... | | 900 |

After posting the preceding entry, the balance in the allowance account would be $1,500, or 3% of total accounts receivable. Note that this method adjusts the existing balance to the desired balance based on a percentage of total receivables outstanding. If, in the example, the allowance account had a $200 debit balance caused by writing off more bad debts than had been estimated previously, the adjusting entry would be for $1,700 in order to bring the allowance account to the desired credit balance of $1,500, or 3% of total receivables.

The most commonly used method for establishing an allowance based on outstanding receivables involves **aging receivables.** Individual accounts are analyzed to determine those not yet due and those past due. Past-due accounts are classified in terms of the length of the period past due. An analysis sheet used in aging accounts receivable is shown below.

**ICO Products, Inc.**
**Analysis of Receivables**
**December 31, 1993**

| Customer | Amount | Not Yet Due | Not More Than 30 Days Past Due | 31-60 Days Past Due | 61-90 Days Past Due | 91-180 Days Past Due | 181-365 Days Past Due | More Than One Year Past Due |
|---|---|---|---|---|---|---|---|---|
| A. B. Andrews ...... | $ 450 | | | $ 450 | | | | |
| B. T. Brooks ........ | 300 | | | | $100 | $200 | | |
| B. Bryant ........... | 200 | | $ 200 | | | | | |
| L. B. Devine ........ | 2,100 | $ 2,100 | | | | | | |
| K. Martinez ......... | 200 | | | | | | | $ 200 |
| M. A. Young ........ | 1,400 | 1,000 | | 100 | 300 | | | |
| Total .............. | $47,550 | $40,000 | $3,000 | $1,200 | $650 | $500 | $800 | $1,400 |

Overdue balances can be evaluated individually to estimate the collectibility of each item as a basis for developing an overall estimate. An alternative procedure is to develop a series of estimated loss percentages and apply these to the different receivables classifications. The calculation of the allowance on the latter basis is illustrated on page 313.

Just as with the previous method based on a percentage of total receivables outstanding, Doubtful Accounts Expense is debited and Allowance for Doubtful Accounts is credited for an amount bringing the allowance account to the required balance. Assuming uncollectibles estimated at $2,870 as shown in the schedule above and a credit balance of $620 in the allowance account before adjustment, the following entry would be made:

| Doubtful Accounts Expense ..................................... | 2,250 | |
| Allowance for Doubtful Accounts ........................... | | 2,250 |

The aging method provides the most satisfactory approach to the valuation of receivables at their net realizable amounts. Furthermore, data developed through aging receivables may be quite useful to management for purposes of credit analysis and control. On the other hand, application of this method may involve considerable time and cost. This

**ICO Products, Inc.**
**Estimated Amount of Uncollectible Accounts**
**December 31, 1993**

| Classification | Balances | Uncollectible Accounts Experience Percentage | Estimated Amount of Uncollectible Accounts |
|---|---|---|---|
| Not yet due ......................... | $40,000 | 2% | $ 800 |
| Not more than 30 days past due ...... | 3,000 | 5% | 150 |
| 31-60 days past due ................ | 1,200 | 10% | 120 |
| 61-90 days past due ................ | 650 | 20% | 130 |
| 91-180 days past due ............... | 500 | 30% | 150 |
| 181-365 days past due .............. | 800 | 50% | 400 |
| More than one year past due ........ | 1,400 | 80% | 1,120 |
| | $47,550 | | $2,870 |

method still involves estimates, and the added refinement achieved by the aging process may not warrant the additional cost. With computer programs, however, the time and cost factors are not as significant as they once were.

**Corrections to Allowance for Doubtful Accounts**    As previously indicated, the allowance for doubtful accounts balance is established and maintained by means of adjusting entries at the close of each accounting period. If the allowance provisions are too large, the allowance account balance will be unnecessarily inflated and earnings will be understated; if the allowance provisions are too small, the allowance account balance will be inadequate and earnings will be overstated.

Care must be taken to see that the allowance balance follows the credit experience of the particular business. The process of aging receivables at different intervals may be employed as a means of checking the allowance balance to be certain that it is being maintained satisfactorily. Such periodic reviews may indicate a need for a correction in the allowance as well as a change in the rate or in the method employed.

When the uncollectible accounts experience approximates the estimated losses, the allowance procedure may be considered satisfactory, and no adjustment is required. When it appears that there has been a failure to estimate uncollectible accounts accurately, resulting in an allowance balance that is clearly inadequate or excessive, an adjustment is in order. Such an adjustment would be considered a change in accounting estimate under APB Opinion No. 20, and the effect would be reported in the current and future periods as an ordinary item on the income statement, usually as an addition to or subtraction from Doubtful Accounts Expense.

The actual write-off of receivables as uncollectible by debits to the allowance account and credits to the receivables account may result temporarily in a debit balance in the allowance account. A debit balance arising in this manner does not mean necessarily that the allowance is inadequate; debits to the allowance account simply predate the end-of-period adjustment for uncollectible accounts. The adjustment, when recorded, should cover uncollectibles already determined as well as those yet to be identified.

**The Impact of Uncollectible Accounts on the Statement of Cash Flows**    As noted in Chapter 6, the amount of reported sales or net income on an accrual basis must be adjusted for the change in accounts receivable balances to derive the corresponding amount of cash flow from operations. The establishment of a provision for bad debts with a corresponding allowance for doubtful accounts and the subsequent write-off of uncol-

## Foreign Debt Crisis

The cover story for the January 10, 1983, issue of *Time* was entitled "The Debt-Bomb Threat." Loans receivable by banks, governments, and international financial institutions from developing countries and Eastern bloc countries totaled $706 billion, up from just $100 billion twelve years before. Poland, Mexico, Brazil, and Argentina had all missed scheduled debt payments. The article described the existing fear that a major default could result in widespread political and economic consequences.

At the time of the article, the Allowance for Possible Credit Losses reported by the major U.S. banks totaled less than ten percent of their questionable foreign loans. As time went by, it became clear that allowances of this magnitude were not enough. The major U.S. banks made significant increases in their allowances in 1987. Citicorp, for example, more than tripled its usual allowance addition with an extra $3 billion related to its at-risk foreign loans. This move caused Citicorp to show a loss for the year, and increased the allowance related to these foreign loans to 26 percent of the loan amounts.

These large additions to the banks' loan loss allowances in 1987 were a major step in defusing the foreign debt crisis. The move seemed to some like just the accounting recognition of what was already known—that a large percentage of the debts would never be repaid. However, the "reserve action," as it was called, noticeably increased the flexibility of banks in negotiations since they had now explicitly acknowledged that they weren't ever going to receive the entire amount of the loans.

Two approaches to debt reduction that have been tried are debt-for-equity swaps and loan-to-bond swaps. In the debt-for-equity swaps, banks exchange their rights under the loans receivable contract for ownership interest in various enterprises in the borrowing country. The loan-to-bond swaps involve banks accepting bonds in exchange for the amounts due on the loans. The bonds often have the same face, or principal, amount as the loans, but the interest rate is reduced. Banks are also selling some of their foreign loans receivable to other lenders. In 1988, Citicorp sold $1 billion of its foreign loans for approximately 73 percent of their face value.

Just as the foreign debt crisis was the major story for U.S. banks in the 1980s, the continuing savings and loan mess will probably be the story of the 1990s. And, as with the foreign debt, the ultimate solution will not be a quick one, but will involve patient compromise over an extended period.

### Questions:

1. *How did banks' large additions to loan loss allowances help ease the foreign debt crisis?*
2. *What is a "debt-for-equity swap?" How can debt-for-equity swaps ease a debt crisis?*

Sources:

Jay Palmer, "The Debt-Bomb Threat," *Time*, January 10, 1983, p. 42.

*Citicorp* 1988 Annual Report.

lectible accounts may impact the reporting of cash flows, depending on whether the direct or indirect method is used and whether the analysis considers *gross* or *net* accounts receivable balances.

Since working with *net* accounts receivable changes is much easier for the indirect method and at least as good for the direct method, that is the approach used in this text. The amount of net change in receivables will always be determinable, either because that is how the receivables are reported in the financial statements or by simply subtracting the appropriate allowance accounts from the *gross* accounts receivable balances.

If the indirect method is used and the receivable balances are reported *net* of the allowance for doubtful accounts, which is the most common situation, any bad debt expense and any write-offs of uncollectible accounts may be ignored. Both the write-off and the estimated bad debt expense have already been netted against the receivable balances.

Similarly, if the direct method is used to compute cash flow from operations and the receivable balances are considered "net," any write-offs of uncollectible accounts can be ignored. The write-off reduces both the allowance account and the receivable account and thus leaves the net balance unchanged. However, with the direct method, sales would have to be reduced by the amount of the bad debt expense for the period to determine cash collected from customers. This is because the bad debt provision reduces the net receivable balance but does not generate any cash.

To illustrate, assume the following data:

|  | Beginning Balances | Ending Balances |
|---|---|---|
| Accounts receivable | $20,000 | $25,000 |
| Allowance for doubtful accounts | 4,000 | 5,000 |
| Net accounts receivable | $16,000 | $20,000 |
| | | |
| Sales for the year | | $1,000,000 |
| Net income for the year | | 100,000 |
| Bad debt expense for the year | | 2,000 |
| Write-off of uncollectible amounts for the year | | 1,000 |
| Cash expenses for the year | | 898,000 |

In order to focus on the impact of uncollectible accounts, the illustration assumes that all operating expenses other than bad debt expense were paid in cash. Also, it is assumed that, with the exception of accounts receivable, there were no changes in the levels of current assets and current liabilities.

Using the above data, the net cash flow provided by operations during the period would be computed as follows:

### Direct Method

| | |
|---|---|
| Sales | $1,000,000 |
| Less:  Net increase in accounts receivable | (4,000) |
| Bad debt expense | (2,000) |
| Cash collected from customers | $ 994,000 |
| Cash expenses | (898,000) |
| Net cash flow provided by operations | $   96,000 |

### Indirect Method

| | |
|---|---|
| Net income | $100,000 |
| Less net increase in accounts receivable | (4,000) |
| Net cash flow provided by operations | $ 96,000 |

The above discussion is summarized in Exhibit 9—1 on page 316.

**Discounts**    Many companies bill their customers at a gross sales price less an amount designated as a *trade discount*. The discount may vary by customer depending on the

**Exhibit 9—1    Guidelines for Considering the Impact of Uncollectible Accounts on the Statement of Cash Flows**

Adjustments with *net* receivable balances:

| Direct Approach | Indirect Approach |
| --- | --- |
| —Adjust for bad debt expense<br>—Ignore write-offs of uncollectible accounts | —Ignore bad debt expense<br>—Ignore write-offs of uncollectible accounts |

volume of business or size of order from the customer. In effect, the trade discount reduces the "list" sales price to the "net" sales price actually charged the customer. This net price is the amount at which the receivable and corresponding revenue should be recorded.

Another type of discount is a **cash discount** or **sales discount** offered to customers by some companies to encourage prompt payment of bills. Cash discounts may be taken by the customer only if payment is made within a specified period of time, generally thirty days or less. Receivables are generally recorded at their gross amounts, without regard to any cash discount offered. If payment is received within the discount period, Sales Discounts (a contra account to Sales) is debited for the difference between the recorded amount of the receivable and the total cash collected. This method, which is simple and widely used, is illustrated below with credit terms of "2/10, n/30" (2% discount if paid within 10 days, net amount due in 30 days).

### Cash Discounts—Gross Method

Sales of $1,000; terms 2/10, n/30:

| | | |
| --- | --- | --- |
| Accounts Receivable | 1,000 | |
|     Sales | | 1,000 |

Payments of $300 received within discount period:

| | | |
| --- | --- | --- |
| Cash | 294 | |
| Sales Discounts | 6 | |
|     Accounts Receivable | | 300 |

Payments of $700 received after discount period:

| | | |
| --- | --- | --- |
| Cash | 700 | |
|     Accounts Receivable | | 700 |

**Sales Returns and Allowances**    In the normal course of business, some goods will be returned by customers and some allowances will have to be made for such factors as goods damaged during shipment, spoiled or otherwise defective goods, or shipment of an incorrect quantity or type of goods. When goods are returned or an allowance is necessary, net sales and accounts receivable are reduced. To illustrate, assume merchandise costing $1,000 is sold and later returned. The return would be recorded in the following manner:

| | | |
| --- | --- | --- |
| Sales Returns and Allowances | 1,000 | |
|     Accounts Receivable | | 1,000 |

While the charge could be made directly to Sales, the use of a separate contra account preserves information that may be useful to management.

## Accounts Receivable as a Source of Cash

Accounts receivable are a part of the normal operating cycle of a business. Cash is used to purchase inventory, which in turn is often sold on account. The receivables are then collected, providing cash to start the cycle over. Frequently the operating cycle takes several months to complete. Sometimes companies need immediate cash and cannot wait for completion of the normal cycle. At other times companies are not in financial stress but want to accelerate the receivable collection process, shift the risk of credit and the effort of collection to someone else, or merely use receivables from customers as a source of financing.

Receivables financing was once looked upon as a desperate measure. In recent years, however, receivables financing has become quite popular for financing leveraged buyouts and for business expansion. As one executive put it, "receivables financing is no longer viewed as last-resort financing but as a legitimate business tool."[4]

Accounts receivable may be converted to cash in one of three ways: (1) **assignment of receivables**, which is a borrowing arrangement with receivables pledged as security on the loan; (2) **factoring receivables**, which is a sale of receivables without recourse for cash to a third party, usually a bank or other financial institution; and (3) the **transfer of receivables with recourse**, which is a hybrid of the other two forms of receivables financing.

**Assignment of Accounts Receivable**    Loans are frequently obtained from banks or other lending institutions by assigning or pledging accounts receivable as security. The loan is evidenced by a written promissory note that provides for either a general assignment of receivables or an assignment of specific receivables.

With a **general assignment**, all accounts receivable serve as collateral on the note. There are no special accounting problems involved. The books simply report the loan (a debit to Cash and a credit to Notes Payable) and subsequent settlement of the obligation (a debit to Notes Payable and a credit to Cash). However, disclosure should be made on the balance sheet, by a parenthetical comment or a note, of the amount and nature of receivables pledged to secure the obligation to the lender.

When there is an **assignment of specific receivables** to a lender, the borrower should transfer the balance of those accounts to a special general ledger control account and clearly identify and account for the individual assigned accounts in the subsidiary ledger. The procedures involved are illustrated in the following example. It is assumed that the assignor (the borrower) collects the receivables, which is often the case.

On July 1, 1993, Provo Mercantile Co. assigns specific receivables totaling $300,000 to Salem Bank as collateral on a $200,000, 12% note. Provo Mercantile does not notify its account debtors and will continue to collect the assigned receivables. Salem assesses a 1% finance charge on assigned receivables in addition to the interest on the note. Provo is to make monthly payments to Salem with cash collected on assigned receivables. The entries on the following page would be made.

If in the preceding example Salem Bank assumes responsibility for collecting the assigned receivables, the account debtors would have to be notified to make their payments to the bank. Salem would then use a liability account (e.g., Payable to Provo Mercantile) to account for cash collections during the period. Since the receivables are still owned by Provo Mercantile, the bank would not record them as assets. Upon full

---

[4]See "Factoring: A Flexible Borrowing Tool," *Small Business Report* (March 1987), p. 50.

## Illustrative Entries for Assignment of Specific Receivables

| Provo Mercantile Co. | Salem Bank |
|---|---|

Issuance of note and assignment of specific receivables on July 1, 1993:

| Cash ................ | 197,000 | | Notes Receivable ...... | 200,000 | |
|---|---|---|---|---|---|
| Finance Charge* ...... | 3,000 | | Finance Revenue* ... | | 3,000 |
| Accounts Receivable— | | | Cash .............. | | 197,000 |
| Assigned ............. | 300,000 | | | | |
|    Notes Payable ...... | | 200,000 | | | |
|    Accounts Receivable | | 300,000 | | | |

*(1% × $300,000)

Collections of assigned accounts during July, $180,000 less cash discounts of $1,000; sales returns in July, $2,000:

| Cash ................ | 179,000 | | |
|---|---|---|---|
| Sales Discounts ....... | 1,000 | | (No Entry) |
| Sales Returns ......... | 2,000 | | |
|    Accounts Receiv- | | | |
|    able—Assigned ..... | | 182,000 | |

Paid Salem Bank amounts owed for July collections plus accrued interest on note to August 1:

| Interest Expense* ..... | 2,000 | | Cash ................ | 181,000 | |
|---|---|---|---|---|---|
| Notes Payable ........ | 179,000 | |    Interest Revenue .... | | 2,000 |
|    Cash .............. | | 181,000 |    Notes Receivable .... | | 179,000 |

*($200,000 × .12 × 1/12)

Collections of remaining assigned accounts during August less $800 written off as uncollectible:

| Cash ................ | 117,200 | | (No Entry) |
|---|---|---|---|
| Allowance for Doubt- | | | |
| ful Accounts .......... | 800 | | |
|    Accounts Receiv- | | | |
|    able—Assigned* .... | | 118,000 | |

*($300,000 − $182,000)

Paid Salem Bank remaining balance owed plus accrued interest on note to September 1:

| Interest Expense* ..... | 210 | | Cash ................ | 21,210 | |
|---|---|---|---|---|---|
| Notes Payable** ...... | 21,000 | |    Interest Revenue* | | 210 |
|    Cash .............. | | 21,210 |    Notes Receivable**... | | 21,000 |

*($21,000 × .12 × 1/12)
**($200,000 − $179,000)

payment of the note plus interest, the bank would remit to Provo Mercantile any cash collections in excess of the note along with any uncollected accounts.

In disclosing the specifically assigned accounts receivable, Provo Mercantile should report them separately as a current asset if they are material. In addition, the equity in assigned accounts should be disclosed parenthetically or in a note. For example, on July 1, Provo Mercantile had $100,000 equity in its assigned receivables ($300,000 − $200,000).

**Factoring Accounts Receivable**    Certain banks, dealers, and finance companies purchase accounts receivable outright on a nonrecourse basis. A **sale of accounts receivable without recourse**[5] is commonly referred to as accounts receivable **factoring**, and the buyer is referred to as a "factor." Customers are usually notified that their bills are payable to the factor, and this party assumes the burden of billing and collecting accounts. The flow of activities involved in factoring is presented in Exhibit 9—2.

**Exhibit 9—2    Flow of Activities Involved in Factoring**

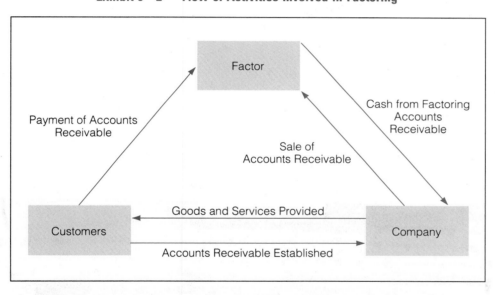

In many cases, factoring involves more than the purchase and collection of accounts receivable. Factoring frequently involves a continuing agreement whereby a financing institution assumes the credit function as well as the collection function. Under such an arrangement, the factor grants or denies credit, handles the accounts receivable records, bills customers, and makes collections. The business unit is relieved of all these activities, and the sale of goods provides immediate cash for business use. Because the factor absorbs the losses from bad accounts and frequently assumes credit and collection responsibilities, the charges associated with factoring generally exceed the interest charges on a loan with an assignment of receivables. Typically the factor will charge a fee of 10% to 30% of the net amount of receivables purchased, except for credit card factoring where the rate is 3%

---

[5]Recourse is defined by the FASB as "the right of a transferee of receivables to receive payment from the transferor of those receivables for (a) failure of the debtors to pay when due, (b) the effects of prepayments, or (c) adjustments resulting from defects in the eligibility of the transferred receivables." *Statement of Financial Accounting Standards No. 77*, "Reporting by Transferors for Transfers of Receivables with Recourse" (December 1983), p. 7.

to 5%. The factor may withhold a portion of the purchase price for possible future charges for customer returns and allowances or other special adjustments. Final settlement is made after receivables have been collected.

When receivables are sold outright, without recourse, Cash is debited, receivables and related allowance balances are closed, and an expense account is debited for factoring charges. When part of the purchase price is withheld by the factor, a receivable from the factor is established pending final settlement. Upon receipt of the total purchase price from the bank or finance company, the factor receivable account is eliminated. To illustrate, assume that $10,000 of receivables are factored, i.e., sold without recourse, to a finance company for $8,500. An allowance for doubtful accounts equal to $300 was previously established for these accounts. This amount will need to be written off along with the accounts receivable being sold. The finance company withheld 5% of the purchase price as protection against sales returns and allowances. The entry to record the sale of the accounts would be:

| | | |
|---|---|---|
| Cash .................................................. | 8,075 | |
| Receivable From Factor ....................................... | 425 | |
| Allowance for Doubtful Accounts ............................ | 300 | |
| Loss From Factoring Receivables ............................ | 1,200 | |
|     Accounts Receivable ....................................... | | 10,000 |

Computations:
Cash = $8,500 − $425 = $8,075;
Factor receivable = $8,500 × 5% = $425;
Factoring loss = ($10,000 − $300) − $8,500 = $1,200

Assuming there were no returns or allowances, the final settlement would be recorded as follows:

| | | |
|---|---|---|
| Cash .................................................. | 425 | |
|     Receivable From Factor ..................................... | | 425 |

**Transfer of Accounts Receivable With Recourse**     The third way that cash can be obtained from accounts receivable financing is by **transferring accounts receivable with recourse**. This is different from factoring, which generally is on a nonrecourse basis. Transferring with recourse means that a transferee (bank or finance company) advances cash in return for accounts receivable, but retains the right to collect from the transferor if debtors (transferor's customers) fail to make payments when due. An important accounting question is whether this type of transaction is a **borrowing transaction** (like an assignment with the receivables as collateral) or a **sale transaction** (like a factoring arrangement). If viewed as a borrowing transaction, a liability should be reported and the difference between the proceeds received and the net receivables transferred is a financing cost (interest). If viewed as a sale, the difference between the amount received from the finance company (the transfer price) and the net amount of the receivables transferred (the gross amount of the receivables adjusted for allowance for doubtful accounts and any finance and service charges) is to be recognized as a gain or loss on the sale, as illustrated previously in the factoring example.

The FASB in Statement No. 77 has concluded that a transfer of receivables with recourse should be accounted for and reported as a sale if all the following conditions are met:

1. The transferor surrenders control of the future economic benefit embodied in the receivables.

2. The transferor's obligation under the recourse provisions can be reasonably estimated.

3. The transferee cannot require the transferor to repurchase the receivables except pursuant to the recourse provisions.[6]

If these conditions are not met, the transfer is reported as a secured loan, i.e., in the same manner as an assignment of receivables discussed previously.

In summary, accounts receivable provide an important source of cash for many companies. The transfer of receivables to third parties in return for cash generally takes the form of an assignment (borrowing with the receivables pledged as collateral) or factoring (a sale without recourse). The financing arrangements are often complex and may involve a transfer of receivables on a recourse basis. Each transaction must be analyzed carefully to see if in form and substance it is a borrowing transaction or a sale transaction, and treated accordingly.

## NOTES RECEIVABLE

A promissory note is an unconditional written promise to pay a certain sum of money at a specified time. The note is signed by the **maker** and is payable to the order of a specified payee or to bearer. Notes usually involve interest, stated at an annual rate and charged on the face amount of the note. Most notes are negotiable notes that are legally transferable by endorsement and delivery.

For reporting purposes, **trade notes receivable** should include only negotiable short-term instruments acquired from trade debtors and not yet due. Trade notes generally arise from sales involving relatively high dollar amounts where the buyer wants to extend payment beyond the usual trade credit period of 30 to 90 days. Also, sellers sometimes request notes from customers whose accounts receivable are past due. Most companies, however, have relatively few trade notes receivable.

**Nontrade notes receivable** should be separately designated on the balance sheet under an appropriate title. For example, notes arising from loans to customers, officers, employees, and affiliated companies should be reported separately from trade notes.

### Valuation of Notes Receivable

Notes receivable are initially recorded at their present value, which may be defined as the sum of future receipts discounted to the present date at an appropriate rate of interest.[7] In a lending transaction, the present value is the amount of cash received by the borrower. When a note is exchanged for property, goods, or services, the present value equals the current cash selling price of the items exchanged. The difference between the present value and the amount to be collected at the due date or maturity date is a charge for interest.

All notes arising in arm's-length transactions between unrelated parties involve an element of interest. However, a distinction as to form is made between interest-bearing and non-interest-bearing notes. An interest-bearing note is written as a promise to pay principal (or face amount) plus interest at a specified rate. In the absence of special valuation problems discussed in the next section, the face amount of an interest-bearing note is the present value upon issuance of the note.

A non-interest-bearing note does not specify an interest rate, but the face amount includes the interest charge. Thus, the present value is the difference between the face

---

[6]*Statement of Financial Accounting Standards No. 77,* "Reporting by Transferors of Transfers of Receivables with Recourse" (December 1983), par. 5.

[7]See Chapter 7 for a discussion of present-value concepts and applications.

amount and the interest included in that amount, sometimes called the implicit (or effective) interest.

In recording receipt of a note, Notes Receivable is debited for the face amount of the note. When the face amount differs from the present value, as is the case with non-interest-bearing notes, the difference is recorded as a premium or discount and amortized over the life of the note. In the example to follow, a note receivable is established with credits to Sales and a discount on notes receivable account. The amount of discount is the implicit interest on the note and will be recognized as interest revenue as the note matures.

To illustrate, assume that High Value Corporation sells goods on January 1, 1993, with a price of $1,000. The buyer gives High Value a promissory note due December 31, 1994. The maturity value of the note includes interest at 10%. Thus, High Value will receive $1,210 ($1,000 × 1.21)[8] when the note is paid. The following entries show the accounting procedures for an interest-bearing note and one written in a non-interest-bearing form.

### Illustrative Entries for Notes

| Interest-Bearing Note<br>Face Amount = Present Value = $1,000<br>Stated Interest Rate = 10% | Non-Interest-Bearing Note<br>Face Amount = Maturity = $1,210<br>No Stated Interest Rate |
|---|---|

To record note received in exchange for goods selling for $1,000:

| 1993 | | | | | | |
|---|---|---|---|---|---|---|
| Jan. 1 | Notes Receivable ...... | 1,000 | | Notes Receivable...... | 1,210 | |
| | Sales .............. | | 1,000 | Sales............... | | 1,000 |
| | | | | Discount on Notes | | |
| | | | | Receivable.......... | | 210 |

To recognize interest earned for one year, $1,000 × .10:

| Dec. 31 | Interest Receivable ... | 100 | | Discount on Notes Re- | | |
|---|---|---|---|---|---|---|
| | Interest Revenue ... | | 100 | ceivable ............ | 100 | |
| | | | | Interest Revenue ... | | 100 |

To record settlement of note at maturity and recognize interest earned for one year; ($1,000 + $100) × .10:

| 1994 | | | | | | |
|---|---|---|---|---|---|---|
| Dec. 31 | Cash ............... | 1,210 | | Cash ............... | 1,210 | |
| | Notes Receivable ... | | 1,000 | Discount on Notes | | |
| | Interest Receivable .. | | 100 | Receivable.......... | 110 | |
| | Interest Revenue ... | | 110 | Notes Receivable... | | 1,210 |
| | | | | Interest Revenue ... | | 110 |

At December 31, 1993, the unamortized discount of $110 on the non-interest-bearing note would be deducted from notes receivable on the balance sheet. If the non-interest-

[8]The amount of $1 due in two years at an annual rate of 10% is $1.21. See Table I, Chapter 7.

bearing note were recorded at face value with no recognition of the interest included therein, the sales price and profit to the seller would be overstated. In subsequent periods interest revenue would be understated. Failure to record the discount would also result in an overstatement of assets.

Although the proper valuation of receivables calls for the amortization procedure just described, exceptions may be appropriate in some situations due to special limitations or practical considerations. The Accounting Principles Board in Opinion No. 21 provided guidelines for the recognition of interest on receivables and payables and the accounting subsequently to be employed. However, the board indicated that this process is not to be regarded as applicable under all circumstances. Among the exceptions are the following:

> . . . receivables and payables arising from transactions with customers or suppliers in the normal course of business which are due in customary trade terms not exceeding approximately one year.[9]

Accordingly, as mentioned earlier, short-term notes and accounts receivable arising from trade sales may be properly recorded at the amounts collectible in the customary sales terms.

Notes, like accounts receivable, are not always collectible. If notes receivable comprise a significant portion of regular trade receivables, a provision should be made for uncollectible amounts and an allowance account established using procedures similar to those for accounts receivable already discussed.

**Special Valuation Problems**    APB Opinion No. 21 was issued to clarify and refine existing accounting practice with respect to receivables and payables. The opinion is especially applicable to nontrade, long-term notes, such as secured and unsecured notes, debentures (bonds), equipment obligations, and mortgage notes. Examples are provided for notes exchanged for cash and for property, goods, or services.

***Notes Exchanged for Cash***    When a note is exchanged for cash, and there are no other rights or privileges involved, the present value of the note is presumed to be the amount of the cash proceeds. The note should be recorded at its face amount and any difference between the face amount and the cash proceeds should be recorded as a premium or discount on the note. The premium or discount should be amortized over the life of the note as illustrated previously for High Value Corporation. The total interest is measured by the difference in actual cash received by the borrower and the total amount to be received in the future by the lender. Any unamortized premium or discount on notes is reported on the balance sheet as a direct addition to or deduction from the face amount of the receivables, thus showing their net present value.

***Notes Exchanged for Property, Goods, or Services***    When a note is exchanged for property, goods, or services in an arm's-length transaction, the present value of the note is usually evidenced by the terms of the note or supporting documents. There is a general presumption that the interest specified by the parties to a transaction represents fair and adequate compensation for the use of borrowed funds.[10] Valuation problems arise, however, when one of the following conditions exists:[11]

---

[9]*Opinions of the Accounting Principles Board, No. 21,* "Interest on Receivables and Payables" (New York: American Institute of Certified Public Accountants, 1971), par. 3(a).

[10]*Ibid.,* par. 12.

[11]*Ibid.*

1. No interest rate is stated.
2. The stated rate does not seem reasonable, given the nature of the transaction and surrounding circumstances.
3. The stated face amount of the note is significantly different from the current cash equivalent sales price of similar property, goods, or services, or from the current market value of similar notes at the date of the transaction.

Under any of the preceding conditions, APB No. 21 requires accounting recognition of the economic substance of the transaction rather than the form of the note. The note should be recorded at (1) the fair market value of the property, goods, or services exchanged or (2) the current market value of the note, whichever is more clearly determinable. The difference between the face amount of the note and the present value is recognized as a discount or premium and amortized over the life of the note.

To illustrate, assume that on July 1, 1993, Timberline Corporation sells a tract of land purchased three years ago at a cost of $250,000. The buyer gives Timberline a 1-year note with a face amount of $310,000 bearing interest at a stated rate of 8%. An appraisal of the land prior to the sale indicated a market value of $300,000, which in this example is considered to be the appropriate basis for recording the sale as follows:

```
1993
July 1   Notes Receivable ...............................   310,000
             Discount on Notes Receivable...................            10,000
             Land...........................................           250,000
             Gain on Sale of Land ..........................            50,000
```

When the note is paid at maturity, Timberline will receive the face value ($310,000) plus stated interest of $24,800 ($310,000 × .08), or a total of $334,800. The interest to be recognized, however, is $34,800—the difference between the maturity value of the note and the market value of the land at the date of the exchange. Thus the effective rate of interest on the note is 11.6% ($34,800 ÷ $300,000).

Assuming straight-line amortization of the discount and that Timberline's year-end is December 31, the following entries would be made to recognize interest revenue and to record payment of the note at maturity:

```
1993
Dec. 31   Interest Receivable .............................   12,400*
          Discount on Notes Receivable ...................    5,000
              Interest Revenue ..............................            17,400

          *$310,000 × .08 × 6/12 = $12,400


1994
June 30   Cash ...........................................   334,800
          Discount on Notes Receivable ...................    5,000
              Notes Receivable..............................           310,000
              Interest Receivable ..........................            12,400
              Interest Revenue .............................            17,400
```

The unamortized discount balance of $5,000 would be subtracted from Notes Receivable on the December 31, 1993, balance sheet.

**Imputing an Interest Rate**   If there is no current market price for either the property, goods or services, or the note, then the present value of the note must be determined by selecting an appropriate interest rate and using that rate to discount future receipts to the present. The imputed interest rate is determined at the date of the exchange and is not altered thereafter.

The selection of an appropriate rate is influenced by many factors, including the credit standing of the issuer of the note and prevailing interest rates for debt instruments of similar quality and length of time to maturity. APB Opinion No. 21 states:

> In any event, the rate used for valuation purposes will normally be at least equal to the rate at which the debtor can obtain financing of a similar nature from other sources at the date of the transaction. The objective is to approximate the rate which would have resulted if an independent borrower and an independent lender had negotiated a similar transaction under comparable terms and conditions with the option to pay the cash price upon purchase or to give a note for the amount of the purchase which bears the prevailing rate of interest to maturity.[12]

To illustrate the process of imputing interest rates, assume that Horrocks & Associates surveyed 800,000 acres of mountain property for the Mountain Meadow Ranch. On December 31, 1993, Horrocks accepted a $45,000 note as payment for services. The note is non-interest-bearing and comes due in three yearly installments of $15,000 each beginning December 31, 1994. Assume there is no market for the note and no basis for estimating objectively the fair market value of the services rendered. After considering the current prime interest rate, the credit standing of the ranch, the collateral available, the terms for repayment, and the prevailing rates of interest for the issuer's other debt, a 10% imputed interest rate is considered appropriate. The note should be recorded at its present value and a discount recognized. The computation is based on Present Value Table IV, Chapter 7, as follows:

| | |
|---|---:|
| Face amount of note . . . . . . . . . . . . . . . . . . . . . . . . . . . . . . . . . . . . . . . . . . . . . . . | $45,000 |
| Less present value of note: | |
| $PV_n = R(PVAF_{\overline{3}\rceil 10\%})$ | |
| $PV_n = \$15,000(2.4869)$ . . . . . . . . . . . . . . . . . . . . . . . . . . . . . . . . . . . . . . . . . . | 37,303* |
| Discount on note . . . . . . . . . . . . . . . . . . . . . . . . . . . . . . . . . . . . . . . . . . . . . . . . . | $ 7,697 |

*Rounded to nearest dollar.

The entry to record the receipt of the note would be:

| 1993 | | | |
|---|---|---:|---:|
| Dec. 31 | Notes Receivable . . . . . . . . . . . . . . . . . . . . . . . . . . . . . . . . . . . | 45,000 | |
| | Discount on Notes Receivable. . . . . . . . . . . . . . . . . . . . . | | 7,697 |
| | Service Revenue . . . . . . . . . . . . . . . . . . . . . . . . . . . . . . . . | | 37,303 |
| | *To record a non-interest-bearing note receivable at its present value based on an imputed interest rate of 10% per year.* | | |

A schedule showing the amortization of the discount on the note is presented below. This type of computation is commonly referred to as the effective interest amortization method.

| | (1)<br>Face Amount<br>Before<br>Current<br>Installment | (2)<br>Unamortized<br>Discount | (3)<br>Net<br>Amount<br>(1) − (2) | (4)<br>Discount<br>Amortization<br>10% × (3) | (5)<br>Payment<br>Received |
|---|---:|---:|---:|---:|---:|
| Dec. 31, 1994 | $45,000 | $7,697 | $37,303 | $3,730 | $15,000 |
| Dec. 31, 1995 | 30,000 | 3,967* | 26,033 | 2,603 | 15,000 |
| Dec. 31, 1996 | 15,000 | 1,364** | 13,636 | 1,364 | 15,000 |
| | | | | $7,697 | $45,000 |

*$7,697 − $3,730 = $3,967
**$3,967 − $2,603 = $1,364

[12]*Ibid.,* par. 13.

At the end of each year, an entry similar to the following would be made:

```
1994
Dec. 31  Cash .........................................  15,000
         Discount on Notes Receivable ....................  3,730
            Interest Revenue................................            3,730
            Notes Receivable ...............................           15,000
            To record the first year's installment on notes re-
            ceivable and recognize interest earned during the
            period.
```

By using these procedures, at the end of the three years the discount will be completely amortized to interest revenue, the face amount of the note receivable will have been collected, and the appropriate amount of service revenue will have been recognized in the year it was earned. At the end of each year, the balance sheet will reflect the net present value of the receivable by subtracting the unamortized discount balance from the outstanding balance in Notes Receivable.

It is necessary to impute an interest rate only when the present value of the receivable cannot be determined through evaluation of existing market values of the elements of the transaction. The valuation and income measurement objectives remain the same regardless of the specific circumstances—to report notes receivable at their net present values and to record appropriate amounts of interest revenue during the collection period of the receivables.

## Notes Receivable as a Source of Cash

As discussed earlier in the chapter, accounts receivable can be a source of immediate cash. A company can also obtain cash by "discounting" notes receivable. The discounting of notes receivable, sometimes called bank discounting, is not to be confused with the discounting of future cash receipts to arrive at present value or with the discount deducted from Notes Receivable on the balance sheet as discussed previously. **Bank discounting** involves the transfer of negotiable notes to a bank or other financial institution willing to exchange such instruments for cash.

When discounting an interest-bearing note, which is the usual situation, the following steps are taken to determine the amount to be received from the bank (the proceeds):[13]

1.  Determine the maturity value of the note:

    Maturity value = Face amount + Interest
    Interest = Face amount × Interest rate × Interest period
    Interest period = Date of note to date of maturity

2.  Determine the amount of discount:

    Discount = Maturity value × Discount rate × Discount period
    Discount period = Date of discount to date of maturity

3.  Determine the proceeds:

    Proceeds = Maturity value − Discount

[13]The same procedures apply to the discounting of a non-interest-bearing note, except that the maturity value does not have to be computed (Step 1), since the face amount equals the maturity value.

Once the proceeds are determined, the transaction can be recorded, recognizing the applicable liability and net interest revenue or expense (if a borrowing transaction) or the gain or loss (if a sale transaction).

If a note is transferred **without recourse**, i.e., the bank assumes the risk of uncollectibility, the transaction should be recorded as a sale, much like the factoring of accounts receivable discussed earlier. If the note is transferred **with recourse**, which is the usual case, the discounting transaction may be recorded as a sale or a borrowing transaction, depending on the terms and conditions. The criteria for classifying a transfer of accounts receivable with recourse, set forth in FASB Statement No. 77 and presented on page 320, also apply to transfers of notes receivable with recourse.

To illustrate the recording of a transfer (discounting) of notes receivable with recourse, assume that Meeker Corporation received a 90-day, $5,000, 10% note from a customer on September 1 to settle a past-due account receivable. The note is discounted at a bank after 10 days at a discount rate of 15%. The transaction would be treated as a sale only if the FASB Statement No. 77 criteria are met. Otherwise, the transfer is recorded as a borrowing transaction. In this example (and in the end-of-chapter material), a 365-day year is assumed, because that is what most financial institutions use. In some applications and in some textbooks, a 360-day year is assumed in order to simplify the computations. Journal entries for both a sale and borrowing transaction are shown on page 328.

Several important points can be observed in the example. First, the loss or net interest expense recognized at the date of discounting ($45) is the difference between the amount charged by the bank to discount the note (in effect, interest expense of $168) and the amount of interest revenue the company would have earned if it had held the note to maturity ($123). Alternatively, the loss or net interest expense is the difference between the face amount of the note ($5,000) and the proceeds received from the bank ($4,955). Depending on how long the note is held prior to discounting and on the difference between the interest rate on the note and the discount rate charged by the bank, it is possible for the proceeds to be greater than the face amount of the note, which would result in a gain or net interest revenue being recorded. For example, if the Meeker Corporation had held the note for 60 days prior to discounting, the entries to record the discounting would be:

| Transaction Recorded as Sale | | | Transaction Recorded as Borrowing | | |
|---|---|---|---|---|---|
| Cash . . . . . . . . . . . . . . . . . . . . | 5,060 | | Cash . . . . . . . . . . . . . . . . . . | 5,060 | |
| Gain on Sale of Note . . . | | 60 | Interest Revenue . . . . . . | | 60 |
| Notes Receivable. . . . . . . | | 5,000 | Obligation on Discounted Notes Receivable . . . . . . . . . . . . . | | 5,000 |

Computations (rounded to nearest dollar):
Maturity value (same) = $5,123
Discount = $5,123 × .15 × $\frac{30}{365}$ = $63
Proceeds = $5,123 − $63 = $5,060
Gain/Interest Revenue = $123 − $63 = $60

As indicated in the Meeker example, when a note is discounted with recourse, the bank will require payment from the company that discounted the note if the maker of the note defaults on payment at maturity (often referred to as **dishonoring** the note). In addition, the bank generally will charge a protest fee, which in the example is $25. Subsequently, the company will attempt to collect from the customer and, if unsuccessful, will eventually write off the note as uncollectible.

### Discounting Notes Receivable With Recourse

| Transaction Recorded as Sale | Transaction Recorded as Borrowing |
|---|---|

Received a 90-day, $5,000, 10% note from a customer on September 1:

| | | | | | |
|---|---|---|---|---|---|
| Notes Receivable......... | 5,000 | | Notes Receivable ........ | 5,000 | |
| Accounts Receivable ... | | 5,000 | Accounts Receivable ... | | 5,000 |

Discounted customer's note at bank on September 11 at a discount rate of 15%:

| | | | | | |
|---|---|---|---|---|---|
| Cash .................... | 4,955 | | Cash .................... | 4,955 | |
| Loss on Sale of Note ..... | 45 | | Interest Expense......... | 45 | |
| Notes Receivable....... | | 5,000 | Obligation on Discoun- ted Notes Receivable .. | | 5,000 |

Computations (rounded to nearest dollar):
  Maturity value = $5,000 + Interest ($5,000 × .10 × $^{90}\!/_{365}$ = $123) = $5,123
  Discount = $5,123 × .15 × $^{80}\!/_{365}$ = $168
  Proceeds = $5,123 − $168 = $4,955
  Loss/Interest Expense = $168 − $123 = $45

If maturity value of note paid to bank by customer on due date, November 30:

| | | | |
|---|---|---|---|
| (No entry) | Obligation on Discounted Notes Receivable......... | 5,000 | |
| | Notes Receivable ...... | | 5,000 |

If customer defaults and bank collects from Meeker Corporation on November 30 the maturity value ($5,123) plus a $25 protest fee:

| | | | | | |
|---|---|---|---|---|---|
| Notes Receivable—Past Due .................... | 5,148 | | Notes Receivable—Past Due .................... | 5,148 | |
| Cash ................. | | 5,148 | Cash ................. | | 5,148 |
| | | | Obligation on Discounted Notes Receivable...........5,000 | | |
| | | | Notes Receivable ...... | | 5,000 |

If the note had been discounted without recourse, the transaction would have been recorded in exactly the same manner as shown for a sale in the example. However, no entries would be required after the discounting transaction is recorded on September 11, since the company has no liability with regard to the note after the transfer.

## PRESENTATION OF RECEIVABLES ON THE BALANCE SHEET

The receivables qualifying as current items may be grouped for presentation on the balance sheet in the following classes: (1) notes receivable—trade debtors, (2) accounts receivable—trade debtors, and (3) other receivables. Alternatively, trade notes and accounts receivable can be reported as a single amount. The detail reported for other

## ZZZZ Best

Barry Minkow started operating his carpet-cleaning business out of the Minkow family garage when he was 15. At its peak six years later, the company, called ZZZZ Best, had a market value of $211 million. On paper, Minkow himself was worth $109 million. Minkow was a celebrity. In February 1987, he was selected as one of the top 100 young entrepreneurs in the United States. He spoke of making ZZZZ Best the General Motors of carpet cleaning. He talked of running for president one day. But, in a press release dated July 3, 1987, ZZZZ Best announced that Minkow had resigned as chief executive officer because of a "severe medical problem." Shortly thereafter, ZZZZ Best filed for Chapter 11 bankruptcy. The rapid growth of ZZZZ Best had been a fraud, and Barry Minkow was eventually sentenced to 25 years in prison.

The major aspect of the fraud involved reporting fictitious receivables and revenue from fire damage restoration jobs. For example, ZZZZ Best filed a registration statement with the SEC in 1985 in which it claimed to have a contract for a $2.3 million restoration job on an eight-story building in Arroyo Grande, California. Unfortunately, Arroyo Grande, a town of 13,000 people and five traffic lights, had no buildings over three stories. On May 19, 1987, *The Wall Street Journal* reported that ZZZZ Best had received a $13.8 million restoration contract for a Dallas job. Again, the job was nonexistent. With bogus revenue and receivables like this, ZZZZ Best was able to report net income for the year ended April 30, 1987, of $5 million on revenue of $50 million, up from $900,000 net income on $4.8 million revenue the year before.

Why didn't the auditor uncover these irregularities? Larry Gray, the partner in charge of auditing ZZZZ Best, did what he was supposed to, but in this case he didn't do it well enough. When ZZZZ Best reported a $7 million contract to restore a building in Sacramento, Gray demanded to see the building. This was difficult since neither the building nor the job existed. However, officials of ZZZZ Best managed to get access to a large office building in Sacramento for a weekend, and Gray was allowed to tour the building to inspect the "finished work." On another occasion, ZZZZ Best reported an $8.2 million restoration contract in San Diego. Again, Gray demanded to see the job site. This time he was led through an unfinished building and told that the work was still ongoing. Things got very complicated for ZZZZ Best when Gray later requested to see the finished job. ZZZZ Best had to spend $1 million to lease the building and hire contractors to finish six of the eight floors in ten days. Gray was led on another tour and wrote a memo saying, "Job looks very good." Gray has subsequently been faulted for looking only at what ZZZZ Best officials chose to show him without making independent inquiries.

### Questions:

1. *ZZZZ Best grossly inflated its operating results by reporting bogus revenue and receivables. What factors prevent a company from continuing to report fraudulent results indefinitely?*
2. *What could the auditor have done to uncover the ZZZZ Best fraud?*

Sources:

Daniel Akst, "How Whiz-Kid Chief of ZZZZ Best Had, and Lost, It All," *The Wall Street Journal*, July 9, 1987: p. 1.

Daniel Akst, "How Barry Minkow Fooled the Auditors," *Forbes*, October 2, 1989: p. 126.

receivables depends on the relative significance of the various items included. Valuation accounts are deducted from the individual receivable balances or combined balances to which they relate. Any long-term trade and nontrade receivables would be reported as "Other noncurrent assets" on the balance sheet.

When notes receivable have been discounted with recourse, a liability (e.g., Obligation on Discounted Notes Receivable) is reported in the balance sheet if the discounting is treated as borrowing. If treated as a sale, no liability is recognized, but a contingent liability should be disclosed in the notes to the financial statements or parenthetically on the balance sheet with notes receivable. If notes are discounted without recourse, there is no contingent liability. If notes or accounts receivable have been pledged to secure a loan, the amount should be disclosed.

Accounts and notes receivable as presented by Holiday Corporation in its 1989 annual report are shown in Exhibit 9—3. An alternative disclosure method would be to show net trade receivables on the balance sheet and present the detailed information in a note to the financial statements. This latter approach is illustrated in Exhibit 9—4 for Cincinnati Milacron Inc.

**Exhibit 9—3    Holiday Corporation and Consolidated Subsidiaries**

Balance Sheets                                    Holiday Corporation and Consolidated Subsidiaries

| (In thousands, except share amounts) | 1989 | 1988 |
|---|---|---|
| **Assets** | | |
| Current assets | | |
| Cash ............................................... | $ 61,771 | $ 65,409 |
| Temporary cash investments, at cost which approximates market ................... | 19,686 | 265,925 |
| Receivables, including notes receivable of $19,053 and $15,621, less allowance for doubtful accounts of $18,275 and $24,672 ........ | 133,883 | 128,050 |

## KEY TERMS

Accounts receivable 307
Aging receivables 312
Allowance method 310
Assignment of receivables 317
Bank discounting 326
Cash discount 316
Direct write-off method 310
Factoring receivables 317
Implicit or effective interest 322

Imputed interest rate 324
Interest-bearing note 321
Negotiable notes 321
Net realizable value 310
Non-interest-bearing note 321
Nontrade receivables 307
Notes receivable 307
Present value 321

Principal or face amount 321
Promissory note 321
Receivables 307
Sales discount 316
Trade discount 315
Trade receivables 307
Transfer of receivables with recourse 317

Exhibit 9—4   Cincinnati Milacron Inc. and Subsidiaries

# Consolidated Balance Sheet
# Cincinnati Milacron Inc. and Subsidiaries
Fiscal year ends on Saturday closest to December 31

| (In thousands) | 1989 | 1988 |
|---|---|---|
| Assets | | |
| Current assets | | |
| Cash and cash equivalents ............................................... | $ 32,894 | $ 17,868 |
| Notes and accounts receivable less allowances ........................... | 198,512 | 235,823 |

**Receivables**

The components of notes and accounts receivable less allowances are shown in the table.

Included in "Notes and accounts receivable less allowances" are install-ment receivables not due within one year of $7.0 million and $15.1 million in 1989 and 1988, respectively.

### Notes and Accounts Receivable Less Allowances

| (In thousands) | 1989 | 1988 |
|---|---|---|
| Notes receivable ......................... | $ 27,493 | $ 44,590 |
| Accounts receivable .................... | 176,469 | 196,461 |
| | 203,962 | 241,051 |
| Less allowances for doubtful accounts .. | 5,450 | 5,228 |
| | $198,512 | $235,823 |

## QUESTIONS

1. Explain how each of the following factors affects the classification of a receivable: (a) the form of a receiva-ble, (b) the source of a receivable, and (c) the ex-pected length of time to maturity or collection.
2. (a) Describe the methods for establishing and main-taining an allowance for doubtful accounts.
   (b) How would the percentages used in estimating uncollectible accounts be determined under each of the methods?
3. In accounting for uncollectible accounts receivable, why is the allowance method, rather than the direct write-off method, required by generally accepted ac-counting principles?
4. An analysis of the accounts receivable balance of $8,702 on the records of Jorgenson, Inc., on Decem-ber 31 reveals the following:

| | |
|---|---|
| Accounts from sales of last three months (appear to be fully collectible)........................... | $7,460 |
| Accounts from sales prior to October 1 (of doubtful value) ........... | 1,312 |
| Accounts known to be worthless ....... | 320 |
| Dishonored notes charged back to customer accounts .................... | 800 |
| Credit balances in customer accounts ... | 1,190 |

(a) What adjustments are required?
(b) How should the various balances be shown on the balance sheet?
5. In what section of the income statement would you report (a) doubtful accounts expense, and (b) sales discounts?
6. How are attitudes regarding the financing of accounts receivable changing? Why do you think this is so?
7. Explain the difference between the general assign-ment of accounts receivable and specific assignment of accounts receivable with regard to (a) collateral and (b) disclosure on financial statements.
8. (a) Distinguish between the practices of (1) assign-ment of accounts receivable, (2) factoring accounts receivable, and (3) transfer of accounts receivable with recourse. (b) Describe the accounting proce-dures to be followed in each case.
9. According to FASB Statement No. 77, what three conditions must be met to record the transfer of re-ceivables with recourse as a sale?
10. The Bockweg Co. enters into a continuing agreement with Goessling Financial Services, whereby the latter company buys without recourse all of the trade receiv-ables as they arise and assumes all credit and collec-tion functions. (a) Describe the advantages that may

accrue to Bockweg Co. as a result of the factoring agreement. (b) Are there any disadvantages? Explain.

11. Comment on the statement, "There is no such thing as a non-interest-bearing note."

12. (a) When should a note receivable be recorded at an amount different from its face amount? (b) Describe the procedures employed in accounting for the difference between a note's face amount and its recorded value.

13. What is meant by imputing a rate of interest? How is such a rate determined?

14. The Lambert Optical Co. discounts at 20% the following three notes at the Security First Bank on July 1 of the current year. Compute the proceeds on each note, rounding amounts to the nearest dollar.

(a) A 90-day, 13% note receivable for $24,000 dated June 1.

(b) A 6-month, 11% note receivable for $16,000 dated May 13 and coming due on November 13.

(c) Its own 4-month note payable dated July 1 with face value of $8,000 and no stated interest rate.

15. Distinguish between accounting procedures for (a) note receivable discounted with recourse that is subsequently dishonored, and (b) a note receivable discounted without recourse that is subsequently dishonored.

16. Identify alternative methods for presenting information on the balance sheet relating to (a) notes receivable discounted, and (b) assigned accounts receivable.

---

## DISCUSSION CASES

### Case 9—1  (Should a company sell on credit?)

Olin Company currently makes only cash sales. Given the number of potential customers who have requested to buy on credit, Olin is considering allowing credit sales. What factors should Olin consider in making the decision whether to allow credit sales?

### Case 9—2  (Accounting for uncollectibles)

During the audit of accounts receivable of Montana Company, the new CEO, Joe Frisco, asked why the company had debited the current year's expense for doubtful accounts on the assumption that some accounts will become uncollectible next year. Frisco believes that the financial statements should be based on verifiable, objective evidence. In his opinion it would be more objective to wait until specific accounts become uncollectible before the expense is recorded. What accounting issues are involved? Which method of accounting for uncollectible accounts would you recommend and why?

### Case 9—3  (Accounting for potential sales returns)

Ultimate Corporation is a computer products supplier. Ultimate sells products to dealers who then sell the products to the end users. Most of Ultimate's competitors require dealers to pay for shipments within 45 to 60 days. Ultimate has followed a more relaxed policy; in 1988 Ultimate's average length of time to collect its receivables was 158 days. (This average collection period can be computed as Average Accounts Receivable Balance/Average Daily Credit Sales). It has been suggested that in return for this lax collection policy, dealers allowed Ultimate to ship more product than the dealers needed, allowing Ultimate to recognize the excess shipments as sales. In 1988, Ultimate attempted to reduce the level of its accounts receivable by stepping up collection efforts. As a result, product returns from dealers increased significantly.

1. Assume that Ultimate's sales for the year were $1,000 with cost of sales being $600. For simplicity, also assume that all of the sales occurred on December 31, and that on average, Ultimate expects about 15 percent of products sold to be returned by dissatisfied dealers or dealers who are unable to sell the products. What adjusting entry, if any, should be made at year-end to reflect the likelihood of future sales returns?
2. An allowance for sales returns is analogous to an allowance for doubtful accounts. Most companies disclose an allowance for doubtful accounts but very few disclose an allowance for sales returns. Why not?
3. What other, more conservative accounting treatment is possible in regard to the potential sales returns?

Source: Tatiana Pouschine, "No Question It Looks Bad" *Forbes*, November 28, 1988: p. 62.

## Case 9—4  (Foreign loan write-offs)

In July 1990, U.S. federal regulators ordered U.S. banks to write off 20% of their $11.1 billion in loans to Brazil and also 20% of their $2.9 billion in loans to Argentina. The action significantly affected the loan loss reserves of the banks. For example, Citicorp was ordered to write off loans totaling $780 million, compared to Citicorp's total loan loss reserve of $3.3 billion. However, it was reported that "the action won't automatically have any impact on bank earnings."

1. Why won't the ordered write-offs automatically impact bank earnings?
2. Might the ordered write-offs have an indirect impact on future bank earnings?
3. What effect would you expect to see on bank stock prices in response to this announcement?

Source: Robert Guenther, "Federal Regulators Order Banks to Take Write-Offs on Loans to Brazil, Argentina" *The Wall Street Journal*, July 12, 1990: p. A3.

## Case 9—5  (Accounts receivable as a source of cash)

Assume you are the treasurer for Fullmer Products Inc. and one of your responsibilities is to ensure that the company always takes available cash discounts on purchases. The corporation needs $150,000 within one week in order to take advantage of current cash discounts. The lending officer at the bank insists on adequate collateral for a $150,000 loan. For various reasons, your plant assets are not available as collateral, but your accounts receivable balance is $205,000. What alternatives would you consider for obtaining the necessary cash?

## Case 9—6  (Selling receivables instead of merchandise)

The following excerpt is from an article printed in *The Wall Street Journal*:

Sears, Roebuck & Co. said it arranged to sell $550 million of customer accounts receivable to a group of 16 institutional investors headed by Continental Illinois National Bank & Trust Co.

Under the plan, the investors will assume ownership of the receivables, representing about 8% of Sears' total receivables outstanding as well as additions resulting from new purchases. The receivables will be sold to the institutional investors without recourse. And they will receive subsequent finance charge income on the accounts.

Edward R. Telling, Sears' chairman, said the agreement calls for the sale by Sears of additional receivables each month with the total to be sold expected to reach $625 million by February 1, 1979. Subject to further negotiations, the total could reach $1 billion by 1983, he added.

The initial $550 million will be sold at 99.015% of face value with Sears receiving an administrative fee from the institutional buyers for handling the accounts. Initially, the fee will equal 5.62% of the unpaid balance.

What aspects appear to be unique in this actual example of the sale of receivables?

# EXERCISES

### Exercise 9—1   (Classifying receivables)

Classify each of the items listed below as: (A) Accounts Receivable, (B) Notes Receivable, (C) Trade Receivable, (D) Nontrade Receivable, or (E) Other (indicate nature of item). Since the classifications are not mutually exclusive, more than one classification may be appropriate. Also indicate whether the item would normally be reported as a current or noncurrent asset assuming a 6-month operating cycle.

1. MasterCard or VISA credit card sale of merchandise to customer.
2. Overpayment to supplier for inventory purchased on account.
3. Insurance claim on automobile accident.
4. Charge sale to regular customer.
5. Advance to sales manager.
6. Interest due on 5-year note from company president, interest payable annually.
7. Acceptance of 3-year note on sale of land held as investment.
8. Acceptance of 6-month note for past-due account arising from the sale of inventory.
9. Eight-month subscription for the sale of common stock.
10. Claim for a tax refund from last year.
11. Prepaid insurance—four months remaining in the policy period.
12. Overpayment by customer of an account receivable.

### Exercise 9—2   (Computing the accounts receivable balance)

The following information, pertaining to the Jumbo Company's first year of operations, is to be used in testing the accuracy of Accounts Receivable, which has a balance of $21,000 at December 31, 1993.

(a)  Collections from customers, $72,000.
(b)  Merchandise purchased, $91,000.
(c)  Ending merchandise inventory, $26,000.
(d)  Goods sell at 50% above cost.
(e)  All sales are on account.

Compute the balance that Accounts Receivable should show and determine the amount of any shortage or overage.

### Exercise 9—3   (Recording credit card sales)

Sue Milano owns a gift shop at the airport. She accepts only cash or VISA and MasterCard credit cards. During the last month, the gift shop had a total of $76,000 in sales. Of this amount, 75% were credit card sales. The bank charges a 3% fee on net credit card sales. Make the monthly summary entry to reflect the above transactions.

### Exercise 9—4   (Recording credit card sales)

Greystone Inn is a fine restaurant specializing in French cuisine. The inn is situated on a picturesque location overlooking Dryden Lake. Greystone Inn accepts only two forms of payment: cash and American Express. The American Express receipts cannot be deposited directly in a checking account but must be submitted to American Express in order to receive payment. During April, sales totaled $90,000; cash sales accounted for only 15% of the total.

1. Make the monthly summary entry to record sales for April.
2. Make the summary entry to record receipt of payment from American Express. The service charge is 4%.

**Exercise 9—5  (Estimating doubtful accounts)**

Accounts Receivable of the Fakler Manufacturing Co. on December 31, 1993, had a balance of $200,000. Allowance for Doubtful Accounts had a $7,500 debit balance. Sales in 1993 were $1,725,000 less sales discounts of $14,000. Give the adjusting entry for estimated doubtful accounts expense under each of the following assumptions:

1. One-half of 1% of 1993 net sales will probably never be collected.
2. Two percent of outstanding accounts receivable are doubtful.
3. An aging schedule shows that $9,500 of the outstanding accounts receivable are doubtful.

**Exercise 9—6  (Journal entries for doubtful accounts)**

Health Care Inc. had gross sales of $155,000 during 1993, 30% of which were on credit. Accounts receivable outstanding at December 31, 1993, totaled $2,800, and the allowance for doubtful accounts had a $200 debit balance. Merchandise in the amount of $2,000 was returned by dissatisfied customers. Give the adjusting entry for doubtful accounts expense, assuming:

1. 1% of net credit sales will be uncollectible.
2. 2½% of current accounts receivable are doubtful.

**Exercise 9—7  (Journal entries for receivable write-offs)**

McGraw Medical Center has received a bankruptcy notice for Phillip Hollister. Hollister owes the medical center $650. The bankruptcy notice indicates that the medical center can't expect to receive payment of any of the $650.

1. Make the journal entry necessitated by receipt of the bankruptcy notice.
2. Six months after the medical center received the bankruptcy notice, Hollister appeared requesting medical treatment. He agreed to pay his old bill in its entirety. Make the journal entry or entries necessary to record receipt of the $650 payment from Hollister.

**Exercise 9—8  (Estimating doubtful accounts—percentage-of-sales method)**

Jenkins, Inc., follows the percentage-of-sales method of estimating doubtful accounts. The following data were gathered by the accounting department:

|  | 1990 | 1991 | 1992 | 1993 |
|---|---|---|---|---|
| Total sales ................ | $1,050,000 | $2,100,000 | $3,600,000 | $6,300,000 |
| Credit sales .............. | 600,000 | 960,000 | 1,950,000 | 3,600,000 |
| Accounts receivable (end-of-year balance) ............. | 186,000 | 234,000 | 360,000 | 750,000 |
| Allowance for doubtful accounts (end-of-year credit balance) ................. | 3,000 | 18,000 | 12,000 | 66,000 |
| Accounts written off ........ | 27,000 | 6,000 | 42,000 | 9,000 |

1. What amounts were debited to expense for 1991, 1992, and 1993?
2. Compute the balance in the valuation account at the beginning of 1990, assuming there has been no change in the percentage of sales used over the four-year period.
3. What explanation can be given for the fluctuating amount of write-off?
4. Why do the actual write-offs fail to give the correct charge to expense?

 **Exercise 9—9  (Aging accounts receivable)**

Blanchard Company's accounts receivable subsidiary ledger reveals the following information:

| Customer | Account Balance Dec. 31, 1993 | Invoice Amounts and Dates | |
|---|---|---|---|
| Allison, Inc.......................... | $ 8,795 | $3,500 | 12/6/93 |
| | | 5,295 | 11/29/93 |
| Banks Bros ........................ | 5,230 | 3,000 | 9/27/93 |
| | | 2,230 | 8/20/93 |
| Barker & Co. ...................... | 7,650 | 5,000 | 12/8/93 |
| | | 2,650 | 10/25/93 |
| Marrin Co. ......................... | 11,285 | 5,785 | 11/17/93 |
| | | 5,500 | 10/9/93 |
| Ring, Inc. .......................... | 7,900 | 4,800 | 12/12/93 |
| | | 3,100 | 12/2/93 |
| West Corp.......................... | 4,350 | 4,350 | 9/12/93 |

Blanchard Company's receivable collection experience indicates that, on the average, losses have occurred as follows:

| Age of Accounts | Uncollectible Percentage |
|---|---|
| 0-30 days | .7% |
| 31-60 days | 1.4% |
| 61-90 days | 3.5% |
| 91-120 days | 10.2% |
| 121 days and over | 60.0% |

The allowance for doubtful accounts credit balance on December 31, 1993, was $2,245 before adjustment.

1. Prepare an accounts receivable aging schedule.
2. Using the aging schedule from part (1), compute the allowance for doubtful accounts balance as of December 31, 1993.
3. Prepare the end-of-year adjusting entry.
4. (a) Where accounts receivable are few in number, such as in this exercise, what are some possible weaknesses in estimating doubtful accounts by the aging method?
   (b) Would the other methods of estimating doubtful accounts be subject to these same weaknesses? Explain.

## Exercise 9—10  (Analysis of allowance for doubtful accounts)

The Transtech Publishing Company follows the procedure of debiting Doubtful Accounts Expense for 2% of all new sales. Sales for four consecutive years and year-end allowance account balances were as follows:

| Year | Sales | Allowance for Doubtful Accounts End-of-Year Credit Balance |
|---|---|---|
| 1990 | $2,100,000 | $21,500 |
| 1991 | 1,975,000 | 35,500 |
| 1992 | 2,500,000 | 50,000 |
| 1993 | 2,350,000 | 66,000 |

1. Compute the amount of accounts written off for the years 1991, 1992, and 1993.
2. The external auditors are concerned with the growing amount in the allowance account. What action do you recommend the auditors take?

## Exercise 9—11    (Receivables and the statement of cash flows)

The following selected information is provided for Lynez Company. All sales are credit sales and all receivables are trade receivables.

| | |
|---|---:|
| Accounts receivable, Jan. 1 net balance | $150,000 |
| Accounts receivable, Dec. 31 net balance | 165,000 |
| Sales for the year | 800,000 |
| Uncollectible accounts written off during the year | 14,000 |
| Bad debt expense for the year | 24,000 |
| Cash expenses for the year | 681,000 |
| Net income for the year | 95,000 |

Based on the above information, answer the following independent questions:

1. Using the *direct* method, compute the net cash flow from operations that Lynez Company would report in its statement of cash flows.
2. Assuming use of the *indirect* method, what adjustments to net income would be required in reporting net cash flow from operations?

## Exercise 9—12    (Accounts receivable as a source of cash)

The Alpha Corporation decides to use accounts receivable as a basis for financing. Its current position is as follows:

| | | | |
|---|---:|---|---:|
| Accounts receivable | $80,000 | Cash overdraft | $    400 |
| Inventories | 81,000 | Accounts payable | 57,500 |

For each case below, prepare a statement of Alpha's current position, assuming cash is obtained as indicated:

1. Cash of $60,000 is borrowed on short-term notes and $35,000 is applied to the payment of creditors; accounts of $70,000 are assigned to secure the loan.
2. Cash of $60,000 is advanced to the company by Beta Finance Co., the advance representing 80% of accounts transferred on a recourse basis. (Assume the transfer meets the FASB conditions to be accounted for as a sale.)
3. Cash of $60,000 is received on factoring of $78,000 of accounts receivable.

## Exercise 9—13    (Accounting for accounts receivable factoring)

On July 15, Mann Company factored $600,000 in accounts receivable for cash of $550,000. The factor withheld 10% of the cash proceeds to allow for possible customer returns or account adjustments. An allowance for doubtful accounts of $80,000 had previously been established by Mann in relation to these accounts.

1. Make the journal entry necessary on Mann's books to record the factoring of the accounts.
2. Make the journal entry necessary on Mann's books to record final settlement of the factoring arrangement. No customer returns or account adjustments occurred in relation to the factored accounts.

## Exercise 9—14    (Accounting for a non-interest-bearing note)

Zobell Corporation sells equipment with a book value of $8,000, receiving a non-interest-bearing note due in three years with a face amount of $10,000. There is no established market value for the equipment. The interest rate on similar obligations is estimated at 12%. Compute the gain or loss on the sale and the discount on notes receivable, and make the necessary entry to record the sale. Also, make the entries to record the amortization of the discount at the end of the first, second, and third year using effective-interest amortization. (Round to the nearest dollar.)

### Exercise 9—15  (Accounting for an interest-bearing note)

High Country, Inc., purchased inventory costing $50,000. Terms of the purchase were 5/10, n/30. In order to take advantage of the cash discount, High Country borrowed $45,000 from Downtown 1st National, signing a 2-month, 12% note. The bank requires monthly interest payments. Make the entries to record the following:

1. Initial purchase of inventory on account
2. Payment to the supplier within the discount period
3. Loan from the bank
4. First month's payment to the bank
5. Second and final payment to the bank

### Exercise 9—16  (Discounting notes—computations)

On December 21, the following notes are discounted by the bank at 15%. Determine the cash proceeds, rounded to the nearest dollar, from discounting each note.

1. 30-day, $4,500, non-interest-bearing note dated December 15.
2. 60-day, $3,380, 9% note dated December 1.
3. 60-day, $15,000, 13% note dated November 6.
4. 90-day, $6,775, 10% note dated November 24.

### Exercise 9—17  (Accounting for notes receivable discounted)

Tandy Company accepted a $20,000, 90-day, 12% interest-bearing note dated September 1, 1993, from a customer for the sale of a piece of machinery. The machinery cost $25,000 and was 50% depreciated. On October 15, 1993, Tandy discounted the note, with recourse, at First National Bank at a 15% discount rate. The customer paid the note at maturity. Make the entries necessary to record the above transactions on Tandy Company's books. Assume the transfer of the note to the bank does not meet FASB criteria for recording as a sale. (Round amounts to the nearest dollar.)

### Exercise 9—18  (Accounting for notes receivable discounted)

S. Atwater received from K. Rogers, on account, a 90-day, 12% note for $8,000, dated June 6, 1993. On July 6, Atwater discounted the note, with recourse, at 15% and recorded the discounting as a sale in accordance with FASB Statement No. 77. The note was not paid at maturity, and the bank charged Atwater with protest fees of $25 in addition to the maturity value of the note. On September 28, 1993, the note was collected by Atwater with interest at 15% from the maturity date to the date of collection. What entries would appear on Atwater's books as a result of the foregoing? (Round amounts to the nearest dollar.)

### Exercise 9—19  (Discounting a note receivable)

On June 1, 1993, Flint Company received a $5,200, 90-day, 11% interest-bearing note from a customer on an overdue account receivable. Flint discounted the note, with recourse, immediately at State Bank at a discount rate of 15%. The discounting transaction did not meet FASB criteria for recording as a sale. At the date of maturity, the bank notified Flint that the note had not been paid and that the amount of the note plus a $25 protest fee had been charged to its account. Flint is unable to collect from the customer.

1. How much money will Flint receive upon discounting the note?
2. What is the effective rate of interest the bank will earn on the note?
3. Prepare the journal entries to record the events described above.

(Round amounts to the nearest dollar.)

# PROBLEMS

## Problem 9—1   (Journal entries and balance sheet presentation)

The balance sheet for the Itex Corporation on December 31, 1992, includes the following receivables balances:

| | | |
|---|---:|---:|
| Notes receivable (including notes discounted with recourse, $15,500) | | $36,500 |
| Accounts receivable | $85,600 | |
| Less allowance for doubtful accounts | 4,150 | 81,450 |
| Interest receivable | | 525 |

Current liabilities reported in the December 31, 1992, balance sheet included:

| | |
|---|---:|
| Obligation on discounted notes receivable | $15,500 |

Transactions during 1993 included the following:

(a) Sales on account were $767,000.
(b) Cash collected on accounts totaled $576,500, which included accounts of $93,000 on which cash discounts of 2% were allowed.
(c) Notes received in settlement of accounts totaled $82,500.
(d) Notes receivable discounted as of December 31, 1992, were paid at maturity with the exception of one $3,000 note on which the company had to pay the bank $3,090, which included interest and protest fees. It is expected that recovery will be made on this note early in 1994.
(e) Customer notes of $60,000 were discounted with recourse during the year, proceeds from their transfer being $58,500. (All discounting transactions were recorded as loans.) Of this total, $48,000 matured during the year without notice of protest.
(f) Customer accounts of $8,720 were written off during the year as worthless.
(g) Recoveries of doubtful accounts written off in prior years were $2,020.
(h) Notes receivable collected during the year totaled $27,000 and interest collected was $2,450.
(i) On December 31, accrued interest on notes receivable was $630.
(j) Uncollectible accounts are estimated to be 5% of the December 31, 1993, accounts receivable balance.
(k) Cash of $35,000 was borrowed from the bank, accounts receivable of $40,000 being pledged on the loan. Collections of $19,500 had been made on these receivables (included in the total given in transaction [b]) and this amount was applied on December 31, 1993, to payment of accrued interest on the loan of $600, and the balance to partial payment of the loan.

**Instructions:**

1. Prepare journal entries summarizing the transactions and information given above.
2. Prepare a summary of current receivables for balance sheet presentation.

## Problem 9—2   (Cost to customers of missing cash discounts)

Duane Kennedy, the chief financial officer for Malott Company, is perplexed about the small number of customers who take the cash discount offered by Malott. The credit terms offered by Malott are 1/10, n/70.

**Instructions:**

1. Explain why so few customers take the cash discount offered by Malott.
2. Assume that the interest rate on short-term borrowing is 15%. Determine which of the following credit terms might induce customers to take cash discounts.

(a) 2/10, n/30       (c) 3/10, n/100
(b) 2/15, n/55       (d) 1/10, n/30

## Problem 9—3   (Accounting for receivables—journal entries)

The following transactions affecting the accounts receivable of Olympic Corporation took place during the year ended January 31, 1993:

| | |
|---|---:|
| Sales (cash and credit) .......................................... | $591,050 |
| Cash received from credit customers ($298,900 was received from customers who took advantage of the discount feature of the corporation's credit terms 2/10, n/30)........................................ | 302,755 |
| Cash received from cash customers ............................... | 205,175 |
| Accounts receivable written off as worthless ....................... | 4,955 |
| Credit memoranda issued to credit customers for sales returns and allowances ...................................................... | 56,275 |
| Cash refunds given to cash customers for sales returns and allowances | 16,972 |
| Recoveries on accounts receivable written off as uncollectible in prior periods (not included in cash amount stated above) ................ | 10,615 |

The following two balances were taken from the January 31, 1992, balance sheet:

| | |
|---|---:|
| Accounts receivable ....................................... | $95,842 |
| Allowance for doubtful accounts ........................... | 9,740  (credit) |

The corporation provides for its net uncollectible account losses by crediting Allowance for Doubtful Accounts for 1½% of net credit sales for the fiscal period.

**Instructions:**

1. Prepare the journal entries to record the transactions for the year ended January 31, 1993.
2. Prepare the adjusting journal entry for estimated uncollectible accounts on January 31, 1993.

## Problem 9—4   (Accounting for cash discounts)

Beebe Company sold goods on account with a sales price of $50,000 on August 17. The terms of the sale were 2/10, n/30.

**Instructions:**

1. Record the sale using the gross method of accounting for cash discounts as illustrated in the text.
2. Record the sale using the net method of accounting for cash discounts. The net method differs from the gross method in that the original sale is recorded at the net amount (gross price minus cash discount). In essence, the net method assumes that the customer will take the cash discount.
3. Assume that payment is received on August 25. Record receipt of the payment using both the gross method and the net method.
4. Assume that payment is received on September 15. Record receipt of the payment using both the gross method and the net method. In making the entry for the net method, you will need to use the account "Cash Discounts Not Taken." Is this account an asset, liability, revenue, or expense?
5. Which method makes more theoretical sense—the gross method or the net method? Why? Why don't more firms use the net method?

## Problem 9—5   (Estimating doubtful accounts expense: sales method vs. receivables method)

During 1993, Lacee Enterprises had gross sales of $247,000. At the end of 1993, Lacee had accounts receivable of $83,000, and a credit balance of $5,600 in the Allowance for Doubtful Accounts. Lacee has used the percent-of-gross-sales method to estimate the Allowance for Doubtful Accounts Expense. For the past several years, the amount estimated to be uncollectible has been 3%.

**Instructions:**

1. Using the percent-of-gross-sales method, estimate the doubtful accounts expense and make any necessary adjusting entries.

2. Assuming that 6% of receivables are estimated to be uncollectible and that Lacee decides to use the percent-of-receivables method to estimate doubtful accounts expense, estimate the doubtful accounts expense and make any adjusting entries.

3. Which of the two methods more accurately reflects the net realizable value of receivables? Explain.

## ▪ Problem 9—6  (Estimating uncollectible accounts by aging receivables)

Rainy Day Company, a wholesaler, uses the aging method to estimate bad debt losses. The following schedule of aged accounts receivable was prepared at December 31, 1993.

| Age of Accounts | Amount |
|---|---|
| 0-30 days | $561,600 |
| 31-60 days | 196,100 |
| 61-90 days | 88,400 |
| 91-120 days | 18,500 |
| More than 120 days | 9,600 |
| | $874,200 |

The following schedule shows the year-end receivables balances and uncollectible accounts experience for the previous five years:

### Loss Experience—Percent of Uncollectible Accounts

| Year | Year-End Receivables | 0-30 days | 31-60 days | 61-90 days | 91-120 days | Over 120 days |
|---|---|---|---|---|---|---|
| 1992 | $780,700 | 0.5% | 1.0% | 10.2% | 49.1% | 78.2% |
| 1991 | 750,400 | 0.4 | 1.1 | 10.0 | 51.2 | 77.3 |
| 1990 | 681,400 | 0.6 | 1.2 | 11.0 | 51.7 | 79.0 |
| 1989 | 698,200 | 0.5 | 0.9 | 10.1 | 52.3 | 78.5 |
| 1988 | 723,600 | 0.4 | 1.0 | 8.9 | 49.2 | 77.6 |

The unadjusted allowance for doubtful accounts balance on December 31, 1993, is $32,796.

**Instructions:**  Compute the correct balance for the allowance account based on the average loss experience for the last five years and prepare the appropriate end-of-year adjusting entry.

## Problem 9—7  (Citicorp loan losses)

The following financial statement data are for Citicorp, the largest bank in the United States (as of December 31, 1988). All amounts are in millions of U.S. dollars.

| | 1988 | 1987 | 1986 | 1985 |
|---|---|---|---|---|
| Provision for Credit Losses (Bad Debt Expense)..................................... | $1,330 | $4,410 | $1,825 | $1,243 |
| Income before income taxes............... | 2,707 | (288) | 1,645 | 1,642 |
| Year-end balance in the Allowance for Credit Losses ..................................... | 4,205 | 4,618 | 1,698 | 1,235 |

The unusually large provision for credit losses in 1987 ($4,410) includes a special one-time provision of $3,000 for troubled foreign loans.

**Instructions:**

1. Compute the amount of loans written off in 1986, 1987, and 1988.

2. Why was there a big increase in bad debt expense in 1987 but no corresponding large increase in the amount of write-offs?
3. Suppose that you are a financial analyst. At the end of 1987 you are asked to forecast Citicorp's 1988 income before taxes. What would your forecast be? Why?

### Problem 9—8   (Bad debts and the statement of cash flows)

Sage Company had a $300,000 balance in Accounts Receivable on January 1. The balance in Allowance for Doubtful Accounts on January 1 was $36,000. Sales for the year totaled $1,700,000. All sales were credit sales. Bad debt expense is estimated to be 2% of sales. Write-offs of uncollectible accounts for the year were $28,000. The balance in Accounts Receivable on December 31 was $345,000. All receivables are trade receivables. Sage uses the *direct* method in preparing its statement of cash flows.

**Instructions:**   What is the amount of cash collected from customers?

### Problem 9—9   (Accounting for assignment of specific accounts receivable)

On July 1, 1993, Balmforth Company assigns specific receivables totaling $200,000 to Rocky Mountain Bank as collateral on a $150,000, 16% note. Balmforth will continue to collect the assigned receivables. In addition to the interest on the note, Rocky Mountain also receives a 2% finance charge, deducted in advance on the $150,000 value of the note. Additional information for Balmforth Company is as follows:

(a)   July collections amounted to $145,000, less cash discounts of $750.
(b)   On August 1, paid the bank the amount owed for July collections plus accrued interest on note to August 1.
(c)   Balmforth collected the remaining assigned accounts during August except for $550 written off as uncollectible.
(d)   On September 1, paid bank the remaining amount owed plus accrued interest.

**Instructions:**   Prepare the journal entries necessary to record the above information on the books of both Balmforth Company and Rocky Mountain Bank.

### Problem 9—10   (Assigning and factoring accounts receivable)

During its second year of operations, Shank Corporation found itself in financial difficulties. Shank decided to use its accounts receivable as a means of obtaining cash to continue operations. On July 1, 1993, Shank factored $75,000 of accounts receivable for cash proceeds of $69,500. No bad debt allowance was associated with these accounts. On December 17, 1993, Shank assigned the remainder of its accounts receivable, $250,000 as of that date, as collateral on a $125,000, 12% annual interest rate loan from Sandy Finance Company. Shank received $125,000 less a 2% finance charge. Additional information is as follows:

| | |
|---|---|
| Allowance for Doubtful Accounts, 12/31/93 ......... | $3,200 (credit) |
| Estimated uncollectibles, 12/31/93................. | 3% of Accounts Receivable |
| Accounts Receivable (not including factored and as-signed accounts), 12/31/93 ....................... | $50,000 |

None of the assigned accounts had been collected by the end of the year.

**Instructions:**

1. Prepare the journal entries to record the receipt of cash from (a) factoring and (b) general assignment of the accounts receivable.
2. Prepare the journal entry necessary to record the adjustment to Allowance for Doubtful Accounts.

3. Prepare the accounts receivable section of Shank's balance sheet as it would appear after the above transactions.
4. What entry would be made on Shank's books when the factored accounts have been collected?

## Problem 9—11    (Discounting notes)

Dival Marketing Corporation completed the following transactions, among others:

| | | |
|---|---|---|
| May | 5 | Received a $5,000, 60-day, 10% note dated May 5 from R. D. Spears, on account. |
| | 24 | Received an $1,800, 90-day, non-interest-bearing note dated May 23 from B. Collins as settlement for unpaid balance of $1,752. |
| | 25 | Had Spears' note discounted at the bank at 13%. |
| June | 7 | Had Collins' note discounted at the bank at 15%. |
| | 25 | Received from J. L. Smith, a customer, a $7,000, 90-day, 12% note dated June 5, payable to J. L. Smith and signed by the Racine Corp. Upon endorsement, gave the customer credit for the maturity value of the note less discount at 13%. |
| | 29 | Received a $3,500, 60-day, 9% note dated June 29 from B. Grady, on account. |
| July | 5 | Received notice from the bank that Spears' note was not paid at maturity. Protest fees of $15 were charged by the bank. |
| | 21 | Received payment from Spears on the dishonored note, including interest at 16% on the balance from maturity date to payment date. |

### Instructions:

1. Give the journal entries to record the above transactions. Assume notes are discounted with recourse and do not meet the FASB criteria for recording as a sale. (Show data used in calculations with each entry; round to the nearest dollar.)
2. Give the adjusting entries required on July 31.

## Problem 9—12    (Accounting for discounted notes)

The following transactions were completed by M. D. Ellis over a three-month period:

| | | |
|---|---|---|
| Nov. | 10 | Received from G. R. Kack, on account, a $5,000, 60-day, 9% note dated Nov. 9. |
| | 11 | Received from M. C. Leckner on account, a $2,100, 60-day, 12% note dated Nov. 10. |
| | 20 | Discounted Leckner's note, without recourse, at the bank at 11%. |
| | 24 | Discounted Kack's note, with recourse, at the bank at 10%. |
| Dec. | 3 | Received a $2,950, 30-day, non-interest-bearing note dated Dec. 1 from M. Ichtemple, crediting Ichtemple's account at face value. |
| | 7 | Discounted Ichtemple's note, with recourse, at the bank at 12%. |
| | 28 | Received from S. E. Dillhunt, a $500, 90-day, 12% note dated Dec. 14 and made by Bell Realty Inc. Gave the customer credit for the maturity value of the note less discount at 10%. |
| | 29 | Received a $4,000, 10-day, 8% note dated Dec. 29 from M. L. Reinhard, on account. |
| Jan. | 10 | Received notice from the bank that Kack's note was not paid at maturity. A protest fee of $15 was charged by the bank. |
| | 22 | Received a $25,000, 120-day, 9% note dated Jan. 22 from V. M. Cherry, on account. |
| | 28 | Received payment on Reinhard's note, including interest at 10%, the legal rate, on the face value from the maturity date. |

### Instructions:

1. Give the entries to record the preceding transactions. Assume that notes discounted with recourse do not meet FASB criteria for recording as a sale. (Show data used in calculations with each entry; round amounts to nearest dollar.)
2. Give the necessary adjusting entries on January 31. Assume all notes discounted are paid when due unless otherwise indicated.

## Problem 9—13  (Discounting notes with and without recourse)

Ladd, Inc., has $162,000 of accounts receivable on July 1, 1992. On that date, Ladd accepts a one-year, $27,000, 11% note from Travis Corporation in settlement of Travis' $27,000 accounts receivable balance. The note and interest are due June 30, 1993. Additional information:

(a)  On November 30, 1992, Ladd discounts the note with First Valley National Bank at 12% interest.
(b)  On June 30, 1993, Travis Corporation dishonors the note and the bank collects the maturity value plus a $150 protest fee from Ladd.
(c)  On August 31, 1993, Travis pays the amount outstanding, including interest since the dishonor date at 11%.

### Instructions:

1.  Prepare the necessary journal entries on Ladd's books assuming the note is considered a borrowing with recourse. (Round to the nearest dollar and compute interest using months rather than days.)
2.  Prepare the necessary journal entries assuming the note is discounted without recourse. (Round to the nearest dollar and compute interest using months rather than days.)

## Problem 9—14  (Accounting for a non-interest-bearing note)

On January 1, 1992, Cache Valley Realty sold a tract of land to three doctors as an investment. The land, purchased ten years ago, was carried on Cache Valley's books at a value of $110,000. Cache Valley received a non-interest-bearing note for $220,000 from the doctors. The note is due December 31, 1993. There is no readily available market value for the land, but the current market rate of interest for comparable notes is 12%.

### Instructions:

1.  Give the journal entry to record the sale of land on Cache Valley's books.
2.  Prepare a schedule of discount amortization for the note with amounts rounded to the nearest dollar.
3.  Give the adjusting entries to be made at the end of 1992 and 1993 to record the effective interest earned.

## Problem 9—15  (Note with below-market interest rate)

On January 1, 1993, the Denver Company sold land that originally cost $400,000 to the Boise Company. As payment, Boise gave Denver a $600,000 note. The note bears an interest rate of 4% and is to be repaid in three annual installments of $200,000 (plus interest on the outstanding balance). The first payment is due on December 31, 1993. The market price of the land is not reliably determinable. The prevailing rate of interest for notes of this type is 14%.

**Instructions:**  Prepare the entries required on Denver's books to record the land sale and the receipt of each of the three payments. Use the effective-interest method of amortizing any premium or discount on the note.

## Problem 9—16  (Factoring receivables)

Freemont Factors provides financing to other companies by purchasing their accounts receivable on a nonrecourse basis. Freemont charges a commission to its clients of 15% of all receivables factored. In addition, Freemont withholds 10% of receivables factored as protection against sales returns or other adjustments. Freemont credits the 10% withheld to Client Retainer and makes payments to clients at the end of each month so that the balance in the retainer is equal to 10% of unpaid receivables at the end of the month. Freemont recognizes its 15% commissions as revenue at the time the receivables are factored. Also, experience has led Freemont to establish an Allowance for Doubtful Accounts of 4% of all receivables purchased.

On January 4, 1993, Freemont purchased receivables from Detmer Company totaling $1,500,000. Detmer had previously established an allowance for doubtful accounts for these receivables of $35,000. By January 31, Freemont had collected $1,200,000 on these receivables.

**Instructions:**

1. Prepare the entries necessary on Freemont's books to record the above information. Freemont makes adjusting entries at the end of every month.
2. Prepare the entries on Detmer's books to record the above information.

# CHAPTER 10

# Inventories–Cost Allocation and Valuation

Regina, Inc., was a fast-growing floor-care company that went public in 1985 and went bankrupt in 1988. Reported earnings climbed from $1.1 million in 1985 to $10.9 million in 1988. Investigation following the bankruptcy filing revealed a massive management fraud. Revenues were being recorded when orders were received rather than when goods were shipped, and fictitious sales invoices were being generated. These two fraudulent activities accounted for an increase in reported revenues of $11.4 million in 1988. In addition to these misstatements, inventory was also manipulated. Cost of goods sold was understated by such methods as failing to record product returns. These manipulations accounted for cost of goods sold being understated by $16 million. The reported income of $10.9 million in 1988 was subsequently changed by investigators to a loss of $16.8 million.

The primary source of revenue for a nonservice enterprise is from the sale of inventory. Because there is normally a period of time that elapses between the purchase and sale of inventory, unsold inventory is frequently a significant element on the balance sheet. Sold inventory, on the other hand, is reported as cost of goods sold on the income statement. As illustrated by the Regina example, the valuation and allocation of inventory can have a material effect on these two primary financial statements.

The principal valuation problems for inventory relate to deciding which costs should be included in inventory and under what circumstances a deviation from historical cost should be used for balance sheet valuation. Typically, until revenue is recognized, usually at time of sale, inventory is valued at cost. When a sale occurs, the inventory cost is allocated to cost of sales. If the inventory cost is the same for all units, the allocation presents no problems. However, if the inventory units were acquired or produced at different costs, a decision must be made as to which costs are charged to cost of goods sold and which costs remain as the valuation of the asset. In addition, if there has been a reduction in the costs of inventory, the use of a valuation method other than historical cost may be required.

This chapter focuses on the various components of cost that are assigned to inventory and also on the cost allocation methods that are employed in practice. Some of these are unique to the United States and they have developed under economic circumstances of changing prices and income tax laws. Chapter 11 presents some additional valuation issues relating to inventory, including the lower-of-cost-or-market rule for adjusting cost valuation downward.

## NATURE OF INVENTORY

The term inventory designates goods held for sale in the normal course of business and, in the case of a manufacturer, goods in production or to be placed in production. The nature of goods classified as inventory varies widely with the nature of business activities, and in some cases includes assets not normally thought of as inventory. For example, land and buildings held for resale by a real estate firm, partially completed buildings to be sold in the future by a construction firm, and marketable securities held for resale by a stockbroker are all properly classified as inventory by the respective firms.

Inventory represents one of the most active elements in business operations, being continuously acquired or produced and resold. A large part of a company's resources is frequently invested in goods purchased or manufactured.

The term **inventory** (or **merchandise inventory**) is generally applied to goods held by a merchandising firm, either wholesale or retail, when such goods have been acquired in a condition for resale. The terms **raw materials**, **goods in process**, and **finished goods** refer to the inventories of a manufacturing enterprise.

### Raw Materials

Raw materials are goods acquired for use in the production process. Some raw materials are obtained directly from natural sources. More often, however, raw materials are purchased from other companies and represent the finished products of the suppliers. For example, newsprint is the finished product of the paper mill but represents raw material to the printer who acquires it.

Although the term raw materials can be used broadly to cover all materials used in manufacturing, this designation is usually restricted to materials that will be physically incorporated in the products being manufactured. Because these materials are used directly in the production of goods, they are frequently referred to as **direct materials**. The term **factory supplies**, or **indirect materials**, is then used to refer to auxiliary materials, i.e., materials that are necessary in the production process but are not directly incorporated in the products. Oils and fuels for factory equipment, cleaning supplies, and similar items fall into this grouping since these items are not incorporated in a product but simply facilitate production as a whole.

Although factory supplies may be summarized separately, they should be reported as a part of a company's inventories since they ultimately will be consumed in the production process. Supplies purchased for use in the delivery, sales, and general administrative functions of the enterprise should not be reported as part of the inventories, but as prepaid expenses.

## Goods in Process

Goods in process, alternately referred to as work in process, consist of materials partly processed and requiring further work before they can be sold. This inventory includes three cost elements: (1) **raw materials**, (2) **direct labor**, and (3) **factory overhead** or **manufacturing overhead**. The cost of materials directly identified with the goods in production is included under (1). The cost of labor directly identified with goods in production is included under (2). The portion of factory overhead assignable to goods still in production forms the third element of cost.

Factory overhead consists of all manufacturing costs other than direct materials and direct labor. It includes factory supplies used and labor not directly identified with the production of specific products. It also includes general manufacturing costs such as depreciation, maintenance, repairs, property taxes, insurance, and light, heat, and power, as well as a reasonable share of the managerial costs other than those relating solely to the selling and administrative functions of the business.

## Finished Goods

Finished goods are the manufactured products awaiting sale. As products are completed, the costs accumulated in the production process are transferred from Goods in Process to the finished goods inventory account. The diagram below illustrates the basic flow of product costs through the inventory accounts of a manufacturer.

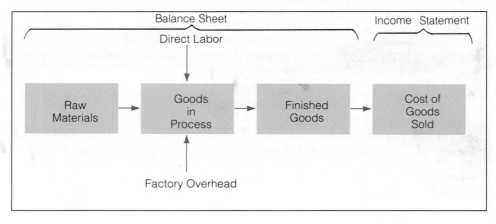

## INVENTORY SYSTEMS

Inventory records may be maintained on either a periodic or perpetual basis. A periodic inventory system requires a physical inventory, i.e., a counting, measuring, or weighing of goods, at the end of the accounting period to determine the quantities on hand. Values are then assigned to the quantities to determine the portion of the recorded costs to be carried forward on the balance sheet as inventory. The entries to adjust the inventories under a periodic inventory system are illustrated in Chapter 3, page 69.

The perpetual inventory system requires the maintenance of records that provide a continuous summary of inventory items on hand. Individual accounts are kept for each class of goods. Inventory increases and decreases are recorded in the individual accounts, the resulting balances representing the amounts on hand. Perpetual records may be kept in terms of quantities only or in terms of both quantities and costs. In a manufacturing organization, a perpetual system applied to inventories requires recording the full movement of goods through individual accounts for raw materials, goods in process, and finished goods. To illustrate, assume the following data for the Bartlett Corporation, a manufacturing company that uses a perpetual inventory system:

| | |
|---|---:|
| Inventories, January 1, 1993: | |
|     Finished goods | $ 45,000 |
|     Goods in process | 29,400 |
|     Raw materials | 21,350 |
| Costs incurred during 1993: | |
|     Raw materials purchased | 107,500 |
|     Raw materials used | 106,500 |
|     Direct labor | 96,850 |
|     Factory overhead | 134,055 |
| Cost of goods completed in 1993 | 340,305 |
| Cost of goods sold in 1993 | 334,305 |
| Inventories, December 31, 1993: | |
|     Finished goods | 51,000 |
|     Goods in process | 26,500 |
|     Raw materials | 22,350 |

Summary entries to record the preceding data for 1993 would be as follows:

| | | | |
|---|---|---:|---:|
| (a) | Raw Materials | 107,500 | |
| |     Accounts Payable | | 107,500 |
| |       *To record purchase of raw materials.* | | |
| (b) | Goods in Process | 106,500 | |
| |     Raw Materials | | 106,500 |
| |       *To record raw materials used in production.* | | |
| (c) | Goods in Process | 96,850 | |
| |     Payroll | | 96,850 |
| |       *To distribute direct labor to goods in process.* | | |
| (d) | Factory Overhead | 134,055 | |
| |     Various accounts (e.g., Liabilities, Accumulated Depreciation, and Prepaid Expenses) | | 134,055 |
| |       *To record factory overhead charges.* | | |
| (e) | Goods in Process | 134,055 | |
| |     Factory Overhead | | 134,055 |
| |       *To apply factory overhead to goods in process.* | | |
| (f) | Finished Goods | 340,305 | |
| |     Goods in Process | | 340,305 |
| |       *To transfer completed goods.* | | |

| (g) | Cost of Goods Sold............................... | 334,305 | |
|---|---|---|---|
| | Finished Goods .................................. | | 334,305 |
| | *To record the cost of goods sold.* | | |

After posting, the inventory and cost of goods sold accounts would appear in the ledger as follows:

**Raw Materials**

| | | | | |
|---|---|---|---|---|
| Jan. 1 | 21,350 | (b) | 106,500 | |
| (a) | 107,500 | | | |
| Dec. 31 | 22,350 | | | |

**Goods in Process**

| | | | | |
|---|---|---|---|---|
| Jan. 1 | 29,400 | (f) | 340,305 | |
| (b) | 106,500 | | | |
| (c) | 96,850 | | | |
| (e) | 134,055 | | | |
| Dec. 31 | 26,500 | | | |

**Finished Goods**

| | | | | |
|---|---|---|---|---|
| Jan. 1 | 45,000 | (g) | 334,305 | |
| (f) | 340,305 | | | |
| Dec. 31 | 51,000 | | | |

**Cost of Goods Sold**

| | | | |
|---|---|---|---|
| (g) | 334,305 | | |

When preparing the income statement for a manufacturing company, it is useful to prepare a separate manufacturing schedule that shows the detail supporting the cost of goods completed and transferred to Finished Goods. An illustration of this schedule, based on the preceding data and additional factory overhead detail, follows:

**Bartlett Corporation**
**Schedule of Cost of Goods Manufactured**
**For the Year Ended December 31, 1993**

| | | |
|---|---|---|
| Direct materials: | | |
| Raw materials inventory, January 1, 1993.............. | $ 21,350 | |
| Purchases ......................................... | 107,500 | |
| Cost of raw materials available for use ............... | $128,850 | |
| Less raw materials inventory, December 31, 1993 ....... | 22,350 | |
| Raw materials used in production....................... | | $106,500 |
| Direct labor ......................................... | | 96,850 |
| Factory overhead: | | |
| Indirect labor....................................... | $ 40,000 | |
| Factory supervision.................................. | 29,000 | |
| Depreciation expense—factory buildings and equipment | 20,000 | |
| Light, heat, and power .............................. | 18,000 | |
| Factory supplies expense ........................... | 15,000 | |
| Miscellaneous factory overhead ..................... | 12,055 | 134,055 |
| Total manufacturing costs............................. | | $337,405 |
| Add goods in process inventory, January 1, 1993......... | | 29,400 |
| | | $366,805 |
| Less goods in process inventory, December 31, 1993 ...... | | 26,500 |
| Cost of goods manufactured ........................... | | $340,305 |

Even when a perpetual system is employed, physical counts of the units on hand should be made at least once a year to confirm the balances on the books. The frequency of physical inventories will vary depending on the nature of the goods, their rate of turnover, and the degree of internal control. A plan for continuous counting of inventory items on a rotation basis is frequently employed. Variations may be found between the recorded amounts and the amounts actually on hand as a result of recording errors, shrinkage, breakage, theft, and other causes. The inventory accounts should be adjusted to agree with the physical count when a discrepancy exists. To illustrate, assume that a physical inventory of raw materials resulted in a value that is $2,500 less than the recorded inventory. The entry to adjust the inventory account would be:

| | | |
|---|---|---|
| Inventory Adjustment..................................... | 2,500 | |
| Raw Materials Inventory ................................. | | 2,500 |

Normal inventory adjustments for shrinkage and breakage are reported as adjustments to cost of goods sold. Abnormal shortages or thefts may be reported separately as operating expenses.

Practically all large trading and manufacturing enterprises and many relatively small organizations have adopted the perpetual inventory system as an integral part of their record keeping and internal control. This system offers a continuous check and control over inventories. Purchasing and production planning are facilitated, adequate inventories on hand are assured, and losses incurred through damage and theft are fully disclosed. The additional costs of maintaining such a system are usually well repaid by the benefits provided to management.

## ITEMS TO BE INCLUDED IN INVENTORY

As a general rule, goods should be included in the inventory of the party holding title. The passing of title is a legal term designating the point at which ownership changes. In some situations, the legal rule may be waived for practical reasons or because of certain limitations in its application. When the rule of passing title is not observed, there should be appropriate disclosure on the statements of the special practice followed and the factors supporting such practice. Application of the legal test under a number of special circumstances is described in the following paragraphs.

### Goods in Transit

When terms of sale are FOB (free on board) shipping point, title passes to the buyer with the loading of goods at the point of shipment. Under these terms, application of the legal rule to a year-end shipment calls for recognition of a sale and an accompanying decrease in goods on hand on the books of the seller. Since title passes at the shipping point, goods in transit at year-end should be included in the inventory of the buyer despite the lack of physical possession. A determination of the goods in transit at year-end is made by a review of the incoming orders during the early part of the new period. The purchase records may be kept open beyond the fiscal period to permit the recognition of goods in transit as of the end of the period, or goods in transit may be recorded by means of an adjusting entry.

When terms of a sale are FOB destination, application of the legal test calls for no recognition of the transaction until goods are received by the buyer. In this case, because of the difficulties involved in ascertaining whether goods have reached their destination at year-end, the seller may prefer to ignore the legal rule and employ shipment as a basis for recognizing a sale and the accompanying inventory decrease.

In some cases, title to goods may pass before shipment takes place. For example, if goods are produced on special customer order, they may be recorded as a sale as soon as they are completed and segregated from the regular inventory. If the sale is recognized upon segregation by the seller, care must be taken to exclude such goods from the seller's inventory. The buyer, on the other hand, could recognize the in-transit goods as a purchase and thus as part of inventory.

### Goods on Consignment

Goods are frequently transferred to a dealer (**consignee**) on a consignment basis. The shipper (**consignor**) retains title and includes the goods in inventory until their sale by the consignee. For example, Caterpillar Tractor Co. often consigns heavy equipment to its dealers. The cost of these items is such that many dealers could not afford to stock an entire inventory line. By consigning the inventory, Caterpillar is increasing its opportunities for generating revenue. Consigned goods are properly reported at the sum of their costs and the handling and shipping costs incurred in their transfer to the consignee. The goods may be separately designated on the balance sheet as merchandise on consignment. The consignee does not own the consigned goods; hence neither consigned goods nor obligations for such goods are reported on the consignee's financial statements. Accounting for consignments is discussed in a later chapter.

Other merchandise owned by a business but in the possession of others, such as goods in the hands of salespersons and agents, goods held by customers on approval, and goods held by others for storage, processing, or shipment, should also be shown as a part of that business' ending inventory.

### Conditional and Installment Sales

Conditional sales and installment sales contracts may provide for a retention of title by the seller until the sales price is fully recovered. Under these circumstances, the seller, who retains title, may continue to show the goods, reduced by the buyer's equity in such goods as established by collections; the buyer, in turn, can report an equity in the goods accruing through payments made. However, in the usual case when the possibilities of returns and defaults are very low, title to the goods should be relinquished and the transaction recorded in terms of the expected outcome. The seller, anticipating completion of the contract and the ultimate passing of title, recognizes the transaction as a regular sale involving deferred collections; the buyer, intending to comply with the contract and acquire title, recognizes the transaction as a regular purchase. Installment sales are discussed in detail in a later chapter.

## DETERMINATION OF INVENTORY COST

After the goods to be included as inventory have been identified, the accountant must assign a dollar value to the physical units. As indicated earlier, the profession has historically favored retention of some measure of cost, generally historical cost for this purpose. Attention is directed in this chapter to identifying the elements that comprise cost, and to a consideration of how to determine the portion of historical costs to be retained as the inventory amount reported on the balance sheet and the amount to be charged against current revenues.

### Items Included in Cost

Inventory costs consist of all expenditures, both direct and indirect, relating to inventory acquisition, preparation, and placement for sale. In the case of raw materials or goods acquired for resale, cost includes the purchase price, freight, receiving, storage, and all other costs incurred to the time goods are ready for sale. Certain expenditures can be traced to specific acquisitions or can be allocated to inventory items in some equitable manner. Other expenditures may be relatively small and difficult to allocate. Such items are normally excluded in the calculation of inventory cost and are thus charged in full against current revenue as period costs.

The charges to be included in the cost of manufactured products have already been mentioned. Proper accounting for materials, labor, and factory overhead items and their identification with goods in process and finished goods inventories is best achieved through adoption of a cost accounting system designed to meet the needs of a particular business unit. Certain costs relating to the acquisition or the manufacture of goods may be considered abnormal and may be excluded in arriving at inventory cost. For example, costs arising from idle capacity, excessive spoilage, and reprocessing are usually considered abnormal items chargeable to current revenue. Only those portions of general and administrative costs that are clearly related to procurement or production should be included in inventory cost.

In practice, companies take different positions in classifying certain costs. For example, costs of the purchasing department, costs of accounting for manufacturing activities, and costs of pensions for production personnel may be treated as inventoriable costs by some companies and period costs by others.

### Discounts as Reductions in Cost

Discounts treated as a reduction of cost in recording the acquisition of goods should similarly be treated as a reduction in the cost assigned to the inventory. Trade discounts are discounts converting a catalog price list to the prices actually charged to a buyer. The discount available may vary with such factors as the quantity purchased. Thus, trade discounts are frequently stated in a series. For example, given trade discount terms based on the quantity ordered of 30/20/10, a customer would be entitled to a discount of either 30%, 30% and 20%, or 30% and 20% and 10%, depending on the size of the order. Each successive discount is applied to the net invoice cost after deducting any earlier discounts. To illustrate, assume that an inventory item is listed in a catalog for $5,000 and a buyer is given terms of 20/10/5. The net invoice price is calculated as follows:

| Discount | Net Invoice Amount |
|---|---|
| $5,000 × 20% = $1,000 | $5,000 − $1,000 = $4,000 |
| $4,000 × 10% = $ 400 | $4,000 − $ 400 = $3,600 |
| $3,600 × 5% = $ 180 | $3,600 − $ 180 = $3,420 |

An alternative approach to the preceding computation is to compute a composite discount rate that can be applied to the initial gross amount. The following computation could be made for the above invoice:

| Discount Rate | × | Percentage of Original Invoice Cost | = | Composite Discount Rate |
|---|---|---|---|---|
| 20% | | 100% | | 20.00% |
| 10% | | 80%(100% − 20%) | | 8.00 |
| 5% | | 72%(80% − 8%) | | 3.60 |
| | | | | 31.60% |

Computation of discount: $5,000 × 31.6% = $1,580 discount

Net price = $5,000 − $1,580 = $3,420

The advantage of the composite approach is that once a composite rate is computed, it can be used directly for all purchases that have the same trade discount terms.

Cost is defined as the list price less the trade discount. No record needs to be made of the discount, and the purchases should be recorded at the net price of $3,420.

**Cash discounts** are discounts granted for payment of invoices within a limited time period. Business use of such discounts has declined in popularity over the past years, although they are still found in some industries. Cash discounts are usually stated as a certain percentage to be allowed if the invoice is paid within a certain number of days, with the full amount due within another time period. For example, 2/10, n/30 (two ten, net thirty) means that 2% is allowed as a cash discount if the invoice is paid within 10 days after the invoice date, but that the full or "net" amount is due within 30 days. Terms of 3/10 eom mean a 3% discount is allowed if the invoice is paid within 10 days after the end of the month in which the invoice is written.

Theoretically, inventory should be recorded at the discounted amount, i.e., the gross invoice price less the allowable discount. This net method reflects the fact that discounts not taken are in effect credit-related expenditures incurred for failure to pay within the discount period. They are recorded in the discounts lost account and reported as a separate item on the income statement. Discounts lost usually represent a relatively high rate of interest. To illustrate, assume a purchase of $10,000 provides for payment on a 2/10, n/30 basis. This means that if the buyer pays for the purchase by the tenth day, only $9,800 must be paid. Twenty days later the full $10,000 is due. Thus, a discount of $200 is earned for 20 days advance payment. The implicit annual interest rate in this arrangement is 36%,[1] clearly a desirable rate even if a loan is necessary to obtain the cash for the advance payment. Failure on the part of management to take a cash discount usually represents carelessness in considering payment alternatives.

Under the gross method of recording discounts, cash discounts are booked only when they are taken. While the net method tracks discounts not taken, the gross method provides no such information and inventory records are maintained at the gross unit price. When a periodic system is used, cash discounts taken are reflected through a contra purchases account, Purchase Discounts. With a perpetual inventory system, discounts are credited directly to Inventory.

Because of its control features, the net method of accounting for purchases is strongly preferred; however, many companies still follow the historical practice of recognizing cash discounts only as payments are made. If the payment is made in the same period the inventory is purchased, use of either method will result in the same net income. However, if inventory is purchased in one period and payment is made in a subsequent period, net income is affected and a proper matching of costs against revenue will not take place. If the net method is used, an adjusting entry should be made at the end of each period to record the discounts lost on unpaid invoices for which the discount period has passed.

The entries required for both the gross and net methods are illustrated on page 355. A perpetual inventory method is assumed.

### Purchase Returns and Allowances

Adjustments to invoice cost are also made when merchandise either is damaged or is of a lesser quality than ordered. Sometimes the merchandise is physically returned to the

[1]   $I = P \times R \times T$
$\$200 = \$10,000 \times R \times {}^{20}\!/_{360}$
$\$200 = \$556 \times R$
$R = {}^{200}\!/_{556}$
$R = 36\%$

| Transaction | Purchases Reported Net | | Purchases Reported Gross | |
|---|---|---|---|---|
| Purchase of merchandise priced at $2,500 less trade discount of 30/20 and a cash discount of 2% $2,500 less 30% = $1,750 $1,750 less 20% = $1,400 $1,400 less 2% = $1,372 | Inventory ........ 1,372 Accounts Payable ........... | 1,372 | Inventory ....... 1,400 Accounts Payable ........... | 1,400 |
| (a) Assuming payment of the invoice within discount period. | Accounts Payable 1,372 Cash ........... | 1,372 | Accounts Payable 1,400 Inventory....... Cash ........... | 28 1,372 |
| (b) Assuming payment of the invoice after discount period. | Accounts Payable 1,372 Discounts Lost ... 28 Cash ........... | 1,400 | Accounts Payable 1,400 Cash ........... | 1,400 |
| (c) Required adjustment at the end of the period assuming that the invoice was not paid and the discount period has lapsed. | Discounts Lost ... 28 Accounts Payable ........... | 28 | No entry required | |

supplier. In other instances, a credit is allowed to the buyer by the supplier to compensate for the damage or the inferior quality of the merchandise. In either case, the liability is reduced and a credit is made directly to the inventory account under a perpetual inventory system, or to a contra purchases account, Purchase Returns and Allowances, under a periodic inventory system.

## TRADITIONAL HISTORICAL COST ALLOCATION METHODS

One of the more difficult issues facing the user of financial statements is understanding the effect of the allocation of specific unit prices, measured at the unit's historical cost at the time of purchase, to cost of goods sold and to inventory. Several methods have evolved to make this allocation between expense and inventory. The methods discussed in this section of the chapter are (1) **specific identification**, (2) **first-in, first-out (FIFO)**, (3) **average cost**, and (4) **last-in, first-out (LIFO)**. Each has certain characteristics that make it preferable under certain conditions. One of them, the last-in, first-out method, was specifically developed as an attempt to reduce the impact of changing prices on net income. All four methods have in common the fact that inventory cost, as defined in this chapter, is allocated between the income statement and the balance sheet. Only the specific identification method determines the cost allocation according to the physical inventory flow. Unless individual inventory items, such as automobiles, are clearly definable, inventory items are exchangeable. Thus, the emphasis in inventory valuation is on the accounting cost allocation, not the physical flow. No adjustment for price changes is made to the total amount to be allocated.

Except for specific identification, all the cost methods are frequently encountered in practice. Many companies use more than one method, applying different methods to different classes of inventory. *Accounting Trends & Techniques* reported the data on page 356 regarding the inventory methods used by the 600 companies surveyed.[2]

A significant increase in the number of companies using LIFO occurred in the 1970s and 1980s. A survey conducted in 1987 of LIFO users reported that of 206 respondents

[2]*Accounting Trends & Techniques*—1990 (New York American Institute of Certified Public Accountants, 1990), p. 105.

## The War in the Gulf

In August of 1990, Iraq invaded Kuwait. For gasoline distributors, this meant that the price they would pay for oil in the future could increase dramatically. For consumers, the effect was more immediate. Within a week, gasoline prices had jumped by as much as 20 cents per gallon. The American public accused gasoline distributors of ripping off consumers by raising the price on gas that was purchased prior to the gulf crisis. Distributors countered by stating that it is replacement cost, not historical cost, that dictates selling price.

### Questions:

1. *Assuming FIFO costing of inventory, what would be the effect of an increased selling price on the income statement of a gasoline distributor?*
2. *What would be the effect on the distributor's statement of cash flows as the firm replaced the inventory with more expensive petroleum products?*
3. *Was the American public correct in claiming that gasoline distributors used the gulf crisis as an opportunity to increase profits?*

| Method | Number Using Identified Method—1989 |
|---|---|
| Last-in, first-out (LIFO) ............................. | 366 |
| First-in, first-out (FIFO) ............................. | 401 |
| Average cost ........................................ | 200 |
| Other................................................ | 48 |
| Total .............................................. | 1,015 |

using LIFO, only 29 companies adopted LIFO before 1970. The other 177 adopted LIFO between 1970 and 1982.[3]

There have been few guidelines developed by the profession to assist companies in choosing among these alternative cost allocation methods. Some accountants have suggested that, conceptually, costs attach to the inventory as they are incurred and thus should follow the inventory to its disposition. This argument suggests that methods that allocate the cost of inventory sold according to the physical flow of goods would be preferred. Other writers have emphasized capital maintenance concepts and suggest the use of methods that provide for maintenance of a physical quantity of inventory before recognizing income from its sale. The following discussion of the allocation methods demonstrates how each method relates to these different viewpoints.

### Specific Identification

Costs may be allocated between goods sold during the period and goods on hand at the end of the period according to the actual cost of specific units. This specific identification method requires a means of identifying the historical cost of each unit of inventory up to

---

[3]James M. Reeve and Keith G. Stanga, "Balance Sheet Impact of Using LIFO: An Empirical Study," *Accounting Horizons,* September 1987, p. 11.

the time of sale. With specific identification, the flow of recorded costs matches the physical flow of goods.

The specific identification method is a highly objective approach to matching historical costs with revenues. As stated in Accounting Research Study No. 13, "There appears to be little theoretical argument against the use of specific identification of cost with units of product if that method of determining inventory cost is practicable."[4] Application of this method, however, is often difficult or impossible. When inventory is composed of a great many items or identical items acquired at different times and at different prices, cost identification procedures are likely to be slow, burdensome, and costly. Furthermore, when units are identical and interchangeable, this method opens the doors to possible profit manipulation through the selection of particular units for delivery. Finally, significant changes in costs during a period may warrant charges to expense on a basis other than past identifiable costs.

### First-in, First-Out Method

The first-in, first-out (FIFO) method is based on the assumption that costs should be charged to expense (cost of goods sold) in the order in which incurred. Inventories are thus stated in terms of the most recent costs. To illustrate the application of this method, assume the following data:

| Jan. | | | | | | |
|---|---|---|---|---|---|---|
| 1 | Inventory | 200 | units at | $10 | = | $ 2,000 |
| 12 | Purchase | 400 | units at | 12 | = | 4,800 |
| 26 | Purchase | 300 | units at | 11 | = | 3,300 |
| 30 | Purchase | 100 | units at | 12 | = | 1,200 |
| | Total | 1,000 | units | | | $11,300 |

A physical inventory on January 31 shows 300 units on hand. The most recent costs would be assigned to the units as follows:

| | | | | |
|---|---|---|---|---|
| Most recent purchase, Jan. 30 | 100 | units at $12 | = | $1,200 |
| Next most recent purchase, Jan. 26 | 200 | units at 11 | = | 2,200 |
| Total | 300 | units | | $3,400 |

If the ending inventory is recorded at $3,400, cost of goods sold is $7,900 ($11,300 − $3,400). Thus, expense is charged with the earliest costs incurred.

In the above example, ending inventory was computed and the cost of goods sold was inferred. A similar procedure can be used to compute cost of goods sold and then infer ending inventory. If 300 units are in ending inventory, then 700 units can be assumed sold. Under the FIFO method, cost of goods sold is computed as follows:

| Jan. | | | | | | |
|---|---|---|---|---|---|---|
| 1 | Inventory | 200 | units at | $10 | = | $2,000 |
| 12 | Purchase | 400 | units at | 12 | = | 4,800 |
| 26 | Purchase | 100 | units at | 11 | = | 1,100 |
| | Total | 700 | units | | | $7,900 |

If cost of goods sold is recorded at $7,900, ending inventory is $3,400 ($11,300 − $7,900). Because the number of units in ending inventory is typically less than the number of units sold, computing ending inventory first requires fewer computations. However, the resulting cost of goods sold and ending inventory figures are the same regardless of which is computed first.

---

[4]Horace G. Barden, *Accounting Research Study No. 13,* "The Accounting Basis of Inventories" (New York: American Institute of Certified public Accountants, 1973) p. 83.

When perpetual inventory accounts are maintained, a form similar to that illustrated below is used to record the cost assigned to units issued and the cost relating to the goods on hand. The columns show the quantities and values of goods acquired, goods issued, and balances on hand. It should be observed that identical values for periodic and perpetual inventories are obtained when FIFO is applied.

FIFO can be supported as a logical and realistic approach to the flow of costs when it is impractical or impossible to achieve specific cost identification. FIFO assumes a cost flow closely paralleling the usual physical flow of goods sold. Expense is charged with costs considered applicable to the goods actually sold; ending inventories are reported in terms of most recent costs—costs closely approximating the current value of inventories at the balance sheet date. FIFO affords little opportunity for profit manipulation because the assignment of costs is determined by the order in which costs are incurred.

## COMMODITY: X (FIFO)

| DATE | RECEIVED | | | ISSUED | | | BALANCE | | |
|---|---|---|---|---|---|---|---|---|---|
| | Quantity | Unit Cost | Total Cost | Quantity | Unit Cost | Total Cost | Quantity | Unit Cost | Total Cost |
| Jan. 1 | | | | | | | 200 | $10 | $2,000 |
| 12 | 400 | $12 | $4,800 | | | | 200 | 10 | 2,000 |
| | | | | | | | 400 | 12 | 4,800 |
| 16 | | | | 200 | $10 | $2,000 | | | |
| | | | | 300 | 12 | 3,600 | 100 | 12 | 1,200 |
| 26 | 300 | 11 | 3,300 | | | | 100 | 12 | 1,200 |
| | | | | | | | 300 | 11 | 3,300 |
| 29 | | | | 100 | 12 | 1,200 | | | |
| | | | | 100 | 11 | 1,100 | 200 | 11 | 2,200 |
| 30 | 100 | 12 | 1,200 | | | 7900 | 200 | 11 | 2,200 |
| | | | | | | | 100 | 12 | 1,200 |

## Average Cost Method

Some companies value inventories using an average cost method that assigns the same average cost to each unit. This cost is computed using a weighted average technique for a periodic system or a moving average technique for a perpetual system.

The **weighted average technique** is based on the assumption that goods sold should be charged at an average cost, such average being influenced or weighted by the number of units acquired at each price. Inventories are stated at the same weighted average cost per unit. Using the cost data in the preceding section, the weighted average cost of a physical inventory of 300 units on January 31 would be as follows:

| Jan. | 1 | Inventory | 200 | units at $10 = | $ 2,000 |
|---|---|---|---|---|---|
| | 12 | Purchase | 400 | units at 12 = | 4,800 |
| | 26 | Purchase | 300 | units at 11 = | 3,300 |
| | 30 | Purchase | 100 | units at 12 = | 1,200 |
| | | Total | 1,000 | units | $11,300 |

Weighted average cost.......................  $11,300 ÷ 1,000 = $11.30
Ending inventory .............................  300 units at $11.30 = $3,390

The ending inventory is recorded at a cost of $3,390; cost of goods sold is $7,910 ($11,300 − $3,390), thus charging expense with a weighted average cost. The calculations above were made for costs of one month. Similar calculations could be developed for a periodic inventory system in terms of data for a quarter or for a year.

When a perpetual inventory system that records both quantities and amounts is used, a variation of the weighted average technique is required. A new weighted average amount is calculated after each purchase, and this amount is used to cost each subsequent sale until another purchase is made. Because this method results in continuous updating of the average, it is referred to as the **moving average technique**. The use of this approach is illustrated below.

### COMMODITY: X (moving average)

| DATE | RECEIVED | | | ISSUED | | | BALANCE | | |
|------|----------|-----------|------------|----------|-----------|------------|----------|-----------|------------|
| | Quantity | Unit Cost | Total Cost | Quantity | Unit Cost | Total Cost | Quantity | Unit Cost | Total Cost |
| Jan.  1 | | | | | | | 200 | $10.00 | $2,000 |
| 12 | 400 | $12 | $4,800 | | | | 600 | 11.33 | 6,800 |
| 16 | | | | 500 | $11.33 | $5,665 | 100 | *11.35 | 1,135 |
| 26 | 300 | 11 | 3,300 | | | | 400 | 11.09 | 4,435 |
| 29 | | | | 200 | 11.09 | 2,218 | 200 | 11.09 | 2,217 |
| 30 | 100 | 12 | 1,200 | | | | 300 | 11.39 | 3,417 |

*Increase in unit cost due to rounding.

On January 12 the new unit cost of $11.33 was found by dividing $6,800, the total cost, by 600, the number of units on hand. Then on January 16, the balance of $1,135 represented the previous balance of $6,800 less $5,665, the cost assigned to the 500 units issued on this date. New unit costs were calculated on January 26 and 30 when additional units were acquired.

With successive recalculations of cost and the use of such different costs during the period, the cost identified with the ending inventory will differ from that determined when cost is assigned to the ending inventory in terms of average cost for all goods available during the period. A periodic inventory and use of the weighted average method resulted in a value for the ending inventory of $3,390; a perpetual inventory and use of the moving average method resulted in a value for the ending inventory of $3,417.

The average cost method can be supported as realistic and as paralleling the physical flow of goods, particularly where there is an intermingling of identical inventory units. Unlike the other inventory methods, the average approach provides the same cost for similar items of equal utility. The method does not permit profit manipulation. Limitations of the average method are that inventory values perpetually contain some degree of influence of earliest costs and that inventory values may lag significantly behind current prices in periods of rapidly rising or falling prices.

### Last-In, First-Out Method—Specific Goods

The last-in, first-out (LIFO) method is based on the assumption that the latest costs of a specific item should be charged to cost of goods sold. Inventories are thus stated at earliest costs. Using the cost data in the preceding section, a physical inventory of 300 units on January 31 would have a cost as follows:

Earliest costs relating to goods, Jan. 1 ............... 200 units at $10   $2,000
Next earliest cost, Jan. 12 ......................... 100 units at  12    1,200
Total .......................................... 300              $3,200

The ending inventory is recorded at a cost of $3,200 and cost of goods sold is $8,100 ($11,300 − $3,200). Thus, expense is charged with the most recently incurred costs.

When perpetual inventories are maintained, it is necessary to calculate costs on a last-in, first-out basis using the cost data on the date of each issue as illustrated below.

## COMMODITY: X (LIFO)

| DATE | RECEIVED | | | ISSUED | | | BALANCE | | |
|---|---|---|---|---|---|---|---|---|---|
| | Quantity | Unit Cost | Total Cost | Quantity | Unit Cost | Total Cost | Quantity | Unit Cost | Total Cost |
| Jan. 1 | | | | | | | 200 | $10 | $2,000 |
| 12 | 400 | $12 | $4,800 | | | | 200 | 10 | 2,000 |
| | | | | | | | 400 | 12 | 4,800 |
| 16 | | | | 400 | $12 | $4,800 | | | |
| | | | | 100 | 10 | 1,000 | 100 | 10 | 1,000 |
| 26 | 300 | 11 | 3,300 | | | | 100 | 10 | 1,000 |
| | | | | | | | 300 | 11 | 3,300 |
| 29 | | | | 200 | 11 | 2,200 | 100 | 10 | 1,000 |
| | | | | | | | 100 | 11 | 1,100 |
| 30 | 100 | 12 | 1,200 | | | *8000* | 100 | 10 | 1,000 |
| | | | | | | | 100 | 11 | 1,100 |
| | | | | | | | 100 | 12 | 1,200 |

It should be noted that LIFO values obtained under a periodic system will usually differ from those determined on a perpetual basis. In the example, a cost of $3,200 was obtained for the periodic inventory, whereas $3,300 was obtained when costs were calculated as goods were issued. This difference results because it was necessary to "dip into" the beginning inventory layer and charge 100 units of the beginning inventory at $10 to the issue of January 16. The ending inventory thus reflects only 100 units at the beginning unit cost.

These temporary liquidations of inventory frequently occur during the year, especially for companies with seasonal business. These liquidations cause monthly reports prepared on the LIFO basis to be unrealistic and meaningless. Because of this, most companies using LIFO maintain their internal records using other inventory methods, such as FIFO or weighted average, and adjust the statements to LIFO at the end of the year with a LIFO allowance account. Burlington Holdings, Inc. (Exhibit 10-1), includes a note to its balance sheet that itemizes its inventories at average cost, and then includes a separate allowance account, identified as "excess of average cost over LIFO," to reduce the inventory to LIFO cost.

Assuming the allowance was used by Burlington Holdings for the first time in 1988, the entry to record the allowance would be as follows:

Cost of Goods Sold ........................................ 43,570
    Excess of Average Cost Over LIFO ...................... 43,570

In 1989 the difference was more, therefore, the adjusting entry would increase the allowance account to its new difference.

Cost of Goods Sold ........................................ 8,162
    Excess of Average Cost Over LIFO ...................... 8,162

## Exhibit 10—1    Burlington Holdings, Inc.—Dollar-Value LIFO Inventory Disclosure

*Inventories:* Inventories are valued at the lower of cost or market. Cost of substantially all components of textile inventories in the United States is determined using the dollar-value last-in, first-out (LIFO) method. All other inventories are valued principally at average cost.

*Note D—Inventories*

Inventories are summarized as follows (in thousands):

|  | 1989 | 1988 |
|---|---|---|
| Inventories at average cost: | | |
| Raw materials | $ 53,615 | $ 64,125 |
| Stock in process | 117,623 | 110,689 |
| Produced goods | 193,665 | 193,589 |
| Dyes, chemicals, and supplies | 20,590 | 20,065 |
|  | $385,493 | $388,468 |
| Less excess of average cost over LIFO | 51,732 | 43,570 |
| Total | $333,761 | $344,898 |

Each year, the allowance would be adjusted in this manner to properly record the LIFO inventory on the financial statements.

**LIFO Conformity Rule**    The LIFO inventory method was developed in the United States during the late 1930s as a method of permitting deferral of illusory inventory profits during periods of rising prices. Petition was made to Congress by companies desiring to use this method for tax purposes, and in the Revenue Act of 1938, it became an acceptable tax method. There was, however, a unique provision attached to the use of the LIFO inventory method. It has become known as the **LIFO conformity rule** and specifies that only those taxpayers who use LIFO for financial reporting purposes may use it for tax purposes. LIFO inventory is the only accounting method that must be reported the same way for tax and book purposes. In the early years, the rule was strictly applied. Companies were not permitted to report inventory values using any other method either in the body of the financial statements or in the attached notes. This provision was to avoid the implication that some value other than LIFO was really a better one. Over time, the IRS has gradually relaxed the conformity rule. In 1981, the IRS regulations were further relaxed by (1) permitting companies to provide non-LIFO disclosures such as those presented by Burlington as long as they are not presented on the face of the income statement, and (2) allowing companies to apply LIFO differently for book purposes than for tax purposes as long as they use some acceptable form of LIFO.[5] Differences between book and tax LIFO inventories arise from different definitions of "LIFO pools" or from different application of market values that are lower than LIFO cost.

Prior to the relaxation of the LIFO conformity rule, the income tax regulations became the governing rules for book purposes. The accounting standards bodies elected not to address the method except to recognize that LIFO was an acceptable inventory method.[6] Now that companies may apply LIFO differently for book and tax purposes, both the SEC and the AICPA have addressed the LIFO issue for financial statement reporting

[5]Treasury Decision 7756, Title 26 CFR 1.472-2(e), (Washington, D.C.: U.S. Government Printing Office, 1981).

[6]*Accounting Research Bulletin No. 43*, "Restatement and Revision of Accounting Research Bulletins" (New York: American Institute of Certified Public Accountants, 1953), Chapter 4, par. 6.

purposes. In July 1981, the SEC issued ASR No. 293 which provided guidelines for companies to follow in making supplemental non-LIFO income disclosures. They also included several examples of what they labeled inappropriate use of the LIFO method. Their concern with LIFO as applied was stated as follows:

> For too long, the application of the LIFO method for financial accounting and reporting has been unduly influenced by the tax application. Most explanations or analyses of LIFO in textbooks and articles have been oriented toward tax implications, rather than financial accounting and reporting. With few exceptions, the accounting profession has deferred to the IRS in this area; indeed many accountants appear to view IRS LIFO regulations as if they were generally accepted accounting principles ("GAAP"). The Commission disagrees with this approach and believes that since LIFO may now be applied differently for book accounting and tax accounting, it is appropriate for the current practices used in the application of LIFO to be examined.[7]

The AICPA responded to this request, and under the direction of the Accounting Standards Executive Committee, appointed a nine-person Task Force on LIFO Inventory Problems to study the area. Their study resulted in the publication in November 1984 of an Issues Paper, "Identification and Discussion of Certain Financial Accounting and Reporting Issues Concerning LIFO Inventories." The task force addressed over fifty separate issues and reported by vote their views on the topic. Although the task force did not have the power to establish definitive accounting standards, the SEC has accepted their report as authoritative pending review of this area by the FASB. Where applicable, the views of the task force will be referenced in the detailed discussion of LIFO that follows.

**Specific-Goods LIFO Pools**   With large and diversified inventories, application of the LIFO procedures to specific goods is extremely burdensome. Because of the complexity and cost involved, companies frequently selected only a few very important inventory items, usually raw materials, for application of the LIFO method. As a means of simplifying the valuation process and extending its applicability to more items, an adaptation of LIFO applied to specific goods was developed and approved by the IRS. This adaptation permitted the establishment of LIFO inventory pools of substantially identical goods. At the end of a period, the quantity of items in the pool is determined, and costs are assigned to those items. Units equal to the beginning quantity in the pool are assigned the beginning unit costs. If the number of units in ending inventory exceeds the number of beginning units, the additional units are regarded as an incremental layer within the pool.

The unit cost assigned to the items in the new layer may be based on any one of the following measurements:

1. Actual costs of earliest acquisitions within the period (LIFO)
2. The weighted average cost of acquisitions within the period
3. Actual costs of the latest acquisitions within the period (FIFO)

Increments in subsequent periods form successive inventory layers. A decrease in the number of units in an inventory pool during a period is regarded as a reduction in the most recently added layer, then in successively lower layers, and finally in the original or base quantity. Once a specific layer is reduced or eliminated, it is not restored.

To illustrate the LIFO valuation process, assume that a company uses three inventory pools. The changes in the pools are as listed below. The inventory calculations that follow the listing are based on the assumption that weighted average costs are used in valuing annual incremental layers.

[7]*Accounting Series Release No. 293*, "The Last-In, First-Out Method of Accounting for Inventories" (Washington, D.C.: U.S. Government Printing Office, 1981), section II.

## Inventory Pool Increments and Liquidations

|  | Inventory Pool A | Inventory Pool B | Inventory Pool C |
|---|---|---|---|
| Inv., Dec. 31, 1992 . . . . . . . . . . . . . | 3,000 @ $6 | 3,000 @ $5 | 2,000 @ $10 |
| Purchases—1993 . . . . . . . . . . . . . | 3,000 @ $7<br>1,000 @ $9 | 2,000 @ $6 | 3,000 @ $11 |
| Total available for sale . . . . . . . . | 7,000 | 5,000 | 5,000 |
| Sales—1993 . . . . . . . . . . . . . . . . | 3,000 | 1,000 | 3,500 |
| Inv., Dec. 31, 1993 . . . . . . . . . . . . | 4,000 | 4,000 | 1,500 |
| Purchases—1994 . . . . . . . . . . . . . | 1,000 @ $8<br>3,000 @ $10 | 2,000 @ $6 | 3,000 @ $11 |
| Total available for sale . . . . . . . . | 8,000 | 6,000 | 4,500 |
| Sales—1994 . . . . . . . . . . . . . . . . | 3,500 | 2,500 | 2,000 |
| Inv., Dec. 31, 1994 . . . . . . . . . . . . | 4,500 | 3,500 | 2,500 |

## Inventory Valuations Using Specific-Goods LIFO Pools

|  | Inventory Pool A | | Inventory Pool B | | Inventory Pool C | |
|---|---|---|---|---|---|---|
| Inv., Dec. 31, 1992 . . . . . . . . . | 3,000 @ $6 | $18,000 | 3,000 @ $5 | $15,000 | 2,000 @ $10 | $20,000 |
| Inv., Dec. 31, 1993 . . . . . . . . . | 3,000 @ $6<br>1,000 @ $7.50[1] | $18,000<br>7,500 | 3,000 @ $5<br>1,000 @ $6 | $15,000<br>6,000 | 1,500 @ $10 | $15,000 |
|  | 4,000 | $25,500 | 4,000 | $21,000 | 1,500 | $15,000 |
| Inv., Dec. 31, 1994 . . . . . . . . . | 3,000 @ $6<br>1,000 @ $7.50<br>500 @ $9.50[2] | $18,000<br>7,500<br>4,750 | 3,000 @ $5<br>500 @ $6 | $15,000<br>3,000 | 1,500 @ $10<br>1,000 @ $11 | $15,000<br>11,000 |
|  | 4,500 | $30,250 | 3,500 | $18,000 | 2,500 | $26,000 |

[1]Cost of units acquired in 1993, $30,000, divided by number of units acquired, 4,000, or $7.50.
[2]Cost of units acquired in 1994, $38,000, divided by number of units acquired, 4,000, or $9.50.

The layer process for LIFO inventories may be further illustrated as shown on page 364.

A new layer was added to Inventory Pool A each year. Previously established layers were reduced in 1994 for Inventory Pool B and in 1993 for Inventory Pool C.

### Last-In, First-Out Method—Dollar Value

Even the grouping of substantially identical items into quantity pools does not produce all the benefits desired from the use of the LIFO method. Technological changes sometimes introduce new products thus requiring the elimination of inventory in old pools, and requiring the establishment of new pools for the new product that no longer qualifies as being substantially identical. For example, the introduction of synthetic fabrics to replace cotton meant that "cotton" pools were eliminated and new "synthetic fabric" pools established. This change resulted in the loss of lower LIFO bases by companies changing the type of fabrics they used. To overcome this type of problem and to further simplify the clerical work involved, the dollar-value LIFO inventory method was developed.[8] Under

---

[8]When new items are introduced, the dollar-value LIFO method does not give the same result as the specific-goods LIFO method. See D. R. Bainbridge, "Is Dollar-Value LIFO Consistent with Authoritative GAAP?" *Journal of Accounting, Auditing, and Finance* (Summer 1984), pp. 334-346, for a discussion as to why dollar-value LIFO may violate the historical cost principle and the concept of financial capital maintenance.

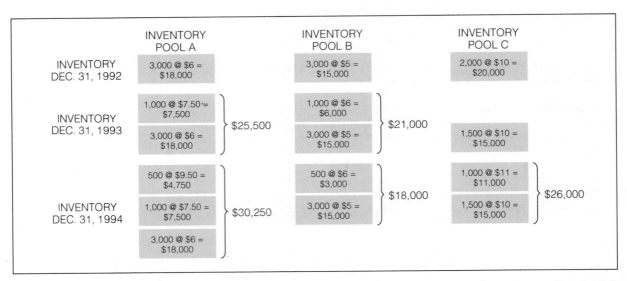

this method, the unit of measurement is the dollar rather than the quantity of goods. All similar items, such as all raw materials for a given line of business, are grouped into a pool, and layers are determined based on total dollar changes. The dollar-value method has become the most widely used adaptation of the LIFO concept. In a survey of LIFO users, Reeve and Stanga found that 95% of the 206 companies responding to their survey used some version of the dollar-value method.[9]

**General Procedures—Dollar-Value LIFO**     All goods in the inventory pool to which dollar-value LIFO is to be applied are viewed as though they are identical items. To determine if the dollar quantity of inventory has increased during the year, it is necessary to value the ending inventory in a pool at the base-year[10] prices and compare the total with that at the beginning of the year, also valued at base-year prices. If the end-of-year inventory at base-year prices exceeds the beginning-of-year inventory at base-year prices, a new LIFO layer is created. If there has been a decrease, a LIFO layer is reduced.

The following four techniques are applied in practice to determine the ending inventory at base-year prices:

1. Double extension (100% of inventory)
2. Double extension index (sample of inventory)
3. Link-chain index (sample of inventory)
4. Externally published index

The income tax regulations specify that the preferred technique is double extension. This technique results in a direct computation of the ending inventory at base-year prices because it requires extending all items in the ending inventory at both the base-year and the end-of-year prices. Because the double extension technique is time-consuming when there are many inventory items, the IRS has permitted the use of an index approach to compute the ending inventory at base-year prices. The IRS has ruled that the preferred index is an internal one developed from a sample of items from the company inventory. Under certain conditions, the IRS has permitted the use of an externally published index.

[9]James M. Reeve and Keith G. Stanga, "The LIFO Pooling Decision: Some Empirical Results from Accounting Practice," *Accounting Horizons,* June 1987, p. 27.

[10]Base-year prices are the prices in effect at the date the LIFO inventory method is adopted by a company. Thus, if a company adopted the LIFO inventory method in 1988, the base year for LIFO computations would be 1988.

In practice, most companies have adopted some form of an index method; therefore, the examples and discussion that follow are based on the use of indexes. Indexes are typically computed by comparing one year's inventory costs with another year's costs. To illustrate, assume a company has in its 1991 ending inventory 20 items at a cost of $1,000 each. If, at the end of 1992, those same 20 items would cost $1,200 each, then the index for 1992 would be computed as follows:

$$\text{Index} = \frac{\text{Inventory cost in 1992 dollars}}{\text{Inventory cost in 1991 dollars}} = \frac{\$24,000}{\$20,000} = 1.20$$

Assume the index numbers and inventories at end-of-year prices for Ahlander Whole-sale Co. are as follows:

| Date | Year-End Price Index* | Inventory at End-of-Year Prices |
|---|---|---|
| December 31, 1990 | 1.00 | $38,000 |
| December 31, 1991 | 1.20 | 54,000 |
| December 31, 1992 | 1.32 | 66,000 |
| December 31, 1993 | 1.40 | 56,000 |
| December 31, 1994 | 1.25 | 55,000 |

*Many published indexes appear as percentages without decimals, e.g., 100, 120, 132, 140, 125.

The effects of adding or deleting inventory layers in this situation can be most easily observed by preparing a work sheet that includes the following steps:

1. Determine the ending inventory in the pool at year-end prices.
2. Convert the ending inventory to base-year prices using the year-end price index.
3. Determine the inventory layers in base-year dollars.
4. Adjust the inventory to dollar-value LIFO layers by applying appropriate indexes to each base-year layer.

The work sheet on page 366 follows these steps and is based on the assumed data for Ahlander.

The following items should be observed in the example:

*December 31, 1991*—With an ending inventory of $45,000 in terms of base prices, the inventory has increased in 1991 by $7,000; however, the $7,000 increase is stated in terms of base-year prices and needs to be restated in terms of 1991 year-end prices which are 120% of the base level.

*December 31, 1992*—With an ending inventory of $50,000 in terms of base prices, the inventory has increased in 1992 by another $5,000; however, the $5,000 increase is stated in terms of base-year prices and needs to be restated in terms of 1992 year-end costs which are 132% of the base level.

*December 31, 1993*—When the ending inventory of $40,000 (expressed in base-year dollars) is compared to the beginning inventory of $50,000 (also expressed in base-year dollars), it is apparent that the inventory has been decreased by $10,000, in base-year terms. Under LIFO procedures, the decrease is assumed to take place in the most recently added layers, reducing or eliminating them. As a result, the 1992 layer, priced at $5,000 in base-year terms, is completely eliminated, and $5,000 of the $7,000 layer from 1991 is

| Date | Inventory at End-of-Year Prices | | Year-End Price Index | | Inventory at Base-Year Prices | Layers in Base-Year Prices | | Incremental Layer Index | | Dollar-Value LIFO Cost |
|------|------|---|------|---|------|------|---|------|---|------|
| December 31, 1990 | $38,000 | ÷ | 1.00 | = | $38,000 | $38,000 | × | 1.00 | = | $38,000 |
| December 31, 1991 | $54,000 | ÷ | 1.20 | = | $45,000 | $38,000 | × | 1.00 | = | $38,000 |
| | | | | | | 7,000 | × | 1.20 | = | 8,400 |
| | | | | | | $45,000 | | | | $46,400 |
| December 31, 1992 | $66,000 | ÷ | 1.32 | = | $50,000 | $38,000 | × | 1.00 | = | $38,000 |
| | | | | | | 7,000 | × | 1.20 | = | 8,400 |
| | | | | | | 5,000 | × | 1.32 | = | 6,600 |
| | | | | | | $50,000 | | | | $53,000 |
| December 31, 1993 | $56,000 | ÷ | 1.40 | = | $40,000 | $38,000 | × | 1.00 | = | $38,000 |
| | | | | | | 2,000 | × | 1.20 | = | 2,400 |
| | | | | | | $40,000 | | | | $40,400 |
| December 31, 1994 | $55,000 | ÷ | 1.25 | = | $44,000 | $38,000 | × | 1.00 | = | $38,000 |
| | | | | | | 2,000 | × | 1.20 | = | 2,400 |
| | | | | | | 4,000 | × | 1.25 | = | 5,000 |
| | | | | | | $44,000 | | | | $45,400 |

eliminated. This leaves only $2,000 of the 1991 layer, plus the base-year amount. The remaining $2,000 of the 1991 layer is multiplied by 1.20 to restate it to 1991 dollars, and is added to the base-year amount to arrive at the ending inventory amount of $40,400.

*December 31, 1994*—The ending inventory of $44,000 in terms of the base prices indicates an inventory increase for 1994 of $4,000; this increase requires restatement in terms of 1994 year-end prices which are 125% of the base level.

As discussed earlier, the Internal Revenue Service allows the incremental LIFO layer to be valued using FIFO, average, or LIFO costing. Thus the incremental index used to compute the new layer may be (1) a beginning-of-year index representing costs in the order of acquisition during the year (LIFO costing); (2) an average index, based on an average purchase price during the year (average costing); or (3) a year-end index, based on the latest acquisition price (FIFO costing).[11]

When FIFO costing is used to value the incremental layer, as in the previous example, the incremental index is the same as the year-end index used to determine if a new layer exists. However, if average or LIFO costing is used to compute the new layer, the incremental index will differ from the year-end index. To illustrate, using data from the preceding example, assume that LIFO costing is used to value incremental inventory layers. The beginning-of-year indexes, representing the earliest purchases in each year, are as follows:

| Date | Price Index Beginning-of-Year Purchases |
|------|------|
| December 31, 1991 | 1.02 |
| December 31, 1992 | 1.21 |
| December 31, 1993 | 1.35 |
| December 31, 1994 | 1.38 |

[11]The Task Force on LIFO Inventory Problems considered this issue from an accounting principles standpoint and unanimously agreed that "the order of acquisition approach (LIFO costing) generally is most compatible with the LIFO objective, but as a practical matter, any of the three pricing approaches consistently applied may be used for financial reporting purposes." *Issues Paper*, "Identification and Discussion of Certain Financial Accounting and Reporting Issues Concerning LIFO Inventories," (New York: American Institute of Certified Public Accountants, 1984), p. 9.

The computation of year-end inventories would then be made as follows:

| Date | Inventory at End-of-Year Prices | | Year-End Price Index | | Inventory at Base-Year Prices | Layers in Base-Year Prices | | Incremental Layer Index | | Dollar-Value LIFO Cost |
|---|---|---|---|---|---|---|---|---|---|---|
| December 31, 1990 | $38,000 | ÷ | 1.00 | = | $38,000 | $38,000 | × | 1.00 | = | $38,000 |
| December 31, 1991 | $54,000 | ÷ | 1.20 | = | $45,000 | $38,000 | × | 1.00 | = | $38,000 |
| | | | | | | 7,000 | × | 1.02 | = | 7,140 |
| | | | | | | $45,000 | | | | $45,140 |
| December 31, 1992 | $66,000 | ÷ | 1.32 | = | $50,000 | $38,000 | × | 1.00 | = | $38,000 |
| | | | | | | 7,000 | × | 1.02 | = | 7,140 |
| | | | | | | 5,000 | × | 1.21 | = | 6,050 |
| | | | | | | $50,000 | | | | $51,190 |
| December 31, 1993 | $56,000 | ÷ | 1.40 | = | $40,000 | $38,000 | × | 1.00 | = | $38,000 |
| | | | | | | 2,000 | × | 1.02 | = | 2,040 |
| | | | | | | $40,000 | | | | $40,040 |
| December 31, 1994 | $55,000 | ÷ | 1.25 | = | $44,000 | $38,000 | × | 1.00 | = | $38,000 |
| | | | | | | 2,000 | × | 1.02 | = | 2,040 |
| | | | | | | 4,000 | × | 1.38 | = | 5,520 |
| | | | | | | $44,000 | | | | $45,560 |

In some cases, the index for the first year of the LIFO layers is not 1.00. This is especially true when an externally generated index is used. When this occurs, it is simpler to convert all inventories to a base of 1.00 rather than to use the index for the initial year of the LIFO layers. The computations are done in the same manner as in the previous example except the inventory is stated in terms of the base year of the index, not the first year of the inventory layers. To illustrate, assume the same facts as stated for the example on page 365 except that the base year of the external index is 1986; in 1990, the index is 1.20; and, in 1991, it is 1.44. The schedule showing the LIFO inventory computations would be modified as follows for the first two years. Note that the inventory cost is the same under either situation.

| Date | Inventory at End-of-Year Prices | | Year-End Price Index | | Inventory at Base = 1.00 (1986 Prices) | Layers in Base = 1.00 (1986 Prices) | | Incremental Layer Index | | Dollar-Value LIFO Cost |
|---|---|---|---|---|---|---|---|---|---|---|
| December 31, 1990 | $38,000 | ÷ | 1.20 | = | $31,667 | $31,667 | × | 1.20 | = | $38,000 |
| December 31, 1991 | $54,000 | ÷ | 1.44 | = | $37,500 | $31,667 | × | 1.20 | = | $38,000 |
| | | | | | | 5,833 | × | 1.44 | = | 8,400 |
| | | | | | | $37,500 | | | | $46,400 |

**Selection of Pools**    The selection of inventory pools is critical in dollar-value LIFO. A company should have a minimum number of pools to benefit most from the use of the LIFO method. For manufacturers and processors, **natural business unit pools** are recommended. If it can be shown that a business has only one natural business unit, one pool may be used for all its inventory, including raw materials, goods in process, and finished goods. If, however, a business enterprise is composed of more than one natural business unit, more than one pool will be required. If the company maintains separate divisions for internal management purposes, has distinct production facilities and processes, or maintains separate income records for different units, more than one business unit pool is inferred. The Income Tax Regulations give the following example of a company with more than one natural business unit pool:

A corporation manufactures, in one division, automatic clothes washers and driers of both commercial and domestic grade as well as electric ranges, mangles, and dishwashers. The corporation manufactures, in another division, radios and television sets. The manufacturing facilities and processes used in manufacturing the radios and television sets are distinct from those used in manufacturing the automatic clothes washers, etc. Under these circumstances, the enterprise would consist of two business units and two pools would be appropriate, one consisting of all of the LIFO inventories entering into the manufacture of clothes washers and driers, electric ranges, mangles, and dishwashers and the other consisting of all of the LIFO inventories entering into the production of radios and television sets.[12]

A manufacturer or processor may choose to use **multiple pools** rather than include all inventory in natural business units. Each pool should consist of inventory items that are substantially similar, including raw materials.

Pools for wholesalers, retailers, etc., are usually defined by major lines, types, or classes of goods. The departments of a retail store are examples of separate pools for these entities. The number and propriety of inventory pools is reviewed periodically by the IRS, and continued use of established pools is subject to the results of the evaluation.

Although it is not necessary for companies to use the same pools for tax and accounting purposes, Reeve and Stanga found that most companies do, even when the IRS regulations require more pools than might be necessary for accounting purposes.[13] In some cases, companies have increased the number of pools to increase income. For example, in 1982 Stauffer Chemical Co. increased its number of LIFO pools for accounting purposes from 8 to 280. In general, the fewer the pools, the lower the ending inventory due to the ability to retain older costs in inventory layers through substitution of decreased inventory for one product with an increase in another. As the number of pools increases, more dipping into layers occurs with a resulting increase in income. In Stauffer's case, the increase in pools resulted in an increase of $16,515,000 in net income, or 13% of earnings.[14] The SEC objected to the change and, in 1984, required Stauffer to restate its financial statements using fewer pools.

The Economic Recovery Tax Act of 1981, and later the Tax Reform Act of 1986, simplified the selection and use of pools for smaller businesses. Any business with average gross receipts not in excess of $5 million for the three most recent taxable years may group their pools in accordance with the 11 general categories of the Consumer Price Index (CPI) or the 15 general categories of the Producer Price Indexes. The company may then use the published index for the category into which its goods are classified to determine its LIFO inventory values.

## COMPARISON OF COST ALLOCATION METHODS

In using first-in, first-out, inventories are reported on the balance sheet at or near current costs. With last-in, first-out, inventories not changing significantly in quantity are reported at more or less fixed amounts relating back to the earliest purchases. Use of the average method generally provides inventory values closely paralleling first-in, first-out values, since purchases during a period are normally several times the opening inventory

---

[12]*Ibid.*, Sec. 1.472.8(b) (2) (ii).

[13]For additional insight into how the selection of pools can be used for tax planning and income determination, see Reeve and Stanga, *op. cit.*, pp. 25-33.

[14]Stauffer Chemical Company, *1982 annual report.*

balance and average costs are thus heavily influenced by current costs. Specific identification can produce any variety of results depending on the desires of management. When the prices paid for merchandise do not fluctuate significantly, alternative inventory methods may provide only minor differences on the financial statements. However, in periods of steadily rising or falling prices, the alternative methods may produce material differences.

Differences in inventory valuations on the balance sheet are accompanied by differences in earnings on the income statement for the period. Use of first-in, first-out in a period of rising prices matches oldest low-cost inventory with rising sales prices, thus expanding the gross profit margin. In a period of declining prices, oldest high-cost inventory is matched with declining sales prices, thus narrowing the gross profit margin. Using an average method, the gross profit margin tends to follow a similar pattern in response to changing prices. On the other hand, use of last-in, first-out in a period of rising prices relates current high costs of acquiring goods with rising sales prices. Thus LIFO tends to have a stabilizing effect on gross profit margins.

The application of the different methods, excluding specific identification, in periods of rising and falling prices is illustrated in the following example. Assume that the Wisconsin Sales Co. sells its goods at 50% over prevailing costs from 1991 to 1994. The company sells its inventories and terminates activities at the end of 1994. Sales, costs, and gross profits using each of the three methods are shown in the following tabulation.

| | FIFO | | Weighted Average* | | LIFO | |
|---|---|---|---|---|---|---|
| **1991:** | | | | | | |
| Sales, 500 units @ $9 | | $4,500 | | $4,500 | | $4,500 |
| Inventory, 200 units | @ $5 $1,000 | | 200 @ $5 | $1,000 | 200 @ $5 $1,000 | |
| Purchases, 500 units | @ $6 3,000 | | 500 @ $6 | 3,000 | 500 @ $6 3,000 | |
| Goods available for sale | $4,000 | | | $4,000 | $4,000 | |
| | | | 200 @ $5.71 | | | |
| Ending Inv., 200 units | @ $6 1,200 | | ($4,000 ÷ 700) | 1,142 | 200 @ $5 1,000 | |
| Cost of goods sold | | 2,800 | | 2,858 | | 3,000 |
| Gross profit on sales | | $1,700 | | $1,642 | | $1,500 |
| **1992:** | | | | | | |
| Sales, 450 units @ $12 | | $5,400 | | $5,400 | | $5,400 |
| Inventory, 200 units | @ $6 $1,200 | | 200 @ $5.71 | $1,142 | 200 @ $5 $1,000 | |
| Purchases, 500 units | @ $8 4,000 | | 500 @ $8 | 4,000 | 500 @ $8 4,000 | |
| Goods available for sale | $5,200 | | | $5,142 | $5,000 | |
| | | | 250 @ $7.35 | | 200 @ $5⎫ | |
| Ending Inv., 250 units | @ $8 2,000 | | ($5,142 ÷ 700) | 1,838 | 50 @ $8⎭ 1,400 | |
| Cost of goods sold | | 3,200 | | 3,304 | | 3,600 |
| Gross profit on sales | | $2,200 | | $2,096 | | $1,800 |
| **1993:** | | | | | | |
| Sales, 475 units @ $10.50 | | $4,988 | | $4,988 | | $4,988 |
| Inventory, 250 units | @ $8 $2,000 | | 250 @ $7.35 | $1,838 | 200 @ $5⎫ | |
| | | | | | 50 @ $8⎭$1,400 | |
| Purchases, 450 units | @ $7 3,150 | | 450 @ $7 | 3,150 | 450 @ $7 3,150 | |
| Goods available for sale | $5,150 | | | $4,988 | $4,550 | |
| | | | 225 @ $7.13 | | 200 @ $5⎫ | |
| Ending Inv., 225 units | @ $7 1,575 | | ($4,988 ÷ 700) | 1,604 | 25 @ $8⎭ 1,200 | |
| Cost of goods sold | | 3,575 | | 3,384 | | 3,350 |
| Gross profit on sales | | $1,413 | | $1,604 | | $1,638 |

|  | FIFO | | Weighted Average* | | LIFO | |
|---|---|---|---|---|---|---|
| **1994:** | | | | | | |
| Sales, 625 units @ $7.50 | | $4,688 | | $4,688 | | $4,688 |
| Inventory, 225 units | @ $7 $1,575 | | 225 @ $7.13 | $1,604 | 200 @ $5 ⎱ | |
| | | | | | 25 @ $8 ⎰ $1,200 | |
| Purchases, 400 units | @ $5 2,000 | | 400 @ $5 | 2,000 | 400 @ $5 2,000 | |
| Cost of goods sold | | 3,575 | | 3,604 | | 3,200 |
| Gross profit on sales | | $1,113 | | $1,084 | | $1,488 |

*Totals in the illustration are calculated to the nearest dollar.

The foregoing transactions are summarized in the table below.

| | | FIFO | | | Weighted Average | | | LIFO | | |
|---|---|---|---|---|---|---|---|---|---|---|
| Year | Sales | Cost of Goods Sold | Gross Profit on Sales | Gross Profit % to Sales | Cost of Goods Sold | Gross Profit on Sales | Gross Profit % to Sales | Cost of Goods Sold | Gross Profit on Sales | Gross Profit % to Sales |
| 1991 | $ 4,500 | $ 2,800 | $1,700 | 37.8% | $ 2,858 | $1,642 | 36.5% | $ 3,000 | $1,500 | 33.3% |
| 1992 | 5,400 | 3,200 | 2,200 | 40.7 | 3,304 | 2,096 | 38.8 | 3,600 | 1,800 | 33.3 |
| 1993 | 4,988 | 3,575 | 1,413 | 28.3 | 3,384 | 1,604 | 32.2 | 3,350 | 1,638 | 32.8 |
| 1994 | 4,688 | 3,575 | 1,113 | 23.7 | 3,604 | 1,084 | 23.1 | 3,200 | 1,488 | 31.7 |
| | $19,576 | $13,150 | $6,426 | 32.8% | $13,150 | $6,426 | 32.8% | $13,150 | $6,426 | 32.8% |

Although the different methods give the same total gross profit on sales for the four-year period, use of first-in, first-out resulted in increased gross profit percentages in periods of rising prices and a contraction of gross profit percentages in periods of falling prices, while last-in, first-out resulted in relatively steady gross profit percentages in spite of fluctuating prices. The weighted average method offered results closely comparable to those obtained by first-in, first-out. Assuming operating expenses at 30% of sales, use of last-in, first-out would result in a net income for each of the four years; first-in, first-out would result in larger net incomes in 1991 and 1992, but net losses in 1993 and 1994. Inventory valuation on the last-in, first-out basis tends to smooth the peaks and fill the troughs of business fluctuations.

## Income Tax Considerations

The preceding comparison of cost methods was made without considering the income tax impact of the method used. As indicated earlier, if a company elects to use LIFO for tax purposes, it must also use some form of LIFO in its financial reports. In a period of inflation, the lower reported profit using LIFO results in lower income taxes. Thus the tax liability on gross profit, assuming a 35% tax rate, for the three illustrated methods over the four-year period would be as follows:

| | Tax Liability | | |
|---|---|---|---|
| | FIFO | Weighted Average | LIFO |
| 1991 | $ 595 | $ 575 | $ 525 |
| 1992 | 770 | 734 | 630 |
| 1993 | 494 | 561 | 573 |
| 1994 | 390 | 379 | 521 |
| Totals | $2,249 | $2,249 | $2,249 |

In this example, a complete cycle of price increases and decreases occurred over the four-year period; thus the total income tax liability for the four years was the same under each method. However, by using LIFO to defer part of the tax during 1991 and 1992, more cash was available to the company for operating purposes. In periods of constantly increasing inflation, the deferral tends to become permanent and is a condition sought by many companies. Whenever inflation starts to accelerate in the United States, many companies begin to report larger net incomes primarily caused by the illusory influence of holding gains. To protect their cash flows, a significant number of companies change to LIFO inventory to reduce their present and future tax liabilities. These changes have to be approved by the Internal Revenue Service and are subject to specific rules governing adoption of the LIFO method. The complexity of some of these rules has deterred other companies from making the change even though the tax consequences promised to be favorable.[15]

When a company changes its method of valuing inventory, the change is accounted for as a change in accounting principle. If the change is to average cost or FIFO, both the beginning and ending inventories can usually be computed on the new basis. Thus the effect of changing inventory methods can be determined and reported in the financial statements as explained in Chapter 21. If the change is *to* LIFO from another method, however, a company's records are generally not complete enough to reconstruct the prior years' inventory layers. Therefore, the base-year layer for the new LIFO inventory is the opening inventory for the year in which LIFO is adopted (also the ending inventory for the year *before* LIFO is adopted). There is no adjustment to the financial statements to reflect the change to LIFO. However, the impact of the change on income for the current year must be disclosed in a note to the statements. In addition, the note should explain why there is no effect on the financial statements. Required disclosures for a change to LIFO are illustrated in the following note from the 1988 annual report of Penn Central Corporation.

---

**Exhibit 10—3    THE PENN CENTRAL CORPORATION—Disclosure of Change to LIFO Method**

---

Effective January 1, 1988, the Company changed its method of valuing a significant component of its building wire inventories from the FIFO to the LIFO method. Management believes the LIFO method will result in a better matching of current costs with current revenues. The effect of the change in 1988 was to decrease both income from continuing operations and net income by $7.4 million, or $.10 per share. The cumulative effect of this accounting change and the pro forma effect on prior years' earnings have not been included because such effects are not reasonably determinable.

At December 31, 1988, $53.8 of inventories were valued using the LIFO method. If the FIFO method had been used, inventories at December 31, 1988, would have been $73.9 million. The FIFO cost of these inventories approximated replacement cost.

---

[15]A survey in 1980 of 213 companies who were not using LIFO indicated many different reasons for their decision. Principal among them were (1) the company had no tax liability, (2) prices were declining in their industry, and (3) the change to LIFO would have an immaterial impact because of rapid inventory turnover. Michael H. Granof and Daniel G. Short, "Why Do Companies Reject Lifo?" *Journal of Accounting, Auditing, and Finance* (Summer 1984), pp. 323-333.

---

## EVALUATION OF LIFO AS A COST ALLOCATION METHOD

Because so many companies have resorted to LIFO as a means of reducing reported income and, consequently, their income tax liability, it is important to identify the advantages and disadvantages of this unique inventory method. It should be noted once again that LIFO is a historical cost allocation method; it assigns the most recent historical cost to expense (cost of goods sold) and the oldest relevant historical cost to inventory. Its ability to match recent historical cost, which approximates current cost, to revenue depends upon the rate of price change, inventory turnover, and frequency of purchase. For example, if the most recent purchase of inventory was two years ago, LIFO, at best, can only assign two-year-old historical cost figures to expense. Because LIFO allocates only historical cost between the balance sheet and income statement, it cannot adjust for changes in the general price level and in specific prices since the acquisition date.

### Major Advantages of LIFO

The advantages of LIFO may be summarized as follows:

**Tax Benefits**     Temporary or permanent deferrals of income taxes can be achieved with LIFO, resulting in current cash savings. These deferrals continue as long as the price level is increasing and inventory quantities do not decline. The improved cash flow enables a company to either decrease its borrowing and reduce interest cost, or invest the savings to produce revenue.

**Better Measurement of Income**     Because LIFO allocates the most recently incurred costs to cost of sales, this method produces an income figure that tends to report only the operating income and defers recognition of the holding gain until prices or quantities decline. The illusory inflation profits discussed earlier tend not to appear as part of net income when LIFO inventory is used.

### Major Disadvantages of LIFO

The disadvantages of LIFO are more subtle than the advantages. Companies adopting LIFO sometimes realize too late that LIFO can produce some severe side effects.

**Reduced Income**     The application of the most recent prices against current revenue produces a decrease in net income in an inflationary period. If management's goal is to maximize reported income, the adoption of LIFO will produce results that are in opposition to that goal.

Investors and other users of financial statements frequently base their evaluations of a company's performance on the "bottom line" or net income. Failure on the part of users to recognize that a lower net income is due to the use of LIFO rather than a decline in operating proficiency may have a depressing effect on the market price of a company's stock. The reduced income may be perceived as a failure on the part of management. Further, the use of LIFO will reduce bonus payments to employees that are based on net income and could reduce the amount of dividends distributed to shareholders.

**Unrealistic Inventory Balances on the Balance Sheet**     The allocation of older inventory costs to the balance sheet can cause a serious understatement of inventory values. Depending on the length of time the LIFO layers have been developing and the severity of the price increase, the reported inventory values can be substantially lower than current replacement values. For example, the Penn Central disclosure on page 371 indicates that if the FIFO method had been used, inventories would be $20.1 million higher in 1988 than the reported LIFO inventory. This is approximately 37.4% of the LIFO valued inventory. Because inventory costs enter into the determination of working capital, the current ratio can be seriously distorted under a LIFO inventory system. Although this discussion of LIFO assumes an inflationary economy, if prices were to decrease, LIFO would produce inventory values higher than current replacement costs. It is fair to assume that should this occur, there would be strong pressure for special action to permit the write-down of inventory balances to replacement cost.

**Unanticipated Profits Created by Failing to Maintain Inventory Quantities**    The income advantages summarized previously will be realized only if inventory quantity levels are maintained. If the ending inventory quantities decline, the old layers of cost eliminated are charged against current revenue. If the inventory costs of these layers are significantly less than the current replacement costs, the reported profit will be artificially increased by the failure to maintain inventory levels.

To avoid the distortion caused by a temporary reduction of LIFO layers at the end of a year, some accountants advocate establishing a replacement allowance that charges the current period for the extra replacement cost expected to be incurred in the subsequent period when the inventory is replenished. However, the use of an allowance for temporary liquidation of LIFO layers, sometimes referred to as the **base-stock method**, is not currently acceptable for financial reporting or tax purposes. The use of this type of allowance on the books could disqualify a company from filing its tax returns on the LIFO basis, and therefore, it is seldom used in practice.

**Unrealistic Flow Assumptions**    The cost assignment resulting from the application of LIFO does not normally approximate the physical movement of goods through the business. One would seldom encounter in practice the actual use or transfer of goods on a last-in, first-out basis.

## SELECTION OF AN INVENTORY METHOD

As indicated in this chapter, companies have many alternative ways to value inventories. Guidelines for the selection of a proper method are very broad, and a company may justify almost any accepted method. After a lengthy study of inventory practices, Horace Barden, retired partner of Ernst and Whinney, concluded his research study by stating:

> . . . one must recognize that no neat package of principles or other criteria exists to substitute for the professional judgment of the responsible accountant. The need for the exercise of judgment in accounting for inventories is so great that I recommend to authoritative bodies that they refrain from establishing rules that, in isolation from the conditions and circumstances that may exist in practice, attempt to determine the accounting treatment to be applied under any and all circumstances.[16]

Many companies use more than one inventory costing method. For example, The Quaker Oats Company uses three different methods and includes the following disclosure in its financial statements:

---

[16]Horace G. Barden, *Accounting Research Study No. 13*, "The Accounting Basis of Inventories" (New York: American Institute of Certified Public Accountants, 1973) p. 141.

## The Steel Industry's LIFO Problem

In the early 1980s, the American steel industry was experiencing severe financial troubles. An increase in foreign competition as well as advancing technology combined to contribute to the decline of industry profits. The demand for domestic steel was down and, as a result, many firms laid off workers. However, the use of the LIFO method of accounting for inventory distorted the actual financial position of many firms as illustrated by the following simple example:

USA Steel Co. has the following LIFO inventory layers on January 1, 1982:

| | |
|---|---|
| Layer 1 | 6,000 tons @ $10 per ton |
| Layer 2 | 5,000 tons @ $15 per ton |
| Layer 3 | 8,000 tons @ $25 per ton |

Assume steel is selling for $50 per ton in 1983 and it costs $35 per ton to produce. Because of a decrease in demand for domestic steel, USA Steel shuts down its production facilities and elects to sell the inventory that is on hand rather than produce additional inventory.

### Questions:

1. *If USA Steel Co. sells 15,000 tons of steel during 1983, what is the gross margin in this simplified example using LIFO?*
2. *What is USA Steel's gross margin if the 15,000 tons of steel had been costed at the current cost of $35 per ton?*
3. *Does the LIFO gross margin accurately depict the financial situation of USA Steel Co.?*
4. *In order for the LIFO inventory method to accurately match current costs with current revenues, what sort of inventory policy must a company have regarding its LIFO layers?*

---

### Exhibit 10—4    The Quaker Oats Company—Disclosure of Inventory Methods

*Inventories.* Inventories are valued at the lower of cost or market, using various cost methods, and include the cost of raw materials, labor and overhead. The percentage of fiscal year-end inventories valued using each of the methods is as follows:

| | 1988 | 1987 | 1986 |
|---|---|---|---|
| Average quarterly cost | 54% | 52% | 51% |
| Last-in, first-out (LIFO) | 29% | 31% | 21% |
| First-in, first-out (FIFO) | 17% | 17% | 28% |

The decision as to which method to use depends on not only the tax consequences but also the nature of the inventories themselves. For inventories other than those valued using LIFO, a company may use a different method for tax purposes than it uses for financial reporting purposes. This creates a temporary difference with respect to cost of goods sold and the resulting net income, which leads to a need for interperiod income tax allocation.

Companies sometimes change their inventory methods, especially as economic conditions change. For instance, several recent research studies have shown that the stock market reacts favorably to companies that elect to adopt the LIFO method.[17] When inventories are a material item, a change in the inventory method by a company may impair comparability of that company's financial statements with prior years' statements and with the financial statements of other entities. Such changes require careful consideration and should be made only when management can clearly demonstrate the preferability of the alternative method. This position was emphasized by the Accounting Principles Board in Opinion No. 20 with the statement, "The burden of justifying other changes rests with the entity proposing the change."[18] If a change is made, complete disclosure of the impact of the change is encouraged by the FASB.

[17]For an example, see Francis L. Stevenson, "New Evidence on LIFO Adoption: The Effects of More Precise Event Dates," *Journal of Accounting Research,* Autumn 1987, pp. 306-316.

[18]*Opinions of the Accounting Principles Board, No. 20,* "Accounting Changes" (New York: American Institute of Certified Public Accountants, 1971), par. 16.

## KEY TERMS

## QUESTIONS

1. What economic conditions make the allocation of inventory costs most difficult?
2. (a) What are the three cost elements entering into goods in process and finished goods? (b) What items enter into factory overhead?
3. Distinguish between raw materials and factory supplies. Why are the terms direct and indirect materials often used to refer to raw materials and factory supplies, respectively?
4. Would you expect to find a perpetual or a periodic inventory system used in each of the following situations?
   (a) Diamond ring department of a jewelry store.
   (b) Computer department of a college bookstore.
   (c) Candy department of a college bookstore.
   (d) Automobile dealership—new car department.
   (e) Automobile dealership—parts department.
   (f) Wholesale dealer of small tools.
   (g) A plumbing supply house—brass fittings department.
5. Under what conditions is merchandise-in-transit legally reported as inventory by the (a) seller? (b) buyer?
6. How should the following items be treated in computing year-end inventory costs: (a) segregated goods? (b) conditional sales?
7. State how you would report each of the following items on the financial statements:
   (a) Manufacturing supplies.
   (b) Goods on hand received on a consignment basis.
   (c) Goods received without an accompanying invoice.
   (d) Goods in stock to be delivered to customers in subsequent periods.
   (e) Goods in hands of agents and consignees.
   (f) Deposits with vendors for merchandise to be delivered next period.
   (g) Goods in hands of customers on approval.
   (h) Defective goods requiring reprocessing.

8. (a) What are the two methods of accounting for cash discounts? (b) Which method is generally preferred? Why?
9. Theoretically, there is little wrong with inventory costing by the specific cost identification method. What objections can be raised to the use of this method?
10. Would you expect to find the specific identification method or some other historical cost flow assumption, such as average cost or LIFO, used for the items noted in Question 4.
11. What advantages are there to using the average cost method of inventory pricing?
12. The Wallace Co. decides to adopt specific goods LIFO as of January 1, 1993, and determines the cost of the different kinds of merchandise carried as of this date. (a) What three different methods may be employed at the end of a period in assigning costs to quantity increases in specific pools? (b) What procedure is employed at the end of each period for quantity decreases of specific items?
13. (a) What is the LIFO conformity rule? (b) How has the rule changed since it was first adopted? (c) How might the changes in the conformity rule affect LIFO inventories reported on the financial statements?
14. Assume a car manufacturer and a discounting retail firm have identical sales and income and that price changes affecting the various factors of production increase at the same rate. The car manufacturer has an inventory turnover rate of 2 times a year and the discounting firm an inventory turnover of 15 times per year. Assume that each firm wants to match an historical cost which approximates current cost against revenue. Which firm will benefit more by changing from FIFO to LIFO?
15. Assume there is no change in the physical quantity of inventory for the current accounting period. During a period of rising prices, which historical cost flow (LIFO or FIFO) will result in the greater dollar value

of ending inventory and the greater dollar value of cost of goods sold? Will the beginning and ending inventory value under LIFO and FIFO be equal? Why or why not?

16. What are the major advantages of dollar-value LIFO over specific goods LIFO?

17. Indexes are used for two different purposes in computing the layers of a dollar-value LIFO pool. Clearly distinguish between these uses and describe how the indexes are applied.

18. The selection of inventory pools is very important in using the dollar-value LIFO method of inventory costing. What factors should be considered in identifying the pools for a specific company?

19. Discuss the advantages and disadvantages of LIFO as a cost allocation method.

---

## DISCUSSION CASES

### Case 10—1  (Should we adopt LIFO?)

You are the controller of the Ford Steel Co. Assume the economy enters a period of rapidly increasing inflation. The turnover of inventory in your company occurs about once every nine months. The inflation is causing revenue to rise more rapidly than the historical cost of the goods sold. Although profits are higher this year than last, you realize that the cost to replace the sold inventory is also higher. You are aware that many companies are changing to the LIFO inventory method, but you are concerned that what goes up will eventually come down, and when prices decline, the LIFO method will result in high profits and taxes. Since declining prices are usually equated with economic recession, it is likely that the higher taxes will have to be paid at a time when revenues are declining.

What factors should you consider before making a change to LIFO? Based on the above considerations, what would you recommend?

### Case 10—2  (What is an inventoriable cost?)

You have been hired by Midwestern Products Co. to work in its accounting department. As part of your assignment, you have been asked to review the inventory costing procedures. In the past, the company has attempted to keep its inventory as low as possible to hedge against future declines in demand. One way of doing this has been to charge off as many costs as can be justified as expenses of the current period. Sales have declined, however, and the controller wants to include as high an ending inventory valuation as possible to show the stockholders a better income figure for the current year. Your study shows the following costs have been consistently treated as period costs for financial reporting purposes:

Depreciation of plant
Fringe payroll benefits for factory personnel
Repairs of equipment
Salaries of foremen
Warehouse rental for storage of finished products
Pension costs for factory personnel
Training program—all employees
Cafeteria costs—all employees
Interest expense
Depreciation and maintenance of fleet of delivery trucks

Which items do you suggest could be deferred by including them as inventoriable costs? Evaluate the wisdom and propriety of making the suggested changes.

## Case 10—3  (Which method shall we use?)

The White Wove Corporation began operations in 1991. A summary of the first quarter appears below.

| | Purchases | |
|---|---|---|
| | **Units** | **Total Cost** |
| January 2 | 250 | $23,250 |
| February 11 | 100 | 9,500 |
| February 20 | 400 | 38,400 |
| March 21 | 200 | 19,600 |
| March 27 | 225 | 22,275 |

| | Other Data | | |
|---|---|---|---|
| | **Sales in Units** | **Sales Price Per Unit** | **Operating Expenses** |
| January | 200 | $140 | $9,575 |
| February | 225 | 142 | 7,820 |
| March | 350 | 145 | 7,905 |

The White Wove Corporation used the LIFO perpetual inventory method and computed an inventory value of $38,300 at the end of the first quarter. Management is considering changing to a FIFO costing method. They have also considered using a periodic system instead of the perpetual system presently being used. You have been hired to assist management in making the decision. What would you advise?

## Case 10—4  (A new use for bricks)

In 1989 an investigation by the United States Department of Justice Criminal Division uncovered a massive fraud perpetrated by top management of Miniscribe Corporation. Miniscribe manufactured and sold computer disk drives. The investigation revealed such practices as shipping bricks in place of disk drives to boost sales and inventory figures. How would shipping bricks boost sales? If sales are inflated this year by selling bricks, what must happen next year to maintain the sales trend?

## Case 10—5  (How well am I really doing?)

Fay Stocks sells oriental rugs. She uses the FIFO method of inventory costing and maintains perpetual inventory records. The inventory available for sale for a particular style of rug is as follows:

| Invoice Date | Current Inventory | Cost |
|---|---|---|
| June 14, 1993 | 4 @ | $1,200 each |
| June 21, 1993 | 3 @ | $1,500 each |
| July 5, 1993 | 6 @ | $1,700 each |

A wealthy customer purchases 3 rugs paying $2,600 for each. Fay immediately replaces those rugs with 3 new rugs at a cost of $1,900 apiece. What is Fay's gross margin from the sale of the rugs? What is Fay's net cash flow from the sale of the rugs and the subsequent purchase of 3 new rugs? Why is there a substantial difference between gross margin and cash flow? What circumstances lead to differences like those illustrated in this case?

## Case 10—6  (Are inventory summaries enough?)

John Craston is presenting information to the audit committee relating to this year's annual financial statements. In discussing inventory, Mr. Craston argues, "There is no need to provide detail as to the components of inventory. A summary figure is all that investors and creditors require. Why should they care if inventory is in the form of raw materials, goods in process, or finished goods?" Information relating to inventory is as follows:

| (in thousands) | 1993 | 1992 |
| --- | --- | --- |
| Raw Materials | $162 | $ 92 |
| Goods in Process | 60 | 65 |
| Finished Goods | 53 | 93 |
| Total | $275 | $250 |

As an owner of 10% of the company's stock, which type of disclosure would you prefer? Why? What information is contained in the detailed inventory figures that cannot be inferred from the summary inventory figure?

---

## EXERCISES

### Exercise 10—1  (Computing cash expenditure for inventory)

Using the following data, compute the total cash expended for inventory in 1993:

| | |
| --- | --- |
| Accounts payable: | |
| January 1, 1993 | $200,000 |
| December 31, 1993 | 240,000 |
| Cost of goods sold—1993 | 900,000 |
| Inventory balance: | |
| January 1, 1993 | 300,000 |
| December 31, 1993 | 200,000 |

### Exercise 10—2  (Passage of title)

The management of Kauer Company has engaged you to assist in the preparation of year-end (December 31) financial statements. You are told that on November 30, the correct inventory level was 150,000 units. During the month of December, sales totaled 50,000 units including 25,000 units shipped on consignment to Towsey Company. A letter received from Towsey indicates that as of December 31, it had sold 12,000 units and was still trying to sell the remainder. A review of the December purchase orders, to various suppliers, shows the following:

| Date of Purchase Order | Invoice Date | Quantity in Units | Date Shipped | Date Received | Terms |
| --- | --- | --- | --- | --- | --- |
| 12-2-93 | 1-3-94 | 10,000 | 1-2-94 | 1-3-94 | FOB shipping point |
| 12-11-93 | 1-3-94 | 8,000 | 12-22-93 | 12-24-93 | FOB destination |
| 12-13-93 | 1-2-94 | 13,000 | 12-28-93 | 1-2-94 | FOB shipping point |
| 12-23-93 | 12-26-93 | 12,000 | 1-2-94 | 1-3-94 | FOB shipping point |
| 12-28-93 | 1-10-94 | 10,000 | 12-31-93 | 1-5-94 | FOB destination |
| 12-31-93 | 1-10-94 | 15,000 | 1-3-94 | 1-6-94 | FOB destination |

Kauer Company uses the "passing of legal title" for inventory recognition. Compute the number of units which should be included in the year-end inventory.

### Exercise 10—3 (Passage of title)

The Young Manufacturing Company reviewed its in-transit inventory and found the following items. Indicate which items should be included in the inventory balance at December 31, 1993. Give your reasons for the treatment you suggest.

(a)  Merchandise costing $2,350 was received on January 3, 1994, and the related purchase invoice was recorded January 5. The invoice showed the shipment was made on December 29, 1993, FOB destination.

(b)  Merchandise costing $625 was received on December 28, 1993, and the invoice was not recorded. The invoice was in the hands of the purchasing agent; it was marked "On consignment."

(c)  A packing case containing a product costing $816 was standing in the shipping room when the physical inventory was taken. It was not included in the inventory because it was marked "Hold for shipping instructions." The customer's order was dated December 18, but the case was shipped and the customer billed on January 10, 1994.

(d)  Merchandise received on January 6, 1994, costing $720 was entered in the purchase register on January 7. The invoice showed shipment was made FOB shipping point on December 31, 1993. Since it was not on hand during the inventory count, it was not included.

(e)  A special machine, fabricated to order for a particular customer, was finished and in the shipping room on December 30. The customer was billed on that date and the machine was excluded from inventory although it was shipped January 4, 1994.

### Exercise 10—4 (Trade and cash discounts)

Olavssen Hardware regularly buys merchandise from Dawson Suppliers and is allowed a trade discount of 20/10/10 from the list price. Olavssen uses the net method to record purchases and discounts. On August 15, Olavssen Hardware purchased material from Dawson Suppliers. The invoice received from Dawson showed a list price of $5,000, and terms of 2/10, n/30. Payment was sent to Dawson Suppliers on August 28. Prepare the journal entries to record the purchase and subsequent payment. (Round to nearest dollar.)

### Exercise 10—5 (Net and gross methods—entries)

On December 3, Hakan Photography purchased inventory listed at $8,600 from Mark Photo Supply. Terms of the purchase were 3/10, n/20. Hakan Photography also purchased inventory from Erickson Wholesale on December 10, for a list price of $7,500. Terms of the purchase were 3/10 eom. On December 16, Hakan paid both suppliers for these purchases. Hakan does not use a perpetual inventory system.

1.  Give the entries to record the purchases and invoice payments assuming that (a) the net method is used, (b) the gross method is used.

2.  Assume that Hakan has not paid either of the invoices at December 31. Give the year-end adjusting entries, if the net method is being used. Also assume that Hakan plans to pay Erickson Wholesale within the discount period.

### Exercise 10—6 (Cost of goods manufactured schedule)

The following cost data has been accumulated for Garrison Mfg. Inc.:

| | |
|---|---|
| Raw Materials—Beginning Inventory | 100 units @ $6.00 |
| Purchases | 85 units @ $7.00 |
| | 110 units @ $7.50 |
| Transferred 215 units to Goods in Process | |
| Goods in Process—Beginning Inventory | 56 units @ $13.50 |
| Direct Labor | $2,500 |
| Factory Overhead | $3,250 |
| Goods in Process—Ending Inventory | 68 units @ $13.75 |

Garrison uses the FIFO method for valuing raw materials inventories. Prepare a cost of goods manufactured schedule for Garrison Mfg. Inc. for the quarter ended March 31, 1993.

### Exercise 10—7  (Inventory computation using different cost flows)

The Webster Store shows the following information relating to one of its products.

| | |
|---|---|
| Inventory, January 1 | 300 units @ $17.50 |
| Purchases, January 10 | 900 units @ $18.00 |
| Purchases, January 20 | 1,200 units @ $18.25 |
| Sales, January 8 | 200 units |
| Sales, January 18 | 600 units |
| Sales, January 25 | 1,000 units |

What are the values of ending inventory under (1) perpetual and (2) periodic methods assuming the cost flows below? (Round unit costs to three decimal places.)

(a)  FIFO
(b)  LIFO
(c)  Average

### Exercise 10—8  (Inventory computation using different cost flows)

Richmond Corporation had the following transactions relating to Product AB during September.

| Date | | | Units | Unit Cost |
|---|---|---|---|---|
| September | 1 | Balance on hand | 500 units | $5.00 |
| | 6 | Purchase | 100 units | 4.50 |
| | 12 | Sale | 300 units | |
| | 13 | Sale | 200 units | |
| | 18 | Purchase | 200 units | 6.00 |
| | 20 | Purchase | 200 units | 4.00 |
| | 25 | Sale | 200 units | |

Determine the ending inventory value under each of the following costing methods:

1. FIFO (perpetual)
2. FIFO (periodic)
3. LIFO (perpetual)
4. LIFO (periodic)

### Exercise 10—9  (Comparison of inventory methods)

Spearman Truck Sales sells semitrailers. The current inventory includes the following five semitrailers (identical except for paint color) along with purchase dates and costs:

| Semitrailer # | Purchase Date | Cost |
|---|---|---|
| 1 | April 4, 1993 | $64,000 |
| 2 | April 12, 1993 | 60,000 |
| 3 | April 12, 1993 | 60,000 |
| 4 | May 3, 1993 | 68,000 |
| 5 | May 12, 1993 | 68,500 |

On May 20, 1993, a trucking firm purchases semitrailer #3 from Spearman for $75,000.

1. Compute the gross margin on this sale assuming Spearman uses:
    (a) FIFO inventory method.
    (b) LIFO inventory method.
    (c) specific identification method.
2. Which inventory method do you think Spearman should use? Why?

### Exercise 10—10   (LIFO inventory computation)

White Farm Supply's records for the first three months of its existence show purchases of Commodity Y2 as follows:

|  | Number of Units | Cost |
|---|---|---|
| August | 5,500 | $29,975 |
| September | 8,000 | 41,600 |
| October | 5,100 | 27,030 |

The inventory at the end of October of Commodity Y2 using FIFO is valued at $36,390. Assuming that none of Commodity Y2 was sold during August and September, what value would be shown at the end of October if LIFO cost was assumed?

### Exercise 10—11   (Inventory computation from incomplete records)

A flood recently destroyed many of the financial records of Riboldi Manufacturing Company. Management has hired you to recreate as much financial information as possible for the month of July. You are able to find out that the company uses a weighted average inventory costing system. You also learn that Riboldi makes a physical count at the end of each month in order to determine monthly ending inventory values. By examining various documents you are able to gather the following information:

| | |
|---|---|
| Ending inventory at July 31 | 50,000 units |
| Total cost of units available for sale in July | $118,800 |
| Cost of goods sold during July | $99,000 |
| Cost of beginning inventory, July 1 | $0.35 per unit |
| Gross margin on sales for July | $101,000 |

| July Purchases | | |
|---|---|---|
| Date | Units | Unit Cost |
| July 4 | 60,000 | $0.40 |
| July 11 | 50,000 | 0.41 |
| July 15 | 40,000 | 0.42 |
| July 16 | 50,000 | 0.45 |

You are asked to provide the following information:

1. Number of units on hand, July 1.
2. Units sold during July.
3. Unit cost of inventory at July 31.
4. Value of inventory at July 31.

### Exercise 10—12   (Computation of beginning inventory)

A note to the financial statements of Alpine Inc. at December 31, 1993, reads as follows:

> Because of the manufacturer's production problems for our Widget Limited line, our inventories were unavoidably reduced. Under the LIFO inventory accounting method currently being used for tax and financial accounting purposes, the net effect of all the inventory changes was to increase pretax income by $1,200,000 over what it would have been had the inventory of Widget Limited been maintained at the normal physical levels on hand at the start of the year.

The unit purchase price of the merchandise was $20 per unit during the year. Alpine Inc. uses the periodic inventory system. Additional data concerning Alpine's inventory was as follows:

| Date | Physical Count of Inventory | LIFO Cost of Inventory |
|------|------------------------------|------------------------|
| January 1, 1993 | 400,000 units | $    ? |
| December 31, 1993 | 300,000 units | $2,900,000 |

1. What was the unit average cost for the 100,000 units sold from the beginning inventory?
2. What was the reported value for the January 1, 1993, inventory?

### Exercise 10—13  (Computation of beginning inventory from ending inventory)

The Killpack Company sells Product N. During a move to a new location, the inventory records for Product N were misplaced. The bookkeeper has been able to gather some information from the sales records, and gives you the data shown below.

July sales: 53,500 units at $10.00.

| July Purchases | | |
|------|------|------|
| Date | Quantity | Unit Cost |
| July  5 | 10,000 | $6.50 |
| July  9 | 12,500 | 6.25 |
| July 12 | 15,000 | 6.00 |
| July 25 | 14,000 | 6.20 |

On July 31, 15,000 units were on hand with a total value of $92,800. Killpack has always used a periodic FIFO inventory costing system. Gross profit on sales for July was $205,875. Reconstruct the beginning inventory (quantity and dollar value) for the month of July.

### Exercise 10—14  (Computing inventory using LIFO pools)

Miller Mfg. applies the LIFO method to specific inventory pools. Information relating to Product OU812 is as follows:

| | |
|---|---|
| Beginning inventory, January 1...................... | 60 units @ $10 each |
| Purchase, February 12 ............................. | 45 units @ $12 each |
| Purchase, February 28 ............................. | 75 units @ $13 each |
| Purchase, March 15................................. | 65 units @ $12.50 each |
| Sales for the first quarter........................... | 135 units |

Compute the ending LIFO inventory value for the first quarter assuming new layers are computed based on:

1. FIFO
2. LIFO
3. Average cost

### Exercise 10—15  (Dollar-value LIFO inventory method)

The Johnson Manufacturing Company manufactures a single product. The managers, Ron and Ken Johnson, decided on December 31, 1991, to adopt the dollar-value LIFO inventory method. The inventory value on that date using the newly adopted dollar-value LIFO method was $500,000. Additional information follows:

| Date | Inventory at Year-End Prices | Year-End Price Index |
|------|------|------|
| Dec. 31, 1992 | $605,000 | 1.10 |
| Dec. 31, 1993 | 597,360 | 1.14 |
| Dec. 31, 1994 | 700,000 | 1.25 |

Compute the inventory value at December 31 of each year using the dollar-value method, assuming incremental layers are costed at year-end prices.

### Exercise 10—16   (Dollar-value LIFO inventory method)

Jennifer Inc. adopted dollar-value LIFO on December 31, 1991. Data for 1991-1994 follows:

Inventory and index on the adoption date, December 31, 1991:
Dollar-value LIFO inventory ...................................... $250,000
Price index at year-end (the base year) ........................... 1.00

Inventory information in succeeding years:

| Date | Inventory at Year-End Prices | Year-End Price Index | Incremental Layer Index |
|------|------|------|------|
| Dec. 31, 1992 | $314,720 | 1.12 | 1.04 |
| Dec. 31, 1993 | 361,800 | 1.20 | 1.14 |
| Dec. 31, 1994 | 353,822 | 1.27 | 1.20 |

1. Compute the inventory value at December 31 of each year under the dollar-value method, assuming new layers are costed at the incremental layer index.
2. Compute the inventory value at December 31, 1994, assuming that dollar-value procedures were adopted at December 31, 1992, rather than in 1991.

### Exercise 10—17   (Impact on profit of failure to replace LIFO layers)

Harrison Lumber Company uses a periodic LIFO method for inventory costing. The following information relates to the plywood inventory carried by Harrison Lumber.

| **Plywood Inventory** | | |
|------|------|------|
| **Date** | **Quantity** | **LIFO Costing Layers** |
| May 1 | 600 sheets | 300 sheets at $ 8.00 |
| | | 225 sheets at $11.00 |
| | | 75 sheets at $13.00 |

| **Plywood Purchases** | |
|------|------|
| May 8 | 115 sheets at $14.00 |
| May 17 | 95 sheets at $15.00 |
| May 29 | 200 sheets at $14.50 |

All sales of plywood during May were at $20 per sheet. On May 31, there were 360 sheets of plywood in the storeroom.

1. Compute the gross profit on sales for May, as a dollar value and as a percent of sales.

2. Assume that because of a lumber strike, Harrison Lumber is not able to purchase the May 29 order of lumber until June 10. Assuming sales remained the same, recompute the gross profit on sales for May, as a dollar value and as a percent of sales.
3. Compare the results of part (1) and part (2) and explain the difference.

## Exercise 10—18   (Gross margin differences—FIFO vs. LIFO)

Assume the Bullock Corporation had the following purchases and sales of its single product during its first 3 years of operation.

| Year | Purchases Units | Unit Cost | Sales Units | Unit Price |
|------|-------|-----------|-------|------------|
| 1 | 10,000 | $10 | 8,000 | $14 |
| 2 | 9,000 | $12 | 9,000 | $17 |
| 3 | 8,000 | $15 | 10,000 | $18 |
|   | 27,000 |  | 27,000 |  |

1. Determine the gross margin for each of the three years assuming FIFO historical cost flow.
2. Determine the gross margin for each of the three years assuming LIFO historical cost flow.
3. Compare the total gross margin over the life of the business. How do the different cost flow assumptions affect the gross margin and cash flows over the life of the business? Does it matter which assumption of cash flow is used?

## Exercise 10—19   (Income differences—FIFO vs. LIFO)

First-in, first-out has been used for inventory valuation by the Atwood Co. since it was organized in 1991. Using the data that follows, redetermine the net incomes for each year on the assumption of inventory valuation on the last-in, first-out basis:

|  | 1991 | 1992 | 1993 | 1994 |
|--|------|------|------|------|
| Reported net income—FIFO basis... | $15,500 | $ 40,000 | $ 34,250 | $ 44,000 |
| Reported ending inventories—FIFO basis ........................... | 61,500 | 102,000 | 126,000 | 120,000 |
| Inventories—LIFO basis ............ | 56,500 | 75,100 | 95,000 | 105,000 |

## Exercise 10—20   (Inventory turnover)

Inventory turnover is a common measure used to indicate how many times inventory is sold during the year. It is calculated by dividing cost of goods sold by average inventory. A related measure, number of days' sales in inventory, indicates how many days, on average, inventory is held before resale. It is computed by dividing 365 days by the inventory turnover. Consider the following information:

|  | 1994 | 1993 |
|--|------|------|
| Cost of goods sold ..................................... | $1,400,000 | $1,200,000 |
| Beginning inventory ..................................... | 200,000 | 150,000 |
| Ending inventory ....................................... | 300,000 | 200,000 |

1. Compute the number of days' sales in inventory for both 1993 and 1994. What can you infer from these numbers?
2. How would you interpret the answer to part (1) if this company were in the business of selling fresh fruit and vegetables? What if this company sold real estate?

## PROBLEMS

### Problem 10—1 (Computing cost of goods sold for a manufacturing firm)

The following information is available for Woodfield Inc.

| | 1995 | 1994 | 1993 |
|---|---|---|---|
| Raw materials: | | | |
|   Beginning inventory | $ 117 | $ ? | $ 100 |
|   Purchases | 391 | 382 | ? |
|   Material available to use | $ ? | $ ? | $ 450 |
|   Ending inventory | 121 | ? | ? |
| Raw materials used | $ ? | $ 390 | $ 325 |
| Direct labor | 325 | ? | 300 |
| Factory overhead | 405 | 411 | ? |
| Total manufacturing costs | $ ? | $1,118 | $1,025 |
| Goods in process, January 1 | 85 | ? | 55 |
| | $1,202 | $ ? | $ ? |
| Goods in process, December 31 | ? | 85 | ? |
| Cost of goods manufactured | $ ? | $ ? | $1,005 |
| Finished goods, January 1 | ? | 92 | 87 |
| | $1,212 | $ ? | $ ? |
| Finished goods, December 31 | ? | 105 | ? |
| Cost of goods sold | $1,122 | $1,095 | $ ? |

**Instructions:** Compute the missing amounts.

### Problem 10—2 (Whose inventory is it?)

Streuling Inc. is preparing its 1993 year-end financial statements. Prior to any adjustments, inventory is valued at $76,050. The following information has been found relating to certain inventory transactions.

(a) Goods valued at $11,000 are on consignment with a customer. These goods are not included in the $76,050 inventory figure.

(b) Goods costing $2,700 were received from a vendor on January 5, 1994. The related invoice was received and recorded on January 12, 1994. The goods were shipped on December 31, 1993, terms FOB shipping point.

(c) Goods costing $8,500 were shipped on December 31, 1993, and were delivered to the customer on January 2, 1994. The terms of the invoice were FOB shipping point. The goods were included in ending inventory for 1993 even though the sale was recorded in 1993.

(d) A $3,500 shipment of goods to a customer on December 31 terms FOB destination was not included in the year-end inventory. The goods cost $2,600 and were delivered to the customer on January 8, 1994. The sale was properly recorded in 1994.

(e) An invoice for goods costing $3,500 was received and recorded as a purchase on December 31, 1993. The related goods, shipped FOB destination, were received on January 2, 1994, and thus were not included in the physical inventory.

(f) Goods valued at $6,500 are on consignment from a vendor. These goods are not included in the year-end inventory figure.

(g) A $6,000 shipment of goods to a customer on December 30, 1993, terms FOB destination, was recorded as a sale in 1993. The goods, costing $3,700 and delivered to the customer on January 6, 1994, were not included in 1993 ending inventory.

**Instructions:**

1. Determine the appropriate accounting treatment for each of the previous items. Justify your answers.
2. Compute the proper inventory amount to be reported on Streuling Inc.'s balance sheet for the year ended December 31, 1993.
3. By how much would the income statement have been misstated if no adjustments were made for the above transactions?

## Problem 10—3  (Inventory computation using different cost flows)

The Gidewall Corporation uses Part 210 in a manufacturing process. Information as to balances on hand, purchases, and requisitions of Part 210 is given in the following table:

| | Quantities | | | Unit Purchase |
| Date | Received | Issued | Balance | Price |
| --- | --- | --- | --- | --- |
| January 8 | — | | 200 | $1.55 |
| January 29 | 200 | — | 400 | 1.70 |
| February 8 | — | 80 | 320 | — |
| March 20 | — | 160 | 160 | — |
| July 10 | 150 | — | 310 | 1.75 |
| August 18 | — | 110 | 200 | — |
| September 6 | — | 75 | 125 | — |
| November 14 | 250 | — | 375 | 2.00 |
| December 29 | — | 200 | 175 | — |

**Instructions:**  What is the closing inventory under each of the following pricing methods? (Round unit costs to three decimal places.)

1. Perpetual FIFO
2. Periodic FIFO
3. Perpetual LIFO
4. Periodic LIFO
5. Moving average
6. Weighted average

## Problem 10—4  (Inventory computation using different cost flows)

Records of the Schwab New Products Co. show the following data relative to Product C:

| March | 2 | Inventory | 325 units at $25.50 |
| | 3 | Sale | 300 units at $37.50 |
| | 6 | Purchase | 300 units at $26.00 |
| | 13 | Purchase | 350 units at $27.00 |
| | 20 | Sale | 200 units at $35.70 |
| | 25 | Purchase | 50 units at $27.50 |
| | 28 | Sale | 125 units at $36.00 |

**Instructions:**  Calculate the inventory balance and the gross profit on sales for the month on each of the following bases:

1. Perpetual FIFO
2. Periodic FIFO
3. Perpetual LIFO
4. Periodic LIFO
5. Moving average (Carry calculations to four decimal places and round to three.)
6. Weighted average

## Problem 10—5  (Inventory calculations—LIFO and FIFO)

The Zerbel Manufacturing Co. was organized in 1992 to produce a single product. The company's production and sales records for the period 1992-1994 are summarized below.

| | Units Produced | | Sales | |
| | No. of Units | Production Costs | No. of Units | Sales Revenue |
|---|---|---|---|---|
| 1992 | 340,000 | $142,800 | 200,000 | $187,000 |
| 1993 | 310,000 | 161,200 | 290,000 | 230,000 |
| 1994 | 270,000 | 153,900 | 260,000 | 221,000 |

**Instructions:**   Calculate the gross profit for each of the three years assuming that inventory values are calculated in terms of:

1. LIFO (average cost used for incremental layers)
2. FIFO

## Problem 10—6  (Computation of LIFO inventory with LIFO pools)

The Bergman Company sells three different products. Five years ago, management adopted the LIFO inventory method and established three specific pools of goods. Bergman values all incremental layers of inventory at the average cost of purchases within the period. Information relating to the three products for the first quarter of 1994 is given below.

| | Product 400 | Product 401 | Product 402 |
|---|---|---|---|
| Purchases: | | | |
| January ..................... | 1,000 @ $12.00 | 500 @ $25 | 5,000 @ $5.30 |
| February..................... | 1,500 @ $12.50 | 250 @ $26 | 4,850 @ $5.38 |
| March ....................... | 1,200 @ $12.25 | — | 3,500 @ $5.45 |
| First quarter sales (units) ....... | 2,850 | 775 | 10,750 |
| January 1, 1994, inventory ....... | 950 @ $11.50 | 155 @ $24 | 3,760 @ $5.00 |

**Instructions:**   Compute the ending inventory value for the first quarter of 1994. (Round unit inventory values to the nearest cent and final inventory values to the nearest dollar.)

## Problem 10—7  (Computation of inventory from balance sheet and transaction data)

A portion of the Stark Company's balance sheet appears as follows:

| | December 31, 1994 | December 31, 1993 |
|---|---|---|
| Assets: | | |
| Cash ......................... | $353,300 | $100,000 |
| Notes receivable ................. | -0- | 25,000 |
| Inventory ....................... | ? | 199,875 |
| Liabilities: | | |
| Accounts payable ............... | ? | 75,000 |

Stark Company pays for all operating expenses with cash, and purchases all inventory on credit. During 1994, cash totaling $471,700 was paid on accounts payable. Operating expenses for 1994 totaled $220,000. All sales are cash sales. The inventory was restocked by purchasing 1,500 units per month and valued by using periodic FIFO. The unit cost of inventory was $32.60 during January 1994 and increased $0.10 per month during the year. Stark sells only one product. All sales are made for $50 per unit. The ending inventory for 1993 was valued at $32.50 per unit.

**Instructions:**

1. Compute the number of units sold during 1994.
2. Compute the December 31, 1994, accounts payable balance.
3. Compute the beginning inventory quantity.
4. Compute the ending inventory quantity and value.
5. Prepare an income statement for 1994 (including a detailed cost of goods sold section and ignoring income taxes).

## Problem 10—8    (Impact of LIFO inventory system)

The Manuel Corporation sells household appliances and uses LIFO for inventory costing. The inventory contains ten different products, and historical LIFO layers are maintained for each of them. The LIFO layers for one of the products, Easy Chef, were as follows at December 31, 1993:

| | |
|---|---|
| 1992 layer | 4,000 @ $90 |
| 1987 layer | 3,500 @ $85 |
| 1983 layer | 1,000 @ $75 |
| 1981 layer | 3,000 @ $48 |

**Instructions:**

1. What was the value of the ending inventory of Easy Chefs at December 31, 1993?
2. How did the December 31, 1993, quantity of Easy Chefs compare with the December 31, 1992, quantity?
3. What was the value of the ending inventory of Easy Chefs at December 31, 1994, assuming that there were 10,800 units on hand?
4. How would income in part (3) be affected if, in addition to the quantity on hand, 1,250 units were in transit to Manuel Corporation at December 31, 1994? The shipment was made on December 26, 1994, terms FOB shipping point. Total invoice cost was $131,250.

## Problem 10—9    (Dollar-value LIFO inventory method)

Steve's Repair Shop began operations on January 1, 1989. After discussing the matter with his accountant, Steve decided dollar-value LIFO should be used for inventory costing. Information concerning the inventory of Steve's Repair Shop is shown below.

| Date | Inventory at Year-End Prices | Year-End Index |
|---|---|---|
| Dec. 31, 1989 | $20,500 | 1.00 |
| Dec. 31, 1990 | 34,000 | 1.18 |
| Dec. 31, 1991 | 55,600 | 1.36 |
| Dec. 31, 1992 | 37,800 | 1.14 |
| Dec. 31, 1993 | 72,250 | 1.72 |
| Dec. 31, 1994 | 53,900 | 2.05 |

**Instructions:**  Compute the inventory value at December 31 of each year under the dollar-value LIFO inventory method, assuming incremental layers are costed at year-end prices.

 ## Problem 10—10    (Dollar-value LIFO inventory method)

The Mietus Company manufactures a single product. The company adopted the dollar-value LIFO inventory method on December 31, 1989. More information concerning Mietus Company is shown on page 390.

*233,000* (handwritten)

Inventory and index on the adoption date, December 31, 1989:
Dollar-value LIFO inventory ....................................... $300,900
Price index at year-end (the base year) ........................... 1.18
Inventory information in succeeding years:

| Date | Inventory at Year-End Prices | Year-End Price Index | Incremental Layer Index |
|------|------------------------------|----------------------|-------------------------|
| Dec. 31, 1990 | $369,600 | 1.320 | 1.240 |
| Dec. 31, 1991 | 420,206 | 1.420 | 1.368 |
| Dec. 31, 1992 | 435,095 | 1.505 | 1.452 |
| Dec. 31, 1993 | 417,073 | 1.543 | 1.515 |
| Dec. 31, 1994 | 451,627 | 1.588 | 1.552 |

*(handwritten annotations: 454608 next to 1990; 487872.00; 596,69262; 123; 596,025.23; 459,543.19; 643,543.19; 717,183.68)*

**Instructions:** Compute the inventory value at December 31 of each year under the dollar-value LIFO inventory method.

### Problem 10—11  (LIFO inventory pools—unit LIFO)

On January 1, 1990, Nolder Company changed its inventory cost flow method from FIFO to LIFO for its raw material inventory. The change was made for both financial statement and income tax reporting purposes. Nolder uses the multiple-pools approach under which substantially identical raw materials are grouped into LIFO inventory pools; weighted average costs are used in valuing annual incremental layers. The composition of the December 31, 1992, inventory for the Class F inventory pool is as follows:

| | Units | Weighted Average Unit Cost | Total Cost |
|------|-------|----------------------------|------------|
| Base year inventory—1990 .................... | 9,000 | $10.00 | $ 90,000 |
| Incremental layer—1991 ..................... | 3,000 | 11.00 | 33,000 |
| Incremental layer—1992 ..................... | 2,000 | 12.50 | 25,000 |
| Inventory, December 31, 1992 ............... | 14,000 | | $148,000 |

Inventory transactions for the Class F inventory pool during 1993 and 1994 were as follows:

1993
Mar.  1    4,800 units were purchased at a unit cost of $13.50 for $64,800.
Sept.  1    7,200 units were purchased at a unit cost of $14.00 for $100,800.

A total of 15,000 units were used for production during 1993.

1994
Jan.  10    7,500 units were purchased at a unit cost of $14.50 for $108,750.
May  15    5,500 units were purchased at a unit cost of $15.50 for $85,250.
Dec.  29    7,000 units were purchased at a unit cost of $16.00 for $112,000.

A total of 16,000 units were used for production during 1994.

**Instructions:**

1. Prepare a schedule to compute the inventory (unit and dollar amounts) of the Class F inventory pool at December 31, 1993. Show supporting computations in good form.
2. Prepare a schedule to compute the cost of Class F raw materials used in production for the year ended December 31, 1993.
3. Prepare a schedule to compute the inventory (unit and dollar amounts) of the Class F inventory pool at December 31, 1994. Show supporting computations in good form.

(AICPA adapted)

### Problem 10—12    (Change from FIFO to LIFO inventory)

The Greenriver Manufacturing Company manufactures two products: Raft and Float. At December 31, 1993, Greenriver used the FIFO inventory method. Effective January 1, 1994, Greenriver changed to the LIFO inventory method. The cumulative effect of this change is not determinable and, as a result, the ending inventory for 1993 for which the FIFO method was used, is also the beginning inventory for 1994 for the LIFO method. Any layers added during 1994 should be costed by reference to the first acquisitions of 1994.

The following information was available from Greenriver inventory records for the two most recent years:

| | Raft | | Float | |
|---|---|---|---|---|
| | Units | Unit Cost | Units | Unit Cost |
| **1993 purchases:** | | | | |
| January 7 | 5,000 | $4.00 | 22,000 | $2.00 |
| April 16 | 12,000 | 4.50 | | |
| November 8 | 17,000 | 5.00 | 18,500 | 2.50 |
| December 13 | 10,000 | 6.00 | | |
| **1994 purchases:** | | | | |
| February 11 | 3,000 | 7.00 | 23,000 | 3.00 |
| May 20 | 8,000 | 7.50 | | |
| October 15 | 20,000 | 8.00 | | |
| December 23 | | | 15,500 | 3.50 |
| **Units on hand:** | | | | |
| December 31, 1993 | 15,000 | | 14,500 | |
| December 31, 1994 | 16,000 | | 13,000 | |

**Instructions:**    Compute the effect on income before income taxes for the year ended December 31, 1994, resulting from the change from the FIFO to the LIFO inventory method.

(AICPA adapted)

# CHAPTER 11

## Inventories–Estimation and Noncost Valuation Procedures

---

**CHAPTER TOPICS**

**Gross Profit Method**

**Retail Inventory Method**

**Valuation at Lower of Cost or Market**

**Purchase Commitments, Trade-Ins, and Repossessions**

**Foreign Currency Inventory Transactions**

**Inventories on the Balance Sheet**

---

In 1989, Hurricane Hugo destroyed numerous businesses in South Carolina. As insurance companies investigated damage claims, they were faced with the problem of placing a value on inventory that had been destroyed or scattered over miles of country. In situations such as this, how can an insurance firm value inventory when that inventory may no longer exist?

This chapter introduces two inventory estimation techniques—the gross profit and the retail inventory methods. Inventory estimation may be necessary whenever it is too costly or it is not possible to physically count the inventory. This may occur when there is a natural disaster, a fire, or a theft, or when monthly financial statements are prepared. The valuation of inventory at the lower of cost or market and foreign currency inventory transactions are also discussed.

# GROSS PROFIT METHOD

The gross profit method of estimating inventory costs is based on an assumed relationship between gross profit and sales. A gross profit percentage is applied to sales to determine cost of goods sold; then, cost of goods sold is subtracted from the cost of goods available for sale to arrive at an estimated inventory balance.

The gross profit method is useful when:

1. A periodic system is in use and inventories are required for interim statements or for the determination of the week-to-week or month-to-month inventory position, and the cost of taking physical inventories would be excessive for such purposes.
2. Inventories have been destroyed or lost by fire, theft, or other casualties, and the specific data required for inventory valuation is not available.
3. It is desired to test or check the validity of inventory figures determined by other means. Such application is referred to as the **gross profit test.**

To be useful, the gross profit percentage used must be a reliable measure of current experience. In developing a reliable rate, reference is made to past rates and these are adjusted for variations considered to exist currently. Past gross profit rates, for example, may require adjustment when inventories are valued at last-in, first-out and significant fluctuations in inventory position and/or prices have occurred. Current changes in cost-price relationships or in the sales mix of specific products also create a need for modifying past rates.

The calculations of cost of goods sold and inventory depend on whether the gross profit percentage is developed and stated in terms of sales or in terms of cost. The procedures to be followed in each case are shown below.

### Example 1    Gross Profit as a Percentage of Sales

Assume sales are $100,000 and goods are sold at a gross profit of 40% of sales. If gross profit is 40% of sales, then cost of goods sold must be 60% of sales.

| Sales...................... | 100% | | Sales...................... | 100% |
|---|---|---|---|---|
| Cost of goods sold ......... | ? | = | Cost of goods sold.......... | 60% |
| Gross profit............... | 40% | | Gross profit............... | 40% |

Cost of goods sold, then, is 60% of $100,000, or $60,000. Goods available for sale less the estimated cost of goods sold gives the estimated cost of the remaining inventory. Assuming the cost of goods available for sale is $85,000, this balance less the estimated cost of goods sold, $60,000, gives an estimated inventory of $25,000.

### Example 2    Gross Profit as a Percentage of Cost (or Markup on Cost)

Assume sales are $100,000 and goods are sold at a gross profit that is 60% of their cost. If sales are made at a gross profit that is 60% of cost, then sales must be equal to the sum of cost, considered 100%, and the gross profit on cost, 60%. Sales, then, are 160% of cost:

| Sales...................... | ? | | Sales...................... | 160% |
|---|---|---|---|---|
| Cost of goods sold ......... | 100% | = | Cost of goods sold.......... | 100% |
| Gross profit............... | 60% | | Gross profit............... | 60% |

To find cost, or 100%, sales may be divided by 160 and multiplied by 100, or sales may simply be divided by 1.60. Cost of goods sold, then, is $100,000 ÷ 1.60 = $62,500. This amount is subtracted from the cost of goods available for sale to determine the estimated inventory. If goods available for sale is $85,000, then ending inventory is estimated to be $22,500 ($85,000 − $62,500).

When various lines of merchandise are sold at different gross profit rates and the product mix is unstable, it may be possible to develop a reliable inventory value only by making separate calculations for each line. Under such circumstances, it is necessary to develop summaries of sales, goods available for sale, and gross profit data for the different merchandise lines.

In order to use the gross profit method, four elements must be determinable: (1) cost of the beginning inventory, (2) cost of net purchases for the period, (3) sales, and (4) a gross profit rate. Given these four elements, an estimate of the ending inventory can be made. A common application of the gross profit method is the estimation of inventory when a physical count is impossible because of the loss or destruction of goods.

For example, assume that on October 31, 1993, a fire in the warehouse of a wholesale distributing company totally destroyed the contents, including many accounting records. Remaining records indicated that the last physical inventory was taken on December 31, 1992, and that the inventory at that date was $329,500. Microfilm bank records of canceled checks disclosed that during 1993, payments to suppliers for inventory items were $1,015,000. Unpaid invoices at the beginning of 1993 amounted to $260,000, and communication with suppliers indicated a balance due at the time of the fire of $315,000. Bank deposits for the ten months amounted to $1,605,000. All deposits came from customers for goods purchased except for a loan of $100,000 obtained from the bank during the year. Accounts receivable at the beginning of the year were $328,000, and an analysis of the available records indicated that accounts receivable on October 31 totaled $275,000. Gross profit percentages on sales for the preceding four years were:

| | | | |
|---|---|---|---|
| 1989 . . . . . . . . . . . . . . . . . . . . . | 28% | 1991 . . . . . . . . . . . . . . . . . . . . . | 23% |
| 1990 . . . . . . . . . . . . . . . . . . . . . | 25% | 1992 . . . . . . . . . . . . . . . . . . . . . | 24% |

From these facts, the inventory in the warehouse at the time of the fire could be estimated as shown below and at the top of page 395.

### Estimate of sales January 1 to October 31, 1993

| | |
|---|---|
| Collection of accounts receivable ($1,605,000 − $100,000) . . . . . . . . . . | $1,505,000 |
| Add accounts receivable balance at October 31, 1993 . . . . . . . . . . . . . . | 275,000 |
| | $1,780,000 |
| Deduct accounts receivable balance at January 1, 1993 . . . . . . . . . . . . . | 328,000 |
| Estimate of sales January 1 to October 31, 1993 . . . . . . . . . . . . . . . . . . . | $1,452,000 |
| Average gross profit percentage on sales for past 4 years: | |
| (.28 + .25 + .23 + .24) ÷ 4 . . . . . . . . . . . . . . . . . . . . . . . . . . . . . . . . . . | 25% |
| Average cost percentage on sales for past 4 years . . . . . . . . . . . . . . . . . . | 75% |
| Estimate of cost of goods sold to October 31, 1993 ($1,452,000 × 75%) . . . . . . . . . . . . . . . . . . . . . . . . . . . . . . . . . . . . . . . . . . . . . . . . . . . . | $1,089,000 |

## RETAIL INVENTORY METHOD

The retail inventory method is widely employed by retail concerns, particularly department stores, to arrive at reliable estimates of inventory position whenever desired. This

**Estimate of inventory on October 31, 1993**

| | | |
|---|---:|---:|
| Inventory, December 31, 1992 ....................... | | $ 329,500 |
| Add: Payments to suppliers—1993................... | $1,015,000 | |
|     Accounts payable to suppliers, October 31, 1993 .. | 315,000 | |
| | $1,330,000 | |
| Deduct accounts payable to suppliers, January 1, 1993 .. | 260,000 | |
| Estimate of purchases January 1 to October 31, 1993 ... | | 1,070,000 |
| Goods available for sale ........................... | | $1,399,500 |
| Estimate of cost of goods sold for 1993 (from above) ... | | 1,089,000 |
| Estimated inventory, October 31, 1993 ............... | | $ 310,500 |

method, like the gross profit method, permits the calculation of an inventory amount without the time and expense of taking a physical inventory or maintaining a detailed perpetual inventory record for each of the thousands of items normally included in a retail inventory. When this method is used, records of goods purchased are maintained at two amounts—cost and retail. The computer has now made it feasible to maintain cost records for the thousands of items normally included in a retail inventory. A cost percentage is computed by dividing the goods available for sale at cost by the goods available for sale at retail. This cost percentage can then be applied to the ending inventory at retail, an amount that can be readily calculated by subtracting sales for the period from the total goods available for sale at retail.

The computation of retail inventory at the end of a month is illustrated by the following example:

| | Cost | Retail |
|---|---:|---:|
| Inventory, January 1..................................... | $30,000 | $45,000 |
| Purchases in January .................................... | 20,000 | 35,000 |
| Goods available for sale ................................ | $50,000 | $80,000 |
| Cost percentage ($50,000 ÷ $80,000) = 62.5% | | |
| Deduct sales for January ................................ | | 25,000 |
| Inventory, January 31, at retail.......................... | | $55,000 |
| Inventory, January 31, at estimated cost ($55,000 × 62.5%) .. | $34,375 | |

The effect of the above procedure is to provide an inventory valuation in terms of average cost. No cost sequence, such as LIFO or FIFO, is recognized in the preceding computation; the percentage of cost to retail for the ending inventory is the same as the percentage of cost to retail for goods sold.

Use of the retail inventory method offers the following advantages:

1. Estimated interim inventories can be obtained without a physical count.
2. When a physical inventory is actually taken for financial statement purposes, it can be taken at retail and then converted to cost without reference to individual costs and invoices, thus saving time and expense.
3. Significant shoplifting losses can be determined and monitored. Since physical counts of inventory costed at retail should agree with the calculated retail inventory, any material difference not accounted for by clerical errors in the company records must be attributable to actual physical loss by shoplifting or employee theft.

Although this method permits the estimation of a value for inventory, errors can occur in accounting for the dual prices and in applying the retail method. Thus a physical count of the inventory to be reported on the annual financial statements is required at least once a year. Retail inventory records should be adjusted for variations shown by the physical count so that records reflect the actual status of the inventory for purposes of future estimates and control.

The accounting entries for the retail inventory method are similar to those made using a periodic inventory system. The retail figures are part of the analysis necessary to compute the cost of the inventory; however, they do not actually appear in the accounts. Thus the following entries would be made to record the inventory data included in the preceding example.

| | | |
|---|---|---|
| Purchases | 20,000 | |
|     Accounts Payable | | 20,000 |
| | | |
| Accounts Receivable | 25,000 | |
|     Sales | | 25,000 |
| | | |
| Inventory | 4,375 | |
| Cost of Goods Sold | 15,625 | |
|     Purchases | | 20,000 |

*To adjust inventory, cost of goods sold, and related accounts.*

## Markups and Markdowns—Conventional Retail

In the earlier inventory calculations, it was assumed that there were no changes in retail prices after the goods were originally recorded. Frequently, however, retail prices do change because of changes in the price level, shifts in consumer demand, or other factors. The following terms are used in discussing the retail method:

1. Original retail—the initial sales price, including the original increase over cost referred to as the initial markup.
2. Additional markups—increases that raise sales prices above original retail.
3. Markup cancellations—decreases in additional markups that do not reduce sales prices below original retail.
4. Net markups—Additional markups less markup cancellations.
5. Markdowns—decreases that reduce sales prices below original retail.
6. Markdown cancellations—decreases in the markdowns that do not raise the sales prices above original retail.
7. Net markdowns—markdowns less markdown cancellations.

To illustrate the use of these terms, assume that goods originally placed for sale are marked at 50% above cost. Merchandise costing $4 a unit, then, is marked at $6, which is the **original retail.** The **initial markup** of $2 is referred to as a "50% markup on cost" or a "33⅓% markup on sales price." In anticipation of a heavy demand for the article, the retail price is subsequently increased to $7.50. This represents an **additional markup** of $1.50. At a later date, the price is reduced to $7. This is a **markup cancellation** of 50 cents and not a markdown since the retail price has not been reduced below the original sales price. But assume that goods originally marked to sell at $6 are subsequently reduced to a sales price of $5. This represents a **markdown** of $1. At a later date, the goods are marked to sell at $5.25. This is a **markdown cancellation** of 25 cents and not a markup, since sales price does not exceed the original retail.

Retail inventory results will vary depending on whether net markdowns are used in computing the cost percentage. When applying the most commonly used retail method, net markups are added to goods available for sale at retail before calculating the cost percentage; net markdowns, however, are not deducted in arriving at the percentage.

This method, sometimes referred to as the conventional retail inventory method, is illustrated in the following example:

**Net markdowns not deducted to calculate cost percentage (conventional retail):**

|  | Cost | Retail |
|---|---|---|
| Beginning inventory | $ 8,600 | $ 14,000 |
| Purchases | 72,100 | 110,000 |
| Additional markups | | 13,000 |
| Markup cancellations | | (2,500) |
| Goods available for sale | $80,700 | $134,500 |
| Cost percentage ($80,700 ÷ $134,500) = 60% | | |
| Deduct: Sales | | $108,000 |
| Markdowns | | 4,800 |
| Markdown cancellations | | (800) |
| | | $112,000 |
| Ending inventory at retail | | $ 22,500 |
| Ending inventory at estimated cost ($22,500 × 60%) | $13,500 | |

The conventional retail method results in a lower cost percentage and, correspondingly, a lower inventory amount and a higher cost of goods sold than would be obtained if net markdowns were deducted before calculating the cost percentage. This latter approach, the average cost retail inventory method, is illustrated below.

**Net markdowns deducted to calculate cost percentage (average cost retail):**

|  | Cost | Retail |
|---|---|---|
| Goods available for sale (conventional retail) | $80,700 | $134,500 |
| Deduct net markdowns | | 4,000 |
| Goods available for sale (average cost retail) | | $130,500 |
| Cost percentage ($80,700 ÷ $130,500) = 61.84% | | |
| Deduct sales | | 108,000 |
| Ending inventory at retail | | $ 22,500 |
| Ending inventory at estimated cost ($22,500 × 61.84%) | $13,914 | |

The lower inventory obtained with the conventional retail method approximates a **lower-of-average-cost-or-market** valuation. The lower-of-cost-or-market concept, discussed in detail later in this chapter, requires recognition of declines in the value of inventory in the period such declines occur. Under the conventional retail method, markdowns are viewed as indicating a decline in the value of inventory and are deducted as a current cost of sales. When markdowns are included in the cost percentage computation, the result is an average cost allocated proportionately between cost of sales and ending inventory. Thus only a portion of the decline in value is charged to the current period. The remainder is carried forward in ending inventory to be charged against future sales.

Markdowns may be made for special sales or clearance purposes, or they may be made as a result of market fluctuations and a decline in the replacement cost of goods. In either case, their omission in calculating the cost percentage is necessary in order to value the inventory at the lower of cost or market. This is illustrated in the two examples that follow.

### Example 1    Markdowns for Special Sales Purposes

Assume that merchandise costing $50,000 is marked to sell for $100,000. To dispose of part of the goods immediately, one-fourth of the stock is marked down $5,000 and is sold. The cost of the ending inventory is calculated as follows:

|  | Cost | Retail |
|---|---|---|
| Purchases ........................................... | $50,000 | $100,000 |
| Cost percentage ($50,000 ÷ $100,000) = 50% |  |  |
| Deduct: Sales ........................................ |  | $ 20,000 |
| Markdowns ..................................... |  | 5,000 |
|  |  | $ 25,000 |
| Ending inventory at retail ............................. |  | $ 75,000 |
| Ending inventory at estimated cost ($75,000 × 50%)........ | $37,500 |  |

If cost, $50,000, had been related to sales price after markdowns, $95,000, a cost percentage of 52.6% would have been obtained, and the inventory, which is three-fourths of the merchandise originally acquired, would have been reported at 52.6% of $75,000, or $39,450. The inventory would thus be stated above the $37,500 cost of the remaining inventory and cost of goods sold would be understated by $1,950. A markdown relating to goods no longer on hand would have been recognized in the development of a cost percentage to be applied to the entire inventory. Reductions in the goods available at sales prices resulting from shortages or damaged goods should likewise be disregarded in calculating the cost percentage.

### Example 2    Markdowns as a Result of Market Declines

Assume that merchandise costing $50,000 is marked to sell for $100,000. With a drop in replacement cost of merchandise to $40,000, sales prices are marked down to $80,000. Three-fourths of the merchandise is sold. The cost of the ending inventory is calculated as follows:

|  | Cost | Retail |
|---|---|---|
| Purchases ........................................... | $50,000 | $100,000 |
| Cost percentage ($50,000 ÷ $100,000) = 50% |  |  |
| Deduct: Sales ........................................ |  | $ 60,000 |
| Markdowns ..................................... |  | 20,000 |
|  |  | $ 80,000 |
| Ending inventory at retail ............................. |  | $ 20,000 |
| Ending inventory at estimated cost ($20,000 × 50%)........ | $10,000 |  |

If cost, $50,000, had been related to sales price after markdowns, $80,000, a cost percentage of 62.5% would have been obtained, and the inventory would have been reported at 62.5% of $20,000, or $12,500. The use of the 50% cost percentage in the example reduces the inventory to $10,000 (¼ × $40,000), a balance providing the usual gross profit in subsequent periods if current prices and relationships between cost and retail prices prevail.

### Freight, Discounts, Returns, and Allowances

In calculating the cost percentage, freight-in should be added to the cost of the purchase; purchase discounts and returns and allowances should be deducted. A purchase return affects both the cost and the retail computations, while a purchase allowance affects only the cost total unless a change in retail price is made as a result of the allowance. Sales returns are proper adjustments to gross sales since the inventory is returned; however, sales discounts and sales allowances are not deducted to determine the estimated ending retail inventory. The deduction is not made because the sales price of an item is added into the computation of the retail inventory when it is purchased and deducted when it is sold, all at the gross sales price. Subsequent price adjustments included in the computation would leave a balance in the inventory account with no inventory on hand to represent it. For example, assume the sales price for 100 units of Product A is $5,000. When these units are sold for $5,000, the retail inventory balance would be zero. Subsequently, if an allowance of $100 is granted to the customer, the allowance would not be included in the computation of the month-end retail inventory balance. It would be recorded on the books, however, in the usual manner: debit Sales Allowances and credit Accounts Receivable.

## Retail Method With Varying Profit Margin Inventories

The calculation of a cost percentage for all goods carried in inventory is valid only when goods on hand can be regarded as representative of the total goods handled. Varying markup percentages and sales of high-margin and low-margin items in proportions that differ from purchases will require separate records and the development of separate cost percentages for different classes of goods. For example, assume that a store operates three departments and that for July the following information pertains to these departments:

|  | Department A | | Department B | | Department C | | Total | |
|---|---|---|---|---|---|---|---|---|
|  | Cost | Retail | Cost | Retail | Cost | Retail | Cost | Retail |
| Beginning inventory........... | $20,000 | $ 28,000 | $10,000 | $15,000 | $16,000 | $ 40,000 | $ 46,000 | $ 83,000 |
| Net purchases ................ | 57,000 | 82,000 | 20,000 | 35,000 | 20,000 | 60,000 | 97,000 | 177,000 |
| Goods available for sale ........ | $77,000 | $110,000 | $30,000 | $50,000 | $36,000 | $100,000 | $143,000 | $260,000 |
| Cost percentage................ | 70% |  | 60% |  | 36% |  | 55% |  |
| Sales........................ |  | 80,000 |  | 30,000 |  | 40,000 |  | 150,000 |
| Inventory at retail ............. |  | $ 30,000 |  | $20,000 |  | $ 60,000 |  | $110,000 |
| Inventory at cost .............. |  | $ 21,000 |  | $12,000 |  | $ 21,600 |  | $ 60,500 |

$54,600

Because of the range in cost percentages from 36% to 70% and the difference in mix of the purchases and ending inventory, the ending inventory balance, using an overall cost percentage, is $5,900 higher ($60,500 − $54,600) than when the departmental rates are used. When material variations exist in the cost percentages by departments, separate departmental rates should be computed and applied.

The retail method is acceptable for income tax purposes, provided the taxpayer maintains adequate and satisfactory records supporting inventory calculations and applies the method consistently on successive tax returns.

## INVENTORY VALUATIONS AT OTHER THAN COST

The basic cost procedures for determining inventory values have been discussed in this and the previous chapter. In some cases, generally accepted accounting principles permit deviations from cost, especially if a write-down of inventory values is warranted. The following sections of this chapter discuss some of these departures from historical cost and the circumstances under which they are appropriate.

## Inventory Valuation at Lower of Cost or Market

The conceptual framework establishes and defines recognition criteria for the elements of the financial statements. The definition of an asset requires that it produce future benefits to the owner. If at any time the monetary value assigned to an asset overstates these future benefits, an adjustment should be made to reflect a loss. Recognition criteria limit the adjustment to situations where the asset value can be estimated and a probable loss exists. The application of these accounting concepts to inventory is known as valuation at the lower of cost or market (LCM).

Currently, generally accepted accounting principles permit recognition of increases in the value of assets above cost only after the increase is realized and/or earned. The current practice of recognizing inventory write-downs before realization but not inventory write-ups until after realization results in inconsistent treatment of value changes.

The American Institute of Certified Public Accountants (AICPA) sanctioned lower-of-cost-or-market valuation in the following statement:

> A departure from the cost basis of pricing the inventory is required when the utility of the goods is no longer as great as its cost. Where there is evidence that the utility of goods, in their disposal in the ordinary course of business, will be less than cost, whether due to physical deterioration, obsolescence, changes in price levels, or other causes, the difference should be recognized as a loss of the current period. This is generally accomplished by stating such goods at a lower level commonly designated as market.[1]

In applying the lower-of-cost-or-market rule, the cost of the ending inventory, as determined under an appropriate cost allocation method, is compared with market value at the end of the period. If market is less than cost, an adjusting entry is made to record the loss and restate ending inventory at the lower value. It should be noted that no adjustment to LIFO cost is permitted for tax purposes; however, for financial reporting purposes, the lower-of-cost-or-market rule applies to all inventories. Application of LCM to LIFO inventories for financial reporting purposes does not violate the "LIFO conformity" rules if IRS approval is obtained.

**Definition of Market**    The term market in "lower of cost or market" is interpreted as replacement cost with upper and lower limits that reflect estimated realizable values. This concept of market was stated by the AICPA as follows:

> As used in the phrase *lower of cost or market,* the term *market* means current replacement cost (by purchase or by reproduction, as the case may be) except that:
> 1. Market should not exceed the net realizable value (i.e., estimated selling price in the ordinary course of business less reasonably predictable costs of completion and disposal); and
> 2. Market should not be less than net realizable value reduced by an allowance for an approximately normal profit margin.[2]

Replacement cost, sometimes referred to as entry cost, includes the purchase price of the product or raw materials plus all other costs incurred in the acquisition or manufacture of goods. Because wholesale and retail prices are generally related, declines in entry costs usually indicate declines in selling prices or exit values. However, exit values do not always respond immediately and in proportion to changes in entry costs. If selling price does not decline, there is no loss in utility and a write-down of inventory values would not

---

[1]*Accounting Research and Terminology Bulletins—Final Edition,* No. 43, "Restatement and Revision of Accounting Research Bulletins" (New York: American Institute of Certified Public Accountants, 1961), Ch. 4, Statement 5.

[2]*Ibid.,* Statement 6.

be warranted. On the other hand, selling prices may decline in response to factors unrelated to replacement costs. Perhaps an inventory item has been used as a demonstrator which reduces its marketability as a new product. Or perhaps an item is damaged in storage or becomes shopworn from excessive handling.

The AICPA definition considers exit values as well as entry costs by establishing a ceiling for the market value at sales price less costs of completion and disposal and a floor for market at sales price less both the costs of completion and disposal and the normal profit margin. The ceiling limitation is applied so the inventory is not valued at more than its net realizable value (NRV). Failure to observe this limitation would result in charges to future revenue that exceed the utility carried forward and an ultimate loss on the sale of the inventory. The floor limitation is applied so the inventory is not valued at less than its net realizable value minus a **normal profit.** The concept of normal profit is a difficult one to measure objectively. Profits vary by item and over time. Records are seldom accurate enough to determine a normal profit by individual inventory item. Despite these difficulties, however, the use of a floor prevents a definition of market that would result in a write-down of inventory values in one period to create an abnormally high profit in future periods.

**Applying Lower-of-Cost-or-Market Method**    Application of the LCM rule to determine the appropriate inventory valuation may be summarized in the following steps:

1. Define pertinent values: cost, replacement cost, upper limit (NRV), lower limit (NRV—normal profit).
2. Determine "market" (replacement cost as modified by upper or lower limits).
3. Compare cost with market (as defined in 2 above), and select the lower amount.

To illustrate these steps, assume that a certain commodity sells for $1; selling expenses are $.20; the normal profit is 25% of sales or $.25. The lower of cost or market as modified by the upper and lower limits is developed in each case as shown in the illustration below.

|  |  |  | **Market** |  |  |  |
|---|---|---|---|---|---|---|
| Case | Cost | Replacement Cost | Lower Limit—Floor (estimated sales price less selling expenses and normal profits) | Upper Limit— Ceiling (estimated sales price less selling expenses) | Market (limited by floor and ceiling values) | Lower of Cost or Market |
| A | $.65 | $ .70 | $.55 | $.80 | $.70 | $.65 |
| B | .65 | .60 | .55 | .80 | .60 | .60 |
| C | .65 | .50 | .55 | .80 | .55 | .55 |
| D | .50 | .45 | .55 | .80 | .55 | .50 |
| E | .75 | .85 | .55 | .80 | .80 | .75 |
| F | .90 | 1.00 | .55 | .80 | .80 | .80 |

A: Market is not limited by floor or ceiling; cost is less than market.
B: Market is not limited by floor or ceiling; market is less than cost.
C: Market is limited to floor; market is less than cost.
D: Market is limited to floor; cost is less than market.
E: Market is limited to ceiling; cost is less than market.
F: Market is limited to ceiling; market is less than cost.

The following dollar line graphically illustrates the floor and ceiling range. B and A replacement costs clearly are within bounds and therefore are defined as market. D and C are below the floor and thus the market is the floor; E and F are above the ceiling and market therefore is the ceiling.

Note that the market value is always the middle value of three amounts: replacement cost, floor, and ceiling.

The lower-of-cost-or-market method may be applied to each inventory item, to the major classes or categories of inventory items, or to the inventory as a whole. Application of this procedure to the individual inventory items will result in the lowest inventory value and is the most commonly used application because it is required for income tax purposes. Once an individual item is reduced to a lower market price, the new market price is considered to be the item's cost for future inventory valuations; cost reductions once made are not restored. Thus detailed inventory records must be adjusted to reflect the new values.

Application of the lower-of-cost-or-market method to inventory classes or to the inventory as a whole produces a more representative valuation and avoids the necessity of adjusting individual inventory items. Because declines in the value of some items are offset by increases in value of other items, the value of the items in the detailed inventory records are not adjusted. To assure that the detailed records agree with the inventory control account, an allowance system similar to that described in Chapter 9 for marketable securities would have to be used.

To illustrate the difference in valuation applications, assume Clarks Men's Store classifies its inventories into three categories: (1) formal wear, (2) casual wear, and (3) sportswear. As shown on page 403, the inventory, on an individual item basis, would be valued at $360,300, a reduction from cost of $29,500. The valuation based on categories and on the total inventory would be $371,300 and $377,300 respectively.

The entry to record the write-down of the inventory on an individual item basis is usually made directly to the inventory control account as follows:

Loss From Decline in Value of Inventory . . . . . . . . . . . . . . . . . . .     29,500
    Inventory . . . . . . . . . . . . . . . . . . . . . . . . . . . . . . . . . . . . . . . . . . . .          29,500
    *Write-down of inventory to market.*

Any subsidiary inventory record would also be reduced for the decline. The loss on the decline in market value may be shown as a separate item in the income statement after cost of goods sold. Alternatively, the loss may be reflected directly in the cost of goods sold section by reporting the ending inventory at market rather than cost. To illustrate the two reporting alternatives shown on page 403, assume that sales for the period totaled $1.2 million and beginning inventory and net purchases were $280,000 and $855,000, respectively.

Separate reporting of the loss has the advantage of providing readers with increased information to forecast operations and cash flows.

Rather than reducing the inventory directly, the inventory control account could be maintained at cost, and an allowance for inventory decline used to record the decline in value. This method would generally be used when inventory is valued on a category or entire inventory basis. The entry to record the write-down using an allowance for the categories of Clarks Men's Store would be as follows:

Loss From Decline in Value of Inventory . . . . . . . . . . . . . . . . . . . . .     18,500
    Allowance for Decline in Value of Inventory . . . . . . . . . . . . . . . .          18,500

**Clarks Men's Store**
**Applications of Lower of Cost or Market**

| Classes and Items | Cost | Market | Cost or Market Whichever Is Lower | | |
| --- | --- | --- | --- | --- | --- |
| | | | Individual Items | Inventory Categories | Total Inventory |
| Formal wear: | | | | | |
| Tuxedos ......... | $ 75,000 | $ 70,000 | $ 70,000 | | |
| Suits ........... | 120,000 | 130,000 | 120,000 | | |
| Dress shirts ...... | 30,000 | 28,000 | 28,000 | | |
| Dress shoes...... | 18,000 | 21,000 | 18,000 | | |
| Total formal wear .. | $243,000 | $249,000 | $236,000 | $243,000 | |
| Casual wear: | | | | | |
| Slacks ........... | $ 39,500 | $ 32,000 | $ 32,000 | | |
| Casual shirts ..... | 26,000 | 23,000 | 23,000 | | |
| Sweaters ........ | 15,000 | 17,000 | 15,000 | | |
| Total casual wear... | $ 80,500 | $ 72,000 | $ 70,000 | $ 72,000 | |
| Sportswear: | | | | | |
| Sport shirts ...... | $ 39,000 | $ 29,000 | $ 29,000 | | |
| Swimming wear.. | 10,000 | 8,000 | 8,000 | | |
| Warm-ups ....... | 17,300 | 19,300 | 17,300 | | |
| Total sportswear ... | $ 66,300 | $ 56,300 | $ 54,300 | $ 56,300 | |
| Total inventory ..... | $389,800 | $377,300 | | | $377,300 |
| | | | $360,300 | $371,300 | $377,300 |

## Inventory Loss Reported Separately

| | | |
| --- | --- | --- |
| Sales ............................................ | | $1,200,000 |
| Cost of goods sold: | | |
| Beginning inventory .............................. | $  280,000 | |
| Purchases ...................................... | 855,000 | |
| Cost of goods available for sale.................... | $1,135,000 | |
| Ending inventory (at cost) ........................ | 389,800 | 745,200 |
| Gross profit...................................... | | $  454,800 |
| Inventory loss due to write-down of cost to market ..... | | 29,500 |
| | | $  425,300 |

## Inventory Loss Included in Cost of Goods Sold

| | | |
| --- | --- | --- |
| Sales ........................................... | | $1,200,000 |
| Cost of goods sold: | | |
| Beginning inventory .............................. | $  280,000 | |
| Purchases ...................................... | 855,000 | |
| Cost of goods available for sale.................... | $1,135,000 | |
| Ending inventory (at market, which is lower than cost) | 360,300 | 774,700 |
| Gross profit...................................... | | $  425,300 |

The allowance account would be reported as an offset to the inventory account on the balance sheet. In subsequent years, it will be adjusted upward or downward depending on the amount required to adjust cost to market. If the required allowance declines, a recovery or gain entry would be recorded. Assume the difference between cost and market for the three categories in the next year is only $9,500. The adjusting entry to record this information in the next year would be as follows:

| | | |
|---|---|---|
| Allowance for Decline in Value of Inventory.................... | 9,000 | |
| Recovery of Decline in Value of Inventory.................... | | 9,000 |

As is true for marketable securities, the recovery is limited by the amount in the allowance account. The category and total inventory applications are not acceptable for income tax purposes.[3]

**Evaluation of Lower-of-Cost-or-Market Rule**    As mentioned earlier, the lower-of-cost-or-market rule is evidence of the concept of accounting conservatism. Its strict application has been applied to avoid valuing inventory on the balance sheet at more than replacement cost. Also as discussed earlier, the AICPA replaced a strict entry valuation with a utility measure that relies partially upon exit prices. If selling prices for the inventory have declined and the decline is expected to hold until the inventory is sold, the adjustment of income in the period of the decline seems justified. The value of the inventory has been impaired, which requires current adjustment. However, care must be taken in using this method not to manipulate income by allowing excessive charges against income in one period to be offset by excessive income in the next period.

Some accountants have argued against the use of cost or market because it violates the cost concept. Market valuations are often subjective and based on expectations. To the extent these expectations are not realized, misleading financial statements will be produced. To illustrate, assume that activities summarized in terms of cost provide the following results over a three-year period:

| | 1992 | | 1993 | | 1994 | |
|---|---|---|---|---|---|---|
| Sales............................ | | $200,000 | | $225,000 | | $250,000 |
| Cost of goods sold: | | | | | | |
| Beginning inventory ............ | $ 60,000 | | $ 80,000 | | $127,500 | |
| Purchases .................... | 120,000 | | 160,000 | | 90,000 | |
| Goods available for sale ........ | $180,000 | | $240,000 | | $217,500 | |
| Less ending inventory .......... | 80,000 | 100,000 | 127,500 | 112,500 | 92,500 | 125,000 |
| Gross profit on sales.............. | | $100,000 | | $112,500 | | $125,000 |
| Operating expenses ............. | | 80,000 | | 90,000 | | 100,000 |
| Net income ...................... | | $ 20,000 | | $ 22,500 | | $ 25,000 |
| Rate of income to sales ........... | | 10% | | 10% | | 10% |

Assume estimates as to the future utility of ending inventories indicated market values as follows:

| 1992 | 1993 | 1994 |
|---|---|---|
| $75,000 | $110,000 | $92,500 |

If the expected decline in selling prices did not occur, inventory valuation at the lower of cost or market would provide the following results.

[3]Many disputes have arisen through the years between taxpayers and the IRS as to what constitutes a recognizable decline in inventory value. An important tax case in this area was settled by the U.S. Supreme Court in 1979. The taxpayer, Thor Power Tool Co., had followed the practice of writing down the value of spare parts inventories that were being held to cover future warranty requirements. Although the sales prices did not decline, the probability of the parts being sold, and thus their net realizable value, decreased as time passed. The write-down to reflect the current decline in value is consistent with the accounting principle of recognizing declines in value as they occur. The Supreme Court, however, ruled that for tax purposes the reduction must await the actual decline in the sales price for the parts in question.

| | 1992 | | 1993 | | 1994 | |
|---|---|---|---|---|---|---|
| Sales .......................... | | $200,000 | | $225,000 | | $250,000 |
| Cost of goods sold: | | | | | | |
| Beginning inventory ............ | $ 60,000 | | $ 75,000 | | $110,000 | |
| Purchases .................... | 120,000 | | 160,000 | | 90,000 | |
| Goods available for sale ........ | $180,000 | | $235,000 | | $200,000 | |
| Less ending inventory ......... | 75,000 | 105,000 | 110,000 | 125,000 | 92,500 | 107,500 |
| Gross profit on sales............. | | $ 95,000 | | $100,000 | | $142,500 |
| Operating expenses ............. | | 80,000 | | 90,000 | | 100,000 |
| Net income .................... | | $ 15,000 | | $ 10,000 | | $ 42,500 |
| Rate of income to sales .......... | | 7.5% | | 4.4% | | 17.0% |

Reduction of an inventory below cost reduces the net income of the period in which the reduction is made and increases the net income of a subsequent period over what it would have been. In the example just given, total net income for the three-year period is the same under either set of calculations. But the reduction of inventories to lower market values reduced the net income for 1992 and for 1993 and increased the net income for 1994. The fact that inventory reductions were not followed by decreases in the sales prices resulted in net income determinations that varied considerably from those that might reasonably have been expected from increasing sales and costs that normally vary with sales volume.

Objection to valuation at the lower of cost or market is also raised on the grounds that it produces inconsistencies in the measurements of both the financial position and the operations of the enterprise. Market decreases are recognized, but increases are not. Although this system does produce some inconsistent application to the upward and downward movement of market, the authors feel that the lower-of-cost-or-market concept is preferable to a strict cost measurement. A loss in the utility of any asset should be reflected in the period the impairment is first recognized and a reasonable estimate of its significance can be determined.

## Valuation of Trade-Ins and Repossessions

When goods are acquired in secondhand condition as a result of repossessions and trade-ins, they should be recorded at their estimated cash purchase prices. In some industries, these prices are defined and made available to dealers. One of the more organized used markets is that for automobiles. A book, published frequently in the various geographical markets of the country, lists low, medium, and high market values for the different models and makes of cars. It also distinguishes between retail and wholesale values. Similar lists are provided for machinery and equipment in some lines. When these publications exist, the prices listed may be used to value repossessed or trade-in inventory.

When published prices are not available, it is more difficult to measure the equivalent cash purchase price of the inventory. Under these conditions, the consistent use of **floor values**—amounts that, after adding reconditioning charges and selling expenses, will permit the recognition of normal profits—would be appropriate.

Accounting for trade-ins is illustrated by the following example: Christensen Department Store sells a new washing machine to a customer for $350 cash and a trade-in of an old washer. It is estimated that a realistic floor value for the trade-in is $50. Reconditioning costs of $30 are incurred after which the trade-in washer is sold for $120, an amount that provides a normal profit. Perpetual inventory records are maintained for trade-ins but not for the regular inventory. The following entries reflect these transactions.

| | | |
|---|---|---|
| Cash ............................................................... | 350 | |
| Trade-In Inventory ............................................. | 50 | |
| Sales ......................................................... | | 400 |

*To record sale of new washer and receipt of old washer as trade-in.*

| | | |
|---|---|---|
| Trade-In Inventory ............................................. | 30 | |
| Cash ......................................................... | | 30 |

*To record cost to recondition trade-in.*

| | | |
|---|---|---|
| Cash ............................................................... | 120 | |
| Sales—Trade-Ins ........................................... | | 120 |

*To record sale of trade-in washing machine.*

| | | |
|---|---|---|
| Cost of Trade-Ins Sold ......................................... | 80 | |
| Trade-In Inventory ......................................... | | 80 |

*To record cost of trade-in washing machine.*

Another approach to valuing trade-in inventories is to establish clearly the sales price of the new inventory being sold, and charge the trade-in inventory for the difference between a cash sales price and the cash required with the trade-in. Assume in the case of the washing machine that the regular cash sales price without a trade-in could be established at $390. The value assigned to the trade-in would thus be $40, the difference between $390 and $350.

Accounting for repossessions requires a slightly different approach. Assume Christensen Department Store sold another washing machine on account for $350 plus interest on the unpaid balance. The customer made principal payments of $200 on the machine and then defaulted on the contract. The machine was repossessed and overhauled at a cost of $40. It was then sold for $150, a price that provided a normal profit of 50% on cost.

The following entries reflect the repossession and subsequent resale:

| | | |
|---|---|---|
| Allowance for Doubtful Accounts ................................... | 90 | |
| Repossessed Inventory .......................................... | 60 | |
| Accounts Receivable .......................................... | | 150 |

*Computation:*

Value of repossession established to permit 50% normal profit on cost (33⅓% on selling price)

| | |
|---|---|
| Selling price ...................................................... | $150 |
| Less profit at 33⅓% of $150 ...................................... | 50 |
| Cost of repossessed goods sold ................................... | $100 |
| Less cost of overhaul ............................................. | 40 |
| Value of repossessed inventory ................................... | $ 60 |

| | | |
|---|---|---|
| Repossessed Inventory ......................................... | 40 | |
| Cash ......................................................... | | 40 |

*To record cost to overhaul repossessed washing machine.*

| | | |
|---|---|---|
| Cash ............................................................... | 150 | |
| Sales—Repossessed Inventory ............................... | | 150 |

*To record sale of repossessed washing machine.*

| | | |
|---|---|---|
| Cost of Repossessed Goods Sold ................................. | 100 | |
| Repossessed Inventory....................................... | | 100 |

*To record cost of repossessed washing machine ($60 + $40).*

## Losses on Purchase Commitments

Purchase commitments are contracts made for the future purchase of goods at fixed prices. No entry is required to record the purchase prior to delivery of the goods. However, when price declines take place subsequent to such commitments and they are outstanding at the end of an accounting period, it is considered appropriate to measure and recognize these losses on the books just as losses on goods on hand are recognized. A decline is recorded by a debit to a special loss account and a credit to either a contra asset account or an accrued liability account, such as Estimated Loss on Purchase Commitments. Acquisition of the goods in a subsequent period is recorded by a credit to Accounts Payable, a debit canceling the credit balance in the contra asset or accrued liability account, and a debit to Purchases for the difference.

For example, assume that Rollins Oat Company entered into a purchase contract on November 1, 1993, for 100,000 bushels of wheat at $3.40 per bushel to be delivered in March of 1994. At the end of 1993, the market price for wheat had dropped to $3.20 per bushel. The entries to record this decline in value and the subsequent delivery of the wheat would be as follows:

```
1993
Dec. 31   Loss on Purchase Commitments ................    20,000
              Estimated Loss on Purchase Commitments .....              20,000

1994
Mar. 31   Estimated Loss on Purchase Commitments .......    20,000
          Purchases....................................   320,000
              Accounts Payable...........................              340,000
```

The loss is thus assigned to the period in which the decline took place, and a subsequent period is charged for no more than the economic utility of the goods it receives. Current loss recognition would not be appropriate when commitments can be canceled, when commitments provide for price adjustment, when hedging transactions[4] prevent losses, or when declines do not suggest reductions in sale prices. No adjustments are customarily made if a recovery occurs prior to delivery.

## FOREIGN CURRENCY INVENTORY TRANSACTIONS

The discussion of inventories thus far has centered around the purchase and valuation of inventories in a domestic environment, that is, within the United States. As noted in Chapter 1, business has become increasingly global in perspective. Exports and imports of materials and finished goods are a significant part of many companies' purchases and sales. Depending on how a purchase or sale transaction is structured, additional gains or losses may occur in foreign inventory transactions because of fluctuations in the currency exchange rates between two countries. This section of the chapter addresses issues associated with foreign currency inventory transactions.

**Foreign currency transactions** are those transactions that involve a buyer and a seller whose financial reporting currencies are different. If a Japanese company sells goods to an American company and the American company is expected to pay for those goods in yen, the result is a foreign currency transaction for the American company. These types of transactions are becoming more commonplace as business activity becomes more global. Consider, for example, the impact of international operations on IBM Corporation. In 1989, IBM reported net income of $3,758 million—income of $4,083 million from foreign operations and a loss of $325 million from domestic operations (see Appendix A). Even if one never leaves the United States, students of accounting must be prepared to deal with the intricacies associated with international business operations.

[4]Purchases or sales entered into for the purpose of balancing, respectively, sales or purchases already made or under contract in order to offset the effects of price fluctuations.

**Silver's Ups and Downs**

In 1979 and 1980, the Hunt brothers from Texas attempted to corner the world's silver market. Their hope was to own enough silver to be able to dictate world prices. They made purchase commitments, which locked in the price they would pay for silver, and for a while, their plan worked. The price of silver rose, and the Hunt brothers used the silver they owned as collateral to purchase more silver.

Their plans were shattered when the price of silver started to decline. From a high in January 1980 of $50.35 an ounce, silver fell to $10.80 in just two months. The silver they were using as collateral decreased in value requiring the Hunt brothers to provide additional collateral. This collateral was in the form of oil, sugar, and real estate, each of which was faring poorly at the time of the silver crash. At the same time, the purchase commitments they had made required them to buy silver at prices higher than the current market value of silver. The Hunt brothers sought protection in bankruptcy court and the scheme eventually cost them approximately $4 billion.

**Questions:**

1. What are the risks associated with making purchase commitments?
2. Why do accounting standards require that price declines subsequent to the purchase commitment but prior to the actual purchase be recorded immediately?
3. Can firms take any action to reduce their exposure to changing prices?

To illustrate the complexities associated with foreign transactions, we will first consider a simple domestic transaction involving the purchase of inventory on account. Suppose that Washington, Inc., purchases $10,000 worth of inventory from California Co. on November 1, 1992, and payment is due on February 1, 1993. The journal entry made by Washington, Inc., on the date of purchase would be:

| | | |
|---|---|---|
| Inventory | 10,000 | |
|     Accounts Payable | | 10,000 |

When the account is paid on February 1, 1993, Washington, Inc., would make the following journal entry:

| | | |
|---|---|---|
| Accounts Payable | 10,000 | |
|     Cash | | 10,000 |

If Washington, Inc., had purchased the inventory from a foreign company, the purchase transaction could be structured to require payment for the purchase either in dollars or in the foreign currency. Denominated currency is the term used to designate the currency to be used for payment. The denomination agreement determines who will bear the risk associated with foreign currency rate changes. If the U.S. dollar is the designated denomination currency for the foreign inventory purchase, Washington, Inc., would treat the purchase as a domestic transaction, and the journal entries for the purchase and the payment would be the same as above. Washington, Inc., would not bear the risk for any exchange rate changes. However, if the invoice had been denominated in a foreign currency, the amount of the invoice would have to be converted from the foreign currency into dollars before a purchase entry could be made. In order to do this, the exchange rate at the date of the transaction must be determined.

## Exchange Rates

As the business environment has become more international, companies have required access to various foreign currencies. As a result, foreign currency markets have developed where currencies of different countries can be bought or sold. *The Wall Street Journal* quotes foreign exchange rates on a daily basis. For example, on May 1, 1990, one French franc was worth $.1776. This rate is termed a **direct quote** in that the foreign currency is stated in terms of how many dollars one unit of foreign currency can purchase. An **indirect quote** is stated as the number of foreign currency units required to purchase one dollar. The indirect quote on May 1, 1990, was 5.6306, i.e., 5.6306 francs could be purchased for $1. Note the following relationship between a direct and indirect quote:

$$\text{Direct quote} = \frac{1}{\text{Indirect quote}}$$

or

$$\$.1776 = \frac{\$1}{5.6306 \text{ francs}}$$

The direct quote will be used throughout this chapter. For accounting purposes, three different terms are used to designate exchange rates as of particular points in time. The first is the **spot rate**, that is, the rate at which currencies can be traded immediately. The second exchange rate is the **historical rate**. The historical rate is the exchange rate in effect on the date of a specific transaction. The third rate, the **current rate**, is the exchange rate in effect on the date the balance sheet is prepared.

The Financial Accounting Standards Board has dealt with foreign currency issues throughout its existence. Currently, the standard that determines the accounting for foreign transactions is *FASB Statement No. 52*, "Foreign Currency Translation." This standard requires the use of the historical rate in recording a purchase or sale of inventory if the transaction is denominated in a foreign currency. The standard requires that any subsequent changes in the exchange rate, as measured by the spot rate and the current rate, be recorded as transaction gains and losses and be reflected in income in the period in which exchange rates changed.

## Measurement of a Purchase Transaction

Assume that Washington, Inc., had purchased the inventory from France Co. and the invoice was denominated in francs with a purchase price of 50,000 francs. Using the exchange rate in effect on the transaction date (assume the direct quote is $.200), Washington, Inc., would make the following journal entry to record the purchase:

```
1992
Nov. 1   Inventory .......................................   10,000
              Accounts Payable (fc) ...........................          10,000
              Purchased inventory from France Co. for 50,000
              francs (50,000 × $.200 = $10,000).
```

The (fc) designation is used for convenience to indicate those items that are denominated in a foreign currency. It is important to recognize, however, that the amounts in the journal entry represent the domestic currency—in this case, dollars.

The impact of a foreign currency inventory purchase is recognized when the liability is paid. If the terms call for payment of the liability on February 1, 1993, Washington, Inc., will have to credit cash on that date, but for how much? Recall that the invoice requires payment in francs—not dollars. Washington, Inc., will have to purchase 50,000 francs from a foreign currency broker. How much will the company be required to pay the broker? The answer depends on the spot rate on that date. If the spot rate is $.215 on February 1, 1993, then Washington, Inc., will have to pay $10,750 to purchase 50,000 francs. The journal entry to record the payment of the liability to France Co. would then be:

```
1993
Feb. 1   Accounts Payable (fc)..............................    10,000
         Exchange Loss.....................................       750
            Cash .........................................               10,750
            Purchased 50,000 francs from broker and paid
            France Co. (50,000 × $.215 = $10,750).
```

Washington, Inc., incurs a loss in this situation because the exchange rate, and thus the number of dollars required to purchase francs, has increased since the initial purchase transaction. On November 1, 1992, Washington, Inc., would have had to pay only $10,000 to purchase 50,000 francs. However, to purchase the same number of francs on February 1, 1993, requires $10,750. The exchange loss would appear on the income statement in the period incurred and is typically classified as "other income or expenses."

This situation could just as easily have resulted in an exchange gain for Washington, Inc. If the exchange rate had declined, then fewer dollars would have been required to purchase 50,000 francs. Suppose the exchange rate for French francs had been $.195 on February 1, 1993. Washington, Inc., would have recorded the following journal entry and recognized an exchange gain:

```
1993
Feb. 1   Accounts Payable (fc)..............................    10,000
            Exchange Gain..................................                  250
            Cash .........................................                9,750
            Purchased 50,000 francs from broker and paid
            France Co. (50,000 × $.195 = $9,750).
```

A second requirement of FASB Statement No. 52 relates to balance sheet adjustments. The pronouncement states that balances denominated in a foreign currency be adjusted to the exchange rate as of the balance sheet date, i.e., the current rate. This requirement is consistent with the matching principle, which states that increases and decreases in assets and liabilities should be recorded in the period in which those increases and decreases occur rather than when cash is paid or received. Continuing the initial example, suppose that Washington, Inc.'s, accounting year ends on December 31 and the exchange rate on December 31, 1992, was $.208. On that date, Washington, Inc., would make the following adjusting entry to record the change in the amount of cash required to pay the liability:

```
1992
Dec. 31   Exchange Loss ...................................    400
             Accounts Payable (fc)..........................              400
             Recognized loss from increase in exchange rate
             [(50,000 francs × $.208) − $10,000 = $400].
```

This journal entry adjusts the liability to its value of $10,400 given the current exchange rate ($.208) and allocates the exchange rate loss to the period in which the change in exchange rates occurred. When the liability is subsequently paid on February 1, 1993, when the exchange rate for francs is $.215, the journal entry would be:

```
1993
Feb. 1  Accounts Payable (fc)...........................  10,400
        Exchange loss ..................................     350
            Cash .......................................           10,750
            Purchased 50,000 francs from broker and paid
            France Co. (50,000 × $.215 = $10,750).
```

Note that the exchange losses of $400 and $350 recorded on December 31 and February 1, respectively, total $750—the same amount that is obtained if no adjusting entry were made. The adjusting entry simply allocates the exchange loss to the appropriate accounting periods.

An obvious question at this point is, Why didn't Washington, Inc., avoid the exchange loss and pay the liability early? If Washington, Inc., knew that exchange rates were going to rise, they probably would have. However, predicting the direction and amount of change in the exchange rate for a particular currency is as difficult as predicting whether the price of a specific stock on the New York Stock Exchange is going to rise or fall, and by how much.

### Measurement of a Sales Transaction

The accounting treatment for sales transactions is similar to that discussed for purchase transactions. The only major difference is that a receivable is denominated in a foreign currency instead of a payable. In the example of a purchase transaction, if exchange rates increased, Washington, Inc., recorded an exchange loss, and if exchange rates decreased, the company recorded a gain. The reverse is true with a sales transaction. If a firm is expecting to receive 10,000 foreign currency units and the value of those units declines, the firm will incur an exchange loss. If the exchange rate should rise, then the value of the foreign currency units will increase and a gain will result.

Consider the following example: On December 1, 1992, American Co. sold inventory to German Inc. for 22,000 German marks. Assume that the exchange rate for marks on that day was $.595, and the exchange rate on December 31, 1992, was $.600. American Co. received a check in full payment of German Inc.'s account on January 15, 1993, when the exchange rate was $.613. American Co. would make the following journal entries to record the above events:

```
1992
Dec.  1  Accounts Receivable (fc).........................  13,090
            Sales ........................................           13,090
            Sold inventory to German Inc. for 22,000 marks
            (22,000 × $.595 = $13,090).

     31  Accounts Receivable (fc).........................     110
            Exchange Gain.................................              110
            Recognized gain from increase in exchange rate
            [(22,000 marks × $.600) − $13,090 = $110].

1993
Jan. 15  Cash (fc) .......................................  13,486
            Exchange Gain.................................              286
            Accounts Receivable (fc) .....................           13,200
            Collected 22,000 marks from German Inc. (22,000
            × $.613 = $13,486).

     15  Cash............................................  13,486
            Cash (fc) .....................................           13,486
            Converted the 22,000 marks received from Ger-
            man Inc. into dollars.
```

The entry on December 1 records the account receivable at its value given the exchange rate on the day of the transaction. On December 31, an adjusting entry is made to recognize that the value of the 22,000 marks that American Co. is entitled to receive has increased. The adjustment increases the receivable balance to \$13,200 (\$13,090 + \$110). When the account is collected on January 15, American Co. receives 22,000 marks, and their value on the date of receipt is \$13,486. Because the exchange rate on January 15 is higher than the December 31 rate, an additional gain of \$286 is recognized when American Co. records receipt of the marks. The 22,000 marks are converted immediately into dollars, and a second entry is made on January 15 to record the conversion. If American Co. had not converted the marks into dollars on the day of their receipt, the company would have been exposing itself to additional risk associated with exchange rate changes.

## INVENTORIES ON THE BALANCE SHEET

It is customary to report both merchandise and manufacturing inventories as current assets even though in some situations, considerable time will elapse before portions of such inventories are realized in cash. Among the items that are generally reported separately under the inventories heading are merchandise inventory or finished goods, goods in process, raw materials, factory supplies, goods and materials in transit, goods on consignment, and goods in the hands of agents and salespersons. Inventories are normally listed in the order of their liquidity. Any advance payments on purchase commitments should be reported separately and should not be included with inventories. Such advances are preferably listed after inventories in the current asset section since they have not entered the inventory phase of the operating cycle.

The inventory valuation procedures used must be disclosed in a note to the financial statements outlining all significant accounting policies followed.[5] The basis of valuation (such as cost or lower of cost or market), together with the method of arriving at cost (LIFO, FIFO, average, or other method), should be indicated. The reader of a statement may assume that the valuation procedures indicated have been consistently applied and financial statements are comparable with those of past periods. If this is not the case, a special note should be provided stating the change in the method and the effects of the change upon the financial statements.

If significant inventory price declines take place between the balance sheet date and the date the financial statements are issued, such declines should be disclosed by parenthetical remark or note. When relatively large orders for merchandise have been placed by the reporting company in a period of widely fluctuating prices, but the title to such goods has not yet passed, such commitments should be described by special note. Information should also be provided concerning possible losses on purchase commitments. Similar information may be appropriate for possible losses on sales commitments.

Replacement costs of inventories may be disclosed in a note to the financial statements. Until such time as market valuation of inventories becomes generally acceptable for reporting purposes, only supplemental disclosure of current values is permitted.

When inventories have been pledged as security on loans from banks, finance companies, or factors, the amounts pledged should be disclosed either parenthetically in the inventory section of the balance sheet or in the notes.

---

[5]*Opinions of the Accounting Principles Board, No. 22*, "Disclosure of Accounting Policies" (New York: American Institute of Certified Public Accountants, 1972), par. 12.

## KEY TERMS

Additional markups 396
Average cost retail inventory method 397
Ceiling limitation 401
Conventional retail inventory method 397
Cost percentage 395
Current rate 409
Denominated currency 408
Direct quote 409
Entry cost 400

Exit values 400
Floor limitation 401
Foreign currency transactions 407
Freight-in 398
Gross profit method 393
Historical rate 409
Indirect quote 409
Initial markup 396
Lower of cost or market (LCM) 400
Markdown cancellations 396

Markdowns 396
Market (in "lower of cost or market") 400
Markup cancellations 396
Net markdowns 396
Net markups 396
Original retail 396
Replacement cost 400
Retail inventory method 394
Spot rate 409

## QUESTIONS

1. What is meant by the term "gross profit test"?
2. Distinguish between: (a) gross profit as a percentage of cost and gross profit as a percentage of sales; (b) the gross profit method of calculating estimated inventory cost and the retail inventory method of calculating estimated inventory cost.
3. What effect would the use of the LIFO inventory method have upon the applicability of the gross profit method of valuing inventory?
4. (a) How are markdowns treated under the conventional retail method? (b) What costing method is approximated by this approach?
5. How does the conventional retail inventory method differ from the average cost retail inventory method?
6. How are purchase discounts and sales discounts treated when using the retail inventory method?
7. Under what circumstances would a decline in replacement cost of an item not justify a departure from the cost basis of valuing an inventory?
8. The use of lower of cost or market is an archaic continuation of conservative accounting. Comment on this view.
9. Why are ceiling and floor limitations on replacement cost considered necessary by the AICPA?

10. The Muhlstein Corporation began business on January 1, 1992. Information about inventories, as of December 31 for three consecutive years, under different valuation methods is shown below. Using this information and assuming that the same method is used each year, you are to choose the phrase which best answers each of the following questions:
    (a) The inventory basis that would result in the highest net income for 1992 is: (1) LIFO cost, (2) FIFO cost, (3) Market, (4) Lower of cost or market.
    (b) The inventory basis that would result in the highest net income for 1993 is: (1) LIFO cost, (2) FIFO cost, (3) Market, (4) Lower of cost or market.
    (c) The inventory basis that would result in the lowest net income for the three years combined is: (1) LIFO cost, (2) FIFO cost, (3) Market, (4) Lower of cost or market.
    (d) For the year 1993, how much higher or lower would net income be on the FIFO cost basis than on the lower-of-cost-or-market basis? (1) $400 higher, (2) $400 lower, (3) $600 higher, (4) $600 lower, (5) $1,000 higher, (6) $1,000 lower, (7) $1,400 higher, (8) $1,400 lower.

| | LIFO Cost | FIFO Cost | Market | Lower of Cost or Market* |
|---|---|---|---|---|
| 1992 | $10,200 | $10,000 | $ 9,600 | $ 8,900 |
| 1993 | 9,100 | 9,000 | 8,800 | 8,500 |
| 1994 | 10,300 | 11,000 | 12,000 | 10,900 |

*FIFO Cost, item-by-item valuation.

11. How does the accounting treatment for losses on purchase commitments differ between actual losses which have already occurred and losses which may occur in the future?

12. What is the justification for valuing trade-ins or re-possessions so that a normal profit can be realized upon their sale?

13. How should repossessed goods be valued for inventory purposes? Give reasons for your answers.

14. Are all transactions with foreign companies classified as foreign currency transactions? If not, what determines if a transaction is a foreign currency transaction?

15. Why does a seller recognize a gain on a foreign currency transaction when exchange rates go up?

16. Why does the FASB require an adjustment to be made on the balance sheet date to reflect exchange rate changes?

17. How would you recommend that the following items be reported on the balance sheet?

(a) Unsold goods in the hands of consignees.
(b) Purchase orders outstanding.
(c) Advance payments on purchase commitments.
(d) Raw materials pledged as security on notes payable to bank.
(e) Raw materials in transit from suppliers, FOB shipping point.
(f) Goods produced by special order and set aside to be picked up by customer.
(g) Finished parts to be used in the assembly of final products.
(h) Office supplies.

## DISCUSSION CASES

### Case 11—1   (Where has the inventory gone?)

Main Street Department Store uses the retail inventory method. Periodically, a physical count is made of the inventory and compared with the book figure computed from the company sales and purchase records. This year the extended valuation of the physical count resulted in a total inventory value 10% lower than the book figure. Jennifer Strack, the controller, is concerned by the variance. A 2% to 3% loss from shoplifting has been tolerated through the years. But 10% is too much. The branch manager, Bryan Smith, who is summoned to account for the discrepancy, insists that the book figures must be wrong. He is confident that the shortage could not be that high but that bookkeeping errors must be at fault. Strack, however, is not satisfied with the explanation and asks Smith to outline specifically what types of errors could have caused such a variance. Prepare Smith's outline for Strack.

### Case 11—2   (Inventory valuation without records)

The Ma & Pa Grocery Store has never kept many records. The proceeds from sales are used to pay suppliers for goods delivered. When the owners, Donald and Alicia Wride, need some cash, they withdraw it from the till without any record being made of it. The Wrides realize that eventually tax returns must be filed, but for three years, "they just haven't got around to it." Finally, the Internal Revenue Service catches up with the Wrides, and an audit of the company records is conducted. The auditor requests the general ledger, special journals, inventory counts, and supporting documentation—very little of which is available. Records of expenditures are extremely sketchy because most expenses are paid in cash. If you were the IRS auditor, what might you do to make a reasonable estimate of income for the company?

### Case 11—3   (Have we really had a loss?)

The Destro Company is experiencing an unusual inventory situation. The replacement cost of its principal product has been declining, but because of a unique market condition, Destro has not had to reduce the selling price of the item. Eric Dona, company controller, is aware that GAAP requires the valuation of inventory at the lower of cost or market. He considers market to be replacement cost, and he is concerned that to reduce the ending inventory to replacement cost will improperly reduce net income for the current period. Has an inventory loss occurred? Discuss.

### Case 11—4    (What value should we place on the clunker?)

The Ritchie Automobile Agency is an exclusive agency for the sales of foreign sports cars. As part of its sales strategy, Ritchie allows liberal trade-in allowances on the sale of its new cars. A used car division of the company sells these trade-ins at a separate location, usually at an amount significantly lower than the trade-in allowance. This division is continually showing large losses because the cars are charged to the division at their trade-in values. John Lund, manager of the used car division, has requested that the costing procedure be changed and that trade-ins be recorded at a price sufficiently below expected retail to allow a reasonable profit to his division. Janet Perry, controller of the agency, acknowledges that some adjustment needs to be made to the inflated trade-in values, but feels that expected retail value should be used without allowance for a profit. What value should be used on the financial statements for the ending inventory of trade-ins? Discuss the reasonableness of this method for internal management evaluations.

### Case 11—5    (Can we avoid losses from exchange rate changes?)

Smith & Sons routinely purchases inventory from Mistuhaki Corp. Because of unpredictability in the foreign currency markets, transactions denominated in yen leave Smith & Sons exposed to the risks associated with exchange rate changes. Identify and discuss methods by which Smith & Sons can reduce its exposure to foreign currency losses.

---

## EXERCISES

### Exercise 11—1    (Inventory loss—gross profit method)

On August 15, 1993, a hurricane damaged a warehouse of Folkman Merchandise Company. The entire inventory and many accounting records stored in the warehouse were completely destroyed. Although the inventory was not insured, a portion could be sold for scrap. Through the use of microfilmed records, the following data is assembled:

| | |
|---|---:|
| Inventory, January 1 | $  275,000 |
| Purchases, January 1-August 15 | 1,385,000 |
| Cash sales, January 1-August 15 | 225,000 |
| Collection of accounts receivable, January 1-August 15 | 1,932,000 |
| Accounts receivable, January 1 | 175,000 |
| Accounts receivable, August 15 | 265,000 |
| Salvage value of inventory | 5,000 |
| Gross profit percentage on sales | 30% |

Compute the inventory loss as a result of the hurricane.

### Exercise 11—2    (Inventory loss—gross profit method)

On June 30, 1993, a flash flood damaged the warehouse and factory of Bend Corporation, completely destroying the work-in-process inventory. There was no damage to either the raw materials or finished goods inventories. A physical inventory taken after the flood revealed the following valuations:

| | |
|---|---:|
| Finished goods | $112,000 |
| Work in process | -0- |
| Raw materials | 52,000 |

The inventory on January 1, 1993, consisted of the following:

| | |
|---|---:|
| Finished goods.................................................... | $120,000 |
| Work in process................................................. | 115,000 |
| Raw materials.................................................... | 28,500 |
| | $263,500 |

A review of the books and records disclosed that the gross profit margin historically approximated 35% of sales. The sales for the first six months of 1993 were $365,000. Raw materials purchases were $96,000. Direct labor costs for this period were $90,000, and factory overhead has historically been applied at 50% of direct labor.

Compute the value of the work-in-process inventory lost at June 30, 1993. Show supporting computations in good form.                                    (AICPA adapted)

### Exercise 11—3  (Retail inventory method)

Hilo Department Store uses the retail inventory method. On December 31, 1993, the following information relating to the inventory was gathered:

| | Cost | Retail |
|---|---:|---:|
| Inventory, January 1, 1993 ............................. | $ 26,550 | $ 45,000 |
| Sales................................................. | | 350,000 |
| Purchases ........................................... | 292,000 | 395,000 |
| Purchase discounts .................................. | 4,200 | |
| Freight-in........................................... | 5,250 | |
| Net markups ......................................... | | 30,000 |
| Net markdowns ...................................... | | 10,000 |
| Sales discounts ..................................... | | 5,000 |

Compute the ending inventory value at December 31, 1993, using the conventional retail inventory method.

### Exercise 11—4  (Retail inventory method)

The Evening Out Clothing Store values its inventory under the retail inventory method at the lower of cost or market. The following data is available for the month of November 1993:

| | Cost | Selling Price |
|---|---:|---:|
| Inventory, November 1 ................................. | $ 53,800 | $ 76,000 |
| Markdowns ........................................... | | 5,700 |
| Markups.............................................. | | 11,200 |
| Markdown cancellations ............................... | | 2,200 |
| Markup cancellations ................................. | | 5,600 |
| Purchases ........................................... | 157,304 | 223,600 |
| Sales................................................ | | 244,000 |
| Purchase returns ..................................... | 3,000 | 3,600 |
| Sales returns........................................ | | 12,000 |
| Sales allowances ..................................... | | 6,000 |

Based upon the data presented above, prepare a schedule in good form to compute the estimated inventory at November 30, 1993, at the lower of cost or market under the retail inventory method.
                                                        (AICPA adapted)

## Exercise 11—5  (Retail inventory method)

The Ivory Tower Bookstore recently received a shipment of accounting textbooks from the publisher. Following the receipt of the shipment, the FASB issued a major new accounting standard that related directly to the contents of one chapter of the text. Portions of this chapter became "obsolete" immediately as a result of the FASB's action. In order to sell the books, the bookstore marked down the selling price and offered a separate supplement covering the new standard, which was provided at no cost by the publisher. Information relating to the cost and selling price of the text for the month of September is given below:

|  | Cost | Retail |
|---|---|---|
| Beginning inventory | $ 1,500 | $ 1,800 |
| Purchases | 24,000 | 29,760 |
| Freight-in | 1,100 | |
| Markdowns | | 2,100 |
| Sales | | 27,500 |

Based on the data given, compute the estimated inventory at the end of the month using the retail inventory method and assuming:

1. lower-of-cost-or-market valuation (conventional retail)
2. average cost valuation

## Exercise 11—6  (Lower-of-cost-or-market valuation)

Determine the proper carrying value of the following inventory items if priced in accordance with the recommendations of the AICPA:

| Item | Cost | Replacement Cost | Sales Price | Selling Expenses | Normal Profit |
|---|---|---|---|---|---|
| Product 561 | $1.85 | $1.82 | $2.30 | $.35 | $.20 |
| Product 562 | .69 | .65 | 1.00 | .30 | .04 |
| Product 563 | .31 | .24 | .59 | .15 | .07 |
| Product 564 | .92 | .84 | 1.05 | .27 | .05 |
| Product 565 | .84 | .82 | 1.00 | .19 | .09 |
| Product 566 | 1.19 | 1.15 | 1.43 | .13 | .09 |

## Exercise 11—7  (Lower-of-cost-or-market valuation)

The following inventory data is available for Alpine Ski Shop at December 31:

|  | Cost | Market |
|---|---|---|
| Skis | $60,000 | $65,000 |
| Boots | 37,500 | 35,000 |
| Ski Equipment | 15,000 | 14,000 |
| Ski Apparel | 12,000 | 13,500 |

1. Determine the value of ending inventory using the lower-of-cost-or-market method applied to (a) individual items and (b) total inventory.
2. Prepare any journal entries required to adjust the ending inventory if lower of cost or market is applied to (a) individual items and (b) total inventory.

### Exercise 11—8   (Lower-of-cost-or-market valuation)

Newcomer, Inc., values inventories at the lower-of-cost-or-market method applied to total inventory. Inventory values at the end of the company's first and second years of operation are presented below.

|          | Ending Inventory | |
|----------|--------|--------|
|          | Cost   | Market |
| Year 1 ............................................... | $58,000 | $53,000 |
| Year 2 ............................................... | 75,000 | 73,800 |

1. Prepare the journal entries necessary to reflect the proper inventory valuation at the end of each year. (Assume Newcomer uses an inventory allowance account.)
2. For Year 1, assume sales were $390,000 and purchases were $320,000. What amount would be reported as cost of goods sold on the income statement for Year 1 if: (a) the inventory decline is reported separately? and (b) the inventory decline is not reported separately?

### Exercise 11—9   (Loss on purchase commitments)

On October 1, 1993, Bush Electronics Inc. entered into a six-month, $520,000 purchase commitment for a supply of Product A. On December 31, 1993, the market value of this material has fallen so that current acquisition of the ordered quantity would cost $453,000. It is anticipated that a further decline will occur during the next three months and that market at date of delivery will be approximately $412,000. What entries would you make on December 31, 1993, and on March 31, 1994, assuming the expected decline in prices does occur?

### Exercise 11—10   (Valuation of trade-in)

Wailea Inc. sells new equipment with a $28,000 list price. Assume that Wailea sells one unit of equipment and accepts a trade-in plus $24,100 in cash. The expected sales price of the reconditioned equipment is $3,500; the reconditioning expenses are estimated to be $500; and normal profit is 30% of the sales price.

1. Prepare the journal entry to record the sale assuming that floor values are used.
2. Prepare the journal entry to record the sale assuming that the sale of new equipment is recorded at its normal list price.
3. Evaluate the entries.

### Exercise 11—11   (Repossessed inventory)

Deppe Equipment Inc. sells its inventory on a time basis. In about 5% of the sales, the customer defaults in the payments and the equipment must be repossessed. Assume that equipment was sold for $21,000 which included interest of $2,250 (the company uses an allowance for unearned finance charges account). The customer defaulted after making payments of $10,350, which included $1,350 interest. The equipment was repossessed and overhauled at a cost of $2,700. It was then sold on a thirty-day account for $16,500, a price that provided a normal profit of 25% on cost. What journal entries would be required to record the repossession and subsequent resale of the equipment?

### Exercise 11—12   (Foreign transaction—purchase)

Guenther's, a German company that supplies your firm with a necessary raw material, recently shipped 10,000 units of the material to your production facility.

1. Prepare the necessary journal entries to record the purchase of the goods and the subsequent payment 30 days later if the selling price on the invoice is $6 per unit.

2. Prepare the necessary journal entries to record the purchase of the goods and the subsequent payment 30 days later if the selling price on the invoice is 4 German marks per unit. The spot rate for German marks on the date of purchase is $1.50, and the rate on the date of payment is $1.60.

### Exercise 11—13  (Foreign transaction—sale)

Meny Yawnas Inc., a Japanese firm, regularly purchases semiconductors from your company, Semiconductors, Inc. An order for 1,000 semiconductors was recently shipped to Meny Yawnas.

1. Prepare the necessary journal entries to record the sale of the semiconductors and the subsequent receipt of payment if the denominated selling price for the goods was $12 per unit.
2. Prepare the necessary journal entries to record the sale of the semiconductors and the subsequent receipt of payment if the denominated selling price for the goods was 120 yen per unit. The spot rate for Japanese yen on the date of sale is $.10, and the rate on the date of payment is $.11.

### Exercise 11—14  (Foreign transaction—purchase)

Koreaco produces automobile transmissions which are then sent to the United States where they are installed in domestically built cars. CarCo, an American auto company, received a shipment of transmissions on December 15, 1992. The transmissions were subsequently paid for on January 30, 1993. The invoice was denominated in Korean won and totaled 5,000,000 won. The relevant exchange rates are as follows:

|  | **Exchange Rates** |
|---|---|
| December 15, 1992 | $.055 |
| December 31, 1992 | .057 |
| January 30, 1993 | .060 |

Provide the necessary journal entries to record the above transactions assuming CarCo's fiscal year-end is December 31.

---

## PROBLEMS

### Problem 11—1  (Inventory fire loss)

Bradshaw Manufacturing began operations five years ago. On August 13, 1993, a fire broke out in the warehouse destroying all inventory and many accounting records relating to the inventory. The information available is presented below. All sales and purchases are on account.

|  | **January 1, 1993** | **August 13, 1993** |
|---|---|---|
| Inventory | $136,250 | |
| Accounts receivable | 130,590 | $116,110 |
| Accounts payable | 88,140 | 122,850 |
| Collection on accounts receivable, January 1-August 13 | | 753,800 |
| Payments to suppliers, January 1-August 13 | | 487,500 |
| Goods out on consignment at August 13, at cost | | 32,500 |

Summary of previous years sales:

|  | **1990** | **1991** | **1992** |
|---|---|---|---|
| Sales | $626,000 | $675,000 | $680,000 |
| Gross profit on sales | 194,060 | 189,000 | 231,200 |

**Instructions:**  Determine the inventory loss suffered as a result of the fire.

## Problem 11—2   (Interim inventory computation—gross profit method)

The following information was taken from the records of the Prairie Company.

| | Jan. 1, 1992-<br>Dec. 31, 1992 | Jan. 1, 1993-<br>Sept. 30, 1993 |
|---|---|---|
| Sales (net of returns) | $2,500,000 | $1,500,000 |
| Beginning inventory | 420,000 | 785,000 |
| Purchases | 2,152,000 | 1,061,000 |
| Freight-in | 116,000 | 72,000 |
| Purchase discounts | 30,000 | 15,000 |
| Purchase returns | 40,000 | 13,000 |
| Purchase allowances | 8,000 | 5,000 |
| Ending inventory | 785,000 | |
| Selling and general expenses | 450,000 | 320,000 |

**Instructions:** Compute by the gross profit method the value to be assigned to the inventory as of September 30, 1993, and prepare an income statement for the nine-month period ending on this date.

## Problem 11—3   (Inventory theft loss)

In December 1993, Bullseye Merchandise Inc. had a significant portion of its inventory stolen. The company determined the cost of inventory remaining to be $45,700. The following information was taken from the records of the company:

| | January 1, 1993<br>to<br>Date of Theft | 1992 |
|---|---|---|
| Purchases | $154,854 | $185,375 |
| Purchase returns and allowances | 7,225 | 8,420 |
| Sales | 251,882 | 261,800 |
| Sales returns and allowances | 2,882 | 2,600 |
| Salaries | 9,600 | 10,800 |
| Rent | 6,480 | 6,480 |
| Insurance | 1,160 | 1,178 |
| Light, heat, and water | 1,361 | 1,525 |
| Advertising | 5,100 | 3,216 |
| Depreciation expense | 1,506 | 1,536 |
| Beginning inventory | 75,291 | 59,040 |

**Instructions:** Estimate the cost of the stolen inventory.

## Problem 11—4   (Retail inventory method)

The Cordon Clothing Store values its inventory under the retail inventory method. The following data is available for 1993:

| | Cost | Selling Price |
|---|---|---|
| Inventory, January 1 | $ 51,053 | $ 79,100 |
| Additional markdowns | | 21,000 |
| Additional markups | | 40,600 |
| Markdown cancellations | | 11,000 |
| Markup cancellations | | 9,000 |
| Purchases | 147,179 | 221,600 |
| Sales | | 246,500 |
| Purchase returns | 4,000 | 6,000 |
| Sales allowances | | 12,000 |
| Freight-in | 14,600 | |

**Instructions:**

1. Prepare a schedule to compute the estimated inventory at December 31, 1993, at the lower of average cost or market under the retail method.
2. Prepare the summary accounting journal entries to record the preceding inventory data (include entries to record the purchases, sales, and closing of inventory to cost of goods sold).
3. What gross profit on sales would be reported on the income statement for 1993?

### ▪ Problem 11—5   (Retail inventory method)

The information below was taken from the records of Trump Inc. for the years 1992 and 1993.

|  | 1993 | 1992 |
|---|---|---|
| Sales ........................................... | $138,600 | $135,600 |
| Sales discounts ......................................... | 1,840 | 1,200 |
| Sales returns.......................................... | 2,100 | 1,600 |
| Freight-in .......................................... | 4,000 | 3,640 |
| Purchases (at cost) ..................................... | 78,000 | 68,560 |
| Purchases (at retail) ................................... | 100,500 | 92,480 |
| Purchase discounts ...................................... | 4,155 | 1,000 |
| Beginning inventory (at cost) ............................ |  | 65,600 |
| Beginning inventory (at retail) ........................... |  | 87,520 |

**Instructions:**   Compute the value of the inventory at the end of 1992 and 1993 using the conventional retail inventory method.

### Problem 11—6   (Retail inventory method)

Johnson & Jones, a pharmaceutical company, has used the retail method for several years. The following limited information is available for the past three years:

|  | 1994 | | 1993 | | 1992 | |
|---|---|---|---|---|---|---|
|  | Cost | Retail | Cost | Retail | Cost | Retail |
| Inventory, Jan. 1 .......... | $ 5,536 | $   ? | $   ? | $   ? | $ 8,255 | $ 14,000 |
| Purchases ................ | 77,809 | 114,750 | 84,500 | ? | 71,000 | 105,000 |
| Net markups ............. |  | ? |  | 13,000 |  | ? |
| Goods available .......... | $   ? | $133,780 | $   ? | $   ? | $   ? | $   ? |
| Cost percentage .......... |  | ? | 64.9% |  | ? |  |
| Deduct: Net markdowns ... |  | 7,750 |  | ? |  | ? |
| Sales ............ |  | ? |  | 132,450 |  | 110,000 |
| Inventory, Dec. 31......... | $ 9,255 | $   ? | $   ? | $ 8,530 | $10,890 | $ 18,000 |

**Instructions:**   Compute the missing amounts from the information given.

###  ▪ Problem 11—7   (Lower-of-cost-or-market valuation)

Witte Inc. carries four items in inventory. The following data is relative to such goods at the end of 1993:

|  |  |  | Per Unit | | | |
|---|---|---|---|---|---|---|
|  | Units | Cost | Replacement Cost | Estimated Sales Price | Selling Cost | Normal Profit |
| **Category 1:** |  |  |  |  |  |  |
| Commodity A | 3,000 | $5.50 | $5.25 | $8.00 | $.90 | $2.00 |
| Commodity B | 1,650 | 6.00 | 6.00 | 9.25 | .80 | 1.25 |

| | | Per Unit | | | |
|---|---|---|---|---|---|
| | Units | Cost | Replacement Cost | Estimated Sales Price | Selling Cost | Normal Profit |
| Category 2: | | | | | | |
| Commodity C | 5,000 | 2.50 | 2.00 | 4.20 | .95 | .50 |
| Commodity D | 3,250 | 7.00 | 7.50 | 7.50 | 1.20 | 1.75 |

**Instructions:**

1. Calculate the value of the inventory under each of the following methods:
   (a) cost
   (b) the lower of cost or market applied to the individual inventory items
   (c) the lower of cost or market applied to the inventory categories
   (d) the lower of cost or market applied to the inventory as a whole

2. Prepare any journal entries necessary to reflect the proper inventory valuation assuming inventory is valued at:
   (a) cost
   (b) the lower of cost or market applied to the individual inventory items
   (c) the lower of cost or market applied to the inventory categories (Use valuation allowance.)
   (d) the lower of cost or market applied to the inventory as a whole

### Problem 11—8   (Lower-of-cost-or-market valuation)

Oriental Sales Co. uses the first-in, first-out method in calculating cost of goods sold for three of the products that Oriental handles. Inventories and purchase information concerning these three products are given for the month of August.

| | | Product A | Product B | Product C |
|---|---|---|---|---|
| Aug. 1 | Inventory | 5,000 units at $6.00 | 3,000 units at $10.00 | 6,500 units at $.90 |
| Aug. 1-15 | Purchases | 7,000 units at $6.50 | 4,500 units at $10.50 | 3,000 units at $1.25 |
| Aug. 16-31 | Purchases | 3,000 units at $8.00 | | |
| Aug. 1-31 | Sales | 10,500 units | 5,000 units | 4,500 units |
| Aug. 31 | Sales Price | $8.00 per unit | $11.00 per unit | $2.00 per unit |

On August 31, Oriental's suppliers reduced their prices from the most recent purchase prices by the following percentages: Product A, 20%; Product B, 10%; Product C, 8%. Accordingly, Oriental decided to reduce its sales prices on all items by 10% effective September 1. Oriental's selling cost is 10% of sales price. Products A and B have a normal profit (after selling costs) of 30% on sales prices, while the normal profit on Product C (after selling costs) is 15% of sales prices.

**Instructions:**

1. Calculate the value of the inventory at August 31, using the lower-of-cost-or-market method (applied to individual items).
2. Calculate the FIFO cost of goods sold for August and the amount of inventory write-off due to the market decline.

### Problem 11—9   (Trade-ins and repossessed inventory)

The Foutz Appliance Company began business on January 1, 1992. The company decided from the beginning to grant allowances on merchandise traded in as partial payment on new sales. During 1993 the company granted trade-in allowances of $64,035. The wholesale value of merchandise traded in was $40,875. Trade-ins recorded at $39,000 were sold for their wholesale value of $27,000 during the year. The following summary entries were made to record annual sales of new merchandise and trade-in sales for 1993:

| | | |
|---|---:|---:|
| Accounts Receivable.................... | 439,890 | |
| Trade-In Inventory...................... | 64,035 | |
| Sales ................................. | | 503,925 |
| Cash ................................. | 27,000 | |
| Loss on Trade-In Inventory .............. | 12,000 | |
| Trade-In Inventory .................... | | 39,000 |

When a customer defaults on the accounts receivable contract, the appliance is repossessed. During 1993 the following repossessions occurred:

| | Original Sales Price | Unpaid Contract Balance |
|---|:---:|:---:|
| On 1992 contracts ......................... | $37,500 | $20,250 |
| On 1993 contracts ......................... | 24,000 | 18,750 |

The wholesale value of these goods is estimated by the trade as follows:

(a)  Goods repossessed during year of sale are valued at 50% of original sales price.
(b)  Goods repossessed in later years are valued at 25% of original sales price.

**Instructions:**

1. At what values should Foutz Appliance report the trade-in and repossessed inventory at December 31, 1993?
2. Give the entry that should have been made to record the repossessions of 1993.
3. Give the entry that is required to correct the trade-in summary entries.

### Problem 11—10   (Inventory transactions—journal entries)

The Olsen Company values its perpetual inventory at the lower of FIFO cost or market. The inventory accounts at December 31, 1992, had the following balances:

| | |
|---|---:|
| Raw Materials................................................. | $ 81,000 |
| Allowance to Reduce Raw Materials Inventory From Cost to Market.... | 4,200 |
| Work in Process ................................................. | 131,520 |
| Finished Goods ................................................. | 205,200 |

The following are some of the transactions that affected the inventory of the Olsen Company during 1993:

Feb. 10    Olsen Company purchases raw materials at an invoice price of $25,000; terms 3/15, n/30. Olsen Company uses the net method of valuing inventories.

Mar. 15    Olsen Company repossesses an inventory item from a customer who was overdue in making payment. The unpaid balance on the sale is $190. The repossessed merchandise is to be refinished and placed on sale. It is expected that the item can be sold for $300 after estimated refinishing costs of $85. The normal profit for this item is considered to be $40.

Apr.  1    Refinishing costs of $80 are incurred on the repossessed item.
     10    The repossessed item is resold for $300 on account, 20% down.

May 30    A sale on account is made of finished goods that have a list price of $740 and a cost of $480. A reduction of $100 off the list price is granted as a trade-in allowance. The trade-in item is to be priced to sell at $80 as is. The normal profit on this type of inventory is 25% of the sales price.

Nov. 30    Olsen Company orders materials to be delivered January 31, 1994, at a cost of $21,600. No discount terms are included.

Dec. 31    The following information is available to adjust the accounts for the annual statements:

     (a)  The market value of the items ordered on November 30 has declined to $18,000.

    (b) The raw materials inventory account has a cost balance of $110,400. Current market value is $101,400.

    (c) The finished goods inventory account has a cost balance of $177,600. Current market value is $189,000.

**Instructions:** Record this information in journal entry form, including any required adjusting entries at December 31, 1993.

## Problem 11—11 (Trade-ins and repossessed inventory)

Good Buy Auto Sales buys and sells automobiles. They deal in both new and used cars and often accept trade-ins, which they recondition and sell. Recently, a young couple traded in their 1971 Mustang convertible for a more conservative 1982 Caprice station wagon. The Caprice had a cash price of $3,500. The couple paid $2,400 in cash plus their Mustang. The Mustang was reconditioned by Good Buy at a cost of $250 and sold for $1,150 to be paid in monthly payments to Good Buy. After three months, the new owner failed to make the monthly payment and the Mustang was repossessed. The defaulted receivable amounted to $1,000. After additional reconditioning of $100, the Mustang was sold for a cash price of $900, yielding a 20 percent profit on cost.

**Instructions:**

1. Prepare the journal entries to record the trade-in of the Mustang and the purchase of the station wagon.
2. Prepare the journal entries to record the reconditioning and sale of the Mustang.
3. Prepare the journal entries to record the repossession of the Mustang and its subsequent reconditioning and resale.

## Problem 11—12 (Foreign transactions)

Charles & Sons, a U.S. computer supplies firm, had the following transactions with foreign companies during December of 1992:

(a) Goldstar Co., Ltd., a Korea-based firm, sold 5,000 computer hard drives to Charles & Sons for 1,000 won per drive on December 12, 1992. Charles & Sons paid the bill on January 13, 1993.

(b) Charles & Sons sold 2,000 computer hard drives to a Swiss firm, Lockner Inc., on December 21, 1992. Lockner Inc. agreed to pay $135 per hard drive. Payment was received by Charles & Sons on February 4, 1993.

(c) Charles & Sons sold 2,400 computer hard drives to Geopacific, Inc., a company with headquarters in Canada, on December 28, 1992. Geopacific was billed 148 Canadian dollars per drive. Payment was received on January 10, 1993.

(d) Charles & Sons received 1,000 printers from Printco, a Japanese company, on December 28, 1992. Printco billed Charles & Sons 4,500 yen per printer. Charles & Sons paid the liability on January 14, 1993.

Relevant exchange rates for the above transactions are as follows:

| | **Exchange Rates** | | |
| --- | --- | --- | --- |
| | **As of Date of Sale or Purchase** | **As of Balance Sheet Date** | **As of Date of Payment or Receipt** |
| Korean won | $ .103 | $ .112 | $ .115 |
| Swiss franc | 1.670 | 1.632 | 1.655 |
| Canadian dollar | .910 | .935 | .905 |
| Japanese yen | .075 | .069 | .073 |

**Instructions:** Prepare the journal entries necessary to record each of the above transactions for the following: (1) date of the original transaction, (2) balance sheet date, and (3) date of payment or receipt of cash.

# CHAPTER 12

# Noncurrent Operating Assets–Acquisition

---

**CHAPTER TOPICS**

**Classification of Noncurrent Operating Assets**

**Valuation of Noncurrent Operating Assets at Acquisition**

**Recognition of Goodwill**

**Recording Noncurrent Operating Assets Under Various Methods of Acquisition**

**Classifying Expenditures as Assets or Expenses**

  **Research and Development Expenditures**

  **Computer Software Costs**

  **Post-Acquisition Expenditures**

---

When Jerry Jones, an Arkansas oil man, purchased the Dallas Cowboys for a rumored $140 million in 1989, he acquired a diverse array of assets. These assets included: miscellaneous football equipment, stadium leases, radio and TV broadcast rights, cable TV rights, luxury stadium suites, player contracts, a lease on the Cowboys' luxurious Valley Ranch training facility, and the Cowboys' NFL franchise rights. Allocation of the purchase price among these assets and defining their useful lives was a difficult and strategic task. When H. R. "Bum" Bright bought the Dallas Cowboys for $85 million in 1984, he allocated half the purchase price to "Players' Contracts," an amortizable asset which, for tax purposes, was written off over four years.[1]

[1]Hal Lancaster, "Football Team's Sale Is Strictly Business," *The Wall Street Journal*, April 18, 1989, p. B1.

Many billions of dollars are invested each year in new property, plant, equipment, and intangible assets. Enterprises must continually make choices as to how they will invest their limited resources to acquire the operating assets needed to reach their goals and objectives. Capital budgets are prepared by management to help evaluate the available alternatives and to identify the priorities for implementation.

Many accounting questions are introduced with the acquisition of assets whose lives and economic benefits extend beyond one year, including:

1. How should the various categories of noncurrent operating assets be recorded on the balance sheet?
2. Which costs should be capitalized as assets and which ones should be recognized as expenses in the period of disbursement?
3. At what amounts should the assets be recorded under various methods of purchase?
4. How should expenditures made subsequent to acquisition be recorded?
5. What recognition should be given to changes in either the value of the dollar or the replacement cost of new assets?

These are the central issues concerning the acquisition of noncurrent operating assets that will be explored in this chapter.

## CLASSIFICATION OF NONCURRENT OPERATING ASSETS

Assets are probable future economic benefits that are controlled by an economic entity and are the result of past events. While the actual form of an asset is not an essential characteristic, it is common to group noncurrent operating assets according to whether they are tangible or intangible.

Tangible noncurrent operating assets include land, buildings, and equipment used in revenue-producing activities. Specific categories of equipment include automobiles and trucks, machinery, patterns and dies, furniture and fixtures, and returnable containers.

Intangible noncurrent operating assets include patents, copyrights, franchises, trademarks, trade names, organization costs, software development costs, and goodwill. While these assets cannot be directly observed, they usually are identified by agreements, contracts, or other documentation.

## VALUATION OF NONCURRENT OPERATING ASSETS AT ACQUISITION

Noncurrent operating assets are recorded initially at cost—the original bargained or cash sales price. In theory, the maximum price an entity should be willing to pay for an operating asset is the present value of the net benefit the entity expects to obtain from the use and final disposition of the asset. In a competitive economy, the market value, or cost, of an asset at acquisition is assumed to reflect the present value of its future benefits.

The cost of property includes not only the original purchase price or equivalent value, but also any other expenditures required in obtaining and preparing it for its intended use. Any taxes, freight, installation, and other expenditures related to the acquisition should be included in the asset's cost. Post-acquisition costs incurred *after* the asset is placed into service are usually expensed rather than added to the acquisition cost. Exceptions to this general rule apply to some major replacements or improvements and will be discussed later in the chapter.

Although most noncurrent operating asset categories have similar acquisition costs, over time accounting practice has identified some specific costs that are included for different asset categories. Exhibits 12—1 and 12—2 below and on page 429 summarize the types of cost normally included as acquisition costs for each major noncurrent asset category.

Because land is a nondepreciable asset, costs assigned to land should be those costs that directly relate to land's unlimited life. Together with clearing and grading costs, costs of removing unwanted structures from newly acquired land are considered part of the cost to prepare the land for its intended use and are added to the purchase price of the land. Government assessments for water lines, sewers, roads, and other such items are considered part of the land's cost since maintenance of these items is the responsibility of the government; thus, to the landowner, they have unlimited life. These types of improvements are distinguished from similar costs for landscaping, parking lots, and interior sidewalks that are installed by the owner and must be replaced over time. These owner-responsible improvements are generally classified as land improvements and are depreciated.

The cost of purchased buildings includes any reconditioning costs necessary before occupancy. Because self-constructed buildings have many unique costs, a separate discussion of self-constructed assets is included later in this chapter.

Equipment costs include freight and insurance charges while the equipment is in transit and any expenditures for testing and installation. Costs for reconditioning purchased used equipment are also part of the asset cost.

**Exhibit 12—1    Acquisition Cost of Tangible Noncurrent Operating Assets**

| Asset | Description | Examples of Acquisition Costs |
|---|---|---|
| Land | Realty used for business purposes. | Purchase price, commissions, legal fees, escrow fees, surveying fees, clearing and grading costs, street and water line assessments. |
| Land Improvements | Items such as landscaping, paving, fencing that improve the usefulness of property. | Cost of improvements, including expenditures for materials, labor, and overhead. |
| Buildings | A structure used to house a business operation. | Purchase price, commissions, reconditioning costs. |
| Equipment | Assets used in the production of goods or in providing services. Examples include automobiles, trucks, machinery, patterns and dies, and furniture and fixtures. | Purchase price, taxes, freight, insurance, installation, and any expenditures incurred in preparing the asset for its intended use, e.g., reconditioning and testing costs. |

Intangible assets also are generally recorded at cost; however, acquisition costs differ between externally purchased intangibles and those that are internally developed. Intangible assets arising from exclusive rights granted by the U.S. Government, such as copyrights, patents, and trademarks, are recorded at their purchase price if externally obtained. Internal research and development costs incurred to generate the items subject to government license are generally expensed as incurred because of the uncertainty as to whether the work will result in a successful product. Only the actual legal and filing costs are included as part of the intangible asset cost for these internally developed items. Any cost to defend the rights in court are added to the intangible asset cost if successful. If not successful, all asset costs related to the rights would be written off as an expense.

Franchise operations have become so common in our everyday life that we often don't realize we are dealing with them. The cost of a franchise includes any sum paid specifically for the franchise right as well as legal fees and other costs incurred in obtaining it. Although the value of a franchise at the time of its acquisition may be substantially in excess of its cost, the amount recorded should be limited to actual outlays. When a franchise is purchased from another company, the amount paid is recorded as the franchise cost.

In forming a corporation, certain organization costs are incurred, including legal fees, promotional costs, stock certificate costs, underwriting costs, and state incorporation fees. The benefits to be derived from these expenditures normally extend beyond the first fiscal period. Because the primary benefits of these start-up costs relate to the first few years of operation, they are usually written off to expense fairly rapidly. Some development stage companies have included such costs as interest, administrative salaries, and taxes as part of organization costs. The Financial Accounting Standards Board concluded that these administrative costs should not be classified as an intangible asset. The same accounting principles should apply to development-stage companies as for mature companies. Only the costs related to the actual formation of the company, as mentioned above, should be included as part of organization costs.[2]

In recent years, the tremendous growth in the computer industry, particularly in microcomputers, has raised some significant accounting issues relating to expenditures for the development and production of computer software. Because these costs have been addressed separately by the FASB, the accounting and reporting issues relating to software development expenditures are discussed in detail later in the chapter.

The most frequently reported intangible asset is goodwill. In the 1990 edition of *Accounting Trends & Techniques,* 367 of the 600 surveyed companies reported goodwill. The next most frequent intangible asset was patents, reported by 62 companies. Goodwill is reported only when it arises from the purchase of another entity for more than the market value of the identifiable net assets. Because of its unique character, it will be discussed in more depth than the other intangibles summarized in Exhibit 12—2.

## Goodwill

Of all the intangible assets, goodwill is perhaps the most controversial. In a general sense, goodwill is often referred to as that intangible something that makes the whole company worth more than its individual parts. In general, goodwill represents all the special advantages, not otherwise identifiable, enjoyed by an enterprise, such as a good name, capable staff and personnel, high credit standing, reputation for superior products and services, and favorable location. From an accounting point of view, goodwill is recognized as the intangible resources, factors, and conditions that allow a business to earn above-normal income with the identifiable assets employed in the business. Above-normal income means a rate of return greater than that normally required to attract investors into a particular type of business.

Goodwill differs from most other assets in that it cannot be exchanged or sold separately from the entity itself. Because goodwill is recorded on the books only as part of an entity acquisition, it is difficult to compare a company that has recorded goodwill with one that hasn't. Merely because a company has not purchased another company does not

[2]*Statement of Financial Accounting Standards No. 7,* ''Accounting and Reporting by Development Stage Enterprises'' (Stamford: Financial Accounting Standards Board, 1975), par. 10.

**Exhibit 12—2    Acquisition Cost of Intangible Noncurrent Operating Assets**

| Asset | Description | Examples of Acquisition Costs |
|---|---|---|
| Copyright | An exclusive right granted by the U.S. government that permits an author to sell, license, or control his/her work. Copyright expires 50 years after the death of the author. | Purchase price, filing and registry fees, cost of subsequent litigation to protect right. Does not include internal research and development costs. |
| Patent | An exclusive right granted by the U.S. government that enables an inventor to control the manufacture, sale, or use of an invention. Legal life is 17 years. | |
| Trademark and Trade Name | An exclusive right granted by the U.S. government that permits the use of distinctive symbols, labels, and designs, e.g., McDonald's golden arches, Levi's pocket patch, Chrysler's star. Legal life is virtually unlimited. | |
| Franchise | An exclusive right or privilege received by a business or individual to perform certain functions or sell certain products or services. | Expenditures made to purchase the franchise. Legal fees and other costs incurred in obtaining the franchise. |
| Organization Costs | Costs incurred in forming a corporation. | Expenditures to organize the corporation: cost of stock certificates, underwriting costs, state incorporation fees. |
| Software Development Costs | Costs incurred in the development of computer software. | Expenditures made after software is determined to be technologically feasible but before it is ready for commercial production. |
| Goodwill | Miscellaneous intangible resources, factors, and conditions that allow a company to earn above-normal income with its identifiable net assets. Goodwill is recorded only when a business entity is acquired by a purchase. | Portion of purchase price that exceeds the sum of the current market value for all identifiable net assets. |

mean it does not have goodwill as defined above. Thus, current accounting principles may result in misleading users of financial statements as far as goodwill is concerned. On the other hand, to allow companies to place a value on their own goodwill would introduce a significant amount of added subjectivity to the financial statements. These difficulties have led some accountants to suggest that all purchased goodwill should be written off to expense as soon as it is acquired. Advocates of this position include the authors of Accounting Research Study No. 10, "Accounting for Goodwill," whose justification for immediate write-off was given as follows:

1. Goodwill is not a resource or property right that is consumed or utilized in the production of earnings. It is the result of expectations of future earnings by investors and thus is not subject to normal amortization procedures.
2. Goodwill is subject to sudden and wide fluctuations. The value has no reliable or continuing relation to costs incurred in its creation.
3. Under existing practices of accounting, neither the cost nor the value of nonpurchased goodwill is reported in the balance sheet. Purchased goodwill has no continuing,

## Accounting for Goodwill: The United States Against the World

Sanford Pensler, a mergers-and-acquisitions investment banker, writing on the editorial page of *The Wall Street Journal*, said: "Would-be U.S. purchasers of U.S. firms are burdened by accounting rules that favor foreign buyers." Mr. Pensler was referring to the requirement that U.S. companies record goodwill acquired in a purchase as an asset and amortize the goodwill against earnings over a period not to exceed 40 years. This goodwill amortization can result in a very significant earnings reduction. Consider the case of the acquisition of Kraft by Philip Morris. The purchase price was $12.9 billion, $11.6 billion of which was recorded as goodwill on Philip Morris' books. These numbers suggest a minimum annual goodwill amortization expense amount of $290 million; for comparison, Kraft's net income in 1987, the year before the purchase, was $489 million. One Arthur Andersen partner was quoted as saying: "Chief executives are compensated based on earnings per share. That makes them very wary about taking a big bite of goodwill."

In contrast, in Great Britain, goodwill is recorded as a direct, one-time reduction in equity; there is no effect on earnings. In Canada, Japan, and West Germany, amortization of goodwill is required for financial reporting, but a corresponding tax deduction is allowed. In essence, taxpayers in these countries are subsidizing the purchases. No tax deduction for goodwill amortization is allowed in the U.S. Of the major industrial countries, only the United States requires goodwill to be charged against earnings for financial reporting purposes but allows no write-off for tax purposes.

### Questions:

1. *Examples such as these are cited as justification for working to arrive at a "harmonization" between the standards of different countries. How might representatives of different countries go about resolving such wide differences in practice?*
2. *"Resolution of accounting standard differences must consider cultural, legal, and business differences among countries." Do you agree with this statement? Can these differences justify different accounting standards in various countries?*

Sources:

Penelope Wang, "The Unlevel Accounting Field," *Forbes*, November 28, 1988, p. 170.

Sanford Pensler, "Accounting Rules Favor Foreign Bidders," *The Wall Street Journal*, March 24, 1988, p. 30.

1988 Annual Report of Philip Morris Companies Inc.

---

separately measurable existence after the combination and is merged with the total goodwill value of the continuing business entity. As such, its write-off cannot be measured with any validity.

4. Goodwill as an asset account is not relevant to an investor. Most analysts ignore any reported goodwill when analyzing a company's status and operations.[3]

This position has been consistently rejected by the accounting principles-setting bodies, and the immediate write-off of purchased goodwill is not permitted under GAAP.

---

[3]George R. Catlett and Norman O. Olson, "Accounting for Goodwill," *Accounting Research Study No. 10* (New York: American Institute of Certified Public Accountants, 1968).

They maintain that a price has been paid for the excess earnings power, and it should be recognized as an asset. Because of the poor connotative image the term *goodwill* has acquired, some companies use more descriptive titles for reporting purposes, such as "Excess of Cost Over Net Assets of Acquired Companies."

In the purchase of a going business, the actual price paid for goodwill usually results from bargaining and compromises between the parties concerned. A basis for negotiation in arriving at a price for goodwill involves many variables, including:

1. The level of projected future income.
2. An appropriate rate of return.
3. Current valuation of the net business assets other than goodwill.

When a lump-sum amount is paid for an established business and no explicit evaluation is made of goodwill, goodwill may still be recognized. In this case the identifiable net assets require appraisal, and the difference between the full purchase price and the value of identifiable net assets can be attributed to the purchase of goodwill. In appraising properties for this purpose, current market values should be sought rather than the values reported in the accounts. Receivables should be stated at amounts estimated to be realized. Inventories and securities should be restated in terms of current market values. Land, buildings, and equipment may require special appraisals in arriving at their present replacement or reproduction values. Intangible assets, such as patents and franchises, should be included at their current values even though, originally, expenditures were reported as expenses or were reported as assets and amortized against revenue. Care should be taken to determine that liabilities are fully recognized. Assets at their current fair market values less the liabilities to be assumed provide the net assets total that together with estimated future earnings are used in arriving at a purchase price.

To the extent possible, the amount paid for any existing company should be related to identifiable assets. If an excess does exist, the use of a term other than goodwill can avoid the implication that only companies that purchase other companies have goodwill.

To illustrate the purchase and recording of an ongoing business, assume that Airnational Corporation purchases the net assets of Speedy Freight Airlines for $675,000 cash. A schedule of net assets for Speedy Freight at the time of acquisition is presented on page 432.

Analysis of the $107,800 difference between the purchase price ($675,000) and the net asset book value ($567,200) reveals the following differences between the recorded costs and market values of the assets:

|  | Cost | Market |
|---|---|---|
| Inventory | $292,000 | $327,000 |
| Investments | 72,000 | 85,000 |
| Land, buildings, and equipment | 489,200 | 504,500 |
| Patents | 7,000 | 12,000 |
| Trademarks and trade names | 9,500 | 10,000 |
| Franchises | | 5,000 |
| Totals | $869,700 | $943,500 |

The identifiable portion of the $107,800 difference amounts to $73,800 ($943,500 − $869,700) and is allocated to the respective assets. The remaining difference of $34,000 is recorded as an intangible asset, Goodwill.

**Speedy Freight Airlines**
**Schedule of Net Assets**
**December 31, 1994**

Assets

| | | |
|---|---:|---:|
| Cash and temporary investments ...................... | $ 21,000 | |
| Receivables ......................................... | 146,000 | |
| Inventory .......................................... | 292,000 | |
| Investments ....................................... | 72,000 | |
| Land, buildings, and equipment (net).................. | 489,200 | |
| Patents, trademarks, and trade names ................. | 16,500 | $1,036,700 |

Liabilities

| | | |
|---|---:|---:|
| Current liabilities .................................... | $286,000 | |
| Long-term debt ...................................... | 183,500 | 469,500 |
| Net assets ......................................... | | $ 567,200 |

The entry to record the purchase is as follows:

| | | |
|---|---:|---:|
| Cash and Temporary Investments.......................... | 21,000 | |
| Receivables ........................................... | 146,000 | |
| Inventory ............................................. | 327,000 | |
| Investments .......................................... | 85,000 | |
| Land, Buildings, and Equipment .......................... | 504,500 | |
| Patents ............................................... | 12,000 | |
| Trademarks and Trade Names ............................ | 10,000 | |
| Franchises ............................................ | 5,000 | |
| Goodwill (excess of market value over cost paid for net assets) ................................................. | 34,000 | |
|    Current Liabilities....................................... | | 286,000 |
|    Long-Term Debt ....................................... | | 183,500 |
|    Cash ................................................. | | 675,000 |

**Negative Goodwill**    Occasionally, the amount paid for another company is less than the fair market value of the net assets of the acquired company. This condition can arise when economic conditions are depressed and where bargain purchases are possible. The accounting profession has discussed from time to time how such negative goodwill should be recorded. Some accountants have suggested that it should be recorded as part of owners' equity.

The APB, however, did not want the total assets to be recorded at an aggregate amount that exceeded cost. The Board decided, therefore, to require the allocation of the excess against all acquired noncurrent assets, except for noncurrent marketable equity securities. If this allocation reduces the noncurrent assets to a zero balance, any remaining excess is credited to a deferred credit account and amortized against revenue over the period benefited.[4]

For example, assume Goodtime, Inc., purchases the net assets of Funtime, Inc., for $500,000. The fair market values of Funtime's assets are as follows:

[4]*Opinions of the Accounting Principles Board No. 16,* "Business Combinations" (New York: American Institute of Certified Public Accountants, 1970), par. 91. Some accountants have suggested that, in a negative goodwill transaction, all acquired assets and liabilities should be recorded at their fair market values and that the entire excess of purchase price over net assets acquired be recorded as a one-time increase to stockholders' equity. See Wig De Moville and A. George Petrie, "Accounting for a Bargain Purchase in a Business Combination," *Accounting Horizons* (September 1989), pp. 38-43.

| | |
|---|---:|
| Cash and temporary investments | $ 75,000 |
| Receivables | 125,000 |
| Inventories | 160,000 |
| Property and equipment | 250,000 |
| Investment in noncurrent marketable equity securities | 75,000 |
| Other investments | 50,000 |
| | $735,000 |

Offsetting the above assets are the following liabilities:

| | |
|---|---:|
| Current liabilities | $ 50,000 |
| Noncurrent liabilities | 125,000 |
| | $175,000 |

The market value of net assets for Funtime is thus $560,000 ($735,000 − $175,000), and the indicated negative goodwill is $60,000 ($560,000 − $500,000). The only noncurrent assets that would meet the Board's criteria for adjustment would be property and equipment and other investments. The allocation of the $60,000 would be performed as follows:

| | Book Value | Allocation of Negative Goodwill According to Relative Book Values | Negative Goodwill Assigned to Individual Assets |
|---|---|---|---|
| Property and equipment | $250,000 | 250,000/300,000 × $60,000 | $50,000 |
| Other investments | 50,000 | 50,000/300,000 × $60,000 | 10,000 |
| | $300,000 | | $60,000 |

The $60,000 negative goodwill is thus allocated $50,000 against property and equipment and $10,000 against other investments. The acquisition is then recorded as follows:

| | | |
|---|---:|---:|
| Cash and Temporary Investments | 75,000 | |
| Receivables | 125,000 | |
| Inventories | 160,000 | |
| Property and Equipment | 200,000 | |
| Investment in Noncurrent Marketable Equity Securities | 75,000 | |
| Other Investments | 40,000 | |
|     Cash | | 500,000 |
|     Current Liabilities | | 50,000 |
|     Noncurrent Liabilities | | 125,000 |
|     *To record acquisition of Funtime, Inc.* | | |

Exhibit 12-3 illustrates a note included in Par Technology Corporation's 1989 annual report describing a negative goodwill transaction.

## RECORDING ACQUISITION OF NONCURRENT OPERATING ASSETS

When an asset is purchased for cash, the acquisition is simply recorded at the amount of cash paid, including all outlays relating to its purchase and preparation for intended use. Assets can be acquired under a number of other arrangements, however, some of which present special problems relating to the cost to be recorded. The acquisition of assets is discussed under the following headings:

1. Assets acquired for a lump-sum purchase price
2. Purchase on deferred payment contract
3. Acquisition under capital lease

4. Acquisition by exchange of nonmonetary assets
5. Acquisition by issuance of securities
6. Acquisition by self-construction
7. Acquisition by donation or discovery

### Exhibit 12—3    Par Technology Corporation—Disclosure of Negative Goodwill Transaction

On July 21, 1988, the Company acquired substantially all of the operating assets and business of the Retail Systems Division of Norand Corporation. . . . The purchase price [was] allocated to the assets and liabilities acquired based on their respective estimated fair values at date of acquisition. The excess of the fair market value over cost was first allocated to reduce the noncurrent assets to zero value. The remainder of the excess over cost . . . was classified as negative goodwill. The negative goodwill is being amortized over three years.

## Assets Acquired for a Lump-Sum Purchase Price

In some purchases, a number of assets may be acquired for one lump sum. Some of the assets in the group may be depreciable, others nondepreciable. Depreciable assets may have different useful lives. If there is to be accountability for the assets on an individual basis, the total purchase price must be allocated among the individual assets. When part of a purchase price can be clearly identified with specific assets, such a cost assignment should be made and the balance of the purchase price allocated among the remaining assets. When no part of the purchase price can be related to specific assets, the entire amount must be allocated among the different assets acquired. Appraisal values or similar evidence provided by a competent independent authority should be sought to support such allocation.

To illustrate the allocation of a joint asset cost, assume that land, buildings, and equipment are acquired for $160,000. Assume further that assessed values for the individual assets as reported on the property tax bill are considered to provide an equitable basis for cost allocation. The allocation is made as shown below.

|  | Assessed Values | Cost Allocation According to Relative Assessed Values | Cost Assigned to Individual Assets |
|---|---|---|---|
| Land ............... | $ 28,000 | 28,000/100,000 × $160,000 | $ 44,800 |
| Buildings ........... | 60,000 | 60,000/100,000 × $160,000 | 96,000 |
| Equipment.......... | 12,000 | 12,000/100,000 × $160,000 | 19,200 |
|  | $100,000 |  | $160,000 |

The entry to record this acquisition, assuming a cash purchase, would be as follows:

| | | |
|---|---|---|
| Land ................................................. | 44,800 | |
| Buildings ............................................. | 96,000 | |
| Equipment............................................ | 19,200 | |
| Cash ................................................. | | 160,000 |

## Purchase on Deferred Payment Contract

The acquisition of real estate or other property frequently involves deferred payment of all or part of the purchase price. The indebtedness of the buyer is usually evidenced by a note, debenture, mortgage, or other contract that specifies the terms of settlement of the obligation. The debt instrument may call for one payment at a given future date or a series of payments at specified intervals. Interest charged on the unpaid balance of the contract should be recognized as an expense.

To illustrate the accounting for a deferred payment purchase contract, assume that land is acquired for $100,000; $35,000 is paid at the time of purchase, and the balance is to be paid in semiannual installments of $5,000 plus interest on the unpaid principal at an annual rate of 10%. Entries for the purchase and for the first payment on the contract are shown below.

| Transaction | Entry | | |
|---|---|---|---|
| **January 2, 1993** | | | |
| Purchased land for $100,000 paying $35,000 down, the balance to be paid in semiannual payments of $5,000 plus interest at 10%. | Land ............. | 100,000 | |
| | Cash ........... | | 35,000 |
| | Note Payable.... | | 65,000 |
| **June 30, 1993** | | | |
| Made first payment. | Interest Expense .. | 3,250 | |
| Amount of Payment: | Note Payable...... | 5,000 | |
| $5,000 + $3,250 (5% of $65,000) = $8,250 | Cash .......... | | 8,250 |

In the preceding example, the contract specified both a purchase price and interest at a stated rate on the unpaid balance. Sometimes, however, a contract may simply provide for a payment or series of payments without reference to interest, or may provide for a stated interest rate that is unreasonable in relation to the market. As indicated in Chapter 9, APB Opinion No. 21, "Interest on Receivables and Payables," requires that in these circumstances, the note, sales price, and cost of the property, goods, or services exchanged for the note should be recorded at the fair market value of the property, goods, or services or at the current market value of the note, whichever value is more clearly determinable.[5] Application of Opinion No. 21 with respect to the seller was illustrated in Chapter 9. The following example illustrates the accounting by the purchaser.

Assume that certain equipment, which has a cash price of $50,000, is acquired under a deferred payment contract. The contract specifies a down payment of $15,000 plus seven annual payments of $7,189 each, or a total price, including interest, of $65,323. Although not stated, the effective interest rate implicit in this contract is 10%, the rate that discounts the annual payments of $7,189 to a present value of $35,000, the cash price less the down payment.[6] As specified in APB Opinion No. 21, if the cash equivalent price, that is, the fair market value of the asset, varies from the contract price because of delayed payments, the difference should be recorded as a discount (contra liability) and amortized over the life of the contract using the implicit or effective interest rate. The entries to record the purchase, the amortization of the discount for the first two years, and the first two payments would be as shown on page 436.

---

[5]The term *notes* is used by the Board in Opinion No. 21 as a general term for contractual rights to receive money or contractual obligations to pay money at specified or determinable dates.

[6]As illustrated in Chapter 7, the effective or implicit interest rate is computed as follows:

$$PV_n = R(PVAF_{\overline{n}|i})$$
$$\$50,000 - \$15,000 = \$7,189(PVAF_{\overline{n}|i})$$
$$PVAF_{\overline{n}|i} = \frac{\$35,000}{\$7,189}$$
$$PVAF_{\overline{n}|i} = 4.8685$$

From Table IV, Chapter 7, the interest rate for the present value of 4.8684 when $n = 7$ is 10%. Additional examples of computing an implicit rate of interest are presented in Chapter 7.

| Transaction | Entry | | |
|---|---|---|---|
| **January 2, 1993**<br>Purchased equipment with a cash price of $50,000 for $15,000 down plus seven annual payments of $7,189 each, or a total contract price of $65,323. | Equipment . . . . . . .<br>Discount on<br>Note Payable . . . . .<br>Note Payable . . .<br>Cash . . . . . . . . . | 50,000<br><br>15,323 | <br><br><br>50,323<br>15,000 |
| **December 31, 1993**<br>Made first payment of $7,189.<br>Amortization of debt discount:<br>10% × $35,000 = $3,500<br>($50,323 − $15,323 = $35,000) | Note Payable . . . . .<br>Cash . . . . . . . . .<br>Interest Expense . .<br>Discount on<br>Note Payable . . . | 7,189<br><br>3,500 | <br>7,189<br><br><br>3,500 |
| **December 31, 1994**<br>Made second payment of $7,189.<br>Amortization of debt discount:<br>10% × $31,311* = $3,131 | Note Payable . . . . .<br>Cash . . . . . . . . .<br>Interest Expense . .<br>Discount on<br>Note Payable . . . | 7,189<br><br>3,131 | <br>7,189<br><br><br>3,131 |

*$50,323 − $7,189 = $43,134   Note payable
 $15,323 − $3,500 = <u>11,823</u>   Discount on note payable
                  <u>$31,311</u>   Present value of note payable at end of first year

When there is no established cash price for the property, goods, or services, and there is no stated rate of interest on the contract, or the stated rate is unreasonable under the circumstances, an imputed interest rate must be used. A discussion of the determination and application of imputed interest rates was included in Chapter 9.

Property is often acquired under a conditional sales contract whereby legal title to the asset is retained by the seller until payments are completed. The failure to acquire legal title may be disregarded by the buyer and the transaction recognized in terms of its substance—the acquisition of an asset and assumption of a liability. The buyer has the possession and use of the asset and must absorb any decline in its value; title to the asset is retained by the seller simply as a means of assuring payment on the purchase contract.

## Acquisition Under Capital Lease

A **lease** is a contractual agreement whereby a **lessee** is granted a right to use property owned by the **lessor** for a specified period of time for a specified periodic cost. Many leases, referred to as **capital leases**, are in effect purchases of property. In such cases, the property should be recorded on the lessee's books as an asset at the present value of the future lease payments. Because lease accounting is a complex area, an entire chapter is devoted to accounting for leases. Even when a lease is not considered to be the same as a purchase and the periodic payments are written off as rental expense, certain lease prepayments or improvements to the property by the lessee may be treated as capital expenditures. Since leasehold improvements, such as partitions in a building, additions, and attached equipment, revert to the owner at the expiration of the lease, they are properly capitalized on the books of the lessee and amortized over the remaining life of the lease. Some lease costs are really expenses of the period and should not be capitalized. These include improvements that are made in lieu of rent, e.g., a lessee builds partitions in a leased warehouse for storage of its product, and the lessor allows the lessee to offset the cost against rental expense for the period. These costs should be expensed by the lessee.

## Acquisition by Exchange of Nonmonetary Assets

In some cases, an enterprise acquires a new asset by exchanging or trading existing non-monetary assets.[7] Generally, the new asset should be valued at its fair market value or at the fair market value of the asset given up, whichever is more clearly determinable.[8] If the nonmonetary asset is used equipment, the fair market value of the new asset is generally more clearly determinable, and therefore used to record the exchange. It should be observed that determining the fair market value of a new asset can sometimes be difficult.

The quoted or list price for an asset is not always a good indicator of the market value and is often higher than the actual cash price for the asset. An inflated list price permits the seller to increase the indicated trade-in allowance for a used asset. The price for which the asset could be acquired in a cash transaction is the fair market value that should be used to record the acquisition.

To illustrate, assume the sticker on the window of a new car sitting in a dealer's showroom lists a total selling price of $13,500. The sticker includes a base price plus an itemized listing of all the options that have been added. If you, as a buyer, approached the dealer with your old clunker as a trade-in, you might be surprised to be offered $2,000 for a car you know is worth no more than $1,000. If you offered to pay cash for the new car with no trade-in, however, you could probably buy it for approximately $12,500, or the list price reduced by the inflated amount of allowance offered for the trade-in. The fair market value of the new asset is thus not the list price of $13,500 but the true cash price of $12,500.

If the nonmonetary asset given up to acquire the new asset is also property or equipment, a disposition of property occurs simultaneously with the acquisition. Because of the need to first discuss depreciation methods and practices before presenting the disposition of assets, the full discussion of acquisition and disposition by exchange is covered in Chapter 13.

## Acquisition by Issuance of Securities

A company may acquire certain property by issuing its own bonds or stocks. When a market value for the securities can be determined, that value is assigned to the asset; in the absence of a market value for the securities, the fair market value of the asset acquired would be used. If bonds or stocks are selling at more or less than par value, Bonds Payable or Capital Stock should be credited at par and the difference recorded as a premium or discount. To illustrate, assume that a company issues 1,000 shares of $25 par stock in acquiring land; the stock is currently selling on the market at $45. An entry should be made as follows:

| | | |
|---|---|---|
| Land .................................................. | 45,000 | |
| Capital Stock ........................................... | | 25,000 |
| Paid-In Capital in Excess of Par .......................... | | 20,000 |

When securities do not have an established market value, appraisal of the acquired assets by an independent authority may be required to arrive at an objective determination of their fair market value. If satisfactory market values cannot be obtained for either the securities issued or the assets acquired, values may have to be established by the board of directors for accounting purposes. The source of the valuation should be disclosed on the

---

[7]Monetary assets are those assets whose amounts are fixed in terms of currency, by contract, or otherwise. Examples include cash and short- or long-term accounts receivable. Nonmonetary assets include all other assets, such as inventories, land, buildings, and equipment.

[8]*Opinions of the Accounting Principles Board No. 29,* "Accounting for Nonmonetary Transactions" (New York: American Institute of Certified Public Accountants, 1973), par. 18.

balance sheet. Assignment of values by the board of directors is normally not subject to challenge unless it can be shown that the board has acted fraudulently. Nevertheless, evidence should be sought to validate the fairness of original valuations, and if, within a short time after an acquisition, the sale of stock or other information indicates that original valuations were erroneous, the affected asset and owners' equity accounts should be adjusted.

Property is frequently acquired in exchange for securities in conjunction with a corporate merger or consolidation. When such combination represents the transfer of properties to a new owner, the combination is designated a *purchase* and the acquired assets are reported at their cost to the new owner. But when such combination represents essentially no more than a continuation of the original ownership in the enlarged entity, the combination is designated a *pooling of interests,* and accounting authorities have approved the practice of recording properties at the original book values as shown on the books of the acquired company. Specific guidelines for distinguishing between a purchase and a pooling of interests are included in APB Opinion No. 16 and are discussed in detail in advanced accounting texts.[9]

## Acquisition by Self-Construction

Sometimes buildings or equipment are constructed by a company for its own use. This may be done to save on construction costs, to utilize idle facilities, or to achieve a higher quality of construction.

Self-constructed assets, like purchased assets, are recorded at cost, including all expenditures incurred to build the asset and make it ready for its intended use. Some considerations in determining the cost of self-constructed assets are discussed in the following sections.

**Overhead Chargeable to Self-Construction**     All costs that can be related to construction should be charged to the assets under construction. There is no question about the inclusion of charges for material and labor directly attributable to the new construction. However, there is a difference of opinion regarding the amount of overhead properly assignable to the construction activity. Some accountants take the position that assets under construction should be charged with no more than the incremental overhead—the increase in a company's total overhead resulting from the special construction activity. Others maintain that overhead should be assigned to construction just as it is assigned to normal operations. This would call for the inclusion of not only the increase in overhead resulting from construction activities but also a pro rata share of the company's fixed overhead.

The argument for limiting overhead charges to incremental amounts is that the cost of construction is actually no more than the extra costs incurred. Charges should not be shifted from normal operations to construction activities. Management is aware of the cost of normal operations and decides to undertake a project on the basis of the anticipated added costs. The position that construction should carry a fair share of the fixed overhead if the full cost of the asset is to be reported is based on the premise that overhead has served a dual purpose during the construction period and this is properly reflected in reduced operating costs. The latter argument may be particularly persuasive if construction takes place during a period of subnormal operations and utilizes what would otherwise represent idle capacity cost, or if construction restricts production or other regular business activities.

---

[9]See, for example, Paul M. Fischer, William James Taylor, and J. Arthur Leer, *Advanced Accounting* (Cincinnati: South-Western Publishing Co., 1990).

The assignment to construction of normal overhead otherwise chargeable to current operations will increase net income during the construction period. The recognition of a portion of overhead is postponed and related to subsequent periods through depreciation expense.

The accounting profession has not been successful in coming to an agreement on this issue. Authors of a research study for the AICPA have suggested the following criterion to help resolve the issue:

> . . . in the absence of compelling evidence to the contrary, overhead costs considered to have "discernible future benefits" for the purpose of determining the cost of inventory should be presumed to have "discernible future benefits" for the purpose of determining the cost of a self-constructed depreciable asset.[10]

This criterion would charge both normal and incremental overhead costs to self-constructed fixed assets and has the advantage of providing consistency within a company in the treatment of overhead costs.

**Saving or Loss on Self-Construction**  When the cost of self-construction of an asset is less than the cost to acquire it through purchase or construction by outsiders, the difference for accounting purposes is not a profit but a savings. The construction is properly reported at its actual cost. The savings will emerge as income over the life of the asset as lower depreciation is charged against periodic revenue. Assume, on the other hand, the cost of self-construction is greater than bids originally received for the construction. There is generally no assurance that the asset under alternative arrangements might have been equal in quality to that which was self-constructed. In recording this transaction, just as in recording others, accounts should reflect those courses of action taken, not the alternatives that might have been selected. However, if there is evidence indicating cost has been materially excessive because of certain construction inefficiencies or failures, and the cost exceeds the fair market value of the asset, the excess is properly recognized as a loss; subsequent periods should not be burdened with charges for depreciation arising from costs that could have been avoided.

**Interest During Period of Construction**  In public utility accounting, interest during a period of construction has long been recognized as a part of asset cost. This practice applies both to interest actually paid and to an implicit interest charge if the public utility uses its own funds. Interest costs, then, are charged to expense through depreciation over the useful life of the asset. Service rates established by regulatory bodies are based on current charges, including depreciation, and thus provide for a recovery of past interest costs.

Generally accepted accounting principles also permit the deferral of certain construction-period interest by nonutility companies. Deferred interest is often referred to as capitalized interest. Only interest costs actually incurred are capitalized, and no implicit interest on internal funds is recognized. The practice of capitalizing interest as part of asset cost is supported on the grounds that interest is a legitimate cost of construction, and the proper matching of revenues and expenses suggests that interest be deferred and charged over the life of the constructed asset. It can also be argued that if buildings or equipment were acquired by purchase rather than by self-construction, a charge for interest during the construction period would be implicit in the purchase price.

Arguments advanced against this practice are:

---

[10]Charles Lamden, Dale L. Gerboth, and Thomas McRae, "Accounting for Depreciable Assets," *Accounting Research Monograph No. 1* (New York: American Institute of Certified Public Accountants, 1975), p. 57.

1. It is difficult to follow cash once it is invested in a firm. Is the interest charge really related to the constructed asset, or is it a payment made to meet general financial needs? Even when a loan is made for specific purposes, it frees cash raised by other means to be used for other projects.
2. To be consistent, implicit interest on all funds used, not just borrowed funds, should be charged to the asset cost. This practice is followed in utility accounting and requires determining a cost of capital for internal funds used, a very difficult task.

Historically, interest capitalization was not a common practice outside the public utility industry. Beginning in the mid-1970s, however, an increasing number of nonutility companies changed their accounting method to a policy of capitalizing interest, an action that tended to increase net income. In 1979, FASB Statement No. 34 was issued recommending limited capitalization of interest cost. If the development of an asset for use or in limited cases, for sale or lease, requires a significant period of time between the initial expenditure related to its development and its readiness for intended use, interest cost on borrowed funds should be capitalized as part of the asset cost.

The amount of interest to be capitalized is:

> . . . that portion of the interest cost incurred during the assets' acquisition periods that theoretically could have been avoided (for example, by avoiding additional borrowings or by using the funds expended for the assets to repay existing borrowings) if expenditures for the assets had not been made.[11]

Capitalization of interest is permitted for assets, such as buildings and equipment, that are being self-constructed for an enterprise's own use and assets that are intended to be leased or sold to others that can be identified as **discrete projects**, that is, projects that can be clearly identified as to the assets involved. The construction project should have the following characteristics before interest charges are capitalized:[12]

1. Costs are separately accumulated.
2. Construction covers an extended period of time.
3. Construction costs are substantial.

Interest should not be capitalized for inventories manufactured or produced on a repetitive basis, for assets that are currently being used, or for assets that are idle and are not undergoing activities to prepare them for use. Thus, real property that is being held for future development does not qualify for interest capitalization.[13]

Once it is determined that the construction project qualifies for interest capitalization, the amount of interest to be capitalized must be determined. The following basic principles govern the computation of capitalized interest:[14]

1. Only **interest expense actually incurred** can be capitalized. There is no provision for including an interest cost on equity capital.
2. The **maximum interest** that can be capitalized is the **total interest expense paid or accrued** for the year. In consolidated companies, this includes all interest paid by the parent and subsidiaries.

---

[11]*Statement of Financial Accounting Standards No. 34*, "Capitalization of Interest Cost" (Stamford: Financial Accounting Standards Board, 1979), par. 12.

[12]Alex T. Arcady and Charles Baker, "Interest Cost Accounting: Some Practical Guidance," *The Journal of Accountancy* (March 1981), p. 64.

[13]*Statement of Financial Accounting Standards No. 34*, par. 10.

[14]All of the items in the list are included in FASB Statement No. 34 except as otherwise noted.

3. Interest charges begin when the first expenditures are made on the project and continue as long as the activities to get the asset ready for its intended use are in progress, and until the asset is completed and actually ready for use.
4. The **average amount of accumulated expenditures** is used as the cost on which to compute the interest charge. This can be computed for each expenditure or can be estimated using the assumption that costs are being incurred evenly over the construction period. Expenditures mean cash disbursements, not accruals.
5. If the construction period covers more than one fiscal period, accumulated expenditures include prior years' capitalized interest.
6. The **interest rates** to be applied to the average accumulated expenditures are applied in a priority order as follows:
   (a) Rate incurred for any debt specifically incurred for funds used on the project.
   (b) **Weighted average interest rate** from all other enterprise borrowings regardless of the use of funds.
7. If borrowed funds are invested awaiting expenditure on the project, revenue from the investment is not offset against the interest expense in determining the actual interest expense incurred, unless the funds came from tax-exempt borrowings.[15]
8. Disclosure must be made of the total interest expense incurred for the period and the portion that was included as a capitalized cost.

The following illustration demonstrates the application of these guidelines. Cutler Industries, Inc., has decided to construct a new computerized assembly plant. It is estimated that the construction period will be two years and that the cost of construction will be $6.4 million. A 12% construction loan for $2 million is obtained at the beginning of construction.

In addition to the construction loan, Cutler has the following outstanding debt during the construction period:

5-year notes payable, 11% interest . . . . . . . . . . . . . . . . . . . . . . . . . . . . . . . .    $ 750,000
Mortgage on other plant, 9% interest . . . . . . . . . . . . . . . . . . . . . . . . . . . . .    1,200,000

Expenditures on the project are incurred evenly during each year, beginning January 1, 1993, and ending on December 31, 1994. The expenditures incurred during 1993 amounted to $3,000,000.

The first step in determining the portion of interest expense to capitalize for Cutler Industries is to determine the total interest paid during the year. This amount becomes the maximum interest that can be capitalized. In the example, the debt described below is assumed to be outstanding during all of 1993 and 1994. The interest paid is computed as follows:

**Computation of Maximum Interest That Can Be Charged Each Year**

| Debt | Amount | Interest Rate | Annual Interest |
|---|---|---|---|
| Construction Loan . . . . . . . . . . . . . . . . . . . . . . . . . | $2,000,000 | 12% | $240,000 |
| Notes Payable . . . . . . . . . . . . . . . . . . . . . . . . . . | 750,000 | 11% | 82,500 |
| Mortgage Payable . . . . . . . . . . . . . . . . . . . . . . . . | 1,200,000 | 9% | 108,000 |
| Maximum Interest . . . . . . . . . . . . . . . . . . . . . . . . | | | $430,500 |

[15]*FASB Technical Bulletin 81-5*, "Offsetting Interest to Be Capitalized with Interest Income" (Stamford: Financial Accounting Standards Board, 1981) as amended by *Statement of Financial Accounting Standards No. 62*, "Capitalization of Interest Cost in Situations Involving Certain Tax-Exempt Borrowings and Certain Gifts and Grants" (Stamford: Financial Accounting Standards Board, 1982).

The next step is to compute a weighted average interest rate on outstanding debt not directly obtained for construction. For Cutler Industries, this rate is computed as follows:

### Computation of Weighted Average Interest Rate

| Non-Construction Debt | Principal | Rate | Interest Cost |
|---|---|---|---|
| Notes Payable ............................. | $ 750,000 | 11% | $ 82,500 |
| Mortgage..................................... | 1,200,000 | 9% | 108,000 |
| | $1,950,000 | 9.8%* | $190,500 |

*Weighted average rate = $190,500 ÷ $1,950,000 = 9.8% (rounded)

The computation of the average accumulated expenditures must be made for each year. This is done by weighting each expenditure by the number of months left in the year after the expenditure is made. Since Cutler Industries incurred its expenditures evenly throughout the year, a simplifying method may be used to compute the average accumulated expenditures; simply average the beginning and ending total accumulated expenditures. The average for Cutler Industries for 1993 and 1994 would be computed as follows. Note that the beginning balance in 1993 is $0, but in 1994, it is $3,180,000, the total expenditures for 1993 plus the capitalized 1993 interest.

### Computation of Weighted Average Accumulated Expenditures—1993

| | |
|---|---|
| Accumulated expenditures, Jan. 1, 1993 ........................... | $ -0- |
| Expenditures incurred during 1993 ............................... | 3,000,000 |
| Accumulated expenditures, Dec. 31, 1993 ........................ | $3,000,000 |
| Average accumulated expenditures—1993 ($3,000,000 ÷ 2) ......... | $1,500,000 |

### Computation of Interest Eligible for Capitalization—1993

$1,500,000 × 12% (rate on construction loan) = $180,000

Since $180,000 is less than the actual interest expense, the $180,000 is capitalized as interest cost.

Assume that the project was completed at the end of 1994 and that expenditures during 1994 totaled $3.2 million, bringing the actual total cost of construction (excluding interest) to $6.2 million.

### Computation of Weighted Average Accumulated Expenditures—1994

| | |
|---|---|
| Accumulated expenditures, Dec. 31, 1993 ........................ | $3,000,000 |
| Interest capitalized—1993 ....................................... | 180,000 |
| Adjusted accumulated expenditures, Dec. 31, 1993* ................ | $3,180,000 |
| Expenditures incurred during 1994 ............................... | 3,200,000 |
| Accumulated expenditures, Dec. 31, 1994 ........................ | $6,380,000 |
| Average accumulated expenditures—1994 [($3,180,000 + $6,380,000) ÷ 2] .................................................................. | $4,780,000 |

*1993 expenditures are considered incurred for all of 1994.

**Computation of Interest Eligible for Capitalization—1994**

---

| | | |
|---|---|---|
| $2,000,000* × 12% | .............................................. | $240,000 |
| 2,780,000** × 9.8% | .............................................. | 272,440 |
| | | $512,440 |

*Amount of construction loan

**$4,780,000 − $2,000,000

Since $512,440 is more than the actual annual interest of $430,500, the actual interest expense is capitalized for 1994.

There are several important observations about this example. In 1993, the interest expense actually incurred exceeded the amount of interest computed on the average accumulated expenditures. The computed interest amount, therefore, was capitalized. In 1994, however, more of the company's internal funds were used for the construction, and the computation of interest that could have been capitalized exceeded the interest actually paid. The interest actually paid, therefore, was capitalized.

The example assumed no new loans were obtained during 1994. If additional monies were borrowed specifically for the project, the rate on the new borrowings would have been applied to expended funds before applying the weighted average rate on all other borrowings.[16] If additional general borrowings were made, a new computation of the weighted average rate would have been necessary. The example also assumed expenditures were made evenly throughout the construction period. If only a few identifiable payments were made, computation of the weighted average accumulated expenditures could have been made by weighting each expenditure separately for the portion of the year during which it was outstanding.

FASB Statement No. 34 requires disclosure of the total interest expense for the year and the amount capitalized. This disclosure can be made either in the body of the income statement or in a note to the statements.

To illustrate these two methods, assume that Cutler Industries reported the 1993 interest information in the income statement and the 1994 information in a note as on the top of page 444.

Another example of note disclosure is presented with the financial statements of IBM Corporation in Appendix A at the back of the book.

The capitalization of interest costs as part of the cost of self-constructed assets has been subject to much criticism. The initial acceptance vote of the FASB was by a 4-3 margin, the minimum acceptable. The conceptual question that still remains is whether the interest added to asset cost truly adds to the expected future benefit of the constructed asset. For now, the profession has specified the conditions where the answer is yes.

## Acquisition by Donation or Discovery

When property is received through donation by a governmental unit or other source, there is no cost that can be used as a basis for its valuation. This type of transaction is

---

[16]An interesting question arises when specific borrowings cover a period shorter than the construction period. FASB Statement No. 34 is unclear whether the interest rate on specific borrowing is applied to the full amount of the loan or to a weighted average of the loan reflecting the period it was outstanding. For a discussion of the implications of these two alternatives, see Kathryn M. Means and Paul M. Karenski, "SFAS 34: A Recipe for Diversity," *Accounting Horizons* (September 1988), pp. 62-67.

**Cutler Industries, Inc.**
**Income Statement**
**For the Year Ended 1993**

| | | |
|---|---:|---:|
| Operating income ..................................... | | $xxx,xxx |
| Other expenses and losses: | | |
|    Interest expense..................................... | $430,500 | |
|    Less capitalized interest .............................. | 180,000 | 250,500 |
| Income before income taxes........................... | | $xxx,xxx |
| Income taxes ......................................... | | xxx,xxx |
| Net income .......................................... | | $xxx,xxx |

**Cutler Industries Notes—1994**

**Note X—Interest expense**

Total interest of $430,500 was capitalized in 1994 as part of the cost of construction for the computerized assembly line building in accordance with the requirements of FASB Statement No. 34.

classified as a **nonreciprocal transfer of a nonmonetary asset.**[17] Even though certain expenditures may have to be made incident to the gift, these expenditures are generally considerably less than the value of the property. Here cost obviously fails to provide a satisfactory basis for asset valuation.

Property acquired through donation should be appraised and recorded at its fair market value.[18] A donation increases owners' equity; therefore, Donated Capital is credited. To illustrate, if the Beverly Hills Chamber of Commerce donates land and buildings appraised at $400,000 and $1,500,000 respectively, the entry on the books of the donee would be:

| | | |
|---|---:|---:|
| Land ................................................. | 400,000 | |
| Buildings ............................................ | 1,500,000 | |
|    Donated Capital ..................................... | | 1,900,000 |

Depreciation of an asset acquired by gift should be recorded in the usual manner, the value assigned to the asset providing the basis for the depreciation charge.

If a gift is contingent upon some act to be performed by the donee, no asset should be reported until the conditions of the gift have been met. At that time, both the increase in assets and in owners' equity should be recognized in the accounts and on the financial statements.

Occasionally, valuable resources are discovered on land already owned. The discovery greatly increases the value of the property. However, because the cost of the land is not affected by the discovery, it is common practice to ignore this increase in value. Similarly, the increase in value for assets that change over time, such as growing timber or aging wine, is ignored in common practice. Failure to recognize these discovery or accretion values ignores the economic reality of the situation and tends to materially understate the assets of the entity. More meaningful decisions probably could be made if the users of the statements were made aware of these changes in value.

---

[17]*Opinions of the Accounting Principles Board No. 29,* par. 3(d).
[18]*Ibid.,* par. 18.

## CLASSIFYING EXPENDITURES AS ASSETS OR EXPENSES

The decision whether a given expenditure is an asset or an expense is one of the many areas in which an accountant must exercise judgment. If the expenditure is expected to benefit future periods, it is by definition an asset. If the expenditure benefits the current period only, it is an expense.

Income cannot be measured fairly unless expenditures are properly classified. For example, an incorrect charge to an equipment account instead of an expense account results in the overstatement of current earnings on the income statement and the overstatement of assets and owners' equity on the balance sheet. As the charge is assigned to operations in subsequent periods, earnings of such periods will be understated; assets and equity on the successive balance sheets will continue to be overstated, although by lesser amounts each year, until the asset is written off and the original error is fully counterbalanced. On the other hand, an incorrect charge to an expense instead of an equipment account results in the understatement of current earnings and the understatement of assets and equity. Earnings of subsequent periods will be overstated in the absence of debits for depreciation or amortization; assets and equity will continue to be understated, although by lesser amounts each year, until the original error is completely offset.

In many companies, not all expenditures for assets that have future benefits are recorded in the noncurrent asset accounts. A lower limit to the definition of an asset expenditure is established to avoid the excessive costs of accounting for relatively small deferred costs. Thus, any expenditure under the established limit is always expensed currently even though future benefits are expected from that expenditure. This practice is justified on the grounds of expediency and materiality. The amount of the limit varies with the size of the company. Limits of $100, $500, and $1,000 are not unusual. This treatment is acceptable as long as it is consistently applied and no material misstatements arise due to unusual expenditure patterns or other causes.

Previous sections of the chapter have described the types of expenditures that typically are recorded as assets and under various types of acquisition arrangements. The remainder of the chapter focuses on areas where some special problems and considerations arise in determining whether an expenditure is an asset or an expense. These areas are: research and development expenditures, computer software development expenditures, and post-acquisition expenditures.

### Research and Development Expenditures

Historically, expenditures for **research and development (R&D)** purposes were reported sometimes as assets and sometimes as expenses. The FASB inherited this problem from the Accounting Principles Board and made this area the subject of its first definitive standard.[19] The Board defined **research activities** as those undertaken to discover new knowledge that will be useful in developing new products, services, or processes or that will result in significant improvements of existing products or processes. **Development activities** involve the application of research findings to develop a plan or design for new or improved products and processes. Development activities include the formulation, design, and testing of products, construction of prototypes, and operation of pilot plants.

In general, the FASB concluded that research and development expenditures should be expensed in the period incurred.[20] This decision was reached after much analysis and

---

[19]*Statement of Financial Accounting Standards No. 2,* "Accounting for Research and Development Costs" (Stamford: Financial Accounting Standards Board, 1974).

[20]*Ibid.,* par. 12.

after many attempts to establish criteria for selectively recording some research and development expenditures as assets and expensing others. Among the arguments for expensing these costs is the frequent inability to find a definite causal relationship between the expenditures and future revenues. Sometimes very large expenditures do not generate any future revenue, while relatively small expenditures lead to significant discoveries that generate large revenues. The Board found it difficult to establish criteria that would distinguish between those research and development expenditures that would most likely benefit future periods and those that would not.

As defined by the FASB in Statement No. 2, research and development costs include those costs of materials, equipment, facilities, personnel, purchased intangibles, contract services, and a reasonable allocation of indirect costs that are related specifically to research and development activities and that have no alternative future uses.[21] Such activities include:

1. Laboratory research aimed at discovery of new knowledge.
2. Searching for applications of new research findings or other knowledge.
3. Conceptual formulation and design of possible product or process alternatives.
4. Testing in search for or evaluation of product or process alternatives.
5. Modification of the formulation or design of a product or process.
6. Design, construction, and testing of preproduction prototypes and models.
7. Design of tools, jigs, molds, and dies involving new technology.
8. Design, construction, and operation of a pilot plant that is not of a scale economically feasible to the enterprise for commercial production.
9. Engineering activity required to advance the design of a product to the point that it meets specific functional and economic requirements and is ready for manufacture.[22]

The Board stipulated, however, that expenditures for certain items having alternative future uses, either in additional research projects or for productive purposes, can be recorded as an asset and allocated against future projects or periods as research and development expenses. This exception permits the deferral of costs incurred for materials, equipment, facilities, and purchased intangibles, but only if an alternative use can be identified.

The Board was very careful to distinguish between research and development expenses and other expenditures that are related to research activities but classified in other categories. These other expenditures are also usually regarded as expenses in the period incurred, but not as research and development expenses. To illustrate how research related expenditures are recorded under current GAAP, assume the Robotics Corporation made the expenditures listed on page 447 during 1993 related to the development of robots for commercial and productive use.

**Evaluation of FASB Position**     Research and development costs vary widely among companies. Many expenditures do have future worth, while others are so highly uncertain as to future worth that recording them as assets is clearly improper. For the FASB to ignore these differences and issue a blanket rule that all research and development expenditures should be handled the same seems arbitrary and without theoretical support. The International Accounting Group studying this area disagreed with the FASB and identified general situations in which they felt deferral of development costs would be justified. Development costs of a project may be deferred to future periods if the five criteria at the bottom of page 447 are satisfied.

[21]*Ibid.*, par. 11.
[22]*Ibid.*, par. 9.

### Robotics Corporation

| Description of Expenditure | Accounting Treatment Per GAAP |
|---|---|
| 1. Purchase of land to construct research facility. | 1. Record as land. |
| 2. Self-construction of building to use in all robotic research. | 2. Record as building and depreciate as R&D expense. |
| 3. Purchase of special equipment to be used solely for the development of a robot for the space program. The equipment is not expected to have any use beyond this project. | 3. Expense immediately as R&D. |
| 4. Purchase of more generalized equipment that can be used for a wide variety of robotic projects. | 4. Record as equipment and depreciate as R&D expense. |
| 5. Research salaries dedicated to improvement of general robotic technology. | 5. Expense immediately as R&D. |
| 6. Purchase of patent for innovative construction of arm and hand segments. | 6. Record as patent and amortize as cost of production. |
| 7. Labor and material costs incurred in building a prototype model of a robot for space travel. | 7. Expense immediately as R&D. |
| 8. Costs to produce ten robots to specified design. | 8. Include in cost of goods manufactured. Report as inventory on balance sheet until sold. |
| 9. Salary of marketing executive assigned to find customers for the space robot. | 9. Expense immediately as marketing expense. |
| 10. Costs of testing the prototype robot under simulated space travel conditions. | 10. Expense immediately as R&D. |
| 11. Legal costs to protect patents purchased. | 11. Record as patent and amortize as cost of production. |
| 12. Legal costs of filing for patent on space robot. | 12. Record as patent and amortize as cost of production. |
| 13. Research costs for Japanese manufacturer who has contracted with Robotics Corporation for research technology. | 13. Record as receivable for contracted amount. |

1. The product or process is clearly defined and the costs attributable to the product or process can be separately identified.
2. The technical feasibility of the product or process has been demonstrated.
3. The management of the enterprise has indicated its intention to produce and market, or use, the product or process.
4. There is a clear indication of a future market for the product or process or, if it is to be used internally rather than sold, its usefulness to the enterprise can be demonstrated.
5. Adequate resources exist, or are reasonably expected to be available, to complete the project and market the product or process.[23]

The FASB recently has shown more flexibility in this area, as evidenced by its standard on accounting for computer software development, which is discussed on page 448.

[23]*International Accounting Standard No. 9,* "Accounting for Research and Development Activities" (London, England: International Accounting Standards Committee, 1978), par. 17.

## Computer Software Development Expenditures

The development of computer software requires little in the way of initial capital investment, and thus has led to the formation of hundreds of small software companies, each developing its own special software programs. Scores of computer magazines advertising these programs have emerged in the last decade as businesses and households have purchased their own micros. Software programs such as *Lotus 1-2-3, Word Perfect, Paradox,* and *Peachtree* have magnified the power of the computer for everyday use. Specialized accounting, tax, architectural, library, medical, educational, and recreational software packages have been developed by these hundreds of companies and marketed throughout the world.

A major accounting question related to the development of computer software has been how to account for the costs of development and production of the finished product. Many companies considered the development costs as research and development and expensed them in the period incurred as required by FASB Statement No. 2, discussed in the previous section. Other companies argued that these costs should be deferred and written off against future revenues. Since these costs were a very significant part of the total expenditures of a software company, the alternate methods used to account for them created considerable differences among the financial statements of the various companies. The FASB, with strong support from the SEC, addressed this issue and in 1985 issued FASB Statement No. 86, "Accounting for the Costs of Computer Software to Be Sold, Leased, or Otherwise Marketed."

The Board's conclusions concerning computer software costs are summarized in Exhibit 12—4.

**Exhibit 12—4    Development of Successful Software**

As demonstrated by Exhibit 12—4, all costs incurred up to the point where technological feasibility is established are to be expensed as research and development. They include costs incurred for planning, designing, and testing activities. Costs incurred after this point up until the product is ready for commercial production, such as further coding, testing, and production of masters, are to be recorded as an intangible asset. Additional costs to actually produce software from the masters and package the software for distribution are inventoriable costs and will be charged against revenue as the product is sold.

Considerable judgment is required to determine when technological feasibility has been established. The Board attempted to assist in the judgment with specific definitions and examples. At a minimum, technological feasibility shall be attained when an enterprise has produced either:[24]

---

[24]*Statement of Financial Accounting Standards No. 86,* "Accounting for the Costs of Computer Software to Be Sold, Leased, or Otherwise Marketed" (Stamford: Financial Accounting Standards Board, 1985), par. 4.

## Research and Development Costs

Baruch Lev, in a 1989 research paper questioning the usefulness of accounting earnings, suggests that the arbitrariness of some accounting rules, such as the expensing of research and development (R&D) outlays, adversely impacts the usefulness of periodic reported earnings. He cites the example of a firm that makes a particularly large R&D outlay. The required accounting treatment will result in a significant drop in reported earnings for the period, whereas the economic effect may be a significant increase in the market value of the firm's stock. Thus, the R&D expensing rule can weaken the relationship between economic profits, as reflected in stock prices, and accounting profits, as measured by periodic earnings.

Earlier research by Hirschey and Weygandt (1985) presents evidence, based on stock market values, that both R&D and advertising expenditures are viewed by stockholders as investments in intangible assets. A rough estimate of the "useful life" of the R&D intangible asset is five to ten years; the useful life for the advertising intangible asset is one to five years.

In addition to illustrating the dissatisfaction with some accounting rules, the case of R&D accounting also illustrates the complex nature of the economic consequences associated with accounting standards. Recall that the notion of economic consequences is that the choice of accounting standards can cause financial statement users to alter their decisions because of the existence of management compensation plans, loan covenant constraints, and regulatory impacts. Before FASB Statement No. 2 was issued, the FASB received many comments predicting that firms would significantly cut back research expenditures in order to avoid the immediate reduction in earnings. Subsequent to the issuance of FASB Statement No. 2, such an impact proved difficult to document. Elliott et al. (1984) summarized and extended conflicting prior research and concluded that R&D expenditures did decrease after the passage of FASB Statement No. 2, but that the decrease may have been a function of the generally unfavorable economic conditions in the U.S. in the mid-1970s.

There are still many who think that the FASB should reexamine the research and development issue. The standards established for the computer software industry (in FASB Statement No. 86) are proposed as a model for the accounting for all R&D costs. As technology and research become even more important, this is an area where changes in accounting standards are likely to take place in the future.

### Questions:

1. *In what ways does the R&D expensing rule reduce the usefulness of financial statements? How does the rule increase the usefulness of financial statements?*
2. *Would you expect that the rule requiring all firms to expense R&D outlays would cause R&D expenditures to decrease? Why or why not?*

Sources:

Baruch Lev, "On the Usefulness of Earnings and Earnings Research: Lessons and Directions from Two Decades of Empirical Research," *Journal of Accounting Research* 27 (Supplemental 1989), pp. 153-192.

Mark Hirschey and Jerry J. Weygandt, "Amortization Policy for Advertising and Research and Development Expenditures," *Journal of Accounting Research* 23 (Spring 1985), pp. 326-335.

John Elliott, Gordon Richardson, Thomas Dyckman, and Roland Dukes, "The Impact of SFAS No. 2 on Firm Expenditures on Research and Development: Replications and Extensions," *Journal of Accounting Research* 22 (Spring 1984), pp. 85-102.

1. A **detail program design** of the software establishing that the necessary skills, hardware, and software technology are available to the enterprise to produce the product (includes coding and testing necessary to resolve uncertainties for high-risk development issues), or
2. **A working model** of the software has been completed and tested.

If an enterprise purchases computer software externally for further development and resale, it should be accounted for in the same manner as described above for internally developed software. While Statement No. 86 does not directly address accounting for costs of computer software that is to be *used* internally by an enterprise as opposed to being *sold* externally, the Board indicated that the limited deferral of software costs would "likely be applied to costs incurred in developing software for internal use as well as for sale or lease to others."[25]

The treatment of computer software development costs by the FASB demonstrates how the more general research and development guidelines of FASB Statement No. 2 may be applied in future specific situations. By establishing two transitional points (technological feasibility and availability for general release to customers), the Board has recognized a separation between costs that are identified as being expenses and those that are assets to be deferred and amortized against future revenues. This treatment seems more in keeping with the approach used by the International Accounting Group for all research and development costs as described earlier.

## Post-Acquisition Expenditures

Over the useful lives of plant assets, regular as well as special expenditures are incurred. Certain expenditures are required to maintain and repair assets; others are incurred to increase their capacity or efficiency or to extend their useful lives. Each expenditure requires careful analysis to determine whether it should be charged to an expense account, or whether it should be assigned to revenue of more than one period, which requires a charge to an asset account or to an accumulated depreciation account. In many cases the answer may not be clear, and the procedure chosen may be a matter of judgment.

The terms maintenance, repairs, betterments, improvements, additions, and rearrangements are used in describing expenditures made in the course of asset use. These are described in the following sections. Exhibit 12—5 summarizes the accounting for these subsequent expenditures.

**Maintenance and Repairs**   Expenditures to maintain plant assets in good operating condition are referred to as maintenance. Among these are expenditures for painting, lubricating, and adjusting equipment. Maintenance expenditures are ordinary and recurring and do not improve the asset or add to its life; therefore, they are recorded as expenses when they are incurred.

Expenditures to restore assets to good operating condition upon their breakdown or to restore and replace broken parts are referred to as repairs. These are ordinary and recurring expenditures that benefit only current operations; thus, they also are debited to expense immediately.

**Renewals and Replacements**   Expenditures for overhauling plant assets are frequently referred to as renewals. Substitutions of parts or entire units are referred to as replacements. If these expenditures are necessary to achieve the original plans and do not change the original estimates of useful life or cash flows, they should be expensed. If, however,

---

[25]*Ibid.,* par. 26.

**Exhibit 12—5    Summary of Expenditures Subsequent to Acquisition**

| Type of Expenditure | Definition | Accounting Treatment |
| --- | --- | --- |
| Maintenance and repairs | Normal cost of keeping property in operating condition. | Expense as incurred. |
| Renewals and replacements: | | |
| 1. No extension of useful life or increase in future cash flows. | Unplanned replacement. Expenditure needed to fulfill original plans. | Expense as incurred. |
| 2. Extends useful life or increases future cash flows. | Improvement resulting from replacement with better component. | Record as an asset by one of two methods:<br>1. If cost of old component is known: Remove cost of old part and its accumulated depreciation, recognizing gain or loss. Defer cost of new component.<br>2. If cost of old component is not known: Deduct cost of new component from accumulated depreciation. |
| Additions and betterments | Expenditures that add to asset usefulness by either extending life or increasing future cash flows. No replacement of component involved. | Add to the cost of an asset. |

these expenditures extend the life of the asset or increase the cash flows generated by the asset, they should be capitalized by either adding them to the asset value or deducting them from accumulated depreciation.

Theoretically, if a part is removed and replaced with a superior part, the cost and accumulated depreciation related to the replaced part should be removed from the accounts, a loss recognized for the undepreciated book value, and the expenditure for the replacement added to the asset value. Often it is not possible to identify the cost related to a specific part of an asset. In these instances, by debiting Accumulated Depreciation, the undepreciated book value is increased without creating a buildup of the gross asset values. When this entry is made, no immediate loss related to the removal of the old asset is recognized.

To illustrate replacements, assume the Mendon Fireworks Company replaces the roof of its manufacturing plant for $40,000 and extends the estimated life of the building by five years. Assume that the original cost of the building was $1,600,000 and it is 3/4 depreciated. If the original roof cost $20,000, the following entry could be made to remove the undepreciated book value of the old roof and record the expenditure for the new one.

| | | |
| --- | --- | --- |
| Buildings (new roof) | 40,000 | |
| Accumulated Depreciation (old roof) | 15,000 | |
| Loss From Replacement of Roof | 5,000 | |
|     Buildings (old roof) | | 20,000 |
|     Cash | | 40,000 |

If Mendon could not identify the cost of the old roof, the following entry would be made:

Accumulated Depreciation ............................... 40,000
    Cash .................................................. 40,000

The book value of the building after the first entry is $435,000 ($1,600,000 − $1,200,000 + $40,000 − $5,000). Assuming the second entry is made, the book value would be $440,000 ($1,600,000 − $1,200,000 + $40,000). The $5,000 additional cost would be reflected in higher depreciation charges over the remaining life of the building.

**Additions and Betterments**   Enlargements and extensions of existing facilities are referred to as **additions**. Changes in assets designed to provide increased or improved services are referred to as **betterments**. If the addition or betterment does not involve a replacement of component parts of an existing asset, the expenditure should be deferred by adding it to the cost of the asset. If a replacement is involved, it is accounted for as discussed in the previous section.

## VALUATION OF ASSETS AT CURRENT VALUES

Throughout this chapter, the valuation of assets has been based on historical costs. As discussed in Chapter 2, FASB Concepts Statement No. 5 identified other measurement attributes that might be used if they were more relevant than historical cost and if their reliability could be improved.[26]

The discussion of current values in accounting ebbs and flows with the economic environment. In the late 1980s, the dramatic bail-out of the savings and loan industry by the federal government highlighted the excesses that can occur when current market values are not reported. Accounting for financial institutions is being scrutinized very carefully by the FASB, and a strong recommendation to report current values on such diverse assets as bond investments and real estate has been made by the SEC. It is likely that this reexamination of the use of current values will spill over to all financial reporting because of its greater relevance to decision makers.

## SUMMARY

The most challenging issue facing accountants in the area of asset acquisitions is deciding which costs should be deferred and matched against future revenue and which should be expensed immediately. Costs to acquire new property items with lives in excess of one fiscal period clearly should be charged against future periods. Accounting for repairs, additions, and similar costs incurred subsequent to the initial acquisition is less clear, and such expenditures must be individually evaluated in light of existing conditions. The historical acquisition cost of an asset is widely accepted as the basis for the gross investment, whether for tangible or intangible assets. Methods for matching these costs against future revenues will be discussed in the next chapter, as well as accounting for the retirement of assets.

[26]*Statement of Financial Accounting Concepts No. 5,* "Recognition and Measurement in Financial Statements of Business Enterprises" (Stamford: Financial Accounting Standards Board, 1984), par. 30.

## KEY TERMS

## QUESTIONS

1. In the balance sheet of many companies, the largest classification of assets in amount is noncurrent operating assets. Name the items, in addition to the amount paid to the former owner or contractor, that may be properly included as part of the acquisition cost of the following property items: (a) land, (b) buildings, and (c) equipment.

2. What acquisition costs are included in (a) copyrights, (b) franchises, and (c) trademarks?

3. How would a trademark worth $5,000,000 be reported on the balance sheet if (a) the trademark were purchased for $5,000,000 or (b) the trademark gradually became identified over the years as a company symbol?

4. How should development stage enterprises report their (a) organization costs and (b) net operating losses?

5. (a) Under what conditions may goodwill be reported as an asset? (b) The Roper Company engages in a widespread advertising campaign on behalf of new products, charging above-normal expenditures to goodwill. Do you approve of this practice? Why or why not?

6. How should negative goodwill be reported in the financial statements?

7. What procedure should be followed to allocate the cost of a lump-sum purchase of assets among specific accounts?

8. What special accounting problems are introduced when a company purchases equipment on a deferred payment contract rather than with cash?

9. (a) Why is the "list price" of an asset often not representative of its fair market value? (b) Under these conditions, how should a fair market value be determined?

10. Gaylen Corp. decides to construct a building for itself and plans to use whatever plant facilities it has to further such construction. (a) What costs will enter into the cost of construction? (b) What two positions can the company take with respect to general overhead allocation during the period of construction? Evaluate each position and indicate your preference.

11. What characteristics must a construction project have before interest can be capitalized as part of the project cost?

12. What are the general guidelines for determining the amount of interest that can be capitalized?

13. What are the principal arguments against capitalizing interest as presently mandated by the FASB?

14. The Parkhurst Corporation acquires land and buildings valued at $250,000 as a gift from Industrial City. The president of the company maintains that since there was no cost for the acquisition, neither cost of the facilities nor depreciation needs to be recognized for financial statement purposes. Evaluate the president's position assuming (a) the donation is unconditional, (b) the donation is contingent upon the employment by the company of a certain number of employees for a ten-year period.

15. Why do some companies expense asset expenditures that are under an established monetary amount?

16. Indicate the effects of the following errors on the balance sheet and the income statement in the current year and succeeding years:
    (a) The cost of a depreciable asset is incorrectly recorded as an expense.
    (b) An expense expenditure is incorrectly recorded as an addition to the cost of a depreciable asset.

17. (a) What type of activities are considered to be research and development activities? (b) Under what conditions, if any, are research and development costs deferred?

18. What conceptual modification to the FASB standard on research and development costs is apparent in the later standard on accounting for computer software development costs?

19. Which of the following items would be recorded as expenses and which would be recorded as assets?

    (a) Cost of installing machinery
    (b) Cost of unsuccessful litigation to protect patent
    (c) Extensive repairs as a result of a fire
    (d) Cost of grading land
    (e) Insurance on machinery in transit
    (f) Bond discount amortization during construction period
    (g) Cost of major unexpected overhaul on machinery
    (h) New safety guards on machinery
    (i) Commission on purchase of real estate
    (j) Special tax assessment for street improvements
    (k) Cost of repainting offices

20. Why are some asset expenditures made subsequent to acquisition recorded as an increase in an asset account and others recorded as a decrease in Accumulated Depreciation?

## DISCUSSION CASES

### Case 12—1 (Where should we charge it?)

Fugate Energy Corp. has recently purchased the assets of a small local company, Gleave Inc., for $556,950 cash. The chief accountant of Fugate has been given the assignment of preparing the journal entry to record the purchase. An investigation disclosed the following information about the assets of Gleave Inc.:

(a) Gleave owned land and a small manufacturing building. The book value of the property on Gleave's records was $115,000. An appraisal for fire insurance purposes had been made during the year. The building was appraised by the insurance company at $175,000. Property tax assessment notices showed that the building's worth was five times the worth of the land.

(b) Gleave's equipment had a book value of $75,000. It is estimated by Gleave that it would take six times the amount of book value to replace the old equipment with new. The old equipment is, on the average, 50% depreciated.

(c) Gleave had a franchise to produce and sell solar energy units from another company in a set geographic area. The franchise was transferred to Fugate as part of the purchase. Gleave carried the asset on its books at $40,000, the unamortized balance of the original cost of $90,000. The franchise is for an unlimited time. Similar franchises are now being sold by the company for $120,000 per geographic area.

(d) Gleave had two excellent research scientists who were responsible for much of the company's innovation in product development. They are each paid $50,000 per year by Gleave. They have agreed to work for Fugate Energy at the same salary.

(e) Gleave held two patents on its products. Both had been fully amortized and were not carried as assets on Gleave's books. Gleave feels they could have been sold separately for $75,000 each.

Evaluate each of the above items and prepare the journal entry that should be made to record the purchase on Fugate's books.

### Case 12—2 (How much does it cost?)

The Bakeman Co. decides to construct a piece of specialized machinery using personnel from the maintenance department. This is the first time the maintenance personnel have been used for this purpose, and the cost accountant for the factory is concerned as to the accounting for costs of the machine. Some of the issues raised by the maintenance department management are highlighted below and on the next page.

(a) The supervisor of the maintenance department has instructed the workers to schedule work so all the overtime hours are charged to the machinery. Overtime is paid at 150% of the regular rate, or at a 50% premium.

(b) Material used in the production of the machine is charged out from the materials storeroom at 125% of cost, the same markup used when material is furnished to subsidiary companies.

(c) The maintenance department overhead rate is applied on maintenance hours. No extra overhead is anticipated as a result of constructing the machine.

(d) The maintenance department personnel are not qualified to test the machine on the production line. This will be done by production employees.

(e) Although the machine will take about one year to build, no extra borrowing of funds will be necessary to finance its construction. The company does, however, have outstanding bonds from earlier financing.

(f) It is expected that the self-construction of the machinery will save the company at least $20,000.

What advice can you give the cost accountant to help in the determination of a proper cost for the machine?

### Case 12—3  (But computer software is my inventory!)

Strategy, Inc., was organized by Elizabeth Durrant and Ramona Morales, two students working their way through college. Both Elizabeth and Ramona had played with computers while in high school and had become very proficient users. Elizabeth had a special ability for designing computer software games that challenged the reasoning power of players. Ramona could see great potential in marketing Elizabeth's products to other computer buffs, and so the two began Strategy. Sales have exceeded expectations, and they have added ten employees to their company to design additional products, debug new programs, and produce and distribute the final software products.

Because of its growing size, increased capital is needed for the company. The partners decide to apply for a $100,000 loan to support the growing cost of research. As part of the documentation to obtain the loan, the bank asks for audited financial statements for the past year. After some negotiation, Mark Dawson, CPA, is hired. Strategy had produced a preliminary income statement that reported net income of $35,000. After reviewing the statements, Dawson indicates that the company actually had a $10,000 loss for the year. The major difference relates to $45,000 of wage and material costs that Strategy had capitalized as an intangible asset but that Dawson determined should be expensed.

"It's all research and development," Dawson insisted.

"But we'll easily recoup it in sales next year," countered Ramona. "I thought you accountants believed in the matching principle. Why do you permit us to capitalize the equipment we're using, but not our software development costs? We'll never look profitable under your requirements."

What major issues are involved in this case? Which position best reflects the FASB Statement relating to software development costs?

### Case 12—4  (Why can't I include the value of that gold on my balance sheet?)

The Ling Company owns several mining claims in Nevada and California. The claims are carried on the books at the cost paid to acquire them ten years ago. At that time, it was estimated that the claims represented ore reserves valued at $250,000, and the price paid for the properties reflected this value. Subsequent mining and exploration activities have indicated values up to four times the original estimate. Additional capital is needed to pursue the claims, and Ling has decided to issue new shares of common stock. The company wants to report the true value of the claims in the financial statements in order to make the stock more attractive to potential investors. The accountant, Jennifer Harrison, realizes that the cost basis of accounting does not permit the recording of discovery values. On the other hand, she believes that to ignore the greatly increased value of the claims would be misleading to users. Isn't there some way the asset values can be increased to better reflect future cash flows arising from the claims?

You are hired as an accounting consultant to assist Ling in its fund raising. What recommendations can you make?

### Case 12—5   (Is it an asset or not?)

The Hunter Company has developed a computerized machine to assist in the production of appliances. It is anticipated that the machine will do well in the marketplace; however, the company lacks the necessary capital to produce the machine. Rosalyn Finch, the secretary-treasurer of the Hunter Company, has offered to transfer land to the company to be used as collateral for a bank loan. Consideration for the transfer is an employment contract for five years and a percentage of any profits earned from sales of the new machine. The title to the land is to be transferred unconditionally. In the event Hunter defaults on the employment contract, a lump-sum cash settlement for lost wages will be paid to Finch.

What are the arguments for and against recording the land as an asset on Hunter's books? Is it a contingent asset? What effect does the provision for a cash settlement in the event of default have on your decision?

### Case 12—6   (Why is my ROA lower than yours?)

Terri Morton has been recently hired as a financial analyst. Terri's first assignment is to analyze why the reported ROA (return on assets) for Arnold Company is so much different than that of Baker Company. Arnold Company develops and markets innovative consumer products. Baker Company is a fabricator of heavy steel products. Both companies have net incomes of $1 million, but Arnold has reported total assets of only $3 million, compared to $6 million for Baker. Terri suspects her new boss is using this assignment to test her understanding of financial statements. Terri's boss did give her one cryptic clue: unrecorded assets. Prepare Terri's analysis.

### Case 12—7   (The asbestos must go, but where do we charge it?)

The FASB's Emerging Issues Task Force (EITF) recently considered the question of how the costs incurred in removing asbestos from buildings should be treated (Issue 89-13). This is a widespread issue since studies indicate that some 20% of buildings in the U.S. contain asbestos. The EITF considered the following specific questions:

1. If a company purchases a building with a known asbestos problem, should the removal costs be expensed or capitalized?
2. If a company discovers an asbestos problem in a building it already owns, should the removal costs be expensed or capitalized?

If you were on the Task Force, how would you rule on these two questions?

### Case 12—8   (Why are the costs of buildings different?)

In FASB Statement No. 34, the FASB called for the capitalization of interest costs associated with projects involving the construction or development of assets extending over a significant time period. Interest capitalized is restricted to the amount of interest actually incurred.

Consider the case of the following two companies that each constructed a building with a total construction cost of $20 million (the costs were incurred evenly over the course of a year) but that chose to finance the construction differently. (See details on the following page.)

As the auditor for both companies, you are asked by your supervisor to prepare a report that calculates the total cost for each building that would be included in each company's financial statements. Because both companies had the option of purchasing the buildings from a contractor rather than constructing them, your report should include your estimate of the price the contractor would have charged and how you explain the discrepancy in the way cost was determined for the two buildings. Conclude your report by proposing a change in the accounting standards that could eliminate this discrepancy.

| | Company A | Company B |
|---|---|---|
| Weighted average accumulated expenditures on building project during the year .................. | $10,000,000 | $10,000,000 |
| Total construction cost of building (excluding interest) ........................................... | 20,000,000 | 20,000,000 |
| Company financing (outstanding at year-end): | | |
| Construction loan (14%)......................... | 20,000,000 | -0- |
| Common stock issue........................... | -0- | 20,000,000 |
| Total construction loan interest during the year (based on average outstanding loan balance) ....... | 1,400,000 | -0- |

# EXERCISES

## Exercise 12—1   (Cost of specific plant items)

The following expenditures were incurred by the Eagle Food Co. in 1993:

| | |
|---|---|
| Purchase of land .............................................. | $300,000 |
| Land survey ...................................................... | 1,500 |
| Fees for search of title for land ....................................... | 350 |
| Building permit ..................................................... | 500 |
| Temporary quarters for construction crews ......................... | 10,750 |
| Payment to tenants of old building for vacating premises ............. | 2,000 |
| Razing of old building ............................................... | 20,000 |
| Excavation of basement.......................................... | 10,000 |
| Special assessment tax for street project .......................... | 2,000 |
| Dividends......................................................... | 5,000 |
| Damages awarded for injuries sustained in construction (no insurance was carried; the cost of insurance would have been $500) ............ | 8,400 |
| Costs of construction .............................................. | 750,000 |
| Cost of paving parking lot adjoining building ....................... | 40,000 |
| Cost of shrubs, trees, and other landscaping ....................... | 18,000 |

What is the cost of the land, land improvements, and building?

## Exercise 12—2   (Determining cost of patent)

Chen King Enterprises Inc. developed a new machine that reduces the time required to insert the fortunes into their fortune cookies. Because the process is considered very valuable to the fortune cookie industry, Chen King had the machine patented. The following expenses were incurred in developing and patenting the machine:

| | |
|---|---|
| Research and development laboratory expenses ...................... | $15,000 |
| Metal used in construction of the machine ........................... | 5,000 |
| Blueprints used to design the machine ............................. | 1,500 |
| Legal expenses to obtain patent ..................................... | 10,000 |
| Wages paid for employees' work on the research, development, and building of the machine (60% of the time was spent in actually building the machine)........................................................ | 30,000 |
| Expense of drawings required by the patent office to be submitted with the patent application......................................................... | 150 |
| Fees paid to government patent office to process application ........... | 500 |

One year later, Chen King Enterprises Inc. paid $12,000 in legal fees to successfully defend the patent against an infringement suit by Dragon Cookie Co.

Give the entries on Chen King's books indicated by the above events. Ignore any amortization of the patent or depreciation of the machine.

## Exercise 12—3  (Correcting organization costs account)

The Salt Air Manufacturing Co. was incorporated on January 1, 1993. In reviewing the accounts in 1994, you find the organization costs account appears as follows:

**ACCOUNT: Organization Costs**

| Item | Debit | Credit | Balance Debit | Balance Credit |
|------|-------|--------|---------------|----------------|
| Incorporation fees | 3,750 | | 3,750 | |
| Legal fees relative to organization | 21,150 | | 24,900 | |
| Stock certificate cost | 6,000 | | 30,900 | |
| Cost of rehabilitating building acquired at end of 1993 | 165,600 | | 196,500 | |
| Advertising expenditures to promote company products in 1993 | 18,000 | | 214,500 | |
| Net loss for 1993 | 25,000 | | 239,500 | |

Give the entry or entries required to correct the account.

## Exercise 12—4  (Purchase of a company)

Hull Company purchased Heaston Company for $750,000 cash. A schedule of the market values of Heaston's assets and liabilities as of the purchase date is given below.

**Heaston Company**
**Schedule of Asset and Liability Market Values**

|  |  |  |
|--|--|--|
| **Assets** | | |
| Cash and temporary investments | $ 5,000 | |
| Receivables | 78,000 | |
| Inventory | 136,000 | |
| Land, buildings, and equipment | 436,000 | $655,000 |
| **Liabilities** | | |
| Current liabilities | $ 80,000 | |
| Long-term debt | 120,000 | 200,000 |
| Net asset market value | | $455,000 |

1. Make the journal entry necessary for Hull Company to record the purchase.
2. Assume that the purchase price is $400,000 cash. Make the journal entry necessary to record the purchase.

## Exercise 12—5  (Lump-sum acquisition)

The Cowan Shipping Co. acquired land, buildings, and equipment at a lump-sum price of $430,000. An appraisal of the assets at the time of acquisition disclosed the following values:

| | |
|--|--|
| Land | $100,000 |
| Buildings | 150,000 |
| Equipment | 250,000 |

What cost should be assigned to each asset?

## Exercise 12—6  (Lump-sum acquisition)

The Boswell Corporation purchased land, a building, a patent, and a franchise for the lump sum of $975,000. A real estate appraiser estimated the building to have a resale value of $400,000 (⅔ of the total worth of land and building). The franchise had no established resale value. The patent was valued by management at $250,000. Give the journal entry to record the acquisition of the assets.

### Exercise 12—7  (Equipment purchase on deferred payment contract)

Andrews Co. purchases equipment costing $110,000 with a down payment of $20,000 and sufficient semiannual installments of $7,000 (which includes interest on the unpaid principal at 10% per year) to pay the balance.

1. Give the entries to record the purchase and the first two semiannual payments.
2. Assume that there was no known cash price and twenty semiannual installments were to be made in addition to the $20,000 down payment. Give the entries to record the purchase and the first two semiannual payments.

### Exercise 12—8  (Exchange of nonmonetary assets)

Baldwin Analysis Inc. purchased a new computer from a dealer. The following data relates to the purchase:

(a)  List price of new computer with trade-in—$45,000
(b)  Cash price of new computer with no trade-in—$41,000
(c)  Baldwin Analysis Inc. received a trade-in allowance (based on list price) of $10,000 on a machine costing $25,000 new and having a present book value of $8,000. The balance of $35,000 was paid in cash.
(d)  The Express Delivery Service charged Baldwin $1,200 to deliver the computer.

Determine the cost to be recorded for the new computer.

### Exercise 12—9  (Lump-sum acquisition with stock)

On January 31, 1993, Cesarino Corp. exchanged 10,000 shares of its $25 par common stock for the following assets:

(a)  A trademark valued at $120,000.
(b)  A building, including land, valued at $650,000 (20% of the value is for the land).
(c)  A franchise right. No estimate of value at time of exchange.

Cesarino Corp. stock is selling at $91 per share on the date of the exchange. Give the entries to record the exchange on Cesarino's books.

### Exercise 12—10   (Purchase of building with bonds and stock)

The Fellingham Co. enters into a contract with the Dice Construction Co. for construction of an office building at a cost of $710,000. Upon completion of construction, the Dice Construction Co. agrees to accept in full payment of the contract price Fellingham Co. 10% bonds with a face value of $300,000 and common stock with a par value of $300,000 and no established fair market value. Fellingham Co. bonds are selling on the market at this time at 104. How would you recommend the building acquisition be recorded?

### Exercise 12—11   (Acquisition of land and building for stock and cash)

Valdilla's Music Store acquired land and an old building in exchange for 50,000 shares of its common stock, par $10, and cash of $80,000. The auditor ascertains that the company's stock was selling on the market at $15 when the purchase was made. The following additional costs were incurred to complete the transaction:

| | |
|---|---|
| Legal cost to complete transaction ................................... | $10,000 |
| Property tax for previous year ....................................... | 30,000 |

| Cost of building demolition | 13,000 |
|---|---|
| Salvage value of demolished building | (6,000) |

What entry should be made to record the acquisition of the property?

### Exercise 12—12    (Cost of self-constructed asset including interest capitalization)

The Brodhead Manufacturing Company has constructed its own special equipment to produce a newly developed product. A bid to construct the equipment by an outside company was received for $620,000. The actual costs incurred by Brodhead to construct the equipment were as follows:

| Direct material | $220,000 |
|---|---|
| Direct labor | 150,000 |

It is estimated that incremental overhead costs for construction amount to 125% of direct labor costs. In addition, fixed costs (exclusive of interest) of $700,000 were incurred during the construction period and allocated to production on the basis of total prime costs (direct labor plus direct material). The prime costs incurred to build the new equipment amounted to 20% of the total prime costs incurred for the period. The company follows the policy of capitalizing all possible costs on self-construction projects.

In order to assist in financing the construction of the equipment, a $300,000, 10% loan was acquired at the beginning of the six-month construction period. The company carries no other debt except for trade accounts payable. Assume expenditures were incurred evenly over the six-month period, and interest charges were to be capitalized in accordance with FASB Statement No. 34. Compute the cost to be assigned to the new equipment.

### Exercise 12—13    (Capitalization of interest)

Lodi Department Stores, Inc., constructs its own stores. In the past, no cost has been added to the asset value for interest on funds borrowed for construction. Management has decided to change its policy and desires to include interest as part of the cost of a new store just being completed. (a) Based on the following information, how much interest would be added to the cost of the store in 1993? (b) In 1994?

| Total construction expenditures: | |
|---|---|
| January 2, 1993 | $200,000 |
| May 1, 1993 | 600,000 |
| November 1, 1993 | 500,000 |
| March 1, 1994 | 700,000 |
| September 15, 1994 | 400,000 |
| December 31, 1994 | 500,000 |
| | $2,900,000 |

| Outstanding company debt: | |
|---|---|
| Mortgage related directly to new store; interest rate 12%; term, five years from beginning of construction | $1,000,000 |
| General bond liability: | |
| Bonds issued just prior to construction of store; interest rate 10% for ten years | $  500,000 |
| Bonds issued previously—8%, mature in five years | $1,000,000 |
| Estimated cost of equity capital | 14% |

### Exercise 12—14    (Interest capitalization decision)

For each of the situations described below, indicate when interest should be capitalized (C) and when it should not be capitalized (NC).

1. King Company is constructing a piece of equipment for its own use. Total construction costs are expected to be $5 million, and the construction period will be 3 months.

2. Ortegren Company is constructing a piece of equipment for sale. Total construction costs are expected to exceed $8 million and the construction period will be about 10 months. This is a special order—Ortegren has never produced a piece of equipment like this before.
3. Lowe Company is constructing a piece of equipment for sale. Total construction costs are expected to exceed $8 million and the construction period will be about 10 months. This particular piece of equipment is Lowe's best seller.
4. Nair Company is constructing a piece of equipment for its own use. Total construction costs are expected to be $6,000, and the construction period will be 10 months.
5. Rittenberg Company is constructing a piece of equipment for its own use. Total construction costs are expected to be $11 million and the construction period will be about 2 years. The forecasted total construction cost is only a very rough estimate because Rittenberg has no system in place to accumulate separately the costs associated with this project.
6. LeClair Company is in the process of renovating its corporate office building. The project will cost $13 million and will take about 15 months. The building will remain in use throughout the project.
7. Ricketts Company owns a piece of undeveloped land. The land originally cost $27 million. Ricketts plans to hold onto the land for 3 to 4 years and then develop it into a vacation resort.

## Exercise 12—15 (Research and development costs)

In 1993 the Jericho Corporation incurred research and development costs as follows:

| | |
|---|---:|
| Materials and equipment | $130,000 |
| Personnel | 100,000 |
| Indirect costs | 50,000 |
| | $280,000 |

These costs relate to a product that will be marketed in 1994. It is estimated that these costs will be recouped by December 31, 1997.

1. What is the amount of research and development costs which should be charged to income in 1993?
2. Assume that of the above costs, equipment of $90,000 can be used on other research projects. Estimated useful life of the equipment is five years, and it was acquired at the beginning of 1993. What is the amount of research and development costs that should be charged to income in 1993 under these conditions? Assume depreciation on all equipment is computed on a straight-line basis.

## Exercise 12—16 (What are the R&D costs?)

Pringle Company has a substantial research department. Below are listed, in chronological order, some of the major activities associated with one of Pringle's research projects.

### Project Started

(a) Purchased special equipment to be used solely for this project.
(b) Purchased general equipment that will be usable in Pringle's normal operations.
(c) Allocated overhead to the project.

### Technological Feasibility Established

(d) Purchased more special equipment to be used solely for this project.
(e) Performed tests on an early model of the product.
(f) Allocated overhead to the project.

**Product Becomes Ready for Production**

(g)  Incurred direct production costs.
(h)  Allocated overhead to the products.

1. For each activity (a) through (h), indicate whether the cost should be capitalized (C), expensed (E), or included in cost of inventory (I).
2. Follow the instructions in (1) assuming that Pringle is a computer software development company.

## Exercise 12—17  (Classifying expenditures as assets or expenses)

One of the most difficult problems facing an accountant is the determination of which expenditures should be deferred as assets and which should be immediately charged off as expenses. What position would you take in each of the following instances?

(a)  Painting of partitions in a large room recently divided into four sections.
(b)  Labor cost of tearing down a wall to permit extension of assembly line.
(c)  Replacement of motor on a machine. Life used to depreciate the machine is 8 years. The machine is 4 years old. Replacement of the motor was anticipated when the machine was purchased.
(d)  Cost of grading land prior to construction.
(e)  Assessment for street paving.
(f)  Cost of tearing down a previously occupied old building in preparation for new construction; old building is fully depreciated.

---

# PROBLEMS

## Problem 12—1  (Correcting noncurrent operating asset valuation)

On December 31, 1993, the Fridley Co. shows the following account for machinery it had assembled for its own use during 1993:

ACCOUNT: Machinery (Job Order #962)

| Item | Debit | Credit | Balance Debit | Balance Credit |
|------|-------|--------|--------|--------|
| Cost of dismantling old machine ............... | 12,480 | | 12,480 | |
| Cash proceeds from sale of old machine ......... | | 10,000 | 2,480 | |
| Raw materials used in construction of new machine ..................................... | 63,000 | | 65,480 | |
| Labor in construction of new machine .......... | 49,000 | | 114,480 | |
| Cost of installation ........................... | 11,200 | | 125,680 | |
| Materials spoiled in machine trial runs........... | 2,400 | | 128,080 | |
| Profit on construction ........................ | 24,000 | | 152,080 | |
| Purchase of machine tools..................... | 16,000 | | 168,080 | |

An analysis of the detail in the account disclosed the following:

(a)  The old machine, which was removed in the installation of the new one, had been fully depreciated.
(b)  Cash discounts received on the payments for materials used in construction totaled $3,000 and these were reported in the purchase discounts account.

(c) The factory overhead account shows a balance of $292,000 for the year ended December 31, 1993; this balance exceeds normal overhead on regular plan activities by approximately $21,200 and is attributable to machine construction.

(d) A profit was recognized on construction for the difference between costs incurred and the price at which the machine could have been purchased.

**Instructions:**

1. Determine the machinery and machine tools balances as of December 31, 1993.
2. Give individual journal entries necessary to correct the accounts as of December 31, 1993, assuming that the nominal accounts are still open.

### Problem 12—2   (Cost classification for a golf course)

The accountant for Stansbury Development Company is uncertain how to record the following costs associated with the construction of a golf course:

(a) Building man-made lakes.
(b) Moving earth around to enhance the "hilliness" of the course.
(c) Planting fairway grass.
(d) Planting trees and shrubs.
(e) Installing an automatic sprinkler system.
(f) Installing golf cart paths.
(g) 50 wooden sandtrap rakes (at $1 each).
(h) Paying attorneys' fees to prepare and file the land title.
(i) Demolishing an old house situated on the site planned for the clubhouse.

**Instructions:**  Indicate which costs should be expensed (E), which should be capitalized and considered to be nondepreciable (CN), and which should be capitalized and depreciated (CD). Include explanations for each classification.

### Problem 12—3   (Acquisition of land and buildings)

The Excelsior Co. planned to open a new store. The company narrowed the possible sites to two lots and decided to take purchase options on both lots while studying traffic densities in both areas. Excelsior paid $6,000 for the option on Lot A and $14,400 for the option on Lot B. After studying traffic densities, Excelsior decided to purchase Lot B. The company opened a single real estate account that shows the following:

| | | |
|---|---|---:|
| Debits: | Option on Lot A | $ 6,000 |
| | Option on Lot B | 14,400 |
| | Payment of balance on Lot B | 155,000 |
| | Title insurance | 2,700 |
| | Assessment for street improvements | 5,100 |
| | Recording fee for deed | 600 |
| | Cost of razing old building on Lot B | 9,000 |
| | Payment for construction of new building | 350,000 |
| Credit: | Sale of salvaged materials from old building | 5,000 |

The salvage value of material obtained from the old building and used in constructing the new building was $10,000. The depreciated value of the old building, as shown by the books of the company from which the purchase was made, was $54,000. The old building was razed immediately after the purchase.

**Instructions:**

1. Determine the cost of the land, listing the items included in the total.
2. Determine the cost of the new building, listing the items included in the total.

## Problem 12—4  (Transactions involving property)

The following transactions were completed by the Space Age Toy Co. during 1993:

Mar.  1    Purchased real property for $628,250, which included a charge of $18,250 representing property tax for March 1-June 30 that had been prepaid by the vendor; 20% of the purchase price is deemed applicable to land, and the balance to buildings. A mortgage of $375,000 was assumed by the Space Age Toy Co. on the purchase. Cash was paid for the balance.

2-30    Previous owners had failed to take care of normal maintenance and repair requirements on the building, necessitating current reconditioning at a cost of $29,600.

May  15    Garages in the rear of the building were demolished, $4,500 being recovered on the lumber salvage. The company proceeded to construct a warehouse. The cost of such construction was $67,600 which was almost exactly the same as bids made on the construction by independent contractors. Upon completion of construction, city inspectors ordered extensive modifications in the buildings as a result of failure on the part of the company to comply with the building safety code. Such modifications, which could have been avoided, cost $9,600.

June  1    The company exchanged its own stock with a fair market value of $40,000 (par $30,000) for a patent and a new toy-making machine. The machine has a market value of $25,000.

July  1    The new machinery for the new building arrived. In addition to the machinery, a new franchise was acquired from the manufacturer of the machinery to produce toy robots. Payment was made by issuing bonds with a face value of $50,000 and by paying cash of $18,000. The value of the franchise is set at $20,000 while the fair market value of the machine is $45,000.

Nov. 20    The company contracted for parking lots and landscaping at a cost of $45,000 and $9,600 respectively. The work was completed and paid for on November 20.

Dec.  31    The business was closed to permit taking the year-end inventory. During this time, required redecorating and repairs were completed at a cost of $7,500.

**Instructions:**  Give the journal entries to record each of the preceding transactions. (Disregard depreciation.)

## Problem 12—5  (Acquisition of land and construction of plant)

The Senger Corporation was organized in June 1993. In auditing the books of the company, you find the land, buildings, and equipment account on the following page.

An analysis of this account and of other accounts disclosed the following additional information:

(a)  The building acquired on June 16, 1993, was valued at $35,000.
(b)  The corporation paid $20,000 for the demolition of the old building, then sold the scrap for $5,000 and credited the proceeds to Miscellaneous Revenue.
(c)  The corporation executives did not participate in the construction of the new building.
(d)  The county real estate tax was for the six-month period ended December 31, 1993, and was assessed by the county on the land.

**Instructions:**  Prepare journal entries to correct the books of the Senger Corporation. Each entry should include an explanation.

**ACCOUNT:** Land, Buildings, and Equipment

| Date | | Item | Debit | Credit | Balance Debit | Balance Credit |
|---|---|---|---|---|---|---|
| 1993 | | | | | | |
| June | 8 | Organization fees paid to the state ................. | 20,000 | | 20,000 | |
| | 16 | Land site and old building .. | 315,000 | | 335,000 | |
| | 30 | Corporate organization costs .................... | 30,000 | | 365,000 | |
| July | 2 | Title clearance fees ........ | 18,400 | | 383,400 | |
| Aug. | 28 | Cost of razing old building | 20,000 | | 403,400 | |
| Sept. | 1 | Salaries of Senger Corporation executives ........... | 36,000 | | 439,400 | |
| | 1 | Cost to acquire patent for special equipment ......... | 60,000 | | 499,400 | |
| Dec. | 12 | Stock bonus to corporate promoters, 2,000 shares of common stock, $40 market value ................... | 80,000 | | 579,400 | |
| | 15 | County real estate tax...... | 14,400 | | 593,800 | |
| | 15 | Cost of new building completed and occupied on this date .................... | 1,500,000 | | 2,093,800 | |

## Problem 12—6   (Acquisition of intangible assets)

In your audit of the books of Dyer Corporation for the year ending September 30, 1993, you found the following items in connection with the company's patents account:

(a)   The company had spent $120,000 during its fiscal year ended September 30, 1992, for research and development costs and debited this amount to its patents account. Your review of the company's cost records indicated the company had spent a total of $141,500 for the research and development of its patents, of which only $21,500 spent in its fiscal year ended September 30, 1991, had been debited to Research and Development Expense.

(b)   The patents were issued on April 1, 1992. Legal expenses in connection with the issuance of the patents of $14,280 were debited to Legal and Professional Fees.

(c)   The company paid a retainer of $15,000 on October 5, 1992, for legal services in connection with an infringement suit brought against it. This amount was debited to Deferred Costs.

(d)   A letter dated October 15, 1993, from the company's attorneys in reply to your inquiry as to liabilities of the company existing at September 30, 1993, indicated that a settlement of the infringement suit had been arranged. The other party had agreed to drop the suit and to release the company from all future liabilities for $20,000. Additional fees due to the attorneys amounted to $1,260.

**Instructions:**   From the information given, prepare correcting journal entries as of September 30, 1993.

## Problem 12—7   (Acquisition of intangible assets)

Transactions during 1993 of the newly organized Stokes Corporation included the following:

Jan.   2   Paid legal fees of $15,000 and stock certificate costs of $5,100 to complete organization of the corporation.

15   Hired a clown to stand in front of the corporate office for two weeks and hand out pamphlets and candy to create goodwill for the new enterprise. Clown cost, $1,000; pamphlets and candy, $500.

Apr.   1   Patented a newly developed process with the following costs:

| | |
|---|---|
| Legal fees to obtain patent .................................. | $28,600 |
| Patent application and licensing fees ....................... | 6,350 |
| Total ............................................... | $34,950 |

It is estimated that in six years other companies will have developed improved processes making the Stokes Corporation process obsolete.

May 1 Acquired both a license to use a special type of container and a distinctive trademark to be printed on the container in exchange for 600 shares of Stokes Corporation no-par common stock selling for $80 per share. The license is worth twice as much as the trademark, both of which may be used for 6 years.

July 1 Constructed a shed for $93,000 to house prototypes of experimental models to be developed in future research projects.

Dec. 31 Salaries for an engineer and a chemist involved in product development totaled $100,000 in 1993.

## Instructions:

1. Give journal entries to record the foregoing transactions. Give explanations in support of your entries. (Ignore amortization of intangible assets.)
2. Present in good form the "Intangible assets" section of the Stokes Corporation balance sheet at December 31, 1993.

### Problem 12—8  (Lump-sum acquisition of noncurrent operating assets)

The Wenatcher Wholesale Company incurred the following expenses in 1993 for a warehouse acquired on July 1, 1993, the beginning of its fiscal year:

| | |
|---|---|
| Cost of land................................................. | $ 90,000 |
| Cost of building ............................................ | 510,000 |
| Remodeling and repairs prior to occupancy .......................... | 67,500 |
| Escrow fee................................................. | 10,000 |
| Landscaping ................................................ | 25,000 |
| Property tax for period prior to acquisition......................... | 15,000 |
| Real estate commission ........................................ | 30,000 |

The company signed a non-interest-bearing note for $500,000 on July 1, 1993. The implicit interest rate is 10%. Payments of $25,000 are to be made semiannually beginning December 31, 1993, for 10 years.

**Instructions:**   Give the required journal entries to record (1) the acquisition of the land and building (assume that cash is paid to equalize the cost of the assets and the present value of the note), and (2) the first two semiannual payments, including amortization of note discount.

### Problem 12—9  (Income statement for computer software company)

The Betterword Company is engaged in developing computer software for the small business and home computer market. Most of the computer programmers are involved in developmental work designed to produce software that will perform fairly specific tasks in a user-friendly manner. Extensive testing of the working model is performed before it is released to production for preparation of masters and further testing. As a result of careful preparation, Betterword has produced several products that have been very successful in the marketplace. The following costs were incurred during 1993:

| | |
|---|---|
| Salaries and wages of programmers doing research .................. | $235,000 |
| Expenses related to projects prior to establishment of technological feasibility .................................................. | 78,400 |
| Expenses related to projects after technological feasibility has been established but before software is available for production .............. | 49,500 |

Amortization of capitalized software development costs from current
and prior years . . . . . . . . . . . . . . . . . . . . . . . . . . . . . . . . . . . . . . . . . . . . . . . . . . . .    $ 26,750
Costs to produce and prepare software for sale . . . . . . . . . . . . . . . . . . . . .    56,300

Additional data for 1993 includes:

Sales of products for the year . . . . . . . . . . . . . . . . . . . . . . . . . . . . . . . . . . . . .    $515,000
Beginning inventory . . . . . . . . . . . . . . . . . . . . . . . . . . . . . . . . . . . . . . . . . . . . . .    142,000
Portion of goods available for sale sold during year . . . . . . . . . . . . . . . . .    60%

**Instructions:** Prepare an income statement for Betterword for the year 1993. Income tax rate is 30%.

### Problem 12—10   (Valuation of property)

At December 31, 1992, certain accounts included in the noncurrent operating assets section of the Rodrigo Company's balance sheet had the following balances:

Land . . . . . . . . . . . . . . . . . . . . . . . . . . . . . . . . . . . . . . . . . . . . . . . . . . . . . . . . . . .    $150,000
Buildings . . . . . . . . . . . . . . . . . . . . . . . . . . . . . . . . . . . . . . . . . . . . . . . . . . . . . . .    805,000
Leasehold improvements . . . . . . . . . . . . . . . . . . . . . . . . . . . . . . . . . . . . . . . .    500,000
Machinery and equipment . . . . . . . . . . . . . . . . . . . . . . . . . . . . . . . . . . . . . . .    600,000

During 1993 the following transactions occurred:

(a) Land site #653 was acquired for $1,350,000. Additionally, to acquire the land, Rodrigo paid a $90,000 commission fee to a real estate agent. Costs of $25,000 were incurred to clear the land. During the course of clearing the land, timber and gravel were recovered and sold for $10,000.

(b) A second tract of land (site #654) with a building was acquired for $700,000. The closing statement indicated that the land value was $510,000 and the building value was $190,000. Shortly after acquisition, the building was demolished at a cost of $30,000. A new building was constructed for $600,000 plus the following costs:

Excavation fees . . . . . . . . . . . . . . . . . . . . . . . . . . . . . . . . . . . . . . . . . . . . . . . . .    $35,000
Architectural design fees . . . . . . . . . . . . . . . . . . . . . . . . . . . . . . . . . . . . . . . .    19,000
Building permit fee . . . . . . . . . . . . . . . . . . . . . . . . . . . . . . . . . . . . . . . . . . . . . .    15,000
Imputed interest on funds used during construction . . . . . . . . . . . . . . . . .    42,000

The building was completed and occupied on September 30, 1993.

(c) A third tract of land (site #655) was acquired for $600,000 and was put on the market for resale.

(d) Extensive work was done to a building occupied by Rodrigo under a lease agreement that expires on December 31, 2002. The total cost of work was $125,000, which consisted of the following:

| | | |
|---|---|---|
| Painting of ceilings . . . . . . . . . . . . . | $ 10,000 | (estimated useful life is one year) |
| Electrical work . . . . . . . . . . . . . . . . . | 35,000 | (estimated useful life is ten years) |
| Construction of extension to current working area . . . . . . . . . . . . . . | 80,000 | (estimated useful life is thirty years) |
| | $125,000 | |

The lessor paid half of the costs incurred in connection with the extension to the current working area.

(e) During December 1993 costs of $65,000 were incurred to improve leased office space. The related lease will terminate on December 31, 1995, and is not expected to be renewed.

(f) A group of new machines was purchased under a royalty agreement which provides for payment of royalties based on units of production for the machines. The invoice price of the machines was $90,000, freight costs were $2,000, unloading charges were $2,500, and royalty payments for 1993 were $13,000.

**Instructions:**

1. Prepare a detailed analysis of the changes in each of the following balance sheet accounts for 1993:

Land
Buildings
Leasehold improvements
Machinery and equipment

(Disregard the related accumulated depreciation accounts.)

2. List the items in the foregoing information which were not used to determine the answer to (1), and indicate where, if at all, these items should be included in Rodrigo's financial statements.

(AICPA adapted)

### Problem 12—11   (Acquisition of noncurrent operating assets)

At December 31, 1993, Arnold Company's noncurrent operating asset accounts had the following balances:

| Category | Cost |
|---|---|
| Land | $  175,000 |
| Buildings | 1,500,000 |
| Machinery and equipment | 1,125,000 |
| Automobiles | 172,000 |
| Leasehold improvements | 216,000 |
| Land improvements | — |

Transactions for 1994 included the following:

Jan.   6   A plant facility consisting of land and a building was acquired from Jesco Corp. in exchange for 25,000 shares of Arnold's common stock. On this date, Arnold's stock had a market price of $50 a share. Current assessed values of land and building for property tax purposes are $187,500 and $562,500, respectively.

Mar. 25   New parking lots, streets, and sidewalks at the acquired plant facility were completed at a total cost of $192,000.

July   1   Machinery and equipment were purchased at a total invoice cost of $325,000, which included $14,000 of sales tax. Additional costs of $10,000 for delivery and $50,000 for installation were incurred.

Aug. 30   Arnold purchased a new automobile for $12,500.

Nov.   4   Arnold purchased for $350,000 a tract of land as a potential future building site.

Dec. 20   A machine with a cost of $17,000 and a remaining book value of $2,975 at date of disposition was scrapped without cash recovery.

**Instructions:**   Prepare a schedule analyzing the changes in each of the noncurrent operating asset accounts during 1994. This schedule should include columns for beginning balance, increase, decrease, and ending balance for each of the noncurrent operating asset accounts.

(AICPA adapted)

### Problem 12—12   (Capitalization of interest)

Oceanwide Enterprises, Inc., is involved in building and operating cruise ships. Each ship is identified as a separate discrete job in the accounting records, and costs are incurred evenly during the construction period. At the end of 1993, Oceanwide correctly reported $5,400,000 as Construction in Progress on the following jobs:

| Ship | Completion Date (end of month) | Accumulated Costs (including 1993 interest) December 31, 1993 |
|------|--------------------------------|--------------------------------------------------------------|
| #340 | October 31, 1993* | $2,300,000 |
| #341 | June 30, 1994 | 1,150,000 |
| #342 | September 30, 1994 | 1,200,000 |
| #343 | January 31, 1995 | 750,000 |

*Ship #340 was completed and ready for use in October 1993 and will be placed in service May 1, 1994.

Labor, material, and overhead costs for 1994 were as follows:

| Ship | Costs | |
|------|-------|---|
| #341 | $1,200,000 | |
| #342 | 1,600,000 | |
| #343 | 2,200,000 | |
| #344 | 810,000 | (construction began May 1) |
| #345 | 360,000 | (construction began Nov. 1) |

Oceanwide had the following general liabilities at December 31, 1994:

12%, 5-year note (maturity date—1996) .......................... $1,000,000
10%, 10-year bonds (maturity date—1998) ...................... 4,000,000

On January 1, 1994, Oceanwide borrowed $1,000,000 specifically for the construction projects. The loan was for 3 years with interest at 13%.

**Instructions:**

1. Compute the maximum interest that can be capitalized in 1994.
2. Compute the weighted average interest rate for the general liabilities for 1994.
3. Compute the weighted average accumulated expenditures for 1994.
4. Compute the interest that Oceanwide should capitalize during 1994.

## Problem 12—13  (Self-construction of equipment)

American Corporation received a $400,000 low bid from a reputable manufacturer for the construction of special production equipment needed by American in an expansion program. Because its own plant was not operating at capacity, American decided to construct the equipment itself and recorded the following production costs related to the construction:

Services of consulting engineer..................................... $ 10,000
Work subcontracted ............................................. 20,000
Materials ...................................................... 200,000
Plant labor normally assigned to production ........................ 65,000
Plant labor normally assigned to maintenance ...................... 100,000
Total ......................................................... $395,000

Management prefers to record the cost of the equipment under the incremental cost method. Approximately 40% of the corporation's production is devoted to government supply contracts, which are all based in some way on cost. The contracts require that any self-constructed equipment be allocated its full share of all costs related to the construction.

The following information also is available:

(a)  The above production labor was for partial fabrication of the equipment in the plant. Skilled personnel were required and were assigned from other projects. The maintenance labor amount

    ($100,000) represents the cost of nonproduction plant employees assigned to the construction project. Had these workers not been assigned to construction, the $100,000 cost would still have been incurred for their idle time.

(b) Payroll taxes and employee fringe benefits are approximately 30% of labor cost and are included in manufacturing overhead cost. Total manufacturing overhead for the year was $5,630,000 including the $100,000 maintenance labor used to construct the equipment.

(c) Manufacturing overhead is approximately 50% variable and is applied on the basis of production labor cost. Production labor cost for the year for the corporation's normal products totaled $6,810,000.

(d) General and administrative expenses include $22,500 of executive salary cost and $10,500 of postage, telephone, supplies, and miscellaneous expenses identifiable with this equipment construction.

### Instructions:

1. Prepare a schedule computing the amount that should be reported as the full cost of the constructed equipment to meet the requirements of the government contracts. Any supporting computations should be in good form.
2. Prepare a schedule computing the incremental cost of the constructed equipment.
3. What is the greatest amount that should be capitalized as the cost of the equipment? Why?

### Problem 12—14 (Summary entries for interest payments)

Clarksville Company reported interest expense in 1993 and 1992 of $350,000 and $300,000, respectively. The balance in Accrued Interest Payable at the end of 1993, 1992, and 1991 was $30,000, $47,000, and $23,000, respectively. In addition, a note to Clarksville's 1993 financial statements included the following:

> Interest costs related to construction in progress are capitalized as incurred. The company capitalized $500,000 and $200,000 of interest costs during the years 1993 and 1992, respectively.

### Instructions:

1. What summary journal entries would be needed to record all information related to interest in 1993 and 1992?
2. How would interest paid be disclosed in Clarksville's statement of cash flows for 1993 and 1992? Clarksville uses the indirect method in reporting cash flow from operating activities.

### Problem 12—15 (Classifying expenditures as assets or expenses)

As of December 31, 1993, W. W. Cole Company's total assets were $325 million and total liabilities were $180 million. Net income for 1993 was $38 million. During 1993, W. W. Cole's chief executive officer had put extreme pressure on employees to meet the profitability goal the CEO had set for them. The goal was to achieve a return on stockholders' equity in 1993 of 25 percent (Net income ÷ Stockholders' equity). The rumor among Cole's employees is that, in order to meet this goal, the accounting for some items may have been overly "aggressive." The following items are of concern:

(a) Research and development costs totaling $18 million were capitalized. None of these costs related to items with alternative uses. The capitalized R&D was assigned a useful life of 6 years; $3 million was written off during 1993.

(b) During the year, a building was acquired in exchange for 5 million shares of Cole common stock. The building was assigned a value of $27 million by the board of directors. At the time of the exchange, Cole common stock was trading on the New York Stock Exchange for $3 per share.

(c) On December 31, equipment was purchased for $1 million in cash and an agreement to pay $3 million per year for the next 8 years—the first payment to be made in one year. The cost of the equipment was recorded at $25 million. The interest rate implicit in the contract was 12%. (Use Present-Value Table IV in Chapter 7.)

(d) Interest of $7 million was capitalized during the year. The only items produced during the year by Cole were routine inventory items.

**Instructions:**

1. Ignoring any concerns raised by items (a) through (d), did W. W. Cole Company meet its profitability goal for the year?
2. After making any adjustments suggested by items (a) through (d), did W. W. Cole meet its profitability goal? (Ignore income taxes.)
3. What should prevent accounting abuses like those described above?

**Problem 12—16   (Classifying expenditures as assets or expenses)**

The Topp Company completed a program of expansion and improvement of its plant during 1993. You are provided with the following information concerning its buildings account:

(a) On October 31, 1993, a 30-foot extension to the present factory building was completed at a contract cost of $108,000.
(b) During the course of construction, the following costs were incurred for the removal of the end wall of the building where the extension was to be constructed:
   (1) Payroll costs during the month of April arising from employees' time spent in removing the wall, $6,940.
   (2) Payments to a salvage company for removing unusual debris, $780.
(c) The cost of the original structure allocable to the end wall was estimated to be $26,400 with accumulated depreciation thereon of $11,100. Topp Company received $7,080 from the construction company for windows and other assorted materials salvaged from the old wall.
(d) The old floor covering was replaced with a new type of long-lasting floor covering at a cost of $5,290. Cost of old floor covering was not available.
(e) The interior of the plant was repainted in new bright colors for a contract price of $5,375.
(f) New and improved shelving was installed at a cost of $1,212. Cost of old shelving was not determinable.
(g) Old electrical wiring was replaced at a cost of $10,218. Cost of the old wiring was determined to be $4,650 with accumulated depreciation to date of $2,055.
(h) New electrical fixtures using fluorescent bulbs were installed. The new fixtures were purchased on the installment plan; the schedule of monthly payments showed total payments of $9,300, which included interest and carrying charges of $720. The old fixtures were carried at a cost of $2,790 with accumulated depreciation to date of $1,200. The old fixtures have no scrap value.

**Instructions:**   Prepare journal entries including explanations for the above information. Briefly justify the asset-vs.-expense decision for each item.

# CHAPTER 13

## Noncurrent Operating Assets–
## Utilization and Retirement

---

**CHAPTER TOPICS**

**Depreciation of Tangible Noncurrent Operating Assets**

**Amortization of Intangible Noncurrent Operating Assets**

**Depletion of Natural Resources**

**Changes in Estimates of Cost Allocation Variables**

**Asset Retirements**

**Balance Sheet Presentation and Disclosure**

---

Blockbuster Video is easily the largest video rental chain in the United States. On May 8, 1989, a Bear, Stearns investment report was released that was critical of many of Blockbuster's accounting practices, including its depreciation policies. The report suggested that the 40-year life Blockbuster used for goodwill was much too long; to quote from the report: "Have you ever seen a 40-year-old videotape store?" Five years was suggested as a more reasonable amortization period. The report also criticized Blockbuster for increasing the depreciation period for videotapes from 9 months to 36 months. Revising both these items to use the shorter amortization periods would have cut Blockbuster's 1988 net income almost in half—from $0.57 per share to $0.32 per share. Release of the Bear, Stearns report caused Blockbuster's stock price to drop from $33.50 to $26.25 in two days, a 22 percent decline. This represented a total decline in market value of approximately $200 million.

Blockbuster's management was understandably upset with the report. The report wasn't "worth the powder to blow it to hell," according to one Blockbuster official.

472

Blockbuster's management pointed out that estimates of asset useful lives are necessarily a matter of judgment and that the estimates Blockbuster used were reasonable. This view was at least partially vindicated when, within six weeks, Blockbuster's stock regained the 22 percent loss.

The lesson from this whole affair is that the smart investor had better know something about depreciation.[1]

A fundamental characteristic of noncurrent operating assets is that they are used to produce revenues over more than one accounting period. Another characteristic common to these assets is that they have limited economic or useful lives. A notable exception to this generalization is land—even farm land can be kept productive indefinitely with proper fertilization and care. All other noncurrent operating assets, however, have limited lives. The economic benefits provided by intangible assets are, in some cases, limited to a period of time specified by law or contract. Other intangible assets tend to decline in usefulness with the passage of time.

In order to match costs with related revenues, the cost of an operating asset (other than land) must be allocated in some manner over the estimated useful life of the asset. In practice, three different terms have evolved to describe this cost allocation process depending on the type of asset involved. The allocation of tangible property costs is referred to as **depreciation**. For mineral and other natural resources, the cost allocation process is appropriately called **depletion**. For intangible assets, such as patents, copyrights, and goodwill, the process is referred to as **amortization**. Sometimes the latter term is used generically to encompass all the other terms. Because the principles underlying each of these terms are similar, they are discussed together in this chapter.

## DEPRECIATION OF NONCURRENT OPERATING ASSETS

Depreciation is the systematic and rational allocation of tangible asset cost over the periods benefited by the use of the asset. There has been a tendency, however, on the part of many readers of financial statements to interpret depreciation accounting as somehow related to the accumulation of a fund for asset replacement. Terminology used in the past, such as "provision for depreciation" and "reserve for depreciation" has contributed toward this misinterpretation. These terms have been replaced by more descriptive terms, e.g., "depreciation expense" and "accumulated depreciation."

The charge for depreciation is the recognition of the declining service potential of an asset. The nature of this charge is no different from those made to recognize the expiration of insurance premiums or patent rights. It is true that revenues equal to or in excess of expenses for a period result in a recovery of these expenses; salary expense is thus recovered by revenues, as is insurance expense, patent amortization, and charges for depreciation. But this does not mean that cash equal to the recorded depreciation will be segregated for property replacement. Revenues may be applied to many uses: to the increase in receivables, inventories, or other working capital items; to the acquisition of new property or other noncurrent items; to the retirement of debt or the redemption of stock; or to the payment of dividends. If a special fund is to be established for the replacement of property, specific authorization by management would be required. Such a fund is seldom found, however, because fund earnings would usually be less than the return from alternative uses of the resources.

Depreciation is also not a technique of asset valuation. The notion of depreciation frequently is motivated by speaking of it as "the decrease in asset value during the year as a

[1]See: Eric Savitz, "An End to Fast Forward?" *Barron's* (December 11, 1989), p. 13; and Dana Wechsler, "Earnings Helper," *Forbes* (June 12, 1989), p. 150.

consequence of business use of the asset." Thinking of depreciation in this way is not correct. The book value of an asset (historical cost less accumulated depreciation) is the asset cost remaining to be allocated to future periods, and not an estimate of the asset's current value.

### Factors Affecting the Periodic Depreciation Charge

Four factors must be recognized in determining the periodic charge for depreciation: (1) **asset cost**, (2) **residual or salvage value**, (3) **useful life**, and (4) **pattern of use**.

**Asset Cost**   The cost of an asset includes all the expenditures relating to its acquisition and preparation for use as described in Chapter 12. The cost of property less the expected residual value, if any, is the depreciable cost or depreciation base, i.e., the portion of asset cost to be charged against future revenues.

**Residual or Salvage Value**   The residual (salvage) value of property is an estimate of the amount that can be realized upon retirement of the asset. This depends on the retirement policy of the company as well as market conditions and other factors. If, for example, the company normally uses equipment until it is physically exhausted and no longer serviceable, the residual value, represented by the scrap or junk that can be salvaged, may be nominal. But if the company normally replaces its equipment after a relatively short period of use, the residual value, represented by the selling price or trade-in value, may be relatively high. From a theoretical point of view, any estimated residual value should be subtracted from cost in arriving at the portion of asset cost to be charged to depreciation.

In practice, however, residual values are frequently ignored in determining periodic depreciation charges. This practice is not objectionable when residual values are relatively small or are not subject to reasonable estimation, and when it is doubtful more useful information will be provided through such refinement.

**Useful Life**   Noncurrent operating assets other than land have a limited useful life as a result of certain physical and functional factors. The **physical factors** that limit the service life of an asset are (1) wear and tear, (2) deterioration and decay, and (3) damage or destruction. Everyone is familiar with the processes of wear and tear that render an automobile, a typewriter, or furniture no longer usable. A tangible asset, whether used or not, also is subject to deterioration and decay through aging. Finally, fire, flood, earthquake, or accident may reduce or terminate the useful life of an asset.

The **functional factors** limiting the lives of these assets are (1) inadequacy and (2) obsolescence. An asset may lose its usefulness when, as a result of altered business requirements or technical progress, it no longer can produce sufficient revenue to justify its continued use. Although the asset is still usable, its inability to produce sufficient revenue has cut short its service life. An example of rapid obsolescence can be observed in the computer industry. The rapid technological changes in this field have rendered perfectly good electronic equipment obsolete for efficient continued use long before the physical asset itself has worn out.

Both physical and functional factors must be considered in estimating the useful life of a depreciable asset. This recognition requires estimating what events will take place in the future and requires careful judgment on the part of the accountant.[2] Physical factors are

---

[2]Although the concept of useful life is generally recognized to be difficult to apply, there has been relatively little written on it in accounting literature. For a thorough discussion of the topic, see Charles Lamden, Dale L. Gerboth, and Thomas McRae, "Accounting for Depreciable Assets," *Accounting Research Monograph No. 1* (New York: American Institute of Certified Public Accountants, 1975), Ch. 5.

more readily apparent than functional factors in predicting asset life. But when functional factors are expected to hasten the retirement of an asset, these also must be recognized.

In practice, many companies as a matter of policy dispose of certain classes of assets after a predetermined period, without regard to the serviceability of individual assets within a class. Company automobiles, for example, may be replaced routinely every two or three years.

The useful life of a depreciable plant asset may be expressed in terms of either an estimated time factor or an estimated use factor. The **time factor** may be a period of months or years; the **use factor** may be a number of hours of service or a number of units of output. The cost of the asset is allocated in accordance with the lapse of time or extent of use. The rate of cost allocation may be modified by other factors, but basically depreciation must be recognized on a time or use basis.

**Pattern of Use**    In order to match asset cost against revenues, periodic depreciation charges should reflect as closely as possible the pattern of use. If the asset produces a varying revenue pattern, then the depreciation charges should vary in a corresponding manner. When depreciation is measured in terms of a time factor, the pattern of use must be estimated. Because of the difficulty in identifying a pattern of use, several somewhat arbitrary methods have come into common practice. Each method represents a different pattern and is designed to make the time basis approximate the use basis. The time factor is employed in two general classes of methods: **straight-line depreciation** and **decreasing-charge depreciation**. When depreciation is measured in terms of a use factor, the units of use must be estimated. The depreciation charge varies periodically in accordance with the services provided by the asset. The use factor is employed in **service-hours depreciation** and in **productive-output depreciation**.

## Recording Periodic Depreciation

The periodic allocation of property costs is made by debiting either a production overhead cost account or a selling or administrative expense account, and crediting an allowance or contra asset account. If the charge is made to a production overhead account, it becomes part of the cost of the finished and unfinished goods inventories and is deferred to the extent inventory has not been sold or completed. If the charge is made to selling or administrative expenses, it is considered a period cost and is written off against revenue as an operating expense of the current period.

The valuation or allowance account that is credited in recording periodic depreciation is commonly titled Accumulated Depreciation. The accumulation of expired cost in a separate account rather than crediting the asset account directly permits identification of the original cost of the asset and the accumulated depreciation. The FASB requires disclosure of both cost and accumulated depreciation for property on the balance sheet or notes to the financial statements. This enables the user to estimate the relative age of all assets and provides some basis for predicting future cash outflows for the replacement of assets.

## Methods of Depreciation

There are a number of different methods for allocating the costs of depreciable assets. The depreciation method used in any specific instance is a matter of judgment and, conceptually, should be selected to most closely approximate the actual pattern of use expected from the asset. In practice, most firms select one depreciation method, such as straight-line, and use it for substantially all their assets. The following methods are described in this chapter:

### Time-Factor Methods

1. Straight-line depreciation
2. Decreasing-charge (accelerated) methods
   (a) Sum-of-the-years-digits depreciation
   (b) Declining-balance depreciation
3. Accelerated cost recovery system (ACRS) and Modified accelerated cost recovery system (MACRS)

### Use-Factor Methods

1. Service-hours depreciation
2. Productive-output depreciation

### Group-Rate and Composite-Rate Methods

1. Group depreciation
2. Composite depreciation

The examples that follow assume the acquisition of a polyurethane plastic molding machine at the beginning of 1993 by Schuss Boom Ski Manufacturing, Inc., at a cost of $100,000 with an estimated residual value of $5,000. The following symbols are used in the formulas for the development of depreciation rates and charges:

C = Asset cost
R = Estimated residual value
n = Estimated life in years, hours of service, or units of output
r = Depreciation rate per period, per hour of service, or per unit of output
D = Periodic depreciation charge

**Time-Factor Methods**   The most common methods of cost allocation are related to the passage of time. In general, a productive asset is used up over time. Possible obsolescence due to technological changes is also a function of time. Of the **time-factor depreciation methods**, straight-line depreciation has been by far the most popular. *Accounting Trends & Techniques* reported that 562 of the 600 companies surveyed used the straight-line method in their 1989 financial statements.[3]

The use of **decreasing-charge depreciation methods**, sometimes referred to as "accelerated depreciation" methods, is based largely on the assumption that there will be rapid reductions in asset efficiency, output, or other benefits in the early years of an asset's life. Such reductions may be accompanied by increased charges for maintenance and repairs. Charges for depreciation decline, then, as the economic advantages afforded through ownership of the asset decline. The most commonly used decreasing-charge methods are sum-of-the-years-digits and some variation of a declining-balance method.

**Straight-Line Depreciation**   **Straight-line depreciation** relates cost allocation to the passage of time and recognizes equal periodic charges over the life of the asset. The allocation assumes equal usefulness per time period, and in applying this assumption, the charge is not affected by asset productivity or efficiency variations. In developing the periodic charge, an estimate is made of the useful life of the asset in terms of months or years. The difference between the asset cost and residual value is divided by the useful life of the asset in arriving at the cost assigned to each time unit.

[3]*Accounting Trends & Techniques* (New York: American Institute of Certified Public Accountants, 1990), p. 261.

Using data for the machine acquired by Schuss Boom Ski Manufacturing (see page 476) and assuming a 5-year life, annual depreciation is determined as follows:

$$D = \frac{C - R}{n}, \text{ or } \frac{\$100,000 - \$5,000}{5 \text{ years}} = \$19,000 \text{ per year}$$

Annual depreciation also can be computed by applying a percentage, or **depreciation rate,** to depreciable cost. The rate is the reciprocal value of the useful life expressed in periods, or r (per period) $= 1 \div n$. In the example, the depreciation rate would be $1 \div 5 = 20\%$, and annual depreciation can be computed as follows:

$$\$95,000 \times 20\% = \$19,000$$

A table summarizing the cost allocation process for the asset in the example, using the straight-line method, follows:

### Asset Cost Allocation—Straight-Line Method

| End of Year | Depreciation Computation | | Amount | Accumulated Depreciation | Asset Book Value |
|---|---|---|---|---|---|
| | | | | | $100,000 |
| 1993 | $95,000 ÷ 5 | = | $19,000 | $19,000 | 81,000 |
| 1994 | 95,000 ÷ 5 | = | 19,000 | 38,000 | 62,000 |
| 1995 | 95,000 ÷ 5 | = | 19,000 | 57,000 | 43,000 |
| 1996 | 95,000 ÷ 5 | = | 19,000 | 76,000 | 24,000 |
| 1997 | 95,000 ÷ 5 | = | 19,000 | 95,000 | 5,000 |
| | Total | | $95,000 | | |

It was indicated earlier that residual value is frequently ignored when it is a relatively minor amount. If this were done in the example, depreciation would be recognized at $20,000 per year instead of $19,000.

**Sum-of-the-Years-Digits Depreciation**   The sum-of-the-years-digits depreciation method provides decreasing charges by applying a series of fractions, each of a smaller value, to depreciable asset cost. Fractions are developed in terms of the sum of the asset life periods. The numerators are the years-digits listed in reverse order. The denominator for the fraction is obtained by adding these digits.

For example, given an asset with a 3-year life, the denominator, which is the same each year, would be 6, the "sum-of-the-years-digits" $(1 + 2 + 3)$. Since the numerators, which decrease each year, are the years-digits in reverse order $(3, 2, 1)$, the fractions would be: $\frac{3}{6}$ for the first year; $\frac{2}{6}$ for the second year; and $\frac{1}{6}$ for the third year. The total of these fractions is 1.00; thus 100% of the depreciable cost is charged to expense at the end of 3 years. The following formula can be used to facilitate computation of the denominator:

$$[(n + 1) \div 2] \times n$$

If useful life is 15 years, the denominator, determined by the formula, is: $[(15 + 1) \div 2] \times 15 = 120$. The fraction applied to depreciable cost in the first year would be $\frac{15}{120}$, in the second year, $\frac{14}{120}$, and so on.

In the Schuss Boom example, useful life is 5 years, and the denominator of the fraction is: $[(5 + 1) \div 2] \times 5 = 15$. Alternatively, the denominator can be found by adding the years-digits ($1 + 2 + 3 + 4 + 5 = 15$). Depreciation using the sum-of-the-years-digits method is summarized in the following table:

**Asset Cost Allocation—Sum-of-the-Years-Digits Method**

| End of Year | Depreciation Computation | | Amount | Accumulated Depreciation | Asset Book Value |
|---|---|---|---|---|---|
| | | | | | $100,000 |
| 1993 | $95,000 × ⁵⁄₁₅ | = | $31,667 | $31,667 | 68,333 |
| 1994 | 95,000 × ⁴⁄₁₅ | = | 25,333 | 57,000 | 43,000 |
| 1995 | 95,000 × ³⁄₁₅ | = | 19,000 | 76,000 | 24,000 |
| 1996 | 95,000 × ²⁄₁₅ | = | 12,667 | 88,667 | 11,333 |
| 1997 | 95,000 × ¹⁄₁₅ | = | 6,333 | 95,000 | 5,000 |
| | | Total | $95,000 | | |

Note that under this method, the annual charge to depreciation expense declines by ¹⁄₁₅ of the depreciation asset base each year, or by $6,333.

***Declining-Balance Depreciation***    The declining-balance depreciation methods provide decreasing charges by applying a constant percentage rate to a declining asset book value. The most popular rates are 1.5 times the straight-line rate, often referred to as "150% declining balance," and 2 times the straight-line rate, often referred to as double-declining-balance depreciation.[4] Residual value is not used in the computations under this method; however, it is generally recognized that depreciation should not continue once the book value is equal to the residual value. The percentage to be used is a multiple of the straight-line rate, calculated for various useful lives as follows:

| Estimated Useful Life in Years | Straight-Line Rate | 1.5 times Straight-Line Rate | 2.0 times Straight-Line Rate |
|---|---|---|---|
| 3 | 33⅓% | 50% | 66⅔% |
| 5 | 20 | 30 | –40 |
| 7 | 14²⁄₇ | 21³⁄₇ | 28⁴⁄₇ |
| 8 | 12½ | 18¾ | 25 |
| 10 | 10 | 15 | ➔20 |
| 20 | 5 | 7½ | 10 |

Depreciation using the double-declining-balance method for the asset described earlier is summarized in the table at the top of page 479.

It should be noted that the rate of 40% is applied to the decreasing book value of the asset each year. This results in a declining amount of depreciation expense. In applying this rate, the book value after 5 years exceeds the residual value by $2,776 ($7,776 − $5,000). This condition arises whenever residual values are relatively low in amount. Since it is impossible to bring a value to zero by using a constant multiplier, most adopters of this method switch to the straight-line method when the remaining annual depreciation computed using straight-line exceeds the depreciation computed by continuing to apply the declining-balance rate. In the above example, the depreciation expense for

[4]The pure declining-balance method computes a constant rate that, when applied to a declining book value, will cause the book value to equal the estimated residual value at the end of the estimated useful life. The formula to arrive at this rate is $1 - \sqrt[n]{R \div C}$, where R is the residual value, C is cost of the asset, and n is the life of the asset. This method is seldom used in practice because it often exceeds the double-declining-balance rate, a limit imposed in the past through the tax code.

| End of Year | Depreciation | | Amount | Accumulated Depreciation | Asset Book Value |
|---|---|---|---|---|---|
| | Computation | | | | |
| | | | | | $100,000 |
| 1993 | $100,000 × 40% | = | $40,000 | $40,000 | 60,000 |
| 1994 | 60,000 × 40 | = | 24,000 | 64,000 | 36,000 |
| 1995 | 36,000 × 40 | = | 14,400 | 78,400 | 21,600 |
| 1996 | 21,600 × 40 | = | 8,640 | 87,040 | 12,960 |
| 1997 | 12,960 × 40 | = | 5,184 | 92,224 | 7,776 |
| | | Total | $92,224 | | |

1997 would be $7,960 if a switch were made from double-declining balance to straight-line. This would reduce the book value of the asset to its $5,000 residual value. In this example, the switch was made in the last year of the asset's life, and the depreciation expense was simply the amount necessary to reduce the asset's book value to its residual value. However, if the asset in the example had a lower residual value, the switch could have been made in the fourth year. For example, assume the asset is expected to have no residual value. The book value under the double-declining-balance method at the end of the third year as shown above is $21,600, thus the straight-line depreciation for Years 4 and 5 would be $10,800 ($21,600 ÷ 2). Since the straight-line depreciation of $10,800 exceeds the double-declining depreciation of $8,640, the straight-line amount would be used for Years 4 and 5.

**Accelerated Cost Recovery System (ACRS)**    The Economic Recovery Tax Act (ERTA) of 1981 introduced an adaptation of the declining-balance depreciation method to be used for income tax purposes. It is referred to as the accelerated cost recovery system (ACRS). Subsequent revisions to the income tax laws have altered the original provisions. Because the Tax Reform Act of 1986 made several significant changes to ACRS, the new system is now referred to as the modified accelerated cost recovery system (MACRS).

The term "cost recovery" was used in the tax regulations to emphasize that ACRS is not a standard depreciation method since the system is not based strictly on asset life or pattern of use. ACRS has largely replaced traditional depreciation accounting for income tax purposes. Its original purpose was to both simplify the computation of tax depreciation and provide for a more rapid write-off of asset cost to reduce income taxes and thus stimulate investment in noncurrent operating assets. Simplification was to be achieved by using one of three cost recovery periods for all assets rather than a specific useful life for each class of asset as previously prescribed by the income tax regulations. In addition, salvage values were to be ignored. A more rapid write-off was achieved by allowing companies to write off most machinery and equipment over 3 to 5 years, and all real estate over 15 years, even though previously prescribed income tax class lives were for much longer periods. The class lives prescribed by the IRS were based on estimates of actual useful lives for specific assets in specific industries.

The subsequent modifications to ACRS by Congress have tended to dampen both of its original objectives, primarily because Congress has become more concerned with increasing tax revenues to offset the rapidly growing federal deficit without increasing income tax rates than with simplification or stimulating growth in the economy. The original three recovery periods have been replaced with six recovery periods for personal property,[5] such as equipment, automobiles, and furniture, and two periods for real property, or buildings. At the same time, the recovery periods for most assets have been extended so that less rapid write-off of asset cost is permitted.

---

[5]Personal property is a general term that encompasses all property other than real property (land and buildings).

Exhibit 13—1 illustrates the cost recovery periods and depreciation methods under MACRS. The exhibit applies to assets purchased after December 31, 1986, the date MACRS became effective. For personal property, the appropriate cost recovery period is determined by reference to the IRS class lives defined in the tax regulations. The real property recovery periods relate to the type of real property involved rather than class lives. ACRS initially provided for a 150% declining-balance depreciation. The 1986 Reform Act increased the number of asset recovery periods and extended the recovery periods for most assets. The effects of these changes were partially offset by changing the method of depreciation for most personal property to the 200% declining-balance method.

**Exhibit 13—1    MACRS Cost Recovery Periods and Depreciation Method**

|  | IRS-Defined Class Lives | MACRS Cost Recovery Period | Depreciation Method | Examples of Business Assets |
|---|---|---|---|---|
| Personal Property | Less than 4 years | 3 years | 200% declining-balance | Small tools |
|  | 4 to < 10 years | 5 years | 200% declining-balance | Cars, trucks, office machinery |
|  | 10 to < 16 years | 7 years | 200% declining-balance | Office furniture, most factory machinery |
|  | 16 to < 20 years | 10 years | 200% declining-balance | Land improvements |
|  | 20 to < 25 years | 15 years | 150% declining-balance | Communication equipment |
|  | More than 25 years | 20 years | 150% declining-balance | Farm buildings |
|  | **Type of Property** |  |  |  |
| Real Property—Buildings | Residential rental | 27.5 years | Straight-line |  |
|  | Nonresidential | 31.5 years | Straight-line |  |

Both the AICPA and FASB expressed opposition to the use of ACRS for financial reporting purposes because of the wide disparity between the recovery periods permitted for income tax purposes and the actual useful lives of the assets. The 1986 Reform Act modifications have reduced this disparity, and in many cases, the MACRS recovery periods may represent reasonable estimates of useful life for financial reporting purposes. However, companies should exercise caution in adopting MACRS rules for financial reporting purposes because of the volatility of income tax laws and regulations.

***Comparison of Time-Factor Methods***    Exhibit 13—2 illustrates the pattern of depreciation expense for the time-factor methods discussed in the preceding sections. Note that when the straight-line method is used, depreciation is a constant or fixed charge each period. When the life of an asset is affected primarily by the lapse of time rather than by the degree of use, recognition of depreciation as a constant charge is generally appropriate. However, net income measurements become particularly sensitive to changes in the volume of business activity. With above-normal activity, there is no increase in the depreciation charge; with below-normal activity, there is no decrease in the depreciation charge.

Straight-line depreciation is a widely used procedure for financial reporting purposes. It is readily understood and frequently parallels asset use. It has the advantage of simplicity and under normal conditions offers a satisfactory means of cost allocation. Normal asset conditions exist when (1) assets have been accumulated over a period of years so that the total of depreciation plus maintenance is comparatively even from period to period, and (2) service potentials of assets are being steadily reduced by functional as well as physical factors. The absence of either of these conditions may suggest the use of some depreciation method other than straight line.

Decreasing-charge methods can be supported as reasonable approaches to cost allocation when the annual benefits provided by an asset decline as it grows older. These methods, too, are suggested when an asset requires increasing maintenance and repairs over its useful life.[6] When straight-line depreciation is employed, the combined charges for depreciation, maintenance, and repairs will increase over the life of the asset; when the decreasing-charge methods are used, the combined charges will tend to be equalized. Exhibit 13—3 illustrates this relationship.

Other factors suggesting the use of a decreasing-charge method include: (1) the anticipation of a significant contribution in early periods with the extent of the contribution to be realized in later periods being less definite; (2) the possibility that inadequacy or obsolescence may result in premature retirement of the asset.

**Exhibit 13—2    Time-Factor Methods: Depreciation Patterns Compared**

[6]The AICPA Committee on Accounting Procedure has stated, "The declining-balance method is one of those which meets the requirements of being 'systematic and rational.' In those cases where the expected productivity or revenue-earning power of the asset is relatively greater during the earlier years of its life, or where maintenance charges tend to increase during the later years, the declining-balance method may well provide the most satisfactory allocation of cost." The Committee would apply these conclusions to other decreasing-charge methods, including the sum-of-the-years-digits method, that produce substantially similar results. See *Accounting Research and Terminology Bulletins—Final Edition*, "No. 44 (Revised), Declining-Balance Depreciation" (New York: American Institute of Certified Public Accountants, 1961), par. 2.

**Exhibit 13—3    Decreasing-Charge Depreciation and Repairs and Maintenance Expense**

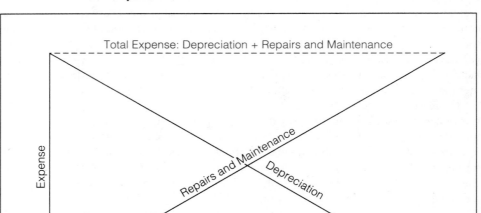

***Depreciation for Partial Periods***    The discussion thus far has assumed that assets were purchased on the first day of a company's fiscal period. In reality, of course, asset transactions occur throughout the year. When a time-factor method is used, depreciation on assets acquired or disposed of during the year may be based on the number of days the asset was held during the period. When the level of acquisitions and retirements is significant, however, companies often adopt a less burdensome policy for recognizing depreciation for partial periods. Some alternatives found in practice include the following:

1. Depreciation is recognized to the nearest whole month. Assets acquired on or before the 15th of the month are considered owned for the entire month; assets acquired after the 15th are not considered owned for any part of the month. Conversely, assets sold on or before the 15th of the month are not considered owned for any part of the month; assets sold after the 15th are considered owned for the entire month.
2. Depreciation is recognized to the nearest whole year. Assets acquired during the first six months are considered held for the entire year; assets acquired during the last six months are not considered in the depreciation computation. Conversely, no depreciation is recorded on assets sold during the first six months, and a full year's depreciation is recorded on assets sold during the last six months.
3. One-half year's depreciation is recognized on all assets purchased or sold during the year. A full year's depreciation is taken on all other assets. This approach is required for tax purposes (ACRS and MACRS).
4. No depreciation is recognized on acquisitions during the year, but depreciation for a full year is recognized on retirements.
5. Depreciation is recognized for a full year on acquisitions during the year, but no depreciation is recognized on retirements.

Alternatives 2 through 5 are attractive because of their simplicity. However, alternative 1 provides greater accuracy, and its use is assumed in the examples and problems in the text except for MACRS problems that require alternative 3.

If a company uses the sum-of-the-years-digits method of depreciation and recognizes partial year's depreciation on assets in the year purchased, the depreciation expense for the second year must be determined by the following allocation procedure. Assume that the asset acquired by Schuss Boom Ski Manufacturing (see page 476) was purchased ¾ of the way through the fiscal year. The computation of depreciation expense for the first two years would be as follows:

```
First year:
  Depreciation for full year (See page 478)................    $31,667
  One-fourth year's depreciation ($31,667 ÷ 4) ............              $ 7,917

Second year:
  Depreciation for balance of first year ($31,667 − $7,917) ...          $23,750
  Depreciation for second full year (See page 478) .........    $25,333
  One-fourth year's depreciation ($25,333 ÷ 4) ............                6,333
  Total depreciation—second year........................              $30,083
```

From this point, each year's depreciation will be ¹⁄₁₅ of the original depreciable asset base ($6,333) less than the previous year. A summary of the depreciation charges for the five-year period is as follows:

|  | Depreciation | Asset Book Value |
|---|---|---|
| Year 1 | $ 7,917 | $92,083 |
| Year 2 | 30,083 | 62,000 |
| Year 3 | 23,750 | 38,250 |
| Year 4 | 17,417 | 20,833 |
| Year 5 | 11,083 | 9,750 |
| Year 6 | 4,750 | 5,000 |
| Total | $95,000 | |

Alternatively, depreciation for Years 2 through 6 can be computed using the standard sum-of-the-years-digits computation with the numerator being the number of years remaining in the asset's useful life as of the beginning of the year. For the second year, the number of years remaining in the asset's useful life at the beginning of the year is 4.75. The depreciation for Year 2 is: $95,000 × 4.75/15 = $30,083.

If a company uses a declining-balance method of depreciation, the computation of depreciation when partial years are involved is relatively straightforward. After the first year's depreciation is computed, the remaining years are calculated in the same manner as illustrated on page 479; a constant percentage is multiplied by a declining book value. Again assuming a purchase ¾ of the way through the fiscal year and the use of alternative 1, the double-declining-balance depreciation expense for the asset described on page 476 would be as follows, assuming a switch to straight-line depreciation in Year 5.

|  |  | Depreciation | Asset Book Value |
|---|---|---|---|
| Year 1 | ($100,000 × .40 × ¼) | $10,000 | $90,000 |
| Year 2 | ($90,000 × .40) | 36,000 | 54,000 |
| Year 3 | ($54,000 × .40) | 21,600 | 32,400 |
| Year 4 | ($32,400 × .40) | 12,960 | 19,440 |
| Year 5 | [($19,440 − $5,000) ÷ 1¾] | 8,251* | 11,189 |
| Year 6 | ($11,189 − $5,000) | 6,189 | 5,000 |
| | Total | $95,000 | |

*rounded

In contrast, the MACRS method for personal property requires use of alternative 3, the half-year convention, and ignores residual value. The cost recovery amounts for the same asset would be as follows:

|        |                          | Cost Recovery Amount | Asset Book Value |
|--------|--------------------------|----------------------|------------------|
| Year 1 | ($100,000 × .40 x ½)     | $ 20,000             | $80,000          |
| Year 2 | ($80,000 × .40)          | 32,000               | 48,000           |
| Year 3 | ($48,000 × .40)          | 19,200               | 28,800           |
| Year 4 | ($28,800 × .40)          | 11,520               | 17,280           |
| Year 5 | ($17,280 ÷ 1.5)          | 11,520               | 5,760            |
| Year 6 | (Remaining book value)   | 5,760                | -0-              |
|        | Total                    | $100,000             |                  |

Even though the asset was purchased ¾ of the way through the year, for tax purposes $20,000 is reported as the cost recovery in the first year rather than $10,000 determined by computing depreciation to the nearest month. Note that a switch to the straight-line method was made in Year 5. If the double-declining-balance method had been applied to this year, only $6,912 ($17,280 × .40) would have been reported rather than $11,520 using straight-line for the remaining 1.5 years.

**Use-Factor Methods**    Use-factor depreciation methods view asset exhaustion as related primarily to asset use or output and provide periodic charges varying with the degree of such service. Service life for certain assets can best be expressed in terms of hours of service; for others, in terms of units of production.

***Service-Hours Method***    Service-hours depreciation is based on the theory that purchase of an asset represents the purchase of a number of hours of direct service. This method requires an estimate of the life of the asset in terms of service hours. Depreciable cost is divided by total service hours in arriving at the depreciation rate to be assigned for each hour of asset use. The use of the asset during the period is measured, and the number of service hours is multiplied by the depreciation rate in arriving at the periodic depreciation charge. Depreciation charges against revenue fluctuate periodically according to the contribution the asset makes in service hours.

Using asset data previously given and an estimated service life of 20,000 hours, the rate to be applied for each service hour is determined as follows:

$$r \text{ (per hour)} = \frac{C - R}{n}, \text{ or } \frac{\$100,000 - \$5,000}{20,000 \text{ hours}} = \$4.75 \text{ per hour}$$

Allocation of asset cost in terms of service hours is summarized in the table at the top of page 485.

It is assumed that the original estimate of service hours is confirmed and the asset is retired after 20,000 hours are reached in the fifth year. Such precise confirmation would seldom be found in practice. Procedures for handling changes in estimates are discussed later in the chapter.

It should be observed that straight-line depreciation resulted in an annual charge of $19,000 regardless of fluctuations in productive activity. When asset life is affected directly by the degree of use, and when there are significant fluctuations in such use in successive periods, the service-hours method, which recognizes hours used instead of hours available for use, normally provides the more equitable charges to operations.

**Asset Cost Allocation—Service-Hours Method**

| End of Year | Service Hours | Depreciation Computation | Amount | Accumulated Depreciation | Asset Book Value |
|---|---|---|---|---|---|
| | | | | | $100,000 |
| 1993 | 3,000 | 3,000 × $4.75 = | $14,250 | $14,250 | 85,750 |
| 1994 | 5,000 | 5,000 × $4.75 = | 23,750 | 38,000 | 62,000 |
| 1995 | 5,000 | 5,000 × $4.75 = | 23,750 | 61,750 | 38,250 |
| 1996 | 4,000 | 4,000 × $4.75 = | 19,000 | 80,750 | 19,250 |
| 1997 | 3,000 | 3,000 × $4.75 = | 14,250 | 95,000 | 5,000 |
| | 20,000 | | $95,000 | | |

**Productive-Output Method**    Productive-output depreciation is based on the theory that an asset is acquired for the service it can provide in the form of production output. This method requires an estimate of the total unit output of the asset. Depreciable cost divided by the total estimated output gives the equal charge to be assigned for each unit of output. The measured production for a period multiplied by the charge per unit gives the charge to be made against revenue. Depreciation charges fluctuate periodically according to the contribution the asset makes in unit output.

Using the previous asset data and an estimated productive life of 2,500,000 units, the rate to be applied for each thousand units produced is determined as follows:

$$r \text{ (per thousand units)} = \frac{C - R}{n}, \text{ or } \frac{\$100,000 - \$5,000}{2,500 \text{ units}} = \$38 \text{ per unit}$$

A table for the productive-output method would be similar to that prepared for the service-hours method.

**Evaluation of Use-Factor Methods**    When quantitative measures of asset use can be reasonably estimated, the use-factor methods provide highly satisfactory approaches to asset cost allocation. Depreciation as a fluctuating charge tends to follow the revenue curve: high depreciation charges are assigned to periods of high activity; low charges are assigned to periods of low activity. When the useful life of an asset is affected primarily by the degree of its use, recognition of depreciation as a variable charge is particularly appropriate.

However, certain limitations in applying the use-factor methods need to be pointed out. Asset performance in terms of service hours or productive output is often difficult to estimate. Measurement solely in terms of these factors could fail to recognize special conditions, such as increasing maintenance and repair costs, as well as possible inadequacy and obsolescence. Furthermore, when service life expires even in the absence of use, a use-factor method may conceal actual fluctuations in earnings; by relating periodic depreciation charges to the volume of operations, periodic operating results may be smoothed out, thus creating a false appearance of stability.

**Group and Composite Methods**    It was assumed in preceding discussions that depreciation expense is associated with individual assets and is applied to each separate unit. This practice is commonly referred to as **unit depreciation**. There may be certain advantages in associating depreciation with a group of assets and applying a single rate to the collective cost of the group at any given time. Group cost allocation procedures are referred to as group depreciation and composite depreciation.[7]

---

[7]These methods are sometimes referred to as multiple-asset methods of depreciation. See Stephen T. Limberg and Bill N. Schwartz, "Should You Use Multiple Asset Accounts?" *The CPA Journal* (October 1981), pp. 25-31.

***Group Depreciation***   When useful life is affected primarily by physical factors, a group of similar items purchased at one time should have the same expected life, but in fact some will probably remain useful longer than others. In recording depreciation on a unit basis, the sale or retirement of an asset before or after its anticipated lifetime requires recognition of a gain or loss. Such gains and losses, however, can usually be attributed to normal variations in useful life rather than to unforeseen disasters and windfalls.

The **group-depreciation** procedure treats a collection of similar assets as a single group. Depreciation is accumulated in a single valuation account, and the depreciation rate is based on the average life of assets in the group. Because the accumulated depreciation account under the group procedure applies to the entire group of assets, it is not related to any specific asset. Thus no book value can be calculated for any specific asset and there are no fully depreciated assets. To arrive at the periodic depreciation charge, the depreciation rate is applied to the recorded cost of all assets remaining in service, regardless of age.

When an item in the group is retired, no gain or loss is recognized; the asset account is credited with the cost of the item and the valuation account is debited for the difference between cost and any salvage. With normal variations in asset lives, the losses not recognized on early retirements are offset by the continued depreciation charges on those assets still in service after the average life has elapsed. Group depreciation is generally computed as an adaptation of the straight-line method, and the illustrations in this chapter assume this approach.[8]

To illustrate, assume that 100 similar machines having an average expected useful life of 5 years are purchased at the beginning of 1993 at a total cost of $2,000,000. Of this group, 30 machines are retired at the end of 1996, 40 at the end of 1997, and the remaining 30 at the end of 1998. Based on the average expected useful life of 5 years, a depreciation charge of 20% is reported on those assets in service each year. The charges for depreciation and the changes in the group asset and accumulated depreciation accounts are summarized below, assuming there was no salvage value at retirement.

**Asset Cost Allocation—Group Depreciation**

| End of Year | Depreciation Expense (20% of Cost) | Asset Debit | Asset Credit | Asset Balance | Accumulated Depreciation Debit | Accumulated Depreciation Credit | Accumulated Depreciation Balance | Asset Book Value |
|---|---|---|---|---|---|---|---|---|
| | | $2,000,000 | | $2,000,000 | | | | $2,000,000 |
| 1993 | $ 400,000 | | | 2,000,000 | | $ 400,000 | $ 400,000 | 1,600,000 |
| 1994 | 400,000 | | | 2,000,000 | | 400,000 | 800,000 | 1,200,000 |
| 1995 | 400,000 | | | 2,000,000 | | 400,000 | 1,200,000 | 800,000 |
| 1996 | 400,000 | | $ 600,000 | 1,400,000 | $ 600,000 | 400,000 | 1,000,000 | 400,000 |
| 1997 | 280,000 | | 800,000 | 600,000 | 800,000 | 280,000 | 480,000 | 120,000 |
| 1998 | 120,000 | | 600,000 | — | 600,000 | 120,000 | — | — |
| | $2,000,000 | $2,000,000 | $2,000,000 | | $2,000,000 | $2,000,000 | | |

It should be noted that the depreciation charge is exactly $4,000 per machine-year. In each of the first four years, 100 machine-years of service[9] are utilized, and the annual

---

[8]The multiple-asset approach may be modified for unusual retirements. In order to preserve the average-life computations, retirements arising from involuntary conversion or other such unusual causes may be recorded at a loss. In order to do this, however, there must be enough detail in the records to approximate the book value of the item at the date of the loss.

[9]It should be observed that in the example the original estimate of an average useful life of 5 years is confirmed in the use of the assets. Such precise confirmation would seldom be the case. In instances where assets in a group are continued in use after their cost has been assigned to operations, no further depreciation charges would be recognized. On the other hand, where all of the assets in a group are retired before their costs have been assigned to operations, a special charge related to such retirement would have to be recognized.

depreciation charge is $400,000. In the fifth year, when only 70 machines are in operation, the charge is $280,000 (20% of $1,400,000). In the sixth year, when 30 units are still in service, a proportionate charge for such use of $120,000 (20% of $600,000) is made.

If the 30 machines retired in 1996 had been sold for $50,000, the entry to record the sale using the group depreciation method would have been as follows:

| | | |
|---|---|---|
| Cash ............................................... | 50,000 | |
| Accumulated Depreciation—Equipment ................... | 550,000 | |
| Equipment ........................................ | | 600,000 |

Because no gain or loss is recognized, the debit to Accumulated Depreciation is the difference between the cost of the equipment and the cash received.

The preceding example assumed that no new assets were added to the group. This is referred to as a "closed" group. Companies may create such a group, for example, for all furniture acquired in a given year. The group method may also be applied to an "open-ended" group. In this case, additions are made to the group, and thus the accounts are never "closed." Assume the previous example is changed to include additions of 20 machines at the end of 1994 at a cost of $425,000, 30 machines at the end of 1997 at a cost of $650,000, and 50 machines at the end of 1998 at a cost of $1,100,000. Assume that all retired machines are from the initial purchase. The charges for the first 6 years under these assumptions are summarized below.

### Asset Cost Allocation—Open-Ended Group Depreciation

| End of Year | Depreciation Expense (20% of Cost) | Asset Debit | Asset Credit | Asset Balance | Accumulated Depreciation Debit | Accumulated Depreciation Credit | Accumulated Depreciation Balance | Asset Book Value |
|---|---|---|---|---|---|---|---|---|
| | | $2,000,000 | | $2,000,000 | | | | $2,000,000 |
| 1993 | $400,000 | | | 2,000,000 | | $400,000 | $ 400,000 | 1,600,000 |
| 1994 | 400,000 | 425,000 | | 2,425,000 | | 400,000 | 800,000 | 1,625,000 |
| 1995 | 485,000 | | | 2,425,000 | | 485,000 | 1,285,000 | 1,140,000 |
| 1996 | 485,000 | | $600,000 | 1,825,000 | $600,000 | 485,000 | 1,170,000 | 655,000 |
| 1997 | 365,000 | 650,000 | 800,000 | 1,675,000 | 800,000 | 365,000 | 735,000 | 940,000 |
| 1998 | 335,000 | 1,100,000 | 600,000 | 2,175,000 | 600,000 | 335,000 | 470,000 | 1,705,000 |

Application of the group-depreciation procedure under circumstances such as the foregoing provides an annual charge that is more closely related to the quantity of productive facilities being used. Gains and losses due solely to normal variations in asset lives are not recognized, and operating results are stated more meaningfully. The convenience of applying a uniform depreciation rate to a number of similar items also may represent a substantial advantage.

**Composite Depreciation**   The basic procedures employed under the group method for allocating the cost of substantially identical assets may be extended to include dissimilar assets. This special application of the group procedure is known as **composite depreciation**. The composite method retains the convenience of the group method, but because assets with varying service lives are aggregated to determine an average life, it is unlikely to provide all the reporting advantages of the group method.

A composite rate is established by analyzing the various assets or classes of assets in use and computing the depreciation as an average of the straight-line annual depreciation as follows:

| Asset | Cost | Residual Value | Depreciable Cost | Estimated Life in Years | Annual Depreciation Expense (Straight-Line) |
|-------|------|----------------|------------------|------------------------|---------------------------------------------|
| A | $ 2,000 | $ 120 | $ 1,880 | 4 | $ 470 |
| B | 6,000 | 300 | 5,700 | 6 | 950 |
| C | 12,000 | 1,200 | 10,800 | 10 | 1,080 |
|   | $20,000 | $1,620 | $18,380 |   | $2,500 |

Composite depreciation rate to be applied to cost: $2,500 ÷ $20,000 = 12.5%

Composite or average life of assets: $18,380 ÷ $2,500 = 7.35 years

It will be observed that a rate of 12.5% applied to the cost of the assets, $20,000, results in annual depreciation of $2,500. Annual depreciation of $2,500 will accumulate to a total of $18,380 in 7.35 years; hence 7.35 years may be considered the composite or average life of the assets. Composite depreciation would be reported in a single accumulated depreciation account. Upon the retirement of an individual asset, the asset account is credited and Accumulated Depreciation is debited with the difference between cost and residual value. As with the group procedure, no gains or losses are recognized at the time individual assets are retired.

After a composite rate has been set, it is ordinarily continued in the absence of significant changes in the lives of assets or asset additions and retirements having a material effect upon the rate. It is assumed in the preceding example that the assets are replaced with similar assets when retired. If they are not replaced, continuation of the 12.5% rate will misstate depreciation charges.

## Historical Cost Versus Current Cost Allocation

A difficult problem in accounting for property utilization arises in determining the periodic charges to revenues in periods of changing prices. In accounting practice, depreciation, depletion, and amortization have traditionally been viewed as an allocation of the acquisition cost over the life of the asset. This meaning can be observed in the definition of depreciation accounting adopted by the Committee on Terminology in the 1940s and still accepted today:

> *Depreciation accounting* is a system of accounting which aims to distribute the cost or other basic value of tangible capital assets, less salvage (if any), over the estimated useful life of the unit (which may be a group of assets) in a systematic and rational manner. It is a process of allocation, not of valuation. *Depreciation for the year* is the portion of the total charge under such a system that is allocated to the year. Although the allocation may properly take into account occurrences during the year, it is not intended to be a measurement of the effect of all such occurrences.[10]

Under this allocation view, the total amount charged against revenue is fixed by the acquisition cost less any estimated residual value. While the pattern of charges may vary with the allocation method used, the total amount charged against revenue cannot exceed the historical cost of the asset. For any group of assets at any given time, the cumulative amount charged against past revenues plus the remaining asset carrying or book value will equal the original acquisition cost adjusted by any additions or betterments.

[10]*Accounting Research and Terminology Bulletins*—Final Edition, "Accounting Terminology Bulletins, No. 1, Review and Resume" (New York: American Institute of Certified Public Accountants, 1961), par. 56.

## College Depreciation: FASB vs. GASB

In August 1987, the FASB issued Statement No. 93 that required all not-for-profit organizations, including public and private colleges and universities, to recognize depreciation in their external financial statements. Prior to the issuance of the statement, more than 90% of colleges and universities had not reported depreciation and many questioned its usefulness. However, the FASB adopted Statement No. 93 with a unanimous vote.

Soon after Statement No. 93 was adopted, the GASB (Governmental Accounting Standards Board), which has responsibility for setting accounting standards for governmental bodies, issued Statement No. 8 that exempted public colleges and universities from the FASB's depreciation rule. A severe issue of comparability arose since public universities would now be reporting under a different set of standards from that of private universities. Some private universities threatened to openly disregard the rule. Others declared their intention to ask Congress to force the FASB to back down. Bond-rating agencies promised not to lower the bond ratings of any institutions that refused to comply with the rule. In the face of all this opposition, the FASB issued Statement No. 99, delaying the effective date of the depreciation standard until January 1990.

The Financial Accounting Foundation (FAF), which oversees both the FASB and the GASB, was faced with a critical jurisdictional dispute. Clearly, the FASB had authority to set accounting standards for business entities. Clearly, the GASB had authority to set accounting standards for governmental entities. However, who had authority to set the standards for those special entities whose ownership could be either public or private, such as hospitals and universities? The FAF originally considered giving jurisdiction over all these special entities to the FASB. This was deemed unacceptable by many governmental officials and they threatened to withdraw their support from the FAF and establish their own independent body for setting governmental accounting standards. In late 1989, the FAF altered its position and gave the GASB authority over financial reporting by all governmental entities. For now, the comparability issue for special entities remains something that will have to be ironed out by the FASB and the GASB on a case-by-case basis.

This case illustrates how jurisdictional issues can significantly impact the setting of accounting standards. As the world community attempts to harmonize international accounting standards in the near future, this type of jurisdictional issue may be the most difficult problem addressed.

### Questions:

1. *What reasons are there for requiring colleges and universities to report depreciation? What arguments could be made against the requirement?*

2. *What dangers are there in jurisdictional disputes of this kind?*

Sources:

Dennis M. Patten, "Battle of the Boards: Identifying the Political Nature of the Standard-Setting Controversies," *Government Accountants Journal* (Fall 1988), p. 3.

News Report, "FAF Alters Position on FASB-GASB Jurisdiction," *Journal of Accountancy* (January 1990), p. 13.

Lee Berton, "Several Private Colleges May Ignore New Accounting Rule on Depreciation," *The Wall Street Journal* (February 4, 1988), p. 24.

As has been discussed previously, there are many accountants who advocate a charge against revenue based on a current asset value, i.e., the **replacement cost** or **current cost**. This allocation approach matches current rather than past costs against current revenues, resulting in a net income figure that better reflects income available for dividends and that is more useful for estimating future cash flows of a business entity. Noncurrent operating assets, like inventories, must be replaced, and that portion of current and future earnings needed for replacement will not be available for distribution to owners or for payments to creditors.

This problem has been recognized as a particularly serious one for utilities, since they must obtain approval from regulatory commissions for any changes in the rates they charge to customers. One of the significant cost factors used in determining the rate base is depreciation. The telecommunications area was especially hard hit in the 1980s as the divestitures arising from the court-ordered breakup of American Telephone and Telegraph Company placed new strains on the pricing structure. The following quotation summarizes the problem as it relates to depreciation:

### Traditional Depreciation Can't Keep Up

Depreciation is a big-ticket issue. The problem is that rapid technological advances and competition among telephone companies are making large portions of their plant and equipment obsolete long before the expiration of useful lives that are calculated under traditional depreciation accounting methods.

For more than a decade, the depreciation charges regulators have allowed telephone companies to pass on to their customers have fallen below what the companies need to recover their investment. The growing depreciation expense now represents by far the largest component of rising phone bills—far outstripping the cost added by divestiture. This has created a gap that some estimate as high as $25 billion between the reserves telephone companies have set aside for depreciation and the amounts they calculate they should have available to replace outmoded equipment. [11]

Historical cost is still the basis for financial statement reporting. However, various attempts have been made to modify the application of historical cost allocation to partially account for the impact of changing prices. Emphasis in this chapter is on the methods used to allocate the historical acquisition cost against revenue.

## AMORTIZATION OF INTANGIBLE ASSETS

The life of an intangible asset is usually limited by the effects of obsolescence, shifts in demand, competition, and other economic factors. Because of the difficulty in estimating such highly uncertain future events, in the past companies sometimes did not amortize the cost of intangible assets but assumed their value was never used up. This practice was frequently followed for trademarks, goodwill, and some franchises. The Accounting Principles Board, however, felt that eventually all intangible assets became of insignificant worth to the company. The Board, therefore, issued Opinion No. 17, requiring that the recorded costs of all intangible assets acquired after October 31, 1970—the effective date of the Opinion—be amortized over the estimated useful life. [12] Many companies do not amortize certain intangibles, notably goodwill, acquired prior to November 1, 1970, although amortization of these assets was encouraged by the Board.

[11]Touche Ross & Co., *Washington Briefing* (January 1986), p. 4.

[12]*Opinions of the Accounting Principles Board, No. 17,* "Intangible Assets" (New York: American Institute of Certified Public Accountants, 1970).

The useful life of an intangible asset may be affected by a variety of factors, all of which should be considered in determining the amortization period. Useful life may be limited by legal, regulatory, or contractual provisions. These factors, including options for renewal or extension, should be evaluated in conjunction with the economic factors noted above and other pertinent information. A patent, for example, has a legal life of 17 years; but if the competitive advantages afforded by the patent are expected to terminate after 5 years, then the patent cost should be amortized over the shorter period.

Although the life of an intangible asset is to be estimated by careful analysis of the surrounding circumstances, a maximum life of 40 years was established for amortization purposes. APB Opinion No. 17 included this limitation as follows:

> The cost of each type of intangible asset should be amortized on the basis of the estimated life of that specific asset and should not be written off in the period of acquisition.
>
> The period of amortization should not, however, exceed forty years. Analysis at the time of acquisition may indicate that the indeterminate lives of some intangible assets are likely to exceed forty years and the cost of those assets should be amortized over the maximum period of forty years, not an arbitrary shorter period.[13]

The requirement that the recorded cost of all intangible assets be amortized and the arbitrary selection of a 40-year life are of questionable theoretical merit. An analysis of the expected future benefits to be derived from a particular asset should be the basis for capitalizing and amortizing the cost of any asset, whether tangible or intangible. However, the very nature of intangible assets makes estimating their useful lives a difficult problem in practice.

The establishment by the APB of a 40-year maximum period for the amortization of intangible assets was not intended to determine the normal write-off period as 40 years. However, for some assets, such as goodwill and franchise costs, 40 years has become the most popular period to use. While it is difficult to determine exactly how long goodwill benefits a company, the amortization period should be established based on sound reasoning, not some arbitrary period of time. Some accountants feel that a five- to ten-year period should be used, because after that period, a company has probably built its own goodwill based on expenditures and actions during that period. Others feel that goodwill should be written off immediately against Equity because of the lack of comparability among companies, some of whom report purchased goodwill and others who do not. The degree of diversity in the amortization of intangible assets, especially goodwill, suggests that further guidelines may be forthcoming in this area.[14]

Amortization, like depreciation, may be charged as an operating expense of the period or allocated to production overhead if the asset is related directly to the manufacture of goods. In practice, the credit entry is often made directly to the asset account rather than to a separate allowance account. This practice is arbitrary, and there is no reason why charges for amortization cannot be accumulated in a separate account in the same manner as depreciation. The FASB requires disclosure of both cost and accumulated depreciation for tangible assets, but does not require similar disclosure for intangible assets. When amortization is recorded in a separate account, such an account is typically called Accumulated Amortization.

---

[13]*Ibid.*, pars. 28-29.

[14]The standard-setting organization for Great Britain considered the goodwill issue in the early 1980s, and issued an official pronouncement in 1984 that recognized two methods of amortizing goodwill: either an immediate write-off against Equity, which was preferred, or an amortization period of no more than 40 years. The second position agrees with the U.S. standard. The first position was carefully considered by the APB, and although it was recommended by the authors of Accounting Research Study No. 10, it was rejected as an acceptable alternative.

Amortization of intangible assets is made evenly in most instances, or on a straight-line allocation basis. APB Opinion No. 17 states:

> The Board concludes that the straight-line method of amortization—equal annual amounts—should be applied unless a company demonstrates that another systematic method is more appropriate.[15]

Although practice favors straight-line amortization, analysis of many intangibles such as patents, franchises, and even goodwill suggests that greater benefit is often realized in the early years of the asset's life than in the later years. In those instances, a decreasing-charge amortization seems justified. Monsanto Company summarized its procedures for amortizing intangibles in the following note:

### Exhibit 13—4    Monsanto Company

*NOTES TO FINANCIAL STATEMENTS*

*Depreciation and Amortization*

|  | 1987 | 1986 | 1985 |
|---|---|---|---|
| Depreciation | $421 | $423 | $477 |
| Amortization of intangible assets... | 225 | 218 | 88 |
| Obsolescence | 33 | 139 | 34 |
| Total | $679 | $780 | $599 |

Intangible assets are recorded at cost less amortization. The components of intangible assets, and their estimated remaining useful lives, were as follows:

|  | Estimated Remaining Life* | 1987 | 1986 |
|---|---|---|---|
| Patents | 6 | $1,057 | $1,234 |
| Goodwill | 35 | 639 | 653 |
| Other intangible assets | 25 | 257 | 257 |
| Total |  | $1,953 | $2,144 |

*Weighted average, in years, at December 31, 1987.

The cost of patents obtained in a business acquisition is initially recorded at the present value of estimated future cash flows resulting from patent ownership. The cost of patents is amortized over their legal lives. Goodwill is the cost of acquired businesses in excess of the fair value of their identifiable net assets, and is amortized over periods of 5 to 40 years. The cost of other intangible assets (principally product rights and trademarks) is amortized over their estimated useful lives.

## DEPLETION OF NATURAL RESOURCES

**Natural resources**, also called **wasting assets**, move toward exhaustion as the physical units representing these resources are removed and sold. The withdrawal of oil or gas, the

[15]*Opinions of the Accounting Principles Board, No. 17*, par. 30.

cutting of timber, and the mining of coal, sulfur, iron, copper, or silver ore are examples of processes leading to the exhaustion of natural resources. Depletion expense is a charge for the using-up of the resources.

## Computing Periodic Depletion

The computation of depletion expense is an adaptation of the productive-output method of depreciation. Perhaps the most difficult problem in computing depletion expense is estimating the amount of resources available for economical removal from the land. Generally, a geologist, mining engineer, or other expert is called upon to make the estimate, and it is subject to continual revision as the resource is extracted or removed.

Developmental costs, such as costs of drilling, sinking mine shafts, and constructing roads should be capitalized and added to the original cost of the property in arriving at the total cost subject to depletion. These costs are often incurred before normal activities begin.

To illustrate the computation of depletion expense, assume the following facts: land containing mineral deposits is purchased at a cost of $5,500,000. The land has an estimated value after removal of the resources of $250,000; the natural resource supply is estimated at 1,000,000 tons. The unit-depletion charge and the total depletion charge for the first year, assuming the withdrawal of 80,000 tons are calculated as follows:

$$\text{Depletion charge per ton} = (\$5,500,000 - \$250,000) \div 1,000,000 = \$5.25$$
$$\text{Depletion charge for the first year} = 80,000 \text{ tons} \times \$5.25 = \$420,000$$

The following entries should be made to record these events:

| | | |
|---|---|---|
| Land ............................................... | 250,000 | |
| Mineral Deposits ...................................... | 5,250,000 | |
| Cash ............................................. | | 5,500,000 |
| *To purchase mineral rights.* | | |
| | | |
| Depletion Expense ..................................... | 420,000 | |
| Accumulated Depletion (or Mineral Deposits) .......... | | 420,000 |
| *To record depletion expense.* | | |

If the 80,000 tons are sold in the current year, the entire $420,000 would be included as part of the cost of goods sold. If only 60,000 tons are sold, $105,000 is reported as part of ending inventory on the balance sheet.

When buildings and improvements are constructed in connection with the removal of natural resources and their usefulness is limited to the duration of the project, it is reasonable to recognize depreciation on such properties on an output basis consistent with the charges to be recognized for the natural resources themselves. For example, assume buildings are constructed at a cost of $250,000; the useful lives of the buildings are expected to terminate upon exhaustion of the natural resource consisting of 1,000,000 units. Under these circumstances, a depreciation charge of $.25 ($250,000 ÷ 1,000,000) should accompany the depletion charge recognized for each unit. When improvements provide benefits expected to terminate prior to the exhaustion of the natural resource, the cost of such improvements should be allocated on the basis of the units to be removed during the life of the improvements or on a time basis, whichever is considered more appropriate.

## Special Problems—Oil and Gas Properties

The preceding discussion relates to depletion of all natural resources. Special problems exist in the oil and gas industry in the determination of the asset cost to be used in computing depletion. Even though apparently valuable property rights are acquired, no one can truly measure their value until exploratory activities have been completed. The nature of oil exploration generally results in several dry wells for each "gusher" that is discovered. The accounting question is, "How should these exploratory costs be recorded? Are they part of the asset cost regardless of their success, or are they a period expense?"

Two methods of accounting have developed to account for exploratory costs. The first method is the full cost approach, and the second method is the successful efforts approach. Under the full cost approach, all exploratory costs are deferred and written off against revenues as depletion expense. Under the successful efforts approach, exploratory costs for unsuccessful projects are expensed, and only exploratory costs for successful projects are deferred as assets. Most large, successful oil companies follow the second approach. For example, Amoco Corporation included the following explanation of its depletion method in the notes to the 1987 financial statements:

### Exhibit 13—5    Amoco Corporation

---

***Costs Incurred in oil and gas producing activities—***
The corporation follows the successful efforts method of accounting. Costs of property acquisition, successful exploratory wells, all development costs (including $CO_2$ and certain other injected materials in enhanced recovery projects), and support equipment and facilities are capitalized. Unsuccessful exploratory wells are expensed when determined to be non-productive. Production costs, overhead, and all exploration costs other than exploratory drilling are charged against income as incurred.

---

For smaller companies, the full cost approach has been popular. This method encourages such companies to continue exploration without the severe penalty of recognizing all costs of unsuccessful projects as immediate expenses. Proponents of the full cost approach argue that often valuable exploratory information is discovered even when a "dry hole" is drilled. The cost of a producing well, therefore, should include these unsuccessful costs. Columbia Gas System, Inc., explains its use of full cost in a note reproduced in Exhibit 13—6.

The issue of how to account for exploratory costs of the oil and gas industry has attracted the attention of the FASB, the SEC, and even the U.S. Congress. When an apparent oil shortage developed in the 1970s, there was strong pressure placed on oil companies to expand their exploration to discover new sources of oil and gas. The FASB was encouraged to identify one of the two alternatives for recording exploratory costs as preferred. In 1977, it selected a form of the successful efforts approach, and issued FASB Statement No. 19, "Financial Accounting and Reporting by Oil and Gas Producing Companies." The smaller companies objected to this standard, arguing that their exploration activities would be less vigorous if they had to immediately expense their drilling costs. In 1979, the SEC issued its own standard that rejected both alternatives, and suggested adoption of a new method it called Reserve Recognition Accounting (RRA). This method was, in reality, a form of **discovery accounting** that would recognize as an asset the value of the reserves rather than their cost. Under public and congressional pressure, the FASB issued its Statement No. 25 that suspended its earlier standard, and effectively permitted again the use of either the full cost or successful efforts approach.[16]

When oil and gas prices declined, the SEC withdrew its support of RRA. However, the commission still favored some form of current-value disclosure. As a result, the FASB issued Statement No. 69 in 1982 which requires oil and gas producing companies to provide supplemental current-value disclosures.

### Exhibit 13—6    Columbia Gas System, Inc.

---

***Oil and Gas Producing Properties.*** The Corporation's subsidiaries engaged in exploring for and developing oil and gas reserves follow the full cost method of accounting. Under this method of accounting, all productive and non-productive costs directly identified with acquisition, exploration and development activities are capitalized in country-wide cost centers. If costs exceed the sum of the estimated present value of the cost centers net future oil and gas revenues and the lower of cost or estimated value of unproved properties, an amount equivalent to the excess is charged to current depletion expense. Gains or losses on the sale or other disposition of oil and gas properties are normally recorded as adjustments to capitalized costs.

---

## CHANGES IN ESTIMATES OF VARIABLES

The allocation of asset costs benefiting more than one period cannot be precisely determined at acquisition because so many of the variables cannot be known with certainty until a future time. Only one factor in determining the periodic charge for depreciation, amortization, or depletion is based on historical information—asset cost. Other factors—residual value, useful life or output, and the pattern of use or benefit—must be estimated. The question frequently facing accountants is how adjustments to these estimates, which arise as time passes, should be reflected in the accounts. As indicated in Chapter 4, a change in estimate is normally reported in the current and future periods rather than as an adjustment of prior periods. This type of adjustment would be made for residual value and useful-life changes. However, a change in the cost allocation method based on a revised expected pattern of use is a change in accounting principle and is accounted for in a different manner. Changes in accounting principles are discussed in a later chapter.

### Change in Estimated Life

To illustrate the procedure for a change in estimated life affecting allocation of asset cost, assume that a company purchased $50,000 of equipment and estimated a 10-year life for depreciation purposes. Using the straight-line method with no residual value, the annual depreciation would be $5,000. After four years, accumulated depreciation would amount to $20,000, and the remaining undepreciated book value would be $30,000. Early in the

---

[16]*Statement of Financial Accounting Standards No. 25,* "Suspension of Certain Accounting Requirements for Oil and Gas Producing Companies," (Stamford: Financial Accounting Standards Board, 1979).

fifth year, a re-evaluation of the life indicates only four more years of service can be expected from the asset. An adjustment must therefore be made for the fifth and subsequent years to reflect the change. A new annual depreciation charge is calculated by dividing the remaining book value by the remaining life of four years. This would result in an annual charge of $7,500 for the fifth through eighth years ($30,000 ÷ 4 = $7,500).

### Asset Cost Allocation—Change in Estimated Life (Straight-Line Method)

| End of Year | Depreciation Computation | Amount | Accumulated Depreciation |
|---|---|---|---|
| 1993 | $50,000 ÷ 10 = | $ 5,000 | $ 5,000 |
| 1994 | $50,000 ÷ 10 = | 5,000 | 10,000 |
| 1995 | $50,000 ÷ 10 = | 5,000 | 15,000 |
| 1996 | $50,000 ÷ 10 = | 5,000 | 20,000 |
| 1997 | ($50,000 − $20,000) ÷ 4 = | 7,500 | 27,500 |
| 1998 | ($50,000 − $20,000) ÷ 4 = | 7,500 | 35,000 |
| 1999 | ($50,000 − $20,000) ÷ 4 = | 7,500 | 42,500 |
| 2000 | ($50,000 − $20,000) ÷ 4 = | 7,500 | 50,000 |
| | | $50,000 | |

A change in the estimated life of an intangible asset is accounted for in the same manner, i.e., the unamortized cost is allocated over the remaining life based on the revised estimate. Because of the uncertainties surrounding the estimation of the life of an intangible asset, frequent evaluation of the amortization period should be made to determine if a change in estimated life is warranted. For example, assume a patent costing $51,000 is being amortized over 17 years. Amortization per year would be $3,000 ($51,000 ÷ 17). If, at the end of 5 years, the patent is estimated to have a remaining life of 4 years, the book value of $36,000 [$51,000 − ($3,000 × 5)] will be amortized over 4 years at $9,000 per year.

### Change in Estimated Units of Production

Another change in estimate occurs in accounting for wasting assets when the estimate of the recoverable units changes as a result of further discoveries, improved extraction processes, or changes in sales prices that indicate changes in the number of units that can be extracted profitably. A revised depletion rate is established by dividing the remaining resource cost balance by the estimated remaining recoverable units.

To illustrate, assume the facts used in the example on page 493. Land is purchased at a cost of $5,500,000 with estimated residual value of $250,000. The original estimated supply of natural resources in the land is 1,000,000 tons. As indicated previously, the depletion rate under these conditions would be $5.25 per ton, and the depletion charge for the first year when 80,000 tons were mined would be $420,000. Assume that in the second year of operation, 100,000 tons of ore are withdrawn, but before the books are closed at the end of the second year, appraisal of the expected recoverable tons indicates a remaining tonnage of 950,000. The new depletion rate and the depletion charge for the second year would be computed as follows:

Cost assignable to recoverable tons as of the beginning of the second year:
Original costs applicable to depletable resources . . . . . . . . . . . . . . . . . $5,250,000
Deduct depletion charge for the first year . . . . . . . . . . . . . . . . . . . . . . .     420,000
Balance of cost subject to depletion . . . . . . . . . . . . . . . . . . . . . . . . . . . $4,830,000

Estimated recoverable tons as of the beginning of the second year:

| | |
|---|---:|
| Number of tons withdrawn in the second year .................. | 100,000 |
| Estimated recoverable tons as of the end of the second year ...... | 950,000 |
| Total recoverable tons as of the beginning of the second year ..... | 1,050,000 |

Depletion charge per ton for the second year = $4,830,000 ÷ 1,050,000 = $4.60
Depletion charge for the second year = 100,000 × $4.60 = $460,000

Sometimes an increase in estimated recoverable units arises from additional expenditures for capital developments. When this occurs, the additional costs should be added to the remaining recoverable cost and divided by the number of tons remaining to be extracted. To illustrate this situation, assume in the preceding example that $525,000 of additional costs had been incurred at the beginning of the second year. The preceding computation of depletion rate and depletion expense would be changed as follows:

Cost assignable to recoverable tons as of the beginning of the second year:

| | |
|---|---:|
| Original costs applicable to depletable resources ................. | $5,250,000 |
| Add additional costs incurred in the second year ................ | 525,000 |
| | $5,775,000 |
| Deduct depletion charge for the first year ...................... | 420,000 |
| Balance of cost subject to depletion ........................... | $5,355,000 |

| | |
|---|---:|
| Estimated recoverable tons as of the beginning of the second year (as above) ................................................. | 1,050,000 |

Depletion charge per ton for the second year = $5,355,000 ÷ 1,050,000 = $5.10
Depletion charge for the second year = 100,000 × $5.10 = $510,000

Accounting is made up of many estimates. The procedures outlined in this section are designed to prevent the continual restating of reported income from prior years. Adjustments to prior-period income figures are made only if actual errors have occurred, not when reasonable estimates have been made that later prove inaccurate.

## Impairment of Tangible and Intangible Asset Values

Events sometimes occur after the purchase of an asset and before the end of its estimated life that impair its value and require an immediate write-down of the asset rather than making a normal allocation over a period of time. This type of **impairment** can occur with any asset, but it occurs with more frequency in relation to goodwill. Excerpts from financial statements of two companies illustrate the varying conditions that can create the need for recording an immediate loss.

### Exhibit 13—7    Amoco Corporation

In 1986, the corporation recorded a $300 million pre-tax charge for impairment of unproved oil and gas properties in addition to normal amortization. The charge is included in depreciation, depletion, and amortization expense in the Consolidated Statement of Income. The charge resulted from a reassessment of unproved acreage in light of changed economic conditions and unfavorable drilling results in certain high-cost areas. On an after-tax basis, the special charge reduced net income by $162 million or $0.63 per share.

**Exhibit 13—8     Inter-City Gas Corporation**

---

Pursuant to this reorganization and as a result of the losses incurred by KeepRite in the past two years, the Company has re-assessed its investment in KeepRite Inc. As a result of this re-assessment, it has been determined that the value of the underlying assets in KeepRite have been impaired by an amount of $4,697,000. Accordingly, the Company has written off goodwill of $4,697,000 as an extraordinary charge against income.

---

The timing for recognizing the impairment of an asset value is a matter of judgment. The authoritative accounting literature does not include a clear statement as to when impairment of assets is to be recognized. Since the publication in 1980 of an AICPA Issues paper, *Accounting for the Inability to Fully Recover the Carrying Amounts of Long-Lived Assets,* the FASB has considered adding this topic to its agenda, but work on the conceptual framework and other more pressing issues delayed an asset impairment project until November 1988. At that time, the FASB Staff was directed to prepare a discussion memorandum that would "focus on long-lived, physical assets with consideration of identifiable, intangible assets to be included in the discussion  document."[17] The discussion memorandum was issued on December 7, 1990, "Accounting for the Impairment of Long-Lived Assets and Identifiable Intangibles."

Continued consideration of reported asset values is necessary to assure that there still are future benefits to justify asset amounts. The write-down of an asset may be classified as an extraordinary item or as a special charge to operations depending upon the materiality of the item and the circumstances surrounding the impairment. The write-down of Amoco Corporation assets was a charge against operations, while the write-down of the goodwill for Inter-City Gas Corporation was an extraordinary charge. In anticipation of more guidance from the FASB on the timing of write-downs for noncurrent operating assets, disclosure of current asset values when they are lower than undepreciated cost would provide important information to users of financial statements. As one writer observed, "I believe such disclosure also would alleviate considerably the surprise that frequently accompanies business failures. A business failure almost always is preceded by a decline in the fair value of the assets of the enterprise."[18]

---

## ASSET RETIREMENTS

Assets may be retired by sale, exchange, or abandonment. Generally, when an asset is disposed of, any unrecorded depreciation or amortization for the period is recorded to the date of disposition. A book value as of the date of disposition can then be computed as the difference between the cost of the asset and its accumulated depreciation. If the disposition price exceeds the book value, a **gain** is recognized. If the disposition price is less than the book value, a **loss** is recorded. The gain or loss is reported on the income statement as "Other revenues and gains" or "Other expenses and losses" in the year of asset disposition. As part of the disposition entry, the balances in the asset and accumulated depreciation accounts for the asset are canceled. The following sections illustrate the asset retirement process under varying conditions.

---

[17]Memorandum to FAF Trustees from Dennis Beresford, "Agenda Decision—Addition of the Project on Impairment of Assets," November 16, 1988.

[18]Walter Schuetze, "Disclosure and the Impairment Question," *Journal of Accountancy* (December 1987), pp. 26-32.

## Asset Retirement by Sale

If the proceeds from the sale of an asset are in the form of cash or a receivable (**monetary asset**), the recording of the transaction follows the order outlined in the previous paragraph. For example, assume that on April 1, 1993, Firestone Supply Co. sells for $43,600 manufacturing equipment that is recorded on the books at cost of $83,600 and accumulated depreciation as of January 1, 1993, of $50,600. The company depreciates its manufacturing equipment on the books using a straight-line, 10% rate. It follows the policy of depreciating its assets to the nearest month.

The following entries would be made to record this transaction:

| | | |
|---|---:|---:|
| Depreciation Expense—Machinery | 2,090 | |
|     Accumulated Depreciation—Machinery | | 2,090 |
|     *To record depreciation for three months in 1993 ($83,600* | | |
|     *× .10 × 3/12).* | | |
| | | |
| Cash | 43,600 | |
| Accumulated Depreciation—Machinery | 52,690 | |
|     Machinery | | 83,600 |
|     Gain on Sale of Machinery | | 12,690* |
|     *To record sale of machinery at a gain.* | | |

*Computation of gain:

| | |
|---|---:|
| Sales price | $43,600 |
| Book value ($83,600 − $52,690) | 30,910 |
| Gain on sale | $12,690 |

The preceding entries could be combined in the form of a single compound entry as follows:

| | | |
|---|---:|---:|
| Cash | 43,600 | |
| Depreciation Expense | 2,090 | |
| Accumulated Depreciation—Machinery | 50,600 | |
|     Machinery | | 83,600 |
|     Gain on Sale of Machinery | | 12,690 |

## Asset Retirement by Exchange for Other Nonmonetary Assets

As indicated in Chapter 12, when operating assets are acquired in exchange for other nonmonetary assets, the new asset acquired is generally recorded at its fair market value or the fair market value of the nonmonetary asset given in exchange, whichever is more clearly determinable. This treatment is referred to as the "general case" and is the more common exchange transaction.

When accounting for exchanges of property, two questions must be asked: (1) Are the assets being exchanged similar in nature? and (2) Are the parties involved in the exchange in the same line of business, i.e., are they both either dealers of the assets or nondealers? If the answers to both of these questions are affirmative, and if the transaction results in a gain, a "special case" approach may be used to record the exchange. The general case will be illustrated first.

The entries required to record the general case for an exchange involving nonmonetary assets are identical to those illustrated in the previous section except that a nonmonetary asset is increased rather than a monetary one. Gains and losses arising from the exchange are recognized when the exchange takes place.

To illustrate, assume in the previous example that the retirement of the described asset was effected by exchanging it for delivery equipment that had a market value of $43,600. The entries would be the same as illustrated except that instead of a debit to Cash,

Delivery Equipment would be debited for $43,600. The gain would still be computed by comparing the book value of the machine and the market value of the asset acquired in the exchange.

| | | |
|---|---:|---:|
| Delivery Equipment........................................ | 43,600 | |
| Depreciation Expense...................................... | 2,090 | |
| Accumulated Depreciation—Machinery ..................... | 50,600 | |
|    Machinery ........................................... | | 83,600 |
|    Gain on Exchange of Machinery .......................... | | 12,690 |

If the machinery's fair market value were more clearly determinable than the value of the delivery equipment, the value of the machinery would be used to compute the gain or loss and to determine the value for the delivery equipment. Assume the delivery equipment is used and has no readily available market price, but the machinery had a market value of $25,000. Under these circumstances, a loss of $5,910 ($30,910 − $25,000) would be indicated, and the combined entry to record the exchange would be as follows:

| | | |
|---|---:|---:|
| Delivery Equipment........................................ | 25,000 | |
| Depreciation Expense...................................... | 2,090 | |
| Accumulated Depreciation—Machinery ..................... | 50,600 | |
| Loss on Exchange of Machinery .......................... | 5,910 | |
|    Machinery ........................................... | | 83,600 |

Often the exchange of nonmonetary assets includes a transfer of cash, since the nonmonetary assets in most exchange transactions do not have equivalent market values. The cash part of the transaction adjusts the market values of the assets received to those of the assets given up. Thus, if in the previous example the exchange of delivery equipment were accompanied by cash of $3,000, the loss would be reduced to $2,910 and the combined entry would be as follows:

| | | |
|---|---:|---:|
| Cash ..................................................... | 3,000 | |
| Delivery Equipment........................................ | 25,000 | |
| Depreciation Expense...................................... | 2,090 | |
| Accumulated Depreciation—Machinery ..................... | 50,600 | |
| Loss on Exchange of Machinery .......................... | 2,910 | |
|    Machinery ........................................... | | 83,600 |

In this example, the exchange involved assets that were dissimilar in nature: delivery equipment and machinery. If the exchange involved similar assets, e.g., a used truck for a new one, the same accounting entries would be required unless the exchange is between two parties in the same line of business. This special case is discussed in the following section.

## Asset Retirement by Exchange of Nonmonetary Assets—Special Case

Not all exchanges of nonmonetary assets have the features to justify the recognition of a gain. Sometimes an exchange of similar assets is made to facilitate one of the parties to the exchange in making a sale to an ultimate consumer. For example, the Tri-City Cadillac dealership has a buyer for a blue Eldorado but has only a red one in stock. Another dealership in a nearby town has a blue Eldorado and is willing to exchange its car for Tri-City's red one. This exchange of similar assets is not intended to be an earnings transaction for either party and, therefore, should not reflect any gain, even if the market values of the cars have increased since they were originally acquired from the manufacturer. Another example of such an exchange would occur if two manufacturing companies exchanged similar equipment that both companies used in the production process.

In both of these illustrations, similar assets were transferred between parties in the same line of business. In the first instance, both parties were dealers of automobiles. In the second example, both parties were nondealers of machines being used in the production process. In neither case was the earning process culminated.

When the Accounting Principles Board studied the exchange of nonmonetary assets issue, it determined that an exception to the general rule was needed when the exchange did not culminate the earning process for either party and a gain was otherwise indicated.[19] The exception provided that **no gain** is to be recognized for these special exchanges unless cash (boot) is received as part of the exchange. If a significant amount of cash is involved in the exchange, the transaction becomes a monetary exchange rather than a nonmonetary one. The Emerging Issues Task Force was asked to determine what is significant, and, in its *Bulletin 86-29*, it concluded that if the cash payment is 25% or more of the fair value of the exchange, the transaction should be considered a monetary exchange with the fair values used to determine a gain or loss. If the cash payment is less than 25%, the party paying the cash records no gain, but the party receiving the cash recognizes a proportionate share of the gain.[20] If the transaction indicates that a loss has occurred, the exception does not apply and the exchange is recorded as illustrated in the previous section. Thus four conditions must exist for the special case to apply:

1. The assets must be similar in nature; i.e., they must be expected to fulfill similar functions in the entity.
2. The parties to the transaction must be in the same line of business; i.e., they must both be dealers or both be nondealers.
3. A gain must be indicated in the transaction; i.e., the market value of the assets surrendered must exceed their book value.
4. If cash is involved, it is less than 25% of the fair value of the exchange.

To illustrate the special case, three examples are included below. In the first example, no cash is involved in the exchange. In the second example, the exchange includes a transfer of cash. The third example illustrates the general case when cash makes up 25% or more of the value of the transaction.

### Example 1    No Cash Involved

---

The Republic Manufacturing Company owns a special molding machine that it no longer uses because of a change in products being manufactured. The machine still has several years of service remaining. Through discussions with other companies in the industry, Republic has located a buyer, Logan Square Company. However, Logan Square is low on funds and suggests an exchange for one of its machines that could be used in Republic's packaging department. It is decided that both machines meet the definition of being similar in use and have the same market values. The following cost and market data relate to the two machines:

---

[19]*Opinions of the Accounting Principles Board, No. 29*, "Accounting for Nonmonetary Transactions," (New York: American Institute of Certified Public Accountants, 1973), pars. 20-23. The "same line of business" test was added by the Emerging Issues Task Force in Issue No. 86-29, "Nonmonetary Transactions: Magnitude of Boot and the Exceptions to the Use of Fair Value," *EITF Abstracts*, October 1, 1987, pp. 275-277.

[20]*EITF Issue No. 86-29*, "Nonmonetary Transactions: Magnitude of Boot and the Exceptions to the Use of Fair Value," *loc. cit.*

|                                          | Republic | Logan |
|------------------------------------------|----------|--------|
| Costs of machines to be exchanged ...................... | $46,000 | $54,000 |
| Book values of machines to be exchanged ................ | 14,000 | 18,000 |
| Market values of machines to be exchanged .............. | 16,000 | 16,000 |

The entry on Republic's books to record the exchange is as follows:

| | | |
|---|---|---|
| Machinery (new) ......................................... | 14,000 | |
| Accumulated Depreciation on Machinery ($46,000 − $14,000) .. | 32,000 | |
| Machinery (old) ....................................... | | 46,000 |

The entry on Logan's books to record the exchange is as follows:

| | | |
|---|---|---|
| Machinery .............................................. | 16,000 | |
| Accumulated Depreciation on Machinery ($54,000 − $18,000) .. | 36,000 | |
| Loss on Exchange of Machinery ........................... | 2,000 | |
| Machinery (old) ....................................... | | 54,000 |

Note that in Republic's entry, the special case is used. All four conditions are present: the machines are similar, both parties are nondealers, the market value of the asset surrendered exceeds its book value (an indicated gain), and no cash is involved. Thus, the value assigned to Republic's newly acquired packaging machine is the book value of its old molding machine.

In Logan's entry, however, the general case is used. The market value of the asset exchanged is less than the book value, so a loss is indicated. The molding machine, therefore, is recorded on Logan's books at its market value, the general-case solution.

## Example 2    Transfer of Cash

Assume the same facts as in Example 1, except that it is decided the molding machine has a market value of $16,000 and the packaging machine is worth $20,000. To make the exchange equal, Republic agrees to pay Logan Square $4,000 cash (20% of the fair value of the exchange) in addition to the molding machine. The entry on Republic's books for Example 2 is as follows:

| | | |
|---|---|---|
| Machinery (new) ......................................... | 18,000 | |
| Accumulated Depreciation on Machinery ($46,000 − $14,000) .. | 32,000 | |
| Machinery (old) ....................................... | | 46,000 |
| Cash .................................................. | | 4,000 |

As was true for Example 1, the facts of this case require Republic to use the special case. The market value of the assets surrendered ($16,000 + $4,000) exceeds their book values ($14,000 + $4,000). A $2,000 gain is thus indicated. The machines are similar in use and the parties are both nondealers. The gain, therefore, is deferred and not recognized. The new machine is recorded at $18,000, the market value of the asset received in the exchange ($20,000) less the deferred gain ($2,000).

In Example 2, the book value of the packaging machine on Logan Square's books is less than the market value, indicating a gain ($20,000 − $18,000, or $2,000). The similar assets and similar parties indicate the special case; however, because Logan Square received less than 25% cash as part of the transaction, generally accepted accounting principles specify that a portion of the $2,000 **indicated gain** should be recognized as having been earned. The amount to be recognized is computed using the following formula:

$$\text{Recognized gain} = \frac{\text{Cash received}}{\text{Cash received} + \text{Market value of acquired asset}} \times \text{Total indicated gain}$$

Using the figures from Example 2, Logan Square, therefore, would recognize $400 of the gain computed as follows:

$$\frac{\$4,000}{\$4,000 + \$16,000} \times \$2,000 = \$400$$

The recorded value of the molding machine on Logan's books is $14,400, the book value of the packaging machine exchanged less the cash received plus the gain recognized, ($18,000 − $4,000 + $400). Another way of computing the recorded value is by deducting the **deferred gain** from the market value of the asset received ($16,000 − $1,600, or $14,400).

The entry on Logan Square's books to record the exchange is as follows:

| | | |
|---|---:|---:|
| Cash ................................................ | 4,000 | |
| Machinery (new) ..................................... | 14,400 | |
| Accumulated Depreciation on Machinery ($54,000 − $18,000) .. | 36,000 | |
|     Machinery (old) ............................... | | 54,000 |
|     Gain on Exchange of Machinery ................. | | 400 |

While the exceptions to the general case seem complex, they occur in relatively rare instances. The general effect of the special case is to defer any indicated gain until the new asset is disposed of through sale, trade, or abandonment.[21]

## Example 3    Transfer of Cash Exceeding 25% of the Fair Value of the Exchange

Assume the same facts as in Example 2, except that it is decided that the molding machine has a market value of $15,000 and that Republic agrees to pay $5,000 cash to make the exchange equal. In this case, the cash equals 25% of the fair value of the exchange ($20,000), so the transaction is considered to be a monetary exchange with recognition of gains and losses. The entry on Republic's books would be:

| | | |
|---|---:|---:|
| Machinery (new) ..................................... | 20,000 | |
| Accumulated Depreciation—Machinery ................. | 32,000 | |
|     Machinery (old) ............................... | | 46,000 |
|     Cash .......................................... | | 5,000 |
|     Gain on Exchange of Machinery ................. | | 1,000 |

The entry on Logan Square's books would be:

| | | |
|---|---:|---:|
| Cash ................................................ | 5,000 | |
| Machinery (new) ..................................... | 15,000 | |
| Accumulated Depreciation—Machinery ................. | 36,000 | |
|     Machinery (old) ............................... | | 54,000 |
|     Gain on Exchange of Machinery ................. | | 2,000 |

Exhibit 13—9 summarizes the accounting for exchanges under the various conditions.

## Retirement by Involuntary Conversion

Sometimes retirement of noncurrent operating assets occurs because of extensive damage caused by such events as fire, earthquake, flood, or condemnation. Retirements caused by

[21]For a further discussion of the special case, see James B. Hobbs and D. R. Bainbridge, "Nonmonetary Exchange Transactions: Clarification of APB Opinion No. 29," *Accounting Review* (January 1982), pp. 171-175.

**Exhibit 13—9     Summary of Retirement or Exchange of Noncurrent Operating Assets**

| Retirement of Assets<br>Exchange of Assets | Recognize<br>All Loss | Recognize<br>All Gain | Recognize<br>No Gain | Recognize<br>Part Gain |
|---|---|---|---|---|
| Market value of assets surrendered < Book value of assets surrendered (loss condition) . . . | X | | | |
| Market value of assets surrendered > Book value of assets surrendered (gain condition): | | | | |
|   1. Dissimilar assets . . . . . . . . . | | X | | |
|   2. Similar assets: | | | | |
|     a. Earning culminated . . . . | | X | | |
|     b. Earning not culminated: | | | | |
|       (1) No cash involved . . . | | | X | |
|       (2) Cash given . . . . . . . . | | | X | |
|       (3) Cash received . . . . . . | | | | X |

Earnings process not culminated for similar assets if:
1. Cash involved < 25% of market value of assets received, and
2. Parties to transaction are both in same line of business.

Effects of above rules on valuation of assets acquired in a retirement or an exchange:
1. If all losses and gains are recognized, the recorded value of all assets received is equal to the market value of the assets surrendered.
2. If no gains are recognized, the recorded value of any nonmonetary asset received is the book value of the asset surrendered plus any cash given.
3. If partial gains are recognized, the recorded value of any nonmonetary asset received is the book value of the asset surrendered less any cash received plus the portion of the gain recognized.

Assumption: Fair market value of assets received and of assets surrendered are equal. If not, use market value of asset that is more clearly evident.

these types of uncontrollable events have been classified as involuntary conversions. Some of these events are insurable risks, and the occurrence of the event triggers reimbursement from an insurance company. If the proceeds exceed the book value of the destroyed assets, a gain is recognized on the books. If the proceeds are less than the book value, a loss is recorded.

If the loss was either not insurable or a company failed to carry insurance on the property, the remaining book value of the asset should be recorded as a loss. Because these types of events are unusual and infrequent, the gains and losses realized are often recorded as an extraordinary item. Of course, if the event has a high probability of recurrence, e.g., a factory built in a low area that frequently experiences flooding, the gain or loss may be classified as an ordinary item.

To illustrate the recording of an involuntary conversion, assume that a flood destroyed a factory building with a $1,200,000 cost and a book value of $350,000. If $400,000 was recovered from the flood insurance policy, the entry to record the gain would be as follows:

| | | |
|---|---|---|
| Receivable From Insurance Company . . . . . . . . . . . . . . . . . . . | 400,000 | |
| Accumulated Depreciation—Building . . . . . . . . . . . . . . . . . . | 850,000 | |
|   Building . . . . . . . . . . . . . . . . . . . . . . . . . . . . . . . . . . . . . . . | | 1,200,000 |
|   Gain on Involuntary Conversion . . . . . . . . . . . . . . . . . . . . . | | 50,000 |

In some cases, the involuntary conversion is caused by government condemnation of private property. Usually such proceedings require the condemning party to pay a fair market value for the assets seized. This generally results in a recognized gain. Some accountants have argued that since these proceeds are often reinvested in similar assets, the gain on such conversion should be deferred by reducing the cost of the new asset. The FASB, however, has indicated that the condemnation and the acquisition of new assets should be viewed as two separate transactions.[22] Thus the gain is recognized on the condemnation, and the new assets are recorded at their acquisition cost.

For example, assume that the Valley Mining Company had land condemned by the state for a state park. The cost of the land to Valley was $50,000. The agreed-upon market value was $260,000. The entry to record the cash receipt would be as follows:

| | | |
|---|---|---|
| Cash | 260,000 | |
| Land | | 50,000 |
| Gain on Condemnation | | 210,000 |

## BALANCE SHEET PRESENTATION AND DISCLOSURE

Tangible noncurrent operating assets, natural resources, and intangible assets are usually shown separately on the balance sheet. As indicated earlier in this chapter, both the gross cost and accumulated depreciation must be disclosed for depreciable assets. Such disclosure is not required for intangible assets and natural resources, and many companies report only net values for these assets. Because of the alternative cost allocation methods available to compute the charges for depreciation, amortization, and depletion, the methods used must be disclosed in the financial statements. Without this information, a user of the statements might be misled in trying to compare the financial results of one company with another. Cost allocation methods are normally reported in the first note to the financial statements, "Significant Accounting Policies." See IBM Corporation's disclosure of its significant accounting policies in Appendix A at the end of the text.

[22]*FASB Interpretation No. 30*, "Accounting for Involuntary Conversions of Nonmonetary Assets to Monetary Assets," (Stamford: Financial Accounting Standards Board, 1979).

## KEY TERMS

Accelerated cost recovery system (ACRS) 479
Amortization 473
Composite depreciation 485
Cost recovery periods 479
Current cost 490
Declining-balance depreciation methods 478
Decreasing-charge depreciation methods 476
Depletion 473
Depreciation 473
Double-declining-balance depreciation 478

Full cost approach 494
Group depreciation 485
Impairment 497
Involuntary conversions 504
Modified accelerated cost recovery system (MACRS) 479
Natural resources 492
Productive-output depreciation 485
Replacement cost 490
Reserve Recognition Accounting (RRA) 494
Residual (salvage) value 474

Service-hours depreciation 484
Similar assets 500
Straight-line depreciation 476
Successful efforts approach 494
Sum-of-the-years-digits depreciation method 477
Time-factor depreciation methods 476
Unit depreciation 485
Use-factor depreciation methods 484
Useful life 474

## QUESTIONS

1. Distinguish among depreciation, depletion, and amortization expenses.
2. What factors must be considered in determining the periodic depreciation charges that should be made for a company's depreciable assets?
3. Distinguish between the functional and physical factors affecting the useful life of a tangible noncurrent operating asset.
4. What role does residual or salvage value play in the various methods of time-factor depreciation?
5. Distinguish between time-factor and use-factor methods of depreciation.
6. The accelerated cost recovery system of depreciation is used for income tax purposes but may not be acceptable for financial reporting. Why is this true?
7. The certified public accountant is frequently called on by management for advice regarding methods of computing depreciation. Although the question arises less frequently, of comparable importance is whether the depreciation method should be based on the consideration of the property items as units, as groups, or as having a composite life.
   (a) Briefly describe the depreciation methods based on recognizing property items as (1) units, (2) groups, or (3) having a composite life.
   (b) Present the arguments for and against the use of each of these methods.
   (c) Describe how retirements are recorded under each of these methods.
8. What arguments can be made for charging more than an asset's historical cost against revenue?
9. What factors determine the period and method for amortizing intangible assets?
10. What procedures must be followed when the estimate of recoverable natural resources is changed due to subsequent development work?
11. Under what circumstances should an asset's remaining book value be written off immediately as a loss?
12. Why is 40 years used as the maximum number of years for amortizing an intangible asset?
13. (a) Distinguish between the "full cost" and "successful efforts" approaches to recording exploratory costs for oil and gas properties.
    (b) The SEC recommended a third approach be followed. What were its distinguishing characteristics?
14. Under what circumstances is a gain or loss recognized when a productive asset is exchanged for a similar productive asset?
15. (a) What are some types of involuntary conversions that can take place with property?
    (b) What are the arguments for and against recognizing gains and losses on such conversions?
16. Machinery in the finishing department of Universal Co., although less than 50% depreciated, has been replaced by new machinery. The company expects to find a buyer for the old machinery, and on December 31 the machinery is in the yard and available for inspection. How should it be reported on the balance sheet?
17. How should property, wasting assets, and intangibles be reported on the balance sheet? What note disclosure should be made for these assets?

## DISCUSSION CASES

### Case 13—1 (We don't need depreciation!)

The managements of two different companies argue that because of specific conditions in their companies, recording depreciation expense should be suspended for 1993. Evaluate carefully their arguments.

(1) The president of Guzman Co. recommends that no depreciation be recorded for 1993 since the depreciation rate is 5% per year, and price indexes show that prices during the year have risen by more than this figure.

(2) The policy of Liebnitz Co. is to recondition its building and equipment each year so that they are maintained in perfect repair. In view of the extensive periodic costs incurred in 1993, officials of the company feel that the need for recognizing depreciation is eliminated.

### Case 13—2 (Why write off goodwill?)

The Nevada Corporation purchased the Stardust Club for $2,000,000, which included $500,000 for goodwill. Nevada Corporation incurs large promotional and advertising expenses to maintain Stardust Club's popularity. As the annual financial statements are being prepared, the CPA of the

Nevada Corporation, Emily Teeson, insists that some of the goodwill be amortized against revenue. Teeson cites APB Opinion No. 17 that requires all intangible assets to be written off over a maximum life of 40 years. Mark Stevenson, the Nevada Corporation controller, feels that amortization of the purchased goodwill in the same periods as heavy expenses are incurred to maintain the goodwill in effect creates a double charge against income of the period. Stevenson argues that no write-off of goodwill is necessary. Indeed, goodwill has increased in value and should even be increased on the books to reflect this improvement. Evaluate the logic of these two positions.

### Case 13—3   (Is it really worth that much?)

International Enterprises, Inc., owns a building in Des Moines, Iowa that was built at a cost of $5,000,000 in 1982. The building was used as a manufacturing facility from 1983-1992. However, economic conditions have made it necessary to consolidate International's operations, and the building has been leased as of January 1, 1993, as a warehouse for ten years at an annual rental of $240,000. Taxes, insurance, and normal maintenance costs are to be paid by the lessee. At the end of the ten-year period, International may offer the lessee a renewal of the lease, or again use the building in its operations. The building is being depreciated on a straight-line basis over a forty-year life.

Petersen & Sons, a CPA firm, is completing the audit for 1993. Julie Ramos, a new staff auditor, has been assigned to review the building accounts and raises a question with Alison Crowther, the senior auditor on the job, concerning the carrying value of the Des Moines building. Julie had written a paper in school concerning accounting for the impairment of noncurrent operating assets. She feels the Des Moines building has been impaired and should be written down in value. Alison is unsure about the current position of the FASB on this issue, and invites Julie to prepare a memorandum recommending a specific write-down amount, with supporting justification. Prepare the memorandum, assuming current interest rates are 10%.

### Case 13—4   (Should alternative methods of depreciation be eliminated?)

The FASB receives recommendations from its advisory board as to areas it should consider for study. Depreciation accounting has not been addressed as a separate topic by the FASB, and several alternative methods are used for recording this expense on the books. Recognizing this situation, assume that a recommendation is made to the Board that a study be made of depreciation accounting with the objective of selecting one method as the only acceptable one. Those making the recommendation reason that only then will comparability in financial statements be achieved. Present the arguments for and against the FASB following the recommendation. If you were a member of the FASB, what would be your position?

### Case 13—5   (Which depreciation method should we use?)

The Atwater Manufacturing Company purchased a new machine especially built to perform one particular function on the assembly line. A difference of opinion has arisen as to the method of depreciation to be used in connection with this machine. Three methods are now being considered:

(a)   The straight-line method
(b)   The productive-output method
(c)   The sum-of-the-years-digits method

List separately the arguments for and against each of the proposed methods from both the theoretical and practical viewpoints.

### Case 13—6   (Should financial reporting follow tax legislation?)

During the 1960s and 1970s, the United States Congress used a tax measure known as the Investment Tax Credit to encourage companies to expand their investment base. Under these provisions, companies received reductions of their tax liabilities based on a percentage of new investments in noncurrent operating assets. This approach was used in lieu of reducing tax rates as a stimulus to expansion. In 1981, the adoption of the ACRS method of cost allocation for noncurrent operating assets added further stimulation to the economy by permitting companies to write off the cost of their property over a shorter than normal period.

In 1986, Congress passed a massive Tax Reform Act that significantly reduced tax rates for all taxpaying entities. At the same time, the Investment Tax Credit was eliminated and the ACRS legislation was replaced by a modified ACRS approach that lengthened the time period for the allocation. These latter provisions reduced the net impact of the reduced tax rates. Because elected government officials do not like to be identified with increased tax rates, there remains the possibility that further modifications to tax accounting for noncurrent operating assets will be made.

Should financial reporting for noncurrent operating assets be affected by tax legislation? Support your answer.

## Case 13—7    (How do we charge that motion picture cost to revenue?)

In today's high tech, high cost entertainment industry, motion pictures often have costs in the tens of millions of dollars. Of course, it is hoped that these movies will be box office winners, and that the revenues will exceed the cost outlay. With first runs, reruns, video reprints, video rentals, etc., it has become increasingly difficult to determine how the initial cost should be amortized against the revenue. Considering this industry and its characteristics, what amortization method would you suggest for these movie production costs?

## Case 13—8    (Is nothing sacred?)

FASB Statement No. 93 required all not-for-profit organizations to compute and report depreciation expense in their external financial statements. Previously, many not-for-profits, including many religious institutions, did not report depreciation expense. Although the implementation date of Statement No. 93 was delayed (by Statement No. 99), and may be delayed again, many are already upset about the idea of depreciating churches. Robert Anthony, a well-known professor of accounting at Harvard University was quoted as saying, "Depreciating cathedrals and churches is stupid." Monsignor Austin Bennett of Brooklyn claimed that the rule would cause "more trouble for American churches than all the sinners in their congregations." Robert K. Mautz in an article "Monuments, Mistakes and Opportunities," *Accounting Horizons*, June 1988, argues that buildings and monuments owned by governments and not-for-profit institutions may be more liabilities than assets because no revenue is generated from them, but they must be maintained. In considering this issue, the following questions and comments were raised in an accounting class:

1. Why do churches prepare external financial statements?
2. It is claimed that requiring churches to record depreciation expense will increase the cost of a church's annual audit. How?
3. One person was quoted in *The Wall Street Journal* as saying, "As some . . . communities change in character, so does the value of the churches. Our depreciation values would have to change every year."

How would you respond to these questions and comments in the class discussion?

Source: Lee Berton, "Is Nothing Sacred? Churches Fight Plan to Alter Accounting," *The Wall Street Journal* (April 16, 1987), p. 1.

## Case 13—9    (Let's take a bath!)

DeAngelo (1988) finds evidence suggesting that when the management of a company is ousted under fire, the new management tends to take an earnings "bath" after gaining control. A "bath" is a large reduction in earnings due to asset write-downs, reorganization charges, discontinuance of segments, and other extraordinary charges.

As an example, The Circle K Corporation declared Chapter 11 bankruptcy and also changed management during fiscal 1990. For the year, Circle K reported a reorganization and restructuring charge of $639 million, consisting primarily of write-downs of long-term assets. This contributed to a net loss for the year of $773 million, compared to average net income for the previous 4 years of about $40 million per year. Why might the new management of a company want to "take a bath" in its first year?

Sources:
Linda DeAngelo, "Managerial Compensation, Information Costs, and Corporate Governance," *Journal of Accounting and Economics* 10 (January 1988), pp. 3-36.
1990 Annual Report of The Circle K Corporation.

### Case 13—10  (But what is a reasonable life for my airplane?)

Airlines are often used as illustrations of firms depreciating the same assets but using different useful life and residual value assumptions. As an example, Continental Airlines depreciates its aircraft over a period of 28 years while Delta Airlines has a policy of depreciating its aircraft, many of which are the same Boeing aircraft Continental uses, over a period of 15 years. What might cause a firm to decide to increase the estimated useful life of a depreciable asset?

## EXERCISES

### Exercise 13—1  (Computation of asset cost and depreciation expense)

A machine is purchased at the beginning of 1993 for $36,000. Its estimated life is 6 years. Freight-in on the machine is $2,000. Installation costs are $1,200. The machine is estimated to have a residual value of $2,000 and a useful life of 40,000 hours. It was used 6,000 hours in 1993.

1. What is the cost of the machine for accounting purposes?
2. Compute the depreciation charge for 1993 using (a) the straight-line method and (b) the service-hours method.

### Exercise 13—2  (Computation of depreciation expense)

The Feng Company purchased a machine for $180,000 on June 15, 1993. It is estimated that the machine will have a 10-year life and a salvage value of $18,000. Its working hours and production in units are estimated at 36,000 and 600,000, respectively. It is the company's policy to take a half-year's depreciation on all assets for which is used the straight-line or double-declining-balance depreciation method in the year of purchase. During 1993, the machine was operated 5,000 hours and produced 70,000 units. Which of the following methods will give the greatest depreciation expense for 1993? (1) double-declining balance; (2) productive-output; or (3) service-hours. (Show computations for all three methods.)

### Exercise 13—3  (Inferring useful lives)

The following information is from the balance sheet of Hampton Company for December 31, 1993, and December 31, 1992:

|  | Dec. 31, 1993 | Dec. 31, 1992 |
|---|---|---|
| Cost—Equipment ............................ | $ 980,000 | $ 980,000 |
| Accumulated Depreciation—Equipment .......... | (550,000) | (330,000) |
| Cost—Buildings ................................ | 2,450,000 | 2,450,000 |
| Accumulated Depreciation—Buildings .......... | (340,000) | (230,000) |

Hampton did not acquire or dispose of any buildings or equipment during 1993. Hampton uses the straight-line method of depreciation.

If residual values are assumed to be 10% of asset cost, what is the average useful life of Hampton's (a) equipment? (b) buildings?

### Exercise 13—4   (Computation of depreciation expense)

Ray Construction purchased a concrete mixer on July 15, 1993. Company officials revealed the following information regarding this asset and its acquisition:

| | |
|---|---:|
| Purchase price | $125,000 |
| Residual value | $18,000 |
| Estimated useful life | 10 years |
| Estimated service hours | 38,000 |
| Estimated production in units | 500,000 yards |

The concrete mixer was operated by construction crews in 1993 for a total of 5,225 hours and it produced 77,000 yards of concrete.

It is company policy to take a half-year's depreciation on all assets for which is used the straight-line or double-declining-balance depreciation method in the year of purchase.

Calculate the resulting depreciation expense for 1993 under each of the following methods and specify which method allows the greatest depreciation expense:

1. Double-declining balance
2. Productive-output
3. Service-hours
4. Straight-line

### Exercise 13—5   (Computation of book and tax depreciation)

Midwest States Manufacturing purchased factory equipment on March 15, 1992. The equipment will be depreciated for financial purposes over its estimated useful life, counting the year of acquisition as one-half year. The company accountant revealed the following information regarding this machine:

| | |
|---|---:|
| Purchase price | $75,000 |
| Residual value | $9,000 |
| Estimated useful life (class life) | 10 years |

1. What amount should Midwest States Manufacturing record for depreciation expense for 1993 using the (a) double-declining-balance method? (b) sum-of-the-years-digits method?
2. Assuming the equipment is classified as 7-year property under the modified accelerated cost recovery system (MACRS), what amount should Midwest States Manufacturing deduct for depreciation on its tax return in 1993?

### Exercise 13—6   (MACRS computation)

The Timpanogas Equipment Company purchases a new piece of factory equipment on May 1, 1993, for $26,500. For income tax purposes, the equipment is classified as a 7-year asset. Because this is similar to the economic life expected for the asset, Timpanogas decides to use the tax depreciation for financial reporting purposes. The equipment is not expected to have any residual value at the end of the seven years. Prepare a depreciation schedule for the life of the asset using the MACRS method of cost recovery.

### Exercise 13—7   (Productive-output depreciation and asset retirement)

Equipment was purchased at the beginning of 1991 for $100,000 with an estimated product life of 300,000 units. The estimated salvage value was $4,000. During 1991, 1992, and 1993, the equipment produced 80,000 units, 120,000 units, and 40,000 units, respectively. The machine was damaged at the beginning of 1994, and the equipment was scrapped with no salvage value.

1. Determine depreciation using the productive-output method for 1991, 1992, and 1993.
2. Give the entry to write off the equipment at the beginning of 1994.

## Exercise 13—8  (Composite depreciation)

The Gold Crolon Co. records show the following assets:

| | Acquired | Cost | Salvage | Estimated Useful Life |
|---|---|---|---|---|
| Machinery .................... | 7/1/92 | $105,000 | $9,000 | 8 years |
| Equipment.................... | 1/1/93 | 33,000 | 1,500 | 5 years |
| Fixtures ...................... | 1/1/93 | 45,000 | 4,500 | 4 years |

For 1993, what is (a) the composite depreciation rate to be applied to cost using the straight-line method and (b) the composite life of the assets?

## Exercise 13—9  (Composite depreciation)

A schedule of machinery owned by Delgado Manufacturing Company is presented below:

| | Total Cost | Estimated Salvage Value | Estimated Life in Years |
|---|---|---|---|
| Machine A ............................ | $700,000 | $70,000 | 12 |
| Machine B ............................ | 200,000 | 20,000 | 8 |
| Machine C ............................ | 40,000 | — | 5 |

Delgado computes depreciation on the straight-line method. Based on the information presented, calculate (a) the composite depreciation rate and (b) the composite life of these assets.

## Exercise 13—10  (Group depreciation—closed group)

The NLG International Co. maintains its tools and dies on a closed group basis. A new group is created for each year's purchase of tools and dies. The assets are depreciated at a 25% rate beginning in the year following the acquisition year. Any gain or loss is deferred until final disposition of the entire group of assets. Assume that for 1992, $150,000 was spent for tools and dies. Disposition of these tools and dies was made as follows (assume that disposals occurred at the beginning of each year):

| Year | Cost | Disposition Cash Price |
|---|---|---|
| 1993 | $ 3,000 | $ 1,500 |
| 1994 | 22,000 | 9,000 |
| 1995 | 53,000 | 22,000 |
| 1996 | 42,000 | 17,500 |
| 1997 | 10,000 | 3,000 |
| 1998 | 20,000 | 2,000 |

Prepare all journal entries required to account for tools and dies for the years 1993-1998. All tools and dies are disposed of by the beginning of 1998.

## Exercise 13—11  (Group depreciation entries—open group)

Lundquist, Inc., uses the group-depreciation method for its furniture account. The depreciation rate used for furniture is 21%. The balance in the furniture account on December 31, 1992, was $125,000, and the balance in Accumulated Depreciation—Furniture was $61,000. The following purchases and dispositions of furniture occurred in the years 1993-1995 (assume that disposals occurred at the beginning of each year):

| | Assets Purchased— | Assets Sold | |
| Year | Cost (Cash) | Cost | Selling Price (Cash) |
|------|------------------|--------|----------------------|
| 1993 | $35,000 | $27,000 | $8,000 |
| 1994 | 27,600 | 15,000 | 6,000 |
| 1995 | 24,500 | 32,000 | 8,000 |

1. Prepare the summary journal entries Lundquist should make each year (1993-1995) for the purchase, disposition, and depreciation of furniture.
2. Prepare a summary of the furniture and accumulated depreciation accounts for the years 1993-1995.

### Exercise 13—12   (Depreciation of special components)

Towsey Manufacturing acquired a new milling machine on April 1, 1988. The machine has a special component that requires replacement before the end of the useful life. The asset was originally recorded in two accounts, one representing the main unit and the other for the special component. Depreciation is recorded by the straight-line method to the nearest month, residual values being disregarded. On April 1, 1994, the special component is scrapped and is replaced with a similar component. This component is expected to have a residual value of approximately 25% of cost at the end of the useful life of the main unit and because of its materiality, the residual value will be considered in calculating depreciation. Specific asset information is as follows:

Main milling machine:
    Purchase price in 1988 ....................................... $52,400
    Residual value ............................................. $4,400
    Estimated useful life ....................................... 10 years
First special component:
    Purchase price ............................................. $10,000
    Residual value ............................................. $250
    Estimated useful life ....................................... 6 years
Second special component:
    Purchase price ............................................. $15,250

What are the depreciation charges to be recognized for the years (a) 1988, (b) 1994, and (c) 1995?

### Exercise 13—13   (Accounting for patents)

The Deep South Co. applied for and received numerous patents at a total cost of $30,345 at the beginning of 1988. It is assumed the patents will be useful evenly during their full legal life. At the beginning of 1990, the company paid $7,875 in successfully prosecuting an attempted infringement of these patent rights. At the beginning of 1993, $25,200 was paid to acquire patents that could make its own patents worthless; the patents acquired have a remaining life of 15 years but will not be used.

1. Give the entries to record the expenditures relative to patents.
2. Give the entries to record patent amortization for the years 1988, 1990, and 1993.

### Exercise 13—14   (Depletion and depreciation expense)

On July 1, 1993, Leadville Mining, a calender-year corporation, purchased the rights to a copper mine. Of the total purchase price, $4,500,000 was appropriately allocable to the copper. Estimated reserves were 600,000 tons of copper. Leadville expects to extract and sell 10,000 tons of copper per month. Production began immediately. The selling price is $20 per ton.

To aid production, Leadville also purchased some equipment on July 1, 1993. The equipment cost $750,000 and has an estimated useful life of 8 years. However, after all the copper is removed from this mine, the equipment will be of no use to Leadville and will be sold for an estimated $30,000.

If sales and production conform to expectations, what is Leadville's depletion expense on this mine and depreciation expense on the new equipment for financial accounting purposes for the calender year 1993?

### Exercise 13—15   (Computation and recording of depletion expense)

Rich Strike Mining sought to increase reserves of a special mineral resource. During 1991, the company purchased a piece of property that was expected to retain some value after removal of the mineral resources was complete. Company records reveal the following:

> In the year 1991:
>> Purchase price for property............................... $4,450,000
>> Estimated supply of mineral resource ..................... 3,640,000 tons
>> Estimated property value after removal of mineral resource .. $650,000
>> Total resource removal this year ......................... 0 tons
> In the year 1992:
>> Developmental costs ..................................... $750,000
>> Total resource removal this year ......................... 0 tons
> In the year 1993:
>> Total resource removal this year ......................... 700,000 tons
> In the year 1994:
>> Estimated total resources to be recovered in future years
>> (based on new discoveries)................................ 3,660,000 tons
>> Additional developmental costs........................... $1,195,800
>> Total resource removal this year ......................... 850,000 tons

Show computations and entries made to recognize depletion for (a) 1993 and (b) 1994.

### Exercise 13—16   (Full cost and successful efforts)

Playfair Company is an oil and gas exploration firm. During 1993, Playfair engaged in 67 different exploratory projects. Only 9 of these projects were successful. The total cost of this exploration effort was $12 million, $2 million of which was associated with the successful projects. As of the end of 1993, production had not yet begun at the successful sites.

1. Using the successful efforts method of accounting for oil and gas exploration costs, how much exploration expense would be shown in Playfair's income statement for 1993? How much of the exploration cost will be capitalized and shown as an asset on Playfair's balance sheet as of December 31, 1993?
2. What would be your answer if Playfair uses the full cost method?

### Exercise 13—17   (Change in estimated useful life)

Zierbel Corporation purchased a machine on January 1, 1988, for $225,000. At the date of acquisition, the machine had an estimated useful life of 15 years with no salvage value. The machine is being depreciated on a straight-line basis. On January 1, 1993, as a result of Zierbel's experience with the machine, it was decided that the machine had an estimated useful life of 10 years from the date of acquisition. What is the amount of depreciation expense on this machine in 1993 using a new annual depreciation charge for the remaining 5 years?

### Exercise 13—18   (Change in estimated useful life)

Pierce Corporation purchased a machine on July 1, 1990, for $180,000. The machine was estimated to have a useful life of 10 years with an estimated salvage value of $10,000. During 1993 it became apparent that the machine would become uneconomical after December 31, 1997, and that the machine would have no scrap value. Pierce uses the straight-line method of depreciation for all machinery. What should be the charge for depreciation in 1993 under a new annual depreciation charge for the remaining life?

**Exercise 13—19  (Recording the sale of equipment with note)**

On December 31, 1993, Blodgett Corporation sold for $10,000 an old machine having an original cost of $50,000 and a book value of $6,000. The terms of the sale were as follows: $4,000 down payment, $3,000 payable on December 31 of the next two years. The agreement of sale made no mention of interest; however, 10% would be a fair rate for this type of transaction. Give the journal entries on Blodgett's books to record the sale of the machine and receipt of the two subsequent payments. (Round to the nearest dollar.)

**Exercise 13—20  (Recording the sale of equipment)**

Schuthess, Inc., purchased equipment costing $220,000 on June 30, 1992, having an estimated life of 5 years and a residual value of $40,000. The company uses the sum-of-the-years-digits method of depreciation and takes one-half year's depreciation on assets in the year of purchase. The asset was sold on December 31, 1994, for $75,000. Give the entry to record the sale of the equipment.

**Exercise 13—21  (Exchange of machinery)**

Assume that Coaltown Corporation has a machine that cost $52,000, has a book value of $35,000, and has a market value of $40,000. The machine is used in Coaltown's manufacturing process. For each of the following situations, indicate the value at which Coaltown should record the new asset and why it should be recorded at that value.

(a)  Coaltown exchanged the machine for a truck with a list price of $43,000.
(b)  Coaltown exchanged the machine with another manufacturing company for a similar machine with a list price of $41,000.
(c)  Coaltown exchanged the machine for a newer model machine from another manufacturing company. The new machine had a list price of $60,000, and Coaltown paid cash of $15,000.
(d)  Coaltown exchanged the machine plus $3,000 cash for a similar machine from Newton Inc., a manufacturing company. The newly acquired machine is carried on Newton's books at its cost of $55,000 with accumulated depreciation of $42,000; its fair market value is $43,000. In addition to determining the value, give the journal entries for both companies to record the exchange.

**Exercise 13—22  (Exchange of truck)**

On January 2, 1993, Bline Delivery Company traded with a dealer an old delivery truck for a newer model. Data relative to the old and new trucks follows:

| | |
|---|---:|
| Old truck: | |
|    Original cost ............................................................ | $12,000 |
|    Accumulated depreciation as of January 2, 1993 .................... | 9,000 |
|    Average published market price ..................................... | 1,700 |
| New truck: | |
|    List price ............................................................. | $15,000 |
|    Cash price without trade-in ......................................... | 14,000 |
|    Cash paid with trade-in ............................................. | 12,700 |

1. Give the journal entries on Bline's books to record the purchase of the new truck.
2. Give the journal entries on Bline's books if the cash paid was $10,700.

**Exercise 13—23  (Exchange of assets)**

The Laughlin Equipment Company exchanged the following assets during 1993. Prepare the journal entries on Laughlin's books for each exchange.

(a)  Exchanged with Loeb Equipment Company (dealer to dealer) a similar machine. Cost of machine exchanged, $25,000; book value of machine exchanged, $13,000; market value of machine exchanged, $15,000. No cash received.

(b) Same as in (a), except received $3,000 cash and machine with market value of $12,000.
(c) Purchased from Baker Manufacturing Company (dealer to nondealer) a new machine with a $50,000 list price. Paid $35,000 cash and a similar used machine; cost of machine exchanged, $40,000; book value of machine exchanged, $12,000; market value of machine exchanged, $10,000.

## PROBLEMS

### Problem 13—1   (Time-factor methods of depreciation)

A delivery truck was acquired by Navarro Inc. for $20,000 on January 1, 1992. The truck was estimated to have a 3-year life and a trade-in value at the end of that time of $5,000. The following depreciation methods are being considered:

(a) Depreciation is to be calculated by the straight-line method.
(b) Depreciation is to be calculated by the sum-of-the-years-digits method.
(c) Depreciation is to be calculated by the 150% declining-balance method.
(d) Depreciation is to be calculated using the modified accelerated cost recovery system for 5-year recovery property.

**Instructions:**   Prepare tables reporting periodic depreciation and asset book value over a 3-year period for each assumption listed.

### Problem 13—2   (Maintenance charges and depreciation of components)

A company buys a machine for $25,400 on January 1, 1991. The maintenance costs for the years 1991-1994 are as follows: 1991, $1,500; 1992, $1,200; 1993, $7,300 (includes $6,100 for cost of a new motor installed in December 1993); 1994, $2,100.

**Instructions:**

1. Assume the machine is recorded in a single account at a cost of $25,400. No record is kept of the cost of the component parts. Straight-line depreciation is used and the asset is estimated to have a useful life of 8 years. It is assumed there will be no residual value at the end of the useful life. What are the total expenses related to the machine for each of the first 4 years?
2. Assume the cost of the frame of the machine was recorded in one account at a cost of $19,600 and the motor was recorded in a second account at a cost of $5,800. Straight-line depreciation is used with a useful life of 10 years for the frame and 4 years for the motor. Neither item is assumed to have any residual value at the end of its useful life. What are the total expenses and losses related to the machine?
3. Evaluate the two methods.

### Problem 13—3   (Depreciation and the steady state)

Lyell Company started a newspaper delivery business on January 1, 1993. On that date, Lyell purchased a small pickup truck for $7,000. Lyell planned to depreciate the truck over 3 years and assumed a $400 residual value. During 1993 and 1994, Lyell's business expanded. On January 1, 1994, Lyell purchased a second truck, identical to the first. On January 1, 1995, Lyell purchased a third truck, again identical to the first two. During 1995, Lyell's growth leveled off. However, on January 1, 1996, Lyell bought another truck to replace the one (purchased in 1993) that had just worn out. All trucks purchased cost the same amount as the first truck.

**Instructions:**

1. Compute depreciation expense for 1993, 1994, 1995, and 1996 using both of the following methods:

   (a) straight-line
   (b) sum-of-the-years-digits

2. What general conclusions can be drawn from your calculations in (1)?

### Problem 13—4  (Group depreciation and asset retirement)

The Wright Manufacturing Co. acquired 20 similar machines at the beginning of 1989 for $75,000. The machines have an average life of 5 years and no residual value. The group-depreciation method is employed in writing off the cost of the machines. They were retired as follows:

| | |
|---|---|
| 2 machines at the end of 1991 | 8 machines at the end of 1993 |
| 4 machines at the end of 1992 | 6 machines at the end of 1994 |

Assume the machines were not replaced.

**Instructions:**   Give the entries to record the retirement of the machines and the periodic depreciation for the years 1989-1994 inclusive.

### Problem 13—5  (Composite depreciation)

Machines are acquired by Siegel Inc. on March 1, 1993, as follows:

| Machines | Cost | Estimated Residual Value | Estimated Life in Years |
|---|---|---|---|
| #301 | $46,000 | $6,000 | 5 |
| #302 | 20,000 | 2,000 | 6 |
| #303 | 20,000 | 4,000 | 8 |
| #304 | 18,000 | 1,500 | 6 |
| #305 | 26,000 | None | 10 |

**Instructions:**

1. Calculate the composite-depreciation rate for this group.
2. Calculate the composite or average life in years for the group.
3. Give the entry to record the depreciation for the year ending December 31, 1993.

### Problem 13—6  (Computation of asset cost and depreciation)

Geneva Corporation, a manufacturer of steel products, began operations on October 1, 1992. The accounting department of Geneva has started the plant asset and depreciation schedule presented on the next page. You have been asked to assist in completing this schedule. In addition to ascertaining that the data already on the schedule is correct, you have obtained from the company's records and personnel the information shown below and on page 517.

(a)  Depreciation is computed from the first of the month of acquisition to the first of the month of disposition.

(b)  Land A and Building A were acquired from a predecessor corporation. Geneva paid $812,500 for the land and building together. At the time of acquisition, the land had an appraised value of $72,000 and the building had an appraised value of $828,000.

(c)  Land B was acquired on October 2, 1992, in exchange for 3,000 newly issued shares of Geneva's common stock. At the date of acquisition, the stock had a par value of $5 per share and a fair value of $25 per share. During October 1992, Geneva paid $15,200 to demolish an existing building on this land so it could construct a new building.

**Geneva Corporation**
**Plant Asset and Depreciation Schedule**
**For the Years Ended September 30, 1993, and September 30, 1994**

| Assets | Acquisition Date | Cost | Salvage | Depreciation Method | Estimated Life in Years | Depreciation Expense Year Ended September 30, 1993 | 1994 |
|---|---|---|---|---|---|---|---|
| Land A .............. | October 1, 1992 | (1) | N/A* | N/A | N/A | N/A | N/A |
| Building A .......... | October 1, 1992 | (2) | $47,500 | Straight-line | (3) | $20,000 | (4) |
| Land B .............. | October 2, 1992 | (5) | N/A | N/A | N/A | N/A | N/A |
| Building B .......... | Under construction | 210,000 to date | — | Straight-line | 30 | — | (6) |
| Donated equipment .. | October 2, 1992 | (7) | 2,000 | Double-declining balance | 10 | (8) | (9) |
| Machinery A ......... | October 2, 1992 | (10) | 5,500 | Sum-of-the years-digits | 10 | (11) | (12) |
| Machinery B ......... | October 1, 1993 | (13) | — | Straight-line | 12 | — | (14) |

*N/A—Not Applicable

(d)  Construction of Building B on the newly acquired land began on October 1, 1993. By September 30, 1994, Geneva had paid $210,000 of the estimated total construction costs of $300,000. Estimated completion and occupancy is July 1995.

(e)  Certain equipment was donated to the corporation by a local university. An independent appraisal of the equipment when donated placed the fair value at $23,000 and the residual value at $2,000.

(f)  Machinery A's total cost of $110,000 includes installation expense of $550 and normal repairs and maintenance of $11,000. Salvage value is estimated at $5,500. Machinery A was sold on April 1, 1994.

(g)  On October 1, 1993, Machinery B was acquired with a down payment of $4,000 and the remaining payments to be made in ten annual installments of $4,000 each beginning October 1, 1994. The prevailing interest rate was 10%.

**Instructions:**   For each numbered item on the plant asset and depreciation schedule, determine the correct amount. (Round each answer to the nearest dollar.)                         (AICPA adapted)

### Problem 13—7  (Accounting for patents)

On January 10, 1986, the Wilkerson Company spent $54,000 to apply for and obtain a patent on a newly developed product. The patent had an estimated useful life of 10 years. At the beginning of 1990, the company spent $18,000 in successfully prosecuting an attempted infringement of the patent. At the beginning of 1991, the company purchased for $40,000 a patent that was expected to prolong the life of its original patent by 5 years. On July 1, 1994, a competitor obtained rights to a patent which made the company's patent obsolete.

**Instructions:**   Give all the entries that would be made relative to the patent for the period 1986-1994, including entries to record the purchase of the patent, annual patent amortization, and ultimate patent obsolescence. (Assume the company's accounting period is the calender year.)

### ▦ Problem 13—8  (Financial statements for mining company)

The Findlay Corp. was organized on January 2, 1993. It was authorized to issue 74,000 shares of common stock, par $50. On the date of organization, it sold 20,000 shares at par and gave the remaining shares in exchange for certain land bearing recoverable ore deposits estimated by geologists at 900,000 tons. The property is deemed to have a value of $2,700,000 with no residual value.

During 1993, purchases of mine buildings and equipment totaled $250,000. During the year, 75,000 tons were mined; 8,000 tons of this amount were on hand unsold on December 31, the balance of the tonnage being sold for cash at $17 per ton. Expenses incurred and paid for during the year, exclusive of depletion and depreciation, were as follows:

| | |
|---|---|
| Mining | $173,500 |
| Delivery | 20,000 |
| General and administrative | 19,500 |

Cash dividends of $2 per share were declared on December 31, payable January 15, 1994.

It is believed that buildings and sheds will be useful only over the life of the mine; hence depreciation is to be recognized in terms of mine output.

**Instructions:**  Prepare an income statement and a balance sheet for 1993. Submit working papers showing the development of statement data. Ignore income taxes.

## Problem 13—9  (Computation of depletion and depreciation)

The Delta Mining Company paid $2,700,000 in 1992 for property with a supply of natural resources estimated at 2,000,000 tons. The estimated cost of restoring the land for use after the resources are exhausted is $225,000. After the land is restored, it will have an estimated value of $325,000. Equipment was purchased at a cost of $825,000. Buildings, such as bunkhouses and a mess hall, were constructed on the site for $175,000. The useful lives of the buildings and equipment are expected to terminate upon exhaustion of the natural resources. Operations were not begun until January 1, 1993. In 1993, resources removed totaled 500,000 tons. During 1994, an additional discovery was made indicating that available resources subsequent to 1994 will total 1,730,000 tons. During 1994, 770,000 tons of resources were removed.

**Instructions:**  Compute the amounts of depletion expense and depreciation expense for 1992, 1993, and 1994.

## Problem 13—10  (Computation of depreciation and depletion)

The following independent situations describe facts concerning the ownership of various assets.

(a)  The Dewey Company purchased a tooling machine in 1983 for $60,000. The machine was being depreciated on the straight-line method over an estimated useful life of 20 years, with no salvage value. At the beginning of 1993, when the machine had been in use for 10 years, Dewey paid $12,000 to overhaul the machine. As a result of this improvement, Dewey estimated that the useful life of the machine would be extended an additional 5 years.

(b)  Emerson Manufacturing Co., a calendar-year company, purchased a machine for $65,000 on January 1, 1991. At the date of purchase, Emerson incurred the following additional costs:

| | |
|---|---|
| Loss on sale of old machinery | $1,500 |
| Freight-in | 500 |
| Installation cost | 2,000 |
| Testing costs prior to regular operation | 400 |

The estimated salvage value of the machine was $5,000 and Emerson estimated that the machine would have a useful life of 20 years, with depreciation being computed on the straight-line method. In January 1993, accessories costing $4,860 were added to the machine in order to reduce its operating costs. These accessories neither prolonged the machine's life nor did they provide any additional salvage value.

(c)  On July 1, 1993, Lund Corporation purchased equipment at a cost of $34,000. The equipment has an estimated salvage value of $3,000 and is being depreciated over an estimated life of eight years under the double-declining-balance method of depreciation. For the six months ended December 31, 1993, Lund recorded one-half year's depreciation.

(d)  The Aiken Company acquired a tract of land containing an extractable natural resource. Aiken is required by its purchase contract to restore the land to a condition suitable for recreational use after it has extracted the natural resource. Geological surveys estimate that the recoverable reserves will be 3,800,000 tons, and that the land will have a value of $500,000 after restoration. Relevant cost information follows:

| | |
|---|---|
| Land ....................................................... | $9,000,000 |
| Estimated restoration costs....................................... | $1,000,000 |
| Tons mined and sold in 1993 ...................................... | 700,000 |

(e) In January 1993, Marcus Corporation entered into a contract to acquire a new machine for its factory. The machine, which had a cash price of $200,000, was paid for as follows:

| | |
|---|---|
| Down payment.............................................. | $ 30,000 |
| Notes payable in 10 equal monthly installments, including interest at 10% ....................................................... | 150,000 |
| 500 shares of Marcus common stock with an agreed value of $50 per share....................................................... | 25,000 |
| Total ..................................................... | $205,000 |

Prior to the machine's use, installation costs of $7,000 were incurred. The machine has an estimated useful life of 10 years and an estimated salvage value of $10,000. The straight-line method of depreciation is used.

**Instructions:** In each case, compute the amount of depreciation or depletion for 1993.

## Problem 13—11 (Depreciation and the cash flow statement)

Hutton Company is a manufacturing firm. Work-in-process and finished goods inventories for December 31, 1993, and December 31, 1992, are listed below.

| | Dec. 31, 1993 | Dec. 31,1992 |
|---|---|---|
| Work-in-process inventory (including depreciation) ...................................... | $ 60,000 | $ 63,000 |
| Finished goods inventory (including depreciation) ...................................... | 131,000 | 120,000 |

Depreciation is a major portion of Hutton's overhead, and the inventories listed above include depreciation in the following amounts:

| | Dec. 31, 1993 | Dec. 31,1992 |
|---|---|---|
| Depreciation included in work-in-process inventory ......................................... | $14,000 | $13,000 |
| Depreciation included in finished goods inventory ......................................... | 30,000 | 32,000 |

Hutton's net income for 1993 was $50,000. General and administrative expenses for the year included $16,000 in depreciation related to non-manufacturing functions.

**Instructions:** Compute net cash flow from operating activities for Hutton Company for 1993. Assume that the levels of all current assets (except for inventories) and all current liabilities were unchanged from beginning of year to end of year.

## Problem 13—12 (Tax depreciation methods and the time value of money)

The following two depreciation methods are acceptable for tax purposes:

(a) Straight-line with a half-year convention. The half-year convention is the assumption that all assets are acquired in the middle of the year. Therefore, a half-year's depreciation is allowed in the first year.

(b) 200% declining-balance with a half-year convention. There is a switchover to straight-line depreciation on the remaining cost when straight-line yields a larger amount than does 200% declining-balance.

On January 1, 1993, Burnet Company purchased a piece of equipment for $500,000. The equipment has an estimated useful life of 5 years and no estimated residual value.

**Instructions:**

1. For tax purposes, depreciation reduces taxes payable by reducing taxable income. If the tax rate is 40%, for example, a $100 depreciation deduction will reduce taxes by $40. Ignoring the time value of money, calculate the total reduction in taxes Burnet will realize through the recovery of the asset cost over the life of the equipment. Assume that the tax rate is 40%. Is the answer the same for each of the acceptable depreciation methods?
2. For each of the acceptable methods, compute the present value (as of January 1, 1993) of the depreciation tax savings. Assume that the appropriate interest rate is 10% and that the tax savings occur at the end of the year. Use the present value tables in Chapter 7.
3. Should a company be required to use the same depreciation method in its financial statements as it uses for tax purposes?

## Problem 13—13    (Exchange of assets)

A review of the books of Lakeshore Electric Co. disclosed that there were five transactions involving gains and losses on the exchange of fixed assets. The transactions were recorded as indicated in the following ledger accounts:

| | Cash | | | | Buildings and Equipment | | |
|---|---|---|---|---|---|---|---|
| (b) | 5,000 | (e) | 1,000 | (a) | 10,000 | (c) | 118,000 |
| (c) | 6,000 | | | (b) | 25,000 | (d) | 850,000 |
| | | | | (d) | 550,000 | | |

| | Accum. Depr.—Buildings and Equipment | | | Intangible Assets | |
|---|---|---|---|---|---|
| (c) | 110,000 | | (e) | 1,000 | |
| (d) | 390,000 | | | | |

| | Gain on Exchange—Buildings and Equipment | | | Loss on Exchange—Buildings and Equipment | |
|---|---|---|---|---|---|
| | | (a) | 10,000 | (c) | 2,000 |
| | | (b) | 30,000 | | |
| | | (d) | 90,000 | | |

Investigation disclosed the following facts concerning these dealer-to-dealer transactions:

(a) Exchanged a piece of equipment with a $50,000 original cost, $20,000 book value, and $30,000 current market value for a piece of similar equipment owned by Highlite Electric that had a $60,000 original cost, $10,000 book value, and a $30,000 current market value.
(b) Exchanged a machine, cost $70,000, book value $10,000, current market value $40,000, for a similar machine, market value $35,000, and $5,000 in cash.
(c) Exchanged a building, cost $150,000, book value $40,000, current market value $30,000, for a building with market value of $24,000 plus cash of $6,000.
(d) Exchanged a factory building, cost $850,000, book value $460,000, current market value $550,000, for equipment owned by Romeo Inc. that had an original cost of $900,000, accumulated depreciation of $325,000, and current market value of $550,000.
(e) Exchanged a patent, cost $12,000, book value $6,000, current market value $3,000 and cash of $1,000 for another patent with market value of $4,000.

**Instructions:**   Analyze each recorded transaction as to its compliance with generally accepted accounting principles. Prepare adjusting journal entries where required.

## Problem 13—14    (Exchange of assets)

The Mutual Development Co. acquired the following assets in exchange for various nonmonetary assets:

1993

Mar. 15   Acquired from another company a computerized lathe in exchange for three old lathes. The old lathes had a total cost of $35,000 and had a remaining book value of $14,000. The new lathe had a market value of $22,000, approximately the same value as the three old lathes.

June   1   Acquired 200 acres of land by issuing 3,000 shares of common stock with par value of $10 and market value of $90. Market analysis reveals that the market value of the stock was a reasonable value for the land.

July  15   Acquired a used piece of heavy, earth-moving equipment, market value $120,000, by exchanging a used molding machine with a market value of $20,000 (book value $8,000; cost $40,000) and land with a market value of $110,000 (cost $40,000). Cash of $10,000 was received by Mutual Development Co. as part of the transaction.

Aug. 15   Acquired a patent, franchise, and copyright for two used milling machines. The book value of each milling machine was $1,500 and each had originally cost $10,000. The market value of each machine is $12,500. It is estimated that the patent and franchise have about the same market values, and the market value of the copyright is 50% of the market value of the patent.

Nov.   1   Acquired from a dealer a new packaging machine for four old packaging machines. The old machines had a total cost of $50,000 and a total remaining book value of $20,000. The new packaging machine has an indicated market value of $30,000, approximately the same value as the four machines.

**Instructions:**   Prepare the journal entries required on Mutual Development Co.'s books to record the exchanges.

## Problem 13—15   (Balance sheet presentation of noncurrent operating assets)

The following account balances pertain to the Liberty Company:

| Account Title | Debit | Credit |
|---|---|---|
| Equipment........................................... | $   675,000 | |
| Goodwill ........................................... | 435,000 | |
| Inventory .......................................... | 90,000 | |
| Land .............................................. | 400,000 | |
| Franchises ......................................... | 260,000 | |
| Cash .............................................. | 65,000 | |
| Accounts Receivable................................ | 137,000 | |
| Buildings .......................................... | 1,400,000 | |
| Patents ............................................ | 15,000 | |
| Notes Receivable ................................... | 456,000 | |
| Accumulated Depreciation—Equipment ............... | | $   365,000 |
| Accounts Payable .................................. | | 147,000 |
| Notes Payable ..................................... | | 1,500,000 |
| Accumulated Depreciation—Buildings ............... | | 385,000 |

Additional information:

(a)   Notes payable in the amount of $600,000 are secured by a direct lien on the building.

(b)   The company uses the sum-of-the-years-digits method of cost allocation for buildings and equipment and uses straight-line for patents, franchises, and goodwill.

(c)   Inventory valuation was made using the retail method.

**Instructions:**   Prepare the land, buildings, and equipment section and the intangible asset section of the balance sheet.

# CHAPTER 14

## Long-Term Investments in Equity Securities and Other Assets

---

**CHAPTER TOPICS**

**Accounting for Long-Term Investments in Stocks**

**The Cost Method**

**The Equity Method**

**Accounting for Long-Term Investments in Funds**

**Reporting Long-Term Investments on the Balance Sheet**

---

The 1980s, termed the "Decade of the Deal," saw more intercorporate investment than any other period in the history of business. The decade culminated with the $24.7 billion purchase of RJR Nabisco by Kohlberg Kravis Roberts.

Companies generally make investments to receive a return *of* the investment as well as to earn a return *on* the investment in the form of dividends, interest, or gains from appreciation upon sale or maturity of the investment. In addition, a company may invest in the stock of another company as a means of diversifying its products or services or to exercise significant influence over that company. For example, if Company A buys most of its raw materials from Company B, Company A may seek to purchase a substantial amount of Company B's stock to ensure a source for its raw materials at favorable prices. Another similar reason is to ensure a distribution outlet for a company's finished product.

The investment in stock of another company represents an ownership interest in the net operating assets of that company. Sometimes an investment involves the acquisition of all the stock of a company, and therefore represents a 100 percent ownership interest in the assets and liabilities of the acquired company. However, 100 percent ownership is not required to effectively control a company. Because of the diversity in ownership of most large corporations, many can be controlled with less than 50 percent ownership.

From the standpoint of the owner, investments are either temporary or long-term. As discussed in Chapter 8, investments are classified as temporary or current only where (1) they are readily marketable and (2) it is management's intent to use them in meeting current cash requirements. The general guideline is whether the investment is expected to be converted to cash within a year or the operating cycle, whichever is longer. Investments not meeting these tests are considered long-term or noncurrent investments and are usually reported on the balance sheet under a noncurrent heading, as illustrated in this chapter and in the balance sheet for IBM Corporation, reproduced in Appendix A.

Long-term investments include a variety of assets. Among the most common are:

1. Equity securities, including both preferred and common stock.
2. Bonds, mortgages, and similar debt instruments.
3. Funds, e.g., for debt retirement, stock redemption, or other special purposes.
4. Miscellaneous items, such as real estate held for appreciation, advances to affiliates, equity in joint ventures and partnerships, and interests in life insurance contracts or in trusts and estates.

The primary emphasis in this chapter will be on accounting for long-term investments in equity securities. Accounting for funds also will be discussed briefly. Accounting for investments in bonds and long-term notes is considered in Chapter 16. Investments in stock rights, warrants, and options are covered in Chapter 17.

## LONG-TERM INVESTMENTS IN EQUITY SECURITIES

One of the characteristics of a free enterprise economy is the considerable level of intercorporate investment. As indicated previously, a corporation may acquire securities of another established corporation for a variety of reasons. Whatever the specific objective, an investment in the securities of another corporate entity is expected to enhance the economic well-being of the acquiring company. The accounting and reporting issues for long-term investments in equity securities (stocks) listed below are discussed in the following sections:

1. Acquisition of stocks
2. Accounting for long-term investments in stocks—consolidation, cost method, and equity method
3. Disclosures for long-term investments in equity securities

### Acquisition of Stocks

The acquisition of long-term investments in stocks follows the same general principles as those for temporary investments in stocks, as explained in Chapter 8.

Shares of stock are usually purchased for cash through stock exchanges (e.g., New York, American, or regional exchanges) and from individuals and institutional investors rather than from the corporations themselves. The investment is recorded at the amount paid, including brokers' commissions, taxes, and other fees incidental to the purchase price. Even when part of the purchase price is deferred, the full cost should be recorded as the investment in stock, with a liability account established for the amount yet to be paid. If stock is acquired in exchange for properties or services instead of cash, the fair market value of the consideration given or the value at which the stock is currently selling,

## Financing a Takeover

In April of 1990, Michael Milken pleaded guilty to charges of manipulating securities markets, evading net capital tax rules, and cheating the government of taxes. Milken was fined $600 million and sentenced to time in federal prison.

During the 1980s, Milken, known as "King of the Junk Bonds," was a major financier of corporate mergers and acquisitions. He used junk bonds—bonds assigned a low grade rating by Moodys and Standard & Poors—to allow companies access to credit markets. As an example, Milken, in conjunction with Drexel, Brunham Lambert, used junk bonds to help finance the decade's biggest takeover, the $24.7 billion takeover of RJR Nabisco by Kohlberg Kravis Roberts.

In addition to using junk bonds to finance takeovers, some corporate raiders spin off the assets of the acquired business to reduce the debt incurred in buying the business. When Merv Griffen purchased Resorts International from Donald Trump, thereby incurring $325 million in additional debt, he had hoped to sell Resorts' casinos in the Bahamas and vacant land in Atlantic City and use the proceeds to reduce the debt. When this strategy failed, Resorts International was forced into bankruptcy.

### Questions:

1. *What are alternative methods for financing corporate takeovers?*
2. *Why would companies finance acquisitions using high-interest junk bonds instead of, for example, stock issuances?*
3. *As junk-bond deals unravel and corporations are unable to make interest and principal payments, who are the big losers? Investors? Suppliers? Bondholders? Management?*
4. *Is spinning off portions of the acquired company in the best interest of shareholders? in the best interest of bondholders?*

Source:   Michael Galen with Dean Foust and Eric Schine, "Guilty, Your Honor," *Business Week*, May 7, 1990.

---

whichever is more clearly determinable, should be used as the basis for recording the investment. If two or more securities are acquired for a lump-sum price, the cost should be allocated to each security in an equitable manner, as illustrated in earlier chapters.

### Accounting for Long-Term Investments in Stocks

In accounting for long-term investments in stocks, one of three basic methods must be used: consolidation, cost, or equity. Which method is appropriate depends on the **control or degree of influence exercised by the acquiring company (investor) over the acquired company (investee).**

**Choosing Among Consolidation, Cost, and Equity Methods**   When one company acquires a majority voting interest in another company through the acquisition of **more than 50 percent** of its voting common stock, the acquiring company has control over the acquired company. The investor and investee are referred to respectively as the parent company and the subsidiary company. Where control exists, the consolidation method is required. This means that the financial statement balances of the parent and subsidiary companies are combined or consolidated for financial reporting purposes even though the companies continue to operate as separate entities. In the consolidation process, any intercompany transactions are eliminated, e.g., any sales and purchases between the parent and subsidiary companies. By eliminating all intercompany transactions, the combined balances or consolidated totals appropriately reflect the financial position and results of operation of the total economic unit. This treatment reflects the fact that majority ownership of common stock assures control by the parent over the decision-making processes of the subsidiary.

Previous accounting standards allowed separate reporting for certain majority-owned subsidiaries if those subsidiaries had "nonhomogeneous" operations, a large minority interest, or a foreign location. Separate reporting by subsidiaries occurred most often when the operations of the subsidiary and parent were significantly different (i.e., nonhomogeneous). Typically, the subsidiary was engaged in finance, insurance, leasing, or real estate, while the parent company was a manufacturer or merchandiser. Examples include General Motors Acceptance Corporation (GMAC) and IBM Credit Corporation, which are finance companies that are wholly owned by General Motors Corp. and IBM Corp., respectively. Traditionally, the financial statements of these subsidiaries were not consolidated with those of their respective parent companies.

With the issuance of Statement of Financial Accounting Standards No. 94, the FASB now requires the consolidation of all majority-owned subsidiaries unless control is temporary or does not rest with the majority owner (as, for instance, where the subsidiary is in legal reorganization or in bankruptcy).[1] Thus, even though a subsidiary has nonhomogeneous operations, a large minority interest, or a foreign location, it should be consolidated. The reporting entity is to be the total economic unit consisting of the parent and all its subsidiaries. Accounting for consolidated entities is covered in advanced accounting texts.[2]

Consolidated financial statements are appropriate only when the investor holds a majority voting interest (more than 50 percent) in the investee. When an investor owns **50 percent or less** of the investee company, the investor may or may not exercise significant influence over the financial and operating decisions of the other company. If conditions indicate that the aquiring company **does exercise significant influence,** the **equity method** of accounting should be used. This method closely parallels the accounting followed when actual control exists, which requires consolidated statements. The equity method is sometimes referred to as a "one-line consolidation."

When the aquiring company **does not exercise significant influence** over the investee, the cost method of accounting should be used. This method recognizes the separate identities of the companies. Since preferred stock is generally nonvoting stock and does not provide for significant influence, the cost method is always used for investments in preferred stock.

The ability of the investor to exercise significant influence over such decisions as dividend distribution and operational and financial administration may be indicated in several ways: e.g., representation on the investee's board of directors, participation in policy-making processes, material intercompany transactions, interchange of managerial personnel, or technological dependency of investee on investor. Another important consideration is the **extent of ownership** by an investor in relation to the concentration of other stockholdings. While it is clear that ownership of over 50 percent of common stock virtually assures control by the acquiring company, ownership of 50 percent or less may

---

[1]*Statement of Financial Accounting Standards No. 94,* "Consolidation of All Majority-Owned Subsidiaries," (Stamford: Financial Accounting Standards Board, 1987).

[2]See, for example, Paul M. Fisher et al., *Advanced Accounting* (Cincinnati: South-Western Publishing Co., 1990).

give effective control if the remaining shares of the stock are widely held, and no significant blocks of stockholders are consistently united in their ownership.

The Accounting Principles Board, in Opinion No. 18, recognized that the degree of influence and control will not always be clear and that judgment will be required in assessing the status of each investment. To achieve a reasonable degree of uniformity in the application of its position, the Board set 20 percent as an ownership standard; the ownership of **20 percent or more** of the voting stock of the company carries the presumption, in the absence of evidence to the contrary, that an investor has the ability to exercise significant influence over that company. Conversely, ownership of **less than 20 percent** leads to the presumption that the investor does not have the ability to exercise significant influence unless such ability can be demonstrated.[3]

In May 1981, the FASB issued Interpretation No. 35 to emphasize that the 20 percent criterion is only a guideline and that judgment is required in determining the appropriate accounting method in cases where ownership is 50 percent or less. Interpretation No. 35 lists five illustrative examples of circumstances that might indicate that the investor does not have significant influence, regardless of the percentage of ownership:[4]

1. Opposition by the investee, such as litigation or complaints to governmental regulatory authorities.
2. An agreement between the investor and investee under which the investor surrenders significant rights as a shareholder.
3. Majority ownership of the investee is concentrated among a small group of shareholders who operate the investee without regard to the views of the investor.
4. The investor needs or wants more financial information to apply the equity method than is available to the investee's other shareholders (for example, the investor wants quarterly financial information from an investee who publicly reports only annually), tries to obtain the information, and fails.
5. The investor tries and fails to obtain representation on the investee's board of directors.

While the FASB examples may be helpful in some cases, evaluating the degree of investor influence is often a very subjective process. As a result, the percentage-of-ownership criterion set forth in APB Opinion No. 18 has been widely accepted as the basis for determining the appropriate method of accounting for long-term investments in equity securities when the investor does not possess absolute voting control.

To summarize, in the absence of persuasive evidence to the contrary, the **cost method** is used when ownership is **less than 20 percent**; the equity method is used when ownership is 20 to 50 percent; the **consolidation method** is used when ownership is **over 50 percent**. These relationships dealing with the effect of ownership interest and control or influence and the proper accounting method to be used are summarized in Exhibit 14—1.[5]

This chapter discusses and illustrates the accounting and reporting issues encountered with the cost and equity methods. The cost method is presented first, followed by the more complex equity method.

---

[3]*Opinions of the Accounting Principles Board No. 18,* "The Equity Method of Accounting for Investments in Common Stock" (New York: American Institute of Certified Public Accountants, 1971).

[4]*FASB Interpretation No. 35,* "Criteria for Applying the Equity Method of Accounting for Investments in Common Stock" (Stamford: Financial Accounting Standards Board, 1981), par. 4.

[5]It should be noted that the FASB has a project on its agenda to consider the reporting entity. This project will review accounting for consolidations and the equity method.

## Off-Balance-Sheet Financing

In 1986, Coca-Cola Co. borrowed $2.4 billion to purchase several large soft drink bottling operations. Then a separate company, Coca-Cola Enterprises, was formed to bottle and distribute Coke throughout the country. Coca-Cola Co. sold 51 percent of Coca-Cola Enterprises to the public and retained a 49 percent ownership. The $2.4 billion in debt incurred to finance the purchase was transferred to the balance sheet of Coca-Cola Enterprises.

While 49 percent ownership does not guarantee control, it does give Coca-Cola Co. significant influence over the bottling company. For example, Coca-Cola Co. determines the price at which it will sell concentrate to Coca-Cola Enterprises and reviews Coca-Cola Enterprises' marketing plan. In addition, Coca-Cola Co.'s chief operating officer is chairman of Coca-Cola Enterprises, and six other current or former Coca-Cola Co. officials are serving on Coca-Cola Enterprises' board of directors.

### Questions:

1. *From an accounting standpoint, what is the significance of owning more than 50 percent of a company's stock?*

2. *Why would the Coca-Cola Co. elect to own less than 50 percent of its distribution network?*

3. *In the consolidation process, the parent and the subsidiary's individual asset and liability account balances are added together and reported on the consolidated financial statements, whereas with the equity method, the net investment is reported as an asset on the investor company's balance sheet. Why would Coca-Cola Co. want to avoid consolidation?*

Source:  *The Wall Street Journal,* October 15, 1986, pp. 1 and 12.

**Exhibit 14—1    Effect of Ownership Interest and Control or Influence on Accounting for Long-Term Investments in Common Stocks**

| Ownership Interest | Control or Degree of Influence | Accounting Method |
|---|---|---|
| More than 50% | Control | Consolidated statements |
| 20% to 50% | Significant influence | Equity method |
| Less than 20% | No significant influence | Cost method |

## The Cost Method

When a long-term investment in another company's stock does not involve either a controlling interest or significant influence, the investment should be accounted for using the cost method. The procedures are essentially the same as those described in Chapter 8 for temporary investments in stocks. The investment is initially recorded at cost including commissions and other related expenditures. Revenue is recognized when dividends are received from the investee. Declines in market value are recognized according to the lower-of-cost-or-market (LCM) valuation rule for all marketable equity securities on a portfolio or aggregate basis. Upon sale of an investment, the difference between the proceeds received and the cost of the investment is recognized as a gain or loss and reported under "Other revenues" or "Other expenses" in the income statement. There is, however, one major difference in accounting for noncurrent versus current equity securities. As explained in the next section, the difference is in the recognition and reporting of changes in market value.

**Temporary Changes in Market Value of Noncurrent Marketable Equity Securities**     As discussed in Chapter 8, current marketable equity securities are valued at LCM, and an allowance account is used to reduce the cost to market. If the market value recovers, the securities may be written back up, but not above original cost. Any change in the allowance account is recognized as a gain or loss in the income statement in the period of change.

When marketable equity securities are classified as long-term investments because it is not management's intent to use the securities as a current source of cash, a somewhat different treatment is required by FASB Statement No. 12.[6] Temporary declines in value of noncurrent marketable equity securities are still reflected in an allowance account, which is deducted from the long-term investment account on the balance sheet. This is the same as for current marketable equity securities. However, the loss on write-down to LCM is treated differently. Stock prices can fluctuate greatly while the stock is being held, and if the investment is to be retained for a long period, the impact of gains or losses on net income from valuation adjustments could be misleading. Therefore, adjustments for temporary changes in value of noncurrent marketable equity securities are not reflected in current income as are adjustments for current marketable equity securities. Instead a **contra stockholders' equity account** is created for changes in noncurrent securities. This account, which in FASB Statement No. 12 is entitled "Net Unrealized Loss on Noncurrent Marketable Equity Securities," is to be deducted from the total stockholders' equity reported in the balance sheet. Both the allowance account that reduces the investment to market and the contra stockholders' equity account should have the same balance at all times. As the market price of the noncurrent equity securities portfolio fluctuates, these accounts will be adjusted to bring the valuation to the lower of aggregate cost or market. When equity securities are sold, the transaction is recorded on the historical cost basis and a gain or loss recognized. Then at year-end, an adjustment is made to the allowance and contra stockholders' equity accounts based on the remaining portfolio of investments. These procedures are illustrated in the following example.

A company carries a noncurrent marketable equity securities portfolio that has a cost of $125,000. Prior to 1992, the portfolio's market value had always exceeded its cost. However, at December 31, 1992, the market value of the securities held has fallen to $110,000. The decline is judged to be temporary. The following entry would be required to reduce the securities valuation from cost to market:

| | | |
|---|---|---|
| Net Unrealized Loss on Noncurrent Marketable Equity Securities | 15,000 | |
| Allowance for Decline in Value of Noncurrent Marketable Equity Securities ............................................. | | 15,000 |

The applicable disclosures on the balance sheet might be shown as follows:

| | | |
|---|---|---|
| Investments: | | |
| Noncurrent investments in marketable equity securities (cost) ............................................. | $125,000 | |
| Less allowance for decline in value of noncurrent marketable equity securities .............................. | (15,000) | 110,000 |
| Total assets ............................................. | | $xxx,xxx |

[6]*Statement of Financial Accounting Standards No. 12,* "Accounting for Certain Marketable Securities" (Stamford: Financial Accounting Standards Board, 1975), par. 9.

Stockholders' Equity:
Total capital stock and retained earnings ............... $xxx,xxx
Less net unrealized loss on noncurrent marketable equity
securities ........................................... (15,000)
Total liabilities and stockholders' equity ................. $xxx,xxx

If during 1993 one of the securities costing $25,000 was sold for $30,000, the transaction would be recorded based on the original cost as follows:

Cash ..................................................... 30,000
    Investment in XYZ Stock (original cost) .................... 25,000
    Gain on Sale of Investment ............................... 5,000

Assume further that no other investment transactions occurred during 1993 and that the aggregate market value of the portfolio at the end of 1993 is $97,000. Therefore, the amount in the allowance account and in the contra equity account would need to be adjusted to $3,000 ($125,000 beginning cost − $25,000 cost of security sold = $100,000 ending cost − $97,000 end-of-year aggregate market value). The entry to reduce the account balances from $15,000 to $3,000 would be:

Allowance for Decline in Value of Noncurrent Marketable Equity
Securities ................................................... 12,000
    Net Unrealized Loss on Noncurrent Marketable Equity Securi-
    ties ...................................................... 12,000

The long-term investments would be shown on the balance sheet at the lower-of-cost-or-market value, $97,000 (cost of $100,000 less allowance of $3,000), and the stockholders' equity contra account would reduce total stockholders' equity by $3,000. Note that the $5,000 gain on the actual sale would be reported as "Other revenues" on the income statement for 1993. Also note that the allowance for decline and net unrealized loss accounts can be adjusted upward, but only to a zero balance. If market exceeds cost, no adjustment above cost is made due to the practice of conservatism in accounting.

**Permanent Declines in Market Value**    Sometimes the market price of stock declines due to economic circumstances that are unlikely to improve. For example, until recently, low oil prices caused the stocks of some oil companies to decrease significantly without much expectation that they would ever recover. If a decline in the market value of an individual security in a noncurrent investment portfolio is judged to be permanent, the cost basis of that security should be reduced by crediting the investment account rather than an allowance account. In addition, the write-down should be recognized as a loss and charged against current income.[7] The new cost basis for the security may not be adjusted upward to its original cost for any subsequent increases in market value.

To illustrate the accounting for a permanent decline, assume that the portfolio of a company at the end of its first year of operations contains the following noncurrent marketable equity securities:

|  | Cost | Market |
|---|---|---|
| Company A ........................................... | $ 50,000 | $ 40,000 |
| Company B ........................................... | 30,000 | 35,000 |
| Company C ........................................... | 100,000 | 60,000 |
| Total ................................................ | $180,000 | $135,000 |

[7] *Ibid.*, par. 21.

On an aggregate basis, the allowance adjustment would be for the difference between cost and market, or $45,000. However, if evaluation of market conditions for the securities of Company C indicates that the decline in value is permanent, the security should be written down to market, which becomes the new cost basis, and a reevaluation made of the total portfolio to determine the need for an allowance. The write-down entry would be as follows:

Recognized Loss From Permanent Decline in Market Value of
Noncurrent Marketable Equity Securities ..................... 40,000
    Long-Term Investments in Marketable Equity Securities......           40,000

The recognized loss account would be closed to Income Summary at the end of the year, reducing net income by $40,000. The portfolio of long-term securities would now appear as follows:

|  | Cost | Market |
|---|---|---|
| Company A ........................................... | $ 50,000 | $ 40,000 |
| Company B ........................................... | 30,000 | 35,000 |
| Company C ........................................... | 60,000 | 60,000 |
| Total ............................................... | $140,000 | $135,000 |

At this point, an adjustment would be required to Net Unrealized Loss and to Allowance for Decline to bring them to a $5,000 balance, which is the remaining difference between total cost and market values.

**Change in Classification Between Current and Noncurrent**    As noted in Chapter 8, if there is a change in the classification of a marketable equity security between current and noncurrent assets, the transfer should be made at the lower of cost or market value of the security at the date of the reclassification. This amount becomes the new cost basis with any loss being recorded in the current period as was done for permanent declines in value.

**Summary of Marketable Equity Securities Valuation**    The valuation of marketable equity securities as discussed on the preceding pages is summarized in the flowchart in Exhibit 14—2. By studying the flowchart carefully in conjunction with the discussion and examples, the decision points and accounting treatment can be more clearly understood.

The Financial Accounting Standards Board, in Statement No. 12, places a high premium on the classification of marketable equity securities. Because the classification is determined on the basis of subjective criteria, e.g., the intent of management to hold or sell, there is concern that the classification can be used to manipulate reported net income. In the authors' opinion, the adoption of a consistent valuation approach for all investments, regardless of their classification, seems preferable to the differentiated treatment for current and noncurrent securities outlined in Statement No. 12.

## The Equity Method

The equity method of accounting for long-term investments in common stock reflects the economic substance of the relationship between the investor and investee rather than the legal distinction of the separate entities. The objective of this method is to reflect the underlying claim by the investor on the net assets of the investee company.

Under the equity method, just as under the cost method, the investment is initially recorded at cost. However, with the equity method, the investment account is periodically adjusted to reflect changes in the underlying net assets of the investee. The investment balance is increased to reflect a proportionate share of the earnings of the investee

**Exhibit 14—2    Flowchart of Valuation for Marketable Equity Securities as Prescribed by FASB Statement No. 12**

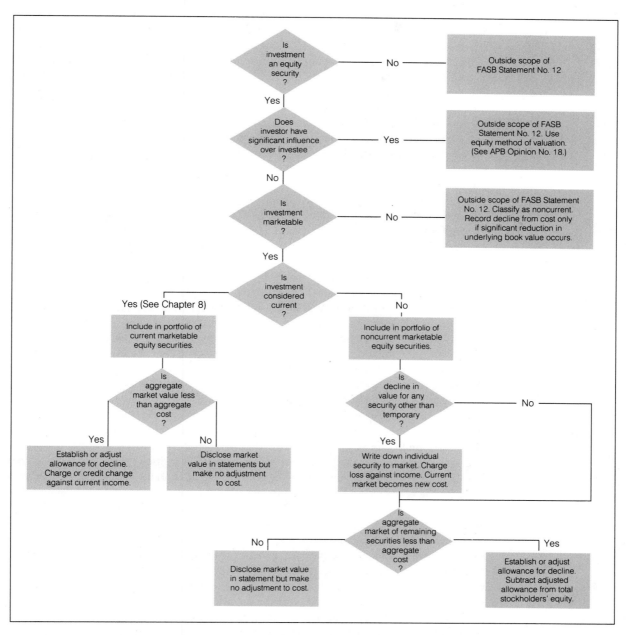

company, or decreased to reflect a share of any losses reported. If preferred stock dividends have been declared by the investee, they must be deducted from income reported by the investee before computing the investor's share of investee earnings or losses. When dividends are received by the investor, the investment account is reduced. Thus, the equity method results in an increase in the investment account when the investee's net assets increase; similarly, the investment account decreases when the investee records a loss or pays out dividends.

**Cost and Equity Methods Compared**     To contrast and illustrate the accounting entries under the cost and equity methods, assume that Powell Corporation purchases 5,000 shares of San Juan Company common stock on January 2 at $20 per share, including commissions and other costs. San Juan has a total of 25,000 shares outstanding; thus, the 5,000 shares represent a 20 percent ownership interest. As discussed earlier in the chapter, the equity method is used when ownership is 20 to 50 percent unless there is persuasive evidence that the investor does not have significant influence over the investee. The appropriate entries under both the cost and equity methods are shown in Exhibit 14—3. The actual method used would depend on the degree of influence exercised by the investor as indicated by a consideration of all relevant factors, as well as the percentage owned. Exhibit 14—3 highlights the basic differences in accounting for long-term investments under the cost and equity methods. Under both methods, the investment is originally recorded at cost. Dividends received are recognized as Dividend Revenue under the cost method and as a reduction in the investment account under the equity method. The investor's percentage of the earnings of the investee company are recorded as income and as an increase to the investment account under the equity method, while no entry is required for this event under the cost method. Under the cost method, an adjustment to lower of cost or market may be required, while no entry is necessary under the equity method. The carrying value under the cost method is cost less any applicable allowance for decline in value; under the equity method, the carrying value is original cost plus any increases from the proportionate share of investee earnings less any dividends received.

**Complexities Under the Equity Method**     When a company is purchased by another company, the purchase price usually differs from the recorded book value of the underlying net assets of the acquired company. For example, assume Snowbird Company purchased 100 percent of the common stock of Ski Resorts International for $8 million, although the book value of Ski Resorts' net assets is only $6.5 million. In effect, Snowbird is purchasing some undervalued assets, above-normal earnings potential, or both.

As explained in Chapter 12, if the purchase price of an ongoing business exceeds the recorded value, the acquiring company must allocate this purchase price among the assets acquired using their current market values as opposed to the amounts carried on the books of the acquired company. If part of the purchase price cannot be allocated to specific assets, that amount is recorded as goodwill. If the purchase price is less than recorded net asset value, the assets acquired must be recorded at an amount less than their carrying value on the books of the acquired company. Whether assets are increased or decreased as a result of the purchase, future income determination will use the new (adjusted) values to determine the depreciation and amortization charges.

When only a portion of a company's stock is purchased and the equity method is used to reflect the income of the partially owned company, an adjustment to the investee's reported income, similar to that just described, may be required. In order to determine whether such an adjustment is necessary, the acquiring company must compare the purchase price of the common stock with the recorded net asset value of the acquired company at the date of purchase. If the purchase price exceeds the investor's share of book value, the computed excess must be analyzed in the same way as described above for a 100 percent purchase. Although no entries to adjust asset values are made on the books of either company, an adjustment to the investee's reported income is required under the equity method for the investor to reflect the economic reality of paying more for the investment than the underlying net book value. If depreciable assets had been adjusted to higher market values on the books of the investee to reflect the price paid by the investor, additional depreciation would have been taken by the investee company. Similarly, if the

### Exhibit 14—3    Comparison of Cost and Equity Methods

| Cost Method | | Equity Method | | |
|---|---|---|---|---|

Jan. 2 Purchased 5,000 shares of San Juan Company common stock at $20 per share:

| | | | | |
|---|---|---|---|---|
| Investment in San Juan Company Stock............... | 100,000 | Investment in San Juan Company Stock............... | 100,000 | |
|    Cash .................. | 100,000 |    Cash .................. | | 100,000 |

Oct. 31 Received dividend of $.80 per share from San Juan Company ($.80 × 5,000 shares):

| | | | | |
|---|---|---|---|---|
| Cash ..................... | 4,000 | Cash ..................... | 4,000 | |
|    Dividend Revenue ........ | 4,000 |    Investment in San Juan Company Stock ......... | | 4,000 |

Dec. 31 San Juan Company announced earnings for the year of $60,000:

| | | | | |
|---|---|---|---|---|
| No Entry | | Investment in San Juan Company Stock............... | 12,000 | |
| | |    Income From Investment in San Juan Company Stock .. | | 12,000 |
| | |    (.20 × $60,000) | | |

Dec. 31 Market value of San Juan Company common stock is $18.50 per share:

| | | | | |
|---|---|---|---|---|
| Net Unrealized Loss on Noncurrent Marketable Equity Securities.............. | 7,500 | No Entry | | |
|    Allowance for Decline in Value of Noncurrent Marketable Equity Securities .. | 7,500 | | | |
|    [($20 − $18.50) × 5,000 shares] | | | | |

Carrying value (book value) of investment at year-end:

| | | | | |
|---|---|---|---|---|
| Cost................................. | $100,000 | Cost..................................... | | $100,000 |
| Less allowance for decline in value .... | 7,500 | Dividend revenue...................... | | (4,000) |
| | | Share of investee earnings ............ | | 12,000 |
| | $ 92,500 | | | $108,000 |

purchase price reflected goodwill, additional amortization would have been required. These adjustments would have reduced the reported income of the investee. To reflect this condition, an adjustment is made by the investor to the income reported by the investee in applying the equity method. This adjustment serves to meet the objective of computing the income reported using the equity method in the same manner as would be done if the company were 100 percent purchased and consolidated financial statements were prepared.

To illustrate, assume that the book value of common stockholders' equity (net assets) of Stewart Inc. was $500,000 at the time Phillips Manufacturing Co. purchased 40% of its common shares for $250,000. Based on a 40% ownership interest, the market value of the net assets of Stewart Inc. would be $625,000 ($250,000 ÷ .40), or $125,000 more than the book value. Assume that a review of the asset values discloses that the market value of depreciable properties exceeds the carrying value of these assets by $50,000. The remaining $75,000 difference ($125,000 − $50,000) is attributed to goodwill. Assume further that the average remaining life of the depreciable assets is 10 years and that goodwill is amortized over 40 years. Phillips Manufacturing Co. would adjust its share of the annual income reported by Stewart Inc. to reflect the additional depreciation and the amortization of goodwill as follows:

$$
\begin{array}{ll}
\text{Additional depreciation } (\$50,000 \times 40\%) \div 10 \text{ years} = & \$2,000 \\
\text{Goodwill amortization } (\$75,000 \times 40\%) \div 40 \text{ years} = & \underline{\phantom{0}750} \\
& \underline{\$2,750}
\end{array}
$$

Each year for the first 10 years, Phillips would make the following entry in addition to entries made to recognize its share of Stewart Inc.'s income and dividends:

| | | |
|---|---|---|
| Income From Investment in Stewart Inc. Stock ................. | 2,750 | |
| Investment in Stewart Inc. Stock ........................... | | 2,750 |

*To adjust share of income on Stewart Inc. common stock for proportionate depreciation on excess market value of depreciable property, $2,000, and for amortization of goodwill from acquisition of the stock, $750.*

After the tenth year, the adjustment would be for $750 until the goodwill amount is fully amortized.

To complete the illustration, assume that the purchase was made on January 2, 1993; Stewart Inc. declared and paid dividends of $70,000 to common stockholders during 1993, and Stewart Inc. reported net income of $150,000 for the year ended December 31, 1993. At the end of 1993, the investment in Stewart Inc. common stock would be reported on the balance sheet of Phillips Manufacturing Co. at $279,250, computed as shown below.

This illustration assumes that the fiscal years of the two companies coincide and that the purchase of the stock is made at the first of the year. If a purchase is made at a time other than the beginning of the year, the income earned up to the date of the purchase is assumed to be included in the cost of purchase. Only income earned by the investee subsequent to acquisition should be recognized by the investor.

**Investment in Stewart Inc. Common Stock**

| | | |
|---|---|---|
| Acquisition cost ........................................ | $250,000 | |
| Add: Share of 1993 earnings of investee company ($150,000 × .40)................................ | 60,000 | $310,000 |
| Less: Dividends received from investee ($70,000 × .40) ... | $ 28,000 | |
| Additional depreciation of undervalued assets ...... | 2,000 | |
| Amortization of unrecorded goodwill .............. | 750 | 30,750 |
| Year-end carrying value of investment (equity in investee company)........................................... | | $279,250 |

The adjustment for additional depreciation and goodwill amortization is needed only when the purchase price is greater than the underlying book value at the date of acquisition. If the purchase price is less than the underlying book value at the time of acquisition, it is assumed that specific assets of the investee are overvalued or that there is negative goodwill as discussed in Chapter 12, and an adjustment is necessary to reduce the depreciation or amortization included in the reported income of the investee. The journal entry to reflect this adjustment is the reverse of the one illustrated previously. The computations would also be similar except that the adjustments for overvalued assets would be added to (instead of subtracted from) the carrying value of the investment.

As noted earlier in the chapter, during the consolidation process, adjustments must be made to eliminate any intercompany sales, costs, and profits. Under the equity method, if the investor and investee are engaged in intercompany revenue-producing activities, similar adjustments must be made to the investment account by the investor to eliminate the effects of intercompany transactions. A more complete description of these intercompany problems is found in advanced accounting texts.

## Changes Between Cost and Equity Methods

Variations in percentage of ownership caused by additional purchases or sales of stock by the investor or by the additional sale or retirement of stock by the investee may require a change in accounting method. For example, if the equity method has been used but subsequent events reduce the investment ownership below 20 percent, a change should be made to the cost method effective for the year when the reduced ownership occurs. Similarly, if the cost method has been used but subsequent acquisitions increase the investment ownership to 20 percent or more, a change should be made to the equity method. The required accounting is different depending on whether the change is from the equity method to the cost method or vice versa.

**Change From Equity to Cost Method**    If an investment in equity securities has been accounted for under the equity method, but circumstances dictate a change to the cost method, no adjustment to the investment account is needed. At the time of change, the carrying amount of the investment, as determined by the equity method for prior years, becomes the new basis for applying the cost method. From that time forward, the investment account would not be adjusted for a proportionate share of investee earnings, nor would any adjustments be made for additional depreciation or amortization of undervalued or unrecorded assets, and dividends received would be credited to a revenue account, not the investment account. Thus, once the equity method is no longer appropriate, the cost method is applied just as in any other situation where the cost method is used.

**Change From Cost to Equity Method**    Accounting for a change from the cost method to the equity method is more complex. A **retroactive adjustment** is required for prior years to reflect the income that would have been reported using the equity method. This adjustment modifies the carrying value of the investment, in effect restating it on an equity basis, as if the equity method had been used during the previous periods that the investment was held. The offsetting entry for the adjustment is to Retained Earnings. From the date of change forward, the equity method is applied normally.

To illustrate, assume that MTI Corporation acquired stock of Excellcior Inc. over the three-year period 1991-1993. Purchase, dividend, and income information for these years are as follows (the purchases were made on the first day of each year):

| Year | Percentage Ownership Acquired | Purchase Price* | Excellcior Inc. Dividends Paid Dec. 31 | Income Earned |
|------|------|------|------|------|
| 1991 | 10% | $ 50,000 | $100,000 | $200,000 |
| 1992 | 5 | 30,000 | 120,000 | 300,000 |
| 1993 | 15 | 117,000 | 180,000 | 400,000 |

*Purchase price equal to underlying book value at date of purchase.

The following entries would be made on the books of MTI Corporation to reflect the cost method for the years 1991 and 1992:

```
1991
Jan.  1   Investment in Excellcior Inc. Stock ................    50,000
              Cash .........................................                50,000
                  To record purchase of 10% interest.

Dec. 31   Cash .........................................    10,000
              Dividend Revenue ............................                10,000
                  To record receipt of dividends from Excellcior
                  Inc. (10% × $100,000).

1992
Jan.  1   Investment in Excellcior Inc. Stock ................    30,000
              Cash .........................................                30,000
                  To record purchase of 5% interest. (Total owner-
                  ship interest is now 15%.)

Dec. 31   Cash .........................................    18,000
              Dividend Revenue ............................                18,000
                  To record receipt of dividends from Excellcior
                  Inc. (15% × $120,000).
```

The additional acquisition of stock at the beginning of 1993 increases ownership to 30%, and a retroactive adjustment to change to the equity method must be made at the time of acquisition. The adjustment is for the difference between the revenue reported using the cost method and that which would have been reported if the equity method had been used. The adjustment would be computed as follows:

| Year | Percentage Ownership | Revenue Recognized—Cost Method | Revenue Recognized—Equity Method | Required Retroactive Adjustment |
|---|---|---|---|---|
| 1991 | 10% | $10,000 | $20,000* | $10,000 |
| 1992 | 15% | 18,000 | 45,000** | 27,000 |
| | | | Total adjustment | $37,000 |

*$200,000 × 10%
**$300,000 × 15%

The following entries would be made on the books of MTI Corporation to reflect the equity method for 1993:

```
1993
Jan.  1   Investment in Excellcior Inc. Stock ..............    117,000
              Cash .........................................                117,000
                  To record purchase of 15% interest. (Total
                  ownership interest is now 30%.)

      1   Investment in Excellcior Inc. Stock ..............    37,000
              Retained Earnings ............................                37,000
                  To retroactively reflect revenue for 1991 and
                  1992 for investment in Excellcior Inc. as if the
                  equity method had been used.

Dec. 31   Investment in Excellcior Inc. Stock ..............    120,000
              Income From Investment in Excellcior Inc. Stock                120,000
                  To record 30% of income earned by Excellcior
                  Inc. using equity method.

      31  Cash .........................................    54,000
              Investment in Excellcior Inc. Stock .............                54,000
                  To record receipt of dividend from Excellcior
                  Inc. using equity method (30% × $180,000).
```

Note that in the previous example the retroactive adjustment restates the investment account to an equity basis. From that point on, the equity method is applied in a normal manner. For simplicity, the illustration assumed a purchase price equal to the underlying book value at date of purchase. If this were not the case, an adjustment to income for depreciation and amortization would be needed as discussed in an earlier section.

## Required Disclosures for Long-Term Investments in Stock

Since the financial position and operating results of the investor can be significantly affected by the method used in accounting for and reporting long-term investments in stocks, it is important that proper disclosures be made. These disclosures may be included parenthetically in the financial statements or more commonly in a note to the financial statements.

FASB Statement No. 12 sets forth disclosure requirements for equity securities accounted for under the cost method and valued at lower of cost or market. These disclosure requirements were discussed and illustrated in Chapter 8.

Because the equity method is generally more complex than the cost method, the disclosures associated with the equity method are usually more detailed. APB Opinion No. 18 provides some recommendations for disclosures applicable to the equity method, including names of investees and the related percentages of ownership interest, and the difference, if any, between the carrying value of the investment and the underlying equity in net assets of the investee.[8] In addition, if an investor has more than 20 percent ownership but chooses not to use the equity method, the reasons for the decision should be disclosed. Similarly, if the equity method is used in cases where there is less than 20 percent ownership, those reasons also should be disclosed.

An example of the type of disclosure often provided by companies relative to their long-term investments in equity securities is presented in Exhibit 14—4. This example is taken from the notes to the 1988 financial statements of The Williams Companies, Inc. Another example is provided in the notes of the IBM Corporation financial statements in Appendix A of the text.

### Exhibit 14—4    The Williams Companies, Inc.

---

*NOTES TO CONSOLIDATED FINANCIAL STATEMENTS*

*1 (In Part): Summary of Significant Accounting Policies*

Principles of Consolidation

The consolidated financial statements include the accounts of The Williams Companies, Inc. (Williams) and all majority owned subsidiaries. Companies in which Williams and its subsidiaries own 20 percent to 50 percent of the voting common stock or otherwise exercise sufficient influence over operating and financial policies of the company are accounted for under the equity method.

---

## Accounting for Long-Term Investments in Stocks Summarized

In summary, the main guidelines for accounting for long-term stock investments are as follows:

[8]*Opinions of the Accounting Principles Board No. 18,* "The Equity Method of Accounting for Investments in Common Stock" (New York: American Institute of Certified Public Accountants, 1971), par. 20.

1. Investments in stock are always initially recorded at cost, which includes commissions and similar expenditures.
2. Revenue is recognized through (a) consolidation when the investor controls the investee or (b) by the cost or equity method, depending on the degree of influence from ownership.
3. If the cost method is used in accounting for long-term marketable equity securities, such securities are valued at the lower of cost or aggregate market, with any temporary write-down reported as a reduction to stockholders' equity rather than charged to income, as is the case for short-term marketable equity securities.
4. If the equity method is used, no valuation adjustment to lower of cost or market is needed. The investment account is increased to reflect a proportionate share of investee income and decreased to reflect investee losses and dividends received from the investee.
5. As with any asset, significant permanent declines in the value of long-term investments are recognized as a loss in the year they occur.
6. When long-term investments are eventually sold, the difference between the carrying value of the investment and the proceeds from the sale is recognized as a realized gain or loss.

## LONG-TERM INVESTMENTS IN FUNDS

Cash and other assets set apart for certain designated purposes are called funds. Some funds are to be used for specific current obligations and are appropriately reported as current assets. Examples of these are petty cash funds, payroll funds, interest funds, dividend funds, and withholding, social security, and other tax funds. Other funds are accumulated over a long term for such purposes as the acquisition or replacement of properties, retirement of long-term debt, the redemption of capital stock, operation of a pension plan, or possible future contingencies. These funds are properly considered noncurrent and are reported under the long-term investment heading.

### Establishment and Accumulation of Funds

A fund may be established through the voluntary action of management, or it may be established as a result of contractual requirements. The fund may be used for a single purpose, such as the redemption of preferred stock, or it may be used for several related purposes, such as the periodic payment of interest on bonds, the retirement of bonds at various intervals, and the ultimate retirement of the remaining bond indebtedness.

When a fund is voluntarily created by management, control of the fund and its disposition are arbitrary matters depending on the wishes of management. When a fund is created through some legal requirement, it must be administered and applied in accordance therewith. Such a fund may be administered by one or more independent trustees under an agreement known as a trust indenture. If the trustee assumes responsibility for fulfillment of the requirement, as may be true for a bond retirement or pension program, neither the fund nor the related liability is carried on the company's books. However, if the indenture does not free the company from further obligation, the fund must be accounted for as if there were no trustee.

When a corporation is required by agreement to establish a fund for a certain purpose, such as the retirement of bonds or the redemption of stock, the agreement generally provides that fund deposits shall (1) be fixed amounts, (2) vary according to gross revenue, net income, or units of product sold, or (3) be equal periodic sums that, together with earnings, will produce a certain amount at some future date. The latter arrangement is based on compound-interest factors, and as noted in Chapter 7, compound interest or annuity tables may be used to determine the equal periodic deposits. For example, in order to accumulate a fund of $100,000 by a series of 5 equal annual deposits at 8% compounded annually, a periodic deposit of $17,045.65 is required.[9]

A schedule can be developed to show the planned fund accumulation through deposits and earnings. Such a schedule is illustrated below.

### Fund Accumulation Schedule

| Year | Earnings on Fund Balance for Year | Amount Deposited in Fund | Total Increase in Fund for Year | Accumulated Fund Total |
|---|---|---|---|---|
| 1 | — | $17,045.65 | $17,045.65 | $ 17,045.65 |
| 2 | $1,363.65 | 17,045.65 | 18,409.30 | 35,454.95 |
| 3 | 2,836.40 | 17,045.65 | 19,882.05 | 55,337.00 |
| 4 | 4,426.96 | 17,045.65 | 21,472.61 | 76,809.61 |
| 5 | 6,144.74 | 17,045.65 | 23,190.39 | 100,000.00 |

Assuming deposits at the end of each year, the table shows a fund balance at the end of the first year of $17,045.65 resulting from the first deposit. At the end of the second year, the fund is increased by (1) earnings at 8% on the investment in the fund during the year, $1,363.65, and (2) the second deposit to the fund, $17,045.65. The total in the fund at this time is $35,454.95. Fund earnings in the following year are based on a total investment of $35,454.95 as of the beginning of the year.

The schedule is developed on the assumption of annual earnings of 8%. However, various factors, such as fluctuations in the earnings rate and gains and losses on investments, may provide earnings that differ from the assumed amounts. If the fund is to be maintained in accordance with the accumulation schedule, deposits must be adjusted for earnings that differ from estimated amounts. Smaller deposits, then, can be made in periods when earnings exceed the assumed rate; larger deposits are necessary when earnings fail to meet the assumed rate.

### Accounting for Funds

A fund is usually composed of cash and securities but could include other assets. The accounting for stock held in a fund is the same as that described earlier in this chapter except the securities are reported as part of the fund balance. The accounting for investments in bonds will be discussed in Chapter 16.

To illustrate the accounting for a fund, assume that a preferred stock redemption fund is established with annual payments to the fund of $20,000. The fund administrator invests 90% of its assets in stock and places the remainder in bank certificates of deposit paying 8% interest. Journal entries for the first year's transactions are as follows:

```
Stock Redemption Fund Cash ............................  20,000
    Cash .................................................       20,000
        Annual fund contribution.
```

[9]This amount can be determined from Table III in Chapter 7. The rent or annual payment for an annuity of $100,000 at 8% for 5 periods is computed as follows:

$$R = \frac{FV_n}{FVAF_n} = \frac{FV_n}{\text{Table III } \overline{5}|8\%} = \frac{\$100,000}{5.8666} = \$17,045.65$$

| Stock Redemption Fund Securities ........................... | 18,000 | |
| Stock Redemption Fund Cash............................... | | 18,000 |
| *Investment of fund cash in securities.* | | |

| Stock Redemption Fund Certificates of Deposit................ | 2,000 | |
| Stock Redemption Fund Cash.............................. | | 2,000 |
| *Investment of fund cash in certificates of deposit.* | | |

| Stock Redemption Fund Cash .............................. | 1,400 | |
| Stock Redemption Fund Revenue ......................... | | 1,400 |
| *Dividends on fund securities.* | | |

| Stock Redemption Fund Cash .............................. | 160 | |
| Stock Redemption Fund Revenue ......................... | | 160 |
| *Interest on certificates of deposit.* | | |

| Stock Redemption Fund Expenses ........................... | 200 | |
| Stock Redemption Fund Cash.............................. | | 200 |
| *Expenses to operate fund.* | | |

At the end of the year, the stock redemption fund assets are as follows:

| Stock redemption fund cash ($1,400 + $160 − $200) .................. | $ 1,360 |
| Stock redemption fund certificates of deposit ......................... | 2,000 |
| Stock redemption fund securities ..................................... | 18,000 |
| Total ......................................................... | $21,360 |

This total amount would be reported under the "investments" heading on the balance sheet.

Stock redemption fund revenue for the year is $1,560 and stock redemption fund expense is $200, resulting in a net income from the fund operation of $1,360. This amount is reported on the income statement as other revenue. When stock is redeemed, the payment is made from Stock Redemption Fund Cash after the securities are converted to cash.

## OTHER LONG-TERM INVESTMENTS

In addition to securities and funds, a company may have other long-term investments. Real estate held as an investment; advances to subsidiaries that are of a long-term nature; deposits made to guarantee contract performance; cash surrender values from life insurance policies; and equity interests in partnerships, trusts, and estates are all examples. Most of these assets either produce current revenues or have a favorable effect on the investor's business in some other way. Cost is generally the underlying basis for these miscellaneous investments, and a gain or loss is recognized upon sale equal to the difference between the sales proceeds and the carrying amount of the investment. When available, market or appraised values may be reported parenthetically.

## REPORTING LONG-TERM INVESTMENTS ON THE BALANCE SHEET

Long-term investments are generally reported on the balance sheet immediately following the current assets classification. The investment section should include only noncurrent investments, with appropriate headings for different long-term investment categories. Cost data should be supplemented by market quotations in parenthetical or note form if market exceeds cost. Information concerning the pledge of long-term investments as collateral on loans or other relevant information should also be provided.

In reporting funds to be applied to specific purposes or paid to specific parties, disclosure should be made by special note of the conditions relative to their establishment and ultimate application. A fund arrearage or other failure to meet contractual requirements should be pointed out; deposit requirements in the succeeding fiscal period should also be disclosed when material. Offset of a fund balance against a liability item is proper only when an asset transfer to a trustee is irrevocable and actually serves to discharge the obligation.

The "Investments" section of a balance sheet is shown below. In practice, some of the detail is often omitted or reported in the notes to the statements.

Investments:
  Affiliated companies:
    Investment in Salt River Co. common stock, reported by the equity method (investment consists of 90,000 shares representing a 40% interest acquired on July 1, 1991, for $1,500,000) ............. $1,548,000
    Advances to Salt River Co. ........................    115,000    $1,663,000
  Miscellaneous stock investments at cost (stock has an aggregate quoted market value of $112,000) .........           100,000
  Stock redemption fund, composed of:
    Cash ......................................    $   15,000
    Stocks and bonds, at cost (aggregate quoted market value, $420,000) ..............................     410,500
    Dividends and interest receivable .................       4,500       430,000
  Investment in land and unused facilities .............           125,000
  Cash surrender value of life insurance carried on officers' lives ......................................            12,500
  Total investments .....................................       $2,330,500

## KEY TERMS

Consolidation method 524

Cost method 525

Equity method 526

Funds 538

Long-term (or noncurrent) investments 523

Parent company 524

Subsidiary company 524

Trust indenture 538

## QUESTIONS

1. (a) Distinguish between long-term (or noncurrent) and short-term (or current) investments.
   (b) List several types of long-term investments.
2. Why might a company invest in the stock of another company?
3. David Giles purchases 1,000 shares of Bart Motors at $90 a share in November, paying his broker $65,000. The market value of the stock on December 31 is $125 a share; Giles has made no further payment to his broker. On this date he shows on his balance sheet Bart Motors stock, $100,000, the difference between market value and the unpaid balance to the broker. Do you approve of this treatment? Explain.
4. What is the general rule used for determining the appropriate method of accounting for investments in equity securities when the investor does not possess absolute voting control?

5. (a) What factors may indicate the ability of an investor owning less than a majority voting interest to exercise significant influence on the investee's operating and financial policies?
   (b) What factors may indicate the investor's inability to exercise significant influence?
6. Distinguish between the method used to account for a temporary decline in the market value of stock under the equity method and under the cost method.
7. How is a permanent decline in the value of long-term stock investments recorded?
8. What adjustment is needed to record the change in classification of an investment in marketable equity securities between current and noncurrent assets?
9. What adjustment is needed when a company switches from (a) the equity method to the cost method and

(b) the cost method to the equity method of valuing securities?

10. What disclosures are recommended in APB Opinion No. 18 when using the equity method?

11. Identify and describe examples of funds that would be listed as current assets and those that would be listed as investments.

12. Describe several items properly reported under the "Investments" heading on the balance sheet.

## DISCUSSION CASES

### Case 14—1 (Classification of investments)

Rainbow Systems, Inc., a chemical processing company, has been operating profitably for many years. On March 1, 1993, Rainbow purchased 40,000 shares of Allied Financial Services Inc. stock for $2,000,000. The 40,000 shares represented 30% of Allied's outstanding stock. Both Rainbow and Allied operate on a fiscal year ending August 31.

For the fiscal year ended August 31, 1993, Allied reported net income of $600,000 earned evenly throughout the year. During May 1993, Allied paid its regular annual cash dividend of $50,000.

What criteria should Rainbow consider in determining whether its investment in Allied should be classified as (a) a current asset or (b) a noncurrent asset? Confine your discussion to the decision criteria for determining the balance sheet classification of the investment.

### Case 14—2 (What is significant influence?)

The Moya Corporation's board of directors has been wrestling with a basic decision concerning its involvement with other business entities. Jim Wallace, President, wants to acquire controlling interest (more than 50%) in several companies that serve as suppliers of basic materials used by Moya and other companies that are distributors of its various products. Gail Brewer, Chair of the Board of Directors, feels part of the capital required to obtain more than 50% ownership should be used to expand Moya's working capital. Brewer argues that significant influence over vital operating decisions can be obtained with far less than 50% of the stock. By reducing the investment cost, more funds can be freed for other vital needs. Both Wallace and Brewer are concerned about the impact of stock acquisitions on company profits, especially the effects of different accounting methods, as more substantial investments in other companies are made. They have come to you as the controller of Moya to shed some light on this issue and to obtain your recommendation as to the direction they should go. What factors would you stress in your answer to them?

### Case 14—3 (Which method of accounting for investments is appropriate?)

International Inc. has ownership of companies in countries all over the world. International is reviewing its methods of accounting for those companies and has asked you to provide input as to whether the cost method, the equity method, or consolidation is appropriate for each of the following subsidiaries. Provide justification for your suggestions.

Subsidiary #1

This subsidiary, MEOil, is an oil company located in the Middle East. A growing anti-American sentiment in the country in which the company is located has led International to remove all non-native employees. There is a growing fear that the government may nationalize MEOil. International Inc. owns 75% of the oil company.

Subsidiary #2

Ecological Inc., a company that produces environmentally safe products, has production facilities in over 10 states. The ownership of the company is widely held, with International Inc. holding the largest block of stock. International has succeeded in placing its president and vice president in two of the five board of directors seats of Ecological Inc. International owns 15% of Ecological Inc.'s outstanding stock.

#### Subsidiary #3

International Inc. recently purchased 100% of the outstanding stock of Harmon National Bank. This subsidiary represents International's first purchase of a nonmanufacturing facility, and management has expressed concern about the comparability of the different accounting methods used by financial institutions.

#### Subsidiary #4

International has been involved in a takeover battle with Beatrix Inc. involving Campton Soups. Beatrix recently purchased 50% of the stock of Campton. International has owned 30% of Campton for five years.

### Case 14—4   (What is the difference in accounting between the cost and equity methods?)

Analogic Corporation, a producer of medical products, disclosed the following investments in affiliates in the notes to its July 31, 1993, financial statement:

|  | 1993 | 1992 |
|---|---|---|
| Investments, at cost ................................. | $ 822,188 | $   50,000 |
| Investments, at equity ............................. | 1,677,181 | 2,009,647 |

Discuss the factors that determine whether Analogic uses the cost or the equity method in accounting for its investment in affiliates. What events are recorded when the cost method is used? What events are recorded when the equity method is used? What does the investment account summarize using the cost method? using the equity method?

### Case 14—5   (How does increased ownership in another company affect our books?)

For the past three years Mapleton Corp. has maintained an investment (properly accounted for and reported upon) in Johnson Co. reflecting a 15% interest in the voting common stock of Johnson. The purchase price was $800,000, and the underlying net equity in Johnson at the date of purchase was $660,000. On January 2 of the current year, Mapleton purchased an additional 10% (total ownership interest is now 25%) of the voting common stock of Johnson for $1,100,000; the underlying net equity of the additional investment at January 2 was $1,000,000. Johnson has been profitable and has paid dividends annually since Mapleton's initial acquisition.

Discuss how this increase in ownership affects the accounting for and reporting on the investment in Johnson. Include in your discussion the adjustments, if any, that must be made to the amount shown prior to the increase in investment to bring the amount into conformity with generally accepted accounting principles. Also include how current and subsequent periods would be reported on.

---

## EXERCISES

### Exercise 14—1   (Accounting methods for long-term investments)

For each of the following independent situations, determine the appropriate accounting method to be used: consolidation, cost, or equity. Explain the rationale for your decision.

1. ATV Company manufactures and sells four-wheel recreational vehicles. It also provides insurance on its products through its wholly-owned subsidiary, RV Insurance Company. *Con*
2. Buy Right Inc. purchased 20,000 shares of Big Supply Company common stock to be held as a long-term investment. Big Supply has 200,000 shares of common stock outstanding. *Cost*
3. Super Tire Manufacturing Co. holds 5,000 shares of the 10,000 outstanding shares of nonvoting preferred stock of Valley Corporation. *equity*
4. Takeover Company owns 15,000 of the 50,000 shares of common stock of Western Supply Company. Takeover has tried and failed to obtain representation on Western's board of directors. *eqp*

5. Espino Inc. purchased 50,000 shares of Independent Mining Company common stock. Independent has a total of 125,000 common shares outstanding.

### Exercise 14—2  (Long-term investments in stocks—cost method)

Prepare journal entries to record the following long-term investment transactions. (Assume that the cost method is used.)

(a) Purchased 4,000 shares of Kat Company common stock at $65.25 per share, which includes brokerage fees of $800.
(b) Received a cash dividend of $2 per share from Kat Company.
(c) Sold 1,000 shares of Kat Company stock at $70 per share, less $600 in brokerage fees.
(d) The end-of-year market value of Kat Company stock is $60.25. The decline in market value is considered temporary.

### Exercise 14—3  (Long-term investments in stocks—equity method)

On January 1, 1993, Biro Corporation purchased 10,000 shares of JWS Corporation common stock for $30 per share, representing the underlying book value at that date. JWS had a total of 40,000 shares of stock outstanding at the acquisition date. Additional transactions and data for the year are as follows:

| | |
|---|---|
| Oct. 31 | JWS paid a $1-per-share dividend. |
| Dec. 31 | JWS reported net income for 1993 of $160,000. |
| Dec. 31 | The market value of JWS Corporation stock is $25 per share. |

Record the above transactions on Biro's books and show how Biro would report its investment in JWS stock on its December 31, 1993, balance sheet.

### Exercise 14—4  (Investment in common stock—cost and equity methods)

On January 10, 1993, Booker Corporation acquired 16,000 shares of the outstanding common stock of Atlanta Company for $800,000. At the time of purchase, Atlanta Company had outstanding 80,000 shares with a book value of $4 million. On December 31, 1993, the following events took place:

(a) Atlanta reported net income of $180,000 for the calendar year 1993.
(b) Booker received from Atlanta a dividend of $0.75 per share of common stock.
(c) The market value of Atlanta Company stock had temporarily declined to $45 per share.

Give the entries that would be required to reflect the purchase and subsequent events on the books of Booker Corporation, assuming (1) the cost method is appropriate; (2) the equity method is appropriate.

### Exercise 14—5  (Investment in common stock—unrecorded goodwill)

Alpha Co. acquired 20,000 shares of Beta Co. on January 1, 1992, at $12 per share. Beta Co. had 80,000 shares outstanding with a book value of $800,000. There were no identifiable undervalued assets at the time of purchase. Beta Co. recorded earnings of $260,000 and $290,000 for 1992 and 1993, respectively, and paid per-share dividends of $1.60 in 1992 and $2.00 in 1993. Assuming a 40-year straight-line amortization policy for goodwill, give the entries to record the purchase in 1992 and to reflect Alpha's share of Beta's earnings and the receipt of the dividends for 1992 and 1993.

### Exercise 14—6  (Investment in common stock—market value different from book value)

On January 3, 1993, McDonald Inc. purchased 40% of the outstanding common stock of Old Farms Co., paying $128,000 when the book value of the net assets of Old Farms equaled $250,000. The difference was attributed to equipment, which had a book value of $60,000 and a fair market value of $100,000, and to buildings, with a book value of $50,000 and a fair market value of $80,000. The remaining useful life of the equipment and buildings was 5 years and 10 years, respectively. During 1993, Old Farms reported net income of $80,000 and paid dividends of $50,000.

Give the journal entries made by McDonald Inc. during 1993 related to its investment in Old Farms.

## Exercise 14—7  (Valuation of long-term marketable equity securities)

The long-term marketable equity securities portfolio for Hill Top Industries contained the following securities at December 31, 1992 and 1993.

1.  Assuming all declines in market value are considered temporary, what is the effect of the changes in market values on the 1992 and 1993 financial statements? Give the valuation entries for these years.

| Marketable Equity Securities (Common Stock) | Initial Cost | Market Value 12/31/92 | Market Value 12/31/93 |
|---|---|---|---|
| Randall Co. ......................... | $10,000 | $12,000 | $15,000 |
| Streuling Co........................ | 7,000 | 3,000 | 2,000 |
| Santana Co........................ | 21,000 | 18,000 | 22,000 |

2.  Assume that at December 31, 1993, management believed that the market value of the Streuling Co. common stock reflected a permanent decline in the value of that stock. Give the entries to be made on December 31, 1993, under this assumption. How would the marketable securities affect the 1993 financial statements?

## Exercise 14—8  (Valuation of long-term marketable equity securities)

Bridgeman Paper Co. reported the following selected balances on its financial statements for each of the four years 1990-1993:

| | 1990 | 1991 | 1992 | 1993 |
|---|---|---|---|---|
| Allowance for Decline in Value of Non-current Marketable Equity Securities ...... | -0- | $25,000 | $18,000 | $30,000 |
| Recognized Loss From Permanent Decline in Market Value of Noncurrent Marketable Equity Securities .............. | -0- | -0- | 4,000 | -0- |
| Allowance for Decline in Value of Current Marketable Equity Securities ........... | -0- | 5,000 | 8,000 | 3,000 |

Based on these balances, reconstruct the valuation journal entries that must have been made each year.

## Exercise 14—9  (Accounting for long-term investments)

During January 1993, P&L Company purchased 5,000 shares of Robison Co. common stock for $10 per share, which reflects the underlying book value at the time of purchase. A commission of $1,000 was also paid. In addition, P&L purchased 8,000 shares of Harris Co. preferred stock for $25 per share, including the commission. Robison Co. has 20,000 shares of common stock outstanding and Harris Co. has 24,000 shares of preferred (nonvoting) stock outstanding.

The following data was obtained during 1993:

| Dividends Paid (Per Share) | |
|---|---|
| Robison Co. ............................... | $0.50 |
| Harris Co.................................... | 2.00 |

| Net Income | |
|---|---|
| Robison Co. ............................... | $ 45,000 |
| Harris Co.................................... | 120,000 |

| Market Value (Per Share) at Dec. 31 | |
|---|---|
| Robison Co. ............................... | $ 9 |
| Harris Co.................................... | 22 |

Give the journal entries required on the books of P&L Company for 1993 to account for the long-term investments in Robison Co. and Harris Co. None of the changes in the market prices of the stocks are considered permanent. Show the balance sheet presentation for the long-term investments.

### Exercise 14—10  (Investment in common stock—equity to cost method)

Porter Co. purchased 50,000 shares of Cannon Manufacturing Co. common stock on July 1, 1992, at $16.50 per share, which reflected book value as of that date. Cannon Manufacturing Co. had 200,000 common shares outstanding at the time of the purchase. Prior to this purchase, Porter Co. had no ownership interest in Cannon. In its second quarterly statement, Cannon Manufacturing Co. reported net income of $168,000 for the six months ended June 30, 1992. Porter Co. received a dividend of $21,000 from Cannon on August 1, 1992. Cannon reported net income of $360,000 for the year ended December 31, 1992, and again paid Porter Co. dividends of $21,000. On January 1, 1993, Porter Co. sold 20,000 shares of Cannon Manufacturing Co. common stock for $17 per share. Cannon reported net income of $372,000 for the year ended December 31, 1993, and paid Porter Co. dividends of $12,000. Give all entries Porter Co. would make in 1992 and 1993 in regard to the Cannon Manufacturing Co. stock.

### Exercise 14—11  (Investment in common stock—equity to cost method)

On January 1, 1992, Medproducts Inc. purchased 50% of Electronico, paying $600,000. On that date, Medproducts' net assets had a book value of $1,100,000. The difference between fair value and book value is attributed to goodwill and is amortized over 20 years. On January 1, 1993, Medproducts sold 80% of its ownership in Electronico (40% of the outstanding stock) for $575,000. Net income and dividends for 1992 and 1993 for Electronico are given below.

| | 1993 | 1992 |
|---|---|---|
| Net income ............................................ | $100,000 | $85,000 |
| Dividends............................................... | 30,000 | 20,000 |

Give the required journal entries made by Medproducts relating to its investment in Electronico for the years 1992 and 1993.

### Exercise 14—12  (Investment in common stock—cost to equity method)

Peterson Inc. purchased 15% of the outstanding common stock of Sunspot Co. on January 1, 1993, when Sunspot's net assets had a book value and fair value of $400,000. Peterson Inc. paid $75,000. Any excess of fair value over cost is attributable to goodwill. Goodwill, when amortized, is amortized over a 40-year period. On January 1, 1994, Peterson purchased an additional 15% of the outstanding stock of Sunspot, paying another $75,000. (Assume net asset book and fair value is still $400,000.) Sunspot's reported income and dividends for 1993 and 1994 are given below.

| | 1994 | 1993 |
|---|---|---|
| Net income ............................................ | $50,000 | $30,000 |
| Dividends............................................... | 40,000 | 30,000 |

Prepare the journal entries made by Peterson during 1993 and 1994 related to its investment in Sunspot Co., including the adjusting entries necessary to reflect the change from the cost to the equity method.

### Exercise 14—13    (Investment in common stock—cost to equity method)

Devers Corporation purchased 5% of the 100,000 outstanding common shares of Milo Inc. on January 1, 1991, for a total purchase price of $7,500. Net assets of Milo Inc. at the time had a book and fair value of $150,000. Net income for Milo Inc. for the year ended December 31, 1991, was $50,000. Devers received dividends from Milo during the year of $1,500. There was no change of Devers' ownership of Milo Inc. during 1992, and Milo reported net income of $70,000 for the year ended December 31, 1992. Devers received dividends of $2,000 from Milo for that year. On January 1, 1993, Devers purchased an additional 20% of Milo Inc.'s common stock or 20,000 shares for a total price of $40,000. Milo Inc.'s net asset book and fair value at the time of the purchase was $200,000. For the year ended December 31, 1993, Milo Inc. reported net income of $100,000; Devers received dividends from Milo Inc. totaling $10,000 for the year ended December 31, 1993.

Prepare journal entries for Devers Corporation to reflect the preceding transactions, including adjusting entries necessary to reflect the change from the cost method to the equity method of accounting for Devers Corporation's investment in Milo Inc.

### Exercise 14—14    (Fund investments)

On December 31, 1992, Haws Corporation set up a stock redemption fund, with an initial deposit of $150,000. On February 1, 1993, Haws Corporation invested $127,500 stock redemption fund cash in 10% preferred stock of Mackay Inc., par value of $75,000. Mackay normally declares and pays dividends on the preferred stock semiannually: March 1 and September 1. On April 1, 1993, Haws exchanged the stock with another investor for 4,000 shares of Lamas Corporation common stock. The market value of the common stock at the date of exchange was $35 per share. Give all the entries necessary to record the preceding transactions assuming semiannual dividends were paid.

### Exercise 14—15    (Fund accumulation schedule)

Fund tables show that 5 annual deposits of $16,379.75 accruing interest at 10% compounded annually will result in a total accumulation of $100,000 immediately after the fifth payment. (1) Prepare a fund accumulation schedule showing the theoretical growth of a property acquisition fund over the 5-year period. (2) Give all of the entries that would appear on the books for the increases in the property acquisition fund balance for the first 3 years.

---

## PROBLEMS

### Problem 14—1    (Investments in common stock)

Arroyo Inc. and the Bell Corp. each have 100,000 shares of no-par common stock outstanding. Universal Inc. acquired 10,000 shares of Arroyo stock and 25,000 shares of Bell stock in 1990. Changes in retained earnings for Arroyo and Bell for 1992 and 1993 are as follows:

|  | Arroyo Inc. | Bell Corp. |
|---|---|---|
| Retained earnings (deficit), January 1, 1992 | $200,000 | $(35,000) |
| Cash dividends, 1992 | (25,000) | — |
|  | $175,000 | $(35,000) |
| Net income, 1992 | 40,000 | 65,000 |
| Retained earnings, December 31, 1992 | $215,000 | $ 30,000 |
| Cash dividends, 1993 | (30,000) | (10,000) |
| Net income, 1993 | 60,000 | 25,000 |
| Retained earnings, December 31, 1993 | $245,000 | $ 45,000 |

**Instructions:**  Give the entries required on the books of Universal Inc. for 1992 and 1993 to account for its investments.

## Problem 14—2   (Long-term investments in stock—equity method)

On January 1, 1993, Compustat Co. bought 30% of the outstanding common stock of Freelance Corp. for $258,000 cash. Compustat Co. accounts for this investment by the equity method. At the date of acquisition of the stock, Freelance Corp.'s net assets had a carrying value of $620,000. Assets with an average remaining life of five years have a current market value that is $130,000 in excess of their carrying values. The remaining difference between the purchase price and the value of the underlying stockholders' equity cannot be attributed to any tangible asset. Compustat Co. has a policy of amortizing goodwill over 40 years. At the end of 1993, Freelance Corp. reports net income of $180,000. During 1993, Freelance Corp. declared and paid cash dividends of $20,000.

**Instructions:**   Give the entries necessary to reflect Compustat Co.'s investment in Freelance Corp. for 1993.

## Problem 14—3   (Investment in common stock)

On July 1 of the current year, Melissa Co. acquired 25% of the outstanding shares of common stock of International Co. at a total cost of $700,000. The underlying equity (net assets) of the stock acquired by Melissa was only $600,000. Melissa was willing to pay more than book value for the International Co. stock for the following reasons:

(a)   International owned depreciable plant assets (10-year remaining economic life) with a current fair value of $60,000 more than their carrying amount.
(b)   International owned land with a current fair value of $300,000 more than its carrying amount.
(c)   Melissa believed International possessed enough goodwill to justify the remainder of the cost. Melissa's accounting policy with respect to goodwill is to amortize it over 40 years.

International Co. earned net income of $540,000 evenly over the current year ended December 31. On December 31, International declared and paid a cash dividend of $105,000 to common stockholders. Both companies close their accounting records on December 31.

**Instructions:**

1. Compute the total amount of goodwill of International Co. based on the price paid by Melissa Co.
2. Prepare all journal entries in Melissa's accounting records relating to the investment for the year ended December 31, under the cost method of accounting.
3. Prepare all journal entries in Melissa's accounting records relating to the investment for the year ended December 31, under the equity method of accounting.

## Problem 14—4   (Accounting for long-term investments—cost and equity methods)

On January 2, 1991, Brozo Company acquired 20% of the 200,000 shares of outstanding common stock of Newberry Corp. for $30 per share. The purchase price was equal to Newberry's underlying book value. Brozo plans to hold this stock as a long-term investment.

The following data is applicable for 1991 and 1992:

|  | 1991 | 1992 |
|---|---|---|
| Newberry dividends (paid Oct. 31) ........................ | $20,000 | $24,000 |
| Newberry earnings ........................................ | 70,000 | 80,000 |
| Newberry stock market price at year-end .................. | 32 | 31 |

On January 2, 1993, Brozo Company sold 10,000 shares of Newberry stock for $31 per share. During 1993, Newberry reported net income of $60,000, and on October 31, 1993, Newberry paid dividends of $10,000. At December 31, 1993, after a significant stock market decline, which is expected to be temporary, Newberry's stock was selling for $22 per share. After selling the 10,000 shares, Brozo does not expect to exercise significant influence over Newberry.

**Instructions:**

1. Make all journal entries for Brozo Company for 1991, 1992, and 1993 assuming the 20% original ownership interest allowed significant influence over Newberry.
2. Make the year-end valuation adjusting entries for Brozo Company for 1991, 1992, and 1993 assuming the 20% original ownership interest did not allow significant influence over Newberry.

## Problem 14—5  (Accounting for marketable equity securities)

The Trans America Trust Co. owns both temporary and long-term investments in marketable equity securities. The following securities were owned on December 31, 1992:

**Temporary Investments**

| Security | Shares | Total Cost | Market Value Dec. 31, 1992 |
|---|---|---|---|
| Albert Groceries, Inc. ..................... | 600 | $ 9,000 | $11,500 |
| West Data, Inc. ......................... | 1,000 | 27,000 | 18,000 |
| Steel Co. .............................. | 450 | 9,900 | 10,215 |

**Long-Term Investments**

| Security | Shares | Total Cost | Market Value Dec. 31, 1992 |
|---|---|---|---|
| Dairy Products ......................... | 2,000 | $ 86,000 | $ 90,000 |
| Vern Movies, Inc. ...................... | 15,000 | 390,000 | 345,000 |
| Disks, Inc. ............................ | 5,000 | 60,000 | 80,000 |

The following transactions occurred during 1993:

(a)  Sold 500 shares of West Data for $9,500.
(b)  Sold 200 shares of Disks, Inc., for $3,000.
(c)  Transferred all of Albert Groceries to long-term portfolio when the total market value was $12,900.
(d)  Transferred the remaining shares of Disks, Inc., to the temporary investment portfolio when the market price was $20 per share. These shares were subsequently sold for $18 per share.

At December 31, 1993, market prices for the remaining securities were as follows:

| Security | Market Price Per Share |
|---|---|
| Albert Groceries Inc. ........................................ | $22 |
| West Data, Inc. ............................................. | 15 |
| Steel Co. .................................................. | 21 |
| Dairy Products ............................................. | 42 |
| Vern Movies, Inc. .......................................... | 28 |

**Instructions:**  Prepare all journal entries necessary to record Trans America Trust Co.'s marketable equity securities transactions and year-end adjustments for 1993. Assume all declines in market value are temporary.

## Problem 14—6  (Valuation of long-term marketable equity securities)

The long-term investment portfolio of Morris Inc. at December 31, 1992, contains the following securities:

Opus Co. common, 3% ownership, 5,000 shares; cost, $100,000; market value, $95,000.

Garrod Inc. preferred, 2,000 shares; cost, $40,000; market value, $43,000.

Sherrill Inc. common, 30% ownership, 20,000 shares; cost, $1,140,000; market value, $1,130,000.

Jennings Co. common, 15% ownership, 25,000 shares; cost, $67,500; market value, $50,000.

**Instructions:**

1. Give the valuation adjustment required at December 31, 1992, assuming market values in the past for the long-term investment portfolio have always exceeded cost and none of the indicated declines in market value are considered permanent.
2. Assume the Jennings Co. common stock market decline is considered permanent. Give the valuation entries required at December 31, 1992, under this change in assumption.
3. Assume the market values for the long-term investment portfolio at December 31, 1993, were as follows:

| | |
|---|---:|
| Opus Co. Common ............................................ | $ 102,000 |
| Garrod Inc. Preferred ........................................ | 43,000 |
| Sherrill Inc. Common ........................................ | 1,115,000 |
| Jennings Co. Common........................................ | 45,000 |

Give the valuation entries at December 31, 1993, assuming all declines in 1992 and 1993 are temporary except for the 1992 decline in Jennings Co. stock.

### Problem 14—7  (Investment in common stock—fair market value less than book value)

MMM Inc. purchased 40% of XYZ Co. on January 4, 1993, for $250,000 when XYZ's book value was $630,000. On that day, the market value of the net assets of XYZ equaled their book values with the following exceptions:

| | **Book** | **Market** |
|---|---:|---:|
| Equipment............................................ | $185,000 | $160,000 |
| Buildings ............................................ | 30,000 | 50,000 |

The equipment has a remaining useful life of 10 years, and the building has a remaining useful life of 20 years. XYZ reported the following related to operations for 1993 and 1994:

| | **Net Income** | **Dividends** |
|---|---:|---:|
| 1993 ............................................ | $ 75,000 | $10,000 |
| 1994 ............................................ | (15,000) | 5,000 |

**Instructions:**   Provide the entries made by MMM Inc. relating to its investment in XYZ for the years 1993 and 1994.

### Problem 14—8  (Change from cost to equity method)

On January 1, 1992, Beans Inc. paid $400,000 for 10,000 shares of Keller Company's voting common stock, which was a 15% interest in Keller. At this date, the net assets of Keller totaled $2 million. The fair values of all of Keller's identifiable assets and liabilities were equal to their book values. Beans did not have the ability to exercise significant influence over the operating and financial policies of Keller. Beans received dividends of $0.70 per share from Keller on October 1, 1992. Keller reported net income of $250,000 for the year ended December 31, 1992.

On July 1, 1993, Beans paid $1,500,000 for 30,000 additional shares of Keller Company's voting common stock, which represents a 25% interest in Keller. The fair value of all Keller's identifiable assets, net of liabilities, was equal to their book values of $4,600,000. As a result of this transaction, Beans has the ability to exercise significant influence over the operating and financial policies of Keller. Beans received a dividend of $0.80 per share from Keller on April 1, 1993, and $1.35 per share from Keller on October 1, 1993. Keller reported net income of $300,000 for the year ended December 31, 1993, and $100,000 for the six months ended December 31, 1993. Beans amortizes goodwill over a 40-year period.

**Instructions:**

1. Determine the amount of income from the investment in Keller Company common stock that should be reported in Beans' income statement for the year ended December 31, 1992.
2. Beans issues comparative financial statements for the years ended December 31, 1993 and 1992. Prepare schedules showing the income or loss that Beans should report from its investment in Keller Company for 1993 and 1992 (restated).

## Problem 14—9  (Investment in common stock—cost to equity to cost method)

Cook Inc. wants to gain a controlling interest in Fox Chemical Co. in order to assure a steady source of a raw material manufactured by Fox. The following transactions occurred with respect to Cook and Fox. Both companies keep their books on a calendar-year basis.

**1989**

Jan.  2    Cook purchased 5,000 shares (5%) of Fox common stock for $10 per share. The assets of Fox had a net carrying value of $800,000. At that date, certain depreciable equipment owned by Fox had a fair market value $30,000 in excess of its carrying value, with an estimated remaining useful life of 10 years. Fox also carried land on its books that had a fair market value $70,000 in excess of its book value. The balance of the excess of the cost of the stock over the underlying equity in net assets was attributable to goodwill, which is amortized over 40 years. (Unless circumstances indicate otherwise, Cook's policy is to amortize any recognized goodwill evenly over a 40-year period from date of acquisition.)

Feb.  15    Cook received a dividend of $3,000 representing a distribution from income earned in 1988.

July  1    Cook purchased 10,000 additional shares of Fox stock for $11 per share. Fox's net income for the first six months of 1989 was $150,000. The net carrying value of Fox stockholders' equity at July 1, 1989, was $890,000. The difference between the fair market value of Fox's depreciable assets and their carrying value at this date was $30,000, and the equipment had an estimated remaining useful life of 9.5 years from the date of purchase. The market value of the land remained $70,000 over book value. Fox had not issued any new stock during the past six months.

Dec.  31    Fox reported net income for the year of $260,000.

**1990**

Feb.  15    Cook received a cash dividend from Fox of $18,000.

Dec.  31    Fox reported net income for the year of $320,000.

**1991**

Jan.  2    Cook purchased 20,000 additional shares of Fox stock for $13 per share, which permitted Cook to exercise significant influence over Fox. At this time, Fox was experiencing a boycott of its products that was expected to last indefinitely. Although the difference between the fair market value of its assets and their carrying values remained the same, Fox's boycott problems detracted from the long-term attractiveness of its shares, and no implied goodwill was included in the purchase price. (There has been no change in the estimated useful lives of depreciable assets from the date of the original purchase on January 2, 1989.)

Feb. 15     Cook received a cash dividend of $49,000 from Fox.
Dec. 31     Fox reported net income of $280,000. In view of Fox's boycott situation, Cook decided to write off remaining goodwill over a period of 10 years, beginning this year.

1992
Feb. 15     Cook received a cash dividend of $39,200 from Fox.
Apr. 1      Cook, after experiencing a series of reversals in the marketplace, ceased manufacturing the product containing the raw material from Fox. On this date, Cook sold 20,000 shares of Fox stock for $12 per share. Cook used the average cost of its investment in Fox in calculating its cost basis per share in the investment. Assume Fox had no income for the first quarter of 1992.
Dec. 31     Fox reported net income of $295,000 for the year ended December 31, 1992.

1993
Feb. 15     Cook received a dividend of $17,700 from Fox.
Mar. 20     Cook sold its remaining 15,000 shares of Fox stock for $11.50 per share.

**Instructions:** Give all the entries necessary to record these transactions on the books of Cook Inc. (Round computations to the nearest dollar.)

## Problem 14—10   (Fund accumulation)

On December 31, 1991, a fund is set up to redeem $50,000 of preferred stock. The fund is guaranteed to earn 8% compounded annually and must generate enough income to enable the company to retire the stock after four payments. The annual installments paid to the fund trustee are $11,096.07. The first deposit is made immediately.

**Instructions:**

1. Give the journal entries in connection with the fund for the years 1991 and 1992. (The company keeps its books on the calendar-year basis.)
2. Assume that on December 31, 1994, the fund balance of $50,000 consisted of $10,000 cash and $40,000 in securities that were purchased in 1993. The securities are sold at the end of 1994 for $48,000. Give all the journal entries that would be made to record the sale of the securities, retire the $50,000 of preferred stock, and liquidate any balance in the fund account.

## Problem 14—11   (Establishing a fund for the retirement of bonds)

Starkson Inc. has elected to establish a bond redemption fund in order to have the necessary funds available to retire a bond that matures in five years. The bonds have a face value of $100,000. Management invests the annual payments into a fund that is guaranteed to return 8% compounded annually.

**Instructions:**

1. What is the amount of the annuity payment management must make each year in order to accumulate $100,000 at the end of five years if the first payment is made today?
2. Prepare a fund accumulation schedule in connection with the redemption fund, assuming the actual rates earned on the funds were 8%, 8.5%, 10%, 8%, and 9% in Years 1-5, respectively.
3. Provide the journal entry to retire the bond at the end of the fifth year. Why didn't the bond redemption fund have exactly $100,000 in it at the end of Year 5?

# PART THREE

## Liabilities and Equity

# CHAPTER 15

## Liabilities–Current and Contingent

---

---

In early 1984, Pennzoil sued Texaco for $14 billion as a result of Texaco's interference in Pennzoil's attempted acquisition of Getty Oil. In December of 1985, a jury awarded $10.5 billion to Pennzoil. The case was appealed in both 1986 and 1987, and in each case, judgment was against Texaco. In December of 1987, Pennzoil and Texaco agreed to settle the litigation by Texaco paying Pennzoil $3 billion in early 1988. At what point during this period did Texaco have a liability?

In this chapter, the general nature of liabilities is discussed as well as how to account for current and contingent liabilities. Subsequent chapters focus on noncurrent liabilities, including bonds, leases, and pensions, that are relatively complex in nature and, in some cases, directly related to asset accounts.

To illustrate the importance of accurately reporting the liabilities of a company, consider the following hypothetical, but realistic, situation.

Judge E. J. Wright is currently deliberating over a type of case that is becoming increasingly common in our society. A suit has been filed by three stockholders against

Transcontinental Corporation alleging that Transcontinental's year-end balance sheet was misleading because it did not accurately reflect the financial position of the company at that date. The stockholders relied on the published financial statements and subsequently lost money on their investments in Transcontinental. Two specific points are at issue. First, Transcontinental chose not to estimate its liability under certain warranty provisions, but instead accounted for warranty expenses on a cash basis. The plaintiffs contend that the warranties were in fact liabilities and should have been reported as such under accrual accounting procedures. Second, Transcontinental did not report a contingent liability relating to a significant, pending lawsuit with a supplier, which Transcontinental subsequently lost. Plaintiffs contend again that this information was material and relevant and should have been disclosed.

Although hypothetical, the above situation is typical of many lawsuits being filed against companies, accountants, underwriters, and financial analysts and advisers. With respect to liabilities, the basic questions are:

- What is a liability?
- When and how should liabilities be measured and disclosed?

These questions relate to definition, recognition, measurement, and reporting addressed by the FASB's conceptual framework, as discussed in Chapter 2.

## DEFINITION OF LIABILITIES

Liabilities have been defined by the FASB as "probable future sacrifices of economic benefits arising from present obligations of a particular entity to transfer assets or provide services to other entities in the future as a result of past transactions or events."[1] This definition contains significant components that need to be explained before individual liability accounts are discussed.

A liability is a result of **past transactions or events**. Thus, a liability is not recognized until incurred. This part of the definition excludes contractual obligations from an exchange of promises if performance by both parties is still in the future. Such contracts are referred to as **executory contracts**. Determining when an executory contract qualifies as a liability is not always easy. For example, the signing of a labor contract that obligates both the employer and the employee does not give rise to a liability in current accounting practice, nor does the placing of an order for the purchase of merchandise. However, under some conditions, the signing of a lease is recognized as an event that requires the current recognition of a liability even though a lease is essentially an executory contract.

A liability must involve a **probable future transfer of assets or services**. Although liabilities result from past transactions or events, an obligation may be contingent upon the occurrence of another event sometime in the future. When occurrence of the future event seems probable, the obligation is defined as a liability. Although the majority of liabilities are satisfied by payment of cash, some obligations are satisfied by transferring other types of assets or by providing services. For example, revenue received in advance requires recognition of an obligation to provide goods or services in the future. Usually, the time of payment is specified by a debt instrument, e.g., a note requiring payment of interest and principal on a given date or series of dates. Some obligations, however, require the transfer of assets or services over a period of time, but the exact dates cannot be determined when the liability is incurred, e.g., obligations to provide parts or service under a warranty agreement.

---

[1]*Statement of Financial Accounting Concepts No. 6,* "Elements of Financial Statements" (Stamford: Financial Accounting Standards Board, December 1985), par. 35.

A liability is the **obligation of a particular entity**, i.e., the entity that has the responsibility to transfer assets or provide services. As long as the payment or transfer is probable, it is not necessary that the entity to whom the obligation is owed be identified. Thus, a warranty to make any repairs necessary to an item sold by an entity is an obligation of that entity even though it is not certain which customers will receive benefits. Generally, the obligation rests on a foundation of legal rights and duties. However, obligations created, inferred, or construed from the facts of a particular situation may also be recognized as liabilities. For example, if a company regularly pays vacation pay or year-end bonuses, accrual of these items as a liability is warranted even though no legal agreement exists to make these payments.

Although the FASB's definition is helpful, the question of when an item is a liability is still not always easy to answer. Examples of areas where there are continuing controversies include the problems associated with off-balance sheet financing, deferred income taxes, leases, pensions, and even some equity securities, such as redeemable preferred stock.[2] Once an item is accepted as having met the definition of a liability, there is still the need to appropriately classify, measure, and report the liability.

## CLASSIFICATION AND MEASUREMENT OF LIABILITIES

For reporting purposes, liabilities are usually classified as **current** or **noncurrent**. The distinction between current and noncurrent liabilities was introduced and explained in Chapter 5, where it was pointed out that the computation of working capital is considered by many to be a useful measure of the liquidity of an enterprise.

### Current Versus Noncurrent Classification

As noted in Chapter 5, the same rules generally apply for the classification of liabilities as for assets. If a liability arises in the course of an entity's normal operating cycle, it is considered current if current assets will be used to satisfy the obligation within one year or one operating cycle, whichever period is longer. On the other hand, bank borrowings, notes, mortgages, and similar obligations are related to the general financial condition of the entity, rather than directly to the operating cycle, and are classified as current only if they are to be paid with current assets within one year.

When debt that has been classified as noncurrent will mature within the next year, the liability should be reported as a current liability in order to reflect the expected drain on current assets. However, if the liability is to be paid by transfer of noncurrent assets that have been accumulated for the purpose of liquidating the liability, the obligation continues to be classified as noncurrent.

### Measurement of Liabilities

The distinction between current and noncurrent liabilities is also an important consideration in the measurement of liabilities. Obviously, before liabilities can be reported on the financial statements, they must be stated in monetary terms. The measurement used for liabilities is the **present value of the future cash outflows** to settle the obligation. Generally, this is the amount of cash required to liquidate the obligation if it were paid today.

If a claim isn't to be paid until sometime in the future, as is the case with noncurrent liabilities, the claim should either provide for interest to be paid on the debt, or the obligation should be reported at the discounted value of its maturity amount. Current obligations that arise in the course of normal business operations are generally due within a short period, e.g., 30-60 days, and normally are not discounted.[3] Thus, trade accounts payable are not discounted even though they carry no interest provision. However, this is an exception to the general rule; most nonoperating business transactions, such as the borrowing of money, purchase of assets over time, and long-term leases, do involve the discounting process. The obligation in these instances is the present value of the future resource outflows.

For measurement purposes, liabilities can be divided into three categories:

1. Liabilities that are definite in amount.
2. Estimated liabilities.
3. Contingent liabilities.

The measurement of liabilities always involves some uncertainty, since a liability, by definition, involves a *future* outflow of resources. However, for the first category above, both the existence of the liability and the amount to be paid are determinable because of a contract, trade agreement, or general business practice. An example of a **liability that is definite in amount** is the principal payment on a note.

The second category includes items that are definitely liabilities, i.e., they involve a definite future resource outflow, but the actual amount of the obligation cannot be established currently. In this situation, the amount of the liability is estimated so that the obligation is reflected in the current period, even though at an approximated value. A warranty obligation that is recorded on an accrual basis is an example of an **estimated liability**.

Generally, liabilities from both of the first two categories are reported on a balance sheet as claims against recorded assets, either as current or noncurrent liabilities, whichever is appropriate. However, items that resemble liabilities but are contingent upon the occurrence of some future event are not recorded until it is probable that the event will occur. Even though the amount of the potential obligation may be known, the actual existence of a liability is questionable, since it is contingent upon a future event for which there is considerable uncertainty. An example of a **contingent liability** is a pending lawsuit. Only if the lawsuit is lost, or is settled out of court, will a liability be recorded. While not recorded in the accounts, some contingent liabilities should be disclosed in the notes to the financial statements, as discussed and illustrated later in the chapter.

## LIABILITIES THAT ARE DEFINITE IN AMOUNT

Representative of liabilities that are definite in amount and reported on the balance sheet are accounts payable, notes payable, and miscellaneous operating payables including salaries, payroll taxes, property and sales taxes, and income taxes. Some liabilities accrue as time passes. Most notable in this category are interest and rent, although the latter is frequently paid in advance. Some of the problems that arise in determining the balances to be reported for liabilities definite in amount are described in the following sections.

### Accounts Payable

Most goods and services in today's economic environment are purchased on credit. The term **accounts payable** usually refers to the amount due for the purchase of materials by a

---

[3]*Opinions of the Accounting Principles Board No. 21*, "Interest on Receivables and Payables" (New York: American Institute of Certified Public Accountants, 1971), par. 3.

manufacturing company or merchandise by a wholesaler or retailer. Other obligations, such as salaries and wages, rent, interest, and utilities, are reported as separate liabilities in accounts descriptive of the nature of the obligation. Accounts payable are usually not recorded when purchase orders are placed but when legal title to the goods passes to the buyer. The rules for the customary recognition of legal passage of title were presented in Chapter 10. If goods are in transit at year-end, the purchase should be recorded if the shipment terms indicate that title has passed. This means that care must be exercised to review the purchase of goods and services near the end of an accounting period to assure a proper cutoff and reporting of liabilities and inventory.

It is customary to report accounts payable at the expected amount of the payment. Because the payment period is normally short, no recognition of interest is required. As indicated in Chapter 10, if cash discounts are available, the liability should be reported net of the expected cash discount. Failure to use the net method in recording purchases usually reports liabilities in excess of the payment finally made, since most companies are careful to take advantage of available cash discounts.

### Short-Term Debt

Companies often borrow money on a short-term basis for operating purposes other than for the purchase of materials or merchandise involving accounts payable. Collectively, these obligations may be referred to as **short-term debt**. In most cases, such debt is evidenced by a **promissory note**, a formal written promise to pay a sum of money in the future, and is usually reflected on the debtor's books as **Notes Payable**.

Notes issued to trade creditors for the purchase of goods or services are called **trade notes payable**. Notes issued to banks or to officers and stockholders for loans to the company, and those issued to others for the purchase of noncurrent operating assets, are called **nontrade notes payable**. It is normally desirable to classify current notes payable on the balance sheet as trade or nontrade, since such information would reveal to statement users the sources of indebtedness and the extent to which the company has relied on each source in financing its activities.

The problems encountered in the valuation of notes payable are the same as those discussed in Chapter 9 with respect to notes receivable. Thus, a short-term note payable is recorded and reported at its present value, which is normally the face value of the note. This presumes that the note bears a reasonable stated rate of interest. However, if a note has no stated rate of interest, or if the stated rate is unreasonable, then the face value of the note would need to be discounted to its present value to reflect the effective rate of interest implicit in the note. This is accomplished by debiting Discount on Notes Payable when the note is issued, and by writing off the discount to Interest Expense over the life of the note, in the same manner as was illustrated for the discount on notes receivable in Chapter 9.

Discount on Notes Payable is a contra account to Notes Payable and would be reported on the balance sheet as follows:

Current liabilities:
Notes payable........................................ $100,000
Less discount on notes payable........................ 10,000   $90,000

### Short-Term Obligations Expected to Be Refinanced

As noted at the beginning of the chapter, omissions or misrepresentation in the reporting of liabilities can create serious problems for users of financial statements. A similar problem can result from the misclassification of liabilities. Since the "current" classification is reserved for those obligations that will be satisfied with current assets within a year, a short-term obligation that is expected to be refinanced on a long-term basis should not be reported as a current liability. This applies to the currently maturing portion of a long-term debt and to all other short-term obligations except those arising in the normal course of operations that are due in customary terms. Similarly, it should not be assumed that a short-term obligation will be refinanced, and therefore classified as a noncurrent liability, unless the refinancing arrangements are secure. Thus, to avoid potential manipulation, the refinancing expectation must be realistic and not just a mere possibility.

An example will illustrate this last point and show the importance of proper classification. Assume that a company borrows a substantial amount of money that it expects to pay back at the end of 5 years. The president of the company signs a 6-month note, which the loan officer at the bank verbally agrees will be renewed "automatically" until the actual maturity date in 5 years. The only current obligation expected is payment of the accrued interest each renewal period. Under these circumstances, the company reports the obligation as noncurrent, except for the accrued interest obligation. Assume further that the loan officer leaves the bank and that the new bank official will not allow the short-term note to be refinanced. The financial picture of the company is now dramatically changed. What was considered a long-term obligation because of refinancing expectations is suddenly a current liability requiring settlement with liquid assets in the near future. This hypothetical situation is similar to what actually happened to Penn Central Railroad before it went bankrupt.

To assist with this problem, the FASB in 1975 issued Statement No. 6, which contains the authoritative guideline for classifying short-term obligations expected to be refinanced. According to the FASB, *both* of the following conditions must be met before a short-term obligation may be properly excluded from the current liability classification.[4]

1. Management must *intend to refinance* the obligation on a long-term basis.
2. Management must *demonstrate an ability to refinance* the obligation.

Concerning the second point, an ability to refinance may be demonstrated by:

(a) Actually refinancing the obligation during the period between the balance sheet date and the date the statements are issued.
(b) Reaching a firm agreement that clearly provides for refinancing on a long-term basis.

The terms of the refinancing agreement should be noncancelable as to all parties and extend beyond the current year. In addition, the company should not be in violation of the agreement at the balance sheet date or the date of issuance, and the lender or investor should be financially capable of meeting the refinancing requirements.

If an actual refinancing does occur before the balance sheet is issued, the portion of the short-term obligation that is to be excluded from current liabilities cannot exceed the proceeds from the new debt or equity securities issued to retire the old debt. For example, if a $400,000 long-term note is issued to partially refinance $750,000 of short-term obligations, only $400,000 of the short-term debt can be excluded from current liabilities.

An additional question relates to the timing of the refinancing. If the obligation is paid prior to the actual refinancing, the obligation should be included in current liabilities on the balance sheet.[5] To illustrate, assume that the liabilities of CareFree Inc. at December 31, 1992, include a note payable for $200,000 due January 15, 1993. The management of CareFree intends to refinance the note by issuing 10-year bonds. The bonds are

---

[4]*Statement of Financial Accounting Standards No. 6*, "Classification of Short-Term Obligations Expected to Be Refinanced" (Stamford: Financial Accounting Standards Board, 1975), pars. 10 and 11.

[5]*FASB Interpretation No. 8*, "Classification of a Short-Term Obligation Repaid Prior to Being Replaced by a Long-Term Security" (Stamford: Financial Accounting Standards Board, 1976), par. 3.

actually issued before the issuance of the December 31, 1992, balance sheet on February 15, 1993. If the bonds were issued prior to payment of the note, the note should be classified as noncurrent on the December 31, 1992, balance sheet. If payment of the note preceded the sale of the bonds, however, the note should be included in current liabilities.

Normally, classified balance sheets are presented that show a total for "current liabilities." If a short-term obligation is excluded from that category due to refinancing expectations, disclosure should be made in the notes to the financial statements. The note should include a general description of the refinancing agreement.

## Miscellaneous Operating Payables

Many miscellaneous payables arise in the course of a company's operating activities. Three of these are specifically discussed in this section. They are indicative of other specific liabilities that could be reported by a given entity. In general, the points made in discussing the definition of liabilities in the opening section of this chapter apply to these miscellaneous operating liabilities.

**Salaries and Wages**    In an ongoing entity, salaries and wages of officers and other employees accrue daily. Normally, no entry is made for these expenses until payment is made. A liability for unpaid salaries and wages is recorded, however, at the end of an accounting period when a more precise matching of revenues and expenses is desired. An estimate of the amount of unpaid wages and salaries is made, and an adjusting entry is prepared to recognize the amount due. Usually, the entire accrued amount is identified as salaries payable with no attempt to identify the withholdings associated with the accrual. When payment is made in the subsequent period, the amount is allocated between the employee and other entities such as government taxing units, unions, and insurance companies.

For example, assume that a company has 15 employees who are paid every two weeks. At December 31, four days of unpaid wages have accrued. Analysis reveals that the 15 employees earn a total of $1,000 a day. Thus the adjusting entry at December 31 would be:

| | | |
|---|---|---|
| Salaries and Wages Expense | 4,000 | |
| Salaries and Wages Payable | | 4,000 |

This entry may be reversed at the beginning of the next period, or when payment is made, Salaries and Wages Payable may be debited for $4,000.

Additional compensation in the form of accrued bonuses or commissions should also be recognized. Bonuses are often based on some measure of the employer's income.

**Payroll Taxes**    Social security and income tax legislation impose four taxes based on payrolls:

1. Federal old-age, survivors', disability, and hospital insurance (tax to both employer and employee).
2. Federal unemployment insurance (tax to employer only).
3. State unemployment insurance (tax to employer only).
4. Individual income tax (tax to employee only, but withheld and paid by employer).

*Federal Old-Age, Survivors', Disability, and Hospital Insurance*    The Federal Insurance Contributions Act (FICA), generally referred to as social security legislation, provides for FICA taxes from both employers and employees to provide funds for federal old-age, survivors', disability, and hospital insurance benefits for certain individuals and members of their families. At one time, only employees were covered by this legislation; however, coverage now includes most individuals who are self-employed.

Provisions of the legislation require an employer of more than one employee, with certain exceptions, to withhold FICA taxes from each employee's wages. The amount of the tax is based on a tax rate and wage base as currently specified in the law. The tax rate and wage base both have increased dramatically since the inception of the social security program in the 1930s. The initial rate of FICA tax was 1% in 1937; the rate in effect for 1990 was 7.65%.[6] During that same period, the annual wages subject to FICA tax increased from $3,000 to $51,300. The taxable wage base is subject to yearly increases based on cost-of-living adjustments in social security benefits.

The employer remits the amount of FICA tax withheld for all employees, along with a matching amount, to the federal government. The employer is required to maintain complete records and submit detailed support for the tax remittance. The employer is responsible for the full amount of the tax even if employee contributions are not withheld.

***Federal Unemployment Insurance***    The Federal Social Security Act and the Federal Unemployment Tax Act (FUTA) provide for the establishment of unemployment insurance plans. Employers with covered workers employed in each of 20 weeks during a calendar year or who pay $1,500 or more in wages during any calendar quarter are affected.

Under present provisions of the law, the federal government taxes eligible employers on the first $7,000 paid to every employee during the calendar year. The rate of tax in effect since 1985 is 6.2%, but the employer is allowed a tax credit limited to 5.4% for taxes paid under state unemployment compensation laws. No tax is levied on the employee. When an employer is subject to a tax of 5.4% or more as a result of state unemployment legislation, the federal unemployment tax, then, is 0.8% of the qualifying wages.

Payment to the federal government is required quarterly. Unemployment benefits are paid by the individual states. Revenues collected by the federal government under the acts are used to meet the cost of administering state and federal unemployment plans as well as to provide supplemental unemployment benefits.

***State Unemployment Insurance***    State unemployment compensation laws are not the same in all states. In most states, laws provide for tax only on employers; but in a few states, taxes are applicable to both employers and employees. Each state law specifies the classes of exempt employees, the number of employees required or the amount of wages paid before the tax is applicable, and the contributions that are to be made by employers and employees. Exemptions are frequently similar to those under the federal act. Tax payment is generally required on or before the last day of the month following each calendar quarter.

Although the normal tax on employers may be 5.4%, states have merit rating or experience plans providing for lower rates based on employers' individual employment experiences. Employers with stable employment records are taxed at a rate in keeping with the limited amount of benefits required for their former employees; employers with less satisfactory employment records contribute at a rate more nearly approaching 5.4% in view of the greater amount of benefits paid to their former employees. Savings under state merit systems are allowed as credits in the calculation of the federal contribution, so the federal tax does not exceed 0.8% even though payment of less than 5.4% is made by an employer entitled to a lower rate under the merit rating system.

---

[6]For illustrative purposes and end-of-chapter exercises and problems, a rate of 7.65% will be used.

***Income Tax***    Federal income tax on the wages of an individual are collected in the period in which the wages are paid. The "pay-as-you-go" plan requires employers to withhold income tax from wages paid to their employees. Most states and many local governments also impose income taxes on the earnings of employees that must be withheld and remitted by the employer. Withholding is required not only of employers engaged in a trade or business, but also of religious and charitable organizations, educational institutions, social organizations, and governments of the United States, the states, the territories, and their agencies, instrumentalities, and political subdivisions. Certain classes of wage payments are exempt from withholding although these are still subject to income tax.

An employer must meet withholding requirements under the law even if wages of only one employee are subject to such withholdings. The amounts to be withheld by the employer are developed from formulas provided by the law or from tax withholding tables made available by the government. Withholding is based on the length of the payroll period, the amount earned, and the number of withholding exemptions claimed by the employee. Taxes required under the Federal Insurance Contributions Act (both employee and employer portions) and income tax that has been withheld by the employer are paid to the federal government at the same time. These combined taxes are deposited in an authorized bank quarterly, monthly, or several times each month depending on the amount of the liability. Quarterly and annual statements must also be filed providing a summary of all wages paid by the employer.

***Accounting for Payroll Taxes***    To illustrate the accounting procedures for payroll taxes, assume that salaries for the month of January for a retail store with 15 employees are $16,000. The state unemployment compensation law provides for a tax on employers of 5.4%. Income tax withholdings for the month are $1,600. Assume FICA rates are 7.65% for employer and employee. Entries for the payroll and the employer's payroll taxes follow:

| | | |
|---|---|---|
| Salaries Expense . . . . . . . . . . . . . . . . . . . . . . . . . . . . . . . . . . . . . . . . . . . . . . . . | 16,000 | |
| FICA Taxes Payable . . . . . . . . . . . . . . . . . . . . . . . . . . . . . . . . . . . . . . . . . . . . | | 1,224 |
| Employees Income Taxes Payable . . . . . . . . . . . . . . . . . . . . . . . . . . . | | 1,600 |
| Cash . . . . . . . . . . . . . . . . . . . . . . . . . . . . . . . . . . . . . . . . . . . . . . . . . . . . . . . . . . | | 13,176 |
| *To record payment of payroll and related employee with- holdings.* | | |
| | | |
| Payroll Tax Expense . . . . . . . . . . . . . . . . . . . . . . . . . . . . . . . . . . . . . . . . . . . . . | 2,216 | |
| FICA Taxes Payable . . . . . . . . . . . . . . . . . . . . . . . . . . . . . . . . . . . . . . . . . . . . | | 1,224 |
| State Unemployment Taxes Payable . . . . . . . . . . . . . . . . . . . . . . . . | | 864 |
| Federal Unemployment Taxes Payable . . . . . . . . . . . . . . . . . . . | | 128 |
| *To record the payroll tax liability of the employer.* | | |

*Computation:*

| | |
|---|---|
| Tax under Federal Insurance Contributions Act (7.65% × $16,000) . . . . . . . | $1,224 |
| Tax under state unemployment insurance legislation (5.4% × $16,000) . . . | 864 |
| Tax under Federal Unemployment Tax Act [0.8% (6.2% − credit of 5.4%) × $16,000] . . . . . . . . . . . . . . . . . . . . . . . . . . . . . . . . . . . . . . . . . . . . . . . . . . . . . . | 128 |
| Total payroll tax expense . . . . . . . . . . . . . . . . . . . . . . . . . . . . . . . . . . . . . . . . | $2,216 |

When tax payments are made to the proper agencies, the tax liability accounts are debited and Cash is credited.

The employer's payroll taxes, as well as the taxes withheld from employees, are based on amounts paid to employees during the period regardless of the basis employed for reporting income. When financial reports are prepared on the accrual basis, the employer will have to recognize both accrued payroll and the employer's payroll taxes relating thereto by adjustments at the end of the accounting period.

For example, assume that the salaries and wages accrued at December 31 were $9,500. Of this amount, $2,000 was subject to unemployment tax and $6,000 to FICA tax. Although the salaries and wages will not be paid until January of the following year, the concept of matching requires these costs to be allocated in the period in which they were incurred. This allocation is accomplished with an adjusting entry. The adjusting entry for the employer's payroll taxes would be as follows:

| | | |
|---|---:|---:|
| Payroll Tax Expense . . . . . . . . . . . . . . . . . . . . . . . . . . . . . . . . . . . . . . . . . . . . . . . . | 583 | |
| FICA Taxes Payable . . . . . . . . . . . . . . . . . . . . . . . . . . . . . . . . . . . . . . . . . . . | | 459 |
| State Unemployment Taxes Payable . . . . . . . . . . . . . . . . . . . . . . . . . . . | | 108 |
| Federal Unemployment Taxes Payable . . . . . . . . . . . . . . . . . . . . . . . . . | | 16 |
| *To accrue the payroll tax liability of the employer.* | | |

*Computation:*

| | |
|---|---:|
| Tax under Federal Insurance Contributions Act (7.65% × $6,000) . . . . . . . . . | $459 |
| Tax under state unemployment insurance legislation (5.4% × $2,000) . . . . . | 108 |
| Tax under Federal Unemployment Tax Act (0.8% × $2,000) . . . . . . . . . . . . . | 16 |
| Total payroll tax expense . . . . . . . . . . . . . . . . . . . . . . . . . . . . . . . . . . . . . . . | $583 |

As was true with the adjusting entry for the salaries and wages discussed on page 560, the preceding entry may be reversed at the beginning of the new period, or the accrued liabilities may be debited when the payments are made to the taxing authorities.

Agreements with employees may provide for payroll deductions and employer contributions for other items, such as group insurance plans, pension plans, savings bonds purchases, or union dues. Such agreements call for accounting procedures similar to those described for payroll taxes.

**Other Tax Liabilities**    There are many different types of taxes imposed on business entities. In addition to the several payroll taxes discussed in the previous section, a company usually must pay property taxes, federal and state income taxes on their earnings, and serve as an agent for the collection of sales taxes. Each of these liabilities has some unusual features that can complicate accounting for them.

***Property Taxes***    Real and personal property taxes are based on the assessed valuation of properties as of a particular date. This has given rise to the view held by courts and others that taxes accrue as of a particular date. Generally, the date of accrual has been held to be the date of property assessment, or **lien date**, and a liability for the full year's property tax can be established at that date. The offset to the liability is a deferred expense, since the tax liability is being established in advance of payment and incurrence of the tax expense. The tax expense is generally recognized as a charge against revenue over the fiscal year of the taxing authority for which the taxes are levied. This procedure relates the tax charge to the period in which the taxes provide benefits through government service. The date for payment of the liability is determined by the taxing authority and is accounted for independently from the monthly recognition of property tax expense.

To illustrate accounting for property taxes, assume that the taxing authority is on a July 1 to June 30 fiscal year, but the entity paying the tax is on a calendar-year basis. Property taxes assessed for the period July 1, 1992, to June 30, 1993, are $60,000, and the full year's tax is to be paid on or before November 15, 1992. The following entry is made by the taxpaying entity at the lien date, July 1, 1992, to accrue property taxes for the year:

| | | |
|---|---:|---:|
| Deferred Property Taxes . . . . . . . . . . . . . . . . . . . . . . . . . . . . . . . . . | 60,000 | |
| Property Taxes Payable . . . . . . . . . . . . . . . . . . . . . . . . . . . . . . . . . | | 60,000 |

Each month, the following entry would be made to recognize the expense:

| | | |
|---|---:|---:|
| Property Tax Expense........................................... | 5,000 | |
|    Deferred Property Taxes ................................... | | 5,000 |

The entry to record payment of the property taxes on November 15, 1992, would be:

| | | |
|---|---:|---:|
| Property Taxes Payable ...................................... | 60,000 | |
|    Cash ................................................. | | 60,000 |

At December 31, 1992, the deferred property tax account would have a debit balance of $30,000, representing the property taxes to be recognized as expenses in 1993. If the tax were due in January 1993, and no payment had been made as of December 31, 1992, Property Taxes Payable would have a $60,000 credit balance, which would be reported as a current liability on the balance sheet.

Although the preceding approach seems to reflect the current definition of liabilities as established by the FASB, some companies recognize the liability ratably over the year rather than on the assessment or lien date. Under this latter approach, a prepaid property tax account is created when the full year's tax is paid before the end of the taxing authority's fiscal year. In the authors' opinion, this practice is not as informative and useful as that illustrated.

**Income Taxes**     Both federal and state governments raise a large portion of their revenue from income taxes assessed against both individuals and corporations. The taxable income of a business entity is determined by applying the tax rules and regulations to the operations of the business. As indicated in Chapter 4, the income tax rules do not always follow generally accepted accounting principles. Thus, the income reported for tax purposes may differ from that reported on the income statement. This difference can give rise to deferred income taxes. The actual amount payable for the current year must be determined after all adjusting entries are made at the close of a fiscal period. Federal and some state income tax regulations require companies to estimate their tax liability and make periodic payments during the year in advance of the final computation and submission of the tax returns. Thus, the amount of income tax liability at year-end is usually much lower than the total tax computed for the year. Because income tax returns are always subject to government audit, a contingent liability exists for any year within the statute of limitations not yet reviewed by the Internal Revenue Service. If an additional liability arises as a result of an audit, the additional assessment should be reported as a liability until the payment is made.

**Sales and Use Taxes**     With the passage of sales and use tax laws by state and local governments, additional duties are required of a business unit. Laws generally provide that the business unit must act as an agent for the governmental authority in the collection from customers of sales tax on the transfers of tangible personal properties. The buyer is responsible for the payment of sales tax to the seller when both buyer and seller are in the same tax jurisdiction; however, the buyer is responsible for the payment of use tax directly to the tax authority when the seller is outside the jurisdiction of such authority. Provision must be made in the accounts for the liability to the government for the tax collected from customers and the additional tax that the business must absorb.

The sales tax payable is generally a stated percentage of sales. The actual sales total and the sales tax collections are usually recorded separately at the time of sale. Cash or Accounts Receivable is debited; Sales and Sales Tax Payable are credited. The amount of sales tax to be paid to the taxing authority is computed on the recorded sales.

## Unearned Revenues

Another category of liabilities that are definite in amount is referred to as unearned revenues. Frequently, these liabilities represent an obligation to provide services rather than tangible resources. Examples of unearned revenue include advances from customers, unearned rent, and unearned subscription revenue for publishing companies. Unearned revenue accounts are classified as current or noncurrent liabilities depending on when the revenue will be earned. When the revenue is earned, e.g., when services are performed, the unearned revenue account is debited and an appropriate revenue account is credited. If advances are refunded without providing goods or services, the liability is reduced by the payment, and no revenue is recognized.

## ESTIMATED LIABILITIES

The amount of an obligation is generally established by contract or accrues at a specified rate. There are instances, however, when an obligation clearly exists on a balance sheet date but the amount ultimately to be paid cannot be definitely determined. Because the amount to be paid is not definite does not mean the liability can be ignored or given a contingent status. The claim must be estimated from whatever data is available. Obligations arising from current operations, for example, the cost of meeting warranties for service and repairs on goods sold, must be estimated when prior experience indicates there is a definite liability. Here, uncertainty as to the amount and timing of expenditures is accompanied by an inability to identify the payees; but the fact that there are charges yet to be absorbed is certain.

Liabilities that are estimated in amount and frequently found on financial statements include the following:

1. Refundable deposits, reporting the estimated amount to be refunded to depositors.
2. Warranties for service and replacements, reporting the estimated future claims by customers as a result of past guarantees of services or products or product part replacements.
3. Customer premium offers, reporting the estimated value of premiums or prizes to be distributed as a result of past sales or sales promotion activities.
4. Tickets, tokens, and gift certificates, reporting the estimated obligations in the form of services or merchandise arising from the receipt of cash in past periods.
5. Compensated absences, reporting the estimated future payments attributable to past services of employees.

## Refundable Deposits

Liabilities of a company may include an obligation to refund amounts previously collected from customers as deposits. Refundable deposits may be classified as current or noncurrent liabilities depending on the purpose of the deposit. If deposits are made to protect the company against nonpayment for future services to be rendered, and the services are expected to be provided over a long period, the deposit should be reported as a noncurrent liability. Utility companies characteristically charge certain customers, such as those renting their homes, a deposit that is held until a customer discontinues the service, usually because of a move.

Another type of customer deposit is one made for reusable containers, such as bottles or drums, that hold the product being purchased. When a sale is recorded, a liability is recognized for the deposit. When a container is returned, a refund or credit is given for the deposit made. Periodically, an adjustment to recognize revenue is recorded for containers not expected to be returned. The asset "containers" and the related accumulated depreciation account should be reduced to eliminate the book value of containers not expected to be returned, and any gain or loss is recognized on the "sale" of the containers.

## Warranties for Service and Replacements

Many companies agree to provide free service on units failing to perform satisfactorily or to replace defective goods. When these agreements, or **warranties**, involve only minor costs, such costs may be recognized in the periods incurred. When these agreements involve significant future costs and when experience indicates a definite future obligation exists, estimates of such costs should be made and matched against current revenues. Such estimates are usually recorded by a debit to an expense account and a credit to a liability account. Subsequent costs of fulfilling warranties are debited to the liability account and credited to an appropriate account, e.g., Cash or Inventory.

To illustrate accounting for warranties, consider the following example. MJW Video & Sound sells compact stereo systems with a two-year warranty. Past experience indicates that 10% of all sets sold will need repairs in the first year, and 20% will need repairs in the second year. The average repair cost is $50 per system. The number of systems sold in 1992 and 1993 was 5,000 and 6,000, respectively. Actual repair costs were $12,500 in 1992 and $55,000 in 1993; it is assumed that all repair costs involved cash expenditures.

| | | | |
|---|---|---:|---:|
| 1992 | Warranty Expense | 75,000 | |
| | Estimated Liability Under Warranties | | 75,000 |
| | *Estimated warranty expense based on systems sold:* | | |
| | *5,000 × .30 × $50 = $75,000.* | | |
| | Estimated Liability Under Warranties | 12,500 | |
| | Cash | | 12,500 |
| | *Cost of actual repairs in 1992.* | | |
| 1993 | Warranty Expense | 90,000 | |
| | Estimated Liability Under Warranties | | 90,000 |
| | *Estimated warranty expense based on systems sold:* | | |
| | *6,000 × .30 × $50 = $90,000.* | | |
| | Estimated Liability Under Warranties | 55,000 | |
| | Cash | | 55,000 |
| | *Cost of actual repairs in 1993.* | | |

Periodically, the warranty liability account should be analyzed to see if the actual repairs approximate the estimate. Adjustment to the percentages used in estimating future warranty obligations will be required if experience differs materially from the estimates. These adjustments are changes in estimates and are reported prospectively, i.e., in current and future periods. If sales and repairs in the preceding example are assumed to occur evenly through the year, analysis of the liability account at the end of 1993 shows the ending balance of $97,500 ($75,000 + $90,000 − $12,500 − $55,000) is reasonably close to the predicted amount of $100,000 based upon the 10% and 20% estimates.

*Computation:*

| | |
|---|---:|
| 1992 sales still under warranty for 6 months: $50 × [5,000(½ × .20)] | $ 25,000 |
| 1993 sales still under warranty for 18 months: $50 × [6,000(½ × .10) + 6,000(.20)] | 75,000 |
| Total | $100,000 |

On occasion, an estimate may differ from actual experience to this point. Misleading financial statements may result if an adjustment is not made. In those instances, an adjustment is made to the liability account in the current period. Continuing the previous example, assume that warranty costs incurred in 1993 were only $35,000. Then the ending balance of $117,500 would be much higher than the $100,000 estimate. If the $17,500 difference was considered to be material, an adjustment to warranty expense would be made in 1993 as follows:

| | | |
|---|---|---|
| Estimated Liability Under Warranties......................... | 17,500 | |
|     Warranty Expense ....................................... | | 17,500 |
|     *Adjustment of estimate for warranty repairs.* | | |

In certain cases, customers are charged special fees for a service or replacement warranty covering a specific period. When fees are collected, an unearned revenue account is credited. The unearned revenue is then recognized as revenue over the warranty period. Costs incurred in meeting the contract requirements are debited to Expense; Cash, Inventory, or another appropriate account is credited. The **service contract** is in reality an insurance contract, and the amount charged for the contract is based on the past repair experience of the company for the item sold. The fee usually is set at a rate that will produce a profit margin on the contract if expectations are realized.

To illustrate accounting for service contracts, assume a company sells 3-year service contracts covering its product. During the first year, $50,000 was received on contracts, and expenses incurred for parts and labor in connection with these contracts totaled $5,000. It is estimated from past experience that the pattern of repairs, based on the total dollars spent for repairs, is 25% in the first year of the contract, 30% in the second year, and 45% in the third year. In addition, it is assumed that sales of the contracts are made evenly during the year. The following entries would be made in the first year:

| | | |
|---|---|---|
| Cash ...................................................... | 50,000 | |
|     Unearned Revenue From Service Contracts ................ | | 50,000 |
|     *Sale of service contracts.* | | |
| | | |
| Unearned Revenue From Service Contracts .................. | 6,250 | |
|     Revenue From Service Contracts.......................... | | 6,250 |
|     *Estimated revenue earned from contracts, 12½% (½ of 25%)* | | |
|     *of $50,000, or $6,250.* | | |
| | | |
| Service Contract Expense ................................. | 5,000 | |
|     Inventory ............................................. | | 5,000 |
|     *Cost of actual repairs made during the year.* | | |

Based on the above entries, a profit of $1,250 on service contracts would be recognized in the first year. If future expectations change, adjustments will be necessary to the unearned revenue account to reflect the change in estimate.

The accounts Estimated Liability Under Warranties and Unearned Revenue From Service Contracts are classified as current or noncurrent liabilities depending on the period remaining on the warranty. Those warranty costs expected to be incurred within one year or unearned revenues expected to be earned within one year are classified as current; the balance as long-term. In the above illustration, the expected revenue percentage for the second year, assuming that sales of the contracts were made evenly during the first year, would be 27½% of the contract price, i.e., 12½% for balance of first year expectations and 15% (½ of 30%) for one-half of the second year expectations, or $13,750. This amount would be classified as current. The remaining 60%, or $30,000, of unearned revenue would be classified as noncurrent.

The method of accounting illustrated above does not recognize any income on the initial sale of the contract, but only as the period of the service contract passes and the actual costs are matched against an estimate of the earned revenue. Alternatively, a company could estimate in advance the cost of the repairs and recognize the difference between the amount of the service contract and the expected repair cost in the period of the contract sale. The choice of which method to use depends on the degree of confidence in the estimated repair cost. As discussed more fully in Chapter 19, revenue recognition varies with the facts involved. When collection is reasonably assured and future costs are known with a high degree of certainty, immediate income recognition is recommended. In the case of service contracts, the uncertainty of future expenses usually dictates use of the deferred revenue method.

## Customer Premium Offers

Many companies offer special premiums to customers to stimulate the regular purchase of certain products. These offers may be open for a limited time or may be of a continuing nature. The premium is normally made available when the customer submits the required number of product labels or other evidence of purchase. In certain instances, the premium offer may provide for an optional cash payment.

If a premium offer expires on or before the end of the company's fiscal period, adjustments in the accounts are not required; premium obligations are fully met and the premium expense account summarizes the full charge for the period. However, when a premium offer is continuing, an adjustment must be made at the end of the period to recognize the liability for future redemptions—Premium Expense is debited and an appropriate liability account is credited. The expense is thus charged to the period benefiting from the premium plan, and current liabilities reflect the claim for premiums outstanding.

To illustrate the accounting for a premium offer, assume the following. Good Foods offers a set of breakfast bowls upon the receipt of 20 certificates, one certificate being included in each package of the cereal distributed by this company. The cost of each set of bowls to the company is $2. It is estimated that only 40% of the certificates will be redeemed. In 1992, the company purchased 10,000 sets of bowls at $2 per set; 400,000 packages of cereal containing certificates were sold at a price of $1.20 per package. By the end of 1992, 30% of the certificates had been redeemed. Entries for 1992 are as follows:

| Transaction | Entry | | |
|---|---|---|---|
| **1992:** | | | |
| Premium purchases: | Premiums—Bowl | | |
| 10,000 sets × $2 = $20,000 | Sets .............. | 20,000 | |
| Sales: | Cash ............. | | 20,000 |
| 400,000 packages × $1.20 = $480,000 | Cash............... | 480,000 | |
| Premium claim redemptions: | Sales ........... | | 480,000 |
| 120,000 certificates, or 6,000 sets | Premium Expense ... | 12,000 | |
| × $2 = $12,000 | Premiums—Bowl | | |
| | Sets ............ | | 12,000 |
| | | | |
| **December 31, 1992:** | | | |
| Coupons estimated redeemable in future periods: | Premium Expense ... | 4,000 | |
| | Estimated Premium | | |
| Total estimated redemptions— | Claims Outstanding | | 4,000 |
| 40% of 400,000 .............. 160,000 | | | |
| Redemptions in 1992 ........ 120,000 | | | |
| Estimated future redemptions  40,000 | | | |
| Estimated claims outstanding: | | | |
| 40,000 certificates, or 2,000 sets | | | |
| @ $2 ...................... $ 4,000 | | | |

The balance sheet at the end of 1992 will show premiums of $8,000 as a current asset and estimated premium claims outstanding of $4,000 as a current liability; the income statement for 1992 will show premium expense of $16,000 as a selling expense.

Experience indicating a redemption percentage that differs from the assumed rate will call for an appropriate adjustment in the subsequent period and the revision of future redemption estimates.

The estimated cost of the premiums may be shown as a direct reduction of sales by recording the premium claim at the time of the sale. This requires an estimate of the premium cost at the time of the sale. For example, in the previous illustration, the summary entry for sales recorded during the year, employing the sales reduction approach, would be as follows:

| | | |
|---|---|---|
| Cash ............................................... | 480,000 | |
| Sales .............................................. | | 464,000 |
| Estimated Premium Claims Outstanding .................. | | 16,000 |

The redemption of premium claims would call for debits to the liability account. Either the expense method or the sales reduction method is acceptable, and both are found in practice.

## Tickets, Tokens, and Gift Certificates Outstanding

Many companies sell tickets, tokens, and gift certificates that entitle the owner to services or merchandise; for example: airlines issue tickets used for travel, local transit companies issue tokens good for fares, and department stores sell gift certificates redeemable in merchandise.

When instruments redeemable in services or merchandise are outstanding at the end of the period, accounts should be adjusted to reflect the obligations under such arrangements. The nature of the adjustment will depend on the entries originally made in recording the sale of the instruments.

Ordinarily, the sale of instruments redeemable in services or merchandise is recorded by a debit to Cash and a credit to a liability account. As instruments are redeemed, the liability balance is debited and Sales or an appropriate revenue account is credited. Certain claims may be rendered void by lapse of time or for some other reason as defined by the sales agreement. In addition, experience may indicate that a certain percentage of outstanding claims will never be presented for redemption. These factors must be considered at the end of the period, when the liability balance is reduced to the balance of the claim estimated to be outstanding and a revenue account is credited for the gain indicated from forfeitures. If Sales or a special revenue account is originally credited on the sale of the redemption instrument, the adjustment at the end of the period calls for a debit to the revenue account and a credit to a liability account for the claim still outstanding.

## Compensated Absences

Compensated absences include payments by employers for vacation, holiday, illness, or other personal activities. Employees often earn paid absences based on the time employed. Generally, the longer an employee works for a company, the longer the vacation allowed, or the more liberal the time allowed for illnesses. At the end of any given accounting period, a company has a liability for earned but unused compensated absences. The matching principle requires that the estimated amounts earned be charged against current revenue, and a liability established for that amount.[7] The difficult part of this accounting treatment is estimating how much should be accrued. In Statement No. 43, the FASB requires a liability to be recognized for compensated absences that (1) have been earned

---

[7]*Statement of Financial Accounting Standards No. 43,* "Accounting for Compensated Absences" (Stamford: Financial Accounting Standards Board, 1980), par. 6.

through services already rendered, (2) vest or can be carried forward to subsequent years, and (3) are estimable and probable.

For example, assume that a company has a vacation pay policy for all employees. If all employees had the same anniversary date for computing time in service, the computations would not be too difficult. However, most plans provide for a flexible employee starting date. In order to compute the liability, a careful inventory of all employees must be made that includes the number of years of service, rate of pay, carryover of unused vacation from prior periods, turnover, and the probability of taking the vacation.

To illustrate the accounting for compensated absences, assume that S&N Corporation has 20 employees who are paid an average of $350 per week. During 1992, a total of 40 vacation weeks were earned by all employees, but only 30 weeks of vacation were taken that year. The remaining 10 weeks of vacation were taken in 1993 when the average rate of pay was $400 per week. The entry to record the accrued vacation pay on December 31, 1992, would be:

| | | |
|---|---|---|
| Wages Expense | 3,500 | |
|   Vacation Wages Payable | | 3,500 |
|     *To record accrued vacation wages ($350 × 10 weeks).* | | |

The above entry assumes that Wages Expense has already been recorded for the 30 weeks of vacation taken during 1992. Therefore, the income statement would reflect the total Wages Expense for the entire 40 weeks of vacation earned during the period. On its December 31, 1992, balance sheet, S&N would report a current liability of $3,500 to reflect the obligation for the 10 weeks of vacation pay that are owed. In 1993, when the additional vacation weeks are taken and the payroll is paid, S&N would make the following entry:

| | | |
|---|---|---|
| Wages Expense | 500 | |
| Vacation Wages Payable | 3,500 | |
|   Cash | | 4,000 |
|     *To record payment at current rates of previously earned vacation time ($400 × 10 weeks).* | | |

Since the vacation weeks are now used, the above entry eliminates the liability. An adjustment to Wages Expense is required because the liability was recorded at the rates of pay in effect during the time the compensation (vacation pay) was earned. However, the cash is being paid at the current rate, which requires an adjustment to Wages Expense. If the rate of pay for the 10 weeks of vacation taken in 1993 had remained the same as the rate used to record the accrual on December 31, 1992, there would not have been an adjustment to Wages Expense. The entry to record payment in 1993 would simply be a debit to the payable and a credit to Cash for $3,500.

An exception to the requirement for accrual of compensated absences, such as vacation pay, is made for sick pay. The FASB decided that sick pay should be accrued only if it vests with the employee, i.e., the employee is entitled to compensation for a certain number of "sick days" regardless of whether the employee is actually absent for that period. Upon leaving the firm, the employee would be compensated for any unused sick time. If the sick pay does not vest, it is recorded as an expense only when actually paid.[8]

Although compensated absences are not deductible for income tax purposes until the vacation, holiday, or illness occurs and the payment is made, they are required by GAAP to be recognized as liabilities on the financial statements.

[8]*Ibid.,* par. 7.

**Frequent Flyer Miles**

As individuals navigate the airways, they may earn frequent flyer miles that, once enough miles are accumulated, can be redeemed for free trips. Rather than account for these bonus miles as they accumulate, airlines typically book a liability only after enough mileage has been accumulated to claim a free ticket. Thus, while experts estimate there are 25 billion miles of free travel resulting from frequent flyer programs, airlines have recognized a liability for approximately only 30 percent, or 7.5 billion miles. The AICPA has argued that with the availability of frequent flyer miles, the earnings process is no longer substantially complete when an airplane ticket is sold. It maintains that a portion of the revenue from each ticket should be deferred, as a "liability reserve," and matched against future periods when the bonus miles are redeemed.

**Questions:**

1. *Do frequent flyer miles meet the definition of a liability?*
2. *If frequent flyer miles are a liability, can the liability be estimated at the time a ticket is sold?*
3. *When should frequent flyer miles be recorded on the books of the airlines: when tickets are sold or as bonus miles are redeemed?*
4. *If airlines are required to make a cumulative catch-up adjustment to account for their frequent flyer liabilities, the effects on the financial statements of many airlines could be catastrophic. Should this factor enter into the decision process of accounting rule makers?*

Source:   Penelope Wang, *Forbes*, June 13, 1988, p. 62.

## CONTINGENT LIABILITIES

A *contingency* is defined in FASB Statement No. 5 as:

> . . . an existing condition, situation, or set of circumstances involving uncertainty as to possible gain . . . or loss . . . to an enterprise that will ultimately be resolved when one or more future events occur or fail to occur.[9]

As defined, contingencies may relate to either assets or liabilities, and to either a gain or loss. In this chapter, attention is focused on **contingent losses** that might give rise to a liability. As mentioned previously, contingent liabilities are distinguishable from estimated liabilities.

Historically, when liabilities were classified as contingent, they were not recorded on the books but were disclosed in notes to financial statements. The distinction between a recorded liability and a **contingent liability** was not always clear. If a legal liability existed and the amount of the obligation was either definite or could be estimated with reasonable certainty, the liability was recorded on the books. If the existence of the obligation depended on the happening of a future event, recording of the liability was deferred until the event occurred. In an attempt to make the distinction more precise, the FASB used three terms in FASB Statement No. 5 to identify the range of possibilities of the event

[9]*Statement of Financial Accounting Standards No. 5*, "Accounting for Contingencies" (Stamford: Financial Accounting Standards Board, 1975), par. 1.

occurring. Different accounting action was recommended for each term. The terms, their definitions, and the accounting actions recommended are as follows:[10]

| Term | Definition | Accounting Action |
|------|-----------|-------------------|
| Probable | The future event or events are likely to occur. | Record the probable event in the accounts if the amount can be reasonably estimated. If not estimable, disclose facts in a note. |
| Reasonably possible | The chance of the future event or events occurring is more than remote but less than likely. | Report the contingency in a note. |
| Remote | The chance of the future event or events occurring is slight. | No recording or reporting unless contingency represents a guarantee. Then note disclosure is required. |

If the happening of an event that would create a liability is **probable**, and if the amount of the obligation can be **reasonably estimated**, the contingency should be recognized as a liability. Some of the liabilities already presented as estimated liabilities may be considered probable contingent liabilities because the existence of the obligation is dependent on some event occurring, e.g., warranties are dependent on the need for repair or service to be given, gift certificates are dependent on the certificate being turned in for redemption, and vacation pay is dependent on a person taking a vacation. These liabilities are not included in this section, however, because historically they have been recognized as recorded liabilities. Other liabilities, such as unsettled litigation claims, self-insurance, and loan guarantees have more traditionally been considered as unrecorded contingent liabilities, and these will be explored separately in the following pages.

Inasmuch as most liabilities have some element of contingency associated with them, the authors feel that the classification "contingent liability" should be reserved for those items that fit into one of the latter two terms, i.e., **reasonably possible** or **remote**. If the happening of the event is probable and the amount of the obligation can be estimated, the liability is no longer a contingent liability, but a recorded estimated liability. Such liabilities meet the definition of liabilities established by the FASB. This approach avoids having to say that some contingent liabilities are recorded and others are not. By this definition, a contingent liability would never be recorded but would be either disclosed in a note or ignored depending on the degree of remoteness of its expected occurrence.

The FASB statement provided no specific guidelines as to how these three terms should be interpreted in probability percentages. Surveys made of statement preparers and users disclosed a great diversity in the probability interpretations of the terms. It is unlikely, therefore, that FASB Statement No. 5 has greatly reduced the diversity in practice in recording some of these contingent items.

## Litigation

An increasing number of lawsuits are being filed against companies and individuals. Lawsuits may result in substantial payments being made to successful plaintiffs. Typically, litigation takes a long time to conclude. Even after a decision has been rendered by a lower court, there are many appeal opportunities available. Thus, both the amount and timing

[10]*Ibid.*, par. 3.

of a loss arising from litigation are generally highly uncertain. Some companies carry insurance to protect them against these losses, so the impact of the losses on the financial statements is minimized. For uninsured risks, however, a decision must be made as to when the liability for litigation becomes probable, and thus a recorded loss. FASB Statement No. 5 identifies several key factors to consider in making the decision. These include:[11]

1. The nature of the litigation.
2. The period when the cause of action occurred. (Liability is not recognized in any period before the cause of action occurred.)
3. Progress of the case in court, including progress between date of the financial statements and their issuance date.
4. Views of legal counsel as to the probability of loss.
5. Prior experience with similar cases.
6. Management's intended response to the litigation.

If analysis of these and similar factors results in the judgment that a loss is probable, and the amount of the loss can be reasonably estimated, the liability should be recorded. A settlement after the balance sheet date but before the statements are issued would be evidence that the loss was probable at the year-end, and would result in a reporting of loss in the current financial statements.

Another area of potential liability involves unasserted claims, i.e., a cause of action has occurred but no claim has yet been asserted. For example, a person may be injured on the property of the company, but as of the date the financial statements are issued, no legal action has been taken; or a violation of a government regulation may occur, but no federal action has yet been taken. If it is probable that a substantiated claim will be filed, and the amount of the claim can be reasonably estimated, accrual of the liability should be made. If the amount cannot be reasonably estimated, note disclosure is required. If assertion of the claim is not judged to be at least reasonably possible, no accrual or disclosure is necessary.

As a practical matter, it should be noted that a company would be very unlikely to record a loss from unasserted claims or from pending litigation unless negotiations for a settlement had been substantially completed. When that is the case, the loss is no longer a contingency, but an estimated loss.

Some companies do not disclose any information regarding potential liabilities from litigation. Others provide a brief, general description of pending litigation, as illustrated in the following note from the 1988 annual report of AMAX Inc.

**Exhibit 15—1    AMAX INC.—Disclosure of Pending Litigation**

---

AMAX INC.

*NOTES TO FINANCIAL STATEMENTS*

*18  (In Part): Contingencies and Commitments*

On January 22, 1988, an AMAX customer filed suit in the United States District Court for the District of Oregon seeking recission of a long-term supply agreement providing for the sale of coal. Additionally, the suit seeks restitution of $17.7 million in prior payments and relief from $14.5 million in present obligations. AMAX believes that the lawsuit is without merit and is opposing it vigorously.

---

[11]*Ibid.*, par. 36.

Sometimes companies provide fairly specific information about pending actions and claims. However, companies must be careful not to increase their chances of losing pending lawsuits, and they generally do not disclose dollar amounts of potential losses, which might be interpreted as an admission of guilt and a willingness to pay a certain amount. For example, Eastman Kodak disclosed the following information in its 1989 annual report in connection with a lawsuit filed by Polaroid Corporation.

---

**Exhibit 15—2     Eastman Kodak Company—Disclosure of Litigation**

---

**Legal Notes**

The action filed by Polaroid Corporation in 1976 in the U.S. District Court in Boston resulted in a decision on October 11, 1985, holding that Kodak's PR-10 instant film and EK4 and EK6 instant cameras infringed seven Polaroid patents and an injunction, effective January 9, 1986, prohibiting further manufacture or sale of such products in the United States. The U.S. Court of Appeals for the Federal Circuit affirmed the decision on April 25, 1986 and the United States Supreme Court denied Kodak's petition for certiorari on October 6, 1986. The case was returned to the U.S. District Court in Boston for trial of the issues of (a) whether Kodak's infringement of any of the patents was willful and deliberate, (b) damages adequate to compensate Polaroid for Kodak's infringement, pre-judgment interest on this amount and whether the damage award should be trebled, (c) whether costs should be taxed against either party, and (d) whether Polaroid is entitled to its reasonable attorney fees. Trial of these issues commenced on May 1, 1989 and concluded on November 20, 1989. Polaroid asserted claims for damages of $3,924,945,000 in lost profits, $2,188,508,000 in pre-judgment interest and increased damages of $7,849,989,000, and also asserted that it should be awarded its attorney fees, costs, and post-judgment interest. Kodak has vigorously contested the amount of damages sought by Polaroid and has asserted that Polaroid's damages should be based on a reasonable royalty and has denied that Polaroid is entitled to increased damages and attorney fees. Damages based on a 5% royalty, for example, could amount to approximately $187 million, including pre-judgment interest. Although the amount of damages eventually to be awarded by the court cannot be reasonably estimated, Kodak, based on the advice of counsel retained to represent it in the case, does not believe that it is likely that the damages awarded against the Company, including pre-judgment interest, will have a material adverse effect on the financial condition of the Company. The amount of the judgment will be charged against future earnings of the Company.

Kodak was involved in other litigation, investigations of a routine nature, and various legal matters during 1989 which are being defended and handled in the ordinary course of business.

---

## Self-Insurance

Some large companies with widely distributed risks may decide not to purchase insurance for protection against the normal business risks of fire, explosion, flood, or damage to other persons or their property. These companies in effect insure themselves against these risks. An accounting question arises as to whether a liability should be accrued and a loss recognized for the possible occurrence of the uninsured risk. Sometimes companies have recorded as an expense an amount equal to the insurance premium that would have been paid had commercial insurance been carried. The FASB considered this specific subject in

### A Reserve, a Liability, or a Commitment?

Other countries of the world do not necessarily follow U.S. GAAP when presenting financial information. For example, Messerschmidt-Boelkow-Blohm GmbH, a West German-based manufacturer of military and commercial aircraft, defense systems, and space systems, disclosed the following three classifications in its December 31, 1988, balance sheet:

|                       | (in thousands of Deutsche marks) |
|-----------------------|---------------------------------:|
| Reserves              | 3,067,518                        |
| Liabilities           | 3,160,265                        |
| Liability commitments | 915,642                          |

Those accounts in the "Reserves" section included pension obligations, deferred taxes, reserves for warranties and obligations relating to personnel, and reserves for deferred overhauls. Accounts classified as "Liabilities" included notes payable, accounts payable, and bank loans payable. Items in the "Liability commitments" section included liabilities resulting from guaranties and warranty agreements.

**Questions:**

1. *Do you perceive a difference between a "Reserve," a "Liability," and a "Liability Commitment"?*
2. *How would the above information be disclosed if the financial statements were prepared in conformance with U.S. GAAP?*
3. *Which method do you think provides more useful information—the West German method or the United States method?*

Source: Messerschmidt—Boelkow-Blohm GmbH 1988 Annual Report.

Statement No. 5, and concluded that no loss or liability should be recorded until the loss has occurred. Fires, explosions, or other casualties are random in occurrence and, as such, are not accruable. Further, they stated that:

> . . . unlike an insurance company, which has a contractual obligation under policies in force to reimburse insurers for losses, an enterprise can have no such obligation to itself and, hence, no liability.[12]

Thus, although an exposed condition does exist, it is a future period that must bear any loss that occurs, not a current period.

### Loan Guarantees

Enterprises sometimes enter into a contract guaranteeing a loan for another enterprise, frequently a subsidiary company, a supplier, or even a favored customer. These guarantees obligate the entity to make the loan payment if the principal borrower fails to make the payment. A similar contingent obligation exists when the payee of a note receivable discounts it at a bank, but is held contingently liable in the event the maker of the note defaults. Discounted notes receivable were discussed in Chapter 9. If the default on the

[12]*Ibid.*, par. 28.

loan or the note is judged to be probable based on the events that have occurred prior to the issuance date of the financial statements, the loss and liability should be accrued in accordance with the general guidelines discussed in this section. Otherwise, note disclosure is required even if the likelihood of making the payment is remote. This exception to not disclosing remote contingencies arose because companies have traditionally disclosed guarantees in notes to the financial statements, and the FASB did not want to reduce this disclosure practice.

## BALANCE SHEET PRESENTATION

The liability section of the balance sheet is usually divided between current and noncurrent liabilities as previously discussed. The nature of the detail to be presented for current liabilities depends on the use to be made of the financial statement. A balance sheet prepared for stockholders might report little detail; on the other hand, creditors may insist on full detail concerning current debts.

Assets are normally recorded in the order of their liquidity, and consistency would suggest that liabilities be reported in the order of their maturity. The latter practice may be followed only to the extent it is practical; observance of this procedure would require an analysis of the different classes of obligations and separate reporting for classes with varying maturity dates.

Liabilities should not be offset by assets to be applied to their liquidation. Disclosure as to future debt liquidation, however, may be provided by an appropriate parenthetical remark or note. Disclosure of liabilities secured by specific assets should also be made by a parenthetical remark or note.

The current liabilities section of a balance sheet prepared on December 31, 1993, might appear as shown below.

| | | |
|---|---:|---:|
| Current liabilities: | | |
| Notes payable: | | |
|    Trade creditors | $12,000 | |
|    Banks (secured by pledge of accounts receivable) | 20,000 | |
|    Officers | 12,500 | $ 44,500 |
| Accounts payable | | 35,250 |
| Current portion of long-term debt | | 10,000 |
| Salaries and wages payable | | 1,250 |
| Income taxes payable | | 6,000 |
| Real and personal property taxes payable | | 1,550 |
| Dividends payable | | 4,500 |
| Other current liabilities: | | |
|    Advances from customers | $ 7,500 | |
|    Estimated warranty costs | 2,500 | 10,000 |
| Total current liabilities | | $113,050 |

Because most of the noncurrent liabilities are discussed in separate chapters that follow, illustration of the details of the noncurrent liabilities section is deferred until Chapter 18 and illustrated with owners' equity. For a further illustration of a liabilities section of a balance sheet, with related notes, see the IBM Corporation financial statements presented in Appendix A at the end of this book.

## KEY TERMS

Compensated absences 569
Contingent liability 557
Liabilities 555

Nontrade notes payable 558
Promissory note 558
Refundable deposits 565

Trade notes payable 558
Unearned revenues 565
Warranties 566

## QUESTIONS

1. Identify the major components included in the definition of liabilities established by the FASB.
2. (a) What is meant by an executory contract? (b) Do these contracts fit the definition of liabilities included in this chapter?
3. Distinguish between current and noncurrent liabilities.
4. At what amount should liabilities generally be reported?
5. Under what conditions would debt that will mature within the next year be reported as a noncurrent liability?
6. Distinguish between the following categories: (a) liabilities that are definite in amount, (b) estimated liabilities, and (c) contingent liabilities.
7. Gross payroll is taxed by both federal and state governments. Identify these taxes and indicate who bears the cost of the tax, the employer or the employee.
8. How should a company account for revenue received in advance for a service contract?
9. Why should a company normally account for product warranties on an accrual basis?
10. What information must a firm accumulate in order to adequately account for estimated liabilities on tickets, tokens, and gift certificates?
11. How should compensated absences be accounted for?
12. How should contingent liabilities that are reasonably possible of becoming liabilities be reported on the financial statements?
13. What factors are important in deciding whether a pending lawsuit should be reported as a liability on the balance sheet?
14. Why does accounting for self-insurance differ from accounting for insurance premiums with outside carriers?

## DISCUSSION CASES

### Case 15—1   (What is a liability?)

Professional athletes regularly sign long-term, multimillion dollar contracts in which they promise to play for a particular team for a specified time period. Owners of these teams often sign long-term leases for the use of playing facilities for a specified time period. GAAP requires the leases to be booked as liabilities but does not require the obligations associated with pro athletes' contracts to be recorded.

Discuss the reasons for the differing treatment of these two seemingly similar events. Do you think the disclosure currently required by GAAP in these instances satisfies the needs of investors and creditors?

### Case 15—2   (Measuring long-term liabilities)

Long-term leases and long-term debt are typically disclosed on the financial statements at their discounted present values. This disclosure recognizes the time value of money. However, the standards related to accounting for deferred income taxes do not involve discounting expected future tax obligations.

Why do you suppose the FASB requires the use of discounting with some long-term liabilities and not with others? Should discounting be required for all long-term liabilities? Provide support for your answer.

## Case 15—3  (Leave my current ratio alone!)

Soto Inc., a closely held corporation, has never been audited and is seeking a large bank loan for plant expansion. The bank has requested audited financial statements. In conference with the president and majority stockholder of Soto, the auditor is informed that the bank looks very closely at the current ratio. The auditor's proposed reclassifications and adjustments include the following:

(a) A note payable issued 4½ years ago matures in six months from the balance sheet date. The auditor wants to reclassify it as a current liability. The controller says no, because "we are probably going to refinance this note with other long-term debt."

(b) An accrual for compensated absences. Again the controller objects because the amount of the pay for these absences cannot be estimated. "Some employees quit in the first year and don't get vacation, and it is impossible to predict which employees will be absent for illness or other causes. Without being able to identify the employees, we can't determine the rate of compensation."

How would you, if you were the auditor, respond to the controller?

## Case 15—4  (When is a loss a loss?)

Chester Company has the following contingencies:

(a) A threat of expropriation exists for one of Chester's manufacturing plants located in a foreign country. Expropriation is deemed to be reasonably possible. Any compensation from the foreign government would be less than the carrying amount (book value) of the plant.

(b) Potential costs exist due to the discovery of a safety hazard related to one of Chester's products. These costs are probable and can be reasonably estimated.

(c) One of Chester's warehouses located at the base of a mountain could no longer be insured against rock-slide losses. No rock-slide losses have occurred.

1. How should Chester report the threat of expropriation of assets? Why?
2. How should Chester report the potential costs due to the safety hazard? Why?
3. How should Chester report the noninsurable rock-slide risk? Why?

(AICPA adapted)

## Case 15—5  (Should a liability be recorded?)

Angela Company is a manufacturer of toys. During the year, the following situations arose:

(a) A safety hazard related to one of its toy products was discovered. It is considered probable that liabilities have been incurred. Based on past experience, a reasonable estimate of the amount of loss can be made.

(b) One of its small warehouses is located on the bank of a river and could no longer be insured against flood losses. No flood losses have occurred after the date that the insurance became unavailable.

(c) This year, Angela began promoting a new toy by including a coupon, redeemable for a movie ticket, in each toy's carton. The movie ticket, which cost Angela $2, is purchased in advance and then mailed to the customer when the coupon is received by Angela. Angela estimated, based on past experience, that sixty percent of the coupons would be redeemed. Forty percent of the coupons were actually redeemed this year, and the remaining twenty percent of the coupons are expected to be redeemed next year.

1. How should Angela report the safety hazard? Why? Do not discuss deferred income tax implications.
2. How should Angela report the noninsurable flood risk? Why?
3. How should Angela account for the toy promotion campaign in this year?

## Case 15—6   (Is it really self-insurance?)

The auditors of Data Retrieval Systems are concerned with how to account for the insurance premiums on a liability policy carried with a large insurance company. Premiums on the policy are based on the average loss experience of Data Retrieval Systems over the past five years. In some years, no insured loss occurs; however, the company follows the practice of recognizing expenses for the premiums paid to the insurance company regardless of actual loss. The senior auditor, Gary Wells, has read FASB Statement No. 5 and argues that the premiums paid are really deposits with the insurance company. Since the premiums are based on the losses actually incurred, income should be charged only when the losses occur, not when the premiums are paid. By charging the premiums to expense, an artificial smoothing of income results, something FASB Statement No. 5 was designed to prevent. Barbara Orton, controller, argues that the premiums are arm's-length payments, that FASB Statement No. 5 applies only to self-insurance, and that the policy carried by Data Retrieval Systems is obviously with an outside carrier. Thus, Orton believes the premiums should be recognized as a valid period expense. As audit manager, you are asked to render your opinion on the matter.

---

# EXERCISES

## Exercise 15—1   (Types of liabilities)

For each of the following scenarios, identify whether the event described is an actual liability, a contingent liability, or not a liability. If you conclude that the event involves an actual liability, determine if the liability is (1) current or noncurrent, and (2) definite in amount or involves an estimate.

(a) Apple Inc. purchased inventory on November 1. The invoice totaled $17,000 and payment is expected to be made within 30 days.

(b) Banana Corp. financed its warehouse facilities with a long-term mortgage that calls for semiannual payments of $7,000. The mortgage's current outstanding balance is $98,000.

(c) Orange Company sells computer systems and supplies. It offers its customers a 30-day, money-back guarantee. In the past, approximately 10% of customers have exercised this return privilege.

(d) Kiwi Industries manufactures and distributes outdoor recreational equipment. An individual recently filed a lawsuit as a result of injuries sustained while using Kiwi equipment. Attorneys for Kiwi feel the chance of losing the case is minimal.

(e) Berry Incorporated, a newly formed company, has an unfunded pension plan that calls for retirement benefits to be paid to employees who retire after a minimum of ten years of employment with the company.

(f) John Townson, a successful entrepreneur, has expressed a desire to establish university scholarships for disadvantaged youth in his community. He has been contacted by numerous universities, but as of yet, nothing firm has been established.

## Exercise 15—2   (Purchase with non-interest-bearing note)

On September 1, 1992, Perfection Manufacturing Co. purchased two new company automobiles from Top Quality Auto Sales. The terms of the sale called for Perfection to pay $20,111 to Top Quality on September 1, 1993. Perfection gave the seller a non-interest-bearing note for that amount. At the date of purchase, the interest rate for short-term loans was 10.5%.

1. Prepare the journal entries necessary on September 1, 1992, December 31, 1992, (year-end adjusting), and September 1, 1993.
2. Show how notes payable would be presented in the December 31, 1992, balance sheet.

### Exercise 15—3  (Recording payroll and payroll taxes)

The Express Company paid one week's wages of $10,600 in cash (net pay after all withholdings and deductions) to its employees. Income tax withholdings were equal to 17% of the gross payroll, and the only other deductions were 7.65% for FICA tax and $160 for union dues. Give the entries that should be made on the books of the company to record the payroll and the tax accruals to be recognized by the employer, assuming that the company is subject to unemployment taxes of 5.4% (state) and 0.8% (federal). Assume that all wages for the week are subject to FICA and unemployment taxes.

### Exercise 15—4  (Monthly payroll entries)

Aggie Co. sells agricultural products. Aggie pays its salespeople a salary plus a commission. The salary is the same for each salesperson, $1,000 per month. The commission varies by length of time of employment, and is a percentage of the company's total gross sales. Each salesperson starts with a commission of 1.0%, which is increased an additional 0.5% for each full year of employment with Aggie, to a maximum of 5.0%. The total gross sales for the month of January were $120,000.

Aggie has six salespeople as follows:

| | No. of Years |
|---|---|
| Frank | 10 |
| Sally | 9 |
| Tina | 8 |
| Barry | 6 |
| Mark | 3 |
| Lisa | 9 mos. |

Assume the FICA rate is 7.65%, the FUTA rate is 6.2%, and the state unemployment rate is 5.4%. (Assume the federal government allows the maximum credit for state unemployment tax paid.) The federal income tax withholding rate is 30%. Compute the January salaries and commissions expense and make any necessary entries to record the payroll transactions.

### Exercise 15—5  (Accounting for property taxes)

On November 20, 1992, Miranda Floral Shop received a property tax assessment of $14,400 for the taxing unit's fiscal year ending June 30, 1993. No entry was made to record the assessment. Later, Miranda's accountant was preparing the yearly financial statements (based on a February 1 to January 31 fiscal year) and came across the property tax assessment. Give the journal entries to record the tax payment (if any) and any adjusting entries necessary on January 31, 1993, assuming:

(a)  The full tax of $14,400 had been paid on January 5, 1993, and charged to expense.
(b)  None of the tax had been paid as of January 31, 1993.
(c)  A portion of the tax ($9,050) had been paid on January 20, 1993, and charged to expense.

### Exercise 15—6  (Warranty liability)

In 1992 Thompson Office Supply began selling a new calculator that carried a two-year warranty against defects. Based on the manufacturer's recommendations, Thompson projects estimated warranty costs (as a percentage of dollar sales) as follows:

| | |
|---|---|
| First year of warranty | 3% |
| Second year of warranty | 8% |

Sales and actual warranty repairs for 1992 and 1993 are presented at the top of page 581.

| | 1992 | 1993 |
|---|---|---|
| Sales | $250,000 | $475,000 |
| Actual warranty repairs | 5,300 | 18,450 |

1. Give the necessary journal entries to record the liability at the end of 1992 and 1993.
2. Analyze the warranty liability account as of the year ending December 31, 1993, to see if the actual repairs approximate the estimate. Should Thompson revise the manufacturer's warranty estimate? (Assume sales and repairs occur evenly throughout the year.)

### Exercise 15—7  (Warranty liability)

Modern Appliance Company's accountant has been reviewing the firm's past television sales. For the past two years, Modern has been offering a special service warranty on all televisions sold. With the purchase of a television, the customer has the right to purchase a three-year service contract for an extra $60. Information concerning past television and warranty contract sales is given below.

**Color-All Model II Television**

| | 1992 | 1993 |
|---|---|---|
| Television sales in units | 460 | 550 |
| Sales price per unit | $400 | $500 |
| Number of service contracts sold | 300 | 350 |
| Expenses relating to television warranties | $3,350 | $9,630 |

Modern's accountant has estimated from past records that the pattern of repairs has been 40% in the first year after sale, 36% in the second year, and 24% in the third year. Give the necessary journal entries related to the service contracts for 1992 and 1993. In addition, indicate how much profit on service contracts would be recognized in 1993. Assume sales of the contracts are made evenly during the year.

### Exercise 15—8  (Premium liability)

Mitchell Cosmetics Company began a sales promotion campaign for a new shampoo on June 30, 1993. Part of this promotion included providing a coupon with each bottle of shampoo sold. Customers can redeem 5 coupons for a hand-held hairdryer. The shampoo is sold for $8.95 per bottle in department stores and beauty salons. Each hairdryer costs Mitchell $7.50. Mitchell estimated that 60% of the coupons issued would be redeemed. For the six months ended December 31, 1993, the following information is available:

| | |
|---|---|
| Bottles of shampoo sold | 180,000 |
| Hairdryers purchased | 13,500 |
| Coupons redeemed | 60,500 |

What is the estimated liability for premium claims outstanding at December 31, 1993?

### Exercise 15—9  (Premium liability)

On June 1, 1993, the National Pet Company began marketing a new dog food created specifically to meet the nutritional requirements of puppies. As a promotion, National was offering a free doghouse to all customers returning the weight seals from the purchase of 1,000 pounds of the new dog food. National estimates that 30% of the weight seals will be returned. At December 31, 1993, the following information was available:

| | |
|---|---|
| Sales (1,650,000 pounds × $.40) | $660,000 |
| Doghouses purchased (495 × $30) | 14,850 |
| Doghouses distributed (265 × $30) | 7,950 |

Give the journal entries to record the sales of dog food, purchase of doghouse premiums, redemption of weight seals, and the estimated liability for outstanding premium offers as of the end of the year.

### Exercise 15—10   (Compensated absence—vacation pay)

The Styles Company employs five people. Each employee is entitled to two weeks' paid vacation every year the employee works for the company. The conditions of the paid vacation are: (a) for each full year of work, an employee will receive two weeks of paid vacation (no vacation accrues for a portion of a year), (b) each employee will receive the same pay for vacation time as the regular pay in the year taken, and (c) unused vacation pay can be carried forward. The following data was taken from the firm's personnel records:

| Employee | Starting Date | Cumulative Vacation Taken as of December 31, 1993 | Weekly Salary |
|---|---|---|---|
| Norm Racine | December 21, 1986 | 11 weeks | $375 |
| Michael Smith | March 6, 1991 | 2 weeks | 500 |
| Phyllis Taylor | August 13, 1992 | none | 350 |
| Brian Hinsman | December 17, 1991 | 3 weeks | 300 |
| Ann Behan | March 29, 1993 | none | 400 |

Compute the liability for vacation pay as of December 31, 1993.

### Exercise 15—11   (Disclosure of contingencies)

Sound Wave, Inc., a manufacturer of electronic greeting cards, has had a lawsuit filed against it by Sounds Good, another manufacturer of electronic greeting cards. The suit alleges patent right infringements by Sound Wave and asks for compensatory damages.

For the following possible situations, determine whether Sound Wave should: (1) report as a liability on the balance sheet and if so, how much, (2) disclose in a note, or (3) do nothing. Give reasons for your answers.

(a)   Sound Wave's legal counsel is convinced that the suit will result in a loss to Sound Wave but isn't sure how much.
(b)   Sound Wave's legal counsel believes an out-of-court settlement is probable and will cost Sound Wave approximately $600,000.
(c)   Sound Wave's legal counsel believes it is reasonably possible that the case will result in a $2,000,000 loss to Sound Wave.
(d)   Sound Wave's legal counsel believes it is probable that the case will result in an undeterminable loss to Sound Wave.
(e)   Sound Wave's legal counsel believes there is a remote chance for a loss to occur.
(f)   The suit hasn't been filed, but Sound Wave's legal counsel has informed management that an unintentional patent infringement has occurred.

### Exercise 15—12   (Contingent losses)

Conrad Corporation sells motorcycle helmets. In 1992, Conrad sold 4 million helmets before discovering a significant defect in the helmet's construction. By December 31, 1992, two lawsuits had been filed against Conrad. The first lawsuit, which Conrad has little chance of winning, is expected to settle out of court for $900,000 in January of 1993. Conrad's attorneys think the company has a fifty-fifty chance of winning the second lawsuit, which is for $400,000. What accounting treatment should Conrad give the pending lawsuits in the year-end financial statements? (Include any necessary journal entries.)

## Exercise 15—13   (Contingent liabilities)

Bell Industries is a multinational company. In preparing the annual financial statements, the auditors met with Bell's attorneys to discuss various legal matters facing the firm. For each of the following independent items, determine the appropriate disclosure.

(a) Bell is being sued by a distributor for breach of contract. The attorneys feel there is a 30% chance of Bell's losing the suit.

(b) One of Bell's subsidiaries has been accused by a federal agency of violating numerous environmental laws. The company faces significant fines if found guilty. The attorneys feel that the subsidiary has complied with all applicable laws and therefore place the probability of incurring the fines at less than 10%.

(c) A subsidiary operating in a foreign country whose government is unstable was recently taken over by the government and nationalized. Bell is negotiating with representatives of that government but company attorneys feel the probability of the company obtaining possession of its assets is approximately 90%.

## Exercise 15—14   (Balance sheet reporting of current liabilities)

Prepare the current liabilities section of the balance sheet for the Ilena Company on December 31, 1992, from the information below.

(a) Short-term notes payable: arising from purchase of goods, $62,680; arising from loans from banks, $20,000, on which marketable securities valued at $26,100 have been pledged as security; arising from short-term advances by officers, $22,600.

(b) Accounts payable arising from purchase of goods, $59,300.

(c) Employees' income taxes payable, $1,584.

(d) First-mortgage serial bonds, $175,000, payable in semiannual installments of $7,000 due on March 1 and September 1 of each year.

(e) Advances received from customers on purchase orders, $4,140.

(f) Estimated expense of meeting warranty-for-service requirements on merchandise sold, $6,480.

## Exercise 15—15   (Recording liabilities)

Bicknell Co. is a retail outlet selling lawn care equipment. During the month of April, the following events occurred:

(a) Sales totaled $60,000 net of sales tax (all on account). The state sales tax rate is 6%.

(b) The cost of inventory sold was $28,000.

(c) Salary expense was $12,000. The FICA rate is 7.65%; income taxes totaled 15% of the gross salary expense; and the state and federal unemployment tax rates are 5.4% and 0.8%, respectively. All salaries are subject to FICA and unemployment taxes.

(d) Inventory costing $35,000 was purchased on account.

(e) Other miscellaneous expenses totaled $15,000, of which $2,500 represents depreciation and $3,000 remained unpaid at the end of the month.

(f) The sales tax and the state unemployment tax were remitted on the last day of the month.

1. Prepare the journal entries to record each of the above events. (Omit explanations.)
2. Prepare a condensed income statement for the month ended April 30, 1993.

## PROBLEMS

### Problem 15—1   (Miscellaneous operating payables)

The Collins Corporation closes its books and prepares financial statements on an annual basis. The following information is gathered by the chief accountant to assist in preparing the liability section of the balance sheet:

(a) Property taxes of $54,000 were assessed on the property in May 1992 for the subsequent period of July 1 to June 30. The payment of taxes is divided into three equal installments—November 1, February 1, and May 1. The November 1 payment was made and charged to Property Tax Expense. No other entries have been made for property taxes relative to the 1992-93 assessment.

(b) The estimated 1992 pretax income for Collins is $629,000. The effective state income tax rate is 10% (applied to pretax income). The effective rate for federal income taxes is estimated at 40% (applied to income after deducting state income taxes). Income tax payments of $280,000 were made by Collins during 1992, including $50,000 as the final payment on 1991 federal income taxes, $20,000 for 1992 estimated state taxes, the balance for 1992 estimated federal taxes.

(c) Taxable sales for 1992 were $7,500,000. The state sales tax rate is 5.5%. Quarterly statements have been filed, and the following tax payments were made with the return.

| | |
|---|---|
| 1st Quarter | $ 96,000 |
| 2nd Quarter | 110,000 |
| 3rd Quarter | 125,000 |

The balance in the sales tax payable account is $81,200 at December 31, 1992.

**Instructions:**

1. Based on the above data, what amounts should be reported on the balance sheet as liabilities at December 31, 1992?
2. Prepare the necessary adjusting entries to record the liabilities.

## Problem 15—2  (Accrued payroll and payroll taxes)

Martina Clothiers' employees are paid on the 5th and 20th of each month for the period ending the last day of the previous month and the 15th of the current month, respectively. An analysis of the payroll on Thursday, November 5, 1993, revealed the following data:

| | Gross Pay | FICA | Federal Income Tax | State Income Tax | Insurance | Net Pay |
|---|---|---|---|---|---|---|
| Office staff salaries ..... | $11,250 | $ 574 | $ 1,200 | $ 450 | $ 270 | $ 8,756 |
| Officers' salaries ....... | 28,500 | 364 | 5,700 | 1,500 | 510 | 20,426 |
| Sales salaries ......... | 18,000 | 712 | 3,600 | 750 | 390 | 12,548 |
| Totals .............. | $57,750 | $1,650 | $10,500 | $2,700 | $1,170 | $41,730 |

It is determined that for the October 31 pay period, no additional employees exceeded the wage base for FICA purposes than had done so in prior pay periods. All of the officers' salaries, 70% of the office staff salaries, and 55% of the sales salaries for the payroll period ending October 31 were paid to employees who had exceeded the wage base for unemployment taxes. Assume the unemployment tax rates in force are as follows: federal unemployment tax, 0.8%, and state unemployment tax, 5.4%.

**Instructions:**   Prepare the adjusting entries that would be required at October 31, the end of Martina's fiscal year, to reflect the accrual of the payroll and any related payroll taxes. Separate salary and payroll taxes expense accounts are used for each of the three employee categories: office staff, officers', and sales salaries.

## Problem 15—3  (Accounting for payroll)

Bags, Inc., a manufacturer of suitcases, has 10 employees. Five of the employees are paid on a salary basis, and five are hourly employees. The employees and their compensations are as follows:

|  | **Annual Salary** |
|---|---|
| Ken Scott (president) ......................................... | $91,500 |
| Tatia Furgins ................................................. | 57,000 |
| Jennifer Poulins .............................................. | 48,750 |
| Robyn Meek .................................................. | 23,800 |
| Kyle Roberts ................................................. | 13,900 |

|  | **Rate Per Hour** |
|---|---|
| Richard Dean (50 hours per week) ............................ | $14.00 |
| Denise Ray (40 hours per week)................................ | 11.50 |
| Dale Frank (40 hours per week) ............................... | 9.75 |
| Bryan Leslie (30 hours per week)............................... | 4.50 |
| Albert Lamb (20 hours per week) ............................. | 3.65 |

The salaried employees are covered by a comprehensive medical and dental plan. The cost of the plan is $45 per employee and is deducted from each paycheck. The hourly employees are covered only by a medical plan. The cost is calculated at 3.5% of gross pay and is deducted from each check. The FICA rate is 7.65%, and FUTA is 6.2%, with the maximum credit for state unemployment allowed. The state unemployment tax is 5.4%. In addition, each of the hourly employees, except Albert, belongs to the Suitcase Workers of America Union. Union dues are $5.65 per month and are deducted and paid on behalf of the hourly employees. The income tax withholding rate is 28% for employees with annual incomes above $29,500 and 15% for employees with annual incomes of $29,500 or less.

Hourly employees are paid weekly on Friday, January 6, 13, 20, and 27. Salaried employees are paid twice a month, on January 13 and 27. Assume that payroll taxes and all employee withholdings and deductions are paid on the 15th and the last day of each month.

**Instructions:**   Make all entries related to Bags, Inc.'s, payroll for January 6 and January 13.

## Problem 15—4   (Tax liability)

Lucille's Cafe, a new business in town, has asked you for help in calculating and recording its property and sales tax liability. On July 1, 1992, Lucille's received notice that property taxes totaling $24,000 were to be paid by October 1, 1992. The property tax was for the period of July 1, 1992, to June 30, 1993. Lucille's Cafe had sales of $89,460 in 1992. This amount included sales tax collections. The sales tax rate in the area is 5%. Sales taxes are due on January 31, 1993.

**Instructions:**

1. Give the entries to record the accrual, monthly expensing, and payment of property taxes. (Give only one example of the monthly recognition of property tax.) What is the December 31, 1992, balance in the deferred property taxes account?
2. Calculate the amount of sales tax payable as of December 31, 1992. Make the entry needed to record this liability at year-end. Also give the entry to record payment of sales tax on January 31, 1993.

## Problem 15—5   (Warranty liability)

High Fidelity Corporation sells stereos under a two-year warranty contract that requires High Fidelity to replace defective parts and provide free labor on all repairs. During 1992, 1,050 units were sold at $900 each. In 1993, High Fidelity sold an additional 900 units at $925. Based on past experience, the estimated two-year warranty costs are $20 for parts and $25 for labor per unit. It is also estimated that 40% of the warranty expenditures will occur in the first year and 60% in the second year.

Actual warranty expenditures were as follows:

| | Warranty Costs 1993 | Warranty Costs 1994 |
|---|---|---|
| Stereos sold in 1992 .................................... | $18,300 | $26,500 |
| Stereos sold in 1993 .................................... | — | 18,100 |

**Instructions:** Assuming sales occurred on the last day of the year for both 1992 and 1993, give the necessary journal entries for the years 1992 through 1994. Analyze the warranty liability account for the year ending December 31, 1994, to see if the actual repairs approximate the estimate. Should High Fidelity revise its warranty estimates?

## Problem 15—6 (Warranty liability)

Monroe Corporation, a client, requests that you compute the appropriate balance of its estimated liability for the product warranty account for a statement as of June 30, 1993.

Monroe Corporation manufactures television tubes and sells them with a six-month warranty under which defective tubes will be replaced without charge. On December 31, 1992, Estimated Liability for Product Warranty had a balance of $510,000. By June 30, 1993, this balance had been reduced to $80,250 by debits for estimated net cost of tubes returned that had been sold in 1992.

The corporation started out in 1993 expecting 8% of the dollar volume of sales to be returned. However, due to the introduction of new models during the year, this estimated percentage of returns was increased to 10% on May 1. It is assumed that no tubes sold during a given month are returned in that month. Each tube is stamped with a date at time of sale so that the warranty may be properly administered. The following table of percentages indicates the likely pattern of sales returns during the six-month period of the warranty, starting with the month following the sale of tubes.

| Month Following Sale | Percentage of Total Returns Expected |
|---|---|
| First ...................................................... | 20% |
| Second .................................................... | 30 |
| Third ...................................................... | 20 |
| Fourth through sixth—10% each month .................. | 30 |
| | 100% |

Gross sales of tubes were as follows for the first six months of 1993:

| Month | Amount | Month | Amount |
|---|---|---|---|
| January ............... | $3,600,000 | April .................. | $2,850,000 |
| February.............. | 3,300,000 | May .................. | 2,000,000 |
| March ............... | 4,100,000 | June ................. | 1,800,000 |

The corporation's warranty also covers the payment of freight cost on defective tubes returned and on the new tubes sent out as replacements. This freight cost runs approximately 10% of the sales price of the tubes returned. The manufacturing cost of the tubes is roughly 80% of the sales price, and the salvage value of returned tubes averages 15% of their sales price. Returned tubes on hand at December 31, 1992, were thus valued in inventory at 15% of their original sales price.

**Instructions:** Using the data given, prepare a schedule for arriving at the balance of the estimated liability for product warranty account and give the proposed adjusting entry.

### Problem 15—7  (Premium liability)

The Village Corp. manufactures a special type of low-suds laundry soap. A dish towel is offered as a premium to customers who send in two proof-of-purchase seals from these soap boxes and a remittance of $2. Data for the premium offer is summarized below.

|  | 1992 | 1993 |
|---|---|---|
| Soap sales ($2.50 per package) ...................... | $2,500,000 | $3,125,000 |
| Dish towel purchases ($2.50 per towel) ............... | $130,000 | $176,250 |
| Number of dish towels distributed as premiums ....... | 50,000 | 70,000 |
| Number of dish towels expected to be distributed in subsequent periods.................................. | 8,500 | 3,000 |

Mailing costs are $0.26 per package.

**Instructions:**

1. Give the entries for 1992 and 1993 to record product sales, premium purchases and redemptions, and year-end adjustments.
2. Present T-accounts with appropriate amounts as of the end of 1992 and 1993.

### Problem 15—8  (Compensated absences)

Sandoval Electronics Inc. has a plan to compensate its employees for certain absences. Each employee can receive five days' sick leave each year plus 10 days' vacation. The benefits carry over for two additional years, after which the provision lapses on a FIFO flow basis. Thus, the maximum accumulation is 45 days. In some cases, the company permits vacations to be taken before they are earned. Payments are made based on current compensation levels, not on the level in effect when the absence time was earned.

| Employee | Days Accrued Jan. 1, 1993 | Daily Rate Jan. 1, 1993 | Days Earned 1993 | Days Taken 1993 | Days Accrued Dec. 31, 1993 | Daily Rate Dec. 31, 1993 |
|---|---|---|---|---|---|---|
| A | 10 | $38 | 15 | 10 | 15 | $40 |
| B | — | 44 | 15 | 10 | 5 | 50 |
| C | 30 | 42 | 7 | 37 | — | Terminated June 15— Rate = $45 |
| D | −5 | 36 | 15 | 20 | −10 | $40 |
| E | 40 | 58 | 15 | 5 | 50 | 70 |
| F | Hired July 1— Rate = $40 | — | 8 | 0 | 8 | 40 |

**Instructions:**

1. How much is the liability for compensated absences at December 31, 1993?
2. Prepare a summary journal entry to record compensation absence payments during the year and the accrual at the end of the year. Assume the payroll liability account is charged for all payments made during the year for both sickness and vacation leaves. The average rate of compensation for the year may be used to value the hours taken except for Employee C, who took leaves at the date of termination. The end-of-year rate should be used to establish the ending liability.

### Problem 15—9  (Contingent liabilities)

The Western Supply Co. has several contingent liabilities at December 31, 1993. The following brief description of each liability is obtained by the auditor:

(a) In May 1992, Western Supply became involved in litigation. In December 1993, a judgment for $800,000 was assessed against Western by the court. Western is appealing the amount of the judgment. Attorneys for Western feel it is probable that they can reduce the assessment on appeal by 50%. No entries have been made by Western pending completion of the appeal process, which is expected to take at least a year.

(b) In July 1993, Morgan County brought action against Western for polluting the Jordan River with its waste products. It is reasonably possible that Morgan County will be successful, but the amount of damages Western might have to pay should not exceed $200,000. No entry has been made by Western to reflect the possible loss.

(c) Western Supply has elected to self-insure its fire and casualty risks. At the beginning of the year, the account Reserve for Insurance had a balance of $2,500,000. During 1993, $750,000 was debited to Insurance Expense and credited to the reserve account. After payment for losses actually sustained in 1993, the reserve account had a balance of $2,800,000 at December 31, 1993. The opening balance was a result of several years of activity similar to 1993.

(d) Western Supply has signed as guarantor for a $50,000 loan by Guaranty Bank to Midwest Parts Inc., a principal supplier to Western. Because of financial problems at Midwest, it is probable that Western Supply will have to pay the $50,000 with only a 40% recovery anticipated from Midwest. No entries have been made to reflect the liability.

**Instructions:**

1. What amount should be reported as a liability on the December 31, 1993, balance sheet?
2. What note disclosure should be included as part of the balance sheet for each of the above items?
3. Prepare the journal entries necessary to adjust Western's books to reflect your answers in (1) and (2).

## Problem 15—10   (Contingencies)

In the introduction to this chapter, the legal history of the case between Pennzoil and Texaco was briefly outlined. Texaco was ordered to pay $10.5 billion to Pennzoil in 1985. Subsequent appeals in 1986 and 1987 affirmed the judgment against Texaco. The two companies agreed in late 1987 to a settlement of $3 billion, and in 1988 Texaco paid Pennzoil.

**Instructions:**

1. In 1984, when the lawsuit was initially filed, how should Texaco have disclosed the event? If a journal entry is required, prepare it.
2. In 1985 following the initial jury award, how should Texaco have disclosed the event? If a journal entry is required, prepare it.
3. In 1986 following the outcome of the appeal, how should Texaco have disclosed the event? If a journal entry is required, prepare it.
4. In 1987 following the $3 billion agreement between Texaco and Pennzoil, how should Texaco have disclosed the event? If a journal entry is required, prepare it.
5. Prepare the journal entry to record Texaco's settlement in 1988.
6. How should Pennzoil have disclosed this event during the years 1984 through 1987?

## Problem 15—11   (Recording and reporting liabilities)

Landon Manufacturing pays its employees on the last day of each month. On December 31, 1993, Landon paid $19,450 in cash to its employees for December salaries and wages. Subject to FICA is $25,000 of the gross payroll for December, and $5,000 is subject to unemployment taxes. The FICA tax rate is 7.65%. The FUTA tax rate is 6.2% and the state unemployment tax rate is 5.7%. The federal government allows the maximum credit for state unemployment tax paid. Payroll and withholding taxes for December are to be paid to the taxing authorities in January 1994. The combined withholding rate for federal, state, and local income taxes is 30%.

Landon has a mortgage of $455,000 for a plant it constructed and completed on September 1, 1990. The entire mortgage balance has been classified as a long-term obligation on the balance sheet. Interest has been paid each September 1, beginning in 1991. The interest is 10% of the outstanding mortgage balance. Beginning September 1, 1994, Landon is required to make annual payments of $46,528, which include both principal and interest.

In addition, Landon has a $15,000, five-year note payable to First Thrift Bank that matures December 31, 1994. Interest is payable on the note at 12% each January 1. Landon management plans to refinance the note when it comes due. A refinancing agreement has been signed with the bank.

On October 1 of each year, Landon pays property taxes in advance and records the payment as an asset. On October 1, 1993, Landon paid property taxes of $13,500 for the 12-month period ending September 30, 1994. The balance in the asset account as of January 1, 1994, was $9,375.

In August of 1993, a lawsuit was filed against Landon. The plaintiff in the lawsuit has asked for $6 million in damages for injuries allegedly resulting from a defective product manufactured by Landon. Landon's legal counsel believes it is probable that the suit will result in a loss to Landon, but the amount of the potential loss cannot be reasonably estimated as of December 31, 1993.

**Instructions:**

1. Make all necessary entries at December 31, 1993, to reflect the above transactions and events.
2. Prepare the liabilities section of Landon's classified balance sheet.

### Problem 15—12   (Accounting for events)

Asbestos Inc. is a manufacturer of heat shields for use in oil refineries. Management has prepared financial statements for the year ended 1993 for review by the auditors. The audit team has questioned several items contained in the financial statements and has asked for your advice concerning the proper treatment of these items. Each of the items being questioned is listed below.

(a)  In November of 1993, attorneys for current and former employees of Asbestos Inc. filed a class action lawsuit alleging that exposure to asbestos has caused significant medical problems. Attorneys for Asbestos Inc. are uncertain as to the outcome of the case. However, similar lawsuits against other firms in the asbestos industry have resulted in significant payments by the employer.

(b)  On January 12, 1994, a fire at a production facility resulted in a number of adjacent buildings (owned by other businesses) being burned. Asbestos' insurance policy does not cover damage to the property of others. Insurance companies for those other businesses have billed Asbestos for the estimated cost of $2.4 million required to restore the damaged buildings.

(c)  One of Asbestos' production plants is located on the shores of Lake Obewankanobe. The lake has been rising for a number of years and the company has installed dikes to prevent flooding. The dikes are currently operating at or near capacity. Weather forecasters have predicted that the lake will rise another 8 inches this coming summer. If this occurs, significant damage will likely result from the dikes being stressed beyond capacity.

(d)  A national magazine printed an article regarding the dangers of asbestos and specifically named Asbestos Inc. as "a killer of innocent victims." Attorneys for Asbestos filed suit for libel and were awarded $1.3 million in damages on December 16, 1993. The newspaper has indicated it would appeal the verdict.

**Instructions:**   Determine how each of the above events should be disclosed on the financial statements of Asbestos Inc. for the year ended December 31, 1993. Provide support for your position.

### Problem 15—13   (Adjusting entries and balance sheet presentation)

The unadjusted trial balance of Sunset Company at December 31, 1992, showed the following account balances:

| | |
|---|---:|
| Sales ............................................................... | $427,000 |
| Mortgage Note Payable ............................................ | 80,000 |
| Bank Notes Payable ............................................... | 10,000 |
| Accounts Payable ................................................. | 19,400 |
| Wages Payable .................................................... | 4,000 |

Additional information:

(a)  The sales account included amounts collected from customers for a 5 percent sales tax. The tax was remitted to the state on January 31, 1993.

(b)  The mortgage note is due on March 1, 1993. Interest at 12 percent has been paid through December 31. Sunset intended at December 31, 1992, to refinance the note on its due date with a new 5-year mortgage note. In fact, on March 1, 1993, Sunset paid $20,000 in cash on the principal balance and refinanced the remaining $60,000.

(c)  The bank notes are due over the next four years. The current portion of the notes is $2,500 at December 31, 1992. Interest of $500 has not been accrued. It is to be paid during 1993.

(d)  On October 1, 1992, a previous employee filed a suit against Sunset, alleging age discrimination and asking for damages of $500,000. At December 31, 1992, Sunset's attorney felt that the likelihood of losing the lawsuit was possible but not probable.

(e)  During 1992, Sunset remitted to the federal government estimated income tax payments of $55,000. The actual taxes for 1992 amounted to $75,000. No accrual has been made as of December 31, 1992.

**Instructions:**

1.  Prepare adjusting journal entries to correct the liability accounts at December 31, 1992. Assume the financial statements will be issued on April 1, 1993.

2.  Prepare the current and noncurrent liability sections of the December 31, 1992, balance sheet.

# CHAPTER 16

## Accounting for Long-Term Debt Securities

---

**CHAPTER TOPICS**

**Nature and Characteristics of Bonds**

**Issuance of Bonds**

**Accounting for Bond Interest**

**Retirement of Bonds at Maturity**

**Early Extinguishment of Debt**

**Valuation and Reporting of Long-Term Debt Securities on the Balance Sheet**

---

Many corporations incurred large amounts of debt in financing expansion in the 1980s. By applying novel techniques, such as deferring interest payments, using gradually increasing interest rates, and making interest payments by issuing additional debt rather than by paying cash, corporations postponed having to service these large amounts of debt. In the 1990s, these strategies are coming back to haunt business executives. Western Union has seen the interest rate on its long-term debt increase to 19.25%. Dr. Pepper/Seven-Up must come up with $84 million in interest payments over and above the $75 million they currently pay annually. As a result of scenarios like these, experts estimate that over $69 billion in bond defaults will occur during the next few years.[1]

[1]Fred R. Bleakley, "Many Firms Find Debt They Piled on in 1980's Is a Cruel Taskmaster," *The Wall Street Journal*, October 9, 1990.

The use of long-term debt securities to finance new products, to expand operations, to acquire other companies, or for a host of other reasons is common practice in today's business environment. This is especially true during periods of low interest rates, allowing companies to use relatively "cheap" money not only for business expansion but also to retire existing higher-cost debt or, in some cases, to retire equity securities. For example, in 1986, interest rates reached their lowest level in over eight years, resulting in a record number of new corporate bond issues. Large new issues of bonds in recent years have also occurred as a result of the significant increase in debt-financed corporate takeovers, or buy-outs.

In addition to bonds, the long-term debt classification includes mortgages, leases, pensions, and other types of long-term obligations. This chapter explains the relative advantages and disadvantages of debt and equity financing, and specifically focuses on how to account for bonds and long-term notes. In discussing bonds, both the liability of the issuer (bonds payable) and the asset of the investor (bond investment) are explained so that the total picture can be seen at one time. Specific issues related to leases are deferred to Chapter 20.

## FINANCING WITH LONG-TERM DEBT

The long-term financing of a corporation is accomplished either through the issuance of long-term debt instruments, usually bonds or notes, or through the sale of additional stock. The issuance of bonds or notes instead of stock may be preferred by management and stockholders for the following reasons:

1. Present owners continue in control of the corporation.
2. Interest is a deductible expense in arriving at taxable income, while dividends are not.
3. Current market rates of interest may be favorable relative to stock market prices.
4. The charge against earnings for interest may be less than the amount of dividends that might be expected by shareholders.

There are, however, certain limitations and disadvantages of financing with long-term debt securities. Debt financing is possible only when a company is in satisfactory financial condition and can offer adequate security to creditors. Furthermore, interest must be paid regardless of the company's earnings and financial position. If a company has operating losses and is unable to raise sufficient cash to meet periodic interest payments, debt security holders may take legal action to assume control of company assets.

A complicating factor is that the distinction between debt and equity securities may become fuzzy. Usually, a debt instrument has a fixed interest rate and a definite maturity date when the principal must be repaid. Also, holders of debt instruments generally have no voting privileges. An equity security, on the other hand, has no fixed repayment obligation or maturity date, and dividends on stock become obligations only after being formally declared by the board of directors of a corporation. In addition, common stockholders generally have voting and other ownership privileges. The problem is that certain convertible debt securities have many equity characteristics, and some preferred stocks have many of the characteristics of debt. This makes it important to recognize the distinction between debt and equity and to provide the accounting treatment that is most appropriate under the specific circumstances.

The FASB has addressed the complications associated with securities that possess features of both debt and equity instruments in a discussion memorandum, "Distinguishing Between Liability and Equity Instruments and Accounting for Instruments with Characteristics of Both." The memorandum addresses such issues as accounting for mandatorily redeemable preferred stock and the creating of a "new" capital element that includes instruments with both debt and equity features.

## ACCOUNTING FOR BONDS

Conceptually, bonds and long-term notes are similar types of financial instruments. There are some technical differences, however. For example, the trust indenture associated with bonds generally provides more extensive detail than the contract terms of a note, often including restrictions on the payment of dividends or incurrence of additional debt. The length of time to maturity is also generally longer for bonds than for notes. Some bonds do not mature for twenty years or longer, while most notes mature in one to five years. Other characteristics of bonds and notes are similar. Therefore, although the discussion that follows deals specifically with bonds, the accounting principles and reporting practices related to bonds can also be applied to long-term notes.

There are three main considerations in accounting for bonds:

1. Recording the issuance or purchase.
2. Recognizing the applicable interest during the life of the bonds.
3. Accounting for the retirement of bonds, either at maturity or prior to the maturity date.

Before these considerations are discussed, the nature of bonds and the determination of bond market prices will be reviewed.

### Nature of Bonds

The power of a corporation to create bond indebtedness is found in the corporation laws of a state and may be specifically granted by charter. In some cases, formal authorization by a majority of stockholders is required before a board of directors can approve a bond issue.

Borrowing by means of bonds involves the issuance of certificates of indebtedness. Bond certificates, commonly referred to simply as "bonds," are frequently issued in denominations of $1,000, referred to as the face amount, par value, or maturity value of the bond, although in some cases, bonds are issued in varying denominations.

The group contract between the corporation and the bondholders is known as the bond indenture. The indenture details the rights and obligations of the contracting parties, indicates the property pledged as well as the protection offered on the loan, and names the bank or trust company that is to represent the bondholders.

Bonds may be sold by the company directly to investors, or they may be underwritten by investment bankers or a syndicate. The underwriters may agree to purchase the entire bond issue or that part of the issue not sold by the company, or they may agree simply to manage the sale of the security on a commission basis, often referred to as a "best efforts" basis.

Most companies attempt to sell their bonds to underwriters to avoid incurring a loss after the bonds are placed on the market. An interesting example of this occurred several years ago when IBM Corporation went to the bond market for the first time and issued a record $1 billion worth of bonds and long-term notes. After the issue was released by IBM to the underwriters, interest rates soared as the Federal Reserve Bank sharply increased its discount rate. The market price of the IBM securities fell, and the brokerage houses and investment bankers participating in the underwriting incurred a loss in excess of $50 million on the sale of the securities to investors.

**Issuers of Bonds**    Bonds and similar debt instruments are issued by private corporations, the United States Government, state, county, and local governments, school districts, and government-sponsored organizations, such as the Federal Home Loan Bank and the Federal National Mortgage Association. The total amount of debt issued by these organizations is now well in excess of $1 trillion.

The U.S. debt includes not only Treasury bonds, but also Treasury bills, which are notes with less than one year to maturity date, and Treasury notes, which mature in one to seven years. Both Treasury bills and Treasury notes are in demand in the marketplace, perhaps even more so in recent years than Treasury bonds.

Debt securities issued by state, county, and local governments and their agencies are collectively referred to as **municipal debt**. A unique feature of municipal debt is that the interest received by investors from such securities is exempt from federal income tax. Because of this tax advantage, "municipals" generally carry lower interest rates than debt securities of other issuers, enabling these governmental units to borrow at favorable interest rates. The tax exemption is in reality a subsidy granted by the federal government to encourage capital investment in state and local governments.

**Types of Bonds**    Bonds may be categorized in many different ways, depending on the characteristics of a particular bond issue. The major distinguishing features of bonds are identified and discussed in the following sections.

**Term Versus Serial Bonds**    Bonds that mature on a single date are called term bonds. When bonds mature in installments, they are referred to as serial bonds. Serial bonds are much less common than term bonds.

**Secured Versus Unsecured Bonds**    Bonds issued by private corporations may be either secured or unsecured. **Secured bonds** offer protection to investors by providing some form of security, such as a mortgage on real estate or a pledge of other collateral. A **first-mortgage bond** represents a first claim against the property of a corporation in the event of the company's inability to meet bond interest and principal payments. A **second-mortgage bond** is a secondary claim ranking only after the claim of the first-mortgage bond or senior issue has been completely satisfied. A **collateral trust bond** is usually secured by stocks and bonds of other corporations owned by the issuing company. Such securities are generally transferred to a trustee, who holds them as collateral on behalf of the bondholders and, if necessary, will sell them to satisfy the bondholders' claim.

Unsecured bonds are not protected by the pledge of any specific assets and are frequently termed debenture bonds, or **debentures**. Holders of debenture bonds simply rank as general creditors along with other unsecured parties. The risk involved in these securities varies with the financial strength of the debtor. Debentures issued by a strong company may involve little risk; debentures issued by a weak company whose properties are already heavily mortgaged may involve considerable risk. Quality ratings for bonds are published by both Moody's and Standard and Poor's investment services companies. For example, Moody's bond ratings range from prime, or highest quality (Aaa) to default (C) for a very high-risk bond. Standard and Poor's range is from AAA to D.

**Registered Versus Bearer (Coupon) Bonds**    Registered bonds call for the registry of the owner's name on the corporation books. Transfer of bond ownership is similar to that for stock. When a bond is sold, the corporate transfer agent cancels the bond certificate surrendered by the seller and issues a new certificate to the buyer. Interest checks are mailed periodically to the bondholders of record. **Bearer** or **coupon bonds** are not recorded in the name of the owner, title to such bonds passing with delivery. Each bond is accompanied by coupons for individual interest payments covering the life of the issue. Coupons are clipped by the owner of the bond and presented to a bank for deposit or collection. The issue of bearer bonds eliminates the need for recording bond ownership changes and preparing and mailing periodic interest checks. But coupon bonds fail to offer the bondholder the protection found in registered bonds in the event the bonds are lost or stolen. In some cases, bonds provide interest coupons but require registry as to principal. Here, ownership safeguards are provided, while the time-consuming routines involved in making interest payments are avoided. Bonds of recent issue are registered rather than coupon bonds.

***Zero-Interest Bonds and Bonds With Variable Interest Rates***    In recent years, some companies have issued long-term debt securities that do not bear interest. Instead, these securities sell at a significant discount that provides an investor with a total interest payoff at maturity. These bonds are known as **zero-interest bonds** or **deep-discount bonds**. Another type of zero-interest bond delays interest payments for a period of time.  For example, Southland Corporation, 7-11's parent company, incurred $4.9 billion in debt in 1987.  The zero-interest bonds postponed interest payments until late in 1990.  At that time, interest of 16.5%, well above the prevailing market rate, had to be paid.

Because of potentially wide fluctuations in interest rates, some bonds and long-term notes are issued with **variable (or floating) interest rates**. Over the life of these obligations, the interest rate changes as prevailing market interest rates increase or decrease. A variable interest rate security reduces the risk to the investor when interest rates are rising, and to the issuer when interest rates are falling.

***Junk Bonds***    High-risk, high-yield bonds issued by companies that are heavily in debt or otherwise in weak financial condition are often referred to as **junk bonds**. These bonds are rated Ba or lower by Moody's investment service and BB or lower by Standard and Poor's.[2] Junk bonds typically yield at least 12%, and some yield in excess of 20%. Some are zero-interest (deep discount) bonds that pay no interest until maturity or pay no interest for the first few years. While junk bonds are generally not an appropriate investment for individuals due to their high risk, they have been a significant segment of the corporate bond market in recent years.

Junk bonds are issued in at least three types of circumstances. First, they are issued by companies that once had high credit ratings but have fallen on hard times. Several companies in the steel industry are included in this category. Second, junk bonds are issued by emerging growth companies, such as Continental Cablevision, that lack adequate cash flow, credit history, or diversification to permit them to issue higher grade (i.e., lower risk) bonds. The third, and largest, category of junk bonds consists of those issued by companies undergoing restructuring, often in conjunction with a leveraged buyout (LBO), discussed later in the chapter. Metromedia Inc. is one of many examples of such companies. In 1990, the market for junk bonds was estimated to exceed $200 billion.

***Convertible and Commodity-Backed Bonds***    Bonds may provide for their conversion into some other security at the option of the bondholder. Such bonds are known as **convertible bonds**. The conversion feature generally permits the owner of bonds to exchange them for common stock. The bondholder is thus able to convert the claim into an

---

[2]Ben Weberman, "High-Grade Junk," *Forbes,* August 21, 1989, p. 115.

## Deferred Interest and Interest Rate Resets

Corporations commonly incur debt in financing the acquisition of other companies or in fighting takeover attacks by competitors. Two strategies often employed involve deferring interest payments and incorporating interest rate resets. For example, Interco Inc. incurred large amounts of debt in 1989 to make itself unattractive as a takeover target. The debt postponed interest payments until 1991 at which time interest was to be paid at 14%. Interco's strategy was to sell a portion of its business, Ethan Allen Inc., to redeem the debt. However, the sale netted $120 million less than expected.

Western Union incurred $500 million in debt that carried with it a reset provision. The provision called for increased interest rates if the bonds were not trading at a specified price. Western Union's reset provision increased interest rates from 16.5% to 19.25% in 1990. While interest expense rose, revenues dropped 28% from 1988 to 1989 as a result of the fax machine's making Western Union's telex service obsolete.

### Questions:

1. What is the significance of debt with respect to company acquisitions?
2. Why would corporations use deferred interest features and interest rate resets?
3. In the case of Interco, how would incurring large amounts of debt be an effective method for fighting a takeover?

Source: "The Junk-Bond Time Bombs Could Go Off," *Business Week*, April 9, 1990, pp. 68-70.

---

ownership interest if corporate operations prove successful and conversion becomes attractive; in the meantime, the special rights of a creditor are maintained. Bonds may also be redeemable in terms of commodities, such as oil or precious metals. These types of bonds are sometimes referred to as commodity-backed bonds or asset-linked bonds.

**Callable Bonds**    Bond indentures frequently give the issuing company the right to call and retire the bonds prior to their maturity. Such bonds are termed callable bonds. When a corporation wishes to reduce its outstanding indebtedness, bondholders are notified of the portion of the issue to be surrendered, and they are paid in accordance with call provisions. Interest does not accrue after the call date.

### Market Price of Bonds

The market price of bonds varies with the safety of the investment and the current market interest rate for similar instruments. When the financial condition and earnings of a corporation are such that payment of interest and principal on bond indebtedness is virtually assured, the interest rate a company must offer to sell a bond issue is relatively low. As the risk factor increases, a higher interest return is necessary to attract investors. The amount of interest paid on bonds is a specified percentage of the face value. This percentage is termed the stated or contract rate. This rate, however, may not be the same as the prevailing or **market rate** for bonds of similar quality and length of time to maturity at the time the issue is sold. Furthermore, the market rate constantly fluctuates. These factors often result in a difference between bond face values and the prices at which the bonds actually sell on the market.

The purchase of bonds at face value implies agreement between the bond stated rate of interest and the prevailing market rate of interest. If the stated rate exceeds the market rate, the bonds will sell at a **premium**; if the stated rate is less than the market rate, the bonds will sell at a **discount**. The bond premium or the bond discount is the amount needed to adjust the stated rate of interest to the actual market rate of interest for that particular bond. Thus, the stated rate adjusted for the premium or the discount on the purchase gives the actual rate of return on the bonds, known as the **market, yield,** or **effective interest rate**. A declining market rate of interest subsequent to issuance of the bonds results in an increase in the market value of the bonds; a rising market rate of interest results in a decrease in their market value.

Bonds are quoted on the market as a percentage of face value. For example, a bond quotation of 96.5 means the market price is 96.5% of face value; thus, the bond is trading at a discount. A bond quotation of 104 means the market price is 104% of face value; thus, the bond is trading at a premium. U.S. Government note and bond quotations are made in 32s rather than 100s. This means that a Government bond selling at 98.16 is selling at $98^{16}/_{32}$, or in terms of decimal equivalents, 98.5%.

The market price of a bond at any date can be determined by discounting the maturity value of the bond and each remaining interest payment at the market rate of interest for similar debt on that date. The present-value tables in Chapter 7 can be used for computing bond market prices.

To illustrate the computation of a bond market price from the tables, assume 10-year, 8% bonds of $100,000 are to be sold on the bond issue date. Further assume that the effective interest rate for bonds of similar quality and maturity is 10%, compounded semiannually. The computation of the market price of the bonds may be divided into two parts:

### Part 1    Present value of principal (maturity value)

| | | |
|---|---|---|
| Maturity value of bonds after 10 years, or 20 semiannual periods . . . . . . . . . . . . . . . . . . . . . . . . . . . . . . . . . . . . . . . . . . . . | $  100,000 | |
| Effective interest rate = 10% per year, or 5% per semiannual period; present value factor (PVF), Table II $\overline{20}|_5$ . . . . . . | ×    .3769 | |
| Present value of $100,000 discounted at 5% for 20 periods | | $37,690 |

### Part 2    Present value of 20 interest payments

| | | |
|---|---|---|
| Semiannual payment, 4% of $100,000 . . . . . . . . . . . . . . . . . . | $    4,000 | |
| Effective interest rate, 10% per year, or 5% per semiannual period; present value of annuity factor (PVAF), Table IV $\overline{20}|_5$ . . . . . . . . . . . . . . . . . . . . . . . . . . . . . . . . . . . . . . . . . . . . | × 12.4622 | |
| Present value of 20, $4,000 payments, discounted at 5% . . | | 49,849 |
| Total present value (market price) of bond . . . . . . . . . . . . . . | | $87,539 |

The market price for the bonds would be $87,539, the sum of the present values of the two parts. Because the effective interest rate is higher than the stated interest rate, the bonds would sell at a $12,461 discount at the issuance date. It should be noted that if the effective rate on these bonds were 8% instead of 10%, the sum of the present values of the two parts would be $100,000, meaning that the bonds would sell at their face amount, or at par. If the effective interest rate were less than 8%, the market price of the bonds would be more than $100,000, and the bonds would sell at a premium.

Specially adapted present-value tables are available to determine directly the price to be paid for bonds if they are to provide a certain return. A portion of such a bond table is illustrated below.

Note that the market price from the bond table for 8% bonds sold to yield 10% in 10 years is $87,539, the same amount as computed using present-value tables. Also, the bond table shows that if the effective interest rate were 8%, the bonds would sell at par, $100,000. If the effective rate were 7.5%, the market price would be $103,476.

The bond table can also be used to determine the effective rate of interest on a bond acquired at a certain price. To illustrate, assume that a $1,000, 8% bond due in 10 years is selling at $951. Reference to the column "10 years" for $95,070 shows an annual return of 8.75% is provided on an investment of $950.70.

### Bond Table
### Values to the Nearest Dollar of 8% Bond for $100,000
### Interest Payable Semiannually

| Yield or Effective Interest | 8 years | 8½ years | 9 years | 9½ years | 10 years |
|---|---|---|---|---|---|
| 7.00 | $106,046 | $106,325 | $106,595 | $106,855 | $107,107 |
| 7.25 | 104,495 | 104,699 | 104,896 | 105,090 | 105,272 |
| 7.50 | 102,971 | 103,100 | 103,232 | 103,360 | 103,476 |
| 7.75 | 101,472 | 101,537 | 101,595 | 101,658 | 101,718 |
| 8.00 | 100,000 | 100,000 | 100,000 | 100,000 | 100,000 |
| 8.25 | 98,552 | 98,494 | 98,437 | 98,372 | 98,325 |
| 8.50 | 97,141 | 97,012 | 96,893 | 96,787 | 96,678 |
| 8.75 | 95,746 | 95,568 | 95,398 | 95,232 | 95,070 |
| 9.00 | 94,383 | 94,147 | 93,920 | 93,703 | 93,496 |
| 9.25 | 93,042 | 92,757 | 92,480 | 92,214 | 91,953 |
| 9.50 | 91,723 | 91,380 | 91,055 | 90,751 | 90,452 |
| 9.75 | 90,350 | 89,960 | 89,588 | 89,238 | 88,902 |
| 10.00 | 89,162 | 88,726 | 88,310 | 87,914 | 87,539 |

## Issuance of Bonds

Bonds may be sold directly to investors by the issuer or they may be sold on the open market through securities exchanges or through investment bankers. Over 50% of bond issues are privately placed with large investors. Regardless of how placed, when bonds are issued (sold), the issuer must record the receipt of cash and recognize the long-term liability. The purchaser must record the payment of cash and the bond investment.

An issuer normally records the bond obligation at its face value—the amount that the company must pay at maturity. Hence, when bonds are issued at an amount other than face value, a bond discount or premium account is established for the difference between the cash received and the bond face value. The premium is added to or the discount is subtracted from the bond face value to report the bonds at their present value. Although an investor could also record the investment in bonds at their face value by using a premium or discount account, traditionally, investors record their bond investments at cost, that is, the face value net of any premium or discount. Cost includes brokerage fees and any other costs incident to the purchase.

Bonds issued or acquired in exchange for noncash assets or services are recorded at the fair market value of the bonds, unless the value of the exchanged assets or services is more clearly determinable. A difference between the face value of the bonds and the cash value of the bonds or the value of the property acquired is recognized as bond discount or bond premium. When bonds and other securities are acquired for a lump sum, an apportionment of such cost among the securities is required.

As indicated earlier, bonds may be issued at par, at a discount, or at a premium. They may be issued on an interest payment date or between interest dates, which calls for the recognition of accrued interest. Each of these situations will be illustrated using the following data: $100,000, 8%, 10-year bonds are issued. Semiannual interest of $4,000 ($100,000 × .08 × $^6/_{12}$) is payable on January 1 and July 1.

**Bonds Issued at Par on Interest Date**    When bonds are issued at par, or face value, on an interest date, there is no premium or discount to be recognized nor any accrued interest at the date of issuance. The appropriate entries for the first year, on the issuer's books and on the investor's books, assuming the data in the preceding paragraph and issuance on January 1 at par value, would be:

| | Issuer's Books | | | Investor's Books | | |
|---|---|---|---|---|---|---|
| Jan. 1 | Cash ............. | 100,000 | | Bond Investment .. | 100,000 | |
| | Bonds Payable .. | | 100,000 | Cash .......... | | 100,000 |
| July 1 | Interest Expense... | 4,000 | | Cash ............ | 4,000 | |
| | Cash .......... | | 4,000 | Interest Revenue | | 4,000 |
| Dec. 31 | Interest Expense... | 4,000 | | Interest Receivable | 4,000 | |
| | Interest Payable.. | | 4,000 | Interest Revenue | | 4,000 |

**Bonds Issued at Discount on Interest Date**    Now assume that the bonds were issued on January 1 but that the effective rate of interest was 10%, requiring recognition of a discount of $12,461 ($100,000 − $87,539). The appropriate entries on January 1 are shown below. The interest entries on July 1 and December 31 are illustrated in a later section that discusses the amortization of discounts and premiums.

| | Issuer's Books | | | Investor's Books | | |
|---|---|---|---|---|---|---|
| Jan. 1 | Cash............. | 87,539 | | Bond Investment.. | 87,539 | |
| | Discount on Bonds | | | Cash.......... | | 87,539 |
| | Payable ......... | 12,461 | | | | |
| | Bonds Payable.. | | 100,000 | | | |

**Bonds Issued at Premium on Interest Date**    Again using the data above, assume that the bonds were sold at an effective interest rate of 7%, resulting in a premium of $7,107. In this case, the entries on January 1 would be:

| | Issuer's Books | | | Investor's Books | | |
|---|---|---|---|---|---|---|
| Jan. 1 | Cash.......... | 107,107 | | Bond Investment | 107,107 | |
| | Premium on | | | Cash ......... | | 107,107 |
| | Bonds Payable | | 7,107 | | | |
| | Bonds Payable | | 100,000 | | | |

**Bonds Issued at Par Between Interest Dates**    When bonds are issued between interest dates, an adjustment is made for the interest accrued between the last interest payment date and the date of the transaction. A buyer of the bonds pays the amount of accrued interest along with the purchase price and then receives the accrued interest plus interest earned subsequent to the purchase date when the next interest payment is made. This practice avoids the problem an issuer of bonds would have in trying to split interest payments for a given period between two or more owners of the securities. To illustrate, if the bonds in the previous example were issued at par on March 1, the appropriate entries would be:

| | Issuer's Books[3] | | | Investor's Books | | |
|---|---|---|---|---|---|---|
| Mar. 1 | Cash .............. | 101,333 | | Bond Investment ... | 100,000 | |
| | Bonds Payable ... | | 100,000 | Interest Receivable .. | 1,333 | |
| | Interest Payable .. | | 1,333* | Cash ............. | | 101,333 |
| | *($100,000 × .08 × 2/12) | | | | | |
| | | | | | | |
| July 1 | Interest Expense ... | 2,667* | | Cash .............. | 4,000 | |
| | Interest Payable .... | 1,333 | | Interest Receivable | | 1,333 |
| | Cash ........... | | 4,000 | Interest Revenue .. | | 2,667 |
| | *($100,000 × .08 × 4/12) | | | | | |

**Bond Issuance Costs**    The issuance of bonds normally involves costs to the issuer for legal services, printing and engraving, taxes, and underwriting. Traditionally, these costs have been either (1) summarized separately as bond issuance costs, classified as deferred charges, and charged to expense over the life of the bond issue, or (2) offset against any premium or added to any discount arising on the issuance and thus netted against the face value of the bonds. The Accounting Principles Board in Opinion No. 21 recommended that these costs be reported on the balance sheet as deferred charges.[4] However, in Statement of Financial Accounting Concepts No. 3, the FASB stated that such costs fail to meet the definition of assets adopted by the Board.[5]    Concepts statements do not establish GAAP, however, and until such time as the FASB addresses this issue, the APB Opinion governs generally accepted practice.

## Accounting for Bond Interest

With coupon bonds, cash is paid by the issuing company in exchange for interest coupons on the interest dates. Payments on coupons may be made by the company directly to bondholders, or payments may be cleared through a bank or other disbursing agent. Subsidiary records with bondholders are not maintained, since coupons are redeemable by bearers. In the case of registered bonds, interest checks are mailed either by the company or its agent. When bonds are registered, the bonds account requires subsidiary ledger support. The subsidiary ledger shows holdings by individuals and changes in such holdings. Checks are sent to bondholders of record as of the interest payment dates.

When bonds are issued at a premium or discount, the market acts to adjust the stated interest rate to a market or effective interest rate. Because of the initial premium or discount, the periodic interest payments made over the bond life by the issuer do not

---

[3]As an alternative, the accrued interest could be initially credited to Interest Expense by the issuer and debited to Interest Revenue by the investor. When the first interest payment is made, the debit to Interest Expense for the issuer, when combined with the initial entry, would result in the proper amount of interest expense being recognized. A similar procedure can be applied by the investor in determining interest revenue.

[4]Opinions of the Accounting Principles Board No. 21, "Interest on Receivables and Payables" (New York: American Institute of Certified Public Accountants, 1971), par. 16.

[5]Statement of Financial Accounting Concepts No. 3, "Elements of Financial Statements of Business Enterprises" (Stamford: Financial Accounting Standards Board, December 1980), par. 161.

represent the total expense for the periods involved. An adjustment to the interest expense asscciated with the cash payment is necessary to reflect the effective interest being incurred on the bonds. This adjustment is referred to as **bond premium** or **discount amortization**. The periodic adjustment of bonds results in a gradual adjustment of the carrying value toward the bond's face value.

A premium on issued bonds recognizes that the stated interest rate is higher than the market interest rate. Amortization of the premium reduces the interest expense below the amount of cash paid. A discount on issued bonds recognizes that the stated interest rate is lower than the market interest rate. Amortization of the discount increases the amount of interest expense above the amount of cash paid.

Two main methods are used to amortize the premium or discount: (1) the straight-line method and (2) the effective-interest method. The straight-line method is explained first, because the computations are simpler. This method is acceptable, however, only when its application results in periodic interest expense that does not differ materially from the amounts that would be reported using the effective-interest method.[6]

**Straight-Line Method**    The straight-line method provides for the recognition of an equal amount of premium or discount amortization each period. The amount of monthly amortization is determined by dividing the premium or discount at purchase or issuance by the number of months remaining to the bond maturity date. For example, if a 10-year, 10% bond issue with a maturity value of $200,000 was sold on the issuance date at 103, the $6,000 premium would be amortized evenly over the 120 months until maturity, or at a rate of $50 per month ($6,000 ÷ 120). If the bonds were sold three months after the issuance date, the $6,000 premium would be amortized evenly over 117 months, or at a rate of $51.28 per month ($6,000 ÷ 117). The amortization period is always the time from original sale to maturity. The premium amortization would reduce both interest expense on the issuer's books and interest revenue on the investor's books. A discount amortization would have the opposite results: both accounts would be increased.

To illustrate the accounting for bond interest using straight-line amortization, consider again the earlier example of the $100,000, 8%, 10-year bonds issued on January 1. When sold at a $12,461 discount, the appropriate entries to record interest on July 1 and December 31 would be as follows:

| | Issuer's Books | | | Investor's Books | |
|---|---|---|---|---|---|
| July 1 | Interest Expense ..... 4,623 | | | Cash ............... 4,000 | |
| | Discount on Bonds | | | Bond Investment.... | 623 |
| | Payable .......... | 623 | | | |
| | Cash............. | 4,000 | | Interest Revenue .. | 4,623 |
| | [$100,000 × .08 × 6/12 = $4,000 cash; $12,461 ÷ 120 × 6 months = $623 (rounded) discount amortization] | | | | |
| Dec. 31 | Interest Expense ..... 4,623 | | | Interest Receivable .. 4,000 | |
| | Discount on Bonds | | | Bond Investment.... | 623 |
| | Payable .......... | 623 | | | |
| | Interest Payable ... | 4,000 | | Interest Revenue .. | 4,623 |

Note that the discount amortization has the effect of increasing the effective interest rate over the life of the bond from the 8% stated rate to the 10% market rate of interest that the bonds were sold to yield. Over the life of the bond, the $12,461 discount will be charged to interest expense for the issuer and recognized as interest revenue by the investor.[7]

---

[6]*Opinions of the Accounting Principles Board No. 21,* par. 15.

[7]Because the amount amortized for each six-month period is identical, many companies make the amortization entry only once a year.

To illustrate the entries that would be required to amortize a bond premium, consider again the situation where the 8% bonds were sold to yield 7%, or $107,107. The $7,107 premium would be amortized on a straight-line basis as follows:

| | Issuer's Books | | | Investor's Books | |
|---|---|---|---|---|---|
| **July 1** | Interest Expense .... 3,645 | | | Cash ............... 4,000 | |
| | Premium on Bonds | | | Bond Investment .. | 355 |
| | Payable ........... 355 | | | | |
| | Cash ............ | | 4,000 | Interest Revenue .. | 3,645 |
| | [$7,107 ÷ 120 × 6 months = $355 (rounded) premium amortization for 6-month period] | | | | |
| **Dec. 31** | Interest Expense .... 3,645 | | | Interest Receivable .. 4,000 | |
| | Premium on Bonds | | | Bond Investment .. | 355 |
| | Payable ........... 355 | | | | |
| | Interest Payable .. | | 4,000 | Interest Revenue .. | 3,645 |

The amortization of the premium has the effect of reducing the amount of interest expense or interest revenue over the life of the bond to the actual yield or market rate of the bonds, 7%.

**Effective-Interest Method**    The effective-interest method of amortization uses a uniform interest rate based on a changing investment balance and provides for an increasing premium or discount amortization each period. In order to use this method, the effective-interest rate for the bonds must be known. This is the rate of interest at bond issuance that discounts the maturity value of the bonds and the periodic interest payments to the market price of the bonds. This rate is used to determine the effective revenue or expense to be recorded on the books.

To illustrate the amortization of a bond discount using the effective-interest method, consider once again the $100,000, 8%, 10-year bonds sold for $87,539, based on an effective-interest rate of 10%.

The discount amortization for the first six months using the effective-interest method would be computed as follows:

| | |
|---|---|
| Investment balance (carrying value) at beginning of first period ........... | **$87,539** |
| Effective rate per semiannual period.................................... | 5% |
| Stated rate per semiannual period...................................... | 4% |
| Interest amount based on carrying value and effective rate ($87,539 × .05) .. | $ 4,377 |
| Interest payment based on par value and stated rate ($100,000 × .04) ..... | 4,000 |
| Discount amortization—difference between interest based on effective rate and stated rate ................................................. | $ 377 |

This difference between the amount paid and the compound interest expense is the discount amortization for the first period using the effective-interest method. For the second semiannual period, the bond carrying value increases by the amount of discount amortized. The amortization for the second semiannual period would be computed as follows:

| | |
|---|---|
| Investment balance (carrying value) at beginning of second period ($87,539 + $377)........................................................ | **$87,916** |
| Interest amount based on carrying value and effective rate ($87,916 × .05).. | $ 4,396 |
| Interest payment based on par value and stated rate ($100,000 × .04) ..... | 4,000 |
| Discount amortization—difference between interest based on effective rate and stated rate ................................................. | $ 396 |

The amount of interest to be recognized each period is computed at a uniform rate on an increasing balance. This results in an increasing discount amortization over the life of the bonds, which is graphically demonstrated and compared with straight-line amortization below.

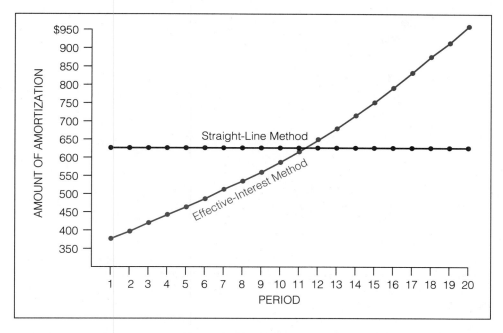

The entries for amortizing the discount would be the same as those shown for straight-line amortization; only the amounts would be different.

Premium amortization would be computed in a similar way except that the interest payment based on the stated interest rate would be higher than the interest amount based on the effective rate. For example, assume that the $100,000, 8%, 10-year bonds were sold on the issuance date for $107,107, thus providing an effective interest rate of 7%. The premium amortization for the first and second six-month periods would be computed as follows (amounts are rounded to the nearest dollar):

| | |
|---|---:|
| Investment balance (carrying value) at beginning of first period . . . . . . . | **$107,107** |
| Effective rate per semiannual period . . . . . . . . . . . . . . . . . . . . . . . . . . . . . . . | 3.5% |
| Stated rate per semiannual period . . . . . . . . . . . . . . . . . . . . . . . . . . . . . . . . . | 4.0% |
| Interest payment based on par value and stated rate ($100,000 × .04). . | $  4,000 |
| Interest amount based on carrying value and effective rate ($107,107 × .035) . . . . . . . . . . . . . . . . . . . . . . . . . . . . . . . . . . . . . . . . . . . . . . . . . . . . . | 3,749 |
| Premium amortization—difference between interest based on stated rate and effective rate . . . . . . . . . . . . . . . . . . . . . . . . . . . . . . . . . . . . . . . . . | $      251 |
| Investment balance (carrying value) at beginning of second period ($107,107 − $251) . . . . . . . . . . . . . . . . . . . . . . . . . . . . . . . . . . . . . . . . . | **$106,856** |
| Interest payment based on par value and stated rate ($100,000 × .04). . | $  4,000 |
| Interest amount based on carrying value and effective rate ($106,856 × .035) . . . . . . . . . . . . . . . . . . . . . . . . . . . . . . . . . . . . . . . . . . . . . . . . . . . . . | 3,740 |
| Premium amortization—difference between interest based on stated rate and effective rate . . . . . . . . . . . . . . . . . . . . . . . . . . . . . . . . . . . . . . . . . | $      260 |

As illustrated, as the investment or liability balance is reduced by the premium amortization, the interest, based on the effective rate, also decreases. The difference between the interest payment and the effective interest amount increases in a manner similar to discount amortization. Bond amortization tables may be prepared to determine the periodic adjustments to the bond carrying value, i.e., the present value of the bond. A partial bond amortization table is illustrated below.

**Amortization of Bond Premium—Effective-Interest Method**
**$100,000, 10-Year Bonds, Interest at 8% Payable Semiannually,**
**Sold at $107,107 to Yield 7%**

| Interest Payment | A<br>Interest Paid<br>(.04 × $100,000) | B<br>Interest Expense<br>(.035 × Bond Carrying Value) | C<br>Premium Amorti-zation<br>(A − B) | D<br>Unamor-tized Premium<br>(D − C) | E<br>Bond Carrying Value<br>($100,000 + D) |
|---|---|---|---|---|---|
| | | | | $7,107 | $107,107 |
| 1 | $4,000 | $3,749 (.035 × $107,107) | $251 | 6,856 | 106,856 |
| 2 | 4,000 | 3,740 (.035 × $106,856) | 260 | 6,596 | 106,596 |
| 3 | 4,000 | 3,731 (.035 × $106,596) | 269 | 6,327 | 106,327 |
| 4 | 4,000 | 3,721 (.035 × $106,327) | 279 | 6,048 | 106,048 |
| 5 | 4,000 | 3,712 (.035 × $106,048) | 288 | 5,760 | 105,760 |

Because the effective-interest method adjusts the stated interest rate to an effective-interest rate, it is theoretically more accurate as an amortization method than is the straight-line method. Note that the total amortization over the life of the bond is the same under either method; only the interim amounts differ. Since the issuance of APB Opinion No. 21, the effective-interest method is the recommended amortization method. However, as stated previously, the straight-line method may be used by a company if the interim results of using it do not differ materially from the amortization using the effective-interest method.

## Cash Flow Effects of Amortizing Bond Premiums and Discounts

The amortization of a bond discount or premium does not involve the receipt or payment of cash and, like other noncash items, must be considered in preparing a statement of cash flows. Recall that when the indirect method is used to report cash flows from operating activities, net income is adjusted for noncash items. When a bond discount is amortized, interest expense reported on the income statement is higher than interest paid, and net income, on a cash basis, is understated. The appropriate adjustment is to add the amount of discount amortization back to net income. The reverse is true in the case of a bond premium. That is, the amount of bond premium amortization is subtracted from net income to arrive at cash flow from operations.

Using the direct method requires conversion of individual accrual-basis revenue and expense items to a cash basis. Thus, to convert interest expense to cash paid for interest, the expense reported on the income statement is decreased by the amount of discount amortization for the period or increased by the amount of premium amortization.

The following example illustrates the adjustments necessary when preparing a statement of cash flows. Assume that in 1993, Rider Co. issued $100,000, 8%, 10-year bonds that sold at a discount of $8,700 (also assume straight-line amortization). In its 1993 income statement, Rider Co. reported interest expense relating to the bonds of $8,870 and net income of $90,000.

Using the indirect method, the amount of discount amortized ($870) is added back to net income. Under the direct method, the amount of the discount is subtracted from reported interest expense to convert that amount to a cash basis as follows: $8,870 interest expense − $870 discount amortization = $8,000 cash paid for interest. In this case, where only one bond issue is involved, cash paid for interest could instead be computed by multiplying the stated interest rate by the face amount of the bonds ($100,000 × .08). A partial statement of cash flow for each method appears below.

| **Indirect Method** | |
| --- | --- |
| Cash flows from operating activities: | |
| Net income ............................................... | $90,000 |
| Adjustments: | |
| Add amortization of bond discount........................... | 870 |

| **Direct Method** | |
| --- | --- |
| Cash flows from operating activities: | |
| Cash payments for interest ................................. | $ 8,000 |

## Retirement of Bonds at Maturity

Bonds always include a specified termination or maturity date. At that time, the issuer must pay the current investors the maturity or face value of the bonds. When bond discount or premium and issuance costs have been properly amortized over the life of the bonds, bond retirement simply calls for elimination of the liability or the investment by a cash transaction, illustrated as follows assuming a $100,000 bond:

| **Issuer's Books** | | | **Investor's Books** | | |
| --- | --- | --- | --- | --- | --- |
| Bonds Payable ...... | 100,000 | | Cash ............... | 100,000 | |
| Cash ............ | | 100,000 | Bond Investment .. | | 100,000 |

There is no recognition of any gain or loss on retirement, since the carrying value is equal to the maturity value, which is also equal to the market value of the bonds at that point in time.

Any bonds not presented for payment at their maturity date should be removed from the bonds payable balance on the issuer's books and reported separately as Matured Bonds Payable; these are reported as a current liability except when they are to be paid out of a bond retirement fund. Interest does not accrue on matured bonds not presented for payment. If a bond retirement fund is used to pay off a bond issue, any cash remaining in the fund may be returned to the cash account.

## Extinguishment of Debt Prior to Maturity

When debt is retired or "extinguished" prior to the maturity date, a gain or loss must be recognized for the difference between the carrying value of the debt security and the amount paid to satisfy the obligation.[8] This gain or loss is classified as an early extinguishment of debt and, according to FASB Statement No. 4, is to be reported as an extraordinary item on the income statement.[9]

[8]*Opinions of the Accounting Principles Board No. 26,* "Early Extinguishment of Debt" (New York: American Institute of Certified Public Accountants, 1972), par. 20.

[9]*Statement of Financial Accounting Standards No. 4,* "Reporting Gains and Losses from Extinguishment of Debt" (Stamford: Financial Accounting Standards Board, 1975), par. 8. Note that an exception to the extraordinary classification is made if the early termination is necessary to satisfy bond retirement (sinking) fund requirements within a one-year period; see *Statement of Financial Accounting Standards No. 64,* "Extinguishment of Debt Made to Satisfy Sinking-Fund Requirements" (Stamford: Financial Accounting Standards Board, 1982), par. 3.

## Circle K Corporation and Financing Covenants

When companies raise money through the issuance of bonds or other long-term debt instruments, debt holders typically require the company to comply with certain conditions, or covenants. The notes to Circle K's 1989 financial statements provide an example of debt covenants:

> The Notes (Senior Secured Notes) require the Company to observe certain financial covenants, including covenants relating to maintenance of a minimum consolidated net worth, a fixed charge coverage ratio, limitations on dividends, purchases of capital stock and a requirement that any successor by merger or similar transaction to the Company have a comparable net worth and assume all the obligations under the Notes.

In addition to using debt to finance expansion, Circle K finances many of its stores through sales and leaseback transactions. These types of transactions represent a form of long-term debt financing and often involve covenants as well. The notes to the 1989 financial statements detail the results of a violation of covenants.

> As of April 30, 1989, the Company was not in compliance with the fixed charge ratio of one of its sale and leaseback transactions involving 250 stores. Because of its non-compliance with such ratio, the Company is required to place $5 million per year into escrow.

### Questions:

1. What is the purpose of debt covenants?
2. What is the purpose of requiring an annual $5 million payment into escrow?
3. If Circle's financial condition is such that it violates its financing covenants, will requiring the company to place $5 million in escrow help to ease the financial strains?
4. Should external auditors be required to determine whether companies are in compliance with their debt covenants?

Source: Circle K 1989 Annual Report

The problems that arise in retiring bonds or other forms of long-term debt prior to maturity are described in the following sections. Bonds may be retired prior to maturity in one of the following ways:

1. Bonds may be **redeemed** by the issuer by purchasing the bonds on the open market or by exercising the call provision that is frequently included in bond indentures;
2. Bonds may be **converted**, i.e., exchanged for other securities; or
3. Bonds may be **refinanced** (sometimes called "refunded") by using the proceeds from the sale of a new bond issue to retire outstanding bonds.

**Redemption by Purchase of Bonds on the Market**   Corporations frequently purchase their own bonds on the market when prices or other factors make such actions desirable. When bonds are purchased, amortization of bond premium or discount and issue costs should be brought up to date. Purchase by the issuer calls for the cancellation of the bond face value together with any related premium, discount, or issue costs as of the purchase date.

To illustrate a bond redemption prior to maturity, assume that $100,000, 8% bonds of Triad Inc. are not held until maturity but are redeemed by the issuer on February 1, 1993, at 97. The carrying value of the bonds on both the issuer's and investor's books is $97,700 as of February 1. Interest payment dates on the bonds are January 31 and July 31. Entries on both the issuer's and investor's books at the time of redemption would be as follows:

---

**Issuer's Books**

---

| | | | |
|---|---|---|---|
| Feb. 1 | Bonds Payable | 100,000 | |
| | Discount on Bonds Payable | | 2,300 |
| | Cash | | 97,000 |
| | Gain on Bond Redemption | | 700 |
| | *To record bond redemption.* | | |

*Computation:*

| | |
|---|---|
| Carrying value of bonds, February 1, 1993 | $97,700 |
| Purchase (redemption) price | 97,000 |
| Gain on redemption | $   700 |

---

**Investor's Books**

---

| | | | |
|---|---|---|---|
| Feb. 1 | Cash | 97,000 | |
| | Loss on Sale of Bonds | 700 | |
| | Investment in Triad Inc. Bonds | | 97,700 |
| | *To record sale of bonds.* | | |

If the redemption had occurred between interest payment dates, adjusting entries would have to be made to recognize the accrued interest and to amortize the bond discount or premium.

**Redemption by Exercise of Call Provision**    A call provision gives the issuer the option of retiring bonds prior to maturity. Frequently the call must be made on an interest payment date, and no further interest accrues on the bonds not presented at this time. When only a part of an issue is to be redeemed, the bonds called may be determined by lot.

The inclusion of call provisions in a bond agreement is a feature favoring the issuer. The company is in a position to terminate the bond agreement and eliminate future interest charges whenever its financial position makes such action feasible. Furthermore, the company is protected in the event of a fall in the market interest rate by being able to retire the old issue from proceeds of a new issue paying a lower rate of interest. A bond contract normally requires payment of a premium if bonds are called. A bondholder is thus offered special compensation if the investment is terminated early.

When bonds are called, the difference between the amount paid and the bond carrying value is reported as a gain or a loss on both the issuer's and investor's books. Any interest paid at the time of the call is recorded as a debit to Interest Expense on the issuer's books and a credit to Interest Revenue on the investor's books. The entries to be made are the same as illustrated previously for the purchase of bonds by the issuer.

**Convertible Bonds**    The issuance of **convertible debt securities**, most frequently bonds, has become increasingly popular.[10] These securities raise specific questions as to the na-

---

[10]Leslie Pittel, "Playing Safe—and Sporty, Too," *Forbes* (October 22, 1984), pp. 248-252.

ture of the securities, i.e., whether they should be considered debt or equity securities, the valuation of the conversion feature, and the treatment of any gain or loss on conversion.

Convertible debt securities usually have the following features:[11]

1. An interest rate lower than the issuer could establish for nonconvertible debt.
2. An initial conversion price higher than the market value of the common stock at time of issuance.
3. A call option retained by the issuer.

The popularity of these securities may be attributed to the advantages to both an issuer and a holder. An issuer is able to obtain financing at a lower interest rate because of the value of the conversion feature to the holder. Because of the call provision, an issuer is in a position to exert influence upon the holders to exchange the debt for equity securities if stock values increase; the issuer has had the use of relatively low interest rate financing if stock values do not increase. On the other hand, the holder has a debt instrument that, barring default, assures the return of investment plus a fixed return and, at the same time, offers an option to transfer his or her interest to equity capital should such transfer become attractive.

Many convertible bond issues place no restriction on when an issuer can call in bonds, and interest accrued on such bonds is sometimes absorbed in a conversion and not paid to the investor. Thus, a company can have the use of interest-free money as a result of calling in bonds prior to the first interest payment. Widespread use of early call provisions in the early 1980s led some investors to demand a provision restricting exercise of the call provision for a specified time period.[12]

Differences of opinion exist as to whether convertible debt securities should be treated by an issuer solely as debt, or whether part of the proceeds received from the issuance of debt should be recognized as equity capital. One view holds that the debt and the conversion privilege are inseparably connected, and therefore the debt and equity portions of a security should not be separately valued. A holder cannot sell part of the instrument and retain the other. An alternate view holds that there are two distinct elements in these securities and that each should be recognized in the accounts: that portion of the issuance price attributable to the conversion privilege should be recorded as a credit to Paid-In Capital; the balance of the issuance price should be assigned to the debt. This would decrease the premium otherwise recognized in the debt or perhaps result in a discount.

These views are compared in the illustration that follows. Assume that 500 ten-year bonds, face value $1,000, are sold at 105, or a total issue price of $525,000 (500 × $1,000 × 1.05). The bonds contain a conversion privilege that provides for exchange of a $1,000 bond for 20 shares of stock, par value $40. The interest rate on the bonds is 8%. It is estimated that without the conversion privilege, the bonds would sell at 96. The journal entries to record the issuance on the issuer's books under the two approaches are at the top of page 636.

The periodic charge for interest will differ depending on which method is employed. To illustrate the computation of interest charges, assume that the straight-line method is used to amortize bond premium or discount. Under the first approach, the annual interest charge would be $37,500 ($40,000 paid less $2,500 premium amortization). Under the second approach, the annual interest charge would be $42,000 ($40,000 paid plus $2,000 discount amortization).

The Accounting Principles Board stated that when convertible debt is sold at a price or with a value at issuance not significantly in excess of the face amount, ". . . no portion

---

[11]*Opinions of the Accounting Principles Board No. 14,* "Accounting for Convertible Debt and Debt Issued with Stock Purchase Warrants" (New York: American Institute of Certified Public Accountants, 1969), par. 3.

[12]Ben Weberman, "The Convertible Bond Scam," *Forbes* (January 19, 1981), p. 92.

### Debt and Equity Not Separated

| | | |
|---|---:|---:|
| Cash | 525,000 | |
|     Bonds Payable | | 500,000 |
|     Premium on Bonds Payable | | 25,000 |

### Debt and Equity Separated

| | | |
|---|---:|---:|
| Cash | 525,000 | |
| Discount on Bonds Payable | 20,000[1] | |
|     Bonds Payable | | 500,000 |
|     Paid-In Capital Arising From Bond Conversion Feature | | 45,000[2] |

*Computations:*

| | |
|---|---:|
| [1]Par value of bonds (500 × $1,000) | $500,000 |
| Selling price of bonds without conversion feature ($500,000 × .96) | 480,000 |
| Discount on bonds without conversion feature | $ 20,000 |
| [2]Total cash received on sale of bonds | $525,000 |
| Selling price without conversion feature | 480,000 |
| Amount applicable to conversion feature (equity portion) | $ 45,000 |

of the proceeds from the issuance . . . should be accounted for as attributable to the conversion feature."[13]

The APB stated that greater weight for this decision was placed on the inseparability of the debt and the conversion option than upon the practical problems of valuing the separate parts. However, the practical problems are considerable. Separate valuation requires asking the question: How much would the security sell for without the conversion feature? In many instances, this question would appear to be unanswerable. Investment bankers responsible for selling these issues are frequently unable to separate the two features for valuation purposes; they contend that the cash required simply could not be raised without the conversion privilege.

There would seem to be strong theoretical support for separating the debt and equity portions of the proceeds from the issuance of convertible debt on the issuer's books. Despite these theoretical arguments, current practice follows APB Opinion No. 14, and no separation is usually made between debt and equity. This is true even when separate values are determinable.

When conversion takes place, a special valuation question must be answered. Should the market value of the securities be used to compute a gain or loss on the transaction? If the convertible security is viewed as debt, then the conversion to equity would seem to be a significant economic transaction and a gain or loss would be recognized. If, however, the convertible security is viewed as equity, the conversion is really an exchange of one type of equity capital for another, and the historical cost principle would seem to indicate that no gain or loss would be recognized. In practice, the latter approach seems to be most commonly followed by both the issuer and investor of the bonds. No gain or loss is recognized either for book or tax purposes. The book value of the bonds is transferred to become the book value of the stock issued. However, this treatment seems inconsistent with APB Opinion No. 14, in which convertible debt is considered to be debt rather than equity.

If an investor views the security as debt, conversion of the debt could be viewed as an exchange of one asset for another. The general rule for the exchange of nonmonetary assets is that the market value of the asset exchanged should be used to measure any gain

---

[13]*Opinions of the Accounting Principles Board No. 14,* par. 12.

or loss on the transaction.[14] If there is no market value of the asset surrendered or if its value is undeterminable, the market value of the asset received should be used. The market value of convertible bonds should reflect the market value of the stock to be issued on the conversion, and thus the market value of the two securities should be similar.

To illustrate bond conversion for the investor recognizing a gain or loss on conversion, assume HiTec Co. offers bondholders 40 shares of HiTec Co. common stock, $20 par, in exchange for each $1,000, 8% bond held. An investor exchanges bonds of $10,000 (carrying value as brought up to date for both investor and issuer, $9,850) for 400 shares of common stock having a market price at the time of the exchange of $26 per share. The exchange is completed at the interest payment date. The exchange is recorded on the books of the investor as follows:

| | | |
|---|---|---|
| Investment in HiTec Co. Common Stock ..................... | 10,400 | |
| Investment in HiTec Co. Bonds ............................ | | 9,850 |
| Gain on Conversion of HiTec Co. Bonds .................... | | 550 |

If the investor chose not to recognize a gain or loss, the journal entry would be as follows:

| | | |
|---|---|---|
| Investment in HiTec Co. Common Stock ...................... | 9,850 | |
| Investment in HiTec Co. Bonds ............................ | | 9,850 |

Similar differences would occur on the issuer's books depending on the viewpoint assumed. If the issuer desired to recognize the conversion of the convertible debt as a significant culminating transaction, the market value of the securities would be used to record the conversion. The HiTec example can be used to illustrate the journal entries for the issuer using this reasoning. The conversion would be recorded as follows:

| | | |
|---|---|---|
| Bonds Payable ......................................... | 10,000 | |
| Loss on Conversion of Bonds............................. | 550 | |
| Common Stock, $20 par ................................. | | 8,000 |
| Paid-In Capital in Excess of Par .......................... | | 2,400 |
| Discount on Bonds Payable.............................. | | 150 |

*Computation:*

| | | |
|---|---|---|
| Market value of stock issued (400 shares at $26)............. | | $10,400 |
| Face value of bonds payable ............................ | $10,000 | |
| Less unamortized discount ............................... | 150 | 9,850 |
| Loss to company on conversion of bonds ................. | | $    550 |

If the issuer did not consider the conversion as a culminating transaction, no gain or loss would be recognized. The bond carrying value would be transferred to the capital stock account on the theory that the company upon issuing the bonds is aware of the fact that bond proceeds may ultimately represent the consideration identified with stock. Thus, when bondholders exercise their conversion privileges, the value identified with the obligation is transferred to the security that replaces it. Under this assumption, the conversion would be recorded as follows:

| | | |
|---|---|---|
| Bonds Payable ......................................... | 10,000 | |
| Common Stock, $20 par ................................. | | 8,000 |
| Paid-In Capital in Excess of Par .......................... | | 1,850 |
| Discount on Bonds Payable.............................. | | 150 |

[14]*Opinions of the Accounting Principles Board No. 29,* "Accounting for Nonmonetary Transactions" (New York: American Institute of Certified Public Accountants, 1973), par. 18.

The profession has not resolved the accounting issues surrounding convertible debt. Although the practice of not recognizing gain or loss on either the issuer's or the investor's books is widespread, it seems inconsistent with the treatment of other items that are transferred by an entity. The economic reality of the transaction would seem to require a recognition of the change in value at least at the time conversion takes place.

**Bond Refinancing**    Cash for the retirement of a bond issue is frequently raised through the sale of a new issue and is referred to as **bond refinancing**, or **refunding**. Bond refinancing may take place when an issue matures, or bonds may be refinanced prior to their maturity when the interest rate has dropped and the interest savings on a new issue will more than offset the cost of retiring the old issue. To illustrate, assume that a corporation has outstanding 12% bonds of $1,000,000 callable at 102 and with a remaining 10-year term, and similar 10-year bonds can be marketed currently at an interest rate of only 10%. Under these circumstances it would be advantageous to retire the old issue with the proceeds from a new 10% issue, since the future savings in interest will exceed by a considerable amount the premium to be paid on the call of the old issue.

The desirability of refinancing may not be so obvious as in the preceding example. In determining whether refinancing is warranted in marginal cases, careful consideration must be given to such factors as the different maturity dates of the two issues, possible future changes in interest rates, changed loan requirements, different indenture provisions, income tax effects of refinancing, and legal fees, printing costs, and marketing costs involved in refinancing.

When refinancing takes place before the maturity date of the old issue, the problem arises as to how to dispose of the call premium and unamortized discount and issue costs of the original bonds. Three positions have been taken with respect to disposition of these items:

1. Such charges are considered a loss on bond retirement.
2. Such charges are considered deferrable and to be amortized systematically over the remaining life of the original issue.
3. Such charges are considered deferrable and to be amortized systematically over the life of the new issue.

Although arguments can be presented supporting each of these alternatives, the APB concluded that "all extinguishments of debt before scheduled maturities are fundamentally alike. The accounting for such transactions should be the same regardless of the means used to achieve the extinguishment."[15] The first position, immediate recognition of the gain or loss, was selected by the Board for all early extinguishment of debt. The Financial Accounting Standards Board considered the nature of this gain or loss and defined it as being an extraordinary item requiring separate income statement disclosure, as indicated earlier.

## VALUATION AND REPORTING OF LONG-TERM DEBT SECURITIES ON THE BALANCE SHEET

Thus far, no reference has been made in this chapter to adjusting investments and liabilities when the debt or investment valuation differs from cost. In Chapter 14, accounting for declines in value of long-term equity securities was presented. There it was noted that

[15]*Opinions of the Accounting Principles Board No. 26*, par. 19.

temporary declines in the market value of equity securities are recognized on the books of the investor by a debit to a contra equity account and a credit to an allowance account. Permanent declines are recognized by a debit to a recognized loss account on the income statement and a credit to the investment account. Debt instruments were not explicitly included in FASB Statement No. 12. However, if a market decline in debt securities is deemed to be permanent, and it is probable that the maturity value will not be paid when due, entries similar to those made for permanent declines in equity securities are normally made on the investor's books. If the market declines are considered temporary, no accounting entries are usually made, but the decline in value is recognized in a note to the financial statements. Entries likewise are not made to reflect increases in the market values of bond investments.

Long-term debt securities are frequently very significant items on the balance sheet of both the investor and the issuer. The valuation and reporting problem for the investor and issuer will be considered separately.

### Reporting Bonds and Long-Term Notes as Investments

The market value of long-term debt varies with changes in the financial strength of the issuing company, changes in the level of interest rates, and shrinkage in the remaining life of the issue. In the absence of material price declines, bonds held as long-term investments are reported on the balance sheet at book value. This book value approaches maturity value as the bonds move closer to maturity. To this extent, then, the accounting can be considered to follow a similar change that is taking place on the market as the bond life is reduced and a correspondingly lower valuation is attached to the difference between the actual rate and the market rate of remaining interest payments. Although investments are usually reported at book value, parenthetical disclosure of the aggregate market value of the securities makes the financial statements more informative.

Data relative to long-term note and bond investments might be reported as follows:

Long-term investments:
Investment in Golden Corp. long-term note, 11%, $50,000 face value,
   due July 1, 1994 (market value, $48,500 at December 31, 1992) . . . . . .    $ 50,000
Investment in Wilkins Co. bonds, 9%, $1,000,000 face value, due
   July 1, 2000 (reported at cost as adjusted for amortized discount) . . . .    982,500

### Reporting Bonds and Long-Term Notes as Liabilities

In reporting long-term debt on the balance sheet, the nature of the liabilities, maturity dates, interest rates, methods of liquidation, conversion privileges, sinking fund requirements, borrowing restrictions, assets pledged, dividend limitations, and other significant matters should be indicated. The portion of long-term debt coming due in the current period should also be disclosed. Bond liabilities are often combined with other long-term debt for balance sheet presentation, with supporting detail disclosed in a note. An example of such a note taken from the 1989 annual report of Motorola, Inc., is presented in Exhibit 16—1. For another illustration of disclosure of long-term debt, see the notes to IBM Corporation's financial statements in Appendix A at the end of this text.

**Exhibit 16—1    Motorola, Inc.—Disclosure of Long-Term Debt**

*NOTES TO CONSOLIDATED FINANCIAL STATEMENTS*
(In millions, except as noted)

*3. Long-term Debt and Credit Facilities*

| December 31 | 1989 | 1988 |
|---|---|---|
| 12% eurodollar notes due 1994 | $ 68 | $ 68 |
| 11½% eurodollar notes due 1997 | 93 | 93 |
| 8⅝% ECU notes due 1992 | 60 | 59 |
| 8% sinking fund debentures due 2007 (callable at 104.0% reducing to 100.0% of the principal amount) | 62 | 62 |
| 6½% industrial revenue bonds due 2014 | 15 | 20 |
| Zero coupon notes due 2009 | 413 | — |
| Capitalized lease obligations | 45 | 46 |
| Other long-term debt | 16 | 30 |
| | 772 | 378 |
| Less current maturities | 17 | 35 |
| Long-term debt | $755 | $343 |

On September 7, 1989 Motorola issued $1.32 billion of zero coupon notes referred to as Liquid Yield Option™ Notes (LYON™), due September 7, 2009, for cash proceeds of $405 million. The LYONs are zero coupon subordinated notes convertible into 4.567 shares of Motorola common stock and have no periodic interest payments. Each note was priced to yield 6% to maturity.

Aggregate maturities and sinking fund requirements for long-term debt, in millions, during the next five years are as follows: 1990, $17; 1991, $16; 1992, $76; 1993, $6; 1994, $69.

The Company has domestic and international credit arrangements for short-term borrowings, generally with banks. On its domestic credit arrangements, it pays commitment fees of approximately ¹⁄₁₀% of the domestic lines of credit. Short-term credit lines totalled $1.95 billion at December 31, 1989, of which $1.11 billion remain unused. Domestic credit arrangements primarily back up the issuance of commercial paper.

Outstanding letters of credit aggregated approximately $99 million at December 31, 1989.

---

## KEY TERMS

Bearer or coupon bonds 595
Bond certificates 593
Bond discount 597
Bond indenture 593
Bond issuance costs 600
Bond premium 597
Callable bonds 596
Commodity-backed bonds or asset-linked bonds 596

Convertible bonds 595
Early extinguishment of debt 605
Effective-interest method 602
Face amount, par value, maturity value 593
Junk bonds 595
Long-term debt 592
Market, yield, or effective-interest rate 597

Registered bonds 594
Secured bonds 594
Serial bonds 594
Stated or contract rate 596
Straight-line method 601
Term bonds 594
Unsecured (debenture) bonds 594
Zero-interest bonds or deep-discount bonds 595

## QUESTIONS

1. What factors should be considered in determining whether cash should be raised by the issuance of bonds or by the sale of additional stock?

2. Distinguish between (a) secured and unsecured bonds, (b) collateral trust and debenture bonds, (c) convertible and callable bonds, (d) coupon and registered bonds, (e) municipal and corporate bonds, and (f) term and serial bonds.

3. What is meant by market rate of interest, stated or contract rate, and effective or yield rate? Which of these rates changes during the lifetime of the bond issue?

4. An investor purchases bonds with a face value of $100,000. Payment for the bonds includes (a) a premium, (b) accrued interest, and (c) brokerage fees. How would each of these charges be recorded and what disposition would ultimately be made of each of these charges?

5. How should bond issuance costs be accounted for on the issuer's books?

6. What amortization method for premiums and discounts on bonds is recommended by APB Opinion No. 21? Why? When can the alternative method be used?

7. Under what conditions would the following statement be true? "The effective-interest method of bond premium or discount amortization for the issuer results in higher net income than would be reported using straight-line amortization."

8. List three ways that bonds are commonly retired prior to maturity. How should the early extinguishment of debt be presented on the income statement?

9. What purpose is served by issuing callable bonds?

10. What are the distinguishing features of convertible debt securities? What questions relate to the nature of this type of security?

11. The conversion of convertible bonds to common stock by an investor may be viewed as an exchange involving no gain or loss, or as a transaction for which market values should be recognized and a gain or loss reported. What arguments support each of these views for the investor and for the issuer?

12. Why do companies find the issuance of convertible bonds a desirable method of financing?

13. What is meant by refinancing or refunding a bond issue? When may refinancing be advisable?

14. How should long-term investments in bonds be recorded and adjusted for significant price changes in periods subsequent to their purchase so that their valuation will be in accordance with GAAP?

## DISCUSSION CASES

### Case 16—1  (Debt or equity financing)

Assume you are a member of the board of directors of Layton Enterprises, a relatively new company in the computer industry. You have just listened to a presentation of the treasurer and an extended discussion among the other board members. The issue is how to raise $13 million of additional funds for company expansion. You must now vote on whether to authorize debt financing through a bond issue or to seek equity financing through additional stock sales. What are the advantages and disadvantages of debt financing versus equity financing? As a member of the board, how would you vote and why?

### Case 16—2  (Accounting for bonds)

Startup Company decided to issue $100,000 worth of 10%, 5-year bonds dated January 1, 1992, with interest payable semiannually on January 1 and July 1 of each year. Due to printing and other delays, Startup was not able to sell the bonds until July 1, 1992. The bonds were sold to yield 12% interest, and they are callable at 102 after January 1, 1994. The company expects interest rates to fall during the next few years and is planning to retire this bond issue and to replace it with a less costly one if the expected decline occurs.

Assume that you have just been hired as the accountant for Startup Company. The financial vice president would like you to identify the accounting issues involved with the bond transaction. You are also asked to explain why the company received less than $100,000 on the sale of the bonds, and to compute the anticipated gain or loss on retirement of the bonds, assuming retirement on July 1, 1994, and use of straight-line amortization.

## Case 16—3  (Is there a loss on conversion?)

Holton Co. recently issued $1,000,000 face value, 8%, 30-year subordinated debentures at 97. The debentures are callable at 103 upon 30 days' notice by the issuer at any time beginning 10 years after the date of issue. The debentures are convertible into $10 par value common stock of the company at the conversion price of $12.50 per share for each $500 or multiple thereof of the principal amount of the debentures ($500 ÷ $12.50 = 40 shares for each $500 of face value).

Assume that no value is assigned to the conversion feature at the date of issue of the debentures. Assume further that 5 years after issue, debentures with a face value of $100,000 and book value of $97,500 are tendered for conversion on an interest payment date when the market price of the debentures is 104 and the common stock is selling at $14 per share. J. K. Biggs, the company accountant, records the conversion as follows:

| | | |
|---|---|---|
| Bonds Payable | 100,000 | |
| Discount on Bonds Payable | | 2,500 |
| Common Stock | | 80,000 |
| Paid-In Capital in Excess of Par | | 17,500 |

Julie Robinson, staff auditor for the company's CPA firm, reviews the transaction and feels the conversion entry should reflect the market value of the stock. According to Robinson's analysis, a loss on the bond conversion of $14,500 should be recognized. Biggs objects to recognizing a loss, so Robinson discusses the problem with the audit manager, K. Ashworth. Ashworth has a different view and recommends using the market value of the debentures as a basis for recording the conversion and recognizing a loss of only $6,500.

Evaluate the various positions. Include in your evaluation the substitute entries that would be made under both Robinson's and Ashworth's proposals.

## Case 16—4  (I like these "no interest" bonds.)

J. R. Chump, president of ProKeeper Industries, is contemplating the issuance of long-term debt to finance plant expansion and renovation. In the past, his company has issued traditional debt instruments that require regular interest payments and a retirement of the principal on the maturity date. However, he has noticed that several competitors have recently issued bonds that either do not require interest payments or defer interest payments for several years. He has asked you, as his chief financial officer, to prepare a summary addressing the following questions:

1. Why would a company issue bonds that require interest payments if bonds that do not require interest payments are being sold in the open market?
2. If the company were to issue 10-year bonds with a face value of $100,000 and the market rate of interest is 10%, what would be the proceeds from the sale if the bonds were zero-coupon bonds? What would be the proceeds if the annual interest payments did not begin for 5 years and the stated rate of interest were 10%? What would be the proceeds if the bonds paid interest annually for 10 years at 10%?
3. What factors must a business consider when determining the interest terms associated with long-term debt?

## Case 16—5  (The battle of Resorts International)

In 1988, Donald Trump and Merv Griffin engaged in a bidding war for Resorts International, an Atlantic City-based casino operation. Griffin eventually purchased the company by issuing $325 million in "secured" junk bonds. This debt was in addition to an already existing "unsecured" debt of $600 million issued by Resorts prior to the takeover.

For 1989, the company's projected cash flow was estimated at $55 million, compared to debt service costs of $133 million. Griffin had hoped to sell other Resorts assets, such as vacant land in Atlantic City or a casino in the Bahamas, to reduce the debt load. These transactions never materialized, leaving Griffin in a cash flow dilemma. Less than a year after issuing the $325 million in new debt, Resorts International filed bankruptcy.

Why would investors purchase the new bond issue when Resorts already had $600 million in outstanding debt? What were the risks to Griffin in planning to sell a portion of Resorts International to reduce the outstanding debt used to finance the original purchase of the company? Who are the big losers when a company like Resorts International goes bankrupt?

Source: Lenny Glynn, "Blowout on the Boardwalk," *Institutional Investor*, December 1989.

## EXERCISES

### Exercise 16—1 (Raising capital with bonds or stock)

Shop Right, Inc., must raise $600,000 for additional working capital. Management wants to choose the method of financing that will result in the higher return per share to the original shareholders. Already issued were 10,000 shares of $60 par common stock. Assume the company can sell an additional 7,500 shares at $80 or it can issue $600,000 in 8% bonds. Earnings before income taxes have historically been approximately $100,000 annually, and it is expected that they will increase by 15% (before additional interest charges) as a result of the additional funds. Assuming an income tax rate of 40%, which method of financing would you recommend? Why? (Show computations.)

### Exercise 16—2 (Computation of market values of bond issues)

What is the market value of each of the following bond issues? (Round to the nearest dollar.)

(a)  10% bonds of $100,000 sold on bond issue date; 10-year life; interest payable semiannually; effective rate, 12%.
(b)  9% bonds of $200,000 sold on bond issue date; 5-year life; interest payable semiannually; effective rate, 8%.
(c)  8% bonds of $150,000 sold 30 months after bond issue date; 15-year life; interest payable semiannually; effective rate, 10%.

### Exercise 16—3 (Selling bonds at par, premium, or discount)

In each of the following independent cases, state whether the bonds were issued at par, a premium, or a discount. Explain your answers.

(a)  Pop-up Manufacturing sold 1,500 of its $1,000, 13% stated-rate bonds when the market rate was 14%.
(b)  Splendor, Inc., sold 500 of its $2,000, 8¾% bonds to yield 9%.
(c)  Cards Corporation issued 1,000 of its 9%, $100 face-amount bonds at an effective rate of 8½%.
(d)  Floppy, Inc., sold 3,000 of its 10% bonds with a face value of $2,500 at a time when the market rate was 9%.
(e)  Cintron Co. sold 5,000 of its 12% contract-rate bonds with stated value of $1,000 at an effective rate of 12%.

### Exercise 16—4 (Zero-coupon bonds)

Allrite Inc. is considering issuing bonds to finance the acquisition of a nationwide chain of distributors of Allrite's products. Allrite is contemplating two different types of bonds to raise the required $30 million purchase price. The first is a traditional 10-year, 10% bond with semiannual interest payments. The second is a 10-year, zero-coupon bond.

Assuming the market rate of interest is 10%, compute the face amount of the bond issuance and the journal entries to record the issuance if (a) a traditional bond is issued, and (b) a zero-coupon bond is issued.

### Exercise 16—5  (Issuance and reacquisition of bonds)

On January 1, 1992, the Housen Company issued 10-year bonds of $500,000 at 102. Interest is payable on January 1 and July 1 at 10%. On April 1, 1993, the Housen Company reacquires and retires 50 of its own $1,000 bonds at 98 plus accrued interest. The fiscal period for the Housen Company is the calendar year.

Prepare entries to record (a) the issuance of the bonds, (b) the interest payments and adjustments relating to the debt in 1992, (c) the reacquisition and retirement of bonds in 1993, and (d) the interest payments and adjustments relating to the debt in 1993. Assume the premium or discount is amortized on a straight-line basis. (Round to the nearest dollar.)

### Exercise 16—6  (Amortization of bond premium or discount)

On January 1, 1992, Terrel Company sold $100,000 of 10-year, 8% bonds at 93.5, an effective rate of 9%. Interest is to be paid on July 1 and December 31. Compute the premium or discount to be amortized in 1992 and 1993 using (a) the straight-line method and (b) the effective-interest method. Make the journal entries to record the amortization when the effective-interest method is used.

---

## PROBLEMS

### Problem 16—1  (Bond issuance and adjusting entries)

On January 1, 1993, Bel Air Company issued bonds with a face value of $1,000,000 and a maturity date of December 31, 2002. The bonds have a stated interest rate of 10%, payable on January 1 and July 1. They were sold to Mercur Company for $885,300, a yield of 12%. It cost Bel Air $30,000 to issue the bonds. This amount was deferred and amortized over the life of the issue using the straight-line method. Assume that both companies have December 31 year-ends and that Bel Air uses the effective-interest method to amortize any premium or discount and Mercur uses the straight-line method.

**Instructions:**

1. Make all entries necessary to record the sale and purchase of the bonds on the two companies' books.
2. Prepare the adjusting entries as of December 31, 1993, for both companies. Assume Mercur is carrying the bonds as a long-term investment.

### Problem 16—2  (Computation of bond market price and amortization of premium or discount)

Signal Enterprises decided to issue $800,000 of 10-year bonds. The interest rate on the bonds is stated at 7%, payable semiannually. At the time the bonds were sold, the market rate had increased to 8%.

**Instructions:**

1. Determine the maximum amount an investor should pay for these bonds. (Round to the nearest dollar.)
2. Assuming that the amount in (1) is paid, compute the amount at which the bonds would be reported after being held for one year. Use two recognized methods of handling amortization of the difference in cost and maturity value of the bonds, and give support to the method you prefer. (Round to the nearest dollar.)

## Problem 16—3  (Premium or discount amortization table)

The Green Co. acquired $20,000 of International Sales Co. 7% bonds, interest payable semiannually, bonds maturing in 5 years. The bonds were acquired at $20,850, a price to return approximately 6%.

**Instructions:**

1. Prepare tables to show the periodic adjustments to the investment account and the annual bond earnings, assuming adjustment by each of the following methods: (a) the straight-line method, and (b) the effective-interest method. (Round to the nearest dollar.)
2. Assuming use of the effective-interest method, give entries for the first year on the books of both companies.

## Problem 16—4  (Amortizing deferred interest bonds)

R. J. Winter Co. recently issued $100,000, 10-year deferred interest bonds. The bonds have a stated rate of 10% and are to be paid in 10 semiannual interest payments beginning 5½ years after the date of issuance. The market rate of interest on the date of issuance was 8%.

**Instructions:**

1. Compute the maximum amount an investor should pay for these bonds. (Round to the nearest dollar.)
2. Prepare a bond amortization schedule for Winter assuming the effective-interest method is used. (Round to the nearest dollar.)

## Problem 16—5  (Cash flow effects of a bond premium)

On January 3, 1993, Datalink Inc. issued $100,000, 10%, 10-year bonds when the market rate of interest was 8%.  The following financial information is available:

| | |
|---|---:|
| Sales . . . . . . . . . . . . . . . . . . . . . . . . . . . . . . . . . . . . . . . . . . . . . . . . . . . . . . . . . . . . . | $300,000 |
| Cost of sales . . . . . . . . . . . . . . . . . . . . . . . . . . . . . . . . . . . . . . . . . . . . . . . . . . . . . | 180,000 |
| Gross profit . . . . . . . . . . . . . . . . . . . . . . . . . . . . . . . . . . . . . . . . . . . . . . . . . . . . . . . | $120,000 |
| Interest expense . . . . . . . . . . . . . . . . . . . . . . . . . . . . . . . . . . . . . . . . . . . . . . . . . . . | ? |
| Depreciation expense . . . . . . . . . . . . . . . . . . . . . . . . . . . . . . . . . . . . . . . . . . . . . . . | 14,500 |
| Other expenses . . . . . . . . . . . . . . . . . . . . . . . . . . . . . . . . . . . . . . . . . . . . . . . . . . . . | 82,000 |
| Net income . . . . . . . . . . . . . . . . . . . . . . . . . . . . . . . . . . . . . . . . . . . . . . . . . . . . . . . . | $    ? |

| | Dec. 31, 1993 | Jan. 1, 1993 |
|---|---:|---:|
| Accounts receivable . . . . . . . . . . . . . . . . . . . . . . . . . . . | $55,000 | $48,000 |
| Inventory . . . . . . . . . . . . . . . . . . . . . . . . . . . . . . . . . . . | 87,000 | 93,000 |
| Accounts payable . . . . . . . . . . . . . . . . . . . . . . . . . . . . . | 60,000 | 58,000 |

All purchases of inventory are on account.  Other expenses are paid for in cash.

**Instructions:**

1. Prepare the journal entry to record the issuance of the bonds on January 3, 1993.
2. Compute (a) the amount of cash paid to bondholders for interest during 1993, (b) the amount of premium amortized during 1993 assuming Datalink uses the straight-line method for amortizing bond premiums and discounts, and (c) the amount of interest expense for 1993.
3. Prepare the "Cash flows from operating activities" section of Datalink's statement of cash flows using (a) the direct method, and (b) the indirect method.

## Problem 16—6  (Bond entries—issuer)

On April 1, 1982, the Quality Tool Company issued $8 million of 7% convertible bonds with interest payment dates of April 1 and October 1. The bonds were sold on July 1, 1982, and mature on April 1, 2002. The bond discount totaled $426,600. The bond contract entitles the bondholders to receive 25 shares of $15 par value common stock in exchange for each $1,000 bond. On April 1, 1992, the holders of bonds with total face value of $1,000,000 exercised their conversion privilege. On July 1, 1992, the Quality Tool Company reacquired bonds, face value $500,000, on the open market. The balances in the capital accounts as of December 31, 1991, were:

| | |
|---|---|
| Common stock, $15 par, authorized 3 million shares, issued and outstanding, 250,000 shares .......................................... | $3,750,000 |
| Paid-in capital in excess of par.................................... | 2,500,000 |

Market values of the common stock and bonds were as follows:

| Date | Bonds (per $1,000) | Common Stock (per share) |
|---|---|---|
| April 1, 1992 | $1,220 | $47 |
| July 1, 1992 | 1,250 | 51 |

**Instructions:**  Prepare journal entries on the issuer's books for each of the following transactions. (Use the straight-line amortization method for the bond discount.)

1. Sale of the bonds on July 1, 1982.
2. Interest payment on October 1, 1982.
3. Interest accrual on December 31, 1982, including bond discount amortization.
4. Conversion of bonds on April 1, 1992. (Assume that interest and discount amortization are correctly shown as of April 1, 1992. No gain or loss on conversion is recognized.)
5. Reacquisition and retirement of bonds on July 1, 1992. (Assume that interest and discount amortization are correctly reported as of July 1, 1992.)

## Problem 16—7  (Bond entries—issuer)

The Tri Arc Company sold $3,000,000 of 9% first-mortgage bonds on October 1, 1985, at $2,873,640 plus accrued interest. The bonds were dated July 1, 1985; interest payable semiannually on January 1 and July 1; redeemable after June 30, 1990, to June 30, 1993, at 101, and thereafter until maturity at 100; and convertible into $100 par value common stock as follows:

Until June 30, 1990, at the rate of 6 shares for each $1,000 bond.
From July 1, 1990, to June 30, 1993, at the rate of 5 shares for each $1,000 bond.
After June 30, 1993, at the rate of 4 shares for each $1,000 bond.

The bonds mature 10 years from their issue date. The company adjusts its books monthly and closes its books as of December 31 each year.

The following transactions occur in connection with the bonds:

1991
July 1    $1,000,000 of bonds were converted into stock, with no gain or loss recognized.

1992
Dec. 31    $500,000 face amount of bonds were reacquired at 99¼ plus accrued interest. These were immediately retired.

1993
July 1    The remaining bonds were called for redemption. For purposes of obtaining funds for redemption and business expansion, a $4,000,000 issue of 7% bonds was sold at 97. These bonds are dated July 1, 1993, and are due in 20 years.

**Instructions:** Prepare in journal form the entries necessary for Tri Arc Company in connection with the preceding transactions, including monthly adjustments where appropriate, as of the following dates. (Round to nearest dollar.)

(1) October 1, 1985
(2) December 31, 1985
(3) July 1, 1991
(4) December 31, 1992
(5) July 1, 1993

(AICPA adapted)

### Problem 16—8   (Bond entries—investor)

On June 1, 1992, Sunderland Inc. purchased, as a long-term investment, 400 of the $1,000 face value, 8% bonds of Stateline Corporation for $369,150. The bonds were purchased to yield 10% interest. Interest is payable semiannually on December 1 and June 1. The bonds mature on June 1, 1997. Sunderland uses the effective-interest method of amortization. On November 1, 1993, Sunderland sold the bonds for $392,500. This amount includes the appropriate accrued interest.

**Instructions:** Prepare a schedule showing the income or loss before income taxes from the bond investment that Sunderland should record for the years ended December 31, 1992, and 1993.

(AICPA adapted)

### Problem 16—9   (Bond entries—investor)

On May 1, 1990, Alpine Co. acquired $40,000 of ZZX Corp. 9% bonds at 97 plus accrued interest. Interest on bonds is payable semiannually on March 1 and September 1, and bonds mature on September 1, 1993.

On May 1, 1991, Alpine Co. sold bonds of $12,000 for 103 plus accrued interest. On July 1, 1992, bonds of $16,000 were exchanged for 2,250 shares of ZZX Corp. no-par common, quoted on the market on this date at $8. Interest was received on bonds to date of exchange.

On September 1, 1993, remaining bonds were redeemed.

**Instructions:** Give journal entries for 1990-1993 to record the foregoing transactions on the books for Alpine Co., including any adjustments that are required at the end of each fiscal year ending on December 31. Assume bond premium or discount amortization by the straight-line method.

### Problem 16—10   (Note payable entries—investor and issuer)

Fitzgerald Inc. issued $750,000 of 8-year, 11% notes payable dated April 1, 1989. Interest on the notes is payable semiannually on April 1 and October 1. The notes were sold on April 1, 1989, to an underwriter for $720,000 net of issuance costs. The notes were then offered for sale by the underwriter, and on July 1, 1989, L. Baum purchased the entire issue as a long-term investment. Baum paid 101 plus accrued interest for the notes. On June 1, 1992, Baum sold the investment in Fitzgerald notes to J. Gott as a short-term investment. Gott paid 96 plus accrued interest for the notes as well as $1,500 for brokerage fees. Baum paid $1,000 brokerage fees to sell the notes. Gott held the investment until April 1, 1993, when the notes were called at 102 by Fitzgerald.

**Instructions:** Prepare all journal entries required: on the books of Fitzgerald Inc. for 1989 and 1993; on the books of Baum for 1989 and 1992; and on the books of Gott for 1992 and 1993. Assume each entity uses the calendar year for reporting purposes and that issue costs are netted against the note proceeds by Fitzgerald. Any required amortization is made using the straight-line method.

### Problem 16—11   (Adjustment of bond investment account)

In auditing the books for the Carmicheal Corporation as of December 31, 1993, before the accounts are closed, you find the following long-term investment account balance:

**ACCOUNT**  Investment in Big Oil 9% Bonds (Maturity Date, June 1, 1997)

| Date | | Item | Debit | Credit | Balance Debit | Balance Credit |
|---|---|---|---|---|---|---|
| 1993 | | | | | | |
| Jan. | 21 | Bonds, $200,000 par, acquired at 102 plus accrued interest ......... | 206,550 | | 206,550 | |
| Mar. | 1 | Proceeds from sale of bonds, $100,000 par and accrued interest .. | | 106,000 | 100,550 | |
| June | 1 | Interest received ................. | | 4,500 | 96,050 | |
| Nov. | 1 | Amount received on call of bonds, $40,000 par, at 101 and accrued interest ........................... | | 41,900 | 54,150 | |
| Dec. | 1 | Interest received ................. | | 2,700 | 51,450 | |

**Instructions:**

1. Give the entries that should have been made relative to the investment in bonds, including any adjusting entries that would be made on December 31, the end of the fiscal year. (Assume bond premium or discount amortization by the straight-line method.)

2. Give the journal entries required at the end of 1993 to correct and bring the accounts up to date in view of the entries actually made.

## Problem 16—12   (Reacquisition of bonds)

Guerra Company issued $500,000 of 12%, 10-year debentures on January 1, 1988. Interest is payable on January 1 and July 1. The entire issue was sold on April 1, 1988, at 102 plus accrued interest. On April 1, 1993, $250,000 of the bond issue was reacquired and retired at 98 plus accrued interest. On June 30, 1993, the remaining bonds were reacquired at 97 plus accrued interest and refunded with $400,000, 9% bonds issue sold at 100.

**Instructions:**   Give the journal entries for 1988 and 1993 (through June 30) on the Guerra Company books. The company's books are kept on a calendar-year basis. (Round to nearest dollar. Assume straight-line amortization of premium or discount.)

## Problem 16—13   (Deferred interest bonds and the selling of assets)

At the beginning of 1991, Wheel R. Dealer purchased the net assets of Consolidated Corp. by issuing 10-year, 10% bonds with a face amount of $100,000,000, with semiannual interest payments made on June 30 and December 31 and no interest payments made until 1996.  Dealer hopes to sell off assets of Consolidated and realize enough cash to buy back the bonds on the open market prior to interest payments becoming due in 1996.  During 1993, Dealer sold net assets with a carrying value of $85,000,000 for $70,000,000 and used the proceeds to retire the bonds issue.

**Instructions:**

1. Prepare the journal entry to record the issuance of the bonds on January 2, 1991, assuming a market rate of 8%.
2. Prepare the journal entry to record the sale of assets.
3. Compute the market value of the bonds on January 3, 1994, the day of retirement, assuming a market rate of 14%.
4. Prepare the journal entry to record the retirement of the bond issue on January 3, 1994, assuming a carrying value of $96,000,000 and the market value as computed in (3) above.
5. Explain how Mr. Dealer can buy his bonds back three years after their initial sale for less than he originally sold them for and without ever having made an interest payment.

### Problem 16—14  (Convertible bonds)

The Robison Co. issued $1,000,000 of convertible 10-year debentures on July 1, 1992. The debentures provide for 9% interest payable semiannually on January 1 and July 1. The discount in connection with the issue was $19,500, which is being amortized monthly on a straight-line basis.

The debentures are convertible after 1 year into 7 shares of the Robison Co.'s $100 par value common stock for each $1,000 of debentures.

On August 1, 1993, $100,000 of debentures were turned in for conversion into common stock. Interest has been accrued monthly and paid as due. Accrued interest on debentures is paid in cash upon conversion.

**Instructions:**  Prepare the journal entries to record the conversion, amortization, and interest in connection with the debentures as of: August 1, 1993, August 31, 1993, and December 31, 1993—including closing entries for end of year. No gain or loss is to be recognized on the conversion. (Round to nearest dollar.)                                                   (AICPA adapted)

### Problem 16—15  (Early extinguishment and conversion of bonds)

On January 1, 1992, Brewster Company issued 2,000 of its 5-year, $1,000 face value, 11% bonds dated January 1 at an effective annual interest rate (yield) of 9%. Interest is payable each December 31. Brewster uses the effective-interest method of amortization. On December 31, 1993, the 2,000 bonds were extinguished early through acquisition in the open market by Brewster for $1,980,000.

On July 1, 1992, Brewster issued 5,000 of its 6-year, $1,000 face value, 10% convertible bonds dated July 1 at an effective annual interest rate (yield) of 12%. Interest is payable every June 30 and December 31. The bonds are convertible at the investor's option into Brewster's common stock at a ratio of 10 shares of common stock for each bond. On July 1, 1993, an investor in Brewster's convertible bonds tendered 1,500 bonds for conversion into 15,000 shares of Brewster's common stock, which had a fair market value of $105 and a par value of $90 at the date of conversion.

**Instructions:**

1. Make all necessary journal entries for the issuer and the investor to record the issuance of both the 11% and the 10% bonds.
2. Make all necessary journal entries to record the early extinguishment of both debt instruments assuming:
    (a) Brewster considered the conversion to be a significant culminating event, and the investors considered their investment in convertible bonds to be debt rather than equity.
    (b) Brewster considered the conversion to be a nonculminating event, and the investors considered their investment in convertible bonds to be equity rather than debt.

# CHAPTER 17

## Owners' Equity–Contributed Capital

---

**CHAPTER TOPICS**

**Nature and Classifications of Capital Stock**

**Preferred and Common Stock Features**

**Issuance of Capital Stock**

**Accounting for Treasury Stock**

**Accounting for Stock Rights, Warrants, and Options**

**Stock Conversions and Stock Splits**

**Balance Sheet Disclosure of Contributed Capital**

---

Microsoft, founded in 1975, was originally best known for developing the operating system used with IBM personal computers and their clones. Microsoft subsequently developed a variety of popular software packages, such as Word, Excel, and Windows. In 1985, Microsoft decided to publicly issue its stock for the first time. Before this time, Microsoft had stock outstanding, but the stock was held by company officials and employees and was not publicly traded. Goldman Sachs, a Wall Street investment banking firm, was selected to be the lead underwriter on the issue. The underwriters provided technical advice as the issue was prepared, bought the shares from the firm, and then resold the shares to the public. For their services, the underwriters on the Microsoft issue received 6.24% of the proceeds.

A key consideration, of course, was what price to charge when issuing the shares. An initial price range of $16 to $19 per share was set, based on Microsoft's earnings per share and the price/earnings ratios for similar firms that already had publicly traded stock. A prospectus describing the company was filed with the SEC (with care taken not to exaggerate, since the SEC is particularly concerned that investors be fully warned of significant risks associated with new issues). Copies of the prospectus were sent to 38,000 brokers and potential investors. The large amount of interest in the Microsoft stock issue resulted in the final offering price being raised to $21 per share. On March 13, 1986, Microsoft shares were first publicly traded, on the over-the-counter market, at $25.75 per share. By the end of the first day of trading, the shares were at $27.75. In June 1990, the stock was trading for a split-adjusted $304 per share.[1]

As the Microsoft example illustrates, firms often seek to raise funds by selling stock to investors. Alternatively, companies may raise capital by generating income and investing those profits back into the business, or they may borrow funds from creditors. The basic accounting equation—**Assets = Liabilities + Owners' Equity**—shows this key relationship. Thus, the assets of an enterprise are provided by creditors and by owners. Assets represent entity resources, while liabilities reflect the creditor claims against those resources. Since the difference between assets and liabilities is owners' equity, the **owners' equity** of an entity represents the residual interest of the owners in the net assets (total assets less total liabilities) of the enterprise.

Reductions in capital result primarily from distributions to owners and business losses. In a proprietorship, the entire owner's equity resulting from investments, withdrawals, and earnings or losses is reflected in a single capital account. Similarly, in a **partnership**, a single capital account for each partner reports the partner's equity resulting from investments, withdrawals, and earnings or losses. In reporting **corporate capital**, however, a distinction is made between (1) investments by owners, called **contributed (paid-in) capital** and (2) increases in net assets arising from earnings, designated as **retained earnings**.

The issues surrounding contributed capital are discussed in this chapter, while those relating to retained earnings are addressed in Chapter 18. Accounting for corporations is emphasized because they are the dominant form of organization in today's economy. Not only are corporations the major source of our national output, but they also provide the majority of employment opportunities. Millions of people hold equity securities (capital stock) in corporations throughout the world.

## NATURE AND CLASSIFICATIONS OF CAPITAL STOCK

A corporation is an artificial entity created by law that has an existence separate from its owners and may engage in business within prescribed limits just as a natural person. Unless the life of a corporation is limited by law, it has perpetual existence. The modern corporation makes it possible for large amounts of resources to be assembled under one management. These resources are transferred to the corporation by individual owners, because they believe they can earn a greater rate of return through the corporation's efficient use of the resources than would be possible from alternative investments. In exchange for these resources, the corporation issues **stock certificates** evidencing ownership interests. Directors elected by stockholders delegate to management responsibility for supervising the use, operation, and disposition of corporate resources.

Business corporations may be created under the incorporating laws of any one of the fifty states or of the federal government. Since the states do not follow a uniform incorporating act, the conditions under which corporations may be created and under which they may operate are somewhat varied.

[1]Bro Uttal, "Inside the Deal That Made Bill Gates $350,000,000," *Fortune,* July 21, 1986, p. 23.

In most states at least three individuals must join in applying for a corporate charter. Application is made by submitting **articles of incorporation** to the secretary of state or other appropriate official. The articles must set forth the name of the corporation, its purpose and nature, the stock to be issued, those persons who are to act as first directors, and other data required by law. If the articles conform to the state's laws governing corporate formation, they are approved and are recognized as the **charter** for the new corporate entity. When stock of a corporation is to be offered or distributed outside the state in which it is incorporated, registration with the Securities and Exchange Commission may be required. The objective of such registration is to ensure that all facts relative to the business and its securities will be adequately and honestly disclosed. A stockholders' meeting is called at which a code of rules or **bylaws** governing meetings, voting procedures, and other internal operations are adopted; a **board of directors** is elected; and the board appoints company administrative officers. Corporate activities may now proceed in conformance with laws of the state of incorporation and charter authorization. A complete record of the proceedings of both the stockholders' and the directors' meetings should be maintained in a minutes book.

When a corporation is formed, a single class of stock, known as **common stock**, is usually issued. Corporations may later find that there are advantages to issuing one or more additional classes of stock with varying rights and priorities. Stock with certain preferences (rights) over the common stock is called **preferred stock**. All shares within a particular class of stock are identical in terms of ownership rights represented.

## Rights of Ownership

Unless restricted or withheld by terms of the articles of incorporation or bylaws, certain basic rights are held by each stockholder. These rights are as follows:

1. To share in distributions of corporate earnings.
2. To vote in the election of directors and in the determination of certain corporate policies.
3. To maintain one's proportional interest in the corporation through purchase of additional capital stock if issued, known as the *preemptive right*. (In recent years, some states have eliminated this right.)
4. To share in distributions of cash or other properties upon liquidation of the corporation.

If both preferred and common stock are issued, the special features of each class of stock are stated in the articles of incorporation or in the corporation bylaws and become a part of the contract between the corporation and its stockholders. One must be familiar with the overall capital structure to understand fully the nature of the equity found in any single class of stock. Frequently, the stock certificate describes the rights and restrictions relative to the ownership interest it represents together with those pertaining to other securities issued. Shares of stock represent personal property and may be freely transferred by their owners in the absence of special restrictions.

## Par or Stated Value of Stock

As indicated, the capital of a corporation is divided between contributed capital and retained earnings. This is an important distinction because readers of financial statements need to know the portion of equity derived from investments by owners as contrasted with the portion of equity that has been earned and retained by the business. The invested or contributed capital may be further classified into (a) an amount forming the corporate **legal capital**, and (b) the balance, if any, in excess of legal capital. The amount of the investment representing the legal capital is reported as **capital stock**. The remaining balance is recognized as **additional paid-in capital**. As discussed in this chapter, and elsewhere in the text, additional paid-in capital may arise from several sources, including the sale of stock at more than par or stated value, treasury stock transactions, and donations of assets. Additional paid-in capital includes all sources of contributed capital other than, or in excess of, legal capital.

The major components of owners' equity for a corporation are shown below. It should be recognized, however, that the definitions and classifications of legal and other capital categories may vary according to state statutes.

Elements of Owners' Equity for a Corporation

Owners' Equity
- Contributed Capital
  - Legal Capital
  - Additional Paid-In Capital
- Retained Earnings

The significance of legal capital is that most state incorporation laws provide that dividends cannot reduce corporate capital below an amount designated as legal capital. Modern corporation laws normally go beyond these limitations and add that legal capital cannot be impaired by the reacquisition of capital stock. Creditors of a corporation cannot hold individual stockholders liable for claims against the company. But with a portion of the corporate capital restricted as to distribution, creditors can rely on the absorption by the ownership group of losses equal to the legal capital before losses are applied to the creditors' equity. As a practical matter, the legal capital of a corporation is generally small in comparison to total capital and does not strongly influence dividend policy nor provide significant creditor protection.

When a value is assigned to each share of stock, whether common or preferred, and is reported on the stock certificate, the stock is said to have a **par value**; stock without such an assigned value is called **no-par** stock. When shares have a par value, the legal capital is normally the aggregate par value of all shares issued and subscribed. When a corporation is authorized to issue stock with a par value, the incorporation laws of most states permit such issue only for an amount equal to or in excess of par. Par value may be any amount, for example, $100, $5, or 25 cents. An amount received on the sale of stock in excess of its par value is recorded in a separate account, such as Paid-In Capital in Excess of Par. The balance in this account is added to capital stock at par in reporting total contributed capital.

From a financial reporting perspective, the concept of par value has little significance. Par value also has virtually no economic significance. Originally, the par value of stock was equal to the market value of the stock at the date of issue. Today, however, most par value stock has only a nominal value; that is, the par value is significantly below its issue or market price. Par value does have legal significance in the historical development of common law and statutory law. But the modern trend is away from par value and an emphasis on legal capital.[2]

When shares are no-par, laws of certain states require that the total consideration received for the shares, even when they are sold at different prices, be recognized as legal capital. Laws of a number of states, however, permit the corporate directors to establish legal capital by assigning an arbitrary value to each share regardless of issue price, although in some instances the value cannot be less than a certain minimum amount. The value fixed by the board of directors or the minimum value required by law is known as the share's **stated value**, and an amount received in excess of stated value is reported in the same manner as an excess over par value, using an appropriate account title, e.g., Paid-In Capital in Excess of Stated Value.

Prior to 1912, corporations were permitted to issue only stock with a par value. In 1912, however, New York State changed its corporation laws to permit the issuance of stock without a par value, and since that time, all other states have followed with similar statutory provisions. Today, a number of stocks listed on the major securities exchanges are no-par. Of 660 common stock issues surveyed in *Accounting Trends & Techniques*, 601 had a par value. Of 195 preferred stock issues, 132 had a par value.[3] Usually, no-par stock must have a stated value for reporting purposes. This makes it very similar to par stock and defines a separation of the stock proceeds between stated value and additional paid-in capital.

## Preferred Stock

When a corporation issues both preferred and common stock, the preference rights attached to preferred stock normally consist of prior claims to dividends. A dividend preference does not assure stockholders of dividends on the preferred issue but simply means that dividend requirements must be met on preferred stock before anything may be paid on common stock. Dividends do not legally accrue; a dividend on preferred stock, as on common stock, requires the ability on the part of the company to make such a distribution as well as appropriate action by the board of directors. When the board of directors fails to declare a dividend on preferred stock at the time such action would be called for, the dividend is said to be "passed." Although preferred stockholders have a prior claim on dividends, such preference is usually accompanied by limitations on the amount of dividends they may receive.

Preferred stock is generally issued with a par value. When preferred stock has a par value, the dividend is stated in terms of a percentage of par value. When preferred stock is no-par, the dividend must be stated in terms of dollars and cents. Thus, holders of 5% preferred stock with a $50 par value are entitled to an annual dividend of $2.50 per share before any distribution is made to common stockholders; holders of $5 no-par preferred stock are entitled to an annual dividend of $5 per share before dividends are paid to common stockholders.

A corporation may issue more than one class of preferred stock. For example, preferred issues may be designated "first preferred" or "second preferred" with the first preferred issue having a first claim on earnings and the second preferred having a second claim on earnings. In other instances, the claim to earnings on the part of several preferred issues may have equal priority, but dividend rates or other preferences may vary. Holders of the

---

[2]For a more complete discussion of the legal significance of par value, see Philip McGough, "The Legal Significance of the Par Value of Common Stock: What Accounting Educators Should Know," *Issues in Accounting Education*, Fall 1988, pp. 330-350.

[3]*Accounting Trends & Techniques—1990* (New York: AICPA, 1990), pp. 186-187.

common stock may receive dividends only after the satisfaction of all preferred dividend requirements.

Other characteristics and conditions are frequently added to preferred stock in the extension of certain advantages or in the limitation of certain rights. For example, preferred stock may be cumulative, participating, convertible, callable, or redeemable. More than one of these characteristics may be applicable to a specific issue of preferred stock.

**Cumulative and Noncumulative Preferred Stock**   When a corporation fails to declare dividends on **cumulative preferred stock**, such dividends accumulate and require payment in the future before any dividends may be paid to common stockholders.

For example, assume that Good Time Corporation has outstanding 100,000 shares of 9% cumulative preferred stock, $10 par. Dividends were last paid in 1990. Total dividends of $300,000 are declared in 1993 by the board of directors. The majority of this amount will be paid to the preferred shareholders as follows:

|  | Dividends to Preferred Shareholders | Dividends to Common Shareholders | Total Dividends |
|---|---|---|---|
| Cumulative dividend for 1991....... | $ 90,000 | — | $ 90,000 |
| Cumulative dividend for 1992....... | 90,000 | — | 90,000 |
| Dividends for 1993 ................ | 90,000 | $30,000 | 120,000 |
| Totals ........................ | $270,000 | $30,000 | $300,000 |

Dividends on cumulative preferred stock that are passed are referred to as **dividends in arrears**. Although these dividends are not a liability until declared by the board of directors, this information is of importance to stockholders and other users of the financial statements. Disclosure of the amount of dividends in arrears is made by special note on the balance sheet.

With **noncumulative preferred stock**, it is not necessary to provide for passed dividends. A dividend omission on preferred stock in any one year means it is irretrievably lost. Dividends may be declared on common stock as long as the preferred stock receives the preferred rate for the current period. Thus, in the previous example, if the preferred stock were noncumulative, the 1993 dividends would be distributed as follows:

|  | Dividends to Preferred Shareholders | Dividends to Common Shareholders | Total Dividends |
|---|---|---|---|
| Dividend passed in 1991 ........... | — | — | — |
| Dividend passed in 1992 ........... | — | — | — |
| Dividends for 1993 ................ | $90,000 | $210,000 | $300,000 |
| Totals ........................ | $90,000 | $210,000 | $300,000 |

Preferred stock contracts normally provide for cumulative dividends. Also, courts have generally held that dividend rights on preferred stock are cumulative in the absence of specific provisions to the contrary.

**Participating Preferred Stock**   Dividends on preferred stock are generally of a fixed amount. However, **participating preferred stock** issues provide for additional dividends to be paid to preferred stockholders after dividends of a specified amount are paid to the common stockholders. For example, additional dividends would be paid to holders of a 6% participating preferred stock after dividends totaling 6% of the par value of the common stock were also paid. Fully participating preferred stock shares equally with common stock in the excess dividends; partially participating preferred stock dividends are capped at some limit. Clearly, a participative provision makes preferred stock less like debt and more like equity. Although once quite common, participating preferred stocks are now relatively rare.

**Convertible Preferred Stock**    Preferred stock is **convertible** when terms of the issue provide that it can be exchanged by its owner for some other security of the issuing corporation. Conversion rights generally provide for the exchange of preferred stock into common stock. Since preferred stock normally has a prior but limited right to earnings, large earnings resulting from successful operations accrue to the common stockholders. The conversion privilege gives the preferred stockholders the opportunity to exchange their holdings for stock in which the rights to earnings are not limited. In some instances, preferred stock may be convertible into bonds, thus allowing investors the option of changing their positions from stockholders to creditors. Convertible preferred issues have become popular with some companies. The journal entries required for stock conversions are illustrated later in the chapter.

**Callable Preferred Stock**    Preferred stock is **callable** when it can be called or redeemed at the option of the corporation. Many preferred issues are callable. The **call price** is usually specified in the original agreement and provides for payment of dividends in arrears as part of the repurchase price. When convertible stock has a call provision, the holders of the stock, at the time of the call, are frequently given the option of converting their holdings into common stock rather than accepting the call price. The decision made by the investor will be based on the market price of the common stock.

**Redeemable Preferred Stock**    Preferred stock is sometimes subject to mandatory redemption requirements or other redemption provisions that give the security overlapping debt and equity characteristics. This type of stock is referred to as **redeemable preferred stock** and is defined as preferred stock that is redeemable at the option of the holder, or at a fixed or determinable price on a specific date, or upon other conditions not solely within the control of the issuer (e.g., redemption upon reaching a certain level of earnings). The FASB currently requires disclosure of long-term obligations, including the extent of redemption requirements for all issues of capital stock that are redeemable at fixed or determinable prices on fixed or determinable dates. Redemption requirements may be disclosed separately for each issue or for all issues combined.[4] The SEC has ruled (in Accounting Series Release No. 268) that firms with publicly traded securities must not include mandatory redeemable preferred stock under the "Stockholders' Equity" heading. Instead, mandatory redeemable preferred is listed above the equity section in a "gray area" between the liabilities and equities.

The entries for reacquiring stock by exercising a call or redemption feature are discussed later in the chapter.

**Asset and Dividend Preferences Upon Corporation Liquidation**    Preferred stock generally takes priority over common stock as to assets distributed upon corporate liquidation. Such a preference, however, cannot be assumed but must be specifically stated in the preferred stock contract. The asset preference for stock with a par value is an amount equal to par, or par plus any amount paid in excess of par; in the absence of a par value, the preference is a stated amount. Terms of the preferred contract may also provide for the full

---

[4]*Statement of Financial Accounting Standards No. 47,* "Disclosure of Long-Term Obligations" (Stamford: Financial Accounting Standards Board, 1981), par. 10c.

## Is It Equity or Is It Debt?

In the field of finance, a debt claim is viewed as one that entitles the debt holders to a fixed payment when company assets are sufficient to meet that payment; if company assets are below that amount, the debt holders get all the assets. An equity claim is viewed as one that entitles the equity holders to all company assets in excess of the debt holders' portion. The definitions of liabilities and equities given by the FASB in its Statement of Accounting Concepts No. 6 embody similar notions—equity is defined as the residual amount of assets left after deducting the liability claims.

Although examples of pure equity (common stock) and pure debt (a bank loan) are easy to distinguish, many securities are in a middle ground and have characteristics of both. For example:

*Preferred Stock*—Preferred stock is very much like debt in that the payments (both dividend and liquidation amounts) are typically capped. However, preferred stock is classified as equity, since the payments aren't guaranteed and have lower priority than debt claims. Mandatory redeemable preferred stock is even more like debt in that the company is obligated to redeem, or pay back, the preferred stock investment just as it is obligated to pay back loans.

*Convertible Debt*—Convertible debt can be exchanged for equity at the option of the debt holder. Whether the debt holder will exercise that option depends on how well the firm does. If it performs well, the debt holder will convert; if it performs poorly, the debt holder will retain the privilege of guaranteed payments under the debt contract. Clearly, as the performance of the firm improves, the convertible debt gradually changes in nature from debt to equity.

*Employee Stock Options*—Since an employee stock option obligates the company to issue its own stock at a specified price in the future, some have suggested that it has some characteristics of a liability. Such options are currently accounted for as equity.

These examples illustrate that the fine line between a liability and an equity can be very blurred. One suggestion for improved disclosure is to have a third category on the right side of the balance sheet where items with elements of both debt and equity would be reported. Mandatory redeemable preferred stock is already treated essentially this way. Another possibility is to have no artificial division between liabilities and equities, but instead list long-term sources of capital according to their mix of debt and equity characteristics—pure long-term debt could be listed first, common stock listed last, and the intermediate items listed in between. The FASB is currently considering how to resolve this issue. One thing is certain—as innovative securities continue to be introduced, the boundary between debt and equity will only get more fuzzy.

### Questions:

1. As described above, it has been suggested that the artificial division between liabilities and equities be removed from the balance sheet. What implications would this have for the income statement?
2. Imagine two companies, A and B. Forty percent of A's financing comes from debt, the remainder comes from equity. B's financing is 99 percent debt and one percent equity. How does the debt of B differ from the debt of A?

Sources:

Clifford C. Woods III and Halsey G. Bullen, "An Overview of the FASB's Financial Instruments Project," *Journal of Accountancy* (November 1989), p. 42.

"Distinguishing Between Liability and Equity Instruments and Accounting for Instruments With Characteristics of Both," FASB Discussion Memorandum (August 21, 1990).

payment of any dividends in arrears upon liquidation, regardless of the retained earnings balance reported by the company. When this is the case and there are insufficient retained earnings, i.e., a deficit, such dividend priorities must be met from paid-in capital of the common stock; the common stockholders receive whatever assets remain after settlement with the preferred group.

## Common Stock

Strictly speaking, there should be but one kind of common stock, representing the residual ownership equity of a company. In recent years, however, a few companies have begun to issue different classes of common stock with different ownership rights. The New York Times Company, for example, has several classes of common stock to appeal to different types of investors. In many ways, these classes of common stock are similar in nature and purpose to preferred stock. For most companies, there is but one class of common stock.

Common stock carries the greatest risk, since common shareholders receive dividends only after preferred dividends are paid. In return for this risk, common stock ordinarily shares in earnings to the greatest extent if the corporation is successful. There is no inherent distinction in voting rights between preferred and common stocks; however, voting rights are frequently given exclusively to common stockholders as long as dividends are paid regularly on preferred stock. Upon failure to meet preferred dividend requirements, special voting rights may be granted to preferred stockholders, thus affording this group a more prominent role in the management. In some states, voting rights cannot be withheld on any class of stock.

## ISSUANCE OF CAPITAL STOCK

In accounting for capital stock, it should be recognized that stock may be:

1. Authorized but unissued.
2. Subscribed for and held for issuance pending receipt of cash for the full amount of the subscription price.
3. Outstanding in the hands of stockholders.
4. Reacquired and held by the corporation for subsequent reissuance.
5. Canceled by appropriate corporation action.

Thus, an accurate record of all transactions involving capital stock must be maintained by a corporation. Separate general ledger accounts are required for each source of capital including each class of stock. In addition, subsidiary records are needed to keep track of individual stockholders and stock certificates.

### Capital Stock Issued for Cash

The issuance of stock for cash is recorded by a debit to Cash and a credit to Capital Stock for the par or stated value.[5] When the amount of cash received from the sale of stock is greater than the par or stated value, the excess is recorded separately as a credit to an additional paid-in capital account. This account is carried on the books as long as the stock to which it relates is outstanding. When stock is retired, the capital stock balance as well as any related additional paid-in-capital balance is generally canceled.

---

[5]The term *Capital Stock* is used in account titles in the text when the class of stock is not specifically designated. When preferred and common designations are given, these are used in the account titles.

To illustrate, assume the Goode Corporation is authorized to issue 10,000 shares of $10 par common stock. On April 1, 1993, 4,000 shares are sold for $45,000 cash. The entry to record the transaction is:

```
1993
April 1   Cash ...........................................    45,000
             Common Stock..................................            40,000
             Paid-In Capital in Excess of Par ...................             5,000
                To record the issuance of 4,000 shares of $10 par
                common stock for $45,000.
```

If, in the example, the common stock were no-par stock but with a $10 stated value, the entry would be the same except that the $5,000 would be designated Paid-In Capital in Excess of Stated Value. Generally, stock is assigned a par or a stated value. However, if there is no such value assigned, the entire amount of cash received on the sale of stock is credited to the capital stock account and there is no additional paid-in capital account associated with the stock. Assuming Goode Corporation's stock were no-par common without a stated value, the entry to record the sale of 4,000 shares for $45,000 would be:

```
1993
April 1   Cash ...........................................    45,000
             Common Stock..................................            45,000
                To record the issuance of 4,000 shares of no-par,
                no-stated-value common stock for $45,000.
```

## Capital Stock Sold on Subscription

Capital stock may be issued on a subscription basis. A **subscription** is a legally binding contract between the subscriber (purchaser of stock) and the corporation (issuer of stock). The contract states the number of shares subscribed, the subscription price, the terms of payment, and other conditions of the transaction. A subscription, while giving the corporation a legal claim for the contract price, also gives the subscriber the legal status of a stockholder unless certain rights as a stockholder are specifically withheld by law or by terms of the contract. Ordinarily, stock certificates evidencing share ownership are not issued until the full subscription price has been received by the corporation.

When stock is subscribed for, Capital Stock Subscriptions Receivable is debited for the subscription price, Capital Stock Subscribed is credited for the amount to be recognized as capital stock when subscriptions have been collected, and a paid-in capital account is credited for the amount of the subscription price in excess of par or stated value.

Capital Stock Subscriptions Receivable is a control account, with individual subscriptions being reported in the subsidiary **subscribers ledger**. A special **subscribers journal** may be used in recording capital stock subscriptions. Subscriptions Receivable is regarded as a current asset when the corporation expects to collect the balance within one year, which is the usual situation. Capital Stock Subscribed and any related paid-in capital accounts are reported as contributed capital in the stockholders' equity section of the balance sheet.

Subscriptions may be collected in cash or in other assets accepted by the corporation. When collections are made, the appropriate asset account is debited and the receivable account is credited. Credits are also made to subscribers' accounts in the subsidiary ledger.

The actual issuance of stock is recorded by a debit to Capital Stock Subscribed and a credit to Capital Stock. The following entries illustrate the recording and issuance of capital stock sold on subscription. It is assumed that the Feitz Corporation is authorized to issue 10,000 shares of $10 par value common stock.

### Recording and Issuance of Capital Stock Sold on Subscription

November 1-30: Received subscriptions for 5,000 shares of $10 par common at $12.50 per share with 50% down, balance due in 60 days.

| | | |
|---|---:|---:|
| Common Stock Subscriptions Receivable . . . . . . . . . . . . . . . . . . . | 62,500 | |
|     Common Stock Subscribed . . . . . . . . . . . . . . . . . . . . . . . . . . . . . | | 50,000 |
|     Paid-in Capital in Excess of Par . . . . . . . . . . . . . . . . . . . . . . . . . | | 12,500 |
| Cash . . . . . . . . . . . . . . . . . . . . . . . . . . . . . . . . . . . . . . . . . . . . . . | 31,250 | |
|     Common Stock Subscriptions Receivable . . . . . . . . . . . . . . . . . . | | 31,250 |

December 1-31: Received balance due on one-half of subscriptions and issued stock to the fully paid subscribers, 2,500 shares.

| | | |
|---|---:|---:|
| Cash . . . . . . . . . . . . . . . . . . . . . . . . . . . . . . . . . . . . . . . . . . . . . . | 15,625 | |
|     Common Stock Subscriptions Receivable . . . . . . . . . . . . . . . . . . | | 15,625 |
| Common Stock Subscribed . . . . . . . . . . . . . . . . . . . . . . . . . . . . . | 25,000 | |
|     Common Stock . . . . . . . . . . . . . . . . . . . . . . . . . . . . . . . . . . . . . . | | 25,000 |

As a result of the preceding transactions, current assets in the December 31 balance sheet would include subscriptions receivable of $15,625. Contributed capital would be reported in the stockholders' equity section of the balance sheet as follows:

**Stockholders' Equity**

| | |
|---|---:|
| Contributed capital: | |
|   Common stock, $10 par, 10,000 shares authorized, 2,500 shares issued | |
|     and outstanding . . . . . . . . . . . . . . . . . . . . . . . . . . . . . . . . . . . . . . . . | $25,000 |
|   Common stock subscribed, 2,500 shares . . . . . . . . . . . . . . . . . . . . . . . . | 25,000 |
|   Paid-in capital in excess of par . . . . . . . . . . . . . . . . . . . . . . . . . . . . . . . | 12,500 |
|   Total contributed capital . . . . . . . . . . . . . . . . . . . . . . . . . . . . . . . . . . . . | $62,500 |

### Subscription Defaults

If a subscriber defaults on a subscription by failing to make a payment when it is due, a corporation may (1) return to the subscriber the amount paid, (2) return to the subscriber the amount paid less any reduction in price or expense incurred on the resale of the stock, (3) declare the amount paid by the subscriber as forfeited, or (4) issue to the subscriber shares equal to the number paid for in full. The practice followed will depend on the policy adopted by the corporation within the legal limitations set by the state in which it is incorporated.

To illustrate the entries under these different circumstances, assume in the Feitz Corporation example described earlier (with subscriptions at $12.50 per share) that one subscriber for 100 shares defaults after making the 50% down payment. Defaulted shares are subsequently resold at $11. The entries to record the default by the subscriber and the subsequent resale of the defaulted shares would be as follows:

1. Assuming the amount paid in is returned to the subscriber:

| | | |
|---|---:|---:|
| Common Stock Subscribed . . . . . . . . . . . . . . . . . . . . . . . . . . . . . | 1,000 | |
| Paid-In Capital in Excess of Par . . . . . . . . . . . . . . . . . . . . . . . . . . | 250 | |
|     Common Stock Subscriptions Receivable . . . . . . . . . . . . . . . . . . . | | 625 |
|     Cash . . . . . . . . . . . . . . . . . . . . . . . . . . . . . . . . . . . . . . . . . . . . . . | | 625 |
| | | |
| Cash . . . . . . . . . . . . . . . . . . . . . . . . . . . . . . . . . . . . . . . . . . . . . . | 1,100 | |
|     Common Stock . . . . . . . . . . . . . . . . . . . . . . . . . . . . . . . . . . . . . . | | 1,000 |
|     Paid-In Capital in Excess of Par . . . . . . . . . . . . . . . . . . . . . . . . . | | 100 |

2. Assuming the amount paid in less the price reduction on the resale is returned to the subscriber:

| | | |
|---|---|---|
| Common Stock Subscribed | 1,000 | |
| Paid-In Capital in Excess of Par | 250 | |
|    Common Stock Subscriptions Receivable | | 625 |
|    Payable to Defaulting Subscriber *(payment withheld pending stock resale)* | | 625 |

| | | |
|---|---|---|
| Cash | 1,100 | |
| Payable to Defaulting Subscriber | 150 | |
|    Common Stock | | 1,000 |
|    Paid-In Capital in Excess of Par | | 250 |

| | | |
|---|---|---|
| Payable to Defaulting Subscriber | 475 | |
|    Cash | | 475 |

3. Assuming the full amount paid in is declared to be forfeited:

| | | |
|---|---|---|
| Common Stock Subscribed | 1,000 | |
| Paid-In Capital in Excess of Par | 250 | |
|    Common Stock Subscriptions Receivable | | 625 |
|    Paid-In Capital From Forfeited Stock Subscriptions | | 625 |

| | | |
|---|---|---|
| Cash | 1,100 | |
|    Common Stock | | 1,000 |
|    Paid-In Capital in Excess of Par | | 100 |

4. Assuming shares equal to the number paid for in full are issued:

| | | |
|---|---|---|
| Common Stock Subscribed | 1,000 | |
| Paid-In Capital in Excess of Par | 125 | |
|    Common Stock | | 500 |
|    Common Stock Subscriptions Receivable | | 625 |

| | | |
|---|---|---|
| Cash | 550 | |
|    Common Stock | | 500 |
|    Paid-In Capital in Excess of Par | | 50 |

## Capital Stock Issued for Consideration Other Than Cash

When capital stock is issued for consideration in the form of property other than cash or for services received, the fair market value of the stock or the fair market value of the property or services, whichever is more objectively determinable, is used to record the transaction. If a quoted market price for the stock is available, that amount should be used as a basis for recording the exchange. Otherwise, it may be possible to determine the fair market value of the property or services received, e.g., through appraisal by a competent outside party.

To illustrate, assume that AC Company issues 200 shares of $100 par value common stock in return for land. The company's stock is currently selling for $150 per share. The entry on AC Company's books would be:

| | | |
|---|---|---|
| Land | 30,000 | |
|    Common Stock | | 20,000 |
|    Paid-In Capital in Excess of Par | | 10,000 |

If, on the other hand, the land has a readily determinable market price of $25,000 but AC Company's common stock has no established fair market value, the transaction would be recorded as follows:

| Land ............................................................... | 25,000 | |
| Common Stock............................................... | | 20,000 |
| Paid-In Capital in Excess of Par ........................... | | 5,000 |

If an objective value cannot be established for either the stock or the property or services received, the board of directors normally has the right to assign values to the securities issued and the assets or services received. These values will stand for all legal purposes in the absence of proof that fraud was involved. However, the assignment of values by the board of directors should be subject to careful scrutiny, because assigning excessive values to the consideration received for stock falsely improves the company's reported financial position. When the value of the consideration cannot be clearly established and the directors' valuations are used in reporting assets and invested capital, the source of the valuations should be disclosed on the balance sheet. When there is evidence that improper values have been assigned to the consideration received for stock, such values should be restated.

### Issuance of Capital Stock in Exchange for a Business

A corporation, upon its formation or at some later date, may be combined with another ongoing business, issuing capital stock in exchange for the net assets acquired. This is referred to as a business combination. In determining the amount of stock to be issued, the fair market value of the stock, as well as the values of the net assets acquired, must be considered.

Frequently the value of the stock transferred by a corporation will exceed the value of the identifiable assets acquired because of a favorable earnings record of the business acquired. If the exchange is accounted for as a purchase, the value of the stock in excess of the values assigned to identifiable assets is recognized as goodwill (see Chapter 12). Under this approach, the retained earnings of the company acquired *do not* become part of the combined retained earnings. On the other hand, if the exchange is treated as a pooling of interests, neither the revaluation of assets nor the recognition of goodwill is recorded. Assets are stated at the amounts previously reported; the retained earnings accounts of the two companies are added together and become the amount of retained earnings for the combined entity. The purchase method assumes that one of the companies is dominant and is acquiring the other company. The pooling-of-interests method assumes equal status and continuity of common ownership. Accounting for business combinations is dealt with in APB Opinion No. 16 and is discussed in detail in advanced accounting texts.

## CAPITAL STOCK REACQUISITION

For a variety of reasons, a company may find it desirable to reacquire shares of its own stock. In 1988, for example, IBM Corporation announced a $2 billion buyback program. Over the past few years, IBM has completed stock purchase programs totaling about 28 million shares. Companies acquire their own stock to:

1. Finance acquisitions.
2. Provide for incentive compensation and employee savings plans.
3. Improve per-share earnings by reducing the number of shares outstanding.
4. Support the market price of the stock.
5. Increase the ratio of debt to equity.
6. Obtain shares for conversion to other securities.
7. Invest excess cash temporarily.

Whatever the reason, a company's stock may be reacquired by exercise of call or redemption provisions, by repurchase of the stock in the open market, or by donation from stockholders. In reacquiring stock, a company must comply with applicable state laws, which can have a significant impact on transactions involving a company's stock. For example, state laws normally provide that the reacquisition of stock must serve a legitimate corporate purpose and must be made without injury or prejudice to the creditors or to the remaining stockholders. Another general restriction relates to the preserving of sufficient legal capital of the corporation.

In accounting for the reacquisition of stock, it should be emphasized that *reacquisitions do not give rise to gain or loss*. A company issues stock to raise capital, which it intends to employ profitably; in reacquiring shares of its stock, the company reduces the capital to be employed in subsequent operations. Gains or losses arise from the operating and investing activities of the business, not from transactions with its shareholders.

A company's stock may be reacquired for immediate retirement or be reacquired and held as treasury stock for subsequent disposition, either eventual retirement or reissuance. Accounting for immediate retirements will be discussed first, followed by accounting for treasury stock transactions.

## Stock Reacquired for Immediate Retirement

If shares of stock are reacquired at par or stated value and then retired, the capital stock account is debited and Cash is credited. However, if the purchase price of the stock exceeds the par or stated value, the excess amount may be: (1) charged to any paid-in capital balances applicable to that class of stock, (2) allocated between paid-in capital and retained earnings, or (3) charged entirely to retained earnings.[6] The alternative used depends on the existence of previously established paid-in capital amounts and on management's preference. To illustrate the application of the alternatives, assume that Interwest Corporation reports the following balances related to an issue of preferred stock:

| | |
|---|---:|
| Preferred Stock ($10 par, 10,000 shares outstanding) ................ | $100,000 |
| Paid-In Capital in Excess of Par .................................... | 10,000 |

Assume Interwest redeems and retires 2,000 shares, or 20%, of the preferred stock at $12.50 per share, or a total purchase price of $25,000. Reductions are made in the preferred stock account for $20,000 (2,000 shares at par of $10) and in the related paid-in capital account for a pro rata share, 20% of $10,000, or $2,000. The remainder of the purchase price, $3,000, is charged to Retained Earnings. The journal entry would be:

| | | |
|---|---:|---:|
| Preferred Stock........................................... | 20,000 | |
| Paid-In Capital in Excess of Par ........................... | 2,000 | |
| Retained Earnings ......................................... | 3,000 | |
|   Cash ................................................. | | 25,000 |

Alternatively, the entire amount paid over par or stated value of the retired shares can be debited to Retained Earnings. In the above example, the entry would be:

| | | |
|---|---:|---:|
| Preferred Stock........................................... | 20,000 | |
| Retained Earnings ......................................... | 5,000 | |
|   Cash ................................................. | | 25,000 |

When a corporation reacquires stock at a price that is less than par or stated value, the difference is credited to a paid-in capital account, not to Retained Earnings. To illustrate, assume Interwest Corporation redeems the 2,000 shares of preferred stock at only $9 per

---

[6]*Opinions of the Accounting Principles Board No. 6,* "Status of Accounting Research Bulletins" (New York: American Institute of Certified Public Accountants, 1965), par. 12a.

share, or a total of $18,000. The preferred stock account is reduced by the par value of the shares, $20,000, and the difference between the debit to Preferred Stock and the amount paid is credited to a paid-in capital account, as illustrated in the following entry:

```
Preferred Stock..........................................    20,000
    Cash ................................................              18,000
    Paid-In Capital From Preferred Stock Reacquisition ..........       2,000
```

If additional shares of preferred stock are subsequently reacquired at amounts in excess of par, the excess can be debited to Paid-In Capital in Excess of Par, Paid-In Capital From Preferred Stock Reacquisition, and/or Retained Earnings.

The preceding discussion and illustrations dealt only with the corporation's books. From the investor's perspective, a stock redemption is recorded by a debit to Cash for the call price received and a credit to the investment account at cost; the difference, if any, is recorded as a gain or loss. Generally, a gain is recognized, since the call price is usually higher than the cost of the investment. Using the first example given for the Interwest Corporation (reacquisition price of $12.50 per share) and assuming only one investor held the 2,000 shares of preferred stock at a cost of $22,000, the entry for the stockholder would be:

```
Cash ................................................    25,000
    Gain on Redemption of Interwest Corporation Preferred Stock       3,000
    Investment in Interwest Corporation Preferred Stock .........    22,000
```

## Treasury Stock

When a company's own stock is reacquired and held in the name of the company rather than formally retired, it is referred to as **treasury stock**. Treasury shares may subsequently be reissued or formally retired. Before discussing how to account for treasury stock, several important features should be noted.

First, treasury stock should not be viewed as an asset; instead, it should be reported as a reduction in total owners' equity.[7] A company cannot have an ownership interest in itself. Furthermore, treasury stock does not confer upon the corporation stockholder rights, e.g., cash dividends or voting rights. Treasury shares may or may not participate in stock dividends or stock splits, depending on the circumstances. The distribution of stock dividends on treasury stock is specifically prohibited by law in some states. In states where such distributions are permitted, stock dividends generally would be distributed on treasury shares only in certain situations, for example when the treasury shares are intended for distribution to employees under a stock option plan. When a stock split alters the par or stated value of all the shares of a particular class of stock, treasury shares would participate in the split.

Second, legal capital is not affected by the acquisition or reissuance of treasury stock. The acquisition of treasury stock decreases the number of shares outstanding, while reissuance increases the number of shares outstanding, but the legal capital is not changed by either the reacquisition or the subsequent reissuance. Third, as noted earlier, there is no income or loss on the reacquisition, reissuance, or retirement of treasury stock. Finally, as illustrated in the next section, Retained Earnings can be decreased by treasury stock transactions, but is never increased by such transactions.

Two methods for recording treasury stock transactions are generally accepted: (1) the **cost method**, where the purchase of treasury stock is viewed as giving rise to a capital element whose ultimate disposition remains to be determined; and (2) the **par (or stated)**

---

[7]Occasionally, however, treasury stock is shown as an asset when shares are acquired in connection with an employee stock option plan.

value method, where the purchase of treasury stock is viewed as effective or "constructive" retirement of outstanding stock.

### Cost Method of Accounting for Treasury Stock

Under the cost method, the purchase of treasury stock is recorded by debiting a treasury stock account for the cost of the purchase and crediting Cash. The cost is determined by the current market price of the stock and is not necessarily tied to the original stock issue price. The balance in the treasury stock account is reported as a deduction from total stockholders' equity on the balance sheet. If treasury stock is subsequently retired, the debit balance in the treasury stock account is eliminated by allocating proportionate amounts to the appropriate capital stock, paid-in capital, and retained earnings accounts, as noted previously. If treasury stock is subsequently sold, the difference between the acquisition cost and the selling price is reported as an increase or decrease in stockholders' equity. If stockholders' equity is increased by the sale of treasury stock, a paid-in capital account, such as Paid-In Capital From Treasury Stock, is credited. If stockholders' equity is decreased, paid-in capital accounts established from previous treasury stock transactions may be debited, or the entire amount may be debited to Retained Earnings.

The cost method of accounting for treasury stock transactions is illustrated in the following example:

1992    Newly organized corporation issued 10,000 shares of common stock, $10 par, at $15:

| Cash..................................................... | 150,000 | |
| Common Stock ....................................... | | 100,000 |
| Paid-In Capital in Excess of Par ....................... | | 50,000 |

Net income for first year of business, $30,000:

| Income Summary..................................... | 30,000 | |
| Retained Earnings ................................... | | 30,000 |

1993    Reacquired 1,000 shares of common stock at $16 per share:

| Treasury Stock ....................................... | 16,000 | |
| Cash............................................. | | 16,000 |

Sold 200 shares of treasury stock at $20 per share:

| Cash............................................. | 4,000 | |
| Treasury Stock....................................... | | 3,200 |
| Paid-In Capital From Treasury Stock .................. | | 800 |

Sold 500 shares of treasury stock at $14 per share:

| Cash............................................. | 7,000 | |
| Paid-In Capital From Treasury Stock ................... | 800 | |
| Retained Earnings ................................... | 200 | |
| Treasury Stock....................................... | | 8,000 |

Retired 300 shares of treasury stock (3% of original issue of 10,000 shares):

| Common Stock ....................................... | 3,000 | |
| Paid-In Capital in Excess of Par........................ | 1,500* | |
| Retained Earnings ................................... | 300* | |
| Treasury Stock (300 × $16) ......................... | | 4,800 |

*As indicated earlier, the entire $1,800 difference between the debit to Common Stock and the cost to acquire the treasury stock may be debited to Retained Earnings.

In the preceding example, if a balance sheet were prepared after the acquisition of the treasury stock but prior to the reissuance and retirement of the stock, the stockholders' equity section would appear as follows:

Stockholders' Equity

| | |
|---|---|
| Contributed capital: | |
|   Common stock | $100,000 |
|   Paid-in capital in excess of par | 50,000 |
|   Total contributed capital | $150,000 |
| Retained earnings | 30,000 |
| Total contributed capital and retained earnings | $180,000 |
| Less treasury stock at cost | 16,000 |
| Total stockholders' equity | $164,000 |

It should be noted that in the example, all treasury stock was acquired at $16 per share. If several acquisitions of treasury stock are made at different prices, the resale or retirement of treasury shares must be recorded using the actual cost to reacquire the shares being sold or retired (specific identification) or on the basis of a cost-flow assumption, such as FIFO or average cost.

**Par (or Stated) Value Method of Accounting for Treasury Stock**    If the par (or stated) value method is used, the purchase of treasury stock is regarded as a withdrawal of a group of stockholders. Similarly, the sale or reissuance of treasury stock, under this approach, is viewed as the admission of a new group of stockholders, requiring entries giving effect to the investment by this group. Thus, the purchase and sale are viewed as two separate and unrelated transactions.

Using the data given for the cost method illustration, the following entries would be made for 1993 under the par value method:

1993    Reacquired 1,000 shares of common stock at $16 per share:

| | | |
|---|---|---|
| Treasury Stock | 10,000 | |
| Paid-In Capital in Excess of Par | 5,000 | |
| Retained Earnings | 1,000 | |
|   Cash | | 16,000 |

Sold 200 shares of treasury stock at $20 per share:

| | | |
|---|---|---|
| Cash | 4,000 | |
|   Treasury Stock | | 2,000 |
|   Paid-In Capital in Excess of Par | | 2,000 |

Sold 500 shares of treasury stock at $14 per share:

| | | |
|---|---|---|
| Cash | 7,000 | |
|   Treasury Stock | | 5,000 |
|   Paid-In Capital in Excess of Par | | 2,000 |

Retired 300 shares of treasury stock:

| | | |
|---|---|---|
| Common Stock | 3,000 | |
|   Treasury Stock | | 3,000 |

Prior to the reissuance or retirement of treasury stock in the example using the par value method, the stockholders' equity section would show:

### Stockholders' Equity

Contributed capital:
Common stock . . . . . . . . . . . . . . . . . . . . . . . . . . . . . . . . . . . . . . . . . . . . .    $100,000
Less treasury stock at par value . . . . . . . . . . . . . . . . . . . . . . . . . . . . . .    10,000
Common stock outstanding . . . . . . . . . . . . . . . . . . . . . . . . . . . . . . . . . .    $ 90,000
Paid-in capital in excess of par . . . . . . . . . . . . . . . . . . . . . . . . . . . . . . .    45,000
Total contributed capital . . . . . . . . . . . . . . . . . . . . . . . . . . . . . . . . . . .    $135,000
Retained earnings . . . . . . . . . . . . . . . . . . . . . . . . . . . . . . . . . . . . . . . . . .    29,000
Total stockholders' equity . . . . . . . . . . . . . . . . . . . . . . . . . . . . . . . . . . .    $164,000

**Evaluating the Cost and Par Value Methods**    Neither the AICPA, through the Accounting Principles Board, nor the FASB has expressed a preference between the two methods of accounting for treasury stock transactions. Although there is theoretical support for each approach, in practice, the cost method is strongly favored because of its simplicity. As noted in the 1990 *Accounting Trends & Techniques,* only 27 of 393 companies that reported treasury stock used some form of par or stated value method.[8]

The following comparison shows the impact on stockholders' equity of the two approaches after all treasury stock transactions have occurred in the illustrative example. Note that total stockholders' equity is the same regardless of which method is used. As shown by the example, however, there may be differences in the relative amounts of contributed capital and retained earnings reported. Note again that Retained Earnings may be decreased by treasury stock transactions, but can never be increased by buying and selling treasury stock.

### Comparison of Stockholders' Equity

|  | Cost Method | Par Value Method |
|---|---|---|
| Contributed capital: |  |  |
| Common stock . . . . . . . . . . . . . . . . . . . . . . . . . . . . . . . . | $ 97,000 | $ 97,000 |
| Paid-in capital in excess of par . . . . . . . . . . . . . . . . . . . | 48,500 | 49,000 |
| Total contributed capital . . . . . . . . . . . . . . . . . . . . . . . | $145,500 | $146,000 |
| Retained earnings . . . . . . . . . . . . . . . . . . . . . . . . . . . . . | 29,500 | 29,000 |
| Total contributed capital and retained earnings . . . . . . | $175,000 | $175,000 |
| Less treasury stock . . . . . . . . . . . . . . . . . . . . . . . . . . . . | -0- | -0- |
| Total stockholders' equity . . . . . . . . . . . . . . . . . . . . . . | $175,000 | $175,000 |

## Donated Treasury Stock

Treasury stock is occasionally acquired by donation from stockholders.  Shares may be donated to enable the company to raise capital by reselling the shares. In other cases, shares may be donated to eliminate a deficit. Ordinarily, all stockholders participate in the donation on a pro rata basis, each party donating a certain percentage of holdings so that relative interests in the corporation remain unchanged.

When treasury stock is donated and the market value of the stock is known, the transaction would be recorded normally, using either the cost or the par value method. Instead of a credit to Cash, however, the credit entry would be to a paid-in capital account, e.g., Donated Capital.

In the absence of an objective basis for valuation, the acquisition of treasury stock by donation may be reported on a corporation's books by a memorandum entry. Upon sale of

[8]*Accounting Trends & Techniques— 1990* (New York: American Institute of Certified Public Accountants, 1990), p. 201.

the donated stock, the entry would be recorded by a debit to Cash and a credit to a paid-in capital account.

## STOCK RIGHTS, WARRANTS, AND OPTIONS

A corporation may issue rights, warrants, or options that permit the purchase of the company's stock for a specified period (the **exercise period**) at a certain price (the **exercise price**). Although the terms *rights, warrants,* and *options* are sometimes used interchangeably, a distinction may be made as follows:

1. Stock rights—issued to existing shareholders to permit them to maintain their proportionate ownership interests when new shares are to be issued. (Some state laws require this preemptive right.)
2. Stock warrants—sold by the corporation for cash, generally in conjunction with another security.
3. Stock options—granted to officers or employees, sometimes as part of a compensation plan.

A company may offer rights, warrants, or options: (1) to raise additional capital, (2) to encourage the sale of a particular class of securities, or (3) as compensation for services received. The exercise period is generally longer for warrants and options than for rights. Warrants and rights may be traded independently among investors, whereas options generally are restricted to a particular person or specified group to whom the options are granted. The accounting considerations relating to stock rights, warrants, and options are described in the following sections.

### Stock Rights

When announcing rights to purchase additional shares of stock, the directors of a corporation specify a date on which the rights will be issued. All stockholders of record on the issue date are entitled to receive the rights. Thus, between the announcement date and the issue date, the stock is said to sell *rights-on.* After the rights are issued, the stock sells *ex-rights,* and the rights may be sold separately by those receiving them from the corporation. An expiration date is also designated when the rights are announced, and rights not exercised by this date are worthless.

**Accounting for Stock Rights by the Issuer**    When rights are issued to stockholders, only a memorandum entry is made on the issuing company's books stating the number of shares that may be claimed under the outstanding rights. This information is required so the corporation may retain sufficient unissued or reacquired stock to meet the exercise of the rights. Upon surrender of the rights and the receipt of payments as specified by the rights, the stock is issued. At this time, a memorandum entry is made to record the decrease in the number of rights outstanding accompanied by an entry to record the stock sale. The entry for the sale is recorded the same as any other issue of stock, with appropriate recognition of the cash received, the par or stated value of the stock issued, and any additional paid-in capital.

Information concerning outstanding rights should be reported with the corporation's balance sheet so that the effects of the future exercise of remaining rights may be determined.

**Accounting for Stock Rights by the Investor**    The receipt of stock rights by a stockholder is comparable to the receipt of a stock dividend (to be discussed fully in Chapter 18). The

## Stock Buybacks in the 1980s

The most significant trend in corporate capital structures during the 1980s was the increasing amount of debt and the decreasing amount of equity. In fact, the combination of takeovers and stock buybacks decreased the amount of New York Stock Exchange-traded stocks by an average of 6.5% per year from 1984 through 1989. This continued the trend of increasing debt ratios (total liabilities/total assets) in the post-World War II period.

Some of the buybacks announced were very large indeed. For example, in November 1989, General Electric announced its intention to spend $10 billion to buy back its own shares. This buyback announcement followed a decade in which GE had spent $19 billion making some significant acquisitions, including the high-profile purchase of RCA. The change in strategy came about because "we don't see value out there to make [further] acquisitions . . . the best bet is our own stock." GE claimed that 60% of the cash needed for the buyback would come from free cash flow (cash flow from operations less capital expenditures and dividend payments), with the rest coming from borrowing.

The most controversial buybacks of the 80s came in the wake of the 508-point stock market crash on October 19, 1987. According to an SEC study, after the crash, 645 companies announced open-market buyback plans totaling $77 billion. These buyback announcements were intended to inspire investor confidence and stop the slide in stock prices. Typical quotes from company executives were:

"It is an acknowledgement of confidence in our current and future value."
"It just underscores our financial stability and sends a signal that we believe in ourselves."

The controversy about these post-crash buyback announcements is that it subsequently became clear that at least some of the announcements had been made purely for their psychological effect and that the actual buybacks were not going to take place. One credit analyst characterized the buyback plans as representing "only a statement of faith, intended to bolster shareholder confidence, rather than a plan of action."

### Questions:

1. *When it announced its stock buyback program in November 1989, General Electric claimed that it would be able to implement the buybacks without raising its debt-to-equity ratio (total liabilities/total equity). Is this possible?*
2. *Many claim that a stock buyback will increase earnings per share. Do you agree?*

Sources:

Christopher Winans, "Stock Market Loses Vital Corporate Crutch," *The Wall Street Journal* (July 23, 1990), p. C1.

Amal Kumar Naj, "General Electric Buy-Back Plan Signals New Tack, Reflects Earnings Optimism," *The Wall Street Journal* (November 20, 1989), p. A3.

Jay Palmer, "Promises, Promises: Or What Happened to All Those Post-Crash Buybacks?" *Barron's* (April 25, 1988), p. 13.

corporation has made no asset distribution, and stockholders' equity remains unchanged. However, a stockholders' investment is now evidenced by shares of stock previously acquired and by rights that have a value of their own when they permit the purchase of shares at less than the market price. These circumstances call for an **allocation of cost** between the shares of stock and the rights. Since the shares and the rights have different values, an apportionment should be made in terms of the relative market values as of the date the rights are issued. Subsequently, the stock and the rights are accounted for separately. Accounting for stock rights by the shareholder is illustrated in the following example.

Assume that in 1992, Northern Supply Co. acquired 100 shares of Telstar Inc.'s common stock at $180 per share. In 1993, Telstar issues rights to purchase 1 share of common at $110 for every 5 shares owned. Northern thus receives 100 rights—1 right for each share owned. However, since 5 rights are required for the acquisition of a single share, the 100 rights enable Northern to subscribe for only 20 new shares. Northern's original investment cost of $18,000 now applies to 2 assets, the shares and the rights. This cost is apportioned on the basis of the relative market values of each security as of the date that the rights are issued to the stockholders.[9] The cost allocation may be expressed as follows:

$$\text{Cost assigned to rights} = \text{Original cost of stock} \times \frac{\text{Market value of rights}}{\text{Market value of stock ex-rights} + \text{Market value of rights}}$$

$$\text{Cost assigned to stock} = \text{Original cost of stock} \times \frac{\text{Market value of stock ex-rights}}{\text{Market value of stock ex-rights} + \text{Market value of rights}}$$

Assume that Telstar Inc.'s common stock is selling ex-rights at $129 per share, and rights are selling at $4 each. The cost allocation would be made as follows:

**To rights:**

$$\$18,000 \times \frac{\$4}{\$129 + \$4} = \$541 \text{ (rounded)}; \$541 \div 100 = \$5.41 \text{ cost per right}$$

**To stock:**

$$\$18,000 \times \frac{\$129}{\$129 + \$4} = \$17,459 \text{ (rounded)}; \$17,459 \div 100 = \$174.59 \text{ cost per share}$$

The following entry may be made to record the allocation:

| | | |
|---|---|---|
| Investment in Telstar Inc. Stock Rights | 541 | |
| Investment in Telstar Inc. Common Stock | | 541 |
| *Received 100 rights permitting the purchase of 20 shares at $110.* | | |

The cost apportioned to the rights is used in determining any gain or loss arising from the sale of rights. Assume that the rights in the preceding example are sold for $4.50 each. The following entry would be made:

| | | |
|---|---|---|
| Cash | 450 | |
| Loss on Sale of Telstar Inc. Stock Rights | 91 | |
| Investment in Telstar Inc. Stock Rights | | 541 |
| *Sold 100 rights at $4.50.* | | |

If the rights are exercised rather than sold, the cost of the new shares acquired consists of the cost assigned to the rights plus the cash that is paid on the exercise of rights. Assume that, instead of selling the rights, Northern Supply Co. exercises its rights to purchase 20 additional shares at $110. The following entry would be made:

---

[9] If the market value of the rights or of the stock is not readily determinable, the market value of the known quantity is used, and the residual purchase price is allocated to the security with the unknown market value.

|  |  |
|---|---|
| Investment in Telstar Inc. Common Stock........................ | 2,741 |
| Investment in Telstar Inc. Stock Rights........................ | 541 |
| Cash .................................................. | 2,200 |

*Exercised rights, acquiring 20 shares at $110.*

Upon exercising the rights, Northern's records show an investment balance of $20,200 consisting of two lots of stock as follows:

|  |  |
|---|---|
| Lot 1 (1992 acquisition) 100 shares: ($17,459 ÷ 100 = $174.59 cost per share, adjusted for stock rights)..................................... | $17,459 |
| Lot 2 (1993 acquisition) 20 shares: ($2,741 ÷ 20 = $137.05 cost per share, acquired through stock rights)............................... | 2,741 |
| Total ................................................. | $20,200 |

These costs provide the basis for calculating gain or loss on subsequent sale of the stock.

Frequently the receipt of rights includes 1 or more rights that cannot be used in the purchase of a whole share. For example, assume that the owner of 100 shares receives 100 rights; 6 rights are required for the purchase of 1 share. Here the holder uses 96 rights in purchasing 16 shares. Several alternatives are available to the holder: allow the remaining 4 rights to lapse; sell the rights and report a gain or a loss on such sale; or supplement the rights held by the purchase of 2 more rights making possible the purchase of an additional share of stock.

If the owner of valuable rights allows them to lapse, it would appear that the cost assigned to such rights should be written off as a loss. This can be supported on the theory that the issuance of stock by the corporation at less than current market price results in a dilution in the equities identified with original holdings. However, when changes in the market price of the stock make the exercise of rights unattractive to all investors and none of the rights can be sold, no dilution has occurred and any cost of rights reported separately should be returned to the investment account.

## Stock Warrants

As noted previously, warrants may be sold in conjunction with other securities as a "sweetener" to make the purchase of the securities more attractive. For example, warrants to purchase shares of a corporation's common stock may be issued with bonds to encourage investors to purchase the bonds. A warrant has value when the exercise price is less than the market value, either present or potential, of the security that can be purchased with the warrants. Warrants issued with other securities may be detachable or nondetachable. **Detachable warrants** are similar to stock rights because they can be traded separately from the security with which they were originally issued. **Nondetachable warrants** cannot be separated from the security they were issued with.

As described in Chapter 16, the Accounting Principles Board in Opinion No. 14 recommended assigning part of the issuance price of debt securities to any detachable stock warrants and classifying it as part of owners' equity.[10] The value assigned to the warrant is determined by a procedure similar to that described for stock rights and is expressed in the following equation:

$$\text{Value assigned to warrants} = \text{Total issue price} \times \frac{\text{Market value of warrant}}{\text{Market value of security without warrant} + \text{Market value of warrant}}$$

[10]*Opinions of the Accounting Principles Board No. 14,* "Accounting for Convertible Debt and Debt Issued with Stock Purchase Warrants" (New York: American Institute of Certified Public Accountants, 1969), par. 16.

Although Opinion No. 14 is directed only to warrants attached to debt, it appears logical to extend the conclusions of that Opinion to warrants attached to preferred stock. Thus, if a market value exists for the warrants at the issuance date, a separate equity account is credited with that portion of the issuance price assigned to the warrants. If the warrants are exercised, the value assigned to the common stock is the value allocated to the warrants plus the cash proceeds from the issuance of the common stock. If the warrants are allowed to expire, the value assigned to the warrants may be transferred to a permanent paid-in capital account.

Accounting for detachable warrants attached to a preferred stock issue is illustrated as follows. Assume the Stewart Co. sells 1,000 shares of $50 par preferred stock for $58 per share. As an incentive to purchase the stock, Stewart Co. gives the purchaser detachable warrants enabling holders to subscribe to 1,000 shares of $20 par common stock for $25 per share. The warrants expire after one year. Immediately following the issuance of the preferred stock, the warrants are selling at $3, and the fair market value of the preferred stock without the warrant attached is $57. The proceeds of $58,000 should be allocated by the Stewart Co. as follows:

$$\text{Value assigned to the warrants} = \$58,000 \times \frac{\$3}{\$57 + \$3} = \$2,900$$

A similar allocation would be made by the investor, and the warrants would subsequently be accounted for in the same manner as stock rights.

The entry on Stewart's books to record the sale of the preferred stock with detachable warrants is:

| | | |
|---|---|---|
| Cash ..................................................... | 58,000 | |
| Preferred Stock, $50 par..................................... | | 50,000 |
| Paid-In Capital in Excess of Par—Preferred Stock ............ | | 5,100 |
| Common Stock Warrants.................................... | | 2,900 |

If the warrants are exercised, the entry to record the issuance of common stock would be:

| | | |
|---|---|---|
| Common Stock Warrants ................................... | 2,900 | |
| Cash ..................................................... | 25,000 | |
| Common Stock, $20 par..................................... | | 20,000 |
| Paid-In Capital in Excess of Par—Common Stock ............ | | 7,900 |

This entry would be the same regardless of the market price of the common stock at the issuance date.

If the warrants in the example were allowed to expire, the following entry would be made:

| | | |
|---|---|---|
| Common Stock Warrants ................................... | 2,900 | |
| Paid-In Capital From Expired Warrants ..................... | | 2,900 |

If warrants are nondetachable, the securities are considered inseparable, and no allocation is made to recognize the value of the warrant. The entire proceeds are assigned to the security to which the warrant is attached. Thus, for nondetachable warrants, the accounting treatment is similar to that for convertible securities, such as convertible bonds. Some accountants feel this inconsistency is not justified, since the economic value of a warrant exists, even if the warrant cannot be traded separately or "detached." This is essentially the same argument made for recognizing the conversion feature of a convertible security. Notwithstanding this argument, a separate instrument does not exist for a nondetachable warrant, and current practice does not require a separate value to be assigned to these warrants.

## Stock Options Issued to Employees

Many corporations have adopted various types of stock option plans giving executives and other employees the opportunity to purchase stock in the employer company. Often these plans are intended as a form of compensation, especially when directed toward or restricted to key executives of a company. These plans are referred to as **compensatory plans**, as contrasted to **noncompensatory plans** that are offered to all full-time employees on an equal basis. Noncompensatory plans generally provide for the purchase of stock at a relatively small discount from the market price of the stock. For example, employees of IBM Corporation are allowed to purchase IBM stock at a 15% discount.

No special accounting problems arise for noncompensatory stock option plans. Stock issued upon the exercise of the options is recorded normally, as an increase in common or preferred stock including any applicable paid-in capital in excess of par or stated value. The issue price is the amount of cash received, i.e., the exercise price.

The major accounting questions associated with compensatory plans include:

1. What amount of compensation expense, if any, should be recognized?
2. When should the compensation expense be recognized, i.e., what period should be charged with the cost?
3. What information should be disclosed relative to stock option plans?

**Measuring Compensation Expense**    For a number of years, the accounting standard in this area has been APB Opinion No. 25, "Accounting for Stock Issued to Employees."[11] Even though APB Opinion No. 25 has been generally accepted for some time, its guidelines have been questioned, perhaps because of perceived inconsistencies in the treatment of various types of stock option plans. Consequently, this is a topic that has been on the FASB's agenda for some time. Even after several years of studying this complex issue, the FASB has been unable to agree on a conceptually valid and practical improvement to the current guidelines of APB Opinion No. 25. The FASB has now decided that the problems of measuring stock compensation cannot be separated from the broader problem of distinguishing between financial instruments that relate to liabilities and those that are a part of equity. Accordingly, the FASB will now consider accounting for stock compensation as a part of the broader agenda item to distinguish between debt and equity instruments.[12]

One of the key issues regarding compensatory stock option plans concerns an appropriate **measurement date**, i.e., the date on which the value of stock options should be determined. Several possibilities exist: (1) the date of adoption of a plan (**plan date**); (2) the date an option is granted to a specific individual grantee (**grant date**); (3) the date on which the grantee may first exercise an option (**exercisable date**); (4) the date the grantee actually exercises an option (**exercise date**); (5) the date the grantee disposes of the stock acquired (**disposal date**); or (6) when variable factors are involved, the date at which both the number of shares and the option price are first known. These dates are not necessarily mutually exclusive. In some cases, for example, the exercisable date may coincide with the exercise date.

The Accounting Principles Board defined the proper measurement date as the first date on which the following are both known: (1) the number of shares that an individual employee is entitled to receive, and (2) the option or exercise price, if any.[13] For "fixed

---

[11]*Opinions of the Accounting Principles Board No. 25,* "Accounting for Stock Issued to Employees" (New York: American Institute of Certified Public Accountants, 1972), par. 7.

[12]For a further discussion of the reexamination of the accounting for stock compensation plans, see Barry P. Robbins, "FASB's Long Look at Stock Compensation Plans," *Journal of Accountancy* (August 1988) p. 60.

[13]*Opinions of the Accounting Principles Board No. 25,* par. 10b.

plans," i.e., plans in which the number of shares and the exercise price are set at the date of grant, the measurement date is generally the date of grant. Plans with variable terms, however, normally use a later measurement date, often the exercisable or exercise date.

The amount of compensation expense to be recognized for a compensatory plan is the amount by which the market price of the stock at the measurement date exceeds the exercise price. Thus, an employer will recognize compensation expense only if the exercise price is less than the market price at the measurement date.

If compensation expense is to be recognized and the amount has been determined, the remaining accounting problem is determining when the compensation expense should be recognized. Generally, the compensation should be charged to the current and future periods in which the employees perform the services for which the options were granted. Past periods should not be adjusted. The grant may specify the period or periods during which the service is to be performed, or it may be inferred from the past patterns of grants or awards. When several periods of employment are involved before the stock is issued, the employer corporation should accrue compensation expense in each period involved. If the measurement date is later than the grant date, the compensation expense for each period prior to the measurement date must be estimated based on the quoted market price of the stock at the end of each period.[14]

As noted, the FASB is currently studying the issues surrounding accounting and reporting for stock option plans in the context of a broader financial reporting issue. As a result, accounting for these plans is in a state of uncertainty. This uncertainty is compounded by frequent changes in the tax laws, some of which make certain types of stock option plans less attractive as a form of compensation. At present, however, the accounting and reporting requirements for stock option plans are those in APB Opinion No. 25. These requirements are illustrated in the following sections. Fixed stock option plans are presented first, followed by variable plans.

**Recording Compensatory Stock Options—Fixed Plans**    To illustrate accounting for compensatory stock options under a fixed plan, assume that on December 31, 1990, the board of directors of the Neff Co. authorized the grant of stock options to supplement the salaries of certain executives. The options permit the purchase of 10,000 shares of $10 par common stock at a price of $47.50. The market price of the stock at the grant date was $50. Options can be exercised beginning January 1, 1993, but only by executives that are still in the employ of the company; the options expire at the end of 1994. All options are exercised on December 31, 1993, when the $10 par common stock is quoted on the market at $60.

In this example, as with most fixed plans, the measurement date is the date of grant, since both the number of shares to be received by employees and the exercise price are known on the grant date. The value of the stock options at the date of the grant (compensation expense) is determined as follows:

| | |
|---|---:|
| Market value of common stock on December 31, 1990, 10,000 shares at $50 | $500,000 |
| Option price, 10,000 shares at $47.50 | 475,000 |
| Value of stock options (compensation expense) | $ 25,000 |

The terms of the grant indicate that the options relate to services to be performed for the period from the grant date to the exercisable date, or for 1991 and 1992.

The following entries are made by the corporation to record the grant of the options, the annual accrual of option rights, and the exercise of the options.

[14]*Ibid.*, par. 13.

| Transaction | Entry |
| --- | --- |
| **December 31, 1990**<br>Grant of compensatory stock options. | (Memorandum entry) Granted options to executives for the purchase of 10,000 shares of common stock at $47.50. Options are exercisable beginning January 1, 1993, providing officers are in the employ of the company on that date. Options expire on December 31, 1994. Value of options on December 31, 1990, is $25,000 (market value of stock, $500,000; option price, $475,000). |
| **December 31, 1991**<br>To record compensation and stock option credit accrual for 1991. Value of stock options, $25,000; period of service covered by plan, 1991 and 1992; cost assigned to 1991: ½ × $25,000 = $12,500. | Executive Compensation Expense 12,500<br>   Credit Under Stock Option Plan          12,500 |
| **December 31, 1992**<br>To record compensation and stock option credit accrual for 1992: ½ × $25,000 = $12,500. | Executive Compensation Expense 12,500<br>   Credit Under Stock Option Plan          12,500 |
| **December 31, 1993**<br>To record exercise of stock options: cash received for stock, 10,000 shares at $47.50, or $475,000; par value of stock issued, 10,000 shares at $10, or $100,000. | Cash ......................... 475,000<br>Credit Under Stock Option Plan .. 25,000<br>   Common Stock ..............   100,000<br>   Paid-In Capital in Excess of Par   400,000 |

The accrued compensation reported in Credit Under Stock Option Plan is properly reported as a part of paid-in capital, because it represents investments of services made by employees that are expected to be paid for by the issuance of capital stock at a reduced price. If options expire through a failure of employees to meet the conditions of the option or through changes in the price of the stock making exercise of options unattractive, the balance of the account should be eliminated by decreasing compensation expense in the period of forfeiture.[15]

**Recording Compensatory Stock Options—Variable Plans**    As noted previously, stock option plans with variable terms generally use the exercisable or exercise date as the measurement date instead of the grant date, since this is usually the earliest date that both the number of shares and the option price can be determined. This presents a problem in recording the compensation expense during the period between the grant date and the exercise date. FASB Interpretation No. 28 addressed this problem and requires the accrual of compensation expense for variable plans in the appropriate service periods.[16] The Interpretation indicates that changes in the market value, either up or down, between the grant date and the measurement date result in a change in the measurement of compensation associated with the options. If a quoted market price is not available, the best estimate of the market value should be used. A catch-up adjustment for the changes in values is to be reflected in the period when the change occurs and the new balance spread over current and future periods.

To illustrate, if the grant provisions offered by Neff Co. were variable and the measurement date occurred after the grant date, different entries would be required than those shown above. Assume that on December 31, 1990, the executives of Neff Co. are given the right to purchase 10,000 shares of $10 par stock at 80% of the market price on

[15]*Ibid.*, par. 15.

[16]*FASB Interpretation No. 28,* "Accounting for Stock Appreciation Rights and Other Variable Stock Option or Award Plans" (Stamford: Financial Accounting Standards Board, 1978).

December 31, 1992, two years after the grant date. December 31, 1992, is the measurement date in this case, since it is the earliest date that the option price is known. To be eligible for the stock, the executives must remain with the company until the exercisable date, December 31, 1993. The market price for the stock is as follows: December 31, 1990, date of grant, $50; December 31, 1991, end of first year of service period, $60; December 31, 1992, end of second year of service period, $65; and December 31, 1993, exercise date, $80.

The following entries and computations would be made to record the annual accruals of option rights and the exercise of the options for the variable stock option plan.

| Transaction | Entry | | |
|---|---|---|---|
| **December 31, 1991** | | | |
| To record estimate of compensation expense accrual for 1991: market price of stock, December 31, 1991, $60; estimated option price, 80% of $60, or $48; estimated value of option per share, $12 ($60 − $48); total compensation, $120,000 ($12 × 10,000). Period of services rendered, three years or $40,000 each year. | Executive Compensation Expense<br>    Credit Under Stock Option Plan | 40,000 | 40,000 |
| **December 31, 1992** | | | |
| To record estimate of compensation expense accrual for 1992: market price of stock, December 31, 1992, $65; estimated option price, 80% of $65, or $52; estimated value of option per share, $13 ($65 − $52); total compensation, $130,000 ($13 × 10,000). Compensation recognized 1991, $40,000. Compensation as adjusted for changes in market values, to be recognized in 1991, $46,667 = ($130,000 ÷ 3 = $43,333) plus $3,334 catch-up from 1991. | Executive Compensation Expense<br>    Credit Under Stock Option Plan | 46,667 | 46,667 |
| **December 31, 1993** | | | |
| To record compensation expense for 1993, as adjusted, and issuance of stock. (See computations.) | Executive Compensation Expense<br>    Credit Under Stock Option Plan | 43,333 | 43,333 |
| | Cash . . . . . . . . . . . . . . . . . . . . . . . .<br>Credit Under Stock Option Plan . . | 520,000<br>130,000 | |
| | Common Stock . . . . . . . . . . . . . . .<br>Paid-In Capital in Excess of Par | | 100,000<br>550,000 |

*Computations:*

| Date | Market Price | Per Share | Compensation Aggregate | Percentage Accrued | Accrued to Date | Accrual of Expense by Year 1991 | 1992 | 1993 |
|---|---|---|---|---|---|---|---|---|
| 12/31/91 | $60 | $12 | $120,000 | 33⅓% | $ 40,000 | $40,000 | | |
| | | | | | 46,667 | | $46,667 | |
| 12/31/92 | $65* | $13 | $130,000 | 66⅔% | $ 86,667 | | | |
| | | | | | 43,333 | | | $43,333 |
| 12/31/93 | $65* | $13 | $130,000 | 100% | $130,000 | | | |

*Measurement date value

It should be noted in the example that the compensation expense accrual of $46,667 recognizes the "catch-up" adjustment for changes in market value in 1992, which is in accordance with Interpretation No. 28. Recall that changes in accounting estimates are generally reflected in the current period or "spread" over current and future periods and that no cumulative effect or "catch-up" adjustment is required per APB Opinion No. 20. If the $10,000 change in estimate in the example had been spread only over the current and future periods, the compensation expense entry for 1992 and 1993 would have been $45,000 in each year ($130,000 − $40,000 = $90,000; $90,000 ÷ 2 = $45,000). Because the example deals with a variable stock option plan and falls specifically under Interpretation No. 28, a catch-up adjustment must be made to the current period, that is, in the period when the change was first determined.

**Stock Appreciation Rights**    One type of variable stock option plan is the granting of stock appreciation rights (SARs). Instead of giving the employee the option to purchase shares at a specified price, SARs award the employee the market value of shares in excess of a specified price.  For example, a SARs plan might award an employee cash or stock equal in value to the excess of the market price of the stock over, say, $35 on December 31, 1992.  If the plan granted the employee 100 SARs and the price of the stock on December 31, 1992, were $42, the employee would receive $700.  The advantage of a SARs plan is that, unlike the exercise of regular stock options, no cash outlay is required by the employee.  SARs are accounted for in the same way as other variable stock option plans.

## Disclosure of Stock Options

When stock option plans are in existence, disclosure should be made as to the status of the option or plan at the end of the reporting period, including the number of shares under option, the option (exercise) price, and the number of shares that were exercisable. Information on options exercised should also be provided, including the number of options exercised and the option price. The notes to the financial statements of IBM Corporation, presented in Appendix A at the end of the book, provide an illustration of disclosures for stock options.

## STOCK CONVERSIONS

As noted earlier, stockholders may be permitted by the terms of their stock agreement or by special action of the corporation to exchange their holdings for stock of other classes. No gain or loss is recognized by the issuer on these conversions, because it is an exchange of one form of equity for another. In certain instances, the exchanges may affect only corporate contributed capital accounts; in other instances, the exchanges may affect both capital and retained earnings accounts.

To illustrate the different conditions, assume that the capital of the Sorensen Corporation on December 31, 1993, is as follows:

| | |
|---|---|
| Preferred stock, $100 par, 10,000 shares | $1,000,000 |
| Paid-in capital in excess of par | 100,000 |
| Common stock, $25 stated value, 100,000 shares | 2,500,000 |
| Paid-in capital in excess of stated value | 500,000 |
| Retained earnings | 1,000,000 |

Preferred shares are convertible into common shares at any time at the option of the shareholder.

### Case 1    Converting One Share of Preferred for Four Shares of Common

Assume the terms of conversion permit the exchange of one share of preferred for four shares of common. On December 31, 1993, 1,000 shares of preferred stock are exchanged for 4,000 shares of common. The amount originally paid for the preferred, $110,000, is now the consideration identified with 4,000 shares of common stock with a total stated value of $100,000. The conversion is recorded by the issuer as follows:

| | | |
|---|---:|---:|
| Preferred Stock, $100 par | 100,000 | |
| Paid-In Capital in Excess of Par | 10,000 | |
|     Common Stock, $25 Stated Value | | 100,000 |
|     Paid-In Capital in Excess of Stated Value | | 10,000 |

### Case 2    Converting One Share of Preferred for Five Shares of Common

Assume terms of conversion permit the exchange of one share of preferred for five shares of common. In converting 1,000 shares of preferred for 5,000 shares of common, an increase in common stock of $125,000 must be recognized, although it is accompanied by a decrease in the preferred equity of only $110,000. The increase in the legal capital related to the issue of common stock is generally accomplished by a debit to Retained Earnings. The conversion on Sorensen's books, then, is recorded as follows:

| | | |
|---|---:|---:|
| Preferred Stock, $100 par | 100,000 | |
| Paid-In Capital in Excess of Par | 10,000 | |
| Retained Earnings | 15,000 | |
|     Common Stock, $25 stated value | | 125,000 |

On the investor's books at the conversion date, an entry would be required to eliminate the cost of the investment in preferred stock and to establish the investment in common stock of Sorensen Corporation. The accounting issue here is similar to the one discussed for convertible bonds. That is, should a gain or loss be recognized on the conversion? If the transaction is viewed as a continuation of the previous investment, then it would be appropriate to record the investment in common stock at the same cost as the preferred stock investment. Since no additional cost has been incurred, this approach is consistent with the cost basis of accounting. Using Case 1 as an example, the entry on the investor's books would be:

| | | |
|---|---:|---:|
| Investment in Sorensen Corp. Common Stock | 110,000 | |
|     Investment in Sorensen Corp. Preferred Stock | | 110,000 |

If, on the other hand, the transaction is viewed as a culminating event and if the market value of the common stock is known, then it would be appropriate to record the investment in the common stock at its current market price and recognize a gain or loss on the conversion. The gain or loss is the difference between the current market price of the common stock and the investment cost of the preferred stock. Assuming, for example, the situation for Case 2 and an objective market price of $24 per share for Sorensen Corp.'s common stock at the conversion date, the entry on the investor's books would be:

| | | |
|---|---:|---:|
| Investment in Sorensen Corp. Common Stock | 120,000 | |
|     Investment in Sorensen Corp. Preferred Stock | | 110,000 |
|     Gain on Conversion | | 10,000 |

The problems relating to the conversion of bonds for capital stock were described in Chapter 16. When either stocks or bonds have conversion rights, the company must be in a position to issue securities of the required class. Unissued or reacquired securities may be maintained by the company for this purpose. Detailed information should be given on the balance sheet or in notes to the financial statements relative to security conversion features as well as the means for meeting conversion requirements.

## STOCK SPLITS AND REVERSE STOCK SPLITS

When the market price of shares is relatively high and it is felt that a lower price will result in more active trading and a wider distribution of ownership, a corporation may authorize the shares outstanding to be replaced by a larger number of shares. For example, 100,000 shares of stock, par value $100, are exchanged for 500,000 shares of stock, par value $20. Each stockholder receives 5 new shares for each share owned. The increase in shares outstanding in this manner is known as a **stock split**. The reverse procedure, replacement of shares outstanding by a smaller number of shares, may be desirable when the price of shares is low and it is felt there may be certain advantages in having a higher price for shares. The reduction of shares outstanding by combining shares is referred to as a **reverse stock split**.

After a stock split or reverse stock split, the capital stock balance for the issue remains the same; however, the change in the number of shares of stock outstanding is accompanied by a change in the par or stated value of the stock. Similarly, the amount of recorded investment for the investor remains the same, but the number of shares and cost per share will be adjusted. The change in the number of shares outstanding, as well as the change in the par or stated value, may be recorded by means of a memorandum entry.

Stock splits are sometimes effected by issuing a large stock dividend. In this case, the par value of the stock is not changed, and an amount equal to the par value of the newly issued shares is transferred to the capital stock account from either additional paid-in capital or from retained earnings. A further discussion of this type of stock split is included in Chapter 18.

## BALANCE SHEET DISCLOSURE OF CONTRIBUTED CAPITAL

Contributed capital and its components should be disclosed separately from Retained Earnings in the balance sheet. Within the contributed capital section, it is important to identify the major classes of stock and the additional paid-in capital. Although it is common practice to report a single amount for additional paid-in capital, separate accounts should be provided in the ledger to identify the individual sources of additional paid-in capital, e.g., paid-in capital in excess of par or stated value, paid-in capital from treasury stock, from forfeited stock subscriptions, or from donations by stockholders.

For each class of stock, a description of the major features should be disclosed, such as par or stated value, dividend preference, or conversion terms. The number of shares authorized, issued, and outstanding should also be disclosed. As an example, the stockholders' equity section and related notes for The New York Times Company is presented on page 653. The balance sheet and accompanying notes for IBM Corporation in Appendix A also illustrate many of these points.

**Exhibit 17—1    The New York Times Company—Reporting Stockholders' Equity**

## THE NEW YORK TIMES COMPANY

|  | 1989 | 1988 |
|---|---|---|
|  | ($000) |  |
| **STOCKHOLDERS' EQUITY** |  |  |
| 5½% Cumulative prior preference stock of $100 par value— authorized 110,000 shares; outstanding: 1989, 26,507 shares; 1988, 26,517 shares | $     2,651 | $    2,652 |
| Serial preferred stock of $1 par value—authorized 200,000 shares—none issued | — | — |
| Common stock of $.10 par value |  |  |
| Class A—authorized 95,000,000 shares; issued: 1989, 87,367,218 shares; 1988, 87,170,818 shares (including treasury shares: 1989, 9,736,233; 1988, 8,364,792) | 8,737 | 8,717 |
| Class B, convertible—authorized 600,000 shares; issued: 1989 and 1988, 581,319 shares (including treasury shares: 1989 and 1988, 139,943) | 58 | 58 |
| Additional capital | 173,230 | 156,050 |
| Earnings reinvested in the business | 1,133,705 | 902,493 |
| Common stock held in treasury, at cost | (251,284) | (194,381) |
| Total stockholders' equity | 1,067,097 | 875,589 |

### *NOTES TO CONSOLIDATED FINANCIAL STATEMENTS*

*12 (In Part): Capital Stock*

The 5½ percent cumulative prior preference stock, which is redeemable at the option of the Company on 30-day's notice at par plus accrued dividends, is entitled to an annual dividend of $5.50 payable quarterly.

The serial preferred stock is subordinate to the 5½ percent cumulative prior preference stock. The Board of Directors is authorized to set the distinguishing characteristics of each series prior to issuance, including the granting of limited or full voting rights; however, the consideration received must be at least $100 per share. No shares of serial preferred stock have been issued.

The Class A and Class B Common Stock are entitled to equal participation in the event of liquidation and in dividend declarations. The Class B Common Stock is convertible at the holders' option on a share-for-share basis into Class A shares. As provided for in the certificate of incorporation, the Class A Common Stock has limited voting rights, including the right to elect 30 percent of the Board of Directors, and the Class A and Class B Common Stock have the right to vote together on reservations of Company stock for stock options, on the ratification of the selection of independent certified public accountants and, in certain circumstances, on acquisitions of the stock or assets of other companies. Otherwise, except as provided by the laws of the State of New York, all voting power is vested solely and exclusively in the holders of the Class B Common Stock.

During 1989 and 1988 the Company repurchased approximately 2,200,000 and 4,200,000 shares of its Class A Common Stock, respectively, at average prices of $28.08 per share in 1989 and $26.99 per share in 1988. In December 1989 the Company announced a continuation of its stock repurchase program up to an additional $50 million.

---

## KEY TERMS

| | | |
|---|---|---|
| Business combination 635 | Owners' equity 624 | Reverse stock split 652 |
| Common stock 625 | Par value 626 | Stated value 627 |
| Compensatory plans 646 | Participating preferred stock 628 | Stock appreciation rights (SARs) |
| Contributed (paid-in) capital 624 | Partnership 624 | 650 |
| Corporation 624 | Pooling of interests 635 | Stock options 641 |
| Cumulative preferred stock 628 | Preferred stock 625 | Stock rights 641 |
| Dividends in arrears 628 | Proprietorship 624 | Stock split 652 |
| Legal capital 626 | Purchase 635 | Stock warrants 641 |
| Noncompensatory plans 646 | Redeemable preferred stock 629 | Treasury stock 637 |
| Noncumulative preferred stock 628 | Retained earnings 624 | |

---

## QUESTIONS

1. What are the basic rights inherent in the ownership of capital stock? What modifications of these basic rights are usually found in preferred stock?
2. What are the two major classifications of contributed capital?
3. Distinguish between cumulative preferred stock and noncumulative preferred stock. If a company with cumulative preferred stock outstanding fails to declare dividends during the year, what disclosure should be made in the financial statements?
4. What is callable preferred stock? Redeemable preferred stock? Convertible preferred stock?
5. The Merrill Co. treats proceeds from capital stock subscription defaults as miscellaneous revenue. (a) Do you approve of this practice? Explain. (b) What alternatives would the Merrill Co. have when dealing with subscription defaults? (c) What limits the choice among the alternatives in (b)?
6. Explain the accounting principle followed in recording the issuance of capital stock in exchange for nonmonetary assets or services.
7. Why might a company purchase its own stock?
8. The Daytime Co. reports treasury stock as a current asset, explaining that it intends to sell the stock soon to acquire working capital. Do you approve of this reporting?
9. (a) What is the basic difference between the cost method and the par value method of accounting for treasury stock? (b) How will total stockholders' equity differ, if at all, under the two methods?
10. There is frequently a difference between the purchase price and the selling price of treasury stock. Why isn't this difference properly shown as an income statement item, especially in view of accounting pronouncements that restrict entries to Retained Earnings?
11. (a) What entries should be made on both the issuer's books and the investor's books when stock rights are issued to stockholders? (b) What entries should be made by both issuer and investor when stock is issued on the exercise of rights? (c) What information, if any, should appear on the company's balance sheet relative to outstanding rights?
12. Distinguish between a compensatory stock option plan and a noncompensatory stock option plan.
13. What determines the measurement date for purposes of a stock option plan valuation?
14. Preferred stockholders of the Lexus Corporation exchange their holdings for no-par common stock in accordance with terms of the preferred stock issue. How should this conversion be reported on the corporation books?
15. The controller of Williams Company contends that the redemption of preferred stock at less than its issuance price should be reported as an increase in Retained Earnings, since redemption at more than issuance price calls for a decrease in Retained Earnings. How would you answer the controller's argument?
16. Define a stock split and identify the major objectives of this corporate action.

---

## DISCUSSION CASES

### Case 17—1    (Should par value be used to determine the amount of contributed capital?)

The Raton Company, in payment for services, issues 5,000 shares of common stock to persons organizing and promoting the company and another 20,000 shares in exchange for properties believed to have valuable mineral rights. The par value of the stock, $10 per share, is used in recording the consideration for the shares. Shortly after organization, the company decides to sell the properties and use the proceeds for another venture. The properties are sold for $265,000. What accounting issues are involved? How would you record the sale of properties and why?

### Case 17—2  (Is the sum of the parts worth more than the whole?)

In 1988, four companies offered investors the opportunity to purchase new securities called "unbundled stock units." These companies (American Express, Dow Chemical, Pfizer, and Sara Lee) argued that the common stock security is undervalued when sold as a single unit. So they proposed to "unbundle" the value represented by common stock and sell three new securities as an alternative to the common stock certificate. The new security package would contain a 30-year bond paying interest at the stock's current dividend rate; a preferred stock that initially would pay no dividends but would match any dividend increases on the company's common stock over the next 30 years; and a security closely resembling a stock warrant that would allow investors to profit from stock appreciation. In effect, the three new securities would provide a package allowing investors to profit explicitly in the same way that common stockholders do with a single security, i.e., from dividends, from dividend increases, and from capital appreciation in the value of common stock. What these companies were counting on is that the value of the three securities would be worth more to investors than common stock sold as a single security.

Why might investors be willing to pay a premium for such a package, i.e., pay more for the three securities than for the single common stock security? What disadvantages can you see for investors in exchanging their common stock for the unbundled stock units?

Source: "Package Deal," *The Wall Street Journal*, December 6, 1988.

### Case 17—3  (Giving something for nothing)

Excerpts from an article appearing in *The Wall Street Journal* are presented as follows:

---

**Dividend News**

**IBM Holders Vote
4-for-1 Stock Split,
Effective May 10**

By a Staff Reporter for *The Wall Street Journal*

SAN DIEGO—International Business Machines Corp. shareholders, as expected, authorized a 4-for-1 split of the company's stock, effective May 10.

At a quiet annual meeting attended by an estimated 1,400 of the computer giant's more than 600,000 shareholders, the split was opposed by less than 1% of the votes cast.

The split, which is expected to make IBM's shares more attractive to small investors, will increase the number of authorized shares to 650 million from 162.5 million. About 583 million shares are expected to be outstanding after the split.

IBM has made numerous stock distributions in recent years so that 100 shares from 1958 ballooned to 1,135 shares at the annual meeting, but the forthcoming split is the first distribution since 1958 that will result in a change in the par value of IBM's shares. The par value will be reduced to $1.25 a share, from $5.00.

Regarding the mechanics of the split, IBM said that current stock certificates will remain in effect. Each shareholder of record May 10 will receive new certificates representing three shares for each held. The new certificates will be mailed around May 31.

---

Source: *The Wall Street Journal*, May 1, 1979, p. 20.

Why did IBM propose the 4-for-1 stock split, and why were the stockholders not opposed to the split? What will the impact be on the owners' equity section of IBM's balance sheet?

### Case 17—4 (Conversion of preferred stock)

Colter Corporation suspended dividend payments on all four classes of capital stock outstanding because of a downturn in the economy. The four classes of stock include: 7% preferred stock, cumulative, $50 par; 5% preferred stock, noncumulative, convertible, $35 par; 9% preferred stock, noncumulative, $80 par; and common stock. Fifteen thousand shares of each class of stock were outstanding. Dividends had been paid through 1990. Colter did not pay dividends in 1991 or 1992. In 1993, the economy improved and a proposal to pay a dividend of $1.50 per share of common stock was made.

You own 100 shares of the 5%, noncumulative, convertible preferred stock and have been thinking of converting those 100 shares to common stock at the existing conversion rate of 3 to 1 (3 shares of common for 1 share of preferred). The rate is scheduled to drop to 2 to 1 at the end of 1993. Because the price of common stock has been rising rapidly, you are trying to decide between retaining your preferred stock or converting to common stock before the price goes higher and the ratio is lowered.

Assuming there is no conversion of preferred stock, how much cash does Colter need to pay the proposed dividend? What are the merits of converting your stock at this time as opposed to waiting until after the dividend is paid and the conversion ratio decreases? Explain the issues involved.

### Case 17—5 (Which kind of bonus would you prefer?)

Many companies have incentive compensation plans whereby executives receive bonuses based on the reported net income of the company. Another kind of incentive plan gives executives options on the company's stock. What are the advantages and disadvantages of an income-based incentive plan? of a stock option plan?

### Case 17—6 (What is a stock warrant worth?)

A stock warrant entitles the owner to buy a specified number of shares of stock at a specified price. Suppose that a certain stock warrant entitled the owner to buy one share of common stock for $50, while the current market price of a share of common stock is $40. Does the warrant have any value? What factors would influence the value of the warrant?

### Case 17—7 (Treasury stock transactions—You can't lose!)

The following is adapted from an article appearing in *Forbes*:

> The board of Hospital Corp. of America authorized the buyback of 12 million of the firm's own shares at a total cost of $564 million. However, after the stock market crash of 1987, HCA's shares were trading at only 31⅛. So, HCA was now out $190.5 million on its investment— right? Common sense would answer yes, but beyond common sense lurks the logic of accounting. According to generally accepted accounting principles, HCA didn't lose a penny on the buyback. Call it a no-risk investment. In this era of stock market volatility, stock buybacks offer firms the opportunity to tell shareholders that they have a terrific investment—without ever having to own up to the bad news if it turns sour.

Consider the criticism in the paragraph above and evaluate the reasonableness of the accounting for treasury stock transactions.

Source: Penelope Wang, "Losses? What Losses?" *Forbes* (February 8, 1988), p. 118.

### Case 17—8 (Fiat's treatment of treasury stock)

The Fiat Group is the largest investor-owned industrial group in Italy. In 1989, Fiat's revenues constituted 3.7% of Italy's gross national product, and Fiat's research and development expenditures were 11.8% of the total R&D in Italy. Fiat is known in the United States primarily for its Fiat, Ferrari, and Alfa Romeo automobiles.

A condensed version of Fiat's 1989 balance sheet is shown at the top of page 706. All amounts are in billions of lire. On December 31, 1989, lire were trading at 1,267 per 1 U.S. dollar.

ASSETS
| | |
|---|---|
| Treasury stock | 321 |
| Other assets | 63,890 |

LIABILITIES AND STOCKHOLDERS' EQUITY
| | |
|---|---|
| Total liabilities | 45,229 |
| Minority interest in consolidated subsidiaries | 3,021 |
| Stockholders' equity | 15,961 |

Note 2 to the financial statements reads as follows (in part): "Treasury stock is accounted for at purchase cost. Repurchased stock is classified as an asset, since it represents an investment of liquidity by Fiat." Explain how Fiat's treatment of treasury stock differs from the treatment prescribed by U.S. generally accepted accounting principles (GAAP). Prepare a restated balance sheet (in lire) for Fiat that conforms with U.S. GAAP.

### Case 17—9    (Debt-to-equity ratio and mandatory redeemable preferred stock)

Below is a summary of the liability and equity section of the balance sheet of The Circle K Corporation as of April 30, 1989. The amounts are in thousands.

| | |
|---|---|
| Current liabilities | $ 350,445 |
| Long-term debt | 1,103,762 |
| Deferred income taxes | 93,045 |
| Other liabilities | 119,792 |
| Mandatory redeemable preferred stock | 47,500 |
| Stockholders' equity | 330,396 |

In the Management Discussion and Analysis portion of the annual report, Circle K reports a "debt-to-equity ratio" of 3.34. Show how Circle K computed this "debt-to-equity ratio." What might be a better name for the ratio? Mandatory redeemable preferred stock is preferred stock that must be redeemed by the issuing firm. What aspects of mandatory redeemable preferred stock are like debt? like equity?

### Case 17—10    (Equity section for Grand Metropolitan)

Grand Metropolitan PLC is based in the United Kingdom. It sells food and dairy products and also operates 1,500 pubs and 450 restaurants in the United Kingdom and Ireland. Grand Metropolitan is best known in the United States for its pet foods (ALPO), its wines and spirits (Smirnoff Vodka, Lancers, Cinzano), and its eyecare products (Pearle Vision).

The equity section from Grand Metropolitan's September 30, 1988, balance sheet is given below. All amounts are in millions of pounds.

| | |
|---|---|
| Called-up share capital | 442.5 |
| Share premium account | 7.2 |
| Revaluation and special reserves | 930.4 |
| Related companies' reserves | 16.4 |
| Profit and loss account | 2,010.2 |
| Minority shareholders' interests | 31.4 |

The revaluation and special reserves account included, among other things, the following items:

(a) Goodwill acquired, (143.7) million pounds.
(b) Surplus on revaluation of property, 643.1 million pounds. This amount resulted from writing up assets to their estimated market values.
(c) Capitalization of brand names, 630.0 million pounds. This amount resulted from recording as an asset the estimated value of brand names.

Refer to Grand Metropolitan's equity section and identify the comparable item to the following: common stock at par, additional paid-in capital, and retained earnings. Of the three items listed as appearing in the revaluation and special reserves section, which, if any, would be acceptable under U.S. accounting principles?

---

# EXERCISES

## Exercise 17—1  (Issuance of common stock)

The Verdero Company is authorized to issue 100,000 shares of $30 par value common stock. Verdero has the following transactions:

(a)  Issued 20,000 shares at par value; received cash.
(b)  Issued 250 shares to attorneys for services in securing the corporate charter and for preliminary legal costs of organizing the corporation. The value of the services was $9,000.
(c)  Issued 300 shares, valued objectively at $10,000, to the corporate promoters.
(d)  Issued 12,500 shares of stock in exchange for buildings valued at $295,000 and land valued at $80,000. (The building was originally acquired by the investor for $250,000 and has $100,000 of accumulated depreciation; the land was acquired for $30,000.)
(e)  Received cash for 6,500 shares of stock sold at $38 per share.
(f)  Issued 8,000 shares at $45 per share; received cash.

1.  Record the above transactions in journal entry form for Verdero Company.
2.  Record the above transactions in journal entry form for the investors.

## Exercise 17—2  (Par and stated values)

At the time of formation, the Buck Corporation was authorized to issue 100,000 shares of common stock. Buck later received cash from the issuance of 25,000 shares at $24.50 per share. Record the entries for the issuance of the common stock under each of the following independent assumptions.

(a)  Stock has a par value of $22 per share.
(b)  Stock has a stated value of $20 per share.
(c)  Stock has no par or stated value.

## Exercise 17—3  (Dividends per share; cumulative and noncumulative features)

The Anderson Company paid dividends at the end of each year as follows: 1991, $150,000; 1992, $240,000; 1993, $560,000. Determine the amount of dividends per share paid on common and preferred stock for each year, assuming independent capital structures as follows:

(a)  300,000 shares of no-par common; 10,000 shares of $100 par, 9% noncumulative preferred.
(b)  250,000 shares of no-par common; 20,000 shares of $100 par, 9% noncumulative preferred.
(c)  250,000 shares of no-par common; 20,000 shares of $100 par, 9% cumulative preferred.
(d)  250,000 shares of $10 par common; 30,000 shares of $100 par, 9% cumulative preferred.

## Exercise 17—4  (Dividends—different classes of stock)

Blank Page Inc. began operations on June 30, 1991, and issued 40,000 shares of $10 par common stock on that date. On December 31, 1991, Blank Page declared and paid $25,600 in dividends. After a vote of the board of directors, Blank Page issued 24,000 shares of 6% cumulative, $12 par, preferred stock on January 1, 1993. On December 31, 1993, Blank Page declared and paid $15,500 in dividends and again on December 31, 1994, Blank Page declared and paid $28,660 in dividends. Determine the amount of dividends to be distributed to each class of stock for each of Blank Page's dividend payments.

### Exercise 17—5　(Computing liquidation amounts)

The stockholders' equity for the Baum Company on July 1, 1993, is given below.

Contributed capital:

| | |
|---|---:|
| Preferred stock, cumulative, $10 stated value, 37,000 shares outstanding, entitled upon involuntary liquidation to $12 per share plus dividends in arrears amounting to $4 per share on July 1, 1993 . . . . . . | $370,000 |
| Common stock, $2 stated value, 90,000 shares outstanding . . . . . . . . | 180,000 |
| Paid-in capital from sale of common stock at more than stated value | 200,000 |
| Retained earnings . . . . . . . . . . . . . . . . . . . . . . . . . . . . . . . . . . . . . . . . . . . . . . . | 56,000 |
| Total stockholders' equity . . . . . . . . . . . . . . . . . . . . . . . . . . . . . . . . . . . . | $806,000 |

Determine the amounts that would be paid to each class of stockholders if the company is liquidated on this date, assuming cash available for stockholders after meeting all of the creditors' claims is (a) $300,000; (b) $500,000; (c) $640,000. *444,000*

*148,000.*

### Exercise 17—6　(Issuance of capital stock)

The Mountain View Company was incorporated on January 1, 1993, with the following authorized capitalization:

20,000 shares of common stock, stated value $50 per share. *1,000,000*

5,000 shares of 7% cumulative preferred stock, par value $15 per share. *75,000*

*5250*

Give the entries required for each of the following transactions:

(a) Issued 12,000 shares of common stock for a total of $672,000 and 3,000 shares of preferred stock at $20 per share.

(b) Subscriptions were received for 2,500 shares of common stock at a price of $52. A 30% down payment is received.

(c) One subscriber defaults for 300 shares of common, and the down payment is retained pending sale of these shares.  *15,600.*

(d) The 300 shares of common are sold at $51 per share. Loss on resale is charged against the account of the defaulting subscriber, and the down payment less the loss is returned to the subscriber.

(e) Collected the remaining amount owed on the stock subscriptions and issued the stock.

(f) The remaining authorized shares of common stock are sold at $57.50 per share.

### Exercise 17—7　(Accounting for defaulted subscriptions)

On January 1, 1993, Leslie Corporation received authorization to issue 200,000 shares of common stock with a par value of $22 per share. The stock was offered at a subscription price of $40 per share, and subscriptions were received for 20,000 shares. Subscriptions were recorded by a debit to Common Stock Subscriptions Receivable and credits to Common Stock Subscribed and to a paid-in capital account. Subsequently, a subscriber who had contracted to purchase 1,500 shares defaulted after paying 40% of the subscription price. Identify four methods of accounting for the default, and give the journal entry to record the default under each method.

### Exercise 17—8　(Acquisition and retirement of stock)

The Steinbeck Company reported the following balances related to common stock as of December 31, 1992:

| | |
|---|---:|
| Common stock, $20 par, 100,000 shares issued and outstanding . . . . . | $2,000,000 |
| Paid-in capital in excess of par . . . . . . . . . . . . . . . . . . . . . . . . . . . . . . . . . . . | 100,000 |

The company purchased and immediately retired 5,000 shares at $26 on August 1, 1993, and 12,000 shares at $18 on December 31, 1993. Give the entries to record the acquisition and retirement of the common stock. (Assume all shares were originally sold at the same price.)

## Exercise 17—9  (Treasury stock: par value and cost methods)

The stockholders' equity of the Thomas Company as of December 31, 1992, was as follows:

> Common stock, $15 par, authorized 275,000 shares; 240,000 shares
> issued and outstanding ......................................... $3,600,000
> Paid-in capital in excess of par.................................. 480,000
> Retained earnings ............................................. 900,000

On June 1, 1993, Thomas reacquired 15,000 shares of its common stock at $16. The following transactions occurred in 1993 with regard to these shares:

> July  1  Sold 5,000 shares at $20.
> Aug. 1  Sold 8,000 shares at $14.
> Sep. 1  Retired 1,000 shares.

1. Using the *cost method* to account for treasury stock:
   (a) Prepare the journal entries to record all treasury stock transactions in 1993.
   (b) Prepare the stockholders' equity section of the balance sheet at December 31, 1993, assuming retained earnings of $1,005,000 (before the effects of treasury stock transactions).

2. Using the *par value method* to account for treasury stock:
   (a) Prepare the journal entries to record all treasury stock transactions in 1993.
   (b) Prepare the stockholders' equity section of the balance sheet at December 31, 1993, assuming retained earnings of $1,005,000 (before the effects of treasury stock transactions).

## Exercise 17—10   (Stock rights)

J. Matson bought 2,000 shares of Layton Mining Co. common stock for $15 per share on April 3, 1992. On June 22, 1993, Layton Mining Co. issued stock rights to its holders of common stock, one right for each share owned. The terms of the exercise required 5 rights plus $15 for each share purchased. Layton stock was selling ex-rights for $19 per share, and the rights have a market value of $1 each. On September 1, 1993, Matson exercised 1,000 rights, and on October 15, 1993, sold the remaining rights at $1.40 each.

What entries would be required to reflect the stock rights transactions in Matson's accounting records?

## Exercise 17—11   (Stock rights)

The Jordan Co. holds stock of Caltex Inc. acquired as follows:

|  | Shares | Total Cost |
|---|---|---|
| Lot A, 1991 ......................................... | 75 | $ 6,000 |
| Lot B, 1992 ......................................... | 125 | 11,000 |

In 1993, Jordan Co. receives 200 rights to purchase Caltex Inc. stock at $75 per share. The shares have a par value of $70. Six rights are required to purchase one share. At issue date, rights had a market value of $4 each and stock was selling ex-rights at $96. Jordan Co. used rights to purchase 30 additional shares of Caltex Inc. Subsequently, the market price of the stock fell to $92, and Jordan Co. allowed the unexercised rights to lapse. Both companies use the first-in, first-out method of identifying stock rights exercised.

1. What entries are required to record the preceding events in Jordan's accounting records?
2. What entries are required to record the preceding events in Caltex's accounting records?

### Exercise 17—12  (Accounting for stock warrants)

The Western Company wants to raise additional equity capital. After analysis of the available options, the company decides to issue 1,000 shares of $20 par preferred stock with detachable warrants. The package of the stock and warrants sells for $90. The warrants enable the holder to purchase 1,000 shares of $25 par common stock at $30 per share. Immediately following the issuance of the stock, the stock warrants are selling at $9 per share. The market value of the preferred stock without the warrants is $85.

1. Prepare a journal entry for Western Company to record the issuance of the preferred stock and the attached warrants.
2. Assuming that all the warrants are exercised, prepare a journal entry for Western to record the exercise of the warrants.
3. Assuming that only 80% of the warrants are exercised, prepare a journal entry for Western to record the exercise and expiration of the warrants.

### Exercise 17—13  (Accounting for compensatory stock options)

The stockholders of the Johnson Co. on December 24, 1986, approved a plan granting certain officers of the company nontransferable options to buy 100,000 shares of no-par common stock at $32 per share. Stock was selling at this time at $40 per share. The option plan provides that the officers must be employed by the company for the next five years, that options can be exercised after January 1, 1992, and that options will expire at the end of 1993. One of the officers who had been granted options for 20,000 shares left the company at the beginning of 1990; remaining officers exercised their rights under the option plan at the end of 1993.

Give the entries that should be made on the books of the corporation at the end of each year for 1986-1993 inclusive. The market price of the stock at January 1, 1992, was $60 per share.

### Exercise 17—14  (Accounting for variable stock option plans)

On March 31, 1990, the board of directors of Allied Industries approved a stock option plan for its twenty executives to purchase 500 shares of $25 par common stock each. The plan further indicated that the executives must remain with the company until March 31, 1993, at which time they could exercise their options. The exercise price is 90% of the market price of the stock on December 31, 1992. All outstanding options expire on December 31, 1994.

Assuming the following stock prices and that all options are exercised on June 27, 1993, give the journal entries for the company for its calendar years 1990, 1991, 1992, and 1993.

| Date | Stock Price |
| --- | --- |
| March 31, 1990 | $30 |
| December 31, 1990 | 35 |
| December 31, 1991 | 45 |
| December 31, 1992 | 42 |
| March 31, 1993 | 45 |
| June 27, 1993 | 46 |

### Exercise 17—15  (Convertible preferred stock)

Stockholders' equity for the Damon Co. on December 31 was as follows:

| | |
| --- | --- |
| Preferred stock, $15 par, 30,000 shares issued and outstanding | $ 450,000 |
| Paid-in capital in excess of par—preferred stock | 90,000 |
| Common stock, $10 par, 150,000 shares issued and outstanding | 1,500,000 |

|  |  |
|---|---|
| Paid-in capital in excess of par—common stock . . . . . . . . . . . . . . . . . . . | 750,000 |
| Retained earnings . . . . . . . . . . . . . . . . . . . . . . . . . . . . . . . . . . . . . . . . . . . . | 1,450,000 |

Preferred stock is convertible into common stock.

1. Give the entry made on Damon Co.'s books assuming 2,000 shares of preferred are converted under each assumption listed:

   (a) Preferred shares are convertible into common on a share-for-share basis.
   (b) Each share of preferred stock is convertible into 4 shares of common.
   (c) Each share of preferred stock is convertible into 1.5 shares of common.

2. Assuming that all the preferred stock is converted into common stock under the conditions in 1a, 1b, and 1c above and that Stadium Inc. owns 45% of Damon Co.'s preferred stock, give the entry made on the books of Stadium Inc. given the following:

   (a) The stock conversion is recorded at the cost of the preferred stock.
   (b) The stock conversion is recorded at the current market price of the common stock. The common stock was selling at $21 per share on the date of conversion.
   (c) The stock conversion is recorded at the current market price of the common stock. The common stock was selling at $11 per share on the date of the conversion.

(Assume all of Damon Co.'s preferred shares were originally acquired by Stadium Inc. at the same price.)

### Exercise 17—16  (Analysis of owners' equity)

From the following information, reconstruct the journal entries that were made by the Rivers Corporation during 1993.

|  | December 31, 1993 | | December 31, 1992 | |
|---|---|---|---|---|
|  | Amount | Shares | Amount | Shares |
| Common stock . . . . . . . . . . . . . . . . . . . . | $175,000 | 7,000 | $150,000 | 6,000 |
| Paid-in capital in excess of par . . . . . . | 54,250 |  | 36,000 |  |
| Paid-in capital from treasury stock . . . . | 1,000 | 200 | — | — |
| Retained earnings . . . . . . . . . . . . . . . . . | 76,500* | — | 49,000 | — |
| Treasury stock . . . . . . . . . . . . . . . . . . . . | 15,000 | 300 | — | — |

*Includes net income for 1993 of $40,000. There were no dividends.

2,500 shares of common stock (issued when the company was formed) were purchased at the beginning of 1993 and were retired later in the year. The cost method is used to record treasury stock transactions.

---

## PROBLEMS

### Problem 17—1  (Journalizing stock transactions)

Vicars Company began operations on January 1. Authorized were 20,000 shares of $10 par value common stock and 4,000 shares of $100 par value convertible preferred stock. The following transactions involving stockholders' equity occurred during the first year of operations:

Jan.  1  Issued 500 shares of common stock to the corporation promoters in exchange for property valued at $17,000 and services valued at $6,000. The property had cost the promoters $9,000 three years before and was carried on the promoters' books at $5,000.

Feb. 23  Issued 1,000 shares of convertible preferred stock with a par value of $100 per share. Each share can be converted to 5 shares of common stock. The stock was issued at a price of $150 per share, and the company paid $6,000 to an agent for selling the shares.

Mar. 10   Sold 3,000 shares of the common stock for $39 per share. Issue costs were $2,500.

Apr. 10   4,000 shares of common stock were sold under stock subscriptions at $45 per share. No shares are issued until a subscription contract is paid in full. No cash was received.

July 14   Exchanged 700 shares of common stock and 140 shares of preferred stock for a building with a fair market value of $51,000. The building was originally purchased for $38,000 by the investors and has a book value of $22,000. In addition, 600 shares of common stock were sold for $24,000 in cash.

Aug. 3   Received payments in full for half of the stock subscriptions and payments on account on the rest of the subscriptions. Total cash received was $140,000. Shares of stock were issued for the subscriptions paid in full.

Sep. 28   Received 10 acres of land from a wealthy stockholder to be used for construction of a new factory. Total cost for Vicars was legal fees of $4,000, but the estimated fair market value of the land was $75,000. The cost of the land to the stockholder was $25,000.

Dec. 1   Declared a cash dividend of $10 per share on preferred stock, payable on December 31 to stockholders of record on December 15, and a $2-per-share cash dividend on common stock, payable on January 5 of the following year to stockholders of record on December 15. (No dividends are paid on unissued subscribed stock.)

Dec. 31   Received notice from holders of stock subscriptions for 800 shares that they would not pay further on the subscriptions since the price of the stock had fallen to $25 per share. The amount still due on those contracts was $30,000. Amounts previously paid on the contracts are forfeited according to the agreements.

Net income for the first year of operations was $60,000.

**Instructions:**

1. Prepare journal entries to record the preceding transactions on Vicars' books.
2. Prepare the stockholders' equity section of the balance sheet at December 31 for Vicars.

## Problem 17—2   (Stockholders' equity transactions and balance sheet presentation)

The Pacific Basin Corporation was organized on September 1, 1993, with authorized capital stock of 200,000 shares of 9% cumulative preferred with a $40 par value and 1,000,000 shares of no-par common stock with a $30 stated value. During the balance of the year, the following transactions relating to capital stock were completed:

Oct. 1   Subscriptions were received for 300,000 shares of common stock at $42, payable $22 down and the balance in two equal installments due November 1 and December 1. On the same date, 16,500 shares of common stock were issued to Jim Williams in exchange for his business. Assets transferred to the corporation were valued as follows: land, $210,000; buildings, $250,000; equipment, $50,000; merchandise, $110,000. Liabilities of the business assumed by the corporation were: mortgage payable, $41,000; accounts payable, $11,000; accrued interest on mortgage, $550. No goodwill is recognized in recording the issuance of the stock for net assets.

3   Subscriptions were received for 120,000 shares of preferred stock at $45, payable $15 down and the balance in two equal installments due November 1 and December 1.

Nov. 1   Amounts due on this date were collected from all common and preferred stock subscribers.

12   Subscriptions were received for 480,000 shares of common stock at $44, payable $22 down and the balance in two equal installments due December 1 and January 1.

Dec. 1   Amounts due on this date were collected from all common stock subscribers and stock fully paid for was issued. The final installment on preferred stock subscriptions was received from all subscribers except one whose installment due on this date was $9,000. State corporation laws provide that the company is liable for the return to the subscriber of the amount received less the loss on the subsequent resale of the stock. Preferred stock fully paid for was issued.

6   Preferred stock defaulted on December 1 was issued for cash at $36. Stock was issued, and settlement was made with the defaulting subscriber.

**Instructions:**

1. Prepare journal entries to record the foregoing transactions.
2. Prepare the contributed capital section of stockholders' equity for the corporation as of December 31.

## Problem 17—3   (Reconstruction of equity transactions)

The Fairfield Company had the following account balances on its balance sheet at December 31, 1993, the end of its first year of operations. All stock was issued on a subscription basis, and the state laws permit the company to retain all partial subscriptions paid by defaulting subscribers.

| | |
|---|---:|
| Common Stock Subscriptions Receivable | $150,000 |
| Common Stock, $25 par | 75,000 |
| Common Stock Subscribed | 225,000 |
| Paid-In Capital in Excess of Par—Common Stock | 40,000 |
| 8% Preferred Stock, $100 par | 100,000 |
| Paid-In Capital in Excess of Par—8% Preferred Stock | 50,000 |
| Paid-In Capital From Default on 8% Preferred Stock Subscriptions (200 shares) | 10,000 |
| 10% Preferred Stock, $50 par | 25,000 |
| Retained Earnings | 20,000 |

The reported net income for 1993 was $55,000.

**Instructions:**   From the data given, reconstruct in summary form the journal entries to record all transactions involving the company's stockholders. Indicate the amount of dividends distributed on each class of stock.

## Problem 17—4   (Comprehensive analysis and reporting of stockholders' equity)

The Gastino Company has two classes of capital stock outstanding: 9%, $20 par preferred and $70 par common. During the fiscal year ending November 30, 1993, the company was active in transactions affecting the stockholders' equity. The following summarizes these transactions:

| Type of Transaction | Number of Shares | Price Per Share |
|---|---|---|
| (a)   Issue of preferred stock | 10,000 | $28 |
| (b)   Issue of common stock | 35,000 | 70 |
| (c)   Reacquisition and retirement of preferred stock | 2,000 | 30 |
| (d)   Purchase of treasury stock—common (reported at cost) | 5,000 | 80 |
| (e)   Stock split—common (par value reduced to $35) | 2 for 1 | |
| (f)   Reissue of treasury stock—common | 5,000 | 52 |

Balances of the accounts in the stockholders' equity section of the November 30, 1992, balance sheet were:

| | |
|---|---:|
| Preferred Stock, 50,000 shares | $1,000,000 |
| Common Stock, 100,000 shares | 7,000,000 |
| Paid-In Capital in Excess of Par—Preferred | 400,000 |
| Paid-In Capital in Excess of Par—Common | 1,200,000 |
| Retained Earnings | 550,000 |

Dividends were paid at the end of the fiscal year on the common stock at $1.20 per share and on the preferred stock at the preferred rate. Net income for the year was $850,000.

**Instructions:** Based on the preceding data, prepare the stockholders' equity section of the balance sheet as of November 30, 1993. (Note: A work sheet beginning with November 30, 1992, balances and providing for transactions for the current year will facilitate the preparation of this section of the balance sheet.)

### Problem 17—5 (Accounting for various capital stock transactions)

The stockholders' equity section of Hastings Inc. showed the following data on December 31, 1992: common stock, $30 par, 300,000 shares authorized, 250,000 shares issued and outstanding, $7,500,000; paid-in capital on common stock, $300,000; credit under stock option plan, $150,000; retained earnings, $480,000. The stock options were granted to key executives and provided them the right to acquire 30,000 shares of common stock at $35 per share. The stock was selling at $40 at the time the options were granted.

The following transactions occurred during 1993:

Mar. 31   Exercised 4,500 options outstanding at December 31, 1992. The market price per share was $44 at this time.

Apr.  1   The company issued bonds of $2,000,000 at par, giving each $1,000 bond a detachable warrant enabling the holder to purchase 2 shares of stock at $40 for a 1-year period. Market values immediately following issuance of the bonds were: $4 per warrant and $998 per $1,000 bond without the warrant.

June 30   The company issued rights to stockholders (1 right on each share, exercisable within a 30-day period) permitting holders to acquire 1 share at $40 with every 10 rights submitted. Shares were selling for $43 at this time. All but 6,000 rights were exercised on July 31, and the additional stock was issued.

Sep. 30   All warrants issued with the bonds on April 1 were exercised.

Nov. 30   The market price per share dropped to $33 and options came due. Since the market price was below the option price, no remaining options were exercised.

### Instructions:

1. Give entries to record the foregoing transactions.
2. Prepare the stockholders' equity section of the balance sheet as of December 31, 1993 (assume net income of $210,000 for 1993).

### Problem 17—6 (Accounting for various capital stock transactions)

Pineview Co., organized on June 1, 1992, was authorized to issue stock as follows:

> 80,000 shares of preferred 9% stock, convertible, $100 par
> 250,000 shares of common stock, $25 stated value

During the remainder of the Pineview Co.'s fiscal year ending May 31, 1993, the following transactions were completed in the order given.

(a)   30,000 shares of preferred stock were subscribed for at $105 and 80,000 shares of common stock were subscribed for at $26. Both subscriptions were payable 30% upon subscription, the balance in one payment.

(b)   The second subscription payment was received, except one subscriber for 6,000 shares of common stock defaulted on payment. The full amount paid by this subscriber was returned, and all of the fully paid stock was issued.

(c)   15,000 shares of common stock were reacquired by purchase at $18. (Treasury stock is recorded at cost.)

(d)   Each share of preferred stock was converted into 4 shares of common stock.

(e)   The treasury stock was exchanged for machinery with a fair market value of $280,000.

(f)  There was a 2-for-1 stock split, and the stated value of the new common stock is $12.50.
(g)  A major stockholder donated 100,000 shares of common stock to the company when the market value was $20 per share.
(h)  Net income was $83,000.

**Instructions:**

1. Give the journal entries to record the foregoing transactions. (For net income, give the entry to close the income summary account to Retained Earnings.)
2. Prepare the stockholders' equity section as of May 31, 1993.

### Problem 17—7   (Issuance, reacquisition, and resale of capital stock)

Tucker Company had the following transactions occur during 1993:

(a)  Issued 8,000 shares of common stock to the founders for land valued at $450,000. Par value of the common stock is $30 per share.
(b)  Issued 5,000 shares of $100 par preferred stock for cash at $110.
(c)  Sold 1,000 shares of common stock to the company president for $60 per share.
(d)  Purchased 400 shares of outstanding preferred stock issued in (b) for cash at par.
(e)  Purchased 500 shares of the outstanding common stock issued in (a) for $55 per share.
(f)  Reissued 150 shares of repurchased preferred stock at $102.
(g)  Reissued 300 shares of reacquired common stock for $58 per share.
(h)  Repurchased 100 shares of the common stock sold in (g) for $53 per share. These same 100 shares were later reissued for $50 per share.

**Instructions:**

1. Prepare the necessary entries to record the preceding transactions involving Tucker preferred stock. Assume that the par value method is used for recording treasury stock.
2. Prepare the necessary entries for the common stock transactions assuming that the cost method is used for recording treasury stock.

### Problem 17—8   (Treasury stock transactions)

Transactions that affected Freeland Company's stockholders' equity during 1993, the first year of operations, are given below.

(a)  Issued 30,000 shares of 9% preferred stock, $20 par, at $26.
(b)  Issued 50,000 shares of $30 par common stock at $33.
(c)  Purchased and immediately retired 4,000 shares of preferred stock at $28.
(d)  Purchased 6,000 shares of its own common stock at $35.
(e)  Reissued 1,000 shares of treasury stock at $37.
(f)  Stockholders donated to the company 4,000 shares of common stock when shares had a market price of $36. One-half of these shares were sold for $38.

No dividends were declared in 1993, and net income for 1993 was $185,000.

**Instructions:**

1. Record each of the transactions. Assume treasury stock acquisitions are recorded at cost.
2. Prepare the stockholders' equity section of the balance sheet at December 31, 1993.

### Problem 17—9   (Accounting for stock options)

The board of directors of the Crisex Company adopted a stock option plan to supplement the salaries of certain executives of the company. Options to buy common stock were granted as follows:

| Date | Employee | Number of Shares | Option Price | Price of Shares at Date of Grant |
|------|----------|------------------|--------------|-----------------------------------|
| Jan. 10, 1990 | Q. L. Peck | 75,000 | $20 | $21 |
| June 30, 1990 | A. G. Byrd | 50,000 | 25 | 26 |
| June 30, 1990 | K. C. Nelson | 20,000 | 25 | 26 |

Options are nontransferable and can be exercised 3 years after date of grant providing the executive is still in the employ of the company. Options expire 2 years after the date they can first be exercised. Nelson left the employ of the company at the beginning of 1992. Stock options were exercised as follows:

| Date | Employee | Number of Shares | Price of Shares at Date of Exercise |
|------|----------|------------------|--------------------------------------|
| Jan. 15, 1993 | Q. L. Peck | 60,000 | $45 |
| Dec. 20, 1993 | Q. L. Peck | 15,000 | 36 |
| Dec. 22, 1993 | A. G. Byrd | 50,000 | 32 |

Stock of the company has a $14 par value. The accounting period for the company is the calendar year.

**Instructions:**   Give all entries that would be made on the books of the company relative to the stock option agreement for the period 1990 to 1993 inclusive.

## Problem 17—10   (Variable stock options)

The Diablo Manufacturing Company adopted an executive stock option plan on January 1, 1990. The plan states that all executives remaining with the firm until the exercisable date would be eligible for the stock. The options are exercisable beginning January 1, 1993, and will expire on December 31, 1993. The option price is to be 75% of the market price on January 1, 1992. The stock price on December 31, 1990, was $90 and on December 31, 1992, was $120. The following information was given for 1993:

| | |
|---|---|
| Change in common stock (par $30) from options exercised............ | $180,000 |
| Change in paid-in capital on common stock from options exercised.... | 450,000 |
| Balance remaining in Credit Under Stock Option Plan................ | 78,750 |

**Instructions:**

1. Compute the following:

   (a) The stock price at January 1, 1992.
   (b) Cash received on options exercised.
   (c) The total number of shares optioned to the executives.
   (d) The executive compensation expense for 1990, 1991, and 1992.

2. Give the journal entries for 1993.

## Problem 17—11   (Analysis of stock transactions)

You have been asked to audit the Greystone Company. During the course of your audit, you are asked to prepare comparative data from the company's inception to the present. You have determined the following:

(a)   Greystone Company's charter became effective on January 2, 1989, when 2,000 shares of no-par common and 1,000 shares of 7% cumulative, nonparticipating, preferred stock were issued. The no-par common stock had no stated value and was sold at $120 per share, and the preferred stock was sold at its par value of $100 per share.

(b) Greystone was unable to pay preferred dividends at the end of its first year. The owners of the preferred stock agreed to accept 2 shares of common stock for every 50 shares of preferred stock owned in discharge of the preferred dividends due on December 31, 1989. The shares were issued on January 2, 1990. The fair market value was $100 per share for common on the date of issue.

(c) Greystone Company acquired all of the outstanding stock of Booth Corporation on May 1, 1991, in exchange for 1,000 shares of Greystone common stock.

(d) Greystone split its common stock 3 for 2 on January 1, 1992, and 2 for 1 on January 1, 1993.

(e) Greystone offered to convert 20% of the preferred stock to common stock on the basis of 2 shares of common for 1 share of preferred. The offer was accepted, and the conversion was made on July 1, 1993.

(f) No cash dividends were declared on common stock until December 31, 1991. Cash dividends per share of common stock were declared as follows:

|      | June 30 | Dec. 31 |
|------|---------|---------|
| 1991 |         | $3.19   |
| 1992 | $1.75   | 2.75    |
| 1993 | 1.25    | 1.25    |

**Instructions:** Prepare schedules that show the computation of:

1. The number of shares of each class of stock outstanding on the last day of each year from 1989 through 1993.
2. Total cash dividends applicable to common stock for each year from 1991 through 1993.

### Problem 17—12  (Auditing stockholders' equity)

You have been assigned to the audit of Belcore Inc., a manufacturing company. You have been asked to summarize the transactions for the year ended December 31, 1993, affecting stockholders' equity and other related accounts. The stockholders' equity section of Belcore's December 31, 1992, balance sheet follows:

**Stockholders' Equity**

Contributed capital:

| | |
|---|---|
| Common stock, $20 par value, 500,000 shares authorized, 90,000 shares issued | $1,800,000 |
| Paid-in capital from treasury stock | 22,500 |
| Paid-in capital in excess of par | 200,000 |
| Total contributed capital | $2,022,500 |
| Retained earnings | 324,689 |
| Total contributed capital and retained earnings | $2,347,189 |
| Less cost of 1,210 shares of treasury stock | 72,600 |
| Total stockholders' equity | $2,274,589 |

You have extracted the following information from the accounting records and audit working papers:

1993

Jan. 15  Belcore reissued 650 shares of treasury stock for $40 per share. The 1,210 shares of treasury stock on hand at December 31, 1992, were purchased in one block in 1992. Belcore used the cost method for recording the treasury shares purchased.

Feb. 2  Sold 90 $1,000, 9% bonds due February 1, 1996, at 103 with one detachable stock purchase warrant attached to each bond. Interest is payable annually on February 1. The fair market value of the bonds without the stock warrants is 97. The detached warrants have a fair value of $60 each and expire on February 1, 1994. Each warrant entitles the holder to purchase 10 shares of common stock at $40 per share.

Mar. 6  Subscriptions for 1,400 shares of common stock were issued at $44 per share, payable 40% down and the balance by March 20.

Mar. 20   The balance due on 1,200 shares was received and those shares were issued. The subscriber who defaulted on the 200 remaining shares forfeited the down payment in accordance with the subscription agreement.

Nov.  1   Exercised 55 stock warrants detached from the bonds.

**Instructions:**   Give journal entries required to summarize the preceding transactions.

# CHAPTER 18

# Owners' Equity–Retained Earnings

---

**CHAPTER TOPICS**

**Factors Affecting Retained Earnings**

**Prior-Period Adjustments**

**Restrictions on Retained Earnings**

**Accounting for Dividends**

**Stock Dividends Versus Stock Splits**

**Quasi-Reorganizations**

**Reporting Stockholders' Equity**

---

Many companies are proud of their record of consecutive years of cash dividend payments. For example, General Electric reports that it has paid cash dividends each year since 1899. Chase Manhattan has a continuous cash dividend stream dating back to 1848. Chemical Bank's record goes back to 1827.

Berkshire Hathaway is one of the few companies that unhesitatingly reports that it does *not* pay cash dividends and has not paid them since 1967. The company prefers to reinvest profits. Berkshire Hathaway is involved in a number of diverse lines of business. Its largest operations are in property and casualty insurance. However, it also produces and sells Kirby vacuums, See's chocolates, and World Book encyclopedias. As might be expected of a company that retains all profits, Berkshire Hathaway has grown rapidly. From 1964 to 1989, its increase in market value averaged 28% per year. During 1989, the company's common stock traded for as high as $8,900 per share—the highest per-share price on the New York Stock Exchange.[1]

Evaluating growth by increase in share price can be misleading. Berkshire Hathaway's share price is high because of real growth, but also because of the absence of stock dividends and stock splits. Most firms use stock dividends or splits to maintain their per-share price in the range that is considered normal, usually between $20 and $80 per share in the United States. For example, IBM common stock traded for $117 per share in June 1990. However, if it hadn't been for a long history of stock dividends (26 stock dividends since 1925, the last being in 1967) and stock splits (13 stock splits since 1926, the latest being a 4-for-1 split in 1979),[2] the per-share price of IBM stock would have been $350,000!

In the previous chapter, owners' equity was defined as the residual ownership interest in the net assets (total assets minus total liabilities) of a business. Owners' equity was further classified into that portion of capital that is contributed by owners and the amount of earnings generated and retained by the enterprise. Chapter 17 discussed the accounting issues associated with contributed capital. The purpose of this chapter is to identify and explain the different types of transactions and events that directly affect retained earnings.

The nature of retained earnings is frequently misunderstood, and this misunderstanding may lead to incorrect impressions in reading and interpreting financial statements. The retained earnings account is essentially the meeting place of balance sheet and income statement accounts. In successive periods, retained earnings are increased by income and decreased by losses and dividends. As a result, the retained earnings balance represents the net accumulated earnings of a corporation. If the retained earnings account were affected *only* by income (losses) and dividends, there would be little confusion in its interpretation. A number of other factors, however, can affect retained earnings.

## FACTORS AFFECTING RETAINED EARNINGS

In addition to earnings or losses and dividends, factors that affect retained earnings include prior-period adjustments for corrections of errors, quasi-reorganizations, and treasury stock transactions (discussed in Chapter 17). The transactions and events that increase or decrease retained earnings may be summarized as follows:

**Retained Earnings**

| Decreases | Increases |
|---|---|
| Prior-period adjustments for overstatements of past earnings | Prior-period adjustments for understatements of past earnings |
| Current net loss | Current net income |
| Dividends | Quasi-reorganizations |
| Treasury stock transactions | |

### Prior-Period Adjustments

In some situations, errors made in past years are discovered and corrected in the current year by an adjustment to the retained earnings account, referred to as a prior-period

[1]1989 Annual Report of Berkshire Hathaway Inc.

[2]*Moody's Industrial Manual,* 1990, Vol. 1, p. 406.

adjustment. There are several types of errors that may occur in measuring the results of operations and the financial status of an enterprise. Accounting errors can result from mathematical mistakes, a failure to apply appropriate accounting procedures, or a misstatement or omission of certain information. In addition, a change from an accounting principle that is not generally accepted to one that is accepted is considered a correction of an error.[3]

Fortunately, most errors are discovered during the accounting period, prior to closing the books. When this is the case, corrections can be made by making adjusting entries directly to the accounts. The corrected balances are then shown on the balance sheet and on the income statement.

Sometimes errors go undetected during the current period, but they are offset by an equal misstatement in the subsequent period; that is, they are **counterbalanced**. When this happens, the under- or overstatement of income in one period is counterbalanced by an equal over- or understatement of income in the next period, and after the closing process is completed for the second year, the retained earnings account is correctly stated. If a counterbalancing error is discovered during the second year, however, it should be corrected at that time.

When errors of past periods are not counterbalancing, retained earnings will be misstated until a correction is made in the accounting records. If the error is material, a prior-period adjustment should be made directly to the retained earnings account.[4] If an error resulted in an understatement of income in previous periods, a correcting entry would be needed to increase retained earnings; if an error overstated income in prior periods, then retained earnings would have to be decreased. These adjustments for corrections in net income of prior periods would typically be shown as a part of the total change in retained earnings as follows:

| | |
|---|---|
| Retained Earnings, unadjusted beginning balance . . . . . . . . . . . . . . . . . . . . . . | $xxx |
| Add or deduct prior-period adjustments . . . . . . . . . . . . . . . . . . . . . . . . . . . . . | xx |
| Retained Earnings, adjusted beginning balance . . . . . . . . . . . . . . . . . . . . . . . | $xxx |
| Add current year's net income or deduct current year's net loss . . . . . . . . . . | xx |
| | $xxx |
| Deduct dividends . . . . . . . . . . . . . . . . . . . . . . . . . . . . . . . . . . . . . . . . . . . . . . . | xx |
| Retained Earnings, ending balance . . . . . . . . . . . . . . . . . . . . . . . . . . . . . . . . . | $xxx |

When errors are discovered, the accountant must be able to analyze the situation and determine what action is appropriate under the circumstances. This calls for an understanding of accounting standards as well as good judgment. Chapter 21 covers in detail the techniques for analyzing and correcting errors.

## Earnings

The primary source of retained earnings is the net income generated by a business. The retained earnings account is increased by net income and is reduced by net losses from business activities. When operating losses or other debits to Retained Earnings produce a debit balance in this account, the debit balance is referred to as a **deficit**.

Corporate earnings originate from transactions with individuals or businesses outside the company. No earnings are recognized for the construction of buildings or other plant assets for a company's own use, even though the cost of such construction is below the market price for similar assets; self-construction at less than the asset purchase price is

---

[3]*Opinions of the Accounting Principles Board No. 20,* "Accounting Changes" (New York: American Institute of Certified Public Accountants, 1971), par. 13.

[4]*Ibid.,* par. 36.

regarded simply as a savings in cost. No increases in retained earnings are recognized from transactions with stockholders involving treasury stock; however, as indicated in Chapter 17, decreases may be recognized. The receipt of assets through donation is not recognized as earnings, but as paid-in capital. The earnings of a corporation may be distributed to the stockholders or retained to provide for expanding operations.

## Dividends

**Dividends** are distributions to the stockholders of a corporation in proportion to the number of shares held by the respective owners. Distributions may take the form of (1) cash, (2) other assets, (3) notes or other evidence of corporate indebtedness, in effect, deferred cash dividends, and (4) stock dividends, i.e., shares of a company's own stock. Most dividends involve reductions in retained earnings. Exceptions include (1) some stock dividends issued in the form of stock splits, which involve a transfer from additional paid-in capital to legal capital, and (2) dividends in corporate liquidation, which represent a return to stockholders of a portion or all of their investment and call for reductions in contributed capital.

Use of the term *dividend* without qualification normally implies the distribution of cash. Dividends in a form other than cash, such as property or stock dividends, should be designated by their special form. Distributions from a capital source other than retained earnings should carry a description of their special origin, e.g., *liquidating dividend* or *dividend distribution of paid-in capital.*

"Dividends paid out of retained earnings" is an expression frequently encountered. Accuracy, however, requires recognition that dividends are paid out of cash, which serves to reduce retained earnings. Earnings of the corporation increase net assets or stockholders' equity. Dividend distributions represent no more than asset withdrawals that reduce net assets. The nature and types of dividends are covered in depth later in the chapter.

## Other Changes in Retained Earnings

The most common changes in retained earnings result from earnings (or losses) and dividends. Other changes may occur, however, resulting from treasury stock transactions or from a quasi-reorganization, which is effected only under special circumstances in which a business seeks a "fresh start."

The remainder of this chapter focuses on accounting for dividends, followed by a discussion of quasi-reorganizations.

## ACCOUNTING FOR DIVIDENDS

Among the powers delegated by the stockholders to the board of directors is the power to control the dividend policy. Whether dividends shall or shall not be paid, as well as the nature and the amount of dividends, are matters that the board determines. In setting dividend policy, the board of directors must answer two questions:

1. Do we have the legal right to declare a dividend?
2. Is a dividend distribution financially advisable?

In answering the first question, the board of directors must observe the legal requirements governing the maintenance of legal capital. The laws of different states range from those making any part of capital other than legal capital available for dividends to those permitting dividends only to the extent of retained earnings and under specified conditions. In most states, dividends cannot be declared in the event of a deficit; in a few states, however, dividends equal to current earnings may be distributed despite a previously accumulated deficit. The availability of capital as a basis for dividends is a determination to be made by the legal counsel and not by the accountant. The accountant must report accurately the sources of each capital increase or decrease; the legal counsel investigates the availability of such sources as bases for dividend distributions.

The board of directors must also consider the second question, i.e., the financial aspect of dividend distributions. The company's cash position relative to present and future cash requirements is a key factor. For example, a corporation may have retained earnings of $500,000. If it has cash of only $150,000, however, cash dividends must be limited to this amount unless it converts certain assets into cash or borrows cash. If the cash required for regular operations is $100,000, the cash available for dividends is then only $50,000. Although legally able to declare dividends of $500,000, the company would be able to distribute no more than one tenth of that amount at this time. Generally, companies pay dividends that are significantly less than the legal amount allowed or the amount of cash on hand.

When a dividend is legally declared and announced, it cannot be revoked. In the event of corporate insolvency after a dividend declaration but prior to payment of the dividend, stockholders have claims as a creditor group to the dividend, and as an ownership group to any assets remaining after all corporate liabilities have been paid. A dividend that was illegally declared, however, is revocable; in the event of insolvency at the time of declaration, such action is nullified and stockholders participate in asset distributions only after creditors have been paid in full.

### Restrictions on Retained Earnings

Although state laws generally permit the distribution of dividends to the extent of retained earnings, other factors may limit the amount of dividends that can be declared. For example, a portion of retained earnings may be restricted as a result of contractual requirements, such as an agreement with creditors that provides for the retention of earnings to ensure repayment of debt at maturity. Retained earnings may also be restricted at the discretion of the board of directors. For example, the board may designate a portion of retained earnings as restricted for a particular purpose, such as expansion of plant facilities.

If restrictions on retained earnings are material, they are generally disclosed in a note to the financial statements. Sometimes, however, the restricted portion of retained earnings is reported on the balance sheet separately from the unrestricted amount that is available for dividends. The restricted portion may be designated as **appropriated retained earnings** and the unrestricted portion as **unappropriated (or free) retained earnings**. When the restrictions are recognized in the accounts, the entry is a debit to the regular retained earnings account and a credit to a special appropriated retained earnings account.

As an example, assume Silverstein Company restricted $100,000 of its $600,000 retained earnings balance for possible plant expansion by making the following entry on January 1, 1993:

```
1993
Jan. 1   Retained Earnings...............................   100,000
             Appropriated Retained Earnings .................           100,000
             To restrict retained earnings for possible plant
             expansion.
```

The balance sheet subsequent to this entry would reflect both retained earnings accounts.

| Appropriated retained earnings . . . . . . . . . . . . . . . . . . . . . . . . | $100,000 | |
| Unappropriated retained earnings . . . . . . . . . . . . . . . . . . . . . | 500,000 | |
| Total retained earnings . . . . . . . . . . . . . . . . . . . . . . . . . . . | | $600,000 |

Once the purpose of the appropriation has been served, the original entry creating the appropriated retained earnings balance is reversed. To illustrate, assume that on June 15, the Silverstein Company decided not to expand its plant and to eliminate the appropriated retained earnings balance. The applicable entry would be:

| June 15 | Appropriated Retained Earnings . . . . . . . . . . . . . . | 100,000 | |
| | Retained Earnings . . . . . . . . . . . . . . . . . . . . . . . . . | | 100,000 |
| | *To discontinue the appropriation of retained* | | |
| | *earnings for plant expansion.* | | |

Note that there is no segregation of funds and no gain or loss involved in the restriction of retained earnings. Whatever the form of disclosure, the main idea behind restrictions on retained earnings is to notify stockholders that some of the assets that might otherwise be available for dividend distribution are being retained within the business for specific purposes. Because the amount of dividends actually paid is usually much less than the retained earnings balance, this is generally not a significant issue.

## Recognition and Payment of Dividends

Three dates are essential in the recognition and payment of dividends: (1) **date of declaration**, (2) **date of record**, and (3) **date of payment**. Dividends are made payable to stockholders of record as of a date following the date of declaration and preceding the date of payment. The liability for dividends payable is recorded on the declaration date and is canceled on the payment date. No entry is required on the record date, but a list of the stockholders is made as of the close of business on this date. These are the persons who receive dividends on the payment date. For example, on November 28, 1990, *The Wall Street Journal* published an announcement that Walt Disney Company had declared a quarterly cash dividend of 14½ cents per share, payable on February 20, 1991, to shareholders of record on January 18, 1991.

Stockholders become aware of a forthcoming dividend upon its declaration and announcement. If stock is sold and a new owner is recognized by the corporation prior to the record date, the dividend is paid to the new owner. If a stock transfer is not recognized by the corporation until after the record date, the dividend will be paid to the former owner, i.e., the shareholder of record. After the record date, stock no longer carries a right to dividends and sells at a lower price or **ex-dividend**.[5] Accordingly, a stockholder is justified in recognizing the corporate dividend action on the record date by debiting a receivable and crediting Dividend Revenue. Upon receipt of the dividend, Cash is debited and the receivable is eliminated. In practice, however, the accrual is frequently omitted, and dividend revenue is recognized when the cash is received.

## Cash Dividends

The most common type of dividend is a **cash dividend**. For the corporation, these dividends involve a reduction in retained earnings and in cash. For the investor, a cash dividend generates cash and is recognized as dividend revenue. Entries to record the declaration and payment of a $100,000 cash dividend by a corporation follow:

---

[5]Stock on the New York Stock Exchange is normally quoted ex-dividend (or ex-rights) four full trading days prior to the record date because of the time required to deliver the stock and to record the stock transfers.

### Declaration of Dividend

| | | |
|---|---|---|
| Dividends (or Retained Earnings) ......................... | 100,000 | |
| Dividends Payable ...................................... | | 100,000 |

### Payment of Dividend

| | | |
|---|---|---|
| Dividends Payable ...................................... | 100,000 | |
| Cash ................................................. | | 100,000 |

An investor owning five percent of the outstanding stock would record the dividend as follows:

### Receipt of Dividend

| | | |
|---|---|---|
| Cash ................................................. | 5,000 | |
| Dividend Revenue ...................................... | | 5,000 |

*Computation:*
$100,000 (total dividends) × .05 (investor's share) = $5,000

As noted previously, the investor could recognize dividend revenue and the corresponding receivable at the date of record. In practice, however, investors typically recognize dividend revenue at the time of receipt.

## Property Dividends

A distribution to stockholders that is payable in some asset other than cash is generally referred to as a property dividend. Frequently the assets to be distributed are securities of other companies owned by the corporation. The corporation thus transfers to its stockholders its ownership interest in such securities. Property dividends occur most frequently in closely held corporations.

This type of transfer is sometimes referred to as a **nonreciprocal transfer to owners,** inasmuch as nothing is received by the company in return for its distribution to the stockholders. These transfers should be recorded using the fair market value (as of the day of declaration) of the assets distributed, and a gain or loss recognized for the difference between the carrying value on the books of the issuing company and the fair market value of the assets.[6] Property dividends are valued at carrying value if the fair market value is not determinable.

To illustrate the entries for a property dividend, assume that the Bigler Corporation owns 100,000 shares in the Tri-State Oil Co., cost $2,000,000, fair market value $3,000,000, or $30 per share, which it wishes to distribute to its stockholders. There are 1,000,000 shares of Bigler Corporation stock outstanding. Accordingly, a dividend of 1/10 of a share of Tri-State Oil Co. stock is declared on each share of Bigler Corporation stock outstanding. The entries for Bigler for the dividend declaration and payment are:

### Declaration of Dividend

| | | |
|---|---|---|
| Dividends (or Retained Earnings) ...................... | 3,000,000 | |
| Property Dividends Payable ......................... | | 2,000,000 |
| Gain on Distribution of Property Dividends............ | | 1,000,000 |

[6]*Opinions of the Accounting Principles Board No. 29,* "Accounting for Nonmonetary Transactions" (New York: American Institute of Certified Public Accountants, 1973), par. 18.

**Payment of Dividend**

Property Dividends Payable ......................... 2,000,000
    Investment in Tri-State Oil Co. Stock .................      2,000,000

An investor owning 5,000 shares of Bigler stock would make the following entry to record the receipt of the property (Tri-State Oil stock) dividend:

**Receipt of Dividend**

Investment in Tri-State Oil Co. Stock ................... 15,000
    Dividend Revenue ..................................      15,000

*Computation:*
5,000 shares × ¹⁄₁₀ = 500 shares
500 shares × $30 per share = $15,000

## Stock Dividends

A corporation may distribute to stockholders additional shares of the company's own stock as a stock dividend. A stock dividend permits the corporation to retain within the business net assets produced by earnings while at the same time offering stockholders additional ownership shares.

**Accounting for Stock Dividends by the Issuer**   A stock dividend usually involves (1) the capitalization of retained earnings, and (2) a distribution of common stock to common stockholders. These distributions are sometimes referred to as "ordinary stock dividends." In other instances, common stock is issued to holders of preferred stock or preferred stock is issued to holders of common stock. These distributions are sometimes referred to as "special stock dividends."

A stock dividend decreases retained earnings while increasing the legal capital of a corporation. In recording the dividend, a debit is made to Retained Earnings and credits are made to appropriate paid-in capital balances. A stock dividend has the same effect as the payment by the corporation of a cash dividend and a subsequent return of the cash to the corporation in exchange for capital stock, as illustrated in a subsequent section.

In distributing stock as a dividend, the issuing corporation must meet legal requirements relative to the minimum amounts to be capitalized. If stock has a par or a stated value, an amount equal to the par or stated value of the shares issued will have to be transferred to capital stock; if stock has no par value and no stated value, the laws of the state of incorporation may provide specific requirements as to the amounts to be transferred, or they may leave such determinations to the corporate directors.

**Accounting for Stock Dividends by the Investor**   From the shareholders' point of view, a stock dividend does not change the proportional ownership interests. Although the number of shares held by each individual stockholder has gone up, there are now a greater total number of shares outstanding, and proportionate interests remain unchanged. This division of equities into a greater number of parts should not be regarded as giving rise to revenue. To illustrate, assume the facts at the top of page 678 for Jeff's Corporation and a shareholder owning 10 shares of stock.

As indicated on page 678, the book value per share would decrease, but total book value would not change. Theoretically, the same relative decrease should occur in the market price as occurred in the book value. In any event, since there is no effect on the underlying book value of the investment, the investor need only make a memorandum entry noting the receipt of additional shares and the new, lower per-share cost basis of the investment.

|  | Prior to 10% Stock Dividend | After 10% Stock Dividend |
|---|---|---|
| Common stock outstanding . . . . . . . . . . . . . . . . . | 10,000 shares | 11,000 shares |
| Total stockholders' equity . . . . . . . . . . . . . . . . . . | $330,000 | $330,000 |
| Company book value per share . . . . . . . . . . . . . | $33 | $30 |
| Individual stockholder book value . . . . . . . . . . . | $330 ($33 × 10 shares) | $330 ($30 × 11 shares) |

**Small Versus Large Stock Dividends**    In accounting for stock dividends, a distinction is made between a small and a large stock dividend.[7] A **small stock dividend** is one in which the number of shares issued is so small in comparison to the number of shares outstanding that it has little impact on the market price per share. As a general guideline, a stock dividend of less than 20%-25% of the number of shares previously outstanding is considered a small stock dividend. Stock dividends involving the issuance of more than 20%-25% are considered **large stock dividends**.[8]

With a small stock dividend, which is the normal situation, the accounting profession recommends that companies transfer from Retained Earnings to capital stock and additional paid-in capital an amount equal to the fair market value of the additional shares at the declaration date. Such a transfer is consistent with the general public's view of a stock dividend as a distribution of corporate earnings at an amount equivalent to the fair market value of the shares received. When a large stock dividend is involved, however, the transfer from Retained Earnings to contributed capital is made at the stock's par value, stated value, or other value as required by law. The following examples illustrate the entries for the declaration and issuance of stock dividends.

Assume that stockholders' equity for the Fuji Company on July 1 is as follows:

| | |
|---|---|
| Common stock, $10 par, 100,000 shares outstanding . . . . . . . . . . . . . . | $1,000,000 |
| Paid-in capital in excess of par . . . . . . . . . . . . . . . . . . . . . . . . . . . . . . . . | 1,100,000 |
| Retained earnings . . . . . . . . . . . . . . . . . . . . . . . . . . . . . . . . . . . . . . . . . . . | 750,000 |

The company declares a 10% stock dividend, or a dividend of 1 share of common for every 10 shares held. The stock is selling on the market on this date at $16 per share. The stock dividend is to be recorded at the market value of the shares issued, or $160,000 (10,000 shares at $16). The entries to record the declaration of the dividend and the issuance of stock by Fuji Company are:

### Declaration of Dividend

| | | |
|---|---|---|
| Retained Earnings . . . . . . . . . . . . . . . . . . . . . . . . . . . . . . . . . . . . . | 160,000 | |
| Stock Dividends Distributable . . . . . . . . . . . . . . . . . . . . . . . . . | | 100,000 |
| Paid-In Capital in Excess of Par . . . . . . . . . . . . . . . . . . . . . . . . | | 60,000 |

### Issuance of Dividend

| | | |
|---|---|---|
| Stock Dividends Distributable . . . . . . . . . . . . . . . . . . . . . . . . . | 100,000 | |
| Common Stock, $10 par . . . . . . . . . . . . . . . . . . . . . . . . . . . . . . . | | 100,000 |

Now assume that the company declares a large stock dividend of 50%, or a dividend of 1 share for every 2 held. Legal requirements call for the transfer to capital stock of an amount equal to the par value of the shares issued. Entries for the declaration of the dividend and the issuance of stock follow:

[7]See *Accounting Research and Terminology Bulletins—Final Edition, No. 43*, "Restatement and Revision of Accounting Research Bulletins," (New York: American Institute of Certified Public Accountants, 1961), Ch. 7, Sec. B.

[8]In *Accounting Series Release No. 124*, the SEC specified that for publicly traded companies, stock dividends of 25% or more should be accounted for as large stock dividends and those of less than 25% as small stock dividends.

**Declaration of Dividend**

| | | |
|---|---|---|
| Retained Earnings | 500,000 | |
| Stock Dividends Distributable | | 500,000 |

**Issuance of Dividend**

| | | |
|---|---|---|
| Stock Dividends Distributable | 500,000 | |
| Common Stock, $10 par | | 500,000 |

**Fractional Share Warrants**    When stock dividends are issued by a company, it may be necessary to issue **fractional share warrants** to certain stockholders. For example, when a 10% stock dividend is issued, a stockholder owning 25 shares can be given no more than 2 full shares; however, the holdings in excess of an even multiple of 10 shares are recognized by issuing a fractional share warrant for one-half share. The warrant for one-half share may be sold, or a warrant for an additional half share may be purchased so that a full share may be claimed from the company. In some instances, the corporation may arrange for the payment of cash in lieu of fractional warrants or it may issue a full share of stock in exchange for warrants accompanied by cash for the fractional share deficiency.

Assume that the Fuji Company in distributing a stock dividend issues fractional share warrants equivalent to 500 shares of $10 par common. The entry for the fractional share warrants issued would be as follows:

| | | |
|---|---|---|
| Stock Dividends Distributable | 5,000 | |
| Fractional Share Warrants Issued | | 5,000 |

Assuming 80% of the warrants are ultimately turned in for shares and the remaining warrants expire, the following entry would be made:

| | | |
|---|---|---|
| Fractional Share Warrants Issued | 5,000 | |
| Common Stock, $10 par | | 4,000 |
| Paid-In Capital From Forfeitures of Fractional Share Warrants | | 1,000 |

**Stock Dividends Versus Stock Splits**    As noted in Chapter 17, a corporation may effect a stock split by reducing the par or stated value of capital stock and increasing accordingly the number of shares outstanding. For example, a corporation with 1,000,000 shares outstanding may split the stock on a 3-for-1 basis. After the split, the corporation will have 3,000,000 total shares outstanding and each stockholder will have 3 shares for every 1 previously held. However, each share now represents only one-third of the capital interest it previously represented; furthermore, each share of stock can be expected to sell for approximately one-third of its previous market price. From an investor's perspective, therefore, a stock split can be viewed the same as a stock dividend. In fact, the accounting for the investor is the same for stock splits as for stock dividends. With an increase in the number of shares, each new share is assigned a portion of the original cost.

Although a stock dividend can be compared to a stock split from the investor's point of view, its effects on corporate capital differ from those of a stock split. A stock dividend results in not only an increase in the number of shares outstanding, but also an increase in the capital stock balance, with no change in the value assigned to each share of stock on the company records; the increase in capital stock outstanding is effected by a transfer from the retained earnings balance, retained earnings available for dividends being permanently reduced by this transfer. A stock split merely divides the existing capital stock balance into more parts, with a reduction in the stated or legal value related to each share; there is no change in the retained earnings balance or the capital stock balance.

Exhibit 18—1 provides a comparative example of the effects of a stock dividend and a stock split, both from the issuing company's perspective and from an investor's perspective.

### Exhibit 18—1    Comparative Example—Stock Dividend Versus Stock Split

#### Stockholders' Equity (Prior to Stock Dividend or Stock Split)

| | |
|---|---:|
| Common stock, 200,000 shares authorized, $5 par, 50,000 shares outstanding .................... | $250,000 |
| Paid-in capital in excess of par ......................................................... | 100,000 |
| Retained earnings ........................................................................ | 200,000 |
| Total stockholders' equity ............................................................... | $550,000 |

#### Issuing Company's Perspective

| Stockholders' Equity After 10% Stock Dividend* | | Stockholders' Equity After 2-for-1 Stock Split | |
|---|---:|---|---:|
| Common stock, 200,000 shares authorized, $5 par, 55,000 shares outstanding ....... | $275,000 | Common stock, 400,000 shares authorized, $2.50 par, 100,000 shares outstanding.... | $250,000 |
| Paid-in capital in excess of par .......... | 175,000 | Paid-in capital in excess of par .......... | 100,000 |
| Retained earnings ..................... | 100,000 | Retained earnings ..................... | 200,000 |
| Total stockholders' equity .............. | $550,000 | Total stockholders' equity .............. | $550,000 |

*Assume market value of $20 per share at declaration date.

#### Investor's Perspective**

| Effect of 10% Stock Dividend | | Effect of 2-for-1 Stock Split | |
|---|---:|---|---:|
| Original investment (1,000 × $15) ........ | $15,000 | Original investment (1,000 × $15) ........ | $15,000 |
| Investment after 10% stock dividend (1,100 × $13.64)*** .................... | $15,000 | Investment after 2-for-1 stock split (2,000 × $7.50) ......................... | $15,000 |

 **Assume an original investment of 1,000 shares at $15 cost per share.
***1,100 × $13.64 = $15,004 = $15,000 (rounded).

**Stock Dividends on the Balance Sheet**    Special disclosure should be provided on the balance sheet when retained earnings have been reclassified as paid-in capital as a result of stock dividends, recapitalizations, or other actions. Information concerning the amount of retained earnings transferred to paid-in capital will contribute to an understanding of the extent to which business growth has been financed through corporate earnings. For example, assume the information for the Fuji Company on page 678 and the transfer to paid-in capital of $500,000 as a result of the 50% stock dividend. The stockholders' equity may be presented as illustrated below.

| | | |
|---|---:|---:|
| Contributed capital: | | |
| Common stock, $10 par, 150,000 shares ............. | $1,500,000 | |
| Paid-in capital in excess of par ..................... | 1,100,000 | $2,600,000 |
| Retained earnings ................................... | $ 750,000 | |
| Less amount transferred to paid-in capital by stock dividend ......................................... | 500,000 | 250,000 |
| Total stockholders' equity ........................... | | $2,850,000 |

### Stock Dividends—Why Do They Exist?

Viewed very simply, stock dividends are purely cosmetic. They should have no effect on the total value of a company, since they involve no inflow or outflow of assets. A stock dividend merely causes the value of the declaring company to be sliced into smaller pieces. For example, a firm with a total market value of $1,000 with 10 shares of stock outstanding (market value of $100 per share) would, after a 100% stock dividend, still have a total market value of $1,000, but now would have 20 shares of stock outstanding (market value of $50 per share).

This cosmetic view of stock dividends makes theoretical sense, but the fact that real companies spend real money (in the form of administrative costs) to enact stock dividends suggests that there must be something more to them. It has been suggested that the accounting treatment of stock dividends makes their declaration a credible way of sending a signal to the market that the firm has favorable future prospects. The reasoning goes like this: A declaration of a stock dividend requires that an amount be transferred from retained earnings to paid-in capital. Since *cash* dividend payments are often restricted to the amount of retained earnings, the reduction in retained earnings occasioned by a *stock* dividend might make it more difficult to declare *cash* dividends in the future. Only firms with favorable future prospects would be likely to declare stock dividends, since they are confident that future earnings will bolster the retained earnings balance, making up for the reduction required by the stock dividend declaration. So, according to this reasoning, a stock dividend declaration is a signal from management that they expect future earnings to be adequate to cover future cash dividend declarations. This view of stock dividends is supported by the fact that, on average, firms' stock prices increase 5% in the days following the announcement of a stock dividend.

#### Question:

*Assume that there is validity to this signaling theory of stock dividends. Which would be a stronger signal— a 20% stock dividend or a 30% stock dividend?*

Source: Josef Lachonishok and Baruch Lev, "Stock Splits and Stock Dividends: Why, Who, and When," *The Journal of Finance* (September 1987), p. 913.

If a balance sheet is prepared after the declaration of a stock dividend but before issue of the shares, Stock Dividends Distributable is reported in the stockholders' equity section as an addition to capital stock outstanding. Through stock dividends, the corporation reduces its retained earnings balance and increases its capital stock.

### Liquidating Dividends

A liquidating dividend is a distribution representing a return to stockholders of a portion of contributed capital. Whereas a normal cash dividend provides a return on investment and is accounted for by reducing Retained Earnings, a liquidating dividend provides a return of investment. A liquidating dividend is accounted for by reducing paid-in capital.

To illustrate, assume the Schwab Corporation declared and paid a cash dividend and a partial liquidating dividend amounting to $150,000. Of this amount, $100,000 represents a regular $10 cash dividend on 10,000 shares of common stock. The remaining $50,000 represents a $5-per-share liquidating dividend, which is recorded as a reduction to Paid-In Capital in Excess of Par. The entries would be:

### Declaration of Dividend

| | | |
|---|---|---|
| Dividends (or Retained Earnings) ........................ | 100,000 | |
| Paid-In Capital in Excess of Par ......................... | 50,000 | |
|     Dividends Payable .................................... | | 150,000 |

### Payment of Dividend

| | | |
|---|---|---|
| Dividends Payable ....................................... | 150,000 | |
|     Cash ............................................... | | 150,000 |

Stockholders should be notified as to the allocation of the total dividend payment, so they can determine the amount that represents revenue and the amount that represents a return of investment. An investor owning 500 shares of Schwab Corporation common stock would record receipt of the dividend as follows:

| | | |
|---|---|---|
| Cash ...................................................... | 7,500 | |
|     Dividend Revenue (500 shares × $10) ...................... | | 5,000 |
|     Investment in Schwab Corp. Common Stock (500 shares × $5) .. | | 2,500 |

## QUASI-REORGANIZATIONS

As noted earlier, a debit balance in the retained earnings account is called a deficit. It may be the result of accumulated losses over a number of years or other significant debits to Retained Earnings. Sometimes a company with a large deficit is forced to discontinue operations and/or enter into bankruptcy proceedings. In some cases, however, where state laws permit, a company may eliminate a deficit through a restatement of invested capital balances. This provides, in effect, a fresh start for the company with a zero retained earnings balance. This is known as a **quasi-reorganization**. The advantage of a quasi-reorganization is that the procedure does not require recourse to the courts as in a formal reorganization or bankruptcy, and there is no change in the legal corporate entity or interruption of business activity.

Quasi-reorganizations are not common, but may be appropriate for a company operating under circumstances that are quite different from those of the past, e.g., a company with new management. Even if operated profitably, the company may take years to eliminate the deficit that was created under a prior management. In the meantime, the corporation generally cannot pay dividends to stockholders. With a quasi-reorganization, however, the accumulated deficit is eliminated. Performance from the reorganization date forward can then be measured and reported without having past mistakes and negative results reflecting unfavorably on the "new" company.

Normally in a quasi-reorganization, assets are revalued to reflect their current market values. This may require significant write-downs of assets against Retained Earnings, thus increasing the deficit. The total deficit is then written off (Retained Earnings is adjusted to a zero balance) against paid-in capital balances, giving the company a new capital structure. The Securities and Exchange Commission provides that any deficit reclassification is to be considered a quasi-reorganization and can only be made if all requisite conditions for a quasi-reorganization are met. Furthermore, the SEC requires that any anticipated accounting changes should be an integral part of the quasi-reorganization, and that the reorganization should not result in a write-up of net assets of the company.[9]

[9]*Staff Accounting Bulletin No. 78,* "Quasi-Reorganizations" (Washington: SEC, August 25, 1988).

To illustrate the nature of a quasi-reorganization, assume TSS Corporation has suffered operating losses for some time, but is now operating profitably and expects to continue to do so. Current and projected income, however, will not be sufficient to eliminate the deficit in the near term. It also appears that plant assets are overstated considering current prices and economic conditions. After receiving permission from state authorities and approval from the shareholders, the board of directors of TSS Corporation decides to restate company assets and paid-in capital balances in order to remove the deficit and make possible the declaration of dividends from profitable operations. A balance sheet for the company just prior to this action is presented below.

**TSS Corporation**
**Balance Sheet**
**June 30, 1993**

| Assets | | | Liabilities and Stockholders' Equity | | |
|---|---|---|---|---|---|
| Current assets ........... | | $ 250,000 | Liabilities ................ | | $ 300,000 |
| Land, buildings, and | | | Common stock, $10 par, | | |
| equipment.............. | $1,500,000 | | 100,000 shares .......... | $1,000,000 | |
| Less accumulated | | | Less deficit ............. | 150,000 | 850,000 |
| depreciation ............. | 600,000 | 900,000 | Total liabilities and | | |
| Total assets.............. | | $1,150,000 | stockholders' equity ...... | | $1,150,000 |

The quasi-reorganization is to be accomplished as follows:

1. Land, buildings, and equipment are to be reduced to their present fair market value of $600,000 by reducing the asset and accumulated depreciation balances by 33⅓%.
2. Common stock is to be reduced to a par value of $5, $500,000 in capital stock thus being converted into "additional paid-in capital."
3. The deficit of $450,000 ($150,000 as reported on the balance sheet increased by $300,000 arising from the write-down of land, buildings, and equipment) is to be applied against the capital from the reduction of the par value of stock.

Entries to record the changes follow:

| Transaction | Entry | | |
|---|---|---|---|
| (1) To write down land, buildings, and equipment and accumulated depreciation balances by 33⅓%. | Retained Earnings ........... <br> Accumulated Depreciation ... <br> Land, Buildings, and Equipment ..................... | 300,000 <br> 200,000 | <br> <br> 500,000 |
| (2) To reduce the common stock balance from $10 par to $5 par and to establish paid-in capital from reduction in stock par value. | Common Stock, $10 par ..... <br> Common Stock, $5 par..... <br> Paid-In Capital From Reduction in Stock Par Value ..... | 1,000,000 | <br> 500,000 <br> 500,000 |
| (3) To apply the deficit after asset devaluation against paid-in capital from reduction in stock par value. | Paid-In Capital From Reduction in Stock Par Value....... <br> Retained Earnings ........ | 450,000 | <br> 450,000 |

The balance sheet after the quasi-reorganization is shown at the top of page 684.

After the quasi-reorganization, the accounting for the company's operations is similar to that for a new company. Earnings subsequent to the quasi-reorganization, however, should be accumulated in a **dated retained earnings account**. On future balance sheets,

**TSS Corporation**
**Balance Sheet**
**June 30, 1993**

| Assets | | | Liabilities and Stockholders' Equity | |
|---|---|---|---|---|
| Current assets .... | | $250,000 | Liabilities .................... | $300,000 |
| Land, buildings, and equipment | $1,000,000 | | Common stock, $5 par, 100,000 shares ...................... | 500,000 |
| Less accumulated depreciation ...... | 400,000 | 600,000 | Paid-in capital from reduction in stock par value ............. | 50,000 |
| Total assets....... | | $850,000 | Total liabilities and stockholders' equity ......... | $850,000 |

retained earnings dated as of the time of account readjustment will inform readers of the date of such action and of the fresh start in earnings accumulation.

Exhibit 18—2 describes the quasi-reorganization undertaken by Genentech Inc., a firm engaged in the development, manufacture, and marketing of genetically engineered products.

**Exhibit 18—2    Genentech Inc.—Note Disclosure of Quasi-Reorganization**

On February 19, 1988, the Company's Board of Directors approved the elimination of the Company's accumulated deficit through an accounting reorganization of its stockholders' equity accounts (quasi-reorganization) effective October 1, 1987. The quasi-reorganization did not involve any revaluation of assets or liabilities, because for similar classes of assets, their fair values were no less than their book values, and for similar classes of liabilities, their book values were no less than their fair values. The effective date of the quasi-reorganization reflected the beginning of the quarter in which the Company received approval for and commenced marketing of its second major product, and as such, marked a turning point in the Company's operations. The accumulated deficit was eliminated by a transfer from additional paid-in capital in an amount equal to the accumulated deficit.

## REPORTING STOCKHOLDERS' EQUITY

In reporting stockholders' equity, it is important to provide readers with information concerning:

1. The sources of stockholders' equity, especially the amount paid in by stockholders (contributed capital) and the amount representing earnings retained in the business (retained earnings).
2. The classes of capital stock, including par or stated values; number of shares authorized, issued, and outstanding; number of shares of treasury stock.
3. Any restrictions on retained earnings.

In addition to the preceding information, the cost (or par value) of treasury stock should be deducted from stockholders' equity. Similarly, any unrealized loss on noncurrent marketable equity securities is to be reported as a contra equity item and deducted in determining total stockholders' equity.

As an illustration, the stockholders' equity section of the balance sheet of Hypothetical Corporation as of December 31, 1993, is presented. Many companies do not provide as much detail in the balance sheet as is illustrated for Hypothetical Corporation. A typical presentation is made in the actual financial statements of IBM Corporation in Appendix A.

Stockholders' Equity

Contributed capital:

| | | |
|---|---:|---:|
| 6% preferred stock, $100 par, cumulative, callable, 5,000 shares authorized and issued ............................................... | $500,000 | |
| Common stock, $5 stated value, 100,000 shares authorized, 60,000 shares issued; treasury stock, 5,000 shares—deducted below ........ | 300,000 | $ 800,000 |
| Paid-in capital in excess of stated value ........................... | $260,000 | |
| Paid-in capital from treasury stock ................................ | 16,000 | 276,000 |
| Total contributed capital ......................................... | | $1,076,000 |
| Retained earnings: | | |
| Appropriated for contingencies (Note X) ......................... | $125,000 | |
| Unappropriated ................................................. | 225,000 | |
| Total retained earnings ......................................... | | 350,000 |
| Total contributed capital and retained earnings ...................... | | $1,426,000 |
| Deduct: Common treasury stock, at cost (5,000 shares acquired at $8) ... | $ 40,000 | |
| Net unrealized loss on noncurrent marketable equity securities .. | 24,000 | 64,000 |
| Total stockholders' equity........................................ | | $1,362,000 |

Readers of financial statements should be provided with an explanation of the changes in individual equity balances during the period. Frequently, such explanation is provided in notes to the financial statements. When stockholders' equity is composed of numerous accounts, as in the preceding example, a statement of changes in stockholders' equity is sometimes presented. An illustrative statement for the Hypothetical Corporation is shown on page 686.

The net ownership equity of a business is an important element. Analyses of the amounts and sources of contributed capital compared to those generated and retained by the company provide useful information for assessing the long-term profitability and solvency of a business. The techniques for analyzing financial statements are discussed in Chapter 22.

---

## KEY TERMS

Appropriated retained earnings 674
Cash dividend 675
Deficit 672
Dividends 673
Liquidating dividend 681
Owners' Equity 671

Prior-period adjustment 671
Property dividend 676
Quasi-reorganization 682
Retained earnings 671
Statement of changes in
   stockholders' equity 685

Stock dividend 677
Stock split 679
Unappropriated (free) retained
   earnings 674

**Hypothetical Corporation**
**Statement of Changes in Stockholders' Equity**
**For the Year Ended December 31, 1993**

| | Preferred Stock | Common Stock | Paid-In Capital | Appropriated Retained Earnings for Contingencies | Unappropriated Retained Earnings | Contra Equity Balances | Total |
|---|---|---|---|---|---|---|---|
| Balances, December 31, 1992 | $300,000 | $300,000 | $260,000* | $ 90,000 | $222,500 | $(20,000) | $1,152,500 |
| Prior-period adjustment—correction of 1991 error, net of tax | | | | | (25,000) | | (25,000) |
| Adjusted balances, December 31, 1992 | $300,000 | $300,000 | $260,000 | $ 90,000 | $197,500 | $(20,000) | $1,127,500 |
| Sale of 2,000 shares of preferred stock in January 1993, at par value | 200,000 | | | | | | 200,000 |
| Sale of 2,500 shares of treasury stock, common, in January 1993, cost $20,000, for $36,000 | | | 16,000 | | | 20,000 | 36,000 |
| Net income for 1993 | | | | | 120,000 | | 120,000 |
| Cash dividends: | | | | | | | |
| Preferred stock, $6 on 5,000 shares, $30,000 | | | | | (57,500) | | (57,500) |
| Common stock, 50¢ on 55,000 shares, $27,500 | | | | | | | |
| Retained earnings appropriated for contingencies | | | | 35,000 | (35,000) | | |
| Purchase of 5,000 shares of common treasury stock @ cost, $8 | | | | | | (40,000) | (40,000) |
| Net unrealized loss on noncurrent marketable equity securities | | | | | | (24,000) | (24,000) |
| Balances, December 31, 1993 | $500,000 | $300,000 | $276,000 | $125,000 | $225,000 | $(64,000) | $1,362,000 |

*From sale of common stock at more than stated value.

## QUESTIONS

1. What is the impact of each of the following transactions or events on retained earnings or total stockholders' equity?

   (a) Operating profits.
   (b) Discovery of an understatement of income in a previous period.
   (c) Release of Retained Earnings Appropriated for Purchase of Treasury Stock upon the sale of treasury stock.
   (d) Issuance of bonds at a premium.
   (e) Purchase of a corporation's own capital stock.
   (f) Increase in a company's earning capacity, assumed to be evidence of considerable goodwill.
   (g) Construction of equipment for a company's own use at a cost less than the prevailing market price of identical equipment.
   (h) Donation to a corporation of its own stock.
   (i) Sale of land, buildings, and equipment at a gain.
   (j) Gain on bond retirement.
   (k) Conversion of bonds into common stock.
   (l) Conversion of preferred stock into common stock.

2. What are the two major considerations of a board of directors in making decisions involving dividend declarations?

3. Very few companies pay dividends in amounts equal to their retained earnings. Why?

4. The following announcement appeared on the financial page of a newspaper:

   The Board of Directors of Benton Co., at their meeting on June 15, 1993, declared the regular quarterly dividend on outstanding common stock of $1.40 per share, payable on July 10, 1993, to the stockholders of record at the close of business June 30, 1993.

   (a) What is the purpose of each of the three dates given in the announcement?
   (b) When would the common stock of Benton Co. normally trade "ex-dividend"?

5. Dividends are sometimes said to have been paid "out of retained earnings." What is wrong with such a statement?

6. The directors of The Dress Shoppe are considering issuance of a stock dividend. They have asked you to answer the following questions regarding the proposed action:

   (a) How is a stock dividend different from a stock split?
   (b) How are stock dividends accounted for by the issuing corporation? by the stockholder?

7. Often, when a company declares a stock dividend, fractional share warrants are issued to certain stockholders. (a) What is a fractional share warrant? (b) What can the stockholder do with fractional share warrants? (c) If the company does not want to issue fractional share warrants, what alternatives are available?

8. At a regular meeting of the board of directors of the Greenwood Corporation, a property dividend payable in the stock of the Mossey Corporation is to be declared. The stock of Mossey Corporation is recorded on the books of the Greenwood Corporation at $190,000; the market value of the stock is $230,000. The question is raised whether the amount to be recorded for the dividend payable should be the book value or the market value. What is the proper accounting treatment?

9. (a) What is a liquidating dividend? (b) Under what circumstances are such distributions made?

10. (a) Why might a company seek a quasi-reorganization? (b) What are the steps in a quasi-reorganization?

11. In reviewing the financial statements of Farmer Inc., a stockholder does not understand the purpose of Appropriation of Retained Earnings for Bond Redemption Fund that has been set up by periodic debits to Retained Earnings. The stockholder is told that this balance will not be used to redeem the bonds at their maturity. (a) What account will be reduced by the payment of the bonds? (b) What purpose is accomplished by the Appropriation of Retained Earnings for Bond Redemption Fund? (c) What disposition is made of the appropriation after the bonds are retired?

## DISCUSSION CASES

### Case 18—1  (Small stock dividends)

The president of Info Company suggests including the following statement in this year's annual report:

On December 18, a 10% common stock dividend was distributed to stockholders, resulting in a transfer of $1,536,000 from Retained Earnings to Common Stock and Capital in Excess of Par.

While the percentage of the stock dividend was the same as the previous year, the sum transferred to stockholders' equity was nearly $80,000 less.

The seeming inconsistency is the result of the requirement of regulatory authorities that the value of stock dividends on the company's books be related to the market value of the stock. As a result, the present year's dividend was valued at $65 per share as compared to $74 per share for last year's stock dividend.

The president feels that this statement would help clarify the apparent inconsistency in the company's dividend policy. As partner for the accounting firm that is performing the annual audit of Info Company, you feel that the president's statement may mislead the readers of the report even though the figures are correct.

State how the stock dividends should be accounted for in a situation such as this one, explaining your reasoning. What criticism, if any, do you have of the terminology used by the president? Explain.

## Case 18—2 (How much should our dividend be?)

Seaside Corp. has paid quarterly dividends of $0.70 per share for the last three years and is trying to continue this tradition. Seaside's balance sheet is as follows:

**Seaside Corp.**
**Balance Sheet**
**December 31, 1993**

| Assets | | Liabilities | |
|---|---|---|---|
| Current assets: | | Current liabilities: | |
| Cash ...................... | $ 50,000 | Accounts payable .......... | $ 520,000 |
| Accounts receivable ........ | 450,000 | Taxes payable ............. | 100,000 |
| Inventory.................. | 1,200,000 | Accrued liabilities .......... | 90,000 |
| Total current assets ....... | $1,700,000 | Total current liabilities ..... | $ 710,000 |
| Investments ................ | 500,000 | Bonds payable ............... | 1,500,000 |
| Land, buildings and equipment | | Total liabilities ............... | $2,210,000 |
| (net) ....................... | 1,600,000 | | |
| | | Stockholders' Equity | |
| | | Common stock ($10 par, 69,000 | |
| | | shares outstanding) ........... | $ 690,000 |
| | | Retained earnings ............. | 900,000 |
| | | Total stockholders' equity ...... | $1,590,000 |
| | | Total liabilities and | |
| Total assets ................. | $3,800,000 | stockholders' equity .......... | $3,800,000 |

Discuss Seaside's possibilities concerning the issuance of dividends.

## Case 18—3 (Cash or stock dividend?)

Best Ski Manufacturer is considering offering a 10% stock dividend rather than its normal cash dividend of $1 per share in the first quarter of 1993. However, some of Best's stockholders have expressed displeasure at the idea and say they strongly prefer cash dividends.

Discuss the issue of a stock dividend as opposed to a cash dividend from the points of view of (a) a stockholder and (b) the board of directors.

## Case 18—4 (Stock splits and stock dividends)

Union and Eastern Corporation has been one of the more popular growth stocks during the past several years. In 1993, its $20 par common stock was selling in the range of $200-$230, with 146,000 shares outstanding. On May 1, 1993, Union and Eastern announced that, effective May 10, 1993, its stock would be split 4-for-1. This was the first time since 1973 that Union and Eastern's stock had been split, although several stock dividends had been issued during the past 20 years. (a) What are the differences between a stock dividend and a stock split both from the standpoint of the investor and the company? (b) What are some possible reasons for Union and Eastern issuing stock dividends prior to 1993?

### Case 18—5   (Are cash dividends relevant?)

On March 23, 1993, the board of directors of Mycroft Company declared a quarterly cash dividend on its $1 par common stock of $0.50 per share, payable on May 10, 1993, to the shareholders of record on April 14, 1993. Before April 9, Mycroft's shares traded in the stock market "with dividend," meaning that the quoted stock price included the right to receive the dividend. After April 9, the shares traded "ex-dividend," meaning that the quoted price did not include the right to receive the dividend. Before April 9, Mycroft's shares were selling for $30 per share. What should happen to Mycroft's stock price on April 9, the ex-dividend date? What should happen to Mycroft's stock price on March 23, the dividend declaration date?

### Case 18—6   (Out of sight, out of mind)

As of 1988, Nippon Steel Corporation was the world's largest steelmaker. Nippon Steel also engages in the engineering and manufacture of electronic equipment, services, and biotechnology. In Note 10 to its 1988 financial statements, Nippon Steel included the following statement: "As is customary practice in Japan, the payment of bonuses to directors and statutory auditors is made out of retained earnings instead of being charged to income of the year." Do you think that this accounting practice encourages or discourages payment of bonuses to directors? Explain.

### Case 18—7   (Asset revaluation in quasi-reorganization)

Mattel manufactures and markets toys. Barbie and Ken are Mattel products, as are Hot Wheels cars. Mattel offered the following description of its 1987 restructuring and quasi-reorganization:

> Effective December 26, 1987, the Company implemented a quasi-reorganization and revalued certain of its assets and liabilities to fair values as of that date. These revaluations resulted in an increase in property, plant and equipment of $83.0 million, a decrease in long-term indebtedness of $5.0 million and an increase in deferred tax liabilities of $19.0 million. The net effect of these adjustments aggregating approximately $69.0 million was credited to additional paid-in capital. Additionally, as of December 26, 1987, the accumulated deficit of approximately $256.0 million and the cumulative translation adjustment of approximately $33.0 million were transferred to additional paid-in capital.

Describe what, if anything, strikes you as being wrong in this description.

---

## EXERCISES

### Exercise 18—1   (Reporting errors from previous periods)

Endicott Company's December 31, 1992, balance sheet reported retained earnings of $86,500, and net income of $124,000 was reported in the 1992 income statement. While preparing financial statements for the year ending December 31, 1993, Tom Dryden, accountant for Endicott Company, discovered that net income for 1992 had been overstated by $22,000 due to an error in recording depreciation expense for 1992. Net income for 1993 was $106,000, and dividends of $30,000 were declared and paid in 1993.

1. What effect, if any, would the $22,000 error made in 1992 have on the company's 1993 financial statements?
2. Compute the amount of retained earnings to be reported in Endicott Company's December 31, 1993, balance sheet.

## Exercise 18—2   (Cash and stock dividends)

On September 30, 1993, Lomax Company issued 4,000 shares of its $5 par common stock in connection with a stock dividend. No entry was made on the stock dividend declaration date. The market value of the stock on the date of declaration was $10 per share. The stockholders' equity accounts of Lomax Company immediately before issuance of the stock dividend shares were as follows:

Common stock, $5 par; 100,000 shares authorized; 40,000 shares
outstanding . . . . . . . . . . . . . . . . . . . . . . . . . . . . . . . . . . . . . . . . . . . . . . . . . . . . . . . .   $200,000
Additional paid-in capital . . . . . . . . . . . . . . . . . . . . . . . . . . . . . . . . . . . . . . . . .    300,000
Retained earnings . . . . . . . . . . . . . . . . . . . . . . . . . . . . . . . . . . . . . . . . . . . . . . . .    350,000

On December 30, 1993, Lomax Company declared a cash dividend of $3.50 per share payable January 5, 1994. Give the necessary entries to record the declaration and payment or issuance of the dividends.

## Exercise 18—3   (Property dividends)

WW Company distributed the following dividends to its stockholders:

(a)  400,000 shares of Shell Corporation stock, carrying value of investment $1,200,000, fair market value $2,300,000.
(b)  230,000 shares of Evans Company stock, a closely held corporation. The shares were purchased by WW three years ago at $5.60 per share, but no current market price is available.

Give the journal entries to account for the declaration and the payment of the dividends.

## Exercise 18—4   (Accounting for property dividends)

Hartz Corporation owned 2,700 shares of Finch Corporation common stock that it had purchased in 1990 for $10 per share. On August 15, 1993, when the value of Finch stock was $25 per share, Hartz declared a property dividend of 1 share of Finch for every 15 shares of Hartz common stock held by stockholders on October 15, 1993. Hartz had 40,500 shares of common outstanding. The Finch shares were distributed on December 15, 1993.

1. Give the necessary journal entries on Hartz's books to record the property dividend.
2. Give the necessary journal entry to record the property dividend on the books of an investor who owns 900 shares of Hartz Corporation common stock.

## Exercise 18—5   (Dividend computations)

Consistent Company has been paying regular quarterly dividends of $1.50 and wants to pay the same amount in the third quarter of 1993. Given the following information, (1) what is the total amount that Consistent will have to pay in dividends in the third quarter in order to pay $1.50 per share, and (2) what is the total amount of dividends to be distributed during the year assuming no equity transactions occur after June 30?

1993
Jan.   1    Shares outstanding, 800,000; $8 par (1,500,000 shares authorized).
Feb.  15   Issued 50,000 new shares at $10.50.
Mar.  31   Paid quarterly dividends of $1.50 per share.
May   12   $1,000,000 of $1,000 bonds were converted to common stock at the rate of 100 shares of stock per $1,000 bond.
June  15   Issued a 15% stock dividend.
        30   Paid quarterly dividends of $1.50 per share.

## Exercise 18—6   (Stock dividends)

The balance sheet of the Carmen Corporation shows the following:

| | |
|---|---:|
| Common stock, $5 stated value, 80,000 shares issued and outstanding . . . . . . . . . . . . . . . . . . . . . . . . . . . . . . . . . . . . . . . . . . . . . . | $400,000 |
| Paid-in capital in excess of stated value . . . . . . . . . . . . . . . . . . . . . . . . . | 800,000 |
| Retained earnings . . . . . . . . . . . . . . . . . . . . . . . . . . . . . . . . . . . . . . . . . . . | 350,000 |

A 25% stock dividend is declared, the board of directors authorizing a transfer from Retained Earnings to Common Stock at the stated value of the shares.

1. Give entries to record the declaration and issuance of the stock dividend.
2. What was the effect of the issuance of the stock dividend on the ownership equity of each stockholder in the corporation?
3. Give entries to record the declaration and issuance of the dividend if the board of directors had elected to transfer an amount from Retained Earnings equal to the market value of the stock ($10 per share).

## Exercise 18—7   (Stock dividends and stock splits)

The capital accounts for Shop Right Market on June 30, 1993, are as follows:

| | |
|---|---:|
| Common stock, $15 par, 40,000 shares . . . . . . . . . . . . . . . . . . . . . . . . . . | $  600,000 |
| Paid-in capital in excess of par . . . . . . . . . . . . . . . . . . . . . . . . . . . . . . . . . | 435,000 |
| Retained earnings . . . . . . . . . . . . . . . . . . . . . . . . . . . . . . . . . . . . . . . . . . . | 2,160,000 |

Shares of the company's stock are selling at this time at $25. What entries would you make in each of the following cases?

(a)   A 10% stock dividend is declared and issued.
(b)   A 50% stock dividend is declared and issued.
(c)   A 3-for-1 stock split is declared and issued.

## Exercise 18—8   (Accounting for stock splits)

Effective December 31, 1993, the stockholders of Interstate Corp. approved a 2-for-1 split of the company's common stock and an increase in authorized common shares from 200,000 (par value $10 per share) to 400,000 shares (par value $5 per share). Interstate's stockholders' equity account immediately before these events is summarized as follows:

| | |
|---|---:|
| Common stock ($10 par, 200,000 shares authorized, 100,000 issued and outstanding) . . . . . . . . . . . . . . . . . . . . . . . . . . . . . . . . . . . . . . . . . . | $1,000,000 |
| Additional paid-in capital—common stock . . . . . . . . . . . . . . . . . . . . . . . . | 150,000 |
| Total contributed capital . . . . . . . . . . . . . . . . . . . . . . . . . . . . . . . . . . . . . . | $1,150,000 |
| Retained earnings . . . . . . . . . . . . . . . . . . . . . . . . . . . . . . . . . . . . . . . . . . . | 1,350,000 |
| Total stockholders' equity . . . . . . . . . . . . . . . . . . . . . . . . . . . . . . . . . . . . . | $2,500,000 |

1. Make the necessary entries to record the stock split for both Interstate and the investors.
2. Prepare the stockholders' equity section of Interstate's December 31, 1993, balance sheet.

## Exercise 18—9   (Stock dividend computation)

The directors of Warehouser Inc., whose $80 par value common stock is currently selling at $100 per share, have decided to issue a stock dividend. Warehouser has authorization for 400,000 shares of common, has issued 220,000 shares, all of which are currently outstanding, and desires to capitalize $2,400,000 of the retained earnings account balance. What percent stock dividend should be issued to accomplish this goal?

### Exercise 18—10   (Accounting for dividends)

The following information has been taken from the balance sheet of Kain Company:

| | |
|---|---:|
| Current assets | $371,250 |
| Investments | 431,400 |
| Common stock (par value $20) | 337,000 |
| Paid-in capital in excess of par | 200,000 |
| Retained earnings | 385,000 |

Prepare the journal entries for the following unrelated transactions:

(a)  A 30% stock dividend is declared and distributed when the market value of the stock is $23 per share.
(b)  Par value of the common stock is reduced to $5, and the stock is split 4-for-1.
(c)  A dividend of 1 share Northern Co. common stock for every share of Kain Company stock is declared and distributed. Northern Co. common stock is carried on the books of Kain Company at a cost of $0.80 per share, and the market value is $1.10 per share.

### Exercise 18—11   (Fractional share warrants)

Groton Company has 500,000 shares of $1 par common stock outstanding. The market price of the shares is $25 per share. In declaring and distributing a 10% stock dividend, Groton initially issued only 46,000 new shares; the other stock dividend shares were not issued, because some investors did not own Groton shares in even multiples of ten. To these stockholders Groton issued fractional share warrants. Prepare all journal entries necessary to record the declaration and distribution of the stock dividend assuming that 90% of the fractional share warrants were ultimately turned in for shares.

### Exercise 18—12   (Restricting retained earnings)

On January 1, 1991, Northwest Manufacturing Corporation issued $20,000,000 of bonds payable. The bond issue agreement with the underwriters required Northwest Manufacturing to appropriate earnings of $1,250,000 at the end of each year until the bonds are retired. During their June 1993 board meeting, the directors decided to change the company's financial structure to include only short-term debt and to drop their present insurance policy in favor of a self-insurance plan. On July 1, 1993, the company retired the bond issue and set up the first annual appropriation for self-insurance for $28,000.

1. Give the entries to record the periodic appropriations under the bond issue agreement for 1991 and 1992 and their cancellation in 1993.
2. Give the entry to record the appropriation for self-insurance.

### Exercise 18—13   (Computation of retained earnings)

The following information has been taken from the accounts of Oviatt Corporation:

| | |
|---|---:|
| Total net income reported since incorporation | $300,000 |
| Total cash dividends paid | 80,000 |
| Capitalized value of stock dividends distributed | 70,000 |
| Paid-in capital from treasury stock | 35,000 |
| Bond discount | 75,000 |
| Appropriation for plant expansion | 100,000 |

Determine the current balance of unappropriated retained earnings.

### Exercise 18—14   (Correcting the retained earnings account)

The retained earnings account for Olausson Corp. shows the following debits and credits. Give all entries required to correct the account. What is the corrected amount of retained earnings?

**Account**    Retained Earnings

| Date | | Item | Debit | Credit | Balance Debit | Balance Credit |
|------|---|------|-------|--------|---------------|----------------|
| Jan. | 1 | Balance ................................... | | | | 263,200 |
| (a) | | Loss from fire............................. | 2,625 | | | 260,575 |
| (b) | | Write-off of goodwill ....................... | 26,250 | | | 234,325 |
| (c) | | Stock dividend........................... | 70,000 | | | 164,325 |
| (d) | | Loss on sale of equipment ................. | 24,150 | | | 140,175 |
| (e) | | Officers' compensation related to income of prior periods—accrual overlooked .......... | 162,750 | | 22,575 | |
| (f) | | Loss on retirement of preferred shares at more than issuance price....................... | 35,000 | | 57,575 | |
| (g) | | Paid-in capital in excess of par ............. | | 64,750 | | 7,175 |
| (h) | | Stock subscription defaults ................ | | 4,235 | | 11,410 |
| (i) | | Gain on retirement of preferred stock at less than issuance price........................ | | 12,950 | | 24,360 |
| (j) | | Gain on early retirement of bonds at less than book value ................................ | | 7,525 | | 31,885 |
| (k) | | Gain on life insurance policy settlement...... | | 5,250 | | 37,135 |
| (l) | | Correction of prior-period error............. | | 25,025 | | 62,160 |

## Exercise 18—15  (Liquidating dividend)

Van Etten Company declared and paid a cash dividend of $4.50 per share on its $1 par common stock.  Van Etten has 100,000 shares of common stock outstanding and total paid-in capital from common stock of $800,000.  As part of the dividend announcement, Van Etten stated that retained earnings served as the basis for only $0.50 of the dividend; investors should consider the remainder to be a return of investment.  Prepare the journal entries necessary on Van Etten's books to record the declaration and distribution of this dividend.

## Exercise 18—16  (Quasi-reorganization)

Hard Luck Corporation has incurred losses from operations for many years. At the recommendation of the newly hired president, the board of directors voted to implement a quasi-reorganization, subject to stockholders' approval. Immediately prior to the quasi-reorganization, on June 30, 1993, Hard Luck's balance sheet was as follows:

| | |
|---|---:|
| Current assets ............................................... | $ 275,000 |
| Property, plant, and equipment (net) ............................ | 675,000 |
| Other assets ................................................ | 100,000 |
| | $1,050,000 |
| | |
| Total liabilities ............................................... | $ 300,000 |
| Common stock ............................................... | 800,000 |
| Additional paid-in capital....................................... | 150,000 |
| Retained earnings ............................................ | (200,000) |
| | $1,050,000 |

The stockholders approved the quasi-reorganization effective July 1, 1993, to be accomplished by a reduction in property, plant, and equipment (net) of $175,000, a reduction in other assets of $75,000, and appropriate adjustment to the capital structure.

1. Prepare the journal entries to record the quasi-reorganization on July 1, 1993.
2. Prepare a new balance sheet after the quasi-reorganization.    (AICPA adapted)

## Exercise 18—17  (Reporting stockholders' equity)

Kenny Co. began operations on January 1, 1992, by issuing at $15 per share one-half of the 950,000 shares of $10 par value common stock that had been authorized for sale. In addition, Kenny has

500,000 shares of $5 par value, 6% preferred shares authorized. During 1992, Kenny had $1,025,000 of net income and declared $237,500 of dividends.

During 1993 Kenny had the following transactions:

Jan. 10   Issued an additional 100,000 shares of common stock for $17 per share.
Apr.  1   Issued 150,000 shares of the preferred stock for $8 per share.
July 19   Authorized the purchase of a custom-made machine to be delivered in January of 1994. Kenny restricted $295,000 of retained earnings for the purchase of the machine.
Oct. 23   Sold an additional 50,000 shares of the preferred stock for $9 per share.
Dec. 31   Reported $1,215,000 of net income and declared a dividend of $645,000 to stockholders of record on January 15, 1994, to be paid on February 1, 1994.

Prepare the stockholders' equity section of Kenny's balance sheet for December 31, 1992, and December 31, 1993.

# PROBLEMS

## Problem 18—1   (Accounting for stock transactions)

TRX Corporation is publicly owned, and its shares are traded on a national stock exchange. TRX has 16,000 shares of $25 stated value common stock authorized. Only 75% of these shares have been issued, and of the shares issued, only 11,000 are outstanding. On December 31, 1992, the stockholders' equity section revealed that the balance in Paid-In Capital in Excess of Stated Value was $140,000, and the retained earnings balance was $110,000. Treasury stock was purchased at an average cost of $37.50 per share.

During 1993, TRX had the following transactions:

Jan. 15   TRX issued, at $55 per share, 800 shares of $50 par, 5% cumulative preferred stock; 2,000 shares are authorized.
Feb.  1   TRX sold 1,500 shares of newly issued $25 stated value common stock at $42 per share.
Mar. 15   TRX declared a cash dividend on common stock of $0.15 per share, payable on April 30 to all stockholders of record on April 1.
Apr. 15   TRX reacquired 200 shares of its common stock for $43 per share. TRX uses the cost method to account for treasury stock.
     30   Employees exercised 1,000 options granted in 1991 under a non-compensatory stock option plan. When the options were granted, each option entitled the employee to purchase 1 share of common stock for $50 per share. On April 30, when the market price was $55 per share, TRX issued new shares to the employees.
May   1   TRX declared a 10% stock dividend to be distributed on June 1 to stockholders of record on May 7. The market price of the common stock was $50 per share on May 1. (Assume treasury shares do not participate in stock dividends.)
     31   TRX sold 150 treasury shares reacquired on April 15 and an additional 200 shares costing $7,500 that had been on hand since the beginning of the year. The selling price was $57 per share.
Sep. 15   The semiannual cash dividend on common stock was declared, amounting to $0.15 per share. TRX also declared the yearly dividend on preferred stock. Both are payable on October 15 to stockholders of record on October 1.

Net income for 1993 was $50,000.

## Instructions:

1. Compute the number of shares and dollar amount of treasury stock at the beginning of 1993.
2. Make the necessary journal entries to record the transactions in 1993 relating to stockholders' equity.
3. Prepare the stockholders' equity section of TRX Corporation's December 31, 1993, balance sheet.

## Problem 18—2  (Accounting for stock transactions)

Brady Company has 30,000 shares of $10 par value common stock authorized and 20,000 shares issued and outstanding. On August 15, 1993, Brady purchased 1,500 shares of treasury stock for $12 per share. (All outstanding shares were issued for $11 per share.) Brady uses the cost method to account for treasury stock. On September 14, 1993, Brady sold 500 shares of the treasury stock for $14 per share.

On October 30, 1993, when the market value of the common stock was $16 per share, Brady declared and distributed 2,000 shares as a "small" stock dividend, 1,500 from unissued shares and 500 from treasury shares. (Assume treasury shares do not participate in stock dividends.)

On December 20, 1993, Brady declared a $1-per-share cash dividend, payable on January 10, 1994, to shareholders of record on December 31, 1993.

## Instructions:

1. Make the entries necessary for Brady to record the above transactions.
2. Assuming that Brady's stockholders' equity consists of only the above mentioned items and that retained earnings was $375,000 as of December 31, 1992 (net income for 1993 was $56,000), prepare the stockholders' equity section of Brady's balance sheet as of December 31, 1993.

(AICPA adapted)

## Problem 18—3  (Accounting for stock transactions)

Ellis Corporation was organized on June 30, 1990. After two and one-half years of profitable operations, the equity section of Ellis's balance sheet was as follows:

| | |
|---|---|
| Contributed capital: | |
| Common stock, $30 par, 600,000 shares authorized, 200,000 shares issued and outstanding | $6,000,000 |
| Paid-in capital in excess of par | 600,000 |
| Retained earnings | 2,800,000 |
| Total stockholders' equity | $9,400,000 |

During 1993, the following transactions affected the stockholders' equity:

Jan. 31   10,000 shares of common stock were reacquired at $32; treasury stock is recorded at cost.
Apr.  1   The company declared a 30% stock dividend. (Applies to all issued stock.)
     30   The company declared a $0.75 cash dividend. (Applies only to outstanding stock.)
June  1   The stock dividend was issued, and the cash dividend was paid.
Aug. 31   All treasury stock was sold at $35.

**Instructions:**  Give journal entries to record the stock transactions.

## Problem 18—4  (Stock dividend and cash dividend)

On January 1, 1993, Homer Company has 100,000 shares of $0.50 par common stock outstanding. The market value of Homer's common stock is $20 per share. Homer's retained earnings balance on January 1 was $580,000. During 1992, Homer declared and paid cash dividends of $0.70 per share.

Net income for 1993 is expected to be $110,000. Homer has a large loan from Garth Bank; part of the loan agreement stipulates that Homer must maintain a minimum retained earnings balance of $400,000.

Homer's board of directors is debating whether to declare a stock dividend. Three proposals have been presented: (1) no stock dividend, (2) a 10% stock dividend, and (3) a 25% stock dividend.

**Instructions:** As a shareholder in Homer Company, which of the three proposals do you favor? Support your answer.

### Problem 18—5 (Stockholders' equity transactions)

The stockholders' equity of the Seasoned Lumber Co. on June 30, 1993, was as follows:

Contributed capital:
| | |
|---|---:|
| 5% preferred stock, $50 par, cumulative, 30,000 shares issued, dividends 5 years in arrears...................................... | $1,500,000 |
| Common stock, $30 par, 100,000 shares issued .................... | 3,000,000 |
| | $4,500,000 |
| Deficit from operations ......................................... | (600,000) |
| Total stockholders' equity ....................................... | $3,900,000 |

On July 1 the following actions were taken:

(a) Common stockholders turned in their old common stock and received in exchange new common stock, 1 share of the new stock being exchanged for every 4 shares of the old. New common stock was given a stated value of $60 per share.
(b) One-half share of the new common stock was issued on each share of preferred stock outstanding in liquidation of dividends in arrears on preferred stock.
(c) The deficit from operations was applied against the paid-in capital arising from the common stock restatement.

Transactions for the remainder of 1993 affecting the stockholders' equity were as follows:

Oct.   1    10,000 shares of preferred stock were called at $55 plus dividends for 3 months at 5%. Stock was formally retired.
Nov. 10    60,000 shares of new common stock were sold at $65.
Dec. 31    Net income for the 6 months ended on this date was $400,000. (Debit Income Summary.) The semiannual dividend was declared on preferred shares, and a $0.75 dividend was declared on common shares, dividends being payable January 20, 1994.

**Instructions:**

1. Record in journal form the foregoing transactions.
2. Prepare the stockholders' equity section of the balance sheet as of December 31, 1993.

### Problem 18—6 (Stockholders' equity transactions)

Seneca Inc. was organized on January 2, 1992, with authorized capital stock consisting of 50,000 shares of 10%, $200 par preferred, and 200,000 shares of no-par, no-stated-value common. During the first 2 years of the company's existence, the following selected transactions took place:

1992
Jan.   2    Sold 10,000 shares of common stock at $16.
       2    Sold 3,000 shares of preferred stock at $216.
Mar.  2    Sold common stock as follows: 10,800 shares at $22; 2,700 shares at $25.
July 10    A nearby piece of land, appraised at $400,000, was acquired for 600 shares of preferred stock and 27,000 shares of common. (Preferred stock was recorded at $216, the balance being assigned to common.)

Dec. 16  The regular preferred and a $1.50 common dividend were declared.
28  Dividends declared on December 16 were paid.
31  The income summary account showed a credit balance of $450,000, which was transferred to Retained Earnings.

1993
Feb. 27  The corporation reacquired 12,000 shares of common stock at $19. The treasury stock is carried at cost. (State law required that an appropriation of retained earnings be made for the purchase price of treasury stock. Appropriations are to be returned to Retained Earnings upon resale of the stock.)
June 17  Resold 10,000 shares of the treasury stock at $23.
July 31  Resold all of the remaining treasury stock at $18.
Sep. 30  The corporation sold 11,000 additional shares of common stock at $21.
Dec. 16  The regular preferred dividend and an $0.80 common dividend were declared.
28  Dividends declared on December 16 were paid.
31  The income summary account showed a credit balance of $425,000, which was transferred to Retained Earnings.

**Instructions:**

1. Give the journal entries to record the foregoing transactions.
2. Prepare the stockholders' equity section of the balance sheet as of December 31, 1993.

## Problem 18—7  (Accounting for stockholders' equity)

A condensed balance sheet for Sharp Tax Inc. as of December 31, 1990, appears below.

Sharp Tax Inc.
Condensed Balance Sheet
December 31, 1990

| Assets | | Liabilities and Stockholders' Equity | |
|---|---|---|---|
| Assets ...................... | $525,000 | Liabilities ..................... | $120,000 |
| | | 8% preferred stock, $100 par.... | 75,000 |
| | | Common stock, $50 par ........ | 150,000 |
| | | Paid-in capital in excess of par .. | 30,000 |
| | | Retained earnings ............. | 150,000 |
| | | Total liabilities and | |
| Total assets ................. | $525,000 | stockholders' equity .......... | $525,000 |

Capital stock authorized consists of 750 shares of 8%, cumulative preferred stock, and 15,000 shares of common stock.

Information relating to operations of the succeeding 3 years follows:

| | 1991 | 1992 | 1993 |
|---|---|---|---|
| Dividends declared on Dec. 20, payable on Jan. 10 of the following year: | | | |
| Preferred stock ....................... | 8% cash | 8% cash | 8% cash |
| Common stock ....................... | $1.00 cash 50% stock | $1.25 cash | $1.00 cash |
| Net income for year ................... | $67,500 | $39,000 | $51,000 |

1992
Feb. 12   Accumulated depreciation was reduced by $72,000 following an income tax investigation. (Assume that this was an error that qualified as a prior-period adjustment.) Additional income tax of $22,500 for prior years was paid.
Mar.  3   Purchased 300 shares of common stock at $54 per share; treasury stock is recorded at cost, and retained earnings are appropriated equal to such costs.

1993
Aug. 10   All the treasury stock was resold at $59 per share and the retained earnings appropriation was canceled.
Sep. 12   By vote of the stockholders, each share of the common stock was exchanged by the corporation for 4 shares of no-par common stock with a stated value of $15.

**Instructions:**

1. Give the journal entries to record the foregoing transactions for the 3-year period ended December 31, 1993.
2. Prepare the stockholders' equity section of the balance sheet as it would appear at the end of 1991, 1992, and 1993.

### Problem 18—8   (Adjustments to retained earnings)

On March 31, 1993, the retained earnings account of Universal Services showed a balance of $19,000,000. The board of directors of Universal made the following decisions during the remainder of 1993 that possibly affect the retained earnings account.

Apr.  1   Universal decided to assume the risk for workers' compensation insurance. The estimated liability for 1993 was $120,000. Also, a fund was set up to cover the estimated liability.
     30   Universal has not experienced even a small fire since 1949; therefore, the board of directors decided to start a self-insurance plan. They decided to start with a $400,000 appropriation.
May 15   A fire did considerable damage to the outside warehouse. It cost $360,000 to repair the warehouse.
Aug. 20   The board of directors received a report from the plant engineer indicating that the company is possibly in violation of pollution control standards. The fine for such a violation is $800,000. As a result of the engineer's report, the board decided to set up a general contingency appropriation for $800,000.
Sep.  1   The company reacquired 80,000 shares of its own stock at $29; treasury stock is recorded at cost. Due to legal restrictions, Universal has to set up an appropriation to cover the cost of the treasury stock.
Dec. 31   The company had to pay an $800,000 fine for pollution control violations and the treasury stock was sold at $31. No workers' compensation was paid during the year.

**Instructions:**   Prepare all the necessary entries to record the transactions.

### Problem 18—9   (Reporting stockholders' equity)

The data at the top of page 748 (presented in alphabetical order) was derived from the accounts of High Country Ranch as of December 31, 1993:

**Instructions:**   From this data, prepare the stockholders' equity section as it would appear on the balance sheet.

| | Debits | Credits |
|---|---|---|
| Accumulated depreciation—buildings ................. | | $ 255,000 |
| Bonds payable ...................................... | | 325,000 |
| Bond retirement fund ............................... | $ 138,000 | |
| Buildings .......................................... | 1,150,000 | |
| Common stock, $10 par (89,000 shares authorized, 63,200 shares issued................................ | | 632,000 |
| Common stock subscribed (4,000 shares) ............. | | 40,000 |
| Current assets ..................................... | 790,200 | |
| Current liabilities—other ........................... | | 270,000 |
| Customer deposits ................................. | | 17,000 |
| Dividends payable—cash ........................... | | 16,000 |
| Income taxes payable............................... | | 43,000 |
| Paid-in capital from treasury stock .................. | | 32,000 |
| Paid-in capital in excess of par...................... | | 24,000 |
| Retained earnings appropriated for contingencies ...... | | 100,000 |
| Retained earnings appropriated for bond retirement fund........................................ | | 138,000 |
| Retained earnings appropriated for purchase of treasury stock ...................................... | | 56,000 |
| Stock dividends distributable (5,040 shares)........... | | 50,400 |
| Treasury stock (4,800 shares at cost) ................ | 56,000 | |
| Unappropriated retained earnings ................... | | 135,800 |
| | $2,134,200 | $2,134,200 |

## Problem 18—10  (Retained earnings and the statement of cash flows)

The following items relate to the activities of Cortland Company for 1993:

(a)  Cash dividends declared and paid on common stock during the year totaled $80,000. In addition, on January 15, 1993, dividends of $15,000 that were declared in 1992 were paid.

(b)  Retained earnings of $130,000 were appropriated during the year in anticipation of a major capital expansion in future years.

(c)  Depreciation expense was $50,000.

(d)  Equipment was purchased for $250,000 in cash.

(e)  Early in the year, a 10% stock dividend was declared and distributed. This stock dividend resulted in the distribution of 50,000 new shares of $1 par common stock. The market value per share before the stock dividend was $40.

(f)  Cash revenues for the year totaled $600,000.

(g)  Cash expenses for the year totaled $320,000.

(h)  Old machinery was sold for its book value of $10,000.

(i)  Near the end of the year, a 2-for-1 stock split was declared. The 550,000 shares of $1 par common stock outstanding at the time were exchanged for 1,100,000 shares with a par value of $0.50.

(j)  Cash dividends totaling $35,000 were declared and paid on preferred stock.

(k)  Land was acquired in exchange for 6,000 shares of $0.50 par common stock. The land had a fair market value of $130,000.

(l)  Assume no changes in current operating receivable and payable balances during the year.

**Instructions:**   Prepare a statement of cash flows for Cortland Company for the year ended December 31, 1993.  Use the indirect method for reporting cash flow from operating activities.

## Problem 18—11  (Quasi-reorganization)

Kennington Copper has experienced several loss years and has plant assets on its books that are overvalued. Kennington plans to revalue its assets downward and eliminate the deficit. At December 31, 1993, the company owns the following plant assets:

| | Cost | Accumulated Depreciation | Book Value | Market Value |
|---|---|---|---|---|
| Land................................ | $ 600,000 | — | $ 600,000 | $300,000 |
| Buildings.......................... | 850,000 | $350,000 | 500,000 | 250,000 |
| Machinery and Equipment ........... | 450,000 | 250,000 | 200,000 | 150,000 |
| | $1,900,000 | $600,000 | $1,300,000 | $700,000 |

The balance sheet on December 31, 1993, reported the following balances in the stockholders' equity section:

| | |
|---|---|
| Common stock, $25 par, 70,000 shares ........................... | $1,750,000 |
| Paid-in capital in excess of par..................................... | 300,000 |
| Retained earnings (deficit)........................................... | (350,000) |
| Total ............................................................... | $1,700,000 |

As part of the reorganization, the common stock is to be canceled and reissued at $10 par.

**Instructions:**

1. Prepare the journal entries to record the quasi-reorganization.
2. Give the plant asset section and stockholders' equity section of the company's balance sheet as they would appear after the entries are posted.

### Problem 18—12    (Balance sheet preparation)

The following trial balance was taken from the books of Miller Manufacturing, a calendar-year corporation, as of April 30, 1993:

**Miller Manufacturing**
**Trial Balance**
**April 30, 1993**

| | Debit | Credit |
|---|---|---|
| Cash ............................................. | $ 310,000 | |
| Accounts Receivable............................... | 800,000 | |
| Finished Goods ................................... | 500,000 | |
| Goods in Process.................................. | 100,000 | |
| Raw Materials.................................... | 750,000 | |
| Land, Buildings, and Equipment ................... | 1,460,000 | |
| Prepaid Expenses ................................ | 5,400 | |
| Sales Returns and Allowances ..................... | 25,000 | |
| Administrative Salaries .......................... | 65,000 | |
| Cost of Goods Sold ............................... | 2,350,000 | |
| Travel Expense................................... | 30,030 | |
| Interest Expense ................................. | 10,570 | |
| Accounts Payable ................................ | | $ 175,000 |
| Notes Payable ................................... | | 100,000 |
| Payroll Payable.................................. | | 6,000 |
| Interest Payable on 6% Bonds ..................... | | 10,000 |
| 6% Preferred Stock, $50 par ...................... | | 1,000,000 |
| Common Stock, $100 par ......................... | | 1,416,000 |
| 6% Bonds Payable (due June 30, 2001) ............. | | 500,000 |
| Sales........................................... | | 2,500,000 |
| Retained Earnings, December 31, 1992 ............. | | 520 |
| Additional Paid-In Capital ........................ | | 698,480 |
| | $6,406,000 | $6,406,000 |

The following transactions have been completed by the company:

(a) The company has purchased various lots of its $100 par value common stock, totaling 840 shares, at an average price of $65.50 per share, for $55,020. In recording these transactions, the company has canceled the stock certificates and debited the common stock account with the par value of $84,000 and credited the paid-in capital account with the $28,980 difference between par and the cash paid.

(b) Additional Paid-In Capital was previously credited for $20 per share on the sale of 15,000 shares of common stock at $120.

(c) 6% bonds with a total face amount of $250,000 falling due on December 31, 1999, were issued on January 1, 1975, at a 10% discount. To June 30, 1991, $16,500 of this discount had been charged against revenues, and as of this date, the entire issue of these bonds was retired at par and the unamortized discount debited to Additional Paid-In Capital.

(d) A new issue of $500,000, 6%, 10-year bonds was sold at par on July 1, 1991. Expenses incurred with respect to this issue in the amount of $20,000 were debited to Additional Paid-In Capital.

**Instructions:**   Prepare a balance sheet as of April 30, 1993, making any corrections necessary in view of the company's treatment of the preceding transactions.                    (AICPA adapted)

## Problem 18—13   (Dividends and stock rights—entries for company and investor)

On April 1, 1992, Estancia Co. purchased 1,000 shares of Cooper Co. common stock, par $10, at $20. On June 1, when the stock was selling for $22 on the open market, Estancia Co. received a 10% stock dividend from Cooper Co. On October 26, Cooper Co. paid Estancia Co. a dividend of $0.75 on the stock and granted a stock right to purchase 1 share at $15 for every 5 shares held. On this date, stock had a market value ex-rights of $22.50, and each right had a value of $1.70; the stock cost was allocated on this basis. On November 15, Estancia Co. sold 120 rights at $1.25 and exercised the remaining rights. On March 3, 1993, Estancia Co. received a cash dividend from Cooper Co. of $1.50 per share. On October 13, Cooper Co. declared a 2-for-1 stock split and, on October 31, declared dividends of $0.40 per share. On December 31, Estancia Co. sold all of its shares in Cooper Co. for $11.50.

**Instructions:**   Prepare all entries for the preceding transactions on the books of (a) Estancia Co. and (b) Cooper Co. (Omit explanations but show computations. Assume these are the only equity transactions for Cooper Co.)

## Problem 18—14   (Reporting stockholders' equity)

The stockholders' equity section of Nilsson Corporation's balance sheet as of December 31, 1992, is as follows:

| | | |
|---|--:|--:|
| Common stock ($5 par, 500,000 shares authorized, 275,000 issued and outstanding) | $1,375,000 | |
| Additional paid-in capital—common stock | 550,000 | |
| Total paid-in capital | | $1,925,000 |
| Unappropriated retained earnings | $1,335,000 | |
| Appropriated retained earnings | 500,000 | |
| Total retained earnings | | 1,835,000 |
| Total stockholders' equity | | $3,760,000 |

Nilsson Co. had the following stockholders' equity transactions during 1993:

Jan. 15   Completed the building renovation for which $500,000 of retained earnings had been restricted. Paid the contractor $485,000, all of which is capitalized.

Mar.  3   Issued 100,000 additional shares of the common stock for $8 per share.

May 18   Declared a dividend of $1.50 per share to be paid on July 31, 1993, to stockholders of record on June 30, 1993.

June 19    Approved additional building renovation to be funded internally. The estimated cost of the project is $400,000, and Retained Earnings are to be restricted for that amount.

July  31    Paid the dividend.

Nov. 12    Declared a property dividend to be paid on December 31, 1993, to stockholders of record on November 30, 1993. The dividend is to consist of 35,000 shares of Hampton Inc. stock that Nilsson purchased for $9 per share. The fair market value of the stock on November 12 is $13 per share.

Dec. 31    Reported $885,000 of net income on the December 31, 1993, income statement. In addition, the stock was distributed in satisfaction of the property dividend. The Hampton stock closed at $14 per share at the end of the day's trading.

**Instructions:**

1.  Make all necessary journal entries for Nilsson to account for the transactions affecting stockholders' equity.
2.  Prepare the December 31, 1993, stockholders' equity section of the balance sheet for Nilsson.

# PART FOUR

## Special Problems in
## Income Determination
## and Reporting

# CHAPTER 19

# Complexities of Revenue Recognition

---

---

Prime Motor Inns, the second largest hotel company in the world, owns and operates numerous hotel chains. In addition, it finances the sales of hotels to investors and, for a fee, manages the hotels' operations. When buyers are unable to service their debt (an event that happens all too often in the sagging hotel industry), Prime often accepts IOUs and continues to book the interest on the unpaid debt as income. Ever the optimist, through 1989 Prime had not provided any estimate for bad debts. In cases such as this, when should revenue be recognized? When the sale is made? When cash is collected?

As discussed and illustrated in Chapter 4, both internal and external users of financial information focus considerable attention on how business activities affect the income statement. Because the financial statements are interrelated, a study of the measurement and recognition of the elements contained in the income statement is also a study of the measurement and recognition of changes in the elements contained in the balance sheet. Thus, while the focus in this chapter is on the recognition of revenue, it also relates to the recognition of assets and liabilities on the balance sheet.

**Recognition** refers to the time when transactions are recorded on the books. The FASB's two criteria for recognizing revenues and gains were identified in Chapter 4 and are repeated here for emphasis. Revenues and gains are generally recognized when:

1. They are realized or realizable, and
2. They have been earned through substantial completion of the activities involved in the earnings process.

Both of these criteria generally are met at the point of sale, which most often occurs when goods are delivered or when services are rendered to customers. Usually, assets and revenues are recognized concurrently. Thus, a sale of inventory results in an increase in Cash or Accounts Receivable and an increase in Sales Revenue. However, assets are sometimes recognized before these revenue recognition criteria are met. In those cases, a liability, Unearned Revenue, is recorded. When the criteria are fully met, revenue is recognized and the liability account is reduced.

While the point-of-sale rule has dominated the interpretation of revenue recognition, there have been notable variations to this rule, especially in specific industries such as construction, real estate, and franchising. Special committees of the AICPA, and later the FASB, have studied these and other areas. For several years, these special studies were conducted under the direction of the AICPA, and publications of the committees' results appeared in the form of **Industry Accounting Guides, Industry Audit Guides,** or **Statements of Position (SOPs)**. These publications have been studied by the FASB and, where deemed desirable, have been incorporated in the literature as Statements of Financial Accounting Standards.[1]

This chapter will explore some of the variations in revenue recognition that have arisen through these special industry studies. The focus of the presentation will be on the revenue recognition variations and not on the detailed accounting procedures for a specific industry. The discussion focuses first on revenue recognition **prior to delivery** of goods or performance of services; second on revenue recognition **after delivery** of goods or performance of services; and finally on methods of accounting for sales before revenue recognition occurs. The special industries referred to are construction, real estate, service, and franchising.

## REVENUE RECOGNITION PRIOR TO DELIVERY OF GOODS OR PERFORMANCE OF SERVICES

Under some circumstances, revenue can be meaningfully reported prior to the delivery of the finished product or completion of a service contract. Usually this occurs when the

[1] In the early 1980s, the FASB issued three research reports dealing with revenue recognition. These reports were used by the FASB in its deliberations leading to Concepts Statement No. 5 and several of the special industry standards. The reports were: (1) Yuji Ijiri, *Recognition of Contractual Rights and Obligations* (Stamford: Financial Accounting Standards Board, 1980); (2) Henry R. Jaenicke, *Survey of Present Practice in Recognizing Revenues, Expenses, Gains and Losses* (Stamford: Financial Accounting Standards Board, 1981); (3) L. Todd Johnson and Reed K. Storey, *Recognition in Financial Statements: Underlying Concepts and Practical Conventions* (Stamford: Financial Accounting Standards Board, 1982).

construction period of the asset being sold or the period of service performance is relatively long, i.e., more than one year. If a company waits until the production or service period is complete to recognize revenue, the income statement may not report meaningfully the periodic achievement of the company. Under this approach, referred to as the completed-contract method, all income from the contract is related to the year of completion, even though only a small part of the earnings may be attributable to effort in that period. Previous periods receive no credit for their efforts; in fact, they may be penalized through the absorption of selling, general and administrative, and other overhead costs relating to the contract but not considered part of the inventory cost.

Percentage-of-completion accounting, an alternative to the completed-contract method, was developed to relate recognition of revenue on long-term construction-type contracts to the activities of a firm in fulfilling these contracts. Similarly, the proportional performance method has been developed to reflect revenue earned on service contracts under which many acts of service are to be performed before the contract is completed. Examples include contracts covering maintenance on electronic office equipment, correspondence schools, trustee services, health clubs, professional services such as those offered by attorneys and accountants, and servicing of mortgage loans by mortgage bankers. Percentage-of-completion accounting and proportional performance accounting are similar in their application. However, some special problems arise in accounting for service contracts. The discussion and examples in the following sections relate first to long-term construction-type contracts, then to the special problems encountered with service contracts.

### General Concepts of Percentage-of-Completion Accounting

Under the percentage-of-completion method, a company recognizes revenues and costs on a contract as it progresses toward completion, rather than deferring recognition of these items until the contract is completed. The amount of revenue to be recognized each period is based on some measure of progress toward completion. This requires an estimate of costs yet to be incurred. Changes in estimates of future costs arise normally, and the necessary adjustments are made in the year the estimates are revised. Thus, the revenues and costs to be recognized in a given year are affected by the revenues and costs already recognized. As work progresses on the contract, the actual costs incurred are charged to inventory. The amount of profit earned each period also is charged to this asset account. Thus, the inventory account is valued at its net realizable value—the sales (or contract) price less the cost to complete the contract and less the unearned profit on the unfinished contract. If a company projects a loss on the contract prior to completion, the full amount of the loss should be recognized immediately. This loss recognition results in a write-down of the asset to its estimated net realizable value. If only a percentage of the loss were recognized, the asset value would exceed the net realizable value. This would violate the lower-of-cost-or-market rule discussed in Chapter 11.

### Necessary Conditions to Use Percentage-of-Completion Accounting

Most long-term construction-type contracts should be reported using the percentage-of-completion method. The guidelines presently in force, however, are not specific as to when a company must use percentage-of-completion and when it must use the alternative completed-contract method. The accounting standards that still govern this area were issued by the Committee on Accounting Procedure in 1955.[2] In January 1981, the Con-

---

[2]Committee on Accounting Procedure, *Accounting Research Bulletin No. 45,* "Long-Term Construction-Type Contracts" (New York: American Institute of Certified Public Accountants, 1955).

struction Contractor Guide Committee of the Accounting Standards Division of the AICPA issued Statement of Position 81-1, "Accounting for Performance of Construction-Type and Certain Production-Type Contracts." In this SOP, the committee strongly recommended which of the two common methods of accounting for these types of contracts should be required, depending on the specific circumstances involved. The committee further stated that the two methods should not be viewed as acceptable alternatives for the same circumstances. The committee identified several elements that should be present if percentage-of-completion accounting is to be used.[3]

1. Dependable estimates can be made of contract revenues, contract costs, and the extent of progress toward completion.
2. The contract clearly specifies the enforceable rights regarding goods or services to be provided and received by the parties, the consideration to be exchanged, and the manner and terms of settlement.
3. The buyer can be expected to satisfy obligations under the contract.
4. The contractor can be expected to perform the contractual obligation.

The completed-contract method should be used only when an entity has primarily short-term contracts, when the conditions for using percentage-of-completion accounting are not met, or when there are inherent uncertainties in the contract beyond the normal business risks.

In February 1982, the FASB issued Statement No. 56 designating the accounting and reporting principles and practices contained in SOP 81-1 and in the AICPA *Audit and Accounting Guide for Construction Contractors* as preferable accounting principles.[4] The Board indicated that it would consider adopting these principles as FASB standards after allowing sufficient time for the principles to be used in practice so that a basis can be provided for determining their usefulness. A critical issue involved in this area is the clear preference in the SOP for using the percentage-of-completion method of accounting.

For many years, the income tax regulations permitted contractors wide latitude in selecting either the percentage-of-completion or completed-contract method. Beginning with the Tax Reform Act of 1986, the tax laws have limited the use of the completed-contract method and have required increased use of the percentage-of-completion method. This results in greater revenues from taxes without increasing the tax rates, and also results in similar revenue recognition treatment for both taxes and financial reporting.

## Measuring the Percentage of Completion

Various methods are currently used in practice to measure the earnings process. They can be conveniently grouped into two categories: input and output measures.

**Input Measures**    Input measures are made in relation to the costs or efforts devoted to a contract. They are based on an established or assumed relationship between a unit of input and productivity. They include the widely used cost-to-cost method and several variations of efforts-expended methods.

---

[3]Construction Contractor Guide Committee of the Accounting Standards Division, AICPA, *Statement of Position 81-1, "*Accounting for Performance of Construction-Type and Certain Production-Type Contracts*"* (New York: American Institute of Certified Public Accountants, 1981), par. 23.

[4]*Statement of Financial Accounting Standards No. 56, "*Designation of AICPA Guide and Statement of Position (SOP) 81-1 on Contractor Accounting and SOP 81-2 Concerning Hospital-Related Organizations as Preferable for Purposes of Applying APB Opinion No. 20*"* (Stamford: Financial Accounting Standards Board, 1982).

***Cost-to-Cost Method***   Perhaps the most popular of the input measures is the cost-to-cost method. Under this method, the degree of completion is determined by comparing costs already incurred with the most recent estimates of total expected costs to complete the project. The percentage that costs incurred bear to total expected costs is applied to the expected net income on the project in arriving at earnings to date. Some of the costs incurred, particularly in the early stages of the contract, should be disregarded in applying this method, because they do not relate directly to effort expended on the contract. These include such items as subcontract costs for work that has yet to be performed and standard fabricated materials that have not yet been installed. One of the most difficult problems in using this method is estimating the costs yet to be incurred. However, this estimation is required in reporting income, regardless of how the percentage of completion is computed.

To illustrate, assume that in January 1992, Strong Construction Company was awarded a contract with a total price of $3,000,000. Strong expected to earn $400,000 profit on the contract, or in other words, total costs on the contract were estimated to be $2,600,000. The construction was completed over a 3-year period, and the following cost data and cost percentages were compiled during that time:

| Year | (1) Actual Cost Incurred | (2) Estimated Cost to Complete | (3) Total Cost (1) + (2) | (4) Cost Percentage (1) ÷ (3) |
|------|--------------------------|-------------------------------|--------------------------|-------------------------------|
| 1992 | $1,092,000 | $1,508,000 | $2,600,000* | 42% |
| 1993 | 832,000 | | | |
| Total | $1,924,000 | 676,000 | 2,600,000* | 74 |
| 1994 | 700,000 | | | |
| Total | $2,624,000 | –0– | 2,624,000** | 100 |

*Estimated total contract cost
**Actual total contract cost

Note that the cost percentage is computed by dividing cumulative actual costs incurred by total cost, an amount that is estimated for the first two years.

***Efforts-Expended Methods***   The efforts-expended methods are based on some measure of work performed. They include labor hours, labor dollars, machine hours, or material quantities. In each case, the degree of completion is measured in a way similar to that used in the cost-to-cost approach: the ratio of the efforts expended to date to the estimated total efforts to be expended on the entire contract. For example, if the measure of work performed is labor hours, the ratio of hours worked to date to the total estimated hours would produce the percentage for use in measuring income earned.

**Output Measures**   Output measures are made in terms of results achieved. Included in this category are methods based on units produced, contract milestones reached, and values added. For example, if the contract calls for units of output, such as miles of roadway, a measure of completion would be a ratio of the miles completed to the total miles in the contract. Architects and engineers are sometimes asked to evaluate jobs and estimate what percentage of a job is complete. These estimates are, in reality, output measures and usually are based on the physical progress made on a contract.

## Accounting for Long-Term Construction-Type Contracts

For both the percentage-of-completion and the completed-contract methods, all direct and allocable indirect costs of the contracts are charged to an inventory account. The difference in recording between the two methods relates to the timing of revenue and expense recognition, that is, when the estimated earned income is recognized with its related effect on the income statement and the balance sheet. During the construction period, the annual reported income under these two accounting methods will differ. However, after the contract is completed, the combined income for the total construction period will be the same under each method of accounting. The balance sheet at the end of the construction and collection period also will be identical.

Usually contracts require progress billings by the contractor and payments by the customer on these billings. The billings and payments are accounted for and reported in the same manner under both methods. The amount of these billings usually is specified by the contract terms and may be related to the costs actually incurred. Generally, these contracts require inspection before final settlement is made. As a protection for the customer, the contract frequently provides for an amount to be retained from the progress payments. This retention is usually a percentage of the progress billings, 10%-20%, and is paid upon final acceptance of the construction. The billings, including any amount to be retained, are debited to Accounts Receivable and credited to a deferred account, Progress Billings on Construction Contracts, that serves as an offset to the inventory account, Construction in Progress. The billing of the contract thus transfers the asset value from inventory to receivables, but because of the long-term nature of the contract, the construction costs continue to be reflected in the accounts.

To illustrate accounting for a long-term construction contract, assume that a dam was constructed over a two-year period commencing in September 1992, at a contract price of $5,000,000. The direct and allocable indirect costs, billings, and collections for 1992, 1993, and 1994 are as follows:

| Year | Direct and Allocable Indirect Costs | Billings Including 10% Retention | Collections |
|------|-------------------------------------|---------------------------------|-------------|
| 1992 | $1,125,000 | $1,000,000 | $ 800,000 |
| 1993 | 2,250,000 | 2,300,000 | 1,900,000 |
| 1994 | 1,125,000 | 1,700,000 | 2,300,000 |

The following entries for the three years would be made on the contractor's books under either the percentage-of-completion or the completed-contract method.

| | 1992 | | 1993 | | 1994 | |
|---|---|---|---|---|---|---|
| Construction in Progress ....... | 1,125,000 | | 2,250,000 | | 1,125,000 | |
| Materials, Cash, etc. ......... | | 1,125,000 | | 2,250,000 | | 1,125,000 |
| *To record costs incurred.* | | | | | | |
| Accounts Receivable.......... | 1,000,000 | | 2,300,000 | | 1,700,000 | |
| Progress Billings on Construc- | | | | | | |
| tion Contracts .............. | | 1,000,000 | | 2,300,000 | | 1,700,000 |
| *To record billings.* | | | | | | |
| Cash ...................... | 800,000 | | 1,900,000 | | 2,300,000 | |
| Accounts Receivable ........ | | 800,000 | | 1,900,000 | | 2,300,000 |
| *To record cash collections.* | | | | | | |

No other entries would be required in 1992 and 1993 under the completed-contract method. In both years, the balance of Construction in Progress exceeds the amount in Progress Billings on Construction Contracts; thus the latter account would be offset against the inventory account in the balance sheet. Because the operating cycle of a company that emphasizes long-term contracts is usually more than one year, all of the preceding balance sheet accounts would be classified as current. The balance sheet at the end of 1993 would disclose the following balances related to the dam construction contract:

Current assets:
  Accounts receivable, including 10% retention fee of
    $330,000 . . . . . . . . . . . . . . . . . . . . . . . . . . . . . . . . . . . . . . . . . . . . .          $600,000
  Construction in progress . . . . . . . . . . . . . . . . . . . . . . . . . . .    $3,375,000
  Less progress billings on construction contracts . . . . . . .     3,300,000      75,000

If the billings exceeded the construction costs, the excess would be reported in the current liability section of the balance sheet.

Under the completed-contract method, the following entries would be made to recognize revenue and costs and to close out the inventory and billings accounts at the completion of the contract:

Progress Billings on Construction Contracts . . . . . . . . . . . . . .    5,000,000
  Revenue From Long-Term Construction Contracts . . . . . .                   5,000,000

Cost of Long-Term Construction Contracts . . . . . . . . . . . . . .    4,500,000
  Construction in Progress . . . . . . . . . . . . . . . . . . . . . . . . . . . .              4,500,000

The first entry represents the billings on the contract that, at the end of the contract, equal the total revenue from the contract. The second journal entry transfers the inventoried cost from the contract to the appropriate expense account on the income statement. The income statement for 1994 would report the gross revenues and the matched costs, thus recognizing the entire $500,000 profit in one year.

**Using Percentage-of-Completion—Cost-to-Cost Method**    If the company used the percentage-of-completion method of accounting, the $500,000 profit would be spread over all three years of construction according to the estimated percentage of completion for each year. Assume that the estimated cost from the beginning of construction was $4,500,000 and that the estimate did not change over the three years. Also assume that the cost-to-cost method of determining percentage of completion is used. The percentage for each year would be calculated as follows:

|  | 1992 | 1993 | 1994 |
| --- | --- | --- | --- |
| (1) Actual cost incurred to date | $1,125,000 | $3,375,000 | $4,500,000 |
| (2) Estimated cost to complete | 3,375,000 | 1,125,000 | –0– |
| (3) Total estimated cost | $4,500,000 | $4,500,000 | $4,500,000 |
| Percentage of completion to date [(1) ÷ (3)] | 25% | 75% | 100% |

These percentages may be used to determine directly the gross profit that should be recognized on the income statement; that is, the income statement for 1992 would report only the gross profit from construction contracts in the amount of $125,000 (estimated income—1992, $500,000 × 25% = $125,000). Preferably, the percentages should be used to determine both revenues and costs. The income statement will then disclose revenues, costs, and the resulting gross profit, a method more consistent with normal income statement reporting. The AICPA Audit and Accounting Guide for Construction Contractors recommended this proportional procedure, and the presentations in this chapter will reflect that recommendation.[5] The procedures are as follows:

[5]Construction Contractor Guide Committee of the Accounting Standards Division, AICPA, *Audit and Accounting Guide for Construction Contractors* (New York: American Institute of Certified Public Accountants, 1980), p. 44.

1. Cumulative revenue to date should be computed by multiplying total estimated contract revenue by the percentage of completion. Revenue for the current period is the difference between the cumulative revenue at the end of the current period and the cumulative revenue recognized in prior periods.

2. Cumulative costs to date should be computed in a manner similar to revenue and should be equal to the total estimated contract cost multiplied by the percentage of completion on the contract. Cost for the current period is the difference between the cumulative costs at the end of the current period and the cumulative costs reported in prior periods.

3. Cumulative gross profit is the excess of cumulative revenue over cumulative costs, and the current period gross profit is the difference between current revenue and current costs.

If the cost-to-cost method is used to estimate earned revenue, the proportional cost for each period will equal the actual cost incurred.

To illustrate, for 1992, 25% of the fixed contract price of $5,000,000 would be recognized as revenue and 25% of the expected total cost of $4,500,000 would be reported as cost. The following revenue recognition entries would be made for each of the three years of the contract. These entries are in addition to the transaction entries illustrated on page 709.

|  | 1992 | | 1993 | | 1994 | |
|---|---|---|---|---|---|---|
| Cost of Long-Term Construction Contracts ..................... | 1,125,000 | | 2,250,000 | | 1,125,000 | |
| Construction in Progress ....... | 125,000 | | 250,000 | | 125,000 | |
| Revenue From Long-Term Construction Contracts ....... | | 1,250,000 | | 2,500,000 | | 1,250,000 |

The gross profit recognized each year is added to the construction in progress account thereby valuing the inventory on the books at its net realizable value. Note that the procedures used in recognizing revenue under the percentage-of-completion method do not affect the progress billings made or the amount of cash collected. These amounts are determined by contract and not by the accounting method used.

Because the construction in progress account contains costs incurred plus recognized profit (which equals total revenues recognized), at the completion of the contract, the balance in this account will exactly equal the amount in Progress Billings on Construction Contracts, since the progress billings account reflects the contract price (or total revenues). The following closing entry would complete the accounting process:

| Progress Billings on Construction Contracts.............. | 5,000,000 | |
|---|---|---|
| Construction in Progress ........................... | | 5,000,000 |

**Using Percentage-of-Completion—Other Methods**   If the cost-to-cost method is not used to measure progress on the contract, the proportional costs recognized under this method may not be equal to the actual costs incurred. For example, assume in 1992 that an engineering estimate measure was used, and 20% of the contract was assumed to be completed. The gross profit recognized would therefore be computed and reported as follows:

| Recognized revenue (20% of $5,000,000)......................... | $1,000,000 |
|---|---|
| Cost (20% of $4,500,000) ...................................... | 900,000 |
| Gross profit (20% of $500,000) ................................ | $ 100,000 |

Because some accountants believed that the amount of cost recognized should be equal to the costs actually incurred, an alternative to the preceding approach was included in

SOP 81-1.[6] Under this **actual cost approach**, revenue is defined as the actual costs incurred on the contract plus the gross profit earned for the period on the contract. Using the data from the previous example, the revenue and costs to be reported on the 1992 income statement would be as follows:

| | |
|---|---:|
| Actual cost incurred to date | $1,125,000 |
| Recognized gross profit (20% of $500,000) | 100,000 |
| Recognized revenue | $1,225,000 |

This contrasts with the $1,000,000 revenue using the **proportional cost approach**. Both approaches report gross profit as $100,000.

In a footnote to this discussion in the SOP, the Committee made it clear that the actual cost approach and the proportional cost approach are equally acceptable. However, because the actual cost approach results in a varying gross profit percentage from period to period whenever the measurement of completion differs from that which would occur if the cost-to-cost method were used, the authors feel that the proportional cost approach is preferable. Unless a different method is explicitly stated, examples and end-of-chapter material will assume the use of the proportional cost approach.

**Revision of Estimates**    In the previous example, it was assumed that the estimated cost did not vary from the beginning of the contract. This rarely would be the case. As estimates change, catch-up adjustments are made in the year of the change. To illustrate the impact of changing estimates, assume that at the end of 1993, it was estimated that the remaining cost to complete the dam was $1,225,000 rather than $1,125,000. This would increase the total estimated cost to $4,600,000, reduce the expected profit to $400,000, and change the percentage of completion at the end of 1993 to 73.37% ($3,375,000 ÷ $4,600,000).

The following analysis shows how this change would affect the revenue and costs to be reported each year assuming that the actual costs in 1994 were $1,175,000.

| | 1992 | 1993 | 1994 |
|---|---:|---:|---:|
| Contract price | $5,000,000 | $5,000,000 | $5,000,000 |
| Actual cost incurred to date | $1,125,000 | $3,375,000 | $4,550,000 |
| Estimated cost to complete | 3,375,000 | 1,225,000 | -0- |
| Total estimated cost | $4,500,000 | $4,600,000 | $4,550,000 |
| Total expected gross profit | $ 500,000 | $ 400,000 | $ 450,000 |
| Percentage of completion to date | 25% | 73.37% | 100% |

| | To Date | Recognized—<br>Prior Years | Recognized—<br>Current Year |
|---|---:|---:|---:|
| 1992 Recognized revenue | | | |
| ($5,000,000 × .25) | $1,250,000 | -0- | $1,250,000 |
| Cost (actual cost) | 1,125,000 | -0- | 1,125,000 |
| Gross profit | $ 125,000 | | $ 125,000 |
| | | | |
| 1993 Recognized revenue | | | |
| ($5,000,000 × .7337) | $3,668,500 | $1,250,000 | $2,418,500 |
| Cost (actual cost) | 3,375,000 | 1,125,000 | 2,250,000 |
| Gross profit | $ 293,500 | $ 125,000 | $ 168,500 |
| | | | |
| 1994 Recognized revenue | $5,000,000 | $3,668,500 | $1,331,500 |
| Cost (actual cost) | 4,550,000 | 3,375,000 | 1,175,000 |
| Gross profit | $ 450,000 | $ 293,500 | $ 156,500 |

[6]*SOP 81-1,* pars. 80 and 81.

The entries to record revenue and cost for the three years given the assumed estimate revision would be as follows:

|  | 1992 | 1993 | 1994 |
|---|---|---|---|
| Cost of Long-Term Construction | | | |
| Contracts .................... | 1,125,000 | 2,250,000 | 1,175,000 |
| Construction in Progress ....... | 125,000 | 168,500 | 156,500 |
| Revenue From Long-Term | | | |
| Construction Contracts ....... | | 1,250,000 | 2,418,500 | 1,331,500 |

In some cases, an increase in total estimated cost can result in recognition of a loss in the year of the increase. Revising the preceding example, assume that at the end of 1993, the estimated cost to complete the dam was $1,495,000 and this was the actual cost incurred in 1994. The following analysis shows how this change in estimated cost would reduce the percentage of completion at the end of 1993 to 69.3%, and the cumulative profit at the end of 1993 to $90,000. Since $125,000 was already recognized as gross profit in 1992, a loss of $35,000 would be recognized in 1993.

|  | 1992 | 1993 | 1994 |
|---|---|---|---|
| Contract price ........................ | $5,000,000 | $5,000,000 | $5,000,000 |
| Actual cost incurred to date ............ | $1,125,000 | $3,375,000 | $4,870,000 |
| Estimated cost to complete............. | 3,375,000 | 1,495,000 | –0– |
| Total estimated cost ................. | $4,500,000 | $4,870,000 | $4,870,000 |
| Total expected gross profit ............. | $ 500,000 | $ 130,000 | $ 130,000 |
| Percentage of completion to date ........ | 25% | 69.3% | 100% |

|  | To Date | Recognized— Prior Years | Recognized— Current Year |
|---|---|---|---|
| **1992 Recognized revenue** | | | |
| ($5,000,000 × .25)........... | $1,250,000 | –0– | $1,250,000 |
| Cost (actual cost)........... | 1,125,000 | –0– | 1,125,000 |
| Gross profit ............... | $ 125,000 | | $ 125,000 |
| **1993 Recognized revenue** | | | |
| ($5,000,000 × .693) ........ | $3,465,000 | $1,250,000 | $2,215,000 |
| Cost (actual cost)........... | 3,375,000 | 1,125,000 | 2,250,000 |
| Gross profit (loss) .......... | $ 90,000 | $ 125,000 | $ (35,000) |
| **1994 Recognized revenue** ........ | $5,000,000 | $3,465,000 | $1,535,000 |
| Cost (actual cost)........... | 4,870,000 | 3,375,000 | 1,495,000 |
| Gross profit ............... | $ 130,000 | $ 90,000 | $ 40,000 |

The entries to record revenue and cost for the three years given the assumed loss estimate in 1993 would be as follows:

|  | 1992 | 1993 | 1994 |
|---|---|---|---|
| Cost of Long-Term Construction | | | |
| Contracts .................... | 1,125,000 | 2,250,000 | 1,495,000 |
| Construction in Progress ....... | 125,000 | 35,000 | 40,000 |
| Revenue From Long-Term | | | |
| Construction Contracts ....... | | 1,250,000 | 2,215,000 | 1,535,000 |

**Reporting Anticipated Contract Losses**    In the example above, an increase in estimated total cost resulted in recognition of a loss in the year the estimate was revised, but overall, the contract resulted in a profit. In some cases, an increase in estimated total cost is so great that a loss on the entire contract is anticipated; that is, total estimated costs are expected to exceed the total revenue from the contract. When a loss on the total contract is anticipated, generally accepted accounting principles require reporting the loss *in its entirety* in the period when the loss is first anticipated. This is true under either the completed-contract or the percentage-of-completion method.

For example, assume that in the earlier dam construction example on page 710, the estimated cost to complete the contract at the end of 1993 was $1,725,000. Because $3,375,000 of costs had already been incurred, the total estimated cost of the contract would be $5,100,000 ($3,375,000 + $1,725,000) or $100,000 more than the contract price.

|  | 1992 | 1993 | 1994 |
|---|---|---|---|
| Contract price | $5,000,000 | $5,000,000 | $5,000,000 |
| Actual cost incurred to date | $1,125,000 | $3,375,000 | $5,100,000 |
| Estimated cost to complete | 3,375,000 | 1,725,000 | –0– |
| Total estimated cost | $4,500,000 | $5,100,000 | $5,100,000 |
| Total expected gross profit (loss) | $ 500,000 | $ (100,000) | $ (100,000) |
| Percentage of completion to date | 25% | 66.18% | 100% |

Using this example, accounting for a contract loss is illustrated first for the completed-contract method, then for the percentage-of-completion method.

***Anticipated Contract Loss—Completed-Contract Method***    If the completed-contract method is used, the recognition of an anticipated contract loss is simple. The amount of the loss is debited to a loss account, and the inventory account, Construction in Progress, is credited by that amount to reduce the inventory to its expected net realizable value. To record the anticipated loss of $100,000 on the dam construction contract, the following entry would be made at the end of 1993:

| Anticipated Loss on Long-Term Construction Contracts | 100,000 | |
| Construction in Progress | | 100,000 |

***Anticipated Contract Loss—Percentage-of-Completion Method***    Recognition of an anticipated contract loss under the percentage-of-completion method is more complex. To properly reflect the entire loss in the year it is first anticipated, the cumulative cost to deduct from cumulative recognized revenue cannot be the actual cost incurred, but must be the cumulative recognized revenue plus the entire anticipated loss. Thus, continuing the dam construction contract example, the cumulative recognized revenue at the end of 1993 would be $3,309,000 (66.18% × $5,000,000), and the cumulative cost at the same date would be $3,409,000 ($3,309,000 + $100,000). Because the example assumes that $125,000 profit was recognized on this contract in 1992, the total loss to be recognized in 1993 is $225,000 ($125,000 + $100,000). The analysis on page 715 reflects the amounts to be reported for each of the three years of the contract life under the anticipated loss assumption.

The entry to record the revenue, costs, and adjustments to Construction in Progress for the loss in 1993 would be as follows:

| Cost of Long-Term Construction Contracts | 2,284,000 | |
| Revenue From Long-Term Construction Contracts | | 2,059,000 |
| Construction in Progress | | 225,000 |

Note that the construction in progress account under both methods would have a balance of $3,275,000 at the end of 1993 computed as shown on page 715.

| | To Date | Recognized—<br>Prior Years | Recognized—<br>Current Year |
|---|---|---|---|
| **1992** Recognized revenue | | | |
| ($5,000,000 × .25)........... | $1,250,000 | –0– | $1,250,000 |
| Cost (actual cost)............ | 1,125,000 | –0– | 1,125,000 |
| Gross profit (loss) ........... | $ 125,000 | | $ 125,000 |
| **1993** Recognized revenue | | | |
| ($5,000,000 × .6618) ........ | $3,309,000 | $1,250,000 | $2,059,000 |
| Cost (recognized revenue plus | | | |
| entire anticipated loss) ...... | 3,409,000 | 1,125,000 | 2,284,000 |
| Gross profit (loss) ........... | $ (100,000) | $ 125,000 | $ (225,000) |
| **1994** Recognized revenue ......... | $5,000,000 | $3,309,000 | $1,691,000 |
| Cost (actual cost)............ | 5,100,000 | 3,409,000 | 1,691,000 |
| Gross profit (loss) ........... | $ (100,000) | $ (100,000) | $ (0) |

Completed-contract method:

**Construction in Progress**

| 1992 cost | 1,125,000 | 1993 loss | 100,000 |
|---|---|---|---|
| 1993 cost | 2,250,000 | | |
| | | | |
| Balance | 3,275,000 | | |

Percentage-of-completion method:

**Construction in Progress**

| 1992 cost | 1,125,000 | 1993 loss | 225,000 |
|---|---|---|---|
| 1992 gross | | | |
| profit | 125,000 | | |
| 1993 cost | 2,250,000 | | |
| Balance | 3,275,000 | | |

**Accounting for Contract Change Orders**    Long-term construction contracts are seldom completed without change orders that affect both the contract price and the cost of performance. Change orders are modifications of an original contract that effectively change the provisions of the contract. They may be initiated by the contractor or the customer, and they include changes in specifications or design, method or manner of performance, facilities, equipment, materials, location site, etc. If the contract price is changed as a result of a change order, future computations are made with the revised expected revenue and any anticipated cost changes that will arise because of the change order. Change orders are often unpriced, that is, the work to be performed is defined, but the adjustment to the contract price is to be negotiated later. If it is probable that a contract price change will be negotiated to at least recover the increased costs, the increased costs may be included with the incurred costs of the period and the revenue may be increased by the same amount.

### Accounting for Long-Term Service Contracts—The Proportional Performance Method

Thus far, the discussion in this chapter has focused on long-term construction-type contracts. As indicated earlier, another type of contract that frequently extends over a long period of time is a **service contract**. An increasing percentage of sales in our economy are classified as sales of services as opposed to sales of goods. When the service to be performed is completed as a single act or over a relatively short period of time, no revenue recognition problems arise. The revenue recognition criteria previously defined apply, and all direct and indirect costs related to the service are charged to expense in the period the revenue is recognized. However, when several acts over a period of time are involved, the same revenue recognition problems illustrated for long-term construction-type contracts arise. Although the FASB has not issued a standard dealing with these contracts, the

Board did issue an Invitation to Comment on a proposed Statement of Position that had been issued by the AICPA's Accounting Standards Division.[7] The discussion on the following pages reflects the recommendations made by the Accounting Standards Division.

The Division recommends that unless the final act of service to be performed is so vital to the contract that earlier acts are relatively insignificant, e.g., the packaging, loading, and final delivery of goods in a delivery contract, revenue should be recognized under the **proportional performance method**.[8] Both input and output measures are identified as possible ways of measuring progress on a service contract. If a contract involves a specified number of identical or similar acts, e.g., the processing of monthly mortgage payments by a mortgage banker, an output measure derived by relating the number of acts performed to the total number of acts to be performed over the contract life is recommended. If a contract involves a specified number of defined but not identical acts, e.g., a correspondence school that provides evaluation, lessons, examinations, and grading, a cost-to-cost input measurement percentage would be applicable. If future costs are not objectively determinable, output measures such as relating sales value of the individual acts to the total sales value of the service contract may be used. If no pattern of performance can be determined, or if a service contract involves an unspecified number of similar or identical acts with a fixed period for performance, e.g., a maintenance contract for electronic office equipment, the Division recommends the use of the straight-line method, i.e., recognizing revenue equally over the periods of performance.

These measures are used to determine what portion of the service contract fee should be recognized as revenue. Generally, the measures are only indirectly related to the pattern of cash collection; however, they are applicable only if cash collection is reasonably assured and if losses from nonpayment can be objectively determined.

The cost recognition problems of service contracts are somewhat different from those of long-term construction-type contracts. Most service contracts involve three different types of costs: (1) initial direct costs related to obtaining and performing initial services on the contract, such as commissions, legal fees, credit investigations, and paper processing; (2) direct costs related to performing the various acts of service; and (3) indirect costs related to maintaining the organization to service the contract, e.g., general and administrative expenses. Initial direct costs generally are charged against revenue using the same input or output measure used for revenue recognition. If the cost-to-cost method of input measurement is used, initial direct costs should be excluded from the cost incurred to date in computing the measure. Only direct costs related to the acts of service are relevant. Direct costs usually are charged to expense as incurred, because they relate directly to the acts for which revenue is recognized. Similarly, all indirect costs should be charged to expense as incurred. As is true for long-term construction-type contracts, any indicated loss on completion of the service contract is to be charged to the period in which the loss is first indicated. If collection of a service contract is highly uncertain, revenue recognition should not be related to performance but to the collection of the receivable using one of the methods described in the latter part of this chapter.

To illustrate accounting for a service contract using the proportional performance method, assume a correspondence school enters into 100 contracts with students for an extended writing course. The fee for each contract is $500, payable in advance. This fee includes many different services such as providing the text material, evaluating written assignments and examinations, and awarding of a certificate. The total initial direct

---

[7]*FASB Invitation to Comment,* "Accounting for Certain Service Transactions" (Stamford: Financial Accounting Standards Board, 1978).

[8]*Ibid.,* pp. 12-13.

costs related to the contracts are $5,000. Direct costs for the lessons actually completed during the period are $12,000. It is estimated that the total direct costs of these contracts will be $30,000. The facts of this case suggest that the cost-to-cost method is applicable, and the following entries would be made to record these transactions:

| | | |
|---|---|---|
| Cash .................................................................. | 50,000 | |
|   Deferred Course Revenue ................................. | | 50,000 |
| Deferred Initial Costs ........................................ | 5,000 | |
|   Cash ................................................... | | 5,000 |
| Contract Costs ............................................ | 12,000 | |
|   Cash ................................................... | | 12,000 |
| Deferred Course Revenue ................................. | 20,000* | |
|   Recognized Course Revenue............................. | | 20,000 |
| Contract Costs ........................................... | 2,000** | |
|   Deferred Initial Costs.................................... | | 2,000 |

Computations:
 *Cost-to-cost percentage: $12,000 ÷ $30,000 = 40%; $50,000 × .40 = $20,000
**$5,000 × .40 = $2,000

The gross profit reported on these contracts for the period would be $6,000 ($20,000 − $12,000 − $2,000). The deferred initial cost and deferred course revenues would normally be reported as current balance sheet deferrals, because the operating cycle of a correspondence school would be equal to the average time to complete a contract or one year, whichever is longer.

## Evaluation of the Proportional Performance Method

As noted, the FASB has not issued a standard on service industries. While the proportional performance method has theoretical support for its adoption, it tends to be extremely conservative, especially during a period of rapid growth in a company's revenues. Since no revenue is recognized until performance of the service has begun, the proportional performance method recognizes no revenue at the critical point of signing a service contract. Thus, in the growing years of a company, use of the proportional performance method will result in large losses being reported even though the operation might be very profitable over time. This can lead to the questionable conclusion that a company is no better off after service contracts are sold than it was before.

An alternative method of recognizing revenue for service contracts would be to recognize part of the revenue upon the signing of the contract, and then spread the balance of the revenue over the contract life using the proportional performance concept. The decision as to how much revenue should be recognized at the beginning of the contract would depend on the nature and terms of the contract, including any forfeiture or cancellation provisions.

## REVENUE RECOGNITION AFTER DELIVERY OF GOODS OR PERFORMANCE OF SERVICES

One of the FASB's two revenue recognition criteria, listed at the beginning of this chapter, states that revenue should not be recognized until the earnings process is substantially completed. Normally, the earnings process is substantially completed by the delivery of goods or performance of services. Collection of receivables is usually routine, and any future warranty costs can be reasonably estimated. In some cases, however, the circumstances surrounding a revenue transaction are such that considerable uncertainty exists as to whether payments will indeed be received. This can occur if the sales transaction is unusual in nature or involves a customer in such a way that default carries little cost or penalty. Under these circumstances, the uncertainty of cash collection suggests that revenue recognition should await the actual receipt of cash. There are at least three different approaches to revenue recognition that depend on the receipt of cash: **installment sales**, **cost recovery**, and **cash**. These methods differ as to the treatment of costs incurred and the timing of revenue recognition. They are summarized and contrasted with the full accrual method in the table below.

| Method | Timing of Revenue and/or Income Recognition | Treatment of Product Costs or Initial Costs Under Service Contracts |
|---|---|---|
| Full accrual | At point of sale. | Charge against revenue at time of sale or rendering of service. |
| Installment sales | At collection of cash. Usually a portion of the cash payment is recognized as income. | Defer to be matched against part of each cash collection. Usually done by deferring the estimated profit. |
| Cost recovery | At collection of cash, but only after all costs are recovered. | Defer to be matched against total cash collected. |
| Cash | At collection of cash. | Charge to expense as incurred. |

These methods are really not alternatives to each other; however, the guidelines for applying them are not well defined. As the uncertainty of the environment increases, generally accepted accounting principles would require moving from the full accrual method to installment sales, cost recovery, and finally, a strict cash approach. The cash method is the most conservative approach, because it would not permit the deferral of any costs, but would charge them to expense as incurred. In the following pages, each of these revenue recognition methods will be discussed and illustrated.

## Installment Sales Method

Traditionally, the most commonly applied method for dealing with the uncertainty of cash collections has been the **installment sales method**. Under this method, income is recognized as cash is collected rather than at the time of sale. This method of accounting was developed after World War II in response to an increasing number of sales contracts that extended the time payment over several years, with full title to the "sold" property being transferred only at the time of final collection. Consumer goods such as electrical appliances, jewelry, automobiles, and recreational equipment were commonly purchased and accounted for in this way. As this method of sales became more popular, and as credit rating evaluations became more sophisticated, the probability of collection on these contracts became more certain. The collection of cash was no longer the critical event, but the point of sale essentially completed the earnings process. Collection costs and the cost of uncollectible accounts could be estimated at the time of sale. Additional protection was afforded the seller because most contracts included a right of repossession. For these reasons, the Accounting Principles Board concluded in 1966 that except for special circumstances, the installment method of recognizing revenue is not acceptable for reporting purposes.[9]

In more recent years, sales of other types of property, such as developed real estate and undeveloped land, also have been made with greatly extended terms. Commonly, these contracts involve little or no down payment, the payments are spread over ten to thirty or forty years, and the probability of default in the early years is high because of a small investment by the buyer in the contract and because the market prices of the property often are unstable. Application of the accrual method to these contracts frequently overstates income in the early years due to the failure to realistically provide for future costs related to the contract, including losses from contract defaults. The FASB considered these types of sales and concluded that accrual accounting applied in these circumstances often results in "front-end loading," i.e., a recognition of all revenue at the time of the sales contract with improper matching of related costs. Thus, the Board has established criteria that must be met before real estate and retail land sales can be recorded using the full accrual method of revenue recognition. If the criteria are not fully met, then the use of the installment sales method, or in some cases the cost recovery or deposit methods, is recommended to reflect the conditions of the sale more accurately.[10] Because the installment sales method often is recommended in new sales environments, it is important for accountants to understand its application.

Accounting for installment sales using the deferred gross profit approach requires determining a gross profit rate for the sales of each year, and establishing an accounts receivable and a deferred revenue account identified by the year of the sale. As collections are made of a given year's receivables, a portion of the deferred revenue equal to the gross profit rate times the collections made is recognized as income. The most common application of this method has been for the sale of merchandise. However, any sale of property or services may be recorded using the concept. The following examples of transactions and journal entries will illustrate this method of recognizing revenue.

**Installment Sales of Merchandise**    Assume that the Riding Corporation sells merchandise on the installment basis and that the uncertainties of cash collection make the use of the installment sales method acceptable. The following data relate to three years of operations. To simplify the presentation, interest charges are excluded from the example.

|  | 1993 | 1994 | 1995 |
|---|---|---|---|
| Installment sales | $150,000 | $200,000 | $300,000 |
| Cost of installment sales | 100,000 | 140,000 | 204,000 |
| Gross profit | $ 50,000 | $ 60,000 | $ 96,000 |
| Gross profit percentage | 33.33% | 30% | 32% |
| Cash collections: | | | |
| 1993 sales | $ 30,000 | $ 75,000 | $ 30,000 |
| 1994 sales | | 70,000 | 80,000 |
| 1995 sales | | | 100,000 |

The entries to record the transactions for 1993 would be as follows:

---

[9]*Opinions of the Accounting Principles Board No. 10*, "Omnibus Opinion—1966" (New York: American Institute of Certified Public Accountants, 1967), par. 12.

[10]*Statement of Financial Accounting Standards No. 66*, "Accounting for Sales of Real Estate" (Stamford: Financial Accounting Standards Board, October 1982).

| | | |
|---|---:|---:|
| Installment Accounts Receivable—1993 .................... | 150,000 | |
|     Installment Sales ........................................ | | 150,000 |
| Cost of Installment Sales ..................................... | 100,000 | |
|     Inventory ............................................... | | 100,000 |
| Cash ...................................................... | 30,000 | |
|     Installment Accounts Receivable—1993 ................. | | 30,000 |
| Installment Sales ........................................ | 150,000 | |
|     Cost of Installment Sales ................................ | | 100,000 |
|     Deferred Gross Profit—1993 ............................. | | 50,000 |
| Deferred Gross Profit—1993............................... | 10,000* | |
|     Realized Gross Profit on Installment Sales ............... | | 10,000 |

*$30,000 × 33.33%

The sales and costs related to sales are recorded in a manner identical with the accounting for sales discussed in Chapter 10. At the end of the year, however, the sales and cost of sales accounts are closed to a deferred gross profit account rather than to Income Summary. The realized gross profit is then recognized by applying the gross profit percentage to cash collections. All other general and administrative expenses are normally written off in the period incurred.

Entries for the next two years are summarized in the schedule below.

| | 1994 | | 1995 | |
|---|---:|---:|---:|---:|
| Installment Accounts Receivable—1994 ...... | 200,000 | | | |
| Installment Accounts Receivable—1995 ...... | | | 300,000 | |
|     Installment Sales ......................... | | 200,000 | | 300,000 |
| Cost of Installment Sales................... | 140,000 | | 204,000 | |
|     Inventory .............................. | | 140,000 | | 204,000 |
| Cash ...................................... | 145,000 | | 210,000 | |
|     Installment Accounts Receivable—1993 .... | | 75,000 | | 30,000 |
|     Installment Accounts Receivable—1994 .... | | 70,000 | | 80,000 |
|     Installment Accounts Receivable—1995 .... | | | | 100,000 |
| Installment Sales ......................... | 200,000 | | 300,000 | |
|     Cost of Installment Sales .................. | | 140,000 | | 204,000 |
|     Deferred Gross Profit—1994.............. | | 60,000 | | |
|     Deferred Gross Profit—1995.............. | | | | 96,000 |
| Deferred Gross Profit—1993 ............... | 25,000[1] | | 10,000[3] | |
| Deferred Gross Profit—1994 ............... | 21,000[2] | | 24,000[4] | |
| Deferred Gross Profit—1995 ............... | | | 32,000[5] | |
|     Realized Gross Profit on Installment Sales .. | | 46,000 | | 66,000 |

Computations:
[1]$75,000 × 33.33% = $25,000
[2]$70,000 × 30% = $21,000
[3]$30,000 × 33.33% = $10,000
[4]$80,000 × 30% = $24,000
[5]$100,000 × 32% = $32,000

Although this method of recording installment sales is the one most commonly followed, it would also be possible to defer both the gross revenue and the gross costs rather than just the net difference. If the latter approach is followed, the resulting entries would be more similar to those illustrated for percentage-of-completion accounting. Each year a portion of the gross revenue and gross costs would be recognized with the difference being the realized gross profit. Both methods produce the same net income.

If a company is heavily involved in installment sales, the operating cycle of the business is normally the period of the average installment contract. Thus, the currently accepted definition of current assets and current liabilities requires the receivables and their related deferred gross profit accounts to be reported in the current asset section of classified balance sheets. The deferred gross profit accounts should be reported as an offset to the related accounts receivable. Thus, at the end of 1993, the current asset section would include the following account balances:

| | | |
|---|---:|---:|
| Installment accounts receivable | $120,000 | |
| Less deferred gross profit | 40,000 | $80,000 |

**Complexities of Installment Sales of Merchandise**    In the previous example, no provision was made for interest. In reality, installment sales contracts always include interest, either expressed or implied. The interest portion of the contract payments is recognized as income in the period in which cash is received, and the balance of the payment is treated as a collection on the installment sale. Thus, if in the example on pages 719-720, the $75,000 collection of 1993 sales in 1994 included interest of $40,000, only $35,000 would be used to compute the realized gross profit from 1993 sales. A complete example involving interest is illustrated in the next section dealing with real estate installment sales.

Additional complexities can arise in installment sales accounting in providing for uncollectible accounts. Because of the right to repossess merchandise in the event of nonpayment, the provision for uncollectible accounts can be less than might be expected. Only the amount of the receivable in excess of the current value of the repossessed merchandise is a potential loss. Accounting for repossessions was discussed in Chapter 11. Theoretically, a proper matching of estimated losses against revenues would require allocating the expected losses over the years of collection. Practically, however, the provision is made and charged against income in the period of the sale. Thus, the accounting entries for handling estimated uncollectible accounts are the same as illustrated in Chapter 9.

**Recognition Issues Involving the Sale of Real Estate—Installment Sales Method**    The installment sales method of accounting often is used for sales of real estate on a long-term contract basis. These sales frequently are characterized by small down payments with long payoff periods on the balance. Usually the seller retains title to the real estate until the final payment is made, thus giving the seller the right of repossession. In an inflationary economy, this right is valuable and, in most cases, means that ultimate collection of the debt, either through payment or repossession, virtually is assured. However, if circumstances reduce the probability of collection or if the market value of the property is unstable, then the installment sales method may be applied, or in extreme cases, the cost recovery method may be required.

To illustrate the accounting for real estate sales using the installment method, assume that Emery Industries Inc. sells land and buildings on January 1, 1993, for $4,000,000. Emery receives a down payment of $300,000 and a promissory note for the remaining $3,700,000 plus interest at 12% to be paid in equal installments of $471,752 at the end of each of the next 25 years. The land has a carrying value on Emery's books at the time of the sale of $200,000, and the buildings have a carrying value of $2,000,000. The sale does not meet the FASB's criteria for the full accrual method of revenue recognition, and the installment method of accounting is assumed to be appropriate. The following entries would be made to record the initial transaction:

```
1993
Jan. 1  Cash.......................................  300,000
        Notes Receivable ...........................  11,793,800¹
            Unearned Interest Revenue ................            8,093,800²
            Real Estate Sales.........................            4,000,000

     1  Cost of Real Estate Sales ....................  2,200,000
            Land.....................................              200,000
            Building (net of accumulated depreciation) ....        2,000,000

     1  Real Estate Sales ...........................  4,000,000
            Cost of Real Estate Sales ...................            2,200,000
            Deferred Gross Profit on Real Estate Sales ....          1,800,000
```

Computations:
¹$471,752 × 25 = $11,793,800
²$11,793,800 − $3,700,000 = $8,093,800

The gross profit percentage for this sale is 45% ($1,800,000 ÷ $4,000,000). This percentage is applied to each cash collection reduced by the amount of interest included in the cash receipt. Thus, $135,000 would be recognized immediately upon receipt of the $300,000 down payment (.45 × $300,000) and the following entry would be made to recognize this profit:

```
1993
Jan. 1  Deferred Gross Profit on Real Estate Sales ..........  135,000
            Realized Gross Profit on Real Estate Sales ........            135,000
```

At the end of the first year, cash of $471,752 will be collected in accordance with the contract terms. Included in this amount is interest earned of $444,000 (.12 × $3,700,000). The remainder of the cash collected, $27,752, is payment on the principal amount of the debt; 45% of this portion of the payment, or $12,488 (.45 × $27,752), also would be recognized as realized gross profit in the first year.

```
1993
Dec. 31  Cash .........................................  471,752
            Notes Receivable ...........................            471,752

     31  Unearned Interest Revenue .....................  444,000
            Interest Revenue............................            444,000

     31  Deferred Gross Profit on Real Estate Sales .........  12,488
            Realized Gross Profit on Real Estate Sales........            12,488
```

The following T-accounts summarize these transactions for the first year before closing entries:

| Notes Receivable | | |
|---|---|---|
| 11,793,800 | | 471,752 |
| Bal.  11,322,048 | | |

| Land | | |
|---|---|---|
| Beg. Bal.  200,000 | | 200,000 |

| Unearned Interest Revenue | | |
|---|---|---|
| 444,000 | | 8,093,800 |
| | Bal. | 7,649,800 |

| Building (net of accumulated depreciation) | | |
|---|---|---|
| Beg. Bal.  2,000,000 | | 2,000,000 |

| Real Estate Sales | |
| --- | --- |
| 4,000,000 | 4,000,000 |

| Deferred Gross Profit on Real Estate Sales | | |
| --- | --- | --- |
| 135,000 | | 1,800,000 |
| 12,488 | | |
| | Bal. | 1,652,512 |

| Cost of Real Estate Sales | |
| --- | --- |
| 2,200,000 | 2,200,000 |

| Realized Gross Profit on Real Estate Sales | | |
| --- | --- | --- |
| | | 135,000 |
| | | 12,488 |
| | Bal. | 147,488 |

| Interest Revenue | |
| --- | --- |
| | 444,000 |

Cash collections in subsequent years would be divided between interest and principal in the same manner, and a portion of the deferred profit would be recognized each year. Because the collections are constant and the interest revenue is declining as the carrying value of the receivable declines, the gross profit recognized would increase each year.

Care must be taken in evaluating a sale of real estate. In some cases, the contract may be, in reality, a financial arrangement or an operating lease, or it may be a deposit on a possible future sale. Revenue should be recognized only after careful evaluation of the contractual arrangements and application of the criteria in FASB Statement No. 66.

## Cost Recovery Method

Under the cost recovery method, no income is recognized on a sale until the cost of the item sold is recovered through cash receipts. All cash receipts, both interest and principal portions, are applied first to the cost of those items sold. Then, all subsequent receipts are reported as revenue. Because all costs have been recovered, the recognized revenue after cost recovery represents income. This method is used only when the circumstances surrounding a sale are so uncertain that earlier recognition is impossible.

Using the information from the Riding Corporation example, assume that collections are so uncertain that the use of the cost recovery method is deemed appropriate. While the entries to record the installment sale, the receipt of cash, and the deferral of the gross profit are identical for both the installment sales and cost recovery methods, the entry for recognizing gross profit differs.

In 1993 no gross profit would be recognized, because the amount of cash collected ($30,000) is less than the cost of the inventory sold ($100,000). The cash collections in 1994 relating to 1993 sales result in total cash receipts exceeding the cost of sales ($30,000 + $75,000 > $100,000). Thus, in 1994 gross profit of $5,000 would be recognized on 1993 sales. The journal entry to recognize this gross profit in 1994 would be:

| | | |
| --- | --- | --- |
| Deferred Gross Profit—1993 . . . . . . . . . . . . . . . . . . . . . . . . . . . . . . . . . . . . | 5,000 | |
|     Realized Gross Profit on Installment Sales . . . . . . . . . . . . . . . . . . . | | 5,000 |

Since the cash collected on 1994 sales ($70,000) is less than the cost of inventory sold ($140,000), no gross profit would be recognized in 1994 on 1994 sales. In 1995 the $30,000 collected in cash from the 1993 sales would all be recognized as gross profit. The cash collected relating to 1994 sales, $80,000, when added to the cash received in 1994, $70,000, exceeds the cost of the 1994 sales of $140,000. Thus, $10,000 of gross profit that was deferred in 1994 will be recognized in 1995. The journal entry to recognize gross profit in 1995 would be as follows:

| | | |
|---|---|---|
| Deferred Gross Profit—1993 ................................. | 30,000 | |
| Deferred Gross Profit—1994 ................................. | 10,000 | |
| Realized Gross Profit on Installment Sales ................. | | 40,000 |

Comparing the amount of gross profit that is recognized using the various revenue recognition methods for the period 1993-1995 indicates how the income statement can be materially impacted by the method used.

| | Gross Profit Recognized | | |
|---|---|---|---|
| Revenue Recognition Method | 1993 | 1994 | 1995 |
| Full accrual ..................................... | $50,000 | $60,000 | $96,000 |
| Installment sales .............................. | 10,000 | 46,000 | 66,000 |
| Cost recovery ................................... | –0– | 5,000 | 40,000 |

To illustrate the accounting entries required under this method when interest is involved, assume that collection on the real estate sales contract for Emery Industries Inc. is felt to be so uncertain that the cost recovery method should be used. Under this method, the $2,200,000 carrying value of the real estate must be collected before any revenue or income is recognized, including any recognition of interest revenue on the contract. The same entries would be made to record the sale, the cost of the sale, and the deferred gross profit on the sale as was done under the installment sales method (page 722). The difference between the carrying value of the property and the down payment received equals the unrecovered cost of $1,900,000 ($2,200,000 − $300,000). Unrecovered cost may also be computed as the net balance that would be reported on the balance sheet as follows:

| | | |
|---|---|---|
| Notes receivable ................................... | | $11,793,800 |
| Less: Unearned interest revenue................... | $8,093,800 | |
| Deferred gross profit ....................... | 1,800,000 | 9,893,800 |
| | | $ 1,900,000 |

When the first annual payment of $471,752 is collected, the following entries would be made:

| 1993 | | | |
|---|---|---|---|
| Dec. 31 | Cash ......................................... | 471,752 | |
| | Notes Receivable ........................... | | 471,752 |
| 31 | Unearned Interest Revenue ..................... | 444,000 | |
| | Unrecognized Interest Revenue ............... | | 444,000 |

Note that the interest revenue for 1993 has been earned through the passage of time, but it is not recognized as revenue because the cost has not yet been recovered. The two separate interest offset accounts clarify this earnings process.

The unrecovered cost would now be $1,428,248 ($1,900,000 − $471,752). This agrees with the balance to be reported on the balance sheet as follows:

| | | |
|---|---|---|
| Notes receivable .................................... | | $11,322,048 |
| Less: Unearned interest revenue................... | $7,649,800 | |
| Deferred gross profit ....................... | 1,800,000 | |
| Unrecognized interest revenue ............... | 444,000 | 9,893,800 |
| Net notes receivable .............................. | | $ 1,428,248 |

By the end of 1996, all but $12,992 of the cost will have been recovered by the cash payments computed as follows:

| | | |
|---|---:|---:|
| Total cost of sold property . . . . . . . . . . . . . . . . . . . . . . . . . . . . . | | $2,200,000 |
| Less payments received: | | |
| Down payment . . . . . . . . . . . . . . . . . . . . . . . . . . . . . . . . . . . . . . . | $300,000 | |
| 1993 payment . . . . . . . . . . . . . . . . . . . . . . . . . . . . . . . . . . . . . . . | 471,752 | |
| 1994 payment . . . . . . . . . . . . . . . . . . . . . . . . . . . . . . . . . . . . . . . | 471,752 | |
| 1995 payment . . . . . . . . . . . . . . . . . . . . . . . . . . . . . . . . . . . . . . . | 471,752 | |
| 1996 payment . . . . . . . . . . . . . . . . . . . . . . . . . . . . . . . . . . . . . . . | 471,752 | 2,187,008 |
| Unrecovered cost . . . . . . . . . . . . . . . . . . . . . . . . . . . . . . . . . . . . | | $    12,992 |

The 1997 payment would result in a cost recovery of the $12,992 and an interest revenue recognition of $458,760. In each of the remaining collection years, the total cash receipt will be recognized as revenue; first allocated to interest revenue until the unrecognized interest revenue is recognized, and then the balance of the collections will be allocated between interest revenue and the gross profit on the real estate sale.

The selection of a revenue recognition method has a great impact on revenue and income, especially in the first year of a sales contract. The following summary shows how income would vary on the real estate sale of Emery Industries Inc. in 1993 depending on which revenue recognition method is used.

| Revenue Recognition Method | Income for 1993 |
|---|---|
| Full accrual . . . . . . . . . . . . . . . . . . . . . . . . . . . . . . . . . . . . . . . . . . . . . . . | $2,244,000[1] |
| Installment sales . . . . . . . . . . . . . . . . . . . . . . . . . . . . . . . . . . . . . . . . . | 591,488[2] |
| Cost recovery . . . . . . . . . . . . . . . . . . . . . . . . . . . . . . . . . . . . . . . . . . . . | –0– |

*Computations:*
[1] $1,800,000 gross profit + $444,000 interest revenue = $2,244,000
[2] $147,488 gross profit + $444,000 interest revenue = $591,488

In subsequent years, only interest revenue is recognized as revenue under the full accrual method, but interest revenue plus a portion of the payment on the principal is recognized under the installment sales method. After four years, all the cash collected is recognized as revenue under the cost recovery method. The graph on page 726 illustrates how revenue for the real estate sale would be recognized over the 25 years assuming all payments were made as scheduled.

## Cash Method

If the probability of recovering product or service costs is remote, the cash method of accounting could be used. Seldom would this method be applicable for sales of merchandise or real estate, because the right of repossession would leave considerable value to the seller. However, the cash method might be appropriate for service contracts with high initial costs and considerable uncertainty as to the ultimate collection of the contract price. Under this method, all costs are charged to expense as incurred, and revenue is recognized as collections are made. This extreme method of revenue and expense recognition would be appropriate only when the potential losses on a contract cannot be estimated with any degree of certainty.

## METHODS OF ACCOUNTING FOR SALES BEFORE RECOGNIZING REVENUE

In addition to the revenue recognition methods discussed in this chapter, some sales arrangements involve an exchange of either goods or monetary assets, such as cash and notes receivable, prior to the point where the earnings process has been completed sufficiently to recognize revenue. Under these circumstances, special accounting procedures

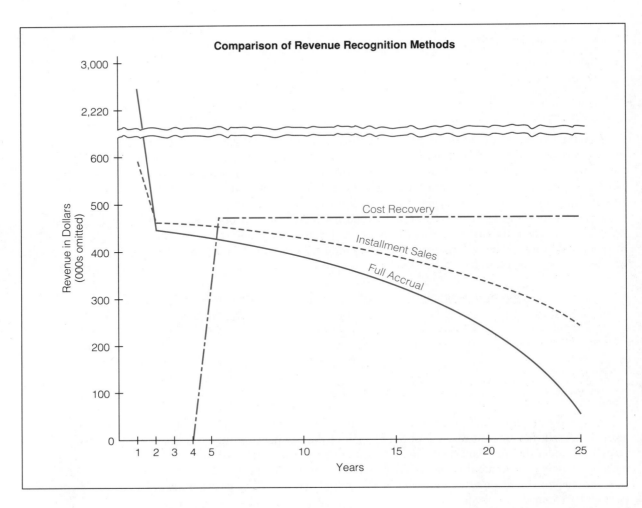

must be applied pending the finalization of the sale and subsequent application of one of the methods of revenue recognition. If monetary assets are received prior to finalization of a sale, the deposit method of accounting should be used. If inventory is exchanged in advance of a sale, consignment accounting procedures should be applied. Each of these methods will be discussed briefly.

## Deposit Method—General

In some cases, cash is collected before a sales contract is sufficiently defined to recognize revenue. This situation frequently arises in real estate sales contracts. For these cases, a method of accounting referred to as the deposit method has been developed.[11] Pending recognition of a sale, the cash received from a buyer is reported as a deposit on the contract and classified among the liabilities on the balance sheet. The property continues to be shown as an asset of the seller, and any related debt on the property continues to be reported as debt of the seller. No revenue or income should be recognized until the sales contract is finalized. At that time, one of the revenue recognition methods illustrated in this chapter may be used, and the deposit account would be closed. If the deposit is forfeited, it should be credited to Income.

[11]*Statement of Financial Accounting Standards No. 66,* pars. 65-67.

## The Savings & Loan Crisis

The estimated cost to taxpayers to bail out failing savings and loan companies has been estimated as high as $500 billion. Reasons for the crisis include mismanagement of resources, management fraud, and unfavorable economic conditions. Another factor contributing to the S&L problems include their revenue recognition techniques.

When a loan is made, the associated loan origination fee, often as high as 6% of the loan principal, immediately is included as revenue. If a financial institution's objective were to increase income for the short term, one strategy would be to loan as much money as possible and collect large loan fees.

The president of one S&L, Texas' Western Savings, elected to follow this strategy. He enticed investors by promising high yields on certificates of deposit that were federally insured. His telephone operations often netted over $20 million in investments per day. Once the money was received from investors, the president would then loan the money to borrowers and collect loan fees as revenue. These fees and other income were the source of a $3 million dividend to the president over a two-year period.

The problem for taxpayers was that the president was making poor loans. Since investors' deposits were federally insured, collectibility of loans was not a major issue for Western. Million-dollar loans were made with no required down payment. Loans were made for more than the full purchase price of properties. As an example, $64 million was loaned to purchase land that two years earlier had sold for $17.2 million. On this particular deal, Western, holding a sixth lien on the property, received $2 million in loan fees.

### Questions:

1. *How can a savings & loan company justify immediately recognizing the loan origination fee as revenue rather than recognizing it over the life of the loan?*
2. *From an accounting point of view, what revenue recognition method should be used when dealing with high-risk loans?*
3. *Why would investors deposit their money in financial institutions that had lending practices like those illustrated in this case?*
4. *Do external auditors have a responsibility to evaluate the loan practices of the financial institutions that they audit?*

Source: "Easy Money," *The Wall Street Journal*, April 27, 1989.

## Deposit Method—Franchising Industry

A special application of the deposit method is found in the franchising industry, one of the fastest growing retail industries of recent years. Franchisors create faster growth by selling various rights to use a name and/or a product to operators (franchisees) who manage independent units as separate entrepreneurs from the franchisor.

Sales of franchises usually include several different services, products, and/or plant assets including: (1) intangible rights to use a trademark or name, (2) property owned by the franchisor, (3) pre-opening services such as helping locate suitable business sites, constructing a building, and training employees, and (4) ongoing services, products, and processes as the operations are carried out. Many revenue recognition problems are present in typical franchises; however, most of them may be solved if the elements are identified separately and accounted for in the same manner as they would be if the sale were a separate transaction. The most troublesome revenue recognition problem has been the initial fee. Typically, the franchisor charges a substantial amount for the right to use the franchise name and to provide for pre-opening services. Sometimes these fees are payable immediately in cash, but typically they include a long-term note receivable. Frequently, liberal refund provisions are included in the agreement, especially in the period prior to opening.

In the early days of franchising agreements, franchisors often reported the initial fee as revenue when the monetary assets were received. Future estimated costs were provided as offsets to the revenue. However, this treatment often resulted in questionable front-end loading of revenue similar to that occurring in the real estate and retail land sale industries. As a result, the AICPA issued an Industry Accounting Guide in 1973 that established revenue recognition guidelines for the franchising industry.[12] The essentials of this guide were later incorporated into FASB Statement No. 45.[13] This standard specifies that no revenue is to be recognized prior to **substantial performance** of the services covered by the initial fee. Until that time, any monetary assets received should be offset by a deposit or deferred credit account, and any costs related to the services rendered should be deferred until revenue is recognized, except that such deferred costs shall not exceed anticipated revenue less estimated additional related costs. Once substantial performance is achieved, revenue should be recognized using the method that best reflects the probability of cash collection, e.g., accrual, installment sales, or cost recovery method. The latter two methods "shall be used to account for franchise fee revenue only in those exceptional cases when revenue is collectible over an extended period and no reasonable basis exists for estimating collectibility."[14]

To illustrate, assume that a franchisor charges new franchisees an initial fee of $25,000. Of this amount, $10,000 is payable in cash when the agreement is signed, and the remainder is to be paid in four annual installments of $3,750 each. This obligation is evidenced by a $15,000, non-interest-bearing note. The agreement provides that the franchisor will assist in locating the site for a building, conduct a market survey to estimate potential income, supervise the construction of a building, and provide initial training to employees. Assume that the franchisee could borrow money at 10%. Thus, the present value of the four $3,750 payments would be $11,887 ($3,750 × 3.1699). The discount of $3,113 ($3,750 × 4 = $15,000 − $11,887) represents interest to be earned over the payment period.

If the down payment is refundable and no services have been rendered at the time the arrangement is made, the deposit method would be used as long as collection on the note is reasonably certain. The following entry would be made to record the transaction:

| | | |
|---|---:|---:|
| Cash | 10,000 | |
| Notes Receivable | 15,000 | |
|    Unearned Interest Revenue | | 3,113 |
|    Deposit on Franchise (or Unearned Franchise Fee) | | 21,887 |

When the initial services are determined to be substantially performed, the revenue recognition method to be used and the resulting journal entries depend on the probability of future cash collection. If the collection of the note is reasonably assured, the full accrual method would be used. Assume that substantial performance of the initial services costs

---

[12]Committee on Franchise Accounting and Auditing, AICPA, *Industry Accounting Guide*, "Accounting for Franchise Fee Revenue" (New York: American Institute of Certified Public Accountants, 1973).

[13]*Statement of Financial Accounting Standards No. 45*, "Accounting for Franchise Fee Revenue" (Stamford: Financial Accounting Standards Board, March 1981).

[14]*Ibid.*, par. 6.

$14,000. The entries to record this event using the full accrual method would be as follows:

| | | |
|---|---|---|
| Cost of Franchise Fee Revenue .............................. | 14,000 | |
|    Cash ..................................................... | | 14,000 |
| Deposit on Franchise (or Unearned Franchise Fee) ............ | 21,887 | |
|    Franchise Fee Revenue.................................... | | 21,887 |

If the collection of the note is doubtful, the installment sales method could be used. In addition to the entries used under the full accrual method, the installment sales method requires the following entries:

| | | |
|---|---|---|
| Franchise Fee Revenue ..................................... | 21,887 | |
|    Cost of Franchise Fee Revenue ........................... | | 14,000 |
|    Deferred Gross Profit on Franchise ........................ | | 7,887 |
| Deferred Gross Profit on Franchise......................... | 3,604* | |
|    Realized Gross Profit on Franchise ........................ | | 3,604 |

*Computation:*
*$7,887 ÷ $21,887 = 36.04% gross profit percentage
.3604 × $10,000 = $3,604

## Consignment Sales

Another method of accounting has developed for when property is exchanged without a transfer of title and without a sales contract being completed. This type of arrangement is referred to as a consignment. Under a consignment, the potential seller, the consignor, delivers merchandise to another party, the consignee, who then acts as an *agent* for the consignor to sell the goods. Title to the merchandise continues to be held by the consignor until a sale is made, at which time title passes to the ultimate purchaser. The consignee usually is entitled to reimbursement for expenses incurred in relation to this arrangement and also is entitled to a commission if a sale is successfully made.

Because title to the merchandise is held by the consignor, but physical possession is held by the consignee, special accounting records must be maintained by the consignor for control purposes. No revenue is recognized until a sale is made by the consignee. Upon shipment of the merchandise by the consignor, a special inventory account is established on the consignor's books to identify the consigned merchandise. Any consignment expenses paid by the consignor are added to the inventory balance as added costs. The consignee does not make an entry for receipt of the inventory in the general ledger; however, memorandum control records usually are kept. Any reimbursable expense paid by the consignee is charged to a receivable account by the consignee and added to the inventory balance by the consignor. When a sale is made, the consignor recognizes the sale as revenue according to one of the revenue recognition methods, and the consignee recognizes the commission as revenue on the transaction.

To illustrate consignment accounting entries, assume that Harrison Products Inc. sends $500,000 worth of goods on consignment to Benson Industries. Shipping costs of $5,000 are paid by Harrison, and reimbursable advertising costs of $20,000 are paid by Benson Industries. By the end of the year, one-half of the goods on consignment are sold for $400,000 cash. A 10% commission is earned by Benson Industries according to the terms of the consignment. The journal entries shown on page 730 would be made on the consignor's and consignee's books.

If the sale by Benson Industries had been on the installment basis, the installment sales entries illustrated earlier in this chapter could have been used in place of the accrual entries illustrated.

| Transaction | Entries on Consignor's Books (Harrison Products Inc.) | | Entries on Consignee's Books (Benson Industries) | |
|---|---|---|---|---|
| (1) Shipment of goods on consignment. | Inventory on Consignment ....   500,000     Finished Goods     Inventory ...... | 500,000 | No entry (memorandum control record) | |
| (2) Payment of expenses by consignor. | Inventory on Consignment ....   5,000     Cash .......... | 5,000 | No entry | |
| (3) Payment of expenses by consignee. | Inventory on Consignment ....   20,000     Consignee     Payable ....... | 20,000 | Consignor Receivable.......   20,000     Cash .......... | 20,000 |
| (4) Sale of merchandise. | No entry | | Cash ...........   400,000     Consignor     Payable ....... | 400,000 |
| (5) Notification of sale to consignor and payment of cash due. | Commission Expense........   40,000 Cash ............   340,000 Consignee Payable ........   20,000     Consignment     Sales Revenue.. Cost of Goods Sold ............   262,500*     Inventory on     Consignment .. | 400,000 262,500 | Consignor Payable .........   400,000     Cash ..........     Commission     Revenue.......     Consignor     Receivable..... | 340,000 40,000 20,000 |

*Computation:
1/2($500,000 + $25,000) = $262,500

## CONCLUDING COMMENTS

This chapter has explored some special problems that arise in recognizing revenue. Some industries such as franchising, construction, and real estate have been used as illustrative of the types of problems that exist in applying the revenue recognition criteria included in currently accepted accounting standards. While recognizing revenue at the point of sale is still the most traditional method, accounting standards provide for flexibility when a different method of revenue recognition provides more meaningful information to users. Percentage-of-completion, proportional performance, installment sales, cost recovery, and deferral through the deposit method are all part of generally accepted accounting principles under specified conditions.

## KEY TERMS

Change orders 715
Completed-contract method 706
Consignment 729
Consignee 729
Consignor 729
Cost recovery method 723

Cost-to-cost method 708
Deposit method 726
Efforts-expended methods 708
Input measures 707
Installment sales method 718
Output measures 708

Percentage-of-completion accounting 706
Proportional performance method 706
Substantial performance 728

## A Problem With Accruing Revenues

Midwestern Companies, a firm specializing in the production and sale of ethanol plants, used accrual accounting to report revenues from the sale of the plants. However, details of the sale of an ethanol plant have left many questioning Midwestern's accounting practices.

An investor in a partnership would pay $15,000 and sign a note for $45,000. After the initial investment, investors were not required to pay any more money as the cash from the operations of the plant would be applied against the note. The company promised that the plant would operate properly and that those purchasing the plant would be provided with customers.

While the firm reported $36.3 million in revenues from the sale of ethanol plants with costs of $12.2 million, they received only $10.8 million in cash. Thus, on a cash basis, the firm was actually operating at a loss for the period.

### Questions:

1. *In selling an ethanol plant, identify the various points at which one could argue that the earnings process is substantially complete. At what point do you think Midwestern was recognizing revenue?*
2. *Did the use of accrual accounting accurately portray the financial performance of Midwestern?*
3. *In your opinion, what revenue recognition method should have been used by Midwestern?*

Source: "Up & Down Wall Street," *Barron's*, March 5, 1984.

## QUESTIONS

1. Under what conditions is percentage-of-completion accounting recommended for construction contractors?
2. Distinguish between the cost-to-cost method and efforts-expended methods of measuring the percentage of completion.
3. Output measures of percentage of completion are sometimes used in preference to input measures. What are some examples of commonly used output measures?
4. What is the relationship between the construction in progress account and the progress billings on construction contracts account? How should these accounts be reported on the balance sheet?
5. When a measure of percentage of completion other than cost-to-cost is used, the amount of cost charged against revenue using the percentage of completion usually will be different from the costs incurred. How do some AICPA committee members recommend handling this situation so that the costs charged against revenue are equal to the costs incurred?
6. The construction in progress account is used to accumulate all costs of construction. What additional item is included in this account when percentage-of-completion accounting is followed?
7. The gross profit percentage reported on long-term construction contracts often varies from year to year. What is the major reason for this variation?
8. How are anticipated contract losses treated under the completed-contract and percentage-of-completion methods?
9. What input and output measures usually are applicable to the proportional performance method for long-term service contracts?
10. The proportional performance method spreads the profit over the periods in which services are being performed. What arguments could be made against this method of revenue recognition for newly formed, service-oriented companies?
11. Distinguish among the three different approaches to revenue recognition that await the receipt of cash. How does the treatment of costs incurred vary depending on the approach used?
12. Under what general conditions is the installment sales method of accounting preferred to the full accrual method?

13. The normal accounting entries for installment sales require keeping a separate record by year of receivables, collections on receivables, and the deferred gross profit percentages. Why are these separate records necessary?

14. Installment sales contracts generally include interest. Contrast the method of recognizing interest revenue from the method used to recognize the gross profit on the sale.

15. Under what conditions would the cash method of recognizing revenue be acceptable for reporting purposes?

16. What special recognition problems arise in accounting for franchise fees?

17. Consignment accounting is primarily a method of accounting for transfers of inventory prior to the point of revenue recognition. Describe the essential elements of this method from the standpoint of (a) the consignor and (b) the consignee.

## DISCUSSION CASES

### Case 19—1  (Recognizing revenue on a percentage-of-completion basis)

As the new controller for Enclave Construction Company, you have been advised that your predecessor classified all revenues and expenses by project, each project being considered a separate venture. All revenues from uncompleted projects were treated as unearned revenue, and all expenses applicable to each uncompleted project were treated as "work in process" inventory. Thus, the income statement for the current year includes only the revenues and expenses related to projects completed during the year.

What do you think about the use of the completed-contract method by the previous controller? What alternative approach might you suggest to company management?

### Case 19—2  (Let's spread our losses too!)

The Abbott Construction Company has several contracts to build sections of freeways, bridges, and dams. Because most of these contracts require more than one year to complete, the accountant, Dave Allred, has recommended use of the percentage-of-completion method to recognize revenue and income on these contracts. The president, Kathy Bahr, isn't quite sure how the accounting method works, and she indicates concern about the impact of this decision on income taxes. Bahr also inquires as to what happens when a contract results in a loss. When told by Allred that any estimated loss must be recognized when it is first identified, Bahr becomes upset. "If it is a percentage-of-completion method and we are recognizing profits as production is finished, why shouldn't we be able to do the same for losses?"

How would you, as the accountant, answer Bahr's concerns?

### Case 19—3  (What is the difference between completed-contract and percentage-of-completion accounting?)

In accounting for long-term contracts (those taking longer than one year to complete), the two methods commonly followed are the percentage-of-completion method and the completed-contract method.

1. Discuss how earnings on long-term contracts are recognized and computed under these two methods.
2. Under what circumstances is it preferable to use one method over the other?
3. Why is earnings recognition as measured by interim billings not generally accepted for long-term contracts?

### Case 19—4  (When is the membership fee earned?)

The Superb Health Studio has been operating for 5 years but is presently for sale. It has opened 50 salons in various cities in the United States. The normal pattern for a new opening is to advertise heavily and sell different types of memberships: 1-year, 3-year, and 5-year. For the initial membership fee, members may use the pool, exercise rooms, sauna, and other recreational facilities without charge. If special courses or programs are taken, additional fees are charged; however, members are granted certain privileges, and the fees are less than those charged to outsiders. In addition, a minimal $10-a-month dues charge is made to all members. Nonmembers may use the facilities; however, they must pay a substantial daily charge for services they receive.

Your client, Dickson Inc., is considering purchasing the chain of health studios, and asks you to give your opinion on its operations. You are provided with financial statements that show a growing revenue and income pattern over the 5-year period. The balance sheet shows that the physical facilities are apparently owned rather than leased. But you are aware that health studios, like all service institutions, have some challenging revenue recognition problems.

What questions would you want answered in preparing your report for Dickson?

## Case 19—5   (When is it revenue?)

Hertzel Advertising Agency handles advertising for clients under contracts that require the agency to develop advertising copy and layouts and place ads in various media, charging clients a commission of 15% of the media cost as its fee. The agency makes advance billings to its clients of estimated media cost plus its 15% commission. Adjustments to these advances usually are small. Frequently both the billings and receipt of cash from these billings occur before the period in which the advertising actually appears in the media.

A conference meeting is held between officers of the agency and the new firm of CPAs recently engaged to perform annual audits. In this meeting, consideration is given to 4 possible points for measuring revenue: (1) at the time the advanced billing is made, (2) when payment is received from the client, (3) in the month when the advertising appears in the media, and (4) when the bill for advertising is received from the media, generally in the month following its appearance. The agency has been following the first method for the past several years on the basis that a definite contract exists and the revenue is earned when billed. When the billing is made, an entry is prepared to record the estimated receivable and liability to the media. Estimated expenses related to the contract are also recorded. Adjusting entries are made later for any differences between the estimated and actual amounts.

As a member of the CPA firm attending this meeting, how would you react to the agency's method of recognizing revenue? Discuss the strengths and weaknesses of each of the 4 methods of revenue recognition and indicate which one you would recommend the agency follow.

## Case 19—6   (Keep shipping, we need the revenue.)

Datarite, a maker of computer hardware systems, sells its products to dealers who, in turn, sell to the final customer. Datarite offers very liberal credit terms and allows its dealers to take up to 90 days to pay. These terms allow dealers to hold larger inventories. As the end of the fiscal year nears, Datarite needs to increase its current ratio and decrease its debt-to-equity ratio in order to avoid violating its debt covenants. The president of the company has asked that all dealers be shipped extra inventory. This will increase both sales and accounts receivable, thereby allowing Datarite to remain in compliance with its debt covenants. The chief financial officer remarks that shipping inventory to dealers that has not been ordered should be accounted for as consigned inventory rather than revenue.

Should the inventory shipments be accounted for as sales or as consigned inventory? Debt covenants exist to protect the interests of creditors. In this instance, are debt covenants effective in monitoring the company's activities?

## Case 19—7   (Which method is appropriate?)

Green Brothers Furniture sells discount furniture and offers easy credit terms. Its margins are not large but it deals in heavy volume. Its customers are often low-income individuals who cannot obtain credit elsewhere. Green Brothers retains the title to the furniture until full payment is received, and it is not uncommon to have 20% of sales be uncollectible.

Green Brothers is considering expansion and has hired an independent auditor to review its financial statements prior to obtaining outside funding. The auditor questions the use of accrual accounting as a method for recognizing revenue and suggests that Green Brothers use the installment sales method. The auditor justifies this by stating that because of the high rate of uncollectibles, the earnings process is not substantially complete at the point of sale. Financial statements adjusted to the installment sales method result in a 17% decrease in net income for the fiscal year just ended.

The chief financial officer for Green Brothers counters that if uncollectibles can be estimated, even if that estimate is high, the use of the accrual method is appropriate. The accountant also notes that restated financial statements showing the lower net income figure will make obtaining external funding much more difficult.

Which method of revenue recognition would you argue that Green Brothers should use? Why? Remember that your decision could affect this company's ability to obtain favorable external financing.

### Case 19—8   (When is the initial franchise fee really earned?)

Magleby Inn sells franchises to independent operators throughout the western part of the United States. The contract with the franchisee includes the following provisions:

(a) The franchisee is charged an initial fee of $25,000. Of this amount, $5,000 is payable when the agreement is signed and a $4,000 non-interest-bearing note is payable at the end of each of the 5 subsequent years.
(b) All the initial franchise fee collected by Magleby Inn is to be refunded and the remaining obligation canceled if, for any reason, the franchisee fails to open the franchise.
(c) In return for the initial franchise fee, Magleby agrees to: assist the franchisee in selecting the location for the business; negotiate the lease for the land; obtain financing and assist with building design; supervise construction; establish accounting and tax records; and provide expert advice over a 5-year period relating to such matters as employee and management training, quality control, and promotion.
(d) In addition to the initial franchise fee, the franchisee is required to pay to Magleby Inn a monthly fee of 2% of sales for recipe innovations and the privilege of purchasing ingredients from Magleby Inn at or below prevailing market prices.

Management of Magleby Inn estimates that the value of the services rendered to the franchisee at the time the contract is signed amounts to at least $5,000. All franchisees to date have opened their locations at the scheduled time and none has defaulted on any of the notes receivable.

The credit ratings of all franchisees would entitle them to borrow at the current interest rate of 10%.

Given the nature of Magleby's agreement with its franchisees, when should revenue be recognized? Discuss the question of revenue recognition for both the initial franchise fee and the additional monthly fee of 2% of sales.

### Case 19—9   (I think they're sales!)

The Rain-Soft Water Company distributes its water softeners to dealers upon their request. The contract agreement with the dealers is that they may have 90 days to sell and pay for the softeners. Until the 90-day period is over, any softeners may be returned at the dealer's expense and with no further obligation on the dealer's part. Past experience indicates that 75% of all softeners distributed on this basis are sold by the dealer. In June, 100 units are delivered to dealers at an average billed price of $800 each. The average cost of the softeners to Rain-Soft is $600. Based on the expected sales, Rain-Soft reports profit of $15,000 [$200 × .75(100)].

You are asked to evaluate the income statement for its compliance with GAAP. What recommendations would you make?

## EXERCISES

### Exercise 19—1  (Completed-contract method)

On December 1, 1993, bids were submitted for a construction project to build a new municipal building and fire station. The lowest bid was $3,980,000, submitted by the Jessop Construction Company. Jessop was awarded the contract. Jessop uses the completed-contract method to report gross profit. The following data is given to summarize the activities on this contract for 1993 and 1994. Give the entries to record these transactions using the completed-contract method.

| Year | Cost Incurred | Estimated Cost to Complete | Billings on Contract | Collections of Billings |
|------|---------------|----------------------------|----------------------|-------------------------|
| 1993 | $1,720,000 | $2,060,000 | $1,350,000 | $1,150,000 |
| 1994 | 2,020,000 | –0– | 2,630,000 | 2,830,000 |

### Exercise 19—2  (Percentage-of-completion analysis)

Espiritu Construction Co. has used the cost-to-cost percentage-of-completion method of recognizing revenue. Tony Espiritu assumed leadership of the business after the recent death of his father, Howard. In reviewing the records, Espiritu finds the following information regarding a recently completed building project for which the total contract was $2,000,000.

| | 1992 | 1993 | 1994 |
|------|------|------|------|
| Gross profit (loss) .......................... | $ 40,000 | $140,000 | $ (20,000) |
| Cost incurred .............................. | 360,000 | ? | 820,000 |

Espiritu wants to know how effectively the company operated during the last 3 years on this project and, since the information is not complete, has asked for answers to the following questions:

1. How much cost was incurred in 1993?
2. What percentage of the project was completed by the end of 1993?
3. What was the total estimated gross profit on the project by the end of 1993?
4. What was the estimated cost to complete the project at the end of 1993?

### Exercise 19—3  (Percentage-of-completion accounting)

The Quality Construction Company was the low bidder on an office building construction contract. The contract bid was $7,000,000, with an estimated cost to complete the project of $6,000,000. The contract period was 34 months starting January 1, 1992. The company uses the cost-to-cost method of estimating earnings. Because of changes requested by the customer, the contract price was adjusted downward to $6,500,000 on January 1, 1993.

A record of construction activities for the years 1992-95 follows:

| Year | Actual Cost— Current Year | Progress Billings | Cash Receipts |
|------|---------------------------|-------------------|---------------|
| 1992 | $2,500,000 | $2,100,000 | $1,800,000 |
| 1993 | 3,300,000 | 3,100,000 | 3,000,000 |
| 1994 | 410,000 | 1,300,000 | 1,000,000 |
| 1995 |  |  | 700,000 |

The estimated cost to complete the contract as of the end of each accounting period is:

| | |
|------|------|
| 1992 ...................................................... | $3,500,000 |
| 1993 ...................................................... | 400,000 |
| 1994 ...................................................... | –0– |

Calculate the gross profit for the years 1992-1994 under the percentage-of-completion method of revenue recognition.

## Exercise 19—4  (Percentage-of-completion analysis)

Smokey International Inc. recently acquired the Kurtz Builders Company. Kurtz has incomplete accounting records. On one particular project, only the information below is available.

|  | 1992 | 1993 | 1994 |
|---|---|---|---|
| Costs incurred during year .................. | $200,000 | $250,000 | ? |
| Estimated cost to complete.................. | 450,000 | 190,000 | –0– |
| Recognized revenue ....................... | 220,000 | ? | ? |
| Gross profit on contract.................... | ? | 10,000 | $(10,000) |
| Contract price............................ | 700,000 |  |  |

Because the information is incomplete, you are asked the following questions assuming the percentage-of-completion method is used, an output measure is used to estimate the percentage completed, and revenue is recorded using the actual cost approach.

1. How much gross profit should be reported in 1992?
2. How much revenue should be reported in 1993?
3. How much revenue should be reported in 1994?
4. How much cost was incurred in 1994?
5. What are the total costs on the contract?
6. What would be the gross profit for 1993 if the cost-to-cost percentage-of-completion method were used rather than the output measure? (Ignore the revenue amount shown for 1992 and gross profit amount reported for 1993.)

## Exercise 19—5  (Reporting construction contracts)

Tara Builders Inc. is building a new home for Margaret Mitchell at a contracted price of $120,000. The estimated cost at the time the contract is signed (January 2, 1993) is $97,000. At December 31, 1993, the total cost incurred is $59,000 with estimated costs to complete of $41,000. Tara has billed $70,000 on the job and has received a $60,000 payment. This is the only contract in process at year-end. Prepare the sections of the balance sheet and the income statement of Tara Builders Inc. affected by these events assuming use of (a) the percentage-of-completion method and (b) the completed-contract method.

## Exercise 19—6  (Percentage of completion using architect's estimates)

Central Iowa Builders Inc. entered into a contract to construct an office building and plaza at a contract price of $10,000,000. Income is to be reported using the percentage-of-completion method as determined by estimates made by the architect. The data below summarizes the activities on the construction for the years 1992-1994. For the years 1992-1994, what entries are required to record this information, assuming the architect's estimate of the percentage completed is used to determine revenue (proportional cost approach)?

| Year | Actual Cost Incurred | Estimated Cost to Complete | Percentage Complete— Architect's Estimate | Project Billings | Collections on Billings |
|---|---|---|---|---|---|
| 1992 | $3,200,000 | $6,000,000 | 25% | $3,300,000 | $3,100,000 |
| 1993 | 4,300,000 | 1,600,000 | 75 | 4,500,000 | 4,000,000 |
| 1994 | 1,550,000 | –0– | 100 | 2,200,000 | 2,900,000 |

## Exercise 19—7  (Completed-contract method)

On January 1, 1992, the Ishikawa Construction Company entered into a 3-year contract to build a dam. The original contract price for the construction was $18,000,000 and the estimated cost was $16,100,000. The following cost data relates to the construction period.

| Year | Cost Incurred | Estimated Cost to Complete | Billings | Cash Collected |
|------|---------------|----------------------------|----------|----------------|
| 1992 | $6,000,000 | $10,000,000 | $6,300,000 | $6,000,000 |
| 1993 | 5,300,000 | 7,400,000 | 5,700,000 | 5,400,000 |
| 1994 | 7,650,000 | –0– | 6,000,000 | 6,600,000 |

Prepare the required journal entries for the 3 years of the contract, assuming Ishikawa uses the completed-contract method.

### Exercise 19—8  (Percentage-of-completion method with change orders)

The Build It Construction Company enters into a contract on January 1, 1993, to construct a 20-story office building for $40,000,000. During the construction period, many change orders are made to the original contract. The following schedule summarizes these changes made in 1993:

| | Cost Incurred—1993 | Estimated Cost to Complete | Contract Price |
|--------|---------------------|-----------------------------|------------------|
| Basic contract........ | $8,000,000 | $28,000,000 | $40,000,000 |
| Change Order #1 .... | 50,000 | 50,000 | 125,000 |
| Change Order #2 .... | –0– | 50,000 | –0– |
| Change Order #3 .... | 300,000 | 300,000 | Still to be negotiated. At least cost. |
| Change Order #4 .... | 125,000 | –0– | 100,000 |

Compute the revenue, costs, and gross profit to be recognized in 1993, assuming use of the cost-to-cost method to determine the percentage completed. (Round percentage to two decimal places.)

### Exercise 19—9  (Service industry accounting)

The Fitness Health Spa charges an annual membership fee of $600 for its services. For this fee, each member receives a fitness evaluation (value $100), a monthly magazine (value $32), and 2-hour's use of the equipment each week. The initial direct costs to obtain the membership are estimated to be $120. The direct cost of the fitness evaluation is $50, and the monthly direct costs to provide the other services are estimated to be $15 per person. In addition, the monthly indirect costs are estimated to average $8 per person. Give the journal entries to record the transactions in 1993 relative to a membership sold on July 1, 1993. The fitness evaluation is given in the first month of membership, and the initial direct cost is to be spread over all direct costs, including the fitness evaluation, using the proportional performance method. (Round percentage of performance to two decimal places and journal entries to the nearest dollar.)

### Exercise 19—10  (Installment sales accounting—real estate)

On January 1, 1993, the Krystyu Realty Company sold property carried in inventory at a cost of $85,000 for $140,000 with terms of 10% down and the balance in annual installments over a 10-year period at 12% interest. Installment payments are to be made at the end of each year.

1. What is the equal annual payment necessary to pay for this property under the stated terms? (Round to nearest dollar.)
2. Give the entries for the first year assuming the installment sales method is used.

### Exercise 19—11  (Installment sales accounting)

Denna Corporation had sales in 1992 of $210,000, in 1993 of $270,000, and in 1994 of $350,000. The gross profit percentage of each year, in order, was 25%, 29%, and 27%. Past history has shown that 10% of total sales are collected in the first year, 40% in the second year, and 30% in the third year. Assuming these collections are made as projected, give the journal entries for 1992, 1993, and 1994, assuming use of the installment sales method. Ignore provisions for doubtful accounts and interest.

**Exercise 19—12   (Installment sales analysis)**

Complete the following table:

|  | 1992 | 1993 | 1994 |
|---|---|---|---|
| Installment sales | $50,000 | $80,000 | $ (7) |
| Cost of installment sales | (1) | (5) | 91,800 |
| Gross profit | (2) | (6) | 28,200 |
| Gross profit percentage | (3) | 25% | (8) |
| Cash collections: |  |  |  |
| 1992 | (4) | 25,000 | 10,000 |
| 1993 |  | 20,000 | 50,000 |
| 1994 |  |  | 45,000 |
| Realized gross profit on installment sales | 1,100 | 10,500 | (9) |

**Exercise 19—13   (Cost recovery method)**

Bailey Bats Inc. had the following sales and gross profit percentages for the years 1992-1995:

|  | Sales | Gross Profit Percentage |
|---|---|---|
| 1992 | $47,000 | 45% |
| 1993 | 45,000 | 42 |
| 1994 | 58,000 | 47 |
| 1995 | 61,000 | 49 |

Historically, 55% of sales are collected in the year of the sale, 30% in the following year, 10% in the third year. Assuming collections are as projected, give the journal entries for the years 1992-1995 assuming the use of the cost recovery method. (Ignore provision for doubtful accounts.) Prepare a table comparing the gross profit recognized for 1992-1995 using the full accrual method and the cost recovery method.

**Exercise 19—14   (Cost recovery analysis)**

Johnson Enterprises uses the cost recovery method for all installment sales. Complete the following table:

|  | 1992 | 1993 | 1994 |
|---|---|---|---|
| Installment sales | $80,000 | $95,000 | (1) |
| Cost of installment sales | (2) | 56,050 | $68,250 |
| Gross profit percentage | 38% | (3) | 35% |
| Cash collections: |  |  |  |
| 1992 sales | 25,600 | 46,400 | 5,600 |
| 1993 sales |  | 22,800 | (4) |
| 1994 sales |  |  | 32,550 |
| Realized gross profit on installment sales | (5) | (6) | 16,050 |

**Exercise 19—15   (Cost recovery method—real estate)**

Pomona Inc. is a land development company. It has acquired 1,000 acres of choice recreational property for $1,200 per acre, and it is selling developed recreational building lots for $5,000 per acre. The improvement costs amount to $1,200 per acre. The land cost, including improvements, is carried on Pomona's books as inventory. In the first year, Pomona sold 30 one-acre lots, 10% down, the balance to be paid over 10 years in annual installments at an interest rate of 10%. Assume the lots were sold on January 1, 1993.

1. Give the entries required for 1993 and 1994 if the cost recovery method is used to recognize revenue.
2. Prove that the balance reported on the December 31, 1994, balance sheet is equal to the unrecovered cost of the land.

### Exercise 19—16   (Franchise accounting)

On September 1, 1993, Jensen Company entered into franchise agreements with three franchisees. The agreements required an initial fee payment of $7,000 plus four $3,000 payments due every 4 months, the first payment due December 31, 1993. The interest rate is 12%. The initial deposit is refundable until substantial performance has been completed. The following table describes each agreement:

| Franchisee | Probability of Full Collection | Services Performed by Franchisor at Dec. 31, 1993 | Total Cost Incurred to Dec. 31, 1993 |
|---|---|---|---|
| A | Likely | Substantially | $ 7,000 |
| B | Doubtful | 25% | 2,000 |
| C | Doubtful | Substantially | 10,000 |

For each franchisee, identify the revenue recognition method that you would recommend considering the circumstances. What amount of revenue and income would be reported in 1993 for the method selected? Assume $10,000 was received from each franchisee during the year.

### Exercise 19—17   (Franchise accounting)

Starbrite Pizzas franchises its name to different people across the country. The franchise agreement requires the franchisee to make an initial payment of $12,000 and sign a $32,000 non-interest-bearing note on the agreement date. The note is to be paid in 4 annual payments of $8,000, each beginning one year from the agreement date. The initial payment is refundable until the date of opening. Interest rates are assumed to be 10%. The franchisor agrees to make market studies, find a location, train the employees, and perform a few other relatively minor services. The following transactions describe the relationship with Libby Loebig, a franchisee:

1993
July   1   Entered into a franchise agreement.
Sep.   1   Completed a market study at a cost of $5,000.
Nov. 15   Found suitable location. Service cost $3,000.

1994
Jan.  10   Completed training program for employees, cost $5,000.
        15   Franchise outlet opened.
July   1   Received first annual payment.

Give Starbrite Pizzas' journal entries in 1993-1994 to record these transactions, including any adjusting entries at December 31, 1993.

### Exercise 19—18   (Consignment accounting)

In 1993, Rawlings Wholesalers transferred goods to a retailer on consignment. The transaction was recorded as a sale by Rawlings. The goods cost $45,000 and normally are sold at a 30% markup. In 1994, $12,000 (cost) of the merchandise was sold by the retailer at the normal markup, and the balance of the merchandise was returned to Rawlings. The retailer withheld a 10% commission from payment. Prepare the journal entry in 1994 to correct the books for 1993, and prepare the correct entries relative to the consignment sale in 1994.

# PROBLEMS

## Problem 19—1   (Construction accounting)

Zamponi's Construction Company reports its income for tax purposes on a completed-contract basis and income for financial statement purposes on a percentage-of-completion basis. A record of construction activities for 1993 and 1994 follows:

| | | 1993 | | 1994 | |
|---|---|---|---|---|---|
| Project | Contract Price | Cost Incurred— 1993 | Estimated Cost to Complete | Cost Incurred— 1994 | Estimated Cost to Complete |
| A | $1,450,000 | $840,000 | $560,000 | $480,000 | –0– |
| B | 1,700,000 | 720,000 | 880,000 | 340,000 | $650,000 |
| C | 850,000 | 160,000 | 480,000 | 431,500 | 58,500 |
| D | 1,000,000 | | | 280,000 | 520,000 |

General and administrative expenses for 1993 and 1994 were $60,000 for each year and are to be recorded as a period cost.

### Instructions:

1. Calculate the income for 1993 and 1994 that should be reported for financial statement purposes.
2. Calculate the income for 1994 to be reported on a completed-contract basis.

## Problem 19—2   (Construction accounting)

The Rushing Construction Company obtained a construction contract to build a highway and bridge over the Snake River. It was estimated at the beginning of the contract that it would take 3 years to complete the project at an expected cost of $50,000,000. The contract price was $60,000,000. The project actually took 4 years, being accepted as completed late in 1994. The following information describes the status of the job at the close of production each year:

| | 1991 | 1992 | 1993 | 1994 | 1995 |
|---|---|---|---|---|---|
| Actual cost incurred .. | $12,000,000 | $18,160,000 | $14,840,000 | $10,000,000 | –0– |
| Estimated cost to complete . . . . . . . . . . . | 38,000,000 | 27,840,000 | 10,555,555 | –0– | –0– |
| Collections on con- tract . . . . . . . . . . . . . . | 12,000,000 | 13,500,000 | 15,000,000 | 15,000,000 | $4,500,000 |
| Billings on contract .. | 13,000,000 | 15,500,000 | 17,000,000 | 14,500,000 | –0– |

### Instructions:

1. What is the revenue, cost, and gross profit recognized for each of the years 1991-1995 under (a) the percentage-of-completion method and (b) the completed-contract method?
2. Give the journal entries for each year assuming that the percentage-of-completion method is used.

## Problem 19—3   (Construction accounting)

The Urban Construction Company commenced doing business in January 1993. Construction activities for the year 1993 are summarized in the table on the next page.

The company is your client. The president has asked you to compute the amounts of revenue for the year ended December 31, 1993, that would be reported under the completed-contract method and the percentage-of-completion method of accounting for long-term contracts.

| Project | Total Contract Price | Contract Expenditures to Dec. 31, 1993 | Estimated Additional Costs to Complete Contracts | Cash Collections to Dec. 31, 1993 | Billings to Dec. 31, 1993 |
|---|---|---|---|---|---|
| A | $ 310,000 | $187,500 | $ 12,500 | $155,000 | $155,000 |
| B | 415,000 | 195,000 | 255,000 | 210,000 | 249,000 |
| C | 350,000 | 310,000 | –0– | 300,000 | 350,000 |
| D | 300,000 | 16,500 | 183,500 | –0– | 4,000 |
| | $1,375,000 | $709,000 | $451,000 | $665,000 | $758,000 |

The following information is available:

(a) Each contract is with a different customer.
(b) Any work remaining to be done on the contracts is expected to be completed in 1994.
(c) The company's accounts have been maintained on the completed-contract method.

**Instructions:**

1. Prepare a schedule computing the amount of revenue, cost, and gross profit (loss) by project for the year ended December 31, 1993, to be reported under (a) the percentage-of-completion method and (b) the completed-contract method. (Round to two decimal places on percentages.)
2. Prepare a schedule under the completed-contract method, computing the amount that would appear in the company's balance sheet at December 31, 1993, for (a) costs in excess of billings and (b) billings in excess of costs.
3. Prepare a schedule under the percentage-of-completion method that would appear in the company's balance sheet at December 31, 1993, for (a) costs and estimated earnings in excess of billings and (b) billings in excess of costs and estimated earnings.

### Problem 19—4 (Construction accounting)

The Kurtz Construction Corporation contracted with the City of Port Huron to construct a dam on the Erie River at a price of $16,000,000. Kurtz expects to earn $1,520,000 on the contract. The percentage-of-completion method is to be used and the completion stage is to be determined by estimates made by the engineer. The following schedule summarizes the activities of the contract for the years 1992-1994:

| Year | Cost Incurred | Estimated Cost to Complete | Engineer's Estimate of Completion | Billings on Contract | Collection on Billings |
|---|---|---|---|---|---|
| 1992 | $4,600,000 | $9,640,000 | 31% | $5,000,000 | $4,500,000* |
| 1993 | 4,500,000 | 5,100,000 | 58 | 6,000,000 | 5,400,000* |
| 1994 | 5,250,000 | –0– | 100 | 5,000,000 | 6,100,000 |

*A 10% retainer accounts for the difference between billings and collections.

**Instructions:**

1. Prepare a schedule showing the revenue, cost, and the gross profit earned each year under the percentage-of-completion method, using the engineer's estimate as the measure of completion to be applied to revenues and costs.
2. Prepare all journal entries required to reflect the contract.
3. Prepare journal entries for 1994, assuming the completed-contract method is used.
4. How would the journal entries in (2) differ if the actual costs incurred were used to calculate cost for the period instead of the engineer's estimate?

## Problem 19—5  (Construction accounting)

Jana Crebs is a contractor for the construction of large office buildings. At the beginning of 1993, 3 buildings were in progress. The following data describes the status of these buildings at the beginning of the year:

| | Contract Price | Costs Incurred to 1/1/93 | Estimated Cost to Complete as of 1/1/93 |
|---|---|---|---|
| Building 1 .................... | $ 4,000,000 | $2,070,000 | $1,380,000 |
| Building 2 .................... | 9,000,000 | 6,318,000 | 1,782,000 |
| Building 3 .................... | 13,150,000 | 3,000,000 | 9,000,000 |

During 1993, the following costs were incurred:

Building 1 $930,000 (estimated cost to complete as of 12/31/93, $750,000)
Building 2 $1,800,000 (job completed)
Building 3 $7,400,000 (estimated cost to complete as of 12/31/93, $2,800,000)
Building 4 $800,000 (contract price, $2,500,000; estimated cost to complete as of 12/31/93, $1,200,000)

### Instructions:

1. Compute the total revenue, costs, and gross profit in 1993. Assume that Crebs uses the cost-to-cost percentage-of-completion method. (Round to two decimal places for percentage completed.)
2. Compute the gross profit for 1993 if Crebs uses the completed-contract method.

## Problem 19—6  (Construction accounting)

The Power Construction Company was the low bidder on a specialized equipment contract. The contract bid was $6,000,000 with an estimated cost to complete the project of $5,300,000. The contract period was 33 months, beginning January 1, 1992. The company uses the cost-to-cost method to estimate profits.

A record of construction activities for the years 1992-1995 follows:

| Year | Actual Cost— Current Year | Progress Billings | Cash Receipts |
|---|---|---|---|
| 1992 | $3,400,000 | $3,200,000 | $3,000,000 |
| 1993 | 2,550,000 | 2,000,000 | 2,000,000 |
| 1994 | 200,000 | 800,000 | 600,000 |
| 1995 | –0– | –0– | 400,000 |

The estimated cost to complete the contract at the end of each accounting period is:

| | |
|---|---|
| 1992 ...................................................... | $2,100,000 |
| 1993 ...................................................... | 150,000 |
| 1994 ...................................................... | –0– |

### Instructions:

1. What is the revenue, cost, and gross profit recognized for each of the years 1992-1994 under the percentage-of-completion method?
2. Give the journal entries for each of the years 1992-1994 to record the information from (1).
3. Give the journal entries in 1995 to record any collections and to close out all construction accounts.

## Problem 19—7  (Construction accounting)

Seattle Boatbuilders was recently awarded a $14,000,000 contract to construct a luxury liner for Cruiseliners Inc. Seattle estimates it will take 42 months to complete the contract. The company uses the cost-to-cost method to estimate profits.

The following information details the actual and estimated costs for the years 1992-1995:

| Year | Actual Cost—Current Year | Estimated Cost to Complete |
|------|-------------------------|----------------------------|
| 1992 | $6,500,000 | $6,800,000 |
| 1993 | 3,300,000 | 3,900,000 |
| 1994 | 2,400,000 | 1,900,000 |
| 1995 | 1,700,000 | –0– |

**Instructions:**

1. Compute the revenue, cost, and gross profit to be recognized for each of the years 1992-1995 under the percentage-of-completion method.
2. Give the journal entries for each of the years 1992-1995 to record the information from (1).

## Problem 19—8  (Installment sales accounting)

London Corporation has been using the cash method to account for income since its first year of operation in 1993. All sales are made on credit with notes receivable given by the customers. The income statements for 1993 and 1994 included the following amounts:

|  | 1993 | 1994 |
|--|------|------|
| Revenues—collection on principal | $32,000 | $50,000 |
| Revenues—interest | 3,600 | 5,500 |
| Cost of goods purchased* | 45,200 | 52,020 |

*Includes increase in inventory of goods on hand of $2,000 in 1993 and $8,000 in 1994.

The balances due on the notes at the end of each year were as follows:

|  | 1993 | 1994 |
|--|------|------|
| Notes receivable—1993 | $62,000 | $36,000 |
| Notes receivable—1994 | –0– | 60,000 |
| Unearned interest revenue—1993 | 7,167 | 5,579 |
| Unearned interest revenue—1994 | –0– | 8,043 |

**Instructions:**   Give the journal entries for 1993 and 1994 assuming the installment sales method was used rather than the cash method.

## Problem 19—9  (Installment sales)

Bain's Furniture sells furniture and electronic items. The majority of its business is on credit, and the following information is available relating to sales transactions for 1992, 1993, and 1994.

|  | 1992 | 1993 | 1994 |
|--|------|------|------|
| Installment sales (net of interest) | $104,000 | $116,000 | $121,000 |
| Gross profit percentage | 38% | 41% | 39% |

| | 1992 | 1993 | 1994 |
|---|---|---|---|
| Cash collections on installment sales: | | | |
| Principal—1992 ......................... | $ 57,200 | $ 29,120 | $ 15,000 |
| Principal—1993 ......................... | | 71,920 | 26,680 |
| Principal—1994 ......................... | | | 76,230 |
| Interest—1992 .......................... | 9,780 | 17,870 | 3,030 |
| Interest—1993 .......................... | | 6,610 | 18,142 |
| Interest—1994 .......................... | | | 6,378 |

**Instructions:** Prepare the journal entries for the years 1992-1994 assuming Bain's uses the installment sales method for revenue recognition and records receivables net of interest.

### Problem 19—10  (Cost recovery accounting—real estate)

After a 2-year search for a buyer, Choapas Inc. sold its idle plant facility to Reeve Company for $700,000 on January 1, 1990. On this date, the plant had a depreciated cost on Choapas' books of $500,000. Under the agreement, Reeve paid $200,000 cash on January 1, 1990, and signed a $500,000 interest-bearing note. The note was payable in installments of $100,000, $150,000, and $250,000 on January 1, 1991, 1992, and 1993, respectively. The note was secured by a mortgage on the property sold. Choapas appropriately accounted for the sale under the cost recovery method, since there was no reasonable basis for estimating the degree of collectibility of the note receivable. Reeve repaid the note with 3 late installment payments, which were accepted by Choapas, as follows:

| Date of Payment | Principal | Interest | Total Payment |
|---|---|---|---|
| July 1, 1991 | $100,000 | $90,000 | $190,000 |
| Dec. 31, 1992 | 150,000 | 75,000 | 225,000 |
| Feb. 1, 1994 | 250,000 | 32,500 | 282,500 |

**Instructions:** Prepare the journal entries required for the years 1990-1994 for the sale and subsequent collections.

### Problem 19—11  (Consignment accounting)

Tingey Industries sells merchandise on a consignment basis to dealers. Shipping costs are chargeable to Tingey, although in some cases, the dealer pays them. The selling price of the merchandise averages 25% above cost of merchandise exclusive of freight. The dealer is paid a 10% commission on the sales price for all sales made. All dealer sales are made on a cash basis. The following consignment sales activities occurred during 1993:

| | | |
|---|---|---|
| Manufacturing cost of goods shipped on consignment...... | | $250,000 |
| Freight costs incurred: | | |
| Paid by Tingey Industries.............................. | $15,000 | |
| Paid by dealer........................................ | 5,000 | 20,000 |
| Sales price of merchandise sold by dealers ............... | | 210,000 |
| Payments made by dealers after deducting commission and freight costs .......................................... | | 139,000 |

**Instructions:**

1. Prepare summary entries on the books of the consignor for these consignment sales transactions.
2. Prepare summary entries on the books of the dealer consignee assuming there is only one dealer involved.
3. Prepare the parts of Tingey Industries' financial statements at December 31, 1993, that relate to these consignment sales.

## Problem 19—12  (Revenue recognition analysis)

The Wasatch Construction Company entered into a $4,500,000 contract in early 1993 to construct a multipurpose recreational facility for the City of Helper. Construction time extended over a 2-year period. The table below describes the pattern of progress payments made by the City of Helper and costs incurred by Wasatch Construction by semiannual periods. Estimated costs of $3,600,000 were incurred as expected.

| Period | Progress Payments for Period | Progress Cost for Period |
|---|---|---|
| (1)  Jan. 1-June 30, 1993 ........................ | $ 750,000 | $ 900,000 |
| (2)  July 1-Dec. 31, 1993 ........................ | 1,050,000 | 1,200,000 |
| (3)  Jan. 1-June 30, 1994 ........................ | 1,950,000 | 1,080,000 |
| (4)  July 1-Dec. 31, 1994 ........................ | 750,000 | 420,000 |
| Total ......................................... | $4,500,000 | $3,600,000 |

The Wasatch Construction Company prepares financial statements twice each year, June 30 and December 31.

### Instructions:

1. Based on the foregoing data, compute the amount of revenue, costs, and gross profit for the 4 semiannual periods under each of the following methods of revenue recognition:
   (a)  Percentage of completion.
   (b)  Completed contract.
   (c)  Installment sales (gross profit only).
   (d)  Cost recovery (gross profit only).
2. Which method do you feel best measures the performance of Wasatch on this contract?

# CHAPTER 20

## Accounting for Leases

---

---

IBM has made numerous long-term commitments, amounting to several billion dollars, to lease office space. Because these lease commitments cannot be canceled, they represent a probable future sacrifice of economic benefits and thus meet the definition of a liability. However, IBM's December 31, 1990, balance sheet, presented in Appendix A, does not report any obligation relating to these lease commitments, even though the company was obligated to pay almost $10 billion in lease payments for 1991 and subsequent years. Why would lease agreements representing definite obligations to pay significant amounts of money not be reported as liabilities? Are there circumstances in which a lease would be reported as a liability? This chapter explores these and other issues associated with leases.

A lease is a contract specifying the terms under which the owner of property, the lessor, transfers the right to use the property to a lessee. Leasing is widely used in our economy as a method of obtaining various kinds of assets. Individuals may lease houses, apartments, automobiles, televisions, appliances, furniture, and almost any other consumer good on the market. Business enterprises lease land, buildings, and almost any type of equipment. For example, The United States Shoe Corporation in its 1989 financial statements reported leased assets including "Plant, warehouse, office and retail shoe facilities as well as certain of its data processing, automotive and production equipment." Indeed, almost any asset that can be acquired through purchase can be obtained through leasing. Of the 600 companies surveyed in the annual AICPA publication, *Accounting Trends & Techniques*, 531 companies, or approximately 90%, reported some form of lease arrangement.[1]

Some leases are simple rental agreements, while others closely resemble a debt-financed purchase of property. A major issue for the accounting profession has been whether this latter type of lease should be accounted for as a rental agreement in accordance with its legal form, or as a purchase of property that reflects the economic substance of the transaction. To illustrate the issue, assume that Monroe Co. decides to acquire equipment costing $10,000. The equipment has a useful life of 5 years with no expected residual value. Monroe Co. can purchase the equipment by issuing a 5-year, 10%, $10,000 note with principal and interest to be paid in 5 equal installments of $2,368. Alternatively, Monroe Co. can lease the asset for 5 years, making 5 annual "rental" payments of $2,368. In substance, the lease is equivalent to purchasing the asset, the only difference being the legal form of the transaction. However, if the lease is accounted for as a simple rental agreement, Monroe Co. will not report the equipment as an asset nor the obligation to the lessor as a liability. Under conditions such as these, recording the transaction as a rental agreement does not reflect the underlying economic substance of acquiring and using the equipment.

As illustrated by this simple example, leasing can be used to avoid reporting a liability on the balance sheet. As discussed in Chapter 16, "off-balance-sheet financing" continues to be a perplexing problem for the accounting profession, and leasing is probably the oldest and most widely used means of keeping debt off the balance sheet. The FASB has attempted to eliminate this practice by requiring leases that meet certain criteria to be treated as capital leases—in effect, debt-financed purchases of property.

## ECONOMIC ADVANTAGES OF LEASING

It would be unfair and incorrect to imply that the only reason companies lease property is to avoid reporting the lease obligation in the financial statements. While the accounting issue is one factor, other financial and tax considerations also play an important role in the leasing decision. While every situation is different, there are two primary advantages to the lessee of leasing over purchasing:

1. **No down payment.** Most debt-financed purchases of property require a portion of the purchase price to be paid immediately by the borrower. This provides added protection to the lender in the event of default and repossession. Lease agreements, in contrast, frequently are structured so that 100% of the value of the property is financed through the lease. This aspect of leasing makes it an attractive alternative to a company that does not have sufficient cash for a down payment or wishes to use available capital for other operating or investing purposes.

2. **Avoids risks of ownership.** There are many risks accompanying the ownership of property. They include casualty loss, obsolescence, changing economic conditions, and physical deterioration. The lessee may terminate a lease, although usually with a

---

[1]*Accounting Trends & Techniques*, 1990 (New York: American Institute of Certified Public Accountants, 1990), p. 171.

certain penalty, and thus avoid assuming the risk of these events. This flexibility is especially important in businesses where innovation and technological change make the future usefulness of particular equipment or facilities highly uncertain. A prime example of this condition in recent years has been the electronics industry with its rapid change in areas such as computer technology, robotics, and telecommunications.

The lessor also may find benefits to leasing its property rather than selling it. Advantages of the lease to the lessor include the following:

1. **Increased sales.** For the reasons suggested in the preceding paragraphs, customers may be unwilling or unable to purchase property. By offering potential customers the option of leasing its products, a manufacturer or dealer may significantly increase its sales volume.
2. **Ongoing business relationship with lessee.** When property is sold, the purchaser frequently has no more dealings with the seller of the property. In leasing situations, however, the lessor and lessee maintain contact over a period of time, and long-term business relationships often can be established through leasing.
3. **Residual value retained.** In many lease arrangements, title to the leased property never passes to the lessee. The lessor benefits from economic conditions that may result in a significant residual value at the end of the lease term. The lessor may lease the asset to another lessee or sell the property and realize an immediate gain. Many lessors have realized significant profits from unexpected increases in residual values.

## NATURE OF LEASES

Leases vary widely in their contractual provisions. Variables include cancellation provisions and penalties, lease term, bargain renewal and purchase options, economic life of assets, residual asset values, minimum lease payments, interest rates implicit in the lease agreement, and the degree of risk assumed by the lessee, including payments of certain costs such as maintenance, insurance, and taxes. These and other relevant facts must be considered in determining the appropriate accounting treatment of a lease.

The many variables affecting lease capitalization have been given precise definitions that must be understood in order to account for the various types of leases found in practice. Each of these variables is defined and briefly discussed below.

### Cancellation Provisions

Some leases may be termed as **noncancellable**, meaning that these lease contracts are cancellable only upon the outcome of some remote contingency or that the cancellation provisions and penalties of these leases are so costly to the lessee that, in all likelihood, cancellation will not occur. Only noncancellable leases are subject to capitalization.

### Lease Term

An important variable in lease agreements is the **lease term**; that is, the time period from the beginning to the end of the lease. The **inception of the lease** is defined as the date of the lease agreement, or the date of an earlier written commitment if all the principal provisions have been negotiated. The **beginning of the lease term** occurs when the lease agreement takes effect, i.e., when the leased property is transferred to the lessee.

The date of the beginning of the lease term may coincide with the date of the inception of the lease. In many cases, however, a considerable amount of time may elapse between the inception date and the beginning of the lease term. For example, property may be constructed by the lessor to the lessee's specifications following the execution of a written agreement specifying all the major provisions for leasing the property to the lessee. The inception of the lease is the date of the agreement to construct the property, but the beginning of the lease term is after the construction is completed and the property is turned over to the lessee.

The **end of the lease term** is the end of the fixed noncancellable period of the lease plus all periods, if any, covered by **bargain renewal options**, or other provisions that, at the inception of the lease strongly indicate that the lease will be renewed.[2] If a bargain purchase option, as defined in the next section, is included in the lease contract, the lease term includes any renewal periods preceding the date of the bargain purchase option. In no case does the lease term extend beyond the date of a bargain purchase option.

## Bargain Purchase Option

Leases often include a provision giving the lessee the right to purchase leased property at some future date. A definite purchase or option price may be specified, although in some cases the price is expressed as the fair market value at the date the option is exercised. If the specified option price is expected to be considerably less than the fair market value at the date the purchase option may be exercised, a **bargain purchase** option is indicated.

## Residual Value

The market value of the leased property at the end of the lease term is referred to as its **residual value**. In some leases, the lease term extends over the entire **economic life of the asset,** or the period in which the asset continues to be productive, and there is little, if any, residual value. In other leases, the lease term is shorter, and a residual value does exist. If the lessee can purchase the asset at the end of the lease term at a materially reduced price from its residual value, a bargain purchase option is present, and it can be assumed that the lessee would exercise the option and purchase the asset.

Some lease contracts require the lessee, or a designated third party, to guarantee a minimum residual value. If the market value at the end of the lease term falls below the **guaranteed residual value**, the lessee or third party must pay the difference. This provision protects the lessor from loss due to unexpected declines in the market value of the asset. For example, assume a piece of equipment is expected to have a $25,000 residual value at the end of the lease term, and the lessee guarantees that amount. However, at the end of the lease term, the residual value is only $15,000. The lessee is obligated to pay the $10,000 difference to the lessor, because the lessor is, in effect, guaranteed the full amount of the residual value that was estimated at the beginning of the lease. The lessee or the third party may buy the property for the $25,000 guaranteed amount, but the terms do not require the purchase. As will be demonstrated later in the chapter, a guarantee of residual value by a third party requires lessees to account for leases differently than would be true if the lessee were making the guarantee.

If there is no bargain purchase option or guarantee of the residual value, the lessor reacquires the property and may offer to renew the lease, lease the asset to another lessee, or sell the property. The actual amount of the residual value is unknown until the end of the lease term; however, it must be estimated at the inception of the lease. The residual value under these circumstances is referred to as the **unguaranteed residual value**.

---

[2]In some lease situations, such as sale-leasebacks, the lessee lends the lessor money to finance the lease or acts as a guarantor for third-party financing. As long as these financial arrangements are in place, the lease-term extends through ordinary renewal option periods. Thus, the lease term for a 10-year lease, with a 10-year ordinary renewal and a 20-year loan on the leased property from the lessee to the lessor, would be 20 years. *Statement of Financial Accounting Standards No. 98,* ''Accounting for Leases: . . . Definition of Lease Term'' (Norwalk: Financial Accounting Standards Board, 1988), par. 22a.

## Minimum Lease Payments

The rental payments required over the lease term plus any amount to be paid for the residual value either through a bargain purchase option or a guarantee of the residual value are referred to as the **minimum lease payments**. If all of these payments are made by the lessee, the minimum lease payments are the same for the lessee and the lessor. However, if a third party guarantees the residual value, the lessee would not include the guarantee as part of the minimum lease payments, but the lessor would.

Rental payments sometimes include charges for such items as insurance, maintenance, and taxes incurred for the leased property. These are referred to as **executory costs**, and they are not included as part of the minimum lease payments. If the lessor includes a charge for profit on these costs, the profit also is considered an executory cost.

To illustrate the computation of minimum lease payments, assume that Dorney Leasing Co. leases road equipment for 3 years at $3,000 per month. Included in the rental payment is $500 per month for executory costs to insure and maintain the equipment. At the end of the 3-year period, Dorney is guaranteed a residual value of $10,000 by the lessee.

Minimum lease payments:

| | |
|---|---:|
| Rental payments exclusive of executory costs ($2,500 × 36)......... | $ 90,000 |
| Guaranteed residual value....................................... | 10,000 |
| Total minimum lease payments................................... | $100,000 |

Because the minimum lease payments are to be made in future periods, the present value of these payments is needed to account for capitalized leases. Two different discount rates must be considered in computing the present value of minimum lease payments: the lessee's incremental borrowing rate and the implicit interest rate. The **incremental borrowing rate** is the rate at which the lessee could borrow the amount of money necessary to purchase the leased asset, taking into consideration the lessee's financial situation and the current conditions in the marketplace. The **implicit interest rate** is the rate that would discount the minimum lease payments to the fair market value of the asset at the inception of the lease. The lessor uses the implicit interest rate in determining the present value of the minimum lease payments. The lessee, however, uses either the implicit rate or the incremental borrowing rate, whichever is lower. If the lessee does not know the implicit rate, the incremental borrowing rate is used.

To illustrate using the Dorney Leasing Co. example, assume that the $3,000 rental payments to Dorney are made at the beginning of each month, the implicit interest rate in the lease contract is 12% per year, and the lessee's incremental borrowing rate is 14%. Assuming the lessee knows the implicit rate, both the lessor and lessee would discount the minimum lease payments using the 12% rate. The present value of the $100,000 minimum lease payments would be:

Present value of 36 payments of $2,500 ($3,000 less executory costs of $500) at 1% interest (12% annual interest divided by 12 months per year) paid at the beginning of each month:

$$PV_n = R(PVAF_{\overline{n-1}|i} + 1)$$
$$PV_n = \$2,500(29.4086^* + 1) \dots\dots\dots\dots\dots\dots\dots\dots\dots\dots\dots\dots \quad \$76,022$$

Present value of $10,000 guaranteed residual value at the end of 3 years at 12% annual interest:

$$PV = A(PVF_{\overline{n}|i})$$
$$PV = \$10,000(0.7118^{**}) \dots\dots\dots\dots\dots\dots\dots\dots\dots\dots\dots\dots \quad 7,118$$

Present value of minimum lease payments .......................... $83,140

*From Table IV, page 256
**From Table II, page 254

The present value of $83,140 would be the selling price or fair market value of the asset at the inception of the lease. The use of present value formulas and tables in discounting minimum lease payments is illustrated later in the chapter.

## LEASE CLASSIFICATION CRITERIA

Leasing was one of the topics on the original agenda of the FASB, and in 1976 the Board issued Statement No. 13, "Accounting for Leases." The objective of the FASB in issuing Statement No. 13 was to reflect the economic reality of leasing by requiring that the majority of long-term leases be accounted for as capital acquisitions by the lessee and sales by the lessor. To accomplish this objective, the FASB identified criteria to determine whether a lease is merely a rental contract, an operating lease, or is, in substance, a purchase of property (a capital lease). In considering this issue, the FASB was concerned with the fact that under the APB pronouncements, leases were often reported differently by the lessee and the lessor. The Board felt that in most cases, there should be consistent treatment between the two parties; i.e., if the lessee treated the agreement as a purchase of property, the lessor should treat it as a sale of property. For this reason, the Board specified four criteria that apply to both the lessee and the lessor, any one of which would identify the lease agreement as a purchase and sale of property or, in other words, a capital lease. Two additional criteria were specified for lessors, both of which must be met before the lease can be treated as a sale by the lessor. The lease classification criteria and their applicability to lessees and lessors are summarized in Exhibit 20—1.

### Exhibit 20—1    Lease Classification Criteria

General criteria applicable to both the lessee and the lessor:

1. The lease transfers ownership of the property to the lessee by the end of the lease term.
2. The lease contains a bargain purchase option.
3. The lease term is equal to 75% or more of the estimated economic life of the leased property.
4. The present value of the minimum lease payments, excluding that portion representing executory costs, equals or exceeds 90% of the fair market value of the property.

Additional criteria applicable to lessors:

5. Collectibility of the minimum lease payments is reasonably predictable.
6. No important uncertainties surround the amount of unreimbursable costs yet to be incurred by the lessor.

Lessee:  Capital lease if any one of criteria 1, 2, 3, or 4 is met.
Lessor:  Capital lease if any one of criteria 1, 2, 3, or 4 is met *and* both 5 and 6 are met.

### Classification Criteria—Lessee and Lessor

The four general criteria that apply to all leases for both the lessee and lessor relate to transfer of ownership, bargain purchase options, economic life, and fair market value. The **transfer of ownership** criterion is met if the lease agreement includes a clause that transfers full ownership of the property to the lessee by the end of the lease term. Of all the classification criteria, transfer of ownership is the most objective and, therefore, the easiest to apply.

The second general criterion is met if the lease contains a **bargain purchase option** that makes it reasonably assured that the property will be purchased by the lessee at some future date. This criterion is more difficult to apply than the first criterion, because the future fair market value of the leased property must be estimated at the inception of the lease and compared with the purchase option price to determine if a bargain purchase is indeed indicated.

The third criterion relates to the **economic life** of the asset. This criterion is met if the lease term is equal to 75% or more of the estimated economic life of the leased property. As defined earlier, the lease term includes renewal periods if renewal seems assured. This criterion is difficult to apply objectively because of the uncertainty of an asset's economic life. Also, it can be easily manipulated to achieve whatever result is desired. An exception to the economic life criterion was made for certain used property. The FASB recognized that used property may be leased near the end of the property's economic life, and this criterion would result in classifying all such leases as capital leases. The Board provided that this criterion would not be applicable to leases occurring in the last 25% of the leased property's economic life. In addition, this criterion cannot apply to land leases, since land has an unlimited life.

The fourth general criterion focuses on the **fair market value** of the property in relation to the provisions of the lease. This criterion is met if, at the beginning of the lease term, the present value of the minimum lease payments equals or exceeds 90% of the fair market value of the leased asset. This criterion was intended to be the key factor in determining the existence of a capital lease. If the lessee is obligated to pay, in present-value terms, almost all of the fair market value of the leased property, the lease is in substance a purchase of the property. But the application of this criterion also has been difficult and subject to manipulation by lessees and lessors. The key variable in this criterion is the discounted minimum lease payments.

Since larger minimum lease payments cause the fair market value criterion to be met, the use of third parties to guarantee residual values has led to a lack of consistency between lessees and lessors in many lease arrangements. Many lessors want to report the lease as a sale and thus recognize income at the inception of the lease. However, lessees generally want to report the lease as a rental contract and gain the advantage of off-balance-sheet financing. Since third-party guarantees are considered minimum lease payments to the lessor but not to the lessee, a careful structuring of the lease terms can allow both parties to achieve their goals.

This variable, more than any other, has been used in lease arrangements to avoid the intent of the FASB to achieve increased consistency in reporting. In fact, a new industry of third-party financing has arisen to take advantage of this difference in defining minimum lease payments between the lessee and the lessor.

The rate used to discount the future minimum lease payments is critical in determining whether the fair market value criterion is met. The lower the discount rate used, the higher the present value of the minimum lease payments and the greater the likelihood that the fair market value criterion of 90% will be met. As explained earlier in the chapter, the FASB specified that the lessor should use the implicit interest rate of the lease agreement. The lessee also uses the lessor's implicit interest rate if it is known and if it is lower than the lessee's incremental borrowing rate. If the lessee cannot determine the lessor's implicit interest rate, the lessee must use its incremental borrowing rate. The use of different discount rates between lessees and lessors is another cause of inconsistent accounting treatment between lessees and lessors.

Because incremental borrowing rates are often higher than the implicit interest rates, and because lessees generally do not want to capitalize leases, many lessees use the borrowing rate and do not attempt to estimate the implicit rate. If there is no residual value, the lessee can determine the implicit rate in most cases, because the market value of the leased asset usually is known. If a residual value exists, however, the lessee must obtain that value from the lessor.

### Additional Classification Criteria—Lessor

In addition to meeting one of the four general criteria, a lease must meet two additional criteria in order to be classified by the lessor as a capital lease.[3] As indicated in Exhibit 20—1, the first of the two lessor-specific criteria relates to **collectibility**. Collection of the minimum lease payments, either from the lessee or a third-party guarantor, must be reasonably predictable.

The second additional criterion requires **substantial completion** of performance by the lessor. This means that any unreimbursable costs yet to be incurred by the lessor under the terms of the lease are known or can be reasonably estimated. This criterion is to be applied at the inception of the lease or at the date the leased asset is acquired by the lessor if acquisition occurs after the inception date. If the leased asset is constructed by the lessor, the criterion is applied at the later of the inception date or the date construction is completed.

### Application of General Lease Classification Criteria

To illustrate the application of the classification criteria specified in FASB Statement No. 13, four different leasing situations are presented in Exhibit 20—2. A summary analysis of each lease also is presented in the exhibit. Following is a brief explanation of the analysis for each of the four leases.

**Lease #1** will be treated as an operating lease by the lessee but as a capital lease by the lessor. The lease does not meet any of the first three general criteria. Since the lessee does not know the implicit interest rate of the lessor, the incremental borrowing rate is used to test for criterion 4. The present value of the minimum lease payments using the incremental borrowing rate is less than 90% of the fair market value of the property; thus criterion 4 is not met for the lessee. Because the lessor uses the implicit interest rate, criterion 4 is met. The two additional criteria applicable to the lessor are also met.

**Lease #2** will be treated as a capital lease by both the lessee and the lessor, because title passes to the lessee at the end of the lease term (criterion 1) and the additional lessor criteria are both met. Because there is a third-party guaranteed residual value, the minimum lease payments are higher for the lessor than the lessee, and criterion 4 is met by the lessor but not by the lessee. Thus, if title had not passed, Lease #2 would be treated as an operating lease by the lessee but a capital lease by the lessor.

**Lease #3** will be treated as a capital lease by the lessee, but as an operating lease by the lessor. The bargain purchase option meets criterion 2, and since the lessee knows the implicit interest rate, both the lessee and lessor computations meet criterion 4. However, since there is some uncertainty as to the collectibility of the rental payments and the amount of lessor costs to be incurred, the lease fails to meet the additional criteria applicable to the lessor.

---

[3]*Statement of Financial Accounting Standards No. 13*, par. 8. If the lease involves real estate, these criteria are replaced by a criterion that requires a transfer of title at the end of the lease term. *Statement of Financial Accounting Standards No. 98*, par. 22c.

**Exhibit 20—2    Application of FASB Statement No. 13 Criteria to Lease Situations**

| Lease Provisions | Lease #1 | Lease #2 | Lease #3 | Lease #4 |
|---|---|---|---|---|
| Cancellable .................................... | No | No | No | Yes |
| Title passes to lessee ............................ | No | Yes | No | Yes |
| Bargain purchase option .......................... | No | No | Yes | No |
| Lease term...................................... | 10 years | 10 years | 8 years | 10 years |
| Economic life of asset .......................... | 14 years | 15 years | 13 years | 12 years |
| Present value of minimum lease payments as a percentage of fair market value—incremental borrowing rate ................................... | 80% | 79% | 95% | 76% |
| Present value of minimum lease payments as a percentage of fair market value—implicit interest rate | 92% | 91% | 92% | 82% |
| Lessee knows implicit interest rate ................ | No | No | Yes | Yes |
| Unguaranteed residual value ..................... | Yes | No | No | No |
| Residual value guaranteed by third party ........... | No | Yes | No | No |
| Present value of minimum lease payments exclusive of third-party guaranteed residual value as a percentage of fair market value—implicit interest rate | 92% | 80% | 92% | 82% |
| Rental payments collectible and lessor costs certain .. | Yes | Yes | No | Yes |
| **Analysis of Leases:** | | | | |
|   Lessee | | | | |
|    Treat as capital lease........................... | No | Yes | Yes | No |
|    Criteria met ................................... | None | 1 | 2 and 4 | must be non- |
|    Use incremental borrowing rate ................. | NA | Yes | No | cancellable |
|    Amortization period ........................... | NA | 15 years | 13 years | |
|   Lessor | | | | |
|    Treat as capital lease........................... | Yes | Yes | No | No |
|    First four criteria met .......................... | 4 | 1 and 4 | 2 and 4 | must be non- |
|    Lessor criteria met............................. | Yes | Yes | No | cancellable |

**Lease #4** will be treated as an operating lease by both the lessee and the lessor. The lease is a cancellable lease, and even though title passes to the lessee at the end of the lease, it would be classified as a rental agreement.

## ACCOUNTING FOR LEASES—LESSEE

All leases as viewed by the lessee may be divided into two types: **operating leases** and **capital leases**. If a lease meets any one of the four classification criteria discussed previously, it is treated as a capital lease. Otherwise, it is accounted for as an operating lease.

Accounting for operating leases involves the recognition of rent expense over the term of the lease. The leased property is not reported as an asset on the lessee's balance sheet nor is a liability recognized for the obligation to make future payments for use of the property. Information concerning the lease is limited to disclosure in notes to the financial statements. Accounting for a capital lease essentially requires the lessee to report on the balance sheet the present value of the future lease payments, both as an asset and a liability. The asset is amortized as though it had been purchased by the lessee. The liability is accounted for in the same manner as would be a mortgage on the property. The difference in the impact of these two treatments on the financial statements often can be significant, as noted in the boxed item on page 762.

## Accounting for Operating Leases—Lessee

Operating leases are considered to be simple rental agreements with debits being made to an expense account as the payments are made. For example, assume the lease terms for manufacturing equipment were $40,000 a year on a year-to-year basis. The entry to record the payment for a year's rent would be:

```
Rent Expense .........................................    40,000
    Cash .............................................              40,000
```

Rent payments frequently are made in advance. If the lease period does not coincide with the lessee's fiscal year, or if the lessee prepares interim reports, a prepaid rent account would be required to record the unexpired portion of rent at the end of the accounting period involved. The prepaid rent account should be adjusted at the end of each period.

**Operating Leases With Varying Rental Payments**    Some operating leases specify rental terms that provide for varying rental payments over the lease term. Most commonly, these types of agreements call for lower initial payments and scheduled rent increases later in the life of the lease. They may even provide an inducement to prospective lessees in the form of a "rent holiday" (free rent). In some cases, however, the lease may provide for higher initial rentals. FASB Statement No. 13 requires that when rental payments vary over the lease term, rental expense be recognized on a straight-line basis "unless another systematic and rational basis is more representative of the time pattern in which use benefit is derived from the leased property, in which case that basis shall be used."[4]

When recording rent expense under these agreements, differences between the actual payments and the debit to expense would be reported as Rent Payable or Prepaid Rent, depending on whether the payments were accelerating or declining. For example, assume the terms of the lease for an aircraft by International Airlines provide for payments of $150,000 a year for the first 2 years of the lease and $250,000 for the next 3 years. The total lease payments for the 5 years would be $1,050,000, or $210,000 a year on a straight-line basis. The required entries in the first 2 years would be:

```
Rent Expense .........................................    210,000
    Cash .............................................              150,000
    Rent Payable .....................................               60,000
```

The entries for each of the last 3 years would be:

```
Rent Expense .........................................    210,000
Rent Payable .........................................     40,000
    Cash .............................................              250,000
```

The portion of Rent Payable due in the subsequent year would be classified as a current liability.

## Accounting for Capital Leases—Lessee

**Capital leases** are considered to be more like a purchase of property than a rental. Consequently, accounting for capital leases by lessees requires entries similar to those required for the purchase of an asset with long-term credit terms. The amount to be recorded as an asset and as a liability is the present value of the future minimum lease payments as previously defined. The discount rates used by lessees to record capital leases are the same as those used to apply the classification criteria previously discussed, i.e., the lower of the

[4]*Ibid.*, par. 15.

implicit interest rate (if known) and the incremental borrowing rate. The minimum lease payments consist of the total rental payments, bargain purchase options, and lessee-guaranteed residual values.

An important exception to the use of the present value of future minimum lease payments as a basis for recording a capital lease was included by the FASB in Statement No. 13 as follows:

> However, if the amount so determined exceeds the fair value of the leased property at the inception of the lease, the amount recorded as the asset and obligation shall be the fair value.[5]

This means that if the leased asset has a determinable sales price, the present value of the future minimum lease payments should be compared with that price. If the sales price is lower, it should be used as the capitalized value of the lease, and an implicit interest rate would have to be computed using the sales price as the capitalized value of the asset.

**Illustrative Entries for Capital Leases**    Assume that Marshall Corporation leases equipment from Universal Leasing Company with the following terms:

Lease period:    5 years, beginning January 1, 1993. Noncancellable.
Rental amount: $65,000 per year payable annually in advance; includes $5,000 to cover executory costs.
Estimated economic life of equipment: 5 years.
Expected residual value of equipment at end of lease period: None.

Because the rental payments are payable in advance, the formula to find the present value of the lease is the annuity-due formula described in Chapter 7. Assuming the Marshall Corporation's incremental borrowing rate and the implicit interest rate on the lease are both 10%, the present value for the lease would be $250,194 computed as follows:[6]

$$PV_n = R(PVAF_{\overline{n-1}|i} + 1)$$
$$PV_n = \$60,000(\text{Table IV}_{\overline{4}|10\%} + 1)$$
$$PV_n = \$60,000(3.1699 + 1)$$
$$PV_n = \$250,194$$

The journal entries to record the lease at the beginning of the lease term would be:

1993
Jan. 1    Leased Equipment ...............................    250,194
                Obligations Under Capital Leases................             250,194[7]
                    To record the lease.

      1    Lease Expense....................................      5,000
           Obligations Under Capital Leases .................     60,000
                Cash ..........................................             65,000
                    To record the first lease payment.

The asset value is amortized in accordance with the lessee's normal method of depreciation for owned assets. The amortization period to be used depends on which of the criteria was used to qualify the lease as a capital lease. If the lease qualified under either of

[5]*Ibid.*, par. 10.

[6]All computations of present value in this chapter will be rounded to the nearest dollar. This will require some adjustment at times to the final figures in the tables to balance the amounts.

[7]It also is possible to record the liability at the gross amount of the payments ($300,000) and offset it with a discount account—Discount on Lease Contract. The net method is more common in accounting for leases by the lessee and will be used in this chapter.

the first two criteria, ownership transfer or bargain purchase option, the economic life of the asset should be used. If the lease qualified under either of the last two criteria, economic life or investment recovery, and the lease term is shorter than the estimated life of the asset, the lease term should be used for amortization purposes. If the lease qualified under a combination of one of the first two criteria and one of the last two criteria, the economic life of the asset should be used for amortization purposes.

In the preceding example, the lease qualifies under the third criterion and presumably the fourth, since the lessor would not lease the asset over its entire economic life if the present value of the lease payments were less than the fair market value of the asset at the inception of the lease. The liability should be reduced each period to produce a constant rate of interest expense on the remaining balance of the obligation. The lessee's incremental borrowing rate, or the lessor's implicit interest rate if lower, is the constant interest rate for the lessee under the provisions of FASB Statement No. 13. Exhibit 20—3 shows how the $60,000 payments (excluding executory costs) would be allocated between payment on the obligation and interest expense. To simplify the schedule, it is assumed that all lease payments after the first payment are made on December 31 of each year. If the payments were made in January, an accrual of interest at December 31 would be required.

**Exhibit 20—3    Schedule of Lease Payments [Five-Year Lease, $60,000 Annual Payments (Net of Executory Costs), 10% Interest]**

| | | Lease Payment | | | |
|---|---|---|---|---|---|
| Date | Description | Amount | Interest Expense* | Principal | Lease Obligation |
| 1-1-93 | Initial balance ........ | | | | $250,194 |
| 1-1-93 | Payment ............. | $ 60,000 | | $ 60,000 | 190,194 |
| 12-31-93 | Payment ............. | 60,000 | $19,019 | 40,981 | 149,213 |
| 12-31-94 | Payment ............. | 60,000 | 14,921 | 45,079 | 104,134 |
| 12-31-95 | Payment ............. | 60,000 | 10,413 | 49,587 | 54,547 |
| 12-31-96 | Payment ............. | 60,000 | 5,453 | 54,547 | –0– |
| | | $300,000 | $49,806 | $250,194 | |

*Preceding lease obligation × 10%.

If the normal company depreciation policy for this type of equipment is straight-line, the required entry at December 31, 1993, for amortization of the leased asset would be:

```
1993
Dec. 31   Amortization Expense on Leased Equipment ........   50,039
              Accumulated Amortization on Leased Equipment ...           50,039
```

> Computation:
> $250,194 ÷ 5 = $50,039

Similar entries would be made for each of the remaining 4 years. Although the credit could be made directly to the asset account, the use of a contra asset account provides the necessary disclosure information about the original lease value and accumulated amortization to date.

In addition to the entry recording amortization, another entry is required at December 31, 1993, to record the second lease payment, including a prepayment of 1994's executory costs. As indicated in Exhibit 20—3, the interest expense for 1993 would be computed by multiplying the incremental borrowing rate of 10% by the initial present value of the obligation less the immediate $60,000 first payment, or ($250,194 − $60,000) × .10 = $19,019.

| 1993 | | |
|---|---|---|
| Dec. 31 | Prepaid Executory Costs............................ | 5,000 | |
| | Obligations Under Capital Leases ................. | 40,981 | |
| | Interest Expense .................................. | 19,019 | |
| | Cash ............................................. | | 65,000 |

Because of the assumption that all lease payments after the first payment are made on December 31, the portion of each payment that represents executory costs must be recorded as a prepayment and charged to lease expense in the following year.

Based on the preceding journal entries and using information contained in Exhibit 20—3, the December 31, 1993, balance sheet of Marshall Corporation would include information concerning the leased equipment and related obligation as illustrated below.

**Marshall Corporation**
**Balance Sheet (Partial)**
**December 31, 1993**

| Assets | | Liabilities | |
|---|---|---|---|
| Current assets: | | Current liabilities: | |
| Prepaid executory costs—leased equipment ........................ | $ 5,000 | Obligations under capital leases, current portion ................... | $ 45,079 |
| Land, buildings, and equipment: | | Noncurrent liabilities: | |
| Leased equipment ................. | $250,194 | Obligations under capital leases, exclusive of $45,079 included in | |
| Less accumulated amortization ..... | 50,039 | current liabilities .................. | $104,134 |
| Net value ......................... | $200,155 | | |

Note that the principal portion of the payment due December 31, 1994, is reported as a current liability on the December 31, 1993, balance sheet.[8]

The income statement would include the amortization on leased property of $50,039, interest expense of $19,019, and executory costs of $5,000 as expenses for the period. The total expense of $74,058 exceeds the $65,000 rental payment made in the first year. As the amount of interest expense declines each period, the total expense will be reduced and, for the last 2 years, will be less than the $65,000 payments (Exhibit 20—4). The total amount debited to expense over the life of the lease will, of course, be the same regardless of whether the lease is accounted for as an operating lease or as a capital lease. If

[8]There have been some theoretical arguments advanced against this method of allocating lease obligations between current and noncurrent liabilities. See Robert J. Swierenga, "When Current Is Noncurrent and Vice Versa," *Accounting Review* (January 1984), pp. 123-130. Professor Swierenga identifies two methods of making the allocation: the "change in present value" (CPV) approach that is used in the example, and the "present value of the next year's payment" (PVNYP) approach that allocates a larger portion of the liability to the current category. A later study shows that the CPV method is followed almost universally in practice. A. W. Richardson, "The Measurement of the Current Portion of Long-Term Lease Obligations—Some Evidence From Practice," *Accounting Review* (October 1985), pp. 744-752. While there is theoretical support for both positions, this text uses the CPV method in chapter examples and problem materials.

a declining-balance method of amortization is used, the difference in the early years between the expense and the payment would be even larger. In addition to this statement disclosure, a note to the financial statements would be necessary to explain the terms of the lease and future rental payments in more detail.

**Exhibit 20—4    Schedule of Expenses Recognized—Capital and Operating Leases Compared**

| Year | Interest | Executory Costs | Amorti-zation | Total | Expenses Recognized—Operating Lease | Difference |
|------|----------|-----------------|---------------|-------|-------------------------------------|------------|
| | | Expenses Recognized—Capital Lease | | | | |
| 1993 | $19,019 | $ 5,000 | $ 50,039 | $ 74,058 | $ 65,000 | $9,058 |
| 1994 | 14,921 | 5,000 | 50,039 | 69,960 | 65,000 | 4,960 |
| 1995 | 10,413 | 5,000 | 50,039 | 65,452 | 65,000 | 452 |
| 1996 | 5,453 | 5,000 | 50,039 | 60,492 | 65,000 | (4,508) |
| 1997 | –0– | 5,000 | 50,038 | 55,038 | 65,000 | (9,962) |
| | $49,806 | $25,000 | $250,194 | $325,000 | $325,000 | $ –0– |

If in this example, the fair market value of the leased asset had been less than $250,194, the exception discussed previously would be applied, and the lower fair market value would be used for the capitalized value of the lease. For example, assume the fair market value, or sales price, of the leased asset is $242,250. By using the present-value tables and the method illustrated in Chapter 7, the implicit interest rate of the lease can be computed as being approximately 12%. A table similar to Exhibit 20—3 could then be constructed using $242,250 as the initial balance and 12% as the interest rate. For complex lease situations involving something other than equal annual lease payments, computation of the implicit rate of interest must be done from the present-value formulas themselves. This computation is facilitated by use of a computer.

**Accounting for Lease With Bargain Purchase Option**    Frequently, the lessee is given the option of purchasing the property at some future date at a bargain price. As discussed previously, the present value of the bargain purchase option is part of the minimum lease payments and should be included in the capitalized value of the lease. Assume in the preceding example that there was a bargain purchase option of $75,000 exercisable after 5 years, and the economic life of the equipment was expected to be 10 years. The other lease terms remain the same. The present value of the minimum lease payments would be increased by the present value of the bargain purchase amount of $75,000 or $46,568 computed as follows:

$$PV = A(PVF_{\overline{n}|i})$$
$$PV = \$75,000(\text{Table II}_{\overline{5}|10\%})$$
$$PV = \$75,000(0.6209)$$
$$PV = \$46,568$$

The total present value of the lease is $296,762 ($250,194 + $46,568). This amount will be used to record the initial asset and liability. The asset balance of $296,762 will be amortized over the asset life of 10 years because of the existence of the bargain purchase option; this makes the transaction, in reality, a sale. The liability balance will be reduced as shown in Exhibit 20—5.

**Exhibit 20—5    Schedule of Lease Payments [Five-Year Lease With Bargain Purchase Option of $75,000 After Five Years, $60,000 Annual Payments (Net of Executory Costs), 10% Interest]**

| Date | Description | Lease Payment Amount | Interest Expense | Principal | Lease Obligation |
|------|-------------|------------|----------|-----------|------------|
| 1-1-93 | Initial balance ........ | | | | $296,762 |
| 1-1-93 | Payment ............. | $ 60,000 | | $ 60,000 | 236,762 |
| 12-31-93 | Payment ............. | 60,000 | $23,676 | 36,324 | 200,438 |
| 12-31-94 | Payment ............. | 60,000 | 20,044 | 39,956 | 160,482 |
| 12-31-95 | Payment ............. | 60,000 | 16,048 | 43,952 | 116,530 |
| 12-31-96 | Payment ............. | 60,000 | 11,653 | 48,347 | 68,183 |
| 12-31-97 | Payment ............. | 75,000 | 6,817 | 68,183 | –0– |
| | | $375,000 | $78,238 | $296,762 | |

At the date of exercising the option, the net balance in the asset account Leased Equipment and its related accumulated amortization account would be transferred to the regular equipment account. The entries at the exercise of the option would be:

```
1997
Dec. 31  Obligations Under Capital Leases ................     68,183
         Interest Expense...............................      6,817
             Cash.......................................             75,000
             To record exercise of bargain purchase option.

         Equipment .....................................    148,381
         Accumulated Amortization on Leased Equipment ...    148,381
             Leased Equipment ..........................            296,762
             To transfer remaining balance in leased asset
             account to equipment account.
```

*Computation:*
Accumulated amortization:
  One-half amortized after 5 years of a 10-year life: $296,762 ÷ 2
  = $148,381

If the equipment is not purchased and the lease is permitted to lapse, a loss in the amount of the net remaining balance in the asset account, less any remaining liabilities, would have to be recognized by the following entry:

```
1997
Dec. 31  Loss From Failure to Exercise Bargain Purchase
             Option .........................................     73,381
         Obligations Under Capital Leases ................     68,183
         Interest Expense...............................      6,817
         Accumulated Amortization on Leased Equipment ...    148,381
             Leased Equipment ..........................            296,762
```

**Accounting for Lease With Lessee-Guaranteed Residual Value**    If the lease terms require the lessee to guarantee a residual value, the lessee treats the guarantee similar to a bargain purchase option and includes the present value of the guarantee as part of the capitalized value of the lease. At the expiration of the lease term, the amount of the guarantee will be reported as a liability under the lease. If the lessee is required to pay the guaranteed amount, the liability will be reduced accordingly. If only part of the guaranteed amount is paid, the difference can be reflected as an adjustment to the current lease expense.

**Accounting for Purchase of Asset During Lease Term**    When a lease does not provide for a transfer of ownership or a purchase option, it is still possible that a lessee may purchase leased property during the term of the lease. Usually the purchase price will differ from the recorded lease obligation at the purchase date. The FASB issued Interpretation No. 26 to cover this situation. The Board decided that no gain or loss should be recorded on the purchase, but the difference between the purchase price and the obligation still on the books should be charged or credited to the acquired asset's carrying value.[9]

To illustrate, assume that on December 31, 1995, rather than making the lease payment due on that date, the lessee purchased the leased property described on page 757 for $120,000. At that date, the remaining liability recorded on the lessee's books is $114,547 (lease obligation of $104,134 + interest payable of $10,413), and the net book value of the recorded leased asset is $100,077, the original capitalized value of $250,194 less $150,117 amortization ($50,039 × 3). The entry to record the purchase on the lessee's books would be:

```
1995
Dec. 31   Interest Expense..................................    10,413
          Obligations Under Capital Leases ................   104,134
          Equipment ......................................   105,530
          Accumulated Amortization on Leased Equipment ...   150,117
             Leased Equipment ............................               250,194
             Cash.........................................               120,000
```

The purchased equipment is capitalized at $105,530, which is the book value of the leased asset, $100,077, plus $5,453, the excess of the purchase price over the carrying value of the lease obligation ($120,000 − $114,547).

## Treatment of Leases on Lessee's Statement of Cash Flows

Operating leases present no special problems to the lessee in preparing a statement of cash flows. The lease payments reduce net income and thus require no adjustment to net income under the indirect method except for any accrued or prepaid rent expense. The cash payments would be reported as operating expense outlays under the direct method.

Adjustments for capital leases by the lessee, however, are more complex. The amortization of leased assets would be treated the same as depreciation, i.e., added to net income under the indirect method and ignored under the direct method. The portion of the cash payment allocated to interest expense would require no adjustment under the indirect method and would be reported as part of the cash payment for interest expense under the direct method. The portion of the cash payment allocated to the lease liability would be reported as a financing outflow under either method. Leases would not be reported as an investment on the statement of cash flows, because the entire arrangement is considered a financing event. If the asset is purchased rather than leased, any down payment made at the purchase date would be reported as an investment in assets with the balance being financed disclosed in the notes to the financial statements. Later payments would be reported as financing cash outflows in the same way lease payments are reported.

---

[9]*FASB Interpretation No. 26, "Accounting for Purchase of a Leased Asset by the Lessee During the Term of the Lease"* (Stamford: Financial Accounting Standards Board, 1978), par. 5.

## Avoiding a Liability

The effect on the financial statements of operating versus capital leases can be significant. One study estimated that if McDonalds were required to capitalize all noncancellable leases that it currently classifies as operating, the company's debt-to-equity ratio would increase 30%. Examining firms in seven different industries, the study concluded that for those firms who use leases extensively, the effect on their return on assets and debt-to-equity ratios would be even more significant. For those firms, the average decrease in the return on total assets was 34% while the debt-to-equity ratio increased by 191%.

With the issuance of FASB Statement No. 13, it was thought that firms would reflect the economic reality of their lease agreements. However, this standard has been relatively ineffective in meeting its objective. Instead of complying with the spirit of the standard, firms seem to have gone to great lengths to structure leases that do not meet the criteria for balance sheet disclosure.

### Questions:

1. *If a major objective of financial statement information is to provide useful information to investors and creditors, are those groups currently receiving financial statements that contain relevant and reliable information regarding leased assets?*

2. *Do you think the FASB has achieved its objective of requiring leases that are, in effect, purchases to be disclosed on the balance sheet?*

3. *It often seems that whenever the FASB provides detailed rules for applying a specific standard, companies spend a great deal of time looking for loopholes in those rules. What can the FASB do to get companies to comply with the intent of a standard?*

4. *If the FASB were to ask you for advice in revising its standard on leasing, what would your advice be?*

Source: Imhoff, Lipe, and Wright, "Operating Leases: Impact of Constructive Capitalization," *Accounting Horizons*, March 1991, pp. 51-63.

## ACCOUNTING FOR LEASES—LESSOR

The lessor in a lease transaction gives up the physical possession of the property to the lessee. If the transfer of the property is considered temporary in nature, the lessor will continue to carry the leased asset as an owned asset on the balance sheet, and the revenue from the lease will be reported as it is earned. Depreciation of the leased asset will be matched against the revenue. This type of lease is described as an **operating lease** and cash receipts from the lessee are treated similar to the operating lease procedures described for the lessee. However, if a lease has terms that make the transaction similar in substance to a sale or a permanent transfer of the asset to the lessee, the lessor should no longer report the asset as though it were owned, but should reflect the transfer to the lessee.

As indicated on page 751, if a lease meets one of the four criteria that apply to both lessees and lessors, plus both of the lessor conditions, collectibility and substantial completion, it is classified by the lessor as a capital lease and recorded as either a direct financing lease or a sales-type lease.

**Direct financing leases** involve a lessor who is primarily engaged in financing activities, such as a bank or finance company. The lessor views the lease as an investment. The revenue generated by this type of lease is interest revenue. **Sales-type leases**, on the other hand, involve manufacturers or dealers who use leases as a means of facilitating the marketing of their products. Thus, there are really two different types of revenue generated by this type of lease: (1) an immediate profit or loss, which is the difference between the cost of the property being leased and its sales price, or fair value, at the inception of the lease, and (2) interest revenue to compensate for the deferred payment provisions.

For either an operating, direct financing, or sales-type lease, a lessor may incur certain costs, referred to as **initial direct costs**, in connection with obtaining the lease. These costs include:[10]

1. Costs to originate a lease that result directly from and are essential to acquire that lease and would not have been incurred if that leasing transaction had not occurred.
2. Certain costs directly related to the following specified activities performed by the lessor for that lease: evaluating the prospective lessee's financial condition; evaluating and recording guarantees, collateral, and other security arrangements; negotiating lease terms; preparing and processing lease documents; and closing the transaction.

Initial direct costs are accounted for differently depending on which of the three types of leases is involved. Exhibit 20—6 summarizes the accounting treatment for initial direct costs. These costs will be discussed further as each type of lease is presented.

**Exhibit 20—6    Accounting for Initial Direct Costs**

| Type of Lease | Accounting Treatment of Costs |
|---|---|
| Operating | Recorded as an asset and amortized over lease term. |
| Direct financing | Recorded as an asset and amortized over lease term with unearned interest so as to produce a constant rate of return on the net investment in the lease. |
| Sales-type | Immediately recognized as reduction in manufacturer's or dealer's profit. |

## Accounting for Operating Leases—Lessor

Accounting for operating leases for the lessor is very similar to that described for the lessee. The lessor recognizes revenue as the payments are received. If there are significant variations in the payment terms, entries will be necessary to reflect a straight-line pattern of revenue recognition. Initial direct costs incurred in connection with an operating lease are deferred and amortized on a straight-line basis over the term of the lease, thus matching them against rent revenue.

To illustrate accounting for an operating lease on the lessor's books, assume that the equipment leased for 5 years by Marshall Corporation (page 756) on January 1, 1993, for $65,000 a year, including executory costs of $5,000 per year, had a cost of $400,000 to the lessor. Initial direct costs of $15,000 were incurred to obtain the lease. The equipment has an estimated life of 10 years, with no residual value. Assuming no purchase or renewal

---

[10]*Statement of Financial Accounting Standards No. 91*, "Accounting for Nonrefundable Fees and Costs Associated With Originating or Acquiring Loans and Initial Direct Costs of Leases" (Stamford: Financial Accounting Standards Board, 1986), par. 24.

options or guarantees by the lessee, the lease does not meet any of the four general classification criteria and would be treated as an operating lease. The entries to record the payment of the initial direct costs and the receipt of rent would be:

```
1993
Jan. 1   Deferred Initial Direct Costs .........................   15,000
            Cash ..............................................            15,000

       1   Cash .............................................   65,000
            Rent Revenue ....................................            65,000
```

Assuming the lessor depreciates the equipment on a straight-line basis over its expected life of 10 years and amortizes the initial direct costs on a straight-line basis over the 5-year lease term, the depreciation and amortization entries at the end of the first year would be:

```
1993
Dec. 31   Amortization of Initial Direct Costs .................   3,000
             Deferred Initial Direct Costs ......................            3,000

       31   Depreciation Expense on Leased Equipment .........   40,000
             Accumulated Depreciation on Leased Equipment ...            40,000
```

Executory costs would be recognized as expense when paid or accrued. If the rental period and the lessor's fiscal year do not coincide, or if the lessor prepares interim reports, an adjustment would be required to record the unearned rent revenue at the end of the accounting period. Amortization of the initial direct costs would be adjusted to reflect a partial year.

## Accounting for Direct Financing Leases

Accounting for direct financing leases for lessors is very similar to that used for capital leases by lessees, but with the entries reversed to provide for interest revenue rather than interest expense and reduction of an asset rather than a liability. In practice, the receivable usually is recorded by the lessor at the gross amount of the lease payments with an offsetting valuation account for the unearned interest revenue, rather than at a net figure as is true for lessee accounting. **Unearned interest revenue** is computed as the difference between the **gross investment** (total lease payments) and the fair market value, or cost, of the leased asset. The difference between the gross investment and the unearned interest revenue is the **net lease investment**.

**Illustrative Entries for Direct Financing Leases**    Referring to the lessee example on page 756, assume that the cost of the equipment to the Universal Leasing Company was the same as its fair market value, $250,194, and the purchase by the lessor had been entered into the account Equipment Purchased for Lease. The entry to record the initial lease would be:

```
1993
Jan. 1   Lease Payments Receivable .......................   300,000
            Equipment Purchased for Lease ..................            250,194
            Unearned Interest Revenue ......................             49,806
```

The first payment would be recorded as follows:

```
Jan. 1   Cash .........................................   65,000
            Lease Payments Receivable .....................            60,000
            Executory Costs ...............................             5,000
```

The lessor is paying the executory costs, but charging them to the lessee. The lessor can record the receipt of the executory costs by debiting Cash and crediting the expense account Executory Costs. As the lessor pays the costs, the expense account is debited. The lessor is serving as a conduit for these costs to the lessee, and will have an expense only if the lessee fails to make the payments.

Interest revenue will be recognized over the lease term as shown in Exhibit 20—7.

**Exhibit 20—7**    **Schedule of Lease Receipts and Interest Revenue [Five-Year Lease, $60,000 Annual Payments (Exclusive of Executory Costs), 10% Interest]**

| Date | Description | Interest Revenue* | Lease Receipt | Lease Payments Receivable | Unearned Interest Revenue |
|---|---|---|---|---|---|
| 1-1-93 | Initial balance ....... | | | $300,000 | $49,806 |
| 1-1-93 | Receipt ............ | | $ 60,000 | 240,000 | 49,806 |
| 12-31-93 | Receipt ............ | $19,019 | 60,000 | 180,000 | 30,787 |
| 12-31-94 | Receipt ............ | 14,921 | 60,000 | 120,000 | 15,866 |
| 12-31-95 | Receipt ............ | 10,413 | 60,000 | 60,000 | 5,453 |
| 12-31-96 | Receipt ............ | 5,453 | 60,000 | –0– | –0– |
| | | $49,806 | $300,000 | | |

*Preceding lease payment receivable less unearned interest revenue × 10%.

At the end of the first year, the following entries would be made to record receipt of the second lease payment, to recognize interest revenue for 1993, and to recognize the advance payment for next year's executory costs as a deferred credit.

```
1993
Dec. 31  Cash .........................................   65,000
              Minimum Lease Payments Receivable ............           60,000
              Deferred Executory Costs .......................            5,000

      31  Unearned Interest Revenue ........................   19,019
              Interest Revenue ...............................           19,019
```

Based on the journal entries, the balance sheet of the lessor at December 31, 1993, will report the lease receivable less the unearned interest revenue as follows:

**Universal Leasing Company**
**Balance Sheet (Partial)**
**December 31, 1993**

Assets

Current assets:
Lease payments receivable ..........................   $ 60,000
Less unearned interest revenue ......................    14,921   $ 45,079
Noncurrent assets:
Lease payments receivable (exclusive of $60,000 included
  in current assets) ....................................   $120,000
Less unearned interest revenue .......................    15,866   $104,134

If a direct financing lease contains a bargain purchase option, the amount of the option is added to the receivable, and the interest included in the option amount is added to the unearned interest revenue account. The periodic entries and computations are made as though the bargain purchase amount was an additional rental payment.

**Lessor Accounting for Direct Financing Lease With Residual Value**    If leased property is expected to have residual value, the gross amount of the expected residual value is added to the receivable account. It does not matter whether the residual value is guaranteed or unguaranteed. If guaranteed, it is treated in the accounts exactly like a bargain purchase option. If unguaranteed, the lessor is expected to have an asset equal in value to the residual amount at the end of the lease term. The estimated residual value is added to the asset account and the interest attributable to the unguaranteed residual value is added to the unearned interest revenue account.

To illustrate the recording of residual values, assume the same facts for the Universal Leasing Company as the example on pages 809-810 except that the asset has a residual value at the end of the 5-year lease term of $75,000 (either guaranteed or unguaranteed) rather than a bargain purchase option. Assume the cost of the equipment to the Universal Leasing Company was again the same as its fair market value, $296,762.

The entries to record this lease and the first payment would be:

```
1993
Jan. 1  Lease Payments Receivable......................   375,000
            Equipment Purchased for Lease ..................             296,762
            Unearned Interest Revenue ......................              78,238

     1  Cash..........................................    65,000
            Lease Payments Receivable .....................              60,000
            Executory Costs................................               5,000
```

The difference between the Lease Payments Receivable of $375,000 and the cost of the equipment leased of $296,762 is the Unearned Interest Revenue of $78,238. The amortization of the unearned interest revenue would be identical to the interest expense computation illustrated in Exhibit 20—5 for the lessee.

At the end of the first year, the lessor would make the following entries:

```
1993
Dec. 31  Cash ..........................................    65,000
             Lease Payments Receivable......................             60,000
             Deferred Executory Costs.......................              5,000

     31  Unearned Interest Revenue ........................    23,676
             Interest Revenue...............................             23,676
```

At the end of the lease term, the lessor would make the following entry to record the recovery of the leased asset assuming the residual value was the same as originally estimated:

```
Equipment..............................................    75,000
Unearned Interest Revenue...............................     6,817
    Lease Payments Receivable ............................             75,000
    Interest Revenue .....................................              6,817
```

The unguaranteed residual value should be reviewed at least annually by the lessor and adjusted for any decline that is considered other than temporary. Any adjustment is accounted for as a change in estimate.

**Initial Direct Costs Related to Direct Financing Lease**    If the lessor incurs any initial direct costs in conjunction with a direct financing lease, those costs are recorded as a separate asset and amortized, along with unearned interest revenue, to produce a constant rate of return on the net lease investment.[11] Because the net lease investment is increased by the initial direct costs, a lower implicit interest rate will be used to compute the amortization. In effect, this treatment spreads the initial costs over the lease term and reduces the amount of interest revenue that would otherwise be recognized.

## Accounting for Sales-Type Leases

Accounting for sales-type leases adds one more dimension to the lessor's revenue, an immediate profit or loss arising from the difference between the sales price of the leased property and the lessor's cost to manufacture or purchase the asset. If there is no difference between the sales price and the lessor's cost, the lease is not a sales-type lease. The lessor also will recognize interest revenue over the lease term for the difference between the sales price and the gross amount of the minimum lease payments. The three values that must be identified to determine these income elements, therefore, can be summarized as follows:

1.  The minimum lease payments as defined previously for the lessee, i.e., rental payments over the lease term net of any executory costs included therein plus the amount to be paid under a bargain purchase option or guarantee of the residual value.
2.  The fair market value of the asset.
3.  The cost or carrying value of the asset to the lessor increased by any initial direct costs to lease the asset.

The manufacturer's or dealer's profit is the difference between the fair market value of the asset [(2) above] and the cost or carrying value of the asset to the lessor [(3) above]. If cost exceeds the fair market value, a loss will be reported. The difference between the gross rentals [(1) above] and the fair market value of the asset [(2) above] is interest revenue and arises because of the time delay in paying for the asset as described by the lease terms. The relationship between these three values can be demonstrated as follows:

(1) Minimum lease payments _____
                                          Financial Revenue
                                             (Interest)
(2) Fair market value of leased asset _____
                                          Manufacturer's or
                                          Dealer's Profit (Loss)
(3) Cost or carrying value of leased asset to lessor _____

To illustrate this type of lease, assume the lessor for the equipment described on page 756 is American Manufacturing Company rather than Universal Leasing. The fair market value of the equipment is equal to its present value (the future lease payments discounted at 10%), or $250,194. Assume the equipment cost American $160,000 and initial direct costs of $15,000 were incurred. The three values and their related revenue amounts would be as shown at the top of page 768.

**Illustrative Entries for Sales-Type Leases**    The interest revenue ($49,806) is the same as that illustrated for a direct financing lease on page 764, and it is recognized over the lease term by the same entries and according to Exhibit 20—7. The manufacturer's profit is recognized as revenue immediately in the current period by including the fair market value of the asset as a sale and debiting the cost of the equipment carried in the finished goods inventory to Cost of Goods Sold. The initial direct costs previously deferred are recog-

---

[11]*Statement of Financial Accounting Standards No. 98*, "Accounting for Leases—Initial Direct Costs of Direct Financing Leases" (Norwalk: Financial Accounting Standards Board, 1988) par. 22i.

(1) Minimum lease payments:
   ($65,000 − $5,000) × 5 _____ $300,000
                                                          $49,806  (Interest Revenue)

(2) Fair market value of
    equipment _____ $250,194
                                                          $75,194  (Manufacturer's Profit)

(3) Cost of leased equipment
    to lessor, plus initial direct
    costs _____ $175,000

nized as an expense immediately by increasing Cost of Goods Sold by the amount expended for these costs. This reduces the amount of immediate profit to be recognized. The reimbursement of executory costs is treated in the same way as illustrated for direct financing leases.

The entries to record this information on American Manufacturing Company's books at the beginning of the lease term would be:

| | | | |
|---|---|---:|---:|
| 1993 | | | |
| Jan. 1 | Lease Payments Receivable......................... | 300,000 | |
| | Cost of Goods Sold .............................. | 175,000 | |
| | Finished Goods Inventory......................... | | 160,000 |
| | Deferred Initial Direct Costs ..................... | | 15,000 |
| | Unearned Interest Revenue ...................... | | 49,806 |
| | Sales ......................................... | | 250,194 |
| 1 | Cash.......................................... | 65,000 | |
| | Lease Payments Receivable ....................... | | 60,000 |
| | Executory Costs................................. | | 5,000 |

The 1993 income statement would include the sales and cost of sales amounts yielding the manufacturer's profit of $75,194 and interest revenue of $19,019. A note to the statements would describe in more detail the nature of the lease and its terms.

In the preceding example, it was implied that the fair market value of the leased equipment was determined by discounting the minimum lease payments at a rate of 10%. Normally, the fair market value is known, and the minimum lease payments are set at an amount that will yield the desired rate of return to the lessor.

**Accounting for Sales-Type Leases With Bargain Purchase Option or Guarantee of Residual Value**    If the lease terms provide for the lessor to receive a lump-sum payment at the end of the lease term in the form of a bargain purchase option or a guarantee of residual value, the minimum lease payments include these amounts. The receivable is thus increased by the gross amount of the future payment, the unearned interest revenue account is increased by the interest on the end-of-lease payment, and sales are increased by the present value of the additional amount.

To illustrate a sales-type lease with a bargain purchase option, assume American Manufacturing was the lessor on the lease described on page 759 and Exhibit 20—5. The initial entries when either a bargain purchase option or a guarantee of residual value of $75,000 is payable at the end of the 5-year lease term would be:

| | | | |
|---|---|---:|---:|
| 1993 | | | |
| Jan. 1 | Lease Payments Receivable......................... | 375,000 | |
| | Cost of Goods Sold .............................. | 175,000 | |
| | Finished Goods Inventory......................... | | 160,000 |
| | Deferred Initial Direct Costs ..................... | | 15,000 |
| | Unearned Interest Revenue ...................... | | 78,238 |
| | Sales ......................................... | | 296,762 |

```
Jan. 1  Cash..........................................  65,000
           Lease Payments Receivable .................          60,000
           Executory Costs............................           5,000
```

Because the lease now includes a bargain purchase option, Sales increases by $46,568 (present value of the bargain purchase amount) over the amount recorded on page 768. The manufacturer's profit is also increased by this amount, and the difference between the $75,000 gross payment and the $46,568 increase in sales is recorded as a $28,432 increase in Unearned Interest Revenue.

**Accounting for Sales-Type Leases With Unguaranteed Residual Value**    When a sales-type lease does not contain a bargain purchase option or a guaranteed residual value, but the economic life of the leased asset exceeds the lease term, the residual value of the property will remain with the lessor. As indicated earlier, this is called an unguaranteed residual value. The only difference between accounting for an unguaranteed residual value and a guaranteed residual value or bargain purchase option is that rather than increasing Sales by the present value of the residual value as was illustrated above, the present value is *deducted* from the cost of the leased equipment. The entry to record the initial lease described above with an unguaranteed residual value, therefore, would be:

```
1993
Jan. 1  Lease Payments Receivable ......................  375,000
        Cost of Goods Sold .............................  128,432
           Finished Goods Inventory.......................         160,000
           Deferred Initial Direct Costs ..................          15,000
           Unearned Interest Revenue .....................          78,238
           Sales .......................................         250,194
```

Note that the gross profit on the transaction is the same regardless of whether the residual value is guaranteed or unguaranteed as demonstrated below.

|  | Guaranteed Residual Value | Unguaranteed Residual Value |
|---|---|---|
| Sales | $296,762 | $250,194 |
| Cost of goods sold | 175,000 | 128,432 |
| Gross profit | $121,762 | $121,762 |

## Sale of Asset During Lease Term

If the lessor sells an asset to the lessee during the lease term, a gain or loss is recognized on the difference between the receivable balance, after deducting any unearned finance charges, and the selling price of the asset. Thus, if the leased asset described in Exhibit 20—7, page 765, is sold on December 31, 1995, for $140,000 before the $60,000 rental payment is made, a gain of $25,453 would be reported. The following journal entry would be made to record the sale:

```
1995
Dec. 31  Unearned Interest Revenue ......................  15,866
         Cash ..........................................  140,000
           Interest Revenue...............................          10,413
           Lease Payments Receivable .....................         120,000
           Gain on Sale of Leased Asset ..................          25,453
```

It should be remembered that although the lessor does recognize a gain or loss on the sale, the lessee defers any gain or loss in the value placed on the purchased asset.

## Treatment of Leases on Lessor's Statement of Cash Flows

Operating leases present no special problems to the lessor in preparing a statement of cash flows except for initial direct costs. The payment of these costs would be reported as an investing cash outflow under all methods. Under the indirect method, the amortization of initial direct costs would be added to net income in the same way income is adjusted for depreciation. Under the direct method, the amortization would be ignored. The lease receipts would be reported as part of net income and would require no adjustment under the indirect method and would be reported as part of the revenue receipts under the direct method.

Capital leases must be analyzed carefully to determine their impact on the statement of cash flows. Financing leases would require adjustments similar to those made by the lessee for capital leases except that for the lendor (lessor), the transaction is viewed as an investing activity rather than a financing activity as was the case for the borrower (lessee). The portion of the receipt that represents interest will be included in net income and requires no adjustment under the indirect method. It would be part of cash inflows from interest under the direct method. The portion of the payment representing the principal would be reported as an investing inflow under either method.

Under sales-type leases, the manufacturer's profit, net of initial direct costs, is reported in net income, but the cash inflow comes as the lease payments are received. Under the indirect method, this requires a deduction from net income for the manufacturer's profit at the inception of the lease. This would automatically occur as the changes in inventory, deferred initial costs, and net lease payments receivable are reflected in the operating section of the statement of cash flows. Since the transaction is being accounted for as a sale, all further receipts under the indirect method are reported as operating inflows, either as interest revenue or as reductions in the net lease payments receivable. Under the direct method, the entire lease receipt would be included in cash flows from operating activities. A summary of the treatment of lease impact on the statement of cash flows is included in Exhibit 20—8.

---

## DISCLOSURE REQUIREMENTS FOR LEASES

The Financial Accounting Standards Board has established specific disclosure requirements for all leases, regardless of whether they are classified as operating or capital leases. The required information supplements the disclosures required in the financial statements and usually is included in a single note to the financial statements. For example, IBM Corporation reports information concerning its operating leases in the note entitled "Rental Expense and Lease Commitments." (See Appendix A at the end of the text.)

The following information is required for all leases that have initial or remaining noncancellable lease terms in excess of one year:

### Lessee

1. Gross amount of assets recorded as capital leases and related accumulated depreciation as of the date of each balance sheet presented by major classes according to the nature of the function.
2. Future minimum rental payments required as of the date of the latest balance sheet presented in the aggregate and for each of the five succeeding fiscal years. These payments should be separated between operating and capital leases. For capital leases, executory costs should be excluded.

### Exhibit 20—8    Summary of Lease Impact on Statement of Cash Flows

| Lessee | Operating Activities Indirect Method | Operating Activities Direct Method | Investing Activities | Financing Activities |
|---|---|---|---|---|
| Operating lease payments.......................... | NI | − Cash | | |
| Capital lease: | | | | |
|     Lease payments—interest ........................... | NI | − Cash | | |
|     Lease payments—principal ......................... | | | | − Cash |
|     Amortization of asset ............................ | + NI | No impact | | |
| **Lessor** | | | | |
| Operating leases: | | | | |
|     Initial direct costs (IDC)............................ | | | − Cash | |
|     Amortization of IDC............................... | + NI | No impact | | |
|     Lease receipts ..................................... | NI | + Cash | | |
| Direct financing lease: | | | | |
|     Initial direct costs.................................. | | | − Cash | |
|     Amortization of IDC............................... | + NI | No impact | | |
|     Lease receipts—interest........................... | NI | + Cash | | |
|     Lease receipts—principal........................... | | | | + Cash |
| Sales-type lease: | | | | |
|     Manufacturer's or dealer's profit (net of IDC) .......... | − NI | No impact | | |
|     Lease receipts—interest........................... | NI | + Cash | | |
|     Lease receipts—principal.......................... | + NI | + Cash | | |

*Key:*
NI = Included in net income
+ NI = Added as an adjustment to net income
− NI = Deducted as an adjustment to net income
+ Cash = Reported as a receipt of cash
− Cash = Reported as a payment of cash

3. Rental expense for each period for which an income statement is presented. Additional information concerning minimum rentals, contingent rentals, and sublease rentals is required for the same periods.
4. A general description of the lease contract including information about restrictions on such items as dividends, additional debt, and further leasing.
5. For capital leases, the amount of imputed interest necessary to reduce the lease payments to present value.

A note accompanying the 1989 financial statements of Vulcan Materials Company, presented in Exhibit 20—9, illustrates the required lessee disclosures for both operating and capital leases.

**Lessor**

1. The following components of the net investment in sales-type and direct financing leases as of the date of each balance sheet presented:
   (a) Future minimum lease payments receivable with separate deductions for amounts representing executory costs and the accumulated allowance for uncollectible minimum lease payments receivable.
   (b) Unguaranteed residual values accruing to the benefit of the lessor.
   (c) Unearned revenue.
   (d) For direct financing leases only, initial direct costs.

## Exhibit 20—9     Vulcan Materials Company—Lessee Disclosures

6. *Leases*

Total rental expense of nonmineral leases, exclusive of rental payments made under leases of one month or less, is summarized as follows (in thousands of dollars):

|  | 1989 | 1988 | 1987 |
|---|---|---|---|
| Minimum rentals | $ 5,260 | $4,202 | $4,399 |
| Contingent rentals (based principally on usage) | 4,896 | 4,764 | 1,643 |
| Total | $10,156 | $8,966 | $6,042 |

Future minimum lease payments under all leases with initial or remaining noncancellable lease terms in excess of one year, exclusive of mineral leases, at December 31, 1989 are as follows (in thousands of dollars):

| Year Ending December 31 | Capital Leases | Operating Leases |
|---|---|---|
| 1990 | $ 929 | $ 6,031 |
| 1991 | 924 | 5,641 |
| 1992 | 2,219 | 5,117 |
| 1993 | 838 | 4,558 |
| 1994 | 833 | 3,955 |
| Remaining years | 1,641 | 10,691 |
| Total minimum lease payments | 7,384 | $35,993 |
| Less: Amount representing interest | 1,967 | |
| Present value of net minimum lease payments (including long-term obligations of $4,979) | $5,417 | |

Lease agreements frequently include renewal options and require that the Company pay for utilities, taxes, insurance and maintenance expense. Options to purchase are also included in some lease agreements, particularly capital leases.

2. Future minimum lease payments to be received for each of the five succeeding fiscal years as of the date of the latest balance sheet presented, including information on contingent rentals.
3. The amount of unearned revenue included in income to offset initial direct costs for each year for which an income statement is prepared.
4. For operating leases, the cost of assets leased to others and the accumulated depreciation related to these assets.
5. A general description of the lessor's leasing arrangements.

An example of lessor disclosure of sales-type and direct financing leases for McDonnell Douglas Corporation is shown in Exhibit 20—10.

## ACCOUNTING FOR SALE-LEASEBACK TRANSACTIONS

A common type of lease arrangement is referred to as a sale-leaseback transaction. Typical of this type of lease is an arrangement whereby one party sells the property to a second party, and then the first party leases the property back. Thus, the seller becomes a seller-lessee and the purchaser a purchaser-lessor. The accounting problem raised by this transaction is whether the seller-lessee should recognize the profit from the original sale immediately or defer it over the lease term. The Financial Accounting Standards Board has

### Exhibit 20—10    McDonnell Douglas Corporation—Lessor Disclosures

McDONNELL DOUGLAS CORPORATION

*NOTES TO CONSOLIDATED FINANCIAL STATEMENTS*
Millions of dollars, except share data

*Finance Receivables and Property on Lease*

The net investment in finance and lease receivables and property on lease consists of the following:

| December 31 | 1989 | 1988 |
|---|---|---|
| Sales type and direct financing leases: | | |
| Minimum lease payments | $2,748 | $2,174 |
| Residual values ($83 guaranteed at December 31, 1989) | 340 | 300 |
| Unearned income | (1,025) | (786) |
| | 2,063 | 1,688 |
| Notes receivable | 664 | 529 |
| | 2,727 | 2,217 |
| Allowances for doubtful receivables | (47) | (44) |
| | 2,680 | 2,173 |
| Investment in operating leases, net of accumulated depreciation of $296 in 1989, $285 in 1988 | 589 | 522 |
| | 3,269 | 2,695 |
| Property held for sale or lease | 4 | 18 |
| | $3,273 | $2,713 |

The aggregate amount of scheduled principal payments and installments to be received on notes and lease receivables and minimum rentals to be received under noncancelable operating leases consist of the following at December 31, 1989:

| | Principal Payments and Installments | Minimum Rentals |
|---|---|---|
| 1990 | $ 588 | $116 |
| 1991 | 479 | 98 |
| 1992 | 479 | 69 |
| 1993 | 466 | 49 |
| 1994 | 316 | 32 |
| After 1994 | 1,084 | 52 |

recommended that if the initial sale produces a profit, it should be deferred and amortized in proportion to the amortization of the leased asset if it is a capital lease or in proportion to the rental payments if it is an operating lease. If the transaction produces a loss because the fair market value of the asset is less than the undepreciated cost, an immediate loss should be recognized.[12]

To illustrate the accounting treatment for a sale at a gain, assume that on January 1, 1993, Hopkins Inc. sells a warehouse having a carrying value of $7,500,000 on its books to Ashcroft Co. for $9,500,000 and immediately leases the warehouse back. The following conditions are established to govern the transaction:

[12]*Ibid.*, pars. 32-33.

1. The land value is less than 25% of the total fair market value.
2. The term of the lease is 10 years, noncancellable. A down payment of $2,000,000 is required plus equal rental payments of $1,071,082 at the beginning of each year.
3. The warehouse has a fair value of $9,500,000 on January 1, 1993, and an estimated economic life of 20 years. Straight-line depreciation is used on all owned assets.
4. The lessee has an option to renew the lease for $100,000 per year for 10 years, the rest of its economic life. Title passes at the end of the lease term.
5. The terms of the lease meet the requirements of FASB Statement No. 66 for sales of real estate.

Analysis of this lease shows that it qualifies as a capital lease under both the third and fourth criteria. Since the land value is less than 25% of the total fair value, the lease is treated as a single depreciable unit (see Appendix 20—1). It meets the third "75% of economic life" criterion because of the bargain renewal option, which makes both the lease term and the economic life of the warehouse 20 years. It meets the fourth "90% of fair market value" criterion, because the present value of the rental payments is equal to the fair market value of the warehouse ($9,500,000).[13] The entries for recording the sale and the leaseback on both the seller-lessee's books and the purchaser-lessor's books for the first year of the lease are shown below and on page 775.

### Hopkins Inc. (Seller-Lessee)

| | | | |
|---|---|---:|---:|
| 1993 | | | |
| Jan. 1 | Cash | 9,500,000 | |
| | Warehouse | | 7,500,000 |
| | Unearned Profit on Sale-Leaseback | | 2,000,000 |
| | *Original sale of warehouse.* | | |
| 1 | Leased Warehouse | 9,500,000 | |
| | Obligations Under Capital Lease | | 6,428,918 |
| | Cash | | 3,071,082 |
| | *Lease of warehouse, including first payment.* | | |
| Dec. 31 | Amortization Expense on Leased Warehouse | 475,000 | |
| | Accumulated Amortization on Leased Warehouse | | 475,000 |
| | *Amortization of warehouse over 20-year period ($9,500,000 ÷ 20).* | | |
| 31 | Interest Expense | 642,892 | |
| | Obligations Under Capital Lease | 428,190 | |
| | Cash | | 1,071,082 |
| | *Second lease payment (interest expense: $6,428,918 × 10% = $642,892).* | | |
| 31 | Unearned Profit on Sale-Leaseback | 100,000 | |
| | Revenue Earned on Sale-Leaseback | | 100,000 |
| | *Recognition of revenue over 20-year life in proportion to the amortization of the leased asset.* | | |

[13]*Computation of present value of lease:*
(a) Present value of 10 years' rentals:
    $R(PVAF_{\overline{10-1}|10\%} + 1) = \$1,071,082 \times 6.7590 = \$7,239,443$.
(b) Present value of second 10 years' rentals:
    $R(PVAF_{\overline{10-1}|10\%} + 1) = \$100,000 \times 6.7590 = \$675,900$, present value at beginning of second 10 years' lease period.
    Present value at beginning of lease, 10 years earlier:
    $A(PVF_{\overline{10}|10\%}) = \$675,900 \times 0.3855 = \$260,559$.
(c) Total present value, $7,239,443 + $260,559 + 2,000,000 down payment = $9,500,000 (rounded).

## Recognizing a Profit From Leasing

In June of 1988, British & Commonwealth PLC (B&C) acquired Atlantic Computers, the world's third largest computer-leasing company. In April of 1990, B&C placed Atlantic Computers into administrative receivership and wrote off its $900 million investment in the company. The reason for the write-off? Atlantic's method of accounting for leases.

Atlantic had developed what was called a "flexlease," which allowed customers to upgrade their computers at specified points during the lease period. The flexlease involved two separate contracts—one with a financing institution and the second with Atlantic. When customers elected to exercise their flex options, Atlantic would take back the equipment, pay off the remainder of the contract to the lender, and sell the equipment in the used computer market.

Even though the original lease arrangement did not meet the criteria for a sales-type lease, Atlantic was estimating the profits to be made from the sale of those computers that would be returned assuming customers exercised their flex options, and recognizing these sales profits when the original lease contract was signed.

### Questions:

1. Is there anything wrong with Atlantic's method of accounting for the profits to be made on the flexleases?

2. When would be the most appropriate time for Atlantic to recognize profits from the sale of a computer that was returned under a flex option?

3. Why would British & Commonwealth PLC get rid of Atlantic rather than simply change the accounting practice?

Source: *Computerworld*, April 30, 1990, p. 99.

---

### Ashcroft Co. (Purchaser-Lessor)

**1993**

**Jan. 1**

| | | |
|---|---|---|
| Warehouse............................... | 9,500,000 | |
|     Cash...................................... | | 9,500,000 |
|        *Purchase of warehouse.* | | |

**1**

| | | |
|---|---|---|
| Cash ...................................... | 3,071,082 | |
| Lease Payments Receivable ................. | 10,639,738 | |
|     Warehouse............................... | | 9,500,000 |
|     Unearned Interest Revenue ................. | | 4,210,820 |
|       *Direct financing leaseback to Hopkins Inc.* | | |
|       *[total receivable = (10 × $1,071,082) +* | | |
|       *(10 × $100,000) = $11,710,820;* | | |
|       *$11,710,820 − $1,071,082 = $10,639,738].* | | |

**Dec. 31**

| | | |
|---|---|---|
| Cash ...................................... | 1,071,082 | |
| Unearned Interest Revenue .................. | 642,892 | |
|     Lease Payments Receivable................ | | 1,071,082 |
|     Interest Revenue........................ | | 642,892 |
|       *Receipt of second lease payment (see com-* | | |
|       *putations for Hopkins Inc.).* | | |

The amortization entries and recognition of the deferred gain on the sale for Hopkins Inc. would be the same each year for the 20-year lease term. The interest expense and interest revenue amounts would decline each year using the effective interest method of computation.

If the lease had not met the criteria, it would have been recorded as an operating lease. The gain on the sale would have been deferred and recognized in proportion to the lease payments. If the initial sale had been at a loss, an immediate recognition of the loss would have been recorded.

## CONCLUDING COMMENT

This chapter has discussed the basics of accounting for leases. Special considerations applicable to real estate leases and leveraged leases are discussed in Appendixes 20—1 and 20—2, respectively, at the end of the chapter. Leveraged leases often are very complex arrangements involving third parties who assist in financing lease transactions.

Comparatively few leases have been capitalized as a result of FASB Statement No. 13 because of the liberal interpretations applied by many companies to the criteria used to define a capital lease. Many modifications and interpretations of the lease standard have been made by the FASB since the standard was first issued in an attempt to reduce the manipulation of the criteria. However, this method of off-balance-sheet financing is still used frequently. The FASB project on financial instruments may address the lease question as part of the larger financing issue. In the meantime, full disclosure of lease arrangements seems to be a minimum requirement to meet the spirit of FASB Statement No. 13.

## Criteria for Classifying Real Estate Leases

A significant percentage of leases involve real estate. If the real estate includes both nondepreciable land and depreciable buildings and equipment, special problems arise in determining how the lease should be treated. Some of the criteria used to evaluate a lease do not apply to leases of land. The FASB treated leases of real estate separately in Statement No. 13. This treatment is summarized in Exhibit 20—11 and in subsequent sections.

### LEASES INVOLVING LAND ONLY OR BUILDINGS ONLY

Leases of land should be classified as capital leases only if title to the land is certain to be transferred in the future or if transfer is reasonably assured based on the existence of a bargain purchase option. Thus, only the first two general criteria listed on page 751 apply to the leasing of land. The third criterion cannot apply because land has an unlimited life. The fourth criterion was not felt to be applicable because under this criterion, no actual ownership transfer is contemplated. Ownership transfer is an important consideration because the residual value of the land to the lessor would be material, since there is no depreciation on land. Leases of land that meet either of the first two general criteria are capitalized on the lessee's books and treated as sales-type or direct financing leases on the lessor's books if both of the lessor's supplementary criteria also are met. Other leases of land are treated as operating leases.

No special problems arise when a lease involves only the building. The four general criteria for lessees and lessors and the two additional criteria for the lessor can be applied as discussed previously.

### LEASES INVOLVING LAND AND BUILDINGS

If a lease involves both land and buildings, the accounting treatment depends on which criteria the lease meets. If it meets either of the first two criteria, both the land and the buildings should be classified as capital leases using the fair market values of the properties to allocate the capital value between them. The building lease portion will be amortized by the lessee and the land will be left at originally allocated cost. The lessor treats the lease as a sale of a single unit and accounts for it as a sales-type or direct financing lease depending on the circumstances.

If the lease does not meet either of the first two criteria, then additional tests are prescribed by the FASB to determine if any portion should be capitalized. If the land fair market value is less than 25% of the total fair value, the lease is treated as a single unit and the third and fourth criteria are applied to the single unit to determine if it should be treated as an operating or a capital lease. The estimated economic life of the building is

**Exhibit 20—11     Flowchart for Treatment of Real Estate Leases**

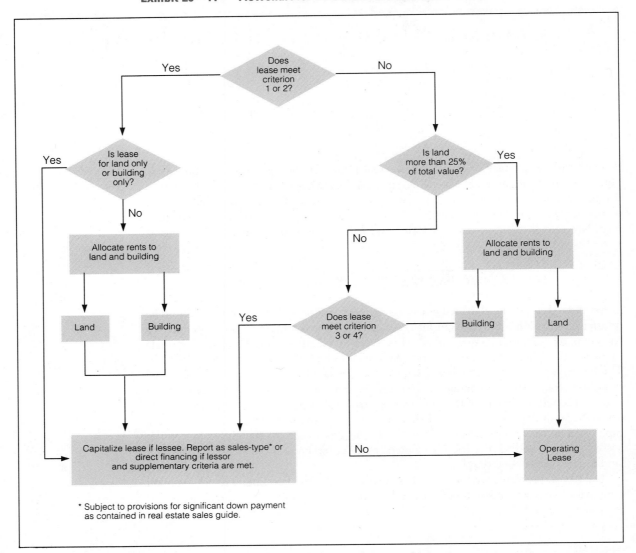

used in applying the third classification criterion. If the fair market value of the land exceeds 25% of the total fair value, the land portion is treated as an operating lease and the third and fourth criteria are applied to the building as a separate unit. If the test is met for the building, the building portion is classified as a capital lease; otherwise, it is treated as an operating lease.

## LEASES INVOLVING REAL ESTATE AND EQUIPMENT

If a lease includes both real estate and equipment, the equipment is considered separately in determining the appropriate classification by the lessee and lessor and is accounted for separately over the term of the lease. The real estate portion of the lease is then classified and accounted for in accordance with the criteria applicable to leases of real estate.

## PROFIT RECOGNITION ON SALES-TYPE REAL ESTATE LEASES

The provisions of profit recognition on sales of real estate have an impact on the lessor's classification of real estate leases. Under the guidelines for sales of real estate, a substantial down payment (approximately 25%) must be made before the profit on the sale can be recognized in full. The FASB amended Statement No. 13 to specify that leases that fail to meet the criteria for full and immediate profit recognition if the real estate had been sold should be classified as operating leases and no immediate profit should be recognized. This amendment does not apply to direct financing leases or sales-type leases where a loss is indicated.

# APPENDIX 20-2

## Leveraged Leases

As indicated in the chapter, there are several potential economic advantages to a lessor in leasing property to others. A lessor who wishes to maximize its ability to lease often has to obtain outside financing for the investment in leased assets. A popular type of lease that has developed over the past twenty-five years to accommodate this type of situation is the **leveraged lease**. There generally are three parties in a leveraged lease: the **lessee**; the **owner-lessor**, or equity participant; and the **third-party, long-term creditor**, or debt participant. Only direct financing leases are treated as leveraged leases.

A leveraged lease generally requires a down payment by the owner-lessor equivalent to 20%-30% of the purchase price. The rest of the financing is provided by the debt participant as a nonrecourse loan on the general credit of the lessor. The interest rate charged on the loan is dependent on the credit rating of the owner-lessor. The owner-lessor enters into the lease arrangement with the lessee, receives rental payments, makes required principal and interest payments on the debt, and recognizes the difference as income. No special accounting is required by the lessee. The lessor records the investment in the leveraged lease net of the nonrecourse debt. The interaction of deferred income taxes, rental payments, and debt-related costs can result in complex accounting entries for the lessor. These complexities are not treated in this text.[14]

[14]For additional discussion and illustrations concerning leveraged leases, see *Statement of Financial Accounting Standards No. 13,* Appendix E, par. 123.

## KEY TERMS

Bargain renewal options 749
Bargain purchase option 749
Capital leases 747
Direct financing leases 762
Executory costs 750
Guaranteed residual value 749
Implicit interest rate 750

Incremental borrowing rate 750
Initial direct costs 763
Lease 746
Lease term 748
Lessee 746
Lessor 746
Leveraged leases 776

Minimum lease payments 750
Net lease investment 764
Operating leases 755
Residual value 749
Sale-leaseback 772
Sales-type leases 763
Unguaranteed residual value 749

## QUESTIONS

1. What are the principal advantages to a lessee in leasing rather than purchasing property?
2. What are the principal advantages to a lessor in leasing rather than selling property?
3. Why is the concept of residual value an important one in capital leases?
4. How is the lease term measured?
5. What criteria must be met before a lease can be properly accounted for as a capital lease on the books of the lessee?
6. The third and fourth criteria for classifying a lease as a capital transaction are not as restrictive as originally intended. Explain how each of these criteria can be circumvented.
7. In determining the classification of a lease, a lessor uses the criteria of the lessee plus two additional criteria. What are these additional criteria and why are they included in the classification of leases by lessors?
8. Under what circumstances are the minimum lease payments for the lessee different from those of the lessor?
9. (a) What discount rate is used to determine the present value of a lease by the lessee? (b) by the lessor?
10. What is the basic difference between an operating lease and a capital lease from the viewpoint of the lessee?
11. If an operating lease requires the payment of uneven rental amounts over its life, how should the lessee recognize rental expense?
12. What amount should be recorded as an asset and a liability for capital leases on the books of the lessee?
13. The FASB has identified a situation in which the present value of future minimum lease payments would not be used as the amount for the initial recording of an asset and liability for lessees under capital leases. Describe this situation and how an interest rate would be calculated for determining interest expense.
14. Why do asset and liability balances for capital leases usually differ after the first year?
15. A capitalized lease should be amortized in accordance with the lessee's normal depreciation policy. What life should be used for lease amortization?

16. The use of the capital lease method for a given lease will always result in a lower net income than the operating lease method. Do you agree? Explain fully.
17. If a lease contains a bargain purchase option, what entries are required on the books of the lessee under each of the following conditions?
    (a) The bargain purchase option is exercised.
    (b) The bargain purchase option is not exercised, and no renewal of the lease is made.
    (c) The bargain purchase option is not exercised, but a renewal of the lease is obtained.
18. (a) How does a capital lease for equipment affect the lessee's statement of cash flows? (b) How would the treatment on the statement of cash flows differ if the contract was identified as a purchase of equipment with a down payment and a long-term note payable for the balance?
19. Distinguish a sales-type lease from a direct financing lease.
20. Under what circumstances would a lessor recognize as interest revenue over the lease term an amount greater than the difference between the gross amount of lease receivables and the cost of the asset to the lessor?
21. Terms of leases may provide for guaranteed residual values by third parties. Why have such agreements been popular in many leasing situations?
22. Unguaranteed residual values accrue to the lessor at the expiration of the lease. How are these values treated in a sales-type lease?
23. Why is the principal portion of a lease receipt of a financing lease treated as an investment inflow on the lessor's books, while the principal portion of a lease payment is treated as a financial cash outflow on the lessee's books?
24. Describe how the manufacturer's profit on a sales-type lease is accounted for by the lessor in a statement of cash flows under both the direct and the indirect methods.
25. Describe the specific lease disclosure requirements for lessees.
26. What disclosure is required by the FASB for lessors under sales-type and direct financing leases?

27. When should the profit or loss be recognized by the seller-lessee in a sale-leaseback arrangement?

*28. Real estate leases can include land and/or buildings. Explain how the four criteria for determining lease capitalization are applied to the following:

(a) Leases involving land only.
(b) Leases involving land and buildings.
(c) Leases involving buildings only.

**29. What characteristics are unique to a leveraged lease?

*Relates to Appendix 20—1                    **Relates to Appendix 20—2

---

## DISCUSSION CASES

### Case 20—1   (How should the lease be recorded?)

Louise Corporation entered into a leasing arrangement with Wilder Leasing Corporation for a certain machine. Wilder's primary business is leasing, and it is not a manufacturer or dealer. Louise will lease the machine for a period of 3 years, which is 50% of the machine's economic life. Wilder will take possession of the machine at the end of the initial 3-year lease. Louise does not guarantee any residual value for the machine.

Louise's incremental borrowing rate is 10%, and the implicit rate in the lease is 8½%. Louise has no way of knowing the implicit rate used by Wilder. Using either rate, the present value of the minimum lease payments is between 90% and 100% of the fair value of the machine at the date of the lease agreement.

Louise has agreed to pay all executory costs directly, and no allowance for these costs is included in the lease payments.

Wilder is reasonably certain that Louise will pay all lease payments, and because Louise has agreed to pay all executory costs, there are no important uncertainties regarding costs to be incurred by Wilder.

1. With respect to Louise (the lessee), answer the following:
   (a) What type of lease has been entered into? Explain the reason for your answer.
   (b) How should Louise compute the appropriate amount to be recorded for the lease or asset acquired?
   (c) What accounts will be created or affected by this transaction, and how will the lease or asset and other costs related to the transaction be matched with earnings?
   (d) What disclosures must Louise make regarding this lease or asset?
2. With respect to Wilder (the lessor), answer the following:
   (a) What type of leasing arrangement has been entered into? Explain the reason for your answer.
   (b) How should this lease be recorded by Wilder, and how are the appropriate amounts determined?
   (c) How should Wilder determine the appropriate amount of earnings to be recognized from each lease payment?
   (d) What disclosures must Wilder make regarding this lease?

(AICPA adapted)

### Case 20—2   (Should we buy or lease?)

The Meeker Machine and Die Company has learned that a sophisticated piece of computer-operated machinery is available to either buy or rent. The machinery will result in 3 employees being replaced, and quality of the output has been tested to be superior in every demonstration. There is no doubt that this machinery represents the latest in technology; however, new inventions and research make it difficult to estimate when the machinery will be made obsolete by new technology. The physical life expectancy of the machine is 10 years; however, the estimated economic life is between 2 and 5 years.

Meeker has a debt-to-equity ratio of .75. If the machine is purchased and the minimum down payment is made, the debt-to-equity ratio will increase to 1.1. The monthly payments if the machine is purchased are 20% lower than the rental payments if it is leased. The incremental borrowing rate for Meeker is 11%. The rate implicit in the lease is 12%. What factors should Meeker consider in deciding how to finance the acquisition of the machine?

## Case 20—3   (How should the leases be classified and accounted for?)

On January 1, Toronto Company, a lessee, entered into three noncancellable leases for new equipment, Lease J, Lease K, and Lease L. None of the three leases transfers ownership of the equipment to Toronto at the end of the lease term. For each of the three leases, the present value at the beginning of the lease term of the minimum lease payments is 75% of the fair value of the equipment to the lessor at the inception of the lease. This excludes that portion of the payments representing executory costs, such as insurance, maintenance, and taxes to be paid by the lessor, including any profit thereon.

The following information is peculiar to each lease:

(a) Lease J does not contain a bargain purchase option; the lease term is equal to 80% of the estimated economic life of the equipment.
(b) Lease K contains a bargain purchase option; the lease term is equal to 50% of the estimated economic life of the equipment.
(c) Lease L does not contain a bargain purchase option; the lease term is equal to 50% of the estimated economic life of the equipment.

1. How should Toronto Company classify each of the 3 leases and why? Discuss the rationale for your answer.
2. What amount, if any, should Toronto record as a liability at the inception of the lease for each of the 3 leases?
3. Assuming that the minimum lease payments are made on a straight-line basis, how should Toronto record each minimum lease payment for each of the 3 leases?

(AICPA adapted)

## Case 20—4   (More leases mean lower profits)

Ultrasound, Inc., has introduced a new line of equipment that may revolutionize the medical profession. Because of the new technology involved, potential users of the equipment are reluctant to purchase the equipment, but they are willing to enter into a lease arrangement as long as they can classify the lease as an operating lease. The new equipment will replace equipment that Ultrasound has been selling in the past. It is estimated that a 25% loss of actual equipment sales will occur as a result of the leasing policy for the new equipment.

Management must decide how to structure the leases so that the lessees can treat them as operating leases. Some members of management want to structure the leases so that Ultrasound, as lessor, can classify the lease as a sales-type lease and thus avoid a further reduction of income. Others feel they should treat the leases as operating leases and minimize the income tax liability in the short term. They are uncertain, however, as to how the financial statements would be affected under these two different approaches. They also are uncertain as to how leases could be structured to permit the lessee to treat the lease as an operating lease and the lessor to treat it as a sales-type lease. You are asked to respond to their questions.

## Case 20—5   (Structuring a lease to avoid liability disclosure)

Johnson Pharmaceuticals is in need of cash. One option being considered by the board of directors is to sell the plant facilities to a group of venture capitalists and then lease the facilities back for a long-term period with the option of repurchasing the plant facilities at the end of the lease.

The chairman has commented that this option will provide Johnson Pharmaceuticals with the needed cash but will result in a large lease liability on the balance sheet. As the chief financial officer, you comment that if the company carefully structures the terms of the lease agreement, it may be able to avoid disclosing the lease liability.

The chairman has asked you to prepare a memo discussing the specific ways in which a lease agreement can be structured so as to avoid disclosing the liability on the balance sheet.

### Case 20—6  (Recognizing profits on a sale-leaseback transaction)

John Carson, president of Carson Enterprises, recently arranged a financing deal with a group of foreign investors whereby he sold his movie company for $13,000,000 and immediately leased the company back, recognizing a $4,000,000 profit on the sale. Mr. Carson has just entered your office to tell you, as his accountant, the good news. After hearing the details of the transaction, you tell Mr. Carson that he must defer recognizing the gain immediately and instead recognize it piecemeal over the term of the lease agreement. Mr. Carson counters that if he had simply sold the company to the investors, he would be able to book the profits. He asks you: "What difference does it make if I lease the company back or not? Shouldn't the sale and the lease be treated as two separate transactions?" How do you respond?

---

# EXERCISES

### Exercise 20—1  (Criteria for capitalizing leases)

Atwater Manufacturing Co. leases its equipment from Westside Leasing Company. In each of the following cases, assuming none of the other criteria for capitalizing leases are met, determine whether the lease would be a capital lease or an operating lease under FASB Statement No. 13. Your decision is to be based only on the terms presented, considering each case independently of the others.

(a) At the end of the lease term, the market value of the equipment is expected to be $20,000. Atwater has the option of purchasing it for $5,000.
(b) The fair market value of the equipment is $75,000. The present value of the lease payments is $71,000 (excluding any executory costs).
(c) Ownership of the property automatically passes to Atwater at the end of the lease term.
(d) The economic life of the equipment is 12 years. The lease term is 9 years.
(e) The lease requires payments of $9,000 per year in advance plus executory costs of $500 per year. The lease period is 3 years, and Atwater's incremental borrowing rate is 12%. The fair market value of the equipment is $28,000.
(f) The lease requires payments of $6,000 per year in advance, which includes executory costs of $500 per year. The lease period is 3 years, and Atwater's incremental borrowing rate is 10%. The fair market value of the equipment is $16,650.

### Exercise 20—2  (Entries for lease—lessor and lessee)

The Doxey Company purchased a machine on January 1, 1993, for $1,250,000 for the express purpose of leasing it. The machine was expected to have a 7-year life from January 1, 1993, no salvage value, and to be depreciated on a straight-line basis. On March 1, 1993, Doxey leased the machine to Mondale Company for $300,000 a year for a 4-year period ending February 28, 1997. Doxey paid a total of $15,000 for maintenance, insurance, and property taxes on the machine for the year ended December 31, 1993. Mondale paid $300,000 to Doxey on March 1, 1993. Doxey retains title to the property and plans to lease it to someone else after the 4-year lease period. Give all the 1993 entries relating to the lease on (a) Doxey Company's books and (b) Mondale Company's books. Assume both sets of books are maintained on the calendar-year basis.

### Exercise 20—3  (Entries for operating lease—lessee)

Jonas Inc. leases equipment on a 5-year lease. The lease payments are to be made in advance as shown in the following schedule.

| January 1, 1993 | $100,000 |
|---|---|
| January 1, 1994 | 100,000 |
| January 1, 1995 | 140,000 |
| January 1, 1996 | 170,000 |
| January 1, 1997 | 210,000 |
| Total | $720,000 |

The equipment is to be used evenly over the 5-year period. For each of the 5 years, give the entry that should be made at the time the lease payment is made to allocate the proper share of rent expense to each period. The lease is classified as an operating lease by Jonas Inc.

### Exercise 20—4   (Entries for lessee)

Bingham Smelting Company entered into a 15-year noncancellable lease beginning January 1, 1993, for equipment to use in its smelting operations. The term of the lease is the same as the expected economic life of the equipment. Bingham uses straight-line depreciation for all plant assets. The provisions of the lease call for annual payments of $290,000 in advance plus $20,000 per year to cover executory costs, such as taxes and insurance, for the 15-year period of the lease. At the end of the 15 years, the equipment is expected to be scrapped. The incremental borrowing rate of Bingham is 10%. The lessor's computed implicit interest rate is unknown to Bingham.

Record the lease on the books of Bingham and give all the entries necessary to record the lease for its first year plus the entry to record the second lease payment on December 31, 1993. (Round to the nearest dollar.)

### Exercise 20—5   (Entries for lease—lessee)

On January 2, 1993, the Jaques Company entered into a noncancellable lease for a new warehouse. The warehouse was built to the Jaques Company's specifications and is in an area where rental to another lessee would be difficult. Rental payments are $300,000 a year for 10 years, payable in advance. The warehouse has an estimated economic life of 20 years. The taxes, maintenance, and insurance are to be paid directly by the Jaques Company, and the title to the warehouse is to be transferred to Jaques at the end of the lease term. Assume the cost of borrowing funds for this type of an asset by Jaques Company is 12%.

1. Give the entry on Jaques' books that should be made at the inception of the lease.
2. Give the entries for 1993 and 1994 assuming the second payment and subsequent payments are made on December 31 and assuming double-declining-balance amortization.

### Exercise 20—6   (Schedule of lease payments)

Carter Construction Co. is leasing equipment from Vasquez Inc. The lease calls for payments of $50,000 a year plus $4,000 a year executory costs for 5 years. The first payment is due on January 1, 1993, when the lease is signed, with the other 4 payments coming due on December 31 of each year. Carter has also been given the option of purchasing the equipment at the end of the lease at a bargain price of $100,000. Carter has an incremental borrowing rate of 10%, the same as the implicit interest rate of Vasquez. Carter has hired you as an accountant and asks for a schedule of its obligations under the lease contract. Prepare a schedule that shows all the lessee's obligations.

### Exercise 20—7   (Entry for purchase by lessee)

The Cordon Enterprise Company leases many of its assets and capitalizes most of the leased assets. At December 31, the company had the following balances on its books in relation to a piece of specialized equipment:

| | |
|---|---|
| Leased Equipment | $70,000 |
| Accumulated Amortization—Leased Equipment | 49,300 |
| Obligations Under Capital Leases | 26,000 |

Amortization has been recorded up to the end of the year, and no accrued interest is involved. At December 31, Cordon decided to purchase the equipment for $32,000 and paid cash to complete the purchase. Give the entry required on Cordon's books to record the purchase.

### Exercise 20—8   (Entry for purchase by lessee)

Smithston Corporation leased a warehouse to Dayplanner Co. on January 1, 1993. The terms of the lease called for annual lease payments to be made at the first of each year. Smithston's implicit interest rate for the transaction is 12%. On July 1, 1995, Dayplanner purchased the warehouse and paid $58,000 to complete the transaction. After the 1995 payment was made, the following balances relating to the leased warehouse were on the books of Smithston as of January 1, 1995:

Lease Payments Receivable . . . . . . . . . . . . . . . . . . . . . . . . . . . . . . . . . . . .    $ 84,500
Unearned Interest Revenue . . . . . . . . . . . . . . . . . . . . . . . . . . . . . . . . . . . .    (18,750)

Prepare the journal entry that should be made by Smithston to record the sale including the accrual of interest through July 1.

### Exercise 20—9   (Computation of implicit interest rate)

Tueller Leasing leases equipment to Tsoi Manufacturing. The fair market value of the equipment is $473,130. Lease payments, excluding executory costs, are $70,000 per year, payable in advance, for 10 years. What is the implicit rate of interest Tueller Leasing should use to record this capital lease on its books?

### Exercise 20—10   (Direct financing lease—lessor)

The Deseret Finance Company purchased a printing press to lease to the Quality Printing Company. The lease was structured so that at the end of the lease period of 15 years, Quality would own the printing press. Lease payments required in this lease were $190,000 (excluding executory costs) per year, payable in advance. The cost of the press to Deseret was $1,589,673, which is also its fair market value at the time of the lease.

1. Why is this a direct financing lease?
2. Give the entry to record the lease transaction on the books of Deseret Finance Company.
3. Give the entry at the end of the first year on Deseret Finance Company's books to recognize interest revenue.

### Exercise 20—11   (Direct financing lease with residual value)

The Massachusetts Casualty Insurance Company decides to enter the leasing business. It acquires a specialized packaging machine for $300,000 cash and leases it for a period of 6 years, after which the machine is returned to the insurance company for disposition. The expected unguaranteed residual value of the machine is $20,000. The lease terms are arranged so that a return of 12% is earned by the insurance company.

1. Calculate the annual rent, payable in advance, required to yield the desired return.
2. Prepare entries for the lessor for the first year of the lease assuming the machine is acquired and the lease is recorded on January 1, 1993. The first lease payment is made on January 1, 1993, and subsequent payments are made each December 31.
3. Assuming the packaging machine is sold by Massachusetts to the lessee at the end of the 6 years for $32,000, give the required entry to record the sale.

### Exercise 20—12   (Table for direct financing lease—lessor)

The Pioche Savings and Loan Company acquires a piece of specialized hospital equipment for $1,500,000 that it leases on January 1, 1993, to a local hospital for $391,006 per year, payable in advance. Because of rapid technological developments, the equipment is expected to be replaced after 4 years. It is expected that the machine will have a residual value of $200,000 to Pioche Savings at the end of the lease term. The implicit rate of interest in the lease is 10%.

1. Prepare a 4-year table for Pioche Savings and Loan similar to Exhibit 20—7 on page 765.
2. How would the table differ if the local hospital guaranteed the residual value to Pioche?

## Exercise 20—13   (Direct financing lease with residual value)

The Mario Automobile Company leases automobiles under the following terms. A 3-year lease agreement is signed in which the lessor receives annual rental of $4,000 (in advance). At the end of the 3 years, the lessee agrees to make up any deficiency in residual value below $3,500. The cash price of the automobile is $13,251. The implicit interest rate is 12%, which is known to the lessee, and the lessee's incremental borrowing rate is 14%. The lessee estimates the residual value at the end of 3 years to be $4,200 and depreciates its automobiles on a straight-line basis.

1. Give the entries on the lessee's books required in the first year of the lease including the second payment on April 30, 1994. Assume the lease begins May 1, 1993, the beginning of the lessee's fiscal year.
2. What balances relative to the lease would appear on the lessee's balance sheet at the end of year 3?
3. Assume the automobile is sold by the lessee for $3,100. Prepare the entries to record the sale and settlement with the lessor.

## Exercise 20—14   (Sales-type lease—lessor)

Salcedo Co. leased equipment to Erickson Inc. on April 1, 1993. The lease is appropriately recorded as a sale by Salcedo. The lease is for an 8-year period ending March 31, 2001. The first of 8 equal annual payments of $175,000 (excluding executory costs) was made on April 1, 1993. The cost of the equipment to Salcedo is $940,000. The equipment has an estimated useful life of 8 years with no residual value expected. Salcedo uses straight-line depreciation and takes a full year's depreciation in the year of purchase. The cash selling price of the equipment is $1,026,900.

1. Give the entry required to record the lease on Salcedo's books.
2. How much interest revenue will Salcedo recognize in 1993?

## Exercise 20—15   (Sales-type lease—lessor)

The Jacinto Leasing and Manufacturing Company uses leases as a means of financing sales of its equipment. Jacinto leased a machine to Hudson Construction for $22,000 per year, payable in advance, for a 10-year period. The cost of the machine to Jacinto was $108,000. The fair market value at the date of the lease was $120,000. Assume a residual value of $0 at the end of the lease.

1. Give the entry required to record the lease on Jacinto's books.
2. How much profit will Jacinto recognize initially on the lease, excluding any interest revenue?
3. How much interest revenue would be recognized in the first year?

## Exercise 20—16   (Effect of lease on reported income—lessee and lessor)

On February 20, 1993, Topham Inc. purchased a machine for $1,200,000 for the purpose of leasing it. The machine is expected to have a 10-year life, no residual value, and is depreciated on the straight-line basis to the nearest month. The machine was leased to Lutts Company on March 1, 1993, for a 4-year period at a monthly rental of $18,000. There is no provision for the renewal of the lease or purchase of the machine by the lessee at the expiration of the lease term. Topham paid $60,000 of commissions associated with negotiating the lease in February 1993.

1. What expense should Lutts record as a result of the lease transaction for the year ended December 31, 1993? Show supporting computations in good form.
2. What income or loss before income taxes should Topham record as a result of the lease transaction for the year ended December 31, 1993? Show supporting computations in good form.

### Exercise 20—17   (Cash flow treatment of capital leases—lessee)

The following information relates to a capital lease between Simpson Electric Co. (lessee) and Harris Manufacturing Inc. (lessor). The lease term began on January 1, 1993. Simpson capitalized the 10-year lease and recorded $90,000 as an asset. The annual lease payment, made at the beginning of each year, is $13,316 at 10% interest. Simpson uses the straight-line method to depreciate its owned assets. How will this lease be reported on Simpson's statement of cash flows for 1993 if the 2nd lease payment is made on December 31, 1993, and Simpson uses the indirect method?

### Exercise 20—18   (Lease disclosures—lessee)

The following lease information was obtained by a staff auditor for a client, Kroller Inc., at December 31, 1993. Indicate how this information should be presented in Kroller's 2-year comparative financial statements. Include any notes to the statements required to meet generally accepted accounting principles. Lease payments are made on December 31 of each year.

| | |
|---|---:|
| Leased building; minimum lease payments per year; 10 years remaining life | $ 45,000 |
| Executory costs per year | 2,000 |
| Capitalized lease value, 12% interest | 343,269 |
| Accumulated amortization of leased building at December 31, 1994 | 114,423 |
| Amortization expense for 1994 | 22,885 |
| Obligations under capital leases; balance at December 31, 1994 | 239,770 |
| Obligations under capital leases; balance at December 31, 1993 | 254,259 |

### Exercise 20—19   (Lease disclosure on the financial statements)

Acme Enterprises leased equipment from Monument Equipment Co. on January 1, 1993. The terms of the lease agreement require 5 annual payments of $20,000 with the first payment being made on January 1, 1993, and each subsequent payment being made on December 31 of each year. Because the equipment has an expected useful life of 5 years, the lease qualifies as a capital lease for Acme. Acme does not know Monument's implicit interest rate and therefore uses its own incremental borrowing rate of 12% to calculate the present value of the lease payments. Acme uses the sum-of-the-years-digits method for amortizing leased assets. The expected salvage value of the leased asset is $0.

1. Prepare a schedule that shows all of the lessee's obligations.
2. Prepare an asset amortization schedule for the leased asset.
3. Compare the amount shown on the year-end balance sheet for the leased asset with that of the lease obligation for the years 1993 through 1997 and explain why the amounts differ.

### Exercise 20—20   (Sale-leaseback accounting)

On July 1, 1993, Baker Corporation sold equipment it had recently purchased to an unaffiliated company for $570,000. The equipment had a book value on Baker's books of $450,000 and a remaining life of 5 years. On that same day, Baker leased back the equipment at $135,000 per year, payable in advance, for a 5-year period. Baker's incremental borrowing rate is 10%, and it does not know the lessor's implicit interest rate. What entries are required for Baker to record the transactions involving the equipment during the first full year assuming the second lease payment is made on June 30, 1994? Ignore consideration of the lessee's fiscal year. The lessee uses the double-declining-balance method of depreciation for similar assets it owns outright.

### Exercise 20—21   (Sale-leaseback transaction)

Smalltown Grocers sold its plant facilities to United Grocers, Inc., for $813,487. United immediately leased the building back to Smalltown for 20 annual payments of $96,000 with the first payment due immediately. The terms of the lease agreement provide a bargain purchase option wherein Smalltown has the option of purchasing the building at the end of the lease term for $100,000. If

United's implicit interest rate is 12% (lower than Smalltown's incremental borrowing rate), prepare the entries that should be made by United to record the purchase of the building and the receipt of the first two payments from Smalltown Grocers assuming this leasing arrangement qualifies as a capital lease for United.

### *Exercise 20—22   (Entries for real estate lease with residual value—lessee)

Atlantus Corporation leases its land and buildings from an investment company. The terms of the lease are as follows:

(a) Lease term is 20 years, after which title to the property can be acquired for 25% of the market value at that date. The estimated remaining life of the building is 30 years.
(b) Annual lease payments payable in advance are $250,000 (excluding executory costs). Expected residual value of the property in 20 years is $800,000.
(c) Assume the current market value of the combined land and buildings is $2,370,945, of which the market value of the land is $350,000. The implicit interest rate of the lease is 10%.

What entries would be required on Atlantus Corporation's books for the first year of the lease? Assume the second lease payment is made on the last day of the first year.

*Relates to Appendix 20—1

### *Exercise 20—23   (Lease of real estate—lessee)

Maycomb Industries leases its land and buildings on a 10-year lease from E. L. Kimball. The property includes 10 acres of land that is used for parking and an amusement area. The market value of the leased land is $500,000, and the market value of the leased buildings is $1,200,000. The annual rent for the property, payable in advance, is $251,516. There is no provision in the lease for Maycomb to purchase the property at the conclusion of the lease. The buildings are estimated to have a 12-year remaining life and are depreciated on a straight-line basis.

1. Does the lease of Maycomb Industries qualify as a capital lease? If yes, what criteria apply?
2. Record the lease on Maycomb's books and give the entries for the first full year of the lease assuming the first payment is made on January 1, 1993, and the second payment is made on December 31, 1993.

*Relates to Appendix 20—1

---

## PROBLEMS

### Problem 20—1   (Entries for capital lease—lessee; lease criteria)

The Miner Company leased a machine on July 1, 1993, under a 10-year lease. The economic life of the machine is estimated to be 15 years. Title to the machine passes to Miner Company at the expiration of the lease, and thus the lease is a capital lease. The lease payments are $83,000 per year, including executory costs of $3,000 per year, all payable in advance annually. The incremental borrowing rate of the company is 10%, and the lessor's implicit interest rate is unknown. The Miner Company uses the straight-line method of amortization and uses the calendar year for reporting purposes.

### Instructions:

1. Give all entries on the books of the lessee relating to the lease for 1993.
2. Assume that the lessor retains title to the machine at the expiration of the lease, that there is no bargain renewal or purchase option, and that the fair market value of the equipment is $575,000 as of the lease date. Using the criteria for distinguishing between operating and capital leases according to FASB Statement No. 13, what would be the amortization expense for 1993?

## Problem 20—2   (Operating lease—lessee and lessor)

Calderwood Industries leases a large specialized machine to the Youngstown Company at a total rental of $1,800,000, payable in 5 annual installments in the following declining pattern: 25% for the first 2 years, 22% in the third year, and 14% in each of the last 2 years. The lease begins January 1, 1993. In addition to the rent, Youngstown is required to pay annual executory costs of $15,000 to cover unusual repairs and insurance. The lease does not qualify as a capital lease for reporting purposes. Calderwood incurred initial direct costs of $15,000 in obtaining the lease. The machine cost Calderwood $2,100,000 to construct and has an estimated life of 10 years with an estimated residual value of $100,000. Calderwood uses the straight-line depreciation method on its equipment. Both companies report on a calendar-year basis.

### Instructions:

1. Prepare the journal entries on Calderwood's books for 1993 and 1997 related to the lease.
2. Prepare the journal entries on Youngstown's books for 1993 and 1997 related to the lease.

## Problem 20—3   (Entries for capital lease—lessee)

Aldridge Enterprises has a long-standing policy of acquiring company equipment by leasing. Early in 1993, the company entered into a lease for a new milling machine. The lease stipulates that annual payments will be made for 5 years. The payments are to be made in advance on December 31 of each year. At the end of the 5-year period, Aldridge may purchase the machine. Company financial records show the incremental borrowing rate to be less than the implicit interest rate. The estimated economic life of the equipment is 12 years. Aldridge uses the calendar year for reporting purposes and uses straight-line depreciation for other equipment. In addition, the following information about the lease is also available:

| | |
|---|---:|
| Annual lease payments | 55,000 |
| Purchase option price | 25,000 |
| Estimated fair market value of machine after 5 years | 75,000 |
| Incremental borrowing rate | 10% |
| Date of first lease payment | Jan. 1, 1993 |

### Instructions:

1. Compute the amount to be capitalized as an asset for the lease of the milling machine.
2. Prepare a schedule that shows the computation of the interest expense for each period.
3. Give the journal entries that would be made on Aldridge's books for the first 2 years of the lease.
4. Assume that the purchase option is exercised at the end of the lease. Give the Aldridge journal entry necessary to record the exercise of the option.

## Problem 20—4   (Entries for capital lease—lessee; guaranteed residual value)

For some time, Balster Inc. has maintained a policy of acquiring company equipment by leasing. On January 1, 1993, Balster entered into a lease with Edgemont Fabricators for a new concrete truck that had a selling price of $265,000. The lease stipulates that annual payments of $52,500 will be made for 6 years. The first lease payment is made on January 1, 1994, and subsequent payments are made on December 31 of each year. Balster guarantees a residual value of $45,890 at the end of the 6-year period. Balster has an incremental borrowing rate of 13%, and the implicit interest rate to Edgemont is 12% after considering the guaranteed residual value. The economic life of the truck is 9 years. Balster uses the calendar year for reporting purposes and uses straight-line depreciation to depreciate other equipment.

### Instructions:

1. Compute the amount to be capitalized as an asset on the lessee's books for the concrete truck.
2. Prepare a schedule showing the reduction of the liability by the annual payments after considering the interest charges.

3. Give the journal entries that would be made on Balster's books for the first 2 years of the lease.
4. Assume that the lessor sells the truck for $35,000 at the end of the 6-year period to a third party. Give the Balster journal entries necessary to record the payment to satisfy the residual guarantee and to write off the leased equipment accounts. Write off any remaining liability to lease expense—adjustment.

### Problem 20—5  (Accounting for direct financing lease—lessee and lessor)

The Trost Leasing Company buys equipment for leasing to various manufacturing companies. On October 1, 1992, Trost leases a press to the Shumway Shoe Company. The cost of the machine to Trost was $196,110, which approximated its fair market value on the lease date. The lease payments stipulated in the lease are $33,000 per year in advance for the 10-year period of the lease. The payments include executory costs of $3,000 per year. The expected economic life of the equipment is also 10 years. The title to the equipment remains in the hands of Trost Leasing Company at the end of the lease term, although only nominal residual value is expected at that time. Shumway's incremental borrowing rate is 10%, and it uses the straight-line method of depreciation on all owned equipment. Both Shumway and Trost have fiscal years ending September 30, and lease payments are made on this date.

**Instructions:**

1. Prepare the entries to record the lease and the first lease payment on the books of the lessor and lessee assuming the lease meets the criteria of a direct financing lease for the lessor and a capital lease for the lessee.
2. Compute the implicit rate of interest of the lessor.
3. Give all entries required to account for the lease on both the lessee's and lessor's books for the fiscal years 1993, 1994, and 1995 [exclusive of the initial entries required in (1)].

### Problem 20—6  (Lease computations—lessee and lessor)

Computer Controls Corporation is in the business of leasing new sophisticated computer systems. As a lessor of computers, Computer Controls purchased a new system on December 31, 1993. The system was delivered the same day (by prior arrangement) to Edwards Investment Company, a lessee. The corporation accountant revealed the following information relating to the lease transaction:

| | |
|---|---|
| Cost of system to Computer Controls | $550,000 |
| Estimated useful life and lease term | 8 years |
| Expected residual value (unguaranteed) | $40,000 |
| Computer Controls' implicit rate of interest | 12% |
| Edwards' incremental borrowing rate | 14% |
| Date of first lease payment | Dec. 31, 1993 |

Additional information is as follows:

(a) At the end of the lease, the system will revert to Computer Controls.
(b) Edwards is aware of Computer Controls' rate of implicit interest.
(c) The lease rental consists of equal annual payments.
(d) Computer Controls accounts for leases using the direct financing method. Edwards intends to record the lease as a capital lease. Both the lessee and the lessor report on a calendar-year basis and elect to depreciate all assets on the straight-line basis.

**Instructions:**

1. Compute the annual rental under the lease. (Round to the nearest dollar.)
2. Compute the amounts of the lease payments receivable and the unearned interest revenue that Computer Controls should disclose at the inception of the lease.
3. What are the total expenses related to the lease that Edwards should record for the year ended December 31, 1993?

## ▒ Problem 20—7 (Sales-type lease—lessor)

Aquatran Incorporated uses leases as a method of selling its products. In early 1993, Aquatran completed construction of a passenger ferry for use on the Upper New York Bay between Manhattan and Staten Island. On April 1, 1993, the ferry was leased to the Manhattan Ferry Line on a contract specifying that ownership of the ferry will transfer to the lessee at the end of the lease period. Annual lease payments do not include executory costs. Other terms of the agreement are as follows:

| | |
|---|---|
| Original cost of the ferry | $1,500,000 |
| Fair market value of ferry at lease date | 2,107,102 |
| Lease payments (paid in advance) | 225,000 |
| Estimated residual value | 78,000 |
| Incremental borrowing rate—lessee | 10% |
| Date of first lease payment | April 1, 1993 |
| Lease period | 20 years |

### Instructions:

1. Compute the amount of financial revenue that will be earned over the lease term and the manufacturer's profit that will be earned immediately by Aquatran.
2. Give the entries to record the lease on Aquatran's books. Compute the implicit rate of interest on the lease.
3. Give the journal entries necessary on Aquatran's books to record the operating of the lease for the first 3 years exclusive of the initial entry. Aquatran's accounting period is the calendar year.
4. Indicate the balance of each of the following accounts at December 31, 1995: Unearned Interest Revenue and Lease Payments Receivable.

## Problem 20—8 (Sales-type lease—lessor)

Universal Enterprises adopted the policy of leasing as the primary method of selling its products. The company's main product is a small jet airplane that is very popular among corporate executives. Universal constructed such a jet for Executive Transport Services (ETS) at a cost of $8,329,784. Financing of the construction was accomplished through borrowings at a 13% rate. The terms of the lease provided for annual advance payments of $1,331,225 to be paid over 20 years with the ownership of the airplane transferring to ETS at the end of the lease period. It is estimated that the plane will have a residual value of $800,000 at that date. The lease payments began on October 1, 1993. Universal incurred initial direct costs of $150,000 in finalizing the lease agreement with ETS. The sales price of similar airplanes is $11,136,734.

### Instructions:

1. Compute the amount of manufacturer's profit that will be earned immediately by Universal.
2. Prepare the journal entries to record the lease on Universal's books at October 1, 1993.
3. Prepare the journal entries to record the lease for the years 1993-1995 exclusive of the initial entry. Universal's accounting period is the calendar year.
4. How much revenue did Universal earn from this lease for each of the first 3 years of the lease?

## Problem 20—9 (Entries for capital lease—lessee and lessor)

The Alta Corporation entered into an agreement with Snowfire Company to lease equipment for use in its ski manufacturing facility. The lease is appropriately recorded as a purchase by Alta and as a sale by Snowfire. The agreement specifies that lease payments will be made on an annual basis. The cost of the machine is reported as inventory on Snowfire's accounting records. Because of extensive changes in ski manufacturing technology, the machine is not expected to have any residual value. Alta uses straight-line depreciation and computes depreciation to the nearest month. After 3 years, Alta purchases the machine from Snowfire.

Annual lease payments do not include executory costs. Other terms of the agreement are as follows:

| | |
|---|---|
| Machine cost recorded in inventory | $3,700,000 |
| Price at purchase option date | 3,250,000 |
| Lease payments (paid in advance) | 710,000 |
| Contract interest rate | 10% |
| Contract date/first lease payment | Oct. 1, 1993 |
| Date of Alta purchase | Oct. 1, 1996 |
| Lease period | 8 years |

**Instructions:**   Prepare journal entries on the books of both the lessee and the lessor as follows:

1. Make entries in 1993 to record the first lease payment, and make adjustments necessary at December 31, the end of each company's fiscal year.
2. Record all entries required in 1994. The companies do not make reversing entries.
3. Prepare the entry in 1996 to record the sale and purchase assuming no previous entries have been made during the year in connection with the lease.

## Problem 20—10   (Accounting for capital lease—lessee and lessor)

The Crosby Equipment Company both leases and sells its equipment to its customers. The most popular line of equipment includes a machine that costs $340,000 to manufacture. The standard lease terms provide for 5 annual payments of $130,000 each (excluding executory costs), with the first payment due when the lease is signed and subsequent payments due on December 31 of each year. The implicit rate of interest in the contract is 10% per year. Dannell Tool Co. leases one of these machines on January 2, 1993. Initial direct costs of $17,000 are incurred by Crosby on January 2, 1993, to obtain the lease. Dannell's incremental borrowing rate is determined to be 12%. The equipment is very specialized, and it is assumed it will have no salvage value after 5 years. Assume the lease qualifies as a capital lease and a sales-type lease for lessee and lessor, respectively. Also assume that both the lessee and the lessor are on a calendar-year basis and that the lessee is aware of the lessor's implicit interest rate.

**Instructions:**

1. Give all entries required on the books of Dannell to record the lease of equipment from Crosby for the year 1993. The depreciation on owned equipment is computed once a year on the straight-line basis.
2. Give entries required on the books of Crosby to record the lease of equipment to Dannell for the year 1993.
3. Prepare the balance sheet section involving lease balances for both the lessee's and lessor's financial statements at December 31, 1993.
4. Determine the amount of expense Dannell will report relative to the lease for 1993 and the amount of revenue Crosby will report for the same period.

## Problem 20—11   (Accounting for leases—lessee and lessor with third-party guarantee)

Atwater Equipment Co. manufactures, sells, and leases heavy construction equipment. England Construction Company, a regular customer, leased equipment on July 1, 1993, that had cost Atwater $252,000 to manufacture. The lease payments are $63,161 beginning on July 1, 1993, and continuing annually, with the last payment being made on July 1, 1997. If England were to purchase the equipment outright, the fair market value would be $291,881. Because of the heavy wear expected on construction equipment, the lease contains a guaranteed residual value clause wherein the lessee guarantees a residual value on June 30, 1998, of $65,000. England contracted with Weathertop Financial Services to serve as a third-party guarantor of the residual value. Atwater's implicit interest rate is 12%, which is lower than England's incremental borrowing rate of 14%.

**Instructions:**

1. Assuming that the equipment reverts to Atwater upon completion of the lease term and that the equipment has an expected useful life of 10 years, prepare the entries that should be made on the books of both Atwater and England in recording the lease on July 1, 1993.

2. Prepare the journal entries that should be made by Atwater and England on July 1, 1994.
3. What financial statement disclosure would be made by Weathertop in its role as a third-party guarantor?

## Problem 20—12   (Accounting for lease—lessee and lessor)

Astle Manufacturing Company manufactures and leases a variety of items. On January 2, 1993, Astle leased a piece of equipment to Haws Industries Co. The lease is for 6 years with an annual amount of $33,500, payable in advance. The lease payment includes executory costs of $1,500 per year. The equipment has an estimated useful life of 9 years, and it was manufactured by Astle at a cost of $120,000. It is estimated that the equipment will have a residual value of $60,000 at the end of the 6-year lease term. There is no provision for purchase or renewal by Haws at the end of the lease term, however, a third party has guaranteed the residual value of $60,000. The equipment has a fair market value at the lease inception of $187,176. The implicit rate of interest in the contract is 10%, the same rate at which Haws can borrow money at its bank. All lease payments after the first one are made on December 31 of each year. Both companies use the straight-line method of depreciation.

### Instructions:

1. Give all the entries relating to the lease on the books of the lessor and lessee for 1993.
2. Show how the lease would appear on the balance sheet of Astle Manufacturing Company and Haws Industries Co. (if applicable) as of December 31, 1993.
3. Assume Astle sold the equipment at the end of the 6-year lease for $70,000. Give the entry to record the sale assuming all lease entries have been properly made.

## Problem 20—13   (Cash flow treatment of capital leases—lessor)

The following information relates to a capital lease between Bradshaw Electric Co. (lessee) and Smoot Manufacturing Inc. (lessor). The lease term began on January 1, 1993. Smoot recorded the lease as a sale and made the following entries related to the lease during 1993. Assume this was the only lease Smoot had during the year.

| | | | | |
|---|---|---|---:|---:|
| Jan. | 1 | Deferred Initial Costs | 4,000 | |
| | | Cash | | 4,000 |
| | 1 | Lease Payments Receivable | 133,156 | |
| | | Cost of Goods Sold | 65,000 | |
| | | Finished Goods Inventory | | 61,000 |
| | | Deferred Initial Costs | | 4,000 |
| | | Sales | | 90,000 |
| | | Unearned Interest Revenue | | 43,156 |
| | 1 | Cash | 13,316 | |
| | | Lease Payments Receivable | | 13,316 |
| Dec. 31 | | Cash | 13,316 | |
| | | Lease Payments Receivable | | 13,316 |
| | 31 | Unearned Interest Revenue | 7,666 | |
| | | Interest Revenue | | 7,666 |

### Instructions:

1. Prepare a partial statement of cash flows for 1993 for Smoot Manufacturing Inc. under the indirect method. Assume Smoot reported net income of $132,666 inclusive of the lease revenue in the above entries.
2. Prepare the partial operating activities section of the statement of cash flows for 1993 for Smoot Manufacturing Inc. under the direct method. Assume that cash provided by operating activities exclusive of the lease transactions is $100,000.

### Problem 20—14   (Disclosure requirements—operating leases)

Jaquar Mining and Manufacturing Company leases from Emory Leasing Company three machines under the following terms:

Machine #1   Lease period—10 years, beginning April 1, 1988.
             Lease payment—$18,000 per year, payable in advance.
Machine #2   Lease period—10 years, beginning July 1, 1992.
             Lease payment—$30,000 per year, payable in advance.
Machine #3   Lease period—15 years, beginning January 1, 1993.
             Lease payment—$12,500 per year, payable in advance.

All of the leases are classified as operating leases.

**Instructions:**   Prepare the note to the 1994 financial statements that would be required to disclose the lease commitments of Jaquar Mining and Manufacturing Company. Jaquar uses the calendar year as its accounting period.

### Problem 20—15   (Sale-leaseback of a building)

On January 3, 1993, Juniper Inc. sold a building with a book value of $1,800,000 to Cedarcrest Industries for $1,757,340. Juniper immediately entered into a leasing agreement whereby Juniper would lease the building back for an annual payment of $260,000. The term of the lease is 10 years, the expected remaining useful life of the building. The first annual lease payment is to be made immediately, and future payments will be made on January 1 of each succeeding year. Cedarcrest's implicit interest rate is 10%.

**Instructions:**

1. Prepare the journal entries that should be made by both Juniper and Cedarcrest on January 3, 1993, relating to this sale-leaseback transaction.
2. Prepare the journal entries that should be made by both parties at the end of 1993 to accrue interest and to amortize the leased building. (Assume a salvage value of $0 and use of the straight-line method.)

# CHAPTER 21

# Accounting Changes and Error Corrections

---

**CHAPTER TOPICS**

**Change in Accounting Estimate**

**Change in Accounting Principle**

**Change in Reporting Entity**

**Accounting for Error Corrections**

---

In 1988, Blockbuster Entertainment, a national video rental chain, changed the amortization period for its videotapes. The change, from 9 months to 36 months, added nearly 20% to Blockbuster's reported net income. The stock market considered this and other liberal accounting policies used by Blockbuster, and the result was a $226 million drop in market value.

As the Blockbuster experience illustrates, the financial statements of companies sometimes report significantly different results from year to year. This may be due to changes in economic circumstances as reflected in the statements. But it may also be due to changes in accounting methods or to corrections of errors in recording past transactions.

Changing the accounting methods used can have a dramatic impact on the financial statements of a company. Because of this impact, one can argue that accounting changes detract from the informational characteristics of *comparability* and *consistency* discussed in Chapter 2. So why are these accounting changes made? The main reasons for such changes may be summarized as follows:

1. A company, as a result of experience or new information, may change its estimates of revenues or expenses, for example, the estimate of uncollectible accounts receivable, or the estimated service lives of depreciable assets.

2. Due to changes in economic conditions, companies may need to change methods of accounting to more clearly reflect the current economic situation.
3. Accounting standard-setting bodies may require the use of a new accounting method or principle, such as new reporting requirements for income taxes.
4. The acquisition or divestiture of companies, which was particularly prevalent in the 1980s, may cause a change in the reporting entity.
5. Management may be pressured to report profitable performance. Making accounting changes can often result in higher net income, thereby reflecting favorably on management.

Whatever the reason, accountants must keep the primary qualitative characteristic of *usefulness* in mind. They must determine if the reasons for accounting changes are appropriate, and then how best to report the changes to facilitate understanding of the financial statements.

The detection of errors in accounting for past transactions presents a similar problem. The errors must be corrected and appropriate disclosures made so that the readers of the financial statements will clearly understand what has happened. The purpose of this chapter is to discuss the different types of accounting changes and error corrections and the appropriate accounting procedures that should be used.

## ACCOUNTING CHANGES

The accounting profession has identified three main categories of accounting changes:[1]

1. Change in accounting estimate
2. Change in accounting principle
3. Change in reporting entity

As pointed out in Chapter 1, a major objective of published financial statements is to provide users with information to help them predict, compare, and evaluate future earning power and cash flows of the reporting entity. When a reporting entity adjusts its past estimates of revenues earned or costs incurred, changes its accounting principles from one method to another, or changes its nature as a reporting entity, it becomes more difficult for a user to predict the future from past historical statements. The basic accounting issue is whether accounting changes should be reported as adjustments of the prior periods' statements, and thus increase their comparability with the current and future statements, or whether the changes should affect only the current and future years.

Several alternatives have been suggested for reporting accounting changes.

1. Restate the financial statements presented for prior periods to reflect the effect of the change. Adjust the beginning retained earnings balance for the current period for the cumulative effect of the change.
2. Make no adjustment to statements presented for prior periods. Report the cumulative effect of the change in the current year as a direct entry to Retained Earnings.
3. Same as (2), except report the cumulative effect of the change as a special item in the income statement instead of directly to Retained Earnings.
4. Report the cumulative effect in the current year as in (3), but also present limited pro forma information for all prior periods included in the financial statements reporting "what might have been" if the change had been made in the prior years.

---

[1]*Opinions of the Accounting Principles Board, No. 20, "Accounting Changes"* (New York: American Institute of Certified Public Accountants, 1971).

5. Make the change effective only for current and future periods with no catch-up adjustment.

Each of these methods for reporting an accounting change has been used by companies in the past, and arguments can be made for each of the various approaches. For example, some accountants argue that accounting principles should be applied consistently for all reported periods. Therefore, if a new accounting principle is used in the current period, the financial statements presented for prior periods should be restated so that the results shown for all reported periods are based on the same accounting principles. Other accountants contend that restating financial statements may dilute public confidence in those statements. Principles applied in earlier periods were presumably appropriate at that time and should be considered final. The only exception would be for changes in a reporting entity. In addition, restating financial statements is costly, requires considerable effort, and is sometimes impossible due to lack of data.

Because of the diversity of practice and the resulting difficulty in user understandability of the financial statements, the Accounting Principles Board issued Opinion No. 20. The Board's objective was to bring increased uniformity to reporting practice. Evidence of compromise exists in the final opinion, as the Board attempted to reflect both its desire to increase comparability of financial statements and to improve user confidence in published financial statements. Depending on the type of accounting change, different accounting treatment is required, as explained in the following sections.

## Change in Accounting Estimate

Contrary to what many people believe, accounting information cannot always be measured and reported precisely. Also, to be reported on a timely basis for decision making, accounting data often must be based on estimates of future events. The financial statements incorporate these estimates, which are based on the best professional judgment given the information available at that time. At a later date, however, additional experience or new facts sometimes make it clear that the estimates need to be revised to more accurately reflect the existing business circumstances. When this happens, a change in accounting estimate occurs.

Examples of areas where changes in accounting estimates often are needed include:

1. Uncollectible receivables
2. Useful lives of depreciable or intangible assets
3. Residual values for depreciable assets
4. Warranty obligations
5. Quantities of mineral reserves to be depleted
6. Actuarial assumptions for pensions or other postemployment benefits
7. Number of periods benefited by deferred costs

Accounting for a change in estimate has already been discussed in Chapter 4 and throughout the text in areas where changes in estimates are common. By way of review, all changes in estimates should be reflected either in the current period or in current and future periods. No retroactive adjustments or pro forma statements are to be prepared for a change in accounting estimate. Changes in estimates are considered to be part of the normal accounting process and not corrections or changes of past periods.

However, disclosures such as the one in Exhibit 21—1, reported by Baker-Hughes Incorporated, are useful in helping readers of financial statements understand the impact of changes in estimates.

**Exhibit 21—1    Baker-Hughes Incorporated—Disclosure of Change in Estimate**

BAKER-HUGHES INCORPORATED

*NOTES TO CONSOLIDATED FINANCIAL STATEMENTS*

*Five—Change in Accounting Estimate:*
During 1989, the Company revised the estimated remaining useful lives of certain rental tools and equipment to more closely reflect expected remaining lives. The effect of this change in accounting estimate resulted in an increase in the Company's income before extraordinary item of $2,220,000, or $.02 per common share, and net income of $2,822,000, or $.02 per common share, for 1989.

## Change in Accounting Principle

A change in accounting principle involves a change from one generally accepted principle or method to another.[2] A change in principle, as defined in APB Opinion No. 20, does not include the initial adoption of an accounting principle as a result of transactions or events that had not occurred (or were immaterial) in previous periods. Also, a change from a principle that is not generally accepted to one that is generally accepted is considered to be an error correction rather than a change in accounting principle.

If an asset is affected by both a change in principle and a change in estimate during the same period, APB Opinion No. 20 requires that the change be treated as a change in estimate rather than a change in principle.[3] For example, if a company changes its depreciation method at the same time it recognizes a change in estimated asset life, this would involve both a change in method and a change in estimate. According to APB Opinion No. 20, such circumstances would be treated as a change in estimate.

As indicated in previous chapters, companies may select among alternative accounting principles to account for business transactions. For example, for financial reporting purposes, a company may depreciate its buildings and equipment using the straight-line depreciation method, the double-declining-balance method, the sum-of-the-years-digits method, or any other consistent and rational allocation procedure. Long-term construction contracts may be accounted for by the percentage-of-completion or the completed-contract method. Inventory may be accounted for using FIFO, LIFO, or other acceptable methods. These alternative methods are often equally available to a given company, but in most instances, criteria for selection among the methods are inadequate. As a result, companies have found it rather easy to justify changing from one accounting principle or method to another.

**Current Recognition of Cumulative Effect of Change in Principle**    The APB concluded that, in general, companies should not change their accounting principles from one period to the next. "Consistent use of accounting principles from one period to another enhances the utility of financial statements to users by facilitating analysis and understanding of comparative accounting data."[4] A company may change its accounting principles, however, if it can justify a change because of a new pronouncement by the authoritative accounting standard-setting body or because of a change in its economic

---

[2]The classification "change in accounting principle" includes changes in methods used to account for transactions. No attempt was made by the APB in Opinion No. 20 to distinguish between a principle and a method.

[3]*Opinions of the Accounting Principles Board, No. 20,* par. 32.

[4]*Ibid.,* par. 15.

circumstances. Just what constitutes an acceptable change in economic circumstances is not clear. It presumably could include a change in the competitive structure of an industry, a significant change in the rate of inflation in the economy, a change resulting from government restrictions due to economic or political crisis, and so forth.

In general, the effect of a change from one accepted accounting principle to another is reflected by **reporting the cumulative effect of the change in the income statement** in the period of the change. This cumulative adjustment is shown as a separate item on the income statement after extraordinary items and before net income.[5] When a change in accounting principle occurs, the financial statements for all prior periods reported for comparative purposes with the current-year financial statements are presented as previously reported. To enhance trend analysis, however, pro forma information also is required to reflect the income before extraordinary items and net income that would have been reported if the new accounting principle had been in effect for the respective prior years. Pro forma earnings per share figures also should be reported.

To illustrate the general treatment of a change in accounting principle, assume Telstar Company, a high-power telescope sales and manufacturing firm, elected in 1993 to change from the double-declining-balance (DDB) method of depreciation to the straight-line method to make its financial reporting more consistent with the majority of its competitors. For tax purposes, assume Telstar had elected to use the straight-line method and will continue to do so. Assume further that Telstar presents comparative income statements for three years, and that the past difference in book and tax depreciation is the only difference in accounting treatment impacting Telstar's financial and taxable income.

These and other assumptions are necessary because, in most instances, a change in accounting principle involves temporary differences between book and tax income, creating the need for interperiod tax allocation. In this chapter, including the end-of-chapter material, the impact of income tax either is ignored or the assumed amounts are provided to simplify the illustrations and focus on the effects of accounting changes and error corrections.

For Telstar, the change to straight-line depreciation for reporting purposes means that tax and book depreciation will be the same in future years. It is assumed, however, that the greater depreciation charged on the books in prior years, as compared to the tax depreciation taken, resulted in a previously recorded deferred tax asset. This and other relevant information for Telstar are presented below.

| Year | Double-Declining-Balance Depreciation | Straight-Line Depreciation | Depreciation Difference | Assumed Tax Effects | Effects on Income (Net of Taxes) |
|---|---|---|---|---|---|
| Prior to 1991 | $163,000 | $ 90,000 | $ 73,000 | $21,900 | $51,100 |
| 1991 | 60,000 | 32,000 | 28,000 | 8,400 | 19,600 |
| 1992 | 65,000 | 35,000 | 30,000 | 9,000 | 21,000 |
| | $288,000 | $157,000 | $131,000 | $39,300 | $91,700 |

The data indicate that depreciation expense for the years prior to 1993 would have been $131,000 ($288,000 − $157,000) less if the straight-line method had been used. Thus, income would have been $131,000 higher, less the applicable assumed income taxes of

[5]IBM Corporation's financial statements (see Appendix A) illustrate the reporting and disclosure of the corporation's adoption of FASB Statement No. 96, "Accounting for Income Taxes." The cumulative effect of this change in accounting principle was reflected in the 1988 income statement along with appropriate note disclosure.

$39,300. Based on these data, the journal entry to record the cumulative effect adjustment and to eliminate the previously recorded deferred tax asset is as follows:

| | | |
|---|---:|---:|
| Accumulated Depreciation ................................. | 131,000 | |
|     Deferred Tax Asset ...................................... | | 39,300 |
|     Cumulative Effect of Change in Accounting Principle........ | | 91,700 |

The $131,000 debit to Accumulated Depreciation represents the excess depreciation charged to the books in prior years. The $39,300 credit would eliminate the previously established deferred tax asset amount. The $91,700 after-tax cumulative effect would be reported in the income statement for 1993, the year of the change.

Continuing the Telstar example, assume that net income for the two preceding years as originally reported was $450,000 in 1991 and $500,000 in 1992, and that all net income in both years was from continuing operations. Using the new depreciation method, in 1993 Telstar reported $560,000 income from continuing operations and an extraordinary gain of $70,000 net of income taxes of $30,000. Following is a partial income statement for 1993 with comparative information for 1992 and 1991.

**Telstar Company**
**Partial Comparative Income Statement**
**For Years Ended December 31**

| | 1993 | 1992 | 1991 |
|---|---:|---:|---:|
| Income from continuing operations ........... | $560,000 | $500,000 | $450,000 |
| Extraordinary gain (net of income taxes of $30,000) ..................................... | 70,000 | | |
| Cumulative effect on prior years of change in accounting principle—change to the straight-line method of depreciation from double-declining-balance method (net of income taxes of $39,300)................................... | 91,700 | | |
| Net income ............................. | $721,700 | $500,000 | $450,000 |

Note that in 1993 the cumulative effect is shown net of tax and as a separate item after the extraordinary item. As explained in Chapter 4, all below-the-line items, such as extraordinary gains or losses and the cumulative effect of a change in accounting principle, are to be reported net of related income taxes. This is referred to as **intraperiod tax allocation**. With this disclosure technique, the appropriate amount of income taxes is associated with income from continuing operations and with the individual below-the-line items reported separately. Also note that the amounts of income from continuing operations for the two prior years are presented as originally reported. In addition, the disclosure of pro forma (as if) income for the prior years is required and would be shown on the face of the income statement (using the assumed data) as follows:

**Pro Forma Income Data**

| | 1992 | 1991 |
|---|---:|---:|
| Net income from continuing operations as previously reported ....................................................... | $500,000 | $450,000 |
| Effect of change in accounting principle (net of tax)........ | 21,000 | 19,600 |
| Pro forma income (restated) ........................... | $521,000 | $469,600 |

Pro forma earnings per share amounts reflecting the revised income figures also would be presented.

In a few cases, past records are inadequate to prepare pro forma statements for individual years. This fact should be disclosed when applicable. For example, a change to the LIFO method of inventory valuation is usually made effective with the beginning inventory in the year of change rather than with some prior year, because of the difficulty in identifying prior-year layers or dollar-value pools. Thus, the beginning inventory in the year of change becomes the same as the previous inventory valued using another costing method, and this becomes the base LIFO layer. No cumulative effect adjustment is required.

**Restatement of Prior Periods for Change in Principle**    If a change in accounting principle is caused by a new pronouncement by an authoritative accounting body, the cumulative effect may be reported retroactively or currently, depending on the instructions contained in the pronouncement. The APB generally favors the reporting procedures described in the previous section, i.e., current recognition of the cumulative effect. However, the Board identified the following four specific changes as being of such a nature that the "advantages of retroactive treatment in prior-period reports outweigh the disadvantages."[6]

1. A change from LIFO method of inventory pricing to another method.
2. A change in the method of accounting for long-term construction contracts.
3. A change to or from the "full cost" method of accounting used in extractive industries.
4. Changes made at the time of an initial distribution of company stock.[7]

In addition to these exceptions, several FASB statements also require retroactive restatement.

In those cases where retroactive restatement is required, the cumulative effect of the change is recorded directly as an adjustment to the beginning retained earnings balance for the earliest year presented. Income statement data reported for comparative purposes also must be adjusted to reflect the new principle.

To illustrate the procedures required for restatement, assume that in 1993 the Forester Company changed from the LIFO inventory costing method to the FIFO method for both financial reporting and income tax purposes. There are no deferred tax consequences because both the old and new methods apply to both financial and tax reporting. However, additional taxes will be payable for prior years as a result of the change in inventory method used for tax purposes. The following data are applicable, and a tax rate of 30% is assumed for all years.

| Year | Pretax Income FIFO | Pretax Income LIFO | Pretax Income Difference | Income Tax Effect (30%) | Effect on Income (Net of Tax) |
|---|---|---|---|---|---|
| Prior to 1991 | $190,000 | $160,000 | $30,000 | $ 9,000 | $21,000 |
| 1991 | 110,000 | 75,000 | 35,000 | 10,500 | 24,500 |
| 1992 | 120,000 | 100,000 | 20,000 | 6,000 | 14,000 |
| Totals—beginning of 1993 | $420,000 | $335,000 | $85,000 | $25,500 | $59,500 |
| 1993 results | $125,000 | $100,000 | $25,000 | $ 7,500 | $17,500 |

[6]*Opinions of the Accounting Principles Board, No. 20,* par. 27.

[7]This exception is available only once for a company, and it may be used for (a) obtaining additional equity capital from investors, (b) effecting business combinations, or (c) registering securities, whenever a company first issues financial statements. *Ibid.,* par. 29.

## The Change From FIFO to LIFO

In 1974, more firms switched their inventory to LIFO than in any other year. As noted in Chapter 10, if LIFO is used for tax purposes, it must also be used for financial reporting purposes. In periods of rising prices, as was the case in 1974, LIFO results in a lower reported net income figure for both financial and tax purposes. Thus, the use of LIFO can result in significant tax savings.

Given these potential savings, one author wondered why more firms didn't switch. Professor Gary Biddle examined 105 firms that did not switch to LIFO during 1974 and estimated that those firms paid, on average, $12 million each in additional taxes simply because they used FIFO rather than LIFO. He concludes by stating, "It is puzzling why so many firms in so many industries have continued to use FIFO."

### Questions:

1. *If inventory costing $100 is purchased by a firm, how much is paid for that inventory if the FIFO inventory method is used? How much if the LIFO method is used?*
2. *Why might firms elect not to switch to LIFO given the tax savings they could receive?*
3. *How is a change to LIFO reported in the financial statements?*

Source:    Gary Biddle, "Paying FIFO Taxes: Your Favorite Charity," *The Wall Street Journal*, January 19, 1981, p. 18.

The entry in 1993 to record the prior-period effects of the change in accounting principle would be:

```
Inventory ..............................................   85,000
    Income Taxes Payable ...................................           25,500
    Retained Earnings ......................................           59,500
```

The $85,000 debit to Inventory adjusts the beginning 1993 inventory to its FIFO cost. The $59,500 reflects the after-tax effect on cost of goods sold in years prior to 1993. Cost of goods sold would have been lower using FIFO and pretax income would have been higher, resulting in additional taxes of $25,500. Assumed comparative income statement data, restated for 1992 and 1991, would be presented as follows:

### Forester Company
### Partial Comparative Income Statement
### For Years Ended December 31

|  | 1993 | 1992 | 1991 |
|---|---|---|---|
| Income before income taxes................. | $125,000 | $120,000 | $110,000 |
| Income taxes (30%)........................ | 37,500 | 36,000 | 33,000 |
| Net income ............................... | $ 87,500 | $ 84,000 | $ 77,000 |
| Earnings per share (10,000 shares outstanding) | $8.75 | $8.40 | $7.70 |

The adjustment for the cumulative effect of the change in principle would be reported in Forester Company's statement of retained earnings. Assuming a beginning retained earnings balance in 1991 of $351,000 and no dividends, a comparative retained earnings statement would appear as shown on page 804.

**Forester Company**
**Comparative Statement of Retained Earnings**
**For Years Ended December 31**

|  | 1993 | 1992 | 1991 |
|---|---|---|---|
| Retained earnings at beginning of year, as previously reported | $473,500 | $403,500 | $351,000 |
| Add adjustment for cumulative effect on prior years of retroactively applying the FIFO method of inventory costing (see Note A) | 59,500 | 45,500 | 21,000 |
| Adjusted retained earnings, beginning of year | $533,000 | $449,000 | $372,000 |
| Net income | 87,500 | 84,000 | 77,000 |
| Retained earnings, end of year | $620,500 | $533,000 | $449,000 |

**Note A** Change in Accounting Principle
Forester Company has changed its inventory costing method from last-in, first-out (LIFO) to first-in, first-out (FIFO), effective January 1, 1993. The new inventory method was adopted to better reflect company earnings and inventory values. The financial statements have been restated to apply the new method retroactively. Because income tax laws permit the use of LIFO for tax purposes only if it is also used for financial reporting, the FIFO method has also been adopted for income tax reporting. As a result, an additional tax liability of $25,500 was incurred for years prior to 1993. The effect of the accounting change on income in 1993 (net of taxes of $7,500) was an increase of $17,500, or $1.75 per share. The net-of-tax effect in 1992 was an increase of $14,000, and in 1991, an increase of $24,500. The retained earnings balances for 1993, 1992, and 1991 have been adjusted to reflect the cumulative effect of retroactively applying the new method of inventory costing, net of applicable taxes.

Note that no pro forma information is required with the retroactive approach, because the statements for prior years are restated directly. If prior-year income statements cannot be presented because of inadequate data, that fact should be disclosed. Under those circumstances, the cumulative effect would be reported only in the retained earnings statement.

### Change in Reporting Entity

Companies sometimes change their structures or report their operations in such a way that the financial statements are, in effect, those of a different reporting entity. Specifically, a change in reporting entity includes: (a) presenting consolidated or combined statements in place of statements of individual companies; (b) changing specific subsidiaries comprising the group of companies for which consolidated statements are presented; (c) changing the companies included in combined financial statements; and (d) a business combination accounted for as a pooling of interests.[8]

Because of the basic objective of comparability, the APB required that financial statements be adjusted retroactively to disclose what the statements would have looked like if the current entity had been in existence in the prior years.

Thus, previous years' financial statements presented for comparison with the current year (the year of change) must be restated to reflect results of operations, financial condition, and cash flows as if the current reporting entity had been in existence in those years. Also, in the period of the change, the financial statements should disclose the nature of, and reasons for, the change, as illustrated in the note included in ALCO Standard Corporation's 1989 annual report, as shown on page 805.

The statements also should disclose the effect of the change on income from continuing operations, net income, and the related earnings per share amounts for all periods presented. Subsequent years' statements do not need to repeat the disclosure.[9] Changes in reporting entities are covered in more depth in advanced accounting texts.

[8]*Ibid.*, par. 12.
[9]*Ibid.*, par. 35.

**Exhibit 21—2    ALCO Standard Corporation—Disclosure of Change in Reporting Entity**

ALCO STANDARD CORPORATION

*NOTES TO CONSOLIDATED FINANCIAL STATEMENTS*

*1 (In Part): Summary of Accounting Policies*

*Consolidation*

All subsidiaries are consolidated and intercompany transactions have been eliminated. The Company adopted Statement of Financial Accounting Standards (SFAS) No. 94 in 1989 and consolidated its wholly-owned finance subsidiaries which were previously accounted for using the equity method. This change in accounting policy was applied retroactively and had no effect on shareholders' equity or net income for any of the years presented. The combined results of the finance subsidiaries' operations included in the Company's consolidated net income were income (loss) of $(326,000) in 1989, $(206,000) in 1988, and $61,000 in 1987. The separate subsidiaries were merged as of September 30, 1989. The surviving finance subsidiary's assets, disclosed in the accompanying balance sheets, exclude intercompany receivables of $13,570,000 in 1989 and $14,658,000 in 1988.

## ERROR CORRECTIONS

Error corrections are not considered accounting changes, but their treatment is specified in APB Opinion No. 20 and reaffirmed in FASB Statement No. 16.[10] In effect, accounting errors made in prior years that have not already been "counterbalanced" or reversed are reported as prior-period adjustments and recorded directly to Retained Earnings. Examples of errors include mathematical mistakes, improper application of accounting principles, or omissions of material facts.

### Kinds of Errors

There are a number of different kinds of errors. Some errors are discovered in the period in which they are made, and these are easily corrected. Others may not be discovered currently and are reflected on the financial statements until discovered. Some errors are never discovered; however, the effects of these errors may be counterbalanced in subsequent periods, and after this takes place, account balances are again accurately stated. Errors may be classified as follows:

1. **Errors discovered currently in the course of normal accounting procedures.** Examples of this type of error are clerical errors, such as an addition error, posting to the wrong account, misstating an account, or omitting an account from the trial balance. These types of errors usually are detected during the regular summarizing process of the accounting cycle and are readily corrected.

2. **Errors limited to balance sheet accounts.** Examples include debiting Marketable Securities instead of Notes Receivable, crediting Interest Payable instead of Notes Payable, or crediting Interest Payable instead of Salaries Payable. Another example is not recording the exchange of convertible bonds for stock. Such errors are frequently discovered and corrected in the period in which they are made. When such errors are

---

[10]*Statement of Financial Accounting Standards No. 16,* "Prior-Period Adjustments" (Stamford: Financial Accounting Standards Board, 1977), p. 5.

not found until a subsequent period, corrections must be made at that time and balance sheet data subsequently restated for comparative reporting purposes.

3. **Errors limited to income statement accounts.** The examples and correcting procedures for this type of error are similar to those in (2). For example, Office Salaries may be debited instead of Sales Salaries. This type of error should be corrected as soon as it is discovered. Even though the error would not affect net income, the misstated accounts should be restated for analysis purposes and comparative reporting.

4. **Errors affecting both income statement accounts and balance sheet accounts.** Certain errors, when not discovered currently, result in the misstatement of net income and thus affect both the income statement accounts and the balance sheet accounts. The balance sheet accounts are carried into the succeeding period; hence, an error made currently and not detected will affect earnings of the future. Such errors may be classified into two groups:

   (a) **Errors in net income that, when not detected, are automatically counterbalanced in the following fiscal period.** Net income amounts on the income statements for two successive periods are inaccurately stated; certain account balances on the balance sheet at the end of the first period are inaccurately stated, but the account balances in the balance sheet at the end of the succeeding period are accurately stated. In this class are errors such as the misstatement of inventories and the omission of adjustments for prepaid and accrued items at the end of the period.

   (b) **Errors in net income that, when not detected, are not automatically counterbalanced in the following fiscal period.** Account balances on successive balance sheets are inaccurately stated until such time as entries are made compensating for or correcting the errors. In this class are errors such as the recognition of capital expenditures as revenue expenditures and the omission of charges for depreciation and amortization.

When errors affecting income are discovered, careful analysis is necessary to determine the required action to correct the account balances. As indicated, most errors will be caught and corrected prior to closing the books. The few material errors not detected until subsequent periods and those that have not already been counterbalanced must be treated as prior-period adjustments.

The following sections describe and illustrate the procedures to be applied when error corrections require prior-period adjustments. It is assumed that each of the errors is material. Errors that are discovered usually affect the income tax liability for a prior period. Amended tax returns are usually prepared either to claim a refund or to pay any additional tax assessment. For simplicity, the examples on the following pages and the exercises and problems ignore the income tax effects of errors.

## Illustrative Example of Error Correction

Assume the Hiedleberg Co. began operations at the beginning of 1991. An auditing firm is engaged for the first time in 1993. Before the accounts are adjusted and closed for 1993, the auditor reviews the books and accounts and discovers the errors summarized on pages 808 and 809. Effects of these errors on the financial statements, before any correcting entries, are indicated as follows: a plus sign ( + ) indicates an overstatement; a minus sign ( − ) indicates an understatement. Each error correction is discussed in the following paragraphs.

**(1) Understatement of Merchandise Inventory**    It is discovered that the merchandise inventory as of December 31, 1991, was understated by $1,000. The effects of the misstatement were as follows:

| Income Statement | Balance Sheet |
|---|---|
| **1991:** Cost of goods sold overstated (ending inventory too low)<br>Net income understated | Assets understated (inventory too low)<br>Retained earnings understated |
| **1992:** Cost of goods sold understated (beginning inventory too low)<br>Net income overstated | Balance sheet items not affected, retained earnings understatement for 1991 being corrected by net income overstatement for 1992 |

Since this type of error counterbalances after two years, no correcting entry is required in 1993.

If the error had been discovered in 1992 instead of 1993, an entry would have been made to correct the account balances so that operations for 1992 would be reported accurately. The beginning inventory for 1992 would have been increased by $1,000, the amount of the asset understatement and Retained Earnings would have been credited for this amount, representing the income understatement in 1991. The correcting entry in 1992 would have been:

| | | |
|---|---|---|
| Merchandise Inventory ...................................... | 1,000 | |
| Retained Earnings ......................................... | | 1,000 |

**(2) Failure to Record Merchandise Purchases**    It is discovered that purchase invoices as of December 28, 1991, for $850 were not recorded until 1992. The goods were included in the inventory at the end of 1991. The effects of failure to record the purchases were as follows:

| Income Statement | Balance Sheet |
|---|---|
| **1991:** Cost of goods sold understated (purchases too low)<br>Net income overstated | Liabilities understated (accounts payable too low)<br>Retained earnings overstated |
| **1992:** Cost of goods sold overstated (purchases too high)<br>Net income understated | Balance sheet items not affected, retained earnings overstatement for 1991 being corrected by net income understatement for 1992 |

Since this is a counterbalancing error, no correcting entry is required in 1993.

If the error had been discovered in 1992 instead of 1993, a correcting entry would have been necessary. In 1992, Purchases was debited and Accounts Payable credited for $850 for merchandise acquired in 1991 and included in the ending inventory of 1991. Retained Earnings would have to be debited for $850, representing the net income overstatement for 1991, and Purchases would have to be credited for the same amount to reduce the purchases balance in 1992. The correcting entry in 1992 would have been:

| | | |
|---|---|---|
| Retained Earnings ............................................. | 850 | |
| Purchases ................................................... | | 850 |

Analysis Sheet to Show Effects

| | At End of 1991 | | | | |
|---|---|---|---|---|---|
| | Income Statement | | Balance Sheet | | |
| | Section | Net Income | Section | | Retained Earnings |
| (1) Understatement of merchandise inventory of $1,000 on December 31,1991. | Cost of Goods Sold     + | − | Current Assets     − | | − |
| (2) Failure to record merchandise purchases on account of $850 in 1991; purchases were recorded in 1992. | Cost of Goods Sold     − | + | Current Liabilities  − | | + |
| (3) Failure to record merchandise sales on account of $1,800 in 1992. (It is assumed that the sales for 1992 were recognized as revenue in 1993.) | | | | | |
| (4) Failure to record accrued sales salaries of $450 on December 31, 1991; expense was recognized when payment was made. | Selling Expense     − | + | Current Liabilities  − | | + |
| (5) Failure to record prepaid taxes of $275 on December 31, 1991; amount was included in Miscellaneous General Expense. | General Expense     + | − | Current Assets     − | | − |
| (6) Failure to record accrued interest on notes receivable of $150 on December 31, 1991; revenue was recognized when collected in 1992. | Other Revenue     − | − | Current Assets     − | | − |
| (7) Failure to record unearned service fees of $225 on December 31, 1992; amounts received were included in Miscellaneous Revenue. | | | | | |
| (8) Failure to record depreciation of delivery equipment. On December 31, 1991, $1,200. | Selling Expense     − | + | Noncurrent Assets     + | | + |
| On December 31, 1992, $1,200. | | | | | |

**(3) Failure to Record Merchandise Sales**    It is discovered that sales on account for the last week of December 1992 for $1,800 were not recorded until 1993. The goods sold were not included in the inventory at the end of 1992. The effects of the failure to report the revenue in 1992 were:

| Income Statement | Balance Sheet |
|---|---|
| **1992:**    Revenue understated (sales too low) | Assets understated (accounts receivable too low) |
| Net income understated | Retained earnings understated |

When the error is discovered in 1993, Sales is debited for $1,800 and Retained Earnings is credited for this amount, representing the net income understatement for 1992. The following entry is made:

| | | |
|---|---|---|
| Sales . . . . . . . . . . . . . . . . . . . . . . . . . . . . . . . . . . . . . . . . . . . | 1,800 | |
| Retained Earnings . . . . . . . . . . . . . . . . . . . . . . . . . . . . . . . . . . | | 1,800 |

of Errors on Financial Statements

| At End of 1992 | | | | At End of 1993 | | | |
| Income Statement | | Balance Sheet | | Income Statement | | Balance Sheet | |
| Section | Net Income | Section | Retained Earnings | Section | Net Income | Section | Retained Earnings |
|---|---|---|---|---|---|---|---|
| Cost of Goods Sold − | + | | | | | | |
| Cost of Goods Sold + | − | | | | | | |
| Sales − | − | Accounts Receivable − | − | Sales + | + | | |
| Selling Expense + | − | | | | | | |
| General Expense − | + | | | | | | |
| Other Revenue + | + | | | | | | |
| Other Revenue + | + | Current Liabilities − | + | Other Revenue − | − | | |
| | | Noncurrent Assets + | + | | | Noncurrent Assets + | + |
| Selling Expense − | + | Noncurrent Assets + | + | | | Noncurrent Assets + | + |

**(4) Failure to Record Accrued Expense** Accrued sales salaries of $450 as of December 31, 1991, were overlooked in adjusting the accounts. Sales Salaries is debited for salary payments. The effects of the failure to record the accrued expense of $450 as of December 31, 1991, were as follows:

| | Income Statement | Balance Sheet |
|---|---|---|
| **1991:** | Expenses understated (sales salaries too low) Net income overstated | Liabilities understated (accrued salaries not reported) Retained earnings overstated |
| **1992:** | Expenses overstated (sales salaries too high) Net income understated | Balance sheet items not affected, retained earnings overstatement for 1991 being corrected by net income understatement for 1992 |

No entry is required in 1993 to correct the accounts for the failure to record the accrued expense at the end of 1991, the misstatement in 1991 having been counterbalanced by the misstatement in 1992. If the error had been discovered in 1992, an entry would have been required to correct the accounts for the failure to record the accrued expense at the end of 1991 if the net income for 1992 is not to be misstated. If accrued expenses are to be properly recorded at the end of 1992, Retained Earnings would be debited for $450, representing the net income overstatement for 1991, and Sales Salaries would be credited for the same amount, representing the amount to be subtracted from salary payments in 1992. The correcting entry made in 1992 would be:

| | | |
|---|---|---|
| Retained Earnings | 450 | |
| Sales Salaries | | 450 |

**(5) Failure to Record Prepaid Expense**    It is discovered that Miscellaneous General Expense for 1991 included taxes of $275 that should have been deferred in adjusting the accounts on December 31, 1991. The effects of the failure to record the prepaid expense were as follows:

| | Income Statement | Balance Sheet |
|---|---|---|
| **1991:** | Expenses overstated (miscellaneous general expense too high) Net income understated | Assets understated (prepaid taxes not reported) Retained earnings understated |
| **1992:** | Expenses understated (miscellaneous general expense too low) Net income overstated | Balance sheet items not affected, retained earnings understatement for 1991 being corrected by net income overstatement for 1992 |

Since this is a counterbalancing error, no entry to correct the accounts is required in 1993.

If the error had been discovered in 1992 instead of 1993, a correcting entry would have been necessary. If prepaid taxes were properly recorded at the end of 1992, Miscellaneous General Expense would have to be debited for $275, the expense relating to operations of 1992, and Retained Earnings would have to be credited for the same amount, representing the net income understatement for 1993. The correcting entry in 1992 would have been:

| | | |
|---|---|---|
| Miscellaneous General Expense | 275 | |
| Retained Earnings | | 275 |

**(6) Failure to Record Accrued Revenue**    Accrued interest on notes receivable of $150 was overlooked in adjusting the accounts on December 31, 1991. The revenue was recognized when the interest was collected in 1992. The effects of the failure to record the accrued revenue were:

| | Income Statement | Balance Sheet |
|---|---|---|
| **1991:** | Revenue understated (interest revenue too low) Net income understated | Assets understated (interest receivable not reported) Retained earnings understated |
| **1992:** | Revenue overstated (interest revenue too high) Net income overstated | Balance sheet items not affected, retained earnings understatement for 1991 being corrected by net income overstatement for 1992 |

Since the balance sheet items at the end of 1992 were correctly stated, no entry to correct the accounts is required in 1993.

If the error had been discovered in 1992 instead of 1993, an entry would have been necessary to correct the account balances. If accrued interest on notes receivable had been properly recorded at the end of 1992, Interest Revenue would have to be debited for $150, the amount to be subtracted from receipts of 1992, and Retained Earnings would have to be credited for the same amount, representing the net income understatement for 1991. The correcting entry in 1992 would have been:

| | | |
|---|---|---|
| Interest Revenue | 150 | |
| Retained Earnings | | 150 |

### (7) Failure to Record Unearned Revenue

Fees of $225 received in advance for miscellaneous services as of December 31, 1992, were overlooked in adjusting the accounts. Miscellaneous Revenue had been credited when fees were received. The effects of the failure to recognize the unearned revenue of $225 at the end of 1992 were as follows:

| | Income Statement | Balance Sheet |
|---|---|---|
| **1992:** | Revenue overstated (miscellaneous revenue too high) | Liabilities understated (unearned service fees not reported) |
| | Net income overstated | Retained earnings overstated |

An entry is required to correct the accounts for the failure to record the unearned revenue at the end of 1992 if the net income for 1993 is not to be misstated. If the unearned revenue were properly recorded at the end of 1993, Retained Earnings would be debited for $225, representing the net income overstatement for 1992, and Miscellaneous Revenue would be credited for the same amount, representing the revenue that is to be identified with 1993. The correcting entry is:

| | | |
|---|---|---|
| Retained Earnings | 225 | |
| Miscellaneous Revenue | | 225 |

### (8) Failure to Record Depreciation

Delivery equipment was acquired at the beginning of 1991 at a cost of $6,000. The equipment has an estimated 5-year life, and depreciation of $1,200 was overlooked at the end of 1991 and 1992. The effects of the failure to record depreciation for 1991 were as follows:

| | Income Statement | Balance Sheet |
|---|---|---|
| **1991:** | Expenses understated (depreciation of delivery equipment too low) | Assets overstated (accumulated depreciation of delivery equipment too low) |
| | Net income overstated | Retained earnings overstated |
| **1992:** | Expenses not affected | Assets overstated (accumulated depreciation of delivery equipment too low) |
| | Net income not affected | Retained earnings overstated |

It should be observed that the misstatements arising from the failure to record depreciation are not counterbalanced in the succeeding year.

Failure to record depreciation for 1992 affected the statements as shown below.

| | Income Statement | Balance Sheet |
|---|---|---|
| **1991:** | Expenses understated (depreciation of delivery equipment too low) | Assets overstated (accumulated depreciation of delivery equipment too low) |
| | Net income overstated | Retained earnings overstated |

When the omission is recognized, Retained Earnings must be decreased by the net income overstatements of prior years and accumulated depreciation must be increased by the depreciation that should have been recorded. The correcting entry in 1993 for depreciation that should have been recognized for 1991 and 1992 is as follows:

| | | |
|---|---|---|
| Retained Earnings ........................................... | 2,400 | |
|     Accumulated Depreciation—Delivery Equipment .............. | | 2,400 |

## SUMMARY OF ACCOUNTING CHANGES AND CORRECTION OF ERRORS

The following summary presents the appropriate accounting procedures applicable to each of the four main categories covered in APB Opinion No. 20. Naturally, accountants must apply these guidelines with judgment and should seek to provide the most relevant and reliable information possible.

**Summary of Procedures for Reporting Accounting Changes and Correction of Errors**

| Category | Accounting Procedures |
|---|---|
| I.  Change in estimate | 1. Adjust only current-period results or current and future periods.<br>2. No separate, cumulative adjustment or restated financial statements.<br>3. No pro forma disclosure needed. |
| II.  Change in accounting principle<br>    a. Current recognition of cumulative effect | 1. Adjust for cumulative effect, i.e., a "catch-up" adjustment in current period as special item in income statement.<br>2. No restated financial statements.<br>3. Pro forma data required showing income and EPS information for all periods presented. |
|     b. Restatement of prior periods | 1. Direct cumulative adjustment to beginning retained earnings balance.<br>2. Restate financial statements to reflect new principle for comparative purposes.<br>3. No pro forma information required, because prior-period statements are changed directly. |
| III.  Change in reported entity | 1. Restate financial statements as though new entity had been in existence for all periods presented. |
| IV.  Error correction | 1. If detected in period error occurred, correct accounts through normal accounting cycle adjustments.<br>2. If detected in a subsequent period, adjust for effect of material errors by making prior-period adjustments directly to Retained Earnings. |

## KEY TERMS

| | | |
|---|---|---|
| Accounting changes 797 | Change in accounting estimate 798 | Change in reporting entity 804 |
| Accounting errors 805 | Change in accounting principle 799 | |

# QUESTIONS

1. How do accounting changes detract from the informational characteristics of comparability and consistency as described in FASB Concepts Statement No. 2?
2. List the three categories of accounting changes and explain briefly why such changes are made.
3. What alternative procedures have been suggested as solutions for reporting accounting changes?
4. (a) List several examples of areas where changes in accounting estimates are often made. (b) Explain briefly the proper accounting treatment for a change in estimate. (c) Why is this procedure considered proper for recording changes in accounting estimates?
5. (a) List several examples of changes in accounting principle that a company may make. (b) Explain briefly the proper accounting treatment for recognizing currently a change in accounting principle.
6. What information should pro forma statements include?
7. Why does a change in accounting principle require justification?
8. (a) When should the effects of a change in accounting principle be reported as a restatement of prior periods? (b) Although no justification was given by the APB for selecting certain items for special treatment, what might be a possible reason?
9. The Stice Company purchased a delivery van in 1990. At the time of purchase, the van's service life was estimated to be 7 years with a salvage value of $500. The company has been using the straight-line method of depreciation. In 1993, the company determined that because of extensive use, the van's service life would be only 5 years with no salvage value. Also, the company has decided to change the depreciation method used from straight-line to the sum-of-the-years-digits method. How would these changes be treated?
10. (a) List the 4 types of changes in reporting entities that might occur. (b) How are these changes treated?

(c) What assumption does the treatment of a change in reporting entity make?
11. Describe the effect on current net income, beginning retained earnings, individual asset accounts, and contra asset accounts when:
    (a) Depreciation is changed from the straight-line method to an accelerated method.
    (b) Depreciation is changed from an accelerated method to the straight-line method.
    (c) Income on construction contracts that had been reported on a completed-contract basis is now reported on the percentage-of-completion basis.
    (d) The valuation of inventories is changed from a FIFO to a LIFO basis.
    (e) It is determined that warranty expenses in prior years should have been 5% of sales instead of 4%.
    (f) The valuation of inventories is changed from a LIFO to a FIFO basis.
    (g) Your accounts receivable clerk has learned that a major customer has declared bankruptcy.
    (h) Your patent lawyer informs you that your rival has perfected and patented a new invention making your product obsolete.
12. (a) How are accounting errors to be treated? (b) What are counterbalancing errors?
13. The Foreign Manufacturing Co. failed to record accrued interest for 1990, $800; 1991, $700; and 1992, $950. What is the amount of overstatement or understatement of retained earnings at December 31, 1993?
14. Goods purchased FOB shipping point were shipped to Merkley & Co. on December 31, 1993. The purchase was recorded in 1993, but the goods were not included in ending inventory. (a) What effect would this error have had on reporting income for 1993 had it not been discovered? (b) What entry should be made on the books to correct this error assuming the books have not yet been closed for 1993?

# DISCUSSION CASES

### Case 21—1  (Accounting changes)

**Situation A**   Tucker Corporation has determined that the depreciable lives of several operating machines are too long and therefore do not fairly match the cost of the assets with the revenues produced. Tucker therefore decides to reduce the depreciable lives of these machines by 3 years.

**Situation B**   Trent Company decides that at the beginning of the year, it will adopt the straight-line method of depreciation for plant equipment. The straight-line method will be used for new acquisitions as well as for the previously acquired plant equipment, which had been accounted for using an accelerated depreciation method.

What types of accounting changes were involved in the two situations? Describe the method of reporting the changes under current GAAP. Where applicable, explain how the reported amounts are computed.

### Case 21—2  (Change in principle or change in estimate?)

Jill Stanton, President of Central Company, is confused about why your accounting firm has recommended that she report certain events as changes in principle instead of changes in estimate, which is what Jill thought they should be. She has asked you for an explanation. Describe a change in an accounting principle and a change in accounting estimate. Explain how each would be reported in the income statement of the period of change.

### Case 21—3  (Why do they make the change?)

An interesting phenomenon can sometimes occur when companies are in danger of not meeting their projected earnings goals. Management suddenly realizes that they have been far too conservative in their previous estimates associated with bad debts, estimated useful lives of equipment, and residual values, to name a few. With this newfound realization, management proceeds to revise these estimates to, as is often stated, "more closely reflect economic reality."

What is the primary difference in financial statement disclosure between a change in estimate and a change in principle? Why do you think managers who are in danger of not meeting their goals would prefer to revise an accounting estimate rather than change an accounting principle?

### Case 21—4  (Continuing that upward trend)

Hornberger Co. has demonstrated a consistently increasing earnings trend over the past ten years. Stockholders have come to expect this steady increase, and management has gone to great lengths to emphasize the smooth growth pattern associated with Hornberger's earnings.

At the year-end board of directors meeting, you, as the chief financial officer, present to the board the preliminary results for the year just ended. These results indicate a slight decline in both income from operations and net income when compared to the previous year. The chairman of the board quickly reviews the firm's earnings history and then suggests the following items for consideration:

(a)  Increase the estimated useful life of the company's plant facilities from 15 to 25 years.
(b)  Change the firm's estimate of bad debts from 4% of credit sales to 2.5% of credit sales.
(c)  Change the firm's amortization period for goodwill from the industry average of 10 years to the maximum allowed by GAAP of 40 years.

These changes will result in income for the period that is slightly higher than that reported for the past year and will continue the upward trend. The board votes on the proposed changes and instructs you to revise the income statement to reflect the changed estimates.

How would each of the above changes be reported in the current year's annual report to shareholders? Why would the chairman of the board suggest changing accounting estimates rather than accounting principles? As the accountant, do you have a responsibility to review management's estimates for reasonableness and to evaluate the motives behind management's decision to change an accounting estimate?

### Case 21—5  (How long can airplanes fly?)

Delta Air Lines depreciates its airplanes over a 15-year period and estimates a salvage value of 10% of the cost of the plane. On the other hand, Pan Am depreciates identical airplanes over a 25-year period and provides for a 15% salvage value. These different assumptions can result in markedly different operating results. For example, if one Boeing 727 costs $10 million, Delta will depreciate $260,000 more per year for 15 years than will Pan Am.

Which company's estimate of useful life more closely reflects reality? Would you feel comfortable as a passenger in an airplane that is 25 years old? Does the fact that Pan Am recently filed for bankruptcy protection provide any information as to why its estimates might be so substantially different from those of financially sound Delta?

---

# EXERCISES

### Exercise 21—1  (Change in estimate and in accounting principle)

Motor Manufacturing purchased a machine on January 1, 1989, for $50,000. At the time, it was determined that the machine had an estimated useful life of 10 years and an estimated residual value of $2,000. The company used the double-declining-balance method of depreciation. On January 1, 1993, the company decided to change its depreciation method from double-declining-balance to straight-line. The machine's remaining useful life was estimated to be 5 years with a residual value of $1,000.

1. Give the entry required to record the company's depreciation expense for 1993.
2. Give the entry, if any, to record the effect of the change in depreciation methods.

### Exercise 21—2  (Change in estimate)

The Curtis Company purchased a machine on January 1, 1990, for $1,500,000. At the date of acquisition, the machine had an estimated useful life of 6 years with no residual value. The machine is being depreciated on a straight-line basis. On January 1, 1993, Curtis determined, as a result of additional information, that the machine had an estimated useful life of 8 years from the date of acquisition with no residual value.

1. Give the journal entry, if any, to record the cumulative effect on prior years of changing the estimated useful life of the machine.
2. What is the amount of depreciation expense on the machine that should be charged to Curtis Company's income statement for the year ended December 31, 1993?

### Exercise 21—3  (Change in accounting estimate)

Albrecht Inc. began business in 1990. An examination of the company's allowance for doubtful accounts reveals the following:

|  | Estimated Bad Debts | Actual Bad Debts |
|---|---|---|
| 1990 | $11,000 | $4,500 |
| 1991 | 13,000 | 6,800 |
| 1992 | 16,500 | 8,950 |
| 1993 | No adjustment yet | 9,500 |

In the past, the company has estimated that 3% of credit sales will be uncollectible. The accountant for Albrecht Inc. has determined that the percentage used in estimating bad debts has been inappropriate. She would like to revise the estimate downward to 1.5%. The president of the company has stated that if the previous estimates of bad debt expense were incorrect, the financial statements should be restated using the more accurate estimate.

1. Assuming credit sales for 1993 are $600,000, provide the adjusting entry to record bad debt expense for the year.
2. What catch-up entry, if any, would be made to correct the inaccurate estimates for previous years?
3. How would you respond to the president's request to restate the prior years' financial statements?

### Exercise 21—4  (Change in accounting estimate)

On January 1, 1993, management of Micro Storage Inc. determined that a revision in the estimates associated with the depreciation of storage facilities was appropriate. These facilities, purchased on January 5, 1991, for $600,000, had been depreciated using the straight-line method with an estimated salvage value of $60,000 and an estimated useful life of 20 years. Management has determined that the storage facilities' expected *remaining* useful life is 10 years and they have an estimated salvage value of $100,000.

1. How much depreciation was recognized by Micro Storage in 1991 and 1992?
2. How much depreciation will be recognized by Micro Storage in 1993 as a result of the changes in estimates?
3. What journal entry is required to account for the change in estimate at the beginning of 1993?

### Exercise 21—5  (Change in accounting principle)

White Lightning Inc. has, in the past, depreciated its computer hardware using the straight-line method assuming a 10% salvage value and an expected useful life of 5 years. As a result of the rapid obsolescence associated with the computer industry, White Lightning has determined that it receives most of the benefit from its computer systems in the first few years of ownership. Therefore, White Lightning proposes changing to the sum-of-the-years-digits method for depreciating its computer hardware. The following information is available regarding all of White Lightning's computer purchases:

|      | Cost |
|------|------|
| 1990 | $40,000 |
| 1991 | 25,000 |
| 1992 | 30,000 |

1. Compute the depreciation taken by White Lightning during 1990, 1991, and 1992. Assume all purchases were made at the beginning of the year.
2. Compute the amount of depreciation expense assuming sum-of-the-years-digits had been used.
3. Prepare the journal entry required to adjust the accounts on January 1, 1993. (Ignore income tax effects.)

### Exercise 21—6  (Change in accounting principle)

High Quality Construction Company has used the completed-contract method of accounting since it began operations in 1986. In 1993, for justifiable reasons, management decided to adopt the percentage-of-completion method.

The following schedule, reporting income for the past 3 years, has been prepared by the company.

|                                              | 1990 | 1991 | 1992 |
|----------------------------------------------|------|------|------|
| Total revenues from completed contracts...   | $500,000 | $1,200,000 | $1,000,000 |
| Less cost of completed contracts ..........  | 350,000 | 925,000 | 760,000 |
| Income from operations ..................    | $150,000 | $ 275,000 | $ 240,000 |
| Extraordinary loss .......................   | -0- | -0- | 45,000 |
| Income ..................................    | $150,000 | $ 275,000 | $ 195,000 |

Analysis of the accounting records disclosed the following income by projects, earned in the years 1990-1992 using the percentage-of-completion method.

|           | 1990 | 1991 | 1992 |
|-----------|------|------|------|
| Project A ............. | $150,000 |  |  |
| Project B ............. | 100,000 | $175,000 |  |
| Project C ............. | 70,000 | 200,000 | $ 10,000 |
| Project D ............. |  | 10,000 | 60,000 |
| Project E ............. |  |  | (40,000) |

Give the journal entry required in 1993 to reflect the change in accounting principle. (Ignore income tax effects.)

### Exercise 21—7  (Change in accounting principle)

Diversified Manufacturing Company decides to change from an accelerated depreciation method it has used for both reporting and tax purposes to the straight-line method for reporting purposes. From the following information, prepare the income statement for the year ended December 31, 1993:

| Year | Net Income as Reported | Excess of Accelerated Depreciation Over Straight-Line Depreciation | Income Effect (Net of Tax) |
|------|------------------------|-------------------------------------------------------------------|----------------------------|
| Prior to 1990 |          | $12,500 | $ 7,500 |
| 1990 | $62,500 | 6,250 | 3,750 |
| 1991 | 54,500 | 7,500 | 4,500 |
| 1992 | 78,000 | 11,250 | 6,750 |
|      |         | $37,500 | $22,500 |

In 1993, net sales were $190,000; cost of goods sold, $92,500; selling expenses, $47,500; and general and administrative expenses, $14,000. The income tax on operating income was $14,400. In addition, Diversified had a tax deductible extraordinary loss of $12,000 net of $8,000 income tax savings.

### Exercise 21—8  (Change in accounting principle involving LIFO)

Assume the change in net income as shown in Exercise 21—7 is the result of a change from the LIFO method of inventory pricing to another method. During 1993, dividends of $17,500 were paid. Based on this information, prepare the retained earnings statement for 1993. The December 31, 1992, retained earnings balance as reported was $260,000.

### Exercise 21—9  (Changes in estimates and accounting principles)

Due to changing economic conditions and to make its financial statements more comparable to those of other companies in its industry, the management of Kelsea Inc. decided in 1993 to review its accounting practices.

On January 1, management decided to change its allowance for uncollectible accounts from 2% to 3½% of its outstanding receivables balance.

On July 1, Kelsea decided to begin using the straight-line method of depreciation on its mainframe computer instead of the sum-of-the-years-digits method. Based on further information, it also was decided that the computer has 10 more years of useful life. Kelsea bought the computer on January 1, 1983, at a cost of $550,000. At that time, Kelsea estimated it would have a 15-year useful life. The computer has no expected salvage value. Prior years' depreciation is as follows:

| | | | |
|------|---------|------|---------|
| 1983 | $68,750 | 1988 | $45,833 |
| 1984 | 64,167 | 1989 | 41,250 |
| 1985 | 59,583 | 1990 | 36,667 |
| 1986 | 55,000 | 1991 | 32,083 |
| 1987 | 50,417 | 1992 | 27,500 |

On October 1, Kelsea determined that starting with the current year, it would depreciate the company's printing press using hours of use as the depreciation base. The press, which had been purchased on January 1, 1980, at a cost of $930,000, was being depreciated for 25 years using the straight-line method. No salvage value was anticipated. It is estimated that this type of press provides 200,000 total hours of use and, as of January 1, 1993, it had been used 76,000 hours. At the end of 1993, the plant manager determined that the press had been run 6,250 hours during the year. Ignore income taxes relating to this change.

1. Evaluate each of the foregoing changes and determine whether it is a change in estimate or a change in accounting principle.
2. Give the journal entries required at December 31, 1993, to account for the above changes. Kelsea's receivable balance at December 31, 1993, was $345,000. Allowance for Doubtful Accounts carried a $1,000 debit balance before adjustment.

### Exercise 21—10   (Accounting errors)

The following errors in the accounting records of the Reed & Kinsey Partnership were discovered on January 10, 1993:

| Year of Error | Ending Inventories Overstated | Depreciation Understated | Accrued Rent Revenue Not Recorded | Accrued Interest Expense Not Recorded |
|---|---|---|---|---|
| 1990 | $20,000 | | $ 6,000 | |
| 1991 | | $5,000 | 22,000 | |
| 1992 | 24,000 | | | $2,000 |

The partners share net income and losses as follows: 40%, Reed; 60%, Kinsey.

1. Prepare a correcting journal entry on January 10, 1993, assuming that the books were closed for 1992.
2. Prepare a correcting journal entry on January 10, 1993, assuming that the books are still open for 1992 and that the partnership uses the perpetual inventory system.

### Exercise 21—11   (Analysis of errors)

State the effect of each of the following errors made in 1992 on the balance sheets and the income statements prepared in 1992 and 1993:

(a)   The ending inventory is understated as a result of an error in the count of goods on hand.
(b)   The ending inventory is overstated as a result of the inclusion of goods acquired and held on a consignment basis. No purchase was recorded on the books.
(c)   A purchase of merchandise at the end of 1992 is not recorded until payment is made for the goods in 1993; the goods purchased were included in the inventory at the end of 1992.
(d)   A sale of merchandise at the end of 1992 is not recorded until cash is received for the goods in 1993; the goods sold were excluded from the inventory at the end of 1992.
(e)   Goods shipped to consignees in 1992 were reported as sales; goods in the hands of consignees at the end of 1992 were not recognized for inventory purposes; sale of such goods in 1993 and collections on such sales were recorded as credits to the receivables established with consignees in 1992.
(f)   The total of one week's sales during 1992 was credited to Gain on Sales—Machinery.
(g)   No depreciation is taken in 1992 for equipment sold in April 1992. The company reports on a calender-year basis and computes depreciation to the nearest month.
(h)   No depreciation is taken in 1992 for equipment purchased in October 1992. The company reports on a calender-year basis and computes depreciation to the nearest month.
(i)   Customer notes receivable are debited to Accounts Receivable.

### Exercise 21—12   (Journal entries to correct accounts)

The first audit of the books for the Balm Corporation was made for the year ended December 31, 1993. In reviewing the books, the auditor discovered that certain adjustments had been overlooked at the end of 1992 and 1993 and also that other items had been improperly recorded. Omissions and other failures for each year are summarized on page 819.

|  | December 31, | |
|---|---|---|
|  | **1992** | **1993** |
| Sales salaries payable ..................................... | $1,300 | $1,100 |
| Interest receivable ........................................ | 325 | 215 |
| Prepaid insurance ........................................ | 450 | 300 |
| Advances from customers.................................. | 1,750 | 2,500 |
| (Collections from customers had been included in sales but should have been recognized as advances from customers, since goods were not shipped until the following year.) | | |
| Equipment................................................ | 1,400 | 1,200 |
| (Expenditures had been recognized as repairs but should have been recognized as cost of equipment; the depreciation rate on such equipment is 10% per year, but depreciation in the year of the expenditure is to be recognized at 5%.) | | |

Prepare journal entries to correct revenue and expense accounts for 1993 and record assets and liabilities that require recognition on the balance sheet as of December 31, 1993. Assume the nominal accounts for 1993 have not yet been closed into the income summary account.

# PROBLEMS

## Problem 21—1   (Change in accounting principle)

Yuki, Inc., acquired the following assets on January 3, 1990:

| Equipment, estimated useful life 5 years; residual value $13,000 ....... | $513,000 |
|---|---|
| Building, estimated useful life 40 years; no residual value ............ | 900,000 |

The equipment has been depreciated using the sum-of-the-years-digits method for the first 3 years. In 1993, the company decided to change the method of depreciation to straight-line. No change was made in the estimated service life or residual value. The company also decided to change the total estimated useful life of the building from 40 to 45 years with no change in the estimated residual value. The building is depreciated on the straight-line method. The company has 200,000 shares of capital stock outstanding. Partial results of operations for 1993 and 1992 are as follows:

|  | **1993** | **1992** |
|---|---|---|
| Income before cumulative effect of change in computing depreciation for 1993; depreciation for 1993 was computed on a straight-line basis for equipment and building* ....... | $890,000 | $856,000 |
| Earnings per share before cumulative effect of change in computing depreciation for 1993........................ | $4.45 | $4.28 |

\* The computations for depreciation expense for 1993 and 1992 for the building were based on the original estimate of useful life of 40 years.

### Instructions:

1. Compute the cumulative effect of the change in accounting principle to be reported in the income statement for 1993, and prepare the journal entry to record the change. (Ignore income tax effects.)
2. Present comparative data for the years 1992 and 1993, starting with income before cumulative effect of accounting change. Prepare pro forma data. (Ignore income tax effects.)

## Problem 21—2   (Accounting changes)

Barney Corporation has released the following condensed financial statements for 1991 and 1992 and has prepared the following proposed statements for 1993:

**Barney Corporation**
**Comparative Balance Sheet**
**December 31**

|  | 1993 | 1992 | 1991 |
|---|---|---|---|
| **Assets** | | | |
| Current assets | $249,000 | $219,000 | $165,000 |
| Land | 60,000 | 45,000 | 30,000 |
| Equipment | 150,000 | 150,000 | 150,000 |
| Accumulated depreciation—equipment | (45,000) | (30,000) | (15,000) |
| Total assets | $414,000 | $384,000 | $330,000 |
| **Liabilities and Stockholders' Equity** | | | |
| Current liabilities | $177,000 | $177,000 | $147,000 |
| Common stock | 60,000 | 60,000 | 60,000 |
| Retained earnings | 177,000 | 147,000 | 123,000 |
| Total liabilities and stockholders' equity | $414,000 | $384,000 | $330,000 |

**Barney Corporation**
**Comparative Income Statement**
**For Years Ended December 31**

|  | 1993 | 1992 | 1991 |
|---|---|---|---|
| Sales | $315,000 | $300,000 | $255,000 |
| Cost of goods sold | $240,000 | $225,000 | $189,000 |
| Other expenses except depreciation | 30,000 | 36,000 | 33,000 |
| Depreciation expense—equipment | 15,000 | 15,000 | 15,000 |
| Total costs | $285,000 | $276,000 | $237,000 |
| Net income | $ 30,000 | $ 24,000 | $ 18,000 |

Barney Corporation acquired the equipment for $150,000 on January 1, 1991, and began depreciating the equipment over a 10-year estimated useful life with no salvage value, using the straight-line method of depreciation. The double-declining-balance method of depreciation, under the same assumptions, would have required the following depreciation expense:

$$1991 \quad 20\% \times \$150,000 = \$30,000$$
$$1992 \quad 20\% \times \$120,000 = \$24,000$$
$$1993 \quad 20\% \times \$\ 96,000 = \$19,200$$

**Instructions:**   In comparative format, prepare a balance sheet and a combined statement of income and retained earnings for 1993, giving effect to the following changes. Ignore any income tax effect. Barney Corporation has 10,000 shares of common stock outstanding. The following situations are independent of each other.

(a)   For justifiable reasons, Barney Corporation changed to the double-declining-balance method of depreciation in 1993. The effect of the change should be included in the net income of the period in which the change was made.

(b)   During 1993, Barney Corporation determined that the equipment was fast becoming obsolete and decided to change the estimated useful life from 10 years to 5 years. The books for 1993 had not yet been closed.

(c)   During 1993, Barney Corporation found that additional equipment, also acquired on January 1, 1991, costing $24,000, had been recorded in the land account and had not been depreciated. This error should be corrected using straight-line depreciation over a 10-year period.

## Problem 21—3  (Change in accounting estimate and principle)

The following information relates to depreciable assets of Brillantez Electronics:

(a)  Machine A was purchased for $30,000 on January 1, 1988. The entire cost was expensed in the year of purchase. The machine had a 15-year useful life and no residual value.

(b)  Machine B cost $105,000 and was purchased January 1, 1989. The straight-line method of depreciation was used. At the time of purchase, the expected useful life was 12 years with no residual value. In 1993, it was estimated that the total useful life of the asset would be only 8 years and that there would be a $5,000 residual value.

(c)  Building A was purchased January 1, 1990, for $600,000. The straight-line method of depreciation was originally chosen. The building was expected to be useful for 20 years and to have zero residual value. In 1993, a change was made from the straight-line depreciation method to the sum-of-the-years-digits method. Estimates relating to the useful life and residual value remained the same.

Income before depreciation expense was $520,000 for 1993. Depreciation on assets other than those described totaled $50,000. Net income for 1992 was $415,000.

**Instructions:**   (Ignore all income tax effects.)

1.  Prepare all entries for 1993 relating to depreciable assets.
2.  Prepare partial income statements for 1992 and 1993. Begin with income before the cumulative effects of any accounting changes. Show all computations.

## Problem 21—4  (Change in estimate and accounting principle)

Johnston Doors began operations on January 4, 1990. During the first month, Johnston purchased the following assets, all of which were depreciated using the straight-line method.

Equipment:    Cost, $48,000; estimated salvage value, $5,000; estimated useful life, 10 years.
Building:       Cost, $85,000; estimated salvage value, $15,000; estimated useful life, 15 years.

At the end of 1993, Johnston reviewed its accounting records and determined that the building should have a total useful life of 20 years. In addition, because of significant wear on the equipment, Johnston proposes changing to the sum-of-the-years-digits method for depreciating equipment.

Johnston also has found that its estimated bad debt expense has been consistently higher than actual bad debts. Management proposes lowering the percentage from 3% of credit sales to 2%. If 2% had been used since 1990, the balance in Allowance for Doubtful Accounts at the beginning of 1993 would have been $3,200 rather than $6,900. Credit sales for 1993 totaled $250,000, and accounts written off as uncollectible during 1993 totaled $5,500.

**Instructions:**   (Ignore income tax effects.)

1.  What is the proper accounting treatment for each of the proposed changes?
2.  Prepare the journal entry necessary to record the cumulative adjustment associated with changing depreciation methods.
3.  Prepare the journal entries necessary to record the depreciation expense for the year for both equipment and buildings.
4.  Prepare the journal entry to record the write-off of accounts deemed uncollectible during 1993 and the adjusting entry at year-end to record the bad debt expense for the period.
5.  What adjustment is made to the allowance account at the beginning of 1993 as a result of changing the bad debt percentage?

## Problem 21—5  (Reporting accounting changes)

Listed at the top of page 822 are three independent, unrelated sets of facts concerning accounting changes.

**Case 1**   The Runyon Development Company determined that the amortization rate on its patents is unacceptably low due to current advances in technology. The company decided at the beginning of 1993 to increase the amortization rate on all existing patents from 10% to 20%. Patents purchased on January 1, 1988, for $3,000,000 had a book value of $1,500,000 on January 1, 1993.

**Case 2**   Cartwright Corporation decided on January 1, 1993, to change its depreciation method for manufacturing equipment from an accelerated method to the straight-line method. The straight-line method is to be used for new acquisitions as well as for previously acquired equipment. It has been determined that the excess of accelerated depreciation over straight-line depreciation for the years 1990 through 1992 totals $343,000.

**Case 3**   On December 31, 1992, Enterprise Inc. owned 35% of the Packard Company, at which time Enterprise reported its investment using the equity method. During 1993, Enterprise increased its ownership in Packard by 25%. Accordingly, Enterprise is planning to prepare consolidated financial statements for Enterprise and Packard for the year ended December 31, 1993.

**Instructions:**   For each of the situations described:

1. Identify the type of accounting change.
2. Explain how the accounting change should be reported in 1993. Where applicable, prepare the journal entries to record the accounting change. (Ignore income tax effects.)
3. Explain the effect of the change on the December 31, 1993, balance sheet and the 1993 income statement.

### Problem 21—6   (Change in accounting principle)

During 1993, All Seasons Company changed its method of depreciating equipment from an accelerated depreciation method to the straight-line method. The following information shows the effect of this change:

| Year | Net Income as Reported | Excess of Accelerated Depreciation Over Straight-Line Depreciation | Assumed Tax Effects |
|---|---|---|---|
| Prior to 1991 |  | $68,000 | $27,200 |
| 1991 | $190,000 | 14,000 | 5,600 |
| 1992 | 210,000 | 17,000 | 6,800 |

**Instructions:**

1. Compute the effect of the change in accounting principle on income (net of tax).
2. Prepare a partial income statement for 1993 assuming income before extraordinary items was $225,000 and an extraordinary loss of $21,600 (net of $14,400 income tax reduction) was incurred. Assume 100,000 shares of common stock are outstanding.
3. Present pro forma income data for the years 1991-1993. Assume 100,000 shares of common stock were outstanding in all years.

### Problem 21—7   (Change in estimate)

On January 3, 1992, Sandy's Fashions, a chain of moderately priced women's clothing, purchased a large quantity of personal computers. The cost of these computers was $120,000. On the date of purchase, Sandy's management estimated that the computers would last approximately 5 years and would have a salvage value at that time of $12,000. The company used the double-declining-balance method to depreciate the computers.

During January of 1993, Sandy's management realized that technological advancements had made the computers virtually obsolete and that they would have to be replaced. Management proposed changing the estimated useful life of the computers to 2 years.

**Instructions:**   Prepare the journal entry necessary at the end of 1993 to record depreciation on the computers.

## Problem 21—8 (Change in accounting principle—LIFO to FIFO)

On January 1, 1993, Overland Inc. decided to change from the LIFO method of inventory costing to the FIFO method. The reported income for the 4 years Overland had been in business was as follows:

| | | | |
|---|---|---|---|
| 1989 | $250,000 | 1991 | $310,000 |
| 1990 | 260,000 | 1992 | 330,000 |

Analysis of the inventory records disclosed that the following inventories were on hand at the end of each year as valued under both the LIFO and FIFO methods.

| | LIFO Method | FIFO Method |
|---|---|---|
| January 1, 1989 | -0- | -0- |
| December 31, 1989 | $228,000 | $256,000 |
| December 31, 1990 | 240,000 | 238,000 |
| December 31, 1991 | 270,000 | 302,000 |
| December 31, 1992 | 288,000 | 352,000 |

The income tax effect of the change in inventory method is assumed to be as follows:

| | | | |
|---|---|---|---|
| 1989 | $ 11,200 | 1991 | $ 13,600 |
| 1990 | (12,000) | 1992 | 12,800 |

**Instructions:**

1. Compute the restated net income for the years 1989-1992.
2. Prepare the retained earnings statement for Overland Inc. for 1993 if the 1992 ending balance had been previously reported at $600,000, 1993 net income using the FIFO method is $360,000, and dividends of $200,000 were paid during 1993.

## Problem 21—9 (Correction of errors)

Twain Textile Corporation is planning an expansion of its current plant facilities. Twain is in the process of obtaining a loan at City Bank. The bank has requested audited financial statements. Twain has never been audited before. It has prepared the following comparative financial statements for the years ended December 31, 1993 and 1992 shown on page 824.

The following facts were disclosed during the audit:

(a) On January 20, 1992, Twain had charged a 5-year fire insurance premium to expense. The total premium amounted to $15,500.

(b) All marketable securities were purchased in 1992. The entire portfolio was properly classified as current and includes only equity securities. The market valuation at the end of each year was as follows:

| | |
|---|---|
| 1992 | $202,500 |
| 1993 | 178,250 |

(c) Over the last two years, the amount of loss due to bad debts has steadily decreased. Twain has decided to reduce the amount of bad debt expense from 2% to 1½% of sales, beginning with 1993. (A charge of 2% has already been made for 1993.)

(d) The inventory account (maintained on a periodic basis) has been in error the last 2 years. The errors were as follows:

1992: ending inventory overstated by $37,750
1993: ending inventory overstated by $49,500

(e) A machine costing $75,000, purchased on January 4, 1992, was incorrectly charged to operating expense. The machine had a useful life of 10 years and a residual value of $12,500. The straight-line depreciation method is used by Twain.

**Twain Textile Corporation**
**Comparative Balance Sheet**
**December 31, 1993 and 1992**

| | 1993 | 1992 |
|---|---|---|
| **Assets** | | |
| Current assets: | | |
| Cash | $ 407,500 | $ 205,000 |
| Accounts receivable | 980,000 | 740,000 |
| Allowance for doubtful accounts | (92,500) | (45,000) |
| Marketable securities (at cost) | 195,000 | 195,000 |
| Inventory | 517,500 | 505,000 |
| Total current assets | $2,007,500 | $1,600,000 |
| Plant assets: | | |
| Property, plant, and equipment | $ 417,500 | $ 423,750 |
| Accumulated depreciation | (304,000) | (266,000) |
| Total plant assets | $ 113,500 | $ 157,750 |
| Total assets | $2,121,000 | $1,757,750 |
| | | |
| **Liabilities and Stockholders' Equity** | | |
| Liabilities: | | |
| Accounts payable | $ 303,500 | $ 490,250 |
| Stockholders' equity: | | |
| Common stock, par value $25; authorized, 30,000 shares; issued and outstanding, 26,000 shares | $ 650,000 | $ 650,000 |
| Retained earnings | 1,167,500 | 617,500 |
| Total stockholders' equity | $1,817,500 | $1,267,500 |
| Total liabilities and stockholders' equity | $2,121,000 | $1,757,750 |

**Twain Textile Corporation**
**Comparative Income Statement**
**For the Years Ended December 31, 1993 and 1992**

| | 1993 | 1992 |
|---|---|---|
| Sales | $2,500,000 | $2,250,000 |
| Cost of goods sold | 1,075,000 | 987,500 |
| Gross margin | $1,425,000 | $1,262,500 |
| Operating expenses | $ 575,000 | $ 512,500 |
| General and administrative expenses | 300,000 | 262,500 |
| | $ 875,000 | $ 775,000 |
| Net income | $ 550,000 | $ 487,500 |

**Instructions:**

1. Prepare the journal entries to correct the books at December 31, 1993. The books for 1993 have not been closed. (Ignore income taxes.)
2. Prepare a schedule showing the computation of corrected net income for the years ended December 31, 1992 and 1993, assuming that any adjustments are to be reported on the comparative statements for the two years. Begin your schedule with the net income for each year. (Ignore income taxes.)

(AICPA adapted)

## Problem 21—10    (Analysis and correction of errors)

A CPA is engaged by the Alpine Corp. in 1993 to examine the books and records and to make whatever corrections are necessary. An examination of the accounts discloses the following:

(a)  Dividends had been declared on December 15 in 1990 and 1991 but had not been entered in the books until paid.

(b)  Improvements in buildings and equipment of $4,800 had been debited to expense at the end of April 1989. Improvements are estimated to have an 8-year life. The company uses the straight-line method in recording depreciation and computes depreciation to the nearest month.

(c)  The physical inventory of merchandise had been understated by $1,500 at the end of 1990 and by $2,150 at the end of 1991.

(d)  The merchandise inventories at the end of 1991 and 1992 did not include merchandise that was then in transit and to which the company had title. These shipments of $1,900 and $2,750 were recorded as purchases in January of 1992 and 1993 respectively.

(e)  The company had failed to record sales commissions payable of $1,050 and $850 at the end of 1991 and 1992 respectively.

(f)  The company had failed to recognize supplies on hand of $600 and $1,250 at the end of 1991 and 1992 respectively.

The retained earnings account appeared as follows on the date the CPA began the examination:

**Account** Retained Earnings

| Date | | Item | Debit | Credit | Balance Debit | Balance Credit |
|---|---|---|---|---|---|---|
| 1990 | | | | | | |
| Jan. ...... | 1 | Balance ..................... | | | | 40,500 |
| Dec. ...... | 31 | Net income for year ............ | | 9,000 | | 49,500 |
| 1991 | | | | | | |
| Jan. ...... | 10 | Dividends paid ............... | 7,500 | | | 42,000 |
| Mar. ...... | 6 | Stock sold—excess over par ..... | | 16,000 | | 58,000 |
| Dec. ...... | 31 | Net loss for year ............... | 5,600 | | | 52,400 |
| 1992 | | | | | | |
| Jan. ...... | 10 | Dividends paid ............... | 7,500 | | | 44,900 |
| Dec. ...... | 31 | Net loss for year ............... | 6,200 | | | 38,700 |

## Instructions:

1. Journalize the necessary corrections.
2. Prepare a statement of retained earnings covering the 3-year period beginning January 1, 1990. The statement should report the corrected retained earnings balance on January 1, 1990, the annual changes in the account, and the corrected retained earnings balances as of December 31, 1990, 1991 and 1992.
3. Set up an account for retained earnings before correction, and post correcting data to this account for part (1). Balance the account, showing the corrected retained earnings as of January 1, 1993.

## Problem 21—11    (Accounting changes and correction of errors)

Stevens Company is in the process of adjusting its books at the end of 1993. Stevens' records reveal the following information:

(a)  Stevens failed to accrue sales commissions at the end of 1991 and 1992 as follows:

$$1991 ................. \quad \$27,000$$
$$1992 ................. \quad 15,333$$

The sales commissions were paid in January of the following year.

(b) On December 31, 1993, Stevens changed its depreciation method for machinery from double-declining-balance to the straight-line method. Stevens has already recorded the 1993 depreciation using the double-declining-balance method. The following information also was provided:

| | Double-Declining-Balance Depreciation | Straight-Line Depreciation | Depreciation Difference |
|---|---|---|---|
| Prior to 1993 | $233,333 | $133,333 | $100,000 |
| 1993 | 40,000 | 33,333 | 6,667 |

(c) Errors in ending inventories for the last 3 years were discovered to be as follows:

| | |
|---|---|
| 1991 ................ | $43,333 understated |
| 1992 ................ | 56,667 understated |
| 1993 ................ | 10,000 overstated |

The incorrect amount has already been recorded for 1993.

(d) Early in 1993, Stevens changed from the percentage-of-completion method of accounting for long-term construction contracts to the completed-contract method. The income for 1993 was recorded using the completed-contract method. The following information also was available:

| | Pretax Income | |
|---|---|---|
| | Percentage of Completion | Completed Contract |
| Prior to 1993 | $583,333 | $166,667 |
| 1993 | 200,000 | 66,667 |

## Instructions:

1. Prepare the necessary journal entries at December 31, 1993, to record the above information. Assume the books are still open for 1993. (Ignore all income tax effects.)
2. Assuming income from continuing operations before taxes of $500,000, taxes of $150,000 on operating income, and no applicable taxes on the cumulative effect of changing depreciation methods, prepare a partial income statement (beginning with income from continuing operations before taxes) for Stevens Company for 1993. (Ignore earnings per share.)
3. Assuming Retained Earnings at the beginning of 1993 was $1,985,000 and that dividends of $125,000 were declared during 1993, prepare a statement of retained earnings for Stevens Company, reflecting appropriate adjustments from (1). Assume no applicable taxes on the cumulative effect of changing to the completed-contract method.

# PART FIVE

## Financial Reporting and Analysis

# CHAPTER 22

# Financial Statement Analysis

---

**CHAPTER TOPICS**

**Objectives of Financial Statement Analysis**

**Comparative Statement Analysis**

**Liquidity Analysis**

**Activity Analysis**

**Profitability Analysis**

**Capital Structure Analysis**

**Segment Information**

**Interim Reporting**

---

As the world economy becomes more integrated, one question facing financial analysts is whether financial ratios can be compared across national boundaries. For example, the average price-earnings ratio for Japanese companies is around 60, while the average for U.S. companies is about 15. A price-earnings ratio in excess of 20 is considered quite high in the U.S. This dramatic variation is a result of differences in the two national economies and in their accounting methods. One of the accounting differences is that Japanese companies generally depreciate their fixed assets over shorter lives than do U.S. companies.[1] The increasing necessity of cross-border financial comparisons will require financial statement users to be even more aware of the assumptions and methods that accountants have used in preparing the numbers.

[1] Arthur Andersen & Co. and Salomon Brothers Inc., ''Valuing Global Securities: Is Accounting Diversity a Mountain or a Molehill?'' (1990).

Accounting provides information to assist various individuals in making economic decisions. A significant amount of information relevant to this purpose is presented in the primary financial statements of companies. Additional useful information is provided by financial data reported by means other than the financial statements. However, as explained in Chapter 2, financial data are only part of the total information needed by decision makers. Nonfinancial information may also be relevant. Thus, the total information spectrum is broader than just financial reporting. It encompasses financial statements, financial reporting by means other than the financial statements, and additional nonfinancial information.

The Financial Accounting Standards Board has restricted its focus to general-purpose external financial reporting by business enterprises. This chapter concentrates on analysis of information in the primary financial statements. Notes are an integral part of financial statements, and significant accounting policies and other information included in notes should be considered carefully in performing an analysis and in evaluating results. Supplementary information should also be considered in interpreting financial statement data.

## OBJECTIVES OF FINANCIAL STATEMENT ANALYSIS

Financial statement analysis is necessary for intelligent decision making. Nearly all businesses prepare financial statements of some type; the form and complexity of the statements vary according to the decisions to be made by those who use them. The owner of a small business might simply list the firm's cash receipts and disbursements and use this to prepare an income tax return. On the other hand, a large corporation's accounting staff spends considerable time in preparing the company's complex financial statements that can be used for many types of decisions.

Whatever their form, financial statements provide information about a business and its operation to interested users. For example, creditors making a lending decision may have questions concerning matters such as a company's sales, net income, and trends for these items, and the changes in cash flows, the relationship of income to sales, and of income to investments. Identifying these relationships requires analysis of data reported on the income statement, the balance sheet, and the statement of cash flows. Internal management is also concerned with analyzing the general-purpose financial statements, but requires additional special information in setting policies and making decisions. Questions may arise on matters such as the performance of various company divisions, the income from sales of individual products, and whether to make or buy product parts and equipment. Decisions on these matters can be made by establishing internal information systems to provide the necessary data. Thus, in analyzing financial data, the nature of analysis and the information needed depend on the decision needs of users and the issues involved.

The analyses of financial data described in this chapter are directed primarily to the informational needs of external users who usually must rely on the financial reports prepared by a company. Many groups are interested in the data found in financial statements, including:

1. Owners—sole proprietor, partners, or stockholders.
2. Management, including board of directors.
3. Creditors.
4. Government—local, state, and federal (including regulatory, taxing, and statistical units).
5. Prospective owners and prospective creditors.
6. Stock exchanges, investment bankers, and stockbrokers.

7. Trade associations.
8. Employees of a business and their labor unions.
9. The general public.

Questions raised by these groups generally can be answered by analyses that develop comparisons and measure relationships between components of financial statements. The analyses will form a basis for decisions made by the user.

Analyses typically are directed toward evaluating four aspects of a business: (1) liquidity, (2) stability, (3) profitability, and (4) growth potential.

Liquidity relates to the ability of an enterprise to pay its liabilities as they mature. Financial statements are analyzed to determine whether a business currently is liquid and whether it could retain its liquidity in a period of adversity. The analysis includes studies of the relationship of current assets to current liabilities, the size and nature of creditor and ownership interests, the protection afforded creditors and owners through sound asset values, and the amounts and trends of net income. Creditors are especially concerned with the liquidity of their debtors.

Stability is measured by the ability of a business to make interest and principal payments on outstanding debt and to pay regular dividends to its stockholders. In judging stability, data concerning operations and financial position are studied. For example, there must be a regular demand for the goods or services sold, and the gross profit on sales must be sufficient to cover operating expenses, interest, and dividends. There should be a satisfactory turnover of assets, and all business resources should be productively employed.

Profitability is measured by the ability of a business to increase its ownership equity from its operations. The nature and amount of income, as well as its regularity and trend, are significant factors affecting profitability.

The growth potential of a company is also of primary importance to stockholders. This element, along with profitability, directly affects future cash flows derived from increased income and/or appreciation in stock values. Growth potential is measured by the expansion and growth into new markets, the rate of growth in existing markets, the rate of growth in earnings per share, and the amount of expenditures for research and development.

An analysis must be directed toward the needs of those for whom it is made. For example, owners are interested in a company's ability to obtain additional capital for current needs and possible expansion. Creditors are interested not only in the position of a business as a going concern but also in its position should it be forced to liquidate.

## ANALYTICAL PROCEDURES

Analytical procedures fall into two main categories: (1) comparisons and measurements based on financial data for two or more periods, and (2) comparisons and measurements based on financial data of only the current fiscal period. The first category includes comparative statements, ratios and trends for data on successive statements, and analyses of changes in the balance sheet, income statement, and statement of cash flows. The second category includes determining current balance sheet and income statement relationships and analyzing earnings and earnings potential. A review of financial data usually requires both types of analyses.

The analytical procedures commonly employed may be identified as: comparative statements, index-number trend series, common-size statements, and analysis of financial statement components. These techniques are described and illustrated in the following sections. It should be emphasized that the analyses illustrated herein are simply guides to the evaluation of financial data. Sound conclusions can be reached only through intelligent use and interpretation of such data. The AC&W Corporation is used as an example throughout the chapter.

## Comparative Statements

Financial data become more meaningful when compared with similar data for preceding periods. Statements reflecting financial data for two or more periods are called comparative statements. Annual data can be compared with similar data for prior years. Monthly or quarterly data can be compared with similar data for previous months or quarters or with similar data for the same months or quarters of previous years.

Comparative data allow statement users to analyze trends in a company, thus enhancing the usefulness of information for decision making. The Accounting Principles Board stated that comparisons between financial statements are most informative and useful under the following conditions:

1. The presentations are in good form; that is, the arrangement within the statements is identical.
2. The content of the statements is identical; that is, the same items from the underlying accounting records are classified under the same captions.
3. Accounting principles are not changed or, if they are changed, the financial effects of the changes are disclosed.
4. Changes in circumstances or in the nature of the underlying transactions are disclosed.[2]

To the extent that the foregoing criteria are not met, comparisons may be misleading. Consistent practices and procedures and reporting periods of equal and regular lengths are also important, especially when comparisons are made for a single enterprise.

Comparative financial statements may be even more useful to investors and others when the reporting format highlights absolute changes in dollar amounts as well as relative percentage changes. Statement users will benefit by considering both amounts as they make their analyses. For example, an investor may decide that any change of 10% or more in a financial statement amount should be investigated further. A 10% change in an amount of $1,000, however, is not as significant as a 5% change in an amount of $100,000. When absolute or relative amounts appear out of line, conclusions, favorable or unfavorable, are not justified until investigation has disclosed reasons for the changes.

The development of data measuring changes taking place over a number of periods is known as horizontal analysis. Using the AC&W Corporation's income statement as an example and a reporting format that discloses dollar and percentage changes, horizontal analysis is illustrated at the top of page 832.

## Index-Number Trend Series

When comparative financial statements present information for more than two or three years, they become cumbersome and potentially confusing. A technique used to overcome this problem is referred to as an index-number trend series.

To compute index numbers, the statement preparer first must choose a base year. This may be the earliest year presented or some other year considered particularly appropriate.

---

[2]*Statement of the Accounting Principles Board No. 4,* "Basic Concepts and Accounting Principles Underlying Financial Statements of Business Enterprises" (New York: American Institute of Certified Public Accountants, 1970), pars. 95-99.

**AC&W Corporation**
**Comparative Income Statement**
**For Years Ended December 31**

| | 1994 | 1993 | 1992 | Increase (Decrease) 1993-1994 Amount | Percent | Increase (Decrease) 1992-1993 Amount | Percent |
|---|---|---|---|---|---|---|---|
| Gross sales .......... | $1,500,000 | $1,750,000 | $1,000,000 | $(250,000) | (14%) | $750,000 | 75% |
| Sales returns ........ | 75,000 | 100,000 | 50,000 | (25,000) | (25%) | 50,000 | 100% |
| Net sales ............ | $1,425,000 | $1,650,000 | $ 950,000 | $(225,000) | (14%) | $700,000 | 74% |
| Cost of goods sold .... | 1,000,000 | 1,200,000 | 630,000 | (200,000) | (17%) | 570,000 | 90% |
| Gross profit on sales .. | $ 425,000 | $ 450,000 | $ 320,000 | $ (25,000) | (6%) | $130,000 | 41% |
| Selling expense ....... | $ 280,000 | $ 300,000 | $ 240,000 | $ (20,000) | (7%) | $ 60,000 | 25% |
| General expense ...... | 100,000 | 110,000 | 100,000 | (10,000) | (9%) | 10,000 | 10% |
| Total operating expenses ............ | $ 380,000 | $ 410,000 | $ 340,000 | $ (30,000) | (7%) | $ 70,000 | 21% |
| Operating income (loss)................ | $ 45,000 | $ 40,000 | $ (20,000) | $ 5,000 | 13% | $ 60,000 | — |
| Other revenue items... | 85,000 | 75,000 | 50,000 | 10,000 | 13% | 25,000 | 50% |
| | $ 130,000 | $ 115,000 | $ 30,000 | $ 15,000 | 13% | $ 85,000 | 283% |
| Other expense items .. | 30,000 | 30,000 | 10,000 | — | — | 20,000 | 200% |
| Income before income tax.................. | $ 100,000 | $ 85,000 | $ 20,000 | $ 15,000 | 18% | $ 65,000 | 325% |
| Income tax .......... | 30,000 | 25,000 | 5,000 | 5,000 | 20% | 20,000 | 400% |
| Net income .......... | $ 70,000 | $ 60,000 | $ 15,000 | $ 10,000 | 17% | $ 45,000 | 300% |

Next, the base-year amounts are all expressed as 100%. The amounts for all other years are then stated as a percentage of the base-year amounts. Index numbers can be computed only when amounts are positive. The set of percentages for several years may thus be interpreted as trend values or as a series of index numbers relating to a particular item. For example, AC&W Corporation had gross sales of $1,000,000 in 1992, $1,750,000 in 1993, and $1,500,000 in 1994. These amounts, expressed in an index-number trend series with 1992 as the base year, would be 100, 175, and 150, respectively.

The index-number trend series technique is a type of horizontal analysis. It can give statement users a long-range view of a firm's financial position, earnings, and cash flow. The user needs to recognize, however, that long-range trend series are particularly sensitive to changing price levels. For example, in the 10 years from 1975 through 1985, the price level in the United States doubled. A horizontal analysis that ignored such a significant change in the price level might suggest that sales or net income had increased during the period when, in fact, no real growth had occurred.

Data expressed in terms of a base year frequently are useful for comparisons with similar data provided by business or industry sources or government agencies. When information used for making comparisons does not employ the same base period, it will have to be restated. Restatement of a base year calls for the expressing of each value as a percentage of the value for the base-year period.

To illustrate, assume the gross sales data for the AC&W Corporation for 1992-1994 are to be compared with a sales index for its particular industry. The industry sales indexes are as follows:

| | 1994 | 1993 | 1992 |
|---|---|---|---|
| (1988 = 100)........................................... | 146 | 157 | 124 |

Recognizing 1992 as the base year, industry sales are restated as follows:

| 1992 | 100 |
|---|---|
| 1993 (157 ÷ 124) | 127 |
| 1994 (146 ÷ 124) | 118 |

Industry sales and net sales for the AC&W Corporation can now be expressed in comparative form as follows:

|  | 1994 | 1993 | 1992 |
|---|---|---|---|
| Industry sales index | 118 | 127 | 100 |
| AC&W Corporation sales index* | 150 | 175 | 100 |

* From comparative income statement on page 1046.

## Common-Size Financial Statements

Horizontal analysis measures changes over a number of accounting periods. Statement users also need data that express relationships within a single period, which is known as **vertical analysis**. Preparation of **common-size financial statements** is a widely used vertical analysis technique. The common-size relationships may be stated in terms of percentages or in terms of ratios. Common-size statements may be prepared for the same business as of different dates or periods, or for two or more business units as of the same date or for the same period.

Common-size financial statements are useful in analyzing the internal structure of a financial statement. For example, a common-size balance sheet expresses each amount as a percentage of total assets, usually expressed as a decimal fraction. A common-size income statement usually shows each revenue or expense item as a percentage of net sales. As an illustration, a comparative balance sheet for AC&W Corporation with each item expressed in both dollar amounts and percentages is shown at the top of page 834. Other types of common-size financial statements, e.g., a common-size retained earnings statement or statement of cash flows, may be prepared. When a supporting schedule shows the detail for a group total, individual items may be expressed as percentages of either the base figure or the group total.

Common-size analysis can also be used when comparing a company with other companies or with an entire industry. Differences in sizes of numbers in the financial statements are neutralized by reducing them to common-size ratios. Industry statistics are frequently published in common-size form, which facilitates making these types of comparisons. When comparing a company with other companies or with industry figures, it is important that the financial data for each company reflect comparable price levels. Furthermore, the financial data should be developed using comparable accounting methods, classification procedures, and valuation bases. Comparisons should be limited to companies engaged in similar activities. When the financial policies of two companies are different, these differences should be recognized in evaluating comparative reports. For example, one company may lease its properties while the other may purchase such items; one company may finance its operations using long-term borrowing while the other may rely primarily on funds supplied by stockholders and by earnings. Financial statements for two companies under these circumstances are not wholly comparable.

All this suggests that comparisons between different companies should be evaluated with care, and should be made with a full understanding of the inherent limitations. Reference was made earlier to the criteria that the Accounting Principles Board identified if comparisons are to be meaningful. Comparability between enterprises is more difficult to obtain than comparability within a single enterprise. Ideally, differences in companies'

**AC&W Corporation**
**Comparative Balance Sheet**
**December 31**

| | 1994 | | 1993 | | 1992 | |
|---|---|---|---|---|---|---|
| | Amount | Common-Size Ratio | Amount | Common-Size Ratio | Amount | Common-Size Ratio |
| **Assets** | | | | | | |
| Current assets .................. | $ 855,000 | .38 | $ 955,500 | .40 | $ 673,500 | .38 |
| Land, buildings, and equipment (net) ......................... | 1,275,000 | .56 | 1,275,000 | .54 | 925,000 | .52 |
| Intangible assets ................ | 100,000 | .04 | 100,000 | .04 | 100,000 | .06 |
| Other assets .................... | 48,000 | .02 | 60,500 | .02 | 61,500 | .04 |
| Total assets.................... | $2,278,000 | 1.00 | $2,391,000 | 1.00 | $1,760,000 | 1.00 |
| **Liabilities** | | | | | | |
| Current liabilities ................ | $ 410,000 | .18 | $ 546,000 | .23 | $ 130,000 | .07 |
| Long-term liabilities—10% bonds.. | 400,000 | .18 | 400,000 | .17 | 300,000 | .17 |
| Total liabilities .................. | $ 810,000 | .36 | $ 946,000 | .40 | $ 430,000 | .24 |
| **Stockholders' Equity** | | | | | | |
| Preferred 6% stock .............. | $ 350,000 | .15 | $ 350,000 | .15 | $ 250,000 | .14 |
| Common stock................... | 750,000 | .33 | 750,000 | .31 | 750,000 | .43 |
| Additional paid-in capital ........ | 100,000 | .04 | 100,000 | .04 | 100,000 | .06 |
| Retained earnings .............. | 268,000 | .12 | 245,000 | .10 | 230,000 | .13 |
| Total stockholders' equity ........ | $1,468,000 | .64 | $1,445,000 | .60 | $1,330,000 | .76 |
| Total liabilities and stockholders' equity ......................... | $2,278,000 | 1.00 | $2,391,000 | 1.00 | $1,760,000 | 1.00 |

financial reports should arise from basic differences in the companies themselves or from the nature of their transactions and not from differences in accounting practices and procedures.

## Other Analytical Procedures

In addition to the financial statement analysis procedures described in the preceding sections, various measures may be developed with respect to specific components of financial statements. Some measurements are of general interest, while others have special significance to particular groups. Creditors, for example, are concerned with the ability of a company to pay its current obligations and seek information about the relationship of current assets to current liabilities. Stockholders are concerned with dividends and seek information relating to earnings that will form the basis for dividends. Managements are concerned with the activity of the merchandise inventory and seek information relating to the number of times goods have turned over during the period. All users are vitally interested in profitability and wish to be informed about the relationship of income to both liabilities and owners' equity.

The computation of percentages, ratios, turnovers, and other measures of financial position and operating results for a period is a form of vertical analysis. Comparison with the same measures for other periods is a form of horizontal analysis. These comparisons can be made within a company's financial statements or with other companies, individually or in industry groups. The measures described and illustrated in the following sections should not be considered all-inclusive; other measures may be useful to various groups, depending on their particular needs. It should be emphasized again that sound conclusions cannot be reached from an individual measurement. But this information, together with adequate investigation and study, may lead to a satisfactory evaluation of financial data.

## Liquidity Analysis

Generally, the first concern of a financial analyst is a firm's liquidity. Will the firm be able to meet its current obligations? If a firm cannot meet its obligations in the short run, it may not have a chance to be profitable or to experience growth in the long run. The two most commonly used measures of liquidity are the current ratio and the acid-test ratio.

**Current Ratio**　　The comparison of current assets with current liabilities is regarded as a fundamental measurement of a company's liquidity. Known as the **current ratio**, or **working capital ratio**, this measurement is computed by dividing total current assets by total current liabilities.

The current ratio is a measure of the ability to meet current obligations. Since it measures liquidity, care must be taken to determine that proper items have been included in the current asset and current liability categories. A ratio of current assets to current liabilities of less than 2 for a trading or manufacturing unit has frequently been considered unsatisfactory. However, because liquidity needs are different for different industries and companies, any such arbitrary measure should not be viewed as meaningful or appropriate in all cases. The table below presents benchmark current ratios for a set of diverse industries:[3]

| Industry (number of firms included) | Median Current Ratio |
|---|---|
| Dairy Farms (303) | 1.9 |
| Blast Furnaces and Steel Mills (550) | 1.8 |
| Electric Utilities (2,167) | 1.8 |
| Grocery Stores (2,183) | 2.2 |
| Jewelry Stores (2,319) | 3.3 |
| Personal Credit Institutions (1,452) | 2.2 |
| Legal Services (2,463) | 2.0 |

A comfortable margin of current assets over current liabilities suggests that a company will be able to meet maturing obligations even in the event of unfavorable business conditions or losses on such assets as marketable securities, receivables, and inventories.

For the AC&W Corporation, current ratios for December 31, 1994, and December 31, 1993, are developed as follows:[4]

| | December 31, 1994 | December 31, 1993 |
|---|---|---|
| Current assets | $855,000 | $955,500 |
| Current liabilities | $410,000 | $546,000 |
| Current ratio | 2.1 | 1.8 |

A current ratio of 2.1 means that AC&W could liquidate its total current liabilities 2.1 times using only its current assets.

The AC&W Corporation increased the current ratio in 1994 from 1.8 to 2.1. If no other information is available, this change may indicate some improvement in AC&W's liquidity position with improved ability to meet its current obligations. This conclusion may be in error, however, since the ratios do not disclose anything about the composition

---

[3]The industry ratios in this table, along with others shown later in the chapter, are from "Industry Norms and Key Business Ratios: 1989-90 Edition," Dun and Bradstreet, Inc. (1990).

[4]Comparative data for more than two years are generally required in evaluating financial trends. Analyses for only two years are given in the examples in this chapter, since these are sufficient to illustrate the analytical procedures involved.

of the current assets. For example, past-due receivables and slow-moving inventories usually are classified as current assets, but they would not represent liquid assets. There is also the possibility, given the business risk in the organization and industry, that these ratios are too high. Assets may be kept unnecessarily liquid and thus not earn the higher returns associated with longer-term investments. Nevertheless, the current ratio is useful in analyzing the liquidity position of the organization. Added meaning is obtained when it is compared with the company's past data and industry standards.

**Acid-Test Ratio**    A test of a company's immediate liquidity is made by comparing the sum of cash, marketable securities, notes receivable, and accounts receivable, commonly referred to as quick assets, with current liabilities. The total quick assets divided by current liabilities gives the acid-test ratio, or quick ratio. Considerable time may be required to convert raw materials, goods in process, and finished goods into receivables and then into cash. A company with a satisfactory current ratio may be in a relatively poor liquidity position when inventories comprise most of the total current assets. This is revealed by the acid-test ratio. In developing the ratio, the receivables and securities included in the total quick assets should be examined closely. In some cases these items actually may be less liquid than inventories.

Usually, a ratio of quick assets to current liabilities of at least 1 is considered desirable. Again, however, special conditions of the particular business must be evaluated. Questions such as the following should be considered: What is the composition of the quick assets? What special requirements are made by current activities upon these assets? How soon are current payables due?

Acid-test ratios for AC&W Corporation are computed as follows:

|  | December 31, | |
|---|---|---|
|  | 1994 | 1993 |
| Quick assets: | | |
| Cash | $ 60,000 | $100,500 |
| Marketable securities | 150,000 | 150,000 |
| Receivables (net) | 420,000 | 375,000 |
| Total quick assets | $630,000 | $625,500 |
| Total current liabilities | $410,000 | $546,000 |
| Acid-test ratio | 1.5 | 1.1 |

**Other Measures of Liquidity**    Other ratios may help to analyze a company's liquidity. For example, it may be useful to show the relationship of total current assets to total assets and the relationship of individual current assets, such as receivables and inventories, to total current assets. In the case of liabilities, it may be useful to show the relationship of total current liabilities to total liabilities and the relationship of individual current liabilities to total current liabilities. Such comparisons may provide information concerning the relative liquidity of total assets and the maturity of total obligations as well as the structure of working capital and shifts within the working capital group.

## Activity Analysis

There are special tests that may be applied to measure how efficiently a firm is utilizing its assets. Several of these measures also relate to liquidity because they involve significant working capital elements, such as receivables, inventories, and accounts payable.

**Accounts Receivable Turnover**    The amount of receivables usually bears a close relationship to the volume of credit sales. The receivable position and approximate collection time may be evaluated by computing the accounts receivable turnover. This rate is determined by dividing net credit sales (or total net sales if credit sales are unknown) by the average trade accounts receivable outstanding during the year. In developing an average receivables amount, monthly balances should be used if available.

Assume in the case of AC&W Corporation that all sales are made on credit, that receivables arise only from sales, and that receivable totals for only the beginning and the end of the year are available. Receivables turnover rates for 1994 and 1993 are computed as follows:

|  | 1994 | 1993 |
|---|---|---|
| Net credit sales | $1,425,000 | $1,650,000 |
| Net receivables: | | |
|   Beginning of year | $ 375,000 | $ 333,500 |
|   End of year | $ 420,000 | $ 375,000 |
| Average receivables [(beginning balance + ending balance) ÷ 2] | $ 397,500 | $ 354,250 |
| Receivables turnover for year | 3.6 times | 4.7 times |

The value computed for receivables turnover represents the average number of sale/collection cycles completed by the firm during the year.

**Number of Days' Sales in Receivables**    Average receivables are sometimes expressed in terms of the **number of days' sales in receivables**, which shows the average time required to collect receivables. Average receivables outstanding divided by average daily credit sales gives the number of days' sales in average receivables. This measure is computed for AC&W Corporation as illustrated below.

|  | 1994 | 1993 |
|---|---|---|
| Average receivables | $ 397,500 | $ 354,250 |
| Net credit sales | $1,425,000 | $1,650,000 |
| Average daily credit sales (net credit sales ÷ 365) | $3,904 | $4,521 |
| Number of days' sales in average receivables (average receivables ÷ average daily credit sales) | 102 days | 78 days |

This same measurement can be obtained by dividing the number of days in the year by the receivables turnover.[5]

In some cases, instead of developing the number of days' sales in average receivables, it may be more useful to report the number of days' credit sales in receivables at the end of the period. This information would be significant in evaluating current position, and particularly the receivable position as of a given date. This information for AC&W Corporation is presented below.

|  | 1994 | 1993 |
|---|---|---|
| Receivables at end of year | $420,000 | $375,000 |
| Average daily credit sales | $ 3,904 | $ 4,521 |
| Number of days' sales in receivables at end of year | 108 days | 83 days |

What constitutes a reasonable number of days in receivables varies with individual businesses. For example, if merchandise is sold on terms of net 60 days, 40 days' sales in receivables would be reasonable; but if terms are net 30 days, a receivable balance equal to

---

[5]A 365-day year is used in this chapter because most banks and other financial institutions use 365 days. For simplicity, ratios are sometimes calculated using a 360-day year.

40 days' sales would indicate slow collections. Typical levels for number of days' sales in receivables for several industries are presented below.

| Industry (number of firms included) | Median Number of Days' Sales in Receivables |
|---|---|
| Dairy Farms (303) | 23.9 days |
| Blast Furnaces and Steel Mills (550) | 44.9 days |
| Electric Utilities (2,167) | 32.9 days |
| Grocery Stores (2,183) | 2.3 days |
| Jewelry Stores (2,319) | 23.4 days |
| Personal Credit Institutions (1,452) | 155.1 days |
| Legal Services (2,463) | 50.0 days |

Sales activity just before the close of a period should be considered when interpreting accounts receivable measurements. If sales are unusually light or heavy just before the end of the fiscal period, this affects total receivables as well as the related measurements. When such unevenness prevails, it may be better to analyze accounts receivable according to their due dates, as was illustrated in Chapter 9.

The problem of minimizing accounts receivable without losing desirable business is important. Receivables often do not earn interest revenue, and the cost of carrying them must be covered by the profit margin. The longer accounts are carried, the smaller will be the percentage return realized on invested capital. In addition, heavier bookkeeping and collection charges and increased bad debts must be considered.

To attract business, credit frequently is granted for relatively long periods. The cost of granting long-term credit should be considered. Assume that a business has average daily credit sales of $5,000 and average accounts receivable of $250,000, which represents 50 days' credit sales. If collections and the credit period can be improved so that accounts receivable represent only 30 days' sales, then accounts receivable will be reduced to $150,000. Assuming a total cost of 10% to carry and service the accounts, the $100,000 decrease would yield annual savings of $10,000.

**Inventory Turnover**    The amount of inventory carried frequently relates closely to sales volume. The inventory position and the appropriateness of its size may be evaluated by computing the **inventory turnover**. The inventory turnover is computed by dividing cost of goods sold by average inventory. Whenever possible, monthly figures should be used to develop the average inventory balance.

Assume that for AC&W Corporation the inventory balances for only the beginning and the end of the year are available. Inventory turnover rates are computed as follows:

|  | 1994 | 1993 |
|---|---|---|
| Cost of goods sold | $1,000,000 | $1,200,000 |
| Inventory: |  |  |
| Beginning of year | $ 330,000 | $ 125,000 |
| End of year | $ 225,000 | $ 330,000 |
| Average inventory [(beginning balance + ending balance) ÷ 2] | $ 277,500 | $ 227,500 |
| Inventory turnover for year | 3.6 times | 5.3 times |

**Number of Days' Sales in Inventories**    Average inventories are sometimes expressed as the **number of days' sales in inventories**. Information is thus afforded concerning the average time it takes to turn over the inventory. The number of days' sales in inventories is calculated by dividing average inventory by average daily cost of goods sold. The number of days' sales also can be obtained by dividing the number of days in the year by the inventory turnover rate. The latter procedure for AC&W Corporation is illustrated below.

|  | 1994 | 1993 |
|---|---|---|
| Inventory turnover for year | 3.6 times | 5.3 times |
| Number of days' sales in average inventory (365 ÷ inventory turnover) | 101 days | 69 days |

As was the case with receivables, instead of developing the number of days' sales in average inventories, it may be more useful to report the number of days' sales in ending inventories. The latter measurement is determined by dividing ending inventory by average daily cost of goods sold. This information is helpful in evaluating the current asset position and particularly the inventory position as of a given date.

A company with departmental classifications for inventories might find it desirable to support the company's inventory measurements with individual department measurements, since there can be considerable variation among departments. A manufacturing company can compute separate turnover rates for finished goods, goods in process, and raw materials. The finished goods turnover is computed by dividing cost of goods sold by average finished goods inventory. Goods in process turnover is computed by dividing cost of goods manufactured by average goods in process inventory. Raw materials turnover is computed by dividing the cost of raw materials used by average raw materials inventory.

The same valuation methods must be employed for inventories in successive periods if the inventory measurements are to be comparable. Maximum accuracy is possible if information relating to inventories and amount of goods sold is available in terms of physical units rather than dollar costs.

The effect of seasonal factors on the size of year-end inventories should be considered in inventory analyses. Inventories may be abnormally high or low at the end of a period. Many companies adopt a fiscal year ending when operations are at their lowest point. This is called a natural business year. Inventories will normally be lowest at the end of such a period, so that the organization can count inventory and complete year-end closing most conveniently. Under these circumstances, monthly inventory balances should be used to arrive at a representative average inventory figure. When a periodic inventory system is employed, monthly inventories may be estimated using the gross profit method, as explained in Chapter 11.

With an increased inventory turnover, the investment necessary for a given volume of business is smaller, and consequently the return on invested capital is higher. This conclusion assumes an enterprise can acquire goods in smaller quantities sufficiently often at no price disadvantage. If merchandise must be bought in very large quantities in order to get favorable prices, then the savings on quantity purchases must be weighed against the additional investment, increased costs of storage, and other carrying charges.

The financial advantage of an increased turnover rate may be illustrated as follows. Assuming cost of goods sold of $1,000,000 and average inventory at cost of $250,000, inventory turnover is 4 times. Assume further that, through careful buying, the same business volume can be maintained with turnover of 5 times, or an average inventory of only $200,000. If interest on money invested in inventory is 10%, the savings on the $50,000 will be $5,000 annually. Other advantages include decreased inventory spoilage and obsolescence, savings in storage cost, taxes, and insurance, and reduction in risk of losses from price declines.

Inventory investments and turnover rates vary among businesses, and each business must be judged in terms of its financial structure and operations. Management must establish an inventory policy that will avoid the extremes of a dangerously low stock, which may impair sales, and an overstocking of goods, involving a heavy capital investment and risks of spoilage and obsolescence, price declines, and difficulties in meeting purchase obligations. The following table lists the average number of days' sales in inventory for several industries:

| Industry (number of firms included) | Average Number of Days' Sales in Inventory |
|---|---|
| Dairy Farms (303) | 103.0 |
| Blast Furnaces and Steel Mills (550) | 48.5 |
| Grocery Stores (2,183) | 26.8 |
| Jewelry Stores (2,319) | 259.8 |

**Asset Turnover**    A measure of the overall efficiency of asset utilization is the ratio of net sales to average total assets, called the asset turnover. This ratio is calculated by dividing net sales by average total assets. With comparative data, judgments can be made concerning the relative effectiveness of asset utilization. A ratio increase may suggest more efficient asset utilization, although a point may be reached where there is a strain on assets and a company is unable to achieve its full sales potential. An increase in average total assets accompanied by a ratio decrease may suggest overinvestment in assets or inefficient utilization.

In developing the asset turnover rate, long-term investments should be excluded from total assets when they make no contribution to sales. On the other hand, a valuation for leased property should be added to total assets to permit comparability between companies owning their properties and those that lease them. If monthly figures for assets are available, they may be used in developing a representative average for total assets employed during the year. Often, however, the beginning-of-year and end-of-year asset totals are used for computing the average. When sales can be expressed in terms of units sold, ratios of sales units to total assets offer more reliable interpretations than sales dollars, since unit sales are not affected by price changes.

Assume that for AC&W Corporation only asset totals for the beginning and end of the year are available and that sales are not expressed in terms of units. Asset turnover ratio is computed as follows:

| | 1994 | 1993 |
|---|---|---|
| Net sales ........................................... | $1,425,000 | $1,650,000 |
| Total assets (excluding long-term investments): | | |
| Beginning of year ................................. | $2,391,000 | $1,760,000 |
| End of year ....................................... | $2,278,000 | $2,391,000 |
| Average total assets [(beginning balance + ending balance) ÷ 2] ......................................... | $2,334,500 | $2,075,500 |
| Asset turnover ..................................... | 0.6 times | 0.8 times |

Asset turnover for several industries is presented below.

| Industry (number of firms included) | Median Asset Turnover |
|---|---|
| Dairy Farms (303) | 0.79 times |
| Blast Furnaces and Steel Mills (550) | 2.04 times |
| Electric Utilities (2,167) | 0.50 times |
| Grocery Stores (2,183) | 5.56 times |
| Jewelry Stores (2,319) | 1.53 times |
| Legal Services (2,463) | 3.53 times |

**Other Measures of Activity**   Turnover analysis, as illustrated for receivables, inventories, and total assets, can also be applied to other assets or groups of assets. For example, current asset turnover is calculated by dividing net sales by average current assets. This figure may be viewed as the number of times current assets are replenished, or as the number of sales dollars generated per dollar of current assets. Similarly, if net sales are divided by average plant assets (land, buildings, and equipment), a plant asset turnover can be computed. This figure measures the efficiency of plant asset management and indicates the volume of sales generated by the operating assets of a company. Increases in turnover rates generally indicate more efficient utilization of assets.

Similar procedures also can be used to analyze specific liabilities. An accounts payable turnover, for example, may be computed by dividing purchases by average payables; the number of days' purchases in accounts payable may be computed by dividing accounts payable by average daily purchases.

Analysis of liabilities in terms of due dates may assist management in cash planning. Useful relationships also can be obtained by comparing specific assets or liabilities with other assets or liabilities, or with asset or liability totals. For example, data concerning the relationship of cash to accounts payable or of cash to total liabilities may be useful.

## Profitability Analysis

Profitability analysis provides evidence concerning the earnings potential of a company and how effectively a firm is being managed. Since the reason most firms exist is to earn profits, the profitability ratios are among the most significant financial ratios. The adequacy of earnings may be measured in terms of (1) the rate earned on sales, (2) the rate earned on average total assets, (3) the rate earned on average common stockholders' equity, and (4) the availability of earnings to common stockholders. Thus, the most popular profitability measurements are profit margin on sales, return-on-investment ratios, and earnings per share.

**Profit Margin on Sales**   The ratio of net income to sales determines the net profit margin on sales. This measurement represents the net income percentage per dollar of sales. The percentage is computed by dividing net income by net sales for a period. For AC&W Corporation, the net profit margin on sales is:

|  | 1994 | 1993 |
| --- | --- | --- |
| Net income | $    70,000 | $    60,000 |
| Net sales | $1,425,000 | $1,650,000 |
| Net profit margin | 4.9% | 3.6% |

This means that for 1994, AC&W generated almost five cents of profit per dollar of sales revenue. Because net income is used in the computation, any extraordinary or irregular items may distort the profit margin rate with respect to normal operating activities. Adjustments may be needed in the analysis to account for such items. A sample of profit margins is presented below.

| Industry (number of firms included) | Median Profit Margin |
| --- | --- |
| Dairy Farms (303) | 6.4% |
| Blast Furnaces and Steel Mills (550) | 3.9% |
| Electric Utilities (2,167) | 6.9% |
| Grocery Stores (2,183) | 1.4% |
| Jewelry Stores (2,319) | 5.0% |
| Legal Services (2,463) | 8.3% |

For merchandising and manufacturing companies, **gross profit margin on sales** is often a significant ratio for evaluating the profitability of a company. In these companies, cost of goods sold is the most significant expense, and careful inventory control is necessary to ensure profitable operations. For AC&W, the gross profit margin on sales is:

| | 1994 | 1993 |
|---|---|---|
| Gross profit on sales | $ 425,000 | $ 450,000 |
| Net sales | $1,425,000 | $1,650,000 |
| Gross profit margin | 29.8% | 27.3% |

**Rate Earned on Average Total Assets**    Overall asset productivity may be expressed as the rate earned on average total assets, also referred to as the **return on investment (ROI)**, or the asset productivity rate. The rate is computed by dividing net income by the average total assets used to produce net income. This rate measures the efficiency in using resources to generate net income. If total assets by months are available, they should be used to develop an average for the year. Frequently, however, the assets at the beginning of the year or the assets at the end of the year are used. In some cases it may be desirable to use net income from operations by excluding revenue from investments, such as interest, dividends, and rents, or from gains or losses resulting from nonoperating transactions. When this is the case, average total assets should be reduced by the investments or other assets. Sometimes comparisons are developed for the rate of operating income to average total assets or the rate of pretax income to average total assets, so that results are not affected by financial management items or by changes in income tax rates.

Rates earned on average total assets for AC&W Corporation are determined as follows:

| | 1994 | 1993 |
|---|---|---|
| Net income | $ 70,000 | $ 60,000 |
| Total assets: | | |
| Beginning of year | $2,391,000 | $1,760,000 |
| End of year | $2,278,000 | $2,391,000 |
| Average total assets [(beginning balance + ending balance) ÷ 2] | $2,334,500 | $2,075,500 |
| Rate earned on average total assets | 3.0% | 2.9% |

An analysis, referred to as the DuPont method, illustrates the factors that affect this ratio. The DuPont method explicitly recognizes that return on average total assets equals the profit margin on sales multiplied by the asset turnover. The formulas for these ratios show clearly why this relationship exists:

$$\text{Profit margin} \times \text{Asset turnover} = \text{Return on average total assets}$$

$$\frac{\text{Net income}}{\text{Sales}} \times \frac{\text{Sales}}{\text{Average total assets}} = \frac{\text{Net income}}{\text{Average total assets}}$$

Sales cancels out of the formula leaving the return-on-assets ratio. Ratios previously computed for the AC&W Corporation in 1994 further illustrate this analysis:

| Profit margin on sales (p. 841) | | Asset turnover (p. 840) | | Rate earned on average total assets (p. 842) |
|---|---|---|---|---|
| 4.9 | × | .6 | = | 3% (rounded) |

This analytical tool helps explain how discount organizations compete with full service companies. Generally, the discount store operates on a relatively small margin and plans for a high turnover of assets, whereas the full service organization has a higher margin but lower turnover.

For example, assume that Company A is a full service organization and Company B is a discount store. Company A has a margin of 22.6% on sales and a total asset turnover of 1.1. Company B has a margin of 4.5% and a turnover of 5.2. Company A's percentage return on assets equals 24.9% (22.6% × 1.1), and Company B's return is 23.4% (4.5% × 5.2). Thus, the return on total assets for Company A is very close to that of Company B, although their asset turnover and profitability ratios are quite different.

**Rate Earned on Average Stockholders' Equity**    Net income may be expressed as the rate earned on average stockholders' equity (or return on stockholders' equity) by dividing net income by average stockholders' equity. In developing this rate, it is preferable to calculate the average stockholders' equity for a year from monthly data, particularly when significant changes have occurred during the year, such as the sale of additional stock, retirement of stock, and accumulation of earnings. Sometimes the beginning or the ending stockholders' equity is used.

For AC&W Corporation, rates earned on average stockholders' equity are as follows:

|  | 1994 | 1993 |
|---|---|---|
| Net income | $   70,000 | $   60,000 |
| Stockholders' equity: |  |  |
| Beginning of year | $1,445,000 | $1,330,000 |
| End of year | $1,468,000 | $1,445,000 |
| Average stockholders' equity [beginning balance + ending balance) ÷ 2] | $1,456,500 | $1,387,500 |
| Rate earned on average stockholders' equity | 4.8% | 4.3% |

As a company's liabilities increase in relationship to stockholders' equity, the spread between the rate earned on average stockholders' equity and the rate earned on average total assets rises. This difference measures the way a company is using leverage in its business financing. The rate earned on average stockholders' equity is important to investors who must reconcile the risk of debt financing with the potentially greater profitability.

**Rate Earned on Average Common Stockholders' Equity**    As a refinement to the rate earned on average stockholders' equity, earnings may be measured in terms of the average common stockholders' equity. The rate earned on average common stockholders' equity is computed by dividing net income after preferred dividend requirements by average common stockholders' equity.

In the case of AC&W Corporation, preferred dividend requirements are 6%. The rate earned on average common stockholders' equity, then, is calculated as follows:

|  | 1994 | 1993 |
|---|---|---|
| Net income | $   70,000 | $   60,000 |
| Less dividend requirements on preferred stock | 21,000 | 21,000 |
| Net income related to common stock | $   49,000 | $   39,000 |
| Common stockholders' equity: |  |  |
| Beginning of year | $1,095,000 | $1,080,000 |
| End of year | $1,118,000 | $1,095,000 |
| Average common stockholders' equity [(beginning balance + ending balance) ÷ 2] | $1,106,500 | $1,087,500 |
| Rate earned on average common stockholders' equity | 4.4% | 3.6% |

**Earnings Per Share**    The Accounting Principles Board in Opinion No. 15 indicated that earnings per share data were of such importance to investors and others that such data should be presented prominently on the income statement. In computing earnings per share on common stock, earnings are first reduced by the prior dividend rights of preferred stock. Computations are made in terms of the weighted average number of common shares outstanding for each period presented. Adjustments are required when a corporation's capital structure includes potentially dilutive securities. If the total potential dilution is material, both primary earnings per share and fully diluted earnings per share must be disclosed. When net income includes below-the-line items, earnings per share should be reported for each major component of income as well as for net income.

For AC&W Corporation, there are no potentially dilutive securities. Earnings per share on common stock is calculated as follows:

|  | 1994 | 1993 |
|---|---|---|
| Net income | $70,000 | $60,000 |
| Less dividend requirements on preferred stock | 21,000 | 21,000 |
| Income related to common stockholders' equity | $49,000 | $39,000 |
| Number of shares of common stock outstanding | 75,000 | 75,000 |
| Earnings per share on common stock | $.65 | $.52 |

**Dividends Per Share**    In addition to earnings per share, many companies report **dividends per share** in the financial statements. This amount is computed simply by dividing cash dividends for the year by the number of shares of common stock outstanding. When a significant number of common shares have been issued or retired during a period, an average should be computed; otherwise, the number of common shares outstanding at the end of the period normally is used. For AC&W Corporation, the number of shares of common stock outstanding has remained constant for the past 3 years. Therefore, the dividends per share are $.35 for 1994 and $.32 for 1993. Another way of analyzing dividends is to compute the dividend payout ratio, or the percentage of net income paid out in dividends. This may be computed by dividing the dividends per share by the earnings per share, or by dividing dividends paid by net income. The dividend payout ratios for AC&W are 54% in 1994 and 62% in 1993.

**Yield on Common Stock**    Dividends per share may be used to compute a rate of return on the market value of common stock. Such a rate, referred to as the **yield on common stock**, or dividend yield, is found by dividing the annual dividends per common share by the latest market price per common share. For AC&W Corporation, the yield on the common stock is computed as follows:

|  | 1994 | 1993 |
|---|---|---|
| Dividends for year per common share | $ .35 | $ .32 |
| Market value per common share at end of year | $10.00 | $6.50 |
| Yield on common stock | 3.5% | 4.9% |

Dividend yields are typically quite low (less than five percent) when compared to the interest yield on debt. Investors in common stock are willing to accept a low dividend yield because they anticipate that the stock will increase in price and result in a capital gain.

**Price-Earnings Ratio**    The market price of common stock may be expressed as a multiple of earnings to evaluate the attractiveness of common stock as an investment. This measurement is referred to as the **price-earnings ratio** and is computed by dividing the market price per share of stock by the annual earnings per share. Instead of using the average market value of shares for the period covered by earnings, the latest market value normally is used. In the United States, price-earnings ratios typically range from 5 to 20. Assuming market values per common share of AC&W Corporation stock at the end of 1994 of $10 and at the end of 1993 of $6.50, price-earnings ratios would be computed as follows:

|  | 1994 | 1993 |
|---|---|---|
| Market value per common share at end of year ............... | $10.00 | $6.50 |
| Earnings per share (calculated on page 844) .................. | $ .65 | $ .52 |
| Price-earnings ratio ........................................ | 15.4 | 12.5 |

As an alternative to the price-earnings ratio, earnings per share can be presented as a percentage of the market price of the stock (earnings-price ratio).

## Capital Structure Analysis

The composition of a company's capital structure has significant implications for stockholders, creditors, potential investors, and potential creditors. Creditors look to the stockholders' equity as a margin of safety. As stockholders' equity increases in relation to total liabilities, the margin of protection to creditors also increases. Should a company have financial difficulty and have to terminate its operations through bankruptcy, the higher the margin of safety, the more probable that creditors will recover their investment in the company.

However, from the perspective of the common stockholders, it is often advantageous to use borrowed capital or preferred stock to expand operations rather than issuing additional common stock. If a company can earn a return on the funds obtained through borrowing or from preferred stock that is greater than the cost of the funds, the excess earnings will benefit the common stockholders through an increase in the return on average common stockholders' equity. This result is commonly referred to as **trading on the equity**, or applying **financial leverage**. On the other hand, if the company earns a return that is less than the cost of the funds, the common stockholders must bear the excess cost. There is a legal obligation to pay interest, and preferred stock dividends usually are cumulative; thus, they must be paid before any distribution to the common stockholders.

To illustrate the impact of financial leverage on common stockholders, assume that a company with 10,000 shares of stock outstanding reports average assets of $500,000 and has no liabilities. The company estimates that its income before income taxes will be $80,000 without any borrowed capital. Income taxes are estimated to be 30% of income; therefore, net income is estimated to be $56,000 ($80,000 − $24,000). This would result in a return on average common stockholders' equity of 11.2% ($56,000 ÷ $500,000).

Exhibit 22—1 illustrates the effects of borrowing an extra million dollars at 12% interest under (1) the assumption the extra funds earn 15% before interest and taxes, or more than the cost of the borrowed funds, and (2) the assumption the extra funds earn 5% before interest and taxes, or less than the cost of the borrowed funds. Using financial leverage favorably under the first assumption results in an increase in the return on average common stockholders' equity from 11.2% to 15.4%. The market would probably react to this increase favorably and the market price of the stock would rise. Additional dividends also could be paid with the increase of $21,000 in net income. On the other hand, the unfavorable result of financial leverage can be seen under the second assumption as the return on average common stockholders' equity decreases from 11.2% to 1.4%. The $49,000 decrease in net income will probably have an unfavorable impact on both the stock's market price and the dividend payments.

The illustration uses borrowed funds that had a tax deductible interest cost attached to them. If the funds had been acquired with preferred stock, the computations would have differed because of the nondeductibility of preferred dividends for income tax purposes. However, the same advantages and disadvantages to the common stockholder apply depending on the relationship between the cost of the funds and the amount that can be earned from the funds.

Stockholders, creditors, and other interested parties often make use of capital structure measurements including the debt-to-equity ratio, number of times interest is earned, fixed charge coverage, and book value per share. These methods are illustrated in the following sections.

### Exhibit 22—1    Financial Leverage

| | Assumption 1 Borrowed Capital Earns 15% | Assumption 2 Borrowed Capital Earns 5% |
|---|---|---|
| Income before interest and taxes: | | |
| Without borrowed funds ............. | $ 80,000 | $ 80,000 |
| On $1,000,000 borrowed ............. | 150,000 | 50,000 |
| | $230,000 | $130,000 |
| Interest (12% x $1,000,000) ............. | 120,000 | 120,000 |
| Income before taxes .................. | $110,000 | $ 10,000 |
| Income taxes (30%) ................... | 33,000 | 3,000 |
| Net income .......................... | 77,000 | $ 7,000 |
| Average common stockholders' equity .. | $500,000 | $500,000 |
| Return on average common stockholders' equity ................................ | 15.4% | 1.4% |

**Ratio of Total Liabilities to Stockholders' Equity**    Creditors' and stockholders' equities may be expressed in terms of total assets or in terms of each other. For example, creditors may have a 40% interest in total assets, and stockholders a 60% interest. This can be expressed as a debt-to-equity ratio of 0.67 to 1.

For AC&W Corporation, the relationship of total liabilities to stockholders' equity is calculated as follows:

| | 1994 | 1993 |
|---|---|---|
| Total liabilities ..................................... | $ 810,000 | $ 946,000 |
| Stockholders' equity ................................. | $1,468,000 | $1,445,000 |
| Ratio of total liabilities to stockholders' equity ......... | 0.55 | 0.65 |

In analyzing the relationship of total liabilities to stockholders' equity, particular note should be made of lease arrangements. Both property rights provided under the leases and the accompanying liabilities should be considered in evaluating the equities and changes in equities from period to period.

Investors generally prefer a higher debt-to-equity ratio to obtain the advantages of financial leverage, while creditors favor a lower ratio to increase the safety of their debt. Typical debt-to-equity ratios are presented at the top of page 847.

| Industry (number of firms included) | Median Debt-to-Equity Ratio |
|---|---|
| Dairy Farms (303) | 0.560 |
| Blast Furnaces and Steel Mills (550) | 1.153 |
| Electric Utilities (2,167) | 1.592 |
| Grocery Stores (2,183) | 0.832 |
| Jewelry Stores (2,319) | 0.578 |
| Personal Credit Institutions (1,452) | 2.015 |
| Legal Services (2,463) | 0.708 |

The DuPont analysis on page 846 can be extended to include the effect of leverage:

$$\begin{array}{ccccc} \text{Profit margin} & & \text{Asset} & \text{Leverage} & \begin{array}{c}\text{Rate earned on}\\\text{average common}\end{array} \\ \text{on sales} & \times & \text{turnover} \times & \text{ratio} & = \begin{array}{c}\text{stockholders' equity}\end{array} \end{array}$$

$$\frac{\begin{array}{c}\text{Net income to}\\\text{common stockholders}\end{array}}{\text{Sales}} \times \frac{\text{Sales}}{\text{Average total assets}} \times \frac{\text{Average total assets}}{\begin{array}{c}\text{Average common}\\\text{stockholders' equity}\end{array}} = \frac{\begin{array}{c}\text{Net income to}\\\text{common stockholders}\end{array}}{\begin{array}{c}\text{Average common}\\\text{stockholders' equity}\end{array}}$$

This formulation illustrates that the return to common stockholders is a function of operating decisions (margin), investing decisions (turnover), and financing decisions (leverage).[6]

**Number of Times Interest Earned**    A measure of the debt position of a company in relation to its earnings ability is the number of times interest is earned. The calculation is made by dividing income before any charges for interest or income tax by the interest requirements for the period. The resulting figure reflects the company's ability to meet interest payments and the degree of safety afforded the creditors. The number of times interest was earned by AC&W Corporation follows:

| | 1994 | 1993 |
|---|---|---|
| Income before income tax | $100,000 | $ 85,000 |
| Add bond interest (10% of $400,000) | 40,000 | 40,000 |
| Amount available in meeting bond interest requirements | $140,000 | $125,000 |
| Number of times bond interest requirements were earned | 3.5 times | 3.1 times |

Pretax income was used in the computation, since income tax applies only after interest is deducted, and it is pretax income that protects creditors.

A computation similar to times interest earned, but more inclusive, is the fixed charge coverage. Fixed charges include such obligations as interest on bonds and notes, lease obligations, and any other recurring financial commitments. The number of times fixed charges are covered is calculated by adding the fixed charges to pretax income and then dividing the total by the fixed charges.

**Book Value Per Share**    Stockholders' equity can be measured by calculating the book value per share, which is the dollar equity in corporate capital of each share of stock. This amount frequently is used by investors in conjunction with the market value per share to evaluate the attractiveness of the stock for investment purposes.

When there is only one class of stock outstanding, the calculation of book value is relatively simple; the total stockholders' equity is divided by the number of shares of stock

[6]For additional disaggregation suggestions, see Thomas L. Selling and Clyde Stickney, "Disaggregating the Rate of Return on Common Shareholders' Equity: A New Approach," *Accounting Horizons*, December 1990, pp. 9-17.

outstanding at the close of the reporting period. When a company is holding treasury stock, its cost is deducted from stockholders' equity and the treasury shares are deducted from the shares issued.

When more than one class of stock is outstanding, a portion of the stockholders' equity must be allocated to the other classes of stock before the book value of the common stock is computed. Usually the par or liquidation value of the other classes of stock is used to make this allocation.

In the case of AC&W Corporation, the par value of the preferred stock is equal to the liquidation value, and there are no preferred dividends in arrears. The book value per share is computed as follows:

|  | 1994 | 1993 |
|---|---|---|
| Common stockholders' equity ........................ | $1,118,000 | $1,095,000 |
| Number of shares of common stock outstanding ....... | 75,000 | 75,000 |
| Book value per share on common stock ............... | $14.91 | $14.60 |

Since the market value of the stock is lower than the book value, many investors would consider AC&W an attractive investment. However, the nature and limitations of the per share book value measurements must be considered in using these data. Carrying values of assets may vary significantly from their present fair values or immediate realizable values. This would directly affect the per share amount that could be realized in the event of a company liquidation.

## Summary of Analytical Measures

Financial ratios, percentages, and other measures are useful tools for analyzing financial statements. They enable statement users to make meaningful judgments about an enterprise's financial condition and operating results. These measures, like financial statements, are more meaningful when compared with similar data for more than one period and with industry averages or other available data. A summary of the major analytical measures discussed in this chapter is presented in Exhibit 22—2.

## USE OF INDUSTRY DATA FOR COMPARATIVE ANALYSIS

As indicated earlier in the chapter, comparisons of common-size information or other measurements may be made over time within a company or with similar companies individually or in industry groups. There are many general and industry sources that can be used to obtain comparative information. The major difficulty in using comparative data is the selection of specific companies or an industry that is similar to the company being examined. The government has established a standard for classifying industries known as the **Standard Industrial Code (SIC)**. Over 800 industries are identified, and general survey information is compiled according to these codes.

If the company being analyzed operates only in one general business area, it usually isn't difficult to find a category for comparison. However, many businesses today are large, complex organizations engaged in a variety of activities that bear little relationship to each other. For example, a company might manufacture airplane engines, operate a real estate business, and manage a professional hockey team. Such companies, referred to as **diversified companies**, or **conglomerates**, operate in multiple industries and do not fit into any one specific industry category. Thus, comparative analysis for a highly diversified company requires either an assumption that the company operates primarily in one area or separate data for each subindustry or segment. Generally, comparisons are more meaningful when separate data for segments are analyzed, and many companies are required to include such data with their financial statements.

**Exhibit 22—2    Summary of Major Analytical Measures**

### Liquidity Analysis

| | | |
|---|---|---|
| (1) Current ratio | $$\frac{\text{Current assets}}{\text{Current liabilities}}$$ | Measures ability to pay short-term debts. |
| (2) Acid-test ratio | $$\frac{\text{Quick assets}}{\text{Current liabilities}}$$ | Measures immediate ability to pay short-term debts. |

### Activity Analysis

| | | |
|---|---|---|
| (3) Accounts receivable turnover | $$\frac{\text{Net credit sales}}{\text{Average accounts receivable}}$$ | Measures receivable position and approximate average collection time. |
| (4) Number of days' sales in receivables | $$\frac{\text{Average accounts receivable}}{\text{Average daily credit sales}}$$ | Measures receivable position and approximate average collection time. |
| (5) Inventory turnover | $$\frac{\text{Cost of goods sold}}{\text{Average inventory}}$$ | Measures appropriateness of inventory levels in terms of time required to sell or "turn over" goods. |
| (6) Number of days' sales in inventories | $$\frac{\text{Average inventory}}{\text{Average daily cost of goods sold}}$$ | Measures appropriateness of inventory levels in terms of time required to sell or "turn over" goods. |
| (7) Asset turnover | $$\frac{\text{Net sales}}{\text{Average total assets}}$$ | Measures effectiveness of asset utilization. |

### Profitability Analysis

| | | |
|---|---|---|
| (8) Net profit margin on sales | $$\frac{\text{Net income}}{\text{Net sales}}$$ | Measures profit percentage per dollar of sales. |
| (9) Gross profit margin on sales | $$\frac{\text{Gross profit}}{\text{Net sales}}$$ | Measures gross profit percentage per dollar of sales. |
| (10) Rate earned on average total assets | $$\frac{\text{Net income}}{\text{Average total assets}}$$ | Measures overall asset productivity. |
| (11) Rate earned on average stockholders' equity | $$\frac{\text{Net income}}{\text{Average stockholders' equity}}$$ | Measures rate of return on average stockholders' equity. |
| (12) Rate earned on average common stockholders' equity | $$\frac{\text{Net income—preferred dividend requirements}}{\text{Average common stockholders' equity}}$$ | Measures rate of return on average common stockholders' equity. |
| (13) Earnings per share | $$\frac{\text{Net income—preferred dividend requirements}}{\text{Weighted average number of shares of common stock outstanding}}$$ | Measures net income per share of common stock. |
| (14) Dividends per share | $$\frac{\text{Dividends on common stock}}{\text{Average number of shares of common stock outstanding}}$$ | Measures dividends per share of common stock. |

## Profitability Analysis (Concluded)

| (15) Yield on common stock | $\dfrac{\text{Dividends per share of common stock}}{\text{Market value per share of common stock}}$ | Measures rate of cash return to stockholders. |
|---|---|---|
| (16) Price-earnings ratio | $\dfrac{\text{Market price per share of common stock}}{\text{Earnings per share of common stock}}$ | Measures investor beliefs about stability of earnings and growth potential. |

## Capital Structure Analysis

| (17) Debt-to-equity ratio | $\dfrac{\text{Total liabilities}}{\text{Stockholders' equity}}$ | Measures use of debt to finance operations. |
|---|---|---|
| (18) Number of times interest is earned | $\dfrac{\text{Income before taxes and interest expense}}{\text{Interest expense}}$ | Measures ability to meet interest payments. |
| (19) Book value per share | $\dfrac{\text{Common stockholders' equity}}{\text{Number of shares of common stock outstanding}}$ | Measures equity per share of common stock. |

## Segment Reporting

When a company is diversified, the different segments of the company often operate in distinct and separate markets, involve different management teams, and experience different growth patterns, profit potentials, and degrees of risk. In effect, the segments of the company behave almost like, and in some cases are, separate companies within an overall corporate structure. Yet, if only total company information is presented for a highly diversified company, the different degrees of risk, profitability, and growth potential for major segments of the company cannot be analyzed and compared.

Recognizing this problem, the FASB issued Statement No. 14, which requires disclosure of selected information for segments of diversified companies.[7] Information to be reported includes revenues, operating profit, and identifiable assets for each significant industry segment of a company. Essentially, a **segment** is considered significant if its sales, profits, or assets are 10% or more of the respective total company amounts. A practical limit of 10 segments is suggested, and at least 75% of total company sales must be accounted for. The segment data may be reported in the audited financial statements or in a separate schedule considered an integral part of the statements. Other provisions of Statement No. 14 require disclosure of revenues from major customers and information about foreign operations and export sales.

Reporting by lines of business presents several problems. For example, how does one determine which business segments should be reported on? Certainly not all companies are organized in the same manner, even if they are engaged in similar business activities. Reporting on a particular division or profit-center in one company may not be comparable to another company. Another problem relates to transfer pricing. Not all companies use the same method of pricing goods or services that are "sold" among the different divisions or units of a company. This could lead to distorted segment profit data. Another related problem is the allocation of common costs among segments of a company. Certain costs, such as general and administrative expenses, are very difficult to assign to particular segments of a company on anything other than an arbitrary basis. This, again, could result in misleading information.

---

[7]*Statement of Financial Accounting Standards No. 14,* "Financial Reporting for Segments of a Business Enterprise" (Stamford: Financial Accounting Standards Board, 1976).

## Market Efficiency

An efficient market is one in which information is reflected rapidly in prices. For example, if the real estate market in a city is efficient, then news of an impending layoff at a major employer in the city should result quickly in lower housing prices because of an anticipated decrease in demand. The major stock exchanges in the United States often are considered to be efficient markets in the sense that information about specific companies or about the economy in general is reflected almost immediately in stock prices. One implication of market efficiency is that, since current stock prices reflect all available information, future movements in stock prices should be unpredictable.

It seems clear that capital markets in the United States are efficient in a general sense, but accumulated evidence suggests the existence of a number of puzzling "anomalies" in the form of predictability in the pattern of stock returns. For example, returns on stock portfolios generally are lower on Monday than on other days of the week. Also, returns are higher than normal on days before holidays and also during the month of January.

From an accounting standpoint, market efficiency relates to the usefulness of so-called "fundamental analysis." Fundamental analysis is the practice of using financial data to calculate the underlying value of a firm and using this underlying value to identify over- and underpriced stocks. The notion of fundamental analysis is in conflict with market efficiency, since the analysis works only if current stock prices do not fully reflect all available accounting information. For this reason, fundamental analysis frequently has been regarded with skepticism by academics. However, recent research has revealed the ability of accounting data to predict future stock returns. Ou and Penman (1989) demonstrate that financial ratios derived from publicly available financial statements can be used to successfully forecast stock returns for the coming year.

### Question:

*Why might accountants be interested in whether stock prices fully reflect the information contained in the financial statements?*

Source:   Jane A. Ou and Stephen H. Penman, "Financial Statement Analysis and the Prediction of Stock Returns," *Journal of Accounting and Economics*, November 1989, p. 295.

In spite of these difficulties, the accounting profession has concluded that segment reporting is necessary to assist readers of financial statements in analyzing and understanding an enterprise's past performance and future prospects and making comparisons with other companies. An example of segment reporting, from the 1988 annual report of Capital Cities/ABC, is presented in Exhibit 22—3.

### Interim Reporting

Statements showing financial position and operating results for intervals of less than a year are referred to as **interim financial statements**. Interim reports are considered essential in providing investors and others with more timely information as to the position and progress of an enterprise. This information is most useful in comparative form because of the relationship it shows to data for similar reporting intervals and to data in the annual report.

Notwithstanding the need for interim reports, there are significant difficulties associated with them. One problem is caused by the seasonal factors of certain businesses. For example, in some companies, revenues fluctuate widely among interim periods; in other businesses, significant fixed costs are incurred during a single period but are to benefit several periods. Not only must costs be allocated to appropriate periods of benefit, but they must be matched against the realized revenues for the interim period to determine a reasonable income measurement.

Exhibit 22—3    Capital Cities/ABC—Segment Reporting

# Notes to Consolidated Financial Statements—(Continued)

## 8. Segment Data

The Company operates the ABC Television Network and eight affiliated television stations, six radio networks and 21 radio stations, and provides programming for cable television. The Company publishes newspapers, shopping guides, various specialized business and consumer periodicals and books; and also distributes information from data bases. Operations are classified into two business segments: Broadcasting and Publishing. There are no product

transfers between segments of the Company, and virtually all of the Company's business is conducted within the United States. Prior to 1986, the Company owned and operated cable television systems. They were classified as a separate business segment and are included below in the Broadcasting segment. Cable television net revenues and income from operations for 1985 were $84,580,000 and $5,206,000, respectively. The segment data follows (000's omitted):

| | 1987 | 1986 | 1985 | 1984 | 1983 |
|---|---|---|---|---|---|
| **Broadcasting** | | | | | |
| Net revenues | $ 3,433,749 | $ 3,153,619 | $ 378,297 | $ 348,106 | $ 302,785 |
| Direct operating costs | 2,680,582 | 2,554,932 | 192,249 | 172,867 | 151,608 |
| Depreciation | 73,730 | 78,952 | 26,711 | 23,257 | 18,889 |
| Total operating costs | 2,754,312 | 2,633,884 | 218,960 | 196,124 | 170,492 |
| Income before amortization of intangible assets | 679,437 | 519,735 | 159,337 | 151,982 | 132,293 |
| Amortization of intangible assets | 46,527 | 45,200 | 8,367 | 7,800 | 7,597 |
| Income from operations | $ 632,910 | $ 474,535 | $ 150,970 | $ 144,182 | $ 124,696 |
| Assets at year-end | $ 4,018,775 | $ 4,186,650 | $ 537,797 | $ 507,433 | $ 455,341 |
| Capital expenditures | 102,425 | 104,278 | 26,327 | 26,370 | 36,782 |
| **Publishing** | | | | | |
| Net revenues | $ 1,006,597 | $ 970,755 | $ 642,583 | $ 591,616 | $ 459,510 |
| Direct operating costs | 822,123 | 778,201 | 482,333 | 438,414 | 342,253 |
| Depreciation | 18,878 | 15,353 | 10,395 | 10,190 | 8,646 |
| Total operating costs | 841,001 | 793,554 | 492,728 | 448,604 | 350,899 |
| Income before amortization of intangible assets | 165,596 | 177,201 | 149,855 | 143,012 | 108,611 |
| Amortization of intangible assets | 18,879 | 18,202 | 11,343 | 9,833 | 4,577 |
| Income from operations | $ 146,717 | $ 158,999 | $ 138,512 | $ 133,179 | $ 104,034 |
| Assets at year-end | $ 908,193 | $ 920,896 | $ 455,274 | $ 430,997 | $ 287,523 |
| Capital expenditures | 13,114 | 48,589 | 45,869 | 26,700 | 10,666 |
| **Consolidated** | | | | | |
| Net revenues | $ 4,440,346 | $ 4,124,374 | $ 1,020,880 | $ 939,722 | $ 762,295 |
| Income from operations | $ 779,627 | $ 633,534 | $ 289,482 | $ 277,361 | $ 228,730 |
| General corporate expense | (33,637) | (30,856) | (11,981) | (9,849) | (8,366) |
| Operating income | 745,990 | 602,678 | 277,501 | 267,512 | 220,364 |
| Interest expense | (190,806) | (185,511) | (22,738) | (27,161) | (14,633) |
| Interest and other income | 8,794 | 5,576 | 22,059 | 28,442 | 18,773 |
| Income before income taxes | $ 563,978 | $ 422,743 | $ 276,822 | $ 268,793 | $ 224,504 |
| Assets employed by segments | $ 4,926,968 | $ 5,107,546 | $ 993,071 | $ 938,430 | $ 742,864 |
| Investments and corporate assets | 451,404 | 83,870 | 891,860 | 269,742 | 310,048 |
| Total assets at year-end | $ 5,378,372 | $ 5,191,416 | $ 1,884,931 | $ 1,208,172 | $ 1,052,912 |

In preparing interim reports, adjustments for accrued items, generally required only at year-end, have to be considered at the end of each interim period. Because of the additional time and extra costs involved to develop complete information, many estimates of expenses are made for interim reports. The increased number of estimates adds an element of subjectivity to these reports.

Another problem is that extraordinary items or the disposal of a business segment will have a greater impact on an interim period's earnings than on the results of operations for an entire year. In analyzing interim financial statements, special attention should be given to these and similar considerations.

Partially because of some of the above problems and partially because of differing views as to the objective of interim reports, there has been a variety of practices in presenting interim financial information. Two prominent viewpoints exist. One viewpoint is that each reporting interval is to be recognized as a separate accounting period. Thus, the results of operations for each interim period are determined in essentially the same manner as for the annual accounting period. Under this approach, the same judgments, estimations, accruals, and deferrals are recognized at the end of each interim period as for the annual period.

The other viewpoint, and the one accepted by the APB in Opinion No. 28, is that the interim period is an integral part of the annual period.[8] Essentially, the revenues and expenses for the total period are allocated among interim periods on some reasonable basis, e.g., time, sales volume, or productive activity.

Under the **integral part of annual period concept**, the same general accounting principles and reporting practices employed for annual reports are to be utilized for interim statements, except modifications may be required so the interim results will better relate to the total results of operations for the annual period. As an example of the type of modification that may be required, assume a company uses the LIFO method of inventory valuation and encounters a situation where liquidation of the base period inventory occurs at an interim date but the inventory is expected to be replaced by the end of the annual period. Under these circumstances, the inventory reported at the interim date should not reflect the LIFO liquidation, and the cost of goods sold for the interim period should include the expected cost of replacing the liquidated LIFO base.[9]

Another example of a required modification deals with a change in accounting principle during an interim period. In general, these changes should follow the provisions of APB Opinion No. 20.[10] However, the FASB has concluded in Statement No. 3 that for any cumulative effect-type change, other than a change to LIFO, if the change is made "in other than the first interim period of an enterprise's fiscal year, the cumulative effect of the change on retained earnings at the beginning of that year shall be included in the determination of net income of the first interim period of the year of change."[11]

Applying generally accepted accounting practices to interim financial statements can become complex. This is an area that is developing to meet the perceived needs of users. For example, the SEC has adopted rules requiring increased disclosure of interim financial information. Interpretations of old standards and the development of new standards will assist in presenting interim financial data that should help investors and others in analyzing and interpreting the financial picture and operating results of a company.

---

[8]*Opinions of the Accounting Principles Board, No. 28,* "Interim Financial Reporting" (New York: American Institute of Certified Public Accountants, 1973), par. 9.

[9]*Ibid.,* par. 14.

[10]*Opinions of the Accounting Principles Board, No. 20,* "Accounting Changes" (New York: American Institute of Certified Public Accountants, 1971).

[11]*Statement of Financial Accounting Standards No. 3,* "Reporting Accounting Changes in Interim Financial Statements" (Stamford: Financial Accounting Standards Board, 1974), par. 4.

## Sources of Industry Data

Whether a company operates in one industry or in several different industries, financial analysis is enhanced if company data can be compared with industry statistics. Ratio information concerning various industries is available from different sources. These sources can be divided into two categories: (1) general sources and (2) specific industry sources. The following two general sources are kept reasonably current and are quite comprehensive:

1. Dun and Bradstreet, Inc., "Key Business Ratios"
2. Robert Morris and Associates, "Annual Statement Studies"

"Key Business Ratios" features 14 financial ratios for over 800 retailing, wholesaling, and manufacturing lines of business. The computations are made using data for over 1 million companies. In addition, common-size statement information is provided for each line of business. "Key Business Ratios" is published annually, but data are collected continuously throughout the year.

The second general source is Robert Morris and Associates "Annual Statement Studies." Ratios for over 350 lines of business are prepared based on data furnished by member banks of Robert Morris and Associates from customer-submitted financial reports. The ratios are presented for 5 years, and additional trend data also are provided. In contrast, the Dun and Bradstreet ratios and common-size data are presented for a single year. Because the submission of data for the Robert Morris publication is on a voluntary basis, the number of companies included in "Annual Statement Studies" is much lower than the number included in Dun and Bradstreet's "Key Business Ratios."

Other general sources of information include limited ratio information published occasionally in business periodicals such as *Forbes, Business Week,* and *Fortune.* This information usually is classified by industry and often includes rankings of factors such as growth and profitability. The annual "Fortune 500" listing and analysis of the 500 largest American companies is perhaps the best known of these sources.

Specific industry sources for comparative data include a large number of industry associations that collect, summarize, and disseminate information about their members. Often this information is of greater use in financial analysis than information from general sources because of its greater detail and more current data.

## INTERPRETATION OF ANALYSES

The analyses discussed in this chapter are designed to help an analyst arrive at certain conclusions with regard to a business. As previously stated, these are merely guides to intelligent interpretation of financial data.

Only those ratios and measurements that will actually assist in arriving at informed conclusions with respect to questions raised need be used. The measurements developed need to be interpreted in terms of the circumstances of a particular enterprise, the accounting methods used, the conditions of the particular industry in which the enterprise operates, and the general business and economic environment. If measurements are to be of maximum value, they must be compared with similar data developed for the particular enterprise for past periods, with standard measurements for the industry as a whole, and with pertinent data relating to general business conditions and price fluctuations affecting the individual enterprise. Only through intelligent use and integration of the foregoing sources of data can financial weaknesses and strengths be identified and reliable opinions be developed concerning business structure, operations, and growth.

# APPENDIX

## Expanded Illustration of Statement of Cash Flows

The basic techniques for preparing a statement of cash flows were explained in Chapter 6. More complex circumstances have been addressed as the topics have come up in subsequent chapters. This appendix presents an expanded problem that illustrates many of the cash flow issues that have been treated in the text.

The following comparative balance sheet for December 31, 1993, and December 31, 1992, is for Willard Company:

**Willard Company**
**Comparative Balance Sheet**
**December 31, 1993 and 1992**

|  | 1993 | 1992 |
|---|---|---|
| **Assets** | | |
| Cash and cash equivalents | $ 62,400 | $ 180,000 |
| Marketable securities (net) | 47,000 | 0 |
| Accounts receivable | 400,000 | 345,000 |
| Allowance for doubtful accounts | (20,000) | (31,000) |
| Inventories | 680,000 | 643,000 |
| Property, plant, and equipment | 810,500 | 743,400 |
| Accumulated depreciation | (229,000) | (228,000) |
| Total assets | $1,750,900 | $1,652,400 |
| **Liabilities** | | |
| Accounts payable | $ 46,000 | $ 103,000 |
| Short-term notes payable | 100,000 | 120,000 |
| Accrued liabilities | 76,500 | 48,000 |
| Bonds payable | 250,000 | 278,000 |
| Discount on bonds payable | (19,600) | (20,800) |
| Deferred income tax liability | 108,000 | 97,000 |
| Total liabilities | $ 560,900 | $ 625,200 |
| **Stockholders' Equity** | | |
| Common stock, $10 par | $ 840,000 | $ 790,000 |
| Paid-in capital in excess of par | 52,000 | 20,000 |
| Unappropriated retained earnings | 268,000 | 217,200 |
| Appropriated retained earnings | 30,000 | 0 |
| Total stockholders' equity | $1,190,000 | $1,027,200 |
| Total liabilities and stockholders' equity | $1,750,900 | $1,652,400 |

Additional information includes:

- —Net income for the year ended December 31, 1993, was $172,300. There were no extraordinary items.
- —During 1993, uncollectible accounts receivable of $26,400 were written off. Bad debt expense for the year was $32,000.
- —During 1993, machinery and land were purchased at a total cost of $115,100.
- —Machinery with a cost of $48,000 and a book value of $4,200 was sold for $3,600.
- —The bonds payable mature at the rate of $28,000 every year.
- —In January 1993, the company issued an additional 1,000 shares of its common stock at $14 per share upon the exercise of outstanding stock options held by key employees.
- —In May 1993, the company declared and issued a 5% stock dividend on its outstanding stock; there were 80,000 shares of stock outstanding at the time and the market value per share was $17.
- —During the year, cash dividends of $20,000 were paid on the common stock.
- —The appropriation of retained earnings was in anticipation of an expected future drop in the market related to goods in inventory.
- —The notes payable relate to operating activities.
- —During 1993, a prior-period adjustment was made to correct an understatement of depreciation on equipment. The amount of the adjustment was $3,500.
- —During the year, marketable securities were purchased for $50,000. As of December 31, 1993, the securities have a market value of $47,000.
- —Depreciation expense for the year totaled $41,300.

The preparation of the statement of cash flows will be illustrated using the indirect method of determining cash flows from operations. The analysis uses T-accounts. The T-accounts are shown on pages 859 and 860. Explanations for the individual adjustments and the related entries that are recorded in the T-accounts are presented below and on subsequent pages. Recall that these entries are only presented to aid in the preparation of the statement of cash flows; they are not actually posted to the accounts. The letter preceding each explanation corresponds with that used in the T-accounts.

(a)  Net income is recorded as follows:

| | | |
|---|---:|---:|
| Cash Flows—Operating .................................. | 172,300 | |
| Unappropriated Retained Earnings ..................... | | 172,300 |

(b)  Cash dividends paid are recorded as follows:

| | | |
|---|---:|---:|
| Unappropriated Retained Earnings ...................... | 20,000 | |
| Cash Flows—Financing ............................... | | 20,000 |

(c)  The 5% stock dividend results in a transfer of retained earnings to common stock at par and to paid-in capital in excess of par. However, the stock dividend has no effect on cash. The amount of the transfer is the number of new shares (80,000 x .05 = 4,000) multiplied by the market value of the shares at the time of the stock dividend ($17):

| | | |
|---|---:|---:|
| Unappropriated Retained Earnings ...................... | 68,000 | |
| Common Stock, $10 par ................................ | | 40,000 |
| Paid-In Capital in Excess of Par ....................... | | 28,000 |

(d)  The recognition that depreciation had been understated in prior periods is recorded by a debit to Retained Earnings and a credit to Accumulated Depreciation. This correction of earnings of prior periods has no effect on cash:

| | | |
|---|---:|---:|
| Unappropriated Retained Earnings ...................... | 3,500 | |
| Accumulated Depreciation............................. | | 3,500 |

(e)  The appropriation of Retained Earnings involves no cash and is recorded as follows:

| | | |
|---|---|---|
| Unappropriated Retained Earnings | 30,000 | |
|    Appropriated Retained Earnings | | 30,000 |

(f)  The purchase of the machinery and land is recorded as follows:

| | | |
|---|---|---|
| Property, Plant, and Equipment | 115,100 | |
|    Cash Flows—Investing | | 115,100 |

(g)  The amount of cash received in the sale was $3,600 and this is shown as cash provided by investing activities. The sale of the machinery involved a loss of $600. Since this loss reduced net income but involved no cash effects beyond the $3,600 received, the $600 must be added to cash flows from operating activities to avoid understating the cash effect of the transaction:

| | | |
|---|---|---|
| Cash Flows—Investing | 3,600 | |
| Accumulated Depreciation | 43,800 | |
| Cash Flows—Operating | 600 | |
|    Property, Plant, and Equipment | | 48,000 |

(h)  Depreciation reduces net income but does not involve cash, so the following adjustment to cash flows is necessary:

| | | |
|---|---|---|
| Cash Flows—Operating | 41,300 | |
|    Accumulated Depreciation | | 41,300 |

(i)  The purchase of the marketable securities is shown as follows:

| | | |
|---|---|---|
| Marketable Securities | 50,000 | |
|    Cash Flows—Investing | | 50,000 |

(j)  A decline in the market value of the marketable securities caused them to be written down. The $3,000 write-down reduced net income but did not involve cash, so its effect on income must be reversed when preparing the statement of cash flows:

| | | |
|---|---|---|
| Cash Flows—Operating | 3,000 | |
|    Marketable Securities | | 3,000 |

(k)  Bonds retired for $28,000 during the year decreased the cash used in financing activities:

| | | |
|---|---|---|
| Bonds Payable | 28,000 | |
|    Cash Flows—Financing | | 28,000 |

(l)  The amortization of bond discount represents another item that reduced net income but did not involve cash. The necessary adjustment to cash flows is as follows:

| | | |
|---|---|---|
| Cash Flows—Operating | 1,200 | |
|    Discount on Bonds Payable | | 1,200 |

(m)  The $11,000 increase in Deferred Income Tax Liability is added back to cash flows provided by operating activities because it represents income taxes recognized as an expense of the current period for which no cash was paid:

| | | |
|---|---|---|
| Cash Flows—Operating | 11,000 | |
|    Deferred Income Tax Liability | | 11,000 |

(n)  The issuance of new common stock is shown as an increase in cash from financing activities:

| | | |
|---|---|---|
| Cash Flows—Financing | 14,000 | |
|    Common Stock, $10 par | | 10,000 |
|    Paid-In Capital in Excess of Par | | 4,000 |

Cash flows from operating activities must be adjusted for changes in the levels of current assets and current liabilities. These adjustments are as follows:

(o)   The simplest way to handle bad debt expense and account write-offs is to make the adjustment using the net receivable balance. If this is done and the indirect method is used, no special adjustments are required:

| | | |
|---|---:|---:|
| Accounts Receivable (net) | 66,000 | |
|    Cash Flows—Operating | | 66,000 |

| | | | |
|---|---|---:|---:|
| (p) | Inventories | 37,000 | |
| |    Cash Flows—Operating | | 37,000 |
| (q) | Accounts Payable | 57,000 | |
| |    Cash Flows—Operating | | 57,000 |
| (r) | Short-Term Notes Payable | 20,000 | |
| |    Cash Flows—Operating | | 20,000 |
| (s) | Cash Flows—Operating | 28,500 | |
| |    Accrued Liabilities | | 28,500 |

After all changes in account balances for the year have been reconciled, the balances in the three cash flows T-accounts are transferred to a summary account. The $117,600 excess credit amount in this summary account represents a net decrease in cash for the year. The final entry records this decrease in the cash account and completes the analysis:

| | | | |
|---|---|---:|---:|
| (t) | Net Decrease in Cash | 117,600 | |
| |    Cash and Cash Equivalents | | 117,600 |

The formal statement of cash flows is prepared using the data in the three cash flows T-accounts.

**Willard Company**
**Statement of Cash Flows**
**For the Year Ended December 31, 1993**

| | | |
|---|---:|---:|
| **Cash flows from operating activities:** | | |
| Net income | $172,300 | |
| Adjustments: | | |
|    Loss on sale of machinery | 600 | |
|    Depreciation expense | 41,300 | |
|    Loss on decline in value of marketable securities | 3,000 | |
|    Amortization of bond discount | 1,200 | |
|    Increase in deferred income tax liability | 11,000 | |
|    Increase in net accounts receivable | (66,000) | |
|    Increase in inventories | (37,000) | |
|    Decrease in accounts payable | (57,000) | |
|    Decrease in short-term notes payable | (20,000) | |
|    Decrease in accrued liabilities | 28,500 | |
| Net cash provided by operating activities | | $ 77,900 |
| **Cash flows from investing activities:** | | |
| Purchase of machinery and land | $(115,100) | |
| Sale of machinery | 3,600 | |
| Purchase of marketable securities | (50,000) | |
| Net cash used in investing activities | | (161,500) |
| **Cash flows from financing activities:** | | |
| Payment of cash dividends | $ (20,000) | |
| Retirement of bonds payable | (28,000) | |
| Issuance of common stock | 14,000 | |
| Net cash used in financing activities | | (34,000) |
| Net decrease in cash | | $(117,600) |
| Cash and cash equivalents, beginning of year | | 180,000 |
| Cash and cash equivalents, end of year | | $ 62,400 |

|      | **Cash Flows—Operating** |     |        |
|------|--------------------------|-----|--------|
| (a)  | 172,300                  | (o) | 66,000 |
| (g)  | 600                      | (p) | 37,000 |
| (h)  | 41,300                   | (q) | 57,000 |
| (j)  | 3,000                    | (r) | 20,000 |
| (l)  | 1,200                    |     |        |
| (m)  | 11,000                   |     |        |
| (s)  | 28,500                   |     |        |
|      | <u>77,900</u>            |     |        |

|      | **Cash Flows—Investing** |     |         |
|------|--------------------------|-----|---------|
| (g)  | 3,600                    | (f) | 115,100 |
|      |                          | (i) | 50,000  |
|      |                          |     | <u>161,500</u> |

|      | **Cash Flows—Financing** |     |        |
|------|--------------------------|-----|--------|
| (n)  | 14,000                   | (b) | 20,000 |
|      |                          | (k) | 28,000 |
|      |                          |     | <u>34,000</u> |

**Cash Flows—Summary**

|        |         |                        |
|--------|---------|------------------------|
| 77,900 |         | Operating              |
|        | 161,500 | Investing              |
|        | 34,000  | Financing              |
| (t) 117,600 |    | Net Decrease in Cash   |
| <u>195,500</u> | <u>195,500</u> | |

| **Cash and Cash Equivalents** |         |     |         |
|-------------------------------|---------|-----|---------|
| Beg. bal.                     | 180,000 | (t) | 117,600 |
| End. bal.                     | 62,400  |     |         |

| **Marketable Securities (net)** |        |     |       |
|---------------------------------|--------|-----|-------|
| Beg. bal.                       | 0      | (j) | 3,000 |
| (i)                             | 50,000 |     |       |
| End. bal.                       | 47,000 |     |       |

| **Accounts Receivable (net)** |         |
|-------------------------------|---------|
| Beg. bal.                     | 314,000 |
| (o)                           | 66,000  |
| End. bal.                     | 380,000 |

| **Inventories** |         |
|-----------------|---------|
| Beg. bal.       | 643,000 |
| (p)             | 37,000  |
| End. bal.       | 680,000 |

| **Property, Plant, and Equipment** |         |     |        |
|------------------------------------|---------|-----|--------|
| Beg. bal.                          | 743,400 | (g) | 48,000 |
| (f)                                | 115,100 |     |        |
| End. bal.                          | 810,500 |     |        |

| **Accumulated Depreciation** |        |           |         |
|------------------------------|--------|-----------|---------|
| (g)                          | 43,800 | Beg. bal. | 228,000 |
|                              |        | (d)       | 3,500   |
|                              |        | (h)       | 41,300  |
|                              |        | End. bal. | 229,000 |

| **Accounts Payable** |        |           |         |
|----------------------|--------|-----------|---------|
| (q)                  | 57,000 | Beg. bal. | 103,000 |
|                      |        | End. bal. | 46,000  |

| **Short-Term Notes Payable** |        |           |         |
|------------------------------|--------|-----------|---------|
| (r)                          | 20,000 | Beg. bal. | 120,000 |
|                              |        | End. bal. | 100,000 |

| **Accrued Liabilities** |           |        |
|-------------------------|-----------|--------|
|                         | Beg. bal. | 48,000 |
|                         | (s)       | 28,500 |
|                         | End. bal. | 76,500 |

| **Bonds Payable** |        |           |         |
|-------------------|--------|-----------|---------|
| (k)               | 28,000 | Beg. bal. | 278,000 |
|                   |        | End. bal. | 250,000 |

| Discount on Bonds Payable | | | |
|---|---|---|---|
| Beg. bal. | 20,800 | (l) | 1,200 |
| End. bal. | 19,600 | | |

| Deferred Income Tax Liability | | | |
|---|---|---|---|
| | | Beg. bal. | 97,000 |
| | | (m) | 11,000 |
| | | End. bal. | 108,000 |

| Common Stock, $10 par | | | |
|---|---|---|---|
| | | Beg. bal. | 790,000 |
| | | (c) | 40,000 |
| | | (n) | 10,000 |
| | | End. bal. | 840,000 |

| Paid-In Capital in Excess of Par | | | |
|---|---|---|---|
| | | Beg. bal. | 20,000 |
| | | (c) | 28,000 |
| | | (n) | 4,000 |
| | | End. bal. | 52,000 |

| Unappropriated Retained Earnings | | | |
|---|---|---|---|
| (b) | 20,000 | Beg. bal. | 217,200 |
| (c) | 68,000 | (a) | 172,300 |
| (d) | 3,500 | | |
| (e) | 30,000 | | |
| | | End. bal. | 268,000 |

| Appropriated Retained Earnings | | | |
|---|---|---|---|
| | | Beg. bal. | 0 |
| | | (e) | 30,000 |
| | | End. bal. | 30,000 |

## KEY TERMS

Accounts receivable turnover 837
Acid-test ratio 836
Asset turnover 840
Book value per share 847
Common-size financial statements 833
Comparative statements 831
Conglomerates 848
Current ratio 835
Debt-to-equity ratio 846
Diversified companies 848
Dividends per share 844
Financial leverage 845
Fixed charge coverage 847

Gross profit margin on sales 842
Growth potential 830
Horizontal analysis 831
Integral part of annual period concept 853
Interim financial statements 851
Inventory turnover 838
Liquidity 830
Natural business year 839
Net profit margin on sales 841
Number of times interest is earned 847
Price-earnings ratio 844
Profitability 830
Quick assets 836

Quick ratio 836
Rate earned on average common stockholder's equity 843
Rate earned on average total assets 842
Rate earned on average stockholders' equity 843
Return on investment (ROI) 842
Segment 850
Stability 830
Trading on the equity 845
Vertical analysis 833
Working capital ratio 835
Yield on common stock 844

## QUESTIONS

1. What groups may be interested in a company's financial statements?
2. What types of questions requiring financial statement analysis might be raised by external users, such as investors and creditors, as contrasted to internal management?
3. What are the factors that one would look for in judging a company's (a) liquidity, (b) stability, (c) profitability, and (d) growth potential?
4. Why are comparative financial statements considered more meaningful than statements prepared for a sin-

gle period? What conditions increase the usefulness of comparative statements?
5. Distinguish between horizontal and vertical analysis. What special purpose does each serve?
6. What information is provided by analysis of comparative statements of cash flows that is not available from analysis of comparative balance sheets and income statements?
7. What is meant by a *common-size* statement? What are its advantages?

8. Mention some factors that may limit the comparability of financial statements of two companies in the same industry.

9. What factors may be responsible for a change in a company's net income from one year to the next?

10. The Black Co. develops the following measurements for 1994 as compared with the year 1993. What additional information would you require before arriving at favorable or unfavorable conclusions for each item?
    (a) Net income has increased by $70,000.
    (b) Sales returns and allowances have increased by $25,000.
    (c) The gross profit rate has increased by 5%.
    (d) Purchase discounts have increased by $5,000.
    (e) Working capital has increased by $85,000.
    (f) Accounts receivable have increased by $150,000.
    (g) Inventories have decreased by $110,000.
    (h) Retained earnings has decreased by $300,000.

11. Distinguish between the current ratio and the acid-test ratio.

12. Balance sheets for the Rich Corporation and the Poor Corporation each show a working capital total of $500,000. Does this indicate that the short-term liquidity of the two corporations is approximately the same? Explain.

13. (a) How is the accounts receivable turnover computed? (b) How is the number of days' purchases in accounts payable computed?

14. (a) How is the merchandise inventory turnover computed? (b) What precautions are necessary in arriving at the basis for the turnover calculation? (c) How would you interpret a rising inventory turnover rate?

15. The ratio of total liabilities to stockholders' equity offers information about the long-term stability of a business. Explain.

16. Indicate how each of the following measurements is calculated and appraise its significance:
    (a) Number of times bond interest requirements were earned.
    (b) Number of times preferred dividend requirements were earned.
    (c) Rate of earnings on average common stockholders' equity.
    (d) Earnings per share on common stock.
    (e) Price-earnings ratio on common stock.
    (f) Dividends per share on common stock.
    (g) Yield on common stock.

17. Briefly explain how the sources of assets, liabilities, and owners' equity affect the rate of return to the residual owners of the organization.

18. Explain how the turnover of assets can affect return on assets.

19. Identify the major financial relationships that reflect the components of the rate of return to the common stockholders.

20. Under what conditions is the rate of return on average total assets equal to the rate of return to the common shareholder?

21. Under what circumstances is the use of industry ratios beneficial in analyzing a company's activity?

22. (a) What are the principal sources of industry data for use in comparative analysis? (b) What are the advantages and disadvantages of each source?

23. In what ways can segment information assist in the analysis of a company's financial statements?

24. Distinguish between the two primary viewpoints concerning the preparation of interim financial statements.

25. Why must investors be careful in interpreting interim reports?

---

## DISCUSSION CASES

### Case 22–1 (How should we finance our expansion?)

The Detweiler Co. is considering expanding its operations. The company's balance sheet at December 31, 1993, is presented at the top of page 862.

Each $1,000 bond is convertible at the option of the bondholder to 15 shares of common stock. The bonds carry an interest rate of 12% and are callable at 100. The company's 1993 income before taxes was $2,200,000 and was $1,520,000 after taxes. The preferred stock is callable at par. The common stock has a market price of $60 per share.

The company's management has identified several alternatives to raise $1,000,000.

(a) Issue additional bonds.
(b) Call in the convertible bonds to force conversion and then issue additional bonds.
(c) Issue additional 8% cumulative preferred stock.
(d) Issue additional common stock.

Evaluate the company's leverage position and discuss the advantages and disadvantages of each alternative.

**Detweiler Co.**
**Balance Sheet**
**December 31, 1993**

| Assets | | Liabilities | |
|---|---|---|---|
| Cash | $ 325,000 | Accounts payable | $ 300,000 |
| Accounts receivable | 525,000 | Bonds payable | 1,100,000 |
| Inventory | 1,150,000 | Total liabilities | $1,400,000 |
| Land | 1,200,000 | | |
| Buildings and equipment (net) | 2,500,000 | Stockholders' Equity | |
| | | Preferred stock, 8% cumulative, $100 par | $ 300,000 |
| | | Common stock, $25 par | 1,000,000 |
| | | Retained earnings | 3,000,000 |
| | | Total stockholders' equity | $4,300,000 |
| | | Total liabilities and stockholders' | |
| Total assets | $5,700,000 | equity | $5,700,000 |

### Case 22—2  (Analyzing earnings)

Royer Donahoe owns two businesses: a drug store and a retail department store.

| | Drug Store | Department Store |
|---|---|---|
| Net sales | $1,050,000 | $670,000 |
| Cost of goods sold | 1,000,000 | 600,000 |
| Average total assets | 50,000 | 200,000 |
| Other expenses | 39,500 | 36,500 |

Which business earns more income? Which business earns a higher return on its investment in total assets? Which business would you consider more profitable?

### Case 22—3  (Can a ratio be too good?)

Tony Christopher is analyzing the financial statements of Shaycole Company and has computed the following ratios:

| | Shaycole | Industry Comparison |
|---|---|---|
| Current ratio | 4.7 | 1.9 |
| Inventory turnover | 14.8 times | 6.1 times |
| Accounts receivable turnover | 27.4 times | 8.7 times |
| Debt-to-equity ratio | .117 | .864 |

Andy Martinez, Tony's colleague, tells Tony that Shaycole looks great. Andy points out that, although Shaycole's ratios deviate significantly from the industry norms, all the deviations suggest that Shaycole is doing better than other firms in its industry. Is Andy right?

### Case 22—4  (Evaluating alternative investments)

Judy Snow is considering investing $10,000 and wishes to know which of two companies offers the better alternative.

The Hoffman Company earned net income of $63,000 last year on average total assets of $280,000 and average stockholders' equity of $210,000. The company's shares are selling on the market at $100 per share; 6,300 shares of common stock are outstanding.

The McMahon Company earned $24,375 last year on average total assets of $125,000 and average stockholders' equity of $100,000. The company's common shares are selling on the market at $78 per share; 2,500 shares are outstanding.

Which stock should Snow buy?

## Case 22—5  (Should the FASB set standards for financial ratios?)

Financial ratios can be computed using many different formulas. In an article in the CPA Journal, one writer recommends that the FASB become involved in identifying common formulas and ratios that would be included in all financial statements. What are the advantages in pursuing such a recommendation? What are the difficulties?

## Case 22—6  (Where do assets go on the income statement?)

Consider the following excerpt from a magazine article about professional baseball:

> "I recall a riveting moment during the lockout when NBC began a television interview with George Steinbrenner by presenting its best guess at the Yankees' 1990 budget—a balance sheet that showed roughly forty-five million dollars in expenses against revenues in excess of a hundred million. Mr. Steinbrenner, invited to comment, claimed the figures were out of whack. "You're way out of line," he said. "In cash flow, the Yankees will be lucky if they break even this year."

Comment on this excerpt from an accountant's perspective. Is it possible for both NBC and Mr. Steinbrenner to be right?

Source: Roger Angell, "The Sporting Scene (Baseball)," The New Yorker, May 21, 1990, p. 75.

---

# EXERCISES

## Exercise 22—1  (Index numbers)

Sales for the Montrek Company for a 5-year period and an industry sales index for this period are listed below. Convert both series into indexes employing 1990 as the base year.

| | **1994** | **1993** | **1992** | **1991** | **1990** |
|---|---|---|---|---|---|
| Sales of Montrek Company (in thousands of dollars) . . . . . . . . . . . . | $8,400 | $9,205 | $8,710 | $8,850 | $8,530 |
| Industry sales index (1982 = 100) . . | 192 | 212 | 200 | 170 | 158 |

## Exercise 22—2  (Comparative cost of goods sold schedule)

Cost of goods sold data for P. Lohner Corporation are presented below. The company's fiscal year ends June 30.

| | **1993-1994** | **1992-1993** |
|---|---|---|
| Inventory, July 1 . . . . . . . . . . . . . . . . . . . . . . . . . . . . . . . . . . . | $ 75,000 | $ 60,000 |
| Purchases . . . . . . . . . . . . . . . . . . . . . . . . . . . . . . . . . . . . . . . | 410,000 | 320,000 |
| Goods available for sale . . . . . . . . . . . . . . . . . . . . . . . . . . . | $485,000 | $380,000 |
| Less inventory, June 30 . . . . . . . . . . . . . . . . . . . . . . . . . . . | 55,000 | 75,000 |
| Cost of goods sold . . . . . . . . . . . . . . . . . . . . . . . . . . . . . . . | $430,000 | $305,000 |

Prepare a comparative schedule of cost of goods sold showing dollar and percentage changes. Round to nearest whole percentage.

## Exercise 22—3  (Vertical analysis)

The financial position of the Islandic Co. at the end of 1994 and 1993 is as follows:

|  | 1994 | 1993 |
|---|---|---|
| **Assets** | | |
| Current assets ......................................... | $ 70,000 | $ 60,000 |
| Long-term investments ............................... | 15,000 | 14,000 |
| Land, buildings, and equipment (net)..................... | 100,000 | 75,000 |
| Intangible assets ..................................... | 10,000 | 10,000 |
| Other assets ......................................... | 5,000 | 6,000 |
| Total assets......................................... | $200,000 | $165,000 |
| **Liabilities** | | |
| Current liabilities ..................................... | $ 30,000 | $ 35,000 |
| Long-term liabilities .................................. | 88,000 | 62,000 |
| Total liabilities ...................................... | $118,000 | $ 97,000 |
| **Stockholders' Equity** | | |
| Preferred 8% stock ................................... | $ 10,000 | $ 9,000 |
| Common stock ....................................... | 54,000 | 42,000 |
| Additional paid-in capital............................... | 5,000 | 5,000 |
| Retained earnings .................................... | 13,000 | 12,000 |
| Total stockholders' equity ............................. | $ 82,000 | $ 68,000 |
| Total liabilities and stockholders' equity ................. | $200,000 | $165,000 |

Prepare a comparative balance sheet including a percentage analysis of component items standardizing each item by total assets. (Common-size statement). Round to nearest whole percentage.

## Exercise 22—4  (Liquidity ratios)

The following data are taken from the comparative balance sheet prepared for the McCabe Resources Company:

|  | 1994 | 1993 |
|---|---|---|
| Cash ................................................ | $ 25,000 | $ 10,000 |
| Marketable securities (net) ............................. | 9,000 | 45,000 |
| Trade receivables (net)................................. | 43,000 | 30,000 |
| Inventories ......................................... | 65,000 | 40,000 |
| Prepaid expenses .................................... | 3,000 | 2,000 |
| Land, buildings, and equipment (net)..................... | 79,000 | 75,000 |
| Intangible assets ..................................... | 10,000 | 15,000 |
| Other assets ......................................... | 2,000 | 8,000 |
| Total assets......................................... | $236,000 | $225,000 |
| Current liabilities ..................................... | $ 80,000 | $ 65,000 |

1. From the data given, compute for 1994 and 1993: (a) the working capital, (b) the current ratio, (c) the acid-test ratio, (d) the ratio of current assets to total assets, and (e) the ratio of cash to current liabilities.
2. Evaluate each of the changes.

## Exercise 22—5  (Analysis of inventory position)

Income statements for the Eldermon Sales Co. show the following:

|                          | **1994**   | **1993**   | **1992**   |
|--------------------------|-----------:|-----------:|-----------:|
| Sales ..................................... | $125,000 | $100,000 | $ 75,000 |
| Cost of goods sold:      |            |            |            |
| Beginning inventory ...................... | $ 30,000 | $ 25,000 | $  5,000 |
| Purchases .............................. | 105,000 | 80,000 | 85,000 |
|                          | $135,000 | $105,000 | $ 90,000 |
| Ending inventory ......................... | 45,000 | 30,000 | 25,000 |
|                          | $ 90,000 | $ 75,000 | $ 65,000 |
| Gross profit on sales...................... | $ 35,000 | $ 25,000 | $ 10,000 |

Give whatever measurements may be developed in analyzing the inventory position at the end of each year. What conclusions would you make concerning the inventory trend?

### Exercise 22–6   (Analysis of accounts payable)

The total purchases of goods by The Gerald Company during 1993 were $720,000. All purchases were on a 2/10, n/30 basis. The average balance in the vouchers payable account was $76,000. Was the company prompt, slow, or average in paying for goods? How many days' average purchases were there in accounts payable, assuming a 365-day year?

### Exercise 22–7   (Inventory turnover)

The following data are taken from the Clayburgh Corporation records for the years ending December 31, 1994, 1993, and 1992.

|                          | **1994**   | **1993**   | **1992**   |
|--------------------------|-----------:|-----------:|-----------:|
| Finished goods inventory ................... | $ 60,000 | $ 40,000 | $ 30,000 |
| Goods in process inventory ................. | 60,000 | 65,000 | 60,000 |
| Raw materials inventory .................... | 60,000 | 40,000 | 35,000 |
| Sales..................................... | 400,000 | 340,000 | 300,000 |
| Cost of goods sold ........................ | 225,000 | 230,000 | 210,000 |
| Cost of goods manufactured ................ | 260,000 | 250,000 | 200,000 |
| Raw materials used in production............ | 150,000 | 130,000 | 120,000 |

1. Compute turnover rates for 1994 and for 1993 for (a) finished goods, (b) goods in process, and (c) raw materials.
2. Analyze the turnover results as to reasonableness and the message they provide to a statement reader.

### Exercise 22–8   (Inventory turnover)

The controller of the Montoya Manufacturing Co. wishes to analyze the activity of the finished goods, goods in process, and raw materials inventories. The following information is produced for the analysis:

| | |
|---|---:|
| Finished goods inventory, 12/31/93.................................... | $112,500 |
| Finished goods inventory, 12/31/94.................................... | 215,000 |
| Goods in process inventory, 12/31/93................................. | 211,000 |
| Goods in process inventory, 12/31/94................................. | 239,000 |
| Raw materials inventory, 12/31/93.................................... | 140,000 |
| Raw materials inventory, 12/31/94.................................... | 175,000 |
| Cost of goods sold, 1994 ........................................... | 245,000 |
| Cost of goods manufactured, 1994 ................................... | 306,000 |
| Cost of materials used, 1994........................................ | 250,000 |

1. Compute the inventory turnovers.
2. Based on the foregoing data and the turnover computations, evaluate the company's control over inventories.

### Exercise 22—9   (Analysis of capital structure)

The Vijay Corporation estimates that pretax earnings for the year ended December 31, 1993, will be $200,000 if it operates without borrowed capital. Income tax is 30% of earnings. Average stockholders' equity for 1993 is $750,000. Assuming that the company is able to borrow $1,200,000 at 12% interest, indicate the effects on net income and return on average stockholders' equity if borrowed capital earns (1) 20%, and (2) 10%. Explain the cause of the variations.

### Exercise 22—10   (Profitability analysis)

The balance sheets for the Fargo Paint Corp. showed long-term liabilities and stockholders' equity balances at the end of each year as follows:

|  | 1994 | 1993 | 1992 |
|---|---|---|---|
| 10% bonds payable.......................... | $   600,000 | $600,000 | $600,000 |
| Preferred 8% stock, $100 par ............... | 600,000 | 400,000 | 400,000 |
| Common stock, $25 par .................... | 1,200,000 | 900,000 | 900,000 |
| Additional paid-in capital.................. | 150,000 | 100,000 | 100,000 |
| Retained earnings ......................... | 300,000 | 100,000 | 50,000 |

Net income was: 1994, $280,000; 1993, $130,000. Using the foregoing data, compute for each year. (Ignore income tax considerations.)

(a)   The rate of earnings on average total stockholders' equity.
(b)   The number of times bond interest requirements were earned.
(c)   The number of times preferred dividend requirements were earned.
(d)   The rate earned on average common stockholders' equity.
(e)   The earnings per share on common stock.

### Exercise 22—11   (Return on stockholders' equity)

Fay Cutler wishes to know which of two companies will yield the greater rate of return on an investment in common stock. Financial information for 1993 for the Joslyn Co. and the Troy Co. is presented below.

|  | Joslyn Co. | Troy Co. |
|---|---|---|
| Net income ......................................... | $   150,000 | $   293,000 |
| Preferred stock (7%) ................................ | 600,000 | 970,000 |
| Common stockholders' equity: |  |  |
| January 1, 1993 ................................. | 1,450,000 | 2,465,000 |
| December 31, 1993 ............................... | 1,350,000 | 2,670,000 |

Determine which company earned the greater return on average common stockholders' equity in 1993.

### Exercise 22—12   (Profitability analysis for two companies)

The following information is obtained from the primary financial statements of two retail companies. One company markets its merchandise in a resort area, the other company is a discount household goods store. Neither company has any interest-bearing debt. By analyzing these data, indicate which company is more likely to be the gift shop and which is the discount household goods store. Support your answer.

|  | Company A | Company B |
|---|---|---|
| Revenue ......................................... | $6,000,000 | $6,000,000 |
| Average total assets ............................ | $1,200,000 | $6,000,000 |
| Net income ...................................... | $   125,000 | $   600,000 |

### Exercise 22—13  (Debt covenants and financing alternatives)

Chasebry Company is in need of another factory building. The building will cost $100,000. Chasebry is considering the following possible financing alternatives to acquire the building:

(a)  Lease the building under an operating lease.
(b)  Issue common stock in the amount of $100,000.
(c)  Negotiate a long-term bank loan for $100,000.
(d)  Negotiate a long-term bank loan for $60,000 and also increase short-term borrowing by $40,000.

Currently, Chasebry has current assets of $150,000, noncurrent assets of $325,000, current liabilities of $60,000, and noncurrent liabilities of $140,000. Under existing loan covenants, Chasebry must maintain a current ratio of 2.0 or more and a debt-to-equity ratio of less than 0.80. Which, if any, of the financing alternatives will allow Chasebry to avoid violating the loan covenants?

### Exercise 22—14  (Analysis of financial data)

For each of the following numbered items, you are to give the lettered financial statement effect(s) for that item. If there is no appropriate response among the effects listed, leave the item blank. If more than one effect is applicable to a particular item, be sure to list *all* applicable letters. (Assume the state statutes do not permit declaration of nonliquidating dividends except from earnings. Also assume that the current ratio is greater than 1:1.)

| Item | Effect |
|---|---|
| 1. Declaration of a cash dividend due in one month on preferred stock. | (a) Reduces working capital. |
| 2. Declaration and distribution of a small stock dividend. | (b) Increases working capital. |
|  | (c) Reduces current ratio. |
| 3. Receipt of a cash dividend, not previously recorded, on stock of another corporation. | (d) Increases current ratio. |
| 4. Passing of a dividend on cumulative preferred stock. | (e) Reduces the dollar amount of total capital stock. |
| 5. Receipt of preferred shares as a dividend on common stock held as a temporary investment. This was not a regularly recurring dividend. The preferred shares are also a temporary investment. | (f) Increases the dollar amount of total capital stock. |
|  | (g) Reduces total retained earnings. |
|  | (h) Increases total retained earnings. |
|  | (i) Reduces equity per share of common stock. |
| 6. Payment of dividend described in (1). | (j) Reduces equity of each common stockholder. |
| 7. Issue of new common shares in a 5-for-1 stock split. |  |

### Exercise 22—15  (Analysis of financial data)

The December 31, 1993, balance sheet of Copepper's Inc. is presented below. These are the only accounts in Copepper's balance sheet. Amounts indicated by a question mark (?) can be calculated from the additional information given.

| Assets | | Liabilities and Stockholders' Equity | |
|---|---|---|---|
| Cash .................... | $ 25,000 | Accounts payable (trade) ... | $    ? |
| Accounts receivable (net) ... | ? | Income taxes payable (current) ...................... | 25,000 |
| Inventory................. | ? | Long-term debt ............ | ? |
| Property, plant, and equipment (net) ................ | 294,000 | Common stock............. | 300,000 |
|  |  | Retained earnings ......... | ? |
|  | $432,000 |  | $    ? |

Additional information is given on page 873.

| | |
|---|---|
| Current ratio (at year-end) .......................................... | 1.5 to 1 |
| Total liabilities divided by total stockholders' equity ............... | .8 |
| Inventory turnover based on sales and ending inventory ............ | 15 times |
| Inventory turnover based on cost of goods sold and ending inventory | 10.5 times |
| Gross margin for 1993 ........................................... | $315,000 |

1. What was Copepper's December 31, 1993 balance in trade accounts payable?
2. What was Copepper's December 31, 1993 balance in retained earnings?
3. What was Copepper's December 31, 1993 balance in the inventory account?

### Exercise 22—16   (Reporting segment information)

Lutz Industries operates in five different industries. From the information given below, determine which segments should be classified as reportable segments according to FASB Statement No. 14. Provide justification for your answer.

**Lutz Industries**
**Information About Company Operations in Different Industries**
**For the Year Ended December 31, 1993**
**(In Millions of Dollars)**

| | Industry 1 | Industry 2 | Industry 3 | Industry 4 | Industry 5 | Total |
|---|---|---|---|---|---|---|
| Revenues ............... | $ 577 | $ 84 | $ 93 | $117 | $ 96 | $ 967 |
| Operating profit ......... | 66 | 11 | 9 | 10 | 10 | 106 |
| Identifiable assets........ | 2,124 | 298 | 328 | 314 | 353 | 3,417 |

### Exercise 22—17   (Interim income statements)

The income statement for the year ended December 31, 1993, of Essex Technology Inc. appears below. Using the yearly income statement and the supplemental information, reconstruct the third-quarter interim statement for Essex.

**Essex Technology Inc.**
**Income Statement**
**For the Year Ended December 31, 1993**

| | |
|---|---|
| Sales ....................................................... | $900,000 |
| Cost of goods sold ........................................... | 560,000 |
| Gross profit on sales.......................................... | $340,000 |
| Operating expenses ........................................... | 96,000 |
| Operating income ............................................ | $244,000 |
| Gain on sale of equipment ..................................... | 28,000 |
| Income from continuing operations before income taxes............. | $272,000 |
| Income taxes ................................................ | 108,800 |
| Income from continuing operations ............................... | $163,200 |
| Extraordinary loss (net of income tax savings of $40,000) ............ | (60,000) |
| Net income ................................................. | $103,200 |

Supplemental information:

(a) Assume a 40% tax rate.
(b) Third-quarter sales were 20% of total sales.
(c) For interim reporting purposes, a gross profit rate of 38% can be justified.
(d) Variable operating expenses are allocated in the same proportion as sales. Fixed operating expenses are allocated based on the expiration of time. Of the total operating expenses, $60,000 relate to variable expenses.

(e) The equipment was sold June 1, 1993.
(f) The extraordinary loss occurred September 1, 1993.

## PROBLEMS

### Problem 22—1  (Comparative statements)

Operations for the Gordo Company for 1994 and 1993 are summarized below:

|  | 1994 | 1993 |
|---|---|---|
| Sales | $500,000 | $450,000 |
| Sales returns | 20,000 | 10,000 |
| Net sales | $480,000 | $440,000 |
| Cost of goods sold | 350,000 | 240,000 |
| Gross profit on sales | $130,000 | $200,000 |
| Selling and general expenses | 100,000 | 120,000 |
| Operating income | $ 30,000 | $ 80,000 |
| Other expenses | 35,000 | 30,000 |
| Income (loss) before income tax | $ (5,000) | $ 50,000 |
| Income tax (refund) | (2,000) | 20,000 |
| Net income (loss) | $ (3,000) | $ 30,000 |

### Instructions:

1. Prepare a comparative income statement showing dollar changes and percentage changes for 1994 as compared with 1993.
2. Prepare a comparative income statement offering a percentage analysis of component revenue and expense items of net sales for each year.
3. Based on the above percentages, prepare an analysis of Gordo's operations for 1994 and 1993.

### Problem 22—2  (Common-size statements)

As of December 31, 1993, balance sheet data for the Stay-Trim Company and the Tone-Up Company follows:

|  | Stay-Trim Company | Tone-Up Company |
|---|---|---|
| **Assets** | | |
| Current assets | $ 51,000 | $ 240,000 |
| Long-term investments | 5,000 | 280,000 |
| Land, buildings, and equipment (net) | 48,000 | 520,000 |
| Intangible assets | 6,000 | 100,000 |
| Other assets | 5,000 | 60,000 |
| Total assets | $115,000 | $1,200,000 |
| **Liabilities** | | |
| Current liabilities | $ 15,000 | $ 180,000 |
| Long-term liabilities | 25,000 | 300,000 |
| Deferred revenues | 5,000 | 70,000 |
| Total liabilities | $ 45,000 | $ 550,000 |
| **Stockholders' Equity** | | |
| Preferred stock | $ 5,000 | $ 100,000 |
| Common stock | 30,000 | 200,000 |
| Additional paid-in capital | 25,000 | 185,000 |
| Retained earnings | 10,000 | 165,000 |
| Total stockholders' equity | $ 70,000 | $ 650,000 |
| Total liabilities and stockholders' equity | $115,000 | $1,200,000 |

**Instructions:**

1. Prepare a comparative common-size statement using the balance sheet data.
2. What analytical conclusions can be drawn from this comparative common-size statement?

## Problem 22—3   (Index numbers)

Sales for Leong Mfg. Co. and its chief competitor, La Ultima Company, and the sales index for the industry are as follows:

|  | 1994 | 1993 | 1992 | 1991 | 1990 |
|---|---|---|---|---|---|
| Sales of Leong Mfg. Co. (in thousands of dollars) ............ | $ 7,000 | $7,280 | $7,735 | $8,450 | $8,385 |
| Sales of La Ultima Company (in thousands of dollars) ............ | $10,100 | $9,690 | $9,975 | $9,785 | $9,880 |
| Industry sales index (1985 = 100) | 140 | 152 | 161 | 144 | 133 |

**Instructions:**

1. Convert the three series to index numbers using 1990 as the base year.
2. Prepare a short report for the management of Leong Mfg. Co. summarizing your findings.

## Problem 22—4   (Computation of various ratios)

The balance sheet data for the Fielding Supply Corp. on December 31, 1993, is as follows:

| Assets | | Liabilities and Stockholders' Equity | |
|---|---|---|---|
| Cash ..................... | $ 120,000 | Notes and accounts payable .. | $ 150,000 |
| Marketable securities ....... | 25,000 | Income tax payable ......... | 40,000 |
| Notes and accounts receivable (net) ................. | 175,000 | Wages and interest payable .. | 10,000 |
|  |  | Dividends payable .......... | 25,000 |
| Inventories ............... | 590,000 | Bonds payable ............. | 380,000 |
| Prepaid expenses .......... | 15,000 | Deferred revenues .......... | 20,000 |
| Bond redemption fund (securities of other companies) | 400,000 | Common stock, $20 par ..... | 1,200,000 |
| Land, buildings, and equipment (net) ................. | 730,000 | Preferred 6% stock, $20 par (noncumulative, liquidating value at par) .............. | 200,000 |
| Intangible assets .......... | 420,000 | Retained earnings appropriated for plant expansion .... | 200,000 |
|  |  | Retained earnings .......... | 250,000 |
| Total assets............... | $2,475,000 | Total liabilities and stockholders' equity ............ | $2,475,000 |

**Instructions:**   From the balance sheet data, compute the following:

1. Amount of working capital.
2. Current ratio.
3. Acid-test ratio.
4. Ratio of current assets to total assets.
5. Ratio of total liabilities to stockholders' equity.
6. Ratio of tangible noncurrent assets to bonds payable.
7. Book value per share of common stock.

## ▚ Problem 22—5   (Liquidity analysis)

The following are comparative data for Sunshine State Equipment, Inc. for the 3-year period 1992-1994.

### Income Statement Data

|  | 1994 | 1993 | 1992 |
|---|---|---|---|
| Net sales | $1,200,000 | $ 900,000 | $1,020,000 |
| Cost of goods sold | 760,000 | 600,000 | 610,000 |
| Gross profit on sales | $ 440,000 | $ 300,000 | $ 410,000 |
| Selling, general, and other expenses | 340,000 | 280,000 | 250,000 |
| Operating income | $ 100,000 | $ 20,000 | $ 160,000 |
| Income tax | 40,000 | 9,000 | 72,000 |
| Net income | $ 60,000 | $ 11,000 | $ 88,000 |
| Dividends paid | 35,000 | 30,000 | 88,000 |
| Net increase (decrease) in retained earnings | $ 25,000 | $ (19,000) | $ 0 |

### Balance Sheet Data

|  | 1994 | 1993 | 1992 |
|---|---|---|---|
| **Assets** | | | |
| Cash | $ 50,000 | $ 40,000 | $ 75,000 |
| Trade notes and accounts receivable (net) | 300,000 | 320,000 | 250,000 |
| Inventory (at cost) | 380,000 | 420,000 | 350,000 |
| Prepaid expenses | 30,000 | 10,000 | 40,000 |
| Land, buildings, and equipment (net) | 760,000 | 600,000 | 690,000 |
| Intangible assets | 110,000 | 100,000 | 125,000 |
| Other assets | 70,000 | 10,000 | 20,000 |
| | $1,700,000 | $1,500,000 | $1,550,000 |
| **Liabilities and Stockholders' Equity** | | | |
| Trade notes and accounts payable | $ 120,000 | $ 185,000 | $ 220,000 |
| Wages, interest, dividends payable | 25,000 | 25,000 | 25,000 |
| Income tax payable | 29,000 | 5,000 | 30,000 |
| Miscellaneous current liabilities | 10,000 | 4,000 | 10,000 |
| 8% bonds payable | 300,000 | 300,000 | 250,000 |
| Deferred revenues | 10,000 | 10,000 | 25,000 |
| Preferred 6% stock, cumulative, $100 par and liquidating value | 200,000 | 200,000 | 200,000 |
| No-par common stock, $10 stated value | 500,000 | 400,000 | 400,000 |
| Additional paid-in capital | 310,000 | 200,000 | 200,000 |
| Retained earnings—appropriated | 90,500 | 60,000 | 60,000 |
| Retained earnings—unappropriated | 105,500 | 111,000 | 130,000 |
| | $1,700,000 | $1,500,000 | $1,550,000 |

## Instructions:

1. From the foregoing data, calculate comparative measurements for the 3 years 1992-1994 as follows (for ratios using averages, assume 1991 figures are the same as 1992):
   (a)  Amount of working capital.
   (b)  Current ratio.
   (c)  Acid-test ratio.
   (d)  Average days' sales in trade receivables at the end of the year (assume a 365-day year and all sales on a credit basis).
   (e)  Trade payables turnover rate for the year.

(f) Inventory turnover rate.
(g) Number of days' sales in the inventory at the end of the year.
(h) Ratio of total liabilities to stockholders' equity.
(i) Ratio of land, buildings, and equipment to bonds payable.
(j) Ratio of stockholders' equity to land, buildings, and equipment.
(k) Book value per share of common stock.
2. Based on the measurements made in (1), evaluate the liquidity position of Sunshine State Equipment, Inc., at the end of 1994 as compared with the end of 1993.

### Problem 22—6   (Profitability analysis)

Use the comparative data for Sunshine State Equipment, Inc., as given in Problem 22—5.

**Instructions:**

1. Compute comparative measurements for the 3 years 1992-1994 as follows:
   (a) Ratio of net sales to average total assets.
   (b) Ratio of net sales to average land, buildings, and equipment.
   (c) Rate earned on net sales.
   (d) Gross profit rate on net sales.
   (e) Rate earned on average total assets.
   (f) Rate earned on average stockholders' equity.
   (g) Number of times bond interest requirements were earned (before income tax).
   (h) Number of times preferred dividend requirements were earned.
   (i) Rate earned on average common stockholders' equity.
   (j) Earnings per share on common stock.
2. Based on the measurements made in (1), evaluate the profitability of Sunshine State Equipment, Inc., for 1994 as compared with 1993 and 1992.

### Problem 22—7   (Analysis of inventory, receivables, and payables)

Inventory and receivable balances and gross profit data for Balboa Arrow Co. appear below.

|  | 1994 | 1993 | 1992 |
|---|---|---|---|
| Balance sheet data: |  |  |  |
| Inventory, December 31 .................... | $100,000 | $ 90,000 | $ 80,000 |
| Accounts receivable, December 31 .......... | 55,000 | 50,000 | 20,000 |
| Accounts payable, December 31 ............ | 70,000 | 50,000 | 45,000 |
| Net purchases............................ | 225,000 | 210,000 | 160,000 |
| Income statement data: |  |  |  |
| Net sales ................................ | $320,000 | $260,000 | $250,000 |
| Cost of goods sold ....................... | 215,000 | 200,000 | 180,000 |
| Gross profit on sales...................... | $105,000 | $60,000 | $70,000 |

**Instructions:**   Assuming a 365-day business year and all sales on a credit basis, compute the following measurements for 1994 and 1993:

1. Receivables turnover rate.
2. Average days' sales in receivables at the end of the year.
3. Inventory turnover rate.
4. Number of days' sales in inventory at the end of the year.
5. Accounts payable turnover rate.

### Problem 22—8   (Profitability analysis of three companies)

Financial information (in thousands of dollars) relating to three different companies follows.

| Item | Company A | Company B | Company C |
|------|-----------|-----------|-----------|
| Net sales ......................... | $ 60,000 | $28,000 | $21,000 |
| Net income ....................... | 9,600 | 1,850 | 360 |
| Net income to common stockholders* | 6,100 | 1,140 | 300 |
| Average balances: | | | |
|    Total assets ..................... | 155,400 | 21,500 | 3,200 |
|    Common stockholders' equity ...... | 61,000 | 11,300 | 1,690 |

\* Net income less preferred stock dividends

**Instructions:**

1. Compute the following ratios:
   (a) Net profit margin on sales.
   (b) Total asset turnover.
   (c) Rate earned on total assets.
   (d) Rate earned on average stockholders' equity.
2. Assume the three companies are (a) a large department store, (b) a large grocery store, and (c) a large utility. Based on the above information, identify each company. Explain your answer.

### Problem 22—9 (Accounting differences and ratio analysis)

The following three ratios have been computed using the financial statements for the year ended December 31, 1993, for Mikemath Company:

$$\text{Current ratio} = (\text{Current assets/Current liabilities})$$
$$= \$80,000 \div \$43,000$$
$$= 1.86$$

$$\text{Debt-to-equity ratio} = (\text{Total liabilities/Stockholders' equity})$$
$$= \$110,000 \div \$125,000$$
$$= 0.88$$

$$\text{Profit margin} = (\text{Net income/Sales})$$
$$= \$45,000 \div \$400,000$$
$$= 0.11$$

The following additional information has been assembled:

(a) Mikemath uses the LIFO method of inventory valuation. Beginning inventory was $36,000 and ending inventory was $43,000. If Mikemath had used FIFO, beginning inventory would have been $48,000 and ending inventory would have been $58,500.
(b) Mikemath's sole depreciable asset was purchased on January 1, 1990. The asset cost $120,000 and is being depreciated over 12 years with no estimated salvage value. Although the 12-year life is within the acceptable range, most firms in Mikemath's industry depreciate similar assets over 7 years.
(c) For 1993, Mikemath adopted FASB Statement No. 106 relating to postretirement benefits other than pensions. As part of the adoption, Mikemath has an $18,000 transition loss. Mikemath has chosen to recognize the entire loss in 1993. Most other firms in Mikemath's industry are amortizing their transition losses over 20 years.

**Instructions:**

1. How would the values for the three ratios computed above differ if Mikemath had used FIFO, depreciated the asset over 7 years, and amortized the transition loss over 20 years? Do not think of these as accounting changes; compute how the financial statements would differ if the alternate accounting methods had been used to begin with. Ignore any income tax effects.
2. What dangers are there in comparing a company's financial ratios with summary industry ratios?

## Problem 22—10   (Reporting segment data)

Abcom Industries operates in several different industries, some of which are appropriately regarded as reportable segments. Total sales for Abcom are $12,000,000 and total common costs are $6,000,000 for 1993. Abcom allocates common costs based on the ratio of a segment's sales to total sales, which is considered an appropriate method of allocation. Additional information regarding the different segments is contained in the following schedule:

|  | Segment 1 | Segment 2 | Segment 3 | Segment 4 | Other Segments |
|---|---|---|---|---|---|
| Contribution to total sales ......... | 23% | 8% | 31% | 28% | 10% |
| Identifiable assets as percent of total company assets .. | 36% | 9% | 32% | 8% | 15% |
| Traceable costs .. | $800,000 | $350,000 | $1,200,000 | $1,000,000 | $650,000 |

**Instructions:**   Prepare a schedule from which operating profit is derived for Abcom Industries. The schedule should conform to the reporting criteria set forth in FASB Statement No. 14.

## Problem 22—11   (Comprehensive analysis of financial data)

The partially condensed balance sheet and income statement for Maxfield Company are shown below.

**Maxfield Company**
**Balance Sheet**
**December 31, 1993**

### Assets

| | |
|---|---|
| Cash ...................................................... | $ 63,000 |
| Trade receivables (net of estimated uncollectibles of $12,000) ......... | 238,000 |
| Inventories ................................................ | 170,000 |
| Prepaid expenses .......................................... | 7,000 |
| Land, buildings, and equipment (net of accumulated depreciation of $182,000) ................................................ | 390,000 |
| Other assets .............................................. | 13,000 |
| | $881,000 |

### Liabilities and Stockholders' Equity

| | |
|---|---|
| Accounts and notes payable—trade ................................ | $ 98,000 |
| Accrued liabilities payable....................................... | 17,000 |
| Income tax payable ............................................ | 18,000 |
| First-mortgage, 7% bonds, due in 2000 ............................ | 150,000 |
| $7 preferred stock—no par value (entitled to $110 per share in liquidation); authorized 1,000 shares; in treasury 400 shares; outstanding 600 shares ......................................... | 108,000 |
| Common stock—no par; authorized 100,000 shares, issued and outstanding 10,000 shares at stated value of $10 per share ............ | 100,000 |
| Paid-in capital in excess of stated value—common stock ............. | 242,000 |
| Retained earnings appropriated for plant expansion ................. | 50,000 |
| Retained earnings appropriated for cost of treasury stock ............. | 47,000 |
| Retained earnings—unappropriated ................................ | 98,000 |
| Cost of 400 shares of treasury stock (preferred) ..................... | (47,000) |
| | $881,000 |

**Maxfield Company**
**Income Statement**
**For the Year Ended December 31, 1993**

|  | Cash | Credit | Total |
|---|---|---|---|
| Gross sales | $116,000 | $876,000 | $992,000 |
| Less: Sales discount | $ 3,000 | $ 12,000 | $ 15,000 |
| Sales returns and allowances | 1,000 | 6,000 | 7,000 |
|  | $ 4,000 | $ 18,000 | $ 22,000 |
| Net sales | $112,000 | $858,000 | $970,000 |
| Cost of goods sold: |  |  |  |
| Inventory of finished goods, January 1 | $ 92,000 |  |  |
| Cost of goods manufactured | 680,000 |  |  |
| Inventory of finished goods, December 31 | (100,000) |  | 672,000 |
| Gross profit on sales |  |  | $298,000 |
| Selling expenses | $173,000 |  |  |
| General expenses | 70,000 |  | 243,000 |
| Income from operations |  |  | $ 55,000 |
| Other additions and deductions (net) |  |  | 3,000 |
| Income before income tax |  |  | $ 58,000 |
| Income tax (estimated) |  |  | 18,000 |
| Net income |  |  | $ 40,000 |

Additional Information:

(a) Working capital at December 31, 1992, was $205,000.
(b) Trade receivables at December 31, 1992, were $220,000 gross, $206,000 net.
(c) Dividends for 1993 have been declared and paid.
(d) There has been no change in amount of bonds outstanding or common stock during 1993.

**Instructions:** Compute the following:

1. Acid-test ratio.
2. Number of days' sales in receivables.
3. Average finished goods turnover.
4. Number of times bond interest was earned (before tax).
5. Number of times preferred dividend was earned.
6. Earnings per share of common stock.
7. Book value per share of common stock.
8. Current ratio.

(AICPA adapted)

**\*Problem 22—12 (Comprehensive statement of cash flows)**

The schedule on page 876 shows the account balances of the Beneficio Corporation at the beginning and end of the fiscal year ended October 31, 1993.

The following information was also available:

(a) All purchases and sales were on account.
(b) Equipment with an original cost of $15,000 was sold for $7,000.
(c) Selling and general expenses include the following:

| Building depreciation | $ 3,750 |
|---|---|
| Equipment depreciation | 25,250 |
| Doubtful accounts expense | 4,000 |
| Interest expense | 18,000 |

| Debits | October 31, 1993 | October 31, 1992 |
|---|---|---|
| Cash and Cash Equivalents | $ 222,000 | $ 50,000 |
| Marketable Securities | 10,000 | 40,000 |
| Accounts Receivable | 148,000 | 100,000 |
| Inventories | 291,000 | 300,000 |
| Prepaid Insurance | 2,500 | 2,000 |
| Land and Building | 195,000 | 195,000 |
| Equipment | 305,000 | 170,000 |
| Discount on Bonds Payable | 8,500 | 9,000 |
| Treasury Stock (at cost) | 5,000 | 10,000 |
| Cost of Goods Sold | 539,000 | |
| Selling and General Expenses | 287,000 | |
| Income Taxes | 35,000 | |
| Loss on Write-down of Marketable Securities | 4,000 | |
| Loss on Sale of Equipment | 1,000 | |
| Total debits | $2,053,000 | $876,000 |

| Credits | October 31, 1993 | October 31, 1992 |
|---|---|---|
| Allowance for Doubtful Accounts | $ 8,000 | $ 5,000 |
| Accumulated Depreciation—Building | 26,250 | 22,500 |
| Accumulated Depreciation—Equipment | 39,750 | 27,500 |
| Accounts Payable | 55,000 | 60,000 |
| Notes Payable—Current | 70,000 | 20,000 |
| Miscellaneous Expenses Payable | 18,000 | 8,700 |
| Taxes Payable | 35,000 | 10,000 |
| Unearned Revenue | 1,000 | 9,000 |
| Notes Payable—Long-Term | 40,000 | 60,000 |
| Bonds Payable—Long-Term | 250,000 | 250,000 |
| Deferred Income Tax Liability | 47,000 | 53,300 |
| Common Stock, $2 par | 359,400 | 200,000 |
| Retained Earnings Appropriated for Possible Building Expansion | 43,000 | 33,000 |
| Unappropriated Retained Earnings | 34,600 | 112,000 |
| Paid-In Capital in Excess of Par Value | 116,000 | 5,000 |
| Sales | 898,000 | |
| Gain on Sale of Marketable Securities | 12,000 | |
| Total credits | $2,053,000 | $876,000 |

(d) A 6-month note payable for $50,000 was issued toward the purchase of new equipment.

(e) The long-term note payable requires the payment of $20,000 per year plus interest until paid.

(f) Treasury stock was sold for $1,000 more than its cost.

(g) During the year, a 30% stock dividend was declared and issued. At the time, there were 100,000 shares of $2 par common stock outstanding. However, 1,000 of these shares were held as treasury stock at the time and were prohibited from participating in the stock dividend. Market price was $10.00 per share at time the dividend was declared.

(h) Equipment was overhauled, extending its useful life at a cost of $6,000. The cost was debited to Accumulated Depreciation—Equipment.

**Instructions:** Prepare a statement of cash flows for the year ended October 31, 1993, using the indirect method of reporting cash flow from operations.                    (AICPA adapted)

*Relates to Appendix

# APPENDIX A

## Illustrative Financial Statements

### REPORT OF MANAGEMENT

Responsibility for the integrity and objectivity of the financial information presented in this Annual Report rests with IBM management. The accompanying financial statements have been prepared in conformity with generally accepted accounting principles, applying certain estimates and judgments as required.

IBM maintains an effective internal control structure. It consists, in part, of organizational arrangements with clearly defined lines of responsibility and delegation of authority, and comprehensive systems and control procedures. We believe this structure provides reasonable assurance that transactions are executed in accordance with management authorization, and that they are appropriately recorded, in order to permit preparation of financial statements in conformity with generally accepted accounting principles and to adequately safeguard, verify and maintain accountability of assets. An important element of the control environment is an ongoing internal audit program.

To assure the effective administration of internal control, we carefully select and train our employees, develop and disseminate written policies and procedures, provide appropriate communication channels, and foster an environment conducive to the effective functioning of controls. We believe that it is essential for the company to conduct its business affairs in accordance with the highest ethical standards, as set forth in the IBM Business Conduct Guidelines. These guidelines, translated into numerous languages, are distributed to employees throughout the world, and re-emphasized through internal programs to assure that they are understood and followed.

Price Waterhouse, independent accountants, are retained to examine IBM's financial statements. Their accompanying report is based on an examination conducted in accordance with generally accepted auditing standards, including a review of the internal control structure and tests of accounting procedures and records.

The Audit Committee of the Board of Directors is composed solely of outside directors, and is responsible for recommending to the Board the independent accounting firm to be retained for the coming year, subject to stockholder approval. The Audit Committee meets periodically and privately with the independent accountants, with our internal auditors, as well as with IBM management, to review accounting, auditing, internal control structure and financial reporting matters.

*John F. Akers*

John F. Akers — Chairman of the Board

*Frank A. Metz, Jr.*

Frank A. Metz, Jr. — Senior Vice President, Finance & Planning

## REPORT OF INDEPENDENT ACCOUNTANTS

To the Stockholders and Board of Directors of
International Business Machines Corporation

January 29, 1991

In our opinion, the accompanying consolidated financial statements, appearing on pages 34, 35, 36, 37 and 43 through 58, present fairly in all material respects the financial position of International Business Machines Corporation and its subsidiaries at December 31, 1990 and 1989, and the results of their operations and their cash flows for each of the three years in the period ended December 31, 1990, in conformity with generally accepted accounting principles. These financial statements are the responsibility of the company's management; our responsibility is to express an opinion thereon based on our audits. We conducted our audits in accordance with generally accepted auditing standards which require that we plan and perform the audit to obtain reasonable assurance about whether such statements are free of material misstatement. An audit includes examining, on a test basis, evidence supporting the amounts and disclosures in the financial statements, assessing the accounting principles used and significant estimates made by management, and evaluating the overall financial statement presentation. We believe that our audits provide a reasonable basis for the opinion expressed above.

As discussed in the note regarding Taxes on page 50, the company changed its method of accounting for income taxes in 1988. We concur with this change.

*Price Waterhouse*

Price Waterhouse
153 East 53rd Street
New York, N.Y. 10022

## CONSOLIDATED STATEMENT OF EARNINGS

| For the year ended December 31: | 1990 | 1989 | 1988 |
|---|---|---|---|
| (Dollars in millions except per share amounts) | | | |
| **Revenue:** | | | |
| Sales | $43,959 | $41,586 | $39,959 |
| Support services | 11,322 | 9,858 | 9,285 |
| Software | 9,952 | 8,424 | 7,927 |
| Rentals and financing | 3,785 | 2,842 | 2,510 |
| | 69,018 | 62,710 | 59,681 |
| **Cost:** | | | |
| Sales | 19,401 | 18,001 | 17,499 |
| Support services | 6,617 | 5,701 | 4,971 |
| Software | 3,126 | 2,694 | 2,110 |
| Rentals and financing | 1,579 | 1,305 | 1,068 |
| | 30,723 | 27,701 | 25,648 |
| **Gross Profit** | 38,295 | 35,009 | 34,033 |
| **Operating Expenses:** | | | |
| Selling, general and administrative | 20,709 | 21,289 | 19,362 |
| Research, development and engineering | 6,554 | 6,827 | 5,925 |
| | 27,263 | 28,116 | 25,287 |
| **Operating Income** | 11,032 | 6,893 | 8,746 |
| **Other Income, principally interest** | 495 | 728 | 996 |
| **Interest Expense** | 1,324 | 976 | 709 |
| **Earnings before Income Taxes** | 10,203 | 6,645 | 9,033 |
| **Provision for Income Taxes** | 4,183 | 2,887 | 3,542 |
| **Net Earnings before Cumulative Effect of Accounting Change** | 6,020 | 3,758 | 5,491 |
| **Cumulative Effect of Change in Accounting for Income Taxes** | — | — | 315 |
| **Net Earnings** | $ 6,020 | $ 3,758 | $ 5,806 |
| Per share amounts: | | | |
| Before cumulative effect of accounting change | $10.51 | $6.47 | $9.27 |
| Cumulative effect of change in accounting for income taxes | — | — | .53 |
| Net earnings | $10.51 | $6.47 | $9.80 |

Average number of shares outstanding:
1990—572,647,906
1989—581,102,404
1988—592,444,409

The notes on pages 43 through 58 are an integral part of this statement.

# CONSOLIDATED STATEMENT OF FINANCIAL POSITION

| At December 31: | 1990 | 1989 |
|---|---|---|
| (Dollars in millions) | | |
| **Assets** | | |
| **Current Assets:** | | |
| Cash | $ 1,189 | $ 741 |
| Cash equivalents | 2,664 | 2,959 |
| Marketable securities, at cost, which approximates market | 698 | 1,261 |
| Notes and accounts receivable—trade, net of allowances | 20,988 | 18,866 |
| Other accounts receivable | 1,656 | 1,298 |
| Inventories | 10,108 | 9,463 |
| Prepaid expenses and other current assets | 1,617 | 1,287 |
| | 38,920 | 35,875 |
| **Plant, Rental Machines and Other Property** | 53,659 | 48,410 |
| Less: Accumulated depreciation | 26,418 | 23,467 |
| | 27,241 | 24,943 |
| **Investments and Other Assets:** | | |
| Software, less accumulated amortization (1990, $5,873; 1989, $4,824) | 4,099 | 3,293 |
| Investments and sundry assets | 17,308 | 13,623 |
| | 21,407 | 16,916 |
| | $87,568 | $77,734 |
| **Liabilities and Stockholders' Equity** | | |
| **Current Liabilities:** | | |
| Taxes | $ 3,159 | $ 2,699 |
| Short-term debt | 7,602 | 5,892 |
| Accounts payable | 3,367 | 3,167 |
| Compensation and benefits | 3,014 | 2,797 |
| Deferred income | 2,506 | 1,365 |
| Other accrued expenses and liabilities | 5,628 | 5,780 |
| | 25,276 | 21,700 |
| **Long-Term Debt** | 11,943 | 10,825 |
| **Other Liabilities** | 3,656 | 3,420 |
| **Deferred Income Taxes** | 3,861 | 3,280 |
| **Stockholders' Equity:** | | |
| Capital stock, par value $1.25 per share | 6,357 | 6,341 |
| Shares authorized: 750,000,000 | | |
| Issued: 1990—571,618,795; 1989—574,775,560 | | |
| Retained earnings | 33,234 | 30,477 |
| Translation adjustments | 3,266 | 1,698 |
| | 42,857 | 38,516 |
| Less: Treasury stock, at cost (Shares: 1990—227,604; 1989—75,723) | 25 | 7 |
| | 42,832 | 38,509 |
| | $87,568 | $77,734 |

The notes on pages 43 through 58 are an integral part of this statement.

## CONSOLIDATED STATEMENT OF CASH FLOWS

| For the year ended December 31: | 1990 | 1989 | 1988 |
|---|---|---|---|
| (Dollars in millions) | | | |
| **Cash Flow from Operating Activities:** | | | |
| Net earnings | $ 6,020 | $ 3,758 | $ 5,806 |
| Adjustments to reconcile net earnings to cash provided from operating activities: | | | |
| Depreciation | 4,217 | 4,240 | 3,871 |
| Amortization of software | 1,086 | 1,185 | 893 |
| Loss (gain) on disposition of investment assets | 32 | (74) | (133) |
| (Increase) in accounts receivable | (2,077) | (2,647) | (2,322) |
| Decrease (increase) in inventory | 17 | (29) | (1,232) |
| (Increase) in other assets | (3,136) | (1,674) | (1,587) |
| Increase in accounts payable | 293 | 870 | 265 |
| Increase in other liabilities | 1,020 | 1,743 | 519 |
| Net cash provided from operating activities | 7,472 | 7,372 | 6,080 |
| **Cash Flow from Investing Activities:** | | | |
| Payments for plant, rental machines and other property | (6,509) | (6,414) | (5,390) |
| Proceeds from disposition of plant, rental machines and other property | 804 | 544 | 409 |
| Investment in software | (1,892) | (1,679) | (1,318) |
| Purchases of marketable securities and other investments | (1,234) | (1,391) | (2,555) |
| Proceeds from marketable securities and other investments | 1,687 | 1,860 | 4,734 |
| Net cash used in investing activities | (7,144) | (7,080) | (4,120) |
| **Cash Flow from Financing Activities:** | | | |
| Proceeds from new debt | 4,676 | 6,471 | 4,540 |
| Payments to settle debt | (3,683) | (2,768) | (3,007) |
| Short-term borrowings less than 90 days—net | 1,966 | 228 | 1,028 |
| Payments to employee stock plans—net | (76) | (29) | (11) |
| Payments to purchase and retire capital stock | (415) | (1,759) | (992) |
| Cash dividends paid | (2,774) | (2,752) | (2,609) |
| Net cash used in financing activities | (306) | (609) | (1,051) |
| **Effect of Exchange Rate Changes on Cash and Cash Equivalents** | 131 | (158) | (201) |
| **Net Change in Cash and Cash Equivalents** | 153 | (475) | 708 |
| **Cash and Cash Equivalents at January 1** | 3,700 | 4,175 | 3,467 |
| **Cash and Cash Equivalents at December 31** | $ 3,853 | $ 3,700 | $ 4,175 |
| **Supplemental Data:** | | | |
| Cash paid during the year for: | | | |
| Income taxes | $ 3,315 | $ 3,071 | $ 3,405 |
| Interest | $ 2,165 | $ 1,605 | $ 1,440 |

The notes on pages 43 through 58 are an integral part of this statement.

## CONSOLIDATED STATEMENT OF STOCKHOLDERS' EQUITY

| | Capital Stock | Retained Earnings | Translation Adjustments | Treasury Stock | Total |
|---|---|---|---|---|---|
| (Dollars in millions) | | | | | |
| **Stockholders' Equity, January 1, 1988** | $6,417 | $29,016 | $2,865 | $ (35) | $ 38,263 |
| **1988** | | | | | |
| Net earnings | | 5,806 | | | 5,806 |
| Cash dividends declared | | (2,609) | | | (2,609) |
| Capital stock issued under employee plans (1,321,697 shares) | 92 | | | | 92 |
| Purchases (8,140,101 shares) and sales (8,117,596 shares) of treasury stock under employee and stockholder plans—net | | (128) | | (1) | (129) |
| Capital stock purchased and retired (8,611,396 shares) | (93) | (899) | | | (992) |
| Tax reductions—employee plans | 26 | | | | 26 |
| Translation adjustments | | | (948) | | (948) |
| **Stockholders' Equity, December 31, 1988** | 6,442 | 31,186 | 1,917 | (36) | 39,509 |
| **1989** | | | | | |
| Net earnings | | 3,758 | | | 3,758 |
| Cash dividends declared | | (2,752) | | | (2,752) |
| Capital stock issued under employee plans (824,026 shares) | 60 | | | | 60 |
| Purchases (8,202,058 shares) and sales (8,423,155 shares) of treasury stock under employee and stockholder plans—net | | (133) | | 29 | (104) |
| Capital stock purchased and retired (16,085,900 shares) | (177) | (1,582) | | | (1,759) |
| Tax reductions—employee plans | 16 | | | | 16 |
| Translation adjustments | | | (219) | | (219) |
| **Stockholders' Equity, December 31, 1989** | 6,341 | 30,477 | 1,698 | (7) | 38,509 |
| **1990** | | | | | |
| Net earnings | | 6,020 | | | 6,020 |
| Cash dividends declared | | (2,774) | | | (2,774) |
| Capital stock issued under employee plans (686,159 shares) | 47 | | | | 47 |
| Purchases (8,448,626 shares) and sales (8,296,745 shares) of treasury stock under employee and stockholder plans—net | | (117) | | (18) | (135) |
| Capital stock purchased and retired (3,842,924 shares) | (43) | (372) | | | (415) |
| Tax reductions—employee plans | 12 | | | | 12 |
| Translation adjustments | | | 1,568 | | 1,568 |
| **Stockholders' Equity, December 31, 1990** | $6,357 | $33,234 | $3,266 | $ (25) | $ 42,832 |

The notes on pages 43 through 58 are an integral part of this statement.

## NOTES TO CONSOLIDATED FINANCIAL STATEMENTS

### Significant Accounting Policies

**Principles of Consolidation**   The consolidated financial statements include the accounts of International Business Machines Corporation and its U.S. and non-U.S. subsidiary companies. Investments in joint ventures and other companies in which IBM does not have control, but has the ability to exercise significant influence over operating and financial policies (generally greater than 20% ownership) are accounted for by the equity method. Other investments are accounted for by the cost method.

**Translation of Non-U.S. Currency Amounts**   For non-U.S. subsidiaries which operate in a local currency environment, assets and liabilities are translated to U.S. dollars at year-end exchange rates. Income and expense items are translated at average rates of exchange prevailing during the year. Translation adjustments are accumulated in a separate component of stockholders' equity. For non-U.S. subsidiaries and branches which operate in U.S. dollars or whose economic environment is highly inflationary, inventories and plant, rental machines and other property are translated at approximate rates prevailing when acquired. All other assets and liabilities are translated at year-end exchange rates. Inventories charged to cost of sales and depreciation are remeasured at historical rates. All other income and expense items are translated at average rates of exchange prevailing during the year. Gains and losses which result from remeasurement are included in earnings.

**Revenue**   Revenue is recognized from sales or sales-type leases when the product is shipped, from software when the program is shipped or as monthly license fees accrue, from support services (primarily maintenance services) over the contractual period or as the services are performed, from rentals under operating leases in the month in which they accrue, and from financing at level rates of return over the term of the lease or receivable.

**Software**   Costs related to the conceptual formulation and design of licensed programs are expensed as research and development. Costs incurred subsequent to establishment of technological feasibility to produce the finished product are generally capitalized. The annual amortization of the capitalized amounts is the greater of the amount computed based on the estimated revenue distribution over the products' revenue-producing lives or the straight-line method, but not in excess of six years. Costs to support or service licensed programs are charged against income as incurred or when related revenue is recognized, whichever occurs first.

**Depreciation**   Plant, rental machines and other property are carried at cost and depreciated over their estimated useful lives using the straight-line method.

**NOTES TO CONSOLIDATED FINANCIAL STATEMENTS**

### Significant Accounting Policies (continued)

**Goodwill**  Goodwill is amortized on a straight-line basis over the periods estimated to be benefited, currently not exceeding five years.

**Retirement Plans and Other Postretirement Benefits**  Current service costs of retirement plans are accrued currently. Prior service costs resulting from improvements in the plans are amortized over the average remaining service period of employees expected to receive benefits. Postretirement health care and life insurance benefits are fully accrued, principally at retirement.

**Selling Expenses**  Selling expenses are charged against income as incurred.

**Income Taxes**  Income tax expense is based on reported earnings before income taxes. Deferred income taxes reflect the impact of temporary differences between the amount of assets and liabilities recognized for financial reporting purposes and such amounts recognized for tax purposes.

In accordance with Statement of Financial Accounting Standards (SFAS) 96, which the company adopted in 1988, these deferred taxes are measured by applying currently enacted tax laws. Deferred investment tax credits are being amortized as a reduction of income tax expense over the average useful life of the applicable classes of property.

**Inventories**  Raw materials, finished goods and work in process are stated at the lower of average cost or market.

**Cash Equivalents**  All highly liquid investments with a maturity of three months or less at date of purchase are considered to be cash equivalents.

| **Non-U.S. Operations** | 1990 | 1989 | 1988 |
|---|---|---|---|
| (Dollars in millions) | | | |
| **At end of year:** | | | |
| Net assets employed: | | | |
| Current assets | $24,337 | $20,361 | $20,005 |
| Current liabilities | 15,917 | 12,124 | 11,481 |
| Working capital | 8,420 | 8,237 | 8,524 |
| Plant, rental machines and other property, net | 11,628 | 9,879 | 9,354 |
| Investments and other assets | 9,077 | 6,822 | 5,251 |
| | 29,125 | 24,938 | 23,129 |
| Long-term debt | 5,060 | 3,358 | 2,340 |
| Other liabilities | 2,699 | 2,607 | 2,505 |
| Deferred income taxes | 2,381 | 1,814 | 1,580 |
| | 10,140 | 7,779 | 6,425 |
| Net assets employed | $18,985 | $17,159 | $16,704 |
| Number of employees | 168,283 | 167,291 | 163,904 |
| | | | |
| **For the year:** | | | |
| Revenue | $41,886 | $36,965 | $34,361 |
| Earnings before income taxes | $ 7,844 | $ 7,496 | $ 7,088 |
| Provision for income taxes | 3,270 | 3,388 | 3,009 |
| Net earnings | $ 4,574 | $ 4,108 | $ 4,079† |
| Investment in plant, rental machines and other property | $ 3,020 | $ 2,514 | $ 2,389 |

† 1988 net earnings before cumulative effect of accounting change for income taxes.

Non-U.S. subsidiaries which operate in a local currency environment account for approximately 90% of the company's non-U.S. revenue. The remaining 10% of the company's non-U.S. revenue is from subsidiaries and branches which operate in U.S. dollars or whose economic environment is highly inflationary.

As the value of the dollar weakens, net assets recorded in local currencies translate into more U.S. dollars than they would have at the previous year's rates. Conversely, as the dollar becomes stronger, net assets recorded in local currencies translate into fewer U.S. dollars than they would have at the previous year's rates. The translation adjustments, resulting from the translation of net assets, amounted to $3,266 million at December 31, 1990, $1,698 million at December 31, 1989, and $1,917 million at December 31, 1988. The changes in translation adjustments since the end of 1988 are a reflection of the strengthening of the dollar in 1989 and the weakening of the dollar in 1990.

Undistributed earnings of non-U.S. subsidiaries included in consolidated retained earnings amounted to $14,388 million at December 31, 1990, $13,207 million at December 31, 1989, and $12,374 million at December 31, 1988. These earnings, which reflect full provision for non-U.S. income taxes, are indefinitely reinvested in non-U.S. operations or will be remitted substantially free of additional tax. Accordingly,

## NOTES TO CONSOLIDATED FINANCIAL STATEMENTS

no material provision has been made for taxes that might be payable upon remittance of such earnings. It is extremely improbable that all these earnings would be remitted to the U.S. Nevertheless, SFAS 96, "Accounting for Income Taxes," requires disclosure of the amount of withholding taxes that would be payable were this unlikely event to occur. Therefore, in response to that requirement, it is estimated that such withholding taxes would be as much as $1,200 million.

### Finance Subsidiaries

The company's wholly owned finance subsidiaries consist of IBM Credit Corporation and several non-U.S. finance subsidiaries. IBM Credit Corporation offers a wide range of financing services for IBM customers and business partners. Financing products, which are directly related to the sale of IBM products, include leases, installment payment loans and remarketer financing. The non-U.S. finance subsidiaries offer lease financing of selected IBM products and in some cases finance installment receivables.

The following schedule depicts the combined financial information for these finance subsidiaries, of which IBM Credit Corporation accounts for more than 70% of the net earnings. These wholly owned subsidiaries are consolidated in the accompanying financial statements. Financing activity in countries in which the company does not have a finance subsidiary is not included.

| Financial position at December 31: | 1990 | 1989 |
|---|---|---|
| (Dollars in millions) | | |
| Assets: | | |
| Cash and cash equivalents | $ 307 | $ 315 |
| Receivables — net | 3,421 | 2,796 |
| Net investment in capital leases | 9,702 | 7,350 |
| Equipment under operating leases — net | 2,082 | 2,030 |
| Other | 499 | 246 |
| Total Assets | $16,011 | $12,737 |

| | 1990 | 1989* |
|---|---|---|
| (Dollars in millions) | | |
| Liabilities and Stockholder's Equity: | | |
| Short-term debt | $ 4,743 | $ 3,482 |
| Deferred taxes and accruals | 1,355 | 1,214 |
| Due to IBM and affiliates | 2,641 | 1,648 |
| Long-term debt | 6,006 | 5,291 |
| Stockholder's equity | 1,266 | 1,102 |
| Total Liabilities and Stockholder's Equity | $16,011 | $12,737 |

| Earnings for the years ended December 31: | 1990 | 1989 | 1988 |
|---|---|---|---|
| (Dollars in millions) | | | |
| Financing and other income | $1,992 | $1,332 | $ 914 |
| Interest and other expenses | 1,649 | 1,098 | 791 |
| Provision for income taxes | 112 | 75 | 26 |
| Net earnings | $ 231 | $ 159 | $ 97† |

*Reclassified to conform with 1990 presentation.

† 1988 net earnings before cumulative effect of accounting change for income taxes.

**Restructuring and Other Actions**    In December 1989, the company announced a series of actions to reduce costs, expenses and structure.

As a result, the 1989 earnings include a charge, recorded in the fourth quarter, of $2,420 million ($1,500 million after tax or $2.58 per share). $1,335 million of this relates to the costs of facility consolidations and capacity reductions and changes in the valuation and recovery periods of special investments. This amount is included in selling, general and administrative expense. Costs of $500 million associated with employee separations and relocations are also included in selling, general and administrative expense.

Costs of $585 million represent a charge related to the adoption of new guidelines to provide for the earlier recognition of costs in both hardware and software due to the pace of technological change and the company's success in shortening its product cycles. These charges are included in research, development and engineering expenses and in cost of software.

In 1988, $870 million was included in selling, general and administrative expense for manufacturing and headquarters consolidations.

**Marketable Securities**    At December 31:

| (Dollars in millions) | 1990 | 1989 |
|---|---|---|
| U.S. government securities | $     92 | $    201 |
| Time deposits and other bank obligations | 373 | 419 |
| Non-U.S. government securities and other fixed-term obligations | 233 | 641 |
| Total | $    698 | $  1,261 |
| Market value | $    698 | $  1,263 |

**Inventories**    At December 31:

| (Dollars in millions) | 1990 | 1989 |
|---|---|---|
| Current inventories: | | |
| Finished goods | $  2,851 | $  2,915 |
| Work in process | 7,051 | 6,394 |
| Raw materials | 206 | 154 |
| Total current inventories | 10,108 | 9,463 |
| Work in process included in plant, rental machines and other property | 1,498 | 1,364 |
| Total inventories | $11,606 | $10,827 |

**NOTES TO CONSOLIDATED FINANCIAL STATEMENTS**

| **Plant, Rental Machines and Other Property**   At December 31: | 1990 | 1989 |
|---|---:|---:|
| (Dollars in millions) | | |
| Land and land improvements | $ 1,645 | $ 1,507 |
| Buildings | 13,792 | 12,333 |
| Plant, laboratory and office equipment | 35,155 | 31,064 |
| | 50,592 | 44,904 |
| Less: Accumulated depreciation | 24,916 | 22,017 |
| | 25,676 | 22,887 |
| Rental machines and parts | 3,067 | 3,506 |
| Less: Accumulated depreciation | 1,502 | 1,450 |
| | 1,565 | 2,056 |
| Total | $27,241 | $24,943 |

| **Investments and Sundry Assets**   At December 31: | 1990 | 1989 |
|---|---:|---:|
| (Dollars in millions) | | |
| Net investment in sales-type leases† | $16,914 | $12,728 |
| Less: Current portion (net) classified as notes and accounts receivable—trade | 5,682 | 4,332 |
| | 11,232 | 8,396 |
| Prepaid pension cost | 1,045 | 655 |
| Installment payment receivables | 896 | 912 |
| Investments in business alliances | 703 | 660 |
| Mortgage investments | 529 | 509 |
| Goodwill, less accumulated amortization (1990, $406; 1989, $283) | 383 | 392 |
| Other investments and sundry assets* | 2,520 | 2,099 |
| Total | $17,308 | $13,623 |

†These leases relate to IBM equipment and are for terms generally ranging from three to five years. Net investment in sales-type leases includes unguaranteed residual values of approximately $1,350 million and $1,100 million at December 31, 1990 and 1989, and is reflected net of unearned income at these dates of approximately $3,600 million and $2,600 million, respectively.

*Includes, at cost, an investment of $400 million in 7.35% preferred stock of MCI Communications Corporation, which is not convertible, nor is it planned to be publicly traded. MCI has the option to redeem all or part of this issue at any time.

| **Long-Term Debt**   At December 31: | Maturities | 1990 | 1989 |
|---|---|---|---|
| (Dollars in millions) | | | |
| **U. S. dollars:** | | | |
| Debentures: | | | |
| 7⅞% convertible, subordinated† | 2004 | $ 1,254 | $ 1,254 |
| 8⅜% | 2019 | 750 | 750 |
| 9⅜% (with sinking fund payments to 2003) | 2004 | 238 | 300 |
| Notes: | | | |
| 5¾% to 7⅝% | 1991-1993 | 354 | 854 |
| 7¾% to 8⅞% | 1991-1995 | 2,370 | 2,470 |
| 9% to 10¼% | 1991-2000 | 2,300 | 2,303 |
| Medium-term note program: 7.5% to 15.0% | 1991-2008 | 890 | 1,057 |
| Other U.S. dollars: 5.0% to 14.7% | 1991-2012 | 508 | 474 |
| | | 8,664 | 9,462 |
| **Other currencies** (average interest rate at December 31, 1990, in parentheses): | | | |
| Swiss francs (6.8%) | 1992-1996 | 1,125 | 317 |
| French francs (10.1%) | 1991-2002 | 736 | 486 |
| Canadian dollars (11.4%) | 1992-1995 | 693 | 443 |
| European currency units (9.0%) | 1992-1995 | 648 | 599 |
| Australian dollars (14.5%) | 1991-1993 | 580 | 539 |
| Japanese yen (5.5%) | 1991-2019 | 532 | 489 |
| Other (10.6%) | 1991-2011 | 684 | 379 |
| | | 13,662 | 12,714 |
| Less: Net unamortized discount | | 15 | 6 |
| | | 13,647 | 12,708 |
| Less: Current maturities | | 1,704 | 1,883 |
| Total | | $11,943 | $10,825 |

Annual maturity and sinking fund requirements in millions of dollars on long-term
debt outstanding at December 31, 1990, are as follows:
1991, $1,704; 1992, $3,658; 1993, $2,277; 1994, $786; 1995, $1,581; 1996 and beyond, $3,656.

†The 7⅞% convertible subordinated debentures are unsecured subordinated obligations of IBM, which are convertible into IBM capital stock at a conversion price of $153.6563 per share. They are redeemable, at the option of the company, as of November 1990 at a price of 103.150% of the principal amount, and at decreasing prices thereafter. Sinking fund payments starting in 1994 are intended to retire 75% of the debentures prior to maturity. There were no conversions of debentures in 1990.

## NOTES TO CONSOLIDATED FINANCIAL STATEMENTS

| Taxes | 1990 | 1989 | 1988 |
|---|---|---|---|
| (Dollars in millions) | | | |
| Earnings before income taxes: | | | |
| U.S. operations | $ 2.359 | $ (851) | $1,945 |
| Non-U.S. operations | 7.844 | 7,496 | 7,088 |
| | $10.203 | $6,645 | $9,033 |
| Provision for income taxes: | | | |
| U.S. operations | $ 913 | $ (501) | $ 533 |
| Non-U.S. operations | 3.270 | 3,388 | 3,009 |
| | 4.183 | 2,887 | 3,542 |
| Social security, real estate, personal property and other taxes | 3.017 | 2,562 | 2,528 |
| Total | $ 7,200 | $5,449 | $6,070 |
| The components of the provision for income taxes are as follows: | | | |
| U.S. Federal: | | | |
| Current | $ 379 | $ 476 | $ 79 |
| Deferred | (44) | (1,247) | (86) |
| Net deferred investment tax credits | (95) | (101) | (125) |
| | 240 | (872) | (132) |
| Non-U.S.: | | | |
| Current | 3,375 | 3,025 | 3,562 |
| Deferred | 446 | 824 | 87 |
| | 3.821 | 3,849 | 3,649 |
| U.S. State and local: | | | |
| Current | 16 | 107 | 12 |
| Deferred | 106 | (197) | 13 |
| | 122 | (90) | 25 |
| Total provision | $ 4,183 | $2,887 | $3,542 |

In 1988, the company implemented Statement of Financial Accounting Standards (SFAS) 96. This standard calls for adjustment of deferred tax assets and liabilities whenever there is a change in enacted tax rates, with a corresponding adjustment being reflected in income tax expense for that period. Previous rules called for recording these assets and liabilities at the current rate, with no subsequent adjustment for tax rate changes.

The cumulative effect of adopting SFAS 96 for the periods ended prior to January 1, 1988, which amounted to a benefit of $315 million, has been included in 1988 net earnings.

Deferred income taxes reflect the impact of temporary differences between the amount of assets and liabilities recognized for financial reporting purposes and such amounts recognized for tax purposes. The principal items making up the deferred tax provision in 1990 included $573 million related to the partial turnaround of deferred tax assets arising from the 1989 U.S. restructuring charge, $343 million for sales-type leases and installment sales, $276 million for deferred software costs, and $173 million for retirement benefits. These amounts were offset by $205 million of deferred tax benefits associated with the alternative minimum tax and $197 million for depreciation. In 1989, the principal items included $904 million related to the restructuring charge and $159 million for deferred inventory overhead, offset by $339 million for sales-type leases and installment sales and $230 million for deferred software costs. In 1988, the principal items included $283 million for sales-type leases and installment sales and $175 million for deferred software costs, offset by $182 million of deferred tax benefits associated with the alternative minimum tax.

Under the rules of SFAS 96, no financial recognition is allowed for net deferred tax assets in excess of the amount that could be recovered as income tax refunds through existing loss carryback or carryforward provisions. Consequently, at December 31, 1990, the company had unrecognized deferred tax assets of approximately $110 million, most of which have carryforwards for substantial periods. The company is also evaluating the potential realization of other deferred tax assets emanating from the continuing transformation of the company. In addition, the company has approximately $190 million of deferred investment tax credits for financial reporting purposes, which will reduce tax expense in future years. For tax purposes, the company has available tax credit carryforwards of approximately $700 million, the majority of which are available indefinitely and may be used to offset future taxes.

The consolidated effective income tax rate was 41.0% in 1990, 43.4% in 1989, and 39.2% in 1988. In 1990, 1989, and 1988, the higher effective tax rate on earnings of non-U.S. operations accounted for 5.9, 12.6, and 6.6 percentage points, respectively, of the difference between the effective rate and the U.S. federal statutory rate of 34.0%.

## NOTES TO CONSOLIDATED FINANCIAL STATEMENTS

**Research, Development and Engineering**   Research, development and engineering expenses amounted to $6,554 million in 1990, $6,827 million in 1989 and $5,925 million in 1988.

Included in these amounts were expenditures of $4,914 million in 1990, $5,201 million in 1989 and $4,419 million in 1988 for a broad program of research and development activities covering basic scientific research in a variety of fields and the application of scientific advances to the development of new and improved products and their uses. The 1989 amount included $375 million associated with the U.S. restructuring. In addition, expenditures for product-related engineering amounted to $1,640 million, $1,626 million and $1,506 million for the same three years.

**Interest Cost**   Interest on borrowings of the company and its subsidiaries amounted to $2,425 million in 1990, $1,853 million in 1989 and $1,321 million in 1988. Of these amounts, $122 million in 1990, $142 million in 1989 and $93 million in 1988 were capitalized. The remainder was charged to cost of rentals and financing and interest expense.

**Lines of Credit**   At December 31, 1990, the company and its subsidiaries had available unused lines of credit with a number of U.S. and non-U.S. banks permitting borrowings, primarily short-term, up to an aggregate of approximately $6,800 million. Interest rates on borrowings would vary from country to country depending on local market conditions.

**Rental Expense and Lease Commitments**   Rental expense, including amounts charged to inventories and fixed assets, amounted to $1,903 million in 1990, $1,765 million in 1989 and $1,566 million in 1988.

Minimum rental commitments, in millions of dollars, under noncancelable leases for 1991 and thereafter are as follows: 1991, $1,558; 1992, $1,342; 1993, $1,161; 1994, $967; 1995, $850; and after 1995, $3,938. These leases are principally for the rental of office premises.

**Other Liabilities**   Other liabilities consist principally of indemnity and retirement plan reserves for non-U.S. employees.

**Financial Instruments**   In March 1990, the Financial Accounting Standards Board issued Statement of Financial Accounting Standards (SFAS) 105. This statement requires disclosure of information about financial instruments with off-balance-sheet risk and about financial instruments with concentrations of credit risk.

As of December 31, 1990, off-balance-sheet risk and concentrations of credit risk were immaterial to the accompanying financial statements. In the normal course of business, the company enters into a variety of forward contracts, options and swaps in order to limit its exposure to loss due to adverse fluctuations in foreign currency exchange and interest rates. These instruments are executed with creditworthy financial institutions and virtually all foreign currency contracts are denominated in currencies of major industrial countries. As foreign currency exchange rates and interest rates fluctuate, gains and losses on these contracts serve as hedges in that they offset losses and gains that would otherwise impact the company's financial results. Costs associated with entering into such contracts are amortized over the life of the instrument and are not material to the company's financial results.

**Retirement Plans** The company and its subsidiaries have retirement plans covering substantially all employees. The total cost of all plans for 1990, 1989 and 1988 was $94 million, $328 million and $460 million, respectively.

Pension cost in 1990 was lower than in 1989 principally due to the growth in the expected return on plan assets exceeding the growth in annual interest and service cost. Pension cost in 1989 was lower than in 1988 principally due to changes in actuarial assumptions in the U.S. and several non-U.S. plans, partially offset by amendments to the U.S. plan.

Annual cost is determined using the Projected Unit Credit actuarial method. Prior service cost is amortized on a straight-line basis over the average remaining service period of employees expected to receive benefits. An assumption is made for modified career average plans that the average earnings base period will be updated to the years prior to retirement.

It is the company's practice to fund amounts for pensions sufficient to meet the minimum requirements set forth in applicable employee benefit and tax laws, and such additional amounts the company may determine to be appropriate from time to time. The assets of the various plans include corporate equities, government securities, corporate debt securities and income-producing real estate.

The tables on page 54 provide information on the status of the U.S. retirement plan, and selected non-U.S. plans which represent approximately 98% of the total non-U.S. accumulated benefit obligations.

*U.S. Plan:* U.S. regular and part-time employees are covered by a noncontributory plan which is funded by company contributions to an irrevocable trust fund, which is held for the sole benefit of employees. Monthly retirement benefits generally represent the greater of a fixed amount per year of service, or a percent of career compensation. For plan purposes, annual compensation before January 1, 1991, is defined as the average annual compensation paid for the years 1981 through 1990. Effective January 1, 1989, benefits become vested upon the completion of five years of service. Prior to January 1, 1989, benefits became vested upon completion of 10 years of service. The number of individuals receiving benefits at December 31, 1990, and December 31, 1989, was 52,895 and 44,701, respectively.

The expected long-term rate of return on plan assets used in the calculation of net periodic pension cost was 9% for 1990, 1989 and 1988. Measurement of the 1990 and 1989 projected benefit obligation was based on an 8½% discount rate and a 5% long-term rate of compensation increase.

*Non-U.S. Plans:* Most subsidiaries and branches outside the U.S. have retirement plans covering substantially all employees, under which funds are deposited under various fiduciary-type arrangements, annuities are purchased under group contracts, or reserves are provided. Retirement benefits are based on years of service and the employee's compensation, generally during a fixed number of years immediately prior to retirement.

**NOTES TO CONSOLIDATED FINANCIAL STATEMENTS**

The ranges of assumptions used for the non-U.S. plans reflect the different economic environments within the various countries. The expected long-term rates of return on plan assets used in the calculation of net periodic pension cost ranged from 5% to 12% in both 1990 and 1989 and from 5% to 11% in 1988. Measurement of the 1990 and 1989 projected benefit obligation was based on discount rates ranging from 4½% to 10% and long-term rates of compensation increase ranging from 3% to 8½%.

| The funded status at December 31 was as follows: | U.S. Plan | | Non-U.S. Plans | |
|---|---|---|---|---|
| | 1990 | 1989 | 1990 | 1989 |
| (Dollars in millions) | | | | |
| Actuarial present value of benefit obligations: | | | | |
| Vested benefit obligation | $(13,112) | $(11,642) | $ (9,022) | $ (6,892) |
| Accumulated benefit obligation | $(13,146) | $(11,708) | $(10,347) | $ (8,056) |
| Projected benefit obligation | $(17,091) | $(15,451) | $(14,338) | $(11,582) |
| Plan assets at fair value | 22,225 | 22,867 | 12,382 | 11,231 |
| Projected benefit obligation less than (in excess of) plan assets | 5,134 | 7,416 | (1,956) | (351) |
| Unrecognized net (gain) loss | (2,665) | (4,902) | 459 | (1,108) |
| Unrecognized prior service cost | 1,323 | 1,092 | 332 | 241 |
| Unrecognized net asset established at January 1, 1986 | (2,747) | (2,951) | (152) | (163) |
| Prepaid (accrued) pension cost recognized in the statement of financial position | $ 1,045 | $ 655 | $ (1,317) | $ (1,381) |

| Net periodic pension cost for the years ended December 31 included the following components: | U.S. Plan | | | Non-U.S. Plans | | |
|---|---|---|---|---|---|---|
| | 1990 | 1989 | 1988 | 1990 | 1989 | 1988 |
| (Dollars in millions) | | | | | | |
| Service cost— | | | | | | |
| benefits earned during the period | $ 573 | $ 562 | $ 579 | $ 575 | $ 501 | $ 482 |
| Interest cost on the projected benefit obligation | 1,309 | 1,194 | 1,120 | 837 | 679 | 648 |
| Return on plan assets— | | | | | | |
| Actual | (160) | (3,950) | (2,058) | 665 | (1,315) | (1,003) |
| Deferred | (1,859) | 2,214 | 456 | (1,644) | 564 | 340 |
| Net amortizations | (253) | (174) | (152) | (5) | 2 | 5 |
| Net periodic pension cost | $ (390) | $ (154) | $ (55) | $ 428 | $ 431 | $ 472 |
| Total net periodic pension cost for all non-U.S. plans | | | | $ 484 | $ 482 | $ 515 |

**Postretirement Benefits**   The company and its U.S. subsidiaries have medical, dental and life insurance plans for retirees, the estimated cost of which is fully accrued, principally at retirement. This cost amounted to $96 million, $303 million and $105 million in 1990, 1989 and 1988, respectively.

Cost was lower in 1990 primarily because of amounts recorded in 1989 as a result of the announced U.S. restructuring. Cost in 1989 was higher than in 1988 primarily for the same reason.

It is the company's practice to fund amounts for postretirement benefits, with an independent trustee, as deemed appropriate from time to time.

Certain of the company's non-U.S. subsidiaries have similar plans for retirees. However, many retirees outside the U.S. are covered by government-sponsored and administered programs. As a result, the cost of company-sponsored programs outside the U.S. is not significant.

In December 1990, the Financial Accounting Standards Board issued Statement of Financial Accounting Standards (SFAS) No. 106, "Employers' Accounting for Postretirement Benefits Other Than Pensions," which requires that the cost of these benefits be recognized in the financial statements over an employee's active working career. The prevalent practice in industry is to account for these costs on a pay-as-you-go (cash) basis. However, the company's current accounting practice of accruing at retirement, along with its funding policy, will significantly mitigate the financial impact of adopting the new standard.

Adoption is required no later than 1993 for U.S. plans and by 1995 for non-U.S. plans, although earlier adoption is encouraged. Adopting the new standard will create a previously unrecognized obligation covering prior years. This transition obligation may be recognized in future financial statements in one of

two ways: (1) by immediate recognition through a cumulative adjustment in the statement of earnings, or (2) on a delayed basis, by amortizing the obligation on a straight-line basis over the average remaining service period of active plan participants.

If the company implements this standard using the delayed recognition basis, the impact on net earnings is expected to be immaterial. If implemented by immediate recognition of the transition obligation, the impact on net earnings will be material in the period adopted.

**Stock Purchase Plan**   In April 1990, stockholders approved the addition of two million shares of capital stock to the 1986 IBM Employees Stock Purchase Plan. Stockholders also approved a new five-year plan, effective July 1, 1990, which authorizes up to fifty million shares of capital stock to be reserved for issuance under the plan. The plan enables employees who are not participants in IBM's stock option programs to purchase IBM's capital stock through payroll deductions of up to 10% of eligible compensation. The price an employee pays for a share of stock is 85% of the average market price on the date the employee has accumulated enough money to buy a share.

During 1990, employees purchased 7,170,973 shares, all of which were treasury shares, for which $679 million was paid to IBM. At December 31, 1990, 47,208,470 shares remain available for purchase.

**Stock Repurchase Programs**   Under programs for purchasing IBM stock, 3,842,924 shares were repurchased during 1990 at a cost of $415 million, 16,085,900 shares were repurchased during 1989 at a cost of $1,759 million and 8,611,396 shares were repurchased during 1988 at a cost of $992 million. The repurchased shares were retired and restored to the status of authorized but unissued shares.

In late 1989, the Board of Directors authorized

## NOTES TO CONSOLIDATED FINANCIAL STATEMENTS

the company to purchase from time to time shares of its capital stock not to exceed $5,000 million. At December 31, 1990, $4,472 million of that authorization remained.

**Long-Term Performance Plan**    The IBM 1989 Long-Term Performance Plan provides for incentive awards to be made to officers and other key employees. The plan is administered by the Executive Compensation Committee of the Board of Directors. The Committee determines the type of award to be granted, which may include stock, a stock option, stock appreciation right (SAR), cash or any combination thereof. The number of shares which are available for granting in each year is limited to .85% of IBM's outstanding capital stock as of December 31 of the preceding year. Any unused amount is carried forward and made available for granting in the subsequent year. Prior to 1989, stock options were issued under the IBM 1986 and predecessor Stock Option Plans.

Options allow the purchase of IBM's capital stock at 100% of the market price on the date of grant and have a maximum duration of 10 years. Payment by the optionee upon exercise of an option may be made using IBM stock as well as cash.

SARs offer eligible optionees the alternative of electing not to exercise the related stock option, but to receive payment in cash and/or stock, equivalent to the difference between the option price and the average market price of IBM stock on the date of exercising the right.

The following table summarizes option activity during 1990 and 1989:

Number of Shares Under Option

|  | 1990 | 1989 |
|---|---|---|
| Balance at January 1 | 20,909,547 | 17,674,645 |
| Options granted | 5,309,140 | 4,629,537 |
| Options exercised | (641,126) | (765,301) |
| Options terminated | (498,977) | (551,675) |
| Options cancelled – SARs exercised | (92,765) | (77,659) |
| Balance at December 31 | 24,985,819 | 20,909,547 |
| Exercisable at December 31 | 14,761,217 | 12,404,456 |

The options exercised were at an average option price of $64.02 per share and $64.66 per share in 1990 and 1989, respectively. The shares under option at December 31, 1990, were at option prices ranging from $55.75 to $159.50 per share. The shares under option at December 31, 1989, were at option prices ranging from $55.25 to $159.50 per share.

There were 835,105 and 1,214,110 unused shares carried forward and made available for granting in the subsequent year as of December 31, 1990 and 1989, respectively.

## Segment Information

IBM is in the field of advanced information technology. The company operates primarily in the single industry segment which offers customers solutions that incorporate information processing systems, software, communications systems and other products and services. This segment represents more than 90% of consolidated revenue, operating profit and identifiable assets. The schedule on the next page shows revenue by industry segments and by classes of similar products or services within the information technology segment.

Financial information by geographic area is summarized on page 58 to provide a better understanding of IBM's operations. Material interdependencies and overlaps exist among IBM's operating units and, therefore, the information may not be indicative of the financial results of, or investments in, the reported areas were they independent organizations.

**Revenue by Industry Segments and Classes of Similar Products or Services**

| | Consolidated | | | U.S. Only | | |
|---|---|---|---|---|---|---|
| | 1990 | 1989[†] | 1988 | 1990 | 1989[†] | 1988 |
| (Dollars in millions) | | | | | | |
| Information technology: | | | | | | |
| Processors* | $16,433 | $16,236 | $15,077 | $ 5,744 | $ 5,941 | $ 5,586 |
| Workstations: | | | | | | |
| Personal systems* | 9,644 | 8,409 | 6,934 | 3,887 | 3,667 | 3,004 |
| Other workstations | 4,312 | 4,169 | 4,550 | 1,492 | 1,509 | 1,745 |
| Peripherals | 13,190 | 11,458 | 11,280 | 5,179 | 4,309 | 4,764 |
| Software | 9,952 | 8,424 | 7,927 | 3,639 | 3,139 | 2,925 |
| Maintenance services | 7,768 | 7,070 | 7,347 | 2,886 | 2,959 | 3,102 |
| Other | 5,791 | 4,938 | 4,470 | 2,377 | 2,215 | 2,103 |
| | 67,090 | 60,704 | 57,585 | 25,204 | 23,739 | 23,229 |
| Federal systems | 1,928 | 2,006 | 2,065 | 1,928 | 2,006 | 2,065 |
| Other business | — | — | 31 | — | — | 26 |
| Total | $69,018 | $62,710 | $59,681 | $27,132 | $25,745 | $25,320 |

[†]Reclassified to conform with 1990 presentation.

*Excludes peripheral functions not embedded, software and maintenance.

While IBM operates primarily in a single industry segment and manages its worldwide business as such, revenue has been categorized into major classes of product.

For purposes of classifying similar information technology products, user programmable equipment having the capability of manipulating data arithmetically or logically and making calculations, in a manner directly addressable by the user through the operation of a stored program, has been classified as processors, except that personal systems are included under workstations. Workstations also include typewriters and other display based terminals. Peripherals include printers, storage and telecommunication devices.

Peripheral functions embedded in processors are classified with processors. Software includes both applications and systems software. Maintenance services consist of separately billed charges for maintenance. Other consists principally of customer solution services, financing revenue and supplies.

Some products logically fit in more than one class and are assigned to a specific class based on a variety of factors. Over time, products tend to overlap, merge into or split from existing classes as a result of changing technologies, market perceptions, and/or customer use. For example, market demand may create requirements for technological enhancements to permit a peripheral product (e.g., printer), to be functionally integrated with a display, a telecommunication device and a processor to form a workstation. Such interchangeability and technological progress tend to make year-to-year comparisons less valid than they would be in an industry less subject to rapid change.

Federal systems consists of specialized information technology products and services primarily for the United States defense, space and other agencies.

Other business consists of training and testing materials for school, home and industrial use offered by Science Research Associates, which was sold by IBM in 1988.

**NOTES TO CONSOLIDATED FINANCIAL STATEMENTS**

| Geographic Areas | 1990 | 1989 | 1988† |
|---|---|---|---|
| (Dollars in millions) | | | |
| **United States** | | | |
| Revenue—Customers | $ 27,132 | $25,745 | $25,320 |
| Interarea transfers | 6,195 | 5,476 | 4,951 |
| Total | $ 33,327 | $31,221 | $30,271 |
| Net earnings | 1,459 | (325) | 1,408 |
| Assets at December 31 | 43,542 | 41,635 | 39,245 |
| **Europe/Middle East/Africa** | | | |
| Revenue—Customers | $ 27,234 | $23,170 | $21,600 |
| Interarea transfers | 976 | 1,101 | 955 |
| Total | $ 28,210 | $24,271 | $22,555 |
| Net earnings | 2,977 | 2,676 | 2,349 |
| Assets at December 31 | 30,689 | 24,732 | 22,745 |
| **Asia Pacific** | | | |
| Revenue—Customers | $ 9,564 | $ 9,202 | $ 8,824 |
| Interarea transfers | 1,496 | 1,673 | 1,837 |
| Total | $ 11,060 | $10,875 | $10,661 |
| Net earnings | 1,151 | 1,296 | 1,394 |
| Assets at December 31 | 8,646 | 7,666 | 7,633 |
| **Americas** | | | |
| Revenue—Customers | $ 5,088 | $ 4,593 | $ 3,937 |
| Interarea transfers | 1,615 | 1,461 | 1,290 |
| Total | $ 6,703 | $ 6,054 | $ 5,227 |
| Net earnings | 420 | 173 | 328 |
| Assets at December 31 | 6,357 | 5,395 | 4,915 |
| **Eliminations** | | | |
| Revenue | $ (10,282) | $ (9,711) | $ (9,033) |
| Net earnings | 13 | (62) | 12 |
| Assets | (1,666) | (1,694) | (1,501) |
| **Consolidated** | | | |
| Revenue | $ 69,018 | $62,710 | $59,681 |
| Net earnings | $ 6,020 | $ 3,758 | $ 5,491 |
| Assets at December 31 | $ 87,568 | $77,734 | $73,037 |

†1988 net earnings before cumulative effect of change in accounting for income taxes.

Non-U.S. subsidiaries which operate in a local currency environment account for approximately 90% of the company's non-U.S. revenue. The remaining 10% is from subsidiaries and branches, predominantly in the Americas, which operate in U.S. dollars or whose economic environment is highly inflationary.

In the Europe/Middle East/Africa area, European operations accounted for approximately 95% of revenue in 1990, 1989 and 1988.

Interarea transfers consist principally of completed machines, subassemblies and parts, and software. Machines, subassemblies and parts transfers are generally priced at cost plus an appropriate service charge. Software transfers represent license fees paid by the non-U.S. subsidiaries. The cost and service charges that relate to fixed asset transfers are capitalized and depreciated by the importing area. Interarea accounts receivable, the unamortized portion of service charges, and the net change during the year in unamortized service charges have been eliminated in consolidation.

## FIVE-YEAR COMPARISON OF SELECTED FINANCIAL DATA

| | 1990 | 1989 | 1988 | 1987 | 1986 |
|---|---|---|---|---|---|
| (Dollars in millions except per share amounts) | | | | | |
| **For the year** | | | | | |
| Revenue | $69,018 | $62,710 | $59,681 | $55,256 | $52,160 |
| Net earnings before cumulative effect of accounting change | 6,020 | 3,758 | 5,491 | 5,258 | 4,789 |
| Per share | 10.51 | 6.47 | 9.27 | 8.72 | 7.81 |
| Cumulative effect of change in accounting for income taxes | — | — | 315 | — | — |
| Per share | — | — | .53 | — | — |
| Net earnings | 6,020 | 3,758 | 5,806 | 5,258 | 4,789 |
| Per share | 10.51 | 6.47 | 9.80 | 8.72 | 7.81 |
| Cash dividends paid | 2,774 | 2,752 | 2,609 | 2,654 | 2,698 |
| Per share | 4.84 | 4.73 | 4.40 | 4.40 | 4.40 |
| Investment in plant, rental machines and other property | 6,548 | 6,410 | 5,431 | 4,312 | 4,644 |
| Return on stockholders' equity | 14.8% | 9.6% | 14.9% | 14.5% | 14.4% |
| **At end of year** | | | | | |
| Total assets | $87,568 | $77,734 | $73,037 | $70,029 | $63,020 |
| Net investment in plant, rental machines and other property | 27,241 | 24,943 | 23,426 | 22,967 | 21,310 |
| Working capital | 13,644 | 14,175 | 17,956 | 18,430 | 15,546 |
| Long-term debt | 11,943 | 10,825 | 8,518 | 7,108 | 6,923 |
| Stockholders' equity | 42,832 | 38,509 | 39,509 | 38,263 | 34,374 |

## SELECTED QUARTERLY DATA

| | Revenue | Gross Profit | Net Earnings | Per Share | | Stock Prices | |
|---|---|---|---|---|---|---|---|
| | | | | Earnings | Dividends | High | Low |
| (Dollars in millions except per share and stock prices) | | | | | | | |
| **1990** | | | | | | | |
| First Quarter | $14,185 | $ 7,857 | $1,037 | $ 1.81 | $1.21 | $109.38 | $ 94.50 |
| Second Quarter | 16,495 | 9,107 | 1,410 | 2.45 | 1.21 | 122.25 | 105.00 |
| Third Quarter | 15,277 | 8,600 | 1,112 | 1.95 | 1.21 | 123.13 | 96.50 |
| Fourth Quarter | 23,061 | 12,731 | 2,461 | 4.30 | 1.21 | 116.00 | 96.25 |
| Total | $69,018 | $38,295 | $6,020 | $10.51 | $4.84 | | |
| **1989** | | | | | | | |
| First Quarter | $12,730 | $ 7,212 | $ 950 | $ 1.61 | $1.10 | $130.88 | $107.63 |
| Second Quarter | 15,213 | 8,481 | 1,340 | 2.31 | 1.21 | 115.75 | 106.25 |
| Third Quarter | 14,305 | 7,900 | 877 | 1.51 | 1.21 | 119.38 | 107.75 |
| Fourth Quarter | 20,462 | 11,416 | 591 | 1.04 | 1.21 | 109.75 | 93.38 |
| Total | $62,710 | $35,009 | $3,758 | $ 6.47 | $4.73 | | |

There were 789,046 stockholders of record at December 31, 1990. During 1990, stockholders received $2,774 million in cash dividends. The regular quarterly cash dividend payable March 9, 1991 will be at the rate of $1.21 per share. This dividend will be IBM's 304th consecutive quarterly cash dividend.

The stock prices reflect the high and low prices for IBM's capital stock on the New York Stock Exchange composite tape for the last two years.

# APPENDIX B

## Glossary

### A

**Accelerated Cost Recovery System (ACRS).** An alternative to traditional depreciation methods introduced for tax purposes in 1981 and subsequently modified. *See* Modified Accelerated Cost Recovery System (MACRS).

**Account.** A record used to classify and summarize the effects of transactions; a separate account is maintained for each asset, liability, owners' equity, revenue, and expense item, showing increases, decreases, and the account balance.

**Account form of balance sheet.** A balance sheet that presents assets on the left-hand side and liabilities and owners' equity on the right-hand side.

**Accounting.** A service activity whose "function is to provide quantitative information, primarily financial in nature, about economic entities that is intended to be useful in making economic decisions—in making reasoned choices among alternative courses of action" (APBO Statement No. 4., par. 40).

**Accounting and Audit Guides.** Publications by special committees of the AICPA that deal with specific industries. These guides not only contain information concerning the auditing of these entities, but also discuss alternative accounting methods that could be used.

**Accounting and Auditing Enforcement Releases (AAERs).** SEC reports of substandard or fraudulent reporting in SEC filings and actions taken against the parties involved.

**Accounting changes.** A general term used to describe the use of different estimates or accounting principles or reporting entities from those used in a prior year.

**Accounting cycle.** *See* Accounting process.

**Accounting errors.** Incorrect accounting treatment resulting from mathematical mistakes, improper application of accounting principles, or omissions of material facts.

**Accounting periods.** The time intervals used for financial reporting; due to the need for timely information, the life of a business or other entity is divided into specific accounting periods for external reporting purposes. One year has been established as the normal reporting period, although some entities also provide interim (e.g., quarterly) statements.

**Accounting Principles Board (APB).** A board of the AICPA that issued opinions establishing accounting standards during the period 1959-1973.

**Accounting process.** The procedures used for analyzing, recording, classifying, and summarizing the information to be presented in accounting reports; also referred to as the accounting cycle.

**Accounting Research Bulletins (ARBs).** The publications of the Committee on Accounting Procedure that established accounting standards during the years 1939-1959.

**Accounting Series Releases (ASRs).** Prior to 1982, the name given to SEC statements dealing with reporting and disclosure requirements in documents filed with the SEC. Such statements are now called Financial Reporting Releases (FRRs).

**Accounting system.** The procedures and methods used, including use of data processing equipment, to collect and report accounting data.

**Accounts receivable.** Trade receivables that are not evidenced by a formal agreement or "note"; accounts receivable are usually unsecured "open accounts" and represent an extension of short-term credit to customers.

**Accounts receivable turnover.** An analytical measurement of how rapidly customers' accounts are being collected. The net accounts receivable formula is net credit sales divided by average accounts receivable for a period.

**Accrual accounting.** A basic assumption that revenues are recognized when earned and expenses are recognized when incurred, without regard to when cash is received or paid.

**Acid-test ratio.** An analytical measurement of the short-term liquidity of an entity. The acid-test ratio formula is quick assets divided by the current liabilities at a specified time.

**Additional markups.** Increases that raise prices above original retail.

**Additional paid-in capital.** The investment by stockholders in excess of the amounts assignable to capital stock as par or stated value as well as invested capital from other sources, such as donations of property or sale of treasury stock.

**Additions.** Expenditures that add to asset usefulness by either extending life or increasing future cash flows. No replacement of components is involved. Additions add to the cost of the asset.

**Adjunct account.** An account used to record additions to a related account. An example is Freight-In, which is added to the purchases account.

**Adjusting entries.** Entries required at the end of each accounting period to update the accounts as necessary and to fully recognize, on an accrual basis, revenues and expenses for the period.

**Aging receivables.** The most commonly used method for establishing an Allowance for Doubtful Accounts based on outstanding receivables. This method involves analyzing individual accounts to determine those not yet due and those past due. Past-due accounts are classified in terms of length of the period past due.

**Allowance method.** A method of recognizing the estimated losses from uncollectible accounts as expenses during the period in which the sales occur; this method is required by GAAP.

**American Accounting Association (AAA).** An organization for accounting academicians. Its role in establishing accounting standards includes research projects to help the FASB and a forum for representing different points of view on various issues.

**American Institute of Certified Public Accountants (AICPA).** A professional organization for CPAs. Membership in the AICPA is voluntary. It publishes a monthly journal, the *Journal of Accountancy*.

**Amortization.** Periodic cost allocation process for intangible assets.

**Annuity.** A series of equal payments (receipts) over a specified number of equal time periods.

**Annuity due.** An annuity that consists of payments (receipts) at the beginning of each period; also known as an annuity in advance.

**Appropriated retained earnings.** The restricted portion of retained earnings.

**Arm's-length transactions.** Exchanges between parties who are independent of each other; a traditional assumption in accounting is that recorded transactions and events are executed between independent parties, each of whom is acting in its own best interests.

**Asset turnover.** *See* Total asset turnover.

**Assets.** The resources of an entity: technically defined by the FASB in Concepts Statement No. 6 as "probable future economic benefits obtained or controlled by a particular entity as a result of past transactions or events."

**Assignment of receivables.** The borrowing of money with receivables pledged as security on the loan.

**Average amount of accumulated expenditures.** A weighted average of the expenditures incurred in the self-construction of an operating asset. Expenditures mean cash disbursements, not accruals. The expenditures are weighted by the portion of the year left after payment is made.

**Average cost method.** An inventory costing method that assigns the same average cost to each unit sold and each item in the inventory. Under a periodic inventory system, the unit cost is a *weighted average* for the entire period. Under a perpetual inventory system, the unit cost is computed as a *moving average* which changes with each new purchase of goods.

**Average cost retail inventory method.** A method of estimating inventory that approximates an average cost valuation.

## B

**Balance sheet.** A statement that reports as of a given point in time the resources (assets) of a business, its obligations (liabilities), and the residual ownership claims against its resources (owners' equity); an alternative title for the statement is the *statement of financial position*.

**Bank discounting.** The process of transferring negotiable notes to a bank or other financial institution in return for cash.

**Bank reconciliation.** A process that identifies differences between the cash balance on the depositor's books and the balance reported on the bank statement. The reconciliation provides information needed to adjust the book balance to a corrected cash amount.

**Bank service charge.** Monthly fee usually charged by a bank to service the depositor's account.

**Bargain purchase option.** A lease provision that allows for the purchase of a leased asset by the lessee at a price significantly lower than the expected fair market value of the leased asset at the date the bargain purchase option can be exercised.

**Bargain renewal option.** A lease provision that allows for renewal of the lease by the lessee at significantly reduced lease payments from the original lease. The bargain terms strongly imply that the lease will be renewed, and the lease term is assumed to extend through the bargain renewal period.

**Bearer or coupon bonds.** Bonds for which owners receive periodic interest by clipping a coupon from the bond and sending it to the issuer as evidence of ownership.

**Betterments.** *See* Additions.

**Bond certificates.** Certificates of indebtedness issued by a company or government agency guaranteeing payment of a principal amount at a specified future date plus periodic interest; usually issued in denominations of $1,000.

**Bond discount.** The difference between the face value and the sales price when bonds are sold below their face value.

**Bond indenture.** The contract between the issuing entity and the bondholders specifying the terms, rights, and obligations of the contracting parties.

**Bond issuance costs.** Costs incurred by the issuer for legal services, printing and engraving, taxes, and underwriting in connection with the sale of a bond.

**Bond premium.** The difference between the face value and the sales price when bonds are sold above their face value.

**Book value per share.** A measure of an entity's value per share of common stock outstanding. The book value per share formula is common stockholders' equity divided by the number of common shares outstanding.

**Business combination.** The combining of two ongoing business entities, usually by the exchange of capital stock for the net assets acquired.

**Business documents.** Business records used as the basis for analyzing and recording transactions; examples include invoices, check stubs, receipts, and similar business papers. They are also referred to as Source documents.

## C

**Callable bonds.** Bonds for which the issuer reserves the right to pay the obligation prior to the maturity date.

**Callable obligation.** A debt instrument that is (1) payable on demand or (2) has a specified due date but is payable on demand if the debtor defaults on the provisions of the loan agreement.

**Capital leases.** A lease that is, in substance, a contract to purchase an asset.

**Capital stock.** The portion of the contribution by stockholders assignable to the shares of stock as par or stated value.

**Capitalized interest.** The amount of interest expenditures included as part of the cost of a self-constructed asset.

**Cash.** Coin, currency, and other items that are acceptable for deposit at face value; serves as a medium of exchange and provides a basis of measurement for accounting.

**Cash-basis accounting.** A system of accounting in which revenues and expenses are recorded as they are received and paid.

**Cash discount.** A reduction in the selling price, allowed if payment is received within a specified period, usually offered to customers to encourage prompt payment.

**Cash dividend.** The payment (receipt) of a dividend in the form of cash.

**Cash equivalents.** Short-term, highly liquid investments that can be converted easily to cash. Generally, only investments with original maturities of three months or less qualify as cash equivalents; U.S. Treasury bills, money market funds, and commercial paper are examples of instruments that are commonly classified as cash equivalents.

**Cash overdraft.** A credit balance in the cash account; results from checks being written for more than the cash amount on deposit; should be reported as a current liability.

**Ceiling limitation.** The net realizable value used as an upper limit in defining market when valuing inventory at the lower of cost or market.

**Certified public accountants (CPAs).** Accountants who have met specified professional requirements and who do not work for a single business enterprise but rather provide a variety of professional services for many different individual and business clients. A key service provided by CPAs is the performance of independent audits of financial statements.

**Change in accounting estimate.** A specific type of accounting change that modifies predictions of future events, e.g., the useful life of a depreciable asset; changes in estimates are to be reflected in current and future periods.

**Change in accounting principle.** A specific type of accounting change that uses a different accounting principle or method from that used previously, e.g., using straight-line depreciation instead of the declining-balance method; generally, changes in principle require the reporting of a cumulative effect of the change in the current year's income statement, as well as "pro forma" information.

**Change in reporting entity.** A specific type of accounting change that reflects financial statements for a different unit of accountability, e.g., after a business merger; a change in reporting entity requires restatement of the financial results of prior periods so as to provide comparative data.

**Change orders.** Modifications to the original terms of a contract.

**Chart of accounts.** A systematic listing of all accounts used by a particular business entity.

**Closing entries.** Entries that reduce all nominal, or temporary, accounts to a zero balance at the end of each accounting period, transferring the preclosing balances to real, or permanent, accounts.

**Committee on Accounting Procedures (CAP).** A committee of the AICPA that issued Accounting Research Bulletins during the period 1939-1959.

**Commodity-backed bonds or asset-linked bonds.** Bonds that may be redeemed in terms of commodities, such as oil or precious metals.

**Common stock.** The class of stock issued by corporations that represents the basic residual ownership interest; allows shareholders the right to vote and to receive dividends if declared, although the right to dividends is generally secondary to that of preferred stock.

**Common-size financial statements.** Financial statements that reflect the components of the financial statement as a percentage of a total, e.g., percentage of total liabilities or total revenues.

**Comparability.** A secondary quality of useful accounting information, based on the premise that information is more useful when it can be related to a benchmark or standard, such as data for other firms within the same industry.

**Comparative statements.** Financial statements reflecting data for two or more periods.

**Compensated absences.** Payments by employers for vacation, holiday, illness, or other personal activities.

**Compensating balances.** The portion of a demand deposit that must be maintained as support for existing borrowing arrangements.

**Compensatory plans.** Stock option plans that are offered to a select group of employees and that provide a form of compensation.

**Completed-contract method.** An accounting method that recognizes revenues and expenses on long-term construction contracts only when completed.

**Composite depreciation.** A method of computing depreciation in which dissimilar assets are aggregated and depreciation is computed for the aggregation based on a weighted average life expectancy.

**Compound interest.** Interest that is computed on the principal amount plus previously accumulated interest.

**Comprehensive income.** A concept of income measurement and reporting that includes all changes in owners' equity except investments by and distributions to owners. Comprehensive income is specifically defined in FASB Concepts Statement No. 5 and is not currently reported in general-purpose financial statements.

**Conceptual framework.** A theoretical foundation underlying accounting standards and practice. Today's framework encompasses the objectives, fundamental concepts, and implementation guidelines described in FASB Concepts Statement Nos. 1-6, as well as traditional assumptions. (See Exhibit 2-1, page 31, and Exhibit 2-7, page 47.)

**Conglomerates.** *See* Diversified companies.

**Conservatism.** A constraint underlying the reporting of accounting information based on the notion that when doubt exists concerning two or more reporting alternatives, users of information are best served by selecting the alternative with the least favorable impact on owners' equity.

**Consigned goods.** Inventory that is physically located at a dealer (consignee); however, the title (ownership) is retained by another entity (consignor) until the consignee sells the inventory.

**Consignee.** An entity that acts as an agent for another party (the consignor) by holding the consignor's inventory in an attempt to sell it. Title to the inventory is retained by the consignor even though physical possession is held by the consignee.

**Consignment.** A transfer of property without a transfer of title and risk of ownership. The recipient of the property (consignee) acts as a selling agent on behalf of the owner (consignor).

**Consignor.** A seller that ships merchandise to a third party (the consignee) but retains title until the inventory is sold by the third party. When the merchandise is subsequently sold, the consignee is typically paid a commission on the sale with the balance from the sale being remitted to the seller.

**Consistency.** A secondary quality of useful accounting information requiring that accounting methods be followed consistently from one period to the next unless conditions indicate that changing to another method would provide more useful information.

**Consolidation method.** An accounting method that combines the financial statement balances of the parent and subsidiary companies as if they were one total economic unit; this method is appropriate where the parent company has control (more than 50 percent of the voting stock) over the subsidiary company.

**Contingent liability.** A potential obligation, the existence of which is uncertain because it is dependent on the outcome of a future event, such as a pending lawsuit. The amount of the potential obligation may or may not be determinable.

**Contra account.** An account used to record subtractions from a related account; sometimes referred to as an "offset account." Examples include Allowance for Doubtful Accounts, which is subtracted from Accounts Receivable, and Accumulated Depreciation, which is subtracted from a plant asset account.

**Contributed capital.** The portion of corporate capital that represents investments by the owners, or stockholders. Also referred to as Paid-in capital.

**Control account.** A general ledger account that summarizes the detailed information in a subsidiary ledger. For example, Accounts Receivable is the control account for the individual customer accounts in the subsidiary accounts receivable ledger.

**Conventional retail inventory method.** A method of estimating inventory that approximates a lower of average cost or market valuation.

**Convertible bonds.** Bonds that provide for conversion into some other security at the option of the stockholder.

**Corporation.** A business entity that is a separate, legal entity owned by its shareholders, who are given stock certificates as evidence of ownership; the owners' equity is divided between contributed capital (capital stock and paid-in capital accounts) and earned capital (retained earnings account).

**Cost effectiveness.** A pervasive constraint underlying the reporting of accounting information; to be cost effective, information must provide benefits in excess of its cost. Analysis of the cost-benefit relationship is an important consideration in selecting or requiring reporting alternatives.

**Cost method.** The method of accounting for long-term investments in the stock of another company where significant influence does not exist (generally less than 20 percent ownership); the initial investment is recorded and maintained at cost with dividends being recognized as revenue when received and no adjustment made for a proportionate share of investee earnings.

**Cost percentage.** Cost of goods available for sale valued at cost divided by the goods available for sale at retail.

**Cost recovery method.** A revenue recognition method which requires recovery of the total cost (investment) prior to the recognition of revenue.

**Cost recovery periods.** A period of time defined by tax legislation over which the cost of noncurrent operating assets may be written off (deducted) for tax purposes. Currently, there are six recovery periods for personal property and two for real estate.

**Cost-to-cost method.** A method for determining the percentage of completion for long-term construction contracts using a ratio of the actual cost incurred to date to the estimated total costs.

**Credit.** An entry on the right side of an account.

**Cumulative effect of a change in accounting principle.** An account that summarizes the net effect on the balance sheet of changing from one accounting principle to another. The effect is disclosed on the income statement as an irregular item net of tax.

**Cumulative preferred stock.** Preferred stock that has a right to receive current dividends as well as any dividends in arrears before common stockholders receive any dividends.

**Current assets.** Cash and resources that are reasonably expected to be converted into cash during the normal operating cycle of a business or within one year, whichever period is longer.

**Current cost.** The current value of an asset (i.e., the current exchange price) as measured by its replacement cost, reproduction cost, sales value, net realizable value, or net present value of future cash flows.

**Current liabilities.** Obligations that are reasonably expected to be paid using current assets or by creating other current liabilities within one year. For operating liabilities, such as accounts payable and accrued liabilities, the time period is extended to cover the operating cycle of a business if the cycle is longer than one year.

**Current market value.** The cash equivalent price that could be obtained currently by selling an asset in an orderly liquidation.

**Current rate.** The exchange rate in effect on the date the balance sheet is prepared.

**Current ratio.** An analytical measurement of the short-term liquidity of an entity. The current ratio formula is current assets divided by current liabilities. Sometimes referred to as the working capital ratio.

**Current replacement cost.** The cash equivalent price that would be paid currently to purchase or replace goods or services.

# D

**Debit.** An entry on the left side of an account.

**Debt securities.** Instruments, such as bonds and notes, issued by corporations and other entities to obtain funds from creditors.

**Debt-to-equity ratio.** A ratio that measures the relationship between the debt and equity of an entity. The debt-to-equity formula is total debt divided by total stockholders' equity.

**Decision usefulness.** The overriding quality or characteristic of accounting information.

**Declining-balance depreciation methods.** A depreciation method providing decreasing periodic charges for depreciation by applying a constant percentage to a declining asset book value.

**Decreasing-charge deprecation methods.** Any method of computing depreciation that provides a decreasing charge against revenue over time. Most common of the decreasing-charge methods are sum-of-the-years-digits depreciation and declining-balance depreciation.

**Deficit.** An excess of dividend payments and losses over net income resulting in a negative (debit) balance in retained earnings.

**Demand deposits.** Funds deposited in a bank that can be withdrawn upon demand.

**Denominated currency.** The currency in which an invoice is stated. For example, an invoice stating that payment is to be made in American dollars is said to be denominated in American dollars.

**Depletion.** The periodic allocation of the cost of natural resources; depletion expense represents a charge for the using-up of the resources and is computed in a manner similar to the productive-output method of depreciation, i.e., cost is divided by estimated total resources available to determine the depletion charge per unit removed or extracted.

**Deposit in transit.** A deposit made near the end of the month and recorded on the depositor's books but that is not received by the bank in time to be reflected on the bank statement.

**Deposit method.** An accounting method which recognizes the receipt of cash and the unearned revenue prior to the completion of a contract.

**Depreciation.** Periodic allocation of the cost of tangible noncurrent operating assets over the periods benefited by use of the asset.

**Development activities.** Application of research findings to develop a plan or design for new or improved products and processes.

**Direct financing leases.** A lease in which the lessor is primarily engaged in financial activities and views the lease activity as an investment.

**Direct method.** An approach to calculating and reporting the net cash flow from operating activities that shows the major operating cash receipts and cash payments. The difference between cash receipts and cash payments is the net cash flow provided (used) by operations.

**Direct quote.** This quote specifies the number of American dollars that can be purchased with one unit of foreign currency. The direct quote for numerous foreign currencies is listed on a daily basis in *The Wall Street Journal.*

**Direct write-off method.** A method of recognizing the actual losses from uncollectible accounts as expenses during the period in which the receivables are determined to be uncollectible; this method is not in accordance with GAAP.

**Discontinued operations.** The disposal of a major segment of a business either through sale or abandonment. The segment may be a product line, a division, or a subsidiary company. The assets and related activities of the segment must be clearly distinguishable from other activities of the company, both physically and operationally.

**Discussion Memorandum.** A document issued by the FASB that identifies the principal issues involved with financial accounting and reporting topics. It includes a discussion of the various points of view as to the resolution of issues, but does not reach a specific conclusion.

**Diversified companies.** Business entities that have a wide variety of product and service lines of business. Sometimes referred to as conglomerates.

**Dividends.** Periodic distributions of earnings in the form of cash, stock, or other property to the stockholders (owners) of a corporation.

**Dividends in arrears.** Dividends on cumulative preferred stock that are passed or not paid. Dividends in arrears must be paid before any dividends can be paid to common stockholders. Disclosure of the amount of dividends in arrears is made in a note to the balance sheet.

**Dividends per share.** A measure of the distribution to stockholders by an entity. The dividends per share formula is the dividends paid to the common shareholders divided by the number of common shares issued and outstanding. Dividends are not paid on treasury stock.

**Dollar-value LIFO inventory method.** An adaptation of the LIFO inventory concept that measures inventory by total dollar amount rather than by individual units. LIFO incremental layers are determined based on total dollar changes.

**Double extension.** A method of determining the valuation of inventory using the dollar-value LIFO method by extending all inventory quantities twice: once at a base-year cost and once at current-year cost.

**Double-declining-balance depreciation.** A decreasing charge depreciation method that uses twice the straight-line depreciation rate as the constant percentage to be applied to the decreasing book value.

**Double-entry accounting.** A system of recording transactions in a way that maintains the equality of the accounting equation: Assets = Liabilities + Owners' Equity.

## E

**Early extinguishment of debt.** The retirement of debt prior to the maturity date of the obligation; any gain or loss arising from early extinguishment of debt must be classified as an extraordinary item on the income statement.

**Earnings.** A new term found in the FASB's concepts statements that is the equivalent of net income without including the effects of changes in accounting principles.

**Economic entity.** A specific reporting unit; a traditional assumption in accounting is that the business enterprise or other reporting unit is viewed as separate and distinct from its owners or other entities.

**Effective rate of interest.** The rate of interest used in compound interest problems; also known as the yield or true rate of interest.

**Effective-interest method.** An amortization method which provides for recognition of an equal rate of amortization of bond premium or discount each period; uses a constant interest rate times a changing investment balance.

**Efforts-expended methods.** Methods for determining the percentage of completion for long-term construction contracts using an estimate of work or service performed. The estimates may be based on labor hours, labor dollars, or estimates of experts.

**Electronic data processing (EDP) systems.** Accounting systems utilizing high-speed computers. Such systems allow great speed and accuracy in processing large amounts of accounting data.

**Emerging Issues Task Force (EITF).** A task force of representatives from the accounting profession and industry created by the FASB to deal with taking timely action on emerging issues of financial reporting. The task force identifies significant emerging issues and develops consensus positions when possible.

**Employee Retirement Income Security Act of 1974 (ERISA).** A legislative act passed by Congress in 1974 that made significant changes in requirements for employer pension plans.

**Entry cost.** The acquisition cost of an asset.

**Equity method.** The method of accounting for long-term investments in the stock of another company where significant influence exists (generally 20-50 percent ownership); the initial investment is recorded at cost but is increased by a proportionate share of investor's income and decreased by dividends and a proportionate share of losses to reflect the underlying claim by the investor on the net assets of the investee company.

**Equity security.** An instrument representing ownership shares, e.g., common stock, or the right to acquire ownership shares (e.g., options).

**Equity-to-debt ratio.** A ratio that measures the relationship between the equity and debt of an entity. The equity-to-debt ratio formula is total stockholders' equity divided by total assets. (See Debt-to-equity ratio.)

**Executory costs.** Costs to maintain property such as repairs, insurance, and taxes. These costs may be paid by the lessee or the lessor. If paid by the lessor, part of each lease payment should be related to the executory costs.

**Exit value.** The value received for an asset when sold.

**Expense recognition.** The process of determining the period in which expenses are to be recorded. Expense recognition is divided into three categories: (1) direct matching, (2) immediate recognition, and (3) systematic and rational allocation.

**Expenses.** Outflows or other using-up of assets or incurrences of liabilities (or a combination of both) from delivering or producing goods, rendering services, or carrying out other activities that constitute the entity's ongoing major or central operations.

**Exposure Draft.** A preliminary statement of a standard that includes specific recommendations made by the FASB. Reaction to the Exposure Draft is requested from the accounting and business community, and the comments received are carefully considered before a Statement of Financial Accounting Standards is issued.

**Extraordinary items.** Gains or losses resulting from events and transactions that are both unusual in nature and infrequent in occurrence or otherwise defined as an extraordinary item per APB Opinion No. 30.

## F

**Face amount, par value, maturity value.** The amount that will be paid on a bond at the maturity date.

**Factoring receivables.** The sale of receivables without recourse for cash to a third party, usually a bank or other financial institution.

**Factory overhead.** All manufacturing costs other than direct materials and direct labor; alternatively referred to as *manufacturing overhead.*

**Feedback value.** A key ingredient of relevant accounting information; helps to confirm or change a decision maker's expectations.

**Financial accounting.** The activity associated with the development and communication of financial information for external users, primarily in the form of general-purpose financial statements.

**Financial Accounting Foundation (FAF).** An organization responsible for selecting members of the FASB, GASB, and their Advisory Councils; also responsible for funding the standard-setting bodies.

**Financial Accounting Standards Advisory Council.** A council that consults with the FASB concerning major policy questions, selects major project task forces to work on specific projects, and conducts such other activities as may be requested by the FASB.

**Financial Accounting Standards Board (FASB).** An independent private organization consisting of seven full-time members with the responsibility of studying accounting issues and establishing accounting standards to govern financial reporting to external users.

**Financial Analysts Federation.** An organization of financial analysts who advise the investing public on the meaning of financial reports.

**Financial capital maintenance.** A concept under which income is defined as the excess of net assets at the end of an accounting period over the net assets at the beginning of the period, excluding effects of transactions with owners.

**Financial Executives Institute (FEI).** A national organization composed of financial executives employed by large corporations. The FEI membership includes treasurers, controllers, and financial vice-presidents.

**Financial leverage.** A measure of an entity's ability to increase profitability to residual shareholders by using borrowed funds whose cost is less than the profit that can be earned with the borrowed funds.

**Financial Reporting Releases (FRRs).** SEC statements dealing with reporting and disclosure requirements in documents filed with the SEC.

**Financing activities.** One of three major categories included in a statement of cash flows; includes transactions and events whereby cash is obtained from or paid to owners and creditors; examples include cash receipts from issuing stocks and bonds and the payment of cash dividends.

**Finished goods.** Manufactured products for which the manufacturing process is complete.

**First-In, First-Out (FIFO) method.** An inventory costing method that assigns historical unit costs to expense (cost of goods sold) in the order in which the costs are incurred.

**Fixed charge coverage.** A measure of the number of times earnings covers the fixed charges of an entity for a period. Fixed charges include interest, lease payments, and specified periodic principal statements.

**Floor limitation.** The net realizable value less a normal profit used as a lower limit in defining market when valuing inventory at the lower of cost or market.

**Foreign currency transactions.** A transaction between two entities wherein the buyer and the seller have different reporting currencies.

**FOB (free on board) destination.** Terms of sale under which title of goods passes to the purchaser at the point of destination.

**FOB (free on board) shipping point.** Terms of sale under which title of goods passes to the purchaser at the point of shipment.

**Freight-in.** Cost of transporting goods from the supplier to the purchaser; part of the cost of inventory.

**Full cost approach.** An amortization approach in the oil and gas industry that defers all exploratory costs and writes them off against revenues as depletion expense.

**Full disclosure principle.** A basic accounting concept which requires that all relevant information be presented in an unbiased, understandable, and timely manner.

**Funds.** Cash and other assets set apart for certain designated purposes.

**Future value.** The amount of cash that will be accumulated in the future if an investment is made today at a certain interest rate.

## G

**Gains.** Increases in equity (net assets) from peripheral or incidental transactions of an entity and from all other transactions and other events and circumstances affecting the entity except those that result from revenues or investments by owners.

**General journal.** An accounting record used to record all business activities for which special journals are not maintained.

**General ledger.** A record of all accounts used by a business. Some accounts in the general ledger, e.g., accounts receivable, are supported by detail contained in subsidiary ledgers. (*See* Control account and Subsidiary ledgers.)

**General-purpose financial statements.** A balance sheet, income statement, statement of cash flows, and usually a statement of changes in retained earnings or in owners' equity.

**Generally accepted accounting principles (GAAP).** Accounting standards recognized by the profession as required in the preparation of financial statements for external users. Currently, the Financial Accounting Standards Board is the principal issuer of generally accepted accounting principles.

**Going concern.** An entity that is expected to continue in existence for the foreseeable future; a traditional assumption in accounting is that an entity is viewed as a going concern in the absence of evidence to the contrary.

**Goods in process.** Inventory of a manufacturer that is partly processed and requires further work before it can be sold. Alternatively referred to as Work in process.

**Goodwill.** The ability of an organization to earn above-normal income. Above-normal income means a rate of return greater than that normally required to attract investors into a particular type of business. Recorded goodwill is the excess amount paid for a company in a business combination over the fair market value of the company's identifiable assets.

**Governmental Accounting Standards Board (GASB).** An independent private organization responsible for establishing standards in the governmental area. Appointed by the Financial Accounting Foundation.

**Gross method.** A method of inventory accounting that records inventory cost before considering purchase discounts.

**Gross profit margin on sales.** A measure of the profitability of sales in relation to the cost of the goods sold. The gross profit margin on sales formula is the gross profit for a financial period divided by sales for the same period.

**Gross profit method.** An inventory estimation technique based on the relationship between gross profit and revenue (sales). The gross profit, as a percentage of sales, is applied to sales to determine cost of goods sold which, in turn, is used to determine the value of the inventory not yet sold.

**Group depreciation.** A method of computing depreciation in which like assets are grouped together and depreciation is computed for the group rather than for individual assets.

**Growth potential.** The capacity of a company to increase sales, net income, and market share in the future. Growth potential is of primary importance to stockholders in valuing a company.

**Guaranteed residual value.** A guarantee by lessee or a third party of a minimum value for the residual value of a leased asset. If the residual value is less than the guarantee, the guarantor must pay the difference to the lessor.

## H

**Historical cost.** The cash equivalent price of goods or services at the date of acquisition.

**Historical rate.** The exchange rate in effect on the date of a specific transaction.

**Horizontal analysis.** Analysis of a company's statements over a number of reporting periods.

## I

**Impairment.** Unexpected reduction in the value of an asset that significantly reduces its current value below its reported value.

**Implicit interest rate.** The interest rate that would discount the minimum lease payments to the fair market value of the asset at the inception of the lease.

**Implicit or effective interest.** The actual interest rate earned or paid on a note, bond, or similar instrument.

**Imprest petty cash system.** A petty cash fund in which all expenditures are documented by vouchers or vendor receipts or invoices.

**Imputed interest rate.** A rate of interest assigned to a note when there is no current market price for either the property, goods or services or the note. The assigned rate of interest is used to discount future receipts or payments to the present in computing the present value of the note.

**Income statement.** A statement that reports a firm's net income for a period of time. The statement summarizes revenues, expenses, gains, and losses. The statement is also called the profit and loss statement or the statement of earnings.

**Income Summary.** A temporary clearing account used at the end of a period to accumulate amounts from closing entries to revenues and expenses. For a corporation, the income summary account is closed to Retained Earnings; for a proprietorship or partnership, it is closed to the appropriate capital accounts.

**Incremental borrowing rate.** The interest rate at which the lessee could borrow the amount of money necessary to purchase the leased asset, taking into consideration the lessee's financial situation and the current conditions in the marketplace.

**Independent audit.** The independent examination of the financial statements to be furnished to external users and issuance of an opinion as to the fairness of the presentation in accordance with generally accepted accounting principles.

**Indirect method.** An approach to calculating and reporting the net cash flow from operating activities that reconciles net income, as reported on the income statement, with net cash flow provided (used) by operations, as shown on the statement of cash flows; net income is adjusted for noncash items, for any gains or losses, and is adjusted from an accrual amount to a cash amount.

**Indirect quote.** The inverse of the direct quote. It indicates the number of foreign currency units that can be purchased with one American dollar.

**Initial direct costs.** Costs such as commissions, legal fees, and preparation of documents that are incurred by the lessor in negotiating and completing a lease transaction.

**Initial markup.** The difference between the initial retail price of merchandise and the original historical cost.

**Input measures.** Measures of the earning process in percentage-of-completion accounting based on cost or efforts devoted to a contract.

**Installment sales method.** A revenue recognition method which recognizes revenue and related expenses as cash is received.

**Institute of Management Accountants (IMA).** An organization of management accountants that is concerned with the development and use of accounting data within the business organization.

**Intangible noncurrent operating assets.** Economic resources with future benefit that are used in the normal operating activity of the organization that cannot be physically observed, e.g., copyrights, patents, trade names, and goodwill.

**Integral part of annual period concept.** A concept of preparing interim financial statements that utilizes the same accounting principles and practices for the interim statements that would be used for the annual statements, except that modifications are permitted to allow the interim results to relate better to the annual statements. An alternate concept would require the interim period to be treated the same way as an annual statement with no flexibility for interim modifications.

**Interest-bearing note.** A note written in a form in which the maker promises to pay the face amount plus interest at a specified rate; in this form, the face amount is usually equal to the present value upon issuance of the note.

**Interest.** The payment (cost) for the use of money; it is the excess cash paid or received over the amount of cash borrowed or loaned.

**Interim financial statements.** Financial statements for a period of time less than one year. Typically, corporations issue quarterly statements that are subject to limited auditor's review.

**Interpolation.** A method of finding future- or present-value table factors when the exact factor does not appear in the table; this method assumes linear relationships.

**Interpretation of a Statement of Financial Accounting Standards.** A supplemental pronouncement that expands the discussion of an existing Statement of Financial Accounting Standards. These are issued by the FASB, and are considered equal in authority to the Statements issued by the FASB.

**Inventory turnover.** An analytical measurement of how rapidly inventories are being used and/or sold during a year. If a company has one inventory, the formula is the cost of goods sold divided by the average inventory. If there are different types of inventory, such as raw materials and work in process, the numerator would be related to the type of inventory. Thus, the numerator for the raw materials inventory would be raw material purchases and the numerator for work in process inventory would be cost of goods completed.

**Inventory.** Assets held for sale in the normal course of business.

**Investing activities.** One of three major categories included in a statement of cash flows; includes transactions and events that occur regularly but that relate only indirectly to the central, ongoing operations of an entity; examples include the purchase or sale of securities or other assets not generally held for resale and the making or collecting of loans to other entities.

**Involuntary conversions.** Retirement of assets caused by uncontrollable events such as fire, earthquake, flood, or condemnation.

## J

**Journals.** Accounting records in which transactions are first entered, providing a chronological record of business activity. (*See* General journal and Special journal.)

**Junk bonds.** High-risk, high-yield bonds issued by companies in a weak financial condition.

# L

**Last-In, First-Out (LIFO) method.** An inventory costing method that assigns the most recent historical unit costs to expense (cost of goods sold) and the oldest unit cost to the asset inventory).

**Lease term.** The noncancellable period of lease designated in the lease contract, plus the period of any bargain renewal periods or other provisions that, at the inception of the lease, strongly indicate that the lease will be renewed.

**Lease.** A contract specifying the terms under which the owner of the property, the lessor, transfers the right to use the property to a lessee.

**Ledgers.** Records used for summarizing the effects of transactions upon individual accounts. A ledger may be in the form of a book of accounts or a computer printout. (*See* General ledger and Subsidiary ledgers.)

**Lessee.** The entity that receives a right to use property under the terms of a lease.

**Lessee.** The party using property that is owned by another party (lessor).

**Lessor.** The owner of leased property who transfers the right to use the property to a second party, the lessee.

**Lessor.** The party who owns property that is used by another party.

**Leveraged lease.** A lease contract usually involving three parties; the lessee, the owner-lessor, and the third-party, a long-term creditor. Only direct financing leases are treated as leveraged leases.

**Liabilities.** The claims of creditors against an entity's resources: technically defined by the FASB as "probable future sacrifices of economic benefits arising from present obligations of a particular entity to transfer assets or provide services to other entities in the future as a result of past transactions or events."

**LIFO allowance.** A valuation account that adjusts a non-LIFO inventory cost to a LIFO cost.

**LIFO conformity rule.** A federal tax regulation that requires the use of LIFO for financial reporting purposes if LIFO is used for income tax purposes.

**LIFO inventory pools.** Classification of inventory into groups of items having common characteristics and then assuming the LIFO cost method for each classification or grouping.

**Liquidating dividend.** A distribution to stockholders representing a return of a portion of contributed capital.

**Liquidity.** The ability of a company to meet it's obligations as they come due.

**Long-term (noncurrent) investments.** Investments that are either not readily marketable or not expected to be converted to cash within a year; these investments are usually reported on the balance sheet under a separate noncurrent heading.

**Long-term debt.** Obligations that are not expected to be paid in cash or other current assets within one year or the normal operating cycle.

**Losses.** Decreases in equity (net assets) from peripheral or incidental transactions of an entity and from all other transactions and other events and circumstances affecting the entity except those that result from expenses or distributions to owners.

**Lower of cost or market (LCM).** Generally accepted method for valuation of certain assets including inventories and marketable equity securities; this method can be applied on an aggregate or individual item basis for inventories but must be applied on an aggregate basis for marketable securities.

# M

**Maintenance.** The normal cost of keeping property in operating condition. Maintenance is charged to expense in the period in which it is incurred.

**Management accounting.** The activity associated with financial reporting for internal users. Information needed for internal decisions may relate to such items as specific product lines, specific financing alternatives, detailed expense classifications, and differences between actual and budgeted revenues and costs.

**Markdown cancellations.** Decreases in the markdowns that do not raise the sales prices above original retail.

**Markdowns.** Decreases that reduce sales prices below original retail.

**Market (lower of cost or market).** The replacement cost adjusted for an upper and/or lower limit that reflects the estimated realizable value.

**Market, yield, or effective interest rate.** The actual rate of interest earned or paid on a bond. Market-related value of pension plan assets. A balance used to calculate the expected return on pension plan assets and the corridor amount. Market-related value can be either fair market value or a calculated value that recognizes changes in fair value in a systematic and rational manner over not more than five years.

**Marketable securities.** Securities that have a day-to-day market and that can be sold on short notice.

**Markup cancellations.** Decreases in additional markups that do not reduce sales prices below original retail.

**Matching principle.** A basic accounting concept that is applied to determine when expenses are recognized (recorded). Under this principle, expenses for a period are determined by associating or "matching" them with specific revenues or a particular time period.

**Materiality.** An important constraint underlying the reporting of accounting information; it determines the threshold for recognition of an item in the financial statements. Materiality decisions focus on the size of a judgment item in a given set of circumstances.

**Minimum lease payments.** The rental payments required over the lease term plus any amount to be paid for the residual value either through a bargain purchase option or a guarantee of residual value.

**Modified Accelerated Cost Recovery System (MACRS).** The accelerated cost recovery system as revised by the Tax Reform Act of 1986. It is applicable for assets acquired after December 31, 1986.

## N

**Natural business year.** A year that ends when a company's operations are at its lowest point. This type of a fiscal year relates primarily to those businesses that have seasonal sales.

**Natural resources.** Assets produced by nature as opposed to those produced by man. They include such wasting assets as oil, gas, timber, and ore deposits.

**Negative goodwill.** The excess of fair market values of a company's net assets over the purchase price for the company in a business combination.

**Negotiable notes.** A note that is legally transferable by endorsement and delivery.

**Net assets.** *See* Owners' equity.

**Net lease investment.** The carrying value of a lease on the lessor's books; equals the difference between total lease payments receivable (gross investment) and unearned interest revenue.

**Net markdowns.** Markdowns less markdown cancellations.

**Net markups.** Additional markups less markup cancellations.

**Net method.** A method of inventory accounting that records inventory net of any purchase discount.

**Net profit margin on sales.** A measure of the profitability of a company that relates net income to the sales of the company. The formula is net income divided by net sales.

**Net realizable value.** The amount of cash expected to be received from the conversion of assets in the normal course of business; net realizable value equals selling price less normal selling costs for inventory and equals gross receivables less the allowance for doubtful accounts for accounts receivable.

**Neutrality.** A key ingredient of reliable accounting information requiring that information be presented in an unbiased manner; relates to the concept of fairness to users.

**Nominal accounts.** Accounts that are closed to a zero balance at the end of an accounting period; they include all income statement accounts (revenues, expenses, gains, and losses) and the dividends account. They are also referred to as Temporary accounts.

**Non-interest-bearing note.** A note written in a form in which the face amount includes an interest charge; in this form, the difference between the face amount and the present value of the note is the implicit or effective interest.

**Noncash investing and financing activities.** Investing and financing transactions that affect an entity's financial position but not the entity's cash flows during the period; an example would be the purchase of land by issuing stock. Significant noncash financing and investing activities should be disclosed separately, not reported in the statement of cash flows.

**Noncash items.** Certain items that are reported on the income statement but that do not affect cash; examples include depreciation on buildings and equipment and amortization of intangibles and bond discount or premium.

**Noncompensatory plans.** Stock option plans that are offered to all employees equally and that are not considered to provide additional compensation.

**Noncumulative preferred stock.** Preferred stock that has no claim on any prior year dividends that may have been "passed."

**Nonreciprocal transfer of a nonmonetary asset.** A transfer of a nonmonetary asset with no sacrifice (cost) incurred by the organization receiving the asset, e.g., donated assets, discovered assets.

**Nontrade notes payable.** A note issued to nontrade creditors for purposes other than to purchase goods or services.

**Nontrade receivables.** Any receivables arising from transactions that are not directly associated with the normal operating activities of a business.

**Normal operating cycle.** The time required for cash to be converted to inventories, inventories into receivables, and receivables ultimately into cash.

**Not-sufficient-funds (NSF) check.** A check that is not honored by a bank because of insufficient cash in the maker's account.

**Notes receivable.** Receivables that are evidenced by a formal written promise to pay a certain sum of money at a specified date.

**Number of times interest is earned.** A measure of the safety for creditors that relates the interest expense to the income before interest. The formula is income before taxes and interest expense divided by interest expense.

## O

**Objective acceleration clause.** A clause in a debt instrument that identifies specific conditions that will cause the debt to be callable immediately.

**Operating activities.** One of three major categories included in a statement of cash flows; includes transactions and events that normally enter into the determination of operating income; examples include selling goods or services and purchasing inventory.

**Operating leases.** Simple rental agreements, usually for a relatively short period of time, for one entity (lessee) to use property that is owned by another entity (lessor).

**Opinions.** Statements of accounting standards issued by the Accounting Principles Board during the period 1959-1973.

**Ordinary annuity.** An annuity that consists of payments (receipts) at the end of each period; also known as an annuity in arrears.

**Original retail.** The initial sales price, including the original increase over cost referred to as the initial markup.

**Output measures.** Measures of the earnings process in percentage-of-completion accounting based on units produced, contract milestones reached, and values added.

**Outstanding checks.** Checks written near the end of the month that have reduced the depositor's cash balance but have not yet cleared the bank as of the bank statement date.

**Owners' equity.** The residual interest in the assets of an entity that remains after deducting its liabilities; sometimes referred to as net assets.

### P

**Paid-in capital.** *See* Contributed capital.

**Par value.** A value that may be assigned to stock by the terms of a corporation's charter; the par value is printed on the stock certificate.

**Parent company.** A company that exercises control over another company, known as a subsidiary, through majority ownership (more than 50 percent) of the subsidiary's voting stock.

**Participating preferred stock.** Preferred stock that provides for additional dividends to be paid to preferred stockholders after dividends of a specified amount are paid to common stockholders. Although once quite common, participating preferred stocks are now relatively rare.

**Partnership.** A business entity owned by two or more people; the owner's equity is recorded in individual partner capital accounts.

**Percentage-of-completion accounting.** An accounting method for long-term construction contracts which recognizes revenue and related expenses prior to delivery of the goods. Recognition is based on either an input or output measure of the earning process.

**Period costs.** Costs that are recognized as expenses during the period in which cash is spent or liabilities are incurred for goods and services that are used up either simultaneously with acquisition or soon after.

**Periodic inventory system.** A method of accounting for inventory in which cost of goods sold is determined and inventory is adjusted to the proper balance at the end of the accounting period, not when inventoriable merchandise is bought or sold. Throughout the period, all purchases of inventoriable merchandise are recorded in the purchases account, and ending inventory is determined by a physical count of merchandise on hand.

**Permanent accounts.** *See* Real (permanent) accounts.

**Perpetual inventory system.** A method of accounting for inventory in which detailed records of each inventory purchase and sale are maintained. This system provides a current record of inventory on hand and cost of goods sold to date.

**Petty cash fund.** A small amount of cash kept on hand for the purpose of making miscellaneous payments.

**Physical capital maintenance.** A concept under which income is defined as the excess of physical productive capacity at the end of an accounting period over the physical productive capacity at the beginning of the period, excluding the effects of transactions with owners.

**Pooling of interests.** A method of accounting for a business combination whereby all the asset, liability, and owners' equity values are combined; under this approach, the retained earnings amounts are added together to become the total retained earnings for the combined entity.

**Post-balance sheet events.** *See* Subsequent events.

**Post-closing trial balance.** A list of all real accounts and their balances after the closing process has been completed.

**Postemployment benefits.** A term used to describe all benefits granted to employees after termination of employment. Includes benefits granted after retirement as well as those benefits granted for any period between the termination of employment and retirement.

**Posting.** The process of summarizing transactions by transferring amounts from the journal to the ledger accounts.

**Predictive value.** A key ingredient of relevant accounting information; helps a decision maker predict future consequences based on information about past transactions and events.

**Preferred stock.** A class of stock that usually confers dividend and liquidation rights that take precedence over those of common stock; preferred stock is often nonvoting stock.

**Present (or discounted) value.** The amount of net future cash inflows or outflows discounted to their present value at an appropriate rate of interest.

**Price-earnings ratio.** A measure of the relationship between the market price of a company's stock and its profitability. The formula is the market price per share of common stock divided by the earnings per share of common stock.

**Price-earnings ratio.** Market price of stock divided by earnings per share.

**Principal or face amount.** The amount, excluding interest, that the maker of a note or the issuer of a bond agrees to pay at the maturity date; this amount is printed on the note or bond contract.

**Prior-period adjustment.** An adjustment made directly to the retained earnings account to correct errors made in prior accounting periods.

**Private Companies Practice Section (PCPS).** A section of the AICPA for firms that do not have clients regulated by the SEC. Membership in the section is voluntary. Periodic peer review is required of all firms with membership in the PCPS.

**Productive-output depreciation.** A use-factor method based on the theory that an asset is acquired for the service it can provide in the form of production output. Depreciable cost is divided by the total estimated output to determine the depreciation rate per unit of output.

**Profitability.** The ability of a company to earn a satisfactory return on its assets.

**Promissory note.** A formal written promise to pay a certain amount of money at a specified future date.

**Property dividend.** The payment (receipt) of a dividend in the form of some asset other than cash.

**Proportional performance method.** An accounting method for recording service revenue and related expenses prior to completion of a service contract.

**Proprietorship.** A business entity owned by one person; the owner's equity is recorded in a single (proprietor) capital account.

**Purchase.** A method of accounting for a business combination whereby the value of the stock in excess of the net assets acquired is recorded as Goodwill; under this approach, the retained earnings of the acquired company do not become part of the combined retained earnings.

## Q

**Quasi-reorganization.** A procedure by which, when permitted by state law, a company eliminates a deficit in retained earnings by restating its invested capital balance; provides a "fresh start" for a company, changing retained earnings from a negative to a zero balance.

**Quick assets.** Assets that are very liquid. They include cash, cash equivalents, marketable securities, and usually accounts receivable. Inventories and prepaid expenses do not qualify as quick assets.

**Quick ratio.** *See* Acid-test ratio.

## R

**Rate earned on average common stockholders' equity.** An analytical measurement of profitability for the residual owners of a company. The formula is net income divided by the average stockholders' equity.

**Rate earned on average total assets.** An analytical measurement of profitability for a company as an entity regardless of the source of funds.

**Rate earned on stockholders' equity.** An analytical measurement of profitability for all stockholders, residual and preferred. The formula is net income divided by average stockholders' equity.

**Raw materials.** Inventory acquired by a manufacturer for use in the production process. Also referred to as *direct materials.*

**Real (permanent) accounts.** Accounts that are not closed to a zero balance at the end of each accounting period; also referred to as Permanent accounts. They include all balance sheet accounts (assets, liabilities, and owners' equity).

**Receivables.** Claims against others for money, goods, or services; usually, receivable claims are settled by the receipt of cash.

**Recognition.** The process of formally recording an item in the accounting records and eventually reporting it in the financial statements; includes both the initial recording of an item and any subsequent changes related to that item.

**Redeemable preferred stock.** Preferred stock that may be redeemed at the option of the holder, or at a fixed price on a specific date, or upon other conditions not solely within the control of the issuer; redemption requirements for this type of stock must be disclosed.

**Refundable deposits.** An obligation of a company to refund amounts previously collected from customers as deposits.

**Registered bonds.** Bonds for which the bondholders' names and addresses are kept on file by the issuing company.

**Relevance.** One of two primary qualities inherent in useful accounting information; essentially information is relevant if it will affect a decision. The key ingredients of relevance are feedback value, predictive value, and timeliness.

**Reliability.** One of two primary qualities inherent in useful accounting information; to be reliable, information must contain the key ingredients of verifiability, neutrality, and representational faithfulness.

**Renewals.** Unplanned replacements of a component of an asset which may or may not extend the asset's useful life or increase future cash flows. If the asset's life is extended or if future cash flows will increase, then a renewal is properly recorded as an asset. If the life of the asset will not increase and no future cash flows are expected as a result of the renewal, then the renewal is charged to expense in the period in which it is incurred.

**Repairs.** Expenditures to restore assets to good operating condition upon their breakdown or to restore and replace broken parts. Repairs benefit only current operations and are expensed immediately.

**Replacement cost.** The cost that would be required to replace an existing asset.

**Replacements.** *See* Renewals.

**Report form of balance sheet.** A balance sheet that presents assets, liabilities, and owners' equity sections in a vertical arrangement.

**Representational faithfulness.** A key ingredient of reliable accounting information requiring that the amounts and descriptions reported in the financial statements reflect the actual results of economic transactions and events.

**Research activities.**  Activities undertaken to discover new knowledge that may be used in developing new products, services, or processes or that may result in significant improvements of existing products or processes.

**Research and development (R&D).**  A functional activity engaged in by a company to discover and develop new products, designs, methods, etc.

**Reserve Recognition Accounting (RRA).**  A method of accounting that recognizes the value of oil and gas reserves rather than their historical cost. RRA was proposed as a method by the SEC, but later withdrawn from active consideration.

**Residual (salvage) value.**  Estimated amount that can be realized upon the retirement of a depreciable asset; sometimes referred to as salvage value.

**Residual value (leased property).**  The value of leased property at the end of the lease term. This value may be retained by the lessor, purchased by the lessee, or sold to a third person.

**Retail inventory method.**  A procedure that converts the retail value of inventory to an estimation of cost by using a cost percentage that reflects the relationship of inventory available for sale valued at retail and cost.

**Retained earnings.**  The portion of owners' equity that represents the net accumulated earnings of a corporation; generally, equal to total owners' equity less contributed capital.

**Retained earnings statement.**  A supplementary financial statement, often combined with the income statement, that shows the change in retained earnings for the period. The most common changes are net income (or loss) and dividends.

**Return on investment (ROI).**  A general term for various analytical measurements of profitability related to input of resources. *See* Rate earned on average common stockholders' equity and Rate earned on average total assets.

**Revenue recognition.**  The process of determining the period in which revenue is recorded. Revenue is generally recognized when it has been realized or is realizable and when it has been earned through substantial completion of the activities involved in the earnings process.

**Revenue recognition principle.**  A basic accounting concept that is applied to determine when revenue should be recognized (recorded). Generally, under this principle, revenues are recognized when two criteria are met: the earnings process is substantially complete and the revenues are realized or realizable.

**Revenues.**  Inflows or other enhancements of assets of an entity or settlements of its liabilities (or a combination of both) from delivering or producing goods, rendering services, or other activities that constitute the entity's ongoing major or central operations.

**Reversing entries.**  Entries made at the beginning of a period that exactly reverse certain adjusting entries made at the end of the previous period. Reversing entries are optional, and their purpose is to facilitate subsequent recording of transactions.

## S

**Sale-leaseback.**  A contractual arrangement in which one party, the seller, sells a leased asset to a second party, and in the same agreement, the seller leases back the property. The seller becomes the seller-lessee and the purchaser the purchaser-lessor. Any profit made on the sale must be deferred and recognized over the lease term. Losses are recognized immediately.

**Sales discount.**  *See* Cash discount.

**Sales-type lease.**  A lease in which the lessor is a manufacturer or dealer utilizing the lease to facilitate the sale of goods.

**Salvage value.**  *See* Residual (salvage) value.

**SEC Practice Section (SECPS).**  A section of the AICPA for firms that have clients that are subject to government regulations through the Securities and Exchange Commission. Membership in the section is voluntary. Periodic peer review is required of all firms with membership in SECPS. Member firms are subject to more regulation than is true for the member firms belonging to the Private Companies Practice Section.

**Secured bonds.**  Bonds for which assets are pledged to guarantee repayment.

**Securities and Exchange Commission (SEC).**  A governmental body created to regulate the issuance and trading of securities by corporations to the general public. As part of this function, the SEC is vitally interested in financial accounting and reporting standards. While this body has the authority to establish accounting standards, it has historically relied heavily on the private sector to perform this function.

**Securities Industry Associates.**  An organization of investment bankers who manage the portfolios of large institutional investors.

**Segment.**  A subdivision of a company that can be identified in relationship to its cash flows, profitability, assets and debt.

**Serial bonds.**  Bonds that mature in a series of installments at future dates.

**Service-hours depreciation.**  A use-factor depreciation method based on the theory that the purchase of an asset represents the purchase of a number of hours of direct service. Depreciable cost is divided by total service hours during the useful life of the asset to determine the depreciation rate per hour.

**Similar assets.**  Assets that are similar in nature and can be exchanged under certain conditions without recognition of a gain on the transfer.

**Simple interest.** Interest that is computed on the principal amount only.

**Solvency.** The ability of an entity to pay all current and long-term debts as they come due.

**Source documents.** *See* Business documents.

**Special journal.** An accounting record used to record a particular type of frequently recurring transaction.

**Specific identification method.** An inventory costing method that assigns the actual cost of the asset to the inventory (unsold) or cost of goods sold (when sold). The cost flow matches the physical flow of the asset.

**Spot rate.** The exchange rate at which currencies can be traded immediately.

**Stability.** The ability of a company to make interest and principal payments on outstanding debt and to pay regular dividends to its stockholders.

**Stable monetary units.** An accounting assumption that the measuring unit maintains constant purchasing power; based on this assumption, U.S. financial statements have traditionally reported items in nominal dollars without adjustment for changes in purchasing power.

**Stated or contract rate.** The rate of interest printed on the bond.

**Stated value.** A value that may be assigned to no-par stock by the board of directors of a corporation; similar in concept to par value.

**Statement of cash flows.** One of three primary financial statements required to be included in the full set of general-purpose statements presented to external users. The statement provides information about the cash receipts (inflows) and cash payments (outflows) of an entity during a period of time. The statement is separated into cash flows from operating, investing, and financing activities.

**Statement of changes in stockholders' equity.** A report that shows the total changes in all stockholders' equity accounts during a period of time; provides a reconciliation of the beginning and ending stockholders' equity amounts.

**Statement of financial position.** *See* Balance sheet.

**Statements of Financial Accounting Concepts.** A set of guidelines established by the FASB to provide a conceptual framework for establishing and administering accounting standards.

**Statements of Financial Accounting Standards (SFAS).** The official statements of the Financial Accounting Standards Board that govern external financial reporting. These statements are prepared after extensive review and discussion by the FASB with the various groups involved in preparing and using general-purpose financial statements.

**Statements of Position.** Statements issued by the Accounting Standards Executive Committee of the AICPA that deal with emerging issues that have not yet been placed on the FASB agenda.

**Stock appreciation rights (SARs).** The right for the holder, typically an employee, to receive an amount equal to the excess of the market value of the issuing company's common stock in excess of a specified price. SARs are often awarded in conjunction with a variable stock option plan.

**Stock dividend.** The payment (receipt) of a dividend in the form of additional shares of a company's own stock.

**Stock options.** Rights granted to officers or employees, sometimes as part of compensation plan; term also may be used interchangeably with stock rights and stock warrants.

**Stock rights.** Rights issued to existing shareholders to permit maintenance of a proportionate ownership interest; term also may be used interchangeably with stock warrants and stock options.

**Stock split.** A reduction in the par or stated value of stock accompanied by a proportionate increase in number of shares outstanding.

**Stock warrants.** Rights sold separately for cash, generally in conjunction with another security; term also may be used interchangeably with stock rights and stock options.

**Straight-line depreciation.** A time-factor method of depreciation that recognizes equal periodic depreciation charges for each year of an asset's useful life.

**Straight-line method.** An amortization method which provides for recognition of an equal amount of bond premium or discount amortization each period.

**Subjective acceleration clause.** A clause in a debt instrument that identified general conditions that can cause the debt to be callable immediately but violation of the conditions cannot be determined objectively.

**Subsequent events.** Events occurring between the balance sheet date and the date financial statements are issued and made available to external users.

**Subsidiary company.** A company that is owned or controlled by another company, known as the parent company.

**Subsidiary ledgers.** A grouping of individual accounts that in total equal the balance of a control account in the general ledger; provides additional detail in support of general ledger balances.

**Substantial performance.** A criterion for recognizing revenue from a franchising agreement which requires that all provisions of the contract agreement be substantially complete before revenue and related expenses may be recognized.

**Successful efforts approach.** An amortization method employed in the gas and oil industry that expenses the cost of unsuccessful projects and records as assets only the exploratory costs for successful oil and gas projects.

**Sum-of-the-years-digits depreciation method.** A depreciation method providing decreasing periodic depreciation charges by applying a series of fractions to the asset cost, where the denominator is the sum of the digits 1 through n, and n equals the asset life in years.

# T

**Tangible noncurrent operating assets.**  Economic resources with future benefit that are used in the normal operating activity of the organization that can be physically observed, e.g., land, buildings, and equipment.

**Technical Bulletins.**  Publications issued by the staff of the FASB that give guidance for specific problems that arise in practice. They are advisory in nature and do not have as much authority as the FASB Statements or Interpretations.

**Technological feasibility.**  The attainment of a detailed program design and working model for computer software.

**Temporary accounts.**  *See* Nominal accounts.

**Temporary investments.**  Investments in securities that: (1) have a ready market, and (2) management intends to sell if the need for cash arises.

**Term bonds.**  Bonds that mature in one lump sum at a specified future date.

**Termination benefits.**  Benefits that arise either from a special amendment to the pension plan that covers only a short period of time, or from the original pension contract that provides special benefits if a certain event, such as a plant closing, occurs.

**Time deposits.**  Funds deposited in a bank that legally require prior notification before they can be withdrawn.

**Time-factor depreciation methods.**  Methods of depreciation in which the factor that measures the declining usefulness of an asset is related to time more than to use. The most widely used depreciation methods, such as straight-line, declining-balance, and ACRS, rely on this factor.

**Timeliness.**  A key ingredient of relevant accounting information; to be relevant and therefore useful for decision making, information must be provided on a timely basis.

**Total asset turnover.**  An analytical measurement of the relationship between asset cost and sales generated by those assets. If a company can generate more sales with the same assets, it will increase its level of profitability. The formula is net sales divided by average total assets.

**Trade discount.**  A reduction in the "list" sales price of an item to the "net" sales price actually charged the customer; trade discounts are generally dependent on the volume of business or size of order from the customer.

**Trade notes payable.**  A note issued to trade creditors for the purchase of goods or services.

**Trade receivables.**  Receivables associated with the normal operating activities of a business, e.g., credit sales of goods or services to customers.

**Trading on the equity.**  *See* Financial leverage.

**Transaction.**  An exchange of goods or services between entities or some other event having an economic impact on a business enterprise.

**Transaction approach.**  A method of determining income by defining the financial statement effects of certain events classified as revenues, gains, expenses, and losses. Also known as the *matching concept*, this is the traditional accounting approach to measuring and defining income.

**Transfer of receivables with recourse.**  A hybrid form of receivables financing; depending on the specific circumstances, these may be treated for accounting purposes as a sale (factoring) transaction or as a borrowing (assignment) transaction.

**Treasury stock.**  Stock issued by a corporation but subsequently reacquired by the corporation and held for possible future reissuance or retirement.

**Trial balance.**  A list of all accounts and their balances; provides a means of testing whether total debits equal total credits for all accounts.

**Trust indenture.**  A legal agreement specifying how a fund should be administered by its trustee(s).

# U

**Unappropriated (free) retained earnings.**  The unrestricted portion of retained earnings.

**Understandability.**  An essential, use-specific quality of accounting information.

**Unearned revenues.**  Liabilities resulting from amounts that are received before they have been earned, e.g., advances from customers or unearned rent.

**Unguaranteed residual value.**  A residual value of leased property that remains with the lessor at the end of the lease term. Since there is no guarantee of the residual value, market factors and asset condition determine the value of the leased asset at the end of the lease.

**Unit depreciation.**  Depreciation computed on an individual asset as opposed to computation on groups of assets.

**Unsecured bonds (debentures).**  Bonds for which no specific collateral has been pledged.

**Use-factor depreciation methods.**  Methods of depreciation in which the factor that measures the declining usefulness of an asset is related to use more than to time. The units-of-production method is the most common depreciation method that emphasizes the use factor.

**Useful life.**  An estimated measure of time or of production capacity a noncurrent operating asset will yield. All noncurrent operating assets, other than land, have a limited useful life. Physical factors such as wear and tear, deterioration, damage or destruction limit the useful life of an asset. Functional factors such as inadequacy or obsolescence may also limit the useful life of an asset.

## V

**Verifiability.**   A key ingredient of reliable accounting information; reported information should be based on objectively determined facts that can be verified by other accountants using the same measurement methods.

**Vertical analysis.**   Analysis of a company's single-year financial statements by comparing elements within the statements with each other and with statement totals.

**Voucher system.**   A system that provides for the control of purchases and cash disbursements. Business documents are used to prepare vouchers in support of all payments by check. The voucher identifies the person authorizing the expenditure, explains the nature of the transaction, and names the affected accounts. Checks are written in payment for each individual voucher.

## W

**Warranties.**   Obligations of a company to provide free service on units failing to perform satisfactorily or to replace defective goods.

**Weighted-average interest rate.**   An interest rate determined by relating interest expenditures for a period with the amount of weighted borrowings during the same period.

**Work in process.**   *See* Goods in process.

**Work sheet.**   A columnar schedule used to summarize accounting data; often used to facilitate the preparation of adjusting entries and financial statements.

**Working capital.**   Current assets less current liabilities; a measure of liquidity.

**Working capital ratio.**   *See* Current ratio.

## Y

**Yield on common stock.**   A measure of the cash return to common stockholders. The formula is dividends per share of common stock divided by market value per share of common stock.

## Z

**Zero-interest bonds or deep-discount bonds.**   Bonds that do not bear interest but instead are sold at significant discounts, providing the investor with a total interest payoff at maturity.

# APPENDIX C

## Index of References to APB and FASB Pronouncements

The following list of pronouncements by the Accounting Principles Board and the Financial Accounting Standards Board (as of September 1, 1991) is provided to give students an overview of the standards issued since 1962 and to reference these standards to the relevant chapters in this book. Earlier pronouncements by the Committee on Accounting Procedures of the AICPA have been largely superseded or amended. In those cases where no change has been made by subsequent standard-setting bodies, the earlier pronouncements are still accepted as official.

### Accounting Principles Board Opinions

| Date Issued | Opinion Number | Title | Chapter References |
|---|---|---|---|
| Nov. 1962 | 1 | New Depreciation Guidelines and Rules | 13 |
| Dec. 1962 | 2 | Accounting for the "Investment Credit"; addendum to Opinion No. 2—Accounting Principles for Regulated Industries | N/A |
| Oct. 1963 | 3 | The Statement of Source and Application of Funds | 6 |
| Mar. 1964 | 4 | Accounting for the "Investment Credit" | N/A |
| Sep. 1964 | 5 | Reporting of Leases in Financial Statements of Lessee | N/A |
| Oct. 1965 | 6 | Status of Accounting Research Bulletins | 17 |
| May 1966 | 7 | Accounting for Leases in Financial Statements of Lessor | 20 |
| Nov. 1966 | 8 | Accounting for the Cost of Pension Plans | N/A |
| Dec. 1966 | 9 | Reporting the Results of Operations | 4 |
| Dec. 1966 | 10 | Omnibus Opinion—1966 | N/A |
| Dec. 1967 | 11 | Accounting for Income Taxes | N/A |
| Dec. 1967 | 12 | Omnibus Opinion—1967 | 13 |
| Mar. 1969 | 13 | Amending Paragraph 6 of APB Opinion No. 9, Application to Commercial Banks | N/A |
| Mar. 1969 | 14 | Accounting for Convertible Debt and Debt Issued with Stock Purchase Warrants | 16, 17 |
| May 1969 | 15 | Earnings per Share | N/A |
| Aug. 1970 | 16 | Business Combinations | N/A |
| Aug. 1970 | 17 | Intangible Assets | 12, 13 |
| Mar. 1971 | 18 | The Equity Method of Accounting for Investments in Common Stock | 14 |
| Mar. 1971 | 19 | Reporting Changes in Financial Position | 6 |
| July 1971 | 20 | Accounting Changes | 21 |
| Aug. 1971 | 21 | Interest on Receivables and Payables | 9, 15 |
| Apr. 1972 | 22 | Disclosures of Accounting Policies | 5 |
| Apr. 1972 | 23 | Accounting for Income Taxes—Special Areas | N/A |
| Apr. 1972 | 24 | Accounting for Income Taxes—Investments in Common Stock Accounted for by the Equity Method (Other than Subsidiaries and Corporate Joint Ventures) | N/A |

## Accounting Principles Board Opinions (Concluded)

| Date Issued | Opinion Number | Title | Chapter References |
|---|---|---|---|
| Oct. 1972 | 25 | Accounting for Stock Issued to Employees | 17 |
| Oct. 1972 | 26 | Early Extinguishment of Debt | 16 |
| Nov. 1972 | 27 | Accounting for Lease Transactions by Manufacturer or Dealer Lessors | 20 |
| May 1973 | 28 | Interim Financial Reporting | 22 |
| May 1973 | 29 | Accounting for Nonmonetary Transactions | 12, 14, 16 |
| June 1973 | 30 | Reporting the Results of Operations | 4, 21 |
| June 1973 | 31 | Disclosures of Lease Commitments by Lessees | 20 |

## Accounting Principles Board Statements

| Date Issued | Statement Number | Title | Chapter References |
|---|---|---|---|
| Apr. 1962 | 1 | Statement by the Accounting Principles Board (on Accounting Research Studies Nos. 1 and 3) | 2 |
| Sep. 1967 | 2 | Disclosure of Supplemental Financial Information by Diversified Companies | 22 |
| June 1969 | 3 | Financial Statements Restated for General Price-Level Changes | N/A |
| Oct. 1970 | 4 | Basic Concepts and Accounting Principles Underlying Financial Statements of Business Enterprises | 2 |

## Financial Accounting Standards Board Statements of Financial Accounting Standards

| Date Issued | Statement Number | Title | Chapter References |
|---|---|---|---|
| Dec. 1973 | 1 | Disclosure of Foreign Currency Translation Information | N/A |
| Oct. 1974 | 2 | Accounting for Research and Development Costs | 12 |
| Dec. 1974 | 3 | Reporting Accounting Changes in Interim Financial Statements | N/A |
| Mar. 1975 | 4 | Reporting Gains and Losses from Extinguishment of Debt | 4, 16 |
| Mar. 1975 | 5 | Accounting for Contingencies | 15 |
| May 1975 | 6 | Classification of Short-Term Obligations Expected to be Refinanced | 5, 15 |
| June 1975 | 7 | Accounting and Reporting by Development Stage Enterprises | 12 |
| Oct. 1975 | 8 | Accounting for the Translation of Foreign Currency Transactions and Foreign Currency Financial Statements | 11 |
| Oct. 1975 | 9 | Accounting for Income Taxes—Oil and Gas Producing Companies | N/A |
| Oct. 1975 | 10 | Extension of "Grandfather" Provisions for Business Combinations | N/A |
| Dec. 1975 | 11 | Accounting for Contingencies—Transition Method | 15 |
| Dec. 1975 | 12 | Accounting for Certain Marketable Securities | 8, 14 |
| Nov. 1976 | 13 | Accounting for Leases | 20 |
| Dec. 1976 | 14 | Financial Reporting for Segments of a Business Enterprise | 22 |
| June 1977 | 15 | Accounting by Debtors and Creditors for Troubled Debt Restructurings | 16 |
| June 1977 | 16 | Prior Period Adjustments | 18 |
| Nov. 1977 | 17 | Accounting for Leases—Initial Direct Costs | 20 |
| Nov. 1977 | 18 | Financial Reporting for Segments of a Business Enterprise—Interim Financial Statements | 22 |
| Dec. 1977 | 19 | Financial Accounting and Reporting by Oil and Gas Producing Companies | 13 |
| Dec. 1977 | 20 | Accounting for Forward Exchange Contracts | N/A |

**Financial Accounting Standards Board Statements of Financial Accounting Standards (Continued)**

| Date Issued | Statement Number | Title | Chapter References |
|---|---|---|---|
| Apr. 1978 | 21 | Suspension of the Reporting of Earnings Per Share and Segment Information by Nonpublic Enterprises | 22 |
| June 1978 | 22 | Changes in the Provisions of Lease Agreements Resulting from Refunding of Tax-Exempt Debt | N/A |
| Aug. 1978 | 23 | Inception of the Lease | 20 |
| Dec. 1978 | 24 | Reporting Segment Information in Financial Statements That Are Presented in Another Enterprise's Financial Report | N/A |
| Feb. 1979 | 25 | Suspension of Certain Accounting Requirements for Oil and Gas Producing Companies | 13 |
| Apr. 1979 | 26 | Profit Recognition on Sales-Type Leases of Real Estate | 20 |
| May 1979 | 27 | Classification of Renewals or Extensions of Existing Sales-Type or Direct Financing Leases | 20 |
| May 1979 | 28 | Accounting for Sales with Leasebacks | 20 |
| June 1979 | 29 | Determining Contingent Rentals | 20 |
| Aug. 1979 | 30 | Disclosures of Information About Major Customers | 22 |
| Sep. 1979 | 31 | Accounting for Tax Benefits Related to U.K. Tax Legislation Concerning Stock Relief | N/A |
| Sep. 1979 | 32 | Specialized Accounting and Reporting Principles and Practices in AICPA Statements of Position and Guides on Accounting and Auditing Matters | 19 |
| Sep. 1979 | 33 | Financial Reporting and Changing Prices | N/A |
| Oct. 1979 | 34 | Capitalization of Interest Cost | 12 |
| Mar. 1980 | 35 | Accounting and Reporting by Defined Benefit Pension Plans | N/A |
| May 1980 | 36 | Disclosure of Pension Information | N/A |
| July 1980 | 37 | Balance Sheet Classification of Deferred Income Taxes | N/A |
| Sep. 1980 | 38 | Accounting for Preacquisition Contingencies of Purchased Enterprises | N/A |
| Oct. 1980 | 39 | Financial Reporting and Changing Prices: Specialized Assets—Mining and Oil and Gas | N/A |
| Nov. 1980 | 40 | Financial Reporting and Changing Prices: Specialized Assets—Timberlands and Growing Timber | N/A |
| Nov. 1980 | 41 | Financial Reporting and Changing Prices: Specialized Assets—Income-Producing Real Estate | N/A |
| Nov. 1980 | 42 | Determining Materiality for Capitalization of Interest Costs | 12 |
| Nov. 1980 | 43 | Accounting for Compensated Absences | 15 |
| Dec. 1980 | 44 | Accounting for Intangible Assets of Motor Carriers | N/A |
| Mar. 1981 | 45 | Accounting for Franchise Fee Revenue | 19 |
| Mar. 1981 | 46 | Financial Reporting and Changing Prices: Motion Picture Films | N/A |
| Mar. 1981 | 47 | Disclosure of Long-Term Obligations | 16 |
| June 1981 | 48 | Revenue Recognition When Right of Return Exists | 19 |
| June 1981 | 49 | Accounting for Product Financing Arrangements | N/A |
| Nov. 1981 | 50 | Financial Reporting in the Record and Music Industry | N/A |
| Nov. 1981 | 51 | Financial Reporting by Cable Television Companies | N/A |
| Dec. 1981 | 52 | Foreign Currency Translation | N/A |
| Dec. 1981 | 53 | Financial Reporting by Producers and Distributors of Motion Picture Films | N/A |
| Jan. 1982 | 54 | Financial Reporting and Changing Prices: Investment Companies | N/A |
| Feb. 1982 | 55 | Determining Whether a Convertible Security Is a Common Stock Equivalent | N/A |
| Feb. 1982 | 56 | Designation of AICPA Guide and Statement of Position (SOP) 81-1 on Contractor Accounting and SOP 81-2 Concerning Hospital-Related Organizations as Preferable for Purposes of Applying APB Opinion 20 | 19 |
| Mar. 1982 | 57 | Related Party Disclosures | N/A |
| Apr. 1982 | 58 | Capitalization of Interest Cost in Financial Statements That Include Investments Accounted for by the Equity Method | N/A |

## Financial Accounting Standards Board Statements of Financial Accounting Standards (Continued)

| Date Issued | Statement Number | Title | Chapter References |
|---|---|---|---|
| Apr. 1982 | 59 | Deferral of the Effective Date of Certain Accounting Requirements for Pension Plans of State and Local Governmental Units | N/A |
| June 1982 | 60 | Accounting and Reporting by Insurance Enterprises | N/A |
| June 1982 | 61 | Accounting for Title Plant | N/A |
| June 1982 | 62 | Capitalization of Interest Cost in Situations Involving Certain Tax-Exempt Borrowings and Certain Gifts and Grants | N/A |
| June 1982 | 63 | Financial Reporting by Broadcasters | N/A |
| Sep. 1982 | 64 | Extinguishments of Debt Made to Satisfy Sinking-Fund Requirements | 16 |
| Sep. 1982 | 65 | Accounting for Certain Mortgage Banking Activities | N/A |
| Oct. 1982 | 66 | Accounting for Sales of Real Estate | 19 |
| Oct. 1982 | 67 | Accounting for Costs and Initial Rental Operations of Real Estate Projects | N/A |
| Oct. 1982 | 68 | Research and Development Arrangements | 16 |
| Nov. 1982 | 69 | Disclosures About Oil and Gas Producing Activities | N/A |
| Dec. 1982 | 70 | Financial Reporting and Changing Prices: Foreign Currency Translation | N/A |
| Dec. 1982 | 71 | Accounting for the Effects of Certain Types of Regulation | N/A |
| Feb. 1983 | 72 | Accounting for Certain Acquisitions of Banking or Thrift Institutions | N/A |
| Aug. 1983 | 73 | Reporting a Change in Accounting for Railroad Track Structures | N/A |
| Aug. 1983 | 74 | Accounting for Special Termination Benefits Paid to Employees | N/A |
| Nov. 1983 | 75 | Deferral of the Effective Date of Certain Accounting Requirements for Pension Plans of State and Local Governmental Units | N/A |
| Nov. 1983 | 76 | Extinguishment of Debt | 16 |
| Dec. 1983 | 77 | Reporting by Transferors for Transfers of Receivables with Recourse | 9 |
| Dec. 1983 | 78 | Classification of Obligations That Are Callable by the Creditor | 5, 16 |
| Feb. 1984 | 79 | Elimination of Certain Disclosures for Business Combinations by Nonpublic Enterprises | N/A |
| Aug. 1984 | 80 | Accounting for Future Contracts | N/A |
| Nov. 1984 | 81 | Disclosure of Postretirement Health Care and Life Insurance Benefits | N/A |
| Nov. 1984 | 82 | Financial Reporting and Changing Prices: Elimination of Certain Disclosures | N/A |
| Mar. 1985 | 83 | Designation of AICPA Guides and Statement of Position on Accounting by Brokers and Dealers in Securities, by Employee Benefit Plans, and by Banks as Preferable for Purposes of Applying APB Opinion 20 | N/A |
| Mar. 1985 | 84 | Induced Conversion of Convertible Debt | 16 |
| Mar. 1985 | 85 | Yield Test for Determining Whether a Convertible Security Is a Common Stock Equivalent | N/A |
| Aug. 1985 | 86 | Accounting for the Costs of Computer Software to Be Sold, Leased, or Otherwise Marketed | 12 |
| Dec. 1985 | 87 | Employers' Accounting for Pensions | N/A |
| Dec. 1985 | 88 | Employers' Accounting for Settlements and Curtailments of Defined Benefit Pension Plans and for Termination Benefits | N/A |
| Dec. 1986 | 89 | Financial Reporting and Changing Prices | N/A |
| Dec. 1986 | 90 | Regulated Enterprises—Accounting for Abandonments and Disallowances of Plant Costs | N/A |
| Dec. 1986 | 91 | Accounting for Nonrefundable Fees and Costs Associated with Originating or Acquiring Loans and Initial Direct Costs of Leases | 20 |
| Aug. 1987 | 92 | Regulated Enterprises—Accounting for Phase-In Plans | N/A |
| Aug. 1987 | 93 | Recognition of Depreciation by Not-for-Profit Organizations | N/A |
| Oct. 1987 | 94 | Consolidation of all Majority-Owned Subsidiaries | 17 |
| Nov. 1987 | 95 | Statement of Cash Flows | 6 |
| Dec. 1987 | 96 | Accounting for Income Taxes | N/A |
| Dec. 1987 | 97 | Accounting and Reporting by Insurance Enterprises for Certain Insurance Enterprises for Certain Long-Duration Contracts and for Realized Gains and Losses from the Sale of Investments | N/A |

### Financial Accounting Standards Board Statements of Financial Accounting Standards (Concluded)

| Date Issued | Statement Number | Title | Chapter References |
|---|---|---|---|
| May 1988 | 98 | Accounting for Leases:<br>• Sale-Leaseback Transactions Involving Real Estate<br>• Sales-Type Leases of Real Estate<br>• Definition of the Lease Term<br>• Initial Direct Costs of Direct Financial Leases | 20 |
| Sep. 1988 | 99 | Deferral of the Effective Date of Recognition of Depreciation by Not-for-Profit Organizations | N/A |
| Dec. 1988 | 100 | Accounting for Income Taxes—Deferral of the Effective Date FASB Statement No. 96 | N/A |
| Dec. 1988 | 101 | Regulated Enterprises—Accounting for the Discontinuation of Application of FASB Statement No. 71 | N/A |
| Feb. 1989 | 102 | Statement of Cash Flows—Exemption of Certain Enterprises and Classification of Cash Flows from Certain Securities Acquired for Resale | N/A |
| Dec. 1989 | 103 | Accounting for Income Taxes—Deferral of Effective Date of FASB Statement No. 96 | N/A |
| Dec. 1989 | 104 | Statement of Cash Flows—Net Reporting of Certain Cash Receipts and Cash Payments and Classification of Cash Flows from Hedging Transactions | N/A |
| Mar. 1990 | 105 | Disclosure of Information about Financial Instruments with Off-Balance-Sheet Risk and Financial Instruments with Concentrations of Credit Risk | 16 |
| Dec. 1990 | 106 | Employers' Accounting for Postretirement Benefits Other Than Pensions | N/A |

### Financial Accounting Standards Board Statements of Financial Accounting Concepts

| Date Issued | Statement Number | Title | Chapter References |
|---|---|---|---|
| Nov. 1978 | 1 | Objectives of Financial Reporting by Business Enterprises | 2 |
| May 1980 | 2 | Qualitative Characteristics of Accounting Information | 2 |
| Dec. 1980 | 3 | Elements of Financial Statements of Business Enterprises | 2 |
| Dec. 1980 | 4 | Objectives of Financial Reporting by Nonbusiness Organizations | N/A |
| Dec. 1984 | 5 | Recognition and Measurement in Financial Statements of Business Enterprises | 2 |
| Dec. 1985 | 6 | Elements of Financial Statements | 2 |

### Selected FASB Exposure Draft

| Date Issued | Title | Chapter References |
|---|---|---|
| June 1991 | Accounting for Income Taxes | N/A |

# INDEX